BUSINESS LAW

TIMOTHY FORT

Everleigh Chair in Business Ethics,
Kelley School of Business, Indiana University

STEPHEN B. PRESSER

Raoul Berger Professor of Legal History &
Professor of Business Law, Kellogg School of Management,
Northwestern University

MAT#41378471

© 2015 LEG, Inc. d/b/a West Academic
444 Cedar Street, Suite 700
St. Paul, MN 55101
1-877-888-1330

West, West Academic Publishing, and West Academic are trademarks
of West Publishing Corporation, used under license.

Printed in the United States of America

MAT#41378471
ISBN: 978-0-314-28648-2

To Susan Graff and to Nancy Nerad—
in mutual gratitude and for a 35-year teacher-student
relationship that is now memorialized as co-authorship.

PREFACE

WHY IS IT THAT ALTHOUGH THE TWO OF US have been teaching Business Law for a combined sixty years, we excitedly walk into each class? It is true that we both love to teach, but our experience hardly seems the exception. Indeed, nearly every Business Law professor we have ever met has the same experience.

Part of the answer might lie in the reaction students have to the course. To be sure, there will always be a student here and there who doesn't view a Legal Environment of Business or a Business Organizations course as his or her favorite. There are quite a few more who have doubts about the course until their first day. Yet, by and large, students also find these courses to be among the most interesting—and useful—they take. Students expect business law to be dull, uninspiring, and, in short, boring. What we and many of our business law colleagues seek to do, however, is to show that business law is about human drama. It is about yearning, emotion, and even revenge. It is, we believe, as fascinating as is the human race itself. Seeing our students begin to sense that, and seeing student skepticism transform into unexpected enthusiasm is, for want of a better word, fun.

The regulation of the business organization by law is America's great contribution to world jurisprudence. And, of course, as David Dudley Field remarked in 1859, as Americans, law is our only sovereign. We have no monarchy, we have no aristocracy, we have no established church. It is the law and the Constitution which holds this republic together, and as Americans we do really believe that ours should be a government of laws, not men (or women), and that our conduct should be guided by a benevolent rule of law. For Americans then, the study of law is not just the story of legal doctrine. It is history. It is philosophy. It is analysis. It is critical thinking. It is communication. It is politics. It is ethics. It is drama. It is even art. How could one not be excited about having the privilege to teach it?

Law touches on so many different parts of our lives that it is, after all, easy to relate to any person's—any student's—daily experience. Students have seen, and sometimes been, the careless driver. They've seen, and sometimes experienced, discrimination. They have had contracts breached and they have wondered if they are really bound to their promises, given their idiosyncratic circumstances. They wonder about how to reign in giant corporations, unruly agents and misguided principals, and they may have even wondered which of the myriad business forms would best suit their entrepreneurial ideas.

We have tried to construct a business law text which captures what we believe to be the intrinsic interest and the immediacy of law. This book has been assembled in a manner that allows the instructor to immerse students in the complex business of business law a bit more fully than can be done in some good business law textbooks that we do admire. We allow cases to run a little longer, believing that in doing so, critical thinking can better emerge within the confines of the richness of the case itself; so too can ethics. In photographs, notes, graphs, and questions, we try also to connect the dots between the law and current events, art, history, and politics.

The collaboration that produced this text is more than three decades long. It dates back to a cold Chicago January day in 1981 when a young law student named Tim Fort sat in Professor Presser's American Legal History course at Northwestern University School of Law, and on the second day of class found himself being grilled on topics pertaining to England's Sir Edward Coke and the relationship between law and religion. (You will see that the same subject matter begins this textbook.) Our relationship developed over the years, as Presser was one of Fort's supervisors during his work toward an unusual PhD in law, management, and theology. We have continued to teach in both management and law schools, and have found this opportunity to work as co-authors to be one of the true high points of our careers.

There are several people we would like to acknowledge. Jim Cahoy has been our terrific editor at West Academic Publishing who has fostered this book and kept us on task, always with grace, humor and enthusiasm. Carol Logie, the creative talent who put this book together, has been fantastic, crafting something truly unusual for a law text, an aesthetically superb book. We are grateful to both of them.

Professor Presser would like to thank his research assistants William O'Hara, Andreas Havajias, and Tiffany Chu, all of whom, in the summer of 2013, drafted large chunks of chapters, and all of whom served as valuable sounding boards for the materials on agency, partnership, LLCs, and corporations. Professor Presser's longtime faculty assistant, Tim Jacobs, performed his usual invaluable services.

Professor Fort would like to thank his research assistants, Lauren Chan and William LeBas at George Washington University School of Law and Jason Allen at the Mauer School of Law at Indiana University. He would also like to recognize four undergraduate students who, as an independent study, took up the challenge to propose graphics, photos, and other art that might capture the attention of students: Amna Bibi, Christopher Oman, Siddhi Salvi, and Danielle Stacey.

Our hope, in assembling these materials, is that those using them will help us, in future editions, better to meet their needs. We welcome any and all suggestions for improvement, and humbly take responsibility for any errors, omissions, or lapses which inevitably creep into such a bold undertaking.

—Stephen B. Presser   — Timothy L. Fort
Chicago, IL   Bloomington, IN

ABOUT THE AUTHORS

STEPHEN PRESSER is the Raoul Berger Professor of Legal History at Northwestern University School of Law, and a Professor of Business Law at Northwestern's Kellogg School of Management, with an appointment in the Management and Strategy Department. He is the co-author of a legal history casebook, the author of a corporations casebook, and the author of a treatise on the law of shareholder liability for corporate debts.

He is a graduate of Harvard College and Harvard Law School, and has frequently been an invited witness before committees of the U.S. Senate and House of Representatives on issues of constitutional law. He has been teaching courses on business organizations to law students and to management students for the last three decades. A course he created for Kellogg, "Law and the Manager," is one of the most popular of Kellogg's highly-ranked Executive Masters of Business Administration program. He is the recipient of many teaching awards from Kellogg and from the Law School, and has twice been a Fulbright Senior Scholar at University College, London.

TIMOTHY FORT holds the Everleigh Chair in Business Ethics at the Kelley School of Business at Indiana University. His primary research identity pertains to issues of ethical corporate culture and the relationship between ethical business and sustainable peace. He has authored five major research books published by Oxford, Cambridge, Yale, and Stanford University Presses. His *Business, Integrity and Peace* won the Best Book Award from the Academy of Management's Social Issues in Business Section. He has also authored two textbooks in the field of business ethics.

Fort holds his PhD from Northwestern University, where he also received his JD. His M.A. and B.A. are from the University of Notre Dame. He has received research awards from The Academy of Management, the Society of Business Ethics, and The Academy of Legal Studies of Business and has served on the editorial board of *The Academy of Management Review*, *Business Ethics Quarterly*, and *The American Business Law Journal*. He has also won teaching awards and recognition at the Doctoral, Executive, and MBA levels.

CHAPTER 10: Products Liability   487

Part 3: Agencies, Partnerships & Limited Liability Entities   591

BUSINESS LAW

Part I

Introduction to Law

CONSTITUTIONAL ISSUES RELEVANT TO BUSINESS

HAD IT NOT BEEN FOR BUSINESSPEOPLE, there might never have been a U.S. Constitution. The idea of limited government was rare at the time of the founding of the United States. Royal monarchies were the norm

rather than constitutional democracies. Even when democracy sought to take root, such as in the French Revolution—which occurred after the American Revolution and was contemporaneous with the writing of the Constitution—democracy gave way to the French Reign of Terror shortly thereafter, and then to Napoleon Bonaparte.

The roots of the U.S. Constitution trace more to England, where the notion of limitations on government power started much earlier. In the 1215 *Magna Carta*, the English King was restricted from punishing "freemen" through rule of law protections. These freemen were the businessmen of the time; feudal barons who had acquired their own strength that the King was forced to recognize. Nearly four hundred years later, Lord Coke, serving as Chief Justice of the Court of Common Pleas, ruled that the King was subject to the laws and did not supersede law through divine right. To have a sense of the language and origins of these limitations, here are excerpts from the *Magna Carta* and from Coke's ruling in Dr. Bonham's Case.

■ KING JOHN OF ENGLAND SIGNS THE MAGNA CARTA; ENGLAND, 1215.

excerpt

SIR EDWARD COKE

Chief Justice of

the King's Bench,

(1552–1634).

Image: Wikimedia Commons

> No FREEMAN shall be taken or imprisoned, or be disseised of his Freehold, or Liberties, or free Customs, or be outlawed, or exiled, or any other wise destroyed; nor will We not pass upon him, nor condemn him, but by lawful judgment of his Peers, or by the Law of the Land. We will sell to no man, we will not deny or defer to any man either Justice or Right.
>
> —*MAGNA CARTA.* § XXIX
>
> AND IT APPEARS IN OUR BOOKS, that in many cases, the common law will *(d)* controul Acts of Parliament, and sometimes adjudge them to be utterly void: for when an Act of Parliament is against common right and reason, or repugnant, or impossible to be performed, the common law will controul it, and adjudge such Act to be void [. . .].
>
> —*DR. BONHAM'S CASE,* 8. Co. Rep. 133b.

This history produced a view of government where rule of law was valued and in which government power was limited. In such a system, individual freedom and liberty flourished. After the American Revolution, the first "Constitution" came in the form of the "Articles of Confederation." The Articles took this notion of freedom from centralized authority and the value of human liberty to such an extreme that the thirteen original colonies found themselves economically bankrupt and militarily vulnerable. And so the debates began, most prominently in **The Federalist Papers,** as to the proper balance of governmental authority, states rights, and individual liberty.

■ THE FEDERALIST PAPERS ARE A SERIES OF 85 ARTICLES AND ESSAYS AUTHORED BY JAMES MADISON, ALEXANDER HAMILTON, JOHN JAY PROMOTING RATIFICATION OF THE UNITED STATES CONSTITUTION.

Those debates gave rise to the U.S. system of government featuring three branches: **Executive** (i.e. the President), **Legislative** (i.e. the Congress), and **Judicial** (i.e the Court system, culminating with the Supreme Court). As a partial explanation for why government can sometimes be slow to act, the rationale for the three-branch system was explicit: each branch would check the other branches and prevent the accumulation of excessive power. Institutional conflict was part of the plan.

Citizens had a say too, though voting had limitations. Initially the definition of who was a citizen empowered to vote meant white, property-owning males. Often, individual citizens did not directly elect statewide or national leaders. Citizens elected legislators, who would then cast votes for the President (the origin of the Electoral College) or Senators. So while citizens did vote, direct popular voting for many major offices did not occur.

The Constitution has been hailed as masterpiece of these kinds of checks and balances and, of course, the exact nature of the balancing has changed over the years. First among those changes was the protection of rights through the Bill of Rights, which created protection against the majority rule of individual and state rights. Over time the right to vote was extended, slavery and segregation ended, and many different doctrines and legal approaches waxed and waned. Yet core to all these developments have been basic principles of limited government, individual rights, and equal justice. Political debates for over two centuries have considered both the proper balance to effectuate the core principles of the Constitution and also the proper touchstones to anchor those debates, such as Courts adhering more to the original intent of the Founders versus viewing the Constitution as an organically evolving document.

I. The Notion of "Limited Government"

SO WHAT EXACTLY does limited government mean? It includes at least four facets: **Federalism and State Powers; The Separation of Powers; Judicial Review,** and **Individual Rights.** Each of these has a particular application for business.

A. FEDERALISM & STATE POWERS

The authors of the Constitution sought to strengthen the national government while also retaining as many state powers as possible. Indeed, the formulation is that the federal government only has those powers designated to it by the Constitution. If such a specific designation has not been made, then the states retain powers. The notion of Federalism, at its heart, recognizes power of both a central authority—the national government—and also state authority, which includes the states themselves of course, but also the many municipalities, counties, and other local governments.

The exercise of certain constitutional powers as interpreted by the Supreme Court has led to a strong central government. Some of these provisions or doctrines includes:

1. *The Supremacy Clause:* The Courts have held that in the case where there is a conflict between federal law and state law, the federal law "preempts" and overrides the state law. This is why there is only, for instance, a federal bankruptcy system as opposed to each state having its own bankruptcy system or why there is one nuclear regulatory system.

2. *The Necessary and Proper Clause:* Courts have interpreted Article 1, Section VIII of the Constitution as authorizing Congress to create laws reasonably related to its enumerated duties. This provides a window for Congress to increase its authoritative reach.

3. *The Commerce Clause:* Congress has always had the authority to regulate interstate commerce, but the definition of interstate commerce has expanded dramatically through court decisions so that now, laws enacted via the Commerce Clause tend to be very difficult to overturn.

4. *Taxing and Spending:* It is central to government that it may impose taxes and spend. Over the history of the United States, that taxing and spending power has grown and become a strong source for federal power.

This list is not exhaustive, but it gives a sense of the fact that the authority of the federal government has expanded through history. That expansion frequently has economic impact.

B. SEPARATION OF POWERS

By setting up a system of checks and balances—implemented by the institutional framework of separation of powers—the framers of the Constitution guaranteed obstacles to government action. This does not mean that the government cannot move quickly. It certainly can move quickly in the time of national security emergencies; it can also apply to domestic issues as well. After the economic scandals of Enron, WorldCom and others, Congress quickly enacted the Sarbanes-Oxley law, a complicated law quickly signed into law by the President.

Having said this, only Congress can pass a law and, with two houses (the House of Representatives and the Senate), this can be difficult. The President must then sign the law, which is then subject to judicial review by the Court system. There are some areas where there are exceptions, such as Presidential Executive Orders, but the President does not have fiat to do anything he wants.

The framers of the Constitution, especially those such as James Madison and Thomas Jefferson (though Jefferson was in France at the time of the Constitution's writing and was skeptical of it) worried that the power of the government to accomplish good also equipped it with the power for more nefarious usage. Given their history of concerns over executive power, the failure of the weak Articles of Confederation, and the commitment to a rule of law approach that required judicial review, the framers sought to pit naturally occurring political ambitions (in each branch of government) against each other to protect individual liberties.

C. JUDICIAL REVIEW

Judicial review was one of the key checks on all branches of government, including not only the executive and legislative but also courts themselves and actions of states, too. That especially became the case over time as the power and authority of the Supreme Court grew. Writing in a different context, legal philosopher Michael Perry has written about the advantages of creating law with an eye toward history: "when consulting a rule, we consult with the dead and by doing so enrich the quality of our conversation."[1] Courts do this as part of their work. They consult past experience and precedent to determine whether a law passes Constitutional or other muster, and they act, for better or for worse, as a pressure against the powers of a Congress or President.

D. INDIVIDUAL RIGHTS

As already suggested, a key reason for all the above limitations of governmental power is the protection of individual rights and liberties. But limitations on governmental powers based on the Constitution were not enough to satisfy many of the framers. Thus to clarify and to strengthen the rights possessed by the people, the framers agreed that immediately after the adoption of the Constitution by the states, there would be a Bill of Rights added to it, specifying rights to worship, speak, and assemble freely; to avoid self-incrimination; and to bear arms. These rights are crucial to the American experience and it is worth setting them out:

The Bill of Rights

AMENDMENT I: Congress shall make no law respecting an establishment of religion, or prohibiting the free exercise thereof; or abridging the freedom of speech, or of the press; or the right of the people peaceably to assemble, and to petition the Government for a redress of grievances.

AMENDMENT II: A well regulated Militia, being necessary to the security of a free State, the right of the people to keep and bear Arms, shall not be infringed.

AMENDMENT III: No Soldier shall, in time of peace be quartered in any house, without the consent of the Owner, nor in time of war, but in a manner to be prescribed by law.

AMENDMENT IV: The right of the people to be secure in their persons, houses, papers, and effects, against unreasonable searches and seizures, shall not be violated, and no Warrants shall issue, but upon probable cause, supported by Oath or affirmation, and particularly describing the place to be searched, and the persons or things to be seized.

---

1   Michael H. Perry; *Morality, Politics, and Law*; 37 (1988).

AMENDMENT V: No person shall be held to answer for a capital, or otherwise infamous crime, unless on a presentment or indictment of a Grand Jury, except in cases arising in the land or naval forces, or in the Militia, when in actual service in time of War or public danger; nor shall any person be subject for the same offence to be twice put in jeopardy of life or limb; nor shall be compelled in any criminal case to be a witness against himself, nor be deprived of life, liberty, or property, without due process of law; nor shall private property be taken for public use, without just compensation.

AMENDMENT VI: In all criminal prosecutions, the accused shall enjoy the right to a speedy and public trial, by an impartial jury of the State and district wherein the crime shall have been committed, which district shall have been previously ascertained by law, and to be informed of the nature and cause of the accusation; to be confronted with the witnesses against him; to have compulsory process for obtaining witnesses in his favor, and to have the Assistance of Counsel for his defence.

AMENDMENT VII: In Suits at common law, where the value in controversy shall exceed twenty dollars, the right of trial by jury shall be preserved, and no fact tried by a jury, shall be otherwise reexamined in any Court of the United States, than according to the rules of the common law.

AMENDMENT VIII: Excessive bail shall not be required, nor excessive fines imposed, nor cruel and unusual punishments inflicted.

AMENDMENT IX: The enumeration in the Constitution, of certain rights, shall not be construed to deny or disparage others retained by the people.

AMENDMENT X: The powers not delegated to the United States by the Constitution, nor prohibited by it to the States, are reserved to the States respectively, or to the people.

II. Federal Government Powers

A. COMMERCE POWER

Does growing some corn in your backyard to eat at your own dinner table constitute interstate commerce? In an important 1942 case, *Wickard v. Filburn*, the Supreme Court said yes. As a way to try to create supports for farmers' prices, Congress established limits on the amount of wheat, among other crops, that could be grown. Mr. Filburn grew some extra wheat, not for sale in the marketplace, but simply to use for food in his own house. Filburn lost the case because the Supreme Court said that Congress had the power to regulate interstate commerce and Filburn's act was interstate commerce. If an activity substantially affects interstate commerce, then Congress can regulate it and if growing some wheat in your own backyard for your own use is by definition interstate commerce, then the range of Congressional authority is vast.

■ FEDERAL INTERSTATE TRAVEL REGULATIONS WERE CITED AS THE BASIS FOR ENDING RACIAL DISCRIMINATION BY STATES AT HOTELS AND MOTELS IN THE U.S.

Image: Atlanta Time Machine

A tremendous number of laws have been passed pursuant to the commerce clause. These include transactions that clearly have a direct impact on commerce, such as trademarks, labor and employment rights, environmental laws, consumer protection and others. It also includes issues one might think are more related to other principles of fairness and equality. For example, the landmark 1964 Civil Rights Act was passed pursuant to the Commerce Clause. Key provisions of this and other Civil Rights Acts made it illegal for businesses to discriminate on the basis of skin color and other attributes. The following case shows the use of the Commerce Clause in these kinds of cases.

Heart of Atlanta Motel v. United States

379 U.S. 241 (1964)

Mr. Justice CLARK delivered the opinion of the Court. . .

1. *The Factual Background and Contentions of the Parties.*

The case comes here on admissions and stipulated facts. Appellant owns and operates the Heart of Atlanta Motel which has 216 rooms available to transient guests. The motel is located on Courtland Street, two blocks from downtown Peachtree Street. It is readily accessible to interstate highways 75 and 85 and state highways 23 and 41. Appellant solicits patronage from outside the State of Georgia through various national advertising media, including magazines of national circulation; it maintains over 50 billboards and highway signs within the State, soliciting patronage for the motel; it accepts convention trade from outside Georgia and approximately 75% of its registered guests are from out of State. Prior to passage of the Act the motel had followed a practice of refusing to rent rooms to Negroes, and it alleged that it intended to continue to do so. In an effort to perpetuate that policy this suit was filed.

The appellant contends that Congress in passing this Act exceeded its power to regulate commerce under [the Commerce Clause]; that the Act violates the Fifth Amendment because appellant is deprived of the right to choose its customers and operate its business as it wishes, resulting in a taking of its liberty and property without due process of law and a taking of its property without just compensation; and, finally, that by requiring appellant to rent available rooms to Negroes against its will, Congress is subjecting it to involuntary servitude in contravention of the Thirteenth Amendment.

The appellees counter that the unavailability to Negroes of adequate accommodations interferes significantly with interstate travel, and that Congress, under the Commerce Clause, has power to remove such obstructions and restraints; that the Fifth Amendment does not forbid reasonable regulation and that consequential damage does not constitute a 'taking' within the meaning of that amendment; that the Thirteenth Amendment claim fails because it is entirely frivolous to say that an amendment directed to the abolition of human bondage and the removal of widespread disabilities associated with slavery places discrimination in public accommodations, beyond the reach of both federal and state law.

* * *

2. The History of the Act.

Congress first evidenced its interest in civil rights legislation in the Civil Rights or Enforcement Act of April 9, 1866. There followed four Acts, with a fifth, the Civil Rights Act of March 1, 1875, culminating the series. In 1883 this Court struck down the public accommodations sections of the 1875 Act in the *Civil Rights Cases*, 109 U.S. 3. No major legislation in this field had been enacted by Congress for 82 years when the Civil Rights Act of 1957 became law. It was followed by the Civil Rights Act of 1960. Three years later, on June 19, 1963, the late President Kennedy called for civil rights legislation in a message to Congress to which he attached a proposed bill. Its stated purpose was

> 'to promote the general welfare by eliminating discrimination based on race, color, religion, or national origin in * * * public accommodations through the exercise by Congress of the powers conferred upon it * * * to enforce the provisions of the fourteenth and fifteenth amendments, to regulate commerce among the several States, and to make laws necessary and proper to execute the powers conferred upon it by the Constitution.'

Bills were introduced in each House of the Congress, embodying the President's suggestion, one in the Senate [. . .] and one in the House [. . .]. However, it was not until July 2, 1964, upon the recommendation of President Johnson, that the Civil Rights Act of 1964, here under attack, was finally passed.

* * *

3. *Title II of the Act.*

This Title is divided into seven sections beginning with § 201(a) which provides that:

> 'All persons shall be entitled to the full and equal enjoyment of the goods, services, facilities, privileges, advantages, and accommodations of any place of public accommodation, as defined in this section, without discrimination or segregation on the ground of race, color, religion, or national origin.'

There are listed in § 201(b) four classes of business establishments, each of which 'serves the public' and 'is a place of public accommodation' within the meaning of § 201(a) 'if its operations affect commerce, or if discrimination or segregation by it is supported by State action.' The covered establishments are:

> '(1) any inn, hotel, motel, or other establishment which provides lodging to transient guests, other than an establishment located within a building which contains not more than five rooms for rent or hire and which is actually occupied by the proprietor of such establishment as his residence;
>
> '(2) any restaurant, cafeteria * * * (not here involved);
>
> '(3) any motion picture house * * * (not here involved);
>
> '(4) any establishment * * * which is physically located within the premises of any establishment otherwise covered by this subsection, or * * * within the premises of which is physically located any such covered establishment * * * (not here involved).'

Section 201(c) defines the phrase 'affect commerce' as applied to the above establishments. It first declares that 'any inn, hotel, motel, or other establishment which provides lodging to transient guests' affects commerce *per se*. Restaurants, cafeterias, etc., in class two affect commerce only if they serve or offer to serve interstate travelers or if a substantial portion of the food which they serve or products which they sell have 'moved in commerce.' Motion picture houses and other places listed in class three affect commerce if they customarily present films, performances, etc., 'which move in commerce.' And the establishments listed in class four affect commerce if they are within, or include within their own premises, an establishment 'the operations of which affect commerce.' Private clubs are excepted under certain conditions. See § 201(e).

Section 201(d) declares that 'discrimination or segregation' is supported by state action when carried on under color of any law, statute, ordinance, regulation or any custom or usage required or enforced by officials of the State or any of its subdivisions.

In addition, § 202 affirmatively declares that all persons 'shall be entitled to be free, at any establishment or place, from discrimination or segregation of any kind on the ground of race, color, religion, or national origin, if such discrimination or segregation is or purports to be required by any law, statute, ordinance, regulation, rule, or order of a State or any agency or political subdivision thereof.'

Finally, § 203 prohibits the withholding or denial, etc., of any right or privilege secured by § 201 and § 202 or the intimidation, threatening or coercion of any person with the purpose of interfering with any such right or the punishing, etc., of any person for exercising or attempting to exercise any such right.

. . .

4. Application of Title II to Heart of Atlanta Motel.

It is admitted that the operation of the motel brings it within the provisions of § 201(a) of the Act and that appellant refused to provide lodging for transient Negroes because of their race or color and that it intends to continue that policy unless restrained.

The sole question posed is, therefore, the constitutionality of the Civil Rights Act of 1964 as applied to these facts. The legislative history of the Act indicates that Congress based the Act on § 5 and the Equal Protection Clause of the Fourteenth Amendment as well as its power to regulate interstate commerce under Art. I, § 8, cl. 3, of the Constitution.

The Senate Commerce Committee made it quite clear that the fundamental object of Title II was to vindicate 'the deprivation of personal dignity that surely accompanies denials of equal access to public establishments.' At the same time, however, it noted that such an objective has been and could be readily achieved 'by congressional action based on the commerce power of the Constitution.' Our study of the legislative record, made in the light of prior cases, has brought us to the conclusion that Congress possessed ample power in this regard, and we have therefore not considered the other grounds relied upon. This is not to say that the remaining authority upon which it acted was not adequate, a question upon which we do not pass, but merely that since the commerce power is sufficient for our decision here we have considered it alone. Nor is § 201(d) or § 202, having to do with state action, involved here and we do not pass upon either of those sections.

* * *

7. *The Power of Congress Over Interstate Travel.*

The power of Congress to deal with these obstructions depends on the meaning of the Commerce Clause. Its meaning was first enunciated 140 years ago by the great Chief Justice John Marshall in *Gibbons v. Ogden*, (1824), in these words:

'The subject to be regulated is commerce; and * * * to ascertain the extent of the power, it becomes necessary to settle the meaning of the word. The counsel for the appellee would limit it to traffic, to buying and selling, or the interchange of commodities * * * but it is something more: it is intercourse * * * between nations, and parts of nations, in all its branches, and is regulated by prescribing rules for carrying on that intercourse.

'To what commerce does this power extend? The constitution informs us, to commerce 'with foreign nations, and among the several States, and with the Indian tribes.'

'It has, we believe, been universally admitted, that these words comprehend every species of commercial intercourse * * *. No sort of trade can be carried on * * * to which this power does not extend.

'The subject to which the power is next applied, is to commerce 'among the several States.' The word 'among' means intermingled * * *.

'* * * [I]t may very properly be restricted to that commerce which concerns more States than one. * * * The genius and character of the whole government seem to be, that its action is to be applied to all the * * * internal concerns (of the Nation) which affect the States generally; but not to those which are completely within a particular State, which do not affect other States, and with which it is not necessary to interfere, for the purpose of executing some of the general powers of the government.

'We are now arrived at the inquiry—What is this power?

'It is the power to regulate; that is, to prescribe the rule by which commerce is to be governed. This power, like all others vested in Congress, is complete in itself, may be exercised to its utmost extent, and acknowledges no limitations, other than are prescribed in the constitution. * * * If, as has always been understood, the sovereignty of Congress * * * is plenary as to those objects (specified in the Constitution), the power over commerce * * * is vested in Congress as absolutely as it would be in a single government, having in its constitution the same restrictions on the exercise of the power as are found in the constitution of the United States. The wisdom and the discretion of Congress, their identity with the people, and the influence which their constituents possess at elections, are, in this, as in many other instances, as that, for example, of declaring war, the sole restraints on which they have relied, to secure them from its abuse. They are the restraints on which the people must often rely solely, in all representative governments.

In short, the determinative test of the exercise of power by the Congress under the Commerce Clause is simply whether the activity sought to be regulated is 'commerce which concerns more States than one' and has a real and substantial relation to the national interest.

. . .

It is said that the operation of the motel here is of a purely local character. But, assuming this to be true, '(i)f it is interstate commerce that feels the pinch, it does not matter how local the operation which applies the squeeze.'

'The power of Congress over interstate commerce is not confined to the regulation of commerce among the states. It extends to those activities intrastate which so affect interstate commerce or the exercise of the power of Congress over it as to make regulation of them appropriate means to the attainment of a legitimate end, the exercise of the granted power of Congress to regulate interstate commerce.

Thus the power of Congress to promote interstate commerce also includes the power to regulate the local incidents thereof, including local activities in both the States of origin and destination, which might have a substantial and harmful effect upon that commerce. One need only examine the evidence which we have discussed above to see that Congress may—as it has—prohibit racial discrimination by motels serving travelers, however 'local' their operations may appear.

> **"ONE NEED ONLY examine the evidence which we have discussed above to see that Congress may—as it has—prohibit racial discrimination by motels serving travelers, however 'local' their operations may appear."**

. . .

We, therefore, conclude that the action of the Congress in the adoption of the Act as applied here to a motel which concededly serves interstate travelers is within the power granted it by the Commerce Clause of the Constitution, as interpreted by this Court for 140 years. It may be argued that Congress could have pursued other methods to eliminate the obstructions it found in interstate commerce caused by racial discrimination. But this is a matter of policy that rests entirely with the Congress not with the courts. How obstructions in commerce may be removed—what means are to be employed—is within the sound and exclusive discretion of the Congress. It is subject only to one caveat-that the means chosen by it must be reasonably adapted to the end permitted by the Constitution. We cannot say that its choice here was not so adapted. The Constitution requires no more.

Affirmed.

THE FLIP SIDE OF THE COMMERCE CLAUSE coin considers what states can do to regulate commerce. If the federal government can regulate most anything pursuant to the Commerce Clause, is there anything left for a state to regulate? Or, does federal power preempt any kind of state action? The answer is that states can regulate businesses as well, but they cannot pass regulations that unduly burden interstate commerce. The courts use a balancing approach to try to achieve this goal. The test asks if the state regulation is necessary and important to a state objective (such as the health and safety of its citizens), if the burden the regulation places on interstate commerce is reasonable, and whether or not the legislation is actually making an effort to favor a local industry over interstate commerce.

The last part of that test is particularly important. Many times a state legislature or local government will seek to pass a law that favors a local business. The executives of the business may be important community leaders or even contributors to campaigns. The employees are the friends, neighbors and voters in the community and strengthening their job security via a thriving business has local benefits. Of course the legislature will not be so obvious as to say "buy from company X," but the impact of the legislation may be exactly that. So the courts will look closely at the impact of state and local legislation to determine whether or not it does, in fact, intrude on interstate commerce.

For example, in a 1970 case, *Pike v. Bruce Church, Inc.*, the U.S. Supreme Court struck down an attempt of the State of Arizona to pack cantaloupes within the state. A company had spent more than $3,000,000 developing 6,400 acres of arid land for agricultural use and ended up producing a product recognized as being very high quality. Because cantaloupes need to get from field to dinner table quickly to prevent spoilage, the company located a packing facility thirty miles away. The problem was that the facility was across the border in California. Arizona wanted to retain production facilities within the State for a variety of reasons, including making sure that Arizona produce—especially high quality produce—was not stamped as a California product and because retaining packing facilities within the state helped employ Arizonans. Thus, the relevant Arizona agency stopped the company from shipping its crop to the California facility, thereby putting $700,000 of produce at risk of never being sold.

The Supreme Court said that such a regulation went too far. It recognized that Arizona did have legitimate interest in making sure to protect the brand of its state's products and to provide employment for people. But citing previous cases, Justice Stewart's opinion held that this was too great of a burden to place on the company and on interstate commerce.

■ IN 1970, THE U.S. SUPREME COURT STRUCK DOWN AN ATTEMPT OF THE STATE OF ARIZONA TO PACK CANTALOUPES WITHIN THE STATE.

Beyond the balancing tests to determine whether states impact interstate commerce, other laws are more straightforward. States cannot tax imports into the country because that is a power specifically reserved to Congress by the Constitution. Taxation itself has limits. All states impose some taxation whether on real estate, sales, or income, but states still must be careful that their taxing does not intrude into interstate commerce. Imposing an income tax on a state resident will not create such a burden, nor will a tax on real estate or sales of real estate. But a sales tax, especially in this Internet age, could create a substantial effect on interstate commerce, and a tax on income earned in the state by a non-resident may raise a question as well.

Amazon.com, LLC v. New York State Dept. of Taxation and Finance
81 A.D. 3d. 183 (2010)

NARDELLI, J.

. . .

Plaintiff Amazon.com, LLC, is a limited liability company incorporated in Delaware, and Amazon Services, LLC is a limited liability company incorporated in Nevada. Neither has offices, employees or property in New York. New York residents order products from Amazon solely through its Web site. Amazon does not have any in-state representatives in New York to assist customers in placing orders, and all technical support telephone calls or e-mails are handled by Amazon's representatives located outside of New York. Products sold by Amazon are shipped directly to customers from fulfillment centers located outside New York.

Amazon, however, has developed a program using entities known as Associates which it allows hundreds of thousands of independent third parties located around the world, many of which have provided Amazon with New York addresses, to advertise the Web site "Amazon.com" on their own Web sites. Visitors to the Affiliates' Web sites can click on the link and immediately be redirected to Amazon.com. If the visitor ends up making a purchase from Amazon on the Amazon.com Web site—and only in that event—the Associate is paid a commission. Any purchase made by the visitor takes place solely with Amazon, and all customer inquiries are handled only by Amazon, its corporate affiliates, or other sellers without any involvement of the Associate.

In the standard operating agreement which governs the relationship between Amazon and its Associates, Amazon expressly disavows any control over their activities or Web site content, except to state that Associates are prohibited from "misrepresent[ing] or embellish[ing]" the relationship between themselves and Amazon.

Co-plaintiff Overstock.com is a Delaware corporation with its principal and only place of business in Utah. As Amazon does, it offers various products over the Internet at discounted prices. Overstock does not have any retail stores or outlets. All goods purchased through Overstock.com are shipped to customers directly via the mail or by common carrier. None of Overstock's employees or representatives live in New York. Like Amazon, Overstock allows owners of other Web sites located around the world to advertise Overstock.com on their own Web sites.

Advertisements on the Web sites of these owners, known as Affiliates, consist of electronic links and banners. When a visitor to the Affiliate's Web site clicks on the link or banner, the visitor's browser navigates to the Overstock.com Web site.

The Master Agreement between Overstock and the Affiliate permits the Affiliate to provide advertising for Overstock in the form of links or banners. Affiliates are paid a commission only when a customer clicks on the link or banner and arrives at Overstock's Web site, and then purchases goods from Overstock. Furthermore, the Master Agreement provides that an Affiliate is only paid a commission if the Affiliate's Web site is the last site visited before Overstock's Web site, and the customer makes a purchase within a specified period of time. After the statute was enacted on April 23, 2008, Overstock suspended its relationships with all of its Affiliates in New York.

. . .

On this appeal Amazon raises three challenges to the statute. It does not pursue its facial claims with the Commerce Clause, but argues that, as applied to it, the statute is unconstitutional because it lacks a "substantial nexus" with in the State. Amazon also argues that the statute violates the Due Process Clause because, facially and as applied, it enacts an irrational and irrebuttable presumption, and is also vague. It lastly argues that the statute violates the Equal Protection Clause because it targets Amazon, one of the world's largest Internet retailers, in bad faith.

Overstock argues that the statute violates the Commerce Clause, both on its face, and as applied to Overstock. It likewise argues that the statute is unconstitutional on its face because it runs afoul of the Due Process Clause because of its vagueness.

. . .

COMMERCE CLAUSE FACIAL CHALLENGE

[The Commerce Clause] of the U.S. Constitution expressly authorizes Congress to "regulate Commerce with foreign Nations, and among the several States." While the Constitution "says nothing about the protection of interstate commerce in the absence of any action by Congress ... the Commerce Clause is more than an affirmative grant of power; it has a negative sweep as well." "'[B]y its own force', [it] prohibits certain state actions that interfere with interstate commerce."

In *Moran Towing Corp.*, the Court of Appeals outlined the four-prong test for determining whether a state tax violates the Commerce Clause. The court stated that the tax will be upheld " '[1] when the tax is applied to an activity with a substantial nexus with the taxing State, [2] is fairly apportioned, [3] does not discriminate against interstate commerce, and [4] is fairly related to the services provided by the State'." As was the situation in Moran, the challenge to the tax in this case only implicates the first prong, i.e., whether the activity involved has a substantial nexus with the taxing State.

The *sine qua non* for the finding that a party has a substantial nexus with New York, and is thus required to collect sales or use taxes, is that it have a physical presence within the state. Nevertheless, "[w]hile a physical presence of the vendor is required, it need not be substantial. "While it must constitute more than a 'slightest presence' "it may be manifested by the presence in the taxing State of the vendor's property or the conduct of economic activities in the taxing State performed by the vendor's personnel or on its behalf."

* * *

"THE WORLD has changed dramatically in the last two decades, and it may be that the physical presence test is outdated. An entity may now have a profound impact upon a foreign jurisdiction solely through its virtual projection via the Internet."

—CHIEF JUDGE JONATHAN LIPPMAN,
New York State Court of Appeals, from
the ruling which prompted Amazon.com's
appeal to the Supreme Court.

Our analysis leads us to the conclusion that on its face the statute does not violate the Commerce Clause. It imposes a tax collection obligation on an out-of-state vendor only where the vendor enters into a business-referral agreement with a New York State resident, and only when that resident receives a commission based on a sale in New York. The statute does not target the out-of-state vendor's sales through agents who are not New York residents. Thus, the nexus requirement is satisfied.

Of equal importance to the requirement that the out-of-state vendor have an in-state presence is that there must be solicitation, not passive advertising. While Tax Law § 1101(3)(8)(vi) creates the presumption that the in-state agent will solicit, it provides the out-of-state vendor with a ready escape hatch or safe harbor. The vendor merely has to include in its contract with the in-state vendor a provision prohibiting the in-state representative from "engaging in any solicitation activities in New York State that refer potential customers to the seller," and the in-state representative must provide an annual certification that it has not engaged in any prohibited solicitation activities as outlined in the memorandum. Thus, an in-state resident which merely acts as a conduit for linkage with the out-of-state vendor will be presumed to have not engaged in activity which would require the vendor to collect sales taxes. Presumably, there are vendors which will be able to execute the annual certification without fear of making a misrepresentation.

On the other hand, the State has a legitimate basis to conclude that many other in-state representatives will engage in direct solicitation, rather than mere advertising. For instance, a document prepared by Amazon explaining the benefits of joining the Associates' program, states, in pertinent part, "Our compensation philosophy is simple: reward Associates for their contributions to our business in unit volume and growth. Amazon is a fast growing business and we want our Associates to grow with us." The overview document goes on to state, "The Performance structure allows you to earn higher fees when you generate a sufficient volume of referrals that result in sales at Amazon.com during a month. *The higher your referrals, the greater your earnings will be.*"

Clearly, Amazon's program, reasonably, is not designed for the passive advertiser, but seeks growth by reliance upon representatives who will look to solicit business. The obligations imposed by the state to collect the tax only arise when the paradigm shifts from advertising to solicitation. Thus, until such time as the out-of-state vendor produces a certification from every one of its New York representatives that they have not engaged in solicitation, the facial challenge based upon the Commerce Clause must fail, since there is a set of circumstances under which the statute would be valid, i.e., when a New York representative uses some form of proactive solicitation which results in a sale by Amazon, and a commission to the representative; and the representative has an in-state presence sufficient to satisfy the substantial nexus test.

. . .

B. TAXING AND SPENDING POWER

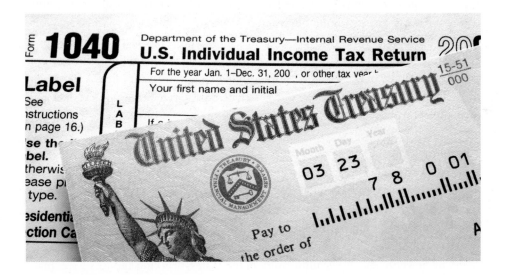

The federal government's authority to tax is well-established and extensive. The limitations on it primarily pertain to making sure that any duties or excise taxes are uniform throughout the country and that there are no import duties on any state. Also, Congress is limited in specifying a group on whom a tax would be levied. For example, Congress cannot impose a tax on anyone who is a chief executive officer of a company or who is a Hollywood star or a professional athlete. Any taxes must be neutrally framed.

Congress also has extensive spending power. In many instances this seems innocuous. Of course, Congress pays the nation's bills—but its spending power can also be used to achieve other regulatory aims or promulgate legislation. An example is that Congress has withheld highway construction money from states if they do not establish certain speed limits. It would be difficult, if not impossible, for Congress to establish a national speed limit, but it can achieve the same result by simply stating that the federal government will not provide money if the states fail to adhere to certain policies. The following case illustrates this kind of Congressional approach.

South Dakota v. Dole

107 S.Ct. 2793 (1987)

Chief Justice REHNQUIST delivered the opinion of the Court.

Petitioner South Dakota permits persons 19 years of age or older to purchase beer containing up to 3.2% alcohol. In 1984 Congress enacted 23 U.S.C. § 158, which directs the Secretary of Transportation to withhold a percentage of federal highway funds otherwise allocable from States "in which the purchase or public possession ... of any alcoholic beverage by a person who is less than twenty-one years of age is lawful." The State sued in United States District Court seeking a declaratory judgment that [the statute] violates the constitutional limitations on congressional exercise of the spending power and violates the Twenty-first Amendment to the United States Constitution. The District Court rejected the State's claims, and the Court of Appeals for the Eighth Circuit affirmed.

* * *

These arguments present questions of the meaning of the Twenty-first Amendment, the bounds of which have escaped precise definition. Despite the extended treatment of the question by the parties, however, we need not decide in this case whether that Amendment would prohibit an attempt by Congress to legislate directly a national minimum drinking age. Here, Congress has acted indirectly under its spending power to encourage uniformity in the States' drinking ages. As we explain below, we find this legislative effort within constitutional bounds even if Congress may not regulate drinking ages directly.

The [Taxing and Spending Clause of the] Constitution empowers Congress to "lay and collect Taxes, Duties, Imposts, and Excises, to pay the Debts and provide for the common Defence and general Welfare of the United States." Incident to this power, Congress may attach conditions on the receipt of federal funds, and has repeatedly employed the power "to further broad policy objectives by conditioning receipt of federal moneys upon compliance by the recipient with federal statutory and administrative directives." The breadth of this power was made clear in *United States v. Butler,* where the Court, resolving a longstanding debate over the scope of the Spending Clause, determined that "the power of Congress to authorize expenditure of public moneys for public purposes is not limited by the direct grants of legislative power found in the Constitution." Thus, objectives not thought to be within Article I's "enumerated legislative fields," may nevertheless be attained through the use of the spending power and the conditional grant of federal funds.

The spending power is of course not unlimited, but is instead subject to several general restrictions articulated in our cases. The first of these limitations is derived from the language of the Constitution itself: the exercise of the spending power must be in pursuit of "the general welfare." In considering whether a particular expenditure is intended to serve general public purposes, courts should defer substantially to the judgment of Congress. Second, we have required that if Congress desires to condition the States' receipt of federal funds, it "must do so unambiguously ..., enabl[ing] the States to exercise their choice knowingly, cognizant of the consequences of their participation." Third, our cases have suggested (without significant elaboration) that conditions on federal grants might be illegitimate if they are unrelated "to the federal interest in particular national projects or programs." Finally, we have noted that other constitutional provisions may provide an independent bar to the conditional grant of federal funds.

South Dakota does not seriously claim that § 158 is inconsistent with any of the first three restrictions mentioned above. We can readily conclude that the provision is designed to serve the general welfare, especially in light of the fact that "the concept of welfare or the opposite is shaped by Congress [...]." Congress found that the differing drinking ages in the States created particular incentives for young persons to combine their desire to drink with their ability to drive, and that this interstate problem required a national solution. The means it chose to address this dangerous situation were reasonably calculated to advance the general welfare. The conditions upon which States receive the funds, moreover, could not be more clearly stated by Congress. And the State itself, rather than challenging the germaneness of the condition to federal purposes, admits that it "has never contended that the congressional action was ... unrelated to a national concern in the absence of the Twenty-first Amendment." Indeed, the condition imposed by Congress is directly related to one of the main purposes for which highway funds are expended-safe interstate travel. This goal of the interstate highway system had been frustrated by varying drinking ages among the States. A Presidential commission appointed to study alcohol-related accidents and fatalities on the Nation's highways concluded that the lack of uniformity in the States' drinking ages created "an incentive to drink and drive" because "young persons commut[e] to border States where the drinking age is lower." By enacting § 158, Congress conditioned the receipt of federal funds in a way reasonably calculated to address this particular impediment to a purpose for which the funds are expended.

. . .

[T]he "independent constitutional bar" limitation on the spending power is not, as petitioner suggests, a prohibition on the indirect achievement of objectives which Congress is not empowered to achieve directly. Instead, we think that the language in our earlier opinions stands for the unexceptionable proposition that the power may not be used to induce the States to engage in activities that would themselves be unconstitutional. Thus, for example, a grant of federal funds conditioned on invidiously discriminatory state action or the infliction of cruel and unusual punishment would be an illegitimate exercise of the Congress' broad spending power. But no such claim can be or is made here. Were South Dakota to succumb to the blandishments offered by Congress and raise its drinking age to 21, the State's action in so doing would not violate the constitutional rights of anyone.

. . .

Here Congress has offered relatively mild encouragement to the States to enact higher minimum drinking ages than they would otherwise choose. But the enactment of such laws remains the prerogative of the States not merely in theory but in fact. Even if Congress might lack the power to impose a national minimum drinking age directly, we conclude that encouragement to state action found in § 158 is a valid use of the spending power. Accordingly, the judgment of the Court of Appeals is
Affirmed.

THE SPENDING AND TAXING AUTHORITY of Congress, and not the Commerce Clause, was identified as the Constitutional justification for the 2010 Health Care Bill (The Patient Protection and Affordable Care Act). Chief Justice Roberts explained in *National Federation of Independent Businesses v. Sebelius*:

Three considerations allay this concern. First, and most importantly, it is abundantly clear the Constitution does not guarantee that individuals may avoid taxation through inactivity. A capitation, after all, is a tax that everyone must pay simply for existing, and capitations are expressly contemplated by the Constitution. The Court today holds that our Constitution protects us from federal regulation under the Commerce Clause so long as we abstain from the regulated activity. But from its creation, the Constitution has made no such promise with respect to taxes.

Whether the mandate can be upheld under the Commerce Clause is a question about the scope of federal authority. Its answer depends on whether Congress can exercise what all acknowledge to be the novel course of directing individuals to purchase insurance. Congress's use of the Taxing Clause to encourage buying something is, by contrast, not new. Tax incentives already promote, for example, purchasing homes and professional educations. Sustaining the mandate as a tax depends only on whether Congress *has* properly exercised its taxing power to encourage purchasing health insurance, not whether it *can*. Upholding the individual mandate under the Taxing Clause thus does not recognize any new federal power. It determines that Congress has used an existing one.

Second, Congress's ability to use its taxing power to influence conduct is not without limits. A few of our cases policed these limits aggressively, invalidating punitive exactions obviously designed to regulate behavior otherwise regarded at the time as beyond federal authority. More often and more recently we have declined to closely examine the regulatory motive or effect of revenue-raising measures. We have nonetheless maintained that "'there comes a time in the extension of the penalizing features of the so-called tax when it loses its character as such and becomes a mere penalty with the characteristics of regulation and punishment.'"

We have already explained that the shared responsibility payment's practical characteristics pass muster as a tax under our narrowest interpretations of the taxing power. Because the tax at hand is within even those strict limits, we need not here decide the precise point at which an exaction becomes so punitive that the taxing power does not authorize it. It remains true, however, that the "'power to tax is not the power to destroy while this Court sits.'"

Third, although the breadth of Congress's power to tax is greater than its power to regulate commerce, the taxing power does not give Congress the same degree of control over individual behavior. Once we recognize that Congress may regulate a particular decision under the Commerce Clause, the Federal Government can bring its full weight to bear. Congress may simply command individuals to do as it directs. An individual who disobeys may be subjected to criminal sanctions. Those sanctions can include not only fines and imprisonment, but all the attendant consequences of being branded a criminal: deprivation of otherwise protected civil rights, such as the right to bear arms or vote in elections; loss of employment opportunities; social stigma; and severe disabilities in other controversies, such as custody or immigration disputes.

By contrast, Congress's authority under the taxing power is limited to requiring an individual to pay money into the Federal Treasury, no more. If a tax is properly paid, the Government has no power to compel or punish individuals subject to it. We do not make light of the severe burden that taxation—especially taxation motivated by a regulatory purpose—can impose. But imposition of a tax nonetheless leaves an individual with a lawful choice to do or not do a certain act, so long as he is willing to pay a tax levied on that choice. The Affordable Care Act's requirement that certain individuals pay a financial penalty for not obtaining health insurance may reasonably be characterized as a tax. Because the Constitution permits such a tax, it is not our role to forbid it, or to pass upon its wisdom or fairness.

C. NATIONAL SECURITY POWER

Fundamental to any government, including the United States, is the obligation to keep the country safe. Simply saying that a government act is justified by national security reasons is not sufficient, but if there is a national security threat, the Congress and the President have significant powers to enact legislation to protect the country. In *The Steel Seizure Case*, Justice Jackson's concurrence famously elaborates a three-part test discussing the abilities of the president and congress to act collectively and separately.

The Steel Seizure Case

343 U.S. 1952 (1952)

Mr. Justice BLACK delivered the opinion of the Court.

. . . In the latter part of 1951, a dispute arose between the steel companies and their employees over terms and conditions that should be included in new collective bargaining agreements. Long-continued conferences failed to resolve the dispute. On December 18, 1951, the employees' representative, United Steelworkers of America, C.I.O., gave notice of an intention to strike when the existing bargaining agreements expired on December 31. The Federal Mediation and Conciliation Service then intervened in an effort to get labor and management to agree. This failing, the President on December 22, 1951, referred the dispute to the Federal Wage Stabilization Board to investigate and make recommendations for fair and equitable terms of settlement. This Board's report resulted in no settlement. On April 4, 1952, the Union gave notice of a nation-wide strike called to begin at 12:01 a.m. April 9. The indispensability of steel as a component of substantially all weapons and other war materials led the President to believe that the proposed work stoppage would immediately jeopardize our national defense and that governmental seizure of the steel mills was necessary in order to assure the continued availability of steel. Reciting these considerations for his action, the President, a few hours before the strike was to begin, issued [the executive order at issue here]. The order directed the Secretary of Commerce to take possession of most of the steel mills and keep them running. The Secretary immediately issued his own possessory orders, calling upon the

Arguing the Powers of the Presidency

"OUR NATIONAL SECURITY and our chances for peace depend on our defense production. Our defense production depends on steel... I have no doubt that if our defense program fails, the danger of war, the possibility of hostile attack, grows that much greater. I would not be faithful to my responsibilities as President if I did not use every effort to keep this from happening."

— PRESIDENT HARRY TRUMAN (left)

"THE PRESIDENT'S POWER, if any, to issue the order must stem either from an act of Congress or from the Constitution itself. There is no statute that expressly authorizes the President to take possession of property as he did here."

— JUSTICE HUGO BLACK (below)

"Harry S. Truman" by Frank Gatteri, United States Army Signal Corps. Image courtesy of the Truman Library via Wikimedia Commons

presidents of the various seized companies to serve as operating managers for the United States. They were directed to carry on their activities in accordance with regulations and directions of the Secretary. The next morning the President sent a message to Congress reporting his action. Twelve days later he sent a second message. Congress has taken no action.

* * *

The President's power, if any, to issue the order must stem either from an act of Congress or from the Constitution itself. There is no statute that expressly authorizes the President to take possession of property as he did here. Nor is there any act of Congress to which our attention has been directed from which such a power can fairly be implied. Indeed, we do not understand the Government to rely on statutory authorization for this seizure. There are two statutes which do authorize the President to take both personal and real property under certain conditions. However, the Government admits that these conditions were not met and that the President's order was not rooted in either of the statutes. The Government refers to the seizure provisions of one of these statutes (§ 201(b) of the Defense Production Act) as "much too cumbersome, involved, and time-consuming for the crisis which was at hand."

■ JUSTICE HUGO BLACK, by Harris & Ewing. Courtesy of the U.S. Library of Congress Prints and Photographs.

Moreover, the use of the seizure technique to solve labor disputes in order to prevent work stoppages was not only unauthorized by any congressional enactment; prior to this controversy, Congress had refused to adopt that method of settling labor disputes. When the Taft-Hartley Act was under consideration in 1947, Congress rejected an amendment which would have authorized such governmental seizures in cases of emergency. Apparently it was thought that the technique of seizure, like that of compulsory arbitration, would interfere with the process of collective bargaining. Consequently, the plan Congress adopted in that Act did not provide for seizure under any circumstances. Instead, the plan sought to bring about settlements by use of the customary devices of mediation, conciliation, investigation by boards of inquiry, and public reports. In some instances temporary injunctions were authorized to provide cooling-off periods. All this failing, unions were left free to strike after a secret vote by employees as to whether they wished to accept their employers' final settlement offer.

It is clear that if the President had authority to issue the order he did, it must be found in some provisions of the Constitution. And it is not claimed that express constitutional language grants this power to the President. The contention is that presidential power should be implied from the aggregate of his powers under the Constitution. Particular reliance is placed on provisions in Article II which say that "the executive Power shall be vested in a President * * *"; that "he shall take Care that the Laws be faithfully executed"; and that he "shall be Commander in Chief of the Army and Navy of the United States."

The order cannot properly be sustained as an exercise of the President's military power as Commander in Chief of the Armed Forces. The Government attempts to do so by citing a number of cases upholding broad powers in military commanders engaged in day-to-day fighting in a theater of war. Such cases need not concern us here. Even though 'theater of war' be an expanding concept, we cannot with faithfulness to our constitutional system hold that the Commander in Chief of the Armed Forces has the ultimate power as such to take possession of private property in order to keep labor disputes from stopping production. This is a job for the Nation's lawmakers, not for its military authorities.

Nor can the seizure order be sustained because of the several constitutional provisions that grant executive power to the President. In the framework of our Constitution, the President's power to see that the laws are faithfully executed refutes the idea that he is to be a lawmaker. The Constitution limits his functions in the lawmaking process to the recommending of laws he thinks wise and the vetoing of laws he thinks bad. And the Constitution is neither silent nor equivocal about who shall make laws which the President is to execute. The first section of the first article says that "All legislative Powers herein granted shall be vested in a Congress of the United States * * *." After granting many powers to the Congress, Article I goes on to provide that Congress may "make all Laws which shall be necessary and proper for carrying into Execution the foregoing Powers and all other Powers vested by this Constitution in the Government of the United States, or in any Department or Officer thereof."

The President's order does not direct that a congressional policy be executed in a manner prescribed by Congress—it directs that a presidential policy be executed in a manner prescribed by the President. The preamble of the order itself, like that of many statutes, sets out reasons why the President believes certain policies should be adopted, proclaims these policies as rules of conduct to be followed, and again, like a statute, authorizes a government official to promulgate additional rules and regulations consistent with the policy proclaimed and needed to carry that policy into execution. The power of Congress to adopt such public policies as those proclaimed by the order is beyond question. It can authorize the taking of private property for public use. It can makes laws regulating the relationships between employers and employees, prescribing rules designed to settle labor disputes, and fixing wages and working conditions in certain fields of our economy. The Constitution did not subject this law-making power of Congress to presidential or military supervision or control.

It is said that other Presidents without congressional authority have taken possession of private business enterprises in order to settle labor disputes. But even if this be true, Congress has not thereby lost its exclusive constitutional authority to make laws necessary and proper to carry out the powers vested by the Constitution "in the Government of the United States, or in any Department or Officer thereof."

The Founders of this Nation entrusted the law making power to the Congress alone in both good and bad times. It would do no good to recall the historical events, the fears of power and the hopes for freedom that lay behind their choice. Such a review would but confirm our holding that this seizure order cannot stand.

The judgment of the District Court is affirmed.

III. Business-Specific Individual Rights

A. PROPERTY RIGHTS

The right to own individual property was a core belief of the founders of the country. Like other individual rights, the Bill of Rights provides explicit protection of the right to own property without interference from the government. The Fifth Amendment tends to be most famous for its right against self-incrimination. One hears defendants in a criminal case say that they refuse to answer a question (from a prosecutor or a Congressional inquiry) on the grounds that their answer might tend to incriminate them. But the Fifth Amendment also has the "Takings Clause."

> No person shall be held to answer for a capital, or otherwise infamous crime, unless on a presentment or indictment of a Grand Jury, except in cases arising in the land or naval forces, or in the Militia, when in actual service in time of War or public danger; nor shall any person be

subject for the same offence to be twice put in jeopardy of life or limb; nor
shall be compelled in any criminal case to be a witness against himself,
nor be deprived of life, liberty, or property, without due process of law;
nor shall private property be taken for public use, without just compensation. (U.S.C. Const. Amend. V.)

The Takings Clause prevents government from seizing one's property unless certain procedures are met. Those procedures entail the government's eminent domain
powers. Let's say that the government wants to build a new highway. The government cannot simply take away your land or your house to build a road through it.
At the same time, the government's civil engineers have undoubtedly conducted
studies so they have a plan for the most efficient (i.e. easier to build with less material) road after taking into account safety concerns (i.e. that the road does not curve
wildly all over the place). All of this is based on which landowners have agreed to
sell their homes and which landowners have refused to sell. Pursuant to the power
of eminent domain, the government can build the road, but it must provide just
compensation to the landowner for taking the land. The following case provides a
traditional example of the interaction between the protections of the Takings Clause
and the government's power of eminent domain.

Berman v. Parker

S48 U.S. 26 (1954)

Mr. Justice DOUGLAS delivered the opinion of the Court.

. . . Congress made a 'legislative determination' that 'owing to technological
and sociological changes, obsolete lay-out, and other factors, conditions existing
in the District of Columbia with respect to substandard housing and blighted areas,
including the use of buildings in alleys as dwellings for human habitation, are injurious to the public health, safety, morals, and welfare, and it is hereby declared to be
the policy of the United States to protect and promote the welfare of the inhabitants
of the seat of the Government by eliminating all such injurious conditions by employing all means necessary and appropriate for the purpose'.

Section 2 goes on to declare that acquisition of property is necessary to eliminate these housing conditions.
* * *

The first project undertaken under the Act relates to Project Area B in South-
west Washington, D.C. In 1950 the Planning Commission prepared and published
a comprehensive plan for the District. Surveys revealed that in Area B, 64.3% of
the dwellings were beyond repair, 18.4% needed major repairs, only 17.3% were
satisfactory; 57.8% of the dwellings had outside toilets, 60.3% had no baths, 29.3%

lacked electricity, 82.2% had no wash basins or laundry tubs, 83.8% lacked central heating. In the judgment of the District's Director of Health it was necessary to redevelop Area B in the interests of public health. The population of Area B amounted to 5,012 persons, of whom 97.5% were Negroes.

The plan for Area B specifies the boundaries and allocates the use of the land for various purposes. It makes detailed provisions for types of dwelling units and provides that at least one-third of them are to be low-rent housing with a maximum rental of $17 per room per month.

After a public hearing, the Commissioners approved the plan and the Planning Commission certified it to the Agency for execution. The Agency undertook the preliminary steps for redevelopment of the area when this suit was brought.

Appellants own property in Area B at 712 Fourth Street, S.W. It is not used as a dwelling or place of habitation. A department store is located on it. Appellants object to the appropriation of this property for the purposes of the project. They claim that their property may not be taken constitutionally for this project. It is commercial, not residential property; it is not slum housing; it will be put into the project under the management of a private, not a public, agency and redeveloped for private, not public, use. That is the argument; and the contention is that appellants' private property is being taken contrary to two mandates of the Fifth Amendment—(1) 'No person shall * * * be deprived of * * * property, without due process of law'; (2) 'nor shall private property be taken for public use, without just compensation.' To take for the purpose of ridding the area of slums is one thing; it is quite another, the argument goes, to take a man's property merely to develop a better balanced, more attractive community. The District Court, while agreeing in general with that argument, saved the Act by construing it to mean that the Agency could condemn property only for the reasonable necessities of slum clearance and prevention, its concept of 'slum' being the existence of conditions 'injurious to the public health, safety, morals and welfare.'

The power of Congress over the District of Columbia includes all the legislative powers which a state may exercise over its affairs. We deal, in other words, with what traditionally has been known as the police power. An attempt to define its reach or trace its outer limits is fruitless, for each case must turn on its own facts. The definition is essentially the product of legislative determinations addressed to the purposes of government, purposes neither abstractly nor historically capable of complete definition. Subject to specific constitutional limitations, when the legislature has spoken, the public interest has been declared in terms well-nigh conclusive. In such cases the legislature, not the judiciary, is the main guardian of the public needs to be served by social legislation, whether it be Congress legislating concerning the District of Columbia. This principle admits of no exception merely because the power of eminent domain is involved. The role of the judiciary in determining whether that power is being exercised for a public purpose is an extremely narrow one.

Public safety, public health, morality, peace and quiet, law and order-these are some of the more conspicuous examples of the traditional application of the police power to municipal affairs. Yet they merely illustrate the scope of the power and do not delimit it. Miserable and disreputable housing conditions may do more than spread disease and crime and immorality. They may also suffocate the spirit by reducing the people who live there to the status of cattle. They may indeed make living an almost insufferable burden. They may also be an ugly sore, a blight on the community which robs it of charm, which makes it a place from which men turn. The misery of housing may despoil a community as an open sewer may ruin a river.

We do not sit to determine whether a particular housing project is or is not desirable. The concept of the public welfare is broad and inclusive. The values it represents are spiritual as well as physical, aesthetic as well as monetary. It is within the power of the legislature to determine that the community should be beautiful as well as healthy, spacious as well as clean, well-balanced as well as carefully patrolled. In the present case, the Congress and its authorized agencies have made determinations that take into account a wide variety of values. It is not for us to reappraise them. If those who govern the District of Columbia decide that the Nation's Capital should be beautiful as well as sanitary, there is nothing in the Fifth Amendment that stands in the way.

Once the object is within the authority of Congress, the right to realize it through the exercise of eminent domain is clear. For the power of eminent domain is merely the means to the end. Once the object is within the authority of Congress, the means by which it will be attained is also for Congress to determine. Here one of the means chosen is the use of private enterprise for redevelopment of the area. Appellants argue that this makes the project a taking from one businessman for the benefit of another businessman. But the means of executing the project are for Congress and Congress alone to determine, once the public purpose has been established. The public end may be as well or better served through an agency of private enterprise than through a department of government-or so the Congress might conclude. We cannot say that public ownership is the sole method of promoting the public purposes of community redevelopment projects. What we have said also disposes of any contention concerning the fact that certain property owners in the area may be permitted to repurchase their properties for redevelopment in harmony with the overall plan. That, too, is a legitimate means which Congress and its agencies may adopt, if they choose.

> **"IF OWNER AFTER OWNER** were permitted to resist these redevelopment programs on the ground that his particular property was not being used against the public interest, integrated plans for redevelopment would suffer greatly."

In the present case, Congress and its authorized agencies attack the problem of the blighted parts of the community on an area rather than on a structure-by-structure basis. That, too, is opposed by appellants. They maintain that since their building does not imperil health or safety nor contribute to the making of a slum or a blighted area, it cannot be swept into a redevelopment plan by the mere dictum of the Planning Commission or the Commissioners. The particular uses to be made of the land in the project were determined with regard to the needs of the particular community. The experts concluded that if the community were to be healthy, if it were not to revert again to a blighted or slum area as though possessed of a congenital disease, the area must be planned as a whole. It was not enough, they believed, to remove existing buildings that were insanitary or unsightly. It was important to redesign the whole area so as to eliminate the conditions that cause slums— the overcrowding of dwellings, the lack of parks, the lack of adequate streets and alleys, the absence of recreational areas, the lack of light and air, the presence of outmoded street patterns. It was believed that the piecemeal approach, the removal of individual structures that were offensive, would be only a palliative. The entire area needed redesigning so that a balanced, integrated plan could be developed for the region, including not only new homes but also schools, churches, parks, streets, and shopping centers. In this way it was hoped that the cycle of decay of the area could be controlled and the birth of future slums prevented. Such diversification in future use is plainly relevant to the maintenance of the desired housing standards and therefore within congressional power.

* * *

The rights of these property owners are satisfied when they receive that just compensation which the Fifth Amendment exacts as the price of the taking.

The judgment of the District Court, as modified by this opinion, is *Affirmed*.

———————————

SOME COMMENTATORS HAVE ARGUED that the Takings Clause protects against other kinds of government actions as well. For example, some have argued that the primarily responsibility of corporations is to maximize profit for their shareholders. That may itself require some elaboration, but assuming that statement to be true, then legislation that permits managers to take into account the impact of corporate actions on non-shareholder constituents, might be considered unconstitutional Takings. The academic or philosophical version of the consideration of non-shareholder constituents is called Stakeholder Theory, and the legal analogues are the Corporate Constituency Statutes. The excerpt from the following law review article by Lynda Oswald sets out this argument:

> Shareholders have a property interest in their shares, for the shares simply represent their ownership of the corporation. It seems almost axiomatic that constituency statutes—at least to the extent that they are ever exercised (and more likely to the extent that a legitimate threat of

exercise exists)—work a very real diminution in the shareholders' interests in their corporation. If managers need no longer act in the best interests of the shareholders, and indeed are permitted to explicitly and deliberately act contrary to those interests, the value of the shareholders' ownership interest in the corporation is reduced, for their claim to residual earnings is weakened. Such statutes cannot be justified as legitimate police power regulations because the complete absence of standards and enforcement mechanisms that uniformly characterizes these statutes makes it clear that the promotion of the common good was neither the motivating factor for legislative action nor the certain outcome of corporate exercises of such statutes [. . .] A very large chunk of societal wealth is thereby rendered bereft of constitutional protection and subject to virtually unlimited state control. Lynda J. Oswald, *Shareholders v. Stakeholders: Evaluating Corporate Constituency Statutes Under the Takings Clause*, 24 J. Corp. L. 1, 2-3 (1998).

B. COMMERCIAL SPEECH & OTHER FIRST AMENDMENT RIGHTS

First Amendment freedoms are perhaps the most well known aspects of the Constitution and its Bill of Rights. Everyone knows that they have the right to speak freely. Everyone has an opinion. Americans also have the right to practice a religion of their choosing and to assemble together. The First Amendment guarantees a free press. These freedoms are central to this country's identity.

Most of the litigation surrounding First Amendment rights concerns just how far these freedoms extend. Are there any limits? Can government restrict these freedoms? If so, how would they do it? What tests must a government meet? No freedom can be completely unencumbered. The right to speak freely does not give a person the right to yell "fire" in a crowded theater (As Justice Holmes famously observed, "[t]he most stringent protection of free speech would not protect a man in falsely shouting fire in a theatre and causing a panic."). The first half of the "free exercise clause"— the portion of the First Amendment that guarantees freedom of religion, states that Congress should not pass laws establishing any kind of preferred religion. While the lines on this "Establishment Clause" have been very difficult to draw, what is reasonably clear is that in order to provide freedom of religious belief, one has to also place limits on the reliance on religious belief—or at least religious action.

Businesses do not face First Amendment issues as frequently as does government. After all, the Constitution is aimed at restricting governmental power rather than business power *per se*. Nevertheless, there are times and places where cases arise.

Continuing with the example of freedom of religion, Title VII of the Civil Rights Act of 1964 (42 U.S.C. § 2000 *et. seq.*) passed under the Commerce Clause, requires that businesses provide "reasonable accommodations" for people to exercise their religion freely, even if this means at work. As the next case illustrates, these issues have caused increasing conflicts for Muslims in the workplace in the aftermath of September 11, 2001.

E.E.O.C. v. Alamo Rent-A-Car, LLC.

432 F. Supp.2d 1006 (D. Arizona 2006)

SILVER, District Judge

Bilan Nur is a Muslim woman who immigrated to the United States from Somalia in 1998. Alamo hired Ms. Nur as a rental agent in November 1999 for a rental agency location on East Washington Street in Phoenix, Arizona. In this position, Ms. Nur rented cars to customers, accepted payment, and answered the telephone; her duties required interaction with clients. Until the events which led to her termination, Ms. Nur's job performance was "fine." While Ms. Nur was employed by Alamo, the company had in effect a "Dress Smart Policy" which promoted a favorable first impression with customers, and expressly prohibited employees from wearing certain clothing and accessories, for example, the wearing of more than one earring, open toe shoes, and half-grown beards. Plaintiff states that the Policy did not expressly prohibit the wearing of head coverings; Alamo counters that the Policy prohibits the wearing of any "garment or item of outer clothing not specifically mentioned in the policy...."

The Muslim holiday of Ramadan began on November 16, 2001. At some point in November 2001, Plaintiff spoke to Alamo's "City Manager" Victor Bellavia and requested permission to wear a head covering at work during the Ramadan holiday. Mr. Bellavia contacted Alamo's Human Resource Manager for the Western Region, Heather Phillips, about Ms. Nur's request for an accommodation to wear a head covering during Ramadan. Ms. Phillips instructed Bellavia that Plaintiff would be allowed to wear a head covering at work in the back of the office, but that she would need to remove the head covering while at the rental counter. Alamo did not excuse Ms. Nur from working at the rental counter during Ramadan.

On December 1, 2001, an Alamo manager. Herman Schilling wrote Ms. Nur a "Counselling [sic] Review," which stated: "You had previously been told by the City Manager that you are not allowed to wear a hat or head covering in your position at work. When I arrived at work this morning you were wearing a veil over your hair and I told you to clock-out and discuss with the City Manager on Sunday." The next day, December 2, 2001, Ms. Nur received another Counseling Review, pursuant to which she was suspended and advised: "You had been previously informed by the city manager that you are not allowed to wear a hat or head covering in your position at work. You were wearing a veil over your hair this morning. You were sent home yesterday for the same violation and will be sent home again today. You need to discuss this issue with the city manager tomorrow." The next day (December 3, 2001), Ms. Nur again received a counseling review. In this review, Mr. Bellavia and LaShunda Brown advised Ms. Nur: "Bilan you have been verbally warned on several different occassion [sic] reguarding [sic] your work uniform. You were also sent home on 12/01-12/02 for failing to comply with company policy. You are been [sic] suspended pending investigation. You are to return on 12/6/01, 8:30 am, to meet with the City Manager."

Also on December 3, 2001, Mr. Bellavia wrote a memorandum to the file summarizing the disciplinary actions taken against Ms. Nur:

> Bilan Nur approached me on Tuesday November 20, 2001 asking me if she was allowed to wear a scarf/head covering during her religious holiday Rhamadan. I informed her that I would run it by Human Resources and let her know if she was allowed to do this. Last year in December of 2000 Sal Vargas [Assistant City Manager] informed her she could not do this and made her take it off. Heather Phillips from Human Resources informed me that she was not allowed to have her head covered do [sic] to the fact its [sic] not part of the uniform policy. I informed this to Bilan and she was not happy with the answer. When the Holiday started she insisted on having her head covered. I informed Heather of the situation and she informed me to warn her that she could not wear it and if she continue [sic] to come to working [sic] wearing it Alamo would then start counseling her immediately. On Saturday December 1, 2001 she came to work not meeting the companies [sic] uniform policy, we counseled her on it and sent her home. On Sunday December 2, 2001 Bilan did not follow the company policy on her uniform and we counseled her again and sent her home. On Monday December 3, 2001 Bilan did not follow company policy with regards to Alamo uniform policy, we counseled her and suspended her three-day [sic] which may result in her termination of employment with Alamo Rent a Car.

Alamo terminated Ms. Nur's employment on December 6, 2001 for violation of company rules. The termination form indicates that Ms. Nur was not eligible for re-hire.

* * *

Alamo contends that EEOC has failed to prove a *prima facie* case of religious discrimination, arguing that Ms. Nur's religious beliefs did not conflict with her job requirements because her "personal practice did not require that she wear a [head covering] at all times during Ramadan." Alamo points to evidence that during

Ramadan in 2000 (the year prior to the Ramadan at issue), Alamo's management asked Ms. Nur to remove her head covering and she complied, and did not assert a religious need to object to the request. Alamo concludes that this evidence supports a question of fact regarding "whether Ms. Nur's religious beliefs are what she is stating in this lawsuit." Similarly, Alamo states that because Ramadan in 2001 began on Friday, November 16 and they say Plaintiff did not request an accommodation permitting her to wear a head covering until Tuesday, November 20, 2001, this could suggest that Ms. Nur's religious beliefs did not actually dictate that she wear a head covering at work under all circumstances. Alamo further states that Plaintiff went to the press with her story immediately after her termination and gave conflicting statements at deposition regarding whether she contacted the press or the press contacted her, arguing this casts doubt on whether Ms. Nur's statement of her religious beliefs is credible.

"[I]t is entirely appropriate, indeed necessary, for a court to engage in analysis of the sincerity—as opposed, of course to the verity—of someone's religious beliefs in ... the Title VII context." Viewed in the light most favorable to Alamo, however, the evidence does not support the existence of a material factual issue regarding the sincerity of Ms. Nur's religious belief at the time of her termination. During Ramadan 2001, Ms. Nur continued to wear a head covering despite warnings from her supervisors that she would be subjected to progressive disciplinary action, and then was terminated because Alamo concluded she had repeatedly violated its official dress policy. Ms. Nur's actions strongly "demonstrate that [s]he attached the utmost religious significance" to her belief that her religion required her to cover her head during Ramadan.

Assistant City Manager Sal Vargas testified that he required Plaintiff to remove her head covering during Ramadan in 2000, which he stated she did do without raising any objection, religious or otherwise. Alamo contends that this fact raises a question about whether Ms. Nur's belief was sincere in 2001. An analysis of the sincerity of Ms. Nur's belief should "be measured by the employee's words and conduct at the time the conflict arose between the belief and the employment requirement." In the Complaint, the EEOC alleges that Alamo discriminated against Ms. Nur with regard to her assertion of her religious belief in November and December 2001, not in 2000. Although there is a dispute of fact regarding whether Ms. Nur was permitted to wear a head covering during Ramadan in 1999 and 2000, that dispute is not relevant to the sincerity of Ms. Nur's belief in the Fall of 2001, when Ms. Nur's assertions of religious belief led to her termination. Alamo further contends that because in 2001 Ramadan began on November 16, and because Alamo asserts that Ms. Nur did not raise the head covering issue with Mr. Bellavia until November 20, this is evidence that might lead a fact finder to infer that Ms. Nur did not wear a head covering at work during the first few days of Ramadan 2001, i.e., between November 16 and November 20. Similarly, Alamo suggests that because Ms. Nur was not first disciplined until December 1, 2001, 15 days into the Ramadan holiday, a reasonable fact finder might infer that Plaintiff had acted consistently

ARTICLE: EQUAL EMPLOYMENT

Alamo Car Rental Guilty of Religious Bias Federal Court Rules In EEOC Lawsuit, EEOC Said Muslim Employee Fired for Wearing Head Scarf Shortly After 9/11 Attacks.

■ STATEMENT RELEASED by the Equal Employment Opportunity Commission.

FURTHER READING:
www.eeoc.gov/eeoc/
newsroom/release/5-30-06.cfm

PHOENIX—IN A LEGAL VICTORY for the U.S. Equal Employment Opportunity Commission (EEOC), Arizona Federal District Court Judge Roslyn Silver ruled that Alamo Car Rental committed post-9/11 backlash discrimination based on religion when it terminated a Somali customer sales representative in December 2001 for refusing to remove her head scarf during the Muslim holy month of Ramadan.

In the first post-9/11 backlash case brought by the EEOC's Phoenix District Office, the court took the unusual step of finding the religious discrimination so clear cut based on the pleadings that it did not need to be resolved by a jury.

"It is extremely rare that a court will find discrimination based solely on the pleadings," said Mary Jo O'Neill, Regional Attorney for the Phoenix District Office. "The court found undisputed evidence that Alamo should have approved this employee's request to wear her head scarf as a religious accommodation or proposed a reasonable alternative."

According to Judge Silver's ruling: "It is undisputed that the accommodation Alamo offered Ms. Nur required her to remove her head covering during Ramadan when she served clients but still required her to serve clients, making it impossible for Ms. Nur to avoid removing her head covering at work." Accordingly, Alamo's proposal would have failed to accommodate Ms. Nur's religious conflict and was not a reasonable accommodation."

The EEOC filed suit in September 2002 (*EEOC v. Alamo Rent -A-Car, LLC; ANC Rental Corporation*, CIV 02 1908 PHX ROS) in the U.S. District Court for the District of Arizona only after exhausting its conciliation efforts to reach a voluntary settlement.

Prior to being fired, charging party Bilan Nur had worked for Alamo since 1999. EEOC's lawsuit asserted that the company had permitted her to wear a head covering for religious reasons during Ramadan in 1999 and 2000. However, following the tragic events of September 11, 2001, Alamo refused to permit Ms. Nur to observe this particular religious belief during December of 2001.

Alamo claimed that it told Ms. Nur that the company dress code prohibited wearing of a scarf. Notwithstanding Alamo's representation, the EEOC found that the company had no such policy. When Ms. Nur refused to remove the religious garment, Alamo disciplined, suspended and terminated her employment following consultation with regional level human resources officials and in-house counsel.

"I am very pleased that the judge believed that Alamo's actions were illegal," said Ms. Nur, who now resides in Minneapolis. "No person should ever have to be forced to choose between her religion and her job. Alamo appeared to understand this before the horrible attacks of September 11, 2001. Then something changed. This has been an incredible nightmare for me and I am very grateful to the EEOC for its efforts to correct this wrong."

Title VII of the Civil Rights Act of 1964 prohibits employers from discriminating against individuals because of their religion in hiring, firing, and other terms and conditions of employment. Employers must reasonably accommodate employees' sincerely held religious beliefs or practices unless doing so would impose an undue hardship on the employer. A reasonable religious accommodation is any adjustment to the work environment that will allow the employee to practice his religion.

with the accommodation Alamo offered prior to December 1, thus eroding Plaintiff's claim that Ms. Nur's religious belief was sincere.

These inferences are not reasonable in the factual context before the Court. Plaintiff testified that when Ramadan began, she started to wear a scarf at work. There is nothing in the record demonstrating that Plaintiff did not wear a head covering at work during Ramadan 2001. The record includes deposition testimony of both Victor Bellavia and LaShunda Brown, who supervised Ms. Nur. Neither Bellavia nor Brown testified that Ms. Nur did not wear a head covering during Ramadan in 2001. In fact, Victor Bellavia's December 3, 2001 memorandum to the file states that "[w]hen the Holiday started [Ms. Nur] insisted on having her head covered." LaShunda Brown testified that Ms. Nur advised her that she wanted to wear a head covering "during Ramadan until after Ramadan was over." The sort of speculation in which Alamo invites the fact finder to indulge does not create a factual dispute for purposes of summary judgment. "When the moving party has carried its burden [for summary judgment], its opponent must do more than simply show that there is some metaphysical doubt as to the material facts." Alamo has not presented specific material facts in the record to reasonably support the inference that Ms. Nur did not wear a head covering during Ramadan 2001, or the further inference that her asserted religious belief was not sincere.

C. Alamo's Burden

Because Plaintiff has proven a *prima facie* case of discrimination, the burden shifts to Alamo to show one of two things: (1) that it initiated good faith efforts to reasonably accommodate Ms. Nur's religious practices; or (2) that it could not reasonably accommodate her without undue hardship.

1. Reasonable Accommodation

Alamo argues that it made a good faith effort to accommodate Ms. Nur and that Ms. Nur accepted the accommodation. Alamo states, without citing authority, that "[w]hen an employer makes a good faith effort to accommodate which an employee accepts, the employer has met its obligation under Title VII." Alamo further argues that "[i]f a jury decides that Ms. Nur agreed that the accommodation was reasonable by agreeing to abide by it, Alamo's duty to accommodate would be fulfilled."

Alamo's assertion that it made efforts to reasonably accommodate Plaintiff lack merit. Alamo must demonstrate that it made "some initial step to reasonably accommodate the religious belief" of Ms. Nur (or show that no reasonable accommodation was possible without undue burden). This obligation requires, at a minimum, that the employer "negotiate with the employee in an effort reasonably to accommodate the employer's religious belief." The accommodation Alamo offered Ms. Nur was that "she would be allowed to wear [a head covering] when she was in the back office ... but when she went to the rental counter to rent cars in the front of the office, she would have to remove it." It is undisputed that the accommodation Alamo offered Ms. Nur required her to remove her head covering during Ramadan when she served clients but still required her to serve clients, making it impossible for Ms. Nur to avoid removing her head covering at work. Accordingly, Alamo's proposal would have failed to accommodate Ms. Nur's religious conflict, and was not a reasonable accommodation. Thus, Alamo failed to uphold its burden to attempt to accommodate Ms. Nur's beliefs, and was left with the alternative burden to show that permitting Ms. Nur to wear a head covering during Ramadan while dealing with clients would impose an undue hardship.

* * *

2. Undue Hardship

* * *

Alamo suggests that permitting Ms. Nur to wear a head covering at the rental counter would result in an undue hardship, concluding simply that "any deviation from [Alamo's] carefully cultivated image is a definite burden." Without supplying any indication of the cost it would have incurred by permitting Ms. Nur to wear a head covering at the rental counter, Alamo simply assumes the question of cost and argues that "the actual issue to be decided [by the jury] is the magnitude of the burden." The record provides no material factual basis for Alamo's conclusions about the cost of "any deviation" from the uniform policy.

Alamo fails to support its assertion of undue burden with anything other than speculation, which is not a basis to establish a genuine issue of material fact. Victor Bellavia testified that it would not have cost Alamo any money to allow Ms. Nur to wear a head scarf while serving customers. Mr. Bellavia did state that allowing Ms. Nur to wear a head covering might have affected the efficiency of Alamo's operations by opening the door for other employees to violate the company uniform policy. Bellavia stated that "[t]he only burden I see is other people wanting to break the uniform policy." However, Mr. Bellavia did not believe that allowing Ms. Nur to wear a head covering at the rental counter would affect the impression she would make on customers, or would it negatively impact customer expectations concerning the level of service or quality of the product they would receive, or otherwise create any type of negative expectations with customers. * * *

V. CONCLUSION

Alamo has not presented genuine issues of material fact concerning either EEOC's *prima facie* case of religious discrimination or Alamo's burden to show that it offered to reasonably accommodate Ms. Nur's religious beliefs or that it could not accommodate those beliefs without undue hardship. Summary judgment has been granted in favor of EEOC on the question of liability.

THESE DAYS most members of the press are corporations. CNN, *The Washington Post*, and *The Huffington Post* are also businesses that seek to be profitable in the practice of journalism. The press frequently has to be aggressive in seeking stories; often people want to hide the truth. Are there restrictions on how far the press can go (in its exercise of the First Amendment Freedom of the Press) with respect to investigating and reporting on government activities? How about with respect to an individual? The following two cases demonstrate examples of these two questions.

New York Times v. U.S.

403 U.S. 713 (1971)

PER CURIAM

Mr. Justice BLACK, with whom Mr. Justice DOUGLAS joins, concurring. I adhere to the view that the Government's case against the Washington Post should have been dismissed and that the injunction against the *New York Times* should have been vacated without oral argument when the cases were first presented to this Court. I believe that every moment's continuance of the injunctions against these newspapers amounts to a flagrant, indefensible, and continuing violation of the First Amendment. Furthermore, after oral argument, I agree completely that we must affirm the judgment of the Court of Appeals for the District of Columbia Circuit and reverse the judgment of the Court of Appeals for the Second Circuit for the reasons stated by my Brothers DOUGLAS and BRENNAN. In my view it is unfortunate that some of my Brethren are apparently willing to hold that the publication of news may sometimes be enjoined. Such a holding would make a shambles of the First Amendment.

> 'THE PEOPLE shall not be deprived or abridged of their right to speak, to write, or to publish their sentiments; and the freedom of the press, as one of the great bulwarks of liberty, shall be inviolable.'

Our Government was launched in 1789 with the adoption of the Constitution. The Bill of Rights, including the First Amendment, followed in 1791. Now, for the first time in the 182 years since the founding of the Republic, the federal courts are asked to hold that the First Amendment does not mean what it says, but rather means that the Government can halt the publication of current news of vital importance to the people of this country.

In seeking injunctions against these newspapers and in its presentation to the Court, the Executive Branch seems to have forgotten the essential purpose and history of the First Amendment. When the Constitution was adopted, many people strongly opposed it because the document contained no Bill of Rights to safeguard certain basic freedoms. They especially feared that the new powers granted to a central government might be interpreted to permit the government to curtail freedom of religion, press, assembly, and speech. In response to an overwhelming public clamor, James Madison offered a series of amendments to satisfy citizens that these great liberties would remain safe and beyond the power of government to abridge. Madison proposed what later became the First Amendment in three parts, two of which are set out below, and one of which proclaimed: 'The people shall not be deprived or abridged of their right to speak, to write, or to publish their sentiments; and the freedom of the press, as one of the great bulwarks of liberty, shall be inviolable.' The amendments were offered to curtail and restrict the general powers granted to the Executive, Legislative, and Judicial Branches two years before in the original Constitution. The Bill of Rights changed the original Constitution into a new charter under which no branch of government could abridge the people's freedoms of press, speech, religion, and assembly. Yet the Solicitor General argues and some members of the Court appear to agree that the general powers of the Government adopted in the original Constitution should be interpreted to limit and restrict the specific and emphatic guarantees of the Bill of Rights adopted later. I can imagine no greater perversion of history. Madison and the other Framers of the First Amendment, able men that they were, wrote in language they earnestly believed could never be misunderstood: 'Congress shall make no law * * * abridging the freedom * * * of the press * * *.' Both the history and language of the First Amendment support the view that the press must be left free to publish news, whatever the source, without censorship, injunctions, or prior restraints.

In the First Amendment the Founding Fathers gave the free press the protection it must have to fulfill its essential role in our democracy. The press was to serve the governed, not the governors. The Government's power to censor the press was abolished so that the press would remain forever free to censure the Government. The press was protected so that it could bare the secrets of government and inform the people. Only a free and unrestrained press can effectively expose deception in government. And paramount among the responsibilities of a free press is the duty to prevent any part of the government from deceiving the people and sending them off to distant lands to die of foreign fevers and foreign shot and shell. In my view, far from deserving condemnation for their courageous reporting, the *New York Times*, the Washington Post, and other newspapers should be commended for serving the purpose that the Founding Fathers saw so clearly. In revealing the workings of government that led to the Vietnam war, the newspapers nobly did precisely that which the Founders hoped and trusted they would do.

* * *

––––––––––––

INDIVIDUALS MAY HAVE A RIGHT to speak freely but do corporations have the same right? Cases on this issue tend to revolve around two kinds of issues. One is with respect to marketing of products. Companies do not have the latitude to say what they wish as to citizens participating in everyday life or the political sphere. For instance, except with respect to violating an established law such as campaign financial disclosures, there are no laws that punish a politician for lying on the campaign trail. The antidote is not prosecution, but debate. Corporations marketing products do not have the same freedom. They may be able to exaggerate about a product, but they cannot lie about it. The following case demonstrates an example of these kinds of issues.

Friedman v. Rogers

440 U.S. I (1971)

Mr. Justice POWELL delivered the opinion of the Court.

The Texas Legislature approved the Texas Optometry Act (Act) in 1969, repealing an earlier law governing the practice of optometry in the State. Section 2.01 of the Act establishes the Texas Optometry Board (Board) and § 2.02 prescribes the qualifications for Board members. The Board is responsible for the administration of the Act, and has the authority to grant, renew, suspend, and revoke licenses to practice optometry in the State. The Act imposes numerous regulations on the practice of optometry, and on several aspects of the business of optometry. Many of the Act's business regulations are contained in § 5.13, which restricts fee splitting by optometrists and forbids an optometrist to allow his name to be associated with any optometrical office unless he is present and practicing there at least half of the hours that the office is open or half of the hours that he practices, whichever is less. Section 5.13(d), at issue here, prohibits the practice of optometry under an assumed name, trade name, or corporate name.

The dispute in this case grows out of the schism between "professional" and "commercial" optometrists in Texas. Although all optometrists in the State must meet the same licensing requirements and are subject to the same laws regulating their practices, they have divided themselves informally into two groups according to their divergent approaches to the practice of optometry. Rogers, an advocate of the commercial practice of optometry and a member of the Board, commenced this action by filing a suit against the other five members of the Board. He sought declaratory and injunctive relief from the enforcement of § 2.02 of the Act, prescribing the composition of the Board, and § 5.13(d) of the Act, prohibiting the practice of optometry under a trade name.

Section 2.02 of the Act requires that four of the six members of the Board must be members of a state organization affiliated with the American Optometric Association (AOA). The only such organization is the Texas Optometric Association (TOA), membership in which is restricted to optometrists who comply with the Code of Ethics of the AOA. Rogers and his fellow commercial optometrists are ineligible for membership in TOA because their business methods are at odds with the AOA Code of Ethics. In his complaint, Rogers alleged that he is deprived of equal protection and due process because he is eligible for only two of the six seats on the Board, and because he is subject to regulation by a Board composed primarily of members of the professional faction. Regarding § 5.13(d), Rogers alleged that while the section prohibits optometrists from practicing under trade names, the prohibition is not extended to ophthalmologists. Rogers claimed that this disparity of treatment denies him the equal protection of the laws, as he is denied the right to conduct his optometrical practice as he has in the past under the name "Texas State Optical."

* * *

II

In holding that § 5.13(d) infringes First Amendment rights, the District Court relied primarily on this Court's decisions in *Bates v. State Bar of Arizona*, 433 U.S. 350 (1977), and *Virginia Pharmacy Board v. Virginia Citizens Consumer Council*, 425 U.S. 748 (1976). A trade name is a form of advertising, it concluded, because after the name has been used for some time, people "identify the name with a certain quality of service and goods." If found specifically "that the Texas State Optical [TSO] name has come to communicate to the consuming public information as to certain standards of price and quality, and availability of particular routine services," and rejected the argument that the TSO name misleads the public as to the identity of the optometrists with whom it deals. Balancing the constitutional interests in the commercial speech in question against the State's interest in regulating it, the District Court held that the prohibition of the use of trade names by § 5.13(d) is an unconstitutional restriction of the "free flow of commercial information."

* * *

In both *Virginia Pharmacy* and *Bates*, we were careful to emphasize that "[s]ome forms of commercial speech regulation are surely permissible." For example, restrictions on the time, place, or manner of expression are permissible provided that "they are justified without reference to the content of the regulated speech, that they serve a significant governmental interest, and that in so doing they leave open ample alternative channels for communication of the information." Equally permissible are restrictions on false, deceptive, and misleading commercial speech.

* * *

Once a trade name has been in use for some time, it may serve to identify an optometrical practice and also to convey information about the type, price, and quality of services offered for sale in that practice. In each role, the trade name is used as part of a proposal of a commercial transaction. Like the pharmacist who desired to advertise his prices in *Virginia Pharmacy*, the optometrist who uses a trade name "does not wish to editorialize on any subject, cultural, philosophical, or political. He does not wish to report any particularly newsworthy fact, or to make generalized observations even about commercial matters." His purpose is strictly business. The use of trade names in connection with optometrical practice, then, is a form of commercial speech and nothing more.

A trade name is, however, a significantly different form of commercial speech from that considered in *Virginia Pharmacy* and *Bates*. In those cases, the State had proscribed advertising by pharmacists and lawyers that contained statements about the products or services offered and their prices. These statements were self-contained and self-explanatory. Here we are concerned with a form of commercial speech that has no intrinsic meaning. A trade name conveys no information about the price and nature of the services offered by an optometrist until it acquires meaning over a period of time by associations formed in the minds of the public between the name and some standard of price or quality. Because these ill-defined associations of trade names with price and quality information can be manipulated by the users of trade names, there is a significant possibility that trade names will be used to mislead the public.

The possibilities for deception are numerous. The trade name of an optometrical practice can remain unchanged despite changes in the staff of optometrists upon whose skill and care and public depends when it patronizes the practice. Thus, the public may be attracted by a trade name that reflects the reputation of an optometrist no longer associated with the practice. A trade name frees an optometrist from dependence on his personal reputation to attract clients, and even allows him to assume a new trade name if negligence or misconduct casts a shadow over the old one. By using different trade names at shops under his common ownership, an optometrist can give the public the false impression of competition among the shops. The use of a trade name also facilitates the advertising essential to large-scale commercial practices with numerous branch offices, conduct the State rationally may wish to discourage while not prohibiting commercial optometrical practice altogether.

> "A TRADE NAME frees an optometrist from dependence on his personal reputation to attract clients, and even allows him to assume a new trade name if negligence or misconduct casts a shadow over the old one."

The concerns of the Texas Legislature about the deceptive and misleading uses of optometrical trade names were not speculative or hypothetical, but were based on experience in Texas with which the legislature was familiar when in 1969 it enacted § 5.13(d). The forerunner of § 5.13(d) was adopted as part of a "Professional Responsibility Rule" by the Texas State Board of Examiners in Optometry in 1959. In a decision upholding the validity of the Rule, the Texas Supreme Court reviewed some of the practices that had prompted its adoption. One of the plaintiffs in that case, Carp, operated 71 optometrical offices in Texas under at least 10 different trade names. From time to time, he changed the trade names of various shops, though the licensed optometrists practicing in each shop remained the same. He purchased the practices of other optometrists and continued to practice under their names, even though they were no longer associated with the practice. In several instances, Carp used different trade names on offices located in close proximity to one another and selling the same optical goods and services. The offices were under common management, and had a common staff of optometrists, but the use of different trade names facilitated advertising that gave the impression of competition among the offices.

The Texas court found that Carp used trade names to give a misleading impression of competitive ownership and management of his shops. It also found that Rogers, a party to this suit and a plaintiff in *Carp*, had used a trade name to convey the impression of standardized optometrical care. All 82 of his shops went under the trade name "Texas State Optical" or "TSO," and he advertised "scientific TSO eye examination[s]" available in every shop. The TSO advertising was calculated as well, the court found, to give "the impression that [Rogers or one of his brothers] is present at a particular office. Actually they have neither been inside nor seen some of their eighty-two offices distributed generally over Texas." Even if Rogers' use and advertising of the trade name were not in fact misleading, they were an example of the use of a trade name to facilitate the large-scale commercialization which enhances the opportunity for misleading practices.

It is clear that the State's interest in protecting the public from the deceptive and misleading use of optometrical trade names is substantial and well demonstrated. We are convinced that § 5.13(d) is a constitutionally permissible state regulation in furtherance of this interest.

A SECOND KIND OF COMMERCIAL SPEECH CASE is with respect to corporations participating in political speech. For many years, Courts have ruled that corporations are "persons" within the eyes of the law with respect to many legal issues. Corporations can own property. They can enter into contracts. They can sue in court and they can be sued. They can lobby Congress for passage of certain legislation. So could they then also participate, as persons, in political campaigns? In the controversial *Citizens United v. Federal Election Commission*, 558 U.S. 310 (2010), Justice Kennedy, writing for the Supreme Court, announced that corporations could provide unlimited donations.

> Our Nation's speech dynamic is changing, and informative voices should not have to circumvent onerous restrictions to exercise their First Amendment rights. Speakers have become adept at presenting citizens with sound bites, talking points, and scripted messages that dominate the 24–hour news cycle. Corporations, like individuals, do not have monolithic views. On certain topics corporations may possess valuable expertise, leaving them the best equipped to point out errors or fallacies in speech of all sorts, including the speech of candidates and elected officials.

Rapid changes in technology—and the creative dynamic inherent in the concept of free expression—counsel against upholding a law that restricts political speech in certain media or by certain speakers. Today, 30–second television ads may be the most effective way to convey a political message. Soon, however, it may be that Internet sources, such as blogs and social networking Web sites, will provide citizens with significant information about political candidates and issues. Yet, § 441b [a statute prohibiting campaign contributions from corporations and unions] would seem to ban a blog post expressly advocating the election or defeat of a candidate if that blog were created with corporate funds. The First Amendment does not permit Congress to make these categorical distinctions based on the corporate identity of the speaker and the content of the political speech. *Citizens United v. Fed. Election Comm'n*, (2010)

C. DUE PROCESS

There are two kinds of due process rights, **substantive** and **procedural**. Substantive due process recognizes certain rights being particularly in need of court protection. Like procedural due process, it arises from the Fourteenth Amendment prohibition that the states may not deprive a person of life, liberty, or property without due process of law. This protection had been guaranteed by the federal government under the Fifth Amendment, but this 1868 Amendment to the Constitution—coming, of course, in the aftermath of the Civil War—essentially authorized the courts to review actions of the individual states on due process terms as well.

The theory of **substantive due process** is that there are certain rights that require particular attention and protection. Thus, if a court finds that these individual rights have been threatened by state action the courts will apply a rigorous standard of review and demand a high level of justification from the state in order to uphold the restriction. The courts determine what rights deserve constitutional protection. Under the "incorporation doctrine," courts determine which of the First Amendment rights have this unique importance. After its ratification the substantive due process cases arose only in a few areas, most prominently with respect to property rights. Indeed substantive due process claims were used to strike down many attempts at economic regulation. The most infamous cases involving economic, substantive due process was the *Lochner* case, which invalidated New York's maximum work-hours requirement for bakers and ushered in an era of *laissez-faire* economic regulation. It is important to note that the Supreme Court no longer regards substantive due process in the same way, and that it effectively overruled *Lochner* in the 1937 case, *West Coast Hotel v. Parrish*.

Today the substantive due process approach has its main importance in cases related to privacy. In the famous case of *Griswold v. Connecticut*, 1965, four of the seven justices grounded their approach to finding a right to privacy (which is not specifically identified in the Constitution) in this substantive due process/fundamental rights area. And the *Griswold* case was the key precedent for the 1973 *Roe v. Wade* decision. Here are some excerpts from those opinions.

excerpts

GRISWOLD v. CONNECTICUT:

" THE FOREGOING CASES suggest that specific guarantees in the Bill of Rights have penumbras, formed by emanations from those guarantees that help give them life and substance. Various guarantees create zones of privacy. The right of association contained in the penumbra of the First Amendment is one, as we have seen. The Third Amendment in its prohibition against the quartering of soldiers 'in any house' in time of peace without the consent of the owner is another facet of that privacy. The Fourth Amendment explicitly affirms the 'right of the people to be secure in their persons, houses, papers, and effects, against unreasonable searches and seizures.' The Fifth Amendment in its Self-Incrimination Clause enables the citizen to create a zone of privacy which government may not force him to surrender to his detriment. The Ninth Amendment provides: 'The enumeration in the Constitution, of certain rights, shall not be construed to deny or disparage others retained by the people.'

We deal with a right of privacy older than the Bill of Rights—older than our political parties, older than our school system. Marriage is a coming together for better or for worse, hopefully enduring, and intimate to the degree of being sacred. It is an association that promotes a way of life, not causes; a harmony in living, not political faiths; a bilateral loyalty, not commercial or social projects. Yet it is an association for as noble a purpose as any involved in our prior decisions.

—*GRISWOLD V. CONNECTICUT, (1965).*

ROE v. WADE:

> THIS RIGHT OF PRIVACY, whether it be founded in the Fourteenth Amendment's concept of personal liberty and restrictions upon state action, as we feel it is, or, as the District Court determined, in the Ninth Amendment's reservation of rights to the people, is broad enough to encompass a woman's decision whether or not to terminate her pregnancy. The detriment that the State would impose upon the pregnant woman by denying this choice altogether is apparent. Specific and direct harm medically diagnosable even in early pregnancy may be involved. Maternity, or additional offspring, may force upon the woman a distressful life and future. Psychological harm may be imminent. Mental and physical health may be taxed by child care. There is also the distress, for all concerned, associated with the unwanted child, and there is the problem of bringing a child into a family already unable, psychologically and otherwise, to care for it. In other cases, as in this one, the additional difficulties and continuing stigma of unwed motherhood may be involved. All these are factors the woman and her responsible physician necessarily will consider in consultation.

— *ROE v. WADE*, 410 U.S. 113, 153, 93 S. Ct. 705, 727, 35 L. Ed. 2d 147 (1973) holding modified by *Planned Parenthood of S.E. Pennsylvania v. Casey*, 505 U.S. 833, 112 S. Ct. 2791, 120 L. Ed. 2d 674 (1992).

The second kind of due process is **procedural due process**. As its name indicates, it focuses on the processes that a government must go through in order to take away a person's right to life, liberty or property. Many of these cases pertain to criminal prosecutions, where there exist due process rights to an attorney, notice that charges (or a lawsuit in a civil case) have been filed against you, a standard that the laws are not too vague (so that one can understand them), and that decisions are supported by evidence. Typically a procedural due process claim must meet three criteria: there must be a deprivation, that deprivation must involve "life, liberty, or property," and it must be without due process of law. One of the most recent and surprising articulations of procedural due process was in the context of excessive punitive damage awards. In *State Farm v. Campell*, the court considered a $145 million dollar punitive award against an insurance company, an amount that far exceeded the compensatory damages suffered by the plaintiffs in a car accident.

State Farm Mutual Insurance Co. v. Campbell

538 U.S. 408 (2003)

Justice KENNEDY delivered the opinion of the Court.

* * *

The courts awarded punitive damages to punish and deter conduct that bore no relation to the Campbells' harm. A defendant's dissimilar acts, independent from the acts upon which liability was premised, may not serve as the basis for punitive damages. A defendant should be punished for the conduct that harmed the plaintiff, not for being an unsavory individual or business. Due process does not permit courts, in the calculation of punitive damages, to adjudicate the merits of other parties' hypothetical claims against a defendant under the guise of the reprehensibility analysis, but we have no doubt the Utah Supreme Court did that here. Punishment on these bases creates the possibility of multiple punitive damages awards for the same conduct; for in the usual case nonparties are not bound by the judgment some other plaintiff obtains.

* * *

[W]e have been reluctant to identify concrete constitutional limits on the ratio between harm, or potential harm, to the plaintiff and the punitive damages award. We decline again to impose a bright-line ratio which a punitive damages award cannot exceed. Our jurisprudence and the principles it has now established demonstrate, however, that, in practice, few awards exceeding a single-digit ratio between punitive and compensatory damages, to a significant degree, will satisfy due process. In *Haslip*, in upholding a punitive damages award, we concluded that an award of more than four times the amount of compensatory damages might be close to the line of constitutional impropriety. We cited that 4-to-1 ratio again in *Gore*. The Court further referenced a long legislative history, dating back over 700 years and going forward to today, providing for sanctions of double, treble, or quadruple damages to deter and punish. While these ratios are not binding, they are instructive. They demonstrate what should be obvious: Single-digit multipliers are more likely to comport with due process, while still achieving the State's goals of deterrence and retribution, than awards with ratios in range of 500 to 1, or, in this case, of 145 to 1.

* * *

The compensatory award in this case was substantial; the Campbells were awarded $1 million for a year and a half of emotional distress. * * *

The punitive award of $145 million, therefore, was neither reasonable nor proportionate to the wrong committed, and it was an irrational and arbitrary deprivation of the property of the defendant. The proper calculation of punitive damages under the principles we have discussed should be resolved, in the first instance, by the Utah courts.

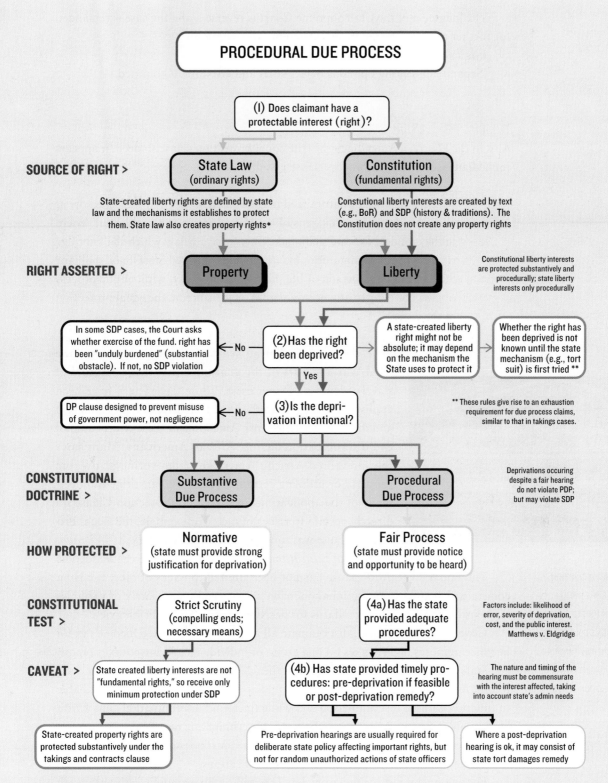

PROCEDURAL DUE PROCESS

(1) Does claimant have a protectable interest (right)?

SOURCE OF RIGHT >

State Law (ordinary rights)

State-created liberty rights are defined by state law and the mechanisms it establishes to protect them. State law also creates property rights*

Constitution (fundamental rights)

Constitutional liberty interests are created by text (e.g., BoR) and SDP (history & traditions). The Constitution does not create any property rights

RIGHT ASSERTED >

Property

Liberty

Constitutional liberty interests are protected substantively and procedurally; state liberty interests only procedurally

In some SDP cases, the Court asks whether exercise of the fund. right has been "unduly burdened" (substantial obstacle). If not, no SDP violation

— No —

(2) Has the right been deprived?

— Yes —

A state-created liberty right might not be absolute; it may depend on the mechanism the State uses to protect it

Whether the right has been deprived is not known until the state mechanism (e.g., tort suit) is first tried **

DP clause designed to prevent misuse of government power, not negligence

— No —

(3) Is the deprivation intentional?

** These rules give rise to an exhaustion requirement for due process claims, similar to that in takings cases.

CONSTITUTIONAL DOCTRINE >

Substantive Due Process

Procedural Due Process

Deprivations occuring despite a fair hearing do not violate PDP; but may violate SDP

HOW PROTECTED >

Normative (state must provide strong justification for deprivation)

Fair Process (state must provide notice and opportunity to be heard)

CONSTITUTIONAL TEST >

Strict Scrutiny (compelling ends; necessary means)

(4a) Has the state provided adequate procedures?

Factors include: likelihood of error, severity of deprivation, cost, and the public interest. Matthews v. Eldgridge

CAVEAT >

State created liberty interests are not "fundamental rights," so receive only minimum protection under SDP

(4b) Has state provided timely procedures: pre-deprivation if feasible or post-deprivation remedy?

The nature and timing of the hearing must be commensurate with the interest affected, taking into account state's admin needs

State-created property rights are protected substantively under the takings and contracts clause

Pre-deprivation hearings are usually required for deliberate state policy affecting important rights, but not for random unauthorized actions of state officers

Where a post-deprivation hearing is ok, it may consist of state tort damages remedy

* States create liberty/property rights either through positive law or by creating a reasonable expectation that an interest will be protected

Chart courtesy Prof. Karl Manheim © 2011

The judgment of the Utah Supreme Court is reversed, and the case is remanded for further proceedings not inconsistent with this opinion.

It is so ordered.

[Separate dissenting opinions by SCALIA and GINSBURG omitted.]

D. EQUAL PROTECTION ISSUES

Also in the Fourteen Amendment lies the equal protection clause. Indeed, it appears immediately after the due process clause just discussed.

> "All persons born or naturalized in the United States, and subject to the jurisdiction thereof, are citizens of the United States and of the State wherein they reside. No State shall make or enforce any law which shall abridge the privileges or immunities of citizens of the United States; nor shall any State deprive any person of life, liberty, or property, without due process of law; nor deny to any person within its jurisdiction the equal protection of the laws."

Historically, of course, the Fourteen Amendment was enacted as a result of the Civil War and part of the guarantee that the institution of slavery would no longer exist. While slavery may have been abolished, first through the 1863 Emancipation Proclamation and then via the Thirteenth Amendment, these efforts did not end discrimination against African Americans. Many laws that prevented African Americans from voting or owning property or utilizing certain services were instituted. Indeed, many of the applications of the Equal Protection Clause do directly pertain to issues of race. For example, the Equal Protection Clause was fundamental to the landmark, 1954 *Brown v. Board of Education*, which struck down segregated schools.

■ THE INSCRIPTION ABOVE THE ENTRANCE OF THE UNITED STATES SUPREME COURT WAS INSPIRED BY THE 14th AMENDMENT EQUAL PROTECTION CLAUSE.

The Equal Protection Clause has not been limited to issues of race. It has become a widely used Constitutional doctrine with an elaborate matrix of variables and various constitutional standards for decision-making and judicial review.

Governments, of course, discriminate all the time. A graduated income tax for instance, imposes higher taxes on one group of individuals and lower taxes on others. States do not allow individuals under the age of sixteen (sometimes other ages) to obtain a drivers license. It is hard to imagine any institution or individual able to function without discrimination and while the term "discrimination" has a troubling connotation these days, one who has a "discriminating taste" is one who tends to have very high standards. And so, the Supreme Court has developed a framework to analyze what discriminations need what justifications.

For example if a discriminatory law is based on an economic rationale (such as the graduated income tax code), then the government needs to demonstrate a rational relationship between the law and the government objective. This rational-basis test tends to be a fairly easy threshold for the government to reach, as the following case indicates.

F.C.C. v. Beach Communications, Inc.

508 U.S. 307 (1993)

Justice THOMAS delivered the opinion of the Court.

* * *

This case arises out of an FCC proceeding clarifying the agency's interpretation of the term "cable system" as it is used in the Cable Act. In this proceeding, the Commission addressed the application of the exemption codified in § 602(7)(B) to satellite master antenna television (SMATV) facilities. Unlike a traditional cable television system, which delivers video programming to a large community of subscribers through coaxial cables laid under city streets or along utility lines, an SMATV system typically receives a signal from a satellite through a small satellite dish located on a rooftop and then retransmits the signal by wire to units within a building or complex of buildings. The Commission ruled that an SMATV system that serves multiple buildings via a network of interconnected physical transmission lines is a cable system, unless it falls within the § 602(7)(B) exemption. Consistent with the plain terms of the statutory exemption, the Commission concluded that such an SMATV system is subject to the franchise requirement if its transmission lines interconnect separately owned and managed buildings or if its lines use or cross any public right-of-way.

Respondents Beach Communications, Inc., Maxtel Limited Partnership, Pacific Cablevision, and Western Cable Communications, Inc.—SMATV operators that would be subject to franchising under the Cable Act as construed by the Commission—petitioned the Court of Appeals for review. The Court of Appeals rejected respondents' statutory challenge to the Commission's interpretation, but a majority of the court found merit in the claim that § 602(7) violates the implied equal protection guarantee of the Due Process Clause. In the absence of what it termed "the predominant rationale for local franchising" (use of public rights-of-way), the court saw no rational basis "[o]n the record," and was "unable to imagine" any conceivable basis, for distinguishing between those facilities exempted by the statute and those SMATV cable systems that link separately owned and managed buildings. The court remanded the record and directed the FCC to provide "additional 'legislative facts' " to justify the distinction.

A report subsequently filed by the Commission failed to satisfy the Court of Appeals. The Commission stated that it was "unaware of any desirable policy or other considerations ... that would support the challenged distinctions," other than those offered by a concurring member of the court. The concurrence had believed it sufficient that Congress *could* have reasoned that SMATV systems serving separately owned buildings are more similar to traditional cable systems than are facilities serving commonly owned buildings, in terms of the problems presented for consumers and the potential for regulatory benefits. In a second opinion, the majority found this rationale to be "a naked intuition, unsupported by conceivable facts or policies," and held that "the Cable Act violates the equal protection component of the Fifth Amendment, insofar as it imposes a discriminatory franchising requirement," The court declared the franchise requirement void to the extent it covers respondents and similarly situated SMATV operators.

Because the Court of Appeals held an Act of Congress unconstitutional, we granted *certiorari*. We now reverse.

II

Whether embodied in the Fourteenth Amendment or inferred from the Fifth, equal protection is not a license for courts to judge the wisdom, fairness, or logic of legislative choices. In areas of social and economic policy, a statutory classification that neither proceeds along suspect lines nor infringes fundamental constitutional rights must be upheld against equal protection challenge if there is any reasonably conceivable state of facts that could provide a rational basis for the classification. Where there are "plausible reasons" for Congress' action, "our inquiry is at an end." This standard of review is a paradigm of judicial restraint. "The Constitution presumes that, absent some reason to infer antipathy, even improvident decisions will eventually be rectified by the democratic process and that judicial intervention is generally unwarranted no matter how unwisely we may think a political branch has acted."

On rational-basis review, a classification in a statute such as the Cable Act comes to us bearing a strong presumption of validity, and those attacking the rationality of the legislative classification have the burden "to negative every conceivable basis which might support it," Moreover, because we never require a legislature to articulate its reasons for enacting a statute, it is entirely irrelevant for constitutional purposes whether the conceived reason for the challenged distinction actually motivated the legislature. Thus, the absence of " 'legislative facts' " explaining the distinction "[o]n the record," has no significance in rational-basis analysis. In other words, a legislative choice is not subject to courtroom fact-finding and may be based on rational speculation unsupported by evidence or empirical data. "'Only by faithful adherence to this guiding principle of judicial review of legislation is it possible to preserve to the legislative branch its rightful independence and its ability to function.' "

* * *

Applying these principles, we conclude that the common-ownership distinction is constitutional. There are at least two possible bases for the distinction; either one suffices. First, Congress borrowed § 602(7)(B) from pre-Cable Act regulations, and although the existence of a prior administrative scheme is certainly not necessary to the rationality of the statute, it is plausible that Congress also adopted the FCC's earlier rationale. Under that rationale, common ownership was thought to be indicative of those systems for which the costs of regulation would outweigh the benefits to consumers. Because the number of subscribers was a similar indicator, the Commission also exempted cable facilities that served fewer than 50 subscribers. In explaining both exemptions, the Commission stated:

> "[N]ot all [systems] can be subject to effective regulation with the resources available nor is regulation necessarily needed in every instance. A sensible regulatory program requires that a division between the regulated and unregulated be made in a manner which best conserves regulatory energies and allows the most cost effective use of available resources. In attempting to make this division, we have focused on subscriber numbers as well as the multiple unit dwelling indicia on the theory that the very small are inefficient to regulate and can safely be ignored in terms of their potential for impact on broadcast service to the public and on multiple unit dwelling facilities on the theory that this effectively establishes certain maximum size limitations."

This regulatory-efficiency model, originally suggested by Chief Judge Mikva in his concurring opinion, provides a conceivable basis for the common-ownership exemption. A legislator might rationally assume that systems serving only commonly owned or managed buildings without crossing public rights-of-way would typically be limited in size or would share some other attribute affecting their impact on the welfare of cable viewers such that regulators could "safely ignor[e]" these systems.

Respondents argue that Congress did not intend common ownership to be a surrogate for small size, since Congress simultaneously rejected the FCC's 50–subscriber exemption by omitting it from the Cable Act. Whether the posited reason for the challenged distinction actually motivated Congress is "constitutionally irrelevant," and, in any event, the FCC's explanation indicates that both common ownership and number of subscribers were considered indicia of "very small" cable systems. Respondents also contend that an SMATV operator could increase his subscription base and still qualify for the exemption simply by installing a separate satellite dish on each building served. The additional cost of multiple dishes and associated transmission equipment, however, would impose an independent constraint on system size.

Furthermore, small size is only one plausible ownership-related factor contributing to consumer welfare. Subscriber influence is another. Where an SMATV system serves a complex of buildings under common ownership or management, individual subscribers could conceivably have greater bargaining power vis-à-vis the cable operator (even if the number of dwelling units were large), since all the subscribers could negotiate with one voice through the common owner or manager. Such an owner might have substantial leverage, because he could withhold permission to operate the SMATV system on his property. He would also have an incentive to guard the interests of his tenants. Thus, there could be less need to establish regulatory safeguards for subscribers in commonly owned complexes. Respondents acknowledge such possibilities, see *id.*, at 44, and we certainly cannot say that these assumptions would be irrational.

There is a second conceivable basis for the statutory distinction. Suppose competing SMATV operators wish to sell video programming to subscribers in a group of contiguous buildings, such as a single city block, which can be interconnected by wire without crossing a public right-of-way. If all the buildings belong to one owner or are commonly managed, that owner or manager could freely negotiate a deal for all subscribers on a competitive basis. But if the buildings are separately owned and managed, the first SMATV operator who gains a foothold by signing a contract and installing a satellite dish and associated transmission equipment on one of the buildings would enjoy a powerful cost advantage in competing for the remaining subscribers: He could connect additional buildings for the cost of a few feet of cable, whereas any competitor would have to recover the cost of his own satellite head-end facility. Thus, the first operator could charge rates well above his cost and still undercut the competition. This potential for effective monopoly power might theoretically justify regulating the latter class of SMATV systems and not the former.

III

The Court of Appeals quite evidently believed that the crossing or use of a public right-of-way is the only conceivable basis upon which Congress could rationally require local franchising of SMATV systems. As we have indicated, however, there are plausible rationales unrelated to the use of public rights-of-way for regulating cable facilities serving separately owned and managed buildings. The assumptions underlying these rationales may be erroneous, but the very fact that they are "arguable" is sufficient, on rational-basis review, to "immuniz[e]" the congressional choice from constitutional challenge.

The judgment of the Court of Appeals is *reversed*, and the case is *remanded* for further proceedings consistent with this opinion.

So ordered.

———————————

NOT ALL DISCRIMINATIONS, however, are so benign, as is the case when a governmental action impacts a suspect class. Suspect classes have been identified as those pertaining to race, religion, and ethnic origin. If the government passes a law that discriminates on these classifications, the Courts demand that the government provide a "compelling state interest" to justify the discrimination. Just as the rational relationship test is relatively easy to pass, the compelling state interest test is very difficult for a state to pass. Indeed, one of the very few cases where the courts have upheld such a discrimination has been in issues of national security and in retrospect, some of these cases might be decided differently today. For instance, the following case involved the constitutionality of an executive order that placed Japanese-American in internment camps during World War II. The case also marks one of the first applications of the strict scrutiny test and relates to the earlier discussion of the President's power in a time of emergency.

Toyosaburo Korematsu v. United States

323 U.S. 214 (1944)

Mr. Justice BLACK delivered the opinion of the Court.

The petitioner, an American citizen of Japanese descent, was convicted in a federal district court for remaining in San Leandro, California, a 'Military Area', contrary to Civilian Exclusion Order No. 34 of the Commanding General of the Western Command, U.S. Army, which directed that after May 9, 1942, all persons of Japanese ancestry should be excluded from that area. No question was raised as to petitioner's loyalty to the United States. The Circuit Court of Appeals affirmed, and the importance of the constitutional question involved caused us to grant *certiorari*.

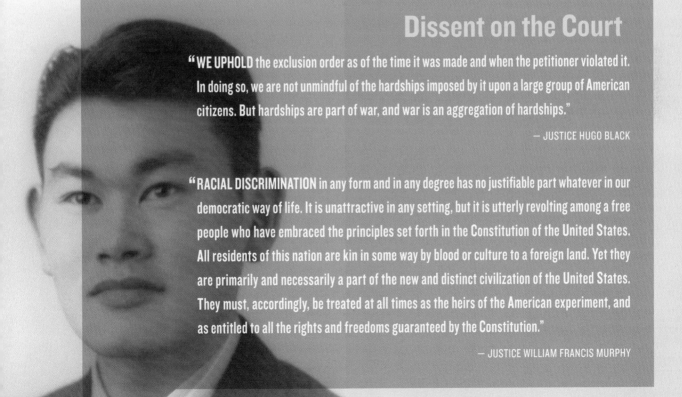

Dissent on the Court

"**WE UPHOLD** the exclusion order as of the time it was made and when the petitioner violated it. In doing so, we are not unmindful of the hardships imposed by it upon a large group of American citizens. But hardships are part of war, and war is an aggregation of hardships."

— JUSTICE HUGO BLACK

"**RACIAL DISCRIMINATION** in any form and in any degree has no justifiable part whatever in our democratic way of life. It is unattractive in any setting, but it is utterly revolting among a free people who have embraced the principles set forth in the Constitution of the United States. All residents of this nation are kin in some way by blood or culture to a foreign land. Yet they are primarily and necessarily a part of the new and distinct civilization of the United States. They must, accordingly, be treated at all times as the heirs of the American experiment, and as entitled to all the rights and freedoms guaranteed by the Constitution."

— JUSTICE WILLIAM FRANCIS MURPHY

< *FRED TOYOSABURO KOREMATSU, photo courtesy of Karen Korematsu and the Fred T. Korematsu Institute*

It should be noted, to begin with, that all legal restrictions which curtail the civil rights of a single racial group are immediately suspect. That is not to say that all such restrictions are unconstitutional. It is to say that courts must subject them to the most rigid scrutiny. Pressing public necessity may sometimes justify the existence of such restrictions; racial antagonism never can.

In the instant case prosecution of the petitioner was begun by information charging violation of an Act of Congress, [. . .] which provides that:

> " * * * whoever shall enter, remain in, leave, or commit any act in any military area or military zone prescribed, under the authority of an Executive order of the President, by the Secretary of War, or by any military commander designated by the Secretary of War, contrary to the restrictions applicable to any such area or zone or contrary to the order of the Secretary of War or any such military commander, shall, if it appears that he knew or should have known of the existence and extent of the restrictions or order and that his act was in violation thereof, be guilty of a misdemeanor and upon conviction shall be liable to a fine of not to exceed $5,000 or to imprisonment for not more than one year, or both, for each offense."

Exclusion Order No. 34, which the petitioner knowingly and admittedly violated was one of a number of military orders and proclamations, all of which were substantially based upon Executive Order [. . .]. That order, issued after we were at war with Japan, declared that "the successful prosecution of the war requires every possible protection against espionage and against sabotage to national-defense material, national-defense premises, and national-defense utilities. * * *"

Here, as in *Hirabayashi*, supra, "* * * we cannot reject as unfounded the judgment of the military authorities and of Congress that there were disloyal members of that population, whose number and strength could not be precisely and quickly ascertained. We cannot say that the war-making branches of the Government did not have ground for believing that in a critical hour such persons could not readily be isolated and separately dealt with, and constituted a menace to the national defense and safety, which demanded that prompt and adequate measures be taken to guard against it."

Like curfew, exclusion of those of Japanese origin was deemed necessary because of the presence of an unascertained number of disloyal members of the group, most of whom we have no doubt were loyal to this country. It was because we could not reject the finding of the military authorities that it was impossible to bring about an immediate segregation of the disloyal from the loyal that we sustained the validity of the curfew order as applying to the whole group. In the instant case, temporary exclusion of the entire group was rested by the military on the same ground. The judgment that exclusion of the whole group was for the same reason a military imperative answers the contention that the exclusion was in the nature of group punishment based on antagonism to those of Japanese origin. That there were members

of the group who retained loyalties to Japan has been confirmed by investigations made subsequent to the exclusion. Approximately five thousand American citizens of Japanese ancestry refused to swear unqualified allegiance to the United States and to renounce allegiance to the Japanese Emperor, and several thousand evacuees requested repatriation to Japan.

We uphold the exclusion order as of the time it was made and when the petitioner violated it. In doing so, we are not unmindful of the hardships imposed by it upon a large group of American citizens. But hardships are part of war, and war is an aggregation of hardships. All citizens alike, both in and out of uniform, feel the impact of war in greater or lesser measure. Citizenship has its responsibilities as well as its privileges, and in time of war the burden is always heavier. Compulsory exclusion of large groups of citizens from their homes, except under circumstances of direst emergency and peril, is inconsistent with our basic governmental institutions. But when under conditions of modern warfare our shores are threatened by hostile forces, the power to protect must be commensurate with the threatened danger.

* * *

■ THOUSANDS OF JAPANESE AMERICANS WERE INTERNED AT THE CAMP IN MANZANAR, CALIFORNIA, MAY 1942.
Photo: Dorothea Lange. Prints and Photographs Division, Library of Congress.

It is said that we are dealing here with the case of imprisonment of a citizen in a concentration camp solely because of his ancestry, without evidence or inquiry concerning his loyalty and good disposition towards the United States. Our task would be simple, our duty clear, were this a case involving the imprisonment of a loyal citizen in a concentration camp because of racial prejudice. Regardless of the true nature of the assembly and relocation centers-and we deem it unjustifiable to call them concentration camps with all the ugly connotations that term implies-we are dealing specifically with nothing but an exclusion order. To cast this case into outlines of racial prejudice, without reference to the real military dangers which were presented, merely confuses the issue. Korematsu was not excluded from the Military Area because of hostility to him or his race. He was excluded because we are at war with the Japanese Empire, because the properly constituted military authorities feared an invasion of our West Coast and felt constrained to take pro*per security* measures, because they decided that the military urgency of the situation demanded that all citizens of Japanese ancestry be segregated from the West Coast temporarily, and finally, because Congress, reposing its confidence in this time of war in our military leaders-as inevitably it must-determined that they should have the power to do just this. There was evidence of disloyalty on the part of some, the military authorities considered that the need for action was great, and time was short. We cannot-by availing ourselves of the calm perspective of hindsight-now say that at that time these actions were unjustified.

Affirmed.

THERE WAS BOTH LEGISLATIVE and judicial reaction to the Japanese Internment cases. In the mid-1980s, Korematsu brought a petition for *coram nobis*, requesting that the court vacate his earlier conviction based on allegations of earlier government misconduct and suppression of evidence. Judge Patel, the district judge in the case, granted the plaintiff's petition and reminded future judges and lawmakers of their constitutional duties in the trying times of war. He wrote,

> As historical precedent [this case] stands as a constant caution that in times of war or declared military necessity our institutions must be vigilant in protecting constitutional guarantees. It stands as a caution that in times of distress the shield of military necessity and national security must not be used to protect governmental actions form close scrutiny and accountability. It stands as a caution that in times of international hostility and antagonisms that our institutions, legislative, executive, and judicial, must be prepared to exercise their authorities to protect all citizens from the petty fears and prejudices that are so easily aroused.

Executive responses began with President Ford's 1976 repeal of Roosevelt's executive order, which began the initial internment. George H.W. Bush also apologized during his presidency saying, "We can never fully right the wrongs of the past. But we can take a clear stand for justice and recognize that serious injustices were done to the Japanese Americans during World War II." Congress also responded with the passage of the Civil Liberties Act of 1988, which provided surviving internees with reparations. For a detailed history of judicial, executive and legislative responses to the cases and Japanese Internment in general, consult Yamamoto, Chon, Izumi, Kang and Wu, *Rights, Race and Reparation: Law and the Japanese American Internment* (2001).

Increasingly, issues of gender and sexual orientation have been brought to the courts under Equal Protection claims; however, they receive slightly different levels of scrutiny—sometimes known as intermediate scrutiny—than other classifications like those based on race or natural origin, which are reviewed under strict scrutiny. To date these have been evaluated under a "substantial interest test" or intermediate scrutiny test, akin to the standards courts apply in Commercial Speech tests. The government must justify its actions by more than a rational interest, but not as dauntingly as a compelling or strict scrutiny interest. The following two cases illustrate the tests the court employs in gender and sexual orientation cases.

Sometimes the government may pass a law that, on its face, is discriminatory, as some of the cases set out above exemplify. At other times, the language of the statute is neutral on its face, but has a "disparate impact." The courts become especially interested in such cases if the disparate impact pertains to a suspect class. Typically, these claims also arise in the Title VII context and courts have developed different tests to determine the scope of the "impact" and the nature of the disparate treatment. The following case shows one of the Supreme Court's most recent analyses of the disparate impact doctrine.

Ricci v. DeStefano

557 U.S. 557 (2009)

Justice KENNEDY delivered the opinion of the Court.

In the fire department of New Haven, Connecticut—as in emergency-service agencies throughout the Nation—firefighters prize their promotion to and within the officer ranks. An agency's officers command respect within the department and in the whole community; and, of course, added responsibilities command increased salary and benefits. Aware of the intense competition for promotions, New Haven, like many cities, relies on objective examinations to identify the best qualified candidates.

In 2003, 118 New Haven firefighters took examinations to qualify for promotion to the rank of lieutenant or captain. Promotion examinations in New Haven (or City) were infrequent, so the stakes were high. The results would determine which firefighters would be considered for promotions during the next two years, and the order in which they would be considered. Many firefighters studied for months, at considerable personal and financial cost.

When the examination results showed that white candidates had outperformed minority candidates, the mayor and other local politicians opened a public debate that turned rancorous. Some firefighters argued the tests should be discarded because the results showed the tests to be discriminatory. They threatened a discrimination lawsuit if the City made promotions based on the tests. Other firefighters said the exams were neutral and fair. And they, in turn, threatened a discrimination lawsuit if the City, relying on the statistical racial disparity, ignored the test results and denied promotions to the candidates who had performed well. In the end the City took the side of those who protested the test results. It threw out the examinations.

Certain white and Hispanic firefighters who likely would have been promoted based on their good test performance sued the City and some of its officials. Theirs is the suit now before us. The suit alleges that, by discarding the test results, the City and the named officials discriminated against the plaintiffs based on their race, in violation of both Title VII of the Civil Rights Act of 1964 and the Equal Protection Clause of the Fourteenth Amendment. The City and the officials defended their actions, arguing that if they had certified the results, they could have faced liability under Title VII for adopting a practice that had a disparate impact on the minority firefighters. The District Court granted summary judgment for the defendants, and the Court of Appeals affirmed.

We conclude that race-based action like the City's in this case is impermissible under Title VII unless the employer can demonstrate a strong basis in evidence that, had it not taken the action, it would have been liable under the disparate-impact statute. The respondents, we further determine, cannot meet that threshold standard. As a result, the City's action in discarding the tests was a violation of Title VII. In light of our ruling under the statutes, we need not reach the question whether respondents' actions may have violated the Equal Protection Clause.

* * *

C

The CSB's decision not to certify the examination results led to this lawsuit. The plaintiffs—who are the petitioners here—are 17 white firefighters and 1 Hispanic firefighter who passed the examinations but were denied a chance at promotions when the CSB refused to certify the test results. They include the named plaintiff, Frank Ricci, who addressed the CSB at multiple meetings.

Petitioners sued the City, Mayor DeStefano, DuBois–Walton, Ude, Burgett, and the two CSB members who voted against certification. Petitioners also named as a defendant Boise Kimber, a New Haven resident who voiced strong opposition to certifying the results. Those individuals are respondents in this Court. Petitioners filed suit [. . .] alleging that respondents, by arguing or voting against certifying the results, violated and conspired to violate the Equal Protection Clause of the

Fourteenth Amendment. Petitioners also filed timely charges of discrimination with the Equal Employment Opportunity Commission (EEOC); upon the EEOC's issuing right-to-sue letters, petitioners amended their complaint to assert that the City violated the disparate-treatment prohibition contained in Title VII of the Civil Rights Act of 1964, as amended.

* * *

II

B

Petitioners allege that when the CSB refused to certify the captain and lieutenant exam results based on the race of the successful candidates, it discriminated against them in violation of Title VII's disparate-treatment provision. The City counters that its decision was permissible because the tests "appear[ed] to violate Title VII's disparate-impact provisions."

Our analysis begins with this premise: The City's actions would violate the disparate-treatment prohibition of Title VII absent some valid defense. All the evidence demonstrates that the City chose not to certify the examination results because of the statistical disparity based on race—i.e., how minority candidates had performed when compared to white candidates. As the District Court put it, the City rejected the test results because "too many whites and not enough minorities would be promoted were the lists to be certified." Without some other justification, this express, race-based decision making violates Title VII's command that employers cannot take adverse employment actions because of an individual's race.

■ THE DECISION IN FAVOR OF THE "NEW HAVEN 20" PROVOKED DEBATE ABOUT RACE-BASED ACTIONS THAT CONTINUES TO IMPACT TITLE VII CASES TO THIS DAY.

Cartoon: Bob Englehart

* * *

The racial adverse impact here was significant, and petitioners do not dispute that the City was faced with a *prima facie* case of disparate-impact liability. On the captain exam, the pass rate for white candidates was 64 percent but was 37.5 percent for both black and Hispanic candidates. On the lieutenant exam, the pass rate for white candidates was 58.1 percent; for black candidates, 31.6 percent; and for Hispanic candidates, 20 percent. The pass rates of minorities, which were approximately one-half the pass rates for white candidates, fall well below the 80–percent standard set by the EEOC to implement the disparate-impact provision of Title VII. Based on how the passing candidates ranked and an application of the "rule of three," certifying the examinations would have meant that the City could not have considered black candidates for any of the then-vacant lieutenant or captain positions.

Based on the degree of adverse impact reflected in the results, respondents were compelled to take a hard look at the examinations to determine whether certifying the results would have had an impermissible disparate impact. The problem for respondents is that a *prima facie* case of disparate-impact liability—essentially, a threshold showing of a significant statistical disparity, and nothing more—is far from a strong basis in evidence that the City would have been liable under Title VII had it certified the results. That is because the City could be liable for disparate-impact discrimination only if the examinations were not job related and consistent with business necessity, or if there existed an equally valid, less-discriminatory alternative that served the City's needs but that the City refused to adopt. We conclude there is no strong basis in evidence to establish that the test was deficient in either of these respects. We address each of the two points in turn, based on the record developed by the parties through discovery—a record that concentrates in substantial part on the statements various witnesses made to the CSB.

* * *

On the record before us, there is no genuine dispute that the City lacked a strong basis in evidence to believe it would face disparate-impact liability if it certified the examination results. In other words, there is no evidence—let alone the required strong basis in evidence—that the tests were flawed because they were not job related or because other, equally valid and less discriminatory tests were available to the City. Fear of litigation alone cannot justify an employer's reliance on race to the detriment of individuals who passed the examinations and qualified for promotions. The City's discarding the test results was impermissible under Title VII, and summary judgment is appropriate for petitioners on their disparate-treatment claim.

* * *

The record in this litigation documents a process that, at the outset, had the potential to produce a testing procedure that was true to the promise of Title VII:

No individual should face workplace discrimination based on race. Respondents thought about promotion qualifications and relevant experience in neutral ways. They were careful to ensure broad racial participation in the design of the test itself and its administration. As we have discussed at length, the process was open and fair.

The problem, of course, is that after the tests were completed, the raw racial results became the predominant rationale for the City's refusal to certify the results. The injury arises in part from the high, and justified, expectations of the candidates who had participated in the testing process on the terms the City had established for the promotional process. Many of the candidates had studied for months, at considerable personal and financial expense, and thus the injury caused by the City's reliance on raw racial statistics at the end of the process was all the more severe. Confronted with arguments both for and against certifying the test results—and threats of a lawsuit either way—the City was required to make a difficult inquiry. But its hearings produced no strong evidence of a disparate-impact violation, and the City was not entitled to disregard the tests based solely on the racial disparity in the results.

Our holding today clarifies how Title VII applies to resolve competing expectations under the disparate-treatment and disparate-impact provisions. If, after it certifies the test results, the City faces a disparate-impact suit, then in light of our holding today it should be clear that the City would avoid disparate-impact liability based on the strong basis in evidence that, had it not certified the results, it would have been subject to disparate-treatment liability.

Petitioners are entitled to summary judgment on their Title VII claim, and we therefore need not decide the underlying constitutional question. The judgment of the Court of Appeals is reversed, and the cases are remanded for further proceedings consistent with this opinion.

It is so ordered.

NOTES AND COMMENTS

I. MOST STUDENTS FIND Constitutional Law the easiest area of law to follow because it is so regularly part of the news. While many courts consider constitutional law issues, especially at the Federal level, the U.S. Supreme Court garners most of the attention. The Supreme Court begins its "year" in October and renders its decision in late Spring/early Summer, especially in June, a calendar that fits nicely into the usual academic year. Try to follow the Supreme Court as it decides what cases to hear, as attorneys for each side make oral arguments, and even as commentators try to determine the outcome of a case based on the questions posed by the Justices. In addition to major national newspapers like *The New York Times* or *Washington Post*, some good sources are *www.scotusblog.com*, *twitter.com/USSupremeCourt*, and *www.supremecourt.gov*.

2. AN ONGOING DEBATE concerning Constitutional interpretation focuses on whether justices should apply the original intent of the framers of the Constitution or whether one should read the Constitution as a developing document. Of course, there are shades of interpretation in between. What do you think is the best way to apply the Constitution to today's issues?

3. IN CHAPTER FOUR, you will see that President Franklin Roosevelt considered asking Congress to change the number of justices from nine to a higher number. What do you think the number of justices on the Court should be and why?

4. THE PRESIDENT NOMINATES individuals to serve on the Supreme Court and the Senate must approve the nominee. Controversies about choices are not new, but in recent years, especially since the 1987 nomination by President Reagan of Robert Bork, the nomination process has featured highly partisan battles with attempts to uncover anything detrimental to a nominee that would preclude a nomination. Thus, questions about whether a nominee had paid social security taxes on a nanny, one whether the nominee had ever used marijuana, or even what videos the nominee checked out of a video stores have been used to question a nominee's credential. What do you believe is relevant to determine whether a nominee is qualified to serve or the Court or not? What allegations go too far? Where would you draw the line?

THE COMMON LAW SYSTEM & COMPARATIVE ALTERNATIVES

THE UNITED STATES, LIKE MANY COUNTRIES with an historical linkage to England, has a common law system. This means that judges play a very strong role in determining the content of the law. In theory, judges are

not supposed to do this; they are supposed to interpret, clarify, and apply the law, but given the structure of the common law system itself, even the most reticent judge will end up making some law. In interpreting, clarifying, and applying the law judges have the power to shape the way it affects the community. Supreme Court Justice Antonin Scalia once described the role of the common law judge as, "playing king—devising, out of the brilliance of one's own mind, those laws that ought to govern mankind."[1]

Most countries follow the civil law system, which does not give the same legal authority to judicial precedent. However, both the United States and the United Kingdom are common law countries. In some cases, countries with a common law system lack a constitution. England, for example, does not have a formal constitution, although others, such as the United States, Australia and India do.

As we will see throughout this book, legislatures have the primary responsibility to make law and, through delegation, administrative agencies as well. For example,

---

1   Antonin Scalia, *"Common-Law Courts in a Civil-Law System: The Role of United States Federal Courts in Interpreting the Constitution and Laws." The Tanner Lectures on Human Values, delivered at Princeton University, March 8-9, 1995.*

in the United States, Congress grants, through legislation, certain authorities to the Food and Drug Administration (FDA) and using those authorities, the FDA can enact regulations that are binding on the people as law. The Executive of the country or state also plays a role in this, not only with respect to enforcing laws (which always has some degree of discretion) but through executive orders.

While courts do not have the ability to draft new legislation like Congress, administrative agencies and the Executive of a country, judges in a common law system can have just as much influence in law-making because of their discretion in interpreting and applying it. No court better exemplifies this influence in law-making than the Supreme Court of the United States. The Supreme Court has the authority to review and determine constitutional issues, and thus it has the power to overturn legislation that it finds unconstitutional. In *Roe v. Wade*, 410 U.S. 113 (1973), the Supreme Court found Texas criminal abortion statutes prohibiting abortions at any stage of pregnancy except to save the life of the mother to be unconstitutional. Instead, the Court decided that states only have the power to regulate abortion procedures past the first trimester of pregnancy. Because the Supreme Court is the highest court in the United States, and the United States is a common law society, any challenge to state abortion laws would have to follow the precedent set in *Roe v. Wade*. Thus, with this decision, the Supreme Court effectively legalized all abortions during the first trimester of pregnancy.

> **IN A COMMON LAW SYSTEM,** any citizen (and some non-citizens) can bring a case to court to determine a legal issue without waiting for a legislature to enact or amend a law, as is the case in civil law societies.

I. The Common Law System

IN A COMMON LAW SYSTEM, any citizen (and some non-citizens) can bring a case to court to determine a legal issue without waiting for a legislature to enact or amend a law, as is the case in civil law societies. This keeps an open, fluid legal system ongoing to change and development. It also enhances individual liberty by keeping in the hands of the individual the opportunity for a grievance to be heard and resolved. Common law systems, particularly the United States, also rely on the jury system. Not all cases are heard by juries, but many are. The United States is one of the few countries that uses juries regularly. The idea behind juries is that cases should be heard by one's peers and not decided by specialists, so as to check against state power and to add legitimacy to legal decisions. This is a strong egalitarian value that further harmonizes the common law system and democracy (though not all democracies utilize the common law system).

At the same time, the common law system has its drawbacks as well. The very nature of individuals being able to file suit means that there is a chance for a lot of lawsuits to be filed. That can clog the system and, indeed, one of the complaints about the system is its slowness. Even in criminal proceedings, when a person's liberty is at stake, it can take up to eight years, as it did in *State v. Patin,* for a case to go to trial without the court violating the defendant's constitutional right to a speedy trial.

State v. Patin

Court of Appeal of Louisiana, Fourth Circuit, 2012 95 So.3d 542

FACTS

Patin and Thomas were charged with shooting Christopher McCrory, Malcolm Green, and Troy Steen on Parc Brittany Court on December 23, 2001. McCrory died as a result of the shooting. Patin became a suspect, and on December 26, 2001, Patin surrendered to the police. Thomas, his brother, accompanied him to the police station and gave a statement. He and Patin were both arrested for the murder. On February 28, 2012, a grand jury returned an indictment charging both of them for the first degree murder of McCrory. They pled not guilty at their arraignment on March 6, 2002. The case was reset for determination of counsel for both defendants, and both defendants appeared with counsel on May 10, 2002. The court held motion hearings on June 14 and July 10, 2002, and at the conclusion of the latter hearing, the court denied the motions to suppress. The court set trial for August 13, 2002.

The matter was reset several times, and on April 20, 2009, the State amended the indictment to charge Thomas and Patin with second degree murder. Counsel for Thomas withdrew; new counsel enrolled in July and filed a motion to sever the trials of Thomas and Patin. The matter was reset several more times, and on August 31, Patin filed a motion to quash the indictment. The court heard the matter on September 10 and denied the motion on statutory grounds. The court held open the opportunity for an evidentiary hearing on each defendants' constitutional claim. On October 28, 2009, after denying the defendants' motion for an evidentiary hearing, the court denied both motions to quash. The court set a trial date of February 1, 2010. Both defendants objected and noted their intent to seek writs, and the court granted the defendants until November 30. On January 4, 2010, the court set the matter for January 13 for the State to indicate which defendant it intended to try first. On January 13, the State elected to try Patin first, and the court ruled that all dates previously set were to remain in effect.

This court granted both Patin's and Thomas' writ applications, vacated the court's denial of their motions to quash, and remanded the cases with the instructions to allow the defendants to present evidence on the issue of prejudice from the delay in going to trial.

On remand, the court heard the matter on February 4, 2010. At the conclusion of the hearing, the court granted both motions to quash only on the issue of the violation of the defendants' constitutional right to speedy trial. The State noted its intent to appeal, and the court stayed the release of the defendants to allow the State time to file its appeal. On February 10, the court denied the defendants' motion for release pending the State's appeal. Both defendants sought writs, which this court granted, ordering the defendants' release. However, the Supreme Court reversed this court's release, ordering a stay of their release until further orders from that Court. The Court then ordered the State to file its appeal "forthwith" and this court to give the State's appeal expedited consideration.

Thomas filed a writ in this court seeking reversal of the trial court's denial of his motion to quash on statutory speedy trial grounds. This court denied writs, noting that it did not have jurisdiction to consider the application because of the State's pending appeal. Thomas sought relief in the Supreme Court. The Court granted the writ. The Court also directed this court to give the appeal expedited consideration. Patin, however, did not seek review of the trial court's denial of his motion to quash on statutory grounds.

On remand, a jury found Thomas not guilty on October 7, 2010. On October 18, 2010, the State amended the bill of indictment to charge Patin with manslaughter, and Patin pled guilty as charged, reserving his right to appeal the trial court's denial of his motion to quash. The court sentenced him to serve ten years at hard labor and granted his motion for appeal.

OPINION

Appellant contends his constitutional right to a speedy trial has been violated because over eight years elapsed between the filing of the first indictment and the filing of his motion to quash. This issue was raised, fully discussed, and rejected by this court in the State's prior appeal of the trial court's granting of the motion to quash. For this reason, the State argues that this issue should not be considered in this appeal, citing the "law of the case" doctrine.

The "law of the case" doctrine is well-settled; when it is applied and the reasons for it were explained... The "law of the case" doctrine applies to all prior rulings or decisions of an appellate court or the Supreme Court in the same case, not merely those arising from the full appeal process. This policy applies to parties who were parties to the case when the former decision was rendered and who thus had their day in court. The reasons for the "law of the case" doctrine is to avoid relitigation of the same issue; to promote consistency of result in the same litigation; and to promote efficiency and fairness to both parties by affording a single opportunity for the argument and decision of the matter at issue. This doctrine is not an inflexible law; thus appellate courts are not absolutely bound thereby and may exercise discretion in application of the doctrine. It should not be applied where it would accomplish an obvious injustice or where the former appellate decision was manifestly erroneous.

In the case at hand, Appellant Patin raises the same constitutional speedy trial claim as was raised in the State's earlier appeal. The record is void of any evidence that he re-urged his motion to quash after the case was remanded and the Supreme Court denied the writ. Additionally, Appellant has failed to present any new evidence for this court to consider.

Considering that this court has already found that Appellant Patin's constitutional right to a speedy trial has not been violated, and he has presented no new evidence to dispute this ruling, this court will not reconsider this matter under the "law of the case" doctrine.

Appellant Patin also argues that his statutory right to a speedy trial has been violated because the State failed to bring him to trial within the statutory limits set forth in La.C.Cr.P. art. 578.

Appellant Patin was originally indicted for first degree murder, a charge to which he was exposed to the death penalty. Pursuant to La.C.Cr.P. art. 578 A(1), trial for a capital case must commence within three years from the date of institution of prosecution. Nonetheless, the time periods set forth in La.C.Cr.P. art. 578 may be suspended by the filing of preliminary pleas (La.C.Cr.P. art. 580) or interrupted by: (1) the defendant's absence for the purpose of avoiding detection, apprehension, or prosecution; (2) the State's inability to try the defendant because he is insane, his presence cannot be obtained by legal process, or for any other reason beyond the State's control; or (3) the defendant's failure to appear in court at a proceeding for which he was given actual notice, proof of which is in the court record.

In cases in which there is interruption, the time limitations set forth in La.C.Cr.P. art. 578 start anew. Once the time limitations... have expired, the trial court shall dismiss the charge upon the defendant's filing of a motion to quash the bill... Nonetheless, according to La.C.Cr.P. art. 580, once a defendant files a motion to quash "or other preliminary plea," the time limitations are suspended until the court rules on the motion, "but in no case shall the state have less than one year after the ruling to commence trial."

In addition, this court has held that the delays caused by Hurricane Katrina constituted a "cause beyond the control of the State" which interrupted the time periods... This court set June 5, 2006, as the date upon which interruption based upon Hurricane Katrina ended.

In the case at hand, the grand jury returned the indictment on October 17, 2002. Appellant Patin filed his first motion to quash the indictment on October 30, 2002, thereby suspending the three-year prescriptive period to bring him to trial. He also filed a motion to adopt for all defendants any pleadings filed by any defendant. The court denied the motion to quash on January 27, 2003, thereby giving the State at least until January 27, 2004 to try him. On July 22, 2003, Appellant filed a second motion to quash, which again suspended the time period. There is no evidence in the record that the court ruled on that particular motion, but on August 20, 2003, Appellant moved to continue his trial. The motion was granted, and at that point, the State had until at least August 20, 2004 to try him. On January 30, 2004, Appellant Patin joined the State in a motion to continue his trial, giving the State until at least January 30, 2005 to try him. On April 20, 2004, Appellant Patin again moved to continue trial, thereby granting the State until April 20, 2005, to try him. Appellant subsequently moved to continue trial on June 17, 2004, and then on January 21, 2005, he joined in a motion to continue trial, giving the State until at least January

21, 2006, to try him. Appellant Patin again moved to continue the trial on March 11, 2005, giving the State until March 11, 2006, to try him.

Hurricane Katrina struck New Orleans on August 29, 2005, and the time limitations of La.C.Cr.P. art. 578 were interrupted… Regarding the constitutional speedy trial claim, and on remand from this court's ruling, the trial court held an evidentiary hearing on February 4, 2010. At the conclusion of which it granted Appellant's and Thomas' motions to quash based upon constitutional grounds. Again, the State could not try the appellant, and it appealed this ruling. This court reversed the quashing of the bill of information on June 27, 2010. This gave the State until June 27, 2011, to try Appellant. In early October 2010, the Appellant Patin filed more preliminary motions, which the court denied on October 14, 2010.

Appellant subsequently pled guilty… on October 18, 2010, approximately eight months before the one-year time limitation that the State obtained pursuant to La.C.Cr.P. art. 580. Thus, we find no merit in Appellant's argument that his statutory right to a speedy trial was violated.

This court fully considered Appellant Patin's constitutional right to speedy trial claim in the 2010 appeal, and he has presented no new evidence to show that this court erred in its 2010 ruling. Thus, pursuant to the "law of the case" doctrine, this court's previous ruling will not be considered. Additionally, we find that Appellant Patin's statutory speedy trial claim has no merit. We further find the trial court did not err by denying Appellant's motion to quash based upon statutory grounds

Accordingly, the findings of the trial court are affirmed.

IN THIS CASE, the defendant's right to a speedy trial was not considered violated after over eight years of pre-trial delays because, under Louisiana state law, in cases where there is an interruption, the statutory time limitations for right to a speedy trial start anew. Furthermore, the "law of the case" doctrine precludes a court from reviewing an issue in a case that has been previously decided by that court or by a higher court.

With many cases, and many of them heard by juries, there is a fear of unpredictability that makes planning difficult in a business context. If one knows what the law is, one can make plans for how to arrange one's business decisions. If the law is unpredictable, it is difficult to make such plans.

In 2012, the U.S. Court of Appeals D.C. Circuit handed down a much anticipated decision that had the potential to adversely affect many small businesses. *AKM, LLC dba Volks Constructors v. Secretary of Labor,* 675 F.3d 752 (2012), arose from a citation from the Occupational Safety and Health Administration for an employer's improper recording of workplace injuries that occurred up to five years ago. The statute of limitations on such citations was previously understood to be six months from the occurrence of a violation.

The importance of precedent tries to address some of these downsides. The Latin term for precedent, *stare decisis*, means: Let the decision stand. In other words, once a court has decided a case, other similar cases in that jurisdiction should be decided the same way. If a court in one jurisdiction determines that a person driving a car over the speed limit is liable for damages when the car injures a pedestrian, a case involving another driver who injures a pedestrian while driving over the speed limit will be decided the same way. However, there are different degrees of legal authority when it comes to cases providing precedent. There is mandatory authority and persuasive authority. Mandatory authority applies in cases where the legal issue has already been decided by a higher court in that jurisdiction or by the Supreme Court of the United States. For example, a trial court in Los Angeles must follow the legal precedent set by the Second District Court of Appeals in California, and the Court of Appeals in California must follow the decisions of the Supreme Court of California. So if the Supreme Court of California has determined liability for that driver who hit a pedestrian, then when a similar case comes up in the Los Angeles County Court, the judge there will be guided by that precedent. As an example, below is a chart indicating the hierarchy of courts in California to help better understand mandatory authority.

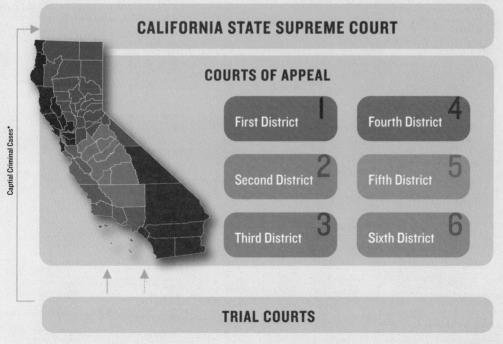

CALIFORNIA STATE SUPREME COURT

COURTS OF APPEAL

First District 1   Fourth District 4

Second District 2   Fifth District 5

Third District 3   Sixth District 6

Capital Criminal Cases*

TRIAL COURTS

* Death Penalty cases are automatically appealed form the superior court to the Supreme Court

—————————— Line of Appeal

- - - - - - - - - - - Line of Discretionary Review

On a state-to-federal level, because of the separation of powers between state and federal law, decisions from federal courts are not binding on state courts, unless the legal issue is pertaining to federal law. Similarly, state court decisions on issues of state law are mandatory authority for federal courts interpreting state law.

Persuasive authority is not binding. Generally speaking, persuasive authority tends to come from the same jurisdiction, and the higher up the court, the more persuasive the authority. However, decisions by lower courts within your jurisdiction can also be considered persuasive. On a federal level, District Court decisions from different districts are not binding on one another but are considered very persuasive. For example, if a case is pending in the Eighth District and the Third District has been known to hand down consistent decisions on antitrust cases, a judge from the Eighth District may find a Third District opinion to be very persuasive.

The following chart provides an easy way of determining when authority is mandatory and when it is persuasive:

Mandatory or Persuasive Authority?

COURT ISSUING DECISION	COURT AFFECTED BY DECISION					
	US SUPREME	FEDERAL APPEALS	FEDERAL DISTRICT	STATE SUPREME	STATE APPELLATE	STATE TRIAL
US SUPREME	M	M	M	M: Fed Q P: State Q	M: Fed Q P: State Q	M: Fed Q P: State Q
FEDERAL APPELLATE	P	M: Same Circuit P: Other Courts	M: Same Circuit P: Other Courts	P	P	P
FEDERAL DISTRICT	P	P	M: Same District P: Other Courts	P	P	P
STATE SUPREME	M : Fed Q P: State Q	M : Fed Q P: State Q	M : Fed Q P: State Q	M	M	M
STATE APPELLATE	P	M: Same State Appellate Ct P: Other Courts	M: Same State Appellate Ct P: Other Courts	P	M: Same State Appellate Ct P: Other Courts	M: Same State Appellate Ct P: Other Courts
STATE TRIAL	P	P	P	P	P	M: Same Court P: Other Courts

In the United States, the American Law Institute publishes a collection of rules that reflect modern common law, called the Restatements. The Restatements cover many areas of law, including torts, contracts, agency, property, and foreign relations of the United States. While courts are not bound by the Restatements, as they reflect the case law of the majority of states and not statutory law, many courts tend to consider the Restatements persuasive authority. It is also interesting to note that the Restatements are drafted by a community of lawyers, judges and scholars, meaning lawyers and legal scholars also have the ability to influence the development of law. While the Restatements are often based on precedent from the majority of states, its drafters also suggest new rules that reflect developments or changes in the legal field.

Precedent in our legal system serves several interests. One is that it does make the law more predictable. If one knows what the law is concerning a situation, then one can know the likely consequences of one's actions. This predictability promotes another interest, which is fairness. As any three year old will realize (and verbally assert), it is manifestly unfair if she gets in trouble for doing the same thing that her sibling just got away with. In a legal setting the sentiment is the same: factually similar cases should be decided similarly. A final interest promoted by precedent is efficiency. This partners with predictability, in that one can efficiently and knowingly undertake actions that accord with the law. In the following case, the Supreme Court found that in the absence of legislation applicable to a particular industry, the parties are entitled to the benefits of *stare decisis*.

Flood v. Kuhn

Supreme Court of the United States, 1972, 407 U.S. 258

BACKGROUND

Curtis Charles Flood, a professional baseball player was 'traded' to another team without his previous knowledge or consent. Flood brought this antitrust suit after being refused the right to make his own contract with another major league team, which is not permitted under the reserve system. The District Court rendered judgment in favor of defendants, and the Court of Appeals affirmed.

The District Court trial took place in May and June 1970. An extensive record was developed. In an ensuing opinion, Judge Cooper first noted that:

> 'Plaintiff's witnesses in the main concede that some form of reserve on play-ers is a necessary element of the organization of baseball as a league sport, but contend that the present all-embracing system is needlessly restrictive and offer various alternatives which in their view might loosen the bonds without sacrifice to the game. . . .

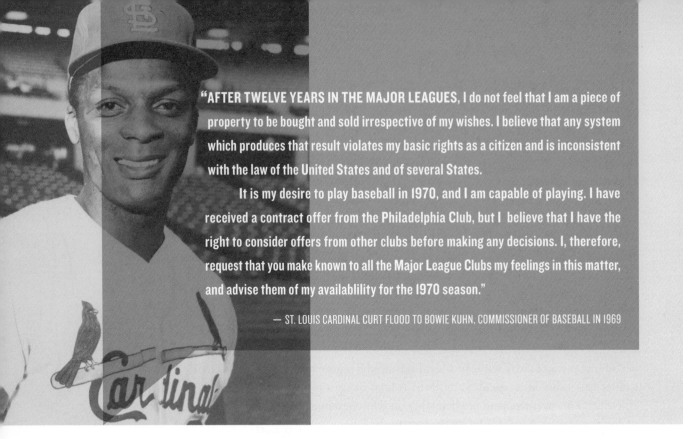

'Clearly the preponderance of credible proof does not favor elimination of the reserve clause. With the sole exception of plaintiff himself, it shows that even plaintiff's witnesses do not contend that it is wholly undesirable; in fact they regard substantial portions meritorious. . . .' 316 F.Supp., at 275-276.

He then held that *Federal Baseball Club v. National League*, 259 U.S. 200 (1922), and *Toolson v. New York Yankees, Inc.*, 346 U.S. 356 (1953), were controlling; that it was not necessary to reach the issue whether exemption from the antitrust laws would result because aspects of baseball now are a subject of collective bargaining; that the plaintiff's state-law claims, those based on common law as well as on statute, were to be denied because baseball was not 'a matter which admits of diversity of treatment,'; that the involuntary servitude claim failed because of the absence of 'the essential element of this cause of action, a showing of compulsory service,' and that judgment was to be entered for the defendants. Judge Cooper included a statement of personal conviction to the effect that 'negotiations could produce an accommodation on the reserve system which would be eminently fair and equitable to all concerned' and that 'the reserve clause can be fashioned so as to find acceptance by player and club.'

On appeal, the Second Circuit felt 'compelled to affirm.' It regarded the issue of state law as one of first impression, but concluded that the Commerce Clause precluded its application. Judge Moore added a concurring opinion in which he predicted, with respect to the suggested overruling of *Federal Baseball* and *Toolson*, that 'there is no likelihood that such an event will occur.'

HOLDING
Mr. Justice BLACKMUN

In view of all this, it seems appropriate now to say that:

1. Professional baseball is a business and it is engaged in interstate commerce.

2. With its reserve system enjoying exemption from the federal antitrust laws, baseball is, in a very distinct sense, an exception and an anomaly. *Federal Baseball* and *Toolson* have become an aberration confined to baseball.

3. Even though others might regard this as 'unrealistic, inconsistent, or illogical,' ... the aberration is an established one, and one that has been recognized not only in *Federal Baseball* and *Toolson*, but in *Shubert*, *International Boxing*, and *Radovich*, as well, a total of five consecutive cases in this Court. It is an aberration that has been with us now for half a century, one heretofore deemed fully entitled to the benefit of *stare decisis*, and one that has survived the Court's expanding concept of interstate commerce. It rests on a recognition and an acceptance of baseball's unique characteristics and needs.

4. Other professional sports operating interstate-football, boxing, basketball, and, presumably, hockey and golf-are not so exempt.

5. The advent of radio and television, with their consequent increased coverage and additional revenues, has not occasioned an overruling of *Federal Baseball* and *Toolson*.

6. The Court has emphasized that since 1922 baseball, with full and continuing congressional awareness, has been allowed to develop and to expand unhindered by federal legislative action. Remedial legislation has been introduced repeatedly in Congress but none has ever been enacted. The Court, accordingly, has concluded that Congress as yet has had no intention to subject baseball's reserve system to the reach of the antitrust statutes. This, obviously, has been deemed to be something other than mere congressional silence and passivity.

7. The Court has expressed concern about the confusion and the retro-activity problems that inevitably would result with a judicial overturning of *Federal Baseball*. It has voiced a preference that if any change is to be made, it come by legislative action that, by its nature, is only prospective in operation.

...

This emphasis and this concern are still with us. We continue to be loath, 50 years after *Federal Baseball* and almost two decades after Toolson, to overturn those cases judicially when Congress, by its positive inaction, has allowed those decisions to stand for so long and, far beyond mere inference and implication, has clearly evinced a desire not to disapprove them legislatively.

Accordingly, we adhere once again to *Federal Baseball* and *Toolson* and to their application to professional baseball. We adhere also to International Boxing and Radovich and to their respective applications to professional boxing and professional football. If there is any inconsistency or illogic in all this, it is an inconsistency and illogic of long standing that is to be remedied by the Congress and not by this Court. If we were to act otherwise, we would be withdrawing from the conclusion as to congressional intent made in *Toolson* and from the concerns as to retrospectivity therein expressed. Under these circumstances, there is merit in consistency even though some might claim that beneath that consistency is a layer of inconsistency.

The petitioner's argument as to the application of state antitrust laws deserves a word. Judge Cooper rejected the state law claims because state antitrust regulation would conflict with federal policy and because national 'uniformity (is required) in any regulation of baseball and its reserved system.' The Court of Appeals, in affirming, stated, '(A) s the burden on interstate commerce outweighs the states' interests in regulating baseball's reserve system, the Commerce Clause precludes the application here of state antitrust law.' As applied to organized baseball, and in the light of this Court's observations and holding in *Federal Baseball*, in *Toolson*, in Shubert, in International Boxing, and in Radovich, and despite baseball's allegedly inconsistent position taken in the past with respect to the application of state law, these statements adequately dispose of the state law claims.

The conclusion we have reached makes it unnecessary for us to consider the respondents' additional argument that the reserve system is a mandatory subject of collective bargaining and that federal labor policy therefore exempts the reserve system from the operation of federal antitrust laws.

We repeat for this case what was said in *Toolson*:

> 'Without re-examination of the underlying issues, the (judgment) below (is) affirmed on the authority of *Federal Baseball* Club of Baltimore v. National League of Professional Baseball Clubs, supra, so far as that decision determines that Congress had no intention of including the business of baseball within the scope of the federal antitrust laws.'

And what the Court said in *Federal Baseball* in 1922 and what it said in *Toolson* in 1953, we say again here in 1972: the remedy, if any is indicated, is for congressional, and not judicial, action.

The judgment of the Court of Appeals is affirmed.

CHANGE AND DEVELOPMENT in the law occurs because no two cases are exactly alike. There will always be cases arising with sets of unique factual details provide room for courts to distinguish a case before it from past precedent.

Butterworth v. National League of Professional Baseball Clubs

Supreme Court of Florida, 1994
644 So.2d 1021

FACTS

This case arose from the unsuccessful attempt of a group of investors to purchase the San Francisco Giants Major League Baseball franchise and relocate it to Tampa Bay, Florida. After the baseball owners voted against approval of the sale to the Tampa investors and the Giants owner signed a contract to sell the franchise to a group of San Francisco investors, Florida Attorney General Robert Butterworth (Attorney General) issued antitrust civil investigative demands (CIDs) to the National League of Professional Baseball Clubs and its president William D. White (National League) pursuant to section 542.28, Florida Statutes (Supp.1992). According to the CIDs, the specific focus of the investigation was "[a] combination or conspiracy in restraint of trade in connection with the sale and purchase of the San Francisco Giants baseball franchise."

The National League petitioned the Circuit Court of the Ninth Judicial Circuit to set aside the CIDs, based upon an assertion that the matters under investigation involved a transaction exempt from the application of both federal and state antitrust laws. The Attorney General filed a response asserting that baseball's antitrust exemption is not applicable to activities relating to the transfer of a baseball franchise. The Attorney General also filed a cross-motion to compel compliance with the CIDs. After receiving written memoranda and hearing argument by the parties, the circuit court issued an order quashing the CIDs. The circuit court determined that "[d]ecisions concerning ownership and location of baseball franchises clearly fall within the ambit of baseball's antitrust exemption." On appeal, the district court affirmed that order and certified the question to this Court.

OPINION

We have for review *Butterworth v. National League of Professional Baseball Clubs*, 622 So.2d 177 (1993), in which the Fifth District Court of Appeal certified the following question to be one of great public importance:

> Does the antitrust exemption for baseball recognized by the United States Supreme Court in *Federal Baseball Club of Baltimore, Inc. v. National League of Professional Baseball Clubs*, 259 U.S. 200 (1922) and its progeny exempt all decisions involving the sale and location of baseball franchises from federal and Florida antitrust law?

We answer the certified question in the negative and quash the decision below because we find that baseball's antitrust exemption extends only to the reserve system.

The United States Supreme Court originally recognized some form of antitrust law exemption for baseball in *Federal Baseball Club, Inc. v. National League of Professional Baseball Clubs*, 259 U.S. 200 (1922). That case involved an antitrust action by a baseball club of the Federal League against the National League and the American League, alleging a conspiracy to monopolize the baseball business. The Supreme Court concluded that the federal antitrust laws were inapplicable because the business at issue, "giving exhibitions of base ball," did not involve interstate commerce. Although the Supreme Court reaffirmed that exemption in the subsequent case of *Toolson v. New York Yankees, Inc.*, 346 U.S. 356 (1953), it did so "[w]ithout re-examination of the underlying issues." Instead, the Supreme Court affirmed the judgments of the courts of appeals in three consolidated cases brought against baseball owners on the authority of *Federal Baseball*, "so far as that decision determines that Congress had no intention of including the business of baseball within the scope of the federal antitrust laws." *Toolson*, 346 U.S. at 357. The Supreme Court noted that Congress "has not seen fit to bring such business under [the antitrust] laws by legislation" and concluded that any such application "should be by legislation." In a later case, the Supreme Court described *Toolson* as "a narrow application of the rule of *stare decisis*." *United States v. Shubert*, 348 U.S. 222 (1955) (finding that business built around the performance of local theatrical productions is subject to antitrust laws).

In response to attempts to extend the reasoning of *Federal Baseball* beyond the context of baseball, the Court specifically limited the antitrust exemption to "the business of organized professional baseball." *Radovich v. National Football League*, 352 U.S. 445 (1957) (refusing to extend the antitrust exemption to football); *Haywood v. National Basketball Ass'n*, 401 U.S. 1204 (1971) ("Basketball ... does not enjoy exemption from the antitrust laws."); *United States v. International Boxing Club*, 348 U.S. 236 (1955) (same as to boxing business).

The Supreme Court directly addressed the baseball exemption for the third and most recent time in *Flood v. Kuhn*, 407 U.S. 258 (1972). In *Flood*, a player challenged professional baseball's reserve system, whereby the player was traded to another franchise without his knowledge or consent. The Supreme Court affirmed the lower court's judgment dismissing the complaint based upon the controlling authority of *Federal Baseball and Toolson*. The Supreme Court also made a number of findings, including the following: professional baseball is a business engaged in interstate commerce; the exemption from antitrust laws is an exception, an anomaly, and an aberration confined to baseball; the exemption is an established one that is entitled to the benefits of *stare decisis;* and any change in the exemption should come through legislative action and should be prospective only in operation.

Based upon the Supreme Court's trilogy of baseball cases, baseball clearly enjoys some form of exemption from antitrust laws. However, there is some disagreement as to the scope of that exemption.

The parties in the instant case view the parameters of the exemption from equally differing perspectives. The Attorney General contends that the exemption only applies to the reserve clause system. The National League asserts that the exemption applies broadly to "the business of baseball," which includes decisions regarding the sale and location of franchises.

Several federal courts have interpreted the scope of the exemption broadly. For example, the United States Court of Appeals for the Seventh Circuit concluded that the "Supreme Court intended to exempt the business of baseball, not any particular facet of that business, from the federal antitrust laws."

However, in a recent decision involving two Pennsylvania citizens who were part of the same investment group as the Tampa Bay investors in the instant case the United States District Court for the Eastern District of Pennsylvania stated that the "antitrust exemption created by *Federal Baseball* is limited to baseball's reserve system. After an extensive analysis of the Supreme Court's baseball trilogy, the *Piazza* court concluded that *Flood* invalidated the rule *stare decisis of Federal Baseball* and *Toolson* and left only the result *stare decisis* under the facts of the case, namely the exemption of baseball's reserve system from federal antitrust law.

Even though the *Piazza* court is the only federal court to have interpreted baseball's antitrust exemption so narrowly, the language of the *Flood* opinion supports such an interpretation. In *Flood*, the Supreme Court itself characterized the trilogy of cases in this manner: "For the third time in 50 years the Court is asked specifically to rule that professional baseball's *reserve system* is within the reach of the federal antitrust laws." In discussing the reasons why the Supreme Court followed *Federal Baseball in Toolson*, the Court cited baseball's development between 1922 and 1953 "upon the understanding that the *reserve system* was not subject to existing federal antitrust laws." In listing its eight findings regarding baseball and the exemption, the Court twice described the exemption as applying to the "reserve system." First, in concluding that baseball's status is "an exception and an anomaly" and that "*Federal Baseball* and *Toolson* have become an aberration confined to baseball," the Court described baseball's "*reserve system* [as] enjoying exemption from federal antitrust laws." Second, the Court concluded that "Congress as yet has had no intention to subject *baseball's reserve system* to the reach of the antitrust statutes."

The Supreme Court also rejected the rationale of *Federal Baseball* when it stated that "professional baseball is a business ... engaged in interstate commerce." The *Piazza* opinion includes a thorough analysis of what this rejection of the analytical underpinnings of *Federal Baseball* means to the precedential value of *Federal Baseball and Toolson*. The court concluded that those cases have no precedential value beyond the particular facts involved, i.e., the reserve clause. The *Piazza* court also noted that the other federal cases which have construed the exemption broadly have not engaged in such an analysis of the Supreme Court's baseball trilogy.

In *Finley*, the Seventh Circuit Court of Appeals rejected the plaintiff's argument that the exemption applies only to the reserve system. The plaintiff argued that the Supreme Court's references to the reserve system in *Flood* supported a narrow interpretation of the exemption. Despite the references in *Flood* to the reserve system, the *Finley* court concluded that the language in the three baseball cases and *Radovich* shows that "the Supreme Court intended to exempt the business of baseball, not any particular facet of that business, from the federal antitrust laws." The United States District Court for the Eastern District of Louisiana agreed with the *Finley* court's interpretation of the baseball exemption and rejected the "cramped view" of the *Piazza* court, even though it found the "reasoning impressive."

There is no question that *Piazza* is against the great weight of federal cases regarding the scope of the exemption. However, none of the other cases have engaged in such a comprehensive analysis of *Flood* and its implications. In fact, many of the cases simply state that baseball is exempt and cite to one or more of the baseball trilogy without any discussion at all. Although the *Finley* opinion does contain analysis and discussion, the court simply cites "business of baseball" language from the baseball trilogy and disregards the Supreme Court's references in *Flood* to the reserve system and its own characterization of the exemption as involving the reserve system. Moreover, *Finley* contains no analysis of what implications the *Flood* findings have on the precedential value of *Federal Baseball* and *Toolson*.

> **THE SUPREME COURT'S "BASEBALL TRILOGY"**
>
> BASEBALL'S ANTITRUST EXEMPTION WAS ESTABLISHED THROUGH DECISIONS IN THREE SUPREME COURT CASES:
>
> - *Federal Baseball Club of Baltimore, Inc. v. National League of Professional Baseball Clubs*
> - *Toolson v. New York Yankees*
> - *Flood v. Kuhn*

The Supreme Court's determination in *Flood* that professional baseball "is engaged in interstate commerce," directly contradicts the determination in *Federal Baseball* that baseball exhibitions are "purely state affairs" and thus do not constitute "commerce among the States." This rejection of the very reason that the Court recognized such an exemption in *Federal Baseball* seriously undercuts the precedential value of both *Federal Baseball* and *Toolson*. Based upon the language and the findings in *Flood*, we come to the same conclusion as the *Piazza* court: baseball's antitrust exemption extends only to the reserve system.

Accordingly, we answer the certified question in the negative, quash the decision below, and remand this case for proceedings consistent with this opinion.

———————————

WHILE PLAINTIFFS in previous antitrust cases involving professional baseball could not prevail in court because of the antitrust exemption for professional baseball, the Florida Supreme Court found differently in this case because the business in question was not the business of baseball (aka the "reserve system") but instead a facet of that business—the sale and purchase of a franchise.

Sometimes, a court will distinguish a case on the basis of law. This is particularly true when an older or outdated law is being relied upon. Over the years, a series of other cases may have chipped away at various principles that, together, had been the basis for a previous decision. But with weakened precedent, the time may finally come for the case to be overturned on the basis of an interpretation of current law.

Lawrence v. City of New York

Supreme Court, Appellate Division,
Second Department, New York, 1981 82 A.D.2d 485

BACKGROUND

On February 2, 1971, plaintiff was employed as a fireman by the New York City Fire Department. While on a break in the backyard of premises where he and other fire fighters had been fighting a fire in the building thereon, plaintiff was struck by a couch pushed or thrown from the building. On or about February 8, 1972, plaintiff brought the within action against the appellant City of New York (hereinafter the city).

Although there was some evidence respecting the failure of the city to have had a lookout stationed on the ground below in preparation for defenestration of smoldering items that might reignite the building, the thrust of plaintiff's case at the trial, limited to the issue of liability, was directed toward the alleged negligence of those who threw or pushed the couch from the building.

At the end of the trial, the jury, in response to interrogatories, held that the negligence of the city had been the proximate cause of the accident, and that plaintiff had not been guilty of contributory negligence nor had he assumed the risk of the incident which caused the injuries.

...

The rule that the employer is not liable for injuries caused solely by the negligence of a servant was first promulgated in England in 1837. Shortly thereafter it became recognized in the United States as well. One of the bases for the **fellow-servant rule** was that it would promote the safety of the public and all servants to make each one watchful of the conduct of others for his own protection. While such reason and others might have been appropriate to small enterprises and shops because of the close contact and acquaintance one workman had with the others, they had little validity in the industrial area where one employee might be injured by the negligence of a

"THE FELLOW SERVANT RULE" was a rule of tort law created in the mid-nineteenth century. It carved out an exception to the well-established rule of *respondeat superior*, and relieved employers of liability for injuries negligently inflicted by any employee upon a "fellow servant." The rule did not exist until 1837, when it was first pronounced in England by Lord Abinger in *Priestley v. Fowler*. In 1842 Chief Justice Lemuel Shaw of Massachiusetts gave the rule its American reception and rationale in the leading case of *Farwell v. Boston & Worcester Rail Road*. By 1880 the rule, in one form or another, was so firmly entrenched in nearly every American jurisdiction that late nineteenth-century treatise writers warned legislatures and courts against tampering with "a rule of the common law, based upon the wisdom and precedents of the ages."

— *The Creation of a Common Law Rule: The Fellow Servant Rule, 1837-1860; University of Pennsylvania Law Review Vol. 139:579.*

co-employee whom he had never seen. According to one writer, the explanation of the rule probably lay in the highly individualistic viewpoint of courts in common law, and their desire to encourage industrial undertakings by making the burden upon employers as light as possible.

Although it is true that slow progress toward imposition of liability upon an employer occurred as a result of decisions in common law cases, the impetus in that direction was greatly accelerated by the passage of workers' compensation acts. In fact it has been held that the fellow-servant rule practically disappeared with workers' compensation.

However, workers' compensation acts, at least in the earlier years, have been held not to cover the injuries of many categories of employees, such as farm laborers. In the absence of remedial legislation, such as workers' compensation laws, courts in many jurisdictions concluded that an employee's action against his employer was still subject, *inter alia*, to the fellow-servant rule defense.

In this State, although it has been held that a New York City policeman and a New York City fireman are not entitled to benefits under the Workers' Compensation Law, the absence of such coverage was not used as a basis for upholding the fellow-servant rule against a member of the city's uniformed officers. Rather... a majority of the Justices of this court hearing the appeal, in applying the fellow-servant rule, did not refer to the absence of Workers' Compensation coverage for the injured policeman...

...However, the Court of Appeals reversed this court's order dismissing the complaint under the fellow-servant rule and reinstated the trial court's judgment in favor of plaintiff. In rejecting the applicability of the fellow-servant doctrine, Judge FULD, writing for the majority, stated that the purpose of section 50–a of the General Municipal Law was to impose liability upon the city for the negligent operation of vehicles by police officers and other municipal officers and thereby overcome the hardship visited upon those who, injured by such negligence, would otherwise be without remedy. According to the majority there was no reason for not extending the relief afforded private persons under 50–a to the police driver's fellow officers as well, since the Legislature had not provided for their exclusion from the provisions of 50–a.

Of particular significance with respect to the case at bar is the strong criticism of the fellow servant rule found in Judge FULD's majority opinion in *Poniatowski*, 241 N.Y.S.2d 770:

> "The inherent injustice of a rule which denies a person, free of fault, the right to recover for injuries sustained through the negligence of another over whose conduct he has no control merely because of the fortuitous circumstance that the other is a fellow officer is manifest. Dean Prosser has characterized the fellow-servant rule as 'wicked' (Prosser, Torts [2d ed., 1955], p. 383), and one court has described it as resulting in 'gross injustice' and as 'callous to human rights'. This may well suggest the desirability of abolishing the rule but we leave decision of that question to the future."

As is evident from both the majority and dissenting opinions of the Court of Appeals in *Poniatowski*, all seven members of this State's highest tribunal had severe reservations about the viability of the fellow servant rule in this era. However, since the majority believed that the rule was not applicable in that case because of the provisions of section 50–a of the General Municipal Law, it left for the future the decision as to whether the rule should be abolished. We strongly believe that such "future" has arrived in the case at bar.

In our opinion this bench has three options, (1) it may determine that the fellow-servant rule is not applicable under an exception to the rule and thus sustain plaintiff's verdict; or (2) it may apply the rule and thus nonsuit the plaintiff; or (3) it may hold that the fellow-servant rule is no longer viable and thus affirm the order and sustain plaintiff's verdict.

With respect to the first two options, it has been stated that because of the great injustice stemming from the application of the fellow-servant rule, courts have been astute to engraft upon it so many modifications that little is left of its original import. It has also been noted that courts have carved out so many exceptions to the applicability of the rule that many have come to be considered as part of the original rule. Amongst the multitudinous number of exceptions to the rule are the nondelegable duty to furnish a safe place to work, the duty to instruct and to warn, the "vice principal rule," the "superior servant rule," the "different department rule," the "dangerous agency rule," *ad infinitum.*

> "THE THEORY...that public policy requires that servants, injured as a result of the negligence of a co-servant, should have no remedy against their masters, because the absence of any remedy will make them more careful of their own safety than they would otherwise be, not only is untenable but is fallacious."

In our opinion it is both illogical and self-defeating to continue a practice of engrafting exception after exception upon a flawed rule of law, which was founded not on natural justice but on an absurd and disingenuous public policy, and which has been universally discredited almost from its inception. Such action might well be compared to the engrafting of roses upon a large weed in the vain hope that the latter will no longer constitute both a threat to beneficial growth in the garden and an eyesore to the landscape. Creating exceptions to the rule does not destroy its lamented and unwanted existence, but instead leaves it readily available for judicial decisions shocking to society's sense of justice.

With respect to the rule itself, the theory upon which it is based, i.e., that public policy requires that servants, injured as a result of the negligence of a co-servant, should have no remedy against their masters, because the absence of any remedy will make them more careful of their own safety than they would otherwise be, not only is untenable but is fallacious. Unlike the relation of the master with a third person which is one of arm's length, the servant is obligated to the former under a bond of fidelity and loyalty. Under the fellow-servant rule the servant, in addition, must be endowed with a prescience and ultra sensory perception in order to forewarn him of the careless propensities of his working counterparts.

"[I]t is indeed strange that we should go on holding that the master is liable to everyone else in the world for the negligent acts of the employee whom he selects, while acting within the scope of his employment, except to the fellow servant or employee, who is usually more apt to be injured than any member of the general public, and who has usually, by the master's orders, been subject to the peril of such negligence on the part of his fellow servant, in the selection of which fellow servant the injured servant had no voice whatever. Such a doctrine shocks our sense of justice. *The general rule of respondeat superior should not any longer contain an exception which is so callous to human rights.*"

Accordingly, I conclude that the fellow servant rule is no longer viable in this State and is hereby abrogated.

The order of the trial court, therefore, should be affirmed insofar as appealed from, without costs or disbursements.

THEN, THERE ARE TIMES when a past law is viewed as simply being wrong or outdated. In such cases, a high court may strike down a law and establish a new line of precedent. A classic example of this occurred in *Brown v. Board of Education.*

Brown v. Board of Education of Topeka, Shawnee County, Kansas

Supreme Court of the United States, 1954   347 U.S. 483

These cases come to us from the States of Kansas, South Carolina, Virginia, and Delaware. They are premised on different facts and different local conditions, but a common legal question justifies their consideration together in this consolidated opinion.

In each of the cases, minors of the Negro race, through their legal representatives, seek the aid of the courts in obtaining admission to the public schools of their community on a nonsegregated basis. In each instance, they have been denied admission to schools attended by white children under laws requiring or permitting segregation according to race. This segregation was alleged to deprive the plaintiffs of the equal protection of the laws under the Fourteenth Amendment. In each of the cases other than the Delaware case, a three-judge federal district court denied relief to the plaintiffs on the so-called 'separate but equal' doctrine announced by this Court in *Plessy v. Ferguson*, 163 U.S. 537. Under that doctrine, equality of treatment is accorded when the races are provided substantially equal facilities, even though these facilities be separate. In the Delaware case, the Supreme Court of Delaware adhered to that doctrine, but ordered that the plaintiffs be admitted to the white schools because of their superiority to the Negro schools.

The plaintiffs contend that segregated public schools are not 'equal' and cannot be made 'equal,' and that hence they are deprived of the equal protection of the laws. Because of the obvious importance of the question presented, the Court took jurisdiction. Argument was heard in the 1952 Term, and reargument was heard this Term on certain questions propounded by the Court.

Mr. Chief Justice WARREN

In the first cases in this Court construing the Fourteenth Amendment, decided shortly after its adoption, the Court interpreted it as proscribing all state-imposed discriminations against the Negro race. The doctrine of "separate but equal" did not make its appearance in this court until 1896 in the case of *Plessy v. Ferguson*, involving not education but transportation. American courts have since labored with the doctrine for over half a century. ***

In the instant cases, that question is directly presented. Here, unlike *Sweatt v. Painter*, there are findings below that the Negro and white schools involved have been equalized, or are being equalized, with respect to buildings, curricula, qualifications and salaries of teachers, and other 'tangible' factors. Our decision, therefore, cannot turn on merely a comparison of these tangible factors in the Negro and white schools involved in each of the cases. We must look instead to the effect of segregation itself on public education.

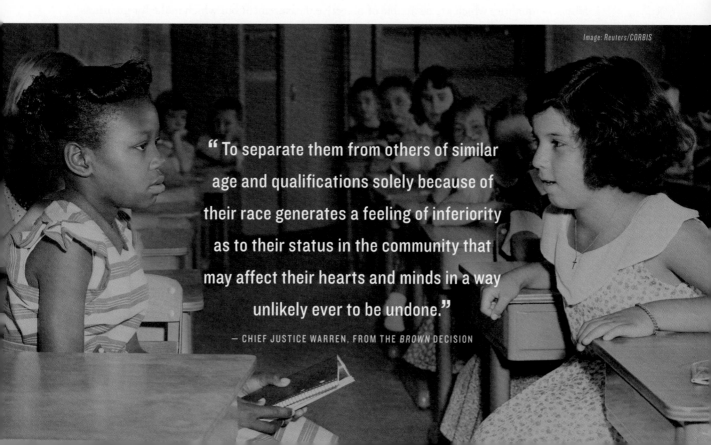

Image: Reuters/CORBIS

" To separate them from others of similar age and qualifications solely because of their race generates a feeling of inferiority as to their status in the community that may affect their hearts and minds in a way unlikely ever to be undone."

— CHIEF JUSTICE WARREN, FROM THE *BROWN* DECISION

In approaching this problem, we cannot turn the clock back to 1868 when the Amendment was adopted, or even to 1896 when *Plessy v. Ferguson* was written. We must consider public education in the light of its full development and its present place in American life throughout the Nation. Only in this way can it be determined if segregation in public schools deprives these plaintiffs of the equal protection of the laws.

Today, education is perhaps the most important function of state and local governments. Compulsory school attendance laws and the great expenditures for education both demonstrate our recognition of the importance of education to our democratic society. It is required in the performance of our most basic public responsibilities, even service in the armed forces. It is the very foundation of good citizenship. Today it is a principal instrument in awakening the child to cultural values, in preparing him for later professional training, and in helping him to adjust normally to his environment. In these days, it is doubtful that any child may reasonably be expected to succeed in life if he is denied the opportunity of an education. Such an opportunity, where the state has undertaken to provide it, is a right which must be made available to all on equal terms.

We come then to the question presented: Does segregation of children in public schools solely on the basis of race, even though the physical facilities and other 'tangible' factors may be equal, deprive the children of the minority group of equal educational opportunities? We believe that it does.

In *Sweatt v. Painter*, in finding that a segregated law school for Negroes could not provide them equal educational opportunities, this Court relied in large part on 'those qualities which are incapable of objective measurement but which make for greatness in a law school.' In *McLaurin v. Oklahoma State Regents*, the Court, in requiring that a Negro admitted to a white graduate school be treated like all other students, again resorted to intangible considerations: '* * * his ability to study, to engage in discussions and exchange views with other students, and, in general, to learn his profession.' Such considerations apply with added force to children in grade and high schools. To separate them from others of similar age and qualifications solely because of their race generates a feeling of inferiority as to their status in the community that may affect their hearts and minds in a way unlikely ever to be undone. The effect of this separation on their educational opportunities was well stated by a finding in the Kansas case by a court which nevertheless felt compelled to rule against the Negro plaintiffs:

> 'Segregation of white and colored children in public schools has a detrimental effect upon the colored children. The impact is greater when it has the sanction of the law; for the policy of separating the races is usually interpreted as denoting the inferiority of the negro group. A sense of inferiority affects the motivation of a child to learn. Segregation with the sanction of law, therefore, has a tendency to (retard) the educational and mental development of Negro children and to deprive them of some of the benefits they would receive in a racial(ly) integrated school system.'

Whatever may have been the extent of psychological knowledge at the time of *Plessy v. Ferguson*, this finding is amply supported by modern authority. Any language in *Plessy v. Ferguson* contrary to this finding is rejected.

We conclude that in the field of public education the doctrine of 'separate but equal' has no place. Separate educational facilities are inherently unequal. Therefore, we hold that the plaintiffs and others similarly situated for whom the actions have been brought are, by reason of the segregation complained of, deprived of the equal protection of the laws guaranteed by the Fourteenth Amendment. This disposition makes unnecessary any discussion whether such segregation also violates the Due Process Clause of the Fourteenth Amendment.

AS SEEN IN *Butterworth v. National League of Professional Baseball Clubs*, 644 So.2d 1021 (1994), *Lawrence v. City of New York*, 82 A.D.2d 485 (1981), and *Brown v. Board of Ed. of Topeka, Shawnee County, Kan.*, 347 U.S. 483 (1954), the common law system in the U.S. provides not only predictability in legal disputes, but also the flexibility for law to evolve with society.

II. Contemporary Comparative Alternatives

CIVIL LAW IS A PRIMARY ALTERNATIVE to the common law system, and its reach is vast. Much of its reach stems from European colonization, apart from England, which follows the common law system. Civil law societies include France, Spain, Portugal, and the Netherlands. If one looks to where those countries colonized, including Latin America, one often finds a civil law tradition. Even in the United States, Louisiana continues to follow a civil law system because of its history as a French settlement.

In a civil law system, judges look only to statutory authority and apply their interpretation of a statute to the facts of a case; prior decisions do not have the binding authority they possess in a common law system. While it may seem like it would be more efficient for judges to apply a single authority to an issue at hand, statutes can be difficult to interpret because of the inherent ambiguity of language, and many different decisions may be reasonably handed down on one legal issue. This makes cases in civil law systems more unpredictable than in common law systems. Another important distinction is the way judges analyze law in the different systems. Judges in civil law societies (particularly in Europe) tend to extrapolate theory from codified laws and use deductive reasoning to come to an appropriate judgment on a case-by-case basis.

Some courts in civil law societies can actually strike down a codified law. Over fifty countries, including Germany, Italy and France have constitutional courts that operate separately from the rest of their courts. Constitutional courts have a monopoly over constitutional review of law and if a codified law is found to be unconstitutional, this specialized court may actually nullify it. In the common law system of the United States, the Supreme Court can only declare a law unconstitutional and choose to not apply it to the case at hand, but it is up to the legislature to amend or nullify it.

Below is a an excerpt from the German Law Journal[2], describing an infamous case heard in the German constitutional court concerning the constitutionality of life imprisonment:

> In the *Life Imprisonment Case* from 1977, the First Senate of the *Bundes-verfassungs-gericht* (German Federal Constitutional Court) was confronted with a challenge to the constitutionality of a sentence of life-long imprisonment without the possibility of parole. Among other asserted constitutional violations the applicant claimed that this complete exclusion from society violated the right to human dignity guaranteed by Article 1 of the Basic Law. The ordinary courts disagreed. Having considered the legislative history behind the framer's abolition of the death penalty, the ordinary courts concluded that the justifications offered in the *Parlamentarisches Rat* (1948 West German constitutional convention) in support of the abolition of capital punishment did not preclude life imprisonment as a substitute.
>
> The First Senate of the Constitutional Court rejected the ordinary courts' interpretive analysis, invoking a standard reminiscent of the American "evolving standard of decency" from the Supreme Court's Eighth Amendment jurisprudence. The Senate explained: "Neither original history nor the ideas and intentions of the framers are of decisive importance ... Since the adoption of the Basic Law [constitution], our understanding of the content, function, and effect of basic rights has deepened ... Current attitudes are important in assessing the constitutionality of life imprisonment."
>
> Thus, freed from the shackles of original intent, the Senate began its analysis with the dramatic proposition that "the free human person and his [or her] dignity are the highest values of the constitutional order." From this foundational value the Court extracted the principle that "it is contrary to human dignity to make persons the mere tools of the state" in the context of criminal justice policy, that the state "cannot turn the offender into an object of crime prevention to the detriment of his constitutionally protected right to social worth and respect." The Court explained that life imprisonment without the possibility of parole violated the constitutional

---

2   Russell Miller, *The Shared Transatlantic Jurisprudence of Dignity*, 4 German Law Journal 9, 929 (2003), available at http://www.germanlawjournal.com/pdfs/Vol04No09/PDF_Vol_04_No_09_925-934_SI_Miller.pdf.

value that holds that every prisoner must possess some hope of regaining his or her freedom: "A sentence of life imprisonment cannot be enforced humanely if the prisoner is denied *a priori* any and every possibility of returning to freedom ... The condemned criminal must be given the chance, after atoning for his crime, to reenter society."

Shortly after the Constitutional Court's ruling the *Bundestag* (federal parliament) amended Germany's *Strafgesetzbuch* (criminal code) to authorize courts to suspend a life sentence when the situation warranted the offender's release from prison. In determining whether or not to release a person sentenced to life imprisonment, the amendments to the statute required courts to consider the personality of the of- fender, his or her behavior in prison, the circumstances of the crime, and his or her capacity to lead a normal life outside prison. These are statutory terms of human dignity, the idea that respect for human dignity particularly requires consideration of the offender's background and the circumstances of his or her crime.

There are some differences between civil law systems and common law systems in terms of the substance of legislation. Governments in a civil law country have a greater range of authority to step into a contractual situation to protect the fairness to either party or to protect the interests of the country as a whole. In common law systems there is a much greater freedom of contract. Whatever two parties decide to include in a contract tends to be enforced unless it violates a law. But in civil law countries the parties do not have to be quite as specific and can rely upon the overarching laws to fill in the blanks of a contractual agreement. Below is a contract law case from France. At issue is a clause in the contract limiting the liability of a transport company.

Case Société Chronopost v. Société Banchereau

Bull. Civ. 2002.IV, no. l2l, p.l29

Given that according to the decision under attack, rendered after remand following the quashing of an earlier decision (22 October 1996, Bull. civ., IV, no. 261), the Banchereau company handed certain documents to the Société Française de Messagerie Internationale (SFMI) addressed to the national office of butchers, meat producers and farmers in order to bid for an allocation of meat, and that since the documents were not delivered the day following their despatch in breach of SFMI's undertaking Banchereau was unable to bid for an allocation; that when Banchereau sued SFMI for damages as compensation for the harm it suffered, SFMI invoked the term of the contract which limited its liability to the cost of the carriage;

On the first ground of the application for review:

Given that Chronopost, successor to SFMI, criticises the judgment below for holding that the obligation it undertook was one "de résultat" or guarantee, whereas, it maintains, although the judges have a sovereign power to interpret contracts containing several terms which must be read together, it is on condition that it takes all such terms into account, and that in simply disregarding the term in Chronopost's general conditions of business that Chronopost will use every effort to deliver its clients' packages within the time laid down, which is characteristic of a mere obligation "de moyens", the court below misinterpreted the contract in breach of article 1134 Code civil;

But given that the court of appeal merely applied the law laid down by the Court of Cassation, this criticism is unacceptable;

But on the second ground of the application for review:

In view of article 1150 Code civil, article 8(II) of the Law of 30 December 1982 (Law no. 82-1153) and articles 1 and 15 of the rules of the contract for the carriage of packages, established by the decree of 4 May 1988, which is applicable:

Given that in declaring that because the contract here contained a specific obligation guaranteeing timeous delivery which could be relied on it was not a contract for the carriage of packages and that in consequence the general law of carriage was inapplicable;

Given that its holding that the clause limiting the carrier's liability was to be treated as not written entails that the statutory limit of compensation, avoidable only on proof of gross negligence on the part of the carrier, falls to be applied, the court of appeal's decision violated the texts cited above;

For these reasons QUASHES the decision of the Court of Appeal of Caen dated 5 January 1999 and remands the case to the Court of Appeal of Rouen.

Com, 9 July 2002, Bull IV no 121: The solution put forward by this judgment has formed the subject of numerous criticisms by legal writers; it has been pointed out that the Rouen court of appeal, which received the court file on the reference back after quashing still did not reach a decision, and that neither the lower courts nor the Cour de Cassation have had to do so since. Without returning expressly to the principle laid down by the commercial chamber on the 22 October 1996 (this case is concerned with the same affair, with the same parties: the judgment is called "Chronopost"), the judgment of the 9 September reduces this solution to much more modest proportions. It substitutes for the clause restricting liability which is nullified (a solution expressly maintained) application of the droit commun of carriage which provides in this case for a legal ceiling of indemnification which corresponds to the total amount of sums provided for in the clause restricting liability. The Cour de Cassation in effect considers that nullity of a clause restrictive of liability which is judged to be abusive and therefore nullified, entails, unless there is grave fault on the part of the carrier, a return not to the rules of the droit commun as the judges at first instance had considered, but application of the provisions of the droit commun of carriage. (A clause contradicting the very essence of a contract - and only such a clause - should be nullified leaving all the other provisions of the contract in existence, including those referring to a contract type capable of having the effect of restricting indemnification of the other contracting party in the same way as the annulled clause would do). However, it should be noted that this solution only applies to cases where a legal ceiling exists to indemnification which prevents return to the application of the rules of the droit commun; and that proof of a grave fault on the part of the other contracting party would in all circumstances entail return to the droit commun of contractual liability.[3]

There are also specific concepts that apply in most civil law countries. One is called "force majeure." This is a principle that eliminates an obligation to perform a contract because of an unpredictable event, such as an earthquake or a hurricane.

Though not necessarily a feature of civil law, per se, bankruptcy in civil law countries tends to result in liquidation of a company rather than a reorganization (as is common in the U.S. and U.K). Consistent with their friendliness to commercial affairs, common law countries tend to have a wider range of security interests that facilitate new forms of business activities than in civil law countries.

It is worth noting that some countries blend aspects of both common law and civil law. The United States, for example, is a blend of both. Its judicial system is, to be sure, based on common law, with a very strong role for the judiciary and a strong presumption of freedom of contract. But as we will see in the chapter on the Uniform Commercial Code, governments also often enacts broad legislation to comprehensively address issues.

While the distinction between common and civil law countries is commonly made, it is worth noting the range of systems utilized by the largest economic actors:

G 20 MEMBER	GENERAL ORIENTATION	NOTABLE CHARACTERISTICS
ARGENTINA	Civil	• No jury trials in Argentina. • Government structure and court system are similar to that of the U.S.
AUSTRALIA	Common	• Australia is a federation of six states, each with their own constitution and three branches of government: the executive, the legislature and the judiciary. • Systems of law of the six states are influential on each other but not binding.

---

3   Bull. Civ. 2002.IV, no. 121, p.129 *Case Société Chronopost v. Société Banchereau*, translated by Tony Weir, University of Texas, © Professor B. S. Markesinis, available at http://www.utexas.edu/law/academics/centers/transnational/work_new/french/case.php?id=1154.

G 20 MEMBER	GENERAL ORIENTATION	NOTABLE CHARACTERISTICS
BRAZIL	Civil	• Federation of 26 states, each with their own constitution and laws. • State constitutions and laws must follow principles established in the Federal Constitution. • Moving towards a trend of incorporating *stare decisis* into legal system.
CANADA	Common	• All provinces of Canada follow the common law system, with the exception of Quebec. • Quebec follows a civil law tradition in private law and follows a common law system in matters of public law. • All legal systems are subject to the Constitution of Canada.
CHINA	Other	• The current constitution of the People's Republic of China was enacted in 1982 and has been revised many times since. • Judiciary lacks transparency because there is no technical separation between the judiciary and the government. • Courts do not review legislation for constitutionality.
FRANCE	Civil	• Dual legal system made up of: Droit Public (public law) and Droit Privé (private law). • Inquisitorial rather than adversarial legal system. • Judges are trained at a national postgraduate school called *"École Nationale de la Magistrature."*

G 20 MEMBER	GENERAL ORIENTATION	NOTABLE CHARACTERISTICS
GERMANY	Civil	• Strong influences from the French legal tradition. • Has trial courts, specialized courts, and constitutional courts. • The constitution is also known as the Basic Law.
INDIA	Common	• Strong influences from the British legal system. • Constitution of India was adopted in 1949 and amended many times. • Civil courts, District courts, State High Courts, and the Supreme Court of India. • Muslim personal law is applied in regular courts. • Customary law may be applied in issues of succession.
INDONESIA	Civil	• Legal system is a mix of customary law and colonial Dutch-Roman law. • Constitutional Court created in 2001. • Predominantly Muslim country with a specialized Religious Court.
ITALY	Civil	• Fixed constitution, meaning it cannot be amended by ordinary laws. • jurisdiction: constitutional courts, ordinary courts, and specialized courts. • Special courts for administrative, auditing, military and fiscal issues.
JAPAN	Civil	• Constitution of Japan was adopted in 1946, following WWII. • Constitution provides 31 articles relating to human rights. • Though a civil law system, judges look heavily to precedent to guide decisions. • Civil law in Japan is highly influenced by German and French civil law. • Oral contracts carry a great deal of weight in Japan.

G 20 MEMBER	GENERAL ORIENTATION	NOTABLE CHARACTERISTICS
MEXICO	Civil	• Constitution provides for three branches of government: the judiciary, the executive and the legislature. • Sources of the law in Mexico according to legal hierarchy are: the Federal Constitution of 1917; International treaties and conventions; federal statutes; codes; doctrine; custom; and, general principles of law.
RUSSIA	Civil	• Current constitution was adopted in 1993. • Three separate court systems: constitutional courts, commercial courts, and courts of general jurisdiction. • Judiciary is autonomous from the legislature and the executive. • Many current judges were educated under the old legal system of the Soviet Union.
SAUDI ARABIA	Other	• Absolute monarchy with no binding written constitution. • Supreme law of the land is Sharia, Islamic law. • While most Islamic states codify parts of Sharia law, Saudi Arabia regards uncodified Sharia law in its entirety as the law of the land. • Sharia court system. • No jury trials. • Lawyers and judges are also part of the country's religious leadership. • The Specialized Criminal Court (non-Sharia) was founded in 2008 for terrorism related offenses.
SOUTH AFRICA	Civil and Common	• Constitution came into force in 1997. • Follows English common law in civil procedure and criminal law and Dutch common law in substantive issues such as contracts, family law, torts. • Has a constitutional court.
SOUTH KOREA	Civil	• Limited jury system for criminal and environmental cases. • Private law is based upon Japan's civil code. • Has a constitutional court.

G 20 MEMBER	GENERAL ORIENTATION	NOTABLE CHARACTERISTICS
TURKEY	Civil	• Judiciary is independent from the executive and the legislature. • Separate jurisdiction over civilian and military matters. • Military court can exercise jurisdiction over civilians during times of martial law. • No juries.
UNITED KINGDOM	Common	• Three legal systems: English law, North Ireland law, and Scots law. • English law and North Ireland law follow common law tradition. • Scots law follows civil law tradition. • Supreme Court of the U.K. is the highest court.
UNITED STATES	Common	• Strongly reinforced separation of powers between the judiciary, the legislature and the executive. • Supreme Court hears constitutional matters.
EUROPEAN UNION	Civil	• Common legislation and regulations are binding on all members of the EU. • Directives from the EU are binding but member states have flexibility to draft their own legislation to put the directive into force nationally.

NOTES AND COMMENTS

I. AS A BUSINESS STUDENT, do you believe that the common law system or a civil law system is more conducive to commerce? What strengths and weaknesses does each have? To be sure, most systems we see are hybrids with a mix of both. As you think about planning a business or operating a business, what features of each attract or concern you?

2. HAS LIVING IN THE SYSTEM of your native country influenced the way you think about deciding issues personally or in a group setting (such as a sorority or fraternity)? For example, does the Constitutional adage "innocent until proven guilty" influence the way you look at issues of right and wrong?

3. DOES PRECEDENT CREATE a good balance of predictability with change or does it unduly inhibit legal changes that match a dynamic business world? Many business people argue strongly both ways, saying on the one hand, that the predictability of precedent allows for good strategic planning, while on the other hand, some argue that law becomes too slow to respond to a changing world. What do you think?

3

ELEMENTS
TO A TRIAL

LAWSUITS CAN'T TAKE PLACE unless certain procedural elements are met. Suppose you're driving to school in New Jersey and suddenly a deer appears in the road. You try to hit the brakes on your car, and they just don't respond.

You end up veering off the road to avoid the deer and hit a tree, sustaining serious injuries. As a result of your injuries, you have incurred thousands of dollars of medical bills and still feel pain in your legs when you walk. To recover for your injuries, you want to sue the Michigan car manufacturer that put defective brakes in your car.

You may have a strong products liability case, but finding the applicable products liability law and establishing that the car manufacturer owed a duty to produce non-defective brakes is only a tiny portion of the battle. You will first have to establish jurisdiction over the Michigan company, find the right venue to bring your case, properly serve the car manufacturer, and sufficiently plead your case. Once all of those elements are satisfied, you can proceed to trial. At trial you must then abide by the requirements of trial procedure, which can include depositions, discovery, and presenting witness testimony. If at any point along the way you fail to abide by the procedural laws governing a trial, a judge may dismiss your case—and in the worst case, you and your attorney may be subject to sanctions. But let's say you satisfy all the elements of a trial and either a judge or a jury finds in your favor. It is almost guaranteed that the car company will file a motion for a new trial or appeal the final judgment. If either is granted, you must then follow post-trial procedures and argue your case all over again.

As you can see, understanding the procedural elements of the law and a trial is just as important if not more important than the substantive law, and it is certainly more cumbersome. The first element any plaintiff will have to satisfy in a lawsuit is establishing jurisdiction—you can't sue the car manufacturer in any court you please. The court must have personal jurisdiction over the defendant or in rem jurisdiction over the property in dispute, and subject matter jurisdiction over the type of dispute.

I. Jurisdiction and Long-Arm Statutes

A. JURISDICTION OF THE COURT

In total, there are 52 court systems in the United States and every court system has its own rules of civil and criminal procedure. Each state, plus the District of Columbia, has its own court system—these make up the state courts. State courts have jurisdiction over substantive state law matters, disputes arising in the state, and persons in the state. Then there is the federal court system. There are 94 federal judicial districts at least one in each state, plus the federal circuit courts. Federal courts are organized by districts and each state is designated a federal district court or circuit court. For example, Alabama, Georgia and Florida make up the 11th Circuit, while Wisconsin, Illinois and Indiana make up the 7th Circuit.

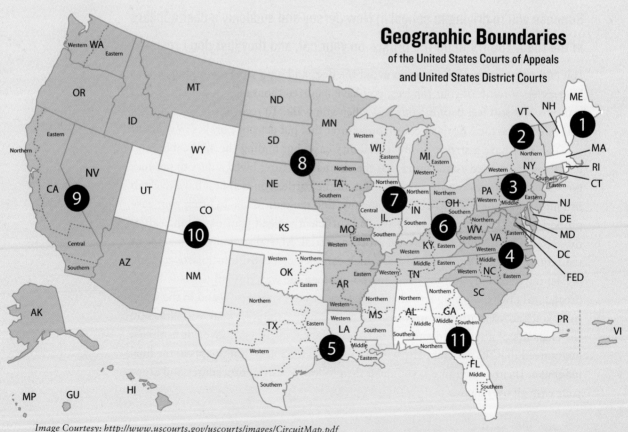

Geographic Boundaries
of the United States Courts of Appeals
and United States District Courts

Image Courtesy: http://www.uscourts.gov/uscourts/images/CircuitMap.pdf

Federal courts have jurisdiction over substantive federal law matters, also known as federal question jurisdiction, and cases that involve citizens of two different states, also known as diversity jurisdiction. A party can also bring a case into the federal court system if the amount in controversy exceeds $75,000.

Within each court system are trial courts where cases are first brought, and appellate courts where trial court decisions are appealed. Trial courts are fact-finding courts, meaning they serve the dual purpose of analyzing both the evidence (facts) presented and the applicable law. Appellate courts, however, do not generally make determinations about the factual elements of a case and consider only the legal questions. Trial court cases are reviewed for legal error and the appellate court will not accept new evidence or retry the case. When a motion for a new trial is granted, it is tried anew in state trial court, not the appellate court.

Two trial courts that can have nationwide jurisdiction over their specialized subject matter are the Court of International Trade, located in New York City, and the U.S. Court of Federal Claims in Washington, D.C. The Court of International Trade hears cases involving international trade and customs issues, while the Court of Federal Claims hears cases where the plaintiff is suing the United States for money damages, disputes over federal contracts, and unlawful takings of private property by the U.S. government (which you will learn more about in Chapter 6).

In addition to trial courts and appellate courts, there are also courts of limited jurisdiction. These courts try minor criminal cases and some civil disputes. Courts of limited jurisdiction usually deal with specialized matters, like tax courts, small claims courts, traffic courts, and probate courts. Courts of limited jurisdiction are used for matters which occur frequently, for small amounts of money, address minor damages, and are best handled by judges familiar with the specific laws. Parties can often represent themselves in courts of limited jurisdiction and therefore do not require attorneys. When decisions of these courts are appealed, the case is tried *de novo* (a new trial, complete with fact-finding) in trial court.

B. PERSONAL JURISDICTION

There are several ways a court can establish personal jurisdiction over a defendant. The first and simplest way is for a defendant to consent to the jurisdiction of the court. At the state level, rules governing personal jurisdiction vary, so it is very important to become familiar with the applicable rules of the state in which you want to bring a case. At the federal level, a court can establish personal jurisdiction over a defendant who enters a general appearance to subject himself to unlimited jurisdiction or one who fails to assert a defense outlined in the Federal Rules of Civil Procedure, FR 12(b)(2)-(5). Failure of a defendant to assert the defense of no personal jurisdiction actually constitutes consent.

Another way for the court to obtain personal jurisdiction over a defendant is if the defendant resides in the forum—the state or district in which the court is located. It is important to note here that contracts will often contain clauses called "forum selection clauses" which require disputes to be settled in a specified forum.

Often contract clauses addressing disputes will opt for alternative dispute resolution mechanisms (most commonly, arbitration). In some cases, the party drafting the contract or the party with more power in the deal-making will insert an arbitration clause that requires the dispute to be settled in a remote location, such as France, to make it unaffordable and undesirable for the other party to bring a dispute. It is an interesting exercise to look through the routine contracts you sign—with your cable provider, cell phone company, even your landlord—to see the forum selection for dispute resolution. You may be surprised by how impractical or seemingly random some of them are.

A residence is considered the state where a person has the intent to remain indefinitely, and an individual's residence can only be changed by establishing a new domicile. Intent to remain can be evidenced by where a defendant pays taxes and votes. When the defendant is a company, the residence of the company is the place of its incorporation. In *Milliken v. Meyer*, a 1940 U.S. Supreme Court case, a state was able to exercise jurisdiction over a temporarily absent citizen because it was shown that the defendant was still enjoying the privileges and protections of being a citizen of the state.

Another way of establishing personal jurisdiction over a defendant is physical presence within the state or district. A defendant is subject to jurisdiction if personally served within the relevant territory, even if he or she is not a citizen of the state. The following case is a landmark case on personal jurisdiction through physical presence.

■ A COPY OF THE NOTICE ATTEMPTING TO PROVIDE MARCUS NEFF WITH SUBSTITUTED SERVICE, PRINTED IN THE *PACIFIC CHRISTIAN ADVOCATE*, ON SAT., DEC. 2, 1865 AND DEC. 9, 1865.

Pennoyer v. Neff

Supreme Court of the United States, 1877 95 U.S. 714

This is an action to recover the possession of a tract of land, of the alleged value of $15,000, situated in the State of Oregon. The plaintiff asserts title to the premises by a patent of the United States issued to him in 1866, under the act of Congress of Sept. 27, 1850, usually known as the Donation Law of Oregon. The defendant claims to have acquired the premises under a sheriff's deed, made upon a sale of the property on execution issued upon a judgment recovered against the plaintiff in one of the circuit courts of the State. The case turns upon the validity of this judgment.

It appears from the record that the judgment was rendered in February, 1866, in favor of J. H. Mitchell, for less than $300, including

Action at Law.

In the Circuit Court of the State of Oregon for the County of Multnomah.

J. H. Mitchell, pl'T vs. Marcus Neff, def't.

TO MARCUS NEFF, defendant: In the name of the State of Oregon, you are hereby commanded to appear in the Circuit Court of the State of Oregon for the county of Multnomah, and answer the complaint filed against you in this action in said court within ten days from the date of the service upon you of this summons, if served within this county; and, within twenty days if served in any other county; and you are notified that in default of such answer, the plaintiff will take judgment against you for the sum of two hundred and fifty-three and 14-100 ($253 14-100) dollars, and accruing interest and for costs and disbursements. By order of Erasmus D. Shattuck, Judge.

MITCHELL & DOLPH,
Att'ys for plaintiff.
2dc11:48w6

(U.S. R. S. 50c.)
Portland, Nov. 30, 1865.

Image: *http://nathenson.org/aalscivpro/teaching-resources/cases-of-note/pennoyer-v-neff/*

costs, in an action brought by him upon a demand for services as an attorney; that, at the time the action was commenced and the judgment rendered, the defendant therein, the plaintiff here, was a non-resident of the State that he was not personally served with process, and did not appear therein; and that the judgment was entered upon his default in not answering the complaint, upon a constructive service of summons by publication.

The Code of Oregon provides for such service when an action is brought against a non-resident and absent defendant, who has property within the State. It also provides, where the action is for the recovery of money or damages, for the attachment of the property of the non-resident. And it also declares that no natural person is subject to the jurisdiction of a court of the State, 'unless he appear in the court, or be found within the State, or be a resident thereof, or have property therein; and, in the last case, only to the extent of such property at the time the jurisdiction attached.' Construing this latter provision to mean, that, in an action for money or damages where a defendant does not appear in the court, and is not found within the State, and is not a resident thereof, but has property therein, the jurisdiction of the court extends only over such property, the declaration expresses a principle of general, if not universal, law. The authority of every tribunal is necessarily restricted by the territorial limits of the State in which it is established. Any attempt to exercise authority beyond those limits would be deemed in every other forum, as has been said by this court, in illegitimate assumption of power, and be resisted as mere abuse. In the case against the plaintiff, the property here in controversy sold under the judgment rendered was not attached, nor in any way brought under the jurisdiction of the court. Its first connection with the case was caused by a levy of the execution. It was not, therefore, disposed of pursuant to any adjudication, but only in enforcement of a personal judgment, having no relation to the property, rendered against a non-resident without service of process upon him in the action, or his appearance therein. The court below did not consider that an attachment of the property was essential to its jurisdiction or to the validity of the sale, but held that the judgment was invalid from defects in the affidavit upon which the order of publication was obtained, and in the affidavit by which the publication was proved.

> **"...EVERY STATE possesses exclusive jurisdiction and sovereignty over persons and property within its territory."**

...

The several States of the Union are not, it is true, in every respect independent, many of the right and powers which originally belonged to them being now vested in the government created by the Constitution. But, except as restrained and limited by that instrument, they possess and exercise the authority of independent States, and the principles of public law to which we have referred are applicable to them. One of these principles is, that every State possesses exclusive jurisdiction and sovereignty over persons and property within its territory. As a consequence, every State has the power to determine for itself the civil *status* and capacities of its inhabitants; to prescribe the subjects upon which they may contract, the forms and solemnities with which their contracts shall be executed, the rights and obligations arising from them, and the mode in which their validity shall be determined and their obligations enforced; and also the regulate the manner and conditions upon which property situated within such territory, both personal and real, may be acquired, enjoyed, and transferred. The other principle of public law referred to follows from the one mentioned; that is, that no State can exercise direct jurisdiction and authority over persons or property without its territory. The several States are of equal dignity and authority, and the independence of one implies the exclusion of power from all others. And so it is laid down by jurists, as an elementary principle, that the laws of one State have no operation outside of its territory, except so far as is allowed by comity; and that no tribunal established by it can extend its process beyond that territory so as to subject either persons or property to its decisions. 'Any exertion of authority of this sort beyond this limit,' says Story, 'is a mere nullity, and incapable of binding such persons or property in any other tribunals.'

But as contracts made in one State may be enforceable only in another State, and property may be held by non-residents, the exercise of the jurisdiction which every State is admitted to possess over persons and property within its own territory will often affect persons and property without it. To any influence exerted in this way by a State affecting persons resident or property situated elsewhere, no objection can be justly taken; whilst any direct exertion of authority upon them, in an attempt to give ex-territorial operation to its laws, or to enforce an ex-territorial jurisdiction by its tribunals, would be deemed an encroachment upon the independence of the State in which the persons are domiciled or the property is situated, and be resisted as usurpation.

Thus the State, through its tribunals, may compel persons domiciled within its limits to execute, in pursuance of their contracts respecting property elsewhere situated, instruments in such form and with such solemnities as to transfer the title, so far as such formalities can be complied with; and the exercise of this jurisdiction in no manner interferes with the supreme control over the property by the State within which it is situated.

So the State, through its tribunals, may subject property situated within its limits owned by non-residents to the payment of the demand of its own citizens against them; and the exercise of this jurisdiction in no respect infringes upon the sovereignty of the State where the owners are domiciled. Every State owes protection to its own citizens; and, when non-residents deal with them, it is a legitimate and just exercise of authority to hold and appropriate any property owned by such non-residents to satisfy the claims of its citizens. It is in virtue of the State's jurisdiction over the property of the non-resident situated within its limits that its tribunals can inquire into that non-resident's obligations to its own citizens, and the inquiry can then be carried only to the extent necessary to control the disposition of the property. If the non-resident have no property in the State, there is nothing upon which the tribunals can adjudicate.

...

ONE CAVEAT TO USING physical presence to obtain personal jurisdiction is that the defendant cannot be tricked into coming into the state. In *Tickle v. Barton*, 95 S.E.2d 427 (W.Va. 1956), the plaintiff's lawyer tricked the defendant into coming into the state by calling Barton and telling him that he was invited to a football banquet that did not really exist. Once Barton arrived in the state, the plaintiff's lawyer served Barton with process. The court held that because the lawyer used false representation to lure Barton into the state and Barton would not have come into that jurisdiction if the lawyer had disclosed his identity and real purpose, the service of process was invalid and there was no personal jurisdiction. Again, note how important it is to follow the rules of procedure—Tickle's case against Barton for injuries in an automobile accident could no longer proceed because of an error in the service of process against the defendant.

As seen in the opinions of *Pennoyer* and *Tickle*, purposeful availment of the protections and privileges of a state, as well as purposeful presence in a state, are enough to establish personal jurisdiction over a defendant. The purposeful presence test was highlighted in a case where a passenger on a plane was served while passing over Arkansas. In *Grace v. Macarthur*, 170 F. Supp. 442 (1959), the defendant was not tricked into being in Arkansas, as he purposefully boarded the plane which would pass through Arkansas. The Supreme Court held that because the airspace above a state is still considered the territory of the state, the defendant's presence in the airplane going over Arkansas was sufficient physical presence and this form of service was valid.

Thinking about the presence of corporations can be tricky. Because the personality of a corporation is a fiction and just a legal tool, it is difficult to determine the purpose or intent of a corporation, its physical presence, and what constitutes an arm of the corporation. Therefore, the courts established a much-needed test in the *International Shoe* case—one of the most important cases to know when thinking about personal jurisdiction of corporations. To establish jurisdiction over corporations, one must look to the activities carried out on its behalf by those who are authorized to act for it.

International Shoe Co. v. State of Washington, Office of Unemployment Compensation and Payment

Supreme Court of the United States, 1945

326 U.S. 310

***

The facts as found by the appeal tribunal and accepted by the state Superior Court and Supreme Court, are not in dispute. Appellant is a Delaware corporation, having its principal place of business in St. Louis, Missouri, and is engaged in the manufacture and sale of shoes and other footwear. It maintains places of business in several states, other than Washington, at which its manufacturing is carried on and from which its merchandise is distributed interstate through several sales units or branches located outside the State of Washington.

Appellant has no office in Washington and makes no contracts either for sale or purchase of merchandise there. It maintains no stock of merchandise in that state and makes there no deliveries of goods in intrastate commerce. During the years from 1937 to 1940, now in question, appellant employed eleven to thirteen salesmen under direct supervision and control of sales managers located in St. Louis. These salesmen resided in Washington; their principal activities were confined to that state; and they were compensated by commissions based upon the amount of their sales. The commissions for each year totaled more than $31,000. Appellant supplies its salesmen with a line of samples, each consisting of one shoe of a pair, which they display to prospective purchasers. On occasion they rent permanent sample rooms, for exhibiting samples, in business buildings, or rent rooms in hotels or business buildings temporarily for that purpose. The cost of such rentals is reimbursed by appellant.

■ THE INTERNATIONAL SHOE FACTORY BUILDING IN ST. LOUIS, MISSOURI.

Photo: Stephen McCaffrey

The authority of the salesmen is limited to exhibiting their samples and soliciting orders from prospective buyers, at prices and on terms fixed by appellant. The salesmen transmit the orders to appellant's office in St. Louis for acceptance or rejection, and when accepted the merchandise for filling the orders is shipped f.o.b. from points outside Washington to the purchasers within the state. All the merchandise shipped into Washington is invoiced at the place of shipment from which collections are made. No salesman has authority to enter into contracts or to make collections.

The Supreme Court of Washington was of opinion that the regular and systematic solicitation of orders in the state by appellant's salesmen, resulting in a continuous flow of appellant's product into the state, was sufficient to constitute doing business in the state so as to make appellant amenable to suit in its courts. But it was also of opinion that there were sufficient additional activities shown to bring the case within the rule frequently stated, that solicitation within a state by the agents of a foreign corporation plus some additional activities there are sufficient to render the corporation amenable to suit brought in the courts of the state to enforce an obligation arising out of its activities there. The court found such additional activities in the salesmen's display of samples sometimes in permanent display rooms, and the salesmen's residence within the state, continued over a period of years, all resulting in a substantial volume of merchandise regularly shipped by appellant to purchasers within the state. The court also held that the statute as applied did not invade the constitutional power of Congress to regulate interstate commerce and did not impose a prohibited burden on such commerce.

Historically the jurisdiction of courts to render judgment *in personam* is grounded on their de facto power over the defendant's person. Hence his presence within the territorial jurisdiction of court was prerequisite to its rendition of a judgment personally binding him. But now that the *capias ad respondendum* has given way to personal service of summons or other form of notice, due process requires only that in order to subject a defendant to a judgment in personam, if he be not present within the territory of the forum, he have certain minimum contacts with it such that the maintenance of the suit does not offend 'traditional notions of fair play and substantial justice.'

Since the corporate personality is a fiction, although a fiction intended to be acted upon as though it were a fact, it is clear that unlike an individual its 'presence' without, as well as within, the state of its origin can be manifested only by activities carried on in its behalf by those who are authorized to act for it. To say that the corporation is so far 'present' there as to satisfy due process requirements, for purposes of taxation or the maintenance of suits against it in the courts of the state, is to beg the question to be decided. For the terms 'present' or 'presence' are used merely to symbolize those activities of the corporation's agent within the state which courts will deem to be sufficient to satisfy the demands of due process. Those demands may be met by such contacts of the corporation with the state of the forum as make it reasonable, in the context of our federal system of government, to require the corporation to defend the particular suit which is brought there. An 'estimate of the inconveniences' which would result to the corporation from a trial away from its 'home' or principal place of business is relevant in this connection.

'Presence' in the state in this sense has never been doubted when the activities of the corporation there have not only been continuous and systematic, but also give rise to the liabilities sued on, even though no consent to be sued or authorization to an agent to accept service of process has been given. Conversely it has been generally recognized that the casual presence of the corporate agent or even his conduct of single or isolated items of activities in a state in the corporation's behalf are not enough to subject it to suit on causes of action unconnected with the activities there. To require the corporation in such circumstances to defend the suit away from its home or other jurisdiction where it carries on more substantial activities has been thought to lay too great and unreasonable a burden on the corporation to comport with due process.

While it has been held in cases on which appellant relies that continuous activity of some sorts within a state is not enough to support the demand that the corporation be amenable to suits unrelated to that activity, there have been instances in which the continuous corporate operations within a state were thought so substantial and of such a nature as to justify suit against it on causes of action arising from dealings entirely distinct from those activities.

Finally, although the commission of some single or occasional acts of the corporate agent in a state sufficient to impose an obligation or liability on the corporation has not been thought to confer upon the state authority to enforce it, other such acts, because of their nature and quality and the circumstances of their commission, may be deemed sufficient to render the corporation liable to suit. True, some of the decisions holding the corporation amenable to suit have been supported by resort to the legal fiction that it has given its consent to service and suit, consent being implied from its presence in the state through the acts of its authorized agents. But more realistically it may be said that those authorized acts were of such a nature as to justify the fiction.

It is evident that the criteria by which we mark the boundary line between those activities which justify the subjection of a corporation to suit, and those which do not, cannot be simply mechanical or quantitative. The test is not merely, as has sometimes been suggested, whether the activity, which the corporation has seen fit to procure through its agents in another state, is a little more or a little less. Whether due process is satisfied must depend rather upon the quality and nature of the activity in relation to the fair and orderly administration of the laws which it was the purpose of the due process clause to insure. That clause does not contemplate that a state may make binding a judgment in personam against an individual or corporate defendant with which the state has no contacts, ties, or relations.

But to the extent that a corporation exercises the privilege of conducting activities within a state, it enjoys the benefits and protection of the laws of that state. The exercise of that privilege may give rise to obligations; and, so far as those obligations arise out of or are connected with the activities within the state, a procedure which requires the corporation to respond to a suit brought to enforce them can, in most instances, hardly be said to be undue.

Applying these standards, the activities carried on in behalf of appellant in the State of Washington were neither irregular nor casual. They were systematic and continuous throughout the years in question. They resulted in a large volume of interstate business, in the course of which appellant received the benefits and protection of the laws of the state, including the right to resort to the courts for the enforcement of its rights. The obligation which is here sued upon arose out of those very activities. It is evident that these operations establish sufficient contacts or ties with the state of the forum to make it reasonable and just according to our traditional conception of fair play and substantial justice to permit the state to enforce the obligations which appellant has incurred there. Hence we cannot say that the maintenance of the present suit in the State of Washington involves an unreasonable or undue procedure.

We are likewise unable to conclude that the service of the process within the state upon an agent whose activities establish appellant's 'presence' there was not sufficient notice of the suit, or that the suit was so unrelated to those activities as to make the agent an inappropriate vehicle for communicating the notice. It is enough that appellant has established such contacts with the state that the particular form of substituted service adopted there gives reasonable assurance that the notice will be actual. Nor can we say that the mailing of the notice of suit to appellant by registered mail at its home office was not reasonably calculated to apprise appellant of the suit.

Only a word need be said of appellant's liability for the demanded contributions of the state unemployment fund. The Supreme Court of Washington, construing and applying the statute, has held that it imposes a tax on the privilege of employing appellant's salesmen within the state measured by a percentage of the wages, here the commissions payable to the salesmen. This construction we accept for purposes of determining the constitutional validity of the statute. The right to employ labor has been deemed an appropriate subject of taxation in this country and England, both before and since the adoption of the Constitution. And such a tax imposed upon the employer for unemployment benefits is within the constitutional power of the states.

Appellant having rendered itself amenable to suit upon obligations arising out of the activities of its salesmen in Washington, the state may maintain the present suit in personam to collect the tax laid upon the exercise of the privilege of employing appellant's salesmen within the state. For Washington has made one of those activities, which taken together establish appellant's 'presence' there for purposes of suit, the taxable event by which the state brings appellant within the reach of its taxing power. The state thus has constitutional power to lay the tax and to subject appellant to a suit to recover it. The activities which establish its 'presence' subject it alike to taxation by the state and to suit to recover the tax.

Affirmed.

NO STATE HAS JURISDICTION over people and property outside the state, unless the claim arises out of minimum contacts with the state and the suit does not offend "traditional notions of fair play and substantial notice" of Due Process. This case resulted in the modern day two-prong test for personal jurisdiction: minimum contacts plus fairness.

While fairness is substantially subject to the discretion of the court, what constitutes minimum contacts?

- **NO JURISDICTION:** Isolated and infrequent contacts, unrelated claim.

- **SPECIFIC JURISDICTION:** Isolated and infrequent contacts, related claim.

- **SPECIFIC JURISDICTION:** Continuous and systematic contacts, related claim.

- **GENERAL JURISDICTION:** Mega contacts, unrelated claim. Based on relationships, direct or indirect, between the forum state and the person whose legal rights are affected; requires a lot of contacts almost to the point of being present in the forum state; i.e. Intel, a nationwide corporation with pervasive advertising.

In some cases, jurisdiction can be extended to nonresidents who cannot be found and served in the jurisdiction's territory. This is made possible through long-arm statutes. When exercising personal jurisdiction under a long-arm statute, courts must ask (1) whether there is a state statute that authorizes it to exercise personal jurisdiction under the circumstances, and (2) whether it would be constitutional under the due process clause to do so. Because long-arm statutes are intended to reach to the limits of due process, the specific categories of jurisdiction conveyed by the long-arm statute are to be interpreted as liberally as the due process clause will allow.

The courts must consider a defendant's general activity within the state, the commission of any of a series of enumerated acts within the state, or the commission of a certain act outside the state causing consequences within it. In *Gray v. American Radiator and Standard Sanitary Corps*, 176 N.E.2d 761 (1961), the court held that personal service outside the state was valid on a safety valve manufacturer in Ohio where the only injury occurred in Illinois. The valve was integrated into a water heater in Pennsylvania and exploded in Illinois, and the Illinois long arm statute read: "a nonresident who, either in person or thorough an agent, commits a tortious act within this State submits to its jurisdiction." Furthermore, agency and consent to service can be appointed or implied by an action. In *Hess v. Pawloski*, 274 U.S. 352 (1927), the Supreme Court upheld a Massachusetts statute that said driving on state roads implied consent to service of process by the state registrar.

Ultimately, the courts have tended to look to any purposeful availment of a state's privileges and protections, and the foreseeability of harm. These two elements are highlighted in the Supreme Court's opinion in the following landmark case.

Worldwide Volkswagen Corp. v. Woodson

Supreme Court of the United States, 1980
444 U.S. 286

Respondents Harry and Kay Robinson purchased a new Audi automobile from petitioner Seaway Volkswagen, Inc. (Seaway), in Massena, N.Y., in 1976. The following year the Robinson family, who resided in New York, left that State for a new home in Arizona. As they passed through the State of Oklahoma, another car struck their Audi in the rear, causing a fire which severely burned Kay Robinson and her two children.

The Robinsons subsequently brought a products-liability action in the District Court for Creek County, Okla., claiming that their injuries resulted from defective design and placement of the Audi's gas tank and fuel system. They joined as defendants the automobile's manufacturer, Audi NSU Auto Union Aktiengesellschaft (Audi); its importer Volkswagen of America, Inc. (Volkswagen); its regional distributor, petitioner World-Wide Volkswagen Corp. (World-Wide); and its retail dealer, petitioner Seaway. Seaway and World-Wide entered special appearances, claiming that Oklahoma's exercise of jurisdiction over them would offend the limitations on the State's jurisdiction imposed by the Due Process Clause of the Fourteenth Amendment.

The facts presented to the District Court showed that World-Wide is incorporated and has its business office in New York. It distributes vehicles, parts, and accessories, under contract with Volkswagen, to retail dealers in New York, New Jersey, and Connecticut. Seaway, one of these retail dealers, is incorporated and has its place of business in New York. Insofar as the record reveals, Seaway and World-Wide are fully independent corporations whose relations with each other and with Volkswagen and Audi are contractual only. Respondents adduced no evidence that either World-Wide or Seaway does any business in Oklahoma, ships or sells any products to or in that State, has an agent to receive process there, or purchases advertisements in any media calculated to reach Oklahoma. In fact, as respondents' counsel conceded at oral argument, there was no showing that any automobile sold by World-Wide or Seaway has ever entered Oklahoma with the single exception of the vehicle involved in the present case.

Despite the apparent paucity of contacts between petitioners and Oklahoma, the District Court rejected their constitutional claim and reaffirmed that ruling in denying petitioners' motion for reconsideration.[5] Petitioners then sought a writ of prohibition in the Supreme Court of Oklahoma to restrain the District Judge, respondent Charles S. Woodson, from exercising *in personam* jurisdiction over them. They renewed their contention that, because they had no "minimal contacts," with the State of Oklahoma, the actions of the District Judge were in violation of their rights under the Due Process Clause.

The Supreme Court of Oklahoma denied the writ, holding that personal jurisdiction over petitioners was authorized by Oklahoma's "long-arm" statute. Although the court noted that the proper approach was to test jurisdiction against both statutory and constitutional standards, its analysis did not distinguish these questions, probably because [the long-arm statute] has been interpreted as conferring jurisdiction to the limits permitted by the United States Constitution.

The Due Process Clause of the Fourteenth Amendment limits the power of a state court to render a valid personal judgment against a nonresident defendant. A judgment rendered in violation of due process is void in the rendering State and is not entitled to full faith and credit elsewhere. Due process requires that the defendant be given adequate notice of the suit, and be subject to the personal jurisdiction of the court. In the present case, it is not contended that notice was inadequate; the only question is whether these particular petitioners were subject to the jurisdiction of the Oklahoma courts.

As has long been settled, and as we reaffirm today, a state court may exercise personal jurisdiction over a nonresident defendant only so long as there exist "minimum contacts" between the defendant and the forum state. The concept of minimum contacts, in turn, can be seen to perform two related, but distinguishable, functions. It protects the defendant against the burdens of litigating in a distant or inconvenient forum. And it acts to ensure that the States through their courts, do not reach out beyond the limits imposed on them by their status as coequal sovereigns in a federal system.

The protection against inconvenient litigation is typically described in terms of "reasonableness" or "fairness." We have said that the defendant's contacts with the forum State must be such that maintenance of the suit "does not offend 'traditional notions of fair play and substantial justice.'" The relationship between the defendant and the forum must be such that it is "reasonable . . . to require the corporation to defend the particular suit which is brought there." Implicit in this emphasis on reasonableness is the understanding that the burden on the defendant, while always a primary concern, will in an appropriate case be considered in light of other relevant factors, including the forum State's interest in adjudicating the dispute; the plaintiff's interest in obtaining convenient and effective relief, at least when that interest is not adequately protected by the plaintiff's power to choose the forum; the interstate judicial system's interest in obtaining the most efficient resolution of controversies; and the shared interest of the several States in furthering fundamental substantive social policies.

The limits imposed on state jurisdiction by the Due Process Clause, in its role as a guarantor against inconvenient litigation, have been substantially relaxed over the years. As we noted... this trend is largely attributable to a fundamental transformation in the American economy:

> "Today many commercial transactions touch two or more States and may involve parties separated by the full continent. With this increasing nationalization of commerce has come a great increase in the amount of business conducted by mail across state lines. At the same time modern transportation and communication have made it much less burdensome for a party sued to defend himself in a State where he engages in economic activity."

The historical developments... of course, have only accelerated in the generation since that case was decided.

Nevertheless, we have never accepted the proposition that state lines are irrelevant for jurisdictional purposes, nor could we, and remain faithful to the principles of interstate federalism embodied in the Constitution. The economic interdependence of the States was foreseen and desired by the Framers. In the Commerce Clause, they provided that the Nation was to be a common market, a "free trade unit" in which the States are debarred from acting as separable economic entities. But the Framers also intended that the States retain many essential attributes of sovereignty, including, in particular, the sovereign power to try causes in their courts. The sovereignty of each State, in turn, implied a limitation on the sovereignty of all of its sister States-a limitation express or implicit in both the original scheme of the Constitution and the Fourteenth Amendment.

Hence, even while abandoning the shibboleth that "[t]he authority of every tribunal is necessarily restricted by the territorial limits of the State in which it is established," we emphasized that the reasonableness of asserting jurisdiction over the defendant must be assessed "in the context of our federal system of government," and stressed that the Due Process Clause ensures not only fairness, but also the "orderly administration of the laws." As we noted in *Hanson v. Denckla*:

> "As technological progress has increased the flow of commerce between the States, the need for jurisdiction over nonresidents has undergone a similar increase. At the same time, progress in communications and transportation has made the defense of a suit in a foreign tribunal less burdensome. In response to these changes, the requirements for personal jurisdiction over nonresidents have evolved from the rigid rule of *Pennoyer v. Neff*, 95 U.S. 714, to the flexible standard of *International Shoe Co. v. Washington*, 326 U.S. 310. But it is a mistake to assume that this trend heralds the eventual demise of all restrictions on the personal jurisdiction of state courts. [Citation omitted.] Those restrictions are more than a guarantee of immunity from inconvenient or distant litigation. They are a consequence of territorial limitations on the power of the respective States."

Thus, the Due Process Clause "does not contemplate that a state may make binding a judgment *in personam* against an individual or corporate defendant with which the state has no contacts, ties, or relations." Even if the defendant would suffer minimal or no inconvenience from being forced to litigate before the tribunals of another State; even if the forum State has a strong interest in applying its law to the controversy; even if the forum State is the most convenient location for litigation, the Due Process Clause, acting as an instrument of interstate federalism, may sometimes act to divest the State of its power to render a valid judgment.

Applying these principles to the case at hand, we find in the record before us a total absence of those affiliating circumstances that are a necessary predicate to any exercise of state-court jurisdiction. Petitioners carry on no activity whatsoever in

Oklahoma. They close no sales and perform no services there. They avail themselves of none of the privileges and benefits of Oklahoma law. They solicit no business there either through salespersons or through advertising reasonably calculated to reach the State. Nor does the record show that they regularly sell cars at wholesale or retail to Oklahoma customers or residents or that they indirectly, through others, serve or seek to serve the Oklahoma market. In short, respondents seek to base jurisdiction on one, isolated occurrence and whatever inferences can be drawn therefrom: the fortuitous circumstance that a single Audi automobile, sold in New York to New York residents, happened to suffer an accident while passing through Oklahoma.

> **"IF FORESEEABILITY were the criterion, a local California tire retailer could be forced to defend in Pennsylvania when a blowout occurs there...or a Florida soft-drink concessionaire could be summoned to Alaska to account for injuries happening there."**

It is argued, however, that because an automobile is mobile by its very design and purpose it was "foreseeable" that the Robinsons' Audi would cause injury in Oklahoma. Yet "foreseeability" alone has never been a sufficient benchmark for personal jurisdiction under the Due Process Clause.

If foreseeability were the criterion, a local California tire retailer could be forced to defend in Pennsylvania when a blowout occurs there; a Wisconsin seller of a defective automobile jack could be haled before a distant court for damage caused in New Jersey; or a Florida soft-drink concessionaire could be summoned to Alaska to account for injuries happening there. Every seller of chattels would in effect appoint the chattel his agent for service of process. His amenability to suit would travel with the chattel...

This is not to say, of course, that foreseeability is wholly irrelevant. But the foreseeability that is critical to due process analysis is not the mere likelihood that a product will find its way into the forum State. Rather, it is that the defendant's conduct and connection with the forum State are such that he should reasonably anticipate being haled into court there. The Due Process Clause, by ensuring the "orderly administration of the laws," gives a degree of predictability to the legal system that allows potential defendants to structure their primary conduct with some minimum assurance as to where that conduct will and will not render them liable to suit.

When a corporation "purposefully avails itself of the privilege of conducting activities within the forum State," it has clear notice that it is subject to suit there, and can act to alleviate the risk of burdensome litigation by procuring insurance, passing the expected costs on to customers, or, if the risks are too great, severing its connection with the State. Hence if the sale of a product of a manufacturer or distributor such as Audi or Volkswagen is not simply an isolated occurrence, but arises from the efforts of the manufacturer or distributor to serve directly or indirectly, the market for its product in other States, it is not unreasonable to subject it to suit in one of those States if its allegedly defective merchandise has there been the source of injury to its owner or to others. The forum State does not exceed its powers under the Due Process Clause if it asserts personal jurisdiction over a corporation that delivers its products into the stream of commerce with the expectation that they will be purchased by consumers in the forum State.

But there is no such or similar basis for Oklahoma jurisdiction over World-Wide or Seaway in this case. Seaway's sales are made in Massena, N. Y. World-Wide's market, although substantially larger, is limited to dealers in New York, New Jersey, and Connecticut. There is no evidence of record that any automobiles distributed by World-Wide are sold to retail customers outside this tristate area. It is foreseeable that the purchasers of automobiles sold by World-Wide and Seaway may take them to Oklahoma. But the mere "unilateral activity of those who claim some relationship with a nonresident defendant cannot satisfy the requirement of contact with the forum State."

In a variant on the previous argument, it is contended that jurisdiction can be supported by the fact that petitioners earn substantial revenue from goods used in Oklahoma. The Oklahoma Supreme Court so found drawing the inference that because one automobile sold by petitioners had been used in Oklahoma, others might have been used there also. While this inference seems less than compelling on the facts of the instant case, we need not question the court's factual findings in order to reject its reasoning.

This argument seems to make the point that the purchase of automobiles in New York, from which the petitioners earn substantial revenue, would not occur *but for* the fact that the automobiles are capable of use in distant States like Oklahoma. Respondents observe that the very purpose of an automobile is to travel, and that travel of automobiles sold by petitioners is facilitated by an extensive chain of Volkswagen service centers throughout the country, including some in Oklahoma. However, financial benefits accruing to the defendant from a collateral relation to the forum State will not support jurisdiction if they do not stem from a constitutionally cognizable contact with that State. In our view, whatever marginal revenues petitioners may receive by virtue of the fact that their products are capable of use in Oklahoma is far too attenuated a contact to justify that State's exercise of *in personam* jurisdiction over them.

Because we find that petitioners have no "contacts, ties, or relations" with the State of Oklahoma, the judgment of the Supreme Court of Oklahoma is *Reversed*.

C. JURISDICTION OVER THE PROPERTY

Other ways to obtain jurisdiction of the defendant are through the property owned by the defendant. *In rem* jurisdiction is when the court exercises its power to determine the status of property located within its territory and judgment is binding on all interest holders. *Quasi-in-rem* jurisdiction is an attempt to obtain personal jurisdiction through attachment of property found within the State, but here recovery is limited to the value of the property. In order to obtain *in rem* or *quasi-in-rem* jurisdiction, the property must (1) be found within the state, (2) property must be attached to the defendant at the outset of the proceeding, and (3) the property can be tangible or intangible (as an example of intangible property, think of bank accounts). Currently, the majority rule is that jurisdiction over attached property requires personal jurisdiction over the property owner.

D. SUBJECT MATTER JURISDICTION

Subject matter jurisdiction is the court's power to hear a case because of the nature of the dispute. It is determined in the state courts by the state constitution, state statutes, and judicial decisions. In the federal courts, it is determined by Article III of the Constitution, federal statutes, and judicial decisions. The aims of diversity jurisdiction in federal courts are to (1) prevent state-court prejudice against out-of-state actors, and (2) implement the constitutional guarantee that citizens of each state are entitled to all privileges of citizens of all states. Exclusive jurisdiction over certain matters is conferred to federal courts by Article III and these cases cannot be heard in state court: Certain securities-law class actions; bankruptcy, patents and copyrights and actions against foreign consuls; actions to recover a fine, penalty or forfeiture under federal law; actions involving certain seizures.

II. Process of a Civil Trial

A. SERVICE

The Due Process Clause of the 14th Amendment requires that the defendant receive adequate notice of litigation. In order for a lawsuit to begin, the plaintiff must give

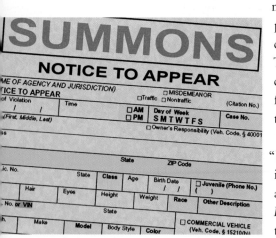

notice to the defendant. This is called service of process and the plaintiff is essentially serving a summons to the defendant to go to court, which includes a copy of the complaint against the defendant. The summons commands the defendant to answer the plaintiff's complaint within a fixed period of time. As we already learned, failure to respond to a claim or assert a defense constitutes consent to jurisdiction of the court to which the defendant was summoned.

One of the requirements of service of process is that it must, "be reasonably calculated under all the circumstances to apprise interested parties of the pendency of the action and afford them an opportunity to present their objections." *Mullane v. Central Hanover Bank & Trust Co.*, 339 U.S. 306, 314 (1950). In *Mullane*, the Supreme Court held that in a lawsuit for judicial settlement of accounts by a trustee of a common trust fund, notice published in a local New York newspaper was sufficient for some parties but not for others. While it may be surprising that such an impersonal method was deemed acceptable, courts continue to increase the standard of service. Here are a few examples of what courts have and have not found to be proper service of process:

Service: Proper or Improper?

- **MCDONALD V. MABEE**, 37 S.Ct. 343 (1917): The Supreme Court held that notice by publication in the last known state of residence was insufficient and required notice by mail to the defendant's last known address.

- **GREENE V. LINDSEY**, 456 U.S. 444 (1982): The Supreme Court found that notice posted on door in a public housing project wasn't sufficient because kids could tear it down and the court required it to be supplemented by notice through mail.

- **DUSENBERRY V. UNITED STATES**, 534 U.S. 161 (2002): The Supreme Court recently held that notice by certified mail to a prisoner was sufficient—even though the prison mail room signed for the letter, not the inmate, and no paper trail verifying the delivery could be found.

- **NATIONAL DEVELOPMENT CO. V. TRIAD HOLDING CORP**, 930 F.2d 253 (1991): The Supreme Court held service on the defendant's housekeeper at his New York City apartment was sufficient even though it was one of twelve homes owned by the defendant. The court said that the service was "reasonably calculated" to provide actual notice. It just so happened that the defendant was at the apartment that day.

- **FASHION PAGE, LTD. V. ZURICH INS. CO.**, 50 N.Y.2d 265 (1980): The Supreme court held that service on the defendant's secretary was sufficient because her testimony showed that she often received service in his absence. The court found this past conduct as evidence of implicit authorization to receive boss's service of process. However, the court noted that her simply saying she could accept, with no past conduct, would not be enough.

- **OMNI CAPITAL INTERNATIONAL V. RUDOLPH WOLFF**, 484 U.S. 97 (1987): The Supreme Court held that foreign defendants conducting business in the U.S. were not amenable to service in any state and were therefore unaccountable to federal law. Congress enacted Rule 4(k)(2) as a response to holding. Federal Rule of Civil Procedure Rule 4(k)(2) states: For a claim that arises under federal law, serving a summons or filing a waiver of service establishes personal jurisdiction over a defendant if: (A) the defendant is not subject to jurisdiction in any state's courts of general jurisdiction; and (B) exercising jurisdiction is consistent with the United States Constitution and laws. The broad language in subsection (B) allows the government flexibility in obtaining jurisdiction over foreign defendants in the U.S.

B. CHOICE OF VENUE

In addition to personal jurisdiction and subject matter jurisdiction, venue must be proper. While state venue is determined by state law and federal venue is determined by federal law, these determinations of venue depend primarily on:

- convenience to the parties

- sensible relationship to the claim

- consideration of judicial economy

These factors are considered by the courts in an effort to prevent "forum shopping," where one party attempts to bring a case in a court solely because he/she believes that court will be favorable to him/her and has no other valid reason for bringing a case in a certain jurisdiction.

C. PLEADINGS

Once personal jurisdiction, subject matter jurisdiction, and venue have been established, the plaintiff must plead his/her case. The function of modern pleading is to provide notice of the nature of a claim or defense. Other traditional functions include giving the court a chance to identify baseless claims in the interest of judicial economy, so the court does not waste any resources on a case that has no merits. The pleading also sets each party's view of the facts, and sets the issues for trial that will be decided by a judge and/or a jury.

The complaint, which includes date, place, injuries, and relief requested, can never be too specific. Attorneys tend to use over-pleading as a strategic move; they want to influence the judge before trial starts. The Federal Rules of Civil Procedure, Rule 8(a) require a pleading to state a claim for relief, and require that it contain:

- a short and plain statement of the grounds for the court's jurisdiction, unless the court already has jurisdiction and the claim needs no new jurisdictional support.

- a short and plain statement of the claim showing that the pleader is entitled to relief.

- a demand for relief sought, which may include relief in the alternative or different types of relief.

It is important to properly plead your case; otherwise, a judge may dismiss it for being too vague or for being baseless. You may not, however, state a claim of relief that contains legal conclusions.

Gillespie v. Goodyear

Supreme Court of North Carolina, 1963
128 S.E.2d 762

Plaintiff alleges she and each of the four individual defendants are citizens and residents of Alamance County, North Carolina; that defendant Goodyear Tire & Rubber Company is a corporation doing business in North Carolina and having a place of business and store in Burlington, North Carolina; and that Goodyear Service Stores is a division of defendant Goodyear Tire & Rubber Company.

The remaining allegations of the complaint and the prayer for relief are as follows:

> On or about May 5, 1959, and May 6, 1959, the defendants, without cause or just excuse and maliciously came upon and trespassed upon the premises occupied by the plaintiff as a residence, and by the use of harsh and threatening language and physical force directed against the plaintiff assaulted the plaintiff and placed her in great fear, and humiliated and embarrassed her by subjecting her to public scorn and ridicule, and caused her to be seized and exhibited to the public as a prisoner, and to be confined in a public jail, all to her great humiliation, embarrassment and harm.

By reason of the defendants' malicious and intentional assault against and humiliation of the plaintiff, the plaintiff was and has been damaged and injured in the amount of $25,000.00.

The acts of the defendants as aforesaid were deliberate, malicious, and with the deliberate intention of harming the plaintiff, and the plaintiff is entitled to recover her actual damages as well as punitive damages from the defendants and each of them.

> 'THEREFORE, the plaintiff prays that she have and recover of the defendants the sum of $25,000.00 as damages and $10,000.00 in addition thereto as punitive damages, and that she have such other and further relief as may be just and proper.'

Separate demurrers were filed by: (1) defendants Goodyear Tire & Rubber Company, Goodyear Service Stores, a division of Goodyear Tire & Rubber Company, and O. J. Hartsell; (2) defendant Robert E. Harden; (3) defendant Melvin Wrenn; (4) defendant Arthur Jones. Although different in phraseology, each demurrer specifies two grounds of objection to the complaint, namely, (1) that the complaint does not state facts sufficient to constitute a cause of action, and (2) that there is a misjoinder of parties and causes of action.

The court entered a separate judgment with reference to each of said four demurrers. In each judgment, after a recital of the said grounds on which the demurrer was based and a recital that the court was of the opinion 'that said demurrer should be sustained,' it was 'ORDERED, ADJUDGED and DECREED that said demurrer be and the same is hereby sustained and the court, in its discretion, grants unto said plaintiff thirty (30) days within which to file amended complaint.'

Plaintiff excepted to each of said four judgments and appealed.

A complaint must contain '(a) plain and concise statement of the facts constituting a cause of action * * *.' 'The cardinal requirement of this statute * * * is that the facts constituting a cause of action, rather than the conclusions of the pleader, must be set out in the complaint, so as to disclose the issuable facts determinative of the plaintiff's right to relief." The cause of action consists of the facts alleged. The statutory requirement is that a complaint must allege the material, essential and ultimate facts upon which plaintiff's right of action is based. 'The law is presumed to be known, but the facts to which the law is to be applied are not known until properly presented by the pleading and established by evidence.'

The facts alleged, but not the pleader's legal conclusions, are deemed admitted when the sufficiency of the complaint is tested by demurrer. 'Where the complaint merely alleges conclusions and not facts, it fails to state a cause of action and is demurrable. However, it is well settled that a complaint must be fatally defective before it will be rejected as insufficient, and 'if in any portion of it or to any extent it presents facts sufficient to constitute a cause of action the pleading will stand.'

When a complaint alleges defendant is indebted to plaintiff in a certain amount and such debt is due, but does not allege in what manner or for what cause defendant became indebted to plaintiff, it is demurrable for failure to state facts sufficient to constitute a cause of action.

'The liability for tort grows out of the violation of some legal duty by the defendant, not arising out of contract, and the complaint should state facts sufficient to show such legal duty and its violation, resulting in injury to the plaintiff. What these facts are must depend upon the elements which go to make up the particular tort complained of, under the substantive law.'

'In an action or defense based upon negligence, it is not sufficient to allege the mere happening of an event of an injurious nature and call it negligence on the part of the party sought to be charged. This is necessarily so because negligence is not a fact in itself, but is the legal result of certain facts. Therefore, the facts which constitute the negligence charged and also the facts which establish such negligence as the proximate cause, or as one of the proximate causes, of the injury must be alleged.'

In *Letterman v. Mica Co.*, 107 S.E.2d 753, a demurrer was sustained on the ground the facts alleged were insufficient to support the plaintiffs' allegation that the injury they sustained was proximately caused by wrongful conduct of the defendants.

As stated by Barnhill, J. in *Parker v. White*, 75 S.E.2d 615, 617: 'The competency of evidence, the form of the issues, and the charge of the court are all controlled in very large measure by the nature of the cause of action alleged by plaintiff. Hence, the trial judge, as well as the defendant, must know the exact right plaintiff seeks to assert or the legal wrong for which he seeks redress before there can be any intelligent trial under the rules of procedure which govern our system of jurisprudence.'

Plaintiff alleges, in a single sentence, that defendant, 'without cause or just excuse and maliciously,' trespassed upon premises occupied by her as a residence, assaulted her and caused her to be seized and confined as a prisoner. The complaint states no facts upon which these legal conclusions may be predicated. Plaintiff's allegations do not disclose what occurred, when it occurred, where it occurred, who did what, the relationships between defendants and plaintiff or of defendants inter se, or any other factual data that might identify the occasion or describe the circumstances of the alleged wrongful conduct of defendants.

A plaintiff must make out his case *secundum allegata*. There can be no recovery except on the case made by his pleadings. Here, there is no factual basis to which the court could apply the law. When considered in the light most favorable to plaintiff, this complaint, in our opinion, falls short of minimum requirements.

In *Stivers v. Baker*, 9 S.W. 491, it was held that a petition alleging the defendant unlawfully assaulted the plaintiff, thereby putting him in great fear, but not stating how the assault was made, stated a mere conclusion of law and was demurrable as not stating facts constituting a cause of action as required by the Kentucky statute. The court, in opinion by Holt, J., points out that a statement of the facts constituting a cause of action 'is not only necessary to enable the opposite party to form an issue, and to inform him of what his adversary intends to prove, but to enable the court to declare the law upon the facts stated. It cannot do so if a mere legal conclusion is stated. The term "assault" has a legal meaning; as much so as the word "trespass." '

The judgments sustaining the demurrers are affirmed on the ground the complaint does not state facts sufficient to constitute any cause of action. It would seem appropriate that plaintiff, in accordance with leave granted in the judgments from which she appealed, now file an amended complaint and therein allege the facts upon which she bases her right to recover.

Affirmed.

AFTER A PLAINTIFF PLEADS THE CASE, the defendant can file a motion to dismiss the claim. There are several reasons for dismissing a claim, and one of them is for failure to state a claim upon which relief can be granted. These motions to dismiss are not often granted, but they do allow the defendant to get out of the suit before incurring any expenses. There are two tests for dismissing a claim for failure to state a claim upon which relief can be granted:

- *Legal Sufficiency:* If the law does not recognize a claim given that all the factual allegations are accepted as true, a motion to dismiss is granted. EAs an example, you don't allege an element of the cause of action you are seeking, the court will find that even if everything in the complaint is true, the case would still be resolved in favor of the defendant.

- *Factual Allegations:* If the is too vague or there are not enough facts alleged to show that claim is plausible, the court will dismiss the claim.

It is important to note that when a plaintiff alleges that the defendant committed fraud, there is a heightened pleading requirement. Fraud itself is a false or misleading statement that induces someone to take action to their detriment. In alleging fraud or mistake, a party must state with particularity the circumstances constituting the fraud or mistake. Malice, intent, knowledge, and other conditions of a person's mind may be alleged generally. The courts have presented four policy reasons for heightened pleadings in fraud cases. These reasons are:

- Protection of reputation (allegations are a very serious matter)

- Deterrence of frivolous or strike suits

- Defense of completed transactions

- Provision of adequate notice

In *Denny v. Barber*, the U.S. Court of Appeals for the Second Circuit held that this heightened pleading requirement was not satisfied because of a lack of specific factual allegations against a bank in a securities fraud case. The court said that the plaintiffs were on "a fishing expedition" for evidence of fraud. Most courts demand that the plaintiff specify the "who, what, when, where and how" of defendant's acts, and there has been a growing trend towards this interpretation.

Even Congress has supported a higher pleading requirement for fraud cases. The Private Securities Litigation Reform Act (PSLRA) says, "[f]acts giving rise to a strong inference that the defendant acted with *scienter* must be stated with particularity." Scienter is the civil court's *mens rea*—a defendant's intention to deceive, manipulate, or defraud. This act was the brainchild of Congress and was created in response to the prevalence of fraud cases. The PSLRA creates a higher burden of pleading for securities fraud in particular. There must be a "strong inference" of scienter requirement, meaning that the complaint must allege facts from which, if true, a reasonable person could infer that scienter is "cogent and at least as compelling as any opposing inference of non-fraudulent intent."

D. ANSWERING A COMPLAINT

After the plaintiff pleads his/her case against the defendant, the defendant must then respond to the complaint by filing an answer. Answers to a complaint generally contain denials, admissions, affirmative defenses, and counterclaims. A denial is when the defendant denies the truth of the complaints alleged against him/her. An admission is when the defendant admits to a fact alleged in the complaint. An affirmative defense is when the defendant admits to the action alleged, but claims it was caused by something else or that he has some recognized legal defense against liability. Lastly a counterclaim is the defendant's own claim against the plaintiff for damages. If the defendant files a counterclaim in the answer to the complaint, the plaintiff must then respond through a reply, which may contain similar elements as an answer to the complaint. Here is a sample answer to a complaint from the Supreme Court of New York:

Sample Complaint

COMPLAINT

Supreme Court of the State of New York
County of Broome

_____ x

John Jones,

    Plaintiff,

                                                         <u>ANSWER</u>

    –vs–   Index No.: 2004-0130

George Smith
    Defendant.

_____ x

As and for his Answer to the Complaint herein, the Defendant, George Smith, respectfully shows and alleges as follows:

1. Admits the truth of the allegations in paragraphs "1" and "2" of the Complaint.

2. Denies knowledge or information suffice to form a belief as to the truth of the allegations of paragraphs "3", "4", "5" and "6" of the Complaint.

3. Denies the allegations of paragraphs "7" and "8" of the Complaint.

4. Denies any and all allegations not heretofore previously admitted or denied.

AS AND FOR FIRST AFFIRMATIVE DEFENSE

5. Defendant repeats and reiterates the allegations contained in paragraphs "1" through "4" as if fully set forth herein.

6. _____
_____
_____

AS AND FOR A SECOND AFFIRMATIVE DEFENSE

7. Defendant repeats and reiterates the allegations contained in paragraphs "1" through "6" as is fully set forth herein

8. _____

_____

_____

Wherefore, Defendant prays that this Court dismiss the Complaint of the Plaintiff herein, with costs and disbursements to the Defendant, together with such other relief the Court finds to be just and proper.

Dated: (Date)

<u>George Smith signature</u>
George Smith, Defendant
125 Main Street
Binghamton, NY 13901
Phone #

TO: John Jones, Plaintiff
32 Adams Street
Vestal, NY 13850

—OR—

Plaintiff's Attorney
Address
City, State, ZIP

<u>VERIFICATIONS</u>

George Smith, being duly sworn, deposes and says:

I am the Defendant in the above entitled action. I have read the foregoing Answer and know the contents thereof. The same are true to my knowledge, except as to matters therein stated to be alleged on information and belief as to those matters, I believe them to be true.

To the best of my knowledge, information and belief, formed after inquiry reasonable under the circumstances, the presentation of these papers or the contentions therein are not frivolous as defined in Subsection (c) of section 130-1.1 of the Rules of the Chief Administrative Judge (22 NYCRR).

<u>George Smith signature</u>
George Smith, Defendant

Sworn to me this (X) day of (month), (year).

<u>William Brown signature</u>
Notary Public

Form: http://www.nycourts.gov/courts/6jd/forms/SRForms/ans_examp.pdf

E. DISCOVERY

The discovery process is considered to be the most cumbersome part of civil cases in the United States. When preparing for trial or even before completion of the pleadings stages, both parties may obtain relevant evidence to build their case– in fact, they have a right to this evidence even if it is in the possession of the opposing side. This procedure is known as discovery.

The purpose of discovery is to preserve relevant information that might not be available at trial, to ascertain and isolate issues that actually are in controversy between the parties, and to find out what testimony and other evidence is available on each of the disputed factual issues. There are also several policy reasons for discovery in the U.S. courts. Discovery helps to promote transparency by making information about government and corporate practice available to a broader set of people than just the parties to a lawsuit. It also permits widespread discovery of the facts before trial, which eliminates an unfair "surprise" at trial. However, the scope of discovery in U.S. courts has become a cause of concern because abuse of the discovery procedure ends up being very pervasive and financially burdensome. Some refer to abuse of the discovery phase as a "fishing expedition."

Discovery can take place through several mechanisms. These include oral depositions, written depositions, interrogatories, document requests, and examinations (both physical and/or mental). Through these mechanisms, parties must present materials that are not legally privileged , that are relevant to any party's claim or defense, including financial information. It is obvious but worth noting that one thing a party is not obligated to disclose is the lawyer's legal strategy for trial.

When the evidence disclosed by the discovery phase makes the verdict clear, a party may move for summary judgment and a judge may make a final and binding determination on the merits. If the judge issues a summary judgment, the case does not need to go to trial.

F. THE TRIAL

If a case goes to trial, there are several stages of which all parties must be aware. First, there is the jury selection. Jury members are selected randomly from the territory of the jurisdiction. However, the parties have a right to conduct a *voir dire* of the selected jury members, which allows the parties a chance to eliminate jurors that are biased and cannot be fair or impartial. This does not mean that the courts allow for any type of discrimination by the attorneys themselves; there must be a valid reason for eliminating a juror, not based solely on race, gender, or religion.

Once the jury has been selected and both attorneys have conducted their *voir dire*s, each side will give its opening statements. During the opening statements, attorneys will present the main factual and legal issues of their clients' cases, which serve as evidence in the trial. Generally, the plaintiff bears the burden of proof because he/she is the one who has instigated the lawsuit—therefore, the plaintiff must prove that the case is a valid one with sufficient evidence to support the alleged wrong. The defendant, on the other hand, will rebut the plaintiff's arguments and evidence, and seek to prove any affirmative defenses that were claimed during the answer to the complaint. If the defendant alleged any counter-claims, this is also the time to present evidence of the harms allegedly committed by the plaintiff. Both sides may present witnesses as part of their arguments.

After the opening statements and after both sides have presented their clients' cases, the plaintiff's attorney has one last chance to make his client's argument and disprove the defendant's case. This is called the rebuttal. At the end of the rebuttal, each side is allowed to make closing arguments.

Closing arguments are the parties' last chances to convince the jury to find in their favor. They will highlight the strengths in their cases while pointing to the weaknesses of the opposing side. Finally, the judge will instruct the jury members as to which laws they must apply when arriving at a verdict. This is called a jury instruction. Then, the jury will enter judgment. Usually this is the final say—the binding decision of the court. However, in some cases the verdict may be overturned by the judge if the judge finds bias or jury misconduct.

NOTES AND COMMENTS

1. CONFLICT OF LAWS, the name of a Law School course that looks to see what courts should hear cases when multiple courts could, in theory, do so, tends to be something of a sleepy subject (granting that there are those who do relish the topic), but it has tremendous importance in today's global economy. Not only may a case be heard in many different states, territories or districts of the United States, it might also be heard in different countries. Because of this, businesses have a significant incentive for determining what courts have jurisdictions over the persons and over the subject matter of a case. They often do this through "choice of law" provisions in contracts, where the agreement states that, in the event of a dispute, the parties agree that the case will be heard in a specific place. Before you click "yes" to the next software you download for Apple or Microsoft, take a look at the actual agreement and you will see this provision. Courts tend to look favorably on such agreements—though not always—as a way to de-clutter court calendars.

2. A FEW DECADES AGO, courts viewed alternate dispute resolution mechanisms suspiciously, viewing such things as the province of the judicial system. But with full court calendars, judges increasing found merit in contract provisions to arbitrate disputes or to agree bring in non-binding mediation efforts. Even television shows like *Judge Judy*, *The People's Court*, or *Judge Joe Brown* provide non-judicial ways to resolve disputes. Together with choice of law provisions, there are ways to decide cases while minimizing court time and legal costs.

ADMINISTRATIVE ASPECTS

THE WORK OF GOVERNMENT, even in ancient times, has always been vast. In the Torah, Moses's father-in-law Jethro advises him to appoint judges who can decide disputes between members of the community in

to reduce the burden on Moses. In ancient Egypt, viziers were appointed by the Pharaoh to supervise specific areas of the government, such as the collection of taxes. Rulers during the Han dynasty in China delegated military power to regional potentates in order to control rebellions.[1]

■ *MOSES TAKES HIS LEAVE OF JETHRO, BY JAN VICTORS, C. 1635*

The result is an administrative structure that requires some set of rules for establishing it, running it, and reviewing it. Of course, the ways governments do each of these three things differ. For instance, one will see a different set of review practices in a totalitarian structure than in a democratic one. The basic questions of how one determines how and what to delegate, how these administrative organizations work, and how decisions they make get reviewed, though, are fundamental.

---

1   Pines, Yuri. *The Everlasting Empire: The Political Culture of Ancient China and Its Imperial Legacy.* Princeton: Princeton University Press, 2012. 24.
Image courtesy of The Yorck Project and Wikimedia Commons.

In the United States, a first division occurs between the Federal and State governments. Each state can have its own unique set of administrative bodies overseeing issues that arise in the state. The state of Iowa will not have an administrative agency concerned with oceanic matters such as what one would find in Florida or Hawaii. But because of the 14th Amendment to the Constitution, the rules that apply to state administrative agencies tend to be very similar to those governing federal agencies. You will remember that the 14th Amendment extends issues of Equal Protection to the states. Federal courts have gradually added rights that are of specific Constitutional importance in reviewing state actions as well. Some of these issues will be covered in this chapter but primarily as illustrations of the issues that apply to most administrative agencies in the country, regardless of the specific administrative source. The 1946 Administrative Procedure Act also sets out a standard way of addressing these kinds of issues.

I. Scope of Regulatory Agencies

ON THE FEDERAL LEVEL there are two types of agencies. One type is comprised of agencies whose heads are part of the Executive Cabinet. The heads of fifteen agencies form the Cabinet, and these agencies are, in order of succession:

- Department of State

- Department of Treasury

- Department of Defense

- Department of Justice

- Department of the Interior

- Department of Agriculture

- Department of Commerce

- Department of Labor

- Department of Health and Human Services

- Department of Housing and Urban Development

- Department of Transportation

- Department of Energy

- Department of Education

- Department of Veterans Affairs

- Department of Homeland Security

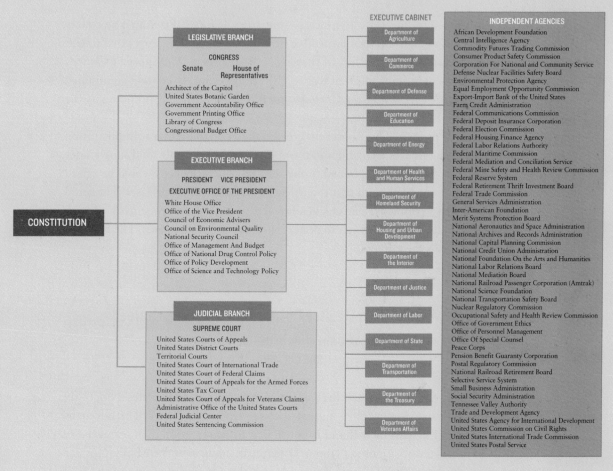

EXECUTIVE CABINET

LEGISLATIVE BRANCH

CONGRESS
Senate   House of
                Representatives

Architect of the Capitol
United States Botanic Garden
Government Accountability Office
Government Printing Office
Library of Congress
Congressional Budget Office

EXECUTIVE BRANCH

PRESIDENT   VICE PRESIDENT

EXECUTIVE OFFICE OF THE PRESIDENT

White House Office
Office of the Vice President
Council of Economic Advisers
Council on Environmental Quality
National Security Council
Office of Management And Budget
Office of National Drug Control Policy
Office of Policy Development
Office of Science and Technology Policy

CONSTITUTION

JUDICIAL BRANCH

SUPREME COURT

United States Courts of Appeals
United States District Courts
Territorial Courts
United States Court of International Trade
United States Court of Federal Claims
United States Court of Appeals for the Armed Forces
United States Tax Court
United States Court of Appeals for Veterans Claims
Administrative Office of the United States Courts
Federal Judicial Center
United States Sentencing Commission

Department of Agriculture
Department of Commerce
Department of Defense
Department of Education
Department of Energy
Department of Health and Human Services
Department of Homeland Security
Department of Housing and Urban Development
Department of the Interior
Department of Justice
Department of Labor
Department of State
Department of Transportation
Department of the Treasury
Department of Veterans Affairs

INDEPENDENT AGENCIES

African Development Foundation
Central Intelligence Agency
Commodity Futures Trading Commission
Consumer Product Safety Commission
Corporation For National and Community Service
Defense Nuclear Facilities Safety Board
Environmental Protection Agency
Equal Employment Opportunity Commission
Export-Import Bank of the United States
Farm Credit Administration
Federal Communications Commission
Federal Deposit Insurance Corporation
Federal Election Commission
Federal Housing Finance Agency
Federal Labor Relations Authority
Federal Maritime Commission
Federal Mediation and Conciliation Service
Federal Mine Safety and Health Review Commission
Federal Reserve System
Federal Retirement Thrift Investment Board
Federal Trade Commission
General Services Administration
Inter-American Foundation
Merit Systems Protection Board
National Aeronautics and Space Administration
National Archives and Records Administration
National Capital Planning Commission
National Credit Union Administration
National Foundation On the Arts and Humanities
National Labor Relations Board
National Mediation Board
National Railroad Passenger Corporation (Amtrak)
National Science Foundation
National Transportation Safety Board
Nuclear Regulatory Commission
Occupational Safety and Health Review Commission
Office of Government Ethics
Office of Personnel Management
Office Of Special Counsel
Peace Corps
Pension Benefit Guaranty Corporation
Postal Regulatory Commission
National Railroad Retirement Board
Selective Service System
Small Business Administration
Social Security Administration
Tennessee Valley Authority
Trade and Development Agency
United States Agency for International Development
United States Commission on Civil Rights
United States International Trade Commission
United States Postal Service

Source: United States Department of State

In addition, there are a number of "independent" agencies established by Congress that are overseen by the executive branch. These would include the Securities Exchange Commission, the National Labor Relations Board, the Federal Reserve Board and the Pension Benefit Guaranty Corporation, among others.

Even though there has been a long history of Cabinet-level administrative agencies in the U.S., it wasn't until after the Great Depression that a number of them proliferated. Most of the agencies came into existence through Congress' power under the commerce clause to regulate matters of interstate commerce. As alluded to in the chapter on Constitutional Law, this proliferation of administrative agencies did not come easily. The federal courts aggressively protected individual rights to private property and state powers under federalism and those rights provided the grounds to strike down regulatory efforts, often under a doctrine of substantive due process.

Yet, after the Great Depression, President Franklin Roosevelt searched for ways to make the economy less susceptible to major financial swings of the market. In doing so, he also sought to use regulatory agencies to institute other oversight that was related to interstate commerce—but stretched its definition. The courts, however, continued to be very protective of individual rights against government intrusion and struck down many of these New Deal efforts. The Supreme Court's actions were undermining much of Roosevelt's strategy and the conflict culminated with *A.L.A. Schechter Poultry Corporation v. United States*, also known as the "sick chicken" case.

Congress, prompted by Roosevelt, created the Food and Drug Administration and authorized it to pass regulations that would make the interstate food supply safer. Some of these regulations pertained to the ways in which chickens would be raised so as to reduce the likelihood that the chickens would contract diseases that could be transported to humans. The chicken farmers protested the costs involved with these regulations, and so filed suit to declare the FDA unconstitutional. The Supreme Court sided with the farmers.

A.L.A. Schechter Poultry Corporation v. United States

Supreme Court of the United States, 1935
295 U.S. 495

New York City is the largest live poultry market in the United States. Ninety-six per cent of the live poultry there marketed comes from other states. Three-fourths of this amount arrives by rail and is consigned to commission men or receivers. Most of these freight shipments (about 75 per cent) come in at the Manhattan Terminal of the New York Central Railroad, and the remainder at one of the four terminals in New Jersey serving New York City. The commission men transact by far the greater part of the business on a commission basis, representing the shippers as agents, and remitting to them the proceeds of sale, less commissions, freight, and handling charges. Otherwise, they buy for their own account. They sell to slaughterhouse operators who are also called market men.

The defendants are slaughterhouse operators of the latter class. A.L.A. Schechter Poultry Corporation and Schechter Live Poultry Market are corporations conducting wholesale poultry slaughterhouse markets in Brooklyn, New York City. Joseph Schechter operated the latter corporation and also guaranteed the credits of the former corporation, which was operated by Martin, Alex, and Aaron Schechter. Defendants ordinarily purchase their live poultry from commission men at the West Washington Market in New York City or at the railroad terminals serving the city, but occasionally they purchase from commission men in Philadelphia. They buy the poultry for slaughter and resale. After the poultry is trucked to their slaughterhouse markets in Brooklyn, it is there sold, usually within twenty-four hours, to retail poultry dealers and butchers who sell directly to consumers. The poultry purchased from defendants is immediately slaughtered, prior to delivery, by shochtim in defendants' employ. Defendants do not sell poultry in interstate commerce.

The 'Live Poultry Code' was promulgated under section 3 of the National Industrial Recovery Act. * * * [I]t was approved by the President on April 13, 1934. Its divisions indicate its nature and scope. The code has eight articles entitled (1) 'purposes,' (2) 'definitions,' (3) 'hours,' (4) 'wages,' (5) 'general labor provisions,' (6) 'administration,' (7) 'trade practice provisions,' and (8) 'general.'

The declared purpose is 'To effect the policies of title I of the National Industrial Recovery Act.' The code is established as 'a code for fair competition for the live poultry industry of the metropolitan area in and about the City of New York.' That area is described as embracing the five boroughs of New York City, the counties of Rockland, Westchester, Nassau, and Suffolk in the state of New York, the counties of Hudson and Bergen in the state of New Jersey, and the county of Fairfield in the state of Connecticut.

The 'industry' is defined as including 'every person engaged in the business of selling, purchasing of resale, transporting, or handling and/or slaughtering live poultry, from the time such poultry comes into the New York metropolitan area to the time it is first sold in slaughtered form,' and such 'related branches' as may from time to time be included by amendment. Employers are styled 'members of the industry,' and the term 'employee' is defined to embrace 'any and all persons engaged in the industry, however compensated,' except 'members.'

The code fixes the number of hours for workdays. It provides that no employee, with certain exceptions, shall be permitted to work in excess of forty hours in any one week, and that no employees, save as stated, 'shall be paid in any pay period less than at the rate of fifty (50) cents per hour.' The article containing 'general labor provisions' prohibits the employment of any person under 16 years of age, and declares that employees shall have the right of 'collective bargaining' and freedom of choice with respect to labor organizations, in the terms of section 7(a) of the act (15 USCA § 707(a). The minimum number of employees, who shall be employed by slaughterhouse operators, is fixed; the number being graduated according to the average volume of weekly sales.

* * *

The President approved the code by an executive order (No. 6675–A) in which he found that the application for his approval had been duly made in accordance with the provisions of title 1 of the National Industrial Recover Act.* * *

Of the eighteen counts of the indictment upon which the defendants were convicted, aside from the count for conspiracy, two counts charged violation of the minimum wage and maximum hour provisions of the code, and ten counts were for violation of the requirement (found in the 'trade practice provisions') of 'straight killing.' This requirement was really one of 'straight' selling. The term 'straight killing' was defined in the code as 'the practice of requiring persons purchasing poultry for resale to accept the run of any half coop, coop, or coops, as purchased by slaughterhouse operators, except for culls. The charges in the ten counts, respectively, were that the defendants in selling to retail dealers and butchers had permitted 'selections of individual chickens taken from particular coops and half coops.'

Of the other six counts, one charged the sale to a butcher of an unfit chicken; two counts charged the making of sales without having the poultry inspected or approved in accordance with regulations or ordinances of the city of New York; two counts charged the making of false reports or the failure to make reports relating to the range of daily prices and volume of sales for certain periods; and the remaining count was for sales to slaughterers or dealers who were without licenses required by the ordinances and regulations of the city of New York.

Mr. Chief Justice HUGHES

The question of chief importance relates to the provisions of the code as to the hours and wages of those employed in defendants' slaughterhouse markets. It is plain that these requirements are imposed in order to govern the details of defendants' management of their local business. The persons employed in slaughtering and selling in local trade are not employed in interstate commerce. Their hours and wages have no direct relation to interstate commerce. The question of how many hours these employees should work and what they should be paid differs in no essential

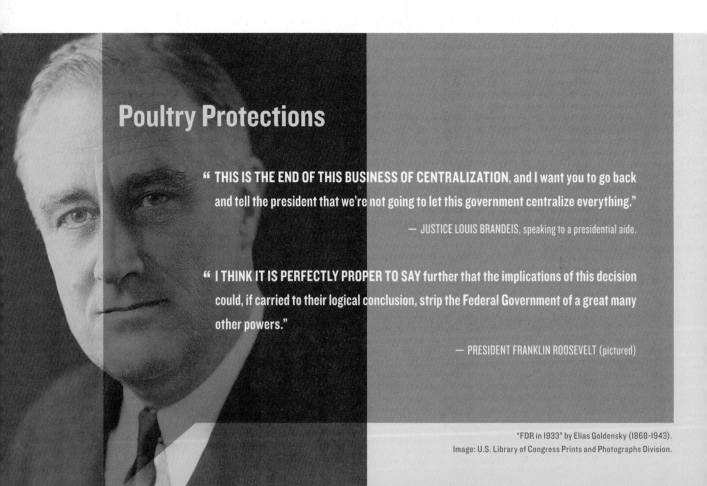

Poultry Protections

❝ **THIS IS THE END OF THIS BUSINESS OF CENTRALIZATION**, and I want you to go back and tell the president that we're not going to let this government centralize everything."

— JUSTICE LOUIS BRANDEIS, speaking to a presidential aide.

❝ **I THINK IT IS PERFECTLY PROPER TO SAY** further that the implications of this decision could, if carried to their logical conclusion, strip the Federal Government of a great many other powers."

— PRESIDENT FRANKLIN ROOSEVELT (pictured)

"FDR in 1933" by Elias Goldensky (1868-1943).
Image: U.S. Library of Congress Prints and Photographs Division.

respect from similar questions in other local businesses which handle commodities brought into a state and there dealt in as a part of its internal commerce. This appears from an examination of the considerations urged by the government with respect to conditions in the poultry trade. Thus, the government argues that hours and wages affect prices; that slaughterhouse men sell at a small margin above operating costs; that labor represents 50 to 60 per cent. of these costs; that a slaughterhouse operator paying lower wages or reducing his cost by exacting long hours of work translates his saving into lower prices; that this results in demands for a cheaper grade of goods: and that the cutting of prices brings about a demoralization of the price structure. Similar conditions may be adduced in relation to other businesses. The argument of the government proves too much. If the federal government may determine the wages and hours of employees in the internal commerce of a state, because of their relation to cost and prices and their indirect effect upon interstate commerce, it would seem that a similar control might be exerted over other elements of cost, also affecting prices, such as the number of employees, rents, advertising, methods of doing business, etc. All the processes of production and distribution that enter into cost could likewise be controlled. If the cost of doing an intrastate business is in itself the permitted object of federal control, the extent of the regulation of cost would be a question of discretion and not of power.

The government also makes the point that efforts to enact state legislation establishing high labor standards have been impeded by the belief that, unless similar action is taken generally, commerce will be diverted from the states adopting such standards, and that this fear of diversion has led to demands for federal legislation on the subject of wages and hours. The apparent implication is that the federal authority under the commerce clause should be deemed to extend to the establishment of rules to govern wages and hours in intrastate trade and industry generally throughout the country, thus overriding the authority of the states to deal with domestic problems arising from labor conditions in their internal commerce.

It is not the province of the Court to consider the economic advantages or disadvantages of such a centralized system. It is sufficient to say that the Federal Constitution does not provide for it. Our growth and development have called for wide use of the commerce power of the federal government in its control over the expanded activities of interstate commerce and in protecting that commerce from burdens, interferences, and conspiracies to restrain and monopolize it. But the authority of the federal government may not be pushed to such an extreme as to destroy the distinction, which the commerce clause itself establishes, between commerce 'among the several States' and the internal concerns of a state. The same answer must be made to the contention that is based upon the serious economic situation which led to the passage of the Recovery Act—the fall in prices, the decline in wages and employment, and the curtailment of the market for commodities. Stress is laid upon the great importance of maintaining wage distributions which would provide the necessary stimulus in starting 'the cumulative forces making for expanding commercial activity.' Without in any way disparaging this motive, it is enough to say that the recuperative efforts of the federal government must be made in a manner consistent with the authority granted by the Constitution.

We are of the opinion that the attempt through the provisions of the code to fix the hours and wages of employees of defendants in their intrastate business was not a valid exercise of federal power.

The other violations for which defendants were convicted related to the making of local sales. Ten counts, for violation of the provision as to 'straight killing,' were for permitting customers to make 'selections of individual chickens taken from particular coops and half coops.' Whether or not this practice is good or bad for the local trade, its effect, if any, upon interstate commerce was only indirect. The same may be said of violations of the code by intrastate transactions consisting of the sale 'of an unfit chicken' and of sales which were not in accord with the ordinances of the city of New York. The requirement of reports as to prices and volumes of defendants' sales was incident to the effort to control their intrastate business.

In view of these conclusions, we find it unnecessary to discuss other questions which have been raised as to the validity of certain provisions of the code under the due process clause of the Fifth Amendment.

On both the grounds we have discussed, the attempted delegation of legislative power and the attempted regulation of intrastate transactions which affect interstate commerce only indirectly, we hold the code provisions here in question to be invalid and that the judgment of conviction must be reversed.

■ JUSTICE OWEN ROBERTS

THIS CASE WAS THE FINAL STRAW for Roosevelt, who then developed a plan to propose to Congress that would change the membership of the Supreme Court. While the justices on the Court could not be removed except for reasons of impeachment, there was (and remains) no set limit on the number of justices who comprise the membership of the Court. So Roosevelt proposed that for every Justice over the age of seventy, another justice would be appointed to the Court. The over-seventy justices were those striking down New Deal legislation, but with a larger Court, Roosevelt believed the votes would tip to his side. Suddenly, or so it seemed, the Court became much more receptive to New Deal measures. In particular, Associate Justice Owen Roberts[2], considered a swing vote on many Supreme Court decisions, changed his views and began voting to uphold Roosevelt's new administrative agencies. The following 1937 case is the one sometimes called "the switch in time that saved the Nine."

----

2   "Owen J. Roberts" by Harris and Ewing. Image: U.S. Library of Congress Prints and Photographs Division

West Coast Hotel Co. v. Parrish

Supreme Court of the United States, 1937
300 U.S. 379

This case presents the question of the constitutional validity of the minimum wage law of the state of Washington.

The act, entitled 'Minimum Wages for Women,' authorizes the fixing of minimum wages for women and minors. It provides:

'Section 1. The welfare of the State of Washington demands that women and minors be protected from conditions of labor which have a pernicious effect on their health and morals. The State of Washington, therefore, exercising herein its police and sovereign power declares that inadequate wages and unsanitary conditions of labor exert such pernicious effect.

'Sec. 2. It shall be unlawful to employ women or minors in any industry or occupation within the State of Washington under conditions of labor detrimental to their health or morals; and it shall be unlawful to employ women workers in any industry within the State of Washington at wages which are not adequate for their maintenance.

'Sec. 3. There is hereby created a commission to be known as the 'Industrial Welfare Commission' for the State of Washington, to establish such standards of wages and conditions of labor for women and minors employed within the State of Washington, as shall be held hereunder to be reasonable and not detrimental to health and morals, and which shall be sufficient for the decent maintenance of women.'

* * *

The appellant conducts a hotel. The appellee Elsie Parrish was employed as a chambermaid and (with her husband) brought this suit to recover the difference between the wages paid her and the minimum wage fixed pursuant to the state law. The minimum wage was $14.50 per week of 48 hours. The appellant challenged the act as repugnant to the due process clause of the Fourteenth Amendment of the Constitution of the United States. The Supreme Court of the state, reversing the trial court, sustained the statute and directed judgment for the plaintiffs. The case is here on appeal.

* * *

Mr. Chief Justice HUGHES

* * *

The principle which must control our decision is not in doubt. The constitutional provision invoked is the due process clause of the Fourteenth Amendment governing the states, as the due process clause invoked in the *Adkins* Case governed Congress. In each case the violation alleged by those attacking minimum wage regulation for women is deprivation of freedom of contract. What is this freedom? The Constitution does not speak of freedom of contract. It speaks of liberty and prohibits the deprivation of liberty without due process of law. In prohibiting that deprivation, the Constitution does not recognize an absolute and uncontrollable liberty. Liberty in each of its phases has its history and connotation. But the liberty safeguarded is liberty in a social organization which requires the protection of law against the evils which menace the health, safety, morals, and welfare of the people. Liberty under the Constitution is thus necessarily subject to the restraints of due process, and regulation which is reasonable in relation to its subject and is adopted in the interests of the community is due process.

This essential limitation of liberty in general governs freedom of contract in particular. More than twenty-five years ago we set forth the applicable principle in these words, after referring to the cases where the liberty guaranteed by the Fourteenth Amendment had been broadly described.

'But it was recognized in the cases cited, as in many others, that freedom of contract is a qualified, and not an absolute, right. There is no absolute freedom to do as one wills or to contract as one chooses. The guaranty of liberty does not withdraw from legislative supervision that wide department of activity which consists of the making of contracts, or deny to government the power to provide restrictive safeguards. Liberty implies the absence of arbitrary restraint, not immunity from reasonable regulations and prohibitions imposed in the interests of the community.'

This power under the Constitution to restrict freedom of contract has had many illustrations. That it may be exercised in the public interest with respect to contracts between employer and employee is undeniable ... In dealing with the relation of employer and employed, the Legislature has necessarily a wide field of discretion in order that there may be suitable protection of health and safety, and that peace and good order may be promoted through regulations designed to insure wholesome conditions of work and freedom from oppression.

The point that has been strongly stressed that adult employees should be deemed competent to make their own contracts was decisively met nearly forty years ago in *Holden v. Hardy, supra*, where we pointed out the inequality in the footing of the parties. We said:

> 'The legislature has also recognized the fact, which the experience of legislators in many states has corroborated, that the proprietors of these establishments and their operatives do not stand upon an equality, and that their interests are, to a certain extent, conflicting. The former naturally desire to obtain as much labor as possible from their employees, while the latter are often induced by the fear of discharge to conform to regulations

which their judgment, fairly exercised, would pronounce to be detrimental to their health or strength. In other words, the proprietors lay down the rules, and the laborers are practically constrained to obey them. In such cases self-interest is often an unsafe guide, and the legislature may properly interpose its authority.'

And we added that the fact 'that both parties are of full age, and competent to contract, does not necessarily deprive the state of the power to interfere, where the parties do not stand upon an equality, or where the public heath demands that one party to the contract shall be protected against himself.' 'The state still retains an interest in his welfare, however reckless he may be. The whole is no greater than the sum of all the parts, and when the individual health, safety, and welfare are sacrificed or neglected, the state must suffer.'

It is manifest that this established principle is peculiarly applicable in relation to the employment of women in whose protection the state has a special interest. That phase of the subject received elaborate consideration in *Muller v. Oregon* (1908), where the constitutional authority of the state to limit the working hours of women was sustained. We emphasized the consideration that 'woman's physical structure and the performance of maternal functions place her at a disadvantage in the struggle for subsistence' and that her physical well being 'becomes an object of public interest and care in order to preserve the strength and vigor of the race.' We emphasized the need of protecting women against oppression despite her possession of contractual rights. We said that 'though limitations upon personal and contractual rights may be removed by legislation, there is that in her disposition and habits of life which will operate against a full assertion of those rights. She will still be where some legislation to protect her seems necessary to secure a real equality of right.' Hence she was 'properly placed in a class by herself, and legislation designed for her protection may be sustained, even when like legislation is not necessary for men, and could not be sustained.' We concluded that the limitations which the statute there in question 'places upon her contractual powers, upon her right to agree with her employer, as to the time she shall labor' were 'not imposed solely for her benefit, but also largely for the benefit of all.'

> **"I AM SO GLAD, not only for myself, but for all the women of the state who have been working for just whatever they could get."**
> —ELSIE PARRISH, PLAINTIFF

This array of precedents and the principles they applied were thought by the dissenting Justices in the *Adkins* Case to demand that the minimum wage statute be sustained. The validity of the distinction made by the Court between a minimum wage and a maximum of hours in limiting liberty of contract was especially challenged. That challenge persists and is without any satisfactory answer. As Chief Justice Taft observed: 'In absolute freedom of contract the one term is as important as the other, for both enter equally into the consideration given and received, a restriction as to the one is not any greater in essence than the other, and is of the same kind. One is the multiplier and the other the multiplicand.' And Mr. Justice Holmes, while recognizing that 'the distinctions of the law are distinctions of degree,' could 'perceive no difference in the kind or degree of interference with liberty, the only matter with which we have any concern, between the one case and the other. The bargain is equally affected whichever half you regulate.'

The minimum wage to be paid under the Washington statute is fixed after full consideration by representatives of employers, employees, and the public. It may be assumed that the minimum wage is fixed in consideration of the services that are performed in the particular occupations under normal conditions. Provision is made for special licenses at less wages in the case of women who are incapable of full service. The statement of Mr. Justice Holmes in the *Adkins* Case is pertinent: 'This statute does not compel anybody to pay anything. It simply forbids employment at rates below those fixed as the minimum requirement of health and right living. It is safe to assume that women will not be employed at even the lowest wages allowed unless they earn them, or unless the employer's business can sustain the burden. In short the law in its character and operation is like hundreds of so-called police laws that have been up-held.' And Chief Justice Taft forcibly pointed out the consideration which is basic in a statute of this character: 'Legislatures which adopt a requirement of maximum hours or minimum wages may be presumed to believe that when sweating employers are prevented from paying unduly low wages by positive law they will continue their business, abating that part of their profits, which were wrung from the necessities of their employees, and will concede the better terms required by the law, and that while in individual cases, hardship may result, the restriction will enure to the benefit of the general class of employees in whose interest the law is passed, and so to that of the community at large.'

> **'THIS STATUTE does not compel anybody to pay anything. It simply forbids employment at rates below those fixed as the minimum requirement of health and right living.'**
>
> —JUSTICE HOLMES, IN THE *ADKINS* CASE—
> THE BASIS FOR THE *PARRISH* DECISION

We think that the views thus expressed are sound and that the decision in the *Adkins* Case was a departure from the true application of the principles governing the regulation by the state of the relation of employer and employed. Those principles have been reinforced by our subsequent decisions …With full recognition of the earnestness and vigor which characterize the prevailing opinion in the *Adkins* Case, we find it impossible to reconcile that ruling with these well-considered declarations. What can be closer to the public interest than the health of women and their protection from unscrupulous and overreaching employers? And if the protection of women is a legitimate end of the exercise of state power, how can it be said that the requirement of the payment of a minimum wage fairly fixed in order to meet the very necessities of existence is not an admissible means to that end? The Legislature of the state was clearly entitled to consider the situation of women in employment, the fact that they are in the class receiving the least pay, that their bargaining power is relatively weak, and that they are the ready victims of those who would take advantage of their necessitous circumstances. The Legislature was entitled to adopt measures to reduce the evils of the 'sweating system,' the exploiting of workers at wages so low as to be insufficient to meet the bare cost of living, thus making their very helplessness the occasion of a most injurious competition. The Legislature had the right to consider that its minimum wage requirements would be an important aid in carrying out its policy of protection. The adoption of similar requirements by many states evidences a deep-seated conviction both as to the presence of the evil and as to the means adapted to check it. Legislative response to that conviction cannot be regarded as arbitrary or capricious and that is all we have to decide. Even if the wisdom of the policy be regarded as debatable and its effects uncertain, still the Legislature is entitled to its judgment.

There is an additional and compelling consideration which recent economic experience has brought into a strong light. The exploitation of a class of workers who are in an unequal position with respect to bargaining power and are thus relatively defenseless against the denial of a living wage is not only detrimental to their health and well being, but casts a direct burden for their support upon the community. What these workers lose in wages the taxpayers are called upon to pay. The bare cost of living must be met. We may take judicial notice of the unparalleled demands for relief which arose during the recent period of depression and still continue to an alarming extent despite the degree of economic recovery which has been achieved. It is unnecessary to cite official statistics to establish what is of common knowledge through the length and breadth of the land. While in the instant case no factual brief has been presented, there is no reason to doubt that the state of Washington has encountered the same social problem that is present elsewhere. The community is not bound to provide what is in effect a subsidy for unconscionable employers. The community may direct its law-making power to correct the abuse which springs from their selfish disregard of the public interest. The argument that the legislation in question constitutes an arbitrary discrimination, because it does not extend to men, is unavailing. This Court has frequently held that the legislative authority, acting within its proper field, is not bound to extend its regulation to all cases which it might possibly reach. The Legislature 'is free to recognize degrees of harm and it may confine its restrictions to those classes of cases where the need is deemed to be clearest.' If 'the law presumably hits the evil where it is most felt, it is not to be overthrown because there are other instances to which it might have been applied.' There is no 'doctrinaire requirement' that the legislation should be couched in all embracing terms. This familiar principle has repeatedly been applied to legislation which singles out women, and particular classes of women, in the exercise of the state's protective power. Their relative need in the presence of the evil, no less than the existence of the evil itself, is a matter for the legislative judgment.

Our conclusion is that the case of *Adkins v. Children's Hospital*, *supra*, should be, and it is, overruled. The judgment of the Supreme Court of the state of Washington is affirmed.

———————

WITH THE NEW DEAL IN PLACE, the alphabet soup of administrative agencies grew to the number and variety that one sees today. Less than ten years after the *West Coast Hotel* case, Congress passed the Administrative Procedure Act that sought to bring common standards to the work of these proliferating administrative agencies. The Act particularly involved agencies' rulemaking, interpretation, and enforcement, including judicial review of agency action.

II. Rulemaking, Lobbying and Capture

LEGISLATURES, whether at the national or state level, will often draft legislation to address a problem. In the legislation, there will be a delegation to the administrative agency to create more specific rules to handle the procedures and content of the rules to apply to actual implementation of the statute. This then results in the rulemaking aspect of administrative agency.

Administrative agencies promulgate thousands of pages of rules pursuant to a statute. In doing so, they must follow the procedures of the APA. The agency will solicit evidence and advice on how best to apply the statute from those who will be affected by the regulations. For example, if the Environmental Protection Agency is tasked with creating the rules to change the standards of air emissions, the EPA would draft a proposed set of rules. In doing so, they would be lobbied by companies and other interest groups as to what those groups think would be the best set of rules. Frequently those organizations have a great deal of experience as to how they and others might be affected. So while on the one hand, it can seem that this lobbying simply tries to create rules that will be most beneficial to the organization, there is also truth to the idea that these corporations and organizations have relevant data and experience. Some may have even started their own programs to limit air emissions and have a model to propose.

There is a difference between formal and informal rulemaking. With each there must be a publication of a notice of proposed rulemaking in the *Federal Register*. But informal rulemaking only requires that the agency offer the opportunity for written comments to the proposed regulation, whereas in formal rulemaking, the agency also must conduct formal hearings in addition to allowing for written comments. Then, when the final rule is published in the *Federal Register*, the formal findings from the hearings must be published along with the rule, whereas in an informal process, only the rule must be published.

Informal rulemaking is, not surprisingly, quicker and more efficient, and most agencies utilize this process in making new regulations. However, some enabling legislation requires that agencies utilize a formal rulemaking process. Section 553(c) of the APA requires that an enabling statute or other legislation that requires all regulations or rules to be enacted by an agency as part of a formal hearing process (including the production of a complete transcript of the proceedings) follow the formal rulemaking process. However, because of the time and expenses of the formal rulemaking process, unless the statute clearly states the type of rulemaking required, courts generally will not find that the law requires formal rulemaking.

Once the rules go into effect, they can still be challenged in the courts, provided that one meets the standards for having the right to challenge the actual implementation of the regulations.

Two other administrative actions require little formality. These are procedural and interpretative rules. These are statements to the public as to how an agency will proceed on various areas and the agency's view or interpretation of the legislation it must apply to cases. Because these "rules" do not constitute actual rulemaking, *per se*, agencies do not have to follow the informal or formal procedures described in the previous paragraph.

The rulemaking aspect of administrative agencies, as well as the issuance of interpretative and procedural rules, is a highly contested area of public policy from several points of view. First, if corporations have a great deal of technical information and lobbying expertise, there is the threat that an administrative agency can be "captured" by the industry. While administrative agencies do have government funding, they may not have sufficient funding to undertake all the scientific analysis that is necessary to make a well-researched rule. They will rely on corporations and organizations, who in turn also fund research (for example, in universities) to study the impact of actions in the area of consideration. This can make for good policy because more information becomes available, but it can also mean that the agency becomes increasingly dependent on those whom they regulate to design the very policies that affect them.

This idea of capture also can apply within an industry. It may be that a particular company has already designed an emissions process while there are several other competing processes out there. If they can persuade their regulating agency to adopt their process rather than a competitor's, the company will obtain a competitive edge over those who now must incur the costs of switching to a different process.

A final issue of the capture theory is that corporations and other organizations have a strong interest in hiring former employees of the agency. When a company hires a former agency employee, it captures the knowledge of the agency's inner workings—along with the employee's ties to former colleagues. These can be utilized to try to influence the rulemaking or interpretation of the rule. This raises issues of the objectivity of the rulemaking process and whether the administrative process simply becomes another battleground for competition between actors in the industry.

The next two articles illustrate this conflict. The first was posted to *The Huffington Post* in 2013 by Bruce Kushnick, Executive Director of the New Networks Institute. He argued strongly that regulatory protections have been weakened by corporate influences working from within the organization to benefit the Telecommunications industry—at the expense of consumers.

Regulatory Capture of the FCC—Time to Clean House

AT&T, WITH THE HELP of Verizon and the cable companies have 'captured' the FCC—and have been able to get the federal agency to create and shape a working group designed specifically to remove all regulations and obligations, close down the Public Switched Telephone Networks (PSTN) and create new digital dead zones.

Think of this as: Imagine taking a company to court and you find out that the judge, most of the jury, and even your lawyer has a direct financial tie to the company you are suing. Think you'll win?

Moreover, AT&T's FCC play is part of a massive, well-choreographed, multi-year state and federal campaign being orchestrated with ALEC, the American Legislative Exchange Council, to remove all regulations and obligations and harm America's communications users—i.e., you, dear reader...

With the *Wall Street Journal* reporting a changing of the guard at the FCC, with FCC Chairman Julius Genachowski and the Republican Commissioner Robert McDowell leaving in the next few months, we need new people who are going to fix, expose and stand up to the corporations, not kowtow to them.

Regulatory Capture and Financial Conflicts of Interest vs. Open Government.

In August 2012, New Networks filed a petition with the FCC outlining how the Technical Advisory Council, (TAC) created a group to 'sunset the PSTN'—meaning shut down America's telecom networks of any regulations or obligations—and that the majority of the TAC members had major, financial conflicts of interest with AT&T and/or Verizon (and Centurylink, formerly Qwest)—the caretakers of America's networks. In fact, AT&T and Verizon are on this Council. Worse, the TAC is using manipulated data supplied by AT&T and the other telcos to bias anyone to their point of view.

...

"Regulatory Capture" is the takeover of a federal agency by the corporations it is regulating and it is not new to the FCC. At a conference in 2010 called Reforming the FCC, its website states that "Former Chair Reed Hundt, (1993-1997) for example, suggested that the acronym 'FCC' stands for 'Firmly Captured by Corporations' while former FCC Chief Economist Tom Hazlett counters that 'FCC' stands for 'Forever Captured by Corporations.'"

Regulatory capture is insidious as the agenda is set by the companies and then uses people and data to support the agenda—regardless of how it will harm those it claims to be helping.

And it is as much about things not discussed, not focused on, not investigated as it is about a proactive corporate position. For example, the TAC could have, as some have advocated, set up a group to create a transition path for moving to a 21st century utility that is open to all competitors, based on IP-enabled services and everyone is upgraded. Or the TAC could have given customers choices—like being able to at least pick a competitive broadband and Internet provider which offers services over the wires coming into the customer's home or office; The Telecom Act of 1996 stated this as a goal. Yet, through capture over the last decade, these same networks are now closed to competition. Instead, this group decided to run with AT&T's-ALEC's plan to close, 'sunset', the PSTN.

What is the PSTN or why you should care?

Before we examine all of the players and their financial ties to the incumbents, AT&T and Verizon, let's go through the timeline of events:

• In 2009, AT&T files comments as part of the National Broadband Plan, claiming that there are two networks—the aging copper networks that supply Plain Old Telephone Service (POTs) and the new shiny broadband network.

This is, of course, pure manipulation as AT&T's broadband service U-Verse is a PSTN-based-copper-to-the-home service; thus the entire network is still based on the POTs-based network.

And let me be clear—as of December 2012, AT&T only had 4.7 million U-Verse Video customers out of 75 million 'locations'—do the math. Thus, AT&T's discussion about the PSTN has been devised to get rid of regulations and obligations over areas that they don't want to do anything with, like upgrade or even provide service.

- Next, in 2009, AT&T gets the FCC to have the Technical Advisory Council (TAC)start a new group dedicated to 'sunsetting' the PSTN.

- Starting before 2010, AT&T, Centurylink (formerly Qwest), Verizon—and the cable companies, as members of the American Legislative Exchange Council, ALEC, create a plan to remove regulations—based on "VOIP" and "Internet Freedom."

  It is evil genius; an effective verbal jujitsu. Their claim is that "VOIP" (Voice-Over-the-Internet Protocol)is the next generation. Phone service based on VOIP is not a telecommunications service, but an 'information service' and the difference in definitions means that VOIP is not regulated the same way.

  Their goal then is to make everything VOIP, removing all obligations and regulation. Thus "IP-based service" is "Internet freedom."Don't you want Internet freedom and innovation? Meanwhile, AT&T's U-Verse phone service, which is VOIP, uses the old copper wiring—so the old networks can support these Internet services today.

- By 2012, as documented by a report by the NRRI, the cabal pulled off a coup and were able to get (as of 2013) 23 states so far to remove basic telecommunications regulations, though it varies by state. AT&T-ALEC et al use 'model' legislation they create and then hand it off to the state ALEC politician members to pass. According to numerous sources, ALEC-based bills will be presented in almost every state again and again until they change the laws.

For an example of the ALEC-state based machinations, we detailed the ALEC-AT&T attack in Wisconsin where AT&T, ALEC and the ALEC member politicians attempted to pass legislation in 2007.

- By 2012, a different ALEC-based piece of 'model legislation' has been able to pass in 19 states, this one designed to close down the rights of municipalities to offer broadband services, even though the phone and cable companies have neglected or refused to do upgraded.

  According to *Business Week*, this ALEC-based bill started almost a decade ago and ALEC's influence is in many other industries as well.

- In August 2012, AT&T laid out the ALEC state-based principles for the Federal plan in a letter to FCC Commissioner Ajit Pai, who has been banging the drum to close down the networks. Pai is a former associate general counsel for Verizon, then went to work for a law firm that handles the telcos' business.

  > IT IS EVIL GENIUS; an effective verbal jujitsu. VOIP is not a telecommunications service but an 'information service' and the difference in definitions means that VOIP is not regulated the same way.

- In August 2012, New Networks filed a petition outlining how the majority of the Technical Advisory Council members have financial conflicts of interest and the FCC is using manipulated data supplied by the companies. It was ignored.

- In November 2012, AT&T files a petition to start the transition to close down the networks and ties it to an extortion plan—if the FCC passes the petition AT&T will spend $14 billion. As we demonstrated, AT&T always uses the promise of broadband deployment to get deregulation then never comes through. In this case, AT&T's numbers are even suspect; probably less than $6 billion will be spent, at best, spread over 3 years.

- In December 2012, the Technical Advisory Council presents their recommendations, which were, of course, to let AT&T et al do what they want.

- In December 2012, the FCC forms a 'Technology Transition Task Force" to close the deal, which is an extension of the work of the TAC.

- In 2012, Commissioner Pai starts banging the drum at conservative, corporate-friendly think tanks, such as the speech given at the Communications Liberty and Innovation Project (CLIP) of Competitive Enterprise Institute, to start the transition.

- In December 2012, Republican Congressmen Greg Walden, whose top 10 campaign contributors include Comcast, AT&T and Verizon and is the Chairman of the House Sub-committee on Telecommunications & Technology, congratulates Pai on the Task Force.

- Expect hearings and a move toward this ALEC-based legislation in 2013, which will be called for by multiple voices—almost all of whom will be heavily backed by the phone and cable companies.

The most disconcerting part, however, is the length and breadth of this massive plan as companies, from AT&T and Verizon's wireless divisions, as well as the three incumbents—AT&T, Verizon and Centurylink—and many of the large cable companies including Comcast—all ALEC members—as well as thousands of state and federal politicians—democrats and republicans—are all working with the same messaging, the same massive budgets. And, as we pointed out, this also includes corporate funded think tanks, non-profits, including minorities, lobbying groups, astroturf groups and a skunkworks coordination team.

The Capture by AT&T *et al* of the FCC

The Technical Advisory Council is the epitome of a stacked jury where the verdict is already in—against you—before the trial even starts.

To start, AT&T and Verizon are on the Council—the two incumbents who control the majority of the U.S. telecommunications networks—wireline and wireless. In this way they don't have to go far to keep their eyes on the progress.

'Friends' of AT&T and Verizon

...The list of TAC members includes:

- Hardware and software vendors including Apple, Motorola, Intel, Cisco and Microsoft all of whom have multiple financial deals with AT&T and Verizon including wireless phones, tablets and technology.

- The cable companies, Comcast, Time Warner and Brighthouse not only sold spectrum to Verizon, but Verizon has a marketing deal with some of them to sell their cable products with Verizon's wireless services.

- Other hardware and consulting companies, from Accenture, Qualcomm, Alcatel-Lucent or Harris all have deals with either Verizon or AT&T or both.

  In fact, the core 16 companies represent about $800 billion dollars in revenues in 2011.

There are a number of other members with conflicts of interest:

- New Venture Partners is an investment firm which is part of the Verizon 4G investment forum.

- Silicon Flatirons is a "Center for law, technology, and entrepreneurship at the University of Colorado;" funders include AT&T, CenturyLink, and Verizon.

- There's also the Von Coalition, which has been lobbying for years to put through ALEC—state-based VOIP legislation. The VON Coalition originally started to when VOIP service was designed to bypass the phone companies, but it and the Coalition has been co-opted and is now funded by AT&T, Google and Microsoft among others. In fact, the Von Coalition has been in California, Colorado, New Hampshire, and Wyoming among other states to do on the state level what the TAC is doing on the Federal level.

  Oh, but it gets worse. The head of the Council, Tom Wheeler, worked for the wireless and cable companies as former head of the cable association and the former head of the wireless association:

  "On the 20th anniversary of the cable television industry (1995), Tom was selected as one of the 20 most influential individuals in the industry's history and on the 25th anniversary of the

cellular telecommunications industry (2008); he was named one of the top 10 innovators in the wireless industry. Tom was President of the National Cable Television Association (NCTA) from 1979 to 1984. After several years as CEO ... he was asked to lead the Cellular Telecommunications & Internet Association (CTIA), where he was CEO until 2004."

TOM WHEELER

More recently, Wheeler works for Core Capital with his focus being wireless. He appears to not care about the telco wires, as told by his own writing. "The PSTN is a casualty of the digital world." His writings are called "Mobile Musings." And he is part of the Open Mobile Video Coalition which is working on "TV Everywhere," which was announced by Comcast and Time Warner. Wheeler is also currently being cited by some as a potential chairman of the FCC when the current chair leaves.

The Other Side? The Mathematics of Regulatory Capture Made Simple.

There is no serious 'other side.' We could identify only 5-7 companies and groups out of about 50, that are pro-wire' and pro PSTN. This includes wireline competitors XO, EarthLink and Level 3, but when added together their revenues are about 1 percent of the core group. This is important as they don't have the financial resources or skunkworks networks that the AT&T-ALEC cabal has.

Missing—Your voice or representation: Ironically, this is a 'technology' council yet the closing down of the networks and the creating of new digital dead zones is a political issue and a customer issue. Those who might actually discuss these points—such as advocates for consumers and customers were not invited to be part of this to give the council 'balance.'

Conclusion: Stop All Proceedings to Close Down the PSTN; Investigate Regulatory Capture and Clean House.

In short, it appears that the Council was set up by AT&T and the telephone and cable companies to close down regulations and obligations and they created a group that was pro wireless and pro VOIP—or more to the point anti-regulation and anti-PSTN.

The FCC will say that they are 'transparent,' data driven and all of those other terms that are political speak but meaningless. The FCC never explored other options like opening the networks or why the utility networks were never properly upgraded or anything that would show that they considered other alternatives to creating new digital dead zones.

Where is the FCC working group for 'structural separation'—i.e.; separating the companies' controls over the utility wires or opening the phone or cable companies' networks to competition? Or separating the wireline and wireless divisions so that they actually compete?

PERSONAL CODA: In 2003, we were a member of the FCC Consumer Advisory Committee. We filed a complaint against the FCC and the Committee in 2005 as we found that the majority of members were either part of the industry—Verizon has been and continues to be on the Committee since its inception—or that the majority of consumer and astroturf groups were also funded by the industry. This is the reason why your phone bills are unreadable, prices continue to rise and many have few, if any, choices for fast broadband in America.

Maybe the new chairman and commissioner should be required to actually care about the public, economic growth and innovation—and clean house—instead of having sections of the FCC captured by the very industry they are supposed to be monitoring and regulating.

THESE ISSUES RAISE ETHICAL QUESTIONS in terms of conflicts of interest. As such, there has also been legislation that affects lobbying and also impacts "the revolving door" between regulator and regulated. The following article, by Nicholas Kusnetz of The Center for Public Integrity, describes the ease with which legislators become lobbyists working in behalf of their biggest corporate donors.

ARTICLE: ETHICAL QUESTIONS

Revolving Door Swings Freely in America's Statehouses
Anything Goes In Some States; Legislators Exploit Loopholes In Others

By Nicholas Kusnetz, March 19, 2013

ON OCTOBER 26, 2011, the Illinois legislature passed a bill that authorized construction of a multi-billion-dollar smart grid and reshaped how utility companies seek approval for raising electricity rates. Consumer groups opposed the measure, saying it was a handout to utilities.

But the final blow for opponents came three months later when former state Rep. Kevin McCarthy, who had pushed the bill through the legislature only to resign after winning its passage, registered his own lobbying firm and signed his first clients. Prominent among them: Commonwealth Edison, one of the state's largest utilities.

"It's hard to believe that there wasn't a quid pro quo for this," said Scott Musser, an Illinois lobbyist for AARP, which opposed the bill.

McCarthy declined to comment. And despite the potential conflict of interest, his move seems to have been in full compliance with state ethics laws. In Illinois and 14 other states, there aren't any laws preventing legislators from resigning one day and registering as lobbyists the next, according to data compiled by the National Conference of State Legislatures.

Most other states impose "cooling off" periods of one or two years during which legislators or government officials are restricted from lobbying or taking certain private-sector jobs. But a review by the State Integrity Investigation found that in several of those states, including Florida, Indiana and Utah, to name a few, the rules are riddled with loopholes, narrowly written or loosely enforced.

And so in many states, it is simply common practice for lawmakers and other officials to cash in on their expertise and connections by lobbying or consulting for the private sector immediately after leaving office. Ethics experts say this "revolving door" erodes public trust in government and corrupts policy-making.

In the most egregious cases, legislators or regulators have set policy that helps a business or industry with whom they have been negotiating for a job once they leave office. Some states do not ban this practice.

"It smells bad, I guess is about the nicest way I can say it," said Peggy Kerns, director of the Center for Ethics in Government at the National Conference of State Legislatures.

Need for Balance

Even advocates of stricter revolving-door laws caution that a balance must be struck. A complete ban on post-employment lobbying or overly restrictive laws preventing other private-sector work could discourage qualified people from serving in public office and unfairly penalize them for their work. The issue can be particularly complicated at the state level, where many legislatures meet for just a few months a year and pay lawmakers modest salaries. Those calling for stronger laws generally support one- or two-year cooling off periods.

But in the absence of such temporary bans, ethics experts say the revolving door between government and the private sector helps elevate the interests of wealthy private clients above those of the public.

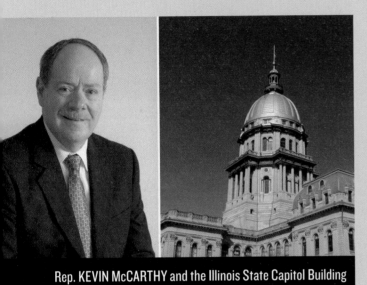

Rep. KEVIN McCARTHY and the Illinois State Capitol Building

"Legislators build up relationships with one another," said Jason Kander, Missouri's new secretary of state, who pushed unsuccessfully for ethics reforms as a state legislator. "It's one thing when that working relationship is beneficial to your constituents — that's how the process is supposed to work. But when that relationship becomes beneficial to paid interests, that's when you cross the ethical line."

From Legislator to Lobbyist

In 2003, Illinois Gov. Rod Blagojevich signed an ethics reform bill that placed limits on post-government employment for certain public officials. The law prevents officials from taking a job if they oversaw a contract with their potential employer while in government. The reform came after the administrator of the Illinois Gaming Board started working for Harrah's casino immediately after resigning from office in 2003. But the law does not prevent a legislator from sponsoring a bill that benefits a company and then resigning in order to work for the firm.

Resigning Early

As Illinois shows, some outgoing legislators resign early rather than serve their full terms. The move usually has little effect on governance as long as the session has ended (most legislatures meet for only part of the year). But in North Carolina, the timing can help circumnavigate the state's six-month cooling off period.

Harold Brubaker, a Republican who had been speaker of the House when the party controlled the legislature in the 1990s, ended his long legislative career by resigning last July after the session ended. "You know when it's time to go," he said in a statement at the time. But the statement also mentioned that he planned to begin lobbying. By stepping down in July, Brubaker will be eligible to lobby his former colleagues as soon as the next legislative session begins, later this month.

Brubaker did not respond to requests for comment.

In September, a local Republican group held an event to honor Brubaker and several legislators attended, including Speaker Thom Tillis, who presented him with an award. A local paper reported that Brubaker's acceptance speech included one request for his former colleagues. "Just remember one thing," Brubaker said, "When I come visit you in the future, just say 'Yes.'"

The move shows that North Carolina's six-month cooling off period, which advocates won only after a hard battle in 2005, is "badly in need of change," said Jane Pinsky, who heads the North Carolina Coalition for Lobbying and Government Reform. State Sen. Richard Stevens stepped down in September and announced he would join a Raleigh law firm, though he said he wasn't sure whether he would lobby the legislature. Such moves "undermine confidence in state government," Pinsky said.

As for Brubaker, by resigning early he was also able to straddle the line with his campaign funds. Lobbyists are barred from making campaign contributions in North Carolina, but there's nothing saying a future lobbyist can't. Brubaker still had about $37,000 left in his campaign account when he announced his intentions, according to campaign finance records, and about six weeks later he sent $6,800 to three former colleagues.

Narrow Rules

Most states do have laws limiting what type of private work public officials can immediately turn to after leaving office, even beyond restrictions on lobbying. But in some states the laws are so narrow or are interpreted so loosely that good-government groups say they fail to prevent many conflicts of interest.

In Indiana, for example, a post-employment rule prohibits officials in the executive branch from taking certain jobs within a year of leaving office and bans for life work on matters they "substantially participated" in while in office. In a 2010 report, The Indianapolis Business Journal examined 27 cases since 2006 and found that the state Ethics Commission enforced the one-year cooling off period in only three of those cases. The commission allowed all the rest to begin their next job immediately, though it did limit the officials from working on certain contracts in 12 cases. Two budget directors, for example, were allowed to work for companies even though they voted on the issuance of bonds involving those companies while in office.

The Journal report was spurred by a revolving-door scandal that led to fines, resignations and

"It smells bad, I guess is about the nicest way I can say it."

—PEGGY KERNS, director of the Center for Ethics in Government at the National Conference of State Legislatures.

even an indictment that is still not settled. In September 2010, Scott Storms left his job as a lawyer and administrative law judge for the Indiana Utility Regulatory Commission to work for Duke Energy, which had been negotiating with the commission over the construction of a cutting-edge coal-powered plant and the deployment of a smart-grid system.

A consumer group raised alarm over the move, and it soon emerged that Storms had conducted hearings involving Duke in the days after the company had offered him a job, in July of 2010. Duke put Storms on leave and Gov. Mitch Daniels fired David Lott Hardy, Storms's boss at the utility commission, after it became clear that Hardy had known of the Duke dealings. After a complaint was brought, the same Ethics Commission that had allowed Storms to go to Duke ended up fining him $12,000 and barring him from future state employment, ruling that Storms had violated conflict of interest rules by working on matters involving Duke while negotiating with the company for a job. Storms denied wrongdoing. Hardy is now awaiting trial on charges of misconduct over the case.

However, the Ethics Commission did not find Storms to have violated the post-employment rule.

While he did oversee issues involving Duke, Storms did not directly regulate the company or issue contracts.

"I'm not going to say the words 'there's nothing wrong with it,'" said David Thomas, the state's inspector general, who investigates ethics issues in the executive branch. But, he added, "The post-employment rule wasn't violated."

The Indianapolis Star said in an August 2011 editorial that the scandal revealed a "pervasive pattern of intimacy between regulatory officers" and Duke, adding that the arrangements were, "unjustifiable by any measure of common sense."

IG Thomas says his office has effectively enforced the law, pointing to 47 cases in which his office, which staffs the Ethics Commission, has issued 117 restrictions since the revolving-door law was enacted in 2005. He said that accusations that his office is too lenient indicate a misunderstanding of the law, which he says imposes a one-year waiting period only if an employee was directly regulating a company or involved in issuing contracts. In a report to the state legislature last year, Thomas recommended against making the revolving-door law more restrictive, pointing to a 2010 federal court ruling that struck down Ohio's cooling off period as too broad.

Julia Vaughn, policy director for Common Cause Indiana, disagrees. She said the attitude that led to the Storms scandal has continued throughout the Daniels administration. "This does go all the way to the top," she said. "It reveals a conspiracy to just get around these laws, that they were considered an inconvenience and that they stood in the way of people who wanted to use their public influence for private gain."

Last summer, Purdue University's board of trustees, most of whom Daniels had appointed, named him the next university president. The inspector general's office said the move would not violate ethics laws. But Vaughn and others have said the case presents clear conflicts of interest and shows the weakness of the state's laws and the Ethics Commission.

"It's been a rubber stamp agency for a long time," Vaughn said. "The law's only as good as the enforcement of it."

The Daniels administration declined to comment for this story, referring questions to the inspector general. But after a Democratic lawmaker filed an ethics complaint in response to Daniels' appointment as Purdue president, a spokeswoman for the governor called it "partisan nonsense."

Loopholes Abound

Even where laws on post-government lobbying exist and are enforced, outgoing public officials have found ways to comply while violating the spirit, government watchdog groups argue. In many cases, lawmakers are prevented from registering as lobbyists for a certain time frame but not from working in an office full of lobbyists and advising them.

"I think that's a slippery area that needs to be closed," said Kerns, of the Center for Ethics in Government. "I don't think any public official should have any kind of a job from a lobbying firm."

Florida has a two-year cooling off period during which ex-legislators cannot lobby their former colleagues. But this hasn't stopped them from working for lobbying firms or from lobbying the executive branch. According to the Orlando Sentinel, at least eight former speakers of the Florida House went on to lobby after leaving the legislature. One of them, John Thrasher, pulled in $1.6 million as a lobbyist in 2008, according to the Sentinel, compared to a state lawmaker's salary of just under $30,000 a year (Thrasher subsequently returned to government as a state senator).

The most recent example is Dean Cannon, who formed his own firm even before leaving office in November, though the firm is not yet registered to lobby. In order to comply with state law, Cannon has said he will focus on lobbying the executive branch and working as a consultant to local governments on political and legislative strategies. His colleague and predecessor as speaker, Larry Cretul, will handle the firm's legislative lobbying.

The arrangement has led some to question the law's effectiveness. Cannon was a strong ally of the Orlando-Orange County Expressway Authority, for example, as it fought last session against a proposal that would have consolidated the agency with several others. Before he left office, the authority invited Cannon to a November meeting to help the agency prepare for the next legislative session. A spokeswoman for the agency told the Sentinel that her company invited Cannon

as the outgoing speaker, but by the time the meeting occurred he had already announced he would soon be lobbying. He has also acknowledged he is seeking a lobbying contract with the authority.

The episode prompted the Sentinel to question Florida's revolving-door law, and its enforcement, in a November editorial. "Floridians can't be blamed," the paper wrote, "for wondering if senators and representatives are making decisions to serve the public interest or to please potential employers."

On Tuesday, the Senate Ethics Committee began work on a sweeping ethics reform bill that could prevent similar moves in the future, either by expanding the cooling off period to include executive branch lobbying or by preventing lawmakers from accepting any work for a firm that lobbies the legislature.

The loophole that allows legislators to work for lobbying firms even applies while they are still in office. One of the side effects of having a part-time legislature, as Florida and nearly all states do, is that many lawmakers often have more lucrative work on the side. According to a report published in July by Integrity Florida, a nonprofit that pushes for ethics reform, 11 lawmakers in the state reported earning money from firms engaged in lobbying in the 2012 session.

Utah's law, passed in 2009, contains perhaps the biggest loophole. While it bans lawmakers from lobbying for one year after leaving office, it exempts anyone lobbying for themselves or for a business they are associated with, as long as lobbying is not the business' primary activity. In 2009, a governor's commission recommended closing the loophole, but a 2010 effort to do just that failed to pass the state House.

Term Limits

Some academics and watchdog groups argue that term limits, which several states have enacted over the past two decades, effectively force more legislators into lobbying jobs. Voters in Michigan approved term limits in 1992, restricting members of the state House to three two-year terms and senators and statewide officials to two four-year terms.

In October, the Detroit Free Press tracked the careers of 291 officials elected from 1992-2004 and found that 71 of them, or nearly one-quarter, ended up either registering as lobbyists or working as consultants or paid advocates. Two former chairs of a House energy committee went to work for utility companies. In the 2009-2010 session, Rep. Kathy Angerer sponsored a bill that would have imposed a two-year cooling off period. The bill failed, however, and Angerer joined AT&T as a lobbyist after the session ended.

Florida's Dean Cannon was limited by term limits, and some proponents of stronger revolving-door laws blame term limits for worsening the revolving door in Missouri and Nebraska as well.

Reforms

Legislators are often reluctant to limit their own options for earning a living. Rep. Jennifer Weiss, a North Carolina Democrat who did not run for re-election in 2012, learned this firsthand when she was part of a group that helped pass the state's revolving-door law.

"I had wanted a year all along," Weiss said, but the group met with too much resistance from legislators on both sides of the aisle, she added, and had to settle for a six-month cooling off period. "People wanted to be able to leave the legislature and lobby, to be blunt."

Similar efforts have failed over the past few years in Idaho, Michigan, Missouri and Illinois, to name a few. Morrison of the Illinois Campaign for Political Reform said his group compromised by pushing for a six-month cooling off period rather than a year, but the initiative has made no progress.

Morrison said Illinois' laws are effective at slowing the revolving door for executive branch officials. And Weiss stressed that a six-month period is better than nothing. While most states do impose some limits, ethics experts say that laws should not completely restrict lawmakers or other officials from moving to the private sector. "They need something else to do," said George Connor, a professor of political science at Missouri State University.

Still, Connor said, loose laws in Missouri allow a pervasive revolving-door culture. The state's outgoing speaker of the House, Steven Tilley, resigned last summer and immediately began a new career in political consulting and lobbying, a step that Connor said has a corrosive effect on governance. "These kinds of relationships cause people to lose sight of the public interest," he said.

One of Tilley's last moves as speaker was to appoint a "blue-ribbon" committee tasked with generating ideas for updating the state's highway system. Tilley, who did not respond to requests for comment, appointed Rod Jetton, a former speaker and now marketing director of a Missouri engineering firm, as co-chair. Also named to the committee was Thomas Dunne, the outgoing chairman and CEO of Fred Weber, Inc., a highway construction company and also one of the first clients that Tilley signed after leaving office.

"It's the smell test," Connor said. "That smells bad."

III. Judicial Enforcement, Review, and Suits

PEOPLE CHALLENGE ADMINISTRATIVE ACTIONS frequently; the judicial system provides an accessible opportunity to do so. An agency's action could be challenged because it violated proper procedures or because it has acted outside of its authority. The underlying law itself may be challenged as being unconstitutional, or because the agency's interpretation of the law is rejected by the courts, which have authority over the agency.

There are hurdles a litigant must pass in order to have a court hear a case for overturning an agency action. Three major issues arise in the enforcement actions of an administrative agency and their ensuing judicial review: due process, standing, and ripeness.

A. DUE PROCESS ISSUES GENERALLY

Like any other government action under the Constitution, administrative agencies must provide basic due process rights. These include giving notice to a person if there is an enforcement action the agency is taking against them. If the IRS seeks to claim money from a taxpayer, it must first provide a notice of the proposed action and an opportunity to appeal the decision. The same is true for other administrative actions.

Due process issues have frequently found their way into the courts when an entitlement is threatened. Examples would include the elimination of welfare benefits, social security, or unemployment compensation. What makes these cases complicated is the fact that some government benefits, such as unemployment compensation, come from state funds as well as the federal government. States may have what is called a durational residency requirement as part of eligibility standards. For example, if a state has no residency requirement, then unemployed individuals may come from all over the nation and immediately seek unemployment benefits, a situation which could cause major financial stress for the state government. Such governments typically want to help its own citizens, but not to create a structure that encourages individuals from other states to take advantage of the government.

The question arises, however, as to how long a person must reside in the state before qualifying for a benefit. Individuals have a right to travel and so if a state's restrictions are too harsh, then the durational residency requirement may violate the person's constitutional due process rights.

Malonado v. Houstoun

United States District Court, E.D. of Pennsylvania, 1997
177 F.R.D. 311

Plaintiffs—Edwin and Maria Delores Maldonado, individually and next as friends of their children and on behalf of all others similarly situated, and a group of associations that represent their interests—have brought this action to challenge the constitutionality of the "multi-tier" durational residency requirement contained in Section 9(5)(ii) of Act 35, codified at 62 P.S. § 432(5)(ii). The defendants in this case are Feather O. Houstoun, the Secretary of the DPW, and Don Jose Stovall, the Executive Director of the Philadelphia County Board of Assistance. The DPW is the executive agency of the Commonwealth vested with responsibility for implementation of the multi-tier durational residency requirement. Stovall is purportedly charged with implementing the multi-tier durational residency requirement in Philadelphia as part of his duties to oversee DPW's cash assistance, food stamp, and medical assistance operations in Philadelphia. Both of these defendants are sued in their official capacities.

This entire action specifically arises out of defendants' implementation and enforcement of Section 9(5)(ii) of Act 35. Section 9(5)(ii) provides:

> Cash assistance for applicants and recipients of aid to families with dependent children who have resided in this Commonwealth for less than twelve months shall not exceed the lesser of the maximum assistance payment that would have been received from the applicant's or recipient's state of prior residence or the maximum assistance payment available to the applicant or recipient in this Commonwealth.

In operation, this provision of Act 35 creates a multi-tier durational residency requirement—referred to as such because the law in effect creates a multitude of benefit levels for otherwise equally situated families. Under the operation of this statute, families who have been residents of Pennsylvania for more than one year receive all of the benefits they would be eligible for under the state plan. Families who have resided in Pennsylvania for less than one year are limited to the amount of cash assistance that they would have received had they remained in their previous state of residence. This means that if a family has moved to Pennsylvania from a state where they would receive cash assistance of only $300 per month, for the first year of their residence in Pennsylvania they can receive no more than $300 monthly in cash benefits, even if they would otherwise be eligible for hundreds more a month under the normal operation of the Commonwealth's welfare program. The multi-tiers arise because long-term residents of Pennsylvania—those with at least one year of residence—will receive a certain amount of benefits under Pennsylvania law; whereas, the short-term residents—those persons with less than one year of residency—will receive varying amounts depending on the law of their prior state of residence. Section 9(5)(ii) is not a lone star in a galaxy of welfare legislation. Indeed, other states have enacted similar provisions.

In this case, the named plaintiffs, Edwin Maldonado, his wife and six children, contend that the operation, implementation and enforcement of Section 9(5)(ii) unconstitutionally discriminates against them because it deprives them of welfare benefits that similarly situated residents of Pennsylvania would receive if they were in the Maldonados' position. In May 1997, the Maldonados moved to Pennsylvania from Guayama, Puerto Rico. The stated reason the family moved to Philadelphia was to receive medical care that would have not been available to them in Puerto Rico. Within seven days of arriving in Philadelphia, the Maldonados applied for welfare benefits.

Because of the operation of Section 9(5)(ii), the Maldonados receive only $304 per month in Temporary Assistance to Needy Families (TANF) benefits rather than the $836 per month that similarly situated families who have lived in Pennsylvania for the past twelve months receive. The difference represents a monthly loss of $532 per month, or 64 percent. Plaintiffs contend that Section 9(5)(ii) deprives them of basic subsistence-level payments because they cannot afford such basic necessities such as shelter, winter heat, clothing, and food on only $304 per month. Moreover, because Mr. and Mrs. Maldonado cannot currently work, they have no way to generate income. The plaintiffs maintain that they cannot afford such basic necessities even though they receive other welfare benefits from Pennsylvania.

For example, the Maldonados receive approximately $720 worth of food stamps per month. The Maldonados also receive medical benefits through the Keystone-Mercy HMO, for which the Commonwealth is being charged $1483.60 per month. The Maldonados also received two special allowances totaling $213, which could be used for Mrs. Maldonado's clothing for job interviews and transportation to prospective employers—interviews which the Commonwealth has determined should not occur until she undergoes and recovers from the eye surgery she needs to be employable. Because Mrs. Maldonado could not work, the Maldonados returned these allowances.

Despite these other benefits, the Maldonados contend that they will be unable to provide for life's basic necessities without a higher monthly cash assistance grant. Indeed, the Maldonados' monthly rent of $350 exceeds their monthly cash assistance, and they do not receive housing assistance. Further, the Maldonados have to pay for utilities such as gas, electricity and the phone. Once again, the Maldonados do not receive assistance for their utilities. The Maldonados also have to provide clothing for themselves and their six children, a cost which is only exacerbated by the fact that they came to Philadelphia from Puerto Rico where there was no need for winter clothing and now they must purchase it. In light of these observations, it is clear that the Maldonados face significant hardship in Pennsylvania due to the fact that they only receive $304 per month.

The Maldonados claim that the disparate treatment they receive by the operation of Section 9(5)(ii) is unconstitutional for three reasons. First, plaintiffs claim that the multi-tier durational residency requirement discriminates against new residents in violation of their fundamental right to travel. Plaintiffs contend that their fundamental right to interstate travel is implicated in this case because (1) Section 9(5)(ii) was enacted in part to deter interstate migration, (2) Section 9(5)(ii) actually deters interstate migration and (3) Section 9(5)(ii) penalizes the right to interstate migration. Because the right to interstate travel is implicated by Section 9(5)(ii), plaintiffs contend that Section 9(5)(ii) is subject to strict scrutiny. As such, plaintiffs argue that Section 9(5)(ii) is unconstitutional because it was enacted for an impermissible purpose and it is not narrowly tailored to serve a compelling government purpose.

Second, plaintiffs claim that Section 9(5)(ii) is unconstitutional because it violates the Equal Protection Clause. Plaintiffs argue that even under the rational review test, Section 9(5)(ii) must fail because no permissible rational purpose supports the distinctions created by the scheme between new residents and longer-term residents, or the distinctions among new residents who moved to Pennsylvania from different states with varied lower benefit levels. As such, the statute violates the Equal Protection Clause.

Finally, plaintiffs contend that Section 9(5)(ii) violates the Privileges and Immunities Clauses of Article IV and the Fourteenth Amendment because it unjustifiably discriminates against new bona fide residents by treating them as Tennesseans of Kentuckians or other out-of-staters, rather than as citizens of Pennsylvania and the United States.

With respect to the preliminary injunction, defendants argue that plaintiffs cannot demonstrate a likelihood of success on the merits, that plaintiffs will not be irreparably harmed, that the Commonwealth will be irreparably harmed, and that the public interest is furthered by this multi-tier durational residency requirement. With respect to the class certification motion, defendants argue that plaintiffs cannot satisfy the commonality, typicality and adequacy of representation requirements of Rule 23(a).

* * *

In a line of cases beginning with *Shapiro*, the Supreme Court has considered whether state durational residency requirements implicated the right to travel and interstate migration to such an extent so as to require the application of the compelling state interest test. In *Shapiro*, the Court found unconstitutional provisions denying welfare assistance to residents who had not resided for at least one year within the jurisdiction of the particular state in which the applicant had applied for benefits. The Court found that such provisions discriminate invidiously by "creat[ing] two classes of needy resident families indistinguishable from each other expect that one is composed of residents who have resided a year or more, and the second of residents who have resided less than a year, in the jurisdiction." The Court found that "any classification which serves to penalize the exercise of that right [to travel] unless shown to promote a compelling state interest, is unconstitutional." The Court could not find any compelling purposes behind the statutes in *Shapiro*.

* * *

The Supreme Court refined the *Shapiro* analysis in two subsequent decisions. In *Memorial Hospital v. Maricopa County,* (1974), the Supreme Court invalidated an Arizona provision requiring a year's residence in a county as a condition of receiving nonemergency medical care at county expense. The Court posed the issue as whether the state's classification "penalized" persons who had recently migrated to the state. If there were such a penalty the provision would be unconstitutional unless supported by a compelling state interest. The Court found that just as the denial of the necessities in life in *Shapiro* operated to penalize recent migrants so did the denial of nonemergency medical care. The Court rejected the state's argument that since some medical services—emergency services—were provided without waiting, the denial of nonemergency medical services could be distinguished from the complete denial as in *Shapiro*. Moreover, the Court, once again, rejected the argument that the state's interest in protecting its financial stability was of a sufficiently compelling nature.

In *Dunn v. Blumstein*, (1972), the Court, relying on *Shapiro*, invalidated a durational residency provision requiring one-year's residence before a new resident could vote. * * *

In sum, *Shapiro* and its progeny establish that a state law implicates the fundamental right to travel and therefore triggers strict scrutiny: (1) when impeding interstate travel is its primary purpose; (2) when its uses a classification which serves to penalize the right to travel; or (3) where it actually deters such travel... The Court must apply the *Shapiro* analysis to the case at bar because it is still binding precedent on this Court due to the fact that it has never been overruled and its facts are similar to this case. * * *

[D]efendants candidly admit that Section 9(5)(ii) was enacted to prevent Pennsylvania from becoming a welfare magnet. In general terms, the welfare magnet theory "postulates that poor people are induced to move to states which pay relatively higher welfare benefits because they want to take advantage of those benefits." * * *

> "THE COMMONWEALTH simply cannot attempt to discourage poor persons from migrating to the Commonwealth in order to prevent the state from becoming a welfare magnet; the law is clear on this point..."

The Supreme Court has repeatedly stated that a law enacted for the purpose of inhibiting migration into state is virtually unconstitutional. Indeed, the Supreme Court has held that "the purpose of inhibiting migration by needy persons into the State is constitutionally impermissible." "If a law has 'no other purpose than to chill the assertion of constitutional rights by penalizing those who choose to exercise them, then it [is] patently unconstitutional.' "

Applying this law, this Court can draw two conclusions about the welfare magnet purpose advanced by the Commonwealth. First, the purpose of preventing the Commonwealth from becoming a welfare magnet is constitutionally impermissible. The Commonwealth simply cannot attempt to discourage poor persons from migrating to the Commonwealth in order to prevent the state from becoming a welfare magnet; the law is clear on this point... The *Shapiro* Court concluded by holding that states "must do more than show that denying welfare benefits to new residents saves money. The saving of welfare costs cannot justify an otherwise invidious classification." Applying this precedent, it is obvious that Pennsylvania's purpose of preventing it from becoming a welfare magnet is constitutionally impermissible.

The second conclusion that this Court reaches, however, is that strict scrutiny should only be applied if the "primary objective" of Section 9(5)(ii) is to deter migration. Thus, the question posed to this Court is whether the "primary objective" of Section 9(5)(ii) is the impermissible purpose of deterrence or the permissible purpose of encouraging work and self-sufficiency... Defendants contend that the primary purpose behind the enactment of Section 9(5)(ii) is to encourage work and self-sufficiency. In support of this position, defendants cite to Section 401 of Act 35 which sets forth the legislative intent for the enactment of Act 35: "It is hereby declared to be the legislative intent to promote the self-sufficiency of all the people of the Commonwealth." It is rare that a Court is provided with such a clear statement of the legislative intent behind a statute.

After considering the purposes that Section 9(5)(ii) was enacted for, the Court concludes that plaintiffs cannot establish that the "primary objective" behind the enactment of Section 9(5)(ii) was to deter migration. The snippets of legislative history and the statement from the DPW do not convince this Court that the primary objective behind the enactment of Section 9(5)(ii) was to deter migration in light of the clear legislative intent of Act 35, which is to encourage self-sufficiency and work. While the Court recognizes that one of the purposes behind Section 9(5)(ii) was to discourage an influx of poor migrants into Pennsylvania, the Court simply cannot find that this was Pennsylvania's primary objective in enacting Section 9(5)(ii). Thus, strict scrutiny will not be applied based on the "primary objective" of the statute.

Plaintiffs also fail to prove that Section 9(5)(ii) actually deters migration. The only evidence that plaintiffs offer in support of their actual deterrence argument is not evidence at all but rather a statement made by the *Shapiro* Court. In *Shapiro*, the Court held that state laws requiring indigent families to wait a year before receiving subsistence level benefits are "well-suited to discourage the influx of poor families in need of assistance." The plaintiffs here, just like the plaintiffs in *Shapiro*, simply offer no empirical evidence that Section 9(5)(ii) will discourage migration. This Court simply cannot rely on speculation and conjecture in deciding whether a statute is potentially unconstitutional. In addition, the little evidence which has been offered indicates that there is no actual deterrence. Indeed, plaintiffs' own witness, Professor Hartman, concluded that poor migrants do not move based on welfare benefits, *i.e.*, welfare benefits simply are not a consideration when poor migrants decide to move. Thus, the Court finds that plaintiffs cannot establish that Section 9(5)(ii) actually deters migration.

Finally, the Court finds that plaintiffs cannot demonstrate that Section 9(5)(ii)'s durational residency requirement results in a "penalty" on the right to interstate migration. To begin, the Supreme Court has made it clear that not every durational residency requirement rises to the level of a penalty and that the parameters of the *Shapiro* penalty analysis are undefined... Thus, the question here is whether the durational residency requirement that limits cash benefits to the level of the state of prior residence but that allows qualified new residents access to food stamps, clothing for job interviews, medical assistance, emergency assistance, and job transportation rises to the level of a *penalty* on the right to interstate migration that would trigger strict scrutiny analysis. This Court concludes that it does not.

In this case, the newcomers to Pennsylvania are not being deprived of the things that are necessary for their very survival, since the plaintiffs and class members are eligible to receive TANF cash assistance benefits, albeit, at a reduced level, food stamps, clothing for job interviews, medical assistance, and job training and transportation, in addition to receiving assistance in finding employment, without regard to any durational residency requirement. In this case, the newcomers receive TANF cash assistance at the same level that they would have received in their state of prior residence. The plaintiffs also receive food stamps ($720 per month) and medical benefits ($1483.60 per month), and are eligible to receive the state's assistance in finding employment. These facts militate against a finding that the multi-tier durational residency requirement imposes a penalty on the plaintiffs' right to interstate migration.

This conclusion is bolstered by the fact that the lower benefits provided do not make new residents any worse off because the new residents receive exactly what they were receiving or would have received in their state of prior residence. Thus, the "penalty" that plaintiffs allege is imposed on them for exercising their right to migrate interstate is not a "penalty" in the traditional sense of the word—a lost benefit that the person would have received had he not exercised some constitutional right…. Because the durational residency requirement of Section 9(5)(ii) dose not operate as a penalty on an individual's right to interstate migration, strict scrutiny is not appropriate. Thus, Section 9(5)(ii) need only be rationally related to a legitimate government purpose to survive the constitutional challenge mounted in the present case.

As stated above, the Commonwealth offers as its legitimate government objectives: (1) "discouraging persons from shopping around for the 'best benefit package of the year' " (2) an intent to encourage employment, self-respect and self-dependency among its welfare recipients, that is to encourage self-reliance over reliance on welfare. The first purpose, of course, is an unconstitutionally impermissible purpose. The Supreme Court has explicitly stated that "the purpose of inhibiting migration by needy persons into the State is constitutionally impermissible." The defendants admit that Section 9(5)(ii) was enacted in part to discourage welfare recipients from shopping around for benefits and to prevent an "influx of indigent people from other states." Because the first purpose is not valid, the Court must turn to the second purpose offered in support of Section 9(5)(ii). This purpose, unlike the first purpose, is clearly a legitimate government objective. The Supreme Court has stated that encouraging work is an "admittedly permissible state objective[]." Thus, the next question to be answered is whether Section 9(5)(ii) is rationally related to a legitimate government purpose.

Although the Supreme Court has stated that encouraging employment is a legitimate government purpose, the Court has also expressly held that a one-year waiting period that is justified as a means of encouraging new residents to seek and obtain employment sooner "provides *no rational basis* for imposing a one-year waiting period restriction on new residents only." Thus, under binding Supreme Court precedent, Section 9(5)(ii)'s one year waiting period simply cannot be justified by claiming that it encourages newcomers to work because it simply is not rationally related to this purpose. Indeed, a close review of how Section 9(5)(ii) would operate indicates that Section 9(5)(ii) must fail because of its inherent irrationality.

To begin, if the goal of the multi-tier durational residency requirement is to promote self-sufficiency, for example by encouraging work, "this logic would also require a similar waiting period for long-term residents of this State." In addition, defendants' justification depends on the wholly unsubstantiated assumptions that newcomers to Pennsylvania are somehow less motivated than more established TANF recipients to seek work and that, when they apply for cash assistance, the members of the latter group but not the former have exhausted any alternatives the Commonwealth has to offer.

Indeed, Section (5)(ii) and its rules and regulations provide for multiple benefit levels for identically situated newcomers. For example, if you had two families, identically situated, arriving in Pennsylvania on the same day, establishing a residence in Pennsylvania and then applying for TANF benefits, but one of the families was from California and one was from Puerto Rico, the family from California would receive the same benefits that a long-term family would receive, and the family from Puerto Rico would receive the limited benefits. At the present time, approximately twenty states have welfare benefits higher then Pennsylvania's benefits; newcomers that come from any of these twenty states would automatically receive the full amount of Pennsylvania TANF cash assistance. In addition, but more surprisingly, the residency requirement appears not to apply to poor migrants from other countries. Hence, new state residents from one of the United States that pays lower benefits will receive less cash assistance than new residents from foreign countries. From these observations, it is manifest that Section 9(5)(ii) is anything but rationally related to achieving its purpose of encouraging newcomers to work. Indeed, large groups of newcomers would automatically receive full benefits upon first arriving in Pennsylvania. This result underscores the irrationality of Section 9(5)(ii).

Because plaintiffs cannot demonstrate that Section 9(5)(ii) is rationally related to its espoused governmental purpose, it appears that Section 9(5)(ii) violates the Equal Protection Clause of the Fourteenth Amendment. Thus, plaintiffs have established a likelihood of success on the merits.

In addition to the deprivation of their right to equal protections, plaintiffs will be irreparably harmed due to the loss of much of their cash assistance benefits... In this case, even if the Maldonados were to receive the full TANF benefits, they would be living at only 37 percent of the poverty line according to official poverty guidelines published by the Department of Health and Human Services. A reduction of their TANF benefits, due to the operation of Section 9(5)(ii), constitutes irreparable harm because they already live on the margin of subsistence. Although the Maldonados as yet have not been pushed into homelessness or rendered unable to feed themselves or their children, Edwin Maldonado testified that he had not yet received his utility bills for which he will receive no assistance in paying. Adding these bills to their monthly rent, and the fact that Mr. Maldonado still has to buy winter clothing for his six children, it becomes clear that the Maldonados will be unable to pay for the basic necessities of life due to the operation of Section 9(5)(ii). Moreover, Edwin and Maria Maldonado are both presently unable to work according to the Commonwealth's own determinations, thus the Maldonados will be unable to earn money to make up for the obvious shortfall in income. Under these circumstances, it is clear that the Maldonados will suffer irreparable harm in the absence of a injunction.

First, it is clearly in the public interest to ensure that all bona fide Pennsylvania residents receive temporary assistance when they are unable to adequately provide for their families and themselves. Second, it is also in the public interest to ensure that Pennsylvanians are not driven into the streets or forced to go without food, shelter or heat due to an unconstitutional statute.

Finally, the defendants have failed to point to any countervailing public interest that would counsel against granting the requested injunctive relief. Indeed, defendants cannot plausibly argue that the multi-tier durational residency requirement advances the public interest because it violates the Equal Protection Clause of the United States Constitution as articulated by the Supreme Court's right to migrate jurisprudence. With this said, the Court finds that the public interest will be furthered by the granting of the preliminary injunction requested herein.

Accordingly, for the foregoing reasons, the Court will grant plaintiffs' motion for class certification. The Court will also grant plaintiffs' motion for a preliminary injunction, it appearing that plaintiffs have a reasonable probability of eventual success on the merits, plaintiffs will sustain immediate and irreparable injury unless a preliminary injunction is issued, greater injury would result by refusing the injunction than by granting such relief, and the public interest would be promoted by the grant of preliminary relief.

Although the Court determines that Section 9(5)(ii) of Act 35 fails to pass constitutional muster under binding Supreme Court precedent, today's decision should not be taken to mean, in any fashion, that the actions of legislature of the Commonwealth of Pennsylvania were undertaken for nefarious purposes. Under our Nation's current welfare laws—which are highly decentralized in the hope that experimentation at the state level will lead to an improvement in these laws, and thus free an untold number of people from their dependency on welfare, durational residency requirements may be needed, and indeed even required, to prevent what has been called the race to the bottom. Without these durational residency requirements, the only option left to a well-intentioned legislature, if it believes that the welfare magnet is correct, is to lower benefits. Thus, the Commonwealth's decision to enact Section 9(5)(ii) cannot be found to have been unreasonable or ill-intentioned, indeed, this Court finds to the contrary. Instead, Section 9(5)(ii) is unconstitutional under binding Supreme Court precedent because it fails to rationally advance the legitimate governmental purposes that underlie it.

B. STANDING AND RIPENESS

The proliferation of administrative agencies assures that governments reach into the daily lives of people. People may debate whether that is a good thing or a bad thing, but that is what tends to happen. And if there is an engagement with the daily lives of citizens then there will inevitably be disputes whether between a taxpayer and the IRS, a small business and the FDA, an entrepreneur wanting to do an initial pubic offering and the SEC, or a larger employer with OSHA. As a practical matter, it is daunting for, say, the average taxpayer to decide to challenge the IRS, or for a tourist to challenge a national park. Administrative agencies remain large governmental organizations with plenty of resources and plenty of lawyers to do battle in the courtroom. Unless the party on the opposing side is a well-funded corporation or individual, the likely payoff of doing battle in litigation is daunting.

At the same time, the United States, like many other well-established democratic countries, has a robust civil society. Indeed, a robust civil society is one of the things that makes a democracy work. In civil society there are hundreds or even thousands of organizations that obtain funding in a variety of different ways (donations from individuals, grants from corporations, foundations, and the government itself, even profit-seeking businesses embedded within the organization) that exist to champion the rights of individuals against government generally, and against administrative agencies particularly. It is not necessarily that these organizations oppose governments *per se*, but that they seek to protect interests that they fear will be excessively limited by governmental action.

So one finds organizations such as the American Civil Liberties Union, which will support individuals whose civil liberties have allegedly been violated so that the individual does not have to foot the bill, or the American Society for the Prevention of Cruelty to Animals, which will investigate and pursue reports of animal cruelty submitted by concerned citizens. In the chapter on Constitutional Law, we saw a recent, famous case of *Citizens United vs. the Federal Election Commission.* This is a classic example of a non-profit organization, Citizen United, taking on an administrative agency.

Questions arise, however, as to whether these groups really meet a judicial standard of "standing" to become involved in the case. To have standing, the person or organization bringing suit needs to show that they suffered an injury in fact. There must be an actual injury to the person or organization, rather than a philosophical or political difference of opinion. For example, a group opposing a new regulation that does not extend the federal government's duty to protect endangered wildlife outside of the U.S. may find moral issues with the regulation, but that does not provide an injury in fact that would allow them to step into the case. In order to get involved in the case, they would have to find an individual who has been injured by the regulation and take up the case on their behalf. If they are unable to find such an individual, the courts will find that they have no standing to bring the case before the courts. The following Supreme Court case illustrates this issue.

Lujan v. Defenders of Wildlife

Supreme Court of the United States, 1992
504 U.S. 555

This case involves a challenge to a rule promulgated by the Secretary of the Interior interpreting § 7 of the Endangered Species Act of 1973 (ESA), 16 U.S.C. § 1536, in such fashion as to render it applicable only to actions within the United States or on the high seas. The preliminary issue, and the only one we reach, is whether respondents here, plaintiffs below, have standing to seek judicial review of the rule.

The ESA seeks to protect species of animals against threats to their continuing existence caused by man. The ESA instructs the Secretary of the Interior to promulgate by regulation a list of those species which are either endangered or threatened under enumerated criteria, and to define the critical habitat of these species. Section 7(a)(2) of the Act then provides, in pertinent part:

> "Each Federal agency shall, in consultation with and with the assistance of the Secretary [of the Interior], insure that any action authorized, funded, or carried out by such agency ... is not likely to jeopardize the continued existence of any endangered species or threatened species or result in the destruction or adverse modification of habitat of such species which is determined by the Secretary, after consultation as appropriate with affected States, to be critical."

In 1978, the Fish and Wildlife Service (FWS) and the National Marine Fisheries Service (NMFS), on behalf of the Secretary of the Interior and the Secretary of Commerce respectively, promulgated a joint regulation stating that the obligations imposed by § 7(a)(2) extend to actions taken in foreign nations. The next year, however, the Interior Department began to reexamine its position. A revised joint regulation, reinterpreting § 7(a)(2) to require consultation only for actions taken in the United States or on the high seas, was proposed in 1983 and promulgated in 1986.

Shortly thereafter, respondents, organizations dedicated to wildlife conservation and other environmental causes, filed this action against the Secretary of the Interior, seeking a declaratory judgment that the new regulation is in error as to the geographic scope of § 7(a)(2) and an injunction requiring the Secretary to promulgate a new regulation restoring the initial interpretation. The District Court granted the Secretary's motion to dismiss for lack of standing. The Court of Appeals for the Eighth Circuit reversed by a divided vote. On remand, the Secretary moved for summary judgment on the standing issue, and respondents moved for summary judgment on the merits. The District Court denied the Secretary's motion, on the ground that the Eighth Circuit had already determined the standing question in this case; it granted respondents' merits motion, and ordered the Secretary to publish a revised regulation. The Eighth Circuit affirmed. We granted certiorari.

Mr. Justice SCALIA

While the Constitution of the United States divides all power conferred upon the Federal Government into "legislative Powers," Art. I, § 1, "[t]he executive Power," Art. II, § 1, and "[t]he judicial Power," Art. III, § 1, it does not attempt to define those terms. To be sure, it limits the jurisdiction of federal courts to "Cases" and "Controversies," but an executive inquiry can bear the name "case" and a legislative dispute can bear the name "controversy." Obviously, then, the Constitution's central mechanism of separation of powers depends largely upon common understanding of what activities are appropriate to legislatures, to executives, and to courts. In *The Federalist* No. 48, Madison expressed the view that "[i]t is not infrequently a question of real nicety in legislative bodies whether the operation of a particular measure will, or will not, extend beyond the legislative sphere," whereas "the executive power [is] restrained within a narrower compass and ... more simple in its nature," and "the judiciary [is] described by landmarks still less uncertain." One of those landmarks, setting apart the "Cases" and "Controversies" that are of the justiciable sort referred to in Article III—"serv[ing] to identify those disputes which are appropriately resolved through the judicial process," —is the doctrine of standing. Though some of its elements express merely prudential considerations that are part of judicial self-government, the core component of standing is an essential and unchanging part of the case-or-controversy requirement of Article III.

Over the years, our cases have established that the irreducible constitutional minimum of standing contains three elements. First, the plaintiff must have suffered an "injury in fact"—an invasion of a legally protected interest which is (a) concrete and particularized and (b) "actual or imminent, not 'conjectural' or 'hypothetical.' Second, there must be a causal connection between the injury and the conduct complained of—the injury has to be "fairly ... trace[able] to the challenged action of the defendant, and not ... th[e] result [of] the independent action of some third party not before the court." Third, it must be "likely," as opposed to merely "speculative," that the injury will be "redressed by a favorable decision."

The party invoking federal jurisdiction bears the burden of establishing these elements... And at the final stage, those facts (if controverted) must be "supported adequately by the evidence adduced at trial."

When the suit is one challenging the legality of government action or inaction, the nature and extent of facts that must be averred (at the summary judgment stage) or proved (at the trial stage) in order to establish standing depends considerably upon whether the plaintiff is himself an object of the action (or forgone action) at issue. If he is, there is ordinarily little question that the action or inaction has caused him injury, and that a judgment preventing or requiring the action will redress it. When, however, as in this case, a plaintiff's asserted injury arises from the government's allegedly unlawful regulation (or lack of regulation) of *someone else*, much more is needed. In that circumstance, causation and redressability ordinarily hinge on the response of the regulated (or regulable) third party to the government action or inaction—and perhaps on the response of others as well. The existence of one or more of the essential elements of standing "depends on the unfettered choices made by independent actors not before the courts and whose exercise of broad and legitimate discretion the courts cannot presume either to control or to predict" and it becomes the burden of the plaintiff to adduce facts showing that those choices have been or will be made in such manner as to produce causation and permit redressability of injury. Thus, when the plaintiff is not himself the object of the government action or inaction he challenges, standing is not precluded, but it is ordinarily "substantially more difficult" to establish.

We think the Court of Appeals failed to apply the foregoing principles in deny-ing the Secretary's motion for summary judgment. Respondents had not made the requisite demonstration of (at least) injury and redressability. Respondents' claim to injury is that the lack of consultation with respect to certain funded activities abroad "increas[es] the rate of extinction of endangered and threatened species." Of course, the desire to use or observe an animal species, even for purely aesthetic purposes, is undeniably a cognizable interest for purpose of standing. "But the 'injury in fact' test requires more than an injury to a cognizable interest. It requires that the party seeking review be himself among the injured." To survive the Secretary's summary judgment motion, respondents had to submit affidavits or other evidence showing, through specific facts, not only that listed species were in fact being threatened by funded activities abroad, but also that one or more of respondents' members would thereby be "directly" affected apart from their " 'special interest' in th[e] subject."

With respect to this aspect of the case, the Court of Appeals focused on the affidavits of two Defenders' members—Joyce Kelly and Amy Skilbred. Ms. Kelly stated that she traveled to Egypt in 1986 and "observed the traditional habitat of the endangered Nile crocodile there and intend[s] to do so again, and hope[s] to observe the crocodile directly," and that she "will suffer harm in fact as the result of [the] American ... role ... in overseeing the rehabilitation of the Aswan High Dam on the Nile ... and [in] develop [ing] ... Egypt's ... Master Water Plan." Ms. Skilbred averred that she traveled to Sri Lanka in 1981 and "observed th[e] habitat" of "endangered species such as the Asian elephant and the leopard" at what is now the site of the Mahaweli project funded by the Agency for International Development (AID), although she "was unable to see any of the endangered species;" "this development project," she continued, "will seriously reduce endangered, threatened, and endemic species habitat including areas that I visited ... [, which] may severely shorten the future of these species;" that threat, she concluded, harmed her because she "intend[s] to return to Sri Lanka in the future and hope[s] to be more fortunate in spotting at least the endangered elephant and leopard." When Ms. Skilbred was asked at a subse-quent deposition if and when she had any plans to return to Sri Lanka, she reiterated that "I intend to go back to Sri Lanka," but confessed that she had no current plans: "I don't know [when]. There is a civil war going on right now. I don't know. Not next year, I will say. In the future."

We shall assume for the sake of argument that these affidavits contain facts showing that certain agency-funded projects threaten listed species—though that is questionable. They plainly contain no facts, however, showing how damage to the species will produce "imminent" injury to Mses. Kelly and Skilbred. That the women "had visited" the areas of the projects before the projects commenced proves nothing. As we have said in a related context, " 'Past exposure to illegal conduct does not in itself show a present case or controversy regarding injunctive relief ... if unaccompanied by any continuing, present adverse effects.' " And the affiants' profession of an "inten[t]" to return to the places they had visited before—where they will presumably, this time, be deprived of the opportunity to observe animals of the endangered species—is simply not enough. Such "some day" intentions—without any description of concrete plans, or indeed even any specification of *when* the some day will be—do not support a finding of the "actual or imminent" injury that our cases require.

> " SUCH 'SOME DAY' INTENTIONS— without any description of concrete plans, or indeed even any specification of *when* the some day will be—do not support a finding of the 'actual or imminent' injury that our cases require."

Besides relying upon the Kelly and Skilbred affidavits, respondents propose a series of novel standing theories. The first, inelegantly styled "ecosystem nexus," proposes that any person who uses *any part* of a "contiguous ecosystem" adversely affected by a funded activity has standing even if the activity is located a great distance away. This approach, as the Court of Appeals correctly observed, is inconsistent with our opinion in *National Wildlife Federation*, which held that a plaintiff claiming injury from environmental damage must use the area affected by the challenged activity and not an area roughly "in the vicinity" of it. It makes no difference that the general-purpose section of the ESA states that the Act was intended in part "to provide a means whereby the ecosystems upon which endangered species and threatened species depend may be conserved." To say that the Act protects ecosystems is not to say that the Act creates (if it were possible) rights of action in persons who have not been injured in fact, that is, persons who use portions of an ecosystem not perceptibly affected by the unlawful action in question.

Respondents' other theories are called, alas, the "animal nexus" approach, whereby anyone who has an interest in studying or seeing the endangered animals anywhere on the globe has standing; and the "vocational nexus" approach, under which anyone with a professional interest in such animals can sue. Under these theories, anyone who goes to see Asian elephants in the Bronx Zoo, and anyone who is a keeper of Asian elephants in the Bronx Zoo, has standing to sue because the Director of the Agency for International Development (AID) did not consult with the Secretary regarding the AID-funded project in Sri Lanka. This is beyond all reason. Standing is not "an ingenious academic exercise in the conceivable," but as we have said requires, at the summary judgment stage, a factual showing of perceptible harm. It is clear that the person who observes or works with a particular animal threatened by a federal decision is facing perceptible harm, since the very subject of his interest will no longer exist. It is even plausible—though it goes to the outermost limit of plausibility—

to think that a person who observes or works with animals of a particular species in the very area of the world where that species is threatened by a federal decision is facing such harm, since some animals that might have been the subject of his interest will no longer exist. It goes beyond the limit, however, and into pure speculation and fantasy, to say that anyone who observes or works with an endangered species, anywhere in the world, is appreciably harmed by a single project affecting some portion of that species with which he has no more specific connection.

...

The most obvious problem in the present case is redressability. Since the agencies funding the projects were not parties to the case, the District Court could accord relief only against the Secretary: He could be ordered to revise his regulation to require consultation for foreign projects. But this would not remedy respondents' alleged injury unless the funding agencies were bound by the Secretary's regulation, which is very much an open question. Whereas in other contexts the ESA is quite explicit as to the Secretary's controlling authority, with respect to consultation the initiative, and hence arguably the initial responsibility for determining statutory necessity, lies with the agencies. When the Secretary promulgated the regulation at issue here, he thought it was binding on the agencies. The Solicitor General, however, has repudiated that position here, and the agencies themselves apparently deny the Secretary's authority. (During the period when the Secretary took the view that § 7(a)(2) did apply abroad, AID and FWS engaged in a running controversy over whether consultation was required with respect to the Mahaweli project, AID insisting that consultation applied only to domestic actions.)

A further impediment to redressability is the fact that the agencies generally supply only a fraction of the funding for a foreign project. AID, for example, has provided less than 10% of the funding for the Mahaweli project. Respondents have produced nothing to indicate that the projects they have named will either be suspended, or do less harm to listed species, if that fraction is eliminated. As in *Simon*, 426 U.S. 26, it is entirely conjectural whether the nonagency activity that affects respondents will be altered or affected by the agency activity they seek to achieve. There is no standing.

...

We hold that respondents lack standing to bring this action and that the Court of Appeals erred in denying the summary judgment motion filed by the United States. The opinion of the Court of Appeals is hereby reversed, and the cause is remanded for proceedings consistent with this opinion.

It is so ordered.

———————————

ADDITIONAL REQUIREMENTS to meet the standing test are that the administrative agency's action caused the injury in fact. This is a test akin to causation in a tort case, where the courts seek to determine that it was the actual administrative agency's action that caused the injury and not other factors.

A final element for judicial review is the concept of ripeness. This is a hard-to-define standard. It arises when courts see an issue brewing, but believe that it is more of a potential legal issue than a matter ready for legal consideration. Three considerations are (1) probability that the predicted harm will take place, (2) hardship to the parties if immediate review is denied, (3) fitness of the record for resolving the legal issues presented (legal issues are fully adjudicated in the early stages while fact issues require development of the facts). Suppose a video store owner finds out that city ordinance makes it illegal to rent adult videos. Because of the theory of ripeness, the store owner can't sue the city and enjoin enforcement of the statute because there is no threatened prosecution or evidence that the law has been applied to the owner's videos. However, if the owner received a warning from a local prosecutor, then the case would be considered ripe.

National Park Hospitality Ass'n v. Department of Interior

Supreme Court of the United States, 2003
538 U.S. 803

The Contract Disputes Act of 1978(CDA) established rules governing disputes arising out of certain Government contracts. After Congress enacted the National Parks Omnibus Management Act of 1998, establishing a comprehensive concession management program for national parks, the National Park Service (NPS) issued implementing regulations including 36 CFR § 51.3, which purports to render the CDA inapplicable to concession contracts. Petitioner concessioners' association challenged § 51.3's validity. The District Court upheld the regulation, concluding that the CDA is ambiguous on whether it applies to concession contracts and finding NPS' interpretation reasonable under *Chevron U.S.A. Inc. v. Natural Resources Defense Council, Inc.*, 467 U.S. 837. The District of Columbia Circuit affirmed, placing no reliance on *Chevron*, but finding NPS' reading of the CDA consistent with both the CDA and the 1998 Act.

The controversy is not yet ripe for judicial resolution. Determining whether administrative action is ripe requires evaluation of (1) the issues' fitness for judicial decision and (2) the hardship to the parties of withholding court consideration. Regarding the hardship inquiry, the federal respondents concede that, because NPS has no delegated rulemaking authority under the CDA, § 51.3 is not a legislative regulation with the force of law. And their assertion that § 51.3 is an interpretative regulation advising the public of the agency's construction of the statutes and rules *which*

it administers is incorrect, as NPS is not empowered to administer the CDA. That task rests with agency contracting officers and boards of contract appeals, as well as the federal courts; and any authority regarding the agency boards' proper arrangement belongs to the Administrator for Federal Procurement Policy. Consequently, § 51.3 is nothing more than a general policy statement designed to inform the public of NPS' views on the CDA's proper application. Thus, § 51.3 does not create "adverse effects of a strictly legal kind," which are required for a hardship showing. Moreover, § 51.3 does not affect a concessioner's primary conduct as it leaves the concessioner free to conduct its business as it sees fit. Moreover, nothing in the regulation prevents concessioners from following the procedures set forth in the CDA once a dispute over a concession contract actually arises. This Court has previously found that challenges to regulations similar to § 51.3 were not ripe for lack of a hardship showing. Petitioner's contention that delaying judicial resolution of the issue will cause real harm because the CDA's applicability *vel non* is a factor taken into account by a concessioner preparing its bids is unpersuasive. Mere uncertainty as to the validity of a legal rule does not constitute a hardship for purposes of the ripeness analysis. As to whether the issue here is fit for review, further factual development would "significantly advance [this Court's] ability to deal with the legal issues presented," even though the question is "purely legal" and § 51.3 constitutes "final agency action" under the Administrative Procedure Act. Judicial resolution of the question presented here should await a concrete dispute about a particular concession contract.

C. EXACTLY WHO GETS SUED?

Under the doctrine of sovereign immunity, the government cannot be sued. For instance, think of the lawsuits that could result in a time of war if injured parties could sue the government. At the same time, sovereign immunity undermines the principle of accountability and, given the impact of administrative actions, Congress often waives sovereign immunity and allows cases to be brought against agencies.

In nearly all such suits against the government, the suit is brought against the agency and not the individual. Even if a suit names the individual who runs the agency, such as the Attorney General, damages demanded in the suit would not be paid by the individual serving as Attorney General, but instead by the government itself. The Supreme Court has established immunity from any tort suit for an administrative official who is acting within the scope of the official's duty for the agency.

Gonzalez v. Reno

United States Court of Appeals, Eleventh Circuit, 2003
325 F.3d 1228

On September 28, 2000, the Gonzalezes commenced this action under *Bivens v. Six Unknown Named Agents of Federal Bureau of Narcotics*, 403 U.S. 388 (1971), by filing a complaint for damages against Attorney General Janet Reno, in her individual capacity; INS Commissioner Doris Meissner, in her individual capacity; Deputy Attorney General Eric Holder, in his individual capacity; INS agent Betty Mills; an unknown number of INS agents whose names are not known; an unknown number of U.S. Border Patrol agents whose names are not known; and an unknown number of U.S. Marshals whose names are not known. In their complaint, the Gonzalezes allege the following facts. On November 25, 1999, six-year-old Elian Gonzalez, a Cuban boy, was found floating on an inner tube off the coast of Fort Lauderdale, Florida. The Coast Guard brought Elian into the United States, and the INS paroled him into the country without inspection, then released him into the custody of his great-uncle, Lazaro Gonzalez ("Lazaro"). Lazaro filed a petition with the INS on behalf of Elian seeking political asylum for the child. Elian also filed a petition for asylum on his own behalf.

On January 5, 2000, INS Commissioner Meissner decided that the INS would not consider the requests for asylum because Elian's father, a Cuban citizen, had requested that Elian be returned to Cuba. On January 7, 2000, Lazaro filed a petition for temporary custody of Elian in the Family Division of the Circuit Court for Miami-Dade County, which was granted pending a full hearing on the matter.

On January 12, 2000, Attorney General Reno affirmed Meissner's decision not to consider the petitions for political asylum. Lazaro challenged Reno's ruling in the United States District Court for the Southern District of Florida, and the court upheld Reno's decision. Lazaro appealed to this court.

"In the course of executing the warrants, the agents allegedly sprayed gas into the residence; broke down the front door with a battering ram and entered the residence without first announcing their presence; sprayed more gas; pointed guns at the occupants of the residence, threatening to shoot; shouted obscenities; and broke doors, furniture, and religious artifacts. As one federal agent pointed a weapon at one of the occupants and Elian, INS agent Betty Mills entered the room with a blanket and seized the child."

Photo: Alan Diaz, Reuters

On April 6, 2000, while that appeal was pending, Elian's father arrived in the United States. On April 12, 2000, the INS instructed Lazaro to bring Elian to Opa Locka Airport, and advised Lazaro that the parole of Elian into his care was being transferred to Elian's father. On April 13, 2000, the circuit court dismissed Lazaro's petition for temporary custody and vacated its prior order granting temporary custody to Lazaro.

On April 19, 2000, a panel of this court entered an order enjoining Elian from departing, or attempting to depart, the United States; enjoining all persons acting on his behalf from aiding, or assisting or attempting to aid or assist, Elian's removal from the United States; and enjoining all officers, agents, and employees of the United States to take such reasonable and lawful measures as necessary to prevent the removal of Elian from the United States. On April 20, 2000, the Gonzalezes began negotiations with Reno, Meissner, and Holder toward the goal of transferring temporary custody of Elian.

Even though it was purporting to negotiate a peaceful transfer of the child, the INS issued an administrative warrant for Elian's arrest on April 21, 2000. The arrest warrant asserted that Elian was within the United States in violation of the immigration laws and could therefore be taken into custody. The INS then obtained a search warrant to enter the Gonzalezes' home and search for Elian.

At approximately 5:15 a.m. on April 22, 2000, armed federal agents arrived at the Gonzalezes' residence to execute the search and arrest warrants. In the course of executing the warrants, the agents allegedly sprayed gas into the residence; broke down the front door with a battering ram and entered the residence without first announcing their presence; sprayed more gas; pointed guns at the occupants of the residence, threatening to shoot; shouted obscenities; and broke doors, furniture, and religious artifacts. As one federal agent pointed a weapon at one of the occupants and Elian, INS agent Betty Mills entered the room with a blanket and seized the child.

Based on the foregoing factual allegations, the Gonzalezes claim in their complaint that the defendants violated their First Amendment rights of freedom of expression and assembly (Count I), their Fourth Amendment rights to be free from unreasonable searches and seizures (Count II), and their Fifth Amendment rights to a liberty interest in personal security and to be free from unnecessary and unreasonable force (Count III). The complaint also claims that the defendants conspired to violate each of these constitutional rights (Counts IV–VI).

Defendants Reno, Meissner, Holder, and Mills moved to dismiss the claims against them arguing that plaintiffs' complaint failed to state a claim against them and that they were entitled to qualified immunity from damages claims in their individual capacity. The district court addressed the defendants' motion to dismiss in an order dated June 5, 2001.

The court dismissed Count I of the complaint without prejudice after concluding that the Gonzalezes failed to allege any facts supporting their theory that the federal agents' entry into their home was undertaken for the purpose of abridging their First Amendment rights. The court dismissed Count III with prejudice after the Gonzalezes conceded in their response that their excessive force claims should be analyzed under Fourth Amendment search and seizure analysis rather than Fifth Amendment substantive due process analysis. The court also dismissed the conspiracy claims in Counts IV–VI.

With respect to the Gonzalezes' Fourth Amendment claims in Count II, the court held that the Gonzalezes lacked standing to challenge the validity of the administrative arrest warrant. The court dismissed the Gonzalezes' Fourth Amendment claims challenging the validity of the search warrant after concluding that the warrant was valid because the magistrate who issued it was presented with a facially valid arrest warrant and an affidavit establishing probable cause to believe that Elian was in the Gonzalezes' home. The court dismissed Betty Mills as a defendant without prejudice because the complaint contained no allegations of excessive force by her. The court denied the motion to dismiss with respect to the excessive force claims against the other federal agents because it found that the Gonzalezes had alleged sufficient facts to support their claim that the federal agents (other than Mills) who executed the warrant at their home used excessive force, in violation of their Fourth Amendment rights.

The court also denied the motion to dismiss with respect to the defense of qualified immunity. The court concluded that the complaint alleged the requisite "causal connection" between the supervisory actions of Reno, Meissner, and Holder and the alleged constitutional violation by the agents on the scene to hold them liable based on their supervisory status, notwithstanding their absence from the scene. The court based this finding on paragraphs 70 and 75 of the complaint, which alleged that Reno, Meissner, and Holder "personally directed and caused a paramilitary raid upon Plaintiffs' residence" and that the agents on the scene "acted under the personal direction of Defendants JANET RENO, DORIS MEISSNER AND ERIC HOLDER."

Reno, Meissner, and Holder now appeal, challenging the district court's rejection of their qualified immunity defense.

A district court's decision to grant or deny the defense of qualified immunity is a question of law which we review *de novo*, accepting the factual allegations in the complaint as true and drawing all reasonable inferences in the plaintiff's favor.

The defense of qualified immunity completely protects government officials performing discretionary functions from suit in their individual capacities unless their conduct violates "clearly established statutory or constitutional rights of which a reasonable person would have known. The purpose of this immunity is to allow government officials to carry out their discretionary duties without the fear of personal liability or harassing litigation, protecting from suit all but the plainly incompetent or one who is knowingly violating the federal law." Because qualified immunity is "an entitlement not to stand trial or face the other burdens of litigation," questions of qualified immunity must be resolved "at the earliest possible stage in litigation." It is therefore appropriate for a district court to grant the defense of qualified immunity at the motion to dismiss stage if the complaint "fails to allege the violation of a clearly established constitutional right."

> "TO RECEIVE qualified immunity, the government official must first prove that he was acting within his discretionary authority. Here, it is clear—and undisputed—that defendants Reno, Meissner, and Holder acted within their discretionary authority."

To receive qualified immunity, the government official must first prove that he was acting within his discretionary authority. Here, it is clear—and undisputed—that defendants Reno, Meissner, and Holder acted within their discretionary authority.

Once the defendants have established that they were acting within their discretionary authority, the burden shifts to the plaintiffs to show that qualified immunity is not appropriate. The Supreme Court has set forth a two part analysis for determining whether qualified immunity is appropriate. The court must first ask "this threshold question: Taken in the light most favorable to the party asserting the injury, do the facts alleged show the officer's conduct violated a constitutional right?" "[I]f a violation could be made out on a favorable view of the parties' submissions, the next, sequential step is to ask whether the right was clearly established."

Our first step, then, is to determine whether the factual allegations in the complaint, if true, establish a constitutional violation by Reno, Meissner, and Holder. The district court properly characterized the complaint as alleging that Reno, Meissner, and Holder are liable in their supervisory capacities only. For purposes of this opinion, therefore, we will assume, without deciding, that the alleged conduct by the agents on the scene—spraying gas into the house, breaking down the front door, pointing guns at plaintiffs, and damaging property—constituted excessive force and deprived plaintiffs of their Fourth Amendment rights to be free from unreasonable searches and seizures. This leaves us with the task of deciding whether the defendants' supervisory actions caused the alleged deprivations of plaintiffs' Fourth Amendment rights.

"It is well established in this circuit that supervisory officials are not liable under [*Bivens*] for the unconstitutional acts of their subordinates 'on the basis of respondeat superior or vicarious liability.' " "The standard by which a supervisor is held liable in her individual capacity for the actions of a subordinate is extremely rigorous." Supervisors "can be held liable under [*Bivens*] when a reasonable person in the supervisor's position would have known that his conduct infringed the constitutional rights of the plaintiffs, and his conduct was causally related to the constitutional violation committed by his subordinate."

"Supervisory liability [under *Bivens*] occurs either when the supervisor personally participates in the alleged constitutional violation or when there is a causal connection between actions of the supervising official and the alleged constitutional violation." A causal connection can be established "when a history of widespread abuse puts the responsible supervisor on notice of the need to correct the alleged deprivation, and he fails to do so," or when the supervisor's improper "custom or policy ... resulted in deliberate indifference to constitutional rights." A causal connection can also be established by facts which support an inference that the supervisor directed the subordinates to act unlawfully or knew that the subordinates would act unlawfully and failed to stop them from doing so.

In examining the factual allegations in the complaint, we must keep in mind the heightened pleading requirements for civil rights cases, especially those involving the defense of qualified immunity. The complaint must allege the relevant facts "with some specificity." "[M]ore than mere conclusory notice pleading is required.... [A] complaint will be dismissed as insufficient where the allegations it contains are vague and conclusory." Moreover, in reviewing a motion to dismiss, we need only accept "well-pleaded facts" and "reasonable inferences drawn from those facts." "[U]nsupported conclusions of law or of mixed fact and law have long been recognized not to prevent a Rule 12(b)(6) dismissal." We must also keep in mind the fact that "[w]e generally accord ... official conduct a presumption of legitimacy."

We now turn to the complaint to determine whether plaintiffs have alleged sufficient facts to establish supervisory liability. Plaintiffs allege that these defendants "personally directed and caused a paramilitary raid upon [their] residence, and had actual knowledge of, and agreed to, and approved of, and acquiesced in, the raid in violation of the Fourth Amendment rights of Plaintiffs herein." Plaintiffs also allege that the agents on the scene "acted under the personal direction of Defendants, JANET RENO, DORIES MEISSNER and ERIC HOLDER, and with the knowledge, agreement, approval, and acquiescence of Defendants, JANET RENO, DORIS MEISSNER and ERIC HOLDER." Finally, plaintiffs allege that these defendants "personally participated in the constitutional violations, and there was clearly a causal connection between their actions and the constitutional deprivation."

These vague and conclusory allegations do not establish supervisory liability. Plaintiffs make bold statements and legal conclusions without alleging any facts to support them. Plaintiffs appeal to the emotions by calling the events that transpired a paramilitary raid, but they do not allege any facts to suggest that the defendants did anything more than personally direct and cause the execution of valid search and arrest warrants. Plaintiffs state that there is a causal connection between these defendants' acts and the excessive force used by the agents on the scene, but they do not allege any facts to support this causal connection. Plaintiffs do not allege that these defendants directed the agents on the scene to spray the house with gas, break down the door with a battering ram, point guns at the occupants, or damage property. Given the presumption of legitimacy accorded to official conduct, it would be unreasonable to draw from the alleged facts the inference that the supervisory defendants directed the agents on the scene to engage in the unconstitutional activity with which they are charged. Instead, the reasonable inference which we must draw from the factual allegations is that the supervisory defendants ordered the execution of valid search and arrest warrants with the expectation that the agents on the scene would execute them in a lawful manner.

In sum, plaintiffs allege that the agents on the scene used excessive force in violation of their Fourth Amendment rights, but they fail to allege any facts which, if true, would establish that the supervisory defendants caused that violation. Because plaintiffs have failed to allege that the supervisory defendants' conduct constituted a constitutional violation, the supervisory defendants are entitled to qualified immunity under the first step in our qualified immunity analysis. The decision of the district court is therefore REVERSED.

HOWEVER, IF AN OFFICIAL ACTS OUTSIDE OF HIS DUTIES—say perhaps leaking information about someone the agency is investigating to the press—then there could be a suit against that individual apart from their protection as an agency official. In *Bivens v. Six Unknown Named Agents of Federal Bureau of Narcotics*, a 1971 Supreme Court case, the Court held that federal officials could be liable for constitutional torts, and found six federal agents to be liable for damages of their actions when they were acting under the "color of authority" conferred upon them due to their administrative positions. In the case, the search and arrest of the plaintiff was extreme. According to the Court, "the agents manacled petitioner in front of his wife and children, and threatened to arrest the entire family. They searched the apartment from stem to stern. Thereafter, petitioner was taken to the federal courthouse in Brooklyn where he was interrogated, booked, and subjected to a visual strip search." There was also a question of whether there even was a valid search warrant to justify the search. The Court held open the possibility, in such cases, of the petitioner being able to recover damages from the officers personally.

IV. Congressional Control of Administrative Agencies

AGENCIES COME INTO EXISTENCE through Congressional legislation, and Congress retains several capabilities of impacting their work. One way of controlling agencies is to change the legislation that affects them. After the terrorist attacks of September 11th, 2001, for instance, the U.S. government undertook changes in its security gathering so that intelligence agencies were better able to communicate with each other. Some of this was achieved through executive orders, but some was also done through legislation.

Actually getting Congress to change legislation or to terminate an agency is very difficult to do. Once in existence, inertia and political pressures make it difficult to end or dramatically change an agency. Recognizing this, Congress will occasionally enact "sunset laws" that call for the automatic ending or review of an agency at a certain time. However it is very rare that this occurs at the federal level because the agencies tend to develop close ties to Congressional constituents. It is much more likely to see agencies eliminated at the state level. In Texas, for example, there is an actual Sunset Advisory Commission which spearheads reviewing, renewing and reforming major state agencies. The Sunset Commission has reviewed over 300 agencies and has eliminated over 70 since 1979.[3] In Maryland, the Program Evaluation Act of 1978 established a system for reviewing and eliminating obsolete or overlapping agencies.

Another way that Congress can control an agency is through its appropriations powers. Even after an agency comes into existence, it has to have money to continue to function. Congress controls appropriations, so Congress could alter the actual funds flowing to the agency.

Finally, undoubtedly the most common, but also the most informal method of Congressional impact on agency action is through direct contact. Elected leaders run for reelection, in part, on the basis of providing constituent services to their electorate. Thus, if a constituent has an issue with the FTC, the constituent may appeal to his or her Congressmen for assistance. This kind of Congressional pressure occurs frequently, but there are also risks for a representative getting too deeply involved in influencing administrative actions. That is particularly true if the representative is acting on behalf of an individual who is not simply a citizen in her district, but a campaign contributor. In *Corporacion Insular de Seguros v. Garcia*, the plaintiff attempted to gain access to communications between a legislator and gubernatorial aides to show

---

3   http://www.utexas.edu/lbj/cpg/docs/f3_2013_sunset.pdf

that the "legislative process was somehow substantively infirm." The Court took a narrow view as to when the facts of a legislative debate can be withheld from the public, especially when the issue did not concern a security issue.

V. Presidential Control of Administrative Agencies

PRESIDENTS IMPACT AGENCIES AS WELL. Perhaps the most common and direct influence is determining who runs the agency. The president appoints leaders and other high-level staff of administrative agencies, usually subject to the approval by Congress. In making such appointments, the president can exercise a great deal of influence on the direction of an agency. A president who campaigns on the promise of tougher enforcement of environmental regulations, for instance, will undoubtedly appoint a similarly motived leader to head the EPA, which will impact the entire organization. On the other hand, a president who believes that the EPA has been overzealous in its work will appoint a leader with those views in mind.

In addition to this power, presidents have required that executive agencies conduct cost-benefit analysis on all proposed regulations and to show that the benefits outweigh the costs. President Obama further ordered executive agencies to quantify costs and benefits. The Office of Management and Budget (OMB) will also review regulatory actions planned in the upcoming year, thus providing another executive opportunity to influence changes. Under President Obama, the OMB issued the Open Government Initiative, which gives the OMB the authority to assist the President in overseeing and coordinating the Administration's legislative and regulatory policies.

VI. Other Controls

BEYOND GOVERNMENTAL CONTROL of administrative agencies, the democratic flow of information that allows debate to occur also can play a significant role. A frustrated citizen may object to the conduct of an agency and use its actions as a basis of a campaign or referendum. The media frequently raises questions about the actions of administrative agencies and has the ability to obtain information about those actions through the usual tools of reviewing *The Federal Register*, reviewing comments and testimony at hearings, or interviewing individuals. The media (and citizens) also can obtain information about the actions of the agencies through the Freedom of Information Act.

The FOIA requires that agencies provide documents to the public unless there is an exemption (such as national security or issues pertaining to agency personnel and their privacy. The following provides a full list of these exemptions:

1. Documents classified as secret in the interest of national defense or foreign policy.

2. Documents related solely to internal personnel rules and practices.

3. Those specifically exempted by other statutes.

4. Trade secrets or privileged or confidential commercial or financial information obtained from a person.

5. Privileged inter-agency or intra-agency memorandum or letter.

6. Personnel, medical or similar file, the release of which would constitute a clearly unwarranted invasion of personal privacy.

7. Documents compiled for law enforcement purposes, the release of which:

    a. could reasonably be expected to interfere with law enforcement proceedings,

    b. would deprive a person of a right to a fair trial or an impartial adjudication,

    c. could reasonably be expected to constitute an unwarranted invasion of personal privacy,

    d. could reasonably be expected to disclose the identity of a confidential source,

    e. would disclose techniques, procedures or guidelines for investigations or prosecutions,

    f. could reasonably be expected to endanger an individual's life or physical safety.

8. Information contained in or related to examination, operating, or condition reports about financial institutions that the SEC regulates or supervises.

9. Documents containing exempt information about gas or oil wells.

Other acts, such as the Government in Sunshine Act, similarly authorize the disclosure of government actions. In the case of the Government in Sunshine Act, there is a general requirement that meetings of multi-member federal agencies must be open to the public and the public must be given advance notice of the meetings. Trying to strike a balance with other important rights, laws such as the Privacy Act also attempt to protect information about individuals supplied to the government.

NOTES AND COMMENTS

1. **A FREQUENT COMPLAINT** is that individuals will work on Congressional staffs or in administrative agencies and then switch to the private sector, where their attractiveness to an employer includes knowing how to navigate the bureaucracy with friends and colleagues in the right places. Of course, citizens have a right to seek employment, and one's life and career experiences are obviously highly relevant to whether one gets a job or not. But there have been efforts to place restrictions on "the revolving door" between government and private industry. One summary of this can be found at *http://www.doi.gov/ethics/post_employment_activities.html*

2. **WHAT IS YOUR VIEW** of doctrines such as standing and ripeness? Does it make sense to you that one has to have suffered some actual injury in order to sue an agency's action? Isn't being a citizen enough? Or does the doctrine preclude even more litigiousness than already exists in the country? Similarly does ripeness inevitably create a situation when an issue is ruled upon when it is too late, once harm is already done? Or, again, does such a doctrine efficiently preclude creatively speculative reasons for bringing one lawsuit after the other?

3. **IF YOU WERE TO WORK** for an administrative agency, which one would you choose? Which one would you least like to work for?

Part 2

Essential Legal Concepts in Business

The Village Lawyer's Office, by Pieter Brueghel the Younger, 1626

5

PROPERTY LAW

THE ANCIENT LAW OF PROPERTY is a rather tame area. Yet private property ownership, one of the fundamental building blocks of free market economics, is essential to conceptions of American Democracy, and has

tremendous vibrancy today in the form of Intellectual Property. Indeed, in emerging market countries or in those where Communist or Socialist regimes formerly governed, some of the first legal reforms generally addressed how to create an enforceable regime of private property rights. With secure property rights, one can own a home and amass wealth. Moreover, one might use real property for a business such as to farm or to extract minerals, or simply as a site to locate an office building or factory.

Private property ownership provides the basis for a financial system that can lend money in the form of mortgages, which in turn can provide the liquid capital to build businesses. And property rights entail transfer rights, so that one can buy, sell, and develop land to facilitate the transfer and exchange of wealth.

I. General Concepts and Classifications of Property Rights

OWNERSHIP OF PRIVATE PROPERTY stands as a counterweight against authoritarian and tyrannical government as well, which is a central reason for why authoritarian governments typically refuse to allow citizens property rights. If individuals (and corporations) own property, there is a limit imposed on the powers of government to do what it will with that property. This becomes another fundamental basis for democracy. In Medieval England, the development of private property through the process of enclosure and the ensuing commercialization of property allowed wealthy landowners to check the power of King John, eventually forcing him to sign the *Magna Carta* in the 1200s.

In short, we owe many of our economic and political freedoms to the history of property law. In the near future, establishing property rights will also be a key to navigating the process of globalization. To begin the study of this ancient concept of property (and, because it is ancient, the rather unusual terminology associated with it) it might be good to set out some different classifications of property.

A. TANGIBLE AND INTANGIBLE

Tangible property is something that one can get one's hands on. It is your house or your car, cell phone, or book. Intangible property is property that you possess and have a right to, but cannot physically touch; others cannot take it away from you without punishment by law. You may well have a paper document that gives you evidence of it, but you are never going to have "it" in your hands. Today, a major example of this comes in the form of various kinds of intellectual property, such as a copyright or trademark. These are as protectable as the oil field you own and drill upon, but it is not something you will physically hold.

B. REAL AND PERSONAL

Real and personal property are both tangible, but the former is something you stand on and the latter is every other kind of tangible property. "Estate" is a term that one frequently finds in property terminology and finds a common reference point in this distinction. Real estate consists of land. You can walk and stand on it. Obviously, you can plow it, drill on it, build on it, or use it for any number of other purposes as well. Buildings—houses, condominiums, and office buildings—are real property as well. While hardly a legal definition *per se*, think of real property as what a real estate agent sells. They sell all of these things, but they don't sell watches, cars, or groceries. These items are personal property. You can put your hands on them—unlike a copyright—but they aren't the ground or a building on the ground.

C. DIVIDED AND UNDIVIDED

A person could have an undivided or divided interest in an item of property. An undivided interest is one where you own and possess all there is to possess of the property. This idea can apply to personal property; for instance, you own a diamond ring without sharing that ownership with anyone else. That constitutes an undivided interest. The same applies to land. You may be the sole owner of a vacation home or an undeveloped piece of land.

On the other hand, you might share the ownership with someone else. The ways in which one can have shared ownership—a divided interest—are almost as many as the human imagination can conceive. You might co-own a bank account with your spouse. You may own an interest in an investment fund only after someone else dies. You may lease an apartment rather than owning a condominium. You may have a right to a seat in a stadium to watch a baseball game rather than owning the seat itself. Each of these stands as an example of a divided interest. Much of property law is about issues that arise with divided interests.

D. LIMITED OR UNLIMITED AS TO TIME

One kind of divided interest splits ownership according to when a person has certain kind of rights. Perhaps the easiest example of this is the life estate, a land ownership concept going back hundreds of years. Suppose a landowner wants to keep the property "in the family" but doesn't know if a child or grandchild will foolishly (at least in the property owner's mind) sell the land. The landowner could carve up ownership in the land according to time. He might give a "life estate" to his child, allowing the use—but not the sale—of the land during the child's life. At the same time the grant of the land would preclude the child from deciding, in her Will, to whom to leave the land after her death. Instead, in accordance with the original landowner's Will, the land might go to a grandchild for the grandchild's life. By doing this, the original landowner could extend his control over the disposition of the land for a hundred years. He can't stretch out the final disposition forever; there is a concept called "the rule against perpetuities" requiring that the land "vest" at some point, but that can be put off for quite a while. This is an example of having a use of land for a limited time period, and if the landowner's grandchild has a second life estate, she owns a property interest even before she gets to enjoy the actual use of the property. The interest is simply contingent on other things (such as the death of the person currently having use of the property). Whoever finally receives the property holds a "remainder" interest during all the time before they come into possession, even while others control the property during the life estates.

There could be many reasons for the landowner's decision to divide up property ownership like this. It could be that he is looking at some expensive tax considerations when the land finally is transferred and wants to delay that transfer with life estates, or he doesn't trust his children's judgement and doesn't want to give them the power (and temptation) to sell the property for money. So the landowner simply gives them the right to live in the family home without having the capacity to sell it. This lack of trust could pertain to the in-law who married the landowner's children, too. While trusting his own children, the landowner may not like the in-law and so wants to make sure the in-law cannot hands on the family heritage. Life estates are one way to do this.

E. FIVE KINDS OF ESTATES—REAL PROPERTY

Recognizing that human imagination can think of many ways to divide up property, there are five key kinds of estates in real property.

I. The first is a FREEHOLD ESTATE. This is an outright ownership of the property which one typically can buy, sell, and develop without asking for permission from anyone else, except as limited by legal restrictions (such as zoning laws) on the use of the land.

2. The second is a LANDLORD-TENANT RELATIONSHIP, where a landowner rents out the property to a tenant. This could be in a residential situation (e.g. an apartment) or it could be for commercial property as well.

Ownership Variations (Concurrent Estates In Land)

Concurrent Estates in Land	Joint Tenancy	Tenancy in Common	Tenancy by Entirety
OWNERSHIP	Undivided Interest	Proportionate and undivided Interest	Undivided Interest
RIGHT OF SURVIVORSHIP	Yes	No	Yes
REQUIRED UNITY	• Unity of Time • Unity of Title • Unity of Possession • Unity of Interest	• Unity of possession	• Unity of Time • Unity of Title • Unity of Possession • Unity of Interest
ESTATE LANGUAGE	"To X and Y as joint tenants with right of survivorship	"To X and Y" (as tenants in common)	"To Husband and Wife"
METHODS OF TERMINATION	Unilaterally severed, then convertible as Tenancy in Common	Freely transferable	Mutually severed, death or divorce
PASSING OF PROPERTY	Upon death, property passes to the remaining joint tenants (operation of law)	Upon death, property passes to heirs	Upon death, property passes to heirs

Source: http://www.cpaexamacademy.com/lessons/regulation-reg/2-0-business-law/2-9-property/

3. A third is a CO-TENANCY. Here a person owns property together with another person. Most often this is an ownership with a family member. Spouses own a house together, or own a joint bank account. Siblings own a farm together. A parent owns an investment fund to pay for college together with the children who will use the funds for their education.

4. A fourth pertains to RIGHTS ABOVE AND BELOW THE GROUND. Ownership of real estate provides some ownership of what is above the ground as well as what is below the surface. Thus a landowner may provide rights to say, a business constructing windmills, that reach up from the ground, or provide rights to a mining company for minerals below that might be extracted.

5. Finally there are INCORPOREAL INTERESTS, which are not only interests such as copyrights and trademarks, but also certain rights with a land-based dimension. Examples of these are easements, which are rights connected to the land, but are not rights in the real estate itself.

II. Ownership Variations

A. FREEHOLD ESTATES

I. FEE SIMPLE: The broadest ownership one can have is a "fee simple," sometimes also called a fee simple absolute. Fee simple ownership means that one owns all the rights associated with the property. One can buy, gift, or sell it. One can develop it. One can subdivide it into successive interests. At death, one can direct the person who will have it next (or if one does not have a Will, then the state will determine who should own it next). It is, in short, the cornerstone of all property rights.

2. LIFE ESTATES: Life estates are a straightforward way to divide up property ownership based on time. The idea is that person will have rights to the property during a period of time, usually a person's life, with the interest then passing to someone else. A life estate always needs to start with someone who has fee simple ownership. That person, the Grantor, then can determine how to divide up ownership of the property.

A conventional life estate would work like this. The Grantor is married with three children. He knows that his wife does not want to move from their home if he were to die. At the same time, for any number of reasons, he does not believe it is a good idea for his wife to have full, fee simple ownership of the property. So, the Grantor executes a deed that states that the Grantor gives the property to his wife for her life and then, at her death, the remainder goes to their children.

This example is overly simplistic, in that surviving spouses have rights to property interests even if the other spouse tries to preclude them from getting them. The exact nature of those rights is complex, but the above example is helpful simply in setting out the ways in which a life estate can be created.

In this simple example, there is a Grantor. One also has a holder of the life estate, the spouse. And one has three people, the children, who have a remainder interest. The children are sometimes called "remaindermen." Because there are multiple parties having interests in the same property, disputes are inevitable. In particular, the question arises as to the nature of rights and duties between the life estate holder and the remainderman.

The simple example of a **Grantor** → **Life Estate Holder** → **Remaindermen** can be varied. When deeding the interests, the grantor could reserve a life estate to himself first, so that the interests would run:

> **Grantor** (as fee simple owner) → **Grantor/Life Estate Holder** → **Spouse/Life Estate Holder** → **Children/Remaindermen**

Another variation would be that the grantor creates a life estate for a term of years. He could establish a "life estate," not for "life," but for a period of, say, fifteen years, after which it then goes to another life estate holder or to a remaindermen.

Estates in Land	Fee Simple	Life Estate	Future Interest
OWNERSHIP RESTRICTED	No	Yes	Yes
DURATION OF OWNERSHIP	Indefinite	Limited to Life	Limited to Future

Source: http://www.cpaexamacademy.com/lessons/regulation-reg/2-0-business-law/2-9-property/

Yet another example is to create a life estate that is not based on the life of the life estate holder. Instead, the "measuring life" is someone else. Perhaps the Grantor's spouse has a significant disability. The Grantor does not want his spouse to face the trauma of having to move. At the same time, the spouse does not have the capacity to make decisions. There are several ways the family could protect the spouse. The family could have the spouse sign a document called a power of attorney, which authorizes someone else to make decisions on her behalf. The family could go into court and have a judge declare that the person is unable to make decisions and have a guardian (usually a family member) appointed for her.

In addition to (or perhaps in lieu of) these steps, the Grantor could simply deed the property to one of his trusted children to use for the life of their mother. In other words, the one child would maintain the property as individuals looking out for another party—the mother—for the rest of her life. Then, at death, the actual ownership of the property would pass to all the children/remaindermen.

Today, many facing this situation might accomplish the same result through the creation of a trust, but one can still utilize the above strategy. A life estate holder's duties with respect to these kind of property as follows:

> "A life tenant is bound to keep the land and the structures comprising the estate 'in as good repair as they were when he took them, not excepting ordinary or natural wear and tear....' The obligation to make ordinary repairs is twofold. The tenant not only has the duty to make the ordinary repairs required to remedy a presently existing condition of substantial disrepair that may have injured the property substantially or permanently, but also has the duty to make any ordinary repairs necessary to prevent the property from progressively declining to the point where its deterioration, and the resultant injury to the inheritance, is substantial or permanent. In discharging the latter duty to make preventive ordinary repairs, for example, 'if a new roof is needed, [the tenant] is bound to put it on; if paint wears off, he is bound to repaint.'
>
> —*Sauner v. Brewer* 220 Conn. 176 (1991).

The Grantor is not restricted to creating only one subsequent life estate at a time. In other words, the Grantor may establish several life estates. Rather than just creating two—one reserved for him and one, then, for his wife—the Grantor could also create successive life estates for all of his children and then, only after all their deaths, provide for the property to pass to a remainderman. How long can this be stretched? Can a Grantor create such a succession of life estates so that the property never "vests" (or becomes a fee simple again)?

The Rule Against Perpetuities was devised to deal with the problem of unvested or life-estates for children ("issue") who had not yet come into being. While the rule seems relatively simple when stated—the estate must vest, if at all, within 21 years of the lives in being—the Rule is one of the most complex (and confusing) parts of property law for law students and even for lawyers.

These ongoing, successive interest issues may sound as if they are purely issues of personal estate planning instead of being connected to business. However, they frequently become deeply involved in business. Suppose, as is often the case with a person who owns a family business, the main asset of a person is their business. At death, inheritance taxes may well be levied against the estate. However, there are innumerable ways to lessen or legally avoid the imposition of such taxes. One way to do so is to structure property ownership so that property does not "vest." Successive life estates help with this.

Another key tool in estate planning that pertains to keeping a business free of inheritance/estate taxes is the use of the marital deduction. In federal law, property passing to a surviving spouse is free from taxation. Of course, the surviving spouse will die sometime (thus triggering taxes), so a business person will want a mix of trying to pass property to the spouse and to others (such as children), with various rights for each. If one does not get the mix right, then taxes may be so significant that a business will need to be sold. Thus, these issues of property ownership can end up making a very big difference to the long-term viability of a family business.

One of the most famous examples involved the necessary sale of the Chicago Cubs to the Tribune Company in order to pay the taxes on the estates of two members of the Wrigley family, famous for Wrigley's chewing gum. Even though the family employed some wealth-shifting techniques to reduce their estate tax liability, ultimately, the heavy tax burden forced the Wrigley heir to sell the Cubs in 1981. Here is the account from the *Chicago Tribune*.*

Estate and Inheritance Taxes of $40 Million Led William Wrigley to Negotiate the Sale of the Chicago Cubs to Tribune Company.

...

WILLIAM WRIGLEY'S estate tax problems resulted in large measure from the fact that his mother died so soon after his father in 1977, and from the fact that he did not want to dilute his controlling interest in either the Cubs or the Wm. Wrigley Jr. Co. These problems were compounded because the estate lacked enough cash or liquid assets to pay taxes.

'Mrs. Wrigley was a number of years younger than Mr. Wrigley,' Bright [Wrigley's attorney] said. 'It was anticipated that she would survive for some period of time, which could have allowed recouping the taxes paid on his estate.'

Phillip Wrigley made a marital gift to his wife of one-half of his estate. That helped reduce the estate and inheritance tax owed on Phillip's estate. But the death of Helen meant that the entire estate was evaluated and taxed as a 'package,' Bright said.

...

The Wrigley Estate did not qualify for substantial deferrals of estate taxes allowed to owners of closely-held businesses because neither the Cubs stock nor the Wrigley Co. stock comprised a sufficiently large portion of the total estate, she added. The government allowed a four-year extension on the payment of the taxes. The maximum estate tax rate it 70 percent on estates of more than $5 million. Included in that 70 per cent are credits for payment of state inheritance taxes.

Bright said there was nothing the Wrigley family could have done to avoid the estate tax problems and still retain control of both the Wrigley Co. and Cubs stock.

Noting that the Cubs have been in the family since 1915, Bright said, 'It was a great family tradition, and it's rather sad that taxes can break it up.'

* Bill Barnhart, "$40 Million Estate Tax Led Wrigley to Sell," *Chicago Tribune*, Jun. 17, 1981

B. CONCURRENT OWNERSHIP

Very often, people own property together with some else. Spouses frequently own their home, bank accounts, cars, and other property together. Parents sometimes share ownership with children. In a partnership, the same usually holds true. Thus, in addition to the possibility of dividing property according to time—such as described in the previous section on life estates—property ownership can be divided between individuals as well. There are two key ways this can be done.

A very common form of joint ownership of property is **joint tenancy**. In a joint tenancy two (or more) parties share four unities in the property. First, they have unity of possession in that they both have an undivided interest in the property. That means that each of them as a right to the entire property. If the property is a $100,000 bank account, they each have a right to the entire $100,000, not just "their half." Thus, if two people are pooling their resources in a joint bank account, they must realize the risk that the other person could walk away with all the money.

A second "unity" is that the parties share title to the property through the same document. Joint tenancy property needs to be created at one time in one document. In most states, there is a formulation that needs to be followed: "As joint tenants and not as tenants in common" needs to be in the title of the document creating the joint tenancy, in part for the exact reasons in the previous example. There is risk associated with a joint tenancy, and courts want to be sure that a person entering into a joint tenancy knows what they are getting into.

Closely related to the second unity, the third unity is Unity of Time. The parties take the property at the same time, the time when the document is created. A joint tenancy arrangement is sometimes referred to as a "poor man's will." This is because a feature of joint tenancy is that the survivor automatically receives the entire interest of the property upon the other co-tenant's death. One does not have to go to Probate Court or to have a will for this to happen. It does so automatically as a feature of the joint tenancy. Thus, a parent might take an already existing bank account and create a new account with one or more of her children's name on it as joint tenants. This creates a new property ownership to the property.

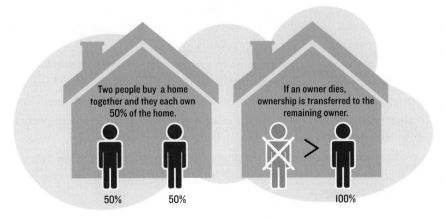

Source: http://hocmn.blogspot.com/2011_03_01_archive.html

The final unity is that of Unity of Interest. This means that the estate owned by each party is of the same type. They each own an interest in a bank account or in real estate.

WHEN THE INEVITABLE disputes arise, they have to be ironed out, and unless there are clear terms or agreements, the parties may have to turn to the court system to resolve these arguments.

Creating a joint tenancy is not particularly difficult. The parties agree that they wish to own the property with the above characteristics and then must physically create it. There must be written documentation of the joint tenancy, unlike a Tenancy in Common, exactly because it has the special features of allowing each tenant to fully take the property and because joint tenancies have a right of survivorship in them.

Death, of course, ends a joint tenancy and the survivor(s) take the remaining interest. While this transfer avoids probate in most states, it does not avoid federal estate taxes. Other ways to sever a joint tenancy are by mutual agreement, any transfer (potentially through a straw man), by petition, and by mortgage in some jurisdictions.

Another common form of joint ownership is a tenancy in common. A tenancy in common has only one of the four unities possessed by a joint tenancy, the unity of possession. Each tenant is entitled to equal use and possession of the property. The interests do not have to be of the same duration. The tenancy is created with two or more parties with interest in the same property. One party may have a one-third interest and the other a two-thirds life estate interest. Unlike joint tenancies, a tenancy in common need not be in writing (unless it pertains to real estate, in which case it must because of the Statute of Frauds). There is no right of survivorship; the parties simply are entitled to their part of the property. In these respects, a tenancy in common is much easier to create, less risky (in that the other co-tenant does not have rights to walk off with the property), and flexible in terms of the kinds of ownership interests contributed to create the co-tenancy.

But that flexibility comes at a cost. When the inevitable disputes arise, they have to be ironed out, and unless there are clear terms or agreements, the parties may have to turn to the court system to resolve these arguments.

While joint tenancies and tenancies in common are the most prominent kinds of co-ownership, there are others. One example is something called Tenancy by the Entirety. In states that authorize these forms of co-ownership, they are limited to arrangements between spouses that cannot be severed either by the other co-tenant or by their creditors. It can only be terminated by mutual agreement, by joint creditors, divorce, or death. At death, the property passes to the remaining tenant. Because of the strictness of these, they are not nearly as common as other forms of joint ownership.

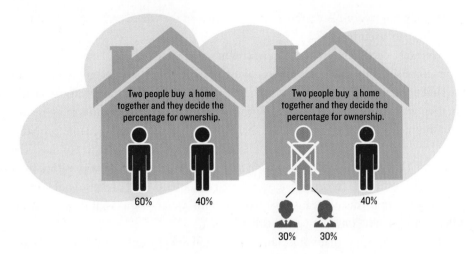

Source: http://superphotoscannerwallpaper.blogspot.com/2012/11/tenants-in-common.html

In addition to these kinds of co-ownership, there are many ways to jointly share ownership once one utilizes more formal business arrangements. As we will see in later chapters, partnerships sometimes utilize some of the above ownership methods, but the larger and more formal the partnership, the more it will rely on partnership agreements that pool interests that are broader than the tenancies described here. Moreover, there are a variety of corporate forms that also allow pooling of interests.

III. Transfer Issues of Real Estate

THE CHAPTER ON CONTRACTS described some of the issues pertaining to transfers of real estate. Most specifically, materials in that chapter described the Statute of Frauds. This anciently rooted legal approach, still valid through the U.S. today, requires that transfers of real estate must be in writing. With real estate, that takes the form of a deed. Title to the land will pass to another person if the deed is validly executed and delivered. There are several kinds of deeds.

The most common deed is called a "warranty deed." As the name implies, these deeds warrant or guarantee that the owner does, in fact, own the property and will defend the authenticity of the title against competing claims or imperfections, even after transfer. A "quitclaim deed" is must less authoritative. With it, the grantor only transfers to another person *whatever interest* that grantor has. The interest may be the same as in a warranty deed, but it also could be nothing. The grantor is not assuring the buyer/grantee anything; she is just conveying whatever she has at the time. Another kind of deed is called a special warranty deed. This does assure some degree of ownership, but only insofar as the grantor is stating that there were no liens placed on the property while the grantor owned the property. The grantor is not assuring the new buyer that there were no liens before the current/transferring owner took possession. With this overview, one can see where each kind of transfer might have its usefulness.

Warranty deeds tend to be the most common for three reasons. First, a new buyer wants to be sure that she is actually receiving property. She is paying good money for the land or house and does not want to be surprised to learn that the grantor/seller did not own what he purported to own. With a warranty deed, the grantor/seller makes a commitment to clear up title in case there is a problem. A second reason, probably more important today, is that a buyer may utilize financing in order to purchase the property. The buyer may get a loan from a bank or other financial entity rather than paying cash outright. In order to cover their risk, a bank will always demand that there is a warranty deed because the bank's funds are at risk as well if the grantor/seller ended up not conveying good title.

The third reason is that banks (and buyers) will not rely only on the seller/grantor to promise to clear up title problems. The banks will demand title insurance. Special insurance companies will insure the property so that, if there is a problem, the insurance company's assets will cover any losses associated with a faulty title. Insurance companies, of course, are in the risk mitigation business so they will not issue a title insurance policy, for which the buyer (or seller) will pay, unless they are very sure that there are, in fact, no problems with the title to the property. The company will hire an attorney to do a title opinion. This will require the attorney to check all the court records to make sure the title is good and clear against other potential deed-holders, and that there are no hidden liens or unreleased mortgages against the property. The attorney will charge a fee to the title company. Of course, then the lawyer also has some malpractice liability—covered as well through insurance—assuring that the title opinion is accurate.

Thus, in most real estate transactions today, there are multiple layers of assurance (and insurance) that a conveyance is a good, lawful, free-of-defects transfer of real estate. At least this is true when banks are involved. When banks are not involved, one party can replicate all the above issues with respect to title insurance by directly dealing with the title insurance company. If one does not want to involve a title insurance company (and pay the premium for the policy), one could simply rely on an attorney's title opinion.

And, in some areas—especially rural ones—occasionally one will still find an older process called an "Abstract of Title." In these cases, someone—usually a lawyer—will put together a history of documents that pertain to the property so that the property owner has all the documents regarding the property in one place. The idea is that everything that has ever been filed related to the property is in that one place, the Abstract, and so one can visually see, read, and review whether or not there are any glitches in the title.

Title insurance options are very difficult to obtain when one is dealing with a quitclaim deed. Quitclaim deeds are more typically executed when the property owner is simply getting out of a situation. In a divorce, one party may quitclaim his interest in the house to the other party. In some cases, a person a hundred years ago may have acquired a small interest in an oil drilling operation and, thereafter, paid little attention to it. The original owner of the fractional interest may have died, as have her children and perhaps even grandchildren, thus creating a hundred individuals who have tiny fractional interests. Then, someone or some company wants to consolidate all the outstanding fractional interests for the company, which may amount to thousands of individual interests. None of these people have any idea as to whether they have good title to the land, and so they will be unwilling to sign any kind of warranty deed. They may be willing to sign, however, a quitclaim deed to convey whatever interest they have. Thus, there are times and places where these kinds of deeds are more useful than others.

A modern example of a quitclaim deed is a deed in lieu of foreclosure. This might occur where a property owner is no longer able to pay the mortgage on the property. It is certainly possible that, if the mortgagee were unable to make the mortgage, he might be unable to pay other bills as well, and those creditors may have filed a lien separately against the property. Rather than face foreclosure, the property owner may simply deed the property to the bank; the property owner will not be in a position to guarantee good title, but he can quitclaim the interest he does have in the property. This may also have tax repercussions resulting from the discharge of indebtedness, depending on the use of the property.

Other, less used forms of property transfer could include a sheriff's deed. If a person has gone through foreclosure, the bank may end up auctioning off its interest in a repossessed home or automobile. Because a foreclosure entails going through the court system, an officer of the government will conduct the auction and then convey the title to the person with the highest bid. That conveyance would be through a sheriff's deed, or some similarly named conveyance, depending on the particular state. A sheriff's deed will typically be another form of a quitclaim deed.

There are also a number of state-specific procedures regarding the registration of title, such as the indexing method for deeds and the state's approach to competing claims between bona fide purchasers. Indexing methods refer to the type of system in place the lawyer or landowner uses to search and see if they have a perfected title. There are two types of systems—the grantor-grantee indexes and tract indexes. Grantor-grantee indexes trace the title through each disposition between persons, and the lawyer or landowner checks to see if the title is perfected by tracing the history of dispositions through each owner. Each piece of land has its own distinct history in the index. Related to this is the idea of notice to subsequent bona-fide purchasers. This area of the law can become complex very quickly, but it suffices to know that there are three types of notice statutes: race, race-notice, and notice statutes. Each system dictates what types of notice and registration are necessary to protect a title against other competing claimants. The case that follows gives an example of a case involving adverse claims.

Board of Education v. Hughes

118 Minn. 404 (Minnesota 1912)

BUNN, J.

Action to determine adverse claims to a lot in Minneapolis. The complaint alleged that plaintiff owned the lot, and the answer denied this, and alleged title in defendant L. A. Hughes. The trial resulted in a decision in favor of plaintiff, and defendants appealed from an order denying a new trial.

The facts are not in controversy and are as follows: On May 16, 1906, Carrie B. Hoerger, a resident of Faribault, owned the lot in question, which was vacant and subject to unpaid delinquent taxes. Defendant L. A. Hughes offered to pay $25 for this lot. His offer was accepted, and he sent his check for the purchase price of this and two other lots bought at the same time to Ed. Hoerger, husband of the owner, together with a deed to be executed and returned. The name of the grantee in the deed was not inserted; the space for the same being left blank. It was executed and acknowledged by Carrie B. Hoerger and her husband on May 17, 1900, and delivered to defendant Hughes by mail. The check was retained and cashed. Hughes filled in the name of the grantee, but not until shortly prior to the date when the deed was recorded, which was December 11, 1910. On April 27, 1909, Duryea & Wilson, real estate dealers, paid Mrs. Hoerger $25 for a quitclaim deed to the lot, which was executed and delivered to them, but which was not recorded until December 21, 1910. On November 19, 1909, Duryea & Wilson executed and delivered to plaintiff a warranty deed to the lot, which deed was filed for record January 27, 1910. It thus appears that the deed to Hughes was recorded before the deed to Duryea & Wilson, though the deed from them to plaintiff was recorded before the deed to defendant.

The questions for our consideration may be thus stated: (1) Did the deed from Hoerger to Hughes ever become operative? (2) If so, is he a subsequent purchaser whose deed was first duly recorded, within the language of the recording act?

1. The decision of the first question involves a consideration of the effect of the delivery of a deed by the grantor to the grantee with the name of the latter omitted from the space provided for it, without express authority to the grantee to insert his own or another name in the blank space. It is settled that a deed that does not name a grantee is a nullity, and wholly inoperative as a conveyance, until the name of the grantee is legally inserted. It is clear, therefore, and this is conceded, that the deed to defendant Hughes was not operative as a conveyance until his name was inserted as grantee.

Defendant, however, contends that Hughes had implied authority from the grantor to fill the blank with his own name as grantee, and that when he did so the deed became operative. This contention must, we think, be sustained. Whatever the rule may have been in the past, or may be now in some jurisdictions, we are satisfied that at the present day, and in this state, a deed which is a nullity when delivered because the name of the grantee is omitted becomes operative without a new execution or acknowledgment if the grantee, with either express or implied authority from the grantor, inserts his name in the blank space left for the name of the grantee. ***

Unquestionably the authorities are in conflict; but this court is committed to the rule that in case of the execution and delivery of a sealed instrument, complete in all respects save that the blank for the name of the grantee is not filled, the grantee may insert his name in the blank space, provided he has authority from the grantor to do so, and, further, that this authority may be in parol, and may be implied from circumstances. We consider this the better rule, and also that it should be and is the law that when the grantor receives and retains the consideration, and delivers the deed in the condition described to the purchaser, authority to insert his name as grantee is presumed. Any other rule would be contrary to good sense and to equity. The same result could perhaps be reached by applying the doctrine of estoppel; but we prefer to base our decision on the ground of implied authority. Clearly the facts in the case at bar bring it within the principle announced, and we hold that Hughes, when he received the deed from Mrs. Hoerger, had implied authority to insert his name as grantee, in the absence of evidence showing the want of such authority. The delay in filling up the blank has no bearing on the question of the validity of the instrument when the blank was filled.

> "THE DELAY in filling up the blank has no bearing on the question of the validity of the instrument when the blank was filled."

It is argued that holding that parol authority to fill the blank is sufficient violates the statute of frauds. This theory is the basis of many of the decisions that conflict with the views above expressed; but we do not think it sound. The cases in this state, and the Wisconsin, Iowa, and other decisions referred to, are abundant authority to the proposition that the authority of the grantee need not be in writing. Our conclusion is, therefore, that the deed to Hughes became operative as a conveyance when he inserted his name as grantee.

2. When the Hughes deed was recorded, there was of record a deed to the lot from Duryea & Wilson to plaintiff, but no record showing that Duryea & Wilson had any title to convey. The deed to them from the common grantor had not been recorded. We hold that this record of a deed from an apparent stranger to the title was not notice to Hughes of the prior unrecorded conveyance by his grantor. He was a subsequent purchaser in good faith for a valuable consideration, whose conveyance was first duly recorded; that is, Hughes' conveyance dates from the time when he filled the blank space, which was after the deed from his grantor to Duryea & Wilson. He was, therefore, a 'subsequent purchaser,' and is protected by the recording of his deed before the prior deed was recorded. The statute cannot be construed so as to give priority to a deed recorded before, which shows no conveyance from a record owner. It was necessary, not only that the deed to plaintiff should be recorded before the deed to Hughes, but also that the deed to plaintiff's grantor should be first recorded.

Our conclusion is that the learned trial court should have held on the evidence that defendant L. A. Hughes was the owner of the lot.

Order *reversed*, and new trial granted.

A. ADVERSE POSSESSION

Less common today than in the past, adverse possession remains a way to obtain ownership to property. Historically, it was more common when the North American continent was being settled and there were large swaths of unoccupied land. At that time, there was a national interest in using property productively. If a landowner—even one who had full, good, exclusive title to property—was so careless about what was going on with the land that he allowed another person to actively use it for twenty consecutive years, then the person using the land could claim it under the concept of adverse possession.

Today, adverse possession has the same requirements and is far less common. The first requirements are that the person claiming ownership through adverse possession has actual and exclusive possession. This means that the person is really using it and living on it to the exclusion of others in the manner that an actual possessor would use the land. The second requirement is that the person's use is "open, visible, and notorious." This simply means the use is being done in a way so that others are aware of it. The person is not putting a sign up on the property and saying it is his; he is building a house on it or farming it or clearly and publicly using the property as if it is his own. The third requirement is that the use is continuous and peaceable for twenty years. The fourth is that the use is hostile and adverse. Additionally, some states require additional elements, such as a claim of right (that the possessor act in good faith) or that the adverse possessor act under the color of title. These requirements seem to conflict with each other: How can ownership be both peaceable and hostile, innocent or acting in good faith but adverse? But the idea is that while the person is making sure that others are not trespassing, no one else is really actively claiming that they, instead, own the land. Further, in calculating the twenty years, "tacking" is allowed as long as the interests of the parties are not adverse to one another. That means that if the person claiming adverse possession (for say eight years) conveys the property to someone else—for instance via intestacy to his child—then that child can count those eight years toward the twenty years necessary to satisfy the requirement.

Today, issues of adverse possession are likely to come up in boundary disputes. Fences are particularly good examples. A neighbor in a subdivision or a farmer or a factory ends up putting a fence just across the boundary and instead builds the fence on the neighbor's land. The neighbor does not say anything and this continues for the twenty-year period. At the end of the twenty years, it is possible for the fence-owner to claim the land the fence is on via adverse possession. The following is an example of just such a case.

Helm v. Clark

244 P.3d 1052 (Wyoming 2010)

KITE, Chief Justice.

* * *

Mr. Clark and the Helms own adjoining agricultural properties in the NE ¼ of Section 12, Township 30 North, Range 119 West, 6th P.M., in Lincoln County, Wyoming. The properties have been in the Clark and Helm families since the 1920s. Mr. Clark's property is north of the Helms' and their respective deeds indicate that the sixteenth section line dividing the NE ¼ and the SE ¼ of the NE ¼ of Section 12 forms their property line, i.e., Mr. Clark owns the NE ¼ NE ¼ and the Helms own the SE ¼ NE ¼. A fence between the properties was built long ago and is south of the actual property line, meaning that part of the Helms' property is fenced in with Mr. Clark's property.

The Helms decided to move the fence to place it on the property line. Mr. Clark objected, and the Helms filed an ejectment action on October 25, 2007. Mr. Clark counterclaimed alleging that he had acquired title to the property north of the fence by adverse possession. The district court held a bench trial and ruled that Mr. Clark had proven the elements of adverse possession and the Helms had not provided a sufficient explanation to establish that Mr. Clark's use was permissive. Consequently, the trial court quieted title in Mr. Clark. The Helms appealed.

* * *

The district court ruled that Mr. Clark had established a *prima facie* case of adverse possession and shifted the burden to the Helms to explain the possession. On appeal, the Helms make a cursory attempt to show the district court incorrectly determined that Mr. Clark had established a *prima facie* case for adverse possession. They assert the district court failed to give proper weight to the facts that they paid taxes on the disputed property and Mr. Clark and his predecessors had executed title instruments affecting their deeded property but had not executed any such instruments affecting the disputed area. In certain cases, each of these factors may be important in determining whether possession is adverse. However, as the district court recognized, the fact that Mr. Clark had not paid taxes on the property is typical when a case involves use to a fence line. The claimant's failure to execute title instruments affecting the disputed property also is not unusual in fence line adverse possession cases. Although these facts weigh against a finding of adverse possession, they are not necessarily determinative.

The district court considered all of the evidence and found Mr. Clark had established a *prima facie* case of adverse possession because the disputed area had been enclosed by a fence with Mr. Clark's property for a very long time, Mr. Clark had used the disputed property for grazing livestock during that time, and the Helms were aware of the discrepancy between the fence and the true boundary. The district court's decision is consistent with prior cases where we have stated that enclosing land in a fence may be sufficient to "raise the flag" of an adverse claim, and "[t] he pasturing of animals within a substantial enclosure is sufficient to establish the elements of adverse possession."

***

B. Boundary Fence or Fence of Convenience

After Mr. Clark presented his *prima facie* case for adverse possession, the burden shifted to the Helms to explain Mr. Clark's possession of the disputed area. They attempted to show that his use of the property was permissive because the fence was located off the property line as a matter of convenience. The placement, type and purpose of a fence are important factors in adverse possession cases. A fence that is intended to be the boundary between properties supports a claim for adverse possession. On the other hand, a fence that is placed in a certain location in order to separate pastures or irrigated meadows from grazing land or because the terrain makes it easier to build the fence in that location rather than on the property line is a fence of convenience. When a fence is located off the property line as a matter of convenience, use by the neighbor is considered permissive and will defeat a claim for adverse possession. The determination of whether a fence establishes a property boundary or is one of convenience is a question of fact.

> "THE DETERMINATION of whether a fence establishes a property boundary or is one of convenience is a question of fact."

The district court rejected the Helms' argument that Mr. Clark's use was permissive and ruled the evidence supported a finding that the fence was a boundary fence rather than a fence of convenience:

> [T]he Clark–Helm fence ... was [not] built as an interior fence. The land on either side of the fence is similar in nature requiring no separation due to the nature of the land. The fence runs from where it intersects with Section 7 [on the east] in a straight-line west over a ridge. Once it goes over the ridge it runs through mixed aspen and evergreen timber where its course meanders somewhat and trees are occasionally used as fence posts. But it is substantial in that it consists of five barbed wires. It runs through serviceberry bushes in places and the wire is off the posts in places in the spring. Trees have fallen over the fence in places. This is the normal condition of a longstanding fence enclosing pasturelands that are located in standing timber and subject to heavy snows. The fences needed to be repaired in the spring as Mr. Clark testified. This does not convert a boundary fence into a fence of convenience.

> [T]he Court finds that the Clark–Helm fence was constructed in the 1920's on a line that ran more or less straight consistent with the fence line located in the south boundary of [the adjacent property to the east in Section 7].... The nature of this fence is consistent with a boundary fence. It is of the same type, if not better, ... as that fence [on the west side of the Helms' property] and a better fence than the Helms' southern boundary fence. It was assumed to be on the surveyed line until about 1968. It is typical of the boundary fences that the Helms and Clarks had even though it may not have been built to modern standards. From 1968 onward the Plaintiffs Helms were aware the Clarks were possessing their property on the other side of the fence yet they failed to take action to stop this possession.

The Helms challenge the district court's finding that the fence was a boundary fence, claiming that Mr. Clark and his predecessors admitted, in a related matter, that a different fence on the eastern boundary of the disputed area was one of convenience. During the trial, the Helms asked the district court to take judicial notice of the record in a case involving a property line dispute between Mr. Clark and his neighbors to the east in Section 7, Township 30 North, Range 118 West, 6th P.M., Lincoln County, Wyoming, Kenneth and Meleese Nebeker. Mr. Clark's father and uncle filed an affidavit in that case. They averred that the Clark/Nebeker fence was off the property line (it was located west of the actual property line so that part of Clark's property was fenced in with Nebekers' property); their father, Ernest L. Clark, had owned the lands on both sides of the fence in Sections 7 and 12; and the "fence was originally put in as a fence of convenience between farm land and hill pasture."

***

C. Nature and Location of Fence/Disputed Area

The Helms challenge the district court's rulings about the nature and location of the Clark/Helm fence. First, they assert the evidence did not establish that the fence was continuous from the eastern border to the western border of the Clark and Helm properties. The district court found that as the fence proceeds west from the eastern border, it generally runs in a straight line until it enters the timber, where "its course meanders somewhat," even using trees as fence posts at times. The trial evidence demonstrated that in some places along its course, the fence line proceeds through timber and dense undergrowth. David Helm testified that it was difficult to follow the fence line in spots because of the vegetation. However, the trial evidence also established that it is a substantial fence, including several barbed wires and gates, Mr. Clark maintained it each spring, and it effectively contained livestock. This evidence is sufficient to support the district court's findings that the Clark/Helm fence was continuous.

The Helms also contest the lack of evidence about the exact location of the fence and, accordingly, the disputed property. Although the record contains ample evidence that the parties and the district court understood the disputed area was that between the recorded property line and the fence, the evidence did not include a survey of the fence or a legal description of the disputed area. An advance plat, which stated that it was "subject to correction and approval" and apparently was not recorded, was admitted into evidence at the trial as Plaintiffs' Exhibit 2. The advance plat showed the recorded property line, the disputed area and the "approximate location of the existing fence line;" however, the fence line was not surveyed and was placed on the map for illustration purposes only. The parties stipulated that, at the eastern boundary, the Clark/Helm fence was approximately 294 feet south of the recorded property line. The record does not, however, contain evidence of the measurements of the disputed area as the fence continued to the west.

Despite the lack of evidence of the exact location and size of the disputed area, the district court concluded:

> The net result is that Defendant Ken Clark and his predecessors have adversely possessed land located north of the fence lines that are the focus of this dispute, the land being of a dimension 235 feet by 1320 feet titled in the Helms[.]

The trial evidence does not support the district court's conclusion because the parties stipulated that the fence was 294 feet off line at the eastern boundary, not 235 feet as the district court found, and there was no evidence as to the measurements of the disputed tract as it continued westward. Given the evidence that the fence meandered, the simple rectangular description given by the district court is not supported by the record.

An adequate legal description is required in adverse possession cases. As a practical matter, without a sufficient legal description, the county clerk will not be able to record the quiet title order and such order will not provide public notice of the ownership of the disputed parcel. Our statutes setting forth the requirements for conveyances of real property interests demonstrate the need for a proper legal description in matters of title to property.

The failure to provide a proper legal description does not, however, undermine the district court's ultimate finding that Mr. Clark proved he adversely possessed the property and was entitled to have title quieted in him. This is true because the parties and the court knew the general location of the property and "[o]nce all the elements of adverse possession are met, the possessor is vested with a fully new and distinct title. No judicial action is necessary." Thus, the proper remedy in this case is to remand for a determination by the district court of the actual legal description of the property adversely possessed by Mr. Clark.

One other issue is raised by the Helms. The record is not very clear on this matter, but the documents from the Clark/Nebeker case and the testimony about those documents suggest that, until sometime in the late 1990s, part of the Helms' property near their northeastern boundary was actually fenced out of Mr. Clark's pasture. The Helms claim the affected area was a small "sliver" of land measuring approximately 50 to 60 feet. The Clark/Nebeker fence was apparently moved to the east in the late 1990s, which caused that portion to be included in Mr. Clark's pasture. The Helms argue, therefore, that Mr. Clark did not meet the ten year statutory requirement for proving adverse possession of this small area. The district court did not make any findings as to the effect of the placement and subsequent relocation of the eastern boundary fence on Mr. Clark's adverse possession claim against the Helms. Because of the imprecision of the discussion of this issue in the record and the fact that Mr. Clark does not address this aspect of the Helms' appeal at all, we do not know whether the evidence supports the Helms' position or whether this aspect of the case was even properly presented to the district court. Consequently, on remand, while determining the exact location of the adversely possessed area, the district court is also charged with determining whether the relocation of the Clark/Nebeker fence had any effect on the disputed area.

Affirmed in part and *reversed* and *remanded* in part for proceedings consistent with this decision.

B. EMINENT DOMAIN—GOVERNMENT CONDEMNATION FOR PUBLIC GOOD

As noted in the chapter on constitutional law, there are times when the government can claim land from a private property owner under the Takings Clause. This is through the government's power of eminent domain. Any exercise of eminent domain powers can create controversy as people generally dislike losing their house or property because of a government decision. But additional issues arise when the government exercise is not for a governmental (public) project, such as building a new road, but is used to enable another private property owner to instead own the property. This could happen, for instance, if the government tries to clear large swaths of land for the building of a sports stadium. The government believes that the building of the sports stadium would be in the public good, but it may be a private stadium owner who ends up profiting from the exercise of eminent domain. The following cases provide examples of the use of eminent domain for public governmental purposes and also for private purposes that have been deemed by the government to be in the public interest.

Kelo v. City of New London, Connecticut

545 US 469 (2005)

Justice STEVENS delivered the opinion of the Court.

I

The city of New London (hereinafter City) sits at the junction of the Thames River and the Long Island Sound in southeastern Connecticut. Decades of economic decline led a state agency in 1990 to designate the City a "distressed municipality." In 1996, the Federal Government closed the Naval Undersea Warfare Center, which had been located in the Fort Trumbull area of the City and had employed over 1,500 people. In 1998, the City's unemployment rate was nearly double that of the State, and its population of just under 24,000 residents was at its lowest since 1920.

These conditions prompted state and local officials to target New London, and particularly its Fort Trumbull area, for economic revitalization. To this end, respondent New London Development Corporation (NLDC), a private nonprofit entity established some years earlier to assist the City in planning economic development, was reactivated. In January 1998, the State authorized a $5.35 million bond issue to support the NLDC's planning activities and a $10 million bond issue toward the creation of a Fort Trumbull State Park. In February, the pharmaceutical company Pfizer Inc. announced that it would build a $300 million research facility on a site immediately adjacent to Fort Trumbull; local planners hoped that Pfizer would draw new business to the area, thereby serving as a catalyst to the area's rejuvenation. After receiving initial approval from the city council, the NLDC continued its planning activities and held a series of neighborhood meetings to educate the public about the process. In May, the city council authorized the NLDC to formally submit its plans to the relevant state agencies for review. Upon obtaining state-level approval, the NLDC finalized an integrated development plan focused on 90 acres of the Fort Trumbull area.

The Fort Trumbull area is situated on a peninsula that juts into the Thames River. The area comprises approximately 115 privately owned properties, as well as the 32 acres of land formerly occupied by the naval facility (Trumbull State Park now occupies 18 of those 32 acres). The development plan encompasses seven parcels. Parcel 1 is designated for a waterfront conference hotel at the center of a "small urban village" that will include restaurants and shopping. This parcel will also have marinas for both recreational and commercial uses. A pedestrian "riverwalk" will originate here and continue down the coast, connecting the waterfront areas of the development. Parcel 2 will be the site of approximately 80 new residences organized into an urban neighborhood and linked by public walkway to the remainder of the development, including the state park. This parcel also includes space reserved for a new U.S. Coast Guard Museum. Parcel 3, which is located immediately north of the Pfizer facility, will contain at least 90,000 square feet of research and development office space. Parcel 4A is a 2.4–acre site that will be used either to support the adjacent state park, by providing parking or retail services for visitors, or to support the nearby marina. Parcel 4B will include a renovated marina, as well as the final stretch of the riverwalk. Parcels 5, 6, and 7 will provide land for office and retail space, parking, and water-dependent commercial uses.

The NLDC intended the development plan to capitalize on the arrival of the Pfizer facility and the new commerce it was expected to attract. In addition to creating jobs, generating tax revenue, and helping to "build momentum for the revitalization of downtown New London," the plan was also designed to make the City more attractive and to create leisure and recreational opportunities on the waterfront and in the park.

The city council approved the plan in January 2000, and designated the NLDC as its development agent in charge of implementation. The city council also authorized the NLDC to purchase property or to acquire property by exercising eminent domain in the City's name. The NLDC successfully negotiated the purchase of most of the real estate in the 90–acre area, but its negotiations with petitioners failed. As a consequence, in November 2000, the NLDC initiated the condemnation proceedings that gave rise to this case.

II

Petitioner Susette Kelo has lived in the Fort Trumbull area since 1997. She has made extensive improvements to her house, which she prizes for its water view. Petitioner Wilhelmina Dery was born in her Fort Trumbull house in 1918 and has lived there her entire life. Her husband Charles (also a petitioner) has lived in the house since they married some 60 years ago. In all, the nine petitioners own 15 properties in Fort Trumbull—4 in parcel 3 of the development plan and 11 in parcel 4A. Ten of the parcels are occupied by the owner or a family member; the other five are held as investment properties. There is no allegation that any of these properties is blighted or otherwise in poor condition; rather, they were condemned only because they happen to be located in the development area.

In December 2000, petitioners brought this action in the New London Superior Court. They claimed, among other things, that the taking of their properties would violate the "public use" restriction in the Fifth Amendment. After a 7–day bench trial, the Superior Court granted a permanent restraining order prohibiting the taking of the properties located in parcel 4A (park or marina support). It, however, denied petitioners relief as to the properties located in parcel 3 (office space).

* * *

III

Two polar propositions are perfectly clear. On the one hand, it has long been accepted that the sovereign may not take the property of *A* for the sole purpose of transferring it to another private party *B*, even though *A* is paid just compensation. On the other hand, it is equally clear that a State may transfer property from one private party to another if future "use by the public" is the purpose of the taking; the condemnation of land for a railroad with common-carrier duties is a familiar example. Neither of these propositions, however, determines the disposition of this case.

***

The disposition of this case therefore turns on the question whether the City's development plan serves a "public purpose." Without exception, our cases have defined that concept broadly, reflecting our longstanding policy of deference to legislative judgments in this field.

***

Viewed as a whole, our jurisprudence has recognized that the needs of society have varied between different parts of the Nation, just as they have evolved over time in response to changed circumstances. Our earliest cases in particular embodied a strong theme of federalism, emphasizing the "great respect" that we owe to state legislatures and state courts in discerning local public needs. For more than a century, our public use jurisprudence has wisely eschewed rigid formulas and intrusive scrutiny in favor of affording legislatures broad latitude in determining what public needs justify the use of the takings power.

IV

Those who govern the City were not confronted with the need to remove blight in the Fort Trumbull area, but their determination that the area was sufficiently distressed to justify a program of economic rejuvenation is entitled to our deference. The City has carefully formulated an economic development plan that it believes will provide appreciable benefits to the community, including—but by no means limited to—new jobs and increased tax revenue. As with other exercises in urban planning and development, the City is endeavoring to coordinate a variety of commercial, residential, and recreational uses of land, with the hope that they will form a whole greater than the sum of its parts. To effectuate this plan, the City has invoked a state statute that specifically authorizes the use of eminent domain to promote economic development. Given the comprehensive character of the plan, the thorough deliberation that preceded its adoption, and the limited scope of our review, it is appropriate for us, as it was in *Berman,* to resolve the challenges of the individual owners, not on a piecemeal basis, but rather in light of the entire plan. Because that plan unquestionably serves a public purpose, the takings challenged here satisfy the public use requirement of the Fifth Amendment.

***

Just as we decline to second-guess the City's considered judgments about the efficacy of its development plan, we also decline to second-guess the City's determinations as to what lands it needs to acquire in order to effectuate the project. "It is not for the courts to oversee the choice of the boundary line nor to sit in review on the size of a particular project area. Once the question of the public purpose has been decided, the amount and character of land to be taken for the project and the need for a particular tract to complete the integrated plan rests in the discretion of the legislative branch."

In affirming the City's authority to take petitioners' properties, we do not minimize the hardship that condemnations may entail, notwithstanding the payment of just compensation. We emphasize that nothing in our opinion precludes any State from placing further restrictions on its exercise of the takings power. Indeed, many States already impose "public use" requirements that are stricter than the federal baseline. Some of these requirements have been established as a matter of state constitutional law, while others are expressed in state eminent domain statutes that carefully limit the grounds upon which takings may be exercised. As the submissions of the parties and their *amici* make clear, the necessity and wisdom of using eminent domain to promote economic development are certainly matters of legitimate public debate. This Court's authority, however, extends only to determining whether the City's proposed condemnations are for a "public use" within the meaning of the Fifth Amendment to the Federal Constitution. Because over a century of our case law interpreting that provision dictates an affirmative answer to that question, we may not grant petitioners the relief that they seek.

The judgment of the Supreme Court of Connecticut is *affirmed*.

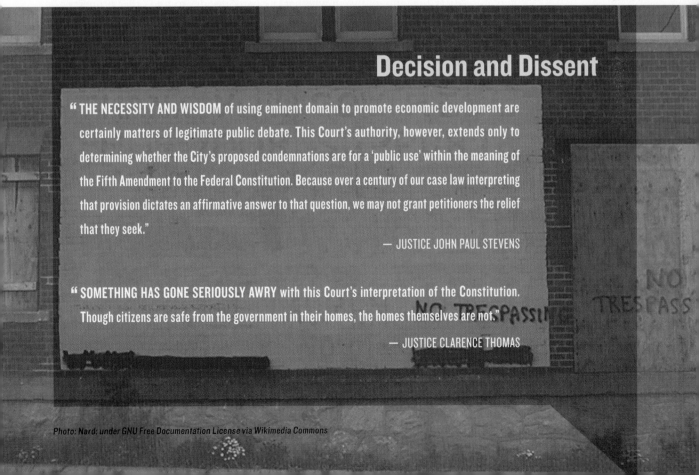

Decision and Dissent

" THE NECESSITY AND WISDOM of using eminent domain to promote economic development are certainly matters of legitimate public debate. This Court's authority, however, extends only to determining whether the City's proposed condemnations are for a 'public use' within the meaning of the Fifth Amendment to the Federal Constitution. Because over a century of our case law interpreting that provision dictates an affirmative answer to that question, we may not grant petitioners the relief that they seek."

— JUSTICE JOHN PAUL STEVENS

" SOMETHING HAS GONE SERIOUSLY AWRY with this Court's interpretation of the Constitution. Though citizens are safe from the government in their homes, the homes themselves are not."

— JUSTICE CLARENCE THOMAS

Photo: Nard; under GNU Free Documentation License via Wikimedia Commons

C. FORECLOSURES

Foreclosures have been around for a very long time, but they became more prominent in the wake of the financial crisis of 2008. A foreclosure can occur through the actions of any creditor. If creditors are owed money, they must find a way to try to recoup their losses. Thus, they may try to locate an asset owned by the debtor that can be used to do so. But they can't just seize the property; they must go through a court process that a secured creditor must go through as well.

A secured creditor has collateral to secure the loan she provides. This could be a bank providing a mortgage to a homeowner or an automobile finance company lending money to buy a car collateralized by the car. If the borrower falls behind on their payments, the creditor typically has to provide notices and a chance for the borrower to repay the loan. Depending on the asset, the notices and workout requirements can be extensive, especially if the asset in question is the borrower's home.

The chart on the following page, from the Federal Housing Finance Agency (FHFA) Office of the Inspector General (OIG) shows the process of home foreclosure from default to eviction[1]. If the borrower cannot repay the loan, she may decide to deed the collateral to the creditor through a deed in lieu of foreclosure. This transfers ownership of the property to the bank or some other creditor. It still may not satisfy the amount owed; whether the bank decides to find other property to seize to have the debt repaid is a judgment call by the creditor. But typically, there is some arrangement between borrower and creditor that, to avoid the expense of a foreclosure court case, the bank will accept the deed for the property and not continue to seek more money from the borrower. The same issues arise out of a "short sale."

If neither of these occurs, then the creditor must file a lawsuit against the borrower for repayment of the debt and to seize the asset. Again, the courts will provide safeguards to protect the debtor, especially with respect to a home, but if the foreclosure case goes to the end, the court will order that the land be sold to satisfy the judgment. The property then goes to a judicial sale, sometimes known as a sheriff's sale, where people can bid on the property. The creditor is allowed to use what they are owed as a price to bid and that is often the highest bid. At that time, a sheriff's deed— or, depending on the state, some other kind of court-generated authority—conveys the property to the bank, which will then attempt to find a buyer for it.

---

1   For more information and state specific procedures, *see*, Federal Housing Finance Agency Office of Inspector General, "An Overview of the Home Foreclosure Process,"*http://fhfaoig.gov/Content/Files/SAR Home Foreclosure Process_0.pdf.*

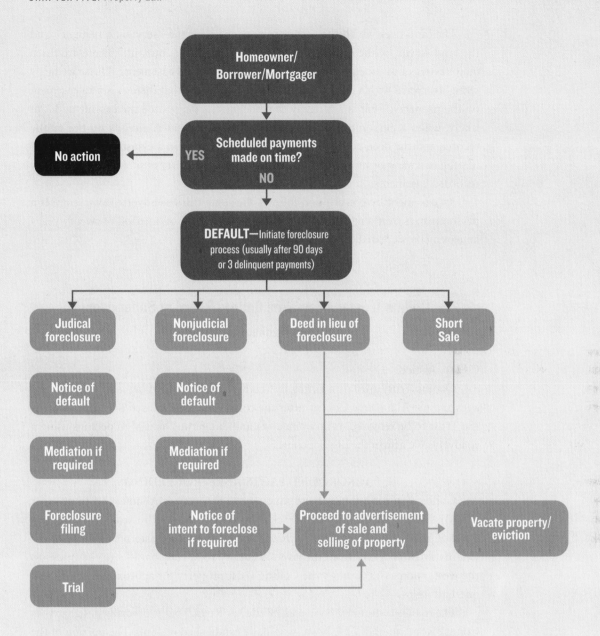

III. Incorporeal Interests—Non Possessory

INCORPOREAL INTERESTS are non-possessory interests. A major example of these is easements. With an easement, one party has the right to travel across another person's party for limited purpose. Utilities use these easements all the time. With nearly any home, easements exist to the phone, cable, and electric companies.

The land over which the easement runs is called the "servient tenement" and the land served by the easement is called the "servient dominant." There are three major types of easement. The most common are express easements. These are fairly straightforward with a clear, usually written agreement that there exists an easement on the property. That is not to say that the parties negotiated the easement. More likely, when a person purchases property, the easement is already on the public records and the deed conveying the property will contain a clause that either specifies the easement or more generally notes that the property is subject to all publicly recorded easements.

An easement by prescription follows the same rules as adverse possession. If a person travels over a neighbor's property continuously for a period of twenty years, an easement is created.

Collins Trust v. Allamakee County Board of Supervisors

599 N.W.2d 460 (Iowa 1999)

CADY, Justice.

Collins Trust appeals a ruling by the district court denying its claim for damages against Allamakee County after the county engineer caused a fence erected by the Trust to be removed as an immediate and dangerous hazard to persons using a roadway. We affirm the district court.

I. BACKGROUND FACTS AND PROCEEDINGS.

Collins Trust is a family trust which owns property in Allamakee County near the Mississippi River. Railroad tracks run north and south through Allamakee County parallel to the Mississippi River and separate the eastern boundary of the Collins Trust property from the river. A county road runs parallel to the tracks to the west, and passes through the Collins Trust property for approximately one and one-half miles.

The road is commonly known as "Red Oak Road," but is officially designated as County Road number 224. It was originally established in 1860. The portion of the road which passes through the Collins Trust property consists of a dirt base, with some areas of gravel.

The County maintains the road at a low level. It has removed downed trees, placed gravel in wet spots, and installed culverts to improve drainage in the area. It does not maintain the road in the winter.

At some point, most likely prior to 1955, there was a train wreck on the tracks running parallel to Red Oak Road in the Trust property. The wreck blocked passage over the traveled portion of Red Oak Road, which caused vehicles using the road to pass around the debris. The debris was never cleared and a curve to the west of the road developed. The curve encroached upon the Collins Trust property, and continued until 1991, when Collins Trust decided to relocate Red Oak Road to its location prior to the train wreck. Collins Trust cleared the debris which covered the original road and installed a barbed wire fence parallel to the original location of the road. The fence was 800 feet long, and crossed the curve created after the train wreck at the north and south ends. Collins Trust also planted walnut tree seedlings within the area enclosed by the newly erected fence.

The county engineer discovered the fence shortly after it was erected and, without providing notice to Collins Trust, directed County employees to remove it. The fencing materials were removed and piled on Collins Trust property. These materials eventually disappeared by theft. None of the walnut seedlings survived.

Collins Trust subsequently brought an action against the Allamakee County Board of Supervisors for damages resulting from the destruction of the fence and trees. Following a bench trial, the district court concluded the curve in the road resulting from the train wreck was acquired by the County by prescription, and the fence crossing the curve in the road was properly removed by the County as an immediate and dangerous hazard to persons or property using the highway.

On appeal Collins Trust claims the district court erred by finding the County acquired the curve in the road by prescriptive easement. It also claims the district court erred by finding the County properly removed the fence as an immediate and dangerous hazard to persons using the road.

***

One recognized method to establish an easement is by prescription. An easement by prescription is created under Iowa law when a person uses another's land under a claim of right or color of title, openly, notoriously, continuously, and hostilely for ten years or more. It is based on the principle of estoppel and is similar to the concept of adverse possession. In fact, we apply the principles of adverse possession to establish a prescriptive easement and use adverse possession to describe an easement by prescription. The fundamental distinction between the two doctrines is an easement by prescription concerns the use of property, while adverse possession deals with the acquisition of title to property by possession.

Collins Trust claims there was insufficient evidence to establish the requirements of an easement by prescription. It argues the use of the curve in the road by the public established neither hostile use of the property nor a claim of right. Additionally, the Trust claims it had no notice of any claim of right until the County removed the fence.

A. Claim of Right.

The hostility and claim of right requirements of a prescriptive easement are closely related. Hostility does not impute ill-will, but refers to declarations or acts revealing a claim of exclusive right to the land. Similarly, a claim of right requires evidence showing an easement is claimed as a right. Thus, mere use of land does not, by lapse of time, ripen into an easement. A party claiming an easement by prescription must prove, independent of use, the easement was claimed as a matter of right.

Although mere use does not constitute hostility or a claim of right, some specific acts or conduct associated with the use will give rise to a claim of right.

The precise evidence to support the requirements of prescriptive easement can vary, and ultimately, each case rests on its own particular facts. However, under our standard of review, we find substantial evidence to support the district court finding that the curve in the road was used hostilely and by a claim of right.

The County not only annually maintained the road for several decades, but also installed and maintained a culvert in the curve of the road to promote drainage. This type of conduct was more than mere use, but was conduct which an owner of land would perform. It is sufficient to support a finding that the County claimed the curve in the road as a right. The fighting question turns to whether there is substantial evidence to support a finding that Collins Trust had express notice of the public's claim.

B. Express Notice.

The open and notorious requirements of a prescriptive easement exist to help place the true owner of land on notice of the adverse use of the land by another. Under Iowa law the owner is required to have "express notice" of any claim of adverse possession. In *Larman,* we determined:

> These requirements ensure the landowner knows another's use of the property is claimed as a right hostile to the landowner's interest in the land. Otherwise, the landowner may incorrectly assume the other's use results merely from the landowner's willingness to accommodate the other's desire or need to use the land.

The notice requirement extends not only to the public use of the land, but also the public's claim to the land independent of use. The notice must either be actual or "from known facts of such nature as to impose a duty to make inquiry which would reveal the existence of an easement."

The record shows the Collins family was very familiar with the road running through its property and used it from time to time over the years. The family was also aware of the train wreck, and knew the road had moved into its property to curve around the wreckage. The family was aware the County maintained the road with its grader equipment and knew a culvert was installed in the curved portion of the road several decades ago. The family also knew the County installed the culvert. This evidence is sufficient to satisfy the "express notice" requirement, not only of the public use of the curve in the road for the last forty years or so, but the public's claim to the easement as well. The public expenditure of funds to maintain and repair the curve in the road over the years was known to Collins Trust and were acts of such a nature to support the public's claim of ownership. Consequently, we find the district court did not err by finding the County acquired the curve in the road by prescriptive easement.

IV. REMOVAL OF FENCE.

A county is permitted to remove obstructions on highways located within its jurisdiction. Our legislature, however, requires the county to first give notice to the owner of the property causing the obstruction before it may be removed, unless the obstruction "constitutes an immediate and dangerous hazard" to persons or property lawfully using the right of way. If an "immediate and dangerous hazard" exists, the county is not required to give notice prior to removal and is not liable for any damages. Additionally, the costs of the removal become the responsibility of the owner of the obstruction.

Collins Trust claims the fence did not constitute an "immediate and dangerous hazard." It maintains travel was not hindered by the fence because the debris had been cleared from the original road and a path was available for motorists to use. Consequently, it asserts the County lost its statutory immunity from liability for damages by failing to provide notice.

> " IF AN 'IMMEDIATE and dangerous hazard' exists, the county is not required to give notice prior to removal and is not liable for any damages. Additionally, the costs of the removal become the responsibility of the owner of the obstruction."

What constitutes an "immediate and dangerous hazard" depends on the facts of each case and is generally a question for the finder of fact. The exception to the notice requirement exists to protect the public, and necessarily considers all the surrounding circumstances including the nature of the hazard and the likelihood of harm if not immediately removed. In this case, the fence was constructed of barbed wire and covered the entire width of the traveled portion of the road. The road was narrow and had no lights or signs to alert motorists of the obstruction or the change in the path of the road. Motorists had become accustomed to using the curve in the road over the years. Furthermore, the fence forced motorists to leave the established roadway and use an alternative, less stable, route created by the Trust. Under these facts, we find substantial evidence to support the determination by the trial court that the fence constituted an "immediate and dangerous hazard" to persons or property using the roadway.

V. CONCLUSION.

We affirm the decision of the district court.

––––––––––––

A THIRD KIND OF EASEMENT is one of necessity. Any property needs to have some kind of public access. Thus, even if no easement is specified, one will be created via the necessity doctrine. The question that follows from this is exactly where that access should be located. It is one thing to claim that one needs access; it is another to determine where that access should be located.

Ashby v. Maechling

365 Mont. 68 (Montana 2010)

Chief Justice MIKE McGRATH delivered the Opinion of the Court.

This case arises from a dispute in which the Ashbys seek an easement by necessity across properties owned by Maechling, Alcosser and Dalton (referred to collectively as Maechlings). The District Court of the Twenty–First Judicial District held that Ashbys had an easement by necessity and defined the scope of the easement. Both sides appeal and we affirm.

***

PROCEDURAL AND FACTUAL BACKGROUND

The property at issue is west of U.S. Highway 93 in northern Ravalli County, Montana, and is bordered on the north by Missoula County. In 1932 Ravalli County acquired tax deed title to a large tract of land that included all of the property now owned by the parties. At that time the West County Line Road, which runs east-west along the Ravalli–Missoula County line, entered the east end of the large Ravalli County tract and provided access to it. In 1934 the County sold to George Jones the property now owned by Maechlings. The County retained the property now owned by Ashbys and sold it to Robert McKenzie in 1935. The Ashbys' tract is 120 acres and lies to the west of Maechlings' property. Maechling and Alcosser own and reside on 30 acres immediately east of Ashbys' land, and Dalton owns and resides on a tract immediately east of Maechling and Alcosser.

No established roads have ever entered the Ashbys' property and no permanent residence or agricultural use was ever established there. There is an irrigation ditch that crosses the parcel, but it has not been developed other than three episodes of logging, one in the 1800s, another in the 1970s and another conducted by Ashbys in 2007.

Ashbys bought their property in late 2004 along with a separate 150 acre parcel from the same seller. They knew at the time of purchase that there was no established access to the property and that their title insurance policy excepted access. Maechlings had for some time prior to 2004 maintained a locked gate on their property at the end of West County Line Road. The Road did not and apparently never has extended to the property now owned by Ashbys. In 2005 Ashbys wrote Maechling and Alcosser claiming an easement by necessity across their land for purposes of logging and offering not to sue them if Maechling and Alcosser sold Ashbys a perpetual non-exclusive easement for $10. Maechlings declined the offer, and this event precipitated Ashbys' claim for interference with the easement.

Ashbys sued in July 2005 seeking to establish that they had an easement by necessity across Maechlings' property to reach their 120–acre parcel, and for damages based upon Maechlings' alleged interference with the claimed easement. In February, 2006 Ashbys moved for summary judgment on the easement issue. In October, 2006 the District Court denied Ashbys' motion on the ground that they had not met their burden to show by clear and convincing evidence that the easement by necessity existed.

In March, 2007 Ashbys again moved for summary judgment, and in June Maechlings also moved for summary judgment. On August 31, 2007 the District Court denied Maechlings' motion for summary judgment and granted summary judgment to Ashbys, holding that West County Line Road is a public road, and that Ashbys have an easement by necessity across Maechlings' land to reach the road. Immediately after the District Court ruling, Ashbys arrived on Maechlings' land at the end of West County Line Road, removed the locked gate and constructed a road to their property across Maechlings' property. Maechlings have not blocked the access since the August 31, 2007, District Court ruling.

> **"Easements by necessity arise from a legal fiction that the owner of a tract of land would not isolate a portion of it without having intended to leave a way of access to the parcel over the lands being severed."**

***

DISCUSSION

We first consider the pivotal issue of whether the District Court properly held that an easement by necessity exists across Maechlings' land to access the Ashby land. Montana law has long recognized the existence of easements by necessity as a species of implied easements. At the same time, easements by necessity are "considered with *extreme* caution" because they deprive the servient tenement owner of property rights "through *mere* implication." Easements by necessity arise from a legal fiction that the owner of a tract of land would not isolate a portion of it without having intended to leave a way of access to the parcel over the lands being severed. Two essential elements of an easement by necessity are unity of ownership and strict necessity. The proponent of the easement by necessity must prove the necessary elements by clear and convincing evidence.

Unity of ownership exists where the owner of a tract of land severs part of the tract without providing an outlet to a public road. A single owner must at one time have owned both the tract to be benefited by the easement and the tract across which the easement would pass. Unity of ownership can originate decades before the judicial determination of whether there is an easement by necessity. The easement by necessity is created by operation of law at the time of severance of the parcels of land.

In this case it is undisputed that in 1932 Ravalli County owned a tract of land referred to as the tax deed parcel that included the land now owned by all parties to this litigation. It is also undisputed that in 1934 the County severed parts of the larger tract to Maechlings' predecessors in interest and then to Ashbys' predecessors in interest. Therefore, the unity of ownership requirement was clearly met.

The element of strict necessity requires that there is no practical access to a public road from the landlocked parcel. Strict necessity must exist at the time the tracts are severed from the original ownership *and* at the time the easement is exercised. A developed way of access to the landlocked parcel need not actually exist at the time of severance, and an easement by necessity is "distinguished from other implied easements on the simple ground that [a developed way] need not be in existence at the time of conveyance...."

In this case the District Court concluded upon a review of the evidence that there was no evidence of any practical road to connect Ashbys' parcel to a public road. Severance of the parcel now owned by Maechlings' landlocked the parcel now owned by Ashbys. No substantial evidence appears to contradict that conclusion.

Maechlings contend that the District Court should have found that quiet title actions brought in 1971 and 2001 extinguished any easement by necessity to serve the Ashby tract. The District Court considered but rejected the contention that the decrees in those two actions extinguished the easement by necessity, finding that while the predecessors to the Ashbys were well known, they were not made parties to the actions. The District Court further found that service by publication upon "all unknown persons" was not effective to bind known individuals who can be identified with reasonable diligence. The District Court therefore properly decided that the prior quiet title actions did not bar the easement.

The dissent argues that Ashbys failed to demonstrate strict necessity because Ravalli County, as the predecessor owner of the relevant parcels, had the power to condemn an easement across the servient property to provide access to a public road. First, this issue should not be considered because, as the dissent acknowledges, it was not raised in the District Court and was noted only in passing on appeal. Second, the primary authority for the condemnation rule is *Leo Sheep Co. v. U.S. Leo Sheep* arose out of the checkerboard land ownership that resulted from grants of alternate sections of Federal land to the Union Pacific Railroad in the 1860s. The United States argued that it had an easement by necessity across lands formerly granted to the Union Pacific but now owned by Leo Sheep Co. to reach a recreation area on Federal land. The Supreme Court held that because the United States could condemn a right of way it could not demonstrate the strict necessity required to secure an easement. Since the Ashbys are not a governmental entity with the power of eminent domain, the *Leo Sheep* case does not resolve the present dispute.

Therefore, since there was clear and convincing evidence of both unity of ownership and strict necessity, the District Court properly concluded that an easement by necessity existed to provide access to the Ashby tract.

The second issue we consider is whether the District Court properly concluded that the West County Line Road is a public road. An easement by necessity exists, if at all, to connect the landlocked tract of land to a public road.

Maechlings contended that the West County Line Road is not a public road and therefore an easement by necessity could not be implied to provide access to it. The District Court received and carefully considered substantial historical evidence as to the nature of the West County Line Road. Based upon this evidence the District Court granted summary judgment to Ashbys, concluding that Ravalli County had declared the Road to be a public highway in 1894, and that the Road was already opened at that time with the exception of a one-half mile section. The District Court also concluded that the Road terminated at the northwest corner of Section 3, on land now owned by Maechlings, but not extending to the land now owned by Ashbys.

Maechlings contended in District Court that the West County Line Road was never properly adopted as a public way. The District Court properly concluded that the Road is a public way and has been since 1894, relying on decisions from this Court recognizing the difficulty of reconstructing the detailed history of county roads created as much as 100 years ago. In *Reid v. Park County*, this Court adopted "the rule that it is sufficient if the [county] record taken as a whole shows that a public road was created. Otherwise the burden on the public in a particular case to prove a public road was created so many years ago may well be insurmountable." Requiring production of documentary evidence of events that occurred long ago can be impracticable, and there is a disputable presumption that official duty has been regularly performed. Discrepancies in the description or location of a road in old county documents are not sufficient to turn a county road into private property.

Here, the fact that the full length of the road was not opened in 1894 does not alter its status as a county road. Mere non-use, even for extended periods of time, is generally insufficient alone to indicate an intent to abandon a public way.

The record in this case, as explained in detail by the District Court's orders, sufficiently established that Ravalli County created and dedicated the West County Line Road as a public road. The District Court was correct in concluding that there were no material facts concerning whether the Road was created and that summary judgment on that issue was appropriate.

We next consider the issue of the scope of Ashbys' easement by necessity. Both sides appeal from the District Court's determination of the scope of the easement. Ashbys contend that the easement should be broader, while Maechlings contend that it is too broad.

The issue arose in the District Court upon Ashbys' motion for partial summary judgment in support of their contention that the scope of the easement is unlimited as long as it serves some use of the property and that use complies with applicable law. Ashbys have not specified any use they contemplate for their land, and in fact disclaim any plans for using it. They similarly did not specify the parameters of the easement by necessity, other than asserting that it must be sufficient to allow them to make any lawful use of the property.

After conducting an evidentiary hearing and after extensive review of the facts and law, the District Court concluded that the scope of the Ashby easement

> is approximately 12–15 feet wide, as it currently exists, for one single-family residential, non-commercial use by owners of the Plaintiffs' Property, their lawful successors and assigns, including recreational access to wildlands on Plaintiffs' property and for irrigation system inspection, repair, maintenance and use, and use by Plaintiffs related to forest thinning and logging consistent with reasonable and responsible forest practices and for no other. All other uses or use by persons other than lawful owners, successors or assigns of Plaintiffs' property shall exceed the scope of this easement and is prohibited. This easement by necessity shall automatically terminate if and when other legal alternate easement access is obtained to Plaintiffs' Property.

Ashbys contend that the scope of their easement must be unlimited in order to serve any use they can lawfully make of the property. Maechlings contend that the easement as decreed is too broad in that it allows use for residential purposes and there has never been a residence on the Ashby property.

* * *

Here, there is no evidence of the actual contemplation of Ravalli County or its purchasers as to the present and future use of the property in 1934. The County acquired the land in a Depression-era tax foreclosure but was able to sell portions of it and return it to the tax rolls a few years later. There is no evidence that the County ever used the property and it is therefore likely that the County's interest and expectation at the time was to realize tax income from the tract. There is evidence that the Ashby land was at that time forested wildland with no established public vehicular access route. The evidence also shows that the Ashby land had been logged in the late 19th century but otherwise had been used, if at all, for wildland recreational purposes. Similarly, the evidence is that at the time of severance the area surrounding the County tax parcel was rural, forested, agricultural and the site of scattered rural residential dwellings.

Therefore, nothing in the history or condition of the property at the time of severance would support a finding that the extent of the implied easement by necessity across the land of the servient estates should be unlimited.

The District Court also properly considered that an easement by necessity, while not unlimited in scope, is not limited to the precise uses and prevailing technology at the time of severance. So, if the severance occurred at a time prior to the general use of motor vehicles and electric power, an easement by necessity may still allow for "reasonable technological developments" as long as the use does not cause unreasonable damage or interference with the rights of the servient estate owner. Thus, modern vehicle access and utility services may be allowed as part of an easement by necessity even though the easement arose as a legal matter before the general use of such improvements.

The District Court here properly recognized these principles and allowed for noncommercial recreational and residential vehicular access by road to the Ashby property. The District Court expressly did not address gates, cattle guards, underground or other utility transmission lines, because "[a]lthough invited to do so by the Court, neither party" addressed those issues.

Ashbys did not provide evidence upon which the District Court might have fashioned different parameters for the easement by necessity. They disclaimed having any specific plans, uses or needs for the property and only asserted that they had the right to do anything that the law allowed and that the easement must accommodate their future decisions, whatever they might be. By that reasoning, such disparate uses as a cattle feed lot, a gravel mine, a dirt track motorcycle racing venue or a high-density subdivision all might be legally permissible on the Ashby tract. It is not reasonable to impose such potential unknown and unlimited burdens on Maechlings' property.

The District Court properly considered the current nature of the area in which the property is located in northern Ravalli County. The area surrounding the Ashby tract is mixed. To the immediate west is Forest Service land. The area is largely rural with scattered, low-intensity residential uses on larger lots or acreage. The District Court's decision to allow one single-family residence on the Ashby property, to be served by the easement, is a reasonable reflection of land use as it has developed in the area. The District Court reached a reasoned and proper decision on the scope of the easement by necessity.

We next consider Ashbys' claim that the District Court erred in not awarding them damages for Maechlings' interference with the easement. Ashbys claim that they are entitled to damages of over $100,000 because Maechlings' rejection of the $10 perpetual easement in 2005 caused them to have to acquire a temporary easement from a third party to conduct the logging on the property in 2007. The District Court granted summary judgment against Ashbys on this claim.

The District Court noted that prior to its ruling in August, 2007, holding that the easement by necessity existed, Ashbys' motion for summary judgment on the existence of the easement had been denied. Further, after August 31, 2007 Ashbys used the easement without interference from Maechlings.

While the essential acts that gave rise to the easement by necessity arose in the 1930s, Ashbys' right to the easement was not established until August 31, 2007. Prior to that time Maechlings could not have wrongfully interfered with Ashbys' easement. We therefore affirm the District Court's determination that Ashbys did not have a claim against Maechlings for interference with the easement by necessity.

The District Court's orders appealed from are affirmed.

RENTS ARE ANOTHER KIND of property interest. There are two main types. One is when the grantor is entitled to a specific dollar amount. This is the most straightforward, with the grantor agreeing to rent a building, an apartment, or some land for a specific amount of money.

A second kind of rent comes from a portion of a product. For instance, many farm leases will provide for the tenant (the person farming the land) to split the profits from the crops grown with the landlord. Here, the rent is in terms of the product itself rather than a specific predetermined amount of money.

As will be seen shortly, licenses have a particularly important use in intellectual property instances, but licenses can be quite simple. A license is the right to use a particular thing for a period of time. A good example is a ticket to a sporting or entertainment event. The ticketholder purchases the right to sit in Section 209, Row ZZ, Seats 3-4. That right exists only for that particular game. One has the right to exclude others from sitting in that seat by contacting the usher to remove a person sitting in the ticketholder's seat. The license for the seat is not assignable, which is one reason why scalping tickets is problematic. However, the ticket/license can also be revoked, especially when the ticketholder is behaving poorly.

■ AN EXAMPLE OF A LICENSE IS A TICKET. A TICKETHOLDER ONLY PURCHASES THE RIGHT TO SIT IN A PARTICULAR SEAT, AND THAT RIGHT EXISTS ONLY FOR THAT EVENT ON THE ASSIGNED DAY AND TIME.

IV. Restrictive Covenants & Zoning

IN MANY SUBDIVISIONS, restrictive covenants limit what property owners can do with their homes. This primarily applies to issues like providing for common fencing, or whether the development allows any fencing at all. It might also apply to the construction of ancillary buildings like decks or storage units or even mailboxes. The idea is that if one is going to living in a housing division, certain rules will follow, often justified as a way of ensuring the property values are not diminished. Typically, these rules are recorded and made part of the public record so that when a person buys a home, the covenants automatically apply.

Renton v. Playtime Theatres, Inc.

475 U.S. 4I (1986)

Justice REHNQUIST delivered the opinion of the Court.

This case involves a constitutional challenge to a zoning ordinance, enacted by appellant city of Renton, Washington, that prohibits adult motion picture theaters from locating within 1,000 feet of any residential zone, single- or multiple-family dwelling, church, park, or school. Appellees, Playtime Theatres, Inc., and Sea-First Properties, Inc., filed an action in the United States District Court for the Western District of Washington seeking a declaratory judgment that the Renton ordinance violated the First and Fourteenth Amendments and a permanent injunction against its enforcement. The District Court ruled in favor of Renton and denied the permanent injunction, but the Court of Appeals for the Ninth Circuit reversed and remanded for reconsideration. We noted probable jurisdiction and now reverse the judgment of the Ninth Circuit.

In May 1980, the Mayor of Renton, a city of approximately 32,000 people located just south of Seattle, suggested to the Renton City Council that it consider the advisability of enacting zoning legislation dealing with adult entertainment uses. No such uses existed in the city at that time. Upon the Mayor's suggestion, the City Council referred the matter to the city's Planning and Development Committee. The Committee held public hearings, reviewed the experiences of Seattle and other cities, and received a report from the City Attorney's Office advising as to developments in other cities. The City Council, meanwhile, adopted Resolution No. 2368, which imposed a moratorium on the licensing of "any business ... which ... has as its primary purpose the selling, renting or showing of sexually explicit materials." The resolution contained a clause explaining that such businesses "would have a severe impact upon surrounding businesses and residences."

In April 1981, acting on the basis of the Planning and Development Committee's recommendation, the City Council enacted Ordinance No. 3526. The ordinance prohibited any "adult motion picture theater" from locating within 1,000 feet of any residential zone, single- or multiple-family dwelling, church, or park, and within one mile of any school. The term "adult motion picture theater" was defined as "[a]n enclosed building used for presenting motion picture films, video cassettes, cable television, or any other such visual media, distinguished or characteri[zed] by an emphasis on matter depicting, describing or relating to 'specified sexual activities' or 'specified anatomical areas' ... for observation by patrons therein."

In early 1982, respondents acquired two existing theaters in downtown Renton, with the intention of using them to exhibit feature-length adult films. The theaters were located within the area proscribed by Ordinance No. 3526. At about the same time, respondents filed the previously mentioned lawsuit challenging the ordinance on First and Fourteenth Amendment grounds, and seeking declaratory and injunctive relief. While the federal action was pending, the City Council amended the ordinance in several respects, adding a statement of reasons for its enactment and reducing the minimum distance from any school to 1,000 feet.

***

In our view, the resolution of this case is largely dictated by our decision in *Young v. American Mini Theatres, Inc., supra.* There, although five Members of the Court did not agree on a single rationale for the decision, we held that the city of Detroit's zoning ordinance, which prohibited locating an adult theater within 1,000 feet of any two other "regulated uses" or within 500 feet of any residential zone, did not violate the First and Fourteenth Amendments. The Renton ordinance, like the one in *American Mini Theatres*, does not ban adult theaters altogether, but merely provides that such theaters may not be located within 1,000 feet of any residential zone, single- or multiple-family dwelling, church, park, or school. The ordinance is therefore properly analyzed as a form of time, place, and manner regulation.

Describing the ordinance as a time, place, and manner regulation is, of course, only the first step in our inquiry. This Court has long held that regulations enacted for the purpose of restraining speech on the basis of its content presumptively violate the First Amendment. On the other hand, so-called "content-neutral" time, place, and manner regulations are acceptable so long as they are designed to serve a substantial governmental interest and do not unreasonably limit alternative avenues of communication.

At first glance, the Renton ordinance, like the ordinance in *American Mini Theatres*, does not appear to fit neatly into either the "content-based" or the "content-neutral" category. To be sure, the ordinance treats theaters that specialize in adult films differently from other kinds of theaters. Nevertheless, as the District Court concluded, the Renton ordinance is aimed not at the *content* of the films shown at "adult motion picture theatres," but rather at the *secondary effects* of such theaters on the surrounding community. The District Court found that the City Council's "*predominate* concerns" were with the secondary effects of adult theaters, and not with the content of adult films themselves. But the Court of Appeals, relying on its decision in *Tovar v. Billmeyer*, held that this was not enough to sustain the ordinance. According to the Court of Appeals, if "*a motivating factor*" in enacting the ordinance was to restrict respondents' exercise of First Amendment rights the ordinance would be invalid, apparently no matter how small a part this motivating factor may have played in the City Council's decision. This view of the law was rejected in *United States v. O'Brien,* the very case that the Court of Appeals said it was applying:

> "It is a familiar principle of constitutional law that this Court will not strike down an otherwise constitutional statute on the basis of an alleged illicit legislative motive....

"...What motivates one legislator to make a speech about a statute is not necessarily what motivates scores of others to enact it, and the stakes are sufficiently high for us to eschew guesswork."

The District Court's finding as to "predominate" intent, left undisturbed by the Court of Appeals, is more than adequate to establish that the city's pursuit of its zoning interests here was unrelated to the suppression of free expression. The ordinance by its terms is designed to prevent crime, protect the city's retail trade, maintain property values, and generally "protec[t] and preserv[e] the quality of [the city's] neighborhoods, commercial districts, and the quality of urban life," not to suppress the expression of unpopular views. See App. to Juris. Statement 90a. As Justice POWELL observed in *American Mini Theatres*, "[i]f [the city] had been concerned with restricting the message purveyed by adult theaters, it would have tried to close them or restrict their number rather than circumscribe their choice as to location."

In short, the Renton ordinance is completely consistent with our definition of "content-neutral" speech regulations as those that "are *justified* without reference to the content of the regulated speech." The ordinance does not contravene the fundamental principle that underlies our concern about "content-based" speech regulations: that "government may not grant the use of a forum to people whose views it finds acceptable, but deny use to those wishing to express less favored or more controversial views."

It was with this understanding in mind that, in *American Mini Theatres*, a majority of this Court decided that, at least with respect to businesses that purvey sexually explicit materials, zoning ordinances designed to combat the undesirable secondary effects of such businesses are to be reviewed under the standards applicable to "content-neutral" time, place, and manner regulations. *** The appropriate inquiry in this case, then, is whether the Renton ordinance is designed to serve a substantial governmental interest and allows for reasonable alternative avenues of communication. It is clear that the ordinance meets such a standard. As a majority of this Court recognized in *American Mini Theatres*, a city's "interest in attempting to preserve the quality of urban life is one that must be accorded high respect." Exactly the same vital governmental interests are at stake here.

***

"[T]he [trial] court heard extensive testimony regarding the history and purpose of these ordinances. It heard expert testimony on the adverse effects of the presence of adult motion picture theaters on neighborhood children and community improvement efforts. The court's detailed findings, which include a finding that the location of adult theaters has a harmful effect on the area and contribute to neighborhood blight, are supported by substantial evidence in the record."

"The record is replete with testimony regarding the effects of adult movie theater locations on residential neighborhoods."

* * *

In sum, we find that the Renton ordinance represents a valid governmental response to the "admittedly serious problems" created by adult theaters. Renton has not used "the power to zone as a pretext for suppressing expression," but rather has sought to make some areas available for adult theaters and their patrons, while at the same time preserving the quality of life in the community at large by preventing those theaters from locating in other areas. This, after all, is the essence of zoning. Here, as in *American Mini Theatres,* the city has enacted a zoning ordinance that meets these goals while also satisfying the dictates of the First Amendment. The judgment of the Court of Appeals is therefore

Reversed.

———————————

AS SOON AS a policy is made, of course, there will be requests for exceptions. These could include requests for a variance from a zoning ordinance or a special use permit.

Willett v. Cerro Gordo County Bd. of Adjustment

490 N.W.2d 556 (Iowa 1992)

SNELL, Justice.

Appellant, Thomas G. Willett, challenges a trial court's summary judgment ruling, which upheld the grant of a special use permit by the appellee, Cerro Gordo County Zoning Board of Adjustment. The board granted a special use permit to Tuttle Asphalt & Paving before Tuttle had received other necessary permits, a requirement under Cerro Gordo County, Iowa, Zoning Ordinance Article 20.2(JJ) and (KK). The trial court found that the requirement was merely a directory obligation, and failure to meet the requirement would not render the special use permit void. We affirm.

On February 25, 1991, Tuttle applied to the board for a special use permit to establish a rock extraction and processing project, a gravel extraction and processing project, and an asphalt plant on land located in Cerro Gordo County, Iowa. The board held a public hearing on the application on April 16, 1991. Following the hearing, the board adopted a resolution granting Tuttle a special use permit for the projects, subject to nine "conditions and/or requirements." Among these was the requirement that "all state and federal requirements must be adhered to."

* * *

County ordinances promulgated pursuant to authority delegated to a local governing body are extensions of state statutes and are to be construed as statutes. The Cerro Gordo County, Iowa, Zoning Ordinance was promulgated pursuant to Iowa Code chapter 358A (1991); the ordinance is an extension of that statute. The principles of statutory construction apply to the Cerro Gordo County, Iowa, Zoning Ordinance.

The parties argue over the import of "must" in the ordinance. The ordinance states that any permit required by any other governmental entity "must be obtained prior to applying for the special use permit." Willett argues that this language places an unavoidable duty on the applicant to obtain all other necessary permits first. Failure to do so would void any special use permit subsequently issued. The board argues that this language is obligatory, but the obligation may be waived by the board because it is merely "directory," not essential to the main objective of the ordinance.

The board's interpretation is derived from our construction of the word "shall" in other statutes. "Shall" and "must" are distinguished by our legislature in Iowa Code chapter 4 (1991), Construction of Statutes. "Shall" imposes a duty; "must" states a requirement. "Duty" and "requirement," however, are not defined in the Iowa Code. "Duty" is a "legal or moral obligation. Obligatory conduct or service. Mandatory obligation to perform." "To require" is to "direct, order, demand, instruct, command, claim, compel, request, need, exact." Both "duty" and "requirement" speak in terms of command and obligation, excluding the idea of discretion. Both direct some type of behavior that is obligatory in nature. As a matter of statutory construction, "shall" and "must" are often treated as synonyms. We find our rules of construction for "shall" to be instructive in our determination of the force of "must" in the Cerro Gordo County, Iowa, Zoning Ordinance.

The ordinance imposes a duty on the applicant to receive all other necessary permits before applying for the special use permit. A duty imposed by statute may be either "mandatory" or "directory." The dichotomy between a mandatory and a directory statute relates to whether a failure to perform the duty will have the effect of invalidating the governmental action that the requirement affects.

In determining whether a statute is mandatory or directory, we look to the nature of the duty in light of the purpose the statute was designed to serve. When the duty imposed by the provision is essential to effect the main purpose of the statute, the provision is mandatory, and failure to perform the duty will invalidate subsequent proceedings. When the duty imposed is not essential to the main statutory objective, however, the provision is directory, and failure to perform the duty will not affect the validity of subsequent proceedings unless prejudice is shown.

Zoning regulation is the local exercise of police power, to promote the "health, safety, morals, comfort, and general welfare [and] to conserve the values of property and encourage the most appropriate use of land...." A special use permit allows property to be put to a purpose that the zoning ordinance conditionally allows. Article 20.1 of the Cerro Gordo County, Iowa, Zoning Ordinance, speaking of special uses, states, "It is recognized that certain uses possess characteristics of such unique and special form as to make impractical their being included automatically in any class of use.... [T]hese uses shall be subject to certain conditions and standards set forth in this Article." Cerro Gordo County, Iowa, Zoning Ordinance Article 20 is designed to promote public health and safety by regulation of special uses expressly permitted in the zone to ensure compatibility with other uses that exist in that zone. The purpose of the special use permit is to bring flexibility to the rigid restrictions of a zoning ordinance, while at the same time controlling troublesome or somewhat incompatible uses by establishing, in advance, standards that admit the use only under certain conditions and standards that must be met.

The requirement that an applicant receive all necessary permits from other governmental entities before applying for the special use permit is not essential to this purpose. First, the resolution adopted by the board conditioned issuance of the special use permit on receipt of all other requisite permits. Neighboring landowners were assured that operations would not begin until all state and federal requirements had been met. Tuttle cannot operate any of the facilities until he has received all necessary permits. To do so would be illegal and would subject Tuttle to injunction to cease operation.

Second, the mandate that the applicant receive the other permits first is a rule of convenience and timing. By enforcing this requirement, the board is assured that other agencies have examined and approved the activity in which the applicant seeks to engage on the site. If the duty is designed to assure "order and promptness" in the proceedings, the statute ordinarily is directory. The function of the Cerro Gordo County, Iowa, Zoning Ordinance requirement is to ensure "order and promptness" in obtaining other permits. We stated in *Taylor*:

> [S]tatutory provisions fixing the time, form and mode of proceedings of public functionaries are directory because they are not of the essence of the thing to be done but are designed to secure system, uniformity and dispatch in public business. Such statutes direct the thing to be done at a particular time but do not prohibit it from being done later when the rights of interested persons are not injuriously affected by the delay.

Third, the duty challenged was imposed on the applicant Tuttle, not the board. When the duty to be construed is not addressed to public officials and does not destroy a right or sacrifice a benefit to the public or individual, then the duty is generally directory. When the duty is directed toward the applicant, not the official, then the official may waive the duty. Willett did not lose any right or benefit by the board's waiver of the requirement. Tuttle was commanded to receive all necessary permits before operation commenced.

Having determined the requirement that an applicant for a special use permit under Cerro Gordo County, Iowa, Zoning Ordinance Article 20.2(JJ) and (KK) receive all other requisite permits before submitting the application is merely directory, the subsequent action of the board will not be void unless prejudice is shown. Willett has not alleged or shown that prejudice resulted from Tuttle's failure to present all other permits to the board with its application. Therefore, the special use permit is not invalid.

Accordingly, we affirm the ruling of the trial court dismissing Willett's petition and entering summary judgment in favor of the Cerro Gordo County Zoning Board of Adjustment.

AFFIRMED.

NOTES AND COMMENTS

1. FROM A PHILOSOPHICAL STANDPOINT, property concepts both underpin and extend beyond the law. Philosophers such as John Locke and, more recently, Thomas Donaldson and Patricia Werhane, have argued that one has a property right in one's labor. Under this formulation, not only might employees have certain humanitarian rights in how to be treated, such rights also claim a kind of property law protection. What do you think? Do you think that one's labor is a kind of property, something that one owns? If not, why? If so, what implications do you think this has for various kinds of service and labor?

2. THE RANGE OF PROPERTY LAW ISSUES, as you have seen, is vast, ranging for personal estate planning and boundary disputes with neighbors to commercial and industrial development via the powers of eminent domain. Do you think it is possible to live happily without private property? What would you lose without property law protections? Would you gain anything?

3. HERE'S A COMMENT YOU WON'T EXPECT. During the 1980s, one of the co-author's colleagues at Northwestern Law School—who also taught Property Law to the other co-author of this textbook—wrote poems to the property law themes. He also invited students to contribute their property poems, even leading some students to write property law lyrics to songs. Why don't you take a stab at this one yourselves?

6

INTELLECTUAL PROPERTY

IN OUR INCREASINGLY technological and mediatized world, copyrights, trademarks, and patents are valuable forms of property and sources of revenue. Companies invest significant capital to develop their brands and protect the symbols of their brands with trademarks. They develop patterns and text, fixed images and moving images, which they secure against copyright infringement. They obtain patents on everything from machinery to chemical formulas for pharmaceuticals. Since whole courses and areas of the law are devoted to IP rights, this book can only give the most cursory treatment of the legal issues involved.

I. General Principles

A. COPYRIGHTS

One of the most basic of intellectual properties is the copyright. Anytime a person creates anything that is in a *fixed media*, that person has a copyright in the property. That is true even of your class notes, and, yes, even your doodles in the margins. You have made an original creation of an idea, even by just writing your notes from a professor's lecture. You then have a copyright in those notes. As a practical matter, the copyrighted material may not be worth enough to sue over if someone, without your permission, were to photocopy them. However with valuable copyrights like songs, photographs, or movies, the stakes quickly grow.

Moreover, there is a question of proving that the materials were used. Indeed, many times, a central issue in copyright is proving who was the original creator of material. One will often see the copyright symbol "©" on printed material indicating that the author claims a copyright on it. That provides some evidence that there is a copyright attached. Even better evidence results if the person obtains a copyright registration proof from the U.S. Copyright Office. One fills out a form and attaches a copy of the material and the U.S. Copyright Office will issue a registration letter indicating that the author has claimed copyright on the material as of the date of the registration. This does not eliminate disputes as to ownership, but it does provide a clear claim of copyright with a government-determined date and time when the claim was made. That itself provides helpful evidence in a copyright dispute.

One occasionally sees in the news an article about someone who claims that they were the original composer of a song that has swept the world (and therefore made a lot of money). The alleged, original composer may then sue to obtain some of the money owed from the unauthorized use of her copyrighted material. More often, though, the controversy is not about the work's origin and the copyright holder, but whether the use is actually an *infringement*. The following case illustrates this kind of issue.

Bridgeport Music v. Dimension Films

410 F.3d 792 (6th Cir. 2005)

RALPH B. GUY, JR., Circuit Judge.

Bridgeport and Westbound claim to own the musical composition and sound recording copyrights in "Get Off Your Ass and Jam" by George Clinton, Jr. and the Funkadelics. We assume, as did the district court, that plaintiffs would be able to establish ownership in the copyrights they claim. There seems to be no dispute either that "Get Off" was digitally sampled or that the recording "100 Miles" was included on the sound track of *I Got the Hook Up*. Defendant No Limit Films, in conjunction with Priority Records, released the movie to theaters on May 27, 1998. The movie was apparently also released on VHS, DVD, and cable television. Fatal to Bridgeport's claims of infringement was the Release and Agreement it entered into with two of the original owners of the composition "100 Miles," Ruthless Attack Muzick (RAM) and Dollarz N Sense Music (DNSM), in December 1998, granting a sample use license to RAM, DNSM, and their licensees. Finding that No Limit Films had previously been granted an oral synchronization license to use the composition "100 Miles" in the sound track of *Hook Up*, the district court concluded Bridgeport's claims against No Limit Films were barred by the unambiguous terms of the Release and Agreement. Although Bridgeport does not appeal from this determination, it is relevant to the district court's later decision to award attorney fees to No Limit Films.

Westbound's claims are for infringement of the sound recording "Get Off." Because defendant does not deny it, we assume that the sound track of *Hook Up* used portions of "100 Miles" that included the allegedly infringing sample from "Get Off." The recording "Get Off" opens with a three-note combination solo guitar "riff" that lasts four seconds. According to one of plaintiffs' experts, Randy Kling, the recording "100 Miles" contains a sample from that guitar solo. Specifically, a two-second sample from the guitar solo was copied, the pitch was lowered, and the copied piece was "looped" and extended to 16 beats. Kling states that this sample appears in the sound recording "100 Miles" in five places; specifically, at 0:49, 1:52, 2:29, 3:20 and 3:46. By the district court's estimation, each looped segment lasted approximately 7 seconds. As for the segment copied from "Get Off," the district court described it as follows:

> The portion of the song at issue here is an arpeggiated chord—that is, three notes that, if struck together, comprise a chord but instead are played one at a time in very quick succession—that is repeated several times at the opening of "Get Off." The arpeggiated chord is played on an unaccompanied electric guitar. The rapidity of the notes and the way they are played produce a high-pitched, whirling sound that captures the listener's attention and creates anticipation of what is to follow.

* * *

Our analysis begins and largely ends with the applicable statute. Section 114(a) of Title 17 of the United States Code provides:

> The exclusive rights of the owner of copyright in a sound recording are limited to the rights specified by clauses (1), (2), (3) and (6) of section 106, and do not include any right of performance under section 106(4).

Section 106 provides:

Subject to sections 107 through 122, the owner of copyright under this title has the exclusive rights to do and to authorize any of the following:

1. to reproduce the copyrighted work in copies or phonorecords;

2. to prepare derivative works based upon the copyrighted work;

3. to distribute copies or phonorecords of the copyrighted work to the public by sale or other transfer of ownership, or by rental, lease, or lending;

4. in the case of literary, musical, dramatic, and choreographic works, pantomimes, and motion pictures and other audiovisual works to perform the copyrighted work publicly;

5. in the case of literary, musical, dramatic, and choreographic works, pantomimes, and pictorial, graphic, or sculptural works, including the individual images of a motion picture or other audiovisual work, to display the copyrighted work publicly; and

6. in the case of sound recordings, to perform the copyrighted work publicly by means of a digital audio transmission.

Section 114(b) states:

(b) The exclusive right of the owner of copyright in a sound recording under clause (1) of section 106 is limited to the right to duplicate the sound recording in the form of phonorecords or copies that directly or indirectly recapture the actual sounds fixed in the recording. The exclusive right of the owner of copyright in a sound recording under clause (2) of section 106 is limited to the right to prepare a derivative work in which the actual sounds fixed in the sound recording are rearranged, remixed, or otherwise altered in sequence or quality. The exclusive rights of the owner of copyright in a sound recording

under clauses (1) and (2) of section 106 do not extend to the making or duplication of another sound recording that consists entirely of an independent fixation of other sounds, even though such sounds imitate or simulate those in the copyrighted sound recording. The exclusive rights of the owner of copyright in a sound recording under clauses (1), (2), and (3) of section 106 do not apply to sound recordings included in educational television and radio programs (as defined in section 397 of title 47) distributed or transmitted by or through public broadcasting entities (as defined by section 118(g)): *Provided,* That copies or phonorecords of said programs are not commercially distributed by or through public broadcasting entities to the general public.

Before discussing what we believe to be the import of the above quoted provisions of the statute, a little history is necessary. The copyright laws attempt to strike a balance between protecting original works and stifling further creativity. The provisions, for example, for compulsory licensing make it possible for "creators" to enjoy the fruits of their creations, but not to fence them off from the world at large. Although musical compositions have always enjoyed copyright protection, it was not until 1971 that sound recordings were subject to a separate copyright. If one were to analogize to a book, it is not the book, i.e., the paper and binding, that is copyrightable, but its contents. There are probably any number of reasons why the decision was made by Congress to treat a sound recording differently from a book even though both are the medium in which an original work is fixed rather than the creation itself. None the least of them certainly were advances in technology which made the "pirating" of sound recordings an easy task. The balance that was struck was to give sound recording copyright holders the exclusive right "to duplicate the sound recording in the form of phonorecords or copies that directly or indirectly recapture the actual sounds fixed in the recording." This means that the world at large is free to imitate or simulate the creative work fixed in the recording so long as an actual copy of the sound recording itself is not made. That leads us directly to the issue in this case. If you cannot pirate the whole sound recording, can you "lift" or "sample" something less than the whole. Our answer to that question is in the negative.

Section 114(b) provides that "[t]he exclusive right of the owner of copyright in a sound recording under clause (2) of section 106 is limited to the right to prepare a derivative work in which the actual sounds fixed in the sound recording are rearranged, remixed, or otherwise altered in sequence or quality." Further, the rights of sound recording copyright holders under clauses (1) and (2) of section 106 "do not extend to the making or duplication of another sound recording that consists *entirely* of an independent fixation of other sounds, even though such sounds imitate or simulate those in the copyrighted sound recording." The significance of this provision is amplified by the fact that the Copyright Act of 1976 added the word "entirely"

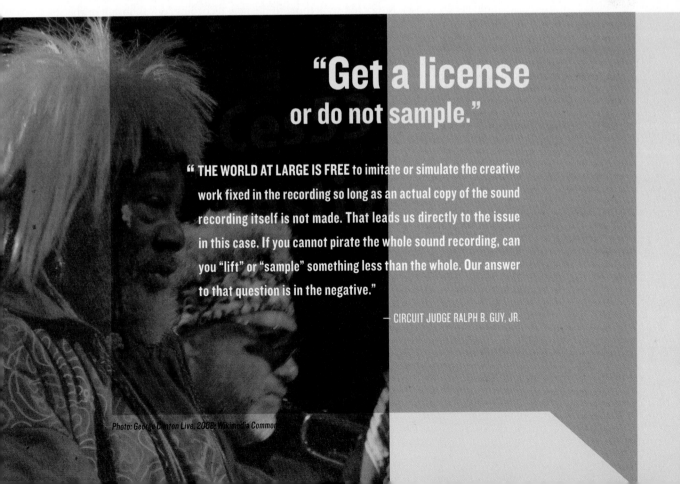

"Get a license
or do not sample."

" **THE WORLD AT LARGE IS FREE** to imitate or simulate the creative work fixed in the recording so long as an actual copy of the sound recording itself is not made. That leads us directly to the issue in this case. If you cannot pirate the whole sound recording, can you "lift" or "sample" something less than the whole. Our answer to that question is in the negative."

— CIRCUIT JUDGE RALPH B. GUY, JR.

Photo: George Clinton Live, 2008; Wikimedia Commons

to this language. In other words, a sound recording owner has the exclusive right to "sample" his own recording. We find much to recommend this interpretation.

To begin with, there is ease of enforcement. Get a license or do not sample. We do not see this as stifling creativity in any significant way. It must be remembered that if an artist wants to incorporate a "riff" from another work in his or her recording, he is free to duplicate the sound of that "riff" in the studio. Second, the market will control the license price and keep it within bounds. The sound recording copyright holder cannot exact a license fee greater than what it would cost the person seeking the license to just duplicate the sample in the course of making the new recording. Third, sampling is never accidental. It is not like the case of a composer who has a melody in his head, perhaps not even realizing that the reason he hears this melody is that it is the work of another which he had heard before. When you sample a sound recording you know you are taking another's work product.

This analysis admittedly raises the question of why one should, without infringing, be able to take three notes from a musical composition, for example, but not three notes by way of sampling from a sound recording. Why is there no *de minimis* taking or why should substantial similarity not enter the equation. Our first answer to this question is what we have earlier indicated. We think this result is dictated by the applicable statute. Second, even when a small part of a sound recording is sampled, the part taken is something of value. No further proof of that is necessary than the fact that the producer of the record or the artist on the record intentionally sampled because it would (1) save costs, or (2) add something to the new recording, or (3) both. For the sound recording copyright holder, it is not the "song" but the sounds that are fixed in the medium of his choice. When those sounds are sampled they are taken directly from that fixed medium. It is a physical taking rather than an intellectual one.

This case also illustrates the kind of mental, musicological, and technological gymnastics that would have to be employed if one were to adopt a *de minimis* or substantial similarity analysis. The district judge did an excellent job of navigating these troubled waters, but not without dint of great effort. When one considers that he has hundreds of other cases all involving different samples from different songs, the value of a principled bright-line rule becomes apparent. We would want to emphasize, however, that considerations of judicial economy are not what drives this opinion. If any consideration of economy is involved it is that of the music industry. As this case and other companion cases make clear, it would appear to be cheaper to license than to litigate.

Since our holding arguably sets forth a new rule, several other observations are in order. First, although there were no existing sound recording judicial precedents to follow, we did not pull this interpretation out of thin air. Several law review and text writers, some of whom have been referenced in this opinion, have suggested that this is the proper interpretation of the copyright statute as it pertains to sound recordings. Since digital sampling has become so commonplace and rap music has become such a significant part of the record industry, it is not surprising that there are probably a hundred articles dealing with sampling and its ramifications. It is also not surprising that the viewpoint expressed in a number of these articles appears driven by whose ox is being gored. As is so often the case, where one stands depends on where one sits. For example, the sound recording copyright holders favor this interpretation as do the studio musicians and their labor organization. On the other hand, many of the hip hop artists may view this rule as stifling creativity. The record companies and performing artists are not all of one mind, however, since in many instances, today's sampler is tomorrow's samplee. The incidence of "live and let live" has been relatively high, which explains why so many instances of sampling go unprotested and why so many sampling controversies have been settled.

Second, to pursue further the subject of stifling creativity, many artists and record companies have sought licenses as a matter of course. Since there is no record of those instances of sampling that either go unnoticed or are ignored, one cannot come up with precise figures, but it is clear that a significant number of persons and companies have elected to go the licensing route. Also there is a large body of pre-1972 sound recordings that is not subject to federal copyright protection. Additionally, just as many artists and companies choose to sample and take their chances, it is likely that will continue to be the case.

> **"THE LEGISLATIVE HISTORY** is of little help because digital sampling wasn't being done in 1971. If this is not what Congress intended or is not what they would intend now, it is easy enough for the record industry, as they have done in the past, to go back to Congress for a clarification or change in the law."

Third, the record industry, including the recording artists, has the ability and know-how to work out guidelines, including a fixed schedule of license fees, if they so choose.

Fourth, we realize we are announcing a new rule and because it is new, it should not play any role in the assessment of concepts such as "willful" or "intentional" in cases that are currently before the courts or had their genesis before this decision was announced.

Finally, and unfortunately, there is no Rosetta stone for the interpretation of the copyright statute. We have taken a "literal reading" approach. The legislative history is of little help because digital sampling wasn't being done in 1971. If this is not what Congress intended or is not what they would intend now, it is easy enough for the record industry, as they have done in the past, to go back to Congress for a clarification or change in the law. This is the best place for the change to be made, rather than in the courts, because as this case demonstrates, the court is never aware of much more than the tip of the iceberg. To properly sort out this type of problem with its complex technical and business overtones, one needs the type of investigative resources as well as the ability to hold hearings that is possessed by Congress.

These conclusions require us to reverse the entry of summary judgment entered in favor of No Limit Films on Westbound's claims of copyright infringement. Since the district judge found no infringement, there was no necessity to consider the affirmative defense of "fair use." On remand, the trial judge is free to consider this defense and we express no opinion on its applicability to these facts.

AFFIRMED in part, *REVERSED* in part, and *REMANDED* for further proceedings consistent with this opinion.

THE UNITED STATES PATENT and Trademark Office provides this summary definition of copyrights:

> **COPYRIGHTS** protect works of authorship, such as writings, music, and works of art that have been tangibly expressed. The Library of Congress registers copyrights which last the life of the author plus 50 years. *Gone With The Wind* (the book and the film), Beatles recordings and video games are all works that are copyrighted.

Fair use is an affirmative defense to copyright infringement and one of the major questions litigated in copyright cases. It also includes issues related to the classroom or use for educational purposes. Can't one just make a copy of an article one thinks interesting and distribute it to a class? Don't the benefits flowing from education allow for such a use? The counter argument is that someone took the time to create that educational material or to write the article that someone finds interesting, and so copying takes away from what they created. Or, more philosophically, as copyrights' cousin – patents – are justified in the Constitution, there is a belief that society as a whole will be better off if creators have the financial incentive to create. If the creator's work will simply be copied for free, then the incentive to create dramatically drops. What about uses that are creative and innovative beyond the sphere of educational use? These questions and considerations create the pressure for the dilemmas associated with fair use.

According to the copyright law, courts are to use four factors in determining whether a use (a copy) is fair use or whether it is an infringement on the author's copyright.

7. The purpose and character of the use, including whether such use is of commercial nature or is for nonprofit educational purposes

8. The nature of the copyrighted work

9. The amount and substantiality of the portion used in relation to the copyrighted work as a whole

10. The effect of the use upon the potential market for, or value of, the copyrighted work

The following two cases set out examples of the parameters of fair use, first in the educational context and the next in copyrighted, musical "sampling."

Marcus v. Rowley

695 F.2d 1171 (9th Cir. 1983)

PFAELZER, District Judge:

I. FACTUAL BACKGROUND

From September 1972 to June 1974, plaintiff, Eloise Toby Marcus was employed by the defendant, San Diego Unified School District ("District") as a teacher of home economics. Plaintiff resigned from the District's employ in 1974 and taught adult education classes intermittently from 1975 to 1980. Shortly after leaving her teaching position with the District, she wrote a booklet entitled "Cake Decorating Made Easy." Plaintiff's booklet consisted of thirty-five pages of which twenty-nine were her original creation. The remaining six pages consisted of material incorporated with the permission of the authors of the materials for which the authors were given appropriate credit.

Plaintiff properly registered the copyright for "Cake Decorating Made Easy" with the Register of Copyrights, and one hundred and twenty-five copies of the booklet were published in the spring of 1975. All of the copies of plaintiff's booklet contained a designation of copyright as evidenced by an encircled "c" followed by "1975 Eloise Marcus." This designation appeared on the table of contents page, the first page, and the page following the cover-title sheet.

Plaintiff sold all but six of the copies of her booklet for $2.00 each to the students in the adult education cake decorating classes which she taught. Plaintiff's profit was $1.00 on the sale of each booklet. Copies of plaintiff's booklet were never distributed to or sold by a bookstore or other outlet. Plaintiff never authorized anyone to copy or reproduce her booklet or any part of it.

Defendant, Shirley Rowley ("Rowley"), teaches food service career classes in the District. In the spring of 1975, she enrolled in one of plaintiff's cake decorating classes and purchased a copy of plaintiff's book. During the following summer, Rowley prepared a booklet entitled "Cake Decorating Learning Activity Package" ("LAP") for use in her food service career classes. The LAP consisted of twenty-four pages and was designed to be used by students who wished to study an optional section of her course devoted to cake decorating. Defendant had fifteen copies of the LAP made and put them in a file so that they would be available to her students. She used the LAP during the 1975, 1976 and 1977 school years. The trial court found that sixty of Rowley's two hundred twenty-five students elected to study cake decorating. The trial court further found that neither Rowley nor the District derived any profit from the LAP.

Rowley admits copying eleven of the twenty-four pages in her LAP from plaintiff's booklet. The eleven pages copied consisted of the supply list, icing recipes, three sheets dealing with color flow and mixing colors, four pages showing how to make and use a decorating bag, and two pages explaining how to make flowers and sugar molds. Four additional pages in defendant's LAP also appear in plaintiff's booklet, but these pages primarily contain information collected by and used with the permission of the Consumer Service Department of the American Institute of Baking[1]. Twenty pages of plaintiff's booklet were not included in Rowley's LAP[2]. Rowley did not give plaintiff credit for the eleven pages she copied, nor did she acknowledge plaintiff as the owner of a copyright with respect to those pages.

Plaintiff learned of Rowley's LAP in the summer of 1977 when a student in plaintiff's adult education class refused to purchase plaintiff's book. The student's son had obtained a copy of the LAP from Rowley's class. After examining Rowley's booklet, the student accused plaintiff of plagiarizing Rowley's work. Following these events, plaintiff made a claim of infringement against Rowley and the District. Both denied infringement and the plaintiff filed suit.

The parties filed cross-motions for summary judgment. The trial court denied both motions for summary judgment and dismissed the case on the merits[3]. The ground for dismissal was that the defendant's copying of the plaintiff's material for nonprofit educational purposes constituted fair use.

* * *

III. THE DOCTRINE OF FAIR USE

* * *

A. *The Purpose and Character of the Use*

The first factor to be considered in determining the applicability of the doctrine of fair use is the purpose and character of the use, and specifically whether the use is of a commercial nature or is for a nonprofit educational purpose. It is uncontroverted that Rowley's use of the LAP was for a nonprofit educational purpose and that the LAP was distributed to students at no charge. These facts necessarily weigh in Rowley's favor. Nevertheless, a finding of a nonprofit educational purpose does not automatically compel a finding of fair use.

This court has often articulated the principle that a finding that the alleged

---

1   The other nine pages of defendant's booklet consisted of the cover, the introduction, and seven pages of lesson plans.

2   These twenty pages consisted of the cover page, the table of contents, two pages on the technique of icing a cake, an explanation of how to make leaves, six pages of lettering designs, eight pages of seasonal designs, and one blank page for notes.

3   The procedural propriety of the trial judge's decision to dismiss the suit rather than to grant one party's motion for summary judgment is not considered here, since, in any event, the case was disposed of on the merits.

infringers copied the material to use it for the same intrinsic purpose for which the copyright owner intended it to be used is strong indicia of no fair use.

This same function test is addressed in the House of Representatives' 1967 Report, specifically in relation to classroom materials. The Report states that, with respect to the fair use doctrine, "[t]extbooks and other material prepared primarily for the school market would be less susceptible to reproduction for classroom use than material prepared for general public distribution."

In this case, both plaintiff's and defendant's booklets were prepared for the purpose of teaching cake decorating, a fact which weighs against a finding of fair use.

Because fair use presupposes that the defendant has acted fairly and in good faith, the propriety of the defendant's conduct should also be weighed in analyzing the purpose and character of the use.

Here, there was no attempt by defendant to secure plaintiff's permission to copy the contents of her booklet or to credit plaintiff for the use of her material even though Rowley's copying was for the most part verbatim. Rowley's conduct in this respect weighs against a finding of fair use.

B. *The Nature of the Copyrighted Work*

The second factor to be weighed is the nature of the copyrighted work. In *Universal City Studios, Inc. v. Sony Corp.*, this court stated that analysis of this factor requires consideration of whether the work is "informational" or "creative." The court stated that "the scope of fair use is greater when informational type works, as opposed to more creative products, are involved." Here, plaintiff's booklet involved both informational and creative aspects. Some pages in her booklet undoubtedly contained information available in other cake decorating books or in recipe books. Other parts of her booklet contained creative hints she derived from her own experiences or ideas; certainly the manner in which plaintiff assembled her book represented a creative expression. Thus, on balance, it does not appear that analysis of this factor is of any real assistance in reaching a conclusion as to applicability of fair use.

C. *The Amount and Substantiality of the Portion Used*

The third factor to be considered is the amount and substantiality of the portion used in relation to the copyrighted work as a whole. Any conclusion with respect to this factor requires analysis of both the quantity and quality of the alleged infringement.

With respect to this factor, this court has long maintained the view that wholesale copying of copyrighted material precludes application of the fair use doctrine. Other courts are in accord with this principle, and two courts have specifically addressed the issue in relation to copying for educational purposes.

* * *

In this case, almost 50% of defendant's LAP was a verbatim copy of plaintiff's booklet and that 50% contained virtually all of the substance of defendant's book. Defendant copied the explanations of how to make the decorating bag, how to mix colors, and how to make various decorations as well as the icing recipes. In fact, the only substantive pages of plaintiff's booklet which defendant did not put into her booklet were hints on how to ice a cake and an explanation of how to make leaves. Defendant argues that it was fair to copy plaintiff's booklet because the booklet contained only facts which were in the public domain. Even if it were true that plaintiff's book contained only facts, this argument fails because defendant engaged in virtually verbatim copying. Defendant's LAP could have been a photocopy of plaintiff's booklet but for the fact that defendant retyped plaintiff's material. This case presents a clear example of both substantial quantitative and qualitative copying.

D. *The Effect of the Use Upon the Potential Market for or Value of the Copyrighted Work*

The final factor to be considered with respect to the fair use defense is the effect which the allegedly infringing use had on the potential market for or value of the copyrighted work. The 1967 House Report points out that this factor is often seen as the most important criterion of fair use, but also warned that it "must almost always be judged in conjunction with the other three criteria." The Report explains that "a use which supplants any part of the normal market for a copyrighted work would ordinarily be considered an infringement." Here, despite the fact that at least one of plaintiff's students refused to purchase her booklet as a result of defendant's copying, the trial court found that it was unable to conclude that the defendant's copying had any effect on the market for the plaintiff's booklet. Even assuming that the trial court's finding was not erroneous, and that that finding must be accepted and weighed in Rowley's favor, it does not alter our conclusion. The mere absence of measurable pecuniary damage does not require a finding of fair use. Fair use is to be determined by a consideration of all of the evidence in the case. Thus, despite the trial court's finding, we conclude that the factors analyzed weigh decisively in favor of the conclusion of no fair use. This conclusion is in harmony with the Congressional guidelines which, as a final point, also merit consideration with respect to the issue of fair use in an educational context.

IV. THE CONGRESSIONAL GUIDELINES

The question of how much copying for classroom use is permissible was of such major concern to Congress that, although it did not include a section on the subject in the revised Act, it approved a set of guidelines with respect to it. The guidelines represent the Congressional Committees' view of what constitutes fair use under the traditional judicial doctrine developed in the case law. The guidelines were designed to give teachers direction as to the extent of permissible copying and to eliminate some of the doubt which had previously existed in this area of the copyright laws.

The guidelines were intended to represent minimum standards of fair use. Thus, while they are not controlling on the court, they are instructive on the issue of fair use in the context of this case.

The guidelines relating to multiple copies for classroom use indicate that such copying is permissible if three tests are met. First, the copying must meet the test of "brevity" and "spontaneity." "Brevity" is defined, for prose, as "[e]ither a complete article, story or essay of less than 2,500 words, or an excerpt from any prose work of not more than 1,000 words or ... 10% of the work, whichever is less ...." Rowley's copying would not be permissible under either of these tests.

The guidelines also provide a separate definition of "brevity" for "special works." "Special works" are works "which often combine language with illustrations and which are intended sometimes for children and at other times for a more general audience." Plaintiff's booklet arguably would fall into this category. The guidelines provide that, notwithstanding the guidelines for prose, " 'special works' may not be reproduced in their entirety; however, an excerpt comprising not more than two of the published pages of such special work and containing not more than 10% of the words found in the text thereof, may be reproduced." Rowley's copying would not be permissible under this test.

Under the guidelines, "spontaneity" requires that "[t]he copying is at the instance and inspiration of the individual teacher, and ... [t]he inspiration and decision to use the work and the moment of its use for maximum teaching effectiveness are so close in time that it would be unreasonable to expect a timely reply to a request for permission." Defendant compiled her LAP during the summer of 1975 and first used it in her classes during the 1975-76 school year. She also used the LAP for the following two school years. Rowley's copying would not meet this requirement either.

The second test under the guidelines is that of "cumulative effect." This test requires that the copied material be for only one course in the school. This aspect of the test would probably be met on these facts. The test also limits the number of pieces which may be copied from the same author and the number of times a teacher may make multiple copies for one course during one term. These latter two tests also appear to be met. The facts indicate that defendant copied only one piece of plaintiff's work. Defendant's conduct, therefore, would satisfy the second test under the guidelines.

The third test requires that each copy include a notice of copyright. As stated, defendant's LAP did not acknowledge plaintiff's authorship or copyright and therefore would not meet this test.

In conclusion, it appears that Rowley's copying would not qualify as fair use under the guidelines. * * *

REVERSED and *REMANDED.*

Campbell v. Acuff-Rose Music, Inc.

<u>510 U.S. 569 (1994)</u>

Justice SOUTER delivered the opinion of the Court.

I

In 1964, Roy Orbison and William Dees wrote a rock ballad called "Oh, Pretty Woman" and assigned their rights in it to respondent Acuff-Rose Music, Inc. Acuff-Rose registered the song for copyright protection.

Petitioners Luther R. Campbell, Christopher Wongwon, Mark Ross, and David Hobbs are collectively known as 2 Live Crew, a popular rap music group. In 1989, Campbell wrote a song entitled "Pretty Woman," which he later described in an affidavit as intended, "through comical lyrics, to satirize the original work...." On July 5, 1989, 2 Live Crew's manager informed Acuff-Rose that 2 Live Crew had written a parody of "Oh, Pretty Woman," that they would afford all credit for ownership and authorship of the original song to Acuff-Rose, Dees, and Orbison, and that they were willing to pay a fee for the use they wished to make of it. Enclosed with the letter were a copy of the lyrics and a recording of 2 Live Crew's song. Acuff-Rose's agent refused permission, stating that "I am aware of the success enjoyed by 'The 2 Live Crews', but I must inform you that we cannot permit the use of a parody of 'Oh, Pretty Woman.' " Nonetheless, in June or July 1989, 2 Live Crew released records, cassette tapes, and compact discs of "Pretty Woman" in a collection of songs entitled "As Clean As They Wanna Be." The albums and compact discs identify the authors of "Pretty Woman" as Orbison and Dees and its publisher as Acuff-Rose.

> Almost a year later, after nearly a quarter of a million copies of the recording had been sold, Acuff-Rose sued 2 Live Crew and its record company, Luke Skyywalker Records, for copyright infringement. The District Court granted summary judgment for 2 Live Crew, reasoning that the commercial purpose of 2 Live Crew's song was no bar to fair use; that 2 Live Crew's version was a parody, which "quickly degenerates into a play on words, substituting predictable lyrics with shocking ones" to show "how bland and banal the Orbison song" is; that 2 Live Crew had taken no more than was necessary to "conjure up" the original in order to parody it; and that it was "extremely unlikely that 2 Live Crew's song could adversely affect the market for the original." * * *

* * *

It is uncontested here that 2 Live Crew's song would be an infringement of Acuff-Rose's rights in "Oh, Pretty Woman," under the Copyright Act of 1976, but for a finding of fair use through parody. From the infancy of copyright protection, some opportunity for fair use of copyrighted materials has been thought necessary to fulfill copyright's very purpose, "[t]o promote the Progress of Science and useful Arts...." For as Justice Story explained, "[i]n truth, in literature, in science and in art, there are, and can be, few, if any, things, which in an abstract sense, are strictly new and original throughout. Every book in literature, science and art, borrows, and must necessarily borrow, and use much which was well known and used before." * * *

In *Folsom v. Marsh*, Justice Story distilled the essence of law and methodology from the earlier cases: "look to the nature and objects of the selections made, the quantity and value of the materials used, and the degree in which the use may prejudice the sale, or diminish the profits, or supersede the objects, of the original work." Thus expressed, fair use remained exclusively judge-made doctrine until the passage of the 1976 Copyright Act, in which Justice Story's summary is discernible:

"§ 107. Limitations on exclusive rights: Fair use

"Notwithstanding the provisions of sections 106 and 106A, the fair use of a copyrighted work, including such use by reproduction in copies or phonorecords or by any other means specified by that section, for purposes such as criticism, comment, news reporting, teaching (including multiple copies for classroom use), scholarship, or research, is not an infringement of copyright. In determining whether the use made of a work in any particular case is a fair use the factors to be considered shall include—

"(1) the purpose and character of the use, including whether such use is of a commercial nature or is for nonprofit educational purposes;

"(2) the nature of the copyrighted work;

"(3) the amount and substantiality of the portion used in relation to the copyrighted work as a whole; and

"(4) the effect of the use upon the potential market for or value of the copyrighted work.

"The fact that a work is unpublished shall not itself bar a finding of fair use if such finding is made upon consideration of all the above factors."

Congress meant § 107 "to restate the present judicial doctrine of fair use, not to change, narrow, or enlarge it in any way" and intended that courts continue the common-law tradition of fair use adjudication. The fair use doctrine thus "permits [and requires] courts to avoid rigid application of the copyright statute when, on occasion, it would stifle the very creativity which that law is designed to foster." * * *

A

The first factor in a fair use enquiry is "the purpose and character of the use, including whether such use is of a commercial nature or is for nonprofit educational purposes." This factor draws on Justice Story's formulation, "the nature and objects of the selections made." The enquiry here may be guided by the examples given in the preamble to § 107, looking to whether the use is for criticism, or comment, or news reporting, and the like. The central purpose of this investigation is to see, in Justice Story's words, whether the new work merely "supersede[s] the objects" of the original creation, or instead adds something new, with a further purpose or different character, altering the first with new expression, meaning, or message; it asks, in other words, whether and to what extent the new work is "transformative." Although such transformative use is not absolutely necessary for a finding of fair use, the goal of copyright, to promote science and the arts, is generally furthered by the creation of transformative works. Such works thus lie at the heart of the fair use doctrine's guarantee of breathing space within the confines of copyright, and the more transformative the new work, the less will be the significance of other factors, like commercialism, that may weigh against a finding of fair use.

* * *

Here, the District Court held, and the Court of Appeals assumed, that 2 Live Crew's "Pretty Woman" contains parody, commenting on and criticizing the original work, whatever it may have to say about society at large. As the District Court remarked, the words of 2 Live Crew's song copy the original's first line, but then "quickly degenerat[e] into a play on words, substituting predictable lyrics with shocking ones ... [that] derisively demonstrat[e] how bland and banal the Orbison song seems to them." Judge Nelson, dissenting below, came to the same conclusion, that the 2 Live Crew song "was clearly intended to ridicule the white-bread original" and "reminds us that sexual congress with nameless streetwalkers is not necessarily the stuff of romance and is not necessarily without its consequences. The singers (there are several) have the same thing on their minds as did the lonely man with the nasal voice, but here there is no hint of wine and roses." * * *

The threshold question when fair use is raised in defense of parody is whether a parodic character may reasonably be perceived. Whether, going beyond that, parody is in good taste or bad does not and should not matter to fair use. As Justice Holmes explained, "[i]t would be a dangerous undertaking for persons trained only to the law to constitute themselves final judges of the worth of [a work], outside of the narrowest and most obvious limits. At the one extreme some works of genius would be sure to miss appreciation. Their very novelty would make them repulsive until the public had learned the new language in which their author spoke.

While we might not assign a high rank to the parodic element here, we think it fair to say that 2 Live Crew's song reasonably could be perceived as commenting on the original or criticizing it, to some degree. 2 Live Crew juxtaposes the romantic musings of a man whose fantasy comes true, with degrading taunts, a bawdy demand for sex, and a sigh of relief from paternal responsibility. The later words can be taken as a comment on the naiveté of the original of an earlier day, as a rejection of its sentiment that ignores the ugliness of street life and the debasement that it signifies. It is this joinder of reference and ridicule that marks off the author's choice of parody from the other types of comment and criticism that traditionally have had a claim to fair use protection as transformative works.[17]

* * *

B

The second statutory factor, "the nature of the copyrighted work," § 107(2), draws on Justice Story's expression, the "value of the materials used." This factor calls for recognition that some works are closer to the core of intended copyright protection than others, with the consequence that fair use is more difficult to establish when the former works are copied. We agree with both the District Court and the Court of Appeals that the Orbison original's creative expression for public dissemination falls within the core of the copyright's protective purposes. This fact, however, is not much help in this case, or ever likely to help much in separating the fair use sheep from the infringing goats in a parody case, since parodies almost invariably copy publicly known, expressive works.

C

The third factor asks whether "the amount and substantiality of the portion used in relation to the copyrighted work as a whole," § 107(3) (or, in Justice Story's words, "the quantity and value of the materials used," are reasonable in relation to the purpose of the copying. Here, attention turns to the persuasiveness of a parodist's justification for the particular copying done, and the enquiry will harken back to the first of the statutory factors, for, as in prior cases, we recognize that the extent of permissible copying varies with the purpose and character of the use. The facts bearing on this factor will also tend to address the fourth, by revealing the degree to which the parody may serve as a market substitute for the original or potentially licensed derivatives.

* * *

The Court of Appeals is of course correct that this factor calls for thought not only about the quantity of the materials used, but about their quality and importance, too. In *Harper & Row*, for example, the Nation had taken only some 300 words out of President Ford's memoirs, but we signaled the significance of the quotations in finding them to amount to "the heart of the book," the part most likely to be newsworthy and important in licensing serialization. We also agree with the Court of Appeals that whether "a substantial portion of the infringing work was copied verbatim" from the copyrighted work is a relevant question, for it may reveal a dearth of transformative character or purpose under the first factor, or a greater likelihood of market harm under the fourth; a work composed primarily of an original, particularly its heart, with little added or changed, is more likely to be a merely superseding use, fulfilling demand for the original.

Where we part company with the court below is in applying these guides to parody, and in particular to parody in the song before us. Parody presents a difficult case. Parody's humor, or in any event its comment, necessarily springs from recognizable allusion to its object through distorted imitation. Its art lies in the tension between a known original and its parodic twin. When parody takes aim at a particular original work, the parody must be able to "conjure up" at least enough of that original to make the object of its critical wit recognizable. What makes for this recognition is quotation of the original's most distinctive or memorable features, which the parodist can be sure the audience will know. Once enough has been taken to assure identification, how much more is reasonable will depend, say, on the extent to which the song's overriding purpose and character is to parody the original or, in contrast, the likelihood that the parody may serve as a market substitute for the original. But using some characteristic features cannot be avoided.

> "WHEN PARODY takes aim at a particular original work, the parody must be able to "conjure up" at least enough of that original to make the object of its critical wit recognizable."

We think the Court of Appeals was insufficiently appreciative of parody's need for the recognizable sight or sound when it ruled 2 Live Crew's use unreasonable as a matter of law. It is true, of course, that 2 Live Crew copied the characteristic opening bass riff (or musical phrase) of the original, and true that the words of the first line copy the Orbison lyrics. But if quotation of the opening riff and the first line may be said to go to the "heart" of the original, the heart is also what most readily conjures up the song for parody, and it is the heart at which parody takes aim. Copying does not become excessive in relation to parodic purpose merely because the portion taken was the original's heart. If 2 Live Crew had copied a significantly less memorable part of the original, it is difficult to see how its parodic character would have come through.

This is not, of course, to say that anyone who calls himself a parodist can skim the cream and get away scot free. In parody, as in news reporting, context is everything, and the question of fairness asks what else the parodist did besides go to the heart of the original. It is significant that 2 Live Crew not only copied the first line of the original, but thereafter departed markedly from the Orbison lyrics for its own ends. 2 Live Crew not only copied the bass riff and repeated it,19 but also produced otherwise distinctive sounds, interposing "scraper" noise, overlaying the music with solos in different keys, and altering the drum beat. This is not a case, then, where "a substantial portion" of the parody itself is composed of a "verbatim" copying of the original. It is not, that is, a case where the parody is so insubstantial, as compared to the copying, that the third factor must be resolved as a matter of law against the parodists.

Suffice it to say here that, as to the lyrics, we think the Court of Appeals correctly suggested that "no more was taken than necessary," but just for that reason, we fail to see how the copying can be excessive in relation to its parodic purpose, even if the portion taken is the original's "heart." As to the music, we express no opinion whether repetition of the bass riff is excessive copying, and we remand to permit evaluation of the amount taken, in light of the song's parodic purpose and character, its transformative elements, and considerations of the potential for market substitution sketched more fully below.

D

The fourth fair use factor is "the effect of the use upon the potential market for or value of the copyrighted work." It requires courts to consider not only the extent of market harm caused by the particular actions of the alleged infringer, but also "whether unrestricted and widespread conduct of the sort engaged in by the defendant ... would result in a substantially adverse impact on the potential market" for the original. The enquiry "must take account not only of harm to the original but also of harm to the market for derivative works."

Since fair use is an affirmative defense, its proponent would have difficulty carrying the burden of demonstrating fair use without favorable evidence about relevant markets. In moving for summary judgment, 2 Live Crew left themselves at just such a disadvantage when they failed to address the effect on the market for rap derivatives, and confined themselves to uncontroverted submissions that there was no likely effect on the market for the original. They did not, however, thereby subject themselves to the evidentiary presumption applied by the Court of Appeals. In assessing the likelihood of significant market harm, the Court of Appeals quoted from language in *Sony* that " '[i]f the intended use is for commercial gain, that likelihood may be presumed. But if it is for a noncommercial purpose, the likelihood must be demonstrated.' " The court reasoned that because "the use of the copyrighted work is wholly commercial, ... we presume that a likelihood of future harm to Acuff-Rose exists." In so doing, the court resolved the fourth factor against 2 Live Crew, just as it had the first, by applying a presumption about the effect of commercial use, a presumption which as applied here we hold to be error.

* * *

We do not, of course, suggest that a parody may not harm the market at all, but when a lethal parody, like a scathing theater review, kills demand for the original, it does not produce a harm cognizable under the Copyright Act. Because "parody may quite legitimately aim at garroting the original, destroying it commercially as well as artistically," the role of the courts is to distinguish between "[b]iting criticism [that merely] suppresses demand [and] copyright infringement[, which] usurps it."

This distinction between potentially remediable displacement and unremediable disparagement is reflected in the rule that there is no protectible derivative market for criticism. The market for potential derivative uses includes only those that creators of original works would in general develop or license others to develop. Yet the unlikelihood that creators of imaginative works will license critical reviews or lampoons of their own productions removes such uses from the very notion of a potential licensing market. "People ask ... for criticism, but they only want praise." Thus, to the extent that the opinion below may be read to have considered harm to the market for parodies of "Oh, Pretty Woman," the court erred.

In explaining why the law recognizes no derivative market for critical works, including parody, we have, of course, been speaking of the later work as if it had nothing but a critical aspect. But the later work may have a more complex character, with effects not only in the arena of criticism but also in protectible markets for derivative works, too. In that sort of case, the law looks beyond the criticism to the other elements of the work, as it does here. 2 Live Crew's song comprises not only parody but also rap music, and the derivative market for rap music is a proper focus of enquiry. Evidence of substantial harm to it would weigh against a finding of fair use, because the licensing of derivatives is an important economic incentive to the creation of originals. Of course, the only harm to derivatives that need concern us, as discussed above, is the harm of market substitution. The fact that a parody may impair the market for derivative uses by the very effectiveness of its critical commentary is no more relevant under copyright than the like threat to the original market.

Although 2 Live Crew submitted uncontroverted affidavits on the question of market harm to the original, neither they, nor Acuff-Rose, introduced evidence or affidavits addressing the likely effect of 2 Live Crew's parodic rap song on the market for a nonparody, rap version of "Oh, Pretty Woman." And while Acuff-Rose would have us find evidence of a rap market in the very facts that 2 Live Crew recorded a rap parody of "Oh, Pretty Woman" and another rap group sought a license to record a rap derivative, there was no evidence that a potential rap market was harmed in any way by 2 Live Crew's parody, rap version. The fact that 2 Live Crew's parody sold as part of a collection of rap songs says very little about the parody's effect on a market for a rap version of the original, either of the music alone or of the music with its lyrics. The District Court essentially passed on this issue, observing that Acuff-Rose is free to record "whatever version of the original it desires;" the Court of Appeals went the other way by erroneous presumption. Contrary to each treatment, it is impossible to deal with the fourth factor except by recognizing that a silent record on an important factor bearing on fair use disentitled the proponent of the defense, 2 Live Crew, to summary judgment. The evidentiary hole will doubtless be plugged on remand.

III

It was error for the Court of Appeals to conclude that the commercial nature of 2 Live Crew's parody of "Oh, Pretty Woman" rendered it presumptively unfair. No such evidentiary presumption is available to address either the first factor, the character and purpose of the use, or the fourth, market harm, in determining whether a transformative use, such as parody, is a fair one. The court also erred in holding that 2 Live Crew had necessarily copied excessively from the Orbison original, considering the parodic purpose of the use. We therefore reverse the judgment of the Court of Appeals and remand the case for further proceedings consistent with this opinion.

If it does nothing else, our electronic age makes it easier to make copies – perfect copies – of items on the Internet. Because copyright law also applies to what is on the Internet, there are significant opportunities for violating copyright law by downloading material online. This pertains to, for instance, music and it also pertains to other items as well as the following two cases illustrate. As you will see, the Digitial Millennium Copyright Act (DMCA), which provides immunity to internet service providers (ISPs) who police copyright infringements, plays a significant role in copyright cases involving online material. Now, one of the significant sources of litigation is not whether infringement has occurred, but whether the ISP is immune from liability.

> Justice Souter attached the lyrics of both songs as appendixes to his majority opinion for the Court. As a result, both songs were reproduced in the United States Reports along with the rest of the opinion, and may now be found in every major law library in the United States.

ALS Scan, Inc. v. ReMarq

239 F.3d 619 (4th Cir. 2001)

NIEMEYER, Circuit Judge:

I

ALS Scan, Inc., a Maryland corporation, is engaged in the business of creating and marketing "adult" photographs. It displays these pictures on the Internet to paying subscribers and also sells them through the media of CD ROMs and videotapes. ALS Scan is holder of the copyrights for all of these photographs.

RemarQ Communities, Inc., a Delaware corporation, is an online Internet service provider that provides access to its subscribing members. It has approximately 24,000 subscribers to its newsgroup base and provides access to over 30,000 newsgroups which cover thousands of subjects. These newsgroups, organized by topic, enable subscribers to participate in discussions on virtually any topic, such as fine arts, politics, religion, social issues, sports, and entertainment. For example, RemarQ provides access to a newsgroup entitled "Baltimore Orioles," in which users share observations or materials about the Orioles. It claims that users post over one million articles a day in these newsgroups, which RemarQ removes after about 8-10 days to accommodate its limited server capacity. In providing access to newsgroups, RemarQ does not monitor, regulate, or censor the content of articles posted in the newsgroup by subscribing members. It does, however, have the ability to filter information contained in the newsgroups and to screen its members from logging onto certain newsgroups, such as those containing pornographic material.

Two of the newsgroups to which RemarQ provides its subscribers access contain ALS Scan's name in the titles. These newsgroups—"alt.als" and "alt.binaries.pictures. erotica.als"—contain hundreds of postings that infringe ALS Scan's copyrights. These postings are placed in these newsgroups by RemarQ's subscribers.

Upon discovering that RemarQ databases contained material that infringed ALS Scan's copyrights, ALS Scan sent a letter, dated August 2, 1999, to RemarQ, stating:

> Both of these newsgroups ["alt.als" and "alt.binaries.pictures.erotica. als"] were created for the sole purpose of violating our Federally filed Copyrights and Tradename. These newsgroups contain virtually all Federally Copyrighted images.... Your servers provide access to these illegally posted images and enable the illegal transmission of these images across state lines.
>
> This is a cease and desist letter. You are hereby ordered to cease carrying these newsgroups within twenty-four (24) hours upon receipt of this correspondence....
>
> America Online, Erol's, Mindspring, and others have all complied with our cease and desist order and no longer carry these newsgroups.
>
>   * * *
>
> Our ALS Scan models can be identified at *http:// www.alsscan.com/ modlinf2.html* [.] Our copyright information can be reviewed at *http:// www.alsscan.com/ copyrite.html* [.]

RemarQ responded by refusing to comply with ALS Scan's demand but advising ALS Scan that RemarQ would eliminate individual infringing items from these newsgroups if ALS Scan identified them "with sufficient specificity." ALS Scan answered that RemarQ had included over 10,000 copyrighted images belonging to ALS Scan in its newsgroups over the period of several months and that

> [t]hese newsgroups have apparently been created by individuals for the
> express sole purpose of illegally posting, transferring and disseminating
> photographs that have been copyrighted by my client through both its
> websites and its CD-ROMs. The newsgroups, on their face from reviewing
> messages posted thereon, serve no other purpose.

When correspondence between the parties progressed no further to resolution of
the dispute, ALS Scan commenced this action, alleging violations of the Copyright
Act and Title II of the DMCA, as well as unfair competition. In its complaint, ALS
Scan alleged that RemarQ possessed actual knowledge that the newsgroups contained infringing material but had "steadfastly refused to remove or block access to
the material." ALS Scan also alleged that RemarQ was put on notice by ALS Scan of
the infringing material contained in its database. In addition to injunctive relief, ALS
Scan demanded actual and statutory damages, as well as attorneys fees. It attached
to its complaint affidavits establishing the essential elements of its claims.

In response, RemarQ filed a motion to dismiss the complaint or, in the alternative, for summary judgment, and also attached affidavits, stating that RemarQ
was prepared to remove articles posted in its newsgroups if the allegedly infringing
articles were specifically identified. It contended that because it is a provider of access
to news-groups, ALS Scan's failure to comply with the DMCA notice requirements
provided it with a defense to ALS Scan's copyright infringement claim.

The district court ruled on RemarQ's motion, stating, "[RemarQ's] motion to
dismiss or for summary judgment is treated as one to dismiss and, as such, is granted." In making this ruling, the district court held: (1) that RemarQ could not be held
liable for *direct* copyright infringement merely because it provided access to a newsgroup containing infringing material; and (2) that RemarQ could not be held liable
for *contributory* infringement because ALS Scan failed to comply with the notice
requirements set forth in the DMCA, 17 U.S.C. § 512(c)(3)(A). This appeal followed.

* * *

III

For its principal argument, ALS Scan contends that it substantially complied with
the notification requirements of the DMCA and thereby denied RemarQ the "safe
harbor" from copyright infringement liability granted by that Act. It asserts that
because its notification was sufficient to put RemarQ on notice of its infringement
activities, RemarQ lost its service-provider immunity from infringement liability. It
argues that the district court's application of the DMCA was overly strict and that
Congress did not intend to permit Internet providers to avoid copyright infringement
liability "merely because a cease and desist notice failed to technically comply with
the DMCA."

RemarQ argues in response that it did not have "knowledge of the infringing
activity as a matter of law," stating that the DMCA protects it from liability because

"ALS Scan failed to identify the infringing works in compliance with the Act, and RemarQ falls within the 'safe harbor' provisions of the Act." It notes that ALS Scan never provided RemarQ or the district court with the identity of the pictures forming the basis of its copyright infringement claim.

These contentions of the parties present the issue of whether ALS Scan complied with the notification requirements of the DMCA so as to deny RemarQ the safe-harbor defense to copyright infringement liability afforded by that Act.

Title II of the DMCA, designated the "Online Copyright Infringement Limitation Act," DMCA, § 201, defines limitations of liability for copyright infringement to which Internet service providers might otherwise be exposed. The Act defines a service provider broadly to include any provider of "online services or network access, or the operator of facilities therefor," including any entity providing "digital online communications, between or among points specified by user, of material of the user's choosing, without modification to the content of the material as sent or received." Neither party to this case suggests that RemarQ is not an Internet service provider for purposes of the Act.

* * *

The DMCA was enacted both to preserve copyright enforcement on the Internet and to provide immunity to service providers from copyright infringement liability for "passive," "automatic" actions in which a service provider's system engages through a technological process initiated by another without the knowledge of the service provider. This immunity, however, is not presumptive, but granted only to "innocent" service providers who can prove they do not have actual or constructive knowledge of the infringement, as defined under any of the three prongs of 17 U.S.C. § 512(c)(1). The DMCA's protection of an innocent service provider disappears at the moment the service provider loses its innocence, i.e., at the moment it becomes aware that a third party is using its system to infringe. At that point, the Act shifts responsibility to the service provider to disable the infringing matter, "preserv[ing] the strong incentives for service providers and copyright owners to cooperate to detect and deal with copyright infringements that take place in the digital networked environment." In the spirit of achieving a balance between the responsibilities of the service provider and the copyright owner, the DMCA requires that a copyright owner put the service provider on notice in a detailed manner but allows notice by means that comport with the prescribed format only "substantially," rather than perfectly. The Act states: "To be effective under this subsection, a notification of claimed infringement must be a written communication provided to the designated agent of a service provider that includes *substantially* the following...." In addition to substantial compliance, the notification requirements are relaxed to the extent that, with respect to multiple works, not all must be identified—only a "representative" list. And with respect to location information, the copyright holder must provide information that is *reasonably* sufficient" to permit the service provider to "locate" this material.

This subsection specifying the requirements of a notification does not seek to burden copyright holders with the responsibility of identifying every infringing work—or even most of them—when multiple copyrights are involved. Instead, the requirements are written so as to reduce the burden of holders of multiple copyrights who face extensive infringement of their works. Thus, when a letter provides notice equivalent to a list of representative works that can be easily identified by the service provider, the notice substantially complies with the notification requirements.

In this case, ALS Scan provided RemarQ with information that (1) identified two sites created for the sole purpose of publishing ALS Scan's copyrighted works, (2) asserted that virtually all the images at the two sites were its copyrighted material, and (3) referred RemarQ to two web addresses where RemarQ could find pictures of ALS Scan's models and obtain ALS Scan's copyright information. In addition, it noted that material at the site could be identified as ALS Scan's material because the material included ALS Scan's "name and/or copyright symbol next to it." We believe that with this information, ALS Scan substantially complied with the notification requirement of providing a representative list of infringing material as well as information reasonably sufficient to enable RemarQ to locate the infringing material. To the extent that ALS Scan's claims about infringing materials prove to be false, RemarQ has remedies for any injury it suffers as a result of removing or disabling noninfringing material.

Accordingly, we reverse the district court's ruling granting summary judgment in favor of RemarQ on the basis of ALS Scan's non-compliance with the notification provisions of 17 U.S.C. § 512(c)(3)(A)(ii) and (iii). Because our ruling only removes the safe harbor defense, we remand for further proceedings on ALS Scan's copyright infringement claims and any other affirmative defenses that RemarQ may have.

* * *

Affirmed in part, reversed in part, and remanded.

A&M Records, Inc. v. Napster

239 F.3d 1004 (9th Cir. 2001)

BEEZER, Circuit Judge:

I

In 1987, the Moving Picture Experts Group set a standard file format for the storage of audio recordings in a digital format called MPEG–3, abbreviated as "MP3." Digital MP3 files are created through a process colloquially called "ripping." Ripping software allows a computer owner to copy an audio compact disk ("audio CD") directly onto a computer's hard drive by compressing the audio information on the CD into the MP3 format. The MP3's compressed format allows for rapid transmission of digital audio files from one computer to another by electronic mail or any other file transfer protocol.

Napster facilitates the transmission of MP3 files between and among its users. Through a process commonly called "peer-to-peer" file sharing, Napster allows its users to: (1) make MP3 music files stored on individual computer hard drives available for copying by other Napster users; (2) search for MP3 music files stored on other users' computers; and (3) transfer exact copies of the contents of other users' MP3 files from one computer to another via the Internet. These functions are made possible by Napster's MusicShare software, available free of charge from Napster's Internet site, and Napster's network servers and server-side software. Napster provides technical support for the indexing and searching of MP3 files, as well as for its other functions, including a "chat room," where users can meet to discuss music, and a directory where participating artists can provide information about their music.

A. Accessing the System

In order to copy MP3 files through the Napster system, a user must first access Napster's Internet site and download[4] the MusicShare software to his individual computer. *See http://www.Napster.com.* Once the software is installed, the user can access the Napster system. A first-time user is required to register with the Napster system by creating a "user name" and password.

B. Listing Available Files

If a registered user wants to list available files stored in his computer's hard drive on Napster for others to access, he must first create a "user library" directory on his computer's hard drive. The user then saves his MP3 files in the library directory, using self-designated file names. He next must log into the Napster system using his user name and password. His MusicShare software then searches his user library and verifies that the available files are properly formatted. If in the correct MP3 format, the names of the MP3 files will be uploaded from the user's computer to the Napster servers. The content of the MP3 files remains stored in the user's computer.

Once uploaded to the Napster servers, the user's MP3 file names are stored in a server-side "library" under the user's name and become part of a "collective directory" of files available for transfer during the time the user is logged onto the Napster system. The collective directory is fluid; it tracks users who are connected in real time, displaying only file names that are immediately accessible.

---

4   1. "To download means to receive information, typically a file, from another computer to yours via your modem . . . . The opposite term is upload, which means to send a file to another computer." *United States v. Mohrbacher*, 182 F.3d 1041, 1048 (9th Cir. 1999) (quoting Robin Williams, Jargon, *An Informal Dictionary of Computer Terms* 170-71 (1993)).

C. Searching For Available Files

Napster allows a user to locate other users' MP3 files in two ways: through Napster's search function and through its "hotlist" function.

Software located on the Napster servers maintains a "search index" of Napster's collective directory. To search the files available from Napster users currently connected to the network servers, the individual user accesses a form in the MusicShare software stored in his computer and enters either the name of a song or an artist as the object of the search. The form is then transmitted to a Napster server and automatically compared to the MP3 file names listed in the server's search index. Napster's server compiles a list of all MP3 file names pulled from the search index which include the same search terms entered on the search form and transmits the list to the searching user. The Napster server does not search the contents of any MP3 file; rather, the search is limited to "a text search of the file names indexed in a particular cluster. Those file names may contain typographical errors or otherwise inaccurate descriptions of the content of the files since they are designated by other users."

To use the "hotlist" function, the Napster user creates a list of other users' names from whom he has obtained MP3 files in the past. When logged onto Napster's servers, the system alerts the user if any user on his list (a "hotlisted user") is also logged onto the system. If so, the user can access an index of all MP3 file names in a particular hotlisted user's library and request a file in the library by selecting the file name. The contents of the hotlisted user's MP3 file are not stored on the Napster system.

D. Transferring Copies of an MP3 file

To transfer a copy of the contents of a requested MP3 file, the Napster server software obtains the Internet address of the requesting user and the Internet address of the "host user" (the user with the available files). The Napster servers then communicate the host user's Internet address to the requesting user. The requesting user's computer uses this information to establish a connection with the host user and downloads a copy of the contents of the MP3 file from one computer to the other over the Internet, "peer-to-peer." A downloaded MP3 file can be played directly from the user's hard drive using Napster's MusicShare program or other software. The file may also be transferred back onto an audio CD if the user has access to equipment designed for that purpose. In both cases, the quality of the original sound recording is slightly diminished by transfer to the MP3 format.

This architecture is described in some detail to promote an understanding of transmission mechanics as opposed to the content of the transmissions. The content is the subject of our copyright infringement analysis.

* * *

IV

We first address plaintiffs' claim that Napster is liable for contributory copyright infringement. Traditionally, "one who, with knowledge of the infringing activity, induces, causes or materially contributes to the infringing conduct of another, may be held liable as a 'contributory' infringer." Put differently, liability exists if the defendant engages in "personal conduct that encourages or assists the infringement."

The district court determined that plaintiffs in all likelihood would establish Napster's liability as a contributory infringer. The district court did not err; Napster, by its conduct, knowingly encourages and assists the infringement of plaintiffs' copyrights.

A. Knowledge

Contributory liability requires that the secondary infringer "know or have reason to know" of direct infringement. The district court found that Napster had both actual and constructive knowledge that its users exchanged copyrighted music. The district court also concluded that the law does not require knowledge of "specific acts of infringement" and rejected Napster's contention that because the company cannot distinguish infringing from noninfringing files, it does not "know" of the direct infringement.

It is apparent from the record that Napster has knowledge, both actual and constructive, of direct infringement. Napster claims that it is nevertheless protected from contributory liability by the teaching of *Sony Corp. v. Universal City Studios, Inc.*. We disagree. We observe that Napster's actual, specific knowledge of direct infringement renders *Sony*'s holding of limited assistance to Napster. We are compelled to make a clear distinction between the architecture of the Napster system and Napster's conduct in relation to the operational capacity of the system.

The *Sony* Court refused to hold the manufacturer and retailers of video tape recorders liable for contributory infringement despite evidence that such machines could be and were used to infringe plaintiffs' copyrighted television shows. *Sony* stated that if liability "is to be imposed on petitioners in this case, it must rest on the fact that *they have sold equipment with constructive knowledge of the fact that their customers may use that equipment to make unauthorized copies* of copyrighted material." The *Sony* Court declined to impute the requisite level of knowledge where the defendants made and sold equipment capable of both infringing and "substantial noninfringing uses."

We are bound to follow *Sony*, and will not impute the requisite level of knowledge to Napster merely because peer-to-peer file sharing technology may be used to infringe plaintiffs' copyrights. We depart from the reasoning of the district court that Napster failed to demonstrate that its system is capable of commercially significant noninfringing uses. The district court improperly confined the use analysis to current uses, ignoring the system's capabilities. Consequently, the district court placed undue weight on the proportion of current infringing use as compared to current and future noninfringing use. Nonetheless, whether we might arrive at a different result is not the issue here. The instant appeal occurs at an early point in the proceedings and "the fully developed factual record may be materially different from that initially before the district court...." Regardless of the number of Napster's infringing versus noninfringing uses, the evidentiary record here supported the district court's finding that plaintiffs would likely prevail in establishing that Napster knew or had reason to know of its users' infringement of plaintiffs' copyrights.

* * *

We agree that if a computer system operator learns of specific infringing material available on his system and fails to purge such material from the system, the operator knows of and contributes to direct infringement. Conversely, absent any specific information which identifies infringing activity, a computer system operator cannot be liable for contributory infringement merely because the structure of the system allows for the exchange of copyrighted material. To enjoin simply because a computer network allows for infringing use would, in our opinion, violate *Sony* and potentially restrict activity unrelated to infringing use.

We nevertheless conclude that sufficient knowledge exists to impose contributory liability when linked to demonstrated infringing use of the Napster system. The record supports the district court's finding that Napster has *actual* knowledge that *specific* infringing material is available using its system, that it could block access to the system by suppliers of the infringing material, and that it failed to remove the material.

B. Material Contribution

Under the facts as found by the district court, Napster materially contributes to the infringing activity. Relying on *Fonovisa*, the district court concluded that "[w]ithout the support services defendant provides, Napster users could not find and download the music they want with the ease of which defendant boasts." We agree that Napster provides "the site and facilities" for direct infringement. The district court correctly applied the reasoning in *Fonovisa*, and properly found that Napster materially contributes to direct infringement.

* * *

V

We turn to the question whether Napster engages in vicarious copyright infringement. Vicarious copyright liability is an "outgrowth" of respondeat superior. In the context of copyright law, vicarious liability extends beyond an employer/employee relationship to cases in which a defendant "has the right and ability to supervise the infringing activity and also has a direct financial interest in such activities."

Before moving into this discussion, we note that *Sony*'s "staple article of commerce" analysis has no application to Napster's potential liability for vicarious copyright infringement. The issues of Sony's liability under the "doctrines of 'direct infringement' and 'vicarious liability' " were not before the Supreme Court, although the Court recognized that the "lines between direct infringement, contributory infringement, and vicarious liability are not clearly drawn." Consequently, when the

Sony Court used the term "vicarious liability," it did so broadly and outside of a technical analysis of the doctrine of vicarious copyright infringement.

A. Financial Benefit

The district court determined that plaintiffs had demonstrated they would likely succeed in establishing that Napster has a direct financial interest in the infringing activity. We agree. Financial benefit exists where the availability of infringing material "acts as a 'draw' for customers. Ample evidence supports the district court's finding that Napster's future revenue is directly dependent upon "increases in userbase." More users register with the Napster system as the "quality and quantity of available music increases." We conclude that the district court did not err in determining that Napster financially benefits from the availability of protected works on its system.

B. Supervision

* * *The ability to block infringers' access to a particular environment for any reason whatsoever is evidence of the right and ability to supervise. Here, plaintiffs have demonstrated that Napster retains the right to control access to its system. Napster has an express reservation of rights policy, stating on its website that it expressly reserves the "right to refuse service and terminate accounts in [its] discretion, including, but not limited to, if Napster believes that user conduct violates applicable law ... or for any reason in Napster's sole discretion, with or without cause."

> **"NAPSTER'S FAILURE to police the system's "premises," combined with a showing that Napster financially benefits from the continuing availability of infringing files on its system, leads to the imposition of vicarious liability.**

To escape imposition of vicarious liability, the reserved right to police must be exercised to its fullest extent. Turning a blind eye to detectable acts of infringement for the sake of profit gives rise to liability.

The district court correctly determined that Napster had the right and ability to police its system and failed to exercise that right to prevent the exchange of copyrighted material. The district court, however, failed to recognize that the boundaries of the premises that Napster "controls and patrols" are limited. Put differently, Napster's reserved "right and ability" to police is cabined by the system's current architecture. As shown by the record, the Napster system does not "read" the content of indexed files, other than to check that they are in the proper MP3 format.

Napster, however, has the ability to locate infringing material listed on its search indices, and the right to terminate users' access to the system. The file name indices, therefore, are within the "premises" that Napster has the ability to police. We recognize that the files are user-named and may not match copyrighted material exactly (for example, the artist or song could be spelled wrong). For Napster to function effectively, however, file names must reasonably or roughly correspond to the material contained in the files, otherwise no user could ever locate any desired music.

As a practical matter, Napster, its users and the record company plaintiffs have equal access to infringing material by employing Napster's "search function."

Our review of the record requires us to accept the district court's conclusion that plaintiffs have demonstrated a likelihood of success on the merits of the vicarious copyright infringement claim. Napster's failure to police the system's "premises," combined with a showing that Napster financially benefits from the continuing availability of infringing files on its system, leads to the imposition of vicarious liability. We address the scope of the injunction in part VIII of this opinion.

* * *

We affirm in part, reverse in part and remand.

B. TRADEMARKS & PATENTS

Patents are specifically protected by Article One, Section 8(8) of the Constitution—"The Congress shall have power...To promote the progress of science and useful arts, by securing for limited times to authors and inventors the exclusive right to their respective writings and discoveries"—and can be broken into three categories: utility patents, design patents, and plant patents. As you will also see, many of the cases resolve the question of when a preliminary injunction—an order that prohibits the company from producing the allegedly infringing product—is an appropriate remedy. The general rule is that the harm must be likely, irreparable and that monetary damages must be unable to remedy the injury.

Utility patents pertain to the way in which manufactured products have their composition or processes uniquely made. These are inventions of new materials for which creators seek patents. These kinds of patents can apply to a wide variety of processes and materials. As the Trademark and Patent Office identifies, these could include fiber optics, computer hardware and medications. If a company creates these new inventions or formulations, it will seek patent protection to prevent competitors from using the patent. Pharmaceutical companies regularly engage in disputes along these lines with respect to other companies in the industry, but more specifically to generic versions of their drugs. Computer companies also compete with each other and in doing so, often mimic successful designs. The line between normal competition and patent infringement can be a thin one. The following famous case is reproduced at length because of its in-depth treatment of this issue and its readily apparent impact on any reader of this book today.

Apple, Inc. v. Samsung Electronics Co., Inc.

678 F.3d 1314 (Fed Cir. 2012)

BRYSON, Circuit Judge.

A

Apple, Inc., is the owner of several design and utility patents pertaining to smart-phones and tablet computers. U.S. Design Patent Nos. D593,087 ("the D'087 patent") and D618,677 ("the D'677 patent") are directed to designs that Apple contends are generally embodied in the iPhone, Apple's popular smartphone. * * * Representative depictions of the designs claimed in the D'087 and D'677 patents are reproduced below:

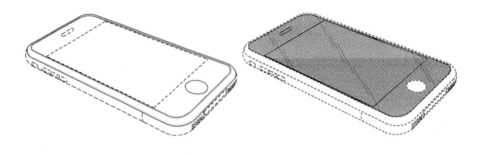

(D'677 Patent, Fig. 1)

Apple also owns U.S. Design Patent No. D504,889 ("the D'889 patent"), which is directed to the design of a tablet computer. * * * Apple claims that its iPad tablet computer embodies the design of the D'889 patent. A figure representing the claimed design shows the following:

(D'889 Patent, Fig.2)

Apple has also asserted U.S. Patent No. 7,469,381 ("the '381 patent"), a utility patent that claims a software feature known as the "bounce-back" feature, which is found on Apple's smartphones and tablets, such as the iPhone and the iPad. The bounce-back feature is activated when the user is scrolling through a document displayed on the device. If the user attempts to scroll past the end of the document, an area beyond the edge of the document is displayed to indicate that the user has reached the document's end. Once the user input ceases (i.e., when the user lifts up the finger that is used for scrolling), the previously visible part of the document "bounces back" into view. * * *

B

Apple filed suit against Samsung on April 15, 2011, alleging, inter alia, infringement of the D'677 and '381 patents. Two months later, Apple amended its complaint and asserted that Samsung was also infringing the D'087 and D' 889 patents. Specifically, Apple claimed that two of Samsung's smartphones, the Galaxy S 4G and the Infuse 4G, which were released on February 23, 2011, and May 15, 2011, respectively, infringed the D'087 and the D'677 patents. Apple also alleged that Samsung's Galaxy Tab 10.1 tablet, which was released in June 2011, infringed the D'889 patent, and that all three devices infringed the '381 patent. On July 1, 2011, Apple moved for a preliminary injunction to block the importation into and sale within the United States of the accused Samsung devices.

* * *

II

"A plaintiff seeking a preliminary injunction must establish that he is likely to succeed on the merits, that he is likely to suffer irreparable harm in the absence of preliminary relief, that the balance of equities tips in his favor, and that an injunction is in the public interest." The decision to grant or deny a preliminary injunction lies within the sound discretion of the district court, and we will not reverse its judgment absent an abuse of that discretion.

In its comprehensive opinion, the district court addressed a large number of legal and factual issues; we have no reason to disagree with the district court on many of those issues, on which the court applied the law correctly or made findings that are not subject to serious challenge, particularly in light of the exacting standard of review that applies to this appeal. We focus our discussion on those aspects of the district court's decision that present close questions or as to which the court committed error that could affect the outcome of this appeal.

The D'677 Patent

The district court held that the design claimed in the D'677 patent was not anticipated or rendered obvious by the prior art. On appeal, Samsung has not made a persuasive case that the district court's conclusion was incorrect. With respect to irreparable harm, however, the district court found that Apple had not shown that it was likely to suffer irreparable injury in the absence of an injunction. The court based its ruling mainly on Apple's failure to show that there was a nexus between the likely infringement of the patented design and Apple's claims of lost market share and brand dilution. On appeal, Apple challenges that ruling on two grounds. First, it contends that it need not show a nexus in order to establish irreparable injury. Second, it contends that even if consumer motives are relevant to the irreparable harm inquiry, the evidence shows that there was a nexus between the asserted infringement and the market injury to Apple.

We hold that the district court was correct to require a showing of some causal nexus between Samsung's infringement and the alleged harm to Apple as part of the showing of irreparable harm. To show irreparable harm, it is necessary to show that the infringement caused harm in the first place. Sales lost to an infringing product cannot irreparably harm a patentee if consumers buy that product for reasons other than the patented feature. If the patented feature does not drive the demand for the product, sales would be lost even if the offending feature were absent from the accused product. Thus, a likelihood of irreparable harm cannot be shown if sales would be lost regardless of the infringing conduct.

* * *

A mere showing that Apple might lose some insubstantial market share as a result of Samsung's infringement is not enough. As the Supreme Court has pointed out, a party seeking injunctive relief must make "a clear showing" that it is at risk of irreparable harm, which entails showing "a likelihood of substantial and immediate irreparable injury." Given our deferential standard of review, we are not prepared to overturn the district court's finding that Apple failed to satisfy its burden of establishing the likelihood of irreparable harm.

Apple argues that the district court erroneously ruled that erosion of a distinctive design could never serve as the basis for a finding of irreparable harm. The district court remarked that "if the introduction of a design-patent-infringing product were sufficient to establish the erosion of design 'distinctiveness,' and therefore irreparable harm, an injunction would presumably issue in every case in which a defendant introduced an infringing product into the market." Contrary to Apple's contention, however, that observation does not reflect a wholesale rejection of design dilution as a theory of irreparable harm, which we agree would have been improper. Instead, the district court went on to note that "Apple has not articulated a theory as to how erosion of 'design distinctiveness' leads to irreparable harm in this case," and that Apple had offered only "conclusory statements and theoretical arguments" in support of its theory. Without "concrete evidence to support its argument," the district court ruled, "Apple has not yet established that this harm to its reputation for innovation is likely to occur." As to Apple's "brand dilution" argument, the district court found that, even assuming "brand dilution" could arise from design patent infringement, "Apple has not demonstrated that brand dilution is likely to occur." The district court's opinion thus makes clear that it did not categorically reject Apple's "design erosion" and "brand dilution" theories, but instead rejected those theories for lack of evidence at this stage of the proceedings.

The district court based its finding as to irreparable harm in part on Apple's delay in seeking preliminary injunctive relief against Samsung's smartphones. Apple objects—and we agree—that the district court should not have faulted Apple for not filing suit as early as 2007, since Apple's design patents had not issued as of that date. Nonetheless, it was reasonable for the district court to consider the issue of delay and to find that Apple had not proceeded as quickly as it could have in seeking preliminary injunctive relief. The district court correctly noted that delay in bringing an infringement action and seeking a preliminary injunction are factors that could suggest that the patentee is not irreparably harmed by the infringement. While the district court rejected the "extreme" position that Apple's failure to seek a preliminary injunction against Samsung's first generation of infringing products precludes it from ever seeking preliminary injunctive relief, the court looked to Apple's "overall diligence in seeking a preliminary injunction," and concluded that, on balance, Apple's "delay in diligently pursuing its infringement claim against Samsung tips in Samsung's favor." We decline Apple's invitation to reject the district court's "delay" analysis altogether, and based on the district court's conclusions as to the nexus and delay factors, we uphold the court's finding that Apple failed to show that it was likely to suffer irreparable harm in the absence of a preliminary injunction.

The D'087 Patent

The district court concluded that the D'087 patent was likely anticipated by the Japanese '638 patent and that Apple had therefore failed to establish a likelihood of success on the merits. The court based its ruling on its conclusion that "the front view of the D'087 patent appears to be substantially similar to the front view of the '638 reference." The court refused to consider any other views of the '638 reference because it found that Apple "never claimed all views of the D'087 patent." That finding was erroneous.

The D'087 patent claims a partial view of the side of the smartphone. The bezel encircling the front face of the patented design extends from the front of the phone to its sides. It is also prominently displayed with solid lines in each figure of the D'087 patent that shows the profile of the device:

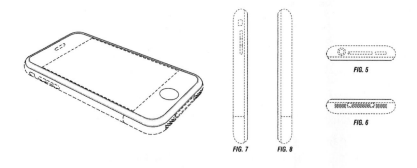

FIG. 7   FIG. 8   FIG. 5   FIG. 6

In that respect, the D'087 patent differs from the D'677 patent, which did not claim a bezel and did not claim any elements of the side view other than the flat front surface (i.e., the side view in the D'677 patent consisted entirely of broken lines). Therefore, the district court erred when it refused to consider the partial side view of the D'087 patent and the resultant flat contour of the front face that the patent disclosed.

Based only on the front view of the patented design, the district court found that the '638 reference raised substantial questions regarding the validity of the D'087 patent. Given our holding that the court misconstrued the full scope of the D'087 patent, that finding cannot stand. Samsung's assertion—that even if the patent claims a portion of the side view, the district court "properly found no material differences between the designs"—finds no support in the record, as the court expressly refused to compare anything more than the front views of the patent in question and the prior art reference. When the claimed portion of the side view is taken into account, the differences between the arched, convex front of the '638 reference distinguish it from the perfectly flat front face of the D'087 patent:

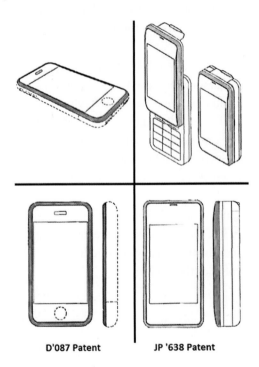

D'087 Patent   JP '638 Patent

We therefore reject the district court's ruling that the D' 087 patent is likely anticipated by the '638 reference.

Notwithstanding our disagreement with the district court on the issue of validity, we uphold the court's order denying relief on the D'087 patent. Because the irreparable harm analysis is identical for both smartphone design patents, and because we have affirmed the district court's finding of no irreparable harm with respect to the D'677 patent, we cannot say that the court abused its discretion when it refused to enjoin Samsung smartphones for infringing the D'087 patent. Consequently, we affirm the court's denial of a preliminary injunction based on the D'087 patent.

The '381 Patent

We also affirm the district court's denial of an injunction based on the '381 patent. The court denied the injunction on the ground that Apple failed to show that it would likely be irreparably harmed by the infringement because it failed to demonstrate that consumer purchasing decisions were based on the presence of the bounce-back feature. Apple again challenges this "consumer motive" requirement. As explained above, we conclude that the district court was correct to require a nexus between infringement of the patent and some market-based injury, be it as a result of consumer preference or some other kind of causal link. Absent such a showing, Apple cannot establish a likelihood of irreparable harm necessary for a preliminary injunction.

Apple relies on evidence that Samsung employees themselves believed that Samsung needed the bounce-back feature to compete with Apple. According to Apple, that internal Samsung evidence is sufficient to establish the requisite nexus. While the evidence that Samsung's employees believed it to be important to incorporate the patented feature into Samsung's products is certainly relevant to the issue of nexus between the patent and market harm, it is not dispositive. That is because the relevant inquiry focuses on the objective reasons as to why the patentee lost sales, not on the infringer's subjective beliefs as to why it gained them (or would be likely to gain them). In light of the deference to which its decision is entitled, we cannot say that the district court erred in refusing to enjoin Samsung's infringement of the '381 patent.

The D'889 Patent

In addressing the D'889 patent, the tablet computer design patent, the district court concluded that Apple had shown that it was likely to suffer irreparable harm from Samsung's alleged infringement. However, the court denied injunctive relief because it found that Apple had failed to establish a likelihood of success on the merits. In particular, it found that Samsung had raised a substantial question as to the validity of the D'889 patent. We sustain the court's finding of a likelihood of irreparable harm, but we hold that the court erred in its analysis of the validity issue.

With respect to irreparable harm, the district court considered the relevant factors, properly weighed them, and concluded that Apple had shown that it was likely to suffer irreparable harm from the sales of Samsung's infringing tablets. The factors included the relative market share of Apple and Samsung and the absence of other competitors in the relevant market. The court also determined, based on evidence submitted by the parties, that design mattered more to customers in making tablet purchases, which helped Apple establish the requisite nexus. The fact that Apple had claimed all views of the patented device and the fact that it was prompt in asserting its patent rights were also properly accorded weight by the court. Given our deferential standard of review, we cannot say that the court abused its discretion when it found that Apple demonstrated a likelihood of irreparable harm.

We disagree with the district court, however, in its conclusion that Apple had failed to show that it was likely to succeed on the merits. The district court concluded that the validity of the D'889 patent was subject to a substantial challenge based on two prior art references: the 1994 Fidler reference and the TC1000 tablet.

| *1994 Fidler Tablet* | *Hewlett–Packard Compaq Tablet TC1000* |

In addressing a claim of obviousness in a design patent, "the ultimate inquiry ... is whether the claimed design would have been obvious to a designer of ordinary skill who designs articles of the type involved." To determine whether "one of ordinary skill would have combined teachings of the prior art to create the same overall visual appearance as the claimed design," the finder of fact must employ a two-step process. First, "one must find a single reference, 'a something in existence, the design characteristics of which are basically the same as the claimed design.' " Second, "other references may be used to modify [the primary reference] to create a design that has the same overall visual appearance as the claimed design." However, the "secondary references may only be used to modify the primary reference if they are 'so related to the primary reference that the appearance of certain ornamental features in one would suggest the application of those features to the other.' "

The district court began its obviousness analysis by finding that the Fidler reference "creates basically the same visual impression as the D'889 patent" because both are rectangular tablets with four evenly rounded corners and a flat reflective surface for the front screen surrounded by a rim on all four sides. The court characterized the back of the Fidler reference as being "essentially flat." It then concluded that although the Fidler reference did not have a flat glass surface, that did not prevent it from creating the same overall visual impression as the D'889 design. The court looked to the TC1000 tablet to supply the missing flat glass screen and the thin rim that surrounds the front face of the device. The court also relied on the testimony of Samsung's expert, who concluded that "a designer of ordinary skill ... would have found it obvious to create the D'889 tablet consisting of a rectangular design with four evenly rounded corners, a relatively thin depth, a smooth back that curves up ... and a flat, clear front surface that extended beyond the edges of the display."

We hold that the district court erred in finding that the Fidler tablet created the same visual impression as the D'889 patent. A side-by-side comparison of the two designs shows substantial differences in the overall visual appearance between the patented design and the Fidler reference:

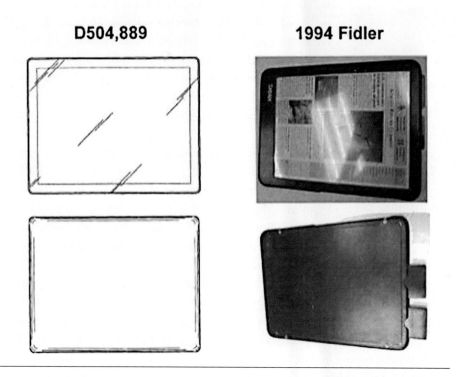

First, the Fidler tablet is not symmetrical: The bottom edge is noticeably wider than the others. More importantly, the frame of the Fidler tablet creates a very different impression from the "unframed" D'889 design. In the Fidler tablet, the frame surrounding the screen contrasts sharply with the screen itself. The Fidler screen appears to sink into the frame, creating a "picture frame" effect and breaking the continuity between the frame and the screen embedded within it. The transparent glass-like front surface of the D'889 patent, however, covers essentially the entire front face of the patented design without any breaks or interruptions. As a result, the D'889 design creates the visual impression of an unbroken slab of glass extending from edge to edge on the front side of the tablet. The Fidler reference does not create such an impression.

There are other noticeable differences between the Fidler tablet and the D'889 patent that contribute to the distinct visual appearance of the two designs. Unlike the D'889 patent, the Fidler reference contains no thin bezel surrounding the edge of the front side. Additionally, one corner of the frame in the Fidler reference contains multiple perforations. Also in contrast to the D'889 patent, the sides of the Fidler reference are neither smooth nor symmetrical; it has two card-like projections extending out from its top edge and an indentation in one of its sides. And the back of the Fidler reference also conveys a visual impression different from that of the D'889 design.

In design patent obviousness analysis, a primary reference must be "something in existence, the design characteristics of which are basically the same as the claimed design in order to support a holding of obviousness." Based on the differences between the Fidler tablet and the D'889 design, we hold that the Fidler tablet does not give the same visual impression as the D'889 patent, and therefore the district court erred in looking to Fidler as the primary reference against the D'889 patent.

'Even assuming that Fidler qualified as a primary reference, the TC1000 secondary reference could not bridge the gap between Fidler and the D'889 design. First, while the TC1000 has a flat glass front, the screen area of that device is surrounded by a gray area that frames the screen. In addition, the perimeter of the TC1000 is encircled by a wide rounded-over metallic rim. And the screen area contains indicator lights in several places, unlike the minimalist design claimed in the D'889 patent. "[T]he teachings of prior art designs may be combined only when the designs are 'so related that the appearance of certain ornamental features in one [design] would suggest the application of those features to the other.' " The TC1000 is so different in visual appearance from the Fidler reference that it does not qualify as a comparison reference under that standard.

Samsung contends that the district court properly focused on overall visual appearance rather than on the "design concepts" highlighted by Apple. In our assessment, however, the district court's error was to view the various designs from too high a level of abstraction. Fidler does not qualify as a primary reference simply by disclosing a rectangular tablet with four evenly rounded corners and a flat back. Rather than looking to the "general concept" of a tablet, the district court should have focused on the distinctive "visual appearances" of the reference and the claimed design. When those visual impressions are compared, it becomes apparent that the Fidler reference, with or without the TC1000, cannot serve to render the D'889 patent invalid for obviousness.

In the alternative, Samsung urges us to consider several other tablet and tablet-like designs as suitable primary references. All of those references consist of rectangular designs with rounded corners dominated by a display area. But those designs all suffer from the same problems as the Fidler reference, because all of them show

> **"IN ADDRESSING a claim of obviousness in a design patent, 'the ultimate inquiry ... is whether the claimed design would have been obvious to a designer of ordinary skill who designs articles of the type involved.' "**

either a thick surrounding frame in which a display is embedded or contain extensive ornamentation on the front of the tablet. The offered designs do not create the same visual impression as Apple's claimed design and thus do not qualify as primary references. In the absence of a qualifying primary reference, we hold that the district court erred in concluding that there is likely to be a substantial question as to the validity of the D'889 patent.

Because the district court found that there is a substantial question as to the validity of the D'889 patent, it did not make any findings with regard to the remaining two questions bearing on whether to issue a preliminary injunction—the balance of hardships and the public interest. The court conducted a detailed assessment of the balance of hardships with respect to the D'677 and '381 patents after finding that they were likely to survive a validity challenge. With respect to the D'889 patent, however, the district court has not determined the extent to which Samsung would be harmed if the sales of Galaxy Tab 10.1 were enjoined, and how the potential harm to Samsung resulting from entering an injunction compares to the potential harm to Apple should the district court deny interim relief. Nor has the district court evaluated the public interest at stake with respect to the sales of Samsung's Galaxy Tab 10.1. Because the district court has not yet weighed the balance of hardships to the parties and the public interest factors, we do not have a sufficient basis for concluding that the failure to enter an injunction was an abuse of discretion. It is normally not appropriate for this court to make such highly factual inquiries for the first time on appeal. That is particularly true for an order granting preliminary relief, as a district court order denying relief can be upheld based on negative findings on fewer than all of the four factors.

* * *

In sum, we affirm the denial of a preliminary injunction with respect to the D'087, D'677, and '381 patents. We vacate the order denying an injunction with respect to the D'889 patent and remand the case to the district court for further proceedings on that portion of Apple's motion for preliminary relief.

Each party shall bear its own costs for this appeal.

AFFIRMED IN PART, VACATED IN PART, and REMANDED

A SECOND KIND OF PATENT is a design patent. These pertain not to the manufacture design of a product that makes it unique; that is covered by Utility Patents, but instead more to the appearance of the product that set it apart, uniquely, from other products. The Patent and Trademark office identifies Star Wars characters, the look of an athletic shoe, or a bicycle helmet as examples.

L.A. Gear v. Thom McAn Shoe Co.

988 F.2d 1117 (Fed. Cir. 1993)

PAULINE NEWMAN, Circuit Judge.

BACKGROUND

In 1987 L.A. Gear designed a line of women's and girls' athletic shoes identified as the L.A. Gear's "Hot Shots" shoes. United States Design Patent No. 299,081 was granted on December 27, 1988 ("the '081 patent"). Figure 4 of the patent is shown:

Although color is not part of the patented design, the colors used on these shoes and their placement are part of the trade dress for which L.A. Gear claims protection from unfair competition.

In the summer and fall of 1987 L.A. Gear exhibited the Hot Shots line of shoes to retailers at trade shows, and announced that these shoes had been selected as L.A. Gear's "hero" or featured shoe line, on which major promotion and advertising would be focused for the ensuing year. There was evidence at trial that L.A. Gear concentrated over seventy percent of its advertising expenditures on these shoes, including television commercials, billboards, and advertisements in magazines and newspapers, at a cost of over five million dollars in 1988. The district court found that the advertising was in color and prominently featured the design of the shoe.

A L.A. Gear Hot Shots shoe is pictured:

This line of shoes was a commercial success, with four million pairs sold by February, 1989. The sales volume was significantly higher than for any of L.A. Gear's other styles. The shoes were sold primarily in department stores, sporting goods stores, and athletic shoe stores, at a retail price ranging from $35 to $60. L.A. Gear testified that it had a policy against sale of its shoes in discount stores.

Melville Corporation sells shoes in discount stores, through its divisions Thom McAn and Meldisco. Thom McAn sells shoes in its own stores, and Meldisco sells shoes in K Mart stores. The Pagoda Trading Company arranges for the manufacture of shoes in the Far East and their importation into the United States.

* * *

I

THE DESIGN PATENT

35 U.S.C. § 171 provides that a patent may be obtained for the ornamental design of an article of manufacture.

> Whoever invents any new, original and ornamental design for an article of manufacture may obtain a patent therefor, subject to the conditions and requirements of this title....

A patented design is ordinarily claimed "as shown," that is, by its drawing.

> The title of the design must designate the particular article. No description, other than a reference to the drawing, is ordinarily required. The claim shall be in formal terms to the ornamental design for the article (specifying name) as shown, or as shown and described. More than one claim is neither required nor permitted.

L.A. Gear charged only Melville with patent infringement, since Pagoda had ceased importation before the issuance of the '081 patent. Melville was held liable for patent infringement with respect to four models of shoes: a women's high top BALLOONS shoe (model no. 78191); a women's high top AEROBIX shoe (model no. 78505); and two girls' high top AEROBIX shoes (models no. 71878 and 76878).

Melville raised defenses of patent invalidity and non-infringement, on the following premises:

Functionality

Melville asserted at trial, and argues on appeal, that the design of the '081 patent is "functional" and that the patent is therefore invalid. Invalidity due to functionality is an affirmative defense to a claim of infringement of a design patent, and must be proved by the party asserting the defense. Applying the presumption of validity, invalidity of a design patent must be established by clear and convincing evidence.

A design patent is directed to the appearance of an article of manufacture. An article of manufacture necessarily serves a utilitarian purpose, and the design of a useful article is deemed to be functional when the appearance of the claimed design is "dictated by" the use or purpose of the article. If the particular design is essential to the use of the article, it can not be the subject of a design patent.

Melville argues that each element comprising the '081 design has a utilitarian purpose: that is, the delta wing provides support for the foot and reinforces the shoelace eyelets; the mesh on the side of the shoe also provides support; the moustache at the back of the shoe provides cushioning for the Achilles tendon and reinforcement for the rear of the shoe; and the position of each of these elements on the shoe is due to its function. However, the utility of each of the various elements that comprise the design is not the relevant inquiry with respect to a design patent. In determining whether a design is primarily functional or primarily ornamental the claimed design is viewed in its entirety, for the ultimate question is not the functional or decorative aspect of each separate feature, but the overall appearance of the article, in determining whether the claimed design is dictated by the utilitarian purpose of the article.

That elements of the '081 design, such as the delta wing or the side mesh, also provide support for the foot does not mean that the specific design of each element, and the combination of these elements into the patented design, is dictated by primarily functional considerations. The elements of the design may indeed serve a utilitarian purpose, but it is the ornamental aspect that is the basis of the design patent.

The district court remarked on the existence of a myriad of athletic shoe designs in which each of the functions identified by Melville as performed by the '081 design elements was achieved in a way other than by the design of the '081 patent. When there are several ways to achieve the function of an article of manufacture, the design of the article is more likely to serve a primarily ornamental purpose. It was not disputed that there were other ways of designing athletic shoes to perform the functions of the elements of the '081 design. In today's marketplace, the primacy of appearance in the design of shoes can not be ignored when analyzing functionality.

The district court found that the '081 design was primarily ornamental, and that the patent was not invalid on the ground of functionality. Clear error has not been shown in this ruling, which is affirmed.

Obviousness

A patented design must meet the substantive criteria of patentability, including non-obviousness in accordance with the law of 35 U.S.C. § 103.

In applying the law of § 103 to the particular facts pertinent to the patented design, obviousness *vel non* is reviewed from the viewpoint of a designer of ordinary skill or capability in the field to which the design pertains. As with utility patents, obviousness is not determined as if the designer had hindsight knowledge of the patented design.

When the patented design is a combination of selected elements in the prior art, a holding of obviousness requires that there be some teaching or suggestion whereby it would have been obvious to a designer of ordinary skill to make the particular selection and combination made by the patentee. The first step in the analysis, when the subject is design, is whether there is "a reference to something in existence, the design characteristics of which are basically the same as the claimed design, in order to support a holding of obviousness." Thus not only the individual elements, but the ornamental quality of the combination must be suggested in the prior art.

Melville offered twenty-two references that were asserted to show or suggest various features of the '081 design, and argues that the '081 design is readily reconstructed from elements found in the prior art. The district court found that all of the elements of the design of the '081 patent were known, but that these particular elements had not previously been combined in a single shoe design. A reconstruction of known elements does not invalidate a design patent, absent some basis whereby a designer of ordinary skill would be led to create this particular design. The district court concluded that there was no teaching or suggestion in the prior art of the appearance of the claimed design as a visual whole. We discern no error in this conclusion or the premises on which it rests. The undisputed commercial success of the patented design, and Appellants' copying thereof, are also relevant to analysis of the obviousness of a design.

The district court's holding that the '081 design patent is not invalid under 35 U.S.C. § 103 is affirmed.

Infringement

In 35 U.S.C. § 289 infringement is defined as unauthorized manufacture or sale of "the patented design, or any colorable imitation thereof." Design patent infringement is a question of fact, to be proven by a preponderance of the evidence.

Design patent infringement requires a showing that the accused design is substantially the same as the claimed design. The criterion is deception of the ordinary observer, such that one design would be confused with the other:

> We hold, therefore, that if, in the eye of an ordinary observer, giving such attention as a purchaser usually gives, two designs are substantially the same, if the resemblance is such as to deceive such an observer, inducing him to purchase one supposing it to be the other, the first one patented is infringed by the other.

In conducting such analysis the patented design is viewed in its entirety, as it is claimed. As for other patented inventions, reference is made to the prior art and the prosecution history in order to give appropriate weight to the factors that contributed to patentability. While the accused design must appropriate the novelty that distinguished the patented design from the prior art, the ultimate question requires determining whether "the effect of the whole design [is] substantially the same."

The district court found that the designs of four models of Melville's accused shoes were "almost a direct copy" of the '081 design. Pictured is the BALLOONS model no. 78191: (*image omitted*).

Substantial similarity is not disputed; indeed, copying is admitted. However, Melville complains that the district court's treatment of the issue of patent infringement was "cursory," in that the court referred, in the part of its opinion relating to patent infringement, to its findings on likelihood of confusion relative to the trade dress issue.

In discussing trade dress, the district court had found that the L.A. Gear shoes and the accused shoes were substantially similar in design, such that the ordinary observer would confuse one with the other. Although design patent analysis requires comparison of the claimed design with the accused articles, Melville has not argued that the patent drawing differs from the embodiment in the L.A. Gear shoe, and has offered no reason why the finding of substantial similarity between the actual shoes was not applicable to the infringement analysis. When the patented design and the design of the article sold by the patentee are substantially the same, it is not error to compare the patentee's and the accused articles directly; indeed, such comparison may facilitate application of the Gorham criterion of whether an ordinary purchaser would be deceived into thinking that one were the other. It was in this context that the district court analyzed likelihood of confusion. No methodological error has been shown in this analysis.

Design patent infringement relates solely to the patented design, and does not require proof of unfair competition in the marketplace or allow of avoidance of infringement by labelling. The district court did not confuse the criteria relevant to these causes of action. Although Melville argues specific differences in features of the four models that were found to infringe the '081 patent, the district court found that "the placement of all the major design elements is the same, creating the same distinctive overall look," and recognized that the novelty resided in the overall appearance of the combination. The court found, in the terms of *Gorham v. White*, that the four infringing models were confusingly similar to the patented design, as viewed by an ordinary observer.

Reversible error has not been shown. The district court's holding of design patent infringement is affirmed.

Willfulness of Infringement

The district court concluded that Melville's patent infringement was not willful, and denied L.A. Gear's request for enhanced damages and attorney fees. Willfulness of infringement is a question of fact, and the district court's finding thereon shall be sustained unless it is clearly in error.

Melville relied on its counsel's obligations under Rule 11 to support its assertion that it had a good faith belief in the invalidity and unenforceability of the '081 patent. L.A. Gear points out, correctly, that a defensive pleading of invalidity or unenforceability may pass muster under Rule 11, yet not provide adequate defense to the charge of willful infringement. Indeed, in this case the pled defense of unenforceability was not pursued at trial; and the only ground asserted for patent invalidity (*i.e.*, functionality) did not present a close question of fact or law.

Melville introduced no evidence of whether it obtained an opinion of counsel that the '081 patent was not valid or not infringed, or any other support for a good faith belief that it was entitled to perform the infringing acts. Although a party to litigation may indeed withhold disclosure of the advice given by its counsel, as a privileged communication, it will not be presumed that such withheld advice was favorable to the party's position. We have held that the assertion of privilege with respect to infringement and validity opinions of counsel may support the drawing of adverse inferences.

Melville presented no evidence to counteract the evidence of copying of the patented design. Indeed, Melville admitted copying, offering as its only justification the proposition that copying is prevalent in the fashion industry, an issue not relevant to patent infringement. The '081 patent issued several months after the complaint for unfair competition under § 43(a) was filed by L.A. Gear. L.A. Gear warned Melville of the impending issuance of the patent. In Avia Group, the defendant was given similar warning of impending patent issuance, yet continued the accused activities after patent issuance. The law imposes an affirmative duty of due care to avoid infringement of the known patent rights of another.

In *Avia Group*, as here, the accused infringer presented no probative evidence of a good faith belief in non-infringement. As in *Avia Group*, Melville's deliberate copying was strong evidence of willful infringement, without any exculpatory evidence to balance the weight. Indeed, the factual situations are not distinguishable on the issue of willfulness. Principles of *stare decisis* require similar rulings on similar facts, and thus it was error to fail to follow *Avia Group*.

The district court's ruling that Melville's infringement was not willful is reversed.

* * *

THE FINAL AREA OF PATENT pertains specifically to plants, which given agricultural issues and other food-related engineering, has become a significant area. Farmers and agricultural companies have been creating hybrid plants for centuries. The framers of the Constitution were aware of this and specifically identified plant breeding as a patentable process. It also applies to flowers as well. One of the bigger issues today concerns issues arising out of genetically modified foods, which expands plant breeding even further. In fact, the Supreme Court has just recently, May 13, 2013, ruled on this issue in the context of plant patents and the doctrine of patent exhaustion.

Bowman v. Monsanto Co.

2013 WL 1942397 (2013)

Justice KAGAN delivered the opinion of the Court.

Under the doctrine of patent exhaustion, the authorized sale of a patented article gives the purchaser, or any subsequent owner, a right to use or resell that article. Such a sale, however, does not allow the purchaser to make new copies of the patented invention. The question in this case is whether a farmer who buys patented seeds may reproduce them through planting and harvesting without the patent holder's permission. We hold that he may not.

I

Respondent Monsanto invented a genetic modification that enables soybean plants to survive exposure to glyphosate, the active ingredient in many herbicides (including Monsanto's own Roundup). Monsanto markets soybean seed containing this altered genetic material as Roundup Ready seed. Farmers planting that seed can use a glyphosate-based herbicide to kill weeds without damaging their crops. Two patents issued to Monsanto cover various aspects of its Roundup Ready technology, including a seed incorporating the genetic alteration.

Monsanto sells, and allows other companies to sell, Roundup Ready soybean seeds to growers who assent to a special licensing agreement. That agreement permits a grower to plant the purchased seeds in one (and only one) season. He can then consume the resulting crop or sell it as a commodity, usually to a grain elevator or agricultural processor. But under the agreement, the farmer may not save any of the harvested soybeans for replanting, nor may he supply them to anyone else for that purpose. These restrictions reflect the ease of producing new generations of Roundup Ready seed. Because glyphosate resistance comes from the seed's genetic material, that trait is passed on from the planted seed to the harvested soybeans: Indeed, a single Roundup Ready seed can grow a plant containing dozens of genetically identical beans, each of which, if replanted, can grow another such plant—and so on and so on. See App. 100a. The agreement's terms prevent the farmer from co-opting that process to produce his own Roundup Ready seeds, forcing him instead to buy from Monsanto each season.

Petitioner Vernon Bowman is a farmer in Indiana who, it is fair to say, appreciates Roundup Ready soybean seed. He purchased Roundup Ready each year, from a company affiliated with Monsanto, for his first crop of the season. In accord with the agreement just described, he used all of that seed for planting, and sold his entire crop to a grain elevator (which typically would resell it to an agricultural processor for human or animal consumption).

Bowman, however, devised a less orthodox approach for his second crop of each season. Because he thought such late-season planting "risky," he did not want to pay the premium price that Monsanto charges for Roundup Ready seed. He therefore went to a grain elevator; purchased "commodity soybeans" intended for human or animal consumption; and planted them in his fields. Those soybeans came from prior harvests of other local farmers. And because most of those farmers also used Roundup Ready seed, Bowman could anticipate that many of the purchased soybeans would contain Monsanto's patented technology. When he applied a glyphosate-based herbicide to his fields, he confirmed that this was so; a significant proportion of the new plants survived the treatment, and produced in their turn a new crop of soybeans with the Roundup Ready trait. Bowman saved seed from that crop to use in his late-season planting the next year—and then the next, and the next, until he had harvested eight crops in that way. Each year, that is, he planted saved seed from the year before (sometimes adding more soybeans bought from the grain elevator), sprayed his fields with glyphosate to kill weeds (and any non-resistant plants), and produced a new crop of glyphosate-resistant—*i.e.*, Roundup Ready—soybeans.

After discovering this practice, Monsanto sued Bowman for infringing its patents on Roundup Ready seed. Bowman raised patent exhaustion as a defense, arguing that Monsanto could not control his use of the soybeans because they were the subject of a prior authorized sale (from local farmers to the grain elevator). The District Court rejected that argument, and awarded damages to Monsanto of $84,456. The Federal Circuit affirmed. It reasoned that patent exhaustion did not protect Bowman because he had "created a newly infringing article." The "right to use" a patented article following an authorized sale, the court explained, "does not include the right to construct an essentially new article on the template of the original, for the right to make the article remains with the patentee." Accordingly, Bowman could not " 'replicate' Monsanto's patented technology by planting it in the ground to create newly infringing genetic material, seeds, and plants."

We granted certiorari to consider the important question of patent law raised in this case and now affirm.

II

The doctrine of patent exhaustion limits a patentee's right to control what others can do with an article embodying or containing an invention. Under the doctrine, "the initial authorized sale of a patented item terminates all patent rights to that item. And by "exhaust[ing] the [patentee's] monopoly" in that item, the sale confers on the purchaser, or any subsequent owner, "the right to use [or] sell" the thing as he sees fit. We have explained the basis for the doctrine as follows: "[T]he purpose of the patent law is fulfilled with respect to any particular article when the patentee has received his reward ... by the sale of the article;" once that "purpose is realized the patent law affords no basis for restraining the use and enjoyment of the thing sold."

Consistent with that rationale, the doctrine restricts a patentee's rights only as to the "particular article" sold; it leaves untouched the patentee's ability to prevent a buyer from making new copies of the patented item. "[T]he purchaser of the [patented] machine ... does not acquire any right to construct another machine either for his own use or to be vended to another." Rather, "a second creation" of the patented item "call[s] the monopoly, conferred by the patent grant, into play for a second time." That is because the patent holder has "received his reward" only for the actual article sold, and not for subsequent recreations of it. If the purchaser of that article could make and sell endless copies, the patent would effectively protect the invention for just a single sale. Bowman himself disputes none of this analysis as a general matter: He forthrightly acknowledges the "well settled" principle "that the exhaustion doctrine does not extend to the right to 'make' a new product."

Unfortunately for Bowman, that principle decides this case against him. Under the patent exhaustion doctrine, Bowman could resell the patented soybeans he purchased from the grain elevator; so too he could consume the beans himself or feed them to his animals. Monsanto, although the patent holder, would have no business interfering in those uses of Roundup Ready beans. But the exhaustion doctrine does not enable Bowman to make *additional* patented soybeans without Monsanto's permission (either express or implied). And that is precisely what Bowman did. He took the soybeans he purchased home; planted them in his fields at the time he thought best; applied glyphosate to kill weeds (as well as any soy plants lacking the Roundup Ready trait); and finally harvested more (many more) beans than he started with. That is how "to 'make' a new product," to use Bowman's words, when the original product is a seed. Because Bowman thus reproduced Monsanto's patented invention, the exhaustion doctrine does not protect him.

Were the matter otherwise, Monsanto's patent would provide scant benefit. After inventing the Roundup Ready trait, Monsanto would, to be sure, "receiv[e] [its] reward" for the first seeds it sells. But in short order, other seed companies could reproduce the product and market it to growers, thus depriving Monsanto of its monopoly. And farmers themselves need only buy the seed once, whether from Monsanto, a competitor, or (as here) a grain elevator. The grower could multiply his initial purchase, and then multiply that new creation, *ad infinitum*—each time profiting from the patented seed without compensating its inventor. Bowman's late-season plantings offer a prime illustration. After buying beans for a single harvest, Bowman saved enough seed each year to reduce or eliminate the need for additional purchases. Monsanto still held its patent, but received no gain from

Bowman's annual production and sale of Roundup Ready soybeans. The exhaustion doctrine is limited to the "particular item" sold to avoid just such a mismatch between invention and reward.

* * *

Bowman principally argues that exhaustion should apply here because seeds are meant to be planted. The exhaustion doctrine, he reminds us, typically prevents a patentee from controlling the use of a patented product following an authorized sale. And in planting Roundup Ready seeds, Bowman continues, he is merely using them in the normal way farmers do. Bowman thus concludes that allowing Monsanto to interfere with that use would "creat[e] an impermissible exception to the exhaustion doctrine" for patented seeds and other "self-replicating technologies."

> "...IF SIMPLE copying were a protected use, a patent would plummet in value after the first sale of the first item containing the invention."

But it is really Bowman who is asking for an unprecedented exception—to what he concedes is the "well settled" rule that "the exhaustion doctrine does not extend to the right to 'make' a new product." Reproducing a patented article no doubt "uses" it after a fashion. But as already explained, we have always drawn the boundaries of the exhaustion doctrine to exclude that activity, so that the patentee retains an undiminished right to prohibit others from making the thing his patent protects. That is because, once again, if simple copying were a protected use, a patent would plummet in value after the first sale of the first item containing the invention. The undiluted patent monopoly, it might be said, would extend not for 20 years (as the Patent Act promises), but for only one transaction. And that would result in less incentive for innovation than Congress wanted. Hence our repeated insistence that exhaustion applies only to the particular item sold, and not to reproductions.

Nor do we think that rule will prevent farmers from making appropriate use of the Roundup Ready seed they buy. Bowman himself stands in a peculiarly poor position to assert such a claim. As noted earlier, the commodity soybeans he purchased were intended not for planting, but for consumption. Indeed, Bowman conceded in deposition testimony that he knew of no other farmer who employed beans bought from a grain elevator to grow a new crop. So a non-replicating use of the commodity beans at issue here was not just available, but standard fare. And in the more ordinary case, when a farmer purchases Roundup Ready seed *qua* seed—that is, seed intended to grow a crop—he will be able to plant it. Monsanto, to be sure, conditions the farmer's ability to reproduce Roundup Ready; but it does not—could not realistically—preclude all planting. No sane farmer, after all, would buy the product without some ability to grow soybeans from it. And so Monsanto, predictably enough, sells Roundup Ready seed to farmers with a license to use it to make a crop. Applying our usual rule in this context therefore will allow farmers to benefit from Roundup Ready, even as it rewards Monsanto for its innovation.

"We think that blame-the-bean defense tough to credit."

" BOWMAN HAS ANOTHER SEEDS-ARE-SPECIAL ARGUMENT: that soybeans naturally "self-replicate or 'sprout' unless stored in a controlled manner," and thus "it was the planted soybean, not Bowman" himself, that made replicas of Monsanto's patented invention... But it was Bowman, and not the bean, who controlled the reproduction (unto the eighth generation) of Monsanto's patented invention."

— JUSTICE ELENA KAGAN

Still, Bowman has another seeds-are-special argument: that soybeans naturally "self-replicate or 'sprout' unless stored in a controlled manner," and thus "it was the planted soybean, not Bowman" himself, that made replicas of Monsanto's patented invention. But we think that blame-the-bean defense tough to credit. Bowman was not a passive observer of his soybeans' multiplication; or put another way, the seeds he purchased (miraculous though they might be in other respects) did not spontaneously create eight successive soybean crops. As we have explained, Bowman devised and executed a novel way to harvest crops from Roundup Ready seeds without paying the usual premium. He purchased beans from a grain eleva-tor anticipating that many would be Roundup Ready; applied a glyphosate-based herbicide in a way that culled any plants without the patented trait; and saved beans from the rest for the next season. He then planted those Roundup Ready beans at a chosen time; tended and treated them, including by exploiting their patented glyphosate-resistance; and harvested many more seeds, which he either marketed or saved to begin the next cycle. In all this, the bean surely figured. But it was Bowman, and not the bean, who controlled the reproduction (unto the eighth generation) of Monsanto's patented invention.

Our holding today is limited—addressing the situation before us, rather than every one involving a self-replicating product. We recognize that such inventions are becoming ever more prevalent, complex, and diverse. In another case, the article's self-replication might occur outside the purchaser's control. Or it might be a necessary but incidental step in using the item for another purpose. We need not address here whether or how the doctrine of patent exhaustion would apply in such circumstances. In the case at hand, Bowman planted Monsanto's patented soybeans solely to make and market replicas of them, thus depriving the company of the reward patent law provides for the sale of each article. Patent exhaustion provides no haven for that conduct.

We accordingly *affirm* the judgment of the Court of Appeals for the Federal Circuit.

TRADEMARKS ARE ANOTHER kind of intellectual property. Trademark protection applies to market-related appearances of products that set them apart. These would include words, names, symbols, sounds and colors. As the USPTO indicates, these can include the roar of the MGM lion, the pink color of Owens-Corning insulation and the shape of the Coca-Cola bottle. Trademark protection can be ongoing; trademarks can be renewed as long as the mark is being used in business. The following case explores trademark and its increasing importance and expansion, particularly in the use of fashion and commerce.

Christian Louboutin S.A. v. Yves Saint Laurent, Inc.

696 F.3d 206 (2d Cir. 2012)

JOSÉ A. CABRANES, Circuit Judge:

This appeal arises out of an action for injunctive relief and enforcement of a trademark brought by Louboutin, together with the corporate entities that constitute his eponymous French fashion house, against YSL, a venerable French fashion institution. Louboutin is best known for his emphasis upon the otherwise-largely-ignored outsole of the shoe. Since their development in 1992, Louboutin's shoes have been characterized by their most striking feature: a bright, lacquered red outsole, which nearly always contrasts sharply with the color of the rest of the shoe.

Christian Louboutin introduced his signature footwear to the fashion market in 1992. Since then, his shoes have grown in popularity, appearing regularly on various celebrities and fashion icons. The District Court concluded, and YSL does not dispute, that "Louboutin [had] invested substantial amounts of capital building a reputation and good will, as well as promoting and protecting Louboutin's claim to exclusive ownership of the mark as its signature in women's high fashion footwear." The

District Court further found that Louboutin had succeeded in promoting his shoes "to the point where, in the high-stakes commercial markets and social circles in which these things matter a great deal, the red outsole became closely associated with Louboutin. Leading designers have said it, including YSL, however begrudgingly." As a result of Louboutin's marketing efforts, the District Court found, the "flash of a red sole" is today "instantly" recognizable, to "those in the know," as Louboutin's handiwork.

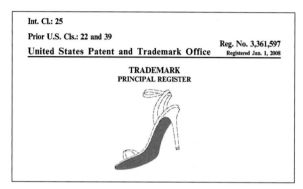

```
Int. Cl.: 25
Prior U.S. Cls.: 22 and 39
                                              Reg. No. 3,361,597
United States Patent and Trademark Office    Registered Jan. 1, 2008

                      TRADEMARK
                  PRINCIPAL REGISTER
```

On the strength of the fashion world's asserted recognition of the red sole, Louboutin on March 27, 2007 filed an application with the PTO to protect his mark (the "Red Sole Mark" or the "Mark"). The trademark was granted in January 2008, and stated: "The color(s) red is/are claimed as a feature of the mark. The mark consists of a lacquered red sole on footwear."

In 2011, YSL prepared to market a line of "monochrome" shoes in purple, green, yellow, and red. YSL shoes in the monochrome style feature the same color on the entire shoe, so that the red version is all red, including a red insole, heel, upper, and outsole. This was not the first time that YSL had designed a monochrome footwear line, or even a line of footwear with red soles; indeed, YSL maintains that since the 1970s it had sold such shoes in red and other colors.

In January 2011, Louboutin avers, his fashion house learned that YSL was marketing and selling a monochrome red shoe with a red sole. Louboutin requested the removal of the allegedly infringing shoes from the market, and Louboutin and YSL briefly entered into negotiations in order to avert litigation.

The negotiations having failed, Louboutin filed this action on April 7, 2011, asserting claims under the Lanham Act, 15 U.S.C. § 1051 *et seq.*, for (1) trademark infringement and counterfeiting, (2) false designation of origin and unfair competition, and (3) trademark dilution, as well as state law claims for (4) trademark infringement, (5) trademark dilution, (6) unfair competition, and (7) unlawful deceptive acts and practices. Louboutin also sought a preliminary injunction preventing YSL from marketing, during the pendency of the action, any shoes, including red monochrome shoes, bearing outsoles in a shade of red identical to the Red Sole Mark, or in any shade which so resembles the Red Sole Mark as to cause confusion among consumers.

* * *

The principal purpose of federal trademark law is to "secure the public's interest in protection against deceit as to the sources of its purchases, [and] the businessman's right to enjoy business earned through investment in the good will and reputation attached to a trade name." * * *

In accordance with these purposes of the Lanham Act, the law provides the owner of a mark with the "enforceable right to exclude others from using [the mark]."

Nevertheless, trademark law is *not* intended to "protect[ ] innovation by giving the innovator a *monopoly* " over a useful product feature. Such a monopoly is the realm of patent law or copyright law, which seek to encourage innovation, and not of trademark law, which seeks to preserve a "vigorously competitive market" for the benefit of consumers.

* * *

C. Single–Color Marks Today

The question of whether a color can be protected as a trademark or trade dress was finally resolved in 1995 by the Supreme Court's decision in *Qualitex*, which involved a claim for trade dress protection of the green-gold color of a dry cleaning press pad. * * * The Court held, among other things, that it could find no "principled objection to the use of color as a mark in the important 'functionality' doctrine of trademark law." It concluded that "color alone, *at least sometimes*, can meet the basic legal requirements for use as a trademark. It can act as a symbol that distinguishes a firm's goods and identifies their source, without serving any other significant function."

III. The "Functionality" Defense

* * *

As set forth below, the test for aesthetic functionality is threefold: At the start, we address the two prongs of the *Inwood* test, asking whether the design feature is either "essential to the use or purpose" or "affects the cost or quality" of the product at issue. Next, if necessary, we turn to a third prong, which is the competition inquiry set forth in *Qualitex*. In other words, if a design feature would, from a traditional utilitarian perspective, be considered "essential to the use or purpose" of the article, or to affect its cost or quality, then the design feature is functional under *Inwood* and our inquiry ends.[5] But if the design feature is not "functional" from a traditional perspective, it must still pass the fact-intensive *Qualitex* test and be shown not to have a significant effect on competition in order to receive trademark protection.

I. The Development of the Aesthetic Functionality Doctrine

* * *

Despite its apparent counterintuitiveness (how can the purely aesthetic be deemed functional, one might ask?), our Court has long accepted the doctrine of aesthetic functionality. We have rejected, however, the circular "important ingredient" test formulated by the *Pagliero* court, which inevitably penalized markholders for their

---

5   15. See, e.g., *Industria Arredamenti Fratelli Saporiti v. Charles Craig, Ltd.*, 725 F.2d 18, 19 (2d Cir.1984) (interlocking design of couch cushions was a visual "label" but served a utilitarian purpose by keeping cushions in place and was therefore functional).

success in promoting their product. Instead, we have concluded that "Lanham Act protection does not extend to configurations of ornamental features which would *significantly* limit the range of competitive designs available." Accordingly, we have held that the doctrine of aesthetic functionality bars protection of a mark that is "necessary to compete in the [relevant] market."

II. A Modern Formulation of the Aesthetic Functionality Doctrine

In 1995, the Supreme Court in *Qualitex* gave its imprimatur to the aesthetic functionality doctrine, holding that "[t]he ultimate test of aesthetic functionality ... is whether the recognition of trademark rights [in an aesthetic design feature] would significantly hinder competition." Six years later, reiterating its *Qualitex* analysis, the Supreme Court in *TrafFix* declared that where "[a]esthetic functionality [is] the central question," courts must "inquire" as to whether recognizing the trademark "would put competitors at a significant non-reputation-related disadvantage."

* * *

In short, a mark is aesthetically functional, and therefore ineligible for protection under the Lanham Act, where protection of the mark *significantly* undermines competitors' ability to compete in the relevant market. In making this determination, courts must carefully weigh "the competitive benefits of protecting the source-identifying aspects" of a mark against the "competitive costs of precluding competitors from using the feature."

Finally, we note that a product feature's successful source indication can sometimes be difficult to distinguish from the feature's aesthetic function, if any. Therefore, in determining whether a mark has an aesthetic function so as to preclude trademark protection, we take care to ensure that the mark's very success in denoting (and promoting) its source does not itself defeat the markholder's right to protect that mark.

Because aesthetic function and branding success can sometimes be difficult to distinguish, the aesthetic functionality analysis is highly fact-specific. In conducting this inquiry, courts must consider both the markholder's right to enjoy the benefits of its effort to distinguish its product and the public's right to the "vigorously competitive market [ ]" protected by the Lanham Act, which an overly broad trademark might hinder. In sum, courts must avoid jumping to the conclusion that an aesthetic feature is functional merely because it denotes the product's desirable source.

III. Aesthetic Functionality in the Fashion Industry

We now turn to the *per se* rule of functionality for color marks in the fashion industry adopted by the District Court—a rule that would effectively deny trademark protection to any deployment of a single color in an item of apparel. As noted above, the *Qualitex* Court expressly held that "sometimes [ ] a color will meet ordinary legal trademark requirements[, a]nd, when it does so, no special legal rule prevents color alone from serving as a trademark." In other words, the Supreme Court specifically forbade the implementation of a *per se* rule that would deny protection for the use of a single color as a trademark in a particular industrial context. *Qualitex* requires an individualized, fact-based inquiry into the nature of the trademark, and cannot be read to sanction an industry-based *per se* rule. The District Court created just such a rule, on the theory that "there is something unique about the fashion world that militates against extending trademark protection to a single color."

Even if *Qualitex* could be read to permit an industry-specific *per se* rule of functionality (a reading we think doubtful), such a rule would be neither necessary nor appropriate here. We readily acknowledge that the fashion industry, like other industries, has special concerns in the operation of trademark law; it has been argued forcefully that United States law does not protect fashion design adequately. Indeed, the case on appeal is particularly difficult precisely because, as the District Court well noted, in the fashion industry, color can serve as a tool in the palette of a designer, rather than as mere ornamentation.

Nevertheless, the functionality defense does not guarantee a competitor "the greatest range for [his] creative outlet," but only the ability to fairly compete within a given market. The purpose of the functionality defense "is to prevent advances in functional design from being *monopolized* by the owner of [the mark] ... in order to encourage competition and the broadest dissemination of useful design features."

In short, "[b]y focusing upon hindrances to legitimate competition, the [aesthetic] functionality test, carefully applied, can accommodate consumers' somewhat conflicting interests in being assured enough product differentiation to avoid confusion as to source and in being afforded the benefits of competition among producers."

IV. The Red Sole Mark

Having determined that no *per se* rule governs the protection of single-color marks in the fashion industry, any more than it can do so in any other industry, we turn our attention to the Red Sole Mark. As we have explained, Part II.A, *ante*, we analyze a trademark infringement claim in two stages, asking first whether the mark "merits protection" and, second, whether the allegedly infringing use of the mark (or a similar mark) is "likely to cause consumer confusion." The functionality defense (including the tripartite aesthetic functionality test) is an affirmative defense that we consider at the second stage of this analysis.

We have stated the basic rule that "[a] certificate of registration with the PTO is *prima facie* evidence that the mark is registered and valid (*i.e.*, protect[a]ble), that the registrant owns the mark, and that the registrant has the exclusive right to use the mark in commerce." As the District Court correctly noted, "Louboutin's certificate of registration of the Red Sole Mark gives rise to a statutory presumption that the mark is valid." But the District Court found, in effect, that YSL had rebutted that presumption by showing that the Red Sole Mark is ineligible for protection because a single color can never achieve trademark protection in the fashion industry. As explained above, that holding was error.

Although, as set forth below, we determine that the Mark as it currently stands is ineligible for protection insofar as it would preclude competitors' use of red outsoles in *all* situations, including the monochromatic use now before us, we conclude that the Mark has acquired secondary meaning—and thus the requisite "distinctness" to merit protection—when used as a red outsole *contrasting* with the remainder of the shoe. Because in this case we determine that the Red Sole Mark merits protection only as modified, and because YSL's use of a red outsole on monochromatic red shoes does not infringe on the Mark as modified, we need not, and do not, reach the issues of customer confusion and functionality at the second stage of the trademark infringement analysis described above.

A. Distinctiveness

We first address whether the Red Sole Mark "merits protection" as a distinctive mark. As discussed above, distinctiveness may be shown either by proof that the mark is itself inherently distinctive, or by showing that the mark has acquired, through use, secondary meaning in the public eye. For the reasons that follow, we hold that the Red Sole Mark has acquired limited secondary meaning as a distinctive symbol that identifies the Louboutin brand, and that it is therefore a valid and protectable mark as modified below.

Although a single color, standing alone, can almost never be inherently distinctive because it does not "almost automatically tell a customer that [it] refer[s] to a brand," a color as used here is certainly capable of acquiring secondary meaning. As the *Qualitex* Court put it,

> over time, customers may come to treat a particular color on a product or its packaging (say, *a color that in context seems unusual*, such as pink on a firm's insulating material or red on the head of a large industrial bolt) as signifying a brand. And, if so, that color would have come to identify and distinguish the goods—*i.e.*, "to indicate" their "source"—much in the way that descriptive words on a product ... can come to indicate a product's origin.

In the case of a single-color mark, therefore, distinctiveness must generally be proved by demonstrating that the mark has acquired secondary meaning.

We see no reason why a single-color mark in the specific context of the fashion industry could not acquire secondary meaning—and therefore serve as a brand or source identifier—if it is used so consistently and prominently by a particular designer that it becomes a symbol, "the primary significance" of which is "to identify the source of the product rather than the product itself."

"The crucial question in a case involving secondary meaning always is whether the public is moved in any degree to buy an article because of its source." "Factors that are relevant in determining secondary meaning include '(1) advertising expenditures, (2) consumer studies linking the mark to a source, (3) unsolicited media coverage of the product, (4) sales success, (5) attempts to plagiarize the mark, and,

(6) length and exclusivity of the mark's use.' " Whether a mark has acquired distinctiveness is "an inherently factual inquiry." Where, as here, the record contains sufficient undisputed facts to resolve the question of distinctiveness—not to speak of facts found by the District Court that are based upon evidence of record and not clearly erroneous—we may do so as a matter of law.

The record before the District Court included extensive evidence of Louboutin's advertising expenditures, media coverage, and sales success, demonstrating both that Louboutin has created a "symbol" within the meaning of *Qualitex*, and that the symbol has gained secondary meaning that causes it to be "uniquely" associated with the Louboutin brand. There is no dispute that Louboutin originated this particular commercial use of the lacquered red color over twenty years ago. As the District Court determined, in findings of fact that are supported by the record and not clearly erroneous, "Louboutin invested substantial amounts of capital building a reputation and good will, as well as promoting and protecting Louboutin's claim to exclusive ownership of the mark as its signature in women's high fashion footwear." And there is no dispute that Louboutin's efforts were successful "to the point where, in the high-stakes commercial markets and social circles in which these things matter a great deal, the red outsole became closely associated with Louboutin," and where unsolicited media attention to that red sole became rampant. Indeed, the Chief Executive Officer of YSL's parent corporation, François–Henri Pinault, himself acknowledged that, "[i]n the fashion or luxury world, it is absolutely clear that we recognize the notoriety of the distinctive signature constituted by the red sole of LOUBOUTIN models in contrast with the general presentation of the model, particularly its upper, and so for all shades of red."

In light of the evidence in the record, including extensive consumer surveys submitted by both parties during the preliminary injunction proceedings, and of the factual findings of the District Court, we think it plain that Louboutin's marketing efforts have created what the able district judge described as "a ... brand with worldwide recognition." By placing the color red "in [a] context [that] seems unusual" and deliberately tying that color to his product, Louboutin has created an identifying mark firmly associated with his brand which, "to those in the know," "instantly" denotes his shoes' source. These findings of fact by the District Court in addressing a motion for a preliminary injunction are not clearly erroneous. We hold that the lacquered red outsole, as applied to a shoe with an "upper" of a different color, has "come to identify and distinguish" the Louboutin brand and is therefore a distinctive symbol that qualifies for trademark protection.

We further hold that the record fails to demonstrate that the secondary meaning of the Red Sole Mark extends to uses in which the sole *does not* contrast with the upper—in other words, when a red sole is used on a monochromatic red shoe. As the District Court observed, "[w]hen Hollywood starlets cross red carpets and high fashion models strut down runways, and heads turn and eyes drop to the celebrities' feet, lacquered red outsoles on *high-heeled, black shoes* flaunt a glamorous statement that *pops out* at once." As clearly suggested by the District Court, it is the *contrast* between the sole and the upper that causes the sole to "pop," and to distinguish its creator.

The evidentiary record further demonstrates that the Louboutin mark is closely associated with contrast. For example, Pinault, the chief executive of YSL's parent company, wrote that the "distinctive signature" of the Mark is in its "contrast with the general presentation of the [shoe], particularly its upper." Of the hundreds of pictures of Louboutin shoes submitted to the District Court, only *four* were monochrome red. And Louboutin's own consumer surveys show that when consumers were shown the YSL monochrome red shoe, of those consumers who misidentified the pictured shoes as Louboutin-made, nearly every one cited the red *sole* of the shoe, rather than its general red color. We conclude, based upon the record before us, that Louboutin has not established secondary meaning in an application of a red sole to a red shoe, but *only* where the red sole contrasts with the "upper" of the shoe. The use of a red lacquer on the outsole of a red shoe of the same color is not a use of the Red Sole Mark.

Because we conclude that the secondary meaning of the mark held by Louboutin extends only to the use of a lacquered red outsole that contrasts with the adjoining portion of the shoe, we modify the Red Sole Mark, pursuant to Section 37 of the Lanham Act, insofar as it is sought to be applied to any shoe bearing the same color "upper" as the outsole. We therefore instruct the Director of the Patent and Trade Office to limit the registration of the Red Sole Mark to only those situations in which the red lacquered outsole contrasts in color with the adjoining "upper" of the shoe.

In sum, we hold that the Red Sole Mark is valid and enforceable as modified. This holding disposes of the Lanham Act claims brought by both Louboutin and YSL because the red sole on YSL's monochrome shoes is neither a use of, nor confusingly similar to, the Red Sole Mark. We therefore affirm the denial of the preliminary injunction insofar as Louboutin could not have shown a likelihood of success on the merits in the absence of an infringing use of the Red Sole Mark by YSL.

B. Likelihood of Confusion and Functionality

Having limited the Red Sole Mark as described above, and having established that the red sole used by YSL is not a use of the Red Sole Mark, it is axiomatic that we need not—and should not—address either the likelihood of consumer confusion or whether the modified Mark is functional.

Rescuecom Corp. v. Google, Inc.

562 F.3d 123 (2d Cir. 2009)

LEVAL, Circuit Judge:

BACKGROUND

As this appeal follows the grant of a motion to dismiss, we must take as true the facts alleged in the Complaint and draw all reasonable inferences in favor of Rescuecom. Rescuecom is a national computer service franchising company that offers on-site computer services and sales. Rescuecom conducts a substantial amount of business over the Internet and receives between 17,000 to 30,000 visitors to its website each month. It also advertises over the Internet, using many web-based services, including those offered by Google. Since 1998, "Rescuecom" has been a registered federal trademark, and there is no dispute as to its validity.

Google operates a popular Internet search engine, which users access by visiting *www.google.com*. Using Google's website, a person searching for the website of a particular entity in trade (or simply for information about it) can enter that entity's name or trademark into Google's search engine and launch a search. Google's proprietary system responds to such a search request in two ways. First, Google provides a list of links to websites, ordered in what Google deems to be of descending relevance to the user's search terms based on its proprietary algorithms. Google's search engine assists the public not only in obtaining information about a provider, but also in purchasing products and services. If a prospective purchaser, looking for goods or services of a particular provider, enters the provider's trademark as a search term on Google's website and clicks to activate a search, within seconds, the Google search engine will provide on the searcher's computer screen a link to the webpage maintained by that provider (as well as a host of other links to sites that Google's program determines to be relevant to the search term entered). By clicking on the link of the provider, the searcher will be directed to the provider's website, where the searcher can obtain information supplied by the provider about its products and services and can perhaps also make purchases from the provider by placing orders.

The second way Google responds to a search request is by showing context-based advertising. When a searcher uses Google's search engine by submitting a search term, Google may place advertisements on the user's screen. Google will do so if an advertiser, having determined that its ad is likely to be of interest to a searcher who enters the particular term, has purchased from Google the placement of its ad on the screen of the searcher who entered that search term. What Google places on the searcher's screen is more than simply an advertisement. It is also a link to the advertiser's website, so that in response to such an ad, if the searcher clicks on the link, he will open the advertiser's website, which offers not only additional information about the advertiser, but also perhaps the option to purchase the goods and services of the advertiser over the Internet. Google uses at least two programs to offer such context-based links: AdWords and Keyword Suggestion Tool.

AdWords is Google's program through which advertisers purchase terms (or keywords). When entered as a search term, the keyword triggers the appearance of the advertiser's ad and link. An advertiser's purchase of a particular term causes the advertiser's ad and link to be displayed on the user's screen whenever a searcher launches a Google search based on the purchased search term.[6] Advertisers pay Google based on the number of times Internet users "click" on the advertisement, so as to link to the advertiser's website. For example, using Google's AdWords, Company Y, a company engaged in the business of furnace repair, can cause Google to display its advertisement and link whenever a user of Google launches a search based on the search term, "furnace repair." Company Y can also cause its ad and link to appear whenever a user searches for the term "Company X," a competitor of Company Y in the furnace repair business. Thus, whenever a searcher interested in purchasing furnace repair services from Company X launches a search of the term X (Company X's trademark), an ad and link would appear on the searcher's screen, inviting the searcher to the furnace repair services of X's competitor, Company Y. And if the searcher clicked on Company Y's link, Company Y's website would open on the searcher's screen, and the searcher might be able to order or purchase Company Y's furnace repair services.

In addition to AdWords, Google also employs Keyword Suggestion Tool, a program that recommends keywords to advertisers to be purchased. The program is designed to improve the effectiveness of advertising by helping advertisers identify keywords related to their area of commerce, resulting in the placement of their ads before users who are likely to be responsive to it. Thus, continuing the example given above, if Company Y employed Google's Keyword Suggestion Tool, the Tool might suggest to Company Y that it purchase not only the term "furnace repair" but also the term "X," its competitor's brand name and trademark, so that Y's ad would appear on the screen of a searcher who searched Company X's trademark, seeking Company X's website.

Once an advertiser buys a particular keyword, Google links the keyword to that advertiser's advertisement. The advertisements consist of a combination of content and a link to the advertiser's webpage. Google displays these advertisements on the search result page either in the right margin or in a horizontal band immediately above the column of relevance-based search results. These advertisements are generally associated with a label, which says "sponsored link." Rescuecom alleges, however, that a user might easily be misled to believe that the advertisements which appear on the screen are in fact part of the relevance-based search result and that the appearance of a competitor's ad and link in response to a searcher's search for Rescuecom is likely to cause trademark confusion as to affiliation, origin, sponsorship, or approval of service. This can occur, according to the Complaint, because Google fails to label

---

6   Although we generally refer to a single advertiser, there is no limit on the number of advertisers who can purchase a particular keyword to trigger the appearance of their ads.

the ads in a manner which would clearly identify them as purchased ads rather than search results. The Complaint alleges that when the sponsored links appear in a horizontal bar at the top of the search results, they may appear to the searcher to be the first, and therefore the most relevant, entries responding to the search, as opposed to paid advertisements.

Google's objective in its AdWords and Keyword Suggestion Tool programs is to sell keywords to advertisers. Rescuecom alleges that Google makes 97% of its revenue from selling advertisements through its AdWords program. Google therefore has an economic incentive to increase the number of advertisements and links that appear for every term entered into its search engine.

Many of Rescuecom's competitors advertise on the Internet. Through its Keyword Suggestion Tool, Google has recommended the Rescuecom trademark to Rescuecom's competitors as a search term to be purchased. Rescuecom's competitors, some responding to Google's recommendation, have purchased Rescuecom's trademark as a keyword in Google's AdWords program, so that whenever a user launches a search for the term "Rescuecom," seeking to be connected to Rescuecom's website, the competitors' advertisement and link will appear on the searcher's screen. This practice allegedly allows Rescuecom's competitors to deceive and divert users searching for Rescuecom's website. According to Rescuecom's allegations, when a Google user launches a search for the term "Rescuecom" because the searcher wishes to purchase Rescuecom's services, links to websites of its competitors will appear on the searcher's screen in a manner likely to cause the searcher to believe mistakenly that a competitor's advertisement (and website link) is sponsored by, endorsed by, approved by, or affiliated with Rescuecom.

The District Court granted Google's 12(b)(6) motion and dismissed Rescuecom's claims. The court believed that our *1–800* decision compels the conclusion that Google's allegedly infringing activity does not involve use of Rescuecom's mark in commerce, which is an essential element of an action under the Lanham Act. The district court explained its decision saying that even if Google employed Rescuecom's mark in a manner likely to cause confusion or deceive searchers into believing that competitors are affiliated with Rescuecom and its mark, so that they believe the services of Rescuecom's competitors are those of Rescuecom, Google's actions are not a "use in commerce" under the Lanham Act because the competitor's advertisements triggered by Google's programs did not exhibit Rescuecom's trademark. The court rejected the argument that Google "used" Rescuecom's mark in recommending and selling it as a keyword to trigger competitor's advertisements because the court read *1–800* to compel the conclusion that this was an internal use and therefore cannot be a "use in commerce" under the Lanham Act.

DISCUSSION

* * *

I. Google's Use of Rescuecom's Mark Was a "Use in Commerce"

Our court ruled in *1–800* that a complaint fails to state a claim under the Lanham Act unless it alleges that the defendant has made "use in commerce" of the plaintiff's trademark as the term "use in commerce" is defined in 15 U.S.C. § 1127. The district court believed that this case was on all fours with *1–800*, and that its dismissal was required for the same reasons as given in *1–800*. We believe the cases are materially different. The allegations of Rescuecom's complaint adequately plead a use in commerce.

In *1–800*, the plaintiff alleged that the defendant infringed the plaintiff's trademark through its proprietary software, which the defendant freely distributed to computer users who would download and install the program on their computer. The program provided contextually relevant advertising to the user by generating pop-up advertisements to the user depending on the website or search term the user entered in his browser. For example, if a user typed "eye care" into his browser, the defendant's program would randomly display a pop-up advertisement of a company engaged in the field of eye care. Similarly, if the searcher launched a search for a particular company engaged in eye care, the defendant's program would display the pop-up ad of a company associated with eye care. The pop-up ad appeared in a separate browser window from the website the user accessed, and the defendant's brand was displayed in the window frame surrounding the ad, so that there was no confusion as to the nature of the pop-up as an advertisement, nor as to the fact that the defendant, not the trademark owner, was responsible for displaying the ad, in response to the particular term searched.

Sections 32 and 43 of the Act, which we also refer to by their codified designations, 15 U.S.C. §§ 1114 & 1125, *inter alia*, impose liability for unpermitted "use in commerce" of another's mark which is "likely to cause confusion, or to cause mistake, or to deceive," § 1114, "as to the affiliation ... or as to the origin, sponsorship or approval of his or her goods [or] services ... by another person." The *1–800* opinion looked to the definition of the term "use in commerce" provided in § 45 of the Act. That definition provides in part that "a mark shall be deemed to be in use in commerce ... (2) on services when it is used or displayed in the sale or advertising of services and the services are rendered in commerce." 15 U.S.C. § 1127. Our court found that the plaintiff failed to show that the defendant made a "use in commerce" of the plaintiff's mark, within that definition.

At the outset, we note two significant aspects of our holding in *1–800*, which distinguish it from the present case. A key element of our court's decision in *1–800* was that under the plaintiff's allegations, the defendant did not use, reproduce, or display the plaintiff's mark *at all*. The search term that was alleged to trigger the pop-up ad was the plaintiff's *website address*. *1–800* noted, notwithstanding the similarities between the website address and the mark, that the website address was not used or claimed by the plaintiff as a trademark. Thus, the transactions alleged to be infringing were not transactions involving use of the plaintiff's trademark. *1–800* suggested in dictum that is highly relevant to our case that had the defendant used the plaintiff's *trademark* as the trigger to pop-up an advertisement, such conduct might, depending on other elements, have been actionable.

Second, as an alternate basis for its decision, *1–800* explained why the defendant's program, which might randomly trigger pop-up advertisements upon a searcher's input of the plaintiff's website address, did not constitute a "use in commerce," as defined in § 1127. In explaining why the plaintiff's mark was not "used or displayed in the sale or advertising of services," *1–800* pointed out that, under the defendant's program, advertisers could not request or purchase keywords to trigger their ads. Even if an advertiser wanted to display its advertisement to a searcher using the plaintiff's trademark as a search term, the defendant's program did not offer this possibility. In fact, the defendant "did not disclose the proprietary contents of [its] directory to its advertising clients...." In addition to not selling trademarks of others to its customers to trigger these ads, the defendant did not "otherwise manipulate which category-related advertisement will pop up in response to any particular terms on the internal directory." The display of a particular advertisement was controlled by the category associated with the website or keyword, rather than the website or keyword itself. The defendant's program relied upon categorical associations such as "eye care" to select a pop-up ad randomly from a predefined list of ads appropriate to that category. To the extent that an advertisement for a competitor of the plaintiff was displayed when a user opened the plaintiff's website, the trigger to display the ad was not based on the defendant's sale or recommendation of a particular trademark.

The present case contrasts starkly with those important aspects of the *1–800* decision. First, in contrast to *1–800*, where we emphasized that the defendant made no use whatsoever of the plaintiff's trademark, here what Google is recommending and selling to its advertisers is Rescuecom's trademark. Second, in contrast with the facts of *1–800* where the defendant did not "use or display," much less sell, trademarks as search terms to its advertisers, here Google displays, offers, and sells Rescuecom's mark to Google's advertising customers when selling its advertising services. In addition, Google encourages the purchase of Rescuecom's mark through its Keyword Suggestion Tool. Google's utilization of Rescuecom's mark fits literally within the terms specified by 15 U.S.C. § 1127. According to the Complaint, Google uses and sells Rescuecom's mark "in the sale ... of [Google's advertising] services ... rendered in commerce."

Google, supported by amici, argues that *1–800* suggests that the inclusion of a trademark in an internal computer directory cannot constitute trademark use. Several district court decisions in this Circuit appear to have reached this conclusion. This over-reads the *1–800* decision. First, regardless of whether Google's use of Rescuecom's mark in its internal search algorithm could constitute an actionable trademark use, Google's recommendation and sale of Rescuecom's mark to its advertising customers are not internal uses. Furthermore, *1–800* did not imply that use of a trademark in a software program's internal directory precludes a finding of trademark use. Rather, influenced by the fact that the defendant was not using the plaintiff's trademark at all, much less using it as the basis of a commercial transaction, the court asserted that the particular use before it did not constitute a use in commerce. We did not imply in *1–800* that an alleged infringer's use of a trademark in an internal software program insulates the alleged infringer from a charge of infringement, no matter how likely the use is to cause confusion in the marketplace. If we were to adopt Google and its amici's argument, the operators of search engines would be free to use trademarks in ways designed to deceive and cause consumer confusion. This is surely neither within the intention nor the letter of the Lanham Act.

Google and its amici contend further that its use of the Rescuecom trademark is no different from that of a retail vendor who uses "product placement" to allow one vender to benefit from a competitors' name recognition. An example of product placement occurs when a store-brand generic product is placed next to a trademarked product to induce a customer who specifically sought out the trademarked product to consider the typically less expensive, generic brand as an alternative. Google's argument misses the point. From the fact that proper, non-deceptive product placement does not result in liability under the Lanham Act, it does not follow that the label "product placement" is a magic shield against liability, so that even a deceptive plan of product placement designed to confuse consumers would similarly escape liability. It is not by reason of absence of a use of a mark in commerce that benign product placement escapes liability; it escapes liability because it is a benign practice which does not cause a likelihood of consumer confusion. In contrast, if a retail seller were to be paid by an off-brand purveyor to arrange product display and delivery in such a way that customers seeking to purchase a famous brand would receive the off-brand, believing they had gotten the brand they were seeking, we see no reason to believe the practice would escape liability merely because it could claim the mantle of "product placement." The practices attributed to Google by the Complaint, which at this stage we must accept as true, are significantly different from benign product placement that does not violate the Act.

Unlike the practices discussed in *1–800*, the practices here attributed to Google by Rescuecom's complaint are that Google has made use in commerce of Rescuecom's mark. Needless to say, a defendant must do more than use another's mark in commerce to violate the Lanham Act. The gist of a Lanham Act violation is an unauthorized use, which "is likely to cause confusion, or to cause mistake, or to deceive as to the affiliation, ... or as to the origin, sponsorship, or approval of ... goods [or] services." We have no idea whether Rescuecom can prove that Google's use of Rescuecom's trademark in its AdWords program causes likelihood of confusion or mistake. Rescuecom has alleged that it does, in that would-be purchasers (or explorers) of its services who search for its website on Google are misleadingly directed to the ads and websites of its competitors in a manner which leads them to believe mistakenly that these ads or websites are sponsored by, or affiliated with Rescuecom. This is particularly so, Rescuecom alleges, when the advertiser's link appears in a horizontal band at the top of the list of search results in a manner which makes it appear to be the most relevant search result and not an advertisement. What Rescuecom alleges is that by the manner of Google's display of sponsored links of competing brands in response to a search for Rescuecom's brand name (which fails adequately to identify the sponsored link as an advertisement, rather than a relevant search result), Google creates a likelihood of consumer confusion as to trademarks. If the searcher sees a different brand name as the top entry in response to the search for "Rescuecom," the searcher is likely to believe mistakenly that the different name which appears is affiliated with the brand name sought in the search and will not suspect, because the fact is not adequately signaled by Google's presentation, that this is not the most relevant response to the search. Whether Google's actual practice is in fact benign or confusing is not for us to judge at this time. We consider at the 12(b)(6) stage only what is alleged in the Complaint.

We conclude that the district court was mistaken in believing that our precedent in 1–800 requires dismissal.

CONCLUSION

The judgment of the district court is vacated and the case is remanded for further proceedings.

THIS BRIEF TOUR OF INTELLECTUAL PROPERTY only touches the surface of the issues currently in play in business and in the courts. This is an exploding area of the law and business pertaining to online navigating tools, search engines, links, frames, and crawlers. The topic of posting and using material online raises issues beyond the *Napster* case about using and protecting copyright material; the Digital Millennium Copyright Act and what rights may be protected. How does one protect key elements of web side such as online trademark issues, domain name registration, and the protection of online content? How do parents interact with the Internet with respect to their children? Other issues arise from conducting business online such as trade secrets, courts obtaining personal jurisdiction of individuals, IP issues arising from email, and the law of virtual property. It is hard to imagine a more vibrant area of the law today.

NOTES AND COMMENTS

1. THE LAW HAS ALWAYS FACED the issue of keeping up with technological developments, especially as they pertain to commerce. As noted in the chapter on common law, the English kings established new court venues to both enhance commercial development and to acquire more power. Intellectual Property stands as a current incarnation of a technological explosion with business applications and it is worth keeping abreast of how the law is changing and what forms of dispute resolution arise. A web source such as *http://www.ip-watch.org* will help you stay current with intellectual property developments from around the globe. Because IP law is "hot," one can also find a good deal of information on the websites of law firms.

2. SECURING INTELLECTUAL PROPERTY protection certainly is valuable, but with it comes responsibilities to protect it. This is not a general statement about ethical duties, but one of protecting one's own legal assets. Especially with respect to trademark and patent protection, the IP owner must be on the outlook for potential infringements that undermine the value of the intellectual property, but also even the legal claim itself. The principles of adverse possession from the previous chapter do not apply directly to IP issues, but they do caution an IP owner that the use of property makes a difference to the courts in determining who has superior rights.

3. SOME BELIEVE THAT IP PROTECTION has gone too far. Some businesses patent business processes that, in the past, would have had nothing particularly unique to them. But because they are modulated through a computer interface, they gain patent law protection. The publisher of this textbook, for example, holds a patent on a business process that ranks attorneys. Anyone, of course, can rank anything one wants, but because of a specified process, manipulated through computer software, West Academic Publishing has a protectable patent. Do you think this is a good thing for the law and for business or do you think examples like this pose problems?

CONTRACTS: COMMON LAW FUNDAMENTALS AND CONCEPTS

EXCHANGE IS FUNDAMENTAL to human society or, for that matter, life itself. The tiniest of plants and animals exchange air, minerals, and water. It should not be surprising then, that human beings extend this naturalistic trait and

extend it socially by exchanging goods and services to meet their wants and needs. Contracts become essential for such social exchanges. For capitalistic societies, the freedom of people to create agreements to reliably facilitate exchange has given rise to a rich, complex body of contract law. In this chapter you will see general concepts and classifications, learn to understand four core elements of contracts, and examine special topics, such as issues concerning written agreements and remedies.

■ *MARRIAGE À-LA-MODE:*

THE MARRIAGE CONTRACT,

William Hogarth (1697–1764)

I. General Concepts and Classifications of Contracts

THERE ARE SEVERAL WAYS to isolate the steps necessary to create a valid contract. For purposes of this book, we look at four:

1. Two Parties Who Have Capacity

2. A Meeting of the Minds

3. Providing Legal Consideration

4. That Does Not Violate Law or Public Policy

As with most areas of the law, there are variations and exceptions to each of these categories. There are also additional provisions that appear. For example, one may have a valid contract—that is, an agreement that meets all four of the above requirements—but the agreement is not enforceable. That may be because of the Statute of Frauds. And so, some commentators will add the requirement that the agreement be in writing as a fifth element of contracts. Sometimes the level of contingency will also be an element. Is there a condition precedent necessary to trigger an obligation to perform, a condition subsequent, or simultaneously occurring conditions?

Both Statute of Frauds and contract contingencies will be discussed in this chapter, but the above four categories adequately handle most contractual situations and provide a straightforward analytical template by which one can determine whether or not a valid, binding contract exists.

Commentators will also group contracts in additional ways (while maintaining the four elements described above). For example, contracts can be described as executed vs. executory, with the latter being a contract containing promises to do something in the future, while the former describes contracts that have already been performed.

Contracts may also be analyzed on the basis of common law rules that apply to all contracts, as well as sales contracts, which apply to commercial transactions. Business people need to be aware of both because some common law contracts also apply to commercial transactions and because the common law principles form the foundational basis for understanding the commercial examples as well. This chapter will look at the foundational common law principles, whereas the following chapter will look at the Uniform Commercial Code, which covers sales contracts, in more detail.

Contracts can also be analyzed in terms of whether they are explicit or implicit, and that difference will help us to understand the first concept of the parties to the contract.

It is worth noting that treatises on contracts, particularly the Second Restatement of Contracts, are often invoked by courts to explain or add support to their legal reasoning. The Restatement, as it is informally referred to, appears throughout contract law, and we will refer to the relevant provisions when discussing various aspects of contract formation and breach. It is important to keep in mind that the last entire Restatement, published in 1981, is supplemented by other materials that deal with areas related to the types contracts we will discuss such as software contracts and employment law. Finally, the Restatement is what it purports to be, a restatement of contract law, meaning it is not binding upon the courts. All references to the Restatement come from Steven Burton and Melvin Eisenberg, ed.s, *Contract Law: Selected Source Materials Annotated* (2011) 149-299.

A. PARTIES TO THE CONTRACT WITH CAPACITY

In many ways the idea that there can be only one party to a contract defies logic. Unless one is utilizing some psychological issues and making contracts with oneself—a New Year's Resolution perhaps—there will always be two or more parties to a contract in some shape or form. The bigger question is whether each party has the capacity to enter into a contract. Because the ability to contract is a linchpin of free market economics, ascertaining capacity is crucial. One of the moral justifications for the free market is that it allows people to freely pursue their interests, including in business. The requirements of a valid, enforceable contract are meant for the institution of contracts to have enough independent fairness so as to let people contract freely for the kinds of business transactions they wish to carry out free from government intervention. If one of the elements of contracts is violated, governmental dispute resolution (i.e. the courts) is available to enforce a contract or to provide remedies, but otherwise, contract is about two or more parties willingly doing business with each other.

■ PUBLICITY PHOTO FROM THE 1930s OF CHILD ACTRESS SHIRLEY TEMPLE SIGNING A HOLLYWOOD FILM CONTRACT.

Image: Corbis

Essential to independent, procedural fairness of contracts is making sure that each party understands what he is doing. Does he understand the contract and its terms? Can he determine the risk he is undertaking? If he doesn't, then there is concern that the person will be taken advantage of and the contract will be unfair.

Courts have created categories to determine the whether there are internal or external impediments to capacity.

I. Internal Impediments to Capacity

An internal impediment to capacity refers to something within the make-up of the individual that prevents her from being able to understand the contracts she might otherwise be able to enter into. There are three major examples. The first is related to a person's age, the second concerns whether they have a mental disability, and the third relates to a temporary impairment, such as being under the influence of alcohol.

a. Internal Impediment to Capacity Due to Age. In most instances, an individual must be 18 years of age to have the capacity to enter into contracts. If a person is under the age of 18 and does enter into a contract, the contract is "voidable." This means that the "child" (actually, the parents or guardians of the child) may cancel the contract.

Three issues arise in these cases: first, who is responsible for determining if the "child" is 18 years of age or not; second, how does a voiding of the contract actually happen; and third, if the minor has accepted some benefits from the contract, how are they handled when the contract is voided?

The following two cases illustrate these points.

Wadge v. Kittleson

12 N.D. 548 (North Dakota 1903)

YOUNG, C. J.

Plaintiff sues upon a promissory note for $225 executed and delivered by the defendant on April 13, 1901, and by its terms due on October 1st thereafter. The defendant, in his answer, admitted the execution of the note, but denied that he is indebted thereon, and alleged as a defense that on the date of the execution of the note he was a minor; that he did not reach his majority until May 12, 1901; that the note was given for a team of horses purchased by him from the plaintiff, and for no other consideration; that on the 4th day of February, 1902, and within one year after reaching his majority, he restored the team to the plaintiff, and rescinded the purchase, and demanded a return of his note. The case was tried to a jury, and a verdict was returned for the plaintiff for the full amount of the note, with interest. Defendant moved for a new trial [...]. This appeal is from the order denying the motion for new trial.

* * *

It is entirely clear, under section 2703, that the contract of a minor who is over 18 years of age is not void, but merely voidable—that is, it is enforceable unless disaffirmed within the period and in the manner provided by the statute; and, further, that his liability rests upon his contract, and not upon a *quantum meruit*. The action was properly brought upon the note.

The evidence wholly fails to show a disaffirmance of the contract. On the contrary, it shows a complete ratification by the defendant after attaining his majority. It appears that when the defendant purchased the team he lacked but 29 days of his majority; that he was the owner of 160 acres of land, which he was then farming, and that he also farmed 480 acres of other land, which he had rented; that after the purchase of the team he used it in plowing his land, harvesting and threshing his crop, and marketing his grain, and for general farming purposes. On two different occasions he promised the plaintiff to pay the note—once in August, and again in

November. On February 4th, thereafter he delivered the team at a livery barn, and served notice on plaintiff that he had disaffirmed the contract upon the ground that he was a minor when he made the purchase. There is no complaint that the team was not in good condition when purchased, or that the sale was in any respect unfair. When the defendant attempted to disaffirm his contract and return the team, one of the horses was practically worthless, and the other was worth not to exceed $30. He retained possession of the team and used it for almost nine months after reaching his majority. The worthless condition of the team was due to his use of the same, and to his abuse and neglect. Upon this state of facts, we are of opinion that the defendant's attempted disaffirmance was without legal effect. The first reason for this conclusion is that after reaching his majority he unequivocally ratified the contract. When he purchased the team he was over 18 years of age. His contract, therefore, under the statute, was not void, but, as we have seen, was voidable at his option— that is, it was enforceable until avoided by a disaffirmance; and it could be disaffirmed only in the manner provided by the statute. He had the right of election for one year after reaching his majority to affirm or disaffirm. He elected to affirm. This is evidenced by nine months' continuous use of the property, and by his promises to pay the note. By affirm-ing the contract after reaching his majority, he lost the right to thereafter disaffirm it. A minor, after reaching his majority, has full capacity to choose for himself, and may, within the statutory period, make his election; but he cannot affirm and thereafter disaffirm his voidable contracts. He is bound by his ratification. Ratifi-cation, when once made, creates no new contract, but merely removes the objection to the voidable contract.

> "A MINOR, after reaching his majority, has full capacity to choose for himself, and may, within the statutory period, make his election; but he cannot affirm and thereafter disaffirm his voidable contracts."

* * *

In this case the retention of the property and its use by the defendant, including his promises to pay the note, all occurring after he reached his majority, constituted a complete ratification of the contract.

* * *

Finding no error in the record, the order appealed from will be *affirmed*. All concur.

———————

Halbman v. Lemke

99 Wis.2d 241 (Supreme Ct. of Wisconsin 1980)

CALLOW, Justice.

On this review we must decide whether a minor who disaffirms a contract for the purchase of a vehicle which is not a necessity must make restitution to the vendor for damage sustained by the vehicle prior to the time the contract was disaffirmed. The court of appeals affirmed the judgment in part, reversed in part, and remanded the cause to the circuit court [...].

This matter was before the trial court upon stipulated facts. On or about July 13, 1973, James Halbman, Jr. (Halbman), a minor, entered into an agreement with Michael Lemke (Lemke) whereby Lemke agreed to sell Halbman a 1968 Oldsmobile for the sum of $1,250. Lemke was the manager of L & M Standard Station in Greenfield, Wisconsin, and Halbman was an employee at L & M. At the time the agreement was made Halbman paid Lemke $1,000 cash and took possession of the car. Arrangements were made for Halbman to pay $25 per week until the balance was paid, at which time title would be transferred. About five weeks after the purchase agreement, and after Halbman had paid a total of $1,100 of the purchase price, a connecting rod on the vehicle's engine broke. Lemke, while denying any obligation, offered to assist Halbman in installing a used engine in the vehicle if Halbman, at his expense, could secure one. Halbman declined the offer and in September took the vehicle to a garage where it was repaired at a cost of $637.40. Halbman did not pay the repair bill.

In October of 1973 Lemke endorsed the vehicle's title over to Halbman, although the full purchase price had not been paid by Halbman, in an effort to avoid any liability for the operation, maintenance, or use of the vehicle. On October 15, 1973, Halbman returned the title to Lemke by letter which disaffirmed the purchase contract and demanded the return of all money theretofore paid by Halbman. Lemke did not return the money paid by Halbman.

The repair bill remained unpaid, and the vehicle remained in the garage where the repairs had been made. In the spring of 1974, in satisfaction of a garageman's lien for the outstanding amount, the garage elected to remove the vehicle's engine and transmission and then towed the vehicle to the residence of James Halbman, Sr., the father of the plaintiff minor. Lemke was asked several times to remove the vehicle from the senior Halbman's home, but he declined to do so, claiming he was under no legal obligation to remove it. During the period when the vehicle was at the garage and then subsequently at the home of the plaintiff's father, it was subjected to vandalism, making it unsalvageable.

Halbman initiated this action seeking the return of the $1,100 he had paid toward the purchase of the vehicle, and Lemke counterclaimed for $150, the amount still owing on the contract. Based upon the uncontroverted facts, the trial court granted judgment in favor of Halbman, concluding that when a minor disaffirms a contract for the purchase of an item, he need only offer to return the property remaining in his hands without making restitution for any use or depreciation. In the order granting judgment, the trial court also allowed interest to the plaintiff dating from the disaffirmance of the contract. On postjudgment motions, the court amended its order for judgment to allow interest to the plaintiff from the date of the original order for judgment, July 26, 1978.

...

II.

The sole issue before us is whether a minor, having disaffirmed a contract for the purchase of an item which is not a necessity and having tendered the property back to the vendor, must make restitution to the vendor for damage to the property prior to the disaffirmance. Lemke argues that he should be entitled to recover for the damage to the vehicle up to the time of disaffirmance, which he claims equals the amount of the repair bill.

Neither party challenges the absolute right of a minor to disaffirm a contract for the purchase of items which are not necessities. That right, variously known as the doctrine of incapacity or the "infancy doctrine," is one of the oldest and most venerable of our common law traditions. Although the origins of the doctrine are somewhat obscure, it is generally recognized that its purpose is the protection of minors from foolishly squandering their wealth through improvident contracts with crafty adults who would take advantage of them in the marketplace. Thus it is settled law in this state that a contract of a minor for items which are not necessities is void or voidable at the minor's option.

Once there has been a disaffirmance, however, as in this case between a minor vendee and an adult vendor, unresolved problems arise regarding the rights and responsibilities of the parties relative to the disposition of the consideration exchanged on the contract. As a general rule a minor who disaffirms a contract is entitled to recover all consideration he has conferred incident to the transaction. In return the minor is expected to restore as much of the consideration as, at the time of disaffirmance, remains in the minor's possession. The minor's right to disaffirm is not contingent upon the return of the property, however, as disaffirmance is permitted even where such return cannot be made.

The return of property remaining in the hands of the minor is not the issue presented here. In this case we have a situation where the property cannot be returned to the vendor in its entirety because it has been damaged and therefore diminished in value, and the vendor seeks to recover the depreciation. Although this court has been cognizant of this issue on previous occasions, we have not heretofore resolved it.

> "ALTHOUGH THE ORIGINS of the doctrine are somewhat obscure, it is generally recognized that its purpose is the protection of minors from foolishly squandering their wealth through improvident contracts with crafty adults who would take advantage of them in the marketplace."

* * *

Here Lemke seeks restitution of the value of the depreciation by virtue of the damage to the vehicle prior to disaffirmance. Such a recovery would require Halbman to return more than that remaining in his possession. It seeks compensatory value for that which he cannot return. Where there is misrepresentation by a minor or willful destruction of property, the vendor may be able to recover damages in tort. But absent these factors, as in the present case, we believe that to require a disaffirming minor to make restitution for diminished value is, in effect, to bind the minor to a part of the obligation which by law he is privileged to avoid.

* * *

Recently the Illinois Court of Appeals came to the same conclusion. In *Weisbrook v. Clyde C. Netzley, Inc.*, 58 Ill.App.3d 862 (1978), a minor sought to disaffirm a contract for the purchase of a vehicle which developed engine trouble after its purchase. In the minor's action the dealer counterclaimed for restitution for use and depreciation. The court affirmed judgment for the minor and, with respect to the dealer's claim for restitution, stated:

> "In the present case, of course, the minor plaintiff never misrepresented his age and, in fact, informed defendant that he was 17 years old. Nor did plaintiff represent to defendant that his father was to be the owner or have any interest in the automobile. There is no evidence in the present case that plaintiff at the time of entering the contract with defendant intended anything more than to enjoy his new automobile. He borrowed the total purchase price and paid it to defendant carrying out the transaction fully at the time of taking delivery of the vehicle. Plaintiff sought to disaffirm the contract and the return of the purchase price only when defendant declined to make repairs to it. In these circumstances we believe the weight of authority would permit the minor plaintiff to disaffirm the voidable contract and that defendant-vendor would not be entitled to recoup any damages which he believes he suffered as a result thereof."

We believe this result is consistent with the purpose of the infancy doctrine.

The decision of the court of appeals is *affirmed*.

SECTIONS 12 AND 14 of the Restatement explain who has the capacity to contract and the effect of the infancy doctrine on the capacity to contract:

§ 12: Capacity to Contract

1.   No one can be bound by contract who has not legal capacity to incur at least voidable contractual duties. Capacity to contract may be partial and its existence in respect to a particular transaction may depend upon the nature of the transaction or upon other circumstances.

2.   A natural person who manifests asset to a transaction has full legal capacity to incur contractual duties thereby unless he is

   a. Under guardianship, or

   b. An infant, or

   c. Mentally ill or defective, or

   d. Intoxicated.

§14: Infants

Unless a statute provides otherwise, a natural person has the capacity to incur only voidable contractual duties until the beginning of the day before the person's eighteenth birthday.

Legislatures' abilities to circumvent the incapacity requirement are especially useful in professions that often involve minors, such as film and television acting. California and New York have both passed laws that make entertainment contracts enforceable if a minor appears before a judge and the judge determines that the minor is capable of understanding and fulfilling his obligations. Upon breach, then, the minor is liable under the contract and cannot attempt to void the agreement by pleading incapacity.[1]

b. Internal Impediment to Capacity Due to Mental Disability. A second kind of internal impediment is due to a mental disability. Depending on whether or not a court has adjudicated a person to have a mental disability that impairs her decision making, a contract may be either void or voidable.

If a Court has adjudicated a person as not having the capacity to handle her own contracts, then any contract the person enters into is void. Instead, her court-appointed guardian or someone who has an approved power of attorney should handle contacts for the person with the impairment. While this rule makes sense insofar as it protects someone who has the disability, it also places a high duty on anyone the person interacts with to take steps to assure that any dealing is with the person's guardian.

---

1   Ethan Bordman, "Lights, Camera, Contract!" 91-Sep. Mich. B.J. 27 (2012). See also, *In Re Applications of Atlantic Recording Corp.*, 192 Misc.2d 622 (2002) (Court, applying the Arts and Cultural Affairs Law § 35.03 2.e., prohibited members of the band Dream Street from voiding a judicially-approved contract in an attempt to keep and perform together under the group's name.).

Some individuals have a degree of incapacity, but not so much so that they require a court proceeding to be declared incapacitated due to mental disease or defect. This could happen in several different ways. Perhaps the most common is when the person and/or family members realize that there is a disability and so simply act for the person either informally (i.e. making sure someone is with the person with the disability at any time when the person is making any kind of serious contract) or formally if the person executes a power-of-attorney.

Powers of attorney authorize and empower another individual to make decisions on behalf of someone else. One does not have to have a disability to have a power of attorney. Married couples often have the power to act on the other's behalf. Advance directives for health care purposes are also examples of a power of attorney.

A common use of a power of attorney that touches upon potential disability issues is when an elderly person executes one to authorize an adult child to act on the elderly person's behalf. That elderly person may know that, as they age, there may come a time when she is no longer able to make decisions for herself and so, while she retains capacity to make contracts (such as a power of attorney itself), she authorizes in advance someone who can act for her.

Two provisions of the Restatement deal with guardianship and mental illness or defect, §§ 13 and 15.

§ 13: Persons Affected by Guardianship

> A person has no capacity to incur contractual duties if his property is under guardianship by reason of an adjudication or mental illness or defect.

§15: Mental Illness or Defect

> 1. A person incurs only voidable contractual duties by entering into a transaction if by reason of a mental illness or defect
>
>> a. He is unable to understand in a reasonable manner the nature and consequences of the transaction, or
>>
>> b. He is unable to act in a reasonable manner in relation to the transaction and the other party has reason to know of his condition.
>
> 2. Where the contract is made on fair terms and the other party is without knowledge of the mental illness or defect, the power of avoidance under Subsection 1. terminates to the extent that the contract has been so performed in whole or in part or the circumstances have so changed that avoidance would be unjust. In such a case a court may rant relief as justice requires.

In cases where a person has not been adjudicated insane, the rules of capacity revert to those applying to age; that is, they are voidable rather than void.

Lloyd v. Jordan

544 So.2d 957 (Alabama 1989)

ADAMS, Justice.

Olivia Lloyd, the widow of George Loring Lloyd, appeals from the probate court's judgment establishing Betty Lou Jordan and Marion F. Pitts as the co-beneficiaries of an annuity purchased by George Loring Lloyd, who allegedly executed a change of beneficiary form before his death naming Olivia Lloyd, not Jordan and Pitts, as the beneficiary of the annuity.

The record reflects that George Lloyd purchased the annuity from the Executive Life Insurance Company of Beverly Hills, California, in September 1983 and named his daughters by a previous marriage, Jordan and Pitts, as co-beneficiaries. George Lloyd also executed a will in June 1985 that devised all of his property to Jordan and Pitts and made no provision for Olivia Lloyd. It appears that although they had divorced after the execution of the will, George Lloyd and Olivia Lloyd remarried in August 1987. Testimony from George Lloyd's physician, however, indicated that Lloyd was showing signs of mental instability and chronic dementia related to hypoxemia in April 1987, and, in fact, he was declared *non compos mentis* in September 1987.

In August 1987, Olivia Lloyd obtained a change of beneficiary form from Executive Life, and George Lloyd allegedly executed the form to change the beneficiary of the annuity to Olivia Lloyd. We note that this change of beneficiary form does not appear in the record. After George Lloyd's death, Jordan and Pitts petitioned the probate court to enter an order designating them as the proper beneficiaries of the annuity on grounds that Lloyd was mentally incompetent and lacked capacity to execute the change of beneficiary form. The issue for our review is whether the probate court erred in its order that Jordan and Pitts be designated beneficiaries of the annuity. The court heard *ore tenus* testimony and, therefore, its judgment will not be disturbed unless it is unsupported by the evidence; this Court "will indulge all favorable presumptions to sustain that court's conclusion, and it will be disturbed on appeal only if shown to be plainly erroneous or manifestly unjust."

Contracts of insane persons are absolutely void and a contract executed before the maker's adjudication of insanity or appointment of a guardian is suspect when it appears that apparent consent to the contract may have been unreal because of mental incapacity:

> "It is essential to the validity of a contract that the parties thereto possess not only the legal status affording capacity to contract, ... but also the mental competence affording capacity to consent. The rule which has been said to be well stated in Corpus Juris Secundum is that to make a valid contract, each party must be of sufficient mental capacity to appreciate the effect of what he is doing, and must also be able to exercise his will with reference thereto. A court of equity guards with jealous

care all contracts with persons of unsound mind. In this connection, it has been said that 'insanity' and 'incompetence' are words of vague and varying import.

"There is no contract where one of the parties was, by reason of physical debility, age, mental aberration, or otherwise, incapable of understanding and appreciating the nature, force, and effect of the agreement he is alleged to have made, as where he was unable to do so because insane, or mentally infirm, or because of incapacity resulting from lunacy, idiocy, senile dementia or imbecility, or any other defect or disease of the mind, whatever the cause, or because suffering from a degree of intoxication precluding rational thought.... However, mere mental weakness falling short of incapacity to appreciate the business in hand will not invalidate a contract, nor will mere mental weakness or unsoundness to some degree, in the absence of fraud or undue influence.

"Physical condition not adversely affecting mental competence is immaterial; and neither age, sickness, extreme distress, nor debility of body will affect the capacity to make a contract if sufficient intelligence remains to understand the transaction." 17 C.J.S. *Contracts* § 1331., at 855-57 (1963).

We recognize, however, that a person's contract will not necessarily be invalidated because he was aged, mentally weak, and feeble in mind; or suffered from loss of memory, senile dementia, fatigue, or ill health.

"Where, however, mental weakness or incapacity is accompanied by other inequitable incidents, it may afford ground for invalidation of the contract, as where, in addition to mental weakness or incapacity, it further appears that there was inadequacy of consideration or a confidential relationship, or fraud, duress, undue influence, imposition, concealment, misrepresentation, overreaching, overexercise of authority, ignorance and want of advice, or even unfairness; mental weakness may render a person more susceptible to these factors." 17 C.J.S. *Contracts* § 1331., at 858-59 (1963).

Consequently, a contract cannot be avoided on ground of mental incapacity or weakness unless it is shown that the incapacity was of such a character that, at the time of execution, "the person had no reasonable perception or understanding of the nature and terms of the contract" or the incapacity was accompanied by, inter alia, undue influence.

Testimony at the trial from George Lloyd's physician indicated that in April 1987, before executing the change of beneficiary form, he was suffering from mental instability and the onset of chronic dementia (mental deterioration or senility). Olivia Lloyd and George Lloyd remarried in August 1987, and, shortly thereafter, Olivia Lloyd obtained the change of beneficiary form for George Lloyd to sign.

We note that Olivia Lloyd testified that she "couldn't say" that George Lloyd "knew what he was doing" on the day he signed the form; and George Lloyd's mental condition was apparently deteriorating to the extent that a guardian was appointed at the time he was declared non compos mentis one month after the execution of the form.

Therefore, we believe that sufficient evidence existed to support the trial court's finding that George Lloyd was incapable of understanding and appreciating the nature and effect of the change of beneficiary form that he signed. Thus, its order that Jordan and Pitts be renamed as beneficiaries of the annuity is not plainly erroneous or manifestly unjust, and it is due to be affirmed.

AFFIRMED.

---

c. Hybrid: Altered Capacity to Contract. A third kind of impediment to capacity stands between internal and external impediments. What if a person under the influence of a prescribed drug makes a contract? The person may be someone who has full capacity to make decisions, but under the influence of given medications for an injury, condition, or surgery, the person no longer retains that capacity. The impediment is partly external—the medication—and partly internal. The following case illustrates this point.

Sparrow v. Demonico

461 Mass. 322 (Massachusetts 2012)

DUFFLY, J.

A family dispute over ownership of what had been the family home in Woburn prompted Frances M. Sparrow to file a complaint in the Superior Court against her sister, Susan A. Demonico, and Susan's husband, David D. Demonico. Prior to trial, the parties resolved their differences by a settlement agreement reached during voluntary mediation.

* * *

We conclude that our evolving standard of contractual incapacity does not in all cases require proof that a party's claimed mental illness or defect was of some significant duration or that it is permanent, progressive, or degenerative; but, without medical evidence or expert testimony that the mental condition interfered with the party's understanding of the transaction, or her ability to act reasonably in relation to it, the evidence will not be sufficient to support a conclusion of incapacity. Because the evidence was insufficient to support a determination of incapacity in this case, we vacate the motion judge's order and remand for entry of an order enforcing the settlement agreement.

BACKGROUND

Sparrow's complaint, filed initially in July, 2003, and later amended, alleged that Sparrow was entitled to a one-half interest in the Woburn property, consistent with the wishes of her (and Susan's) now-deceased mother, under theories of constructive and resulting trusts. Susan, who resided in the Woburn property at the time of the mediation, and David, who had been separated from Susan for several years and was no longer residing with her, asserted that they were the sole owners of the property, as reflected in a deed, and denied that Sparrow had any interest in it.

* * *

On the date of the scheduled mediation, Susan drove from her home to David's residence. From there, David drove them to the location of the mediation session because, in David's view, Susan was not capable of driving to the mediation. The mediation began at approximately 9 A.M. and ended at 3 P.M. The judge, crediting David's testimony, found:

> "Susan was having a breakdown that day, according to David, and was slurring her words, although she had not had any alcoholic beverages on that day. She became less coherent throughout the day, was crying and out of control.... They left the mediation before it was over as Susan could not handle it."

The judge noted Susan's testimony that she had been taking a medication, Zoloft, prior to the mediation, but that she had stopped taking the medication at some point before the mediation, and that she cried much of the day; he specifically credited Susan's testimony that she "was out of control emotionally during the mediation" and found also that "she was not thinking rationally" on that day.

As noted, both sides were represented by counsel throughout the mediation. At some point before they departed from the mediation session, the Demonicos authorized their attorney to execute a settlement agreement on their behalf. According to the terms of a written agreement titled, "Memorandum of Settlement," which was signed by Sparrow, her attorney, and the Demonicos's attorney, and witnessed by the mediator, the Demonicos agreed to pay Sparrow "the settlement amount of $100,000" from the proceeds of the sale of the property, which would occur "as soon as practicable," and in any event within a specified timeframe. The agreement also set forth other affirmative requirements regarding the marketing and sale of the property.

DISCUSSION

A settlement agreement is a contract and its enforceability is determined by applying general contract law. It has been long established that a contract is voidable by a person who, due to mental illness or defect, lacked the capacity to contract at the time of entering into the agreement. The burden is on the party seeking to void the contract to establish that the person was incapacitated at the time of the transaction.

A. Standard For Determining Contractual Incapacity.

As Justice Holmes observed, it is a question of fact whether a person was competent to enter into a transaction—that is, whether the person suffered from "insanity" or "was of unsound mind, and incapable of understanding and deciding upon the terms of the contract." In *Reed v. Mattapan Deposit & Trust Co.*, 198 Mass. 306, 314 (1908), we described this inquiry as the "true test" of mental incapacity:

> "IT HAS BEEN LONG established that a contract is voidable by a person who, due to mental illness or defect, lacked the capacity to contract at the time of entering into the agreement.

> "But while great mental weakness of the individual may exist without being accompanied by an entire loss of reason, and mental incapacity in one case is not necessarily so in another, in such an inquiry the true test is, was the party whose contract it is sought to avoid in such a state of insanity at the time as to render him incapable of transacting the business. When this fact is established the contract is voidable by the lunatic or his representatives, and it is no defense under our decisions that the other party acted fairly and without knowledge of his unsoundness or of any circumstances which ought to have put him upon inquiry."

We applied this test, also known as the "cognitive test," without significant modification for fifty years thereafter.

Over time, however, the traditional test for contractual incapacity, both in Massachusetts, and in other jurisdictions evolved to incorporate an increased understanding of the nature of mental illness in its various forms. Based on this understanding, we adopted a second, alternative test for incapacity.

In *Krasner v. Berk, 319 N.E.2d 897*, we recognized that there may be circumstances when, although a party claiming incapacity has some, or sufficient, understanding of the nature and consequences of the transaction, the contract would still be voidable where, "by reason of mental illness or defect, [the person] is unable to act in a reasonable manner in relation to the transaction and the other party has reason to know of his condition." This modern test—also described as an "affective" or "volitional" test—recognizes that competence can be lost, not only through cognitive disorders, but through affective disorders that encompass motivation or exercise of will.

Under this modern, affective test, "[w]here a person has some understanding of a particular transaction which is affected by mental illness or defect, the controlling consideration is whether the transaction in its result is one which a reasonably competent person might have made." Also relevant to the inquiry in these circumstances is whether the party claiming mental incapacity was represented by independent, competent counsel.

B. *Evidence of Contractual Incapacity.*

* * *

The Demonicos …[that] Susan's incapacity without showing a permanent, degenerative, progressive, or long-standing mental illness. They point to evidence that Susan's asserted mental impairment arose and was limited to the period of the mediation session, and argue that this evidence was sufficient to support a conclusion of incapacity, despite the lack of medical evidence or expert testimony as to the nature of Susan's mental impairment and its effect on her decision-making ability.

We have not previously addressed whether medical evidence is required to establish an incapacity to contract, and the Demonicos have not directed our attention to case law in other jurisdictions that would support their contention. In our prior decisions concerning the issue of incapacity to contract, however, evidence of mental illness or defect has been presented consistently through medical evidence, including the testimony of physicians and mental health providers or experts, in addition to lay testimony. Moreover, in other contexts, we have held that a lay witness is not competent to give an opinion as to mental condition. Expanding on this analysis, we conclude that medical evidence is necessary to establish that a person lacked the capacity to contract due to the existence of a mental condition.

* * *

Here, there was lay evidence, credited by the judge, that Susan's speech was "slurr[ed]," that she was in a state of uncontrollable crying, and that she had experienced an inability to focus or "think rationally" throughout the day of the mediation. Susan testified also that she had recently discontinued taking the prescribed medication Zoloft. However, she presented no medical evidence regarding a diagnosis that would have required her to take the medication, or the effect, if any, that ceasing to take the medication would have had on her medical or mental condition. There was also no evidence that Susan's condition at the mediation was related to or caused by her discontinuing the medication.

* * *

The evidence did not support a conclusion that, under the traditional test for incapacity, Susan was incapable of understanding the nature and quality of the transaction, or of grasping its significance. Indeed, based on Susan's testimony, she understood at the time that she was participating in a mediation to discuss settlement of the lawsuit; she was aware that the subject of the mediation was to resolve the dispute regarding the family home in Woburn; she participated in the mediation and listened to the arguments of counsel; and she "couldn't believe how things [were] turning out."

It is apparent from Susan's testimony that, even if she suffered from a transient mental defect, or "breakdown" as the judge concluded, she had at least some understanding of the nature of the transaction and was aware of its consequences.

Under the modern test to establish Susan's incapacity, the evidence was similarly insufficient. There was no evidence that the settlement agreement was unreasonable, or that a reasonably competent person would not have entered into it.

CONCLUSION

Because the evidence does not support a conclusion that Susan lacked the mental capacity to authorize settlement on the day of the mediation, it was error to deny Sparrow's motion to enforce the agreement. The order denying the motion to enforce the mediated settlement agreement is vacated. The case is remanded to the Superior Court for entry of an order that the settlement agreement be enforced.

So ordered.

NOW, LET US TAKE THIS point one step further and say that the diminution of capacity occurred through the legal consumption of alcohol or prescription. The following case illustrates this point.

Williamson v. Matthews

379 So.2d 1245 (Alabama 1980)

PER CURIAM.

This is an appeal from an order denying appellant Williamson injunctive relief seeking to cancel a deed and to set aside a sale of property from Williamson to the Matthews. We reverse and remand.

The Matthews learned from members of their family that Williamson wanted to sell her home. Her mortgage was in default, and the mortgagee was threatening foreclosure. There was some evidence to the effect that Williamson wanted to get enough equity to help her finance a mobile home. When they went to Williamson's house to inquire about it, Williamson showed the Matthews through the house. Bobby Matthews asked Williamson how much she wanted for it. Williamson told the Matthews to come back the next day. It is at this point that the parties are in disagreement. The Matthews contend that Williamson offered to sell her equity for $1,700, and Williamson contends that she offered to sell her equity for $17,000, and that the Matthews agreed to pay off the mortgage. It is undisputed that on September 27, 1978, the parties went to attorney Arthur J. Cook's office to execute a contract for the sale of the property. The contract of sale stated the purchase price to be $1,800 ($100 increase reflecting an agreement between the parties concerning some of the furniture in the home) plus the unpaid balance of the mortgage. Attorney Cook testified that he read the terms of the sale to both parties.

The parties then met on October 10, 1978, at attorney Larry Keener's office to sign the deed and to close a loan from appellee Family Savings Federal Credit Union to the Matthews so that the Matthews could buy the property from Williamson. Appellee The Brooklyn Savings Bank was about to foreclose the mortgage on Williamson's property. Keener disbursed part of the loan proceeds to Williamson. Williamson signed the deed to the property.

This Court was advised at oral argument that further disbursement of funds has been held up pending final disposition of this appeal.

Immediately after the sale, Williamson became concerned that she had not received her full consideration and consulted an attorney.

Two days later, on October 12, 1978, Williamson filed a petition for injunctive relief alleging inadequate consideration and mental weakness. The trial court granted Williamson a temporary restraining order preventing the sale from being completed, but at a full hearing on the petition for injunctive relief, the court denied Williamson the relief she requested. Williamson moved for and was granted a rehearing and further testimony was taken on the issue of Williamson's alleged mental weakness. Following the rehearing, the court issued a final order, again denying Williamson injunctive relief. This appeal followed.

...

Although in the case at bar there is no proof of suppression of fact, presentation of falsehood, abuse of confidence, fiduciary relationship between the parties, over-reaching, or undue influence, the Court in Judge did not limit "this something else" besides mere inadequacy of consideration to these factors alone.

Williamson contends that the "something else" in the case at bar is mental weakness, either due to some form of permanent mental incapacity or due to intoxication. Of course, the contracts of an insane person are absolutely void. Williamson, however, is not contending that she was insane at the time of the contract, but rather is contending that she had a mental incapacity, which coupled with inadequacy of consideration requires the setting aside of the transaction.

Our rule in such a case is that a party cannot avoid, free from fraud or undue influence, a contract on the ground of mental incapacity, unless it be shown that the incapacity was of such a character that, at the time of execution, the person had no reasonable perception or understanding of the nature and terms of the contract.

Our rule regarding incapacity due to intoxication is much the same. The drunkenness of a party at the time of making a contract may render the contract voidable, but it does not render it void; and to render the contract voidable, it must be made to appear that the party was intoxicated to such a degree that he was, at the time of the contracting, incapable of exercising judgment, understanding the proposed engagement, and of knowing what he was about when he entered into the contract sought to be avoided. Proof merely that the party was drunk on the day the sale was executed does not per se, show that he was without contractual capacity; there must be some evidence of a resultant condition indicative of that extreme impairment of the faculties which amounts to contractual incapacity.

The burden was therefore cast on Williamson to show, by clear and convincing evidence, that she was incapable, at the time of execution, of executing the contract for sale and of executing the deed.

We hold that Williamson met this burden. The testimony elicited at trial by Williamson's attorney charted a history of aberrative behavior. A Mrs. Logan, Williamson's mother, provided lengthy testimony about her daughter's past aberrations. Additionally, Dr. Fredric Feist provided expert testimony regarding Williamson at the rehearing. He stated that she showed signs of an early organic brain syndrome due to her excessive drinking, that she had emotional problems, that he thought that some of her brain cells were destroyed, and that her ability to transact business had been impaired.

Indulging the usual presumption due the trial court, we nevertheless hold that, under the facts of this case, it appears to us that Williamson was not, at the time of execution, capable of fully and completely understanding the nature and terms of the contract and of the deed. Williamson's contention that she was intoxicated supports this holding. Testimony was admitted from various witnesses to the effect that Williamson had a history of drinking, that she still had the problem at the time she executed the contract, and that she had in fact taken a couple of drinks before leaving for the meeting in attorney Arthur Cook's office. We do not hold that Williamson was so intoxicated as to render her incapable of contracting. However, numerous factors combine to warrant the conclusion that she was operating under diminished capacity. Testimony showed that Williamson's capacity to transact business was impaired, that she had a history of drinking, that she had been drinking the day she conducted negotiations, and that she had an apparent weakened will because she was pressured by the possibility of an impending foreclosure. Moreover, Williamson made complaint to an attorney only hours after the transaction. These factors are combined with a gross inadequacy of consideration.

No mitigating factors exist to the contrary. No right of any intervening third party is involved. Further disbursement of the loan proceeds has been frozen until final disposition of this appeal. No hardship is worked upon any party.

Although the evidence was presented before the trial court *ore tenus*, and in such a case where there is evidence to support the trial court's judgment, this Court will not ordinarily reverse that judgment unless there is a showing of plain and palpable error or manifest injustice. We consider that the record supports a finding in this case of such manifest injustice as to require a reversal of the judgment.

We recognize that two able and conscientious attorneys handled parts of the transaction. They are in no wise responsible for, nor were they aware of, the factors which prompt us to require a reversal of this case.

REVERSED AND REMANDED.

TORBERT, C. J., and BLOODWORTH, FAULKNER, ALMON and EMBRY, JJ., concur.

THE RESTATEMENT is not very kind to those whose incapacity results from alcohol consumption. Section 16 provides,

§ 16 Intoxicated Persons

> A person incurs only voidable contractual duties by entering into a transaction if the other party has reason to know that by reason of intoxication.
>
> > a. He is unable to understand in a reasonable manner the nature and consequences of the transaction, or
> >
> > b. He is unable to act in a reasonable manner in relation to the transaction.

2. External Impediments to Capacity

There are times when a person's capacity is removed because of an outside force.

a. Duress. With duress, there is some kind of outside pressure placed on the person that makes independent judgment impossible. Think of someone holding a gun to another person's head, demanding that he sign a document that will benefit the gun-holder. The person told to sign the contract is under duress. He no longer has the capacity to independently determine whether the contract he is told to sign is in his best interests or not.

Two kinds of duress trigger different legal rules with respect to whether the contract is void or voidable. If the threat made to the person is sufficient to cause a reasonable person to believe that her physical well being (or that of loved one or friend) is jeopardized, then the "contract' signed is void. In the example above, a gun is being pointed to the person's head. As long as the gun and the person holding it are reasonably perceived to be a real threat, then the contract is void even if it turns out later that the gun was fake or unloaded and that the individual had no intention of perpetrating any harm. What matters is the reasonable belief of the person under duress.

One can vary the example, though, so that there is a threat, but not one that creates a void contract. What if there is a threat, but the exact nature of potential harm is not as great or is questionable? What if a petite gymnast from the women's Olympic team threatens to beat up an All-Pro, NFL linebacker? Unless there is some evidence that the gymnast is also holding a weapon or is a highly skilled martial arts devotee, the threat to the linebacker may create a voidable contract, but certainly not one that is, per se, void. For that matter, as sketched in the example, it may not qualify for any special treatment.

The point is that, for any kind of duress, the test goes to the reasonable belief in the threat by the person allegedly under duress. Depending on the exact threat, the external impediment to the person's capacity may lead to a void or voidable contract, or may have no impact on capacity at all. Before turning to the cases, the Restatement handles claims of contractual duress in sections 174 through 176.

§ 174: When Duress by Physical Compulsion Prevents Formation of a Contract

If conduct that appears to be a manifestation of assent by a party who does not intend to engage in that conduct is physically compelled by duress, the conduct is not effective as a manifestation of assent.

§ 175: When Duress by Threat Makes a Contract Voidable

1. If a party's manifestation of assent is induced by an improper threat by the other party that leaves the victim no reasonable alternative, the contract is voidable by the victim.

2. If a party's manifestation of assent is induced by one who is not a party to the transaction, the contract is voidable by the victim unless the other party to the transaction in good faith and without reason to know of the duress either gives value or relies materially on the transaction.

§ 176: When a Threat is Improper

1. A threat is improper if

   a. What is threatened is a crime or a tort, or the threat itself would be a crime or a tort if it resulted in obtaining property,

   b. What is threatened is a criminal persecution,

   c. What is threatened is the use of civil process and the threat is made in bad faith, or

   d. The threat is a breach of the duty of good faith and fear dealing under a contract with the recipient

2. A threat is improper if the resulting exchange is not on fair terms, and

   a. The threatened act would harm the recipient and would not significantly benefit the parry making the threat,

   b. The effectiveness of the threat inducing the manifestation of assent is significantly increased by prior unfair dealing by the party making the threat, or

   c. What is threatened is otherwise a use of power for illegitimate ends.

The following case illustrate these points.

Eckstein v. Eckstein

28 Md.App. 757 (Maryland Ct. of Special Appeals 1978)

LISS, JUDGE.

Judith Eckstein, appellant (hereinafter "wife"), and Donald Eckstein, appellee (hereinafter "husband"), were married in Maryland on May 25, 1968. The wife had one daughter from a previous marriage, Kimberly, who was adopted by the husband after their marriage; and a second daughter, Donna, was born to the Ecksteins. At the time of the separation between the parties the children were eight and six years old respectively. The wife had a history of mental disturbances, and in September of 1973, she sought professional help from a psychiatrist, Dr. Gultken Ovacik. During the course of her sessions with Dr. Ovacik, in January of 1974, the wife was committed to the Prince George's Hospital Psychiatric Ward for treatment, where she remained confined for a period of 46 days. Dr. Ovacik, who continued to see her at the hospital, testified that her last visit with him during that period was April 3, 1974, at which time she advised him that she was not going to see him again because her husband objected to her seeing a psychiatrist. She did not see him again until July 21, 1975. The doctor testified that he found the wife to be suffering from a reactive depression when he saw her in April of 1974 and that the condition had not changed when he saw her in July of 1975. Her history indicated that she had attempted suicide four or five times and that she was hospitalized on at least three occasions as a result of these attempts. Dr. Ovacik indicated that in his opinion she was suffering from the reactive depression well before he first saw her in September of 1973.

The marriage was hardly an idyll of matrimonial bliss, and the parties separated temporarily on a number of occasions. During one of these separations in 1971, the husband had his lawyer, a Mr. Leitch, prepare a separation and property settlement agreement; and on April 13, 1971, the husband took the wife who had no counsel and was not given an opportunity to consult counsel to his lawyer's office. The wife signed the agreement, and later that afternoon, she took an overdose of prescribed drugs and was hospitalized. The husband communicated with her by phone while she was in the hospital, and a reconciliation ensued. Several other separations had occurred between the parties and during one such period (in November of 1970), the wife employed an attorney who prepared a separation agreement more favorable to her than the one she ultimately signed but which her husband refused to sign.

On the evening of February 1, 1975, the wife left the marital abode in the parties' jointly owned 1973 Volkswagen van with only the clothes on her back. She had no funds and the husband promptly closed the couple's joint bank account. The wife consulted Legal Aid but was advised that she did not qualify for their assistance. Shortly after the wife left her husband, he discovered her whereabouts and the location of the van and with the assistance of the wife's stepfather seized and secreted the van.

The husband refused the wife's request to visit or communicate with her children and refused to give her her clothing. He told her that she could see her children and take her clothes only if she signed a separation agreement prepared by Mr. Leitch, his attorney. Subsequent events disclosed that the agreement was almost an exact duplicate of the one she signed in 1971 after which she attempted suicide.

On February 10, 1975, she was directed by her husband to go to Mr. Leitch's office; she had no money to employ counsel. At Mr. Leitch's office she was advised that her husband was in the suite but would not talk to her in person. A copy of the separation agreement was given to her to read. She asked several questions of Mr. Leitch who testified that he did not recollect what the questions were but that he refused to give her any advice because he was representing her husband. He asked her if she wanted to talk to her husband and put him on an inter-office phone to discuss the matter with her. The husband also admitted that the wife asked several questions about the agreement but stated that he could not remember what the inquiries were and he did not answer them. The wife testified that her husband told her that if she did not sign the agreement he would get her for desertion, that she would never see her children again, and that she would get nothing neither her clothes nor the van unless she signed the agreement as written. No changes were made in the document, and the wife signed the agreement in Mr. Leitch's office. Immediately after signing, her clothes were surrendered to her and she was given the keys to the Volkswagen van.

The separation agreement provided that the wife give custody of the children to her husband. She agreed to deed to her husband her interest in the jointly owned home of the parties. She agreed to assign to her husband her interest in a jointly owned new 1975 Chevrolet van; she received the Volkswagen. She waived alimony, support, maintenance, court costs, attorney's fees, and any right of inheritance in her husband's estate. She was to receive one-half of the income tax refunds due the parties, of which her share would be approximately $1,000. She was paid $1100 at the time of the execution of the agreement. The husband agreed to retain the wife on his health insurance policy until they were divorced. The wife was to receive any of their furniture which she desired.

On February 10, 1976, the husband filed a bill of complaint in the Circuit Court for Prince George's County in which he prayed the court to grant him a divorce a *vinculo matrimonii* on the ground of voluntary separation and to require specific performance of the third and fourth paragraphs of the property settlement agreement executed by the parties on February 10, 1975. These paragraphs concerned the exchange of the titles to the two vans owned by the parties.

The wife filed an answer in which she prayed that the court grant the divorce but alleged lack of mental capacity on her part and coercion, duress, fraud, breach of contract, lack of consideration and gross overreaching on the part of the husband in securing the execution of the agreement, and requested that the court set aside the property settlement between the parties. She also sought custody of the minor children and counsel fees. The trial court, with the approval of both parties, treated the answer filed by the wife as a cross-bill of complaint seeking affirmative relief. At the conclusion of two days of testimony, the trial court granted the husband's prayer for a divorce a vinculo; granted him custody of the minor children, with visitation rights to the wife; and upheld the validity of the separation and property agreement. All the prayers for relief of the wife were denied, and her cross-bill of complaint was dismissed.

* * *

A separation agreement, being a contract between the parties, is subject to the same general rules governing other contracts.

* * *

Any agreement, contract, or deed obtained by oppressing a person by threats regarding the safety or liberty of himself, or his property, or a member of his family so as to deprive him of the free exercise of his will and prevent the mutuality of assent required for a valid contract may be avoided on the ground of duress.

* * *

The circumstances surrounding the signing of the agreement were bizarre, to say the least: We have already described what occurred between the husband and wife prior to her going to the office of her husband's attorney. When she arrived at Mr. Leitch's office, the agreement was in the process of being typed; the deed transferring her interest in the home had already been prepared. The wife raised several questions concerning the agreement, but neither the attorney nor the husband would answer them. The latter both admitted in their testimony that she raised some such questions, but, neither could remember what they were. When she told her husband that she would not sign the agreement, which was identical with the one she repudiated in 1971, he repeated his threats that she would get nothing neither her van, nor her clothes, nor the right to see or communicate with her children. No changes at all were made in the agreement as prepared by Mr. Leitch.

It is significant, we believe, that when under the circumstances she capitulated and signed the agreement, Mr. Leitch immediately delivered to her, in cash, the $1100 she was to receive for her interest in the property, and her clothes and the van were surrendered to her. These facts indicate to us a strong determination by the husband and his lawyer to pressure the wife into then and there executing the agreement.

* * *

We conclude that it was irregular for the husband and his counsel to prepare a complicated legal document and deeds conveying to the husband her interest in jointly held property without at least offering her an opportunity to have her questions answered by her own legal advisor. It was, we believe, improper to submit the documents to her on a take it or leave it basis and to coerce her signature by withholding her property and threatening to prevent her from seeing or communicating with her children. We might well have reached that conclusion even if the evidence was clear that the wife was a competent, stable, knowledgeable woman; but when, as here, it is obvious that the husband and his lawyer were dealing with an emotionally and mentally unstable individual, we think that the conclusion that the execution of the agreement was obtained by duress is inescapable. With no funds, no lawyer, no clothes, no transportation, and no viable alternative, it is not surprising that the wife capitulated and signed the agreement. We cannot accept that action, under all the circumstances, as one taken by her of her own free will.

---

2. Undue Influence. Undue influence tends to be more subtle than situations of physical duress. In these kinds of cases, one individual reposes so much confidence in another person that they essentially give away their capacity to contract. Suppose, for example, that a parent has three children. Two of the children live far away, while one lives close by the parent and does an enormous amount of work for the parent, especially as the parent ages. More and more, the parent looks to the nearby child to make decisions on the parent's behalf. Increasingly, the parent begins to defer to the children's discretion. The parent still has the capacity to make decisions, but they increasingly rely on this trusted child.

At some point, the child starts to recommend the parent make decisions and enter into contracts that are not in the best interest of the parent, but instead of the child. At this point, the trusted relationship turns into one where there is undue influence. Under §177 of the Restatement, undue influence occurs when:

1. Undue influence is unfair persuasion of a party who is under the domination of the person exercising the persuasion or who by virtue of the relation between them is justified in assuming that the person will not act in a manner inconsistent with his welfare.

2. If a party's manifestation of assent is induced by undue influence by the other party, the contract is voidable by the victim.

3. If a party's manifestation of assent is induced by one who is not a party to the transaction, the contract is voidable by the victim unless the other party to the transaction in good faith and without reason to know of the undue influence either gives value or relies materially on the transaction.

B. MEETING OF THE MINDS

I. Explicit Contracts

Explicit contracts are easy to see and to analyze because, as the category indicates,

their explicitness makes them visible with ascertainable promises. With explicit contracts, terms are clearly negotiated with each party promising to do something.

An explicit contract does not have to be in writing. A simple exchange of promises between two people can form a contract without anything being in writing. There are some contracts that are only enforceable if they are in writing, such as contracts for real estate, but what a written contract helps with most is evidence. What, exactly, did the parties promise to do? If the contract is merely verbal or implied through actions, there is a chance for ambiguity and potential conflict as each party remembers their promises a bit differently. A writing helps to make clear what both parties promised in the event they have to go to a third party—such as a judge—to enforce the contract.

2. Implied Contracts

Implied contracts can be harder to analyze. They typically involve a set of promises, requests, or statements by one party and then some kind of action by another. A key question, then, becomes whether there was an actual agreement or not between the two parties. Another issue arises when one person undertakes an action to benefit the other party and whether the benefitted party will obtain some kind of "unjust enrichment" by not providing some kind of compensation to the other party.

The Restatement actually understands the meeting of the minds as implicit in the concept of mutual assent, discussed below, and refers to this concept in sections 17 through 23.

a. **By Conduct.** If Jennifer were to say to Richard, "I will give you $100 to paint my house," there is no contract. This would be construed as an offer. Richard has some options at this point. One of them is to paint the house within a reasonable time. Let's say he does this right away. If he does, he provides a benefit to Jennifer and performs the actions for which she has indicated she is willing to pay $100. Richard's actions constitute an implied acceptance; his actions manifest his assent. Section 19 of the Restatement provides, in relevant part, that, "the conduct of a party is not effective as a manifestation of his assent unless he intends to engage in the conduct and knows or has reason to know that the other party may infer from his conduct that he assents."

b. **Quasi-Contract & Unilateral Contracts.** All contracts require an offer and acceptance for the formation of a contract. However, in the case of unilateral contracts, the party accepts the offer by performing. Unilateral contracts arise in a myriad of situations; examples arise frequently in the area of prizes and contests, where contestants attempt to claim prizes based upon a company's advertised offer. In these cases, the person performing—i.e. the person accepting the offer—is not compelled to act, but will receive compensation for completing the task before any revocation by the offeror. The restatement handles these cases under section 45:

§ 45: Option Contract Created by Part Performance or Tender

1. When an offeree to accept by rendering a performance and does not invite a promissory acceptance, an option contract is created when the offeree tenders or begins the invited performance or tenders a beginning of it.

2. The offeror's duty of performance under any option contract so created is conditional on completion or tender of the invited performance in accordance with the terms of the offer.

Another area where these disputes arise frequently is in the area of employment law. Courts have been divided about whether an employee handbook constitutes an offer to contract on those terms with an employee and whether an employee can accept by beginning to perform. The case below explores the contractual and policy ramifications courts weigh when determining whether to acknowledge or vitiate these contracts.

Anderson v. Douglas & Lomason Co.

540 N.W.2d 277 (Iowa 1995)

TERNUS, Justice.

Defendant, Douglas & Lomason Company (DLC), discharged plaintiff, Terry Anderson, for taking a box of pencils. ... On Anderson's first day of work at DLC he attended a six hour orientation session for new employees. He was informed that DLC had a progressive discipline policy and he was given a fifty-three page employee handbook which included these policies. Anderson read only the first few pages of the handbook; he admits he never read the provisions on progressive discipline.

DLC fired Anderson after three years of employment. His termination was based on an incident which occurred as he was leaving the plant one day. Company personnel stopped his pickup and asked to search it. Anderson gave permission and the workers found a box of company pencils. As a result, they also asked to search his home and garage. Anderson consented and a subsequent search revealed no company property. However, that same day, DLC asked Anderson to resign. He refused and was immediately fired.

Anderson responded by filing this breach-of-contract action against DLC. He claims DLC did not follow the progressive discipline policies outlined in its handbook for unauthorized possession of company property. These progressive discipline policies require a written warning for the first offense, a three-day suspension without pay for the second offense, and discharge for the third offense. Because this was not Anderson's third offense, he claims DLC could not fire him.

DLC filed a motion for summary judgment claiming the handbook did not constitute a contract and therefore Anderson was employed at-will. First, DLC contended the handbook was never communicated to or accepted by Anderson because he did not read it. Second, DLC argued the handbook was not definite enough to constitute an offer. DLC cited two reasons for its vagueness claim: the handbook contains no written guarantees that discharge will occur only for cause or under certain conditions—the rules are mere guidance; and the manual contains a written disclaimer. The district court granted the employer's summary judgment motion without explanation in a calendar entry.

* * *

The central issue presented by this dispute is whether DLC's issuance of a handbook created an employment contract. This question arises because Iowa employment relationships are presumed to be at-will: In the absence of a valid employment contract either party may terminate the relationship without consequence. Indeed, the doctrine of employment at-will is merely a gap-filler, a judicially created presumption utilized when parties to an employment contract are silent as to duration. To understand our interpretation of employment contracts, particularly the nexus between the at-will doctrine and employee handbooks, we provide a brief overview.

* * *

Despite the universal acceptance of the employment-at-will doctrine, legislatures and courts have restricted its application. For example, federal labor law gave rise to union contracts that include just cause discharge provisions. Similarly, public employees are protected from arbitrary dismissal under civil service statutes.

Reflecting the perceived need to protect employees from the harshness of the at-will doctrine, courts began to erode the doctrine with exceptions. These exceptions generally fell within three categories: 1. discharges in violation of public policy, 2. discharges in violation of employee handbooks constituting a unilateral contract, and 3. discharges in violation of a covenant of good faith and fair dealing. However, Iowa's strong support of the at-will presumption is demonstrated by our reluctance to undermine the rule with exemptions.

We have cation of a "well-recognized and defined public policy of the State," and employee handbooks that meet the requirements for a unilateral contract. We have consistently rejected recognition of a covenant of good faith and fair dealing.

Our prior handbook decisions concerned only "for-cause" provisions. However, we explicitly left room for future expansion: an employment handbook may guarantee an employee that discharge will occur "only for cause *or under certain conditions*." We now hold "or under certain conditions" to include progressive disciplinary procedures. Such provisions are enforceable if they are part of an employment contract. We must now determine whether Anderson's handbook constitutes an enforceable contract. If it does not, we presume the parties intended a contract at will.

C. *Unilateral Contract Approach.*

When considering whether a handbook creates a contract we utilize unilateral contract theory. A unilateral contract consists of an offeror making a promise and an offeree rendering some performance as acceptance. An employee handbook is a unilateral contract when three elements are present: 1. the handbook is sufficiently definite in its terms to create an *offer*; 2. the handbook is communicated to and accepted by the employee so as to constitute *acceptance*; and 3. the employee provides *consideration*.

As with any contract, the party who seeks recovery on the basis of a unilateral contract has the burden to prove the existence of a contract. Therefore, Anderson has the burden to prove DLC's handbook created an enforceable contract. We begin our analysis with a discussion of the communication aspect of the acceptance element of Anderson's claim.

III. *Was the Employee Manual Communicated Even Though Anderson Never Read the Progressive Discipline Policies Upon Which He Now Relies?*

Anderson read only a few pages of the employee manual; he did not read the provisions on progressive discipline. DLC contends that under these circumstances, there can be no acceptance. We disagree. DLC distributed its employee handbook to new employees. We think Anderson's receipt of the handbook is sufficient communication.

Although we apply the traditional requirement of communication in ordinary contexts, [that the offeree must know of the offer] an employment contract based upon an employee handbook "does not always follow the traditional model." We believe important policies, which are confined to employee handbook cases, dictate a narrow divergence.

Where a contract is based upon an employee handbook distributed to all employees, the contract is not an individually negotiated agreement; it is a standardized agreement between the employer and a class of employees. We analogize to the interpretation of standardized contracts: "A standardized agreement 'is interpreted wherever reasonable as treating alike all those similarly situated, without regard to their knowledge or understanding of the standard terms of the writing.' "

Therefore, we hold it unnecessary that the particular employee seeking to enforce a promise made in an employee manual have knowledge of the promise. Although this holding is a departure from traditional 'bargain-theory' contract analysis, we think it produces "the salutary result that all employees, those who read the handbook and those who did not, are treated alike." Moreover, our deviation from traditional contract theory is consistent with the spirit of the judicially created at-will presumption: It is a common law presumption created in response to statutory and societal demands.

Our decision also finds support in other jurisdictions. Thus, the fact that Anderson did not read the employee manual does not prevent him from relying on the promises contained in the manual in this breach-of-contract action.

IV. *Did the Handbook's Progressive Discipline Procedures Constitute an Offer?*

We now consider whether DLC's handbook constituted an offer to Anderson to utilize progressive disciplinary procedures. We believe this aspect of the analysis should be conducted according to traditional contract theory.

"The standard is what a normally constituted person would have understood [the words] to mean, when used in their actual setting." We adopt the following analysis: "The test for an offer is whether it induces a reasonable belief in the recipient that he can, by accepting, bind the sender."

When objectively examining the handbook to determine intent to create an offer, we look for terms with precise meaning that provide certainty of performance. This is a definiteness inquiry: if an offer is indefinite there is no intent to be bound.

* * *

When considering whether a handbook is objectively definite to create a contract we consider its language and context. Our analysis of case law reveals three factors to guide this highly fact-intensive inquiry: 1. Is the handbook in general and the progressive disciplinary procedures in particular mere guidelines or a statement of policy, or are they directives?; 2. Is the language of the disciplinary procedures detailed and definite or general and vague?; and 3. Does the employer have the power to alter the procedures at will or are they invariable? We ask these questions to determine whether an employee is reasonably justified in understanding a commitment has been made.

Here, the text of the disciplinary procedures contains language of command: "The following action is prohibited, and the penalties for violation of these Shop Rules *shall* be as follows [progressive discipline steps are then listed]." However, the introduction to the section of the handbook containing the disciplinary procedures states twice that the rules "have been designed for the *information and guidance* of all employees." Second, the procedures themselves are fairly specific. There are four categories that describe in detail the offenses included in each category. In addition, the discipline for each category is also specific: for unauthorized possession of company property, the first offense requires a written warning, the second offense a three day unpaid suspension and the third offense results in discharge. Finally, DLC retained the power to alter the procedures at will. We need not decide whether these factors alone result in a sufficiently definite offer, however, because we must also consider the effect of DLC's disclaimer.

2. Handbook Disclaimer.

A disclaimer can prevent the formation of a contract by clarifying the intent of the employer not to make an offer. "In the context of employee handbooks, the essential purpose of a disclaimer is to claim at-will status for the employment relationship by repudiating or denying liability for statements expressed in the handbook." Although in theory disclaimers protect employers, many courts have imposed requirements that make it more difficult to give effect to them.

For example, many jurisdictions require the disclaimer be "clear and conspicuous" to be enforceable and negate any contractual relationship between an employer and employee. While we have never considered whether a disclaimer in an employee handbook must be clear and conspicuous, our court of appeals has implicitly endorsed a conspicuous requirement by holding a disclaimer "[p]rominently displayed in the first page" of a handbook prevented the formation of a contract.

The requirement that a disclaimer be conspicuous has given rise to much litigation. Compare cases holding disclaimer clear and conspicuous. [*Explanatory footnotes omitted.*] While the factual nature of the definiteness inquiry is partially to blame, too often such litigation is the product of illusory judicial standards.

We think such uncertainty is unnecessary. A disclaimer should be considered in the same manner as any other language in the handbook to ascertain its impact on our search for the employer's intent. Therefore, we reject any special requirements for disclaimers; we simply examine the language and context of the disclaimer to decide whether a reasonable employee, reading the disclaimer, would understand it to mean that the employer has not assented to be bound by the handbook's provisions.

> **"A DISCLAIMER should be considered in the same manner as any other language in the handbook to ascertain its impact on our search for the employer's intent."**

Similar to our consideration of handbook language in general, we believe two factors guide our inquiry. First, is the disclaimer clear in its terms: does the disclaimer state that the handbook does not create any rights, or does not alter the at-will employment status? Second, is the coverage of the disclaimer unambiguous: what is the scope of its applicability? Here the disclaimer appears on page fifty-three, the last page of the handbook, two inches below the preceding paragraph:

> This Employee Handbook is not intended to create any contractual rights in favor of you or the Company. The Company reserves the right to change the terms of this handbook at any time.

When examining the disclaimer we first consider the text employed. In no uncertain terms DLC's disclaimer states the handbook "is not intended to create *any* contractual rights." We believe DLC's disclaimer is clear in its disavowal of any intent to create a contract.

Second, we examine the scope of the disclaimer. There is nothing about the location of DLC's disclaimer or the language used to suggest that the disclaimer does not apply to the progressive discipline policies. The disclaimer is found in the handbook itself and unequivocally applies to the entire employee handbook.

We think a reasonable person reading the handbook could not believe that DLC has assented to be bound to the provisions contained in the manual. Thus, we hold DLC's handbook is not sufficiently definite to constitute a valid offer.

VI. *Summary.*

We hold as a matter of law no contract existed between Anderson and DLC. Anderson was employed at-will. Therefore, the trial court correctly granted summary judgment to DLC.

AFFIRMED.

---

3. Mutual Assent

Contracts are about two parties (or more) entering into an agreement that they believe to be in their best interest. Contracts are about freedom of choice and mutual benefit in creating relationship with reciprocal rights and duties. The heart of contracts is that the parties agree on what those rights and duties. They understand that one party will pay money, and the other party will paint the fence. What is crucial is their "mutual assent" To the arrangement. As we will see in the following chapter on the Uniform Commercial Code, there can be some kinds of sales issues where there does not have to be a perfect meeting of the minds. But whether there is a pure meeting of the minds or not, there does need to be a valid offer and a valid acceptance.

The following two sections deal with mutual assent through offer and acceptance. In sections 17 through 70 of the Restatement, the drafters cover manifestations of assent in general, the making of offers, the duration of the offeree's power to accept, and the acceptance of offers. These provisions are too numerous to reprint here, but if you have questions about the concepts explored below, the rules of the Restatement and their comments may provide helpful guidance.

I. Offer. The first step in analyzing any contract is determining whether an offeror (the person making the offer) is actually making an offer or not. To make a valid offer, the offeror must create a reasonable expectation in the mind of an offeree that an offer is being made on the basis of sufficiently concrete terms. Central to an offer, then, is a communication between the parties. The most straightforward form of such a communication is if the offeror simply states, verbally or in writing, that they wish to enter into a contract. And so, if one person says to another, I will give you $100 to paint my house if you do it this afternoon, one has created a reasonable expectation in the mind of the offeree than an offer is being extended to her on the basis of the offered terms. The same result would be the case if the offeree put in writing the same statement. In at least two ways, however, things can get more complicated.

One way is when there is a statement of interest in entering into a contract, but it is not conveyed to the offeree. Sticking with the same example as above, if the offeror said to a third party, Jill, "I would love for Bill to paint my house and I would give him $100 if he did it today" a reasonable expectation would not be created in Bill's mind that an offer had been

CENTRAL TO AN OFFER, then, is a communication between the parties. The most straightforward form of such a communication is if the offeror simply states, verbally or in writing, that they wish to enter into a contract.

made to him to paint the house unless Jill happens to be his agent. Similarly, if the offeror made a general statement that "it would be worth $100 to have my house painted today," there again would not be a reasonable expectation created in the mind of the offeree that an actual offer is being extended unless there is some additional action accompanying the words; say, for example, the offeror waving $100 in Bill's face when making the general statement.

In addition to making the statement to an intended party, the second key issue is whether the terms of the offer are sufficiently firm to form the basis of a contract. If a retailer posts an advertisement claiming "we'll give you the best deal in town," that will not be sufficiently certain for a customer to bind the business to a specific price for a specific item. Advertisements for sale (or to solicit an application) have frequently been the cause of litigation in offer cases, as the following cases demonstrate.

Lefkowitz v. Great Minneapolis Surplus Store

251 Minn. 188 (Minnesota 1957)

MURPHY, Justice.

This is an appeal from an order of the Municipal Court of Minneapolis denying the motion of the defendant for amended findings of fact, or, in the alternative, for a new trial. The order for judgment awarded the plaintiff the sum of $138.50 as damages for breach of contract.

This case grows out of the alleged refusal of the defendant to sell to the plaintiff a certain fur piece which it had offered for sale in a newspaper advertisement. It appears from the record that on April 6, 1956, the defendant published the following advertisement in a Minneapolis newspaper:

'Saturday 9 A.M. Sharp 3 Brand New Fur Coats Worth to $100.00
First Come First Served $1 Each'

On April 13, the defendant again published an advertisement in the same newspaper as follows:

> *'Saturday 9 A.M. 2 Brand New Pastel Mink 3-Skin Scarfs Selling for.$89.50*
> *Out they go Saturday. Each ... $1.00*
> *1 Black Lapin Stole Beautiful, worth $139.50 ... $1.00*
> *First Come First Served'*

The record supports the findings of the court that on each of the Saturdays following the publication of the above-described ads the plaintiff was the first to present himself at the appropriate counter in the defendant's store and on each occasion demanded the coat and the stole so advertised and indicated his readiness to pay the sale price of $1. On both occasions, the defendant refused to sell the merchandise to the plaintiff, stating on the first occasion that by a 'house rule' the offer was intended for women only and sales would not be made to men, and on the second visit that plaintiff knew defendant's house rules.

■ DETAIL FROM A PERIOD NEWSPAPER ADVERTISEMENT FOR THE GREAT MINNEAPOLIS SURPLUS STORE.

The trial court properly disallowed plaintiff's claim for the value of the fur coats since the value of these articles was speculative and uncertain. The only evidence of value was the advertisement itself to the effect that the coats were 'Worth to $100.00,' how much less being speculative especially in view of the price for which they were offered for sale. With reference to the offer of the defendant on April 13, 1956, to sell the '1 Black Lapin Stole * * * worth $139.50 * * *' the trial court held that the value of this article was established and granted judgment in favor of the plaintiff for that amount less the $1 quoted purchase price.

＊ ＊ ＊

There are numerous authorities which hold that a particular advertisement in a newspaper or circular letter relating to a sale of articles may be construed by the court as constituting an offer, acceptance of which would complete a contract.

The test of whether a binding obligation may originate in advertisements addressed to the general public is 'whether the facts show that some performance was promised in positive terms in return for something requested.'

The authorities above cited emphasize that, where the offer is clear, definite, and explicit, and leaves nothing open for negotiation, it constitutes an offer, acceptance of which will complete the contract. The most recent case on the subject is *Johnson v. Capital City Ford Co.,* La.App., 85 So.2d 75, in which the court pointed out that a newspaper advertisement relating to the purchase and sale of automobiles may constitute an offer, acceptance of which will consummate a contract and create an obligation in the offeror to perform according to the terms of the published offer.

Whether in any individual instance a newspaper advertisement is an offer rather than an invitation to make an offer depends on the legal intention of the parties and the surrounding circumstances. We are of the view on the facts before us that the offer by the defendant of the sale of the Lapin fur was clear, definite, and explicit, and left nothing open for negotiation. The plaintiff having successful managed to be the first one to appear at the seller's place of business to be served, as requested by the advertisement, and having offered the stated purchase price of the article, he was entitled to performance on the part of the defendant. We think the trial court was correct in holding that there was in the conduct of the parties a sufficient mutuality of obligation to constitute a contract of sale.

2. The defendant contends that the offer was modified by a 'house rule' to the effect that only women were qualified to receive the bargains advertised. The advertisement contained no such restriction. This objection may be disposed of briefly by stating that, while an advertiser has the right at any time before acceptance to modify his offer, he does not have the right, after acceptance, to impose new or arbitrary conditions not contained in the published offer.

Affirmed.

Steinberg v. Chicago Medical School

69 Ill.2d 320 (Illinois 1977)

DOOLEY, Justice:

Robert Steinberg received a catalog, applied for admission to defendant, Chicago Medical School, for the academic year 1974-75, and paid a $15 fee. He was rejected. Steinberg filed a class action against the school claiming it had failed to evaluate his application and those of other applicants according to the academic criteria in the school's bulletin. According to the complaint, defendant used nonacademic criteria, primarily the ability of the applicant or his family to pledge or make payment of large sums of money to the school.

The 1974-75 bulletin distributed to prospective students contained this statement of standards by which applicants were to be evaluated:

> "Students are selected on the basis of scholarship, character, and motivation without regard to race, creed, or sex. The student's potential for the study and practice of medicine will be evaluated on the basis of academic achievement, Medical College Admission Test results, personal appraisals by a pre-professional advisory committee or individual instructors, and the personal interview, if requested by the Committee on Admissions."

* * *

The real question… on this appeal is: Can the facts support a charge of breach of contract?

On motion to dismiss we accept as true all well-pleaded facts. Count I alleges Steinberg and members of the class to which he belongs applied to defendant and paid the $15 fee, and that defendant, through its brochure, described the criteria to be employed in evaluating applications, but failed to appraise the applications on the stated criteria. On the contrary, defendant evaluated such applications according to monetary contributions made on behalf of those seeking admission.

A contract, by ancient definition, is "an agreement between competent parties, upon a consideration sufficient in law, to do or not to do a particular thing."

An offer, an acceptance, and consideration are basic ingredients of a contract. Steinberg alleges that he and others similarly situated received a brochure describing the criteria that defendant would employ in evaluating applications. He urges that such constituted an invitation for an offer to apply, that the filing of the applications constituted an offer to have their credentials appraised under the terms described by defendant, and that defendant's voluntary reception of the application and fee constituted an acceptance, the final act necessary for the creation of a binding contract.

This situation is similar to that wherein a merchant advertises goods for sale at a fixed price. While the advertisement itself is not an offer to contract, it constitutes an invitation to deal on the terms described in the advertisement. Although in some cases the advertisement itself may be an offer (see *Lefkowitz v. Great Minneapolis Surplus Store, Inc., supra* (1957), usually it constitutes only an invitation to deal on the advertised terms. Only when the merchant takes the money is there an acceptance of the offer to purchase.

Here the description in the brochure containing the terms under which an application will be appraised constituted an invitation for an offer. The tender of the application, as well as the payment of the fee pursuant to the terms of the brochure, was an offer to apply. Acceptance of the application and fee constituted acceptance of an offer to apply under the criteria defendant had established.

Consideration is a basic element for the existence of a contract. Any act or promise which is of benefit to one party or disadvantage to the other is a sufficient consideration to support a contract. The application fee was sufficient consideration to support the agreement between the applicant and the school.

Defendant contends that a further requisite for contract formation is a meeting of the minds. But a subjective understanding is not requisite. It suffices that the conduct of the contracting parties indicates an agreement to the terms of the alleged contract. Williston, states in his work on contracts:

> "In the formation of contracts it was long ago settled that secret intent was immaterial, only overt acts being considered in the determination of such mutual assent as that branch of the law requires. During the first half of the nineteenth century there were many expressions which

> seemed to indicate the contrary. Chief of these was the familiar cliché, still reechoing in judicial dicta, that a contract requires the 'meeting of the minds' of the parties." (1 Williston, *Contracts* sec. 22, at 46-48 (3d ed. 1957).)

Here it would appear from the complaint that the conduct of the parties amounted to an agreement that the application would be evaluated according to the criteria described by defendant in its literature. Defendant urges [that] *People ex rel. Tinkoff v. Northwestern University*), 333 Ill.App. 224, (1947), controls. There the plaintiff alleged that since he met the stated requirement for admission, it was the obligation of the university to accept him. Plaintiff was first rejected because he was 14 years of age. He then filed a mandamus action, and subsequently the university denied his admission, apparently because of the court action. That decision turned on the fact that Northwestern University, a private educational institution, had reserved in its charter the right to reject any applicant for any reason it saw fit. Here, of course, defendant had no such provision in its charter or in the brochure in question. But, more important, Steinberg does not seek to compel the school to admit him. The substance of his action is that under the circumstances it was defendant's duty to appraise his application and those of the others on the terms defendant represented.

A medical school is an institution so important to life in society that its conduct cannot be justified by merely stating that one who does not wish to deal with it on its own terms may simply refrain from dealing with it at all.

As the appellate court noted in a recent case in which this defendant was a party:

> "A contract between a private institution and a student confers duties upon both parties which cannot be arbitrarily disregarded and may be judicially enforced.

Here our scope of review is exceedingly narrow. Does the complaint set forth facts which could mean that defendant contracted, under the circumstances, to appraise applicants and their applications according to the criteria it described? This is the sole inquiry on this motion to dismiss. We believe the allegations suffice and affirm the appellate court in holding count I stated a cause of action.

Count III alleges that, with intent to deceive and defraud plaintiffs, defendant stated in its catalogs it would use certain criteria to evaluate applications; that these representations were false in that applicants were selected primarily for monetary considerations; that plaintiffs relied on said representations and were each thereby induced to submit their applications and pay $15 to their damage.

> **"A MEDICAL SCHOOL is an institution so important to life in society that its conduct cannot be justified by merely stating that one who does not wish to deal with it on its own terms may simply refrain from dealing with it at all."**

These allegations support a cause of action for fraud. Misrepresentation of an existing material fact coupled with scienter, deception, and injury are more than adequate. *Roth v. Roth*, 45 Ill.2d 19, (1970), succinctly stated when a misrepresentation may constitute fraud:

> "A misrepresentation in order to constitute a fraud must consist of a statement of material fact, false and known to be so by the party making it, made to induce the other party to act, and, in acting, the other party must rely on the truth of the statement. (*Roda v. Berko*, 401 Ill. 335.)"

Plaintiff's allegations meet the test of common law fraud.

Not to be ignored is defendant's modus operandi as described in *DeMarco v. University of Health Sciences*, 40 Ill.App.3d 474, 481-82(1976):

> "An analysis of those exhibits shows that in 1970, at least 64 out of 83 entering students had pledges made in their behalves totalling $1,927,900. The pledges varied in amounts from $1400 to $100,000 and averaged $30,123. In 1971, at least 55 out of 83 students had pledges made in their behalves totalling $1,893,000. The pledges varied in amounts from $3000 to $100,000 and averaged $34,418. In 1972, at least 73 out of an entering class of 92 had contributions made in their behalves totalling $3,111,000. The pledges varied in amounts from $20,000 to $100,000 and averaged $42,603. In 1973, at least 78 out of 91 students had contributions made in their behalves totalling $3,749,000. The pledges varied in amounts from $10,000 to $100,000 and averaged $48,064. In addition, there were amounts pledged and partial payments made for students who did not enter or dropped out shortly after entering."

It is immaterial here that the misrepresentation consisted of a statement in the medical school catalog, referring to future conduct, that "the student's potential for the study and practice of medicine will be evaluated on the basis of academic achievement, Medical College Admission Test results, personal appraisals by a pre-professional advisory committee or individual instructors, and the personal interview, if requested by the Committee on Admissions." We concede the general rule denies recovery for fraud based on a false representation of intention or future conduct, but there is a recognized exception where the false promise or representation of future conduct is alleged to be the scheme employed to accomplish the fraud. Such is the situation here.

Here an action for fraud is consistent with the recognition of a contract action. The law creates obligations "on the ground that they are dictated by reason and justice." The right to recover on a "constructive contract," although phrased in contract terminology, is not based on an agreement between parties but is an obligation created by law. "Such contracts are contracts merely in the sense that (they) * * * are created and governed by the principles of equity." So here the facts of this situation mandate that equity imply an obligation by the defendant. We note this since the circumstances before us justify a contract action, as well as a fraud action, or, in the event no contract in fact can be proven, an action on an implied-in-law obligation of the defendant.

---

2. Acceptance. Because contracts require a mirror image in order to be valid, the offeree (the person accepting the offer) has three choices when an offer is extended to him.

1. Accept the offer, which creates a contract

2. Reject the offer

3. Reject the offer and make a counteroffer instead.

The first two choices are straightforward. Either a contract is formed on the basis of the offered terms (to which the offeree agrees) or nothing happens if the contract is rejected. A counteroffer, however, reverses the relationship between the parties. Now the original offeree becomes the offeror because the counteroffer is exactly that: another offer. Acceptance can occur either by performance or by the acceptance of the promise. Both require notification to the offeror.

Given the speed of communication today, the so-called mailbox rule has lost some of its relevance. But its can still rear its head and its logic lies behind subsequent policy. Put simply, for the most part, communications of components of an offer and acceptance become effective when they are received by the other party. An offer is effective when the offeree receives it (so that a reasonable expectation is raised in the mind of the offeree that an offer is being made to them that the offeree can accept). The same rule is true for a rejection (made by the offeree) or a revocation (made by the offeror). Because a counteroffer is a combination of a rejection (by the offeree) with a follow-on new offer, the rule still holds that the counteroffer becomes effective when received by the offeree.

The wrinkle comes with an acceptance. It is deemed effective when the offeree says "yes" and does something to send that acceptance to the offeror, such as placing a letter indicating the acceptance in the mail (with proper postage, etc.) Then the offeree changes her mind. She mails an acceptance (immediately effective) and then calls up the offeree and rejects the offer before the acceptance reaches the offeror. Which is effective? In such cases, courts generally revert to is the rule of whichever is received first. But bear in mind, that this simplifies the mailbox rule quite a bit and many nuances await. The following case illustrates some of this nuance.

If you are interested in the law governing electronic transmissions, consult the Uniform Electronic Transactions Act (UETA) promulgated by the National Conference of Commissioners on Uniform State Laws (NCCUSL), now the Uniform Law Commission. Forty-seven states, the District of Columbia, and the Virgin Islands have enacted the code, and New York, Washington and Illinois have similar state laws.

Sementa v. Tylman

230 Ill.App.3d 701 (Ill. Ct. App. 1992)

Justice DUNN delivered the opinion of the court:

* * *

Sementa and Tylman are both engaged in the practice of dentistry. In January 1989, Sementa and Tylman entered into several written agreements pursuant to which Sementa purchased Tylman's dental practice in Lombard for a price of $215,000. In addition, Tylman was to work as a consultant in the office until December 31, 1994, unless the parties mutually agreed to an earlier termination date or one of them died, and was to receive compensation for his services. Tylman also agreed to refrain from practicing dentistry within a five-mile radius of his former office and soliciting patients of that office during the period of his independent contractor agreement with Sementa and for two years thereafter.

On April 16, 1990, Sementa filed a complaint alleging that Tylman had breached the above restrictive covenant by practicing dentistry within five miles of the Lombard office. Tylman filed a separate action against Sementa on June 20, 1990. He alleged that Sementa had failed to make certain payments due under the January 1989 agreements. The circuit court subsequently consolidated the two suits.

* * *

On April 4, Tylman's attorney presented a document titled "Agreed Order" to the trial court. This document set forth terms of a proposed settlement between Sementa and Tylman and contained the signatures of both. Over the objection of Sementa's attorney, the trial judge entered the order and stated that the document was "complete and regular on its face." The trial judge also stated that if Sementa's attorney had a valid objection, he could move to have the agreed order vacated.

On May 1, 1991, Sementa filed a motion to vacate the April 4 judgment order. Sementa's motion and Tylman's response contained affidavits establishing the following undisputed facts. On December 27, 1990, Tylman's attorney, John Garrow, sent a letter to Sementa's attorney, John McCluskey. The letter stated that Tylman's motion to vacate the December 6 stipulated dismissal order or to enforce the alleged verbal settlement agreement was enclosed. The letter also stated that Tylman would agree to a clause which would allow either party to terminate the agreement as of the beginning of 1992, 1993, or 1994. If Tylman terminated the agreement, he would be required to pay $15,000 to Sementa if the termination was to take effect in 1992, $10,000 for 1993, and $5,000 for 1994. The letter also stated that, in general, Tylman was willing to offer the same proposal contained in Garrow's letter of December 7, 1990.

On December 31, 1990, McCluskey delivered the document titled "Agreed Order" to Garrow's office. Sementa had signed the document earlier that day. At the bottom of the document, next to Sementa's signature, there was a signature line with Tylman's name printed below. The "agreed order" was seven pages long. Among other things, it stated that the independent contractor agreement could not be terminated until January 1, 1993. If Tylman wished to terminate the agreement as of that date, he would be required to pay Sementa $10,000, amortized over the period of remaining payments under the independent contractor and equipment lease agreements. If he wished to terminate the agreement as of January 1, 1994, he would be required to pay $2,000, amortized in a similar manner.

Enclosed with the "agreed order" was a check for $30,321.94 made payable to Tylman. Sementa wrote the words "Pursuant to Agreed Order" on the lower left corner of the check. Tylman cashed the check on January 3, 1991, but crossed out the above phrase.

On January 14, 1991, Garrow sent another letter to Sementa. This letter states that Tylman "was willing to settle this matter at any time upon the conditions set forth in my letter to you dated December 27, 1990." McCluskey informed Garrow that this proposal was not acceptable to Sementa.

When Garrow and McCluskey met at the Du Page County courthouse on March 28, 1991, Garrow showed him the "agreed order" dated December 31, 1990, which Tylman had now signed. McCluskey then telephoned Sementa, who was no longer willing to settle the case on those terms. This was the first notice Sementa had that Tylman had signed the agreement. According to Tylman's affidavit, he signed the "agreed order" on January 11, 1991. The attorneys were told to return to court on April 4 because the judge was not available on March 28.

The trial judge denied the motion to vacate. He ruled that, by accepting the check on January 3, Tylman created a contract between the parties. Sementa now appeals.

Tylman initially argues that this court has no jurisdiction to consider this appeal because it involves a consent order. * * * This issue may properly be considered because it does involve a judicial determination as to whether the parties agreed to the entry of the judgment. To rule otherwise would leave a party without effective recourse in the event that a trial court erroneously ruled that he or she had consented to the entry of a judgment order.

Tylman next argues that the "agreed order" is not a final and appealable order because it states that the court retains jurisdiction for the purpose of enforcing all agreements between the parties. * * * [W]e conclude that it is final and appealable and reject Tylman's jurisdictional challenge.

Sementa contends that his December 31, 1990, "agreed order" was an offer that Tylman rejected several times prior to his purported March 28, 1991, acceptance, thereby rendering that acceptance invalid. The law of contracts is applicable to settlement agreements. Settlement agreements are binding only if there is an offer, an acceptance, and a meeting of the minds as to the terms of the agreement.

There is no dispute that the December 31, 1990, "agreed order" was an offer from Sementa to Tylman. The January 14, 1991, letter from Garrow to McCluskey proposed settlement on different terms than Sementa had proposed in the "agreed order." It therefore constituted a counteroffer. Responding to an offer with a counteroffer constitutes a rejection of the original offer. A rejected offer cannot be revived by a later acceptance.

Tylman contends that he accepted the terms of the "agreed order" by signing it on January 11, 1991. There is no acceptance, however, until the offeree notifies the offeror of the acceptance or at least employs reasonable diligence in attempting to do so. (Restatement (Second) of Contracts § 56 (1981).)The record reveals that Tylman made no effort to notify Sementa of his "acceptance" until March 28, 1991, long after he rejected the offer by making the January 14 counteroffer. accordingly, there was no valid acceptance of Sementa's December 31 settlement proposal.

Tylman argues that Sementa ratified the December 31 agreed order by paying himself over $6,000 pursuant to it. This would not, however, remove the requirement of acceptance of the agreement by Tylman. The record reveals that no valid acceptance ever took place.

The trial court's conclusion that Tylman accepted the terms of the December 31 proposal by cashing the check was also erroneous. Under some circumstances, a tendered contract may be accepted if the offeree accepts benefits under the contract. Here, however, although Sementa placed the words "Pursuant to Agreed Order" on the check, the agreed order did not specifically provide for a payment in that amount to Tylman. Instead, it provided that the sum due Tylman under the independent contractor agreement would be determined later. Thus, Tylman would not have been aware that he was accepting a benefit under the agreed order by cashing the check. Furthermore, by crossing out the above phrase before cashing the check, Tylman indicated he was not manifesting any intention to accept the terms of the "agreed order." We therefore conclude that Tylman's acceptance of the check did not constitute an acceptance of the terms of the agreed order.

* * *

For the above reasons, the judgment of the circuit court of Du Page County is reversed, and the cause is remanded for further proceedings.

Reversed and remanded.

C. CONSIDERATION

The third requirement for a valid contract is consideration. Consideration is a legal term of art. It does not mean that the parties treat each other with respect and courtesy as the commonly used definition of consideration would suggest. Instead, consideration, for legal purposes, means that each party has given up something of value in order to bind each other to the contract. Consideration does not attempt to evaluate whether a bargain was fair or not, or that each party gave up roughly equally valuable items or performed equally valuable services, but it does ask if both parties gave up something of "legal value."

Like the sections on offer and acceptance, the Restatement covers a much broader range of concepts than we will in this text. Sections 71 through 109 set forth the requirements that there be consideration, contracts under seal. To begin, though, let us look at § 71:

§ 71: Requirement of Exchange: Types of Exchange:

1. To constitute consideration, a performance or a return promise must be bargained for.

2. A performance or return promise is bargained for if it is sought by the promisor in exchange for his promise and is given by the promisee in exchange for that promise.

3. The performance may consist of

   a. an act other than a promise, or

   b. a forbearance, or

   c. the creation, modification, or destruction of a legal relation.

4. The performance or return promise may be given to the promisor or to some other person. It may be given by the promisee or by some other person.

l. General Framework

The general test for whether the consideration test has been met is whether consideration is mutual—that both parties have given up something—and that what they have given up is determined to be of adequate, legal value. These tend to merge together because what typically happens is if one party did not, in fact, provide something of adequate legal value, there is no mutuality of exchange.

Let's assume that Mike is teaching a business law class and says that he will give $100,000 to anyone who gets up and walks around the room. Several students take him up on the offer and then demand the $100,000. There are two parties, both of them presumably have capacity, and there is a meeting of the minds as to the identity of the parties and the terms of the agreement. But would courts enforce a contract for $100,000 for walking around a (presumably small) room? More likely, the Court would say that the contract lacks consideration. There is not adequate legal value given by simply getting up and walking around the room.

On the other hand, let's say Mike promised that he would give $1,000 if any member of the class ran a marathon. Several students do just that, and then demand payment. Courts may well hold this to be consideration on the part of both parties. Certainly offering $1,000 rather than $100,000 makes is more likely to determine this as a real offer as opposed to some kind of playful joke, but more importantly, the effort of running a marathon is far greater than that required for walking around the room.

A business person may already have a duty to perform some action. This raises the question of whether the person can demand additional consideration for something that he is already obligated to do.

Yerovick v. AAA

461 Mich. 732 (Michigan 2000)

MICHAEL F. CAVANAGH, J.

* * *

FACTS

Plaintiff's minor daughter was injured in an automobile accident when the driver of the vehicle in which she was riding negligently collided with another vehicle. At the time of the accident, plaintiff was a participant in the Michigan United Food and Commercial Workers Unions and Food Employers Health and Welfare Fund. The fund is a self-funded employee welfare benefit plan created and administered pursuant to the Employee Retirement Income Security Act (ERISA) [...]. Plaintiff also had a no-fault policy issued by defendant AAA.

Plaintiff filed this action on behalf of her daughter against both defendants, seeking payment of medical expenses. The fund had initially denied coverage, claiming plaintiff had failed to execute a subrogation agreement. The fund claimed this was required by the plan's subrogation clause. Plaintiff eventually signed the "Subrogation Agreement and Assignment" form, and the fund paid $6,832 in medical expense benefits. The AAA also denied coverage, claiming that plaintiff's policy contained a coordination of benefits clause that made the fund primarily responsible for medical expenses from the accident. Plaintiff also filed a negligence claim seeking noneconomic damages against the driver of the vehicle in which her daughter was riding. That case was settled for $20,000.

Plaintiff and the fund each filed motions for summary disposition in the trial court, essentially advancing the same position. The fund argued that, pursuant to the plan, plaintiff was required to reimburse the fund the $6,832 it had paid for medical expenses out of her third-party tort recovery. Plaintiff and the fund agreed that if such reimbursement were required, it would result in plaintiff paying her own medical expenses, contrary to the provisions of the no-fault act. Plaintiff and the fund argued that the AAA should be responsible for paying for the medical expenses. The AAA argued that the language of the subrogation agreement between plaintiff and the fund did not support a right to reimbursement and limited reimbursement to situations where plaintiff recovered medical expenses from a third-party suit. The trial court granted the motions for summary disposition and ordered the AAA to repay plaintiff any sums she paid to reimburse the fund. The Court of Appeals affirmed.

THE SUBROGATION AGREEMENT

At issue in this case is the interpretation of the plan agreement between the fund and plaintiff. Specifically, we must answer whether the fund was entitled to a refund from plaintiff for medical expenses. The fund provided plaintiff with a plan booklet that laid out the rights, benefits, and duties of the parties. Under the "General Provisions" section, the plan provided a subsection entitled "Third Party Subrogation." The fund argues that, under this section, plaintiff was required to sign further documents ensuring its rights to subrogation, reimbursement, repayment, and assignment.

* * *

> [Y]ou or your dependants will have certain responsibilities to the Plan. When you or your eligible dependent submit a claim to this Plan for injuries, the Fund Office will have you complete a form requesting information as to how the injuries occurred and the identity of any potentially responsible third parties. At the request of the Fund Office, *you must also sign any other documents* and do whatever else is reasonably necessary *to secure this Plan's right of subrogation.* You must not do anything to impair or negate this Plan's right of subrogation; *if* any of your acts or omissions to act compromise this Plan's right of subrogation, this Plan will seek *reimbursement* of all appropriate benefits paid directly to you....
>
> If you recover lost wage benefits from another source, e.g. from an individual who caused the injury which resulted in your receiving Time Loss Weekly Benefits, the Plan has the *right to seek repayment from you* [....] [Court's note: Emphasis added.]

Under this plan, the fund declared "subrogation" rights in order to recover from a third party medical expense benefits it paid. In contrast, it declared the right to "repayment" from plaintiff for lost wage benefits it paid in the event that plaintiff recovered the lost wages "from any other source."

* * *

Although the agreement provides that the fund may "recover *from the person who caused the injury*," the fund seeks to recover instead from plaintiff. It has done so by arguing that the second agreement signed by plaintiff required plaintiff to repay, reimburse, subrogate, and assign sums and rights to the fund. It is agreed that plaintiff signed the second agreement-that greatly expanded her duties under the plan agreement-only after the fund conditioned the payment of medical expenses on her signing the second agreement.

Under the plan agreement, the fund was entitled to seek recovery from the negligent driver for the medical expenses it paid. Plaintiff, in return, was required to sign documents necessary to secure the fund's right of subrogation. Plaintiff was also required to provide any information requested regarding the injuries and the identity of the tortfeasor. *If* plaintiff impaired that right of "subrogation," the fund could *then* seek reimbursement. Plaintiff has done nothing to hinder or obstruct the fund's rights of subrogation. Plaintiff did not sue the tortfeasor for medical expenses or any economic damages. Instead, plaintiff recovered from the tortfeasor purely noneconomic damages for pain and suffering. The fund does not claim that it has paid noneconomic damages. It does not claim that it had a right of subrogation for noneconomic damages, only for benefits it paid. It paid only medical expense benefits. Nor does the plan agreement provide that it may seek reimbursement from plaintiff for medical expenses from plaintiff's noneconomic damage recovery. Under the language of the plan agreement, the fund's right of reimbursement is triggered only if the plaintiff impairs or negates the fund's right of subrogation. This was not triggered. In fact, the fund may step into plaintiff's shoes and sue the negligent driver for medical expenses incurred, because plaintiff has yet to seek them.

> **"AN ESSENTIAL ELEMENT of a contract is legal consideration. Under the preexisting duty rule, it is well settled that doing what one is legally bound to do is not consideration for a new promise."**

Moreover, the fund might have, but did not, place language in the plan agreement requiring reimbursement of medical expenses from plaintiff. Instead, it sought only subrogation as defined in the second paragraph. Therefore, it has no right to reimbursement from plaintiff for medical expenses. This view is strengthened by examining the final paragraph quoted from the plan agreement where the fund demanded "repayment" from the *plaintiff* for lost wage benefits, in contrast to the "subrogation" clause, which allows recovery from the *person who caused the injury* for medical expense benefits.

The fund argues that subrogation *and* reimbursement rights are triggered whenever a plan participant recovers monies for the same injury or accident from a third party. It also urges that we should apply an "arbitrary and capricious" standard of review to the fund's interpretation of the plan agreement, citing *Firestone Tire & Rubber Co. v. Bruch*, 489 U.S. 101(1989). Even under such a standard, we cannot read into the plan agreement that which does not exist. The fund had the opportunity to write into its agreement repayment or reimbursement rights. It did not.

Whether the second agreement entitled the fund to reimbursement is irrelevant to our analysis because the fund was under a preexisting duty to pay plaintiff's medical expenses and could not require her to take on additional duties absent additional consideration.

PREEXISTING DUTY RULE

An essential element of a contract is legal consideration. Under the preexisting duty rule, it is well settled that doing what one is legally bound to do is not consideration for a new promise. This rule bars the modification of an existing contractual relationship when the purported consideration for the modification consists of the performance or promise to perform that which one party was already required to do under the terms of the existing agreement.

In this case, the plan agreement provided that the fund had a preexisting duty to pay plaintiff's medical expenses. This promise was conditioned upon the fund's right of subrogation being protected. As stated, these rights were protected.

Although the parties focus on the second agreement, we find it is void for lack of consideration. Plaintiff was required only to sign documents ensuring the fund's right of subrogation as defined by the fund. The second agreement instead attempted to add to plaintiff's duties and burdens. The second agreement added an obligation to "repay" sums paid by the fund out of "any judgment or settlement" she received. The next paragraph required her to "reimburse" the fund out of any recovery she received. Although the third paragraph included subrogation rights, we will not interpret the language to allow greater rights or duties than those in the original plan agreement. The final paragraphs added assignments of plaintiff's claims and rights to the fund. The result is that plaintiff took on additional obligations, without consideration, in order to be paid that which she was already owed. All such additional obligations are unenforceable.

CONCLUSION

The original plan agreement between plaintiff and the fund required the fund to pay plaintiff's medical expenses as long as its right of subrogation was protected. Absent a breach by plaintiff, the fund had no rights of reimbursement for medical expense benefits from plaintiff. We hold that the preexisting duty rule barred the fund from requiring plaintiff to take on additional burdens, without consideration, in order to get paid that which she was owed. Because the second contract was invalid for lack of consideration, we hold that the fund was not entitled to a reimbursement from plaintiff. We, therefore, reverse the Court of Appeals affirmance of the trial court's grant of summary disposition and order defendant fund to repay to the plaintiff any sums plaintiff paid to reimburse the fund.

2. Detrimental Reliance

Borrowing from a Uniform Commercial Code concept, Courts also use a test of whether one party detrimentally relied on another person's promises as consideration to bind a contract. Suppose a university asked a professor to teach an additional class. The professor had planned to continue work as a consultant with a client but would not have time to both teach the class and continue the consulting assignment. The university offered extra compensation for teaching the class and so the professor declined to continue the consulting assignment. Then the university decided not to offer the class. In such a case, the professor had detrimentally relied on the promises of the university and could enforce the terms of the contract because of that detrimental reliance.

In the Restatement, § 90 defines a "Promise Reasonably Inducing Action or Forbearance as,

1. A promise which the promisor should reasonably expect to induce action or forbearance on the part of the promisee or a third person and which does induce such action or forbearance is binding if injustice can be avoided only by enforcement of the promise. The remedy granted for breach may be limited as justice requires.

2. A charitable subscription or a marriage settlement is binding under Subsection 1. without proof that the promise induced action or forbearance.

The second subdivision states that a gift to charity or a marriage settlement does not have to produce action in order to bind the parties based on reliance. For an example of a charitable subscription case, see Justice Cardozo, writing in *Allegheny College v. National Chautauqua County Bank*, 247 N.Y. 369 (1927), which first announced the rule now codified in subsection two.

3. Statutory Exceptions

There are some statutory exceptions to the requirement of consideration. The more common examples today are covered in the following chapter on the Uniform Commercial Code and pertain to business-related sales contracts where the consideration will be inferred. The rationale for such cases draws heavily on the notions of detrimental reliance just described. There are also some older rules concerning "seals" and "waivers" where if a party is deemed to have provided consideration by undertaking a unique act, which while interesting, take us a bit too far afield from a more focused treatment of consideration.

———————————

D. LEGAL PURPOSE AND PUBLIC POLICY CONSTRAINTS

Even if the parties agree to a contract, that does not mean that the contract is valid. To be a valid contract, it must also not be for a purpose that violates the law or public policy. At the extreme, this makes complete sense: we would not want the court system to enforce a "contract" for murder or a conspiracy to commit theft. But beyond those self-evident kinds of prohibited contracts, there are others that are more nuanced. The Restatement sections holding contracts unenforceable on the grounds of public policy are, again, numerous, and are set out in sections 178 to 199, including a presumption that one cannot collect damages on these void contracts (§197). Sections 178 and 179 lay out the basic framework:

§ 178: When a Term Is Unenforceable on Grounds of Public Policy

1. A promise or other term of an agreement is unenforceable on grounds of public policy if legislation provides that it is unenforceable or the interest in its enforcement is clearly outweighed in the circumstances by a public policy against the enforcement of such terms.

2. In weighing the interest in the enforcement of a term, account is taken of

   a. the parties justified expectations,

   b. any forfeiture that would result if enforcement were denied, and

   c. any special public interest in the enforcement of the particular term.

3. In weighing a public policy against enforcement of a term, account is taken of

   a. the strength of that policy as manifested by legislation or judicial decisions,

   b. the likelihood that a refusal to enforce the term will further that policy,

   c. the seriousness of any misconduct involved and the extent to which it was deliberate, and

   d. the directness of the connection between that misconduct and the term.

§ 179: Bases of Public Policies Against Enforcement

A public policy against the enforcement of promises or other terms may be derived by the court from

   a. legislation relevant to such a policy, or

■ A VALID CONTRACT CANNOT VIOLATE A LAW OR PUBLIC POLICY.

  b. the need to protect some aspect of the public welfare, as is the case for the judicial policies against, for example,

  i. restraint of trade (§§ 186-188),

  ii. impairment of family relations (§§ 189-191), and

  iii. interference with other protected interests (§§ 192-196, 356).

I. Prohibition Against Illegal Contracts

While the contract to murder raises no questions about validity—clearly, it is invalid—the more likely cases to arise are those where a contract violates a requirement of a license or regulation. This might include building or continuing to run a casino after a legislature has revoked a license to operate or allowed a license to expire. Without an authorization, casino gambling would be illegal, and so contracts to continue the business would be unenforceable. Another example would be a contract to build a building or to expand a building without having received permission from a zoning authority. The following case exemplifies these kinds of unenforceability of contract based on conflict with an existing law or regulation.

Jimerson v. Tetlin Native Corp.

144 P.3d 470 (Alaska 2006)

MATTHEWS, Justice.

The Tetlin Native Corporation (TNC) is a village corporation formed pursuant to ANCSA and organized as an Alaska business corporation. On July 17, 1996, TNC transferred approximately 643,174 acres of its land to the Tetlin Tribal Council. This left TNC with 100,000 acres of land.

Subsequently, the appellants, Shirley Jimerson and Ramona David, conducted a campaign to recall TNC's board of directors. The campaign was successful, and on January 12, 1999, Jimerson and David were elected to the board.

On March 15, 1999, TNC and Jimerson and David, as directors and individual shareholders (collectively Jimerson), filed a complaint in Alaska Superior Court in Fairbanks against certain shareholders and directors of TNC. The complaint alleged breach of fiduciary duties and wrongful transfer of TNC land, and requested $257,200,000 in damages and declaratory and injunctive relief. On April 20, 1999, the case was removed to the United States District Court for the District of Alaska.

On August 6, 1999, the Jimerson board was recalled. The new board passed a resolution that TNC dismiss all law suits brought by the Jimerson board. On October 6, 1999, TNC moved to dismiss without prejudice all claims it had against the shareholders and former and current directors of TNC. The district court denied TNC's motion to dismiss and urged the parties to reach a settlement.

The court's advice bore fruit, and the parties reached a settlement agreement. In August 2001 the district court approved the agreement and entered judgment on it. The settlement agreement acknowledged that TNC shareholders may not have been fully informed regarding dissenters' rights in the 1996 land transfer and provided for

> [a] transfer of a portion of Tetlin Native Corporation's remaining lands ... to a new corporation to be formed by dissenting shareholders ... who elect to transfer their shares of Tetlin Native Corporation ANCSA stock back to the corporation in exchange for shares in the new corporation.

In May 2003 Jimerson filed a motion in district court to enforce the settlement agreement. TNC opposed the motion and moved for relief from the judgment, contending that the district court lacked subject-matter jurisdiction. The district court concluded that the case presented no substantial federal question and declared the judgment based on the settlement agreement void for lack of jurisdiction. The case was then remanded to the superior court.

On February 23, 2004, Jimerson filed a motion in the superior court to enforce the settlement agreement. TNC opposed the motion, arguing that the settlement agreement was unenforceable as against public policy for three reasons: 1. the agreement provided for an exchange of shares in violation of ANCSA's prohibition on alienation, 2. the agreement violated the Alaska Corporations Code, and 3. the attorney for plaintiffs had a conflict of interest.

On June 18, 2004, the superior court denied Jimerson's motion to enforce the settlement agreement on the grounds that the agreement was unenforceable because it violated ANCSA's prohibition on alienation.

Jimerson appeals this denial.

III. DISCUSSION

We have adopted the Restatement principle that "[a] promise or other term of an agreement is unenforceable on grounds of public policy if legislation provides that it is unenforceable...." This court has "no power, either in law or in equity, to enforce an agreement which directly contravenes a legislative enactment."

The issue before this court is whether the transaction contemplated by the settlement agreement is prohibited by ANCSA. The settlement agreement transferred a portion of TNC's remaining land to a new corporation and then allowed "dissenting shareholders" to "transfer their shares of Tetlin Native Corporation ANCSA stock back to the corporation in exchange for shares in the new corporation."

When Congress enumerates exceptions to a rule, we can infer that no other exceptions apply. Section 7(h)1.c. lists three exceptions that allow stock to be transferred to a Native or a descendent of a Native: 1. pursuant to a court decree of separation, divorce, or child support, 2. if the stock limits the holder's ability to practice his or her profession, or 3. as an *inter vivos* gift to certain relatives. Section 7(h)2. permits shares to escheat to the corporation if the holder has no heirs, and permits a corporation to repurchase shares transferred by the laws of intestate succession to a person who is not a Native or descendant of a Native. The transaction contemplated by the settlement agreement does not fall within any of these exceptions. We therefore infer that no exception applies for transfer of ANCSA stock back to a Native corporation in exchange for stock in a newly created corporation.

* * *

We AFFIRM the superior court's denial of Jimerson's motion for enforcement of the settlement agreement.

---

2. Public Policy Issues

Contracts that violate public policy present the same issues, and are unenforceable for the same reasons, as contracts that violate the law. The challenging part about these kinds of issues is knowing when they will arise. Like many common law instances, there may not be a preexisting law that a contract would clearly violate. Instead, the "agreement" between the parties raises questions that the courts find themselves very uncomfortable with and that they are therefore unwilling to enforce for "public policy" reasons. Those reasons become law in and of themselves, but the examples continue to often be referred to as violating public policy even though precedent has established them as controlling law for decades. Three examples are unconscionable contracts, covenants not to compete, and waivers of liability.

a. Unconscionability. Beginning in the 1960s, marked by the adoption of adhesion analysis in *Steven v. Fidelity & Casualty Co.*, 58 Cal.2d 862 (1962), courts faced litigation where a company (for example, Sears) was attempting to enforce a contract. The contract in this benchmark case was between the company and an individual who was buying a home appliance, such as a washer or dryer. Many of the customers purchasing the appliance were poorly educated immigrants who were often illiterate and unable to speak or write English. They also bought the appliance on an installment basis, so that they paid a set amount each month. The contracts provided that if the customer missed a payment, the interest rate on the outstanding balance would rise significantly. As a result, the customer was often unable to continue to pay the loan and the appliance was eventually seized by the company.

In reaction, courts developed the idea of "unconscionability." In other words, the terms of the contract so shocked the conscience as to make them unenforceable. More specifically, the standards developed by the court were that if there were grossly unequal bargaining positions and the terms of the contract were so one-sided and unfair as to shock the conscience, the court may view the objectionable terms of the contract as unenforceable. Restatement § 208 allows courts to refuse to enforce unconscionable contracts in part or in whole. "The determination that a contract or term is or is not unconscionable is made in the light of its setting, purpose or effect. Relevant factors include weaknesses in the contracting process like those involved in more specific rules as to contractual capacity, fraud, and other invalidating causes; the policy also overlaps with rules which render particular bargains or terms unenforceable on grounds of public policy" (§ 208, comment a).

It is worth noting that it is very unlikely that someone reading this book would be in a position to claim that they have been so unfairly treated by a company that they can trigger the unconscionability doctrine. One reason is that students in a college or graduate school are not in the category of poor and illiterate consumers who are unable to read the terms. Yes, it is true that, a student (or a professor!) has limited bargaining potential compared to Microsoft. Yet, one can read the contract. One can find a lawyer. One can walk away from unfair terms.

---

b. Covenants Not to Compete. Courts take a balancing approach to covenants not to compete. The fact that there is a balancing approach should put students on notice because there are times when these agreements could inhibit employment mobility. The idea behind a covenant not to compete is that a company spends time and money training employees or, in a takeover case, may be spending money to buy out another company. The employers do not want an employee to take the knowledge and training they have gained, move to a competitor, and compete with the company. Thus, companies will include in the employee's contract a provision that says that the employee is precluded from taking another job with a competing firm for a period of time. The most attractive new employer for an employee, of course, is one that values exactly the experience and knowledge learned by being in the same or similar industry, and so these covenants can unexpectedly inhibit one's mobility.

Courts recognize the property interest companies have in investing in their employees and so will, indeed, enforce these covenants. They also recognize the importance of freedom of contract, including the freedom to work with whomever one wants to work. So, courts will evaluate these covenants on the basis of the geographical and time restrictions that prevent an employee from working elsewhere. These considerations had one set of applications prior to the Internet and its undermining of geographic significance; today, there is another set of considerations that reflect the realities of an Internet-influenced world. The following two cases set out these examples. Sections 186, 187, and 188 govern restraints on trade, and they square with the types of factors listed in the following cases.

Kennedy v. Metropolitan Life Ins. Co.

759 So.2d 362 (Mississippi 2000)

PRATHER, Chief Justice, for the Court:

STATEMENT OF THE CASE

Phillip Dewayne Kennedy ("Kennedy") worked as an insurance agent for Metropolitan Life Insurance Company ("Met Life") for over six years. In the process, Kennedy became one of the top life insurance salesmen in the Tupelo District. On August 4, 1995, Kennedy submitted his resignation to Shelby Ware ("Ware"), district manager of Met Life, and became associated with Massachusetts Mutual Insurance Company ("Mass Mutual").

Following Kennedy's departure, Ware initiated on behalf of Met Life an investigation into whether Kennedy had violated the non-competition terms of an employment contract that Kennedy had signed on January 27, 1989. Met Life concluded that Kennedy had in fact violated his non-competition agreement, and Met Life filed suit against Kennedy on September 20, 1995. Following trial, the Chancellor rejected Kennedy's argument that the non-competition agreement was contrary to public policy, and he further found that Kennedy had violated the terms of the agreement. The Chancellor awarded Met Life damages for lost premium income, as well as attorney's fees in enforcing the agreement. Feeling aggrieved, Kennedy timely appealed to this Court.

* * *

Non-competition agreements have been viewed by this Court as "restrictive contracts [which] are in restraint of trade and individual freedom and are not favorites of the law." Only when such agreements are reasonable will they be considered valid and upheld by this Court. The validity and the enforceability of a non-competition agreement are largely predicated upon the reasonableness and specificity of its terms, primarily, the duration of the restriction and its geographic scope. The burden of proving the reasonableness of these terms is on the employer.

The non-competition provision in the present case provided that:

> 1. During and for 18 months following my voluntary or involuntary termination of employment with Metropolitan, I will not directly or indirectly perform any act or make any statement which would tend to divert from Metropolitan any trade or business with any customer, be it a person, a company, or an organization, to whom I previously sold insurance offered by or through Metropolitan; nor will I advise or induce any customer

of Metropolitan, be it a person, a company or an organization, to reduce, replace, lapse, surrender or cancel any insurance obtained from or
through Metropolitan.

Kennedy argues that he did not violate the aforementioned provision, given that
the evidence at trial established that all of his Met Life clients who switched to Mass
Mutual had done so of their own volition and without advice or encouragement on
his part. The record supports Kennedy's assertions in this regard.

Howard Carnes, who had been friends with Kennedy for eight years, testified
that he learned that Kennedy was no longer a Met Life employee from talking to his
wife. Carnes testified that, upon learning the news, he decided to drop his Met Life
policy and obtain coverage with Mass Mutual "because I wanted (Kennedy) to be my
agent." Carnes testified that Kennedy took no actions at all to influence his decision
to switch his coverage to Mass Mutual, and that the decision was his alone. Carnes
did acknowledge on cross-examination, however, that Kennedy had processed his
application with Mass Mutual, including arranging a physical examination.

Kenneth Clowers, who is married to Kennedy's sister-in-law, testified that he
had known Kennedy for approximately five years. Clowers testified that he learned
of Kennedy's departure from Met Life at a "family get together" and that he decided
to switch his coverage to Mass Mutual due to family loyalty and due to his satisfaction with Kennedy's service as an agent. Clowers testified that the decision to switch
coverage was "totally" his own and that Kennedy had done nothing to influence that
decision. In fact, Clowers testified that Kennedy had "actually tried to get me to keep
the policy, but like I said, I don't have any loyalty to a company. I have a loyalty to a
brother-in-law." Clowers acknowledged on cross examination that, once he decided
to switch his coverage to Mass Mutual, Kennedy arranged for him to do so.

Brenda Matthews testified that she knew Kennedy through his status as her Met
Life insurance agent for several years. Matthews testified that she learned of Kennedy's having left Met Life when she called Met Life to inquire about her coverage.
The Met Life representatives informed Matthews that Kennedy no longer worked
there, although they did not inform her where he was working. Matthews testified
that she then called Kennedy's wife "because I knew them personally." Matthews
testified that "they were acquaintances, but friends if need be" and that she felt she
was close enough to Kennedy to call his wife. Matthews testified that "I decided if he
wasn't there (at Met Life) I didn't want to be there because of the fact of who he was,
and I could depend on him and call him and he would be there for me." Matthews
further testified that "it was my request that he come to my house, and he did. And
it was my request that he show me what he had, because I was not going to keep the
insurance that I already had any way."

Joyce McGar provided very similar testimony, testifying that she had known
Kennedy for 10 years and that she called him when she heard he was no longer employed at Met Life. McGar testified that Kennedy had done nothing to induce her
to make this decision.

Kennedy also emphasizes that, at the time he quit his position, he had approximately 1,000 policyholders on the books at Met Life. Of these 1,000 policyholders, Met Life only presented evidence that twenty-one switched their coverage to Mass Mutual. Moreover, as noted *supra,* all policyholders who testified at trial indicated that it was their decision alone to switch their coverage to Mass Mutual and that Kennedy did not advise them to do so.

Met Life does not dispute that the aforementioned customers contacted Kennedy of their own volition, and Met Life instead argues that Kennedy violated the agreement by helping these customers to obtain Mass Mutual policies once they contacted him. Specifically, Met Life argues that:

> The non-competition provisions at issue prohibited Kennedy from "directly or indirectly perform(ing) any act or mak(ing) any statement which would tend to divert from Metropolitan any trade or business with any customer ... to whom (he had) previously sold insurance." Kennedy contends that he did not violate these prohibitions because he did not solicit the customers who changed their policies to Mass Mutual; rather, he argues, since these customers contacted Kennedy and allegedly desired to continue to do business with him, he can not be found to have diverted Met Life's business. Nevertheless, Kennedy admitted that once contacted, he prepared premium quotations for the customers, prepared applications for coverage with Mass Mutual, prepared replacement coverage notices to MetLife, collected initial premiums and delivered their new Mass Mutual policies. The chancellor found that Kennedy's participation in the change of coverage as stated above constituted activities which "would tend to divert" business with such insurance clients and, therefore, violated the language of the non-competition agreement.

* * *

This Court agrees with Met Life that a non-compete provision which prohibits an ex-employee from accepting business with his former customers may, in appropriate cases, constitute a reasonable and enforceable non-compete provision. However, this Court concludes that the non-competition provision in the present case is ambiguous in that, unlike the provisions in *Kemper* and *Girard,* the provision in the present case does not expressly prohibit Kennedy from "accepting" business with a former employee. Instead, as noted *supra,* the provision in the present case rather ambiguously provides that:

> 1. During and for 18 months following my voluntary or involuntary termination of employment with Metropolitan, I will not directly or indirectly perform any act or make any statement which would tend to divert from Metropolitan any trade or business with any customer, be it a person, a company, or an organization, to whom I previously sold insurance offered by or through Metropolitan; nor will I advise

> or induce any customer of Metropolitan, be it a person, a company
> or an organization, to reduce, replace, lapse, surrender or cancel any
> insurance obtained from or through Metropolitan.

In the view of this Court, the language of this particular non-compete provision is subject to differing interpretations. One arguable interpretation of the provision is that it prohibits the selling of any insurance by Kennedy to his former customers, even if the customer decided to change his coverage on his own volition. Another reasonable interpretation of the provision, however, is that the provision merely prohibits Kennedy from inducing or advising his former customers to change their coverage to Mass Mutual.

The agreement ambiguously prohibits Kennedy from "perform(ing) any act or make any statement which would tend to divert from Met Life any trade or business with any customer." Given these ambiguities, it is apparent that Kennedy was placed in a very uncertain position when he was contacted by his former customers who were seeking to switch their coverage. Kennedy could have reasonably concluded that, since these former customers had already decided to switch their coverage, and had initiated contact with him, he would not be violating the provisions of the non-compete agreement by accepting their business.

This Court also notes that there is no evidence in the record that Kennedy encouraged a single policy holder to switch coverage from Met Life to Mass Mutual.[2] The record supports a conclusion that Kennedy was attempting to comply with the requirements of the non-compete provision, as he understood the requirements to be. Moreover, as noted earlier, Kennedy had issued over one thousand active policies at the time of his departure from Met Life, and Met Life only sought damages for twenty-one of these policies. While neither of these factors is, by any means, dispositive, this Court concludes that an enforcement of the non-compete agreement against Kennedy would be particularly unfair under the facts of the present case.

---

2 As noted *supra*, Kenneth Clowers testified that Kennedy tried to talk him out of switching his coverage to Mass Mutual.

Market Access Int'l, Inc. v. KMD Media, LLC

72 Va.Cir. 355 (Vir. Cir. Ct. 2006)

JONATHAN C. THACHER, Circuit Court Judge.

* * *

Plaintiff Market Access is an Arlington-based company that provides marketing, trade association conference planning, and training seminars for government and private industry personnel in the field of homeland security. Plaintiff Homeland Defense Journal, Inc. (HDJI) produces and distributes trade publications relating to homeland security and information technology security.

Market Access contracted with Defendant Pro-Media to sell advertising space in its publications. Under this agreement, Pro-Media agreed not to compete with the Plaintiff by selling or promoting publications that competed with Market Access' publications. The agreement also included a non-disclosure provision preventing Pro-Media from disclosing Market Access' proprietary client database.

Plaintiffs allege that Defendant Silverberg, who was hired to be the managing editor of Homeland Defense Journal, conspired with Market Access consultant Wandres, Pro-Media, and others to create a competing publication to Market Access' planned homeland security newsletter, alternatively called *Homeland Security Today* or *HSToday*. As part of the alleged conspiracy, Plaintiffs contend that the Defendants organized Defendant KMD as a means of publishing a print magazine called *HSToday* and a web site bearing the same name.

Count II of Plaintiff's Second Amended Motion for Judgment alleges Breach of Contract. Plaintiffs allege that Defendant Pro-Media breached its duties under the non-competition portion of its agreement with Market Access. The relevant non-compete language contained in the parties agreement is as follows:

> "Under this agreement, Sales Representative shall not compete with Company, directly or indirectly in the sale or promotion of products that directly compete with Company's existing publication, *Homeland Defense Journal*, for one year following the termination of this agreement.....Company acknowledges that the primary business area of Sales Representative is the representation of several military publications (both in the U.S. and abroad), and that Sales Representative will continue to represent publications of this nature during the scope of this agreement...."

Defendant Pro-Media demurrers on the grounds that the non-compete agreement is unenforceable as a matter of law.

* * *

In considering whether non-competition agreements are enforceable as a matter of law the Virginia Supreme Court has ruled that such an agreement may be enforced if the agreement is 1. narrowly drawn to protect an employer's business interest, is 2. not unduly burdensome on an employee's ability to earn a living, and 3. is not against public policy. In Virginia, non-competition agreements are viewed as disfavored restraints on trade and thus the burden of proof that the agreement is reasonable and any ambiguities in the agreement are construed against the party seeking to enforce the agreement. Central to the analysis considering the reasonableness of these agreements is whether there are reasonable limits on duration, geographic area and whether the scope of the restrictions is narrowly tailored to protect the employer's interest. Any non-competition agreement that is overbroad is unenforceable as a matter of law.

* * *

Virginia courts are hesitant to enforce non-competition agreements that essentially prohibit a person from seeking employment in his or her chosen field. For that reason, many non-competition agreements contain geographical provisions limiting the area where the employee is not permitted to seek competing work to the area the business can expect to "reach." Where a business is regional in scope this is relatively easy, but with the advent of the Internet and the nationalization of everything from products to ideas, this has become substantially more difficult. *Homeland Defense Journal* holds itself out as a national publication, and indeed homeland security itself is an issue that often lends itself to discussion on the national level.

Pro-Media argues that the lack of any geographic limitation renders the non-competition agreement unenforceable as a matter of law because it essentially infers a worldwide restriction. The analysis conducted by the Virginia Supreme Court in the *Omniplex, Motion Control,* and *Simmons* cases does not support this contention. While in each of these cases the lack of geographic limitations was a part of the analysis, it was by no means solely determinative of the issue of whether the agreements were enforceable as a matter of law.

The Virginia Supreme Court has upheld non-competition agreements that are narrowly-drawn even when they encompass a larger geographic area. In *Blue Ridge Anesthesia & Critical Care, Inc. v. Gidick*, 239 Va. 369 (1990), a non-competition agreement that spanned four states—Virginia, North Carolina, West Virginia, and Maryland, as well as the District of Columbia—was not considered overbroad. The plaintiff company sold and serviced critical care and anesthesia equipment in that region and the Court noted that the agreement did not prohibit former employees from selling similar equipment outside the designated territory, nor did it prohibit the former employees from selling different medical equipment within the company's territory.

In *Roanoke Engineering Sales Co. v. Rosenbaum*, 223 Va. 548 (1982), the Virginia Supreme Court held that a three-year, multi-state non-competition agreement was not overbroad because the former employee had knowledge of the employer's business interests in all its branches. The Court said the agreement was "coterminous" with the territory in which the firm did business and was therefore not overbroad.

What can be garnered from the analysis of each of these cases is that when the competition at issue is direct and the agreements are narrowly drawn to prohibit such direct competition the non-competition agreements are more likely to be enforceable.

> **"WHEN THE COMPETITION at issue is direct and the agreements are narrowly drawn to prohibit such direct competition the non-competition agreements are more likely to be enforceable."**

While the language of the non-competition agreement at issue clearly does not contain language limiting the geographic scope of the agreement, the language of the agreement does limit the duration of the non-compete agreement to one year and limits the prohibited activities to those in direct competition with *Homeland Defense Journal.*

The mere fact that there is no geographic limitation is not fatal to the enforceability of the non-compete agreement between Market Access and Pro-Media. The language of the agreement contemplates Pro-Media's continued relationships with other military publications and only specifically Pro-Media's activities to those that would directly compete with Market Access' *Homeland Defense Journal* publication. Thus it does not prohibit Pro-Media from continuing to work in its field in a manner the Virginia Supreme Court found objectionable in *Omniplex or Motion Control.* Nor does the one year limitation on direct competition with *Homeland Defense Journal* appear unreasonable considering the Court's analysis in *Rosenbaum.* The terms of the non-competition agreement at issue appear to be narrowly tailored to protect Market Access' legitimate business interests while not prohibiting Pro-Media from competing in its chosen field. The non-compete agreement at issue also appears to be narrowly tailored so that it does not offend public policy.

CONCLUSION

The Court disagrees with the contention that the non-competition agreement between Market Access and Pro-Media is unenforceable as a matter of law. Therefore Pro-Media's Demurrer to Count II alleging Breach of Contract [non-compete agreements] by Pro-Media is overruled. Attached to this opinion is an order reflecting the Court's ruling.

E. OTHER ISSUES

Even if a contract is valid—that is, it complies with all the above steps—its enforceability may still be in question. These additional issues pertain to the requirement that some agreements be in writing Those issues are considered under what is known as the Statute of Frauds. Even if the contracts do not have to be in writing, issues arise when a contract is, in fact, put into writing and the parties indicate that it is meant to be a final agreement with no outside evidence to determine the agreement's meeting. This prohibition on outside evidence is known as the "parol evidence rule."

I. Statute of Frauds

The rationale behind the Statute of Frauds was that the subject matter of some contracts was so important—and so important to protect from fraudulent activities—so as to require them to be in writing. The statute of frauds served two related functions: an evidentiary and a commemorative role. Requiring writings for certain transactions, like those for the sale of land, gave the court and the parties the ability to prove the existence of a contract without resorting to implied or oral contracts. Related is the notion that some transactions are so important, or may become effective at such a distant time, that courts have decided they must specifically impress the importance of obligations on the parties by requiring a writing. Chapter 5, Sections 100 through 124, cover the Statute of Frauds; § 100 defines the scope of the statute:

1. The following classes of contracts are subject to a statute, commonly called the Statute of Frauds, forbidding enforcement unless there is a written memorandum or an applicable exception:

   a. a contract of an executor or administrator to answer for a duty of his decedent (the executor-administrator provision);

   b. a contract to answer for the duty of another (the suretyship provision);

   c. a contract made upon consideration of marriage (the marriage provision);

   d. a contract for the sale of an interest in land (the land contract provision);

   e. a contract that is not to be performed within one year from the making thereof (the one-year provision).

2. The following classes of contracts, which were traditionally subject to the Statute of Frauds, are now governed by Statute of Frauds provisions of the Uniform Commercial Code:

   a. a contract for the sale of goods for the price of $500 or more (Uniform Commercial Code § 2-201);

   b. a contract for the sale of securities (Uniform Commercial Code § 8-319);

   c. a contract for the sale of personal property not otherwise covered, to the extent of enforcement by way of action or defense beyond $5,000 in amount or value of remedy (Uniform Commercial Code § 1-206).

  3. In addition the Uniform Commercial Code requires a writing signed by the debtor for an agreement which creates or provides for a security interest in personal property or fixtures not in the possession of the secured party.

  4. Statutes in most states provide that no acknowledgment or promise is sufficient evidence of a new or continuing contract to take a case out of the operation of a statute of limitations unless made in some writing signed by the party to be charged, but that the statute does not alter the effect of any payment of principal or interest.

  5. In many states other classes of contracts are subject to a requirement of a writing.

a. Real Estate Related. Real estate is the main subject matter for the application of the Statute of Frauds. Any transfer of real estate requires that the contract be in writing. This applies, of course, to a conveyance of ownership from one person to the other,

which is called a transfer of fee simple ownership. It is nearly impossible to sell or buy real estate outright without it being in writing. If one has a mortgage on the property, any lender will insist that the mortgagor's right to the property be in writing; otherwise the mortgagee's security interest is in jeopardy. One cannot record any ownership of the real estate without a writing; indeed, a "deed" is a writing necessary to have in order for land ownership to be recorded in a government office. And without such a recording, one's ownership interest would be in jeopardy anyway. Of a more ambiguous nature are leases. These, too, are subject to the Statute of Frauds, but many leases are informal, oral agreements that are never reduced to writing. The following is a contemporary, but typical, Statute of Frauds and real estate analysis.

Ayalla v. Southridge

37 Kan.App.2d 312 (Kan. Ct. App. 2007)

GREEN, P.J.

* * *

Ayalla sued Southridge Presbyterian for breach of contract. Ayalla set forth the following allegations in support of her claim.

Southridge Presbyterian, owner of a residential home, offered to sell it for the amount of $134,500. On April 25, 2005, Ayalla viewed the home. Ayalla made a written offer to purchase the home for $130,000 on April 26, 2005. The written offer was made on a residential real estate sale contract form furnished by Southridge Presbyterian's real estate agent, Jim Henderson. Ayalla gave Henderson a check for $1,000 as an earnest money deposit. Henderson later negotiated the closing costs with Mike Pyper, Ayalla's mortgage broker.

On April 28, 2005, Henderson orally notified Pyper that Southridge Presbyterian had accepted Ayalla's offer. Pyper left a message with Ayalla's nephew regarding Southridge Presbyterian's acceptance. The following day, Henderson orally told Ayalla personally of Southridge Presbyterian's acceptance. Henderson and Ayalla agreed to meet on May 1, 2005, to complete the paperwork, and Ayalla made plans to take that day off work. Based on Southridge Presbyterian's oral acceptance, Ayalla scheduled a home inspection to take place on May 2 or 3.

Ayalla and her friends and family gathered together on May 1 to celebrate. Before her scheduled meeting with Henderson, however, he called and told Ayalla that Southridge Presbyterian had accepted a higher offer of $142,500 from the Hamiltons.

Ayalla alleged that this event caused anguish and monetary damages in the amount of $12,900. Ayalla's damages calculation consisted of $12,500 for the loss of the benefit of her bargain, $200 for her lost wages on May 1, and $200 for her legal expenses. In her petition, Ayalla requested a preliminary injunction, specific performance of the contract, restitution based on Southridge Presbyterian's unjust enrichment, monetary damages in the amount of $12,900, and other such relief the court deemed appropriate.

Following the filing of Ayalla's petition, Southridge Presbyterian moved to dismiss Ayalla's action based on the statute of frauds. Ayalla alleged in her answer to Southridge Presbyterian's motion to dismiss that the sale contract, which was prepared and signed by Henderson on behalf of Southridge Presbyterian, was a sufficient memorandum to satisfy the statute of frauds. Ayalla further alleged that Southridge Presbyterian engaged in fraud when it failed to disclose Ayalla's accepted offer to the Hamiltons. The trial court denied the motion due to the existence of outstanding discovery.

Following the completion of discovery, Southridge Presbyterian moved for summary judgment based on the statute of frauds. Ayalla argued at the summary judgment hearing that the sale contract containing Henderson's signature satisfied the statute of frauds. Ayalla admitted that she never received a signed contract from Southridge Presbyterian but maintained that Henderson's oral acceptance on behalf of Southridge Presbyterian was sufficient to render her written offer an enforceable agreement. The trial court granted Southridge Presbyterian's motion, finding that no enforceable contract under the statute of frauds existed between the parties for the sale of the property.

* * *

STATUTE OF FRAUDS

Ayalla asserts two main theories in support of her argument regarding the statute of frauds: 1. that an enforceable agreement existed between herself and Southridge Presbyterian based on Henderson's oral acceptance of her written offer; and 2. that the sale contract, which was signed by Henderson, was sufficient to satisfy the statute of frauds.

Southridge Presbyterian contends that no written agreement existed between itself and Ayalla for the sale of the real estate; therefore, the statute of frauds precludes relief.

Enacted to prevent fraud and injustice, the statute of frauds requires that an enforceable contract for the sale of real estate be in writing and signed by the party against whom enforcement is sought.

* * *

Based on the statute of frauds, the trial court determined that no enforceable agreement existed between the parties. The court stated the following:

> "[T]here is no evidence of any contract ever signed by anyone on behalf of Southridge Presbyterian Church to sell [Ayalla] that property.... [Henderson's] signature did not say that Southridge Presbyterian was making any specific offer to [Ayalla] to sell the property. All it did was say that this form contract which is a pre-printed form is a form approved by the Kansas City Regional Association of Realtors and that Remax Realty who had printed up this document had not changed it from the form contract that had been approved."

The trial court continued, "[t]he form [contract] was never signed by anyone representing Southridge Presbyterian. Accordingly[,] it has not been signed by the party against whom it is to be charged."

* * *

Because Southridge Presbyterian has asserted the defense of the statute of frauds, the only material fact is whether the parties' alleged agreement was evidenced by a writing signed by Southridge Presbyterian. Ayalla admitted that Henderson's signature on the sale contract did not evidence Southridge Presbyterian's agreement to sell her the house. Moreover, Ayalla failed to show that Henderson was properly authorized by Southridge Presbyterian to act in the capacity of the seller. Further, Ayalla conceded that she did not receive a signed contract from Southridge Presbyterian. As a result, the only material fact is not in dispute.

Next, we turn to the question of whether Southridge Presbyterian was entitled to judgment as a matter of law. Because the issue of whether an alleged contract satisfies the statute of frauds involves the interpretation of a statute, this court's review is unlimited.

Citing *Van Dyke v. Glover*, 326 Ark. 736 (1996), Ayalla first asserts that the oral acceptance of a written offer satisfies the statute of frauds. In *Van Dyke*, however, the written offer was made and signed by the party to be charged. Here, the written offer was made by Ayalla and was never signed by Southridge Presbyterian. The essential point in the trial court's ruling was the absence of a memorandum signed by Southridge Presbyterian as the party against whom Ayalla was seeking enforcement of the alleged oral agreement. As a result, *Van Dyke* does not support Ayalla's position.

Ayalla also argues that parties may bind themselves to an enforceable contract even though they contemplate the future execution of a formal instrument as evidence of their agreement. * * *

These cases do not aid Ayalla because they do not negate the requirement that an agreement for the sale of real estate must be evidenced by a writing signed by the party to be charged. Rather, the principle and cases simply indicate that under some circumstances, parties may bind themselves to an enforceable contract before they reduce their agreement to a formal instrument. In two of the cases cited by Ayalla, this principle was applicable when the parties had created a signed memorandum of the agreement but contemplated the future creation of a more formal instrument. In the third case cited by Ayalla, the statute of frauds was not applicable to the transaction. In the last case cited, the court held that the oral contract was *not* enforceable because it had not been reduced to a signed writing.

> **"AN AGREEMENT for the sale of real estate must be evidenced by a writing signed by the party to be charged."**

Ayalla next argues that the sale contract, signed by Henderson, was sufficient to satisfy the statute of frauds. According to Ayalla, the sale contract satisfies the writing requirement, and Henderson's signature satisfies the requirement that the writing be signed by the party to be charged.

The trial court correctly explained to Ayalla that Henderson's signature on the sale contract did not satisfy the signature requirement of the statute of frauds. As the trial court noted, Henderson signed the sale contract in a box that was designed to certify the form as containing, without addition or deletion, the language approved by the Kansas City Regional Association of Realtors. Notably, Henderson signed the sale contract before he had even informed Southridge Presbyterian of Ayalla's offer. Henderson's signature was not meant to be an acceptance of Ayalla's offer but simply a certification that the form was an approved real estate contract form.

Ayalla also argues in her brief that her actions indicate a contract was formed and cites *Reznik v. McKee, Trustee*, 216 Kan. 659, 673 (1975), for the principle that a court may determine the existence and terms of a contract based on a combination of written instruments and the parties' actions in connection with the writings. The trial court ruled that no enforceable agreement existed between Ayalla and Southridge Presbyterian because the signature requirement of the statute of frauds had not been satisfied. This argument by Ayalla, therefore, does not advance her position because it does not negate the absence of a writing signed by Southridge Presbyterian.

---

b. Employment Contracts. The Statute of Frauds also applies to two other kinds of cases. The first are employment contracts that cannot be performed in less than a year. The application of this rule can be counterintuitive. The Statute of Frauds requirement does not apply to a contract "for life" because it is possible for the contract to be performed within one year (because the employee could die within a year). A contract for a day less than a year also does not apply because the time period specified is, by definition, less than a year. However, a contract for two years would be subject to the Statute of Frauds.

Parker v. Crider Poultry Inc.

275 Ga. 361 (Georgia 2002)

BENHAM, Justice.

Appellant Jeffrey Parker formerly served as president and chief executive officer of appellees Crider, Inc., and Crider Poultry. In May 1998, while serving in those positions, Parker sent a letter resigning his positions effective August 1998. The Crider corporations filed suit against him seeking repayment of a bonus advanced to Parker and damages for an alleged breach of fiduciary duty. Parker filed a counterclaim in which he claimed appellees had breached his employment agreement by refusing to honor the three-month notice period set out in the parties' agreement by either permitting him to work for the three months between the date of his notice and the effective date of his resignation, or by paying him his salary for the three-month period. The trial court granted partial summary judgment to appellees on the counterclaim and the Court of Appeals affirmed the trial court's action. We granted Parker's petition for a writ of certiorari to the Court of Appeals, asking whether the Court of Appeals erred when it held that Parker could not recover on his claim for breach of the notice provision.

1. Both the trial court and the Court of Appeals based their judgments on the interplay between the Statute of Frauds[3] and a letter drafted and signed by W.A. Crider, Jr., on behalf of the Crider corporations, and counter-signed by appellant Parker. The letter set forth the base salary to be paid Parker, the formula for computing an incentive bonus, appellant's title and starting date, other benefits, and provided "Three months notice for either party." Citing *Gatins v. NCR Corp.*, 180 Ga.App. 595 (1986), the trial court determined that appellant's claim failed because the letter agreement did not comply with the Statute of Frauds since "a writing with an indefinite term does not comply with the statute." The Court of Appeals affirmed the trial court's judgment on the ground that the letter agreement was a contract that the Statute of Frauds required to be in writing because "the performance of [Parker's] employment agreement was not to be completed within one year" since he had submitted his letter of resignation more than two years after he had started working for Crider. Our review of the law leads us to conclude that both courts erred in their determination that the employment agreement between Parker and the Crider corporations fell within the Statute of Frauds.

The letter agreement did not state the duration of the term of employment. An employment contract containing no definite term of employment is terminable at the will of either party. A contract of employment of indefinite duration does not fall within the Statute of Frauds. This is so because, at its inception, a contract of employment for an indefinite duration is an agreement capable of being performed within one year, and the possibility of performance of the contract within one year is sufficient to remove it from the Statute of Frauds. The number of years the parties operate under an employment contract of indefinite duration does not affect the applicability of the Statute of Frauds. Thus, the Court of Appeals erred when it determined that the employment agreement relied upon by Parker was within the Statute of Frauds because Parker had completed over a year of employment under the contract before the dispute arose. The trial court misplaced its reliance when it cited Gatins because that case is distinguishable in that the contracts sought to be enforced therein were not to be performed within one year of their making and therefore had to be in writing under the Statute of Frauds. When a contract is required to be in writing, the writings relied upon must contain the entire agreement.

2. Because of their separate determinations that the Statute of Frauds was applicable to Parker's employment agreement, neither the trial court nor the Court of Appeals addressed the merits of Parker's assertion that the Crider corporations breached the employment agreement when they did not adhere to the three-months' notice provision. While an employee with an employment agreement of indefinite

---

3   The Statute of Frauds is codified at OCGA § 13-5-30 and provides that certain types of obligations must be in writing and signed by the party to be charged in order for the obligation to be binding on the promisor. The obligation pertinent to the case at bar is found in subsection (5) of the statute: "Any agreement that is not to be performed within one year from the making thereof" must be in writing and signed by the party to be charged in order to be binding on the promisor.

duration may not successfully pursue a wrongful termination claim upon termination of employment, the employee has a claim for breach of contract if the employer had agreed to give notice of termination but did not. In the case at bar, Parker sent a letter to W.A. Crider, Jr., on May 7, 1998, informing Crider that

> This serves as my written notice of my intention to exercise, under our agreement, my option to resign my position by providing three months notice to you. Therefore, I resign as President/CEO of Crider, Inc. and Crider Poultry, Inc. ninety days from this date or on Wednesday, August 5, 1998.

In his deposition, Parker testified that he recognized Crider had the authority to determine whether Parker worked during the three-month period between notice and resignation, that Crider accepted the resignation immediately on May 7, and that Parker did not return to work at Crider during the three-month period. It is unclear whether Parker's failure to work at Crider during the notice period was due to the fact that Crider accepted the notice of resignation and made it effective on the day of receipt, thereby effectively terminating Parker's employment without giving the required three months' notice, or whether Parker made the decision not to report to work for the three-month period, thereby effectively terminating his employment without giving the required three-months' notice. In light of the unresolved factual issue, summary judgment was inappropriate, making erroneous both the trial court's grant of summary judgment to appellees on Parker's counterclaim, and the Court of Appeals' affirmance of that judgment.

Judgment reversed.

All the Justices concur, except FLETCHER, C.J., who concurs in the judgment only in Division 2.

———————————

c. Suretyship. The other, additional kind of case is suretyship. Today, this might be more commonly known as co-signing a loan for another person. Anytime a person is obligating himself to pay the debt of another, it must be in writing in order to be enforceable.

Webb Manufacturing Co. v. Sinoff

449 PA.Super. 534 (Penn. Super. Ct. 1996)

HUDOCK, Judge:

* * *

This case commenced on September 30, 1994 when Webb Manufacturing Company (Webb) filed a complaint alleging that Brad Sinoff and Larry Sinoff (Sinoffs), on behalf of Apple Marketing, entered a contract to purchase goods and services. Webb averred that Sinoffs "in their capacity as principles [sic] of Apple Marketing" guaranteed to pay for the goods and services supplied by Webb in the event that Apple Marketing could not pay for them. Webb further averred that Sinoffs guaranteed the payment for the goods and services to induce Webb to enter such contract. Webb claimed that without Sinoffs' personal guarantee, it would not have agreed to ship the goods to Apple Marketing.

On April 7, 1995, Sinoffs filed preliminary objections in the nature of a demurrer claiming that Webb's claim was barred by the Statute of Frauds. Sinoffs also claimed that Webb could not recover against them individually since they conspicuously entered the contract in their capacity as agents of Apple Marketing.

* * *

The trial court concluded that Webb could not recover from Sinoffs in their personal capacity because it "failed to produce any written promise by [Sinoffs] to pay the debt of Apple Marketing[ ]" and thus failed to meet the requirements of the Statute of Frauds. Without evidence that Sinoffs executed a written agreement to personally answer for the debt of Apple Marketing, the trial court concluded that Webb's breach of contract claim was unenforceable under the Statute of Frauds.

The pertinent provision of the Pennsylvania Statute of Frauds is found at 33 P.S. section 3, which provides in pertinent part:

> No action shall be brought ... whereby to charge the defendant, upon any special promise, to answer for the debt or default of another, unless the agreement upon which such action shall be brought, or some memorandum or note thereof, shall be in writing, and signed by the party to be charged therewith, or some other person by him authorized.

We have previously explained the purpose of this rule:

> Promises to pay the debt of another must be in writing for at least two reasons. The first is *evidentiary*. The second, *cautionary*.

> Like other provisions of the statute [of frauds], the suretyship provision serves an evidentiary function. Indeed, Williston suggested that

> the circumstance that 'the promisor has received no benefit from the transaction ... may make perjury more likely, because while in the case of one who has received something the circumstances themselves which are capable of proof show probable liability, in the case of a guaranty nothing but the promise is of evidentiary value.' Furthermore, though in many instances the surety is paid by the principal for his undertaking, in others the surety's motivation is purely gratuitous and, 'as the lack of any benefit received by the guarantor increases the hardship of his being called upon to pay, it also increases the importance of being very sure that he is justly charged.'

> In addition to its evidentiary role, the provision serves a cautionary function. By bringing home to the prospective surety the significance of his act, it guards against ill-considered action. Otherwise, he might lightly undertake the engagement, unwisely assuming that there is only a remote possibility that the principal will not perform his duty....

The suretyship provision of the Statute of Frauds is a nonwaivable affirmative defense which may serve as the basis for a demurrer and a judgment on the pleadings.

The suretyship provision of the Statute of Frauds, however, does not apply if the main object of the promisor is to serve his own pecuniary or business purpose. This exception, known as the "leading object" or "main purpose" rule, "applies whenever a promisor, in order to advance some pecuniary or business purpose of his own, purports to enter into an oral agreement even though that agreement may be in the form of a provision to pay the debt of another." The Restatement (Second) of Contracts [§ 116] explains the rationale of this exception:

> Where the surety-promisor's main purpose is his own primary or business advantage, the gratuitous or sentimental element often present in suretyship is eliminated, the likelihood of disproportion in the values exchanged between promisor and promisee is reduced, and the commercial context commonly provides evidentiary safeguards. Thus there is less need for cautionary or evidentiary formality than in other cases of suretyship.

* * *

In cases where the promisor is a shareholder or officer of a corporation whose debt he has personally guaranteed, courts consider the percentage of the shareholder/guarantor's corporate ownership as a significant, although not sole criteria. For example, in *Acme Equipment Company Inc. v. Allegheny Steel Corporation,* 207 Pa.Super. 436 (1966), Rudy Valentino, the President and owner of 25% of Allegheny Steel Corporation, orally guaranteed to Acme Equipment Company that he would pay the debt incurred by Allegheny. When Acme attempted to enforce the oral guarantee, the trial court entered a compulsory nonsuit in favor of Valentino since the promise fell within the Statute of Frauds. On appeal, this Court examined whether Valentino made the promise for his own pecuniary interest. We explained:

> Although the [Statute of Frauds] does not apply if the main object of the promisor is to serve his own pecuniary or business purpose, ... the statute is not rendered inapplicable merely because a stockholder may indirectly receive some gain when he promises to pay the debt of a corporation. In *Bayard v. Pennsylvania Knitting Mills Corp.*, 290 Pa. 79, 84 (1927), the Supreme Court stated: "Ordinarily, the interest which a stockholder has is not individual, for he cannot be held for the corporate debts, and, if a promise to indemnify its creditor is made, the statute of frauds applies. * * * The mere fact that such person is concerned in promoting the financial success of the company is not sufficient to justify the treating of the promise of guaranty as an original undertaking. * * * "

* * *

In the present case the trial court did not consider whether the Sinoffs made the alleged oral guarantee for their own pecuniary or business ends. The court concluded that Webb admitted in paragraph 8 of its complaint that it contracted with Apple Marketing and not Sinoffs in their individual capacity. Paragraph 8 of Webb's complaint read:

> 8. [Appellees] Larry Sinoff and Brad Sinoff, in their capacity as principles [sic] of Apple Marketing, guaranteed the above-referenced bill in the event that Apple Marketing did not pay for said goods and/or services as was agreed. [Court's emphasis]

The trial court concluded that the "leading object" exception did not apply as a matter of law since Webb averred in paragraph eight that Sinoffs acted in their capacity as principals of Apple Marketing.

* * *

After examining the complaint in its entirety, we find Webb pled sufficient facts to raise the "leading object" exception to the Statute of Frauds, thus preventing the entry of a demurrer. Webb averred that Sinoffs made the guarantee "in the event that Apple Marketing did not pay for said goods and/or services as was agreed." Webb further averred that: "[Sinoffs] guaranteed the above-referenced bill in order to induce [Appellant] Webb Manufacturing to sell said goods and/or services to Apple Marketing." Cognizant of the standard that a demurrer may only be sustained when it is clear and free from doubt that the law will not permit recovery by the plaintiff upon the facts averred in the complaint, and that all doubts must be resolved against granting the demurrer, we find that the trial court erred in granting Sinoffs' demurrer. Accepting as true Webb's averment that it would not have sold Apple Marketing goods and services without Sinoffs' personal guarantee, Webb asserted sufficient facts to raise the "leading object" exception to the Statute of Frauds. If further facts are adduced when the parties replead or during discovery or at trial which prove that Sinoffs guaranteed Apple Marketing's debts for their personal benefit, Webb may prevent the lack of a written agreement and the Statute of Frauds from barring its ability to enforce the oral agreement. We find the facts of *Grant R. Wright, Inc. v. Haworth Energy Resources, Inc.*, 337 Pa.Super. 115 (1984), analogous.

* * *

The trial court should not have dismissed Webb's complaint with prejudice when there was insufficient evidence as to Sinoffs' motive in making the alleged oral guarantee to pay Apple Marketing's debt. We recognize, as we did in *Grant R. Wright, Inc. v. Haworth Energy Resources, Inc., supra*, that Webb may be unable to prove that the leading object exception applies in this case at the time of trial. However, at this stage of the proceedings, we find that the trial court should not have granted Sinoffs' demurrer on the basis of the Statute of Frauds when there were sufficient facts pled to raise the defense.

Order *reversed*. Case remanded for further proceedings consistent with this opinion. Jurisdiction is relinquished.

[JAMIESON, Judge, concurring omitted.]

─────────────

2. Parol Evidence Rule

In most contracts, the parties negotiate before reaching a final agreement. If a dispute arises, there can be ambiguity, at times, about what was actually agreed and what may have been discussed, but superseded by the final agreement. A way to handle this is to put the contract in writing and then to indicate that what is in writing constitutes the final agreement between the parties. When that happens, the Parol Evidence Rule is triggered. This Rule says that only the terms in writing control the agreement between the parties and outside evidence cannot be introduced to indicate any additional terms negotiated between the parties. Here is how the Restatement (§ 213) describes the rule:

§ 213: Effect of Integrated Agreement on Prior Agreements (Parol Evidence Rule)

1. A binding integrated agreement discharges prior agreements to the extent that it is inconsistent with them.

2. A binding completely integrated agreement discharges prior agreements to the extent that they are within its scope.

3. An integrated agreement that is not binding or that is voidable and avoided does not discharge a prior agreement. But an integrated agreement, even though not binding, may be effective to render inoperative

a term which would have been part of the agreement if it had not been integrated.

For example, suppose that you were buying a car. After haggling with the dealer, you are ready to sign the agreement, which contains a statement that the agreement constitutes the entire agreement between the parties. But you can't resist trying to add in one more item to "seal the deal.' So you get the saleperson to agree to add in free car servicing for a period of three years. A few months later, you take your car to the dealer's service wing to ask for a free oil change and they refuse because it was not part of the agreement. The salesperson feigns ignorance. The argument escalates and you end up in court. Who will win?

According to the Parol Evidence Rule, the dealer probably wins because you are trying to enforce a term that, pursuant to the contract you signed, is not in a contract that constitutes the entire agreement between the parties. Thus, the Parol Evidence rule has real consequences in contract disputes, as the following case also illustrates.

There are exceptions to the Parol Evidence Rule. One exception would be to prove fraud. A second common exception is to resolve an ambiguity. Sometimes contracts can have conflicting terms. Like some syllabi in courses, a performance date may be different in separate parts of the agreement. The only way one could determine which is the correct one would be to introduce evidence outside of the agreement. The following case combines a discussion of parol evidence with the role of clarifying exterior testimony. It is also important to note that parol evidence is not just limited to speech, but that it is considered any evidence exterior to the "four corners" of the agreement. While traditionally at common law, it was extremely difficult to introduce parol evidence when the contract lacked ambiguous language. As the following case shows, courts have progressively treated this presumption more leniently.

Lapierre v. Cabral

122 N.H. 301 (New Hampshire 1982)

KING, Chief Justice.

The issues presented in this case are whether the trial court erred in concluding that the contract between the plaintiff and a third party was assignable to the defendant and in refusing to admit parol evidence regarding possible financing conditions applicable to the plaintiff's and the defendant's contract of assignment. While we rule that the court should have admitted parol evidence, we find that the defendant did not sustain his burden of proof, and therefore, we affirm.

The plaintiff, Roland Lapierre, is a real estate developer in Nashua, New Hampshire, and the defendant, Richard Cabral, was also extensively engaged in the real estate business for many years.

On November 10, 1977, Lapierre and Guerrette Real Estate, Inc. of Nashua (Guerrette) entered into a written agreement in which Guerrette gave Lapierre an option to purchase land and buildings located on Main Street in Nashua for $200,000, with a schedule of installment payments to be secured by a first mortgage on the Main Street property. The contract was subject to an existing lease with Cabral which was to expire on July 8, 1979. As lessee, Cabral had expended about $15,000 on leasehold improvements that could not be taken to any other location.

Simultaneously with the execution of the option to purchase, Guerrette and Lapierre entered into a purchase-and-sale agreement for the same property. On July 17, 1978, the parties amended the option agreement, extending the period for payments and providing for the subordination of the mortgage to a purchase money or development mortgage which Lapierre placed on the property.

By instrument dated October 16, 1978, Lapierre assigned his option to purchase the Main Street property as well as two deposits totaling $15,000 he had already paid to Guerrette to Cabral. The assignment of the option contract provided that the closing was to take place on or before October 16, 1978. Cabral would then have the obligation to pay Lapierre the sum of $25,000. Under the agreement, Cabral would have no right to assign the option without the written consent of Lapierre. Additionally, the writing included a clause stating that the instrument represented all agreements between the parties.

On April 9, 1979, Guerrette and Lapierre executed a further amendment to the purchase-and-sale agreement which increased the payment at closing from $100,000 to $150,000, extended the term to pay off the mortgage and increased the amount of the interest.

Lapierre made demands upon Cabral in April 1979, for the $25,000, but no payment was made, and at the expiration of the option on July 8, 1979, the $15,000 paid by Lapierre to Guerrette was forfeited. Both Lapierre and Cabral were aware that the option to purchase the real estate had to be exercised by June 8, 1979. Cabral never exercised the option, and Lapierre said he found out that Cabral was not going through with the deal when Cabral leased space elsewhere. Consequently, Lapierre brought an action against Cabral for breach of their assignment contract. The Master (*Margaret Q. Flynn*, Esq.) found for the plaintiff, and her finding was approved by the Superior Court (*Bean*, J.).

At trial, the defendant alleged that because the plaintiff had arranged all the financing terms for the purchase of the property with Guerrette, that Guerrette had relied on the plaintiff's credit, thereby making the option personal to the plaintiff and not assignable to the defendant. The master found that the option was assignable, and we agree.

The option contract between the plaintiff and Guerrette contained words of assignability, and that language constitutes some evidence that the contract was assignable. The existence of financing terms in the plaintiff's option contract with Guerrette does not necessarily indicate that Guerrette relied on the plaintiff's personal credit. The words of assignability must control, absent any evidence that the parties intended the contract to be unassignable. The master, therefore, properly concluded that the option was validly assigned to the defendant.

The defendant also claims that the assignment contract between the defendant and the plaintiff did not satisfy the Statute of Frauds because no closing date was expressed in the writing. Even assuming that the payment date stated in the writing was not intended as a closing date, the writing still satisfies the Statute of Frauds.

The Statute of Frauds requires that contracts for the purchase of real estate be in writing, RSA 506:1, and that the writing express the essential terms of the contract. Because the purchase price, the identity of the parties, and a description of the real estate were expressed in writing, the parties' contract does not violate the Statute of Frauds. Time for performance is not an essential term under the Statute of Frauds.

The defendant finally alleges that the master erred by excluding evidence attempting to prove that the parties' option contract was conditioned on the defendant's ability to obtain 100% financing for the purchase of the property. The master heard the defendant's evidence on this issue, but then concluded that the evidence was inadmissible. Although we disagree with the master's decision that the parol evidence rule precluded the admission of this evidence, we agree with the master's decision that the defendant failed to meet his burden of proof as to the existence of a financing condition.

We agree with the trial court that no ambiguity existed in the writing sufficient to justify admission of parol evidence. In the absence of an ambiguity, the plain meaning rule prohibits the admission of parol evidence "that would contradict the plain meaning of the terms of the contract." Although this court has liberally defined "ambiguity" to include an ambiguity not apparent on the face of the instrument or an ambiguity not capable of resolution by mere examination of the instrument, this case does not involve an assertion of ambiguity.

The trial court failed to consider other aspects of the parol evidence rule. Even absent an ambiguity, parol evidence can be admitted in certain instances to prove the existence of terms or conditions not expressed in the writing.

The first step in determining whether parol evidence is admissible is to consider whether the writing is a total integration and completely expresses the agreement of the parties. Even when an integration clause is included in the writing, as in this case, this court will allow the admission of parol evidence to prove that the writing was not a total integration. *See* In *Steinfield [v. Madnock Mills]*, 81 N.H. at 185, this court held that the parties' intent to create a total integration can be proved by the circumstances surrounding the writing; "[t]he document alone will not suffice."

> **"THE FIRST STEP in determining whether parol evidence is admissible is to consider whether the writing is a total integration and completely expresses the agreement of the parties."**

The integration clause, however, is some evidence that the parties intended the writing to be a total integration. Ultimately, the issue of whether the writing is a total integration is an issue of fact determined by the trier of fact.

If a party proves the absence of a total integration, parol evidence is admissible to prove a term not inconsistent with the writing.

In the instant case, the parol evidence concerning the financing condition should have been admitted, notwithstanding the possibility that the contract might have been a total integration or that the additional term might have been interpreted as inconsistent with the writing. Exceptions to the parol evidence rule allow the admission of parol evidence even in instances where there is a total integration and a lack of an ambiguity. For that reason, the defendant's evidence concerning the possibility that the parties' assignment contract was conditioned on his ability to obtain satisfactory financing for the eventual purchase of the property should have been admitted.

After hearing the evidence, the master stated that even if the parol evidence were admissible, the defendant would fail to meet his burden of proof. The burden of persuasion depends on the weight and credibility of the evidence and therefore is an issue for the trier of fact. Although the defendant produced some evidence that his purchase of the property would not take place unless he obtained 100% financing, the defendant did not prove that his obligation to make payment under the assignment contract was likewise conditioned. We cannot find, therefore, that the master committed reversible error by finding that the parties had not intended their assignment contract to be conditioned on the defendant's ability to obtain financing.

Affirmed.

All concurred.

---

3. Remedies

Having a court determine that the other party improperly breached a contract is of limited value unless you can obtain some kind of remedy to alleviate your damages and to justify bringing suit in event of a breach. Three types of damages are available in contract cases—expectancy, reliance, and restitution damages. Each compensates the non-breaching party with reference to a particular interest that party maintained in the transaction. Expectancy means that the court puts the party in the same place they would have been had the breach not occurred. Reliance compensates the party to the extent that they spent money in reliance on the contract. Restitution (alternatively referred to as *quantum meruit*) compensates the non-breaching party by depriving the breaching party of their advantage in order to avoid unjust enrichment. While sometimes, the non-breaching party's expenditures will equal the breaching parties enrichment, it is important to remember that restitution and reliance focus on different parties and the results of the frustrated transaction.

Three types of damages are available in contract cases: *Expectancy, Reliance,* and *Restitution Damages.*

a. **Legal Remedies.** Legal damages are money damages. The aim of the court is to ascertain what amount of money should be paid by the breaching party. For instance, a contractor who agrees to build a house for a client who later attempts to repudiate the contract could potentially recover the profit they would have earned if the house was never completed, the amount they spent in constructing the house, or the value of the house if it was completed and the buyers attempted to occupy the property. Different damage values may also determine the type of legal strategy a client may employ as they attempt to maximize their recovery. Sections 344 and 345 of the Restatement provide a brief overview (for the rest, see §§ 344-385):

§ 344: Purposes Of Remedies

Judicial remedies under the rules stated in this Restatement serve to protect one or more of the following interests of a promisee:

   a. his "expectation interest," which is his interest in having the benefit of his bargain by being put in as good a position as he would have been in had the contract been performed,

   b. his "reliance interest," which is his interest in being reimbursed for loss caused by reliance on the contract by being put in as good a position as he would have been in had the contract not been made, or

   c. his "restitution interest," which is his interest in having restored to him any benefit that he has conferred on the other party.

§ 345: Judicial Remedies Available

The judicial remedies available for the protection of the interests stated in § 344 include a judgment or order

   a. awarding a sum of money due under the contract or as damages,

   b. requiring specific performance of a contract or enjoining its non-performance,

   c. requiring restoration of a specific thing to prevent unjust enrichment,

   d. awarding a sum of money to prevent unjust enrichment,

   e. declaring the rights of the parties, and

   f. enforcing an arbitration award.

The following case illustrates a court awarding restitution-based damages. Remember, restitution is determined by the undue benefit to the defendant and not by the plaintiff's expense. As the case will also make clear, there is some confusion in the case law about the relation of unjust enrichment, *quantum meruit*, and the idea of "off contract" recovery.

Certified Fire Protection, Inc. v. Precision Construction, Inc.

283 P.3d 250 (Nevada 2012)

By the Court, PICKERING, J.:

* * *

Respondent/cross-appellant Precision Construction, Inc., a general contractor pursuing a contract for a warehouse construction project in 2005, solicited bids from subcontractors for the design and installation of an early suppression, fast response sprinkler system. Certified picked up a set of plans detailing the sprinkler system's requirements and, in mid-November, submitted a bid of $480,000. Precision notified Certified that it had won the bid, and Precision entered into a contract with the owner to complete the project.

On December 5, Certified obtained a copy of the subcontract along with a set of construction plans and sprinkler system specifications. The subcontract's provisions required Certified to complete the preliminary design drawings of the sprinkler system within two weeks and to obtain a certificate naming Precision as an additional insured. Over the next few weeks, Precision asked Certified several times to sign the subcontract and provide the additional-insured certificate.

Certified objected to the subcontract as imposing terms that differed from the bid specifications. It complained that the unanticipated terms changed the scope of work—including the size of pipes to be used, the placement of the fire riser, and the two-week time frame for producing drawings—and that it would have to amend its bid accordingly. Certified also took exception to some of the generic contractual provisions, including the additional-insured requirement.

On December 20, Precision notified all subcontractors, including Certified, that construction was under way. Certified hired Ron Dusky to draft the sprinkler system designs and, sometime in mid-January 2006, Dusky began drafting the designs. On January 19, with the subcontract still unsigned, Certified submitted a $33,575 progress bill to Precision, representing that it had completed seven percent of its work. But the design drawings apparently were still unfinished (or at least undelivered) because six days later, Precision wrote Doug Sartain, Certified's owner, requesting the sprinkler plans "ASAP" and advising that Precision would not process the progress payment without a signed subcontract. The next day, January 26, Precision again contacted Sartain, asking whether Certified planned to continue with the project and notifying him that its delay in submitting the plans was delaying the whole project.

On January 27, Certified reiterated its objections to the subcontract but assured Precision that it had begun the fire protection drawings. Certified completed the design work and submitted the sprinkler system drawings on February 1. Precision and Certified communicated several more times about getting the subcontract signed, and, on February 8, Precision learned that the drawings contained errors that needed correcting. It again asked Certified about the unsigned subcontract.

On February 16, Precision terminated its relationship with Certified for refusing to sign the subcontract, for not providing the additional-insured endorsement, and for incorrect designs. At Precision's request, Certified submitted an itemized billing for the work it had performed; its bill reported costs of $25,185.04, which included design work and permit fees for the project. Precision deemed the costs too high and never paid. Certified placed a mechanic's lien on the property and sued to recover for its design-related work. Certified's complaint sought to foreclose the mechanic's lien and damages for unjust enrichment, *quantum meruit*, and breach of contract.

* * *

"Basic contract principles require, for an enforceable contract, an offer and acceptance, meeting of the minds, and consideration." A meeting of the minds exists when the parties have agreed upon the contract's essential terms. Which terms are essential "depends on the agreement and its context and also on the subsequent conduct of the parties, including the dispute which arises and the remedy sought"[W]hether a contract exists is [a question] of fact, requiring this court to defer to the district court's findings unless they are clearly erroneous or not based on substantial evidence."

Certified argues that the progress bill it sent to Precision established the price term and Precision's urging that Certified get started on the designs established the scope of work for the express design-work-only contract it claims. But the record does not establish that Precision agreed to pay a sum certain for the design—related work. Certified's $33,575 progress bill—which represented seven percent of the whole subcontract—went unpaid, and Precision told Certified it would not make a progress payment until the whole subcontract had been executed. Beyond this, witness testimony established that a party in Precision's position would not execute a contract for only design drawings; such drawings are specifically tailored for the company rendering them and not useful to another installer. Thus, Certified's argument that Precision was parceling out the work—with Certified doing the designs only—makes no sense.

Not only were price and scope of work terms missing from the claimed design-work contract, the parties never agreed to a time for performance. Certified objected to Precision's proposed two-week timeline for producing the design drawings as "not realistic," and the parties never agreed to another time frame. That the time-for-performance term mattered is demonstrated by Precision's repeated prompting of Certified to complete the designs and Certified's refusal to bind itself to Precision's desired two-week turnaround. "When essential terms such as these have yet to be agreed upon by the parties, a contract cannot be formed."

And while the district court's judgment on partial findings does not reference a design-only contract, the record substantially supports its conclusion that no enforceable contract existed.

B.

Next, Certified argues that absent an express contract, it should be able to recover under a theory of implied contract, either by *quantum meruit* or unjust enrichment.

Certified confessedly is confused by *quantum meruit* and unjust enrichment, noting that "the distinction between the two theories in Nevada is unclear." "One source of confusion is that *quantum meruit* is a cause of action in two fields: restitution and contract."

Quantum meruit historically was one of the common counts—a subspecies of the writ of *indebitatus* or general *assumpsit*—available as a remedy at law to enforce implied promises or contracts. A party who pleaded *quantum meruit* sought recovery of the reasonable value, or "as much as he has deserved" for services rendered.

Thus, *quantum meruit*'s first application is in actions based upon contracts implied-in-fact. A contract implied-in-fact must be "manifested by conduct"; it "is a true contract that arises from the tacit agreement of the parties." To find a contract implied-in-fact, the fact-finder must conclude that the parties intended to contract and promises were exchanged, the general obligations for which must be sufficiently clear. It is at that point that a party may invoke *quantum meruit* as a gap-filler to supply the absent term. Where such a contract exists, then, *quantum meruit* ensures the laborer receives the reasonable value, usually market price, for his services.

Certified maintains that it had an implied contract with Precision for the design-related work. As discussed above, however, substantial evidence supports the district court's finding that there was no contract, express or implied, for the design work standing alone. There are simply too many gaps to fill in the asserted contract for *quantum meruit* to take hold. Precision never agreed to a contract for only design-related work, the parties never agreed to a price for that work, and they disputed the time of performance. When Precision selected Certified, it did so on the basis that Certified would design *and install* the fire suppression system, not that it would draft the designs and leave installation to someone else. The evidence established that design drawings are installer-specific and so not useful to a replacement subcontractor. Accordingly, the district court properly denied recovery in *quantum meruit* for an implied-in-fact contract.

Quantum meruit's other role is in providing restitution for unjust enrichment: "Liability in restitution for the market value of goods or services is the remedy traditionally known as *quantum meruit*." "'Where unjust enrichment is found, the law implies a quasi-contract which requires the defendant to pay to plaintiff the value of the benefit conferred. In other words, the defendant makes restitution to the plaintiff in *quantum meruit*.'"

When a plaintiff seeks "as much as he ... deserve [s]" based on a theory of restitution (as opposed to implied-in-fact contract), he must establish each element of unjust enrichment. *Quantum meruit*, then, is "the usual measurement of enrichment in cases where nonreturnable benefits have been furnished at the defendant's request, but where the parties made no enforceable agreement as to price."

Unjust enrichment exists when the plaintiff confers a benefit on the defendant, the defendant appreciates such benefit, and there is " 'acceptance and retention by the defendant of such benefit under circumstances such that it would be inequitable for him to retain the benefit without payment of the value thereof.' Thus—contrary to Certified's argument—a pleading of *quantum meruit* for unjust enrichment does not discharge the plaintiffs obligation to demonstrate that the defendant received a benefit from services provided.

"[B]enefit" in the unjust enrichment context can include "services beneficial to or at the request of the other," "denotes any form of advantage," and is not confined to retention of money or property. But while "[r]estitution may strip a wrong-doer of all profits gained in a transaction with [a] claimant ... principles of unjust enrichment will not support the imposition of a liability that leaves an innocent recipient worse off ... than if the transaction with the claimant had never taken place."

> **"Pleading of *quantum meruit* for unjust enrichment does not discharge the plaintiffs obligation to demonstrate that the defendant received a benefit from services provided."**

That is the state of our law, too. In *Thompson v. Herrmann*, 91 Nev. 63, 68 (1975), this court concluded that "[t]he basis of recovery on *quantum meruit* ... is that a party has received from another a benefit which is unjust for him to retain without paying for it." In that case, the defendant was to build a dam for the plaintiffs but the defendant's preliminary work failed to meet state regulations and thus was rendered useless. Because the plaintiffs were required to hire a new laborer to completely rebuild the dam to code, this court held that the defendant could not recover on his counterclaim under a theory of *quantum meruit* because he had provided no benefit to the plaintiffs, i.e., while he began the work the plaintiffs requested, he ultimately provided no advantage to them.

Here, the district court found that Precision had not "unjustly retain[ed] any money or property because no work performed could be utilized by the replacement fire sprinkler subcontractor," and that included the sprinkler designs. Every one of Certified's witnesses admitted as much on cross-examination. Thus, Certified's owner, Doug Sartain, testified that Certified installed nothing at the job site and its preparatory work could not be utilized by the replacement subcontractor. Gary Wooldridge, Certified's project manager, confirmed Sartain's statements that the design work and permitting performed by Certified could not be used by their replacement subcontractor (though he did say the water flow test could have been utilized). Finally, Ron Dusky, the man who drafted the plans, stated in his deposition (which was read into the record) that the designs Certified submitted contained mistakes that would have required one to two weeks to remedy. This was never done. Certified submitted no evidence of an ascertainable advantage Precision drew from the work it performed. It was incomplete, incorrect, and late. Therefore, we agree with the district court that Certified cannot recover in *quantum meruit* or unjust enrichment.

III.

[The court concludes that the lower court did not abuse its discretion in refusing to award Precision attorney's fees]

Accordingly, we affirm.

We concur: CHERRY, C.J., and GIBBONS, J.

A SECOND KIND OF LEGAL REMEDY is reliance. When focusing on reliance interests, the court attempts to isolate the particular expense the party that began performance expended in reliance on the contract. Courts pay particular attention to fixed costs and if the party incurred losses based in particular reliance on the contract. The reliance on the contract must also be reasonable in order to induce reliance. The following case is one of the most famous illustrations of misplaced reliance and the limitations on recovery for fixed costs.

Chicago Coliseum v. Dempsey

265 Ill.App. 542 (Ill. App. Ct. 1932)

MR. JUSTICE WILSON delivered the opinion of the court.

Chicago Coliseum Club, a corporation, as plaintiff, brought its action against William Harrison Dempsey, known as Jack Dempsey, to recover damages for breach of a written contract executed March 13, 1926, but bearing date of March 6 of that year.

Plaintiff was incorporated as an Illinois corporation for the promotion of general pleasure and athletic purposes and to conduct boxing, sparring and wrestling matches and exhibitions for prizes or purses. The defendant William Harrison Dempsey was well known in the pugilistic world and, at the time of the making and execution of the contract in question, held the title of world's Champion Heavy Weight Boxer.

Under the terms of the written agreement, the plaintiff was to promote a public boxing exhibition in Chicago, or some suitable place to be selected by the promoter, and had engaged the services of one Harry Wills, another well known boxer and pugilist, to engage in a boxing match with the defendant Dempsey for the championship of the world. By the terms of the agreement Dempsey was to receive $10, receipt of which was acknowledged, and the plaintiff further agreed to pay to Dempsey the sum of $300,000 on the 5th day of August 1926,--$500,000 in cash at least 10 days before the date fixed for the contest, and a sum equal to 50 per cent of the net profits over and above the sum of $2,000,000 in the event the gate receipts should exceed that amount. In addition the defendant was to receive 50 per cent of the net revenue derived from moving picture concessions or royalties received by the plaintiff, and defendant agreed to have his life and health insured in favor of the plaintiff in a manner and at a place to be designated by the plaintiff. Defendant further agreed not to engage in any boxing match after the date of the agreement and prior to the date on which the contest was to be held. Certain agreements previously entered into by the defendant with one Floyd Fitzsimmons for a Dempsey-Wills boxing match were declared to be void and of no force and effect. Certain other mutual agreements were contained in the written contract which are not necessary in a consideration of this case.

March 6, 1926, the plaintiff entered into an agreement with Harry Wills, in which Wills agreed to engage in a boxing match with the Jack Dempsey named in the agreement hereinbefore referred to. Under this agreement the plaintiff, Chicago Coliseum Club was to deposit $50,000 in escrow in the National City Bank of New York City, New York, to be paid over to Wills on the 10th day prior to the date fixed for the holding of the boxing contest. Further conditions were provided in said contract with Wills, which, however, are not necessary to set out in detail. There is no evidence in the record showing that the $50,000 was deposited nor that it has ever been paid, nor is there any evidence in the record showing the financial standing of the Chicago Coliseum Club, a corporation, plaintiff in this suit. This contract between the plaintiff and Wills appears to have been entered into several days before the contract with Dempsey.

March 8, 1926, the plaintiff entered into a contract with one Andrew C. Weisberg, under which it appears that it was necessary for the plaintiff to have the services of an experienced person skilled in promoting boxing exhibitions and that the said Weisberg was possessed of such qualifications and that it was necessary for the plaintiff to procure his help in the promoting of the exhibition. It appears further from the agreement that it was necessary to incur expenditures in the way of traveling expenses, legal services and other costs in and about the promotion of the boxing match, and Weisberg agreed to investigate, canvass and organize the various hotel associations and other business organizations for the purpose of securing accommodations for spectators and to procure subscriptions and contributions from such hotels and

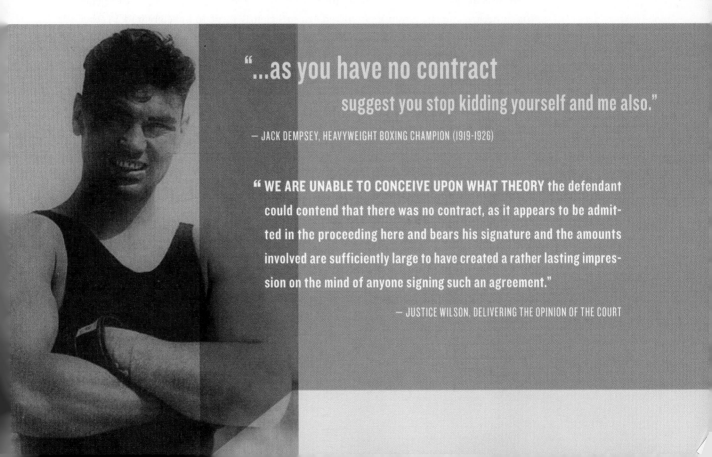

"...as you have no contract suggest you stop kidding yourself and me also."

— JACK DEMPSEY, HEAVYWEIGHT BOXING CHAMPION (1919-1926)

" WE ARE UNABLE TO CONCEIVE UPON WHAT THEORY the defendant could contend that there was no contract, as it appears to be admitted in the proceeding here and bears his signature and the amounts involved are sufficiently large to have created a rather lasting impression on the mind of anyone signing such an agreement."

— JUSTICE WILSON, DELIVERING THE OPINION OF THE COURT

associations and others for the erection of an arena and other necessary expense in order to carry out the enterprise and to promote the boxing match in question. Under these agreements Weisberg was to furnish the funds for such purposes and was to be reimbursed out of the receipts from the sale of tickets for the expenses incurred by him, together with a certain amount for his services.

Both the Wills contract and the Weisberg contract are referred to at some length, inasmuch as claims for damages by plaintiff are predicated upon these two agreements. Under the terms of the contract between the plaintiff and Dempsey and the plaintiff and Wills, the contest was to be held during the month of September, 1926.

July 10, 1926, plaintiff wired Dempsey at Colorado Springs, Colorado, stating that representatives of life and accident insurance companies would call on him for the purpose of examining him for insurance in favor of the Chicago Coliseum Club, in accordance with the terms of his contract, and also requesting the defendant to begin training for the contest not later than August 1, 1926. In answer to this communication plaintiff received a telegram from Dempsey, as follows:

> "President Chicago Coliseum Club Chgo Entirely too busy training for my coming Tunney match to waste time on insurance representatives stop as you have no contract suggest you stop kidding yourself and me also —Jack Dempsey."

We are unable to conceive upon what theory the defendant could contend that there was no contract, as it appears to be admitted in the proceeding here and bears his signature and the amounts involved are sufficiently large to have created a rather lasting impression on the mind of anyone signing such an agreement. It amounts, however, to a repudiation of the agreement and from that time on Dempsey refused to take any steps to carry out his undertaking. It appears that Dempsey at this time was engaged in preparing himself for a contest with Tunney to be held at Philadelphia, Pennsylvania, sometime in September, and on August 3, 1926, plaintiff, as complainant, filed a bill in the superior court of Marion county, Indiana, asking to have Dempsey restrained and enjoined from engaging in the contest with Tunney, which complainant was informed and believed was to be held on the 16th day of September, and which contest would be in violation of the terms of the agreement entered into between the plaintiff and defendant at Los Angeles, March 13, 1926.

* * *

During the proceeding in the circuit court of this county it was sought to introduce evidence for the purpose of showing damages, other than nominal damages, and in view of the fact that the case has to be retried, this court is asked to consider the various items of expense claimed to have been incurred and various offers of proof made to establish damages for breach of the agreement. Under the proof offered, the question of damages naturally divides itself into the four following propositions:

1st. Loss of profits which would have been derived by the plaintiff in the event of the holding of the contest in question;

2nd. Expenses incurred by the plaintiff prior to the signing of the agreement between the plaintiff and Dempsey;

3rd. Expenses incurred in attempting to restrain the defendant from engaging in other contests and to force him into a compliance with the terms of his agreement with the plaintiff; and

4th. Expenses incurred after the signing of the agreement and before the breach of July 10, 1926.

Proposition 1: **Plaintiff offered to prove by one Mullins that a boxing exhibition between Dempsey and Wills held in the City of Chicago on September 22, 1926, would bring a gross receipt of $3,000,000, and that the expense incurred would be $1,400,000, leaving a net profit to the promoter of $1,600,000.**

The court properly sustained an objection to this testimony. The character of the undertaking was such that it would be impossible to produce evidence of a probative character sufficient to establish any amount which could be reasonably ascertainable by reason of the character of the undertaking. The profits from a boxing contest of this character, open to the public, is dependent upon so many different circumstances that they are not susceptible of definite legal determination. The success or failure of such an undertaking depends largely upon the ability of the promoters, the reputation of the contestants and the conditions of the weather at and prior to the holding of the contest, the accessibility of the place, the extent of the publicity, the possibility of other and counter attractions and many other questions which would enter into consideration. Such an entertainment lacks utterly the element of stability which exists in regular organized business. This fact was practically admitted by the plaintiff by the allegation of its bill filed in the Marion county court of Indiana asking for an injunction against Dempsey. Plaintiff in its bill in that proceeding charged, as follows:

> "That by virtue of the premises aforesaid, the plaintiff will, unless it secures the injunctive relief herein prayed for, suffer great and irreparable injury and damages, not compensable by any action at law in damages, the damages being incapable of commensuration, and plaintiff, therefore, has no adequate remedy at law."

Compensation for damages for a breach of contract must be established by evidence from which a court or jury are able to ascertain the extent of such damages by the usual rules of evidence and to a reasonable degree of certainty. We are of the opinion that the performance in question is not susceptible of proof sufficient to satisfy the requirements and that the damages, if any, are purely speculative.

Proposition 2: **Expenses incurred by the plaintiff prior to the signing of the agreement between the plaintiff and Dempsey.**

The general rule is that in an action for a breach of contract a party can recover only on damages which naturally flow from and are the result of the act complained of. The Wills contract was entered into prior to the contract with the defendant and was not made contingent upon the plaintiff's obtaining a similar agreement with the defendant Dempsey. Under the circumstances the plaintiff speculated as to the result of his efforts to procure the Dempsey contract. It may be argued that there had been negotiations pending between plaintiff and Dempsey which clearly indicated an agreement between them, but the agreement in fact was never consummated until sometime later. The action is based upon the written agreement which was entered into in Los Angeles. Any obligations assumed by the plaintiff prior to that time are not chargeable to the defendant. Moreover, an examination of the record discloses that the $50,000 named in the contract with Wills, which was to be payable upon a signing of the agreement, was not and never has been paid. There is no evidence in the record showing that the plaintiff is responsible financially, and, even though there were, we consider that it is not an element of damage which can be recovered for breach of the contract in question.

Proposition 3: **Expenses incurred in attempting to restrain the defendant from engaging in other contests and to force him into a compliance with the terms of his agreement with the plaintiff.**

After the repudiation of the agreement by the defendant, plaintiff was advised of defendant's match with Tunney which, from the evidence, it appears, was to take place in Philadelphia in the month of September and was in direct conflict with the terms of the agreement entered into between plaintiff and defendant. Plaintiff's bill, filed in the superior court of Marion county, Indiana, was an effort on the part of the plaintiff to compel defendant to live up to the terms of his agreement. The chancellor in the Indiana court entered his decree, which apparently is in full force and effect, and the defendant in violating the terms of that decree, after personal service, is answerable to that court for a violation of the injunctional order entered in said proceeding. The expenses incurred, however, by the plaintiff in procuring that decree are not collectible in an action for damages in this proceeding; neither are such similar expenses as were incurred in the trips to Colorado and Philadelphia, nor the attorney's fees and other expenses thereby incurred. The plaintiff having been informed that the defendant intended to proceed no further under his agreement, took such steps at its own financial risk. There was nothing in the agreement regarding attorney's fees and there was nothing in the contract in regard to the services of the defendant from which it would appear that the action for specific performance would lie. After the clear breach of contract by the defendant, the plaintiff proceeded with this character of litigation at its own risk. We are of the opinion that the trial court properly held that this was an element of damages which was not recoverable.

Proposition 4: **Expenses incurred after the signing of the agreement and before the breach of July 10, 1926.**

After the signing of the agreement plaintiff attempted to show expenses incurred by one Weisberg in and about the furtherance of the project. Weisberg testified that he had taken an active part in promoting sports for a number of years and was in the employ of the Chicago Coliseum Club under a written contract during all of the time that his services were rendered in furtherance of this proposition. This contract was introduced in evidence and bore the date of March 8, 1926. Under its terms Weisberg was to be reimbursed out of the gate receipts and profits derived from the performance. His compensation depended entirely upon the success of the exhibition. Under his agreement with the plaintiff there was nothing to charge the plaintiff unconditionally with the costs and expenses of Weisberg's services. The court properly ruled against the admissibility of the evidence.

We find in the record, however, certain evidence which should have been submitted to the jury on the question of damages sustained by the plaintiff. The contract on which the breach of the action is predicated shows a payment of $10 by the plaintiff to the defendant and the receipt acknowledged. It appears that the stadium located in the South Park District, known as Soldier's Field, was considered as a site for the holding of the contest and plaintiff testified that it paid $300 to an architect for plans in the event the stadium was to be used for the performance. This item of damage might have been made more specific and may not have been the best evidence in the case but, standing alone, it was sufficient to go to the jury. There were certain elements in regard to wages paid assistant secretaries which may be substantiated by evidence showing that they were necessary in furtherance of the undertaking. If these expenses were incurred they are recoverable if in furtherance of the general scheme. The defendant should not be required to answer in damages for salaries paid regular officials of the corporation who were presumed to be receiving such salaries by reason of their position, but special expenses incurred are recoverable. The expenses of Hoffman in going to Colorado for the purpose of having Dempsey take his physical examination for insurance, if before the breach and reasonable, are recoverable. The railroad fares for those who went to Los Angeles for the purpose of procuring the signing of the agreement are not recoverable as they were incurred in a furtherance of the procuring of the contract and not after the agreement was entered into. The services of Shank in looking after railroad facilities and making arrangements with the railroad for publicity and special trains and accommodations were items which should be considered and if it develops that they were incurred in a furtherance of the general plan and properly proven, are items for which the plaintiff should be reimbursed.

The items recoverable are such items of expense as were incurred between the date of the signing of the agreement and the breach of July 10, 1926, by the defendant and such as were incurred as a necessary expense in furtherance of the performance. Proof of such items should be made subject to the usual rules of evidence.

For the reasons stated in this opinion the judgment of the circuit court is reversed and the cause remanded for a new trial.

Judgment reversed and cause remanded.

HEBEL, P. J., and FRIEND, J., concur.

FINALLY, EXPECTANCY DAMAGES try to provide parties with what they would have received had the contract been completed, or literally "the benefit of the bargain." The following case involves a lengthy comparison of expectancy, reliance, and restitution interests and the social and public policy reasons militating towards and against these forms of recovery. The case draws on what is known, informally, as the "Hairy Hand" case, a classic contract case.

Sullivan v. O'Connor

363 Mass. 579 (Massachusetts 1973)

KAPLAN, Justice.

The plaintiff patient secured a jury verdict of $13,500 against the defendant surgeon for breach of contract in respect to an operation upon the plaintiff's nose. The substituted consolidated bill of exceptions presents questions about the correctness of the judge's instructions on the issue of damages.

The declaration was in two counts. In the first count, the plaintiff alleged that she, as patient, entered into a contract with the defendant, a surgeon, wherein the defendant promised to perform plastic surgery on her nose and thereby to enhance her beauty and improve her appearance; that he performed the surgery but failed to achieve the promised result; rather the result of the surgery was to disfigure and deform her nose, to cause her pain in body and mind, and to subject her to other damage and expense. The second count, based on the same transaction, was in the conventional form for malpractice, charging that the defendant had been guilty of negligence in performing the surgery. Answering, the defendant entered a general denial.

On the plaintiff's demand, the case was tried by jury. At the close of the evidence, the judge put to the jury, as special questions, the issues of liability under the two counts, and instructed them accordingly. The jury returned a verdict for the plaintiff on the contract count, and for the defendant on the negligence count. The judge then instructed the jury on the issue of damages.

As background to the instructions and the parties' exceptions, we mention certain facts as the jury could find them. The plaintiff was a professional entertainer, and this was known to the defendant. The agreement was as alleged in the declaration. More particularly, judging from exhibits, the plaintiff's nose had been straight, but long and prominent; the defendant undertook by two operations to reduce its prominence and somewhat to shorten it, thus making it more pleasing in relation to the plaintiff's other features. Actually[,] the plaintiff was obliged to undergo three operations, and her appearance was worsened. Her nose now had a concave line to about the midpoint, at which it became bulbous; viewed frontally, the nose from bridge to midpoint was flattened and broadened, and the two sides of the tip had lost symmetry. This configuration evidently could not be improved by further surgery. The plaintiff did not demonstrate, however, that her change of appearance had resulted in loss of employment. Payments by the plaintiff covering the defendant's fee and hospital expenses were stipulated at $622.65.

The judge instructed the jury, first, that the plaintiff was entitled to recover her out-of-pocket expenses incident to the operations. Second, she could recover the damages flowing directly, naturally, proximately, and foreseeably from the defendant's breach of promise. These would comprehend damages for any disfigurement of the plaintiff's nose-that is, any change of appearance for the worse-including the effects of the consciousness of such disfigurement on the plaintiff's mind, and in this connection the jury should consider the nature of the plaintiff's profession. Also consequent upon the defendant's breach, and compensable, were the pain and suffering involved in the third operation, but not in the first two. As there was no proof that any loss of earnings by the plaintiff resulted from the breach, that element should not enter into the calculation of damages.

By his exceptions the defendant contends that the judge erred in allowing the jury to take into account anything but the plaintiff's out-of-pocket expenses (presumably at the stipulated amount). The defendant excepted to the judge's refusal of his request for a general charge to that effect, and, more specifically, to the judge's refusal of a charge that the plaintiff could not recover for pain and suffering connected with the third operation or for impairment of the plaintiff's appearance and associated mental distress.

The plaintiff on her part excepted to the judge's refusal of a request to charge that the plaintiff could recover the difference in value between the nose as promised and the nose as it appeared after the operations. However, the plaintiff in her brief expressly waives this exception and others made by her in case this court overrules the defendant's exceptions; thus she would be content to hold the jury's verdict in her favor.

We conclude that the defendant's exceptions should be overruled.

It has been suggested on occasion that agreements between patients and physicians by which the physician undertakes to effect a cure or to bring about a given result should be declared unenforceable on grounds of public policy. But there are many decisions recognizing and enforcing such contracts, and the law of Massachusetts has treated them as valid, although we have had no decision meeting head on the contention that they should be denied legal sanction. These causes of action are, however, considered a little suspect, and thus we find courts straining sometimes to read the pleadings as sounding only in tort for negligence, and not in contract for breach of promise, despite sedulous efforts by the pleaders to pursue the latter theory.

It is not hard to see why the courts should be unenthusiastic or skeptical about the contract theory. Considering the uncertainties of medical science and the variations in the physical and psychological conditions of individual patients, doctors can seldom in good faith promise specific results. Therefore it is unlikely that physicians of even average integrity will in fact make such promises. Statements of opinion by the physician with some optimistic coloring are a different thing, and may indeed have therapeutic value. But patients may transform such statements into firm promises in their own minds, especially when they have been disappointed in the event, and testify in that sense to sympathetic juries. If actions for breach of promise can be readily maintained, doctors, so it is said, will be frightened into practising 'defensive medicine.' On the other hand, if these actions were outlawed, leaving only the possibility of suits for malpractice, there is fear that the public might be exposed to the enticements of charlatans, and confidence in the profession might ultimately be shaken. See Miller, *The Contractual Liability of Physicians and Surgeons*, 1953 Wash.L.Q. 413, 416-423. The law has taken the middle of the road position of allowing actions based on alleged contract, but insisting on clear proof. Instructions to the jury may well stress this requirement and point to tests of truth, such as the complexity or difficulty of an operation as bearing on the probability that a given result was promised.

> "CONSIDERING the uncertainties of medical science and the variations in the physical and psychological conditions of individual patients, doctors can seldom in good faith promise specific results.

If an action on the basis of contract is allowed, we have next the question of the measure of damages to be applied where liability is found. Some cases have taken the simple view that the promise by the physician is to be treated like an ordinary commercial promise, and accordingly that the successful plaintiff is entitled to a standard measure of recovery for breach of contract-'compensatory' ('expectancy') damages, an amount intended to put the plaintiff in the position he would be in if the contract had been performed, or, presumably, at the plaintiff's election, 'restitution' damages, an amount corresponding to any benefit conferred by the plaintiff upon the defendant in the performance of the contract disrupted by the defendant's breach. Thus in *Hawkins v. McGee*, 84 N.H. 114 [the infamous "Hairy Hand" case made even more famous by the classic law school movie *The Paperchase* (1973)], the defendant doctor was taken to have promised the plaintiff to convert his damaged hand by means of an operation into a good or perfect hand, but the doctor so operated as to damage the hand still further. The court, following the usual expectancy formula, would have asked the jury to estimate and award to the plaintiff the difference between the value of a good or perfect hand, as promised, and the value of the hand after the operation. (The same formula would apply, although the dollar result would be less, if the operation had neither worsened nor improved the condition of the hand.) If the plaintiff had not yet paid the doctor his fee, that amount would be deducted from the recovery. There could be no recovery for the pain and suffering of the operation, since that detriment would have been incurred even if the operation had been successful; one can say that this detriment was not 'caused' by the breach. But where the plaintiff by reason of the operation was put to more pain that he would have had to endure, had the doctor performed as promised, he should be compensated for that difference as a proper part of his expectancy recovery. It may be noted that on an alternative count for malpractice the plaintiff in the Hawkins case had been nonsuited; but on ordinary principles this could not affect the contract claim, for it is hardly a defence to a breach of contract that the promisor acted innocently and without negligence. The New Hampshire court further refined the *Hawkins* analysis in McQuaid v. Michou, 85 N.H. 299, all in the direction of treating the patient-physician cases on the ordinary footing of expectancy.

Other cases, including a number in New York, without distinctly repudiating the *Hawkins* type of analysis, have indicated that a different and generally more lenient measure of damages is to be applied in patient-physician actions based on breach of alleged special agreements to effect a cure, attain a stated result, or employ a given medical method. This measure is expressed in somewhat variant ways, but the substance is that the plaintiff is to recover any expenditures made by him and for other detriment (usually not specifically described in the opinions) following proximately and foreseeably upon the defendant's failure to carry out his promise. This, be it noted, is not a 'restitution' measure, for it is not limited to restoration of the benefit conferred on the defendant (the fee paid) but includes other expenditures, for example, amounts paid for medicine and nurses; so also it would seem according to its logic to take in damages for any worsening of the plaintiff's condition due to the breach. Nor is it an 'expectancy' measure, for it does not appear to contemplate recovery of the whole difference in value between the condition as promised and the condition actually resulting from the treatment. Rather the tendency of the formulation is to put the plaintiff back in the position he occupied just before the parties entered upon the agreement, to compensate him for the detriments he suffered in reliance upon the agreement. This kind of intermediate pattern of recovery for breach of contract is discussed in the suggestive article by Fuller and Perdue, *The Reliance Interest in Contract Damages*, 46 Yale L.J. 52, 373, where the authors show that, although not attaining the currency of the standard measures, a 'reliance' measure has for special reasons been applied by the courts in a variety of settings, including noncommercial settings.

For breach of the patient-physician agreements under consideration, a recovery limited to restitution seems plainly too meager, if the agreements are to be enforced at all. On the other hand, an expectancy recovery may well be excessive. The factors, already mentioned, which have made the cause of action somewhat suspect, also suggest moderation as to the breadth of the recovery that should be permitted. Where, as in the case at bar and in a number of the reported cases, the doctor has been absolved of negligence by the trier, an expectancy measure may be thought harsh. We should recall here that the fee paid by the patient to the doctor for the alleged promise would usually be quite disproportionate to the putative expectancy recovery. To attempt, moreover, to put a value on the condition that would or might have resulted, had the treatment succeeded as promised, may sometimes put an exceptional strain on the imagination of the fact finder. As a general consideration, Fuller and Perdue argue that the reasons for granting damages for broken promises to the extent of the expectancy are at their strongest when the promises are made in a business context, when they have to do with the production or distribution of goods or the allocation of functions in the market place; they become weaker as the context shifts from a commercial to a noncommercial field.

There is much to be said, then, for applying a reliance measure to the present facts, and we have only to add that our cases are not unreceptive to the use of that formula in special situations. We have, however, had no previous occasion to apply it to patient-physician cases.

The question of recovery on a reliance basis for pain and suffering or mental distress requires further attention. We find expressions in the decisions that pain and suffering (or the like) are simply not compensable in actions for breach of contract. The defendant seemingly espouses this proposition in the present case. True, if the buyer under a contract for the purchase of a lot of merchandise, in suing for the seller's breach, should claim damages for mental anguish caused by his disappointment in the transaction, he would not succeed; he would be told, perhaps, that the asserted psychological injury was not fairly foreseeable by the defendant as a probable consequence of the breach of such a business contract. But there is no general rule barring such items of damage in actions for breach of contract. It is all a question of the subject matter and background of the contract, and when the contract calls for an operation on the person of the plaintiff, psychological as well as physical injury may be expected to figure somewhere in the recovery, depending on the particular circumstances. The point is explained in *Stewart v. Rudner*, 349 Mich. 459. Again, it is said in a few of the New York cases, concerned with the classification of actions for statute of limitations purposes, that the absence of allegations demanding recovery for pain and suffering is characteristic of a contract claim by a patient against a physician, that such allegations rather belong in a claim for malpractice. These remarks seem unduly sweeping. Suffering or distress resulting from the breach going beyond that which was envisaged by the treatment as agreed, should be compensable on the same ground as the worsening of the patient's condition because of the breach. Indeed it can be argued that the very suffering or distress 'contracted for'-that which would have been incurred if the treatment achieved the promised result-should also be compensable on the theory underlying the New York cases. For that suffering is 'wasted' if the treatment fails. Otherwise stated, compensation for this waste is arguably required in order to complete the restoration of the status quo ante.

In the light of the foregoing discussion, all the defendant's exceptions fail: the plaintiff was not confined to the recovery of her out-of-pocket expenditures; she was entitled to recover also for the worsening of her condition, and for the pain and suffering and mental distress involved in the third operation. These items were compensable on either an expectancy or a reliance view. We might have been required to elect between the two views if the pain and suffering connected with the first two operations contemplated by the agreement, or the whole difference in value between the present and the promised conditions, were being claimed as elements of damage. But the plaintiff waives her possible claim to the former element, and to so much of the latter as represents the difference in value between the promised condition and the condition before the operations.

Plaintiff's exceptions waived.

Defendant's exceptions *overruled*.

---

b. Equitable Remedies. In addition to legal damages, courts can craft equitable solutions as well. These damages, as we have already seen, go beyond financial compensation. In these cases, the courts recognize that money will not make the parties whole. There is a specific thing to be had or an event to be avoided that is the essence of the contract. Setting forth the availability of specific performance and injunctive relief, described below, the Restatement provides:

§ 357: Availability of Specific Performance And Injunction

1. Subject to the rules stated in §§ 359-69, specific performance of a contract duty will be granted in the discretion of the court against a party who has committed or is threatening to commit a breach of the duty.

2. Subject to the rules stated in §§ 359-69, an injunction against breach of a contract duty will be granted in the discretion of the court against a party who has committed or is threatening to commit a breach of the duty if

   a. the duty is one of forbearance, or

   b. the duty is one to act and specific performance would be denied only for reasons that are inapplicable to an injunction.

For a further rules, see Restatement §§ 358-369.

I. Specific Performance

Sometimes, the contract the parties make concerns something unique. Perhaps, one party bid on the rocking chair used by President Kennedy. If the other party does not deliver the contract, money damages will only go so far to remedy the situation. The party who bid for the rocking chair wants THAT rocking chair. Not money to buy another rocking chair, not even another rocking chair, but the rocking chair that President Kennedy used. This would be a case made for specific performance because the party bidding for the rocking chair would petition to the court to require that the breaching party deliver THAT rocking chair.

These examples also occur with real estate and with performances for special talents. When one is shopping for houses to live in and to raise a family in, one is not simply looking for a collection of rooms underneath a roof. One looks for the house that will be a home. There may be something unique and appealing about the particular unit so that, if the seller breaches and does not perform the contracted conveyance, the suit would likely ask not just for money damages, but for the conveyance of THAT home.

■ PRESIDENT
JOHN F. KENNEDY IN
THE FAMOUS OVAL OFFICE
ROCKING CHAIR.
Image: Abbie Rowe.
White House Photographs.
John F. Kennedy Presidential
Library and Museum, Boston.

To use one final example, suppose the contract is for a particularly talented individual to play a basketball game or to sing a concert. For instance, one of the authors of this text was born on the same day—same day and year—as the late Michael Jackson. The author also happens to be a singer. However, if when Mr. Jackson was alive, he was contracted to sing a concert and came down with a cold and refused to perform, it would not do for him to suggest that this book's author replace him even if Mr. Jackson also said that he might throw in some money to cover any difference in quality of performance. A fan who purchased a ticket to hear Mr. Jackson perform would not be satisfied; the fan wanted to hear Michael Jackson, not someone else.

One area where specific performance arises frequently is within the context of land conveyances, particularly because land is not fungible and may have unique properties that cannot be compensated by monetary damages. The following case also discusses the doctrine of privity, which allows third-party beneficiaries to sue on the contract despite the fact that they were not parties to the original transaction if the transaction was made for their benefit. Privity claims most often arise in situations involving wills and loans, where parties believe that a contract intended to benefit them should entitle them to sue for specific performance. As the next case illustrates, though, specific performance is subject to the usual requirements of contract formation.

2. Injunction

Another common equitable remedy is an injunction. An injunction is a court action that stops any further action from occurring. The following case shows how injunctions are used to prevent an irreparable injury from occurring. In such cases, money damages do not remedy the aggrieved party; stopping the problematic action is necessary because the prospective damage might be irreparable. However, courts are reluctant to compel performance of an action even in cases where they will prohibit another type of action. The following case explores the connection between injunctive relief and specific performance. For another case involving enjoining performance, see *Chicago Colliseum v. Dempsey,* supra.

Florida Panthers Hockey Club, Ltd. v.
Miami Sports and Exhibition Authority

939 F.Supp 855 (S.D. Florida 1996)

ORDER GRANTING PLAINTIFF'S EMERGENCY MOTION
FOR PRELIMINARY INJUNCTION

K. MICHAEL MOORE, District Judge.

THIS CAUSE came before the Court upon Plaintiff's Emergency Motion for Preliminary Injunction (filed August 7, 1996).

THE COURT has considered the Motion, responses, and the pertinent portions of the record. The Court heard this case as an emergency matter and held a hearing on August 22, 1996. For the reasons set forth below, the Court GRANTS the Plaintiff's motion for preliminary injunction.

I. BACKGROUND

On August 7, 1996, Plaintiff The Florida Panthers Hockey Club, Ltd. (the "Panthers") commenced this action against Defendants Miami Sports and Exhibition Authority ("MSEA") and the City of Miami (the "City"). Count I of the Panthers' complaint seeks a declaration of its rights under a license agreement between the Panthers and non-party Leisure Management International. Counts II through IV seek injunctive relief and damages arising out of alleged violations of Section 2 of the Sherman Act.

II. FINDINGS OF FACT

The Panthers is a franchise of the National Hockey League ("NHL"). MSEA is an independent and autonomous authority of the City. MSEA owns the Miami Arena, and the City owns the land upon which the Miami Arena is situated.

On October 10, 1986, MSEA, Decoma Miami Associates, Ltd. ("DMAL") and the City entered into a Land Lease Agreement for the construction of the Miami Arena. On October 19, 1986, MSEA and DMAL executed a contract entitled "Miami Arena Contract" which set forth the rights and obligations of the parties in connection with the operation of the Miami Arena. On December 13, 1990, MSEA and DMAL entered into the First Amendment to the Miami Arena Contract. The Miami Arena Contract and the First Amendment will be referred to collectively as "the Miami Arena Contract." On October 19, 1986, DMAL hired Leisure Management International ("LMI") as an independent contractor to discharge some of DMAL's responsibilities, including the responsibility for entering into agreements for the use of the Miami Arena.

On April 2, 1993, LMI, on DMAL's behalf, entered into a license agreement with the South Florida Hockey Club, Ltd., the predecessor to the Panthers. On June 21, 1993, LMI and the Panthers entered into a First Amendment to the Panthers

License. The Panthers License and the First Amendment will be referred to collectively as "the Panthers License." The Panthers License provided for an initial term of two hockey seasons but gave the Panthers, at its sole discretion, four one-year options to extend the Panthers License.

Under the Panthers License, the Panthers had to exercise its option to renew for the 1996–1997 hockey season on or before August 1, 1995. The Panthers elected not to exercise its option for the 1996–1997 season and advised MSEA to that effect by letter dated May 31, 1995. In that letter, the Panthers advised MSEA, "This is to

Image: iStock

advise you that because of the extremely unfavorable economic terms of the License Agreement, we don't wish to exercise the second one-year option (for the 1996–1997 season). However, if the economic terms of a new License Agreement for the Miami Arena could be obtained which were comparable to those economic terms presently granted to the Miami Heat basketball team, we would seriously consider remaining in the Miami Arena for that subsequent season."

John Blaisdell, president of LMI, testified that LMI, on DMAL's behalf, and the Panthers began negotiating a new license agreement. On May 30, 1996, LMI and DMAL entered into an agreement entitled "Second Amendment to License Agreement" (the "Panthers License Amendment"). Blaisdell testified that the terms of the Panthers License Amendment continued to favor MSEA tremendously. Blaisdell further testified that the Panthers License Amendment did not include any material changes from the Panthers License; rather, the terms and conditions of the Panthers License Amendment substantially conformed to the Panthers License. No evidence was offered to the contrary.

By letter dated June 7, 1996, MSEA rejected the Second Amendment to the License Agreement. In that letter, MSEA indicated that "... we do not believe that the proposed amendments are in the best economic interests of MSEA nor [sic] consistent with the accomplishment of our public purpose. In addition, it is our conclusion that the proposed terms are not reasonably necessary to the operation of the Miami Arena. Instead, we believe that MSEA will be better served by a license[,] which commences on August 1, 1996, and expires on July 31, 2006. We reject paragraphs 3, 4, 5 and 6 of the proposed amendments." By letter dated July 9, 1996, MSEA directed the Panthers to vacate the Miami Arena by July 15, 1996.

* * *

The question of whether the Plaintiff has a substantial likelihood of success on the merits for the contract claim focuses on whether MSEA has an obligation not to unreasonably withhold consent of the Panthers License Amendment. The Court finds that MSEA does have such an obligation.

The Plaintiff contends that the Panthers License Amendment contains substantially similar terms and conditions as the Panthers License and continues to be a boon for MSEA. The Plaintiff argues that MSEA, therefore, cannot unreasonably withhold consent of the Panthers License Amendment and that a preliminary injunction is required to compel approval.

MSEA counters that the Panthers License Amendment is a "personal services" contract and, thus, is not subject to a suit for specific performance. While a personal services contract cannot be enforced by injunction or specific performance, the Panthers License Amendment is not such a contract. The Panthers License Amendment is a lease agreement and such an agreement may be subject to specific performance. The Court, therefore, finds that the remedy of specific performance is available. Certainly, specific performance is only available if it appears from the agreement that the rights and obligations of the parties with respect to the terms and conditions of the contract and the actions to be taken by the parties are clear, definite and certain.

MSEA also counters that, since the Panthers failed to exercise its option to renew the Panthers License, the agreement was effectively cancelled. Further, MSEA argues that cancellation of the Panthers License meant that the Panthers could not enter into a new license agreement. The Court finds MSEA's argument misleading insofar as MSEA delegated to DMAL the "full and exclusive" power and authority to "negotiate, execute, and perform" contracts including licenses. Therefore, even if the Panthers License was cancelled upon the Plaintiff's failure to exercise its option, DMAL/LMI could enter into a new agreement with the Panthers or any other party who desired to use the Miami Arena.

DMAL's power and authority to enter into contracts for the use of the Miami Arena is limited if the contract involves an Owner Affiliate or "schedule[s] events or performances in the Arena for more than 20 days during any one Operating Year." In those instances, MSEA's approval of the contract is required. However, the standard for MSEA approval is clearly defined in and limited under the Miami Arena Contract. Section 7.4 of the Miami Arena Contract provides, in pertinent part:

> Such Owner approval shall
>
> i.   be given by the Chairman of Owner or his designees,
>
> ii. not be unreasonably withheld and
>
> iii. be subject to the standards for Owner review and approval set forth in Exhibit D.6.4.

The relevant portions of Exhibit D.6.4 provides:

> Upon receipt of any matter submitted by Operator for review and approval ... Owner shall review the same and shall promptly (but in any event with ten (10) calendar days after such receipt) give Operator notice of Owner's approval or disapproval, setting forth in detail all reasons

for any disapproval. Owner's right to disapprove any such matter submitted shall be limited to the elements thereof 1. which do not conform substantially to matters previously approved, or in the case of contracts, which contain material provisions less favorable to Owner and Operator than were contained in drafts previously approved by Owner, 2. which are new elements not previously presented and Operator is unable to demonstrate, in the reasonable judgment of the Owner that such new element is reasonably necessary for performance of the Work, or 3. which depict matters that are violations of this Contract or applicable Legal Requirements. (Emphasis added).

MSEA argues that provision D.6.4 is inapplicable to the situation and that MSEA had an unfettered right to disapprove the Panthers License Amendment. The Court rejects this argument. Provision D.7.4 incorporates the standard set forth in D.6.4 for Owner approval, and D.6.4 clearly places limits on an Owner's right to disapprove a contract. MSEA, therefore, may not unconditionally choose not to follow these standards.

MSEA also argues that it should be allowed to disapprove the Panthers License Amendment because it was negotiated by entities that are owned, in whole or in part, by the same person, H. Wayne Huizenga. It should be noted that the Miami Arena Contract expressly contemplates that DMAL will enter into contracts with its affiliates. In those instances in which DMAL enters into a contract with its affiliates, MSEA is required to approve the contract pursuant to the standards set forth in D.6.4 and D.7.4 of the Miami Arena Contract. Accordingly, MSEA cannot now argue that such a contract is impermissible.

MSEA also argues that this dispute is simply a matter of contract negotiations and, accordingly, the Court should not get involved in negotiations between these parties. The Court finds that, once DMAL/LMI and the Panthers submitted the Panthers License Amendment for approval, MSEA's rights and obligations to be a part of the negotiations and to approve the Panthers License Amendment became fixed. Since MSEA is unable to identify any term or condition which is materially different or adverse to MSEA, the Court finds that MSEA's withholding approval of the Panthers License Amendment is unreasonable. Therefore, based on the foregoing, the Court finds that the Plaintiff has established a substantial likelihood of success on the merits.

B. Substantial Threat of Irreparable Harm

MSEA argues that the harm to the Panthers is economic in nature. MSEA relies on *United States v. Jefferson County*, 720 F.2d 1511(11th Cir.1983) for the proposition that: "[m]ere injuries, however substantial, in terms of money, time and energy necessarily expended in the absence of a stay are not enough. The possibility that adequate compensatory or other corrective relief will be available at a later date, in the ordinary course of litigation, weighs heavily against a claim of irreparable harm."

The Court, however, disagrees with MSEA that the irreparable harm is merely economic in nature and that money damages can adequately compensate the Panthers should it ultimately succeed on the merits. The overwhelming evidence presented establishes that the Panthers' existence and success rests, in large part, on the interest and loyalty of the fans. As William Torrey and Brian Burke testified, the potential harm to the Panthers is incalculable and extends beyond the financial injury. If the Panthers cannot play in the Miami Arena, it may lose home game advantage and may lose goodwill among its fans. Further, the Panthers' relationship with the NHL may be adversely affected.

C. Balancing the Harm

The inquiry under the third prong of a preliminary injunction motion requires the Court to determine whether the threatened injury to the movant outweighs the harm that an injunction may cause to the non-movant. The Court is satisfied that the Plaintiff has demonstrated its potential injury outweighs any harm the injunction may cause to MSEA. Indeed, the Panthers License Amendment, in all likelihood, will extend for only two years and will allow MSEA to collect substantial revenues from the use of the Miami Arena which otherwise would be lost if MSEA did not approve the Panthers License Amendment. Whatever other inexplicable reasons MSEA may have for failing to approve the Panthers License Amendment, it is abundantly clear to the Court the MSEA's disapproval is to its own economic disadvantage.

D. The Public Interest

The Court finds that an injunction would not disserve the public. Indeed, professional sports serves the public interest and, in this particular instance, the Panthers Lease Amendment provides economic benefits to the public.

III. CONCLUSION

Based on the foregoing, it is ORDERED AND ADJUDGED as follows:

1. Plaintiff's Emergency Motion for Preliminary Injunction is GRANTED.

2. Defendant MSEA is hereby enjoined from preventing the Panthers from utilizing the Miami Arena in accordance with the terms and conditions set forth in the Panthers License Amendment dated May 30, 1996.

3. Plaintiff is directed to deposit a bond in the sum of Ten Thousand Dollars ($10,000.00) with sureties to be approved by the Court. Said bond shall be deposited with the Clerk of Court no later than 10 a.m. on August 26, 1996.

4. Copies of this Order may be served by the Panthers, its employees, or its agents upon any individual or corporate entity that may be subject to this Order.

5. The Court retains jurisdiction of this matter for all purposes including the enforcement of this Order, should enforcement prove necessary.

3. Rewriting the Contract

A final example of an equitable remedy is when the court steps in or refuses to re-write a contract that the party claims is unfair. Courts tend to favor and protect the autonomy of parties to contract freely. However, sometimes the court concludes that equity necessitates revisions—sometimes these revisions are known as "the blue pencil rule." Restatement § 155 allows parties to reform the written expression of a contract when there is mistake by both parties; other sections also implicitly endorse the ability of the court to rewrite a contract, including allowing the court to strike some or all of an unconscionable contract (§ 208). The following case presents a dialogue between the majority and dissent about the propriety of revising the language of a contract. As you read this case, also think about all the principles we have covered in this chapter and consider whether you find the arguments about the autonomy of parties or the equitable powers of the courts to enforce fair bargains more persuasive.

Wilkie v. Auto-Owners Ins. Co.

469 Mich. 4I (Michigan 2003)

TAYLOR, J.

This case involves a dispute between Auto-Owners Insurance Company and its insureds, Janna L. Frank and the decedent, Paul K. Wilkie, regarding under-insured-motorist coverage. Defendant Auto-Owners argues that plaintiffs Frank and Wilkie's recoveries from Auto-Owners are limited under the terms of the policy to $50,000 each. Frank and Wilkie argue that they are each owed $75,000. The trial court and Court of Appeals agreed with Frank and Wilkie. We reverse.

I. FACTS

On April 17, 1996, Janna Frank was driving east on Maple Rapids Road in Clinton County, with Paul Wilkie as a passenger. At the same time, Stephen Ward was driving west on Maple Rapids Road. Witnesses described his driving as erratic shortly before his vehicle crossed the center line and collided with Frank's car, injuring her and causing the deaths of Ward and Wilkie.

Ward's vehicle was insured under a Citizens Insurance Company no-fault automobile-insurance policy having limits of $50,000. Wilkie's estate and Frank shared this sum, with each receiving $25,000. Wilkie's vehicle was insured under an Auto-Owners no-fault automobile-insurance policy that provided, in addition to the mandatory coverages required under Michigan's no-fault automobile-insurance statute an optional coverage described as underinsured-motorist coverage. Speaking generally, this coverage was intended to supplement insurance proceeds received by the insured from the tortfeasor had the tortfeasor not been underinsured.

This added coverage had limits of $100,000 for each person to a total of $300,000 for each occurrence, and also provided that Auto-Owners' liability was limited to the amount by which these limits exceeded the underinsured motorist's own insurance coverage. The policy clearly stated that the Auto-Owners' limits of liability were not to be increased because of the number of persons injured, claims made, or automobiles involved in the accident.

Auto-Owners did not contest that the accident was Ward's fault and agreed that both Wilkie's and Frank's damages were at least $100,000. Disputed, however, was the total amount due from Auto-Owners to Wilkie and Frank. Auto-Owners asserted that it only owed Wilkie and Frank $50,000 each. As it understood the contract terms, the $100,000 policy limit would be reduced by the $50,000 coverage of the Ward policy. Wilkie and Frank, for their part, claimed that Auto-Owners owed each of them $75,000. They reasoned that, having equally split the Ward policy limits of $50,000, only the $25,000 they received should have been subtracted from the $100,000 policy limit to determine the amount each was due.

Unable to reach a resolution of this dispute, Wilkie and Frank sought declaratory relief against Auto-Owners in the Clinton Circuit Court. The plaintiffs moved for summary disposition predicated on their understanding of the contract's requirements. The trial court granted their motion and ruled that only the amount actually received by each of them, $25,000, and not the entire amount of Ward's policy limits, $50,000, should be set off against the amount available to them, $100,000, under the underinsured-motorist provision. Thus, according to the trial court, Wilkie and Frank were each entitled to $75,000 from Auto-Owners.

* * *

Under the language of the underinsurance policy at issue here, the insurer agreed to pay $100,000 for each person to a total of $300,000 for each occurrence for bodily or compensatory damages to individuals covered by the policy if each person would have been entitled to recover all those sums from the other driver, but was precluded from doing so because the other driver was underinsured. The insurer's liability was then limited by a provision that states that the amount by which the $100,000 for each person to a total of $300,000 for each occurrence exceeds the total limits available to the owner or operator of the underinsured vehicle will determine the amount to be paid. Further clarity is given to this clause by the next provisions, which say that the amounts available are not increased because of the claims made or persons injured.

The Court of Appeals, as urged by the plaintiffs, approached this language by holding that ¶ 4a.1. of the contract was ambiguous because it could be "reasonably understood in differing ways." That is, ¶ 4a.1. of the contract could be interpreted to direct that the $100,000 from the Auto-Owners policy be reduced by either $50,000 or $25,000, depending on how one chose to read it. That being the case, the Court construed the contract against its drafter, Auto-Owners. The Court's ambiguity analysis of the language of ¶ 4a.1. is, at best, questionable because the language appears clearer than the Court found it to be. Paragraph 4a.1. states that the limit of liability for underinsured-motorist coverage shall not exceed "the amount by which the Underinsured Motorist Coverage limits stated in the Declarations exceeds the *total limits* of all bodily injury liability bonds and policies *available to the owner* or operator of the underinsured automobile...." (Emphasis added.) In this case, the underinsured-motorist coverage limit stated in Auto Owner's declaration is $100,000. The *total limit* of all bodily-injury liability policies *available to the owner* of the underinsured automobile, i.e., Ward, is $50,000. Therefore, the amount by which the underinsured-motorist-coverage limits stated in the declarations exceeds the total limits of all bodily-injury policies available to the owner of the underinsured automobile is clearly $50,000, not $75,000. Contrary to the contention of Court of Appeals, this provision cannot be "reasonably understood" to be referring to the amount actually received by the claimant because the provision specifically refers to the *total* available to the *owner*. Yet, whatever the merits of the Court of Appeals analysis, the panel's conclusion is fatally undermined when ¶ 4a. 1. is read, as it must be, with ¶¶ 4b.2. and 3.. These later paragraphs settle any perceived ambiguity in ¶ 4a.1. by stating that the amounts to be paid will not be increased because of claims made, suits brought, or persons injured. Interpreting this provision to mean that each plaintiff is entitled to $75,000 would increase the limit of liability "because of" the number of claims brought or persons injured, which is clearly contrary to the plain language of ¶¶ 4b.2. and 3..

Quite simply, if ¶ 4a.1. appears ambiguous by itself, when read with ¶ ¶ 4b.2. and 3. the ambiguity is eliminated. That being the case, the insurance contract at issue is unambiguous and should be enforced as its terms dictate. Thus, no consideration of the doctrine of construing the contract against the drafter is appropriate.

B

The Court of Appeals, in declining to give the contract the construction ¶¶ 4b.2. and 3. compel, also relied on the argument that to allow such a construction would defy the insured's reasonable expectations, which, as the Court characterized them, would be that no change in the amount due would be occasioned by the vicissitudes of such things as claims made or persons injured.

This approach, where judges divine the parties' reasonable expectations and then rewrite the contract accordingly, is contrary to the bedrock principle of American contract law that parties are free to contract as they see fit, and the courts are to enforce the agreement as written absent some highly unusual circumstance, such as a contract in violation of law or public policy. This Court has recently discussed, and reinforced, its fidelity to this understanding of contract law in *Terrien v. Zwit*, 467 Mich. 56 (2002). The notion, that free men and women may reach agreements regarding their affairs without government interference and that courts will enforce those agreements, is ancient and irrefutable. It draws strength from common-law roots and can be seen in our fundamental charter, the United States Constitution, where government is forbidden from impairing the contracts of citizens, art. I,

§ 10, cl. 1. Our own state constitutions over the years of statehood have similarly echoed this limitation on government power. It is, in short, an unmistakable and ineradicable part of the legal fabric of our society. Few have expressed the force of this venerable axiom better than the late Professor Arthur Corbin, of Yale Law School, who wrote on this topic in his definitive study of contract law, *Corbin on Contracts*, as follows:

> One does not have "liberty of contract" unless organized society both forbears and enforces, forbears to penalize him for making his bargain and enforces it for him after it is made. [15 Corbin, Contracts (Interim ed.), ch. 79, § 1376, p. 17.]

> In contrast to this legal pedigree extending over the centuries, the rule of reasonable expectations is of recent origin. Moreover, it is antagonistic to this understanding of the rule of law, and is, accordingly, in our view, invalid as an approach to contract interpretation.

"THE NOTION, that free men and women may reach agreements regarding their affairs without government interference and that courts will enforce those agreements, is ancient and irrefutable."

The rule of reasonable expectations had innocent origins in 1970. Professor Robert E. Keeton of Harvard Law School wrote an article entitled *Insurance law rights at variance with policy provisions*, […] in which he examined and attempted to rationalize a number of cases in which the results appeared to defy the principle that contracts will be construed according to their unambiguous terms. To explain this phenomenon, as best he could, he concluded that certain courts would evidently not enforce clear contract language in the face of one of the parties' "reasonable expectations" of coverage. As Professor Keeton described it:

> The objectively reasonable expectations of the applicants and intended beneficiaries regarding the terms of insurance contracts will be honored even though painstaking study of the policy provision would have negated those expectations.

Whether Professor Keeton intended this analysis to spawn a frontal assault on the ability of our citizens to manage, by contract, their own affairs, it had that effect because numerous courts, to one degree or another, adopted some form of the rule.

* * *

The rule of reasonable expectations clearly has no application to unambiguous contracts. That is, one's alleged "reasonable expectations" cannot supersede the clear language of a contract. Therefore, if this rule has any meaning, it can only be that, if there is more than one way to reasonably interpret a contract, i.e., the contract is ambiguous, and one of these interpretations is in accord with the reasonable expectations of the insured, this interpretation should prevail. However, this is saying no more than that, if a contract is ambiguous and the parties' intent cannot be discerned from extrinsic evidence, the contract should be interpreted against the insurer. In other words, when its application is limited to ambiguous contracts, the rule of reasonable expectations is just a surrogate for the rule of construing against the drafter. As the Court of Appeals has recently explained:

> Well-settled principles of contract interpretation require one to first look to a contract's plain language. If the plain language is clear, there can be only one reasonable interpretation of its meaning and, therefore, only one meaning the parties could reasonable expect to apply. If the language is ambiguous, longstanding principles of contract law require that the ambiguous provision be construed against the drafter. Applied in an insurance context, the drafter is always the insurer. Thus, it appears that the "rule of reasonable expectations" is nothing more than a unique title given to traditional contract principles applied to insurance contracts....

* * *

The rights and duties of parties to a contract are derived from the terms of the agreement. As this Court has previously stated, "The general rule [of contracts] is that competent persons shall have the utmost liberty of contracting and that their agreements voluntarily and fairly made shall be held valid and enforced in the courts." Under this legal principle, the parties are generally free to agree to whatever they like, and, in most circumstances, it is beyond the authority of the courts to interfere with the parties' agreement. Respect for the freedom to contract entails that we enforce only those obligations actually assented to by the parties. We believe that the rule of reasonable expectations markedly fails in this respect. The words of Justice Kavanagh bear repeating:

> [T]he expectation that a contract will be enforceable other than according to its terms surely may not be said to be reasonable. If a person signs a contract without reading all of it or without understanding it, under some circumstances that person can avoid its obligations on the theory that there was no contract at all for there was no meeting of the minds.

> But to allow such a person to bind another to an obligation not covered by the contract as written because the first person thought the other was bound to such an obligation is neither reasonable nor just.

Accordingly, we hold that the rule of reasonable expectations has no application in Michigan, and those cases that recognized this doctrine are to that extent overruled.

IV. CONCLUSION

We reverse the judgment of the Court of Appeals and find the insurance contract between Auto-Owners and Wilkie unambiguously limited Auto-Owners' liability to $50,000 each for Wilkie and Frank.

NOTES AND COMMENTS

I. THE NOTION OF CONTRACTS has had great impact on a variety of fields beyond the law. Economics and finance scholars often focus statistics models on contracting parties and seek to determine the most efficient and optimal outcomes and terms. The same holds true with ethics scholarship, which draws upon social contract principles to determine what individuals (and society) believes to be fair and just. Thus, in addition to mastering the elements of contracts from this chapter, bear in mind that the concepts and principles have analogues that apply in a wider variety of areas.

2. ONE OF THE CHALLENGES OF CONTRACTS is the balance between what two parties agree to and what society allows. Or, to put this into economic terms, how does a contract handle externalities? To put into ethical terms, what is the social contract within which negotiated contracts become permissible? How much outside monitoring do you think should apply to the agreements made between individual parties? As long as the two parties agree, should the law, society, and others leave the agreement alone or not? At what level should we consider social norms that govern contracts: locally, nationally or globally?

3. SOME OF THE ANSWERS to these questions are addressed in the following chapter where an effort has been made to create a uniform set of rules for contracts involving sales that also leaves open considerable room for individual contractors to flexibly do business. Keep the above thoughts in mind when looking at the next chapter on the Uniform Commercial Code.

CONTRACTS: THE UNIFORM COMMERCIAL CODE

IN THE LATE 1930s, there was an increasing awareness of the need for a more uniform set of laws governing exchanges. Prior to the twentieth century, individual state contract law, which of course can vary from state to state, controlled exchanges. But with an increasingly interdependent country and commerce flowing regularly across state borders, there was a need to provide more predictable laws so that businesspersons could effectively plan their affairs. The UCC was first passed into law in 1952. Since then, every state (except Louisiana) has enacted it, as well as the District of Columbia and the Virgin Islands. There have been several subsequent amendments as well, such as those in 1987 to address the rising importance of leases and in 2003 to address electronic commerce.

The Code is an effort of the National Conference of Commissioners on Uniform State Laws and the American Law Institute. Gathering some of the nation's top scholars, these organizations propose a uniform set of laws; that is, these proposals are not law until adopted. It is up to the states to decide whether or not to enact them.

The Code has the following Articles:

1. General Provisions and Definitions

2. Sales (Article 2) and Leases (Article 2A)

3. Negotiable Instruments

4. Bank Deposits and Collections (Article 4) and Funds Transfers (Article 4A)

5. Letters of Credit

6. Bulk Transfers

7. Warehouse Receipts, Bills of Lading and Other Documents of Title

8. Investment Securities

9. Secured Transactions

10. Effective Date and Repealer

11. Effective Date and Transitions

From the above list one can tell that the scope of the UCC is vast. Negotiable Instruments and Secured Transactions each merit a separate course in Law Schools. Because this textbook does not aim to cover all the legal issues that can pertain to business, but instead, the most common ones, we limit our coverage to Article 2 on Sales. This is the UCC version of contract law. Much of it mirrors what we have already seen concerning contracts, but there are some important variations.

The UCC's aim is to make clearer and simpler the laws governing sales contracts. The UCC achieves this aim, by having a common statute governing sales applicable to nearly all of the states. If the UCC did only that, it would make the law more predictable for businesses. But the UCC does more than this. It takes notice of a well-developed market that provides a great deal of information to business-people and judges alike. With a goal of facilitating business transactions, the UCC pragmatically provides multiple procedures for filling in gaps in a contract. Is the price missing on a contract? The court could read it in by resorting to information from market prices. Do standardized contract forms conflict with each other? The court, within some limits as pertaining to "material terms" can read them in a way to form the contract. Does the contract need to be modified? New consideration is not a requirement.

Thus, the UCC does make contracts easier to occur, but it is in the final analysis still a work of contract law. The basic provisions of contract law already covered in this book still apply. What this chapter will do is to identify some key provisions and variations from the common law of contracts. The following chart provides a way to start on that analysis.

TOPIC	CHARACTERISTICS	VARIATION
MERCHANTS EXCEPTION	Particular Rules When Both Parties Are Merchants	Does Not Exist in Common Law
CONTRACT TERMS	Open Price, Delivery, Price, BOTF; Firm Offers	Much reliance on business customs for merchants to fill in the blanks; More liberal as well for non-merchants, but generally return to a meeting of minds
WRITINGS	Statute of Frauds: For Merchants: 10 Day confirming, Special Manufacturing Rule; For Non-Merchants: $500 rule enforceable if admitted in court or pleadings, partial performance Parol Evidence Rule: Course of Dealing, Trade Usage, Course of Performance	Common Law has much stricter application on both Statute of Frauds and Parol Evidence Rule
CONSIDERATION	Similar Except with respect to modification of contract	Pre-existing duty variance and Firm Offer
REMEDIES	Expectation Damages	More Targeted

I. Merchants Rules

ARTICLE 2 OF THE UCC applies to the sale of goods as opposed to real estate or services (though there can be times when there is a mix of real estate or services with goods). Thus, it has a wide application. However it also has specific provisions that apply when both the parties are merchants. What is a merchant? Section 2-104 defines a merchant in one of three ways: (1) if the person deals of the kind involved in the contract (such as wholesaler, retailer, or manufacturer, (2) If the person holds himself out has having unique skills and knowledge relevant to the transaction, and (3) if the a person employs someone as an intermediary (such as an agent or broker) who is an agent. It is important to note that the determination of a merchant depends on the transaction, not the person himself. For example, a retailer of bicycles may be a merchant with respect to buying bikes, helmets, and other related items from a supplier, but not a merchant at all when buying a business suit.

Special rules for merchants apply throughout the UCC. Major ones will be covered in the appropriate section.

The following case discusses issues of defining a merchant—in this case a farmer—as well as several other provisions of the UCC, which will be discussed later in this chapter.

Brooks Cotton Company, Inc. v. Bradley F. Williams

April 23, 2012.

381 S.W.3d 414, 77 UCC Rep.Serv.2d 493

OPINION

J. STEVEN STAFFORD, J.

Defendant/Appellant Bradley F. Williams is a cotton and soybean farmer with a high school education. According to Plaintiff/Appellee Brooks Cotton Company, Inc. ("Brooks Cotton"), on or about August 5, 2010, Mr. Williams entered into a oral contract to sell his 2010 cotton production to Brooks Cotton. The alleged contract was recorded in the Brooks Cotton purchase book on August 6, 2010 and provided that Mr. Williams would sell his entire 1000 acre cotton production to Brooks Cotton. The price allegedly agreed upon was $0.20 per pound over the guaranteed government loan amount of $0.542 per pound, totaling $0.742 per pound of cotton. At the time of the alleged agreement, Mr. Williams had not yet harvested his cotton. According to the record, Mr. Williams ultimately produced approximately 1206 bales of cotton in 2010. If the contract had been performed as allegedly agreed, the total contract price for Mr. Williams' cotton would have been approximately $446,000.00. Brooks Cotton sent written confirmation of the alleged agreement to Mr. Williams on or about September 4, 2010, nearly thirty days after the contract was allegedly agreed to on the phone. Mr. Williams asserts that he never entered into an oral contract with Brooks Cotton, although he did not call or write Brooks Cotton to object to the written terms sent to him.

Mr. Williams did not deliver all of his 2010 cotton production to Brooks Cotton. On October 30, 2010, Mr. Williams partially performed on the alleged oral contract, delivering 307 bales of the estimated 1206 bales of cotton produced by his farm in 2010. Mr. Williams refused to deliver the remaining cotton, asserting that there was not a valid contract between Mr. Williams and Brooks Cotton. On or about November 18, 2010, Brooks Cotton filed a Complaint for Specific Performance, Injunctive Relief, and Damages against Mr. Williams. An injunction hearing was held on November 30, 2010. Mr. Williams testified at the hearing regarding his experience and skills in marketing cotton, stating that he had been a cotton farmer for approximately twenty-five years. Mr. Williams testified that, in the majority of the years prior to 2010, he had entered into a contract with Brooks Cotton to sell his cotton crop. In most of those years, however, Mr. Williams agreed to the contract in person at Brooks Cotton's office after the cotton had been harvested, rather than over the telephone prior to the harvest. Mr. Williams did testify that he was familiar with the practice of "booking" cotton over the phone, as he had previously "booked" his cotton with Brooks Cotton in 2003. Mr. Williams testified, however, that he did not "book" his cotton with Brooks Cotton in August 2010, but that he merely called to discuss cotton prices. In addition, Mr. Williams explained his process for determining the price at which he will sell his cotton, wherein he reviews the selling price of his cotton crop in the previous three years. Although Mr. Williams testified that he receives daily texts regarding the price of cotton, he explained that he was not familiar with the common practice of "hedging" engaged in by many cotton merchants. David Brooks of Brooks Cotton explained that hedging is a common practice in the cotton trade. In addition, Mr. Williams testified that he never uses his potential cotton crop as collateral on loans to finance the cotton crop, instead relying on various equipment and land. Mr. Williams went on to testify that he owed approximately $400,000.00 to the bank in loans, but that he had approximately $40,000.00 in bank accounts due to his off-season construction work. Based on the testimony, the court issued a preliminary injunction on the sale of Mr. Williams' 2010 production of cotton.

* * *

The central issue presented in this interlocutory appeal is whether a farmer, such as Mr. Williams, may be considered a merchant under the UCC In this case, Mr. Williams' designation as a merchant is critical to the outcome of the lawsuit. If Mr. Williams is considered a merchant, then the merchant exception to the Statute of Frauds applies and the case can proceed; if Mr. Williams cannot be considered a merchant, regardless of whether he entered into an oral contract with Brooks Cotton, an oral contract will not be sufficient to bind him.

Generally contracts need not be in writing to be enforceable, unless they are of the kind that the Statute of Frauds or other law requires to be written. One type of contract that must be in writing is a contract for the sale of goods priced over $500.00:

> **"THE CENTRAL ISSUE presented in this interlocutory appeal is whether a farmer, such as Mr. Williams, may be considered a merchant under the UCC."**

Except as otherwise provided in this section, a contract for sale of goods for the price of five hundred dollars ($500) or more is not enforceable by way of action or defense unless there is some writing or record sufficient to indicate that a contract for sale has been made between the parties and signed by the party against whom enforcement is sought or by his authorized agent or broker. A writing or record is not insufficient because it omits or incorrectly states a term agreed upon but the contract is not enforceable under this paragraph beyond the quantity of goods shown in such writing or record.

It is undisputed that the alleged contract for the sale of Mr. Williams' 2010 cotton production far exceeded $500.00. Accordingly, unless an exception applies, the Statute of Frauds requires that the contract be in writing to be enforceable. However, the UCC provides an exception to this rule in situations where both parties are merchants:

> Between merchants if within a reasonable time a writing or record in confirmation of the contract and sufficient against the sender is received and the party receiving it has reason to know its contents, it satisfies the requirements of subsection (1) against such party unless written notice of objection to its contents is given within ten (10) days after it is received.

Accordingly, for Mr. Williams to be bound by any oral contract, this Court must first determine whether he is a "merchant" for purposes of the UCC Statute of Frauds. The question of what is required to be considered a merchant for purposes of the Statute of Frauds is a question of first impression in this State. * * * [I]t is clear that the framers of the UCC intended the term merchant to encompass three distinct classes. Accordingly, for an individual to be considered a merchant he or she must either be:

1. A person who deals in goods of the kind;

2. A person who by his occupation holds himself out as having knowledge or skill peculiar to the practices or goods involved in the transaction; or

3. A person who employs an agent or broker or other intermediary who by his occupation holds himself out as having such knowledge or skill.

Indeed, many other states have adopted this definition of "merchant" based on the plain language of the statute. While this definition is instructive, it does not end the inquiry into whether a farmer is one who "deals in goods" or who "by his occupation holds himself out as having knowledge or skill peculiar to the practices or goods involved in the transaction." Accordingly, we must look beyond the plain language of the statute in order to determine whether a farmer is a merchant under the UCC Statute of Frauds.

* * *

It is not sufficient ... that one hold himself out as having knowledge or skill peculiar to the practices or goods involved, he must [b]y his occupation so hold himself out. Accordingly, a person cannot be considered a 'merchant' simply because he is a braggart or has a high opinion of his knowledge in a particular area. We conclude that a farmer does not solely [b]y his occupation hold himself out as being a professional cotton merchant.

The remaining thing which a farmer might do to be considered a merchant is to become a dealer in goods. Although there was evidence which indicated that the appellee here had a good deal of knowledge, this is not the test. There is not one shred of evidence that appellee ever sold anyone's cotton but his own. He was nothing more than an astute farmer selling his own product. We do not think this was sufficient to make him a dealer in goods.

> "A PERSON cannot be considered a 'merchant' simply because he is a braggart or has a high opinion of his knowledge in a particular area."

* * *

We find the Colorado case of *Colorado–Kansas Grain Co. v. Reifschneider*, 817 P.2d 637 (Colo.Ct.App.1991), to be particularly instructive. In determining that a farmer may be considered a merchant with regard to the Statute of Frauds, the Colorado Court of Appeals stated:

> In considering the question at issue, we note that the cases which hold that farmers may be merchants reflect on the fact that today's farmer is involved in far more than simply planting and harvesting crops. Indeed, many farmers possess an extensive knowledge and sophistication regarding the purchase and sale of crops on the various agricultural markets. Often, they are more aptly described as agri-businessmen.

Having determined that a farmer could be a merchant for purposes of the Statute of Frauds, the court went on to determine whether the particular farmer in the case should be considered a merchant. In doing so, the court articulated the following test:

> In reaching its determination, a trier of fact should consider the following as well as any other relevant factors: (1) the length of time the farmer has been engaged in the practice of selling his product to the marketers of his product; (2) the degree of business acumen shown by the farmer in his dealings with other parties; (3) the farmer's awareness of the operation and existence of farm markets; and (4) the farmer's past experience with or knowledge of the customs and practices which are unique to the particular marketing of the product which he sells.

Accordingly, the court found that because the farmer at issue had twenty years of experience selling corn, the farmer could be considered a "person who deals in goods of the kind." In addition, the court held that the farmer's extensive experience and knowledge of the futures market "supports [a] determination that he 'by his occupation [held] himself out as having knowledge or skill peculiar to the practices or goods involved in the transaction.' "

* * *

We conclude that the framers of the UCC did not intend to exclude all farmers from the category of merchants, simply because a farmer's primary occupation is the cultivation, rather than the sale, of crops. The sale of crops is as integral to the business of commercial farming as the cultivation. The framers included crops in their definition of goods. Therefore, the framers clearly intended to include those that sell crops commercially in the definition of merchant, so long as that person either "deals in goods of the kind" or who "by his occupation holds himself out as having knowledge or skill peculiar to the practices or goods involved in the transaction." In addition, the definition of merchant is broadly construed for purposes of the Statute of Frauds, encompassing "almost every person in business," including an experienced commercial farmer.

Based on the foregoing, we cannot conclude that the framers intentionally intended to omit experienced commercial farmers from the category of merchants. Accordingly, we adopt the rule that a farmer may be considered a merchant for the purposes of the merchant exception to the Statute of Frauds, when the farmer possesses sufficient expertise in not only the cultivation, but also the sale of crops. However, the determination of whether a particular farmer is a merchant is a mixed question of fact and law, which must be determined on a case-by-case basis, taking into account "the individual experience and activities of the person involved." Accordingly, we reverse the trial court's determination that "Tennessee's farmer[s]," as a whole, are considered merchants for purposes of the Statute of Frauds. Instead, trial courts should consider the following, nonexhaustive, criteria in determining whether a particular farmer is a merchant for purposes of the Statute of Frauds:

(1) the length of time the farmer has been engaged in the practice of selling his product to the marketers of his product; (2) the degree of business acumen shown by the farmer in his dealings with other parties; (3) the farmer's awareness of the operation and existence of farm markets; and (4) the farmer's past experience with or knowledge of the customs and practices which are unique to the particular marketing of the product which he sells.

Applying the above factors to Mr. Williams, we note that several factors weigh in favor of a determination that Mr. Williams was a merchant for purposes of the Statute of Frauds. First, Mr. Williams testified that he had been a cotton farmer for approximately twenty-five years and that throughout the years, he sold both his and his landlord's cotton production. Next, Mr. Williams testified that he had previously engaged in oral crop "booking," a practice that other farmers testified was common in the cotton trade. Mr. Williams also testified that he determined when to sell his cotton, and at what price, by using a three-year history of his cotton sales, as well as daily notifications about the price of cotton on the cotton market. Mr. Williams also testified that he receives periodicals about cotton farming, such as *Cotton Grower*.

However, some factors weigh against a determination that Mr. Williams is a merchant for purposes of the Statute of Frauds. First, Mr. Williams testified that he does not engage in the practice of hedging; indeed, Mr. Williams testified that he was unaware of what the term "hedging" meant. However, the testimony of Mr. Brooks, as well as the depositions of several other area farmers, established that hedging is a practice that is unique and integral to the marketing of cotton. In addition, though Mr. Williams testified that he had previously orally booked his cotton with Brooks Cotton, his testimony shows that he had only engaged in this practice once over the last several years. Further, the record is unclear whether the periodicals Mr. Williams receives deal with the cotton trade, or solely with cotton farming.

* * *

IV. CONCLUSION

The judgment of the Chancery Court of Crockett County is affirmed in part, reversed in part, and remanded for further proceedings in accordance with this opinion. Costs are taxed equally to Appellant Bradley F. Williams, and his surety, and to Appellee Brooks Cotton Company, Inc., for all of which execution may issue if necessary.

II. Contract Terms

IN COMMON LAW a contract required a meeting of the minds. The offer and acceptance of the contract needed to be, if not the mirror-image of each other, very close to that. The UCC relaxes this requirement. As noted above, provided there is a manifestation of intent that the parties desired to enter into a contract with each other, Section 2-204(3) (and 2A-204(3) for leases) permits a court to read terms into the contract in order to give the contract effect. Thus if a contract calls for the sale and conveyance of 1,000 widgets, but fails to state the sales price, the court can consult the market in order to determine the typical price for widgets of similar quality.

The same holds true for delivery. Perhaps the parties entered into an agreement, but failed to designate the time and place of delivery. By consulting normal trade usage and custom, the court could read into a contract where and when a delivery of a product would take place. Bear in mind, of course, that most transactions already do this as the parties work through missing elements themselves. But there are times and places where the ambiguity gives rise to a lawsuit in which the court is called upon to interpret the contract.

Cartamundi USA, Inc. v. Bunky's Enterprises, Inc.

Superior Court of Connecticut, Judicial District of New Haven.
No. CV096006382S. Aug. 16, 2012.

LINDA K. LAGER, Judge.

In January 2008, Gress obtained a license on behalf of Bunky's to use the "Terminator™" name as well as images for the purpose of a collectible card game he created known as "Terminator 2–Judgment Day." Gress negotiated with Cartamundi's employee Rosemary Mills (Mills), an account manager and sales executive, over a period of months regarding the manufacture of the game which he had designed. On June 9, 2008 she sent him proposal #70095 (the June 9th proposal) which contained information pertaining to the collation of the product, the quantity, packaging, assembly and pricing (exhibit 1). The collation, packaging, assembly, delivery, quantity and payment terms were set forth on page 2 of the June 9th proposal. The proposal also included eighteen numbered paragraphs under the title "Printing Trade Customs" as well as a section entitled "Additional Terms and Conditions."

On June 16, 2008, Mills e-mailed to Gress what she described as "a corrected formal" containing a revised second page for proposal #70095 (exhibit 6) (corrected formal). The correction pertained to the collation of "rare" and "ultra rare" cards. Collation refers to the assembly of the cards into final packaging. Initially, the cards are printed in large sheets, referred to as forms, and then cut into single cards. According to the proposal, there were going to be two forms of common cards and one form of rare and ultra rare cards (exhibits 1, 6). Cartamundi then would assemble the cards according to the collation terms agreed to by the parties. Those terms are set forth in the section of the proposal titled "PACKAGING/DELIVERY" on the second page.

The June 9th proposal stated that each "case" would contain two packs with a rare card and one pack with a ultra rare card inserted in lieu of a common card while the "corrected formal" stated that each "POP" would contain two packs with a rare card and one pack with a ultra rare card inserted in lieu of a common card. A "POP" is a display box. Each POP was to contain 30 packs of five cards each or 150 cards. A case would consist of ten to twelve POPs or 1500 to 1800 cards. The second page of the corrected formal specified that the order quantity was 100,000 booster packs and 1,000 starter boxes. The second page also contained a production schedule and the payment terms.

On June 19, 2008, Gress authorized Cartamundi in writing to proceed with the production as specified in the corrected formal. Gress also paid the required 50% down in advance of production by way of a check drawn on Bunky's account in the amount of $17,110.00 dated June 25, 2008 (exhibit D). Production then commenced. A master set of pre-press proofs was sent to Gress who returned it to Cartamundi without any markings. Cartamundi manufactured the game in conformance with the terms of the corrected formal. On or about August 15, 2008, Cartamundi shipped a few cases of the finished product to Gress who was attending a convention. At that time Gress opened up a number of packs in order to create a card catalogue but was unable to put together a full set of cards from the packs that he opened. As a result, he believed certain cards were missing. He never complained to Cartamundi in writing about missing cards although he did complain, in an undated letter, about the ratio of rare and ultra rare cards per display box (exhibit 7).

The completed order remains in Cartamundi's warehouse. An invoice that was sent to the defendant for the balance due of $17,110.00 (exhibit 2) has not been paid. Additional pertinent facts will be set forth below.

II.

* * *

"A contract for sale of goods may be made in any manner sufficient to show agreement, including conduct by both parties which recognizes the existence of such a contract." UCC § 2–204(1). "Unless otherwise unambiguously indicated by the language or circumstances, (a) an offer to make a contract shall be construed as inviting acceptance in any manner and by any medium reasonable under the circumstances." UCC § 2–206(1). Even if the document that Gress signed on June 19, 2008 and returned to Cartamundi was the June 9th proposal rather than the corrected formal, it is clear that Bunky's accepted the terms of the corrected formal and ordered 100,000 booster packs and 1,000 starter boxes to be packed in display boxes (POPs) containing 30 packs of five cards each with each POP containing two packs with a rare card and one pack with an ultra rare card inserted in lieu of a common card. Bunky's demonstrated its assent by its payment of 50% down as required by the terms of the parties' contract, its provision to Cartamundi of the artwork and its review of the pre-press proofs.

> "A CONTRACT FOR sale of goods may be made in any manner sufficient to show agreement, including conduct by both parties which recognizes the existence of such a contract."

The June 16, 2008 e-mail from Mills, including her cover letter and the attached first two pages of proposal #70095 as corrected, followed by the submission of Gress's signature on proposal #70095 on June 19, 2008 and Bunky's issuance of a check in the requisite amount on June 25, 2008, provides ample documentary evidence of the existence and essential terms of the contract. The fact that Cartamundi manufactured and packaged the game in conformance with the terms of the corrected formal is also evidence of the terms of the agreement.

Alternatively, if the terms of the "corrected formal" are different from those "offered or agreed upon" there is still a valid contract pursuant to UCC § 2–207. "This section is intended to address two typical situations, one in which agreement has already been reached by the parties, either orally or through informal writings, and is later followed by a formal confirmation containing both terms agreed upon and additional terms not discussed or in which a wire or letter expressed and intended as a confirmation of an agreement adds further minor suggestions or proposals." The exceptions contained in UCC § 2–207(2) do not apply because the June 9th proposal did not expressly limit acceptance to the terms of that offer, the terms of the "corrected formal" did not materially alter the contract and Bunky's did not object within a reasonable time after receiving the e-mail from Mills specifying the changes to the collation of the rare and ultra rare cards.

The only difference between the June 9th proposal and the "corrected formal" concerns the packaging of the rare and ultra rare cards. Under the collation terms of the corrected formal, more of the rare and ultra rare cards would be packaged than under the collation terms of the June 9th proposal. Thus the different collation terms were beneficial, not harmful, to Bunky's and did not materially alter the contract. UCC § 2–207(2)(b). See 2 Anderson, Uniform Commercial Code (3d ed.1997) § 2–207:81. Furthermore, the UCC presumes that different or additional terms will be included in the contract. Assuming, without deciding, that Bunky's did not assent to the change in the collation terms, Bunky's has failed to establish "that, under the circumstances, it cannot be presumed that a reasonable merchant would have consented to the additional term." A "profession of surprise" is not enough.

III.

Under Texas law, the elements of a breach of contract claim are: (1) the existence of a valid contract between plaintiff and defendant; (2) the plaintiff's performance or tender of performance; (3) the defendant's breach of the contract; and (4) the plaintiff's damage as a result of the breach. Connecticut law is similar. The court has determined that there was a valid contract between Cartamundi and Bunky's. The evidence establishes that Cartamundi performed the contract by producing and assembling the card packages in conformance with the terms of the corrected formal and by sending a partial shipment to Gress on or about August 15, 2008. Whether Bunky's breached the contract and the measure of damages is governed by the UCC and not the common law.

Bunky's has alleged by way of special defense and counterclaim that Cartamundi provided non-conforming goods which it rejected under UCC § 2–602. Under Texas law, "nonconformity is defined in terms of the contract of sale: goods are conforming or conform to the contract when they are in accordance with the obligations under the contract."

Bunky's had the burden of establishing that the game as manufactured was nonconforming. Bunky's has taken the position that the game did not conform to industry standards because Gress was unable to catalogue a full set of cards from the packs that he opened from the partial shipment that had been sent to the convention and because there was an incorrect ratio of rare and ultra rare cards.

Texas law provides that while "the terms of a contract may be explained and supplemented through trade usage ... it may not be used to contradict an express term [of the contract] ... The existence and scope of trade usage must be proved as facts." Cartamundi's vice-president Stephen Venable testified that there are no printing industry standards regarding collectible cards. Gress testified that according to his understanding of the practices of the trade of collectible cards, individuals would purchase an entire display box (i.e., a POP) in order to have a better chance of getting all the cards for the game. He also testified that his goal with respect to this game was that an individual would be able to get every card by purchasing two to three display boxes.

The evidence is insufficient to establish both the existence and scope of trade usage. The express contract terms regarding the collation of the POPs are clear. There is no credible evidence of implied terms that are inconsistent with the contract's express terms. The evidence establishes that Cartamundi tendered the goods in conformance with the terms of the contract, exhibits 5, 8, at the time and place Bunky's had specified. The court concludes as a matter of fact that the goods were conforming within the meaning of UCC § 2–106. Accordingly, the second special defense and the counterclaim fail.

IV.

Having determined that Cartamundi tendered conforming goods to Bunky's, the court must next determine whether Bunky's accepted or wrongfully rejected the goods. UCC § 2–703. UCC § 2–606(1)(b) provides that acceptance of goods occurs when a buyer fails to effectively reject goods, after a reasonable opportunity for inspection, in the manner provided by UCC § 2–602. "Rejection of goods must be within a reasonable time after their delivery or tender. It is ineffective unless the buyer seasonably notifies the seller." UCC § 2–602(1). Under Texas law, whether rejection is timely is "highly fact specific."

Cartamundi maintains that Bunky's waived any right to reject the goods because it did not provide any notice within fifteen days of the partial delivery made on or about August 15, 2008 as required by paragraph 16 of the "Printing Trade Customs" that were part of the contract. It is not necessary to address this issue because the evidence fails to establish that Bunky's, acting in good faith, clearly and unambiguously rejected the goods which, in all respects, conformed to the contract. Although Gress testified that he did not receive the run of cards that he had expected because he was unable to fully catalogue the cards based on the partial delivery to the convention, his undated written notification to Cartamundi concerning a "bad run" only referenced the ratio of rare and ultra rare cards to common cards (exhibit 7). Cartamundi reviewed those complaints and followed up on the issue of card ratios in e-mails dated September 3 and 5, 2008 explaining that the collation conformed to the contract. There is no documentary evidence of any follow-up to this exchange.

Bunky's did not return the cards that were delivered to Gress at the convention. Gress not only opened the packs to put together a card catalogue but he also gave packs of cards to potential customers at the convention. Gress and his wife opened additional packs following the convention in an effort to catalogue the cards. These were reasonable uses consistent with ownership.

Based on the credible evidence, the court concludes that Bunky's accepted the goods within the meaning of UCC § 2–606 and never made an effective rejection within the meaning of UCC § 2–602. "Once acceptance of goods occurs, [t]he buyer must pay at the contract rate for any goods accepted.

V.

Since Bunky's accepted conforming goods, it was obligated to pay the contract price to Cartamundi. Bunky's did not pay the balance of the invoice (exhibit 2). Cartamundi is entitled to damages for the contract price, along with incidental damages. UCC § 2–708(1) damages are inadequate in this case because Cartamundi has produced a speciality item, a collectible card game, that cannot be resold to another buyer.

The evidence establishes that, due to Bunky's breach, Cartamundi is owed the remaining principal amount of $17,110.00. Cartamundi is also entitled to recover "commercially reasonable charges ... resulting from the breach," as incidental damages. Paragraph 16 of the "Printing Trade Customs" incorporated in the contract provides for a "service charge of 1 1/2% per month" to be "added to all invoice due more than 30 days." Bunky's was invoiced on August 29, 2008 (exhibit 2). The service charge, calculated at $256.65 a month for a period of 47.5 months, totals $12,190.87.

JUDGMENT

Based on the foregoing, judgment shall enter in favor of the plaintiff Cartamundi USA, Inc. and against the defendant Bunky's Enterprises, Inc., on the complaint and in favor of the counterclaim defendant Cartamundi USA, Inc. and against the counterclaim plaintiff Bunky's Enterprises, Inc. on the counterclaim. Damages are awarded on the complaint in the amount of $29,300.87. Upon satisfaction of the judgment, Cartamundi shall release the goods to Bunky's if so demanded. In the exercise of its discretion, the court declines to award prejudgment and postjudgment interest. Cartamundi may submit a bill of costs in accordance with Connecticut law.

QUANTITY IS ONE TERM where courts are more hesitant to draw upon the market. Many sources exist to determine the price of an item. Trade usage and custom help a great deal to determine delivery points. But quantity is something determined more between the specific buyer and seller than by the market. Even here, however, Section 2-306(1) will allow courts to read quantity terms for certain kinds of "output" contracts. These are contracts where a buyer agrees to buy all the seller's production (or output) of a product or where a seller agrees satisfy all of the buyer's need for a product, say for a component part the buyer needs for subsequent manufacture of a finished product. In such cases, the court can find evidence of what the quantity term would be.

Section 2-207 has caused more than a few headaches for law students, business law students, and even lawyers and businesspeople. It is sometimes called "The Battle of the Forms." The reality is that in today's business environment, contracts are formed by the exchange of forms prepared by each party's lawyer. The offeror sends over a form and the buyer sends back its form to accept, except of course, the buyer's form does not have identical terms to that of the seller's. At common law, this would not create a contract, because there would be no mirror image. However, the UCC provides a (complicated) procedure for putting these forms, as inconsistent as they may be, together to form a contract. The basic rules are as follows.

First, if the offeree sends an acceptance within a reasonable time, then a contract is formed even if has terms in it that are different from those set out by the offeror. An exception is if the offeree explicitly says that there is no contract unless the offeror accepts those differing terms. If that requirement is included, then there is no contract. But if the offeree does not require that the offeror specifically accept those terms, then those terms, again even if they differ from those of the offeror, become part of the contract.

Assuming we have gotten this far, how does one navigate the problem that terms in the contract conflict with each other? The UCC says that the additional terms are proposals to be added to the contract unless they materially alter the contract or if seasonable notice has already been given objecting to the terms.

Finally, the court will look at the conduct of the parties. If the parties are acting like they have a contract, the court will find that they do have a contract on the basis of the terms in which they do agree plus any other terms that can be ascertained from other sections of the UCC.

It does not take long for the number of disputes that can arise out of Section 2-207 to multiply. On exactly what terms are the parties agreeing by their conduct? What is a seasonable notice of objection? What constitutes a material alteration? This final question may be the one most litigated. The following case provides an example.

Orkal Industries, LLC v. Array Connector Corporation

Supreme Court, Appellate Division, Second Department, New York.
July 5, 2012.

The plaintiff, a limited liability company located in New York, purchased airplane-related products from the defendant, a corporation located in Florida, by transmitting purchase orders for the products. The defendant confirmed the orders with "customer order acknowledgment" forms that contained a forum selection clause, purportedly placing any contractual disputes in a Florida court. Although the plaintiff never expressly objected to the forum selection clause, in February 2010, the plaintiff commenced this action against the defendant in New York. The complaint alleged five causes of action seeking damages, inter alia, for unpaid commissions. As relevant here, the third and fourth causes of action were premised on transactions to which the forum selection clause purportedly applied. The defendant moved, among other things, for summary judgment dismissing the complaint based upon the forum selection clause contained in its customer order acknowledgment forms. In an order dated November 30, 2010, the Supreme Court, in effect, granted those branches of the defendant's motion which were for summary judgment dismissing the complaint. In an order dated May 16, 2011, the Supreme Court, upon reargument, vacated the determination in the order dated November 30, 2010, in effect, granting those branches of the defendant's motion which were for summary judgment dismissing the first and second causes of action, thereupon denied those branches of the motion, severed the first and second causes of action, and removed those causes of action to the District Court, Nassau County. Furthermore, upon reargument, the Supreme Court adhered to its prior determination granting those branches of the defendant's motion which were, in effect, for summary judgment dismissing the third, fourth, and fifth causes of action. The plaintiff appeals from both the order dated November 30, 2010, and so much of the order dated May 16, 2011, as, upon reargument, severed the first and second causes of action, removed those causes of action to the District Court, and adhered to its prior determination granting those branches of the defendant's motion which were, in effect, for summary judgment dismissing the third and fourth causes of action.

Pursuant to additional terms of a contract between merchants become part of the parties' contract unless they are, inter alia, specifically objected to within a reasonable time, or unless the additional terms materially alter the contract. The party opposing the inclusion of the additional terms bears the burden of proving that the additional terms are material changes and, thus, are rendered nonbinding.

New York and Florida forums, the defendant's inclusion of a forum selection clause in its customer order acknowledgment forms constitutes a material alteration to the parties' initial contracts. Therefore, upon reargument, the Supreme Court should have denied those branches of the defendant's motion which were, in effect, for summary judgment dismissing the third and fourth causes of action.

In contrast to the third and fourth causes of action, the first and second causes of action pertained to purchase orders where forum selection was not an issue. The Supreme Court severed those causes of action from this action, and removed them to the District Court, as the amount in controversy did not exceed the $15,000 jurisdictional limit of the District Court. In light of our determination that the third and fourth causes of action, each of which seeks damages in excess of the District Court's $15,000 jurisdictional limit, should not have been summarily dismissed, the first and second causes of action should be removed back to the Supreme Court, Nassau County, for the judicial economy of litigating all of the parties' disputes in a single forum.

The defendant's remaining contentions either are without merit or have been rendered academic by our determination.

IN WORKING THROUGH the Battle of the Forms, as well as other sections of the UCC, it is important for a businessperson (and their lawyer) to bear in mind problems that can be associated with too much rule-making and too onerous a set of contractual requirements. The authors once knew a businessperson who bragged that his lawyer was so tough that no one would sign the contract she drafted. That is not a tough lawyer; that's a dumb lawyer. A businessperson won't make any money if no one will sign a contract with them.

III. Writings

THE UCC has several important provisions pertaining to writing. Section 2-205 (and 2A-205 for leases) provides for a "firm offer." These are a kind of option contract where the offeror keeps the offer open for a specific period of time, not more than three months. If an offeror makes a firm offer, they are not able to revoke it as they typically would be able to do prior to acceptance. This can be enforced even without consideration for leaving the offer open. The key is the offeror indicating that this is a firm offer.

The Statute of Frauds, you'll remember, applies at common law to contracts for real estate, suretyship, and services lasting more than one year. The UCC adds provisions that contracts for more than five hundred dollars ($500) are not enforceable unless they are in writing or some other record establishes the specifics of the contract. Not surprisingly, if the parties sign a contract and the contract provides that any modifications are to be in writing, this triggers the writing requirement. The $500 requirement can make for some closer questions. If a contract was subject to the Statute of Frauds (i.e. it was for more than $500) but the modification reduces it under $500, the modification does not need to be in writing. The following case looks at a similar issue from the other point of view.

June G. Ashton Interiors v. Stark Carpet Corporation

Appellate Court of Illinois, First District, Fourth Division.
March 20, 1986.

Justice JIGANTI delivered the opinion of the court:

The plaintiff, June G. Ashton Interiors (Ashton), brought this action against the defendant, Stark Carpet Corporation (Stark), for breach of a written contract entered into on August 9, 1982, for the purchase of carpeting to be installed in the home of a client of Ashton. Stark counterclaimed for the balance due under the contract in the amount of $6,292. The trial court entered judgment in favor of Ashton in the amounts of $6,292, a refund of her deposit paid under the contract, and $3,891, a recovery of her lost resale profits if the contract had been performed. Stark now appeals claiming that the trial court erred in entering judgment against it as there was no material breach of the contract and the goods were otherwise conforming. Also, Stark argues that the trial court erred in denying its counterclaim for damages incurred as a result of Ashton's wrongful cancellation of the contract.

Ashton had been an interior decorator for nearly 24 years. For the past 14 years she had been self-employed and had owned the interior decorating business known as June G. Ashton Interiors. In May of 1982 Ashton was commissioned by one of her clients to acquire carpeting for the client's home. Specifically, Ashton was asked to locate carpeting for two areas of the home: the first-floor entrance hall or foyer and stairway abutting the entrance hall, and the second-floor hallway. Ashton subsequently contacted Stark and consulted with its salesperson, Ken Gosh, about her client's carpet requirements. She selected the yarns that were to be dyed and woven to her specifications. During these preliminary discussions, Ashton was informed that the carpeting would be delivered within four to five months from the date the orders were placed.

Based on these discussions two confirmation orders for the carpeting were prepared by Stark's salesperson on July 15, 1983. The first confirmation order specified carpeting for the stairway and second-floor hall runner. In addition, part of this carpet order was to be cut into a small area rug to be placed in the upper hallway. The second confirmation order was for two area rugs for the first-floor foyer and the second-floor hallway. The orders indicated that delivery was to be F.O.B. New York.

On August 19, 1982, two purchase orders were prepared by Ashton for the two lots of carpeting described in the confirmation orders. These purchase orders directed Stark to ship both lots of carpeting to Camelot Carpet, Stark's Chicago warehouse and to tag the carpets, "Ashton/Mrs. McCormick." Ashton signed the confirmation orders and paid a 50% deposit on the carpeting in two separate checks, one in the amount of $2,932.50 and the other $3,359.50. Printed on one of the purchase orders was a delivery date of "approximately four to five months." Ashton testified that at trial that she was assured by Stark's salesperson, Ken Gosh, that the carpeting would be delivered within four to five months from the date the orders were placed. She stated that she also wrote this delivery information on her copy of one of the confirmation orders.

Ashton testified that her next contact with Stark was in late November when she inquired as to the date her carpeting would be delivered. Stark's salesperson, Ken Gosh, stated he would check with New York on the status of her carpeting. At the request of her client, Ashton on December 10, 1982, again telephoned Gosh to determine the status of the carpeting and its expected delivery date. He told Ashton that the carpeting would not be in before the end of the year but that it was "on the waters." Ashton interpreted this statement to mean that the carpeting was in the process of being shipped to her from England where the carpeting was being woven.

Ashton's next contact with Stark was on February 3, 1983, at the request of her client. She again spoke with Ken Gosh and told him that her client wanted to cancel the orders because the goods had not yet been received. Later that same day, Ashton was contacted by Stark's regional manager, Paul Adams, concerning her attempt to cancel the carpeting orders. Adams told Ashton that the information that the carpeting was "on the waters" was erroneous. Adams indicated that he would check on the status of her carpeting and would try to get some firm information on delivery dates from the mill in order to arrange a revised delivery schedule. Adams testified that at this time the mills had not yet started to weave the carpeting.

On February 7, Ashton received a call from Adams informing her that he had called the mill in England and had worked out a revised delivery schedule. He stated that Stark would receive the order for the foyer and stairway carpeting in Chicago on February 18. The balance of the goods would follow on February 25. A letter dated February 8, 1983, signed by Paul Adams, confirmed the substance of their February 7 telephone conversation and the agreed-upon revised delivery schedule.

The next communication with Stark occurred on February 18 when Ashton stated that she called Adams concerning the stairway carpeting that was to arrive that day. She stated that she was informed by Adams that the first lot of carpeting was still in New York. In contrast, Adams testified that the first lot of stairway and foyer carpeting had arrived at Camelot Carpet in Chicago on February 18. Adams stated that at this time he informed Ashton that the carpeting had arrived but she stated that she did not wish to receive the goods at that time until all the carpeting had arrived.

Sometime between February 18 and February 25, Ashton again telephoned Adams to determine whether the first lot of carpeting had been delivered on February 18 as scheduled, and whether the second lot of carpeting would also arrive in New York on February 25. According to Ashton, Adams informed her that the first lot of carpeting had arrived in Chicago but that the second lot of carpeting, the area rugs, was still in New York and the borders were not attached to the rugs and would therefore require two more weeks to be assembled and delivered to Chicago. He told Ashton that he could fly the carpets to Chicago in one day. On February 25, Ashton informed Adams that she was cancelling the carpet orders pursuant to her client's request. Adams testified that the second lot of carpeting was shipped to Chicago and arrived on February 26.

On February 28, Ashton, despite her cancellation on February 25, went to Camelot Carpet to locate the carpeting. She stated that if the carpeting had been delivered, she would have accepted it despite the late delivery. She asked for the carpeting tagged "Ashton/Mrs. McCormick." However, only the first lot of carpeting, the stairway carpeting, which she was told by the warehouseman had arrived on February 24, was located. At this time, the small area rug had not yet been cut from the first lot of carpeting as specified in the purchase order. The second lot of carpeting could not be located and Ashton was informed that Camelot Carpet did not have it. Later that same day Ashton telephoned Stark to cancel the carpeting orders. She confirmed this cancellation in a letter sent to the president of Stark, in which she also demanded a refund of the deposit she had already paid to Stark under the contract.

The next communication occurred on March 9 when Ashton received a mailgram from the president of Stark stating that the second lot of carpeting was still in New York and that it would be approximately three days before the carpeting would be completed and flown to Chicago. Adams testified that this information was erroneous and the second lot of carpeting was in fact in Chicago at that time. There was testimony that the area rug which was to be cut from the first lot of stairway carpeting was cut sometime after March 17. The second lot of carpeting was still to be assembled. Ashton testified that her contract with her client for the carpeting was cancelled, although she was able to partially replace the order and obtain a $400 commission. She stated that if the original contract for the carpeting had been performed she would have gotten approximately $4,300 in commission.

Ashton brought this action against Stark alleging that Stark had breached its contract with her by failing to timely deliver the carpeting she had ordered from it. The trial court entered judgment in favor of Ashton finding that the February 8 letter from Stark to Ashton was a modification of the original August 9 contract and established firm dates of delivery of the carpeting to Chicago. Consequently, as Stark did not deliver the carpet to Ashton in accordance with the modified contract, Stark's failure to perform the contract, as modified, was a breach of the contract, thereby entitling Ashton to recover damages. Accordingly, Ashton was awarded $10,583 in damages, less the $400 commission Ashton had secured.

We first consider whether the February 8 letter, setting forth the February 18 and February 25 delivery dates, was a modification to the August 9, 1982, contract. The August 9, 1982, contract did not specify exact dates for the delivery of the carpeting, but rather, stated that delivery was to be within approximately four to five months from the date the order was placed. On February 3, nearly six months after the order had been made, Ashton attempted to cancel the contract because of Stark's failure to deliver the carpeting. Stark then agreed on February 7, confirmed by letter dated February 8, to deliver both lots of carpeting to Chicago on February 18 and February 25. In the February 8 letter, Stark stated that the carpeting would "arrive in Chicago no later than" the specified date and that it would assume the expense of flying the goods directly to Chicago. The letter also stated that Stark would assure that this schedule was maintained.

The instant contract is subject to the provisions of the Uniform Commercial Code (UCC) as adopted in Illinois. Under the UCC, an agreement modifying a contract needs no consideration to be binding but must be in writing signed by the party against which enforcement is sought. The February 8 letter signed by Stark constituted a written confirmation of the carpeting delivery schedule orally agreed upon on February 7 thereby satisfying the requirements of the UCC to be a modification of the contract.

The trial court's finding that the parties intended the February 8 letter to modify the original contract and to establish definite and binding delivery dates is supported by the evidence. Ashton had testified that she had repeatedly contacted Stark about the expected delivery dates of the carpeting. After six months had elapsed from the time the orders had been made, Ashton on February 3 notified Stark that pursuant to her client's request she intended to cancel the contract because of the delays in delivery. Ashton agreed not to cancel the contract after she received written confirmation by Stark that the carpeting would be delivered to Chicago no later than February 18 and February 25. This testimony together with the language used in the February 8 letter could reasonably be found to accomplish a binding modification of the original contract. In addition to modifying the delivery schedule for the carpeting, the original contract had specified Stark's delivery to be F.O.B. New York. In the February 8 letter, Stark agreed to assume the responsibility to deliver the carpeting to Chicago by the specified dates.

The next question this court must consider is whether the trial court's finding that Stark's failure to timely deliver conforming goods, in accordance with the contract, as modified, constituted a material breach of the contract. Considering the first lot of carpeting, there was evidence presented that it was not timely delivered on February 18, as specified under the contract as modified. In addition, the carpeting was not conforming to the terms of the contract as an area rug had not been cut from the carpeting and was not completed until March 17. Further, the second lot of carpeting which was scheduled for delivery in Chicago on February 25 was still in New York and unassembled on March 9, eight months after the original contract had been entered into and nearly two weeks after the delivery date under the modified contract. While Stark presented conflicting testimony that the first lot of carpeting arrived in Chicago on February 18 and the second lot on February 26, it was clear that Stark never informed Ashton as to the arrival of the carpeting in Chicago. Nevertheless, it was for the trial court to assess the credibility of the witnesses and determine the weight to be given their testimony. From the evidence presented at trial it was reasonable for the trial court to infer that both lots of carpeting were not delivered in accordance with the contract as modified.

Under section 2–507 of the UCC, proper tender is a condition to the buyer's duty to accept the goods and to pay for them. If the tender of delivery fails in any respect to conform to the contract, the buyer may cancel the entire contract and is entitled to a return of any money paid by him and to recover damages. (Ill.Rev.Stat.1983, ch. 26, pars. 2–601(a), 2–711(1), and 2–715.) We conclude that Stark materially breached its contract by failing to timely deliver the carpeting to Ashton. The evidence at trial established that time of delivery was imperative. Ashton had attempted to cancel the original contract solely because of delay in delivery. Stark agreed in the February 8 contract modification to deliver the carpeting by February 18 and February 25 to Chicago. Stark was aware that Ashton's client had wanted to cancel the original contract because of the late delivery. Stark was therefore aware of Ashton's need for timely performance and the reasons for and importance of the delivery schedule agreed to on February

> **"IF THE TENDER of delivery fails in any respect to conform to the contract, the buyer may cancel the entire contract and is entitled to a return of any money paid by him and to recover damages."**

8. Thus, a two to three week delay in delivering the carpeting constituted a material breach of contract.

Stark argues that despite any breach in its performance Ashton cannot cancel the contract because she did not allow it to cure the late delivery. Under section 2–508 where a buyer rejects a non-conforming tender, a seller will be allowed a further reasonable time after the time for performance has passed to substitute a conforming tender if he seasonably notifies the buyer of his intention to cure. Ashton cancelled on February 25. She went to the warehouse on February 28 in the hopes that she could still recover the carpeting and salvage her contract with her client. On February 28, the second lot of carpeting could not be located. Later that day, Ashton telephoned Stark to cancel the carpeting as she believed that the second lot of carpeting was not in Chicago. Stark never notified Ashton of any intention to cure in response to her February 28 telephone call and letter cancelling the carpeting. Adams stated that all of the carpeting was in Chicago on February 26. However, Stark never informed Ashton of its arrival. Its first contact with Ashton was on March 9. The notice on March 9 does not constitute a "seasonable" notice of its intention to cure and Stark did not show that it was in a position to cure since it informed her that the second lot of carpeting was still in New York and unassembled and there was evidence that the area rug was still to be cut from the first lot of carpeting.

Furthermore, there is no merit to Stark's argument that tender of delivery to Ashton occurred on February 25 when the second lot of carpeting was placed on a common carrier in New York. As we discussed earlier, the February 8 agreement modified the original contract terms which provided that shipment of the carpeting would be F.O.B. New York. Under the contract as modified, Stark agreed to deliver the carpeting to Chicago on February 25; therefore, the contract became a destination contract which required Stark to "put and hold conforming goods at the buyer's disposition [at the destination] and give the buyer any notification reasonably necessary to enable him to take delivery." Therefore, even if we accepted Stark's evidence that the second lot of carpeting arrived in Chicago on February 26, Stark had to make the goods physically available to Ashton at the destination so that she could take possession of them. This Stark failed to do. Ashton went to Stark's warehouse in Chicago on February 28 to take delivery of both lots of carpeting. It became Stark's duty to produce the carpets. Stark failed to make these carpets available to Ashton. Stark argues that its failure to locate the carpeting was due to Ashton's failure to present proper tagging instructions which were necessary to locate the carpet. However, it was Stark's duty to give Ashton any specific instructions which would be necessary for her to take delivery. Stark did not inform Ashton of the importance of the tagging numbers to locate the carpeting. Even after Ashton telephoned Stark on February 28, Stark still did not inform her about the procedures for locating the carpeting nor the importance of the tagging identification numbers. Under these circumstances, Stark did not give Ashton the reasonable notice necessary to take delivery.

For the foregoing reasons, the judgment of the circuit court of Cook County is affirmed.

CONSISTENT WITH ITS APPROACH to support contracts, the writing requirement need not be instantaneous. It can be met with a written confirmation within a reasonable time. If the seller is making "specially manufactured" goods for the buyer, an oral agreement can be enforced unless the goods can be easily sold elsewhere.

The Uniform Electronic Transactions Act and the Electronic Signatures in Global and National Commerce Act both make clear that email and other electronic signatures can meet the requirements of the Statute of Frauds.

At common law, the Parol Evidence Rule would not allow for provisions that are not reduced to writings within the contract itself unless there is some ambiguity or to prove fraud or a defense. Under the UCC, trade usage would be allowed beyond the terms of the contract, as would other contemporaneous terms unless it is clear that no additional terms could, indeed, be added.

IV. Consideration

WE HAVE ALREADY SEEN that a firm offer does not require consideration to make it binding. The UCC follows this rule with one exception: the UCC also provides that modifications of contracts, which under common law would require new consideration to be binding, need not have additional consideration provided that it is done in good faith.

V. Remedies

THE UCC'S APPROACH to damages is to put the parties into the position they would have been had the contract been performed. This expectation model includes compensatory damages, but does not trigger punitive damages.

The goal of putting the parties into the position they would have been had the contract been performed does not require just one approach. For example, if a buyer is insolvent, the seller can stop delivery or reclaim goods; if a buyer is solvent, the seller can sue for the price of goods or resell the goods and get cover damages, which is the market price at the time of performance less paid contract price plus incidental damages, less expenses saved because of the breach. The following case demonstrates how this works.

Kabbalah Jeans, Inc. v. CN USA International Corp.

Supreme Court, Kings County, New York.
March 24, 2010.

CAROLYN E. DEMAREST, J.

Upon the foregoing papers, in this action by plaintiff Kabbalah Jeans, Inc. (plaintiff) against defendant CN USA International Corp. (defendant) for breach of contract, defendant moves for summary judgment dismissing plaintiff's complaint, which consists of a first cause of action for return of a $26,606.40 deposit and a second cause of action for loss of profits in the amount of $100,000, as against it. Defendant, by its motion, also seeks summary judgment in its favor in the amount of $135,480 on its first counterclaim for breach of contract, its second counterclaim for repudiation, and its third counterclaim for price.

Plaintiff, a distributor of clothing, claims that it had a meeting in February 2008 with defendant, a manufacturer, wherein the parties agreed that plaintiff would purchase certain custom made clothing items from defendant to be manufactured by defendant for plaintiff at its overseas factory. The first purchase order generated by defendant was dated March 12, 2008, and reflected that defendant was to manufacture and deliver to plaintiff by April 2, 2008 and April 8, 2008 certain custom clothing items for $39,772.80. The purchase order explicitly stated, in language immediately to the left of the total price for the goods ordered, that defendant was "not responsible for delays in delivery." Although these goods arrived late, plaintiff paid defendant the full price for these goods.

On April 24, 2008, a second purchase order was generated by defendant, reflecting an agreement by defendant to manufacture at its overseas factory certain custom clothing items, which consisted of men's button-down fashion shirts, for an agreed upon total price of $60,480. The quantities, descriptions, and prices of the goods ordered were listed in this purchase order. However, there was no expected date of delivery listed in this purchase order. As with the earlier purchase order, this purchase order explicitly stated, in language immediately to the left of the total price for the goods ordered, that defendant was "not responsible for delays in delivery ."

A third purchase order dated May 2, 2008, which was generated by defendant, reflected that plaintiff ordered additional custom clothing items to be manufactured by defendant at its overseas factory for the total price of $101,606.40. This purchase order listed the quantities, descriptions, and prices for these items, but did not list any delivery date. As with the two earlier purchase orders, this purchase order explicitly stated, in language immediately to the left of the total price for the goods ordered, that defendant was "not responsible for delays in delivery."

On May 2, 2008, plaintiff paid a deposit in the amount of $26,606 .40 (consisting of a payment of $11,088 and a credit from a prior transaction in the sum of $15,518.40) toward the amounts due and owing under the April 24, 2008 and May

2, 2008 purchase orders. Despite the absence of a delivery date in the April 24, 2008 and May 2, 2008 purchase orders, plaintiff claims that there was a conversation between it and defendant, in which defendant represented that the merchandise would be available for pick up by plaintiff at defendant's warehouse facility on or before Father's Day of 2008 (i.e., June 15, 2008).

Defendant manufactured the custom clothing items listed on the two purchase orders for plaintiff and tendered delivery of these goods to plaintiff. Defendant asserts that this tender of delivery of the goods to plaintiff occurred on June 26, 2008. Plaintiff refused to accept the goods or to pay defendant the $135,480 balance due for the goods based upon the ground that the goods had not been delivered by Father's Day.

Since defendant refused to return plaintiff's deposit and demanded that plaintiff pay the balance of the purchase price, plaintiff, on July 29, 2008, filed this action against defendant. Plaintiff's complaint alleges that defendant breached the agreement with it by failing to timely deliver the goods by Father's Day 2008. Plaintiff's first cause of action seeks the return of plaintiff's deposit in the sum of $26,606.40. Plaintiff's second cause of action seeks to recover lost profits in the amount of $100,000 based upon defendant's breach of the agreement. Defendant has interposed an answer, which asserts three counterclaims, seeking the $135,480 balance due and owing from plaintiff under the purchase orders for the goods. Defendant's first counterclaim alleges a breach of contract by plaintiff, defendant's second counterclaim alleges a repudiation by plaintiff, and defendant's third counterclaim seeks recovery of the price from plaintiff.

Defendant, in support of its motion, asserts that it manufactured and delivered the goods in accordance with the terms of the contract, as set forth in the purchase orders, and that plaintiff has breached the contract by failing to accept the goods and tender payment of the balance of the purchase price. In opposition to defendant's motion, plaintiff has submitted the affidavit of its vice president, Jacobov, who asserts that clothing is seasonal, and that plaintiff had ordered the merchandise from defendant for the summer season. Plaintiff claims that defendant orally represented that the goods would be delivered by Father's Day 2008, and that the delivery was late because it was delivered approximately two to three weeks into the summer season. Plaintiff asserts that due to this delay, most of its customers had cancelled their orders, and that since the merchandise was of a seasonal nature, it would not be saleable at a profit to it due to defendant's late delivery.

Since the parties are merchants as that term is defined in Uniform Commercial Code (UCC) 2–104(1), and the transactions at issue are for the sale of goods as defined in UCC 2–105(1), the transactions are covered by UCC article 2 which governs the sale of goods. UCC 2–201(2) provides:

> "Between merchants if within a reasonable time a writing in confirmation
> of the contract and sufficient against the sender is received and the party
> receiving it has reason to know its contents, it satisfies the requirements
> of [the Statute of Frauds for the sale of goods for the price of $500 or

more] against such party unless written notice of objection to its contents is given within ten days after it is received."

Thus, writings in confirmation of a contract between a seller and a buyer which contain sufficient terms satisfy the requirements of the Statute of Frauds unless written notice of objection to its contents is given within 10 days after they are received. Such a contract, as memorialized in purchase orders, will be enforced if not objected to within such 10–day period.

Here, the purchase orders, which both contained the names of the buyer and seller, the date, the price of the goods, a description of the goods, the quantity of the goods, the unit prices of the goods, and the total price of the goods constitute writings in confirmation of a contract for the sale of goods sufficient to satisfy the Statute of Frauds, provided that no written notice of objection was given as to the contents of the purchase orders within 10 days of receipt. Plaintiff was, therefore, obliged "to make written objection [if] there [wa]s an intent to disavow it."

It is undisputed that plaintiff received the purchase orders and that plaintiff did not object to their contents within 10 days of such receipt. In addition, plaintiff admits, in its complaint and deposition testimony, that a contract for sale was made Plaintiff acknowledges that these purchase orders reflect the terms of the contract.

> "A written [purchase] order following an oral agreement is the usual and recognized contract between the parties" The purchase orders were the final expression of the parties' agreement with respect to the terms that were included therein when the buyer failed to object in writing as required by UCC 2–201.

Pursuant to UCC 2–601(a), a buyer may reject goods if the goods or the tender of delivery fail in any respect to conform to the contract. Here, however, there was no term in the contract, as evidenced by the written purchase orders, requiring the delivery to take place by a certain date.

Pursuant to UCC 2–309(1), where the time for delivery is not agreed upon, it shall be a reasonable time. As discussed above, however, plaintiff alleges that a date no later than Father's Day 2008 was orally agreed upon, and that defendant did not deliver the goods until June 26, 2008, approximately one week after Father's Day (or, as alleged in plaintiff's complaint, until July 2, 2008, approximately two weeks after Father's Day). Even assuming that this delivery term was orally agreed upon, the unambiguous terms of the purchase orders stated that defendant was not responsible for any delays in delivery. Shlomi Skaf (Skaf), plaintiff's principal owner, at his deposition, confirmed that this disclaimer language was present on the purchase orders. Jacobov (who, as noted above, is plaintiff's vice president) testified, at his deposition, that he understood this phrase in the purchase orders to mean that defendant was "not responsible for delays." Skaf further testified, at his deposition, that he "saw [this language] but ... didn't pay attention to it" Thus, pursuant to the written contractual terms, as memorialized in the purchase orders, the mere one or two-week delay in defendant's delivery of the goods would not entitle plaintiff to reject the goods.

Plaintiff contends that this notation in the purchase orders regarding a delay in delivery should not be considered a contract term because the purchase orders were delivered after the oral agreement to buy the goods was made, and because the purchase orders were never signed by it. As set forth above, however, UCC 2–201 does not require that the written memorialization occur at the same time as the alleged oral agreement or that the buyer sign the purchase order where it otherwise complies with that section and where no objection to the purchase order is made within 10 days.

Plaintiff further argues that the delay disclaimer language in the purchase orders nevertheless should not be found to be a contract term based upon its allegation that the oral agreement mandated delivery on or before Father's Day 2008. This argument must be rejected. UCC 2–202 provides:

> "Terms with respect to which the confirmatory memoranda of the parties agree or which are otherwise set forth in a writing intended by the parties as a final expression of their agreement with respect to such terms as are included therein may not be contradicted by evidence of any prior agreement or of a contemporaneous oral agreement but may [only] be explained or supplemented ... by course of dealing or usage of trade ... or by course of performance ...; and ... by evidence of consistent additional terms."

While plaintiff claims that it is the custom and usage of the industry that if merchandise is not received by a deadline date, the sale is deemed to be cancelled, it has submitted no evidentiary proof of any such custom and usage. Indeed, the agreement as to the delivery date alleged by plaintiff cannot be established by course of dealing or performance or usage of trade since the prior March 12, 2008 purchase order was delivered late and accepted by plaintiff. Moreover, plaintiff's assertion that this delivery date was a time is of the essence date which, if not met, permitted it to reject the goods, would constitute an inconsistent additional term contradicting the purchase orders since (as discussed above) they explicitly permitted a delay in delivery by defendant. The parol evidence rule embodied in UCC 2–202 bars the introduction of any such proof of an alleged oral agreement between the parties that would vary the terms of the purchase orders, which were the final written expression of the parties' contract.

Plaintiff also argues that the delay disclaimer is vague because it does not state whether the delay may be occasioned by the fault and neglect on the part of defendant or must be occasioned by a catastrophe that is not within the control of defendant. This argument is unavailing. The plain meaning of this language encompasses all delays and is not limited to any particular source. Moreover, as noted above, Jacobov testified, at his deposition, that he understood that the meaning of this phrase was that defendant was not responsible for delays, and did not claim that he understood it to be limited to particular instances or causes of delay.

By establishing that the parties had a contract and that plaintiff owed money on the contract, defendant has made out a *prima facie* case that it was not liable for breach of contract, but, rather, that plaintiff had breached its contract with it by refusing to accept the goods. It was, therefore, incumbent upon plaintiff to proffer evidentiary proof, in admissible form, sufficient to raise a triable issue of fact, which it has failed to do. Consequently, inasmuch as defendant has demonstrated that it did not breach the terms of the contract, as memorialized by the purchase orders, and that plaintiff has breached the contract by wrongfully refusing to accept the goods tendered by it, plaintiff is not entitled to a return of its $26,606.40 deposit nor lost profits. Thus, summary judgment dismissing plaintiff's first and second causes of action must be granted.

Defendant, in support of its counterclaims, asserts that plaintiff wrongfully rejected the goods and breached the contract between them. Pursuant to UCC 2–703, where the buyer wrongfully rejects goods, and if the breach is of the whole contract, then with respect to the whole undelivered balance, the aggrieved seller is entitled to resell and recover damages under UCC 2–706, recover damages for non-acceptance under UCC 2–708, or, in a proper case, recover the price pursuant to UCC 2–709.

Here, defendant has not resold the goods under UCC 2–706 nor does it seek the difference between the market price at the time and place for tender and the unpaid contract price under UCC 2–708. Rather, defendant seeks to recover the balance of the contract price of $135,480. Pursuant to UCC 2–709(1)(b), when the buyer fails to pay the price, the seller may recover the price "of goods identified to the contract if the seller is unable after reasonable effort to resell them at a reasonable price or the circumstances reasonably indicate that such effort will be unavailing."

UCC 2–709(2) provides:

> "Where the seller sues for the price [it] must hold for the buyer any goods which have been identified to the contract and are still in [its] control except that if resale becomes possible [it] may resell them at any time prior to the collection of the judgment. The net proceeds of any such resale must be credited to the buyer and payment of the judgment entitles [it] to any goods not resold."

In support of its third counterclaim to recover the price, defendant has submitted its answer, verified by its president, in which it asserts that the clothing items, which it was induced to manufacture for plaintiff, were special, custom, and/or unique, that it is unable to resell these goods, and that circumstances reasonably indicate that an effort by it to resell the goods would be unavailing. Plaintiff, in its opposition papers, does not deny or refute these assertions. Indeed, plaintiff does not dispute that the dress shirts were manufactured for it at its request and, in fact, asserts that due to the seasonal nature of the shirts, they would not be readily saleable at a profit.

Thus, defendant is entitled to recover the contract balance of $135,480 from plaintiff in accordance with UCC 2–709. Although defendant's third counterclaim alleges storage costs, defendant has not provided any evidence of specific incidental damages incurred by it nor does it request incidental damages in its motion. Since the court finds that defendant is entitled to summary judgment in its favor in the amount of $135,480 on its third counterclaim for price, defendant's motion, insofar as it also seeks summary judgment in its favor in the amount of $135,480 based upon its first counterclaim for breach of contract and its second counterclaim for repudiation, is duplicative and rendered moot.

Accordingly, defendant's motion for summary judgment dismissing plaintiff's first and second causes of action, and for summary judgment in its favor on its third counterclaim for price in the amount of $135,480, is granted.

This constitutes the decision, order, and judgment of the court.

THE BUYER'S REMEDIES in the case of a breach are to reject any non-conforming goods or to accept non-conforming goods and sue for the difference in value between the two. The buyer can also sue for specific performance. The following cases demonstrate these options. As with other UCC cases, notice how fact-specific these cases can be.

MEMC Electronic Materials, Inc., et al. v. BP Solar International, Inc.

Court of Special Appeals of Maryland.
Dec. 3, 2010.

EYLER, JAMES R., J.

Appellee, a manufacturer of solar energy products, makes photovoltaic panels (also known as solar panels) that are used to convert sunlight into electricity. Appellant is in the business of selling wafers, polysilicon, and other silicon raw feedstock. In 1996, appellee purchased silicon powder from appellant, previously a waste by-product of appellant's polysilicon production process, in order to determine whether the silicon powder, inexpensive at the time, could be used to lower manufacturing costs.

Silicon powder proved useful in reducing costs, and it created a competitive advantage for appellee. Consequently, in 1997, the parties entered into a written, one and a half page sales agreement for the purchase of silicon powder for a two-year period running from April 1, 1997, through March 30, 1999. The agreement required appellant to supply appellee with four MT of silicon powder per month at a price of $3.00 per kilogram. Over the two-year period, appellee sent purchase orders confirming quantity, price, shipping, and other details, and appellant sent the appropriate invoices.

In March 1998, the parties extended this agreement through December 31, 2000. The extension increased the amount of silicon powder to ten MT per month at a price of $3.25 per kilogram, beginning January 1, 1999, and continuing through the end of the contract. Again, confirming purchase orders and subsequent invoices were issued.

Between 2001 and 2004, the parties entered into less formal documented arrangements. These supply agreements were generally consummated through and documented by e-mail exchanges. Each time, after agreement, the parties would follow the usual sequence of purchase orders, invoices, and contractual performance.

Ultimately, anticipating imminent shortages in the market for silicon feedstock supplies, appellee recognized a need to secure long term contracts for the supply of silicon powder. As a result, Pat Barron, appellee's Frederick warehouse manager, was authorized to arrange a long term supply contract with appellant. Herein lies the dispute. It is uncontested that several e-mails were exchanged between August 4, 2004, and November 9, 2004, concerning a long term supply contract between the parties. A printed copy of each e-mail was admitted into evidence. The primary dispute concerns the legal significance of those e-mails.

On August 4, 2004, Mr. Barron e-mailed Sanjeev Lahoti, appellant's product manager, requesting a "quotation (e-mail is fine) for 300 MT of powder per year for calendar years 2005 through 2007. Upon receipt, BP Solar will forward our purchase agreement for these quantities." Mr. Lahoti's September 17 response stated:

> After reviewing our options we want to commit 150MT of powder per year for the next 3 years. The pricing for 2005 would be $3.50/kg. Pricing for 2006 and 2007 would be negotiated in October of the previous year. MEMC would offer to BP any additional quantity available for the following year at th[at] time.

Thereafter, on September 27, 2004, Mr. Barron and Mr. Lahoti discussed, via telephone, the arrangement or contemplated arrangement between the parties. In an e-mail later the same day to Bill Poulin, plant manager at BP Solar's Frederick plant, on which Mr. Lahoti was copied, Mr. Barron described this conversation as follows:

> I had a phone conversation with Sanjeev this morning clarifing [*sic*] the MEMC proposal below. Sanjeev indicates that the 150MT is essentially the *minimum* available for each calendar year 2005-2007. Since this is scrap material for MEMC, their engineering staff has been tasked with improving yield and this is their target based on current levels of production. Sanjeev anticipates the available quantity of powder will be larger (especially in 2005) but did not want to quote a figure higher than their budgeted targets. He has confirmed BP Solar's "right of first refusal" for all quantities of powder they produce. Pricing can be negotiated during MEMC's visit in October.

In his responsive e-mail the following day, Mr. Lahoti stated, "I agree with Pat's comments below. I look forward to meeting you and Pat during our visit."

Two weeks later, on October 13, 2004, Mr. Barron e-mailed Mr. Lahoti asking for confirmation on price. The e-mail stated:

> I hope MEMC felt as poitive [*sic*] about our meeting as we did. As a follow up, you mentioned that you felt you could do better on the pricing of the powder going forward. If you would please send me something in writing, I can begin moving things on this end in terms of a purchase agreement. As stated earlier, BP Solar will commit to taking all quantities available in 2005 and would like to have a right of first refusal in 2006-2007.

On November 9, 2004, Mr. Barron e-mailed Mr. Lahoti concerning purchase orders for the 2005 and 2006 shipments of silicon powder. He stated:

> BP Solar has submitted to MEMC our purchase orders #22692 and #22693 for silicon powder to cover calendar years 2005 and 2006. We are not limiting the quantities we would purchase as we will take all the powder that is available under our agreement of right-of-first-refusal (see below). However, I had to put a quantity on the purchase order so I used the same volume that we have been receiving this year. Again, we will take whatever quantities you have available and adjust the PO accordingly.

> We would also like to give MEMC a purchase order for our 2007 requirements. Does that work for you?

Following this series of e-mail conversations, appellant shipped nearly 224 MT of silicon powder during 2005. The last shipment occurred on December 30, 2005.

In late February 2006, appellee contacted appellant because it had not received any shipments since December. Upon inquiry, appellee was informed that appellant was experimenting with ways to recycle its silicon powder in its process, and therefore, it had only minimal excess powder. In essence, appellant advised appellee that it should not rely on further shipments. Accordingly, appellee filed suit, seeking damages for breach of a contract allegedly formed through the parties' e-mail exchange.

Prior to trial, appellant moved for summary judgment, arguing that as a matter of law, the parties had never reached the clear meeting of the minds necessary to form a contract. The motion was denied. Appellant argued then and throughout the trial that appellee had changed its position, during the pleading and discovery process, as to the terms of the alleged contract. During the trial, appellant continued its stance that the e-mails did not evidence a meeting of the minds. At the close of appellee's case, and at the close of all evidence, appellant moved for judgment, reasserting its argument that appellee could not make up its own mind regarding the terms of the alleged contract and could not prove a clear meeting of the minds. These motions were also denied.

After a two-week trial, the jury found that the parties entered into a contract by which appellant was obligated to supply appellee with silicon powder for the years 2005-07. The jury further found that appellant breached this contract. Consequently, it awarded damages in the amount of $8,849,447 as partial cover damages that resulted from appellant's failure to supply appellee with silicon powder in 2007.

Additional facts will be incorporated as necessary to complete our discussion.

QUESTIONS PRESENTED

Appellant presents a number of issues for our review, which we condense and restate as follows:

> 1) Whether appellant preserved for review its challenge to the sufficiency of the writings under the Statute of Frauds and, if so, whether the printed copies of the e-mails are sufficient to satisfy the Statute.

> 2) Whether any writing, sufficient under the Statute of Frauds, supported BP's claim to the third year of its alleged three-year contract.

> 3) Whether there was sufficient evidence to support the jury's damages award, based on expert opinions concerning "reasonable price" that were speculative, at variance with the Maryland Uniform Commercial Code, and premised on a contract theory that the jury was permitted to disregard.

> 4) Whether the trial court abused its discretion by allowing introduction of certain evidence as "routine practice" under Maryland Rule 5-406, where the "practice" was not relevant to any issue in the case.

* * *

1. CHALLENGE TO SUFFICIENCY OF WRITINGS UNDER THE STATUTE OF FRAUDS

A. Preservation of Issue for Appeal

In seeking reversal of the trial court's judgment, appellant argues that the parties attempted to negotiate an agreement for 2007 but never reached agreement. Consequently, there was not and could not be a confirmatory writing that would satisfy the merchants' exception because there was no agreement to confirm. Appellant notes that appellee never sent a purchase order for silicon powder for 2007, as it did for the years 2005 and 2006. Preliminarily, appellee responds by arguing that appellant failed to preserve this challenge for review by neglecting to argue this specific point in its two motions for judgment.

Appellant presents its arguments in the abstract and does not tie them to a particular ruling by the court. We assume, as does appellee, that the alleged basis for error is the denial of appellant's motions for judgment, pursuant to Maryland Rule 2-519, on the ground that the Statute was not satisfied. A motion for judgment must "state with particularity all reasons why the motion should be granted." Maryland Rule 2-519(a). In that respect, it is well-settled that "[f]ailure to state a reason [why the motion for judgment should be granted] serves to withdraw the issue from appellate review." ("[I]n order to preserve an issue for appellate review, the moving party must have, in to [sic] making the motion either at the close of the plaintiff's case or after all the evidence, stated with particularity all reasons why the motion should be granted.")

With respect to the breach of contract count, appellant argued in support of its first motion that (1) there was no definitive offer and acceptance because Mr. Lahoti's e-mail dated September 28, 2004 merely served to confirm Mr. Barron's understanding of the negotiations, and (2) appellee's breach of contract claim was barred by a one-year statute of limitations provision included in the parties' 1997 supply agreement. In support of its renewed motion at the close of all the evidence, appellant incorporated its earlier arguments and, in addition, argued that because the alleged contract did not include a price, a damage award could only be supported by testimony regarding a reasonable price at the time of delivery pursuant to § 2-305 of the Maryland Uniform Commercial Code ("MD UCC"). Thus, according to appellant, the absence of such testimony required the jury to speculate on the issue and, therefore, warranted judgment in its favor regarding appellee's claim for cover damages.

On the record before us, it is apparent that none of these arguments pertain to appellant's current contention on appeal that no writing by appellee was sufficient to satisfy the merchants' exception to the Statute of Frauds. Consequently, this issue is not properly preserved for appellate review.

B. The Writings Satisfy the Statute of Frauds and Its Merchants' Exception

Assuming appellant's argument is preserved, we conclude it is without merit. Commercial Law Section 2-201(1) of the MD UCC provides:

> [A] contract for the sale of goods for the price of $500 or more is not enforceable by way of action or defense unless there is some writing sufficient to indicate that a contract for sale has been made between the parties and signed by the party against whom enforcement is sought or by his *337 authorized agent or broker. A writing is not insufficient because it omits or incorrectly states a term agreed upon but the contract is not enforceable under this paragraph beyond the quantity of goods shown in such writing.

Thus, the Statute effectively requires a writing that (1) is sufficient to indicate a contract for sale of goods of $500 or more between the parties; (2) is signed by the party against whom enforcement is sought; and (3) contains a quantity term. The rule also provides an exception for merchants, which states that a writing in confirmation of the contract and sufficient against the sender that is received by a party who has reason to know of its contents satisfies the requirements of subsection (1) against the receiving party unless written notice of objection is given within ten days of receipt. We conclude that the e-mail exchange between the parties satisfies both the requirements of the Statute and the merchants' exception.

As noted above, appellant argues that there was no writing that satisfied the Statute of Frauds pertaining to the 2007 calendar year. To this point, appellant argues that it "never signed any writing sufficient to indicate that a contract for sale of silicon powder for three years was ever made between itself and [appellee]." Moreover, appellant points to the fact that appellee sent purchase orders in 2005 and 2006 that satisfied the merchants' exception for those years, but failed to send a purchase order for 2007. With respect to the November 9, 2004 e-mail from Mr. Barron to Mr. Lahoti, appellant argues that this writing is merely representative of ongoing negotiations and does not "indicate that a contract for sale has been made for 2007, nor is it [confirmative] of a contract for 2007."

Here, however, the question regarding whether there was a contract and, if so, its terms, was left to the jury. Appellant does not challenge the court's determination that whether a contract existed was a jury question; its challenge is limited to the requirements of the Statute of Frauds. With respect to quantity, there was evidence that the parties agreed to a specific quantity or a minimum quantity with a right of first refusal of output or an agreement to buy output. The jury was instructed as to the relevant contract principles, including considerations relevant to an output contract.

After reviewing all of the documents and testimonial evidence, the jury determined that the parties entered into a three-year contract that covered the 2007 calendar year. The relevant question on the verdict sheet, which the jury answered in the affirmative, was: "Do you find that the parties entered into a contract by which MEMC was obligated to supply BP Solar with silicon powder for calendar years 2005, 2006, and 2007?" Thus, we do not know the terms of the contract as found by the jury, except to the extent we can infer them from the damages awarded.

Appellee's position during trial was that it had the right to appellant's output with a minimum quantity. It claimed damages for the years 2004-2007, consisting of cover damages under CL § 2-712, non-delivery damages under CL § 2-713, and consequential and incidental damages under CL § 2-715. The verdict sheet reveals that the damages awarded were only for "partial cover damages." The jury awarded "0" damages for "non-delivery damages," "consequential damages," and "incidental damages." Christopher Rosenthal and Mr. Winegarner, appellee's expert witnesses, opined, *inter alia*, as to the amount of cover damages for the year 2007, calculated at a contract price of $8.00 per kilogram, assuming a contract existed between the parties herein. The witnesses applied that price to the amount of silicon purchased from other suppliers by appellee in that year, and compared it to the actual price paid by appellee in that year. Because the amount awarded by the jury as cover damages matched the amount of cover damages claimed for the year 2007, as testified to by appellee's experts, appellant infers that the jury found that appellant was obligated to make its output available to appellee at a contract price of $8.00 per kilogram, and it awarded the entire amount claimed.

On appeal, appellant does not raise any issue regarding the initial jury instructions or the verdict sheet. As a result, appellant's argument that the Statute of Frauds was unsatisfied because there was no contract that could be confirmed in writing must necessarily fail. The jury determined there was a contract. Thus, what we must determine is whether there was a legally sufficient confirmatory writing.

While underlying facts may be disputed in a given case, when resolved, the ultimate decision as to whether a writing satisfies the Statute's requirements is a question of law. We review decisions involving application of Maryland statutory law for legal correctness under a *de novo* standard of review.

Here, the printed e-mails constitute a sufficient writing under the Statute. Maryland law recognizes that a series of communications can satisfy the Statute's requirements. In addition, e-mail communications can amount to a sufficient writing under the Statute. In that regard, if so intended, a typed name is a sufficient signature as an agent of the party against whom enforcement is sought.

Furthermore, the purpose of the Statute is to avoid fraud-not to prevent enforcement of legitimate transactions. Consequently, in regard to that purpose, we have stated that the Statute is intended to prevent successful fraud [through] inducing the enforcement of contracts that were never in fact made. It is not to prevent the performance or enforcement of oral contracts that have in fact been made; it is not to create a loophole of escape for dishonest repudiators. Therefore, we should always be satisfied with "some note or memorandum" that is adequate, when considered with the admitted facts, the surrounding circumstances, and all explanatory and corroborative and rebutting evidence, to convince the court that there is no serious possibility of consummating a fraud by enforcement.

This purpose has guided our examination of the sufficiency of particular writings under the Statute:

The Statute of Frauds was not enacted to afford persons a means of evading just obligations; ... nor was it adopted to enable defendants to interpose the Statute as a bar to a contract fairly, and admittedly, made.... Therefore, if after a consideration of the surrounding circumstances, the pertinent facts and all the evidence in a particular case, the court concludes that enforcement of the agreement will not subject the defendant to fraudulent claims, the purpose of the Statute will best be served by holding the note or memorandum sufficient even though it is ambiguous or incomplete.

> "THUS, even an incomplete writing can be sufficient so long as the court is satisfied that enforcement of the agreement will not advance a fraudulent claim.

Thus, even an incomplete writing can be sufficient so long as the court is satisfied that enforcement of the agreement will not advance a fraudulent claim.

With these principles in mind, we turn to the last requirement, that the writing contain a quantity term, which was the subject of much dispute at the trial court level. Though the verdict sheet does not reveal the precise terms of the contract that the jury found, it is evident that the e-mails support a finding of a specific minimum quantity (150 MT) with a right of first refusal of output or an agreement to buy output. In either event, appellant was obligated to make its output available to appellee. As discussed, the writing requirement in the Statute of Frauds is designed to prevent fraud, not prevent enforcement of legitimate transactions. With respect to the quantity term, because of the factual uncertainty as to the terms of any contract, the jury had to resolve that issue. Once resolved, we look to the writing to see if it contains a quantity term because the contract cannot be enforced beyond the quantity stated.

Here, Mr. Lahoti's September 17, 2004 e-mail committed appellant to 150 MT per year for three years. Thereafter, Mr. Baron's September 27 e-mail clarifying the proposal as to quantity stated that 150 MT was the minimum amount of silicon powder available for 2005-07, and that appellee held a right of first refusal for all excess quantities produced. Mr. Lahoti's responsive e-mail of September 28 served as confirmation of the terms by stating "I agree with Pat's comment's below." Thus, taken together, these e-mails represent the parties' reciprocal agreement that appellant would make its output available to appellee and would supply a minimum amount. Therefore, the September 28 e-mail served as a writing sufficient to satisfy the quantity term of the contract.

Finally, we note that the e-mail dated September 27 from Mr. Barron to Mr. Lahoti and Mr. Poulin satisfies the merchants' exception. That e-mail, especially in light of Mr. Lahoti's September 28 reply, serves as the required confirmatory e-mail under the exception. Thereafter, neither Mr. Lahoti nor any agent of appellant sent written notice of objection within ten days as required by the Statute. Consequently, the September 27 e-mail satisfies the merchants' exception to the Statute.

As a result, we reject appellant's argument that the Statute of Frauds bars appellee's claim as to the year 2007.

* * *

JUDGMENT AFFIRMED. COSTS TO BE PAID BY APPELLANT.

NOTES AND COMMENTS

1. ARTICLE 2 OF THE UCC applies to the sale of goods. Should the scope of the UCC be extended to all contracts, such as for services?

....

2. ONE OF THE MAIN ARGUMENTS for the UCC, and other similar uniform statutes, is that they provide more systemic reliability for businesses to rely upon. Do you agree? Would businesses be better off with each state and territory to have its own set of laws? Does the same analogy, however you come out on the previous question, apply globally as well? What would be the pros and cons of a uniform contracts system worldwide?

....

3. WHILE THE UCC aims to make uniform, to systematize, and to use market information sources to "fill in the blanks" and find business contracts, all so that commerce can operate more predictably and efficiently, the UCC remains a complex document. Determining who is a merchant or how remedies are calculated often gets into rarefied legal air. Should the UCC be made even more straight-forward so that it is more accessible to business people? How would you go about doing this?

TORTS

IMAGINE THAT, after college, you continued to law school. You are now graduated and are practicing law in a small town and living in a house across from a local college. Your alma mater did not have fraternities and sororities, but they play a major role in the college you now live next to.

Your small house is on the intersection of a major street, Euclid Avenue, and Eighth Street, a very small road that dead-ends at a swampy area about two hundred yards away. Beyond the swampy area is the town's wastewater treatment plant.

Directly across Euclid Avenue, near your house, is the college's football field and track. Less than a hundred yards up the street and a small hill is the college fraternity complex. Your house is at the bottom of this hill.

Apparently, when one of the fraternity brothers becomes "lavaliered, pinned, or engaged," his brothers strip the romantically-committed fellow to his underwear, consume large quantities of alcohol and carry him down the Euclid Avenue hill. Aiming to take him onto Eighth Street, they aren't usually in a condition to navigate very carefully, so they always end up crossing over onto your hilly yard. They then continue to stagger down Eighth Street with the elevated brother's girlfriend following along, carrying his clothes.

When they reach their destination, they toss the guy into the smelly swamp, cheer, and sing some kind of traditional song. The stinking brother emerges from the swamp and embraces his girlfriend.

You, having no experience with fraternities and sororities, are at a complete loss as to this ritual, but it happens with regularity. What also occurs regularly is the entourage stumbling when crossing—i.e. trespassing—over your property.

What if they fall? What if they drop the guy ~~aloft~~ over their heads and he is seriously injured? Could any of the injured parties sue you? All you have done is watch, bewildered, as they performed this odd ritual, but are your finances, home, and even your pet dog subject to being seized and sold because of the recklessness of the fraternity guys?

The answer is that you might be at risk and this chapter will help you to understand why.

I. Negligence

A. THE PRIMA FACIE CASE

Business people and business students tend to become frustrated about tort cases. These are the cases where one can see million dollar judgments to compensate a victim—and even larger "punitive" damages that provide money to the victim beyond what damages the victim actually incurred.

Tort cases are comprised of a "prima facie" case. In other words, the case at hand must pass initial tests to be able to get into a court of law. However, even if a case passes these initial tests, it does not mean that the plaintiff will win the case. It simply means that there is a good enough case to file the case in court and start the trial process.

There are times when a plaintiff files a "frivolous case." These are cases that have so little—if any—merit, that courts believe that there is no reason to continue the case. In some situations, "frivolous cases" are filed primarily to harass the defendant, hopefully (from the plaintiff's standpoint) to be enough of a nuisance to get some settlement from the defendant, who would rather not spend the time and expense of going through the court process.

Examples of a frivolous case are meritless complaints, unnecessarily stalling litigation, deliberate disobedience of court orders, and the failure to produce evidence during the discovery process. Courts have several tools at their disposal to address these issues, including very straightforward ones such as directly challenging lawyers to move the trial process along or threatening lawyers (or litigants) with contempt of court sanctions (which can result in jail). In addition, the court can consider making one of the parties pay for all the costs of the case, including sometimes, the other side's attorney's fees. The following case provides an example of how the court handles the costs of a frivolous case.

Roadway Express, Inc. v. Piper

U.S. Supreme Court, 1980 447 U.S. 752

In 1975, two former employees and one unsuccessful applicant (plaintiffs) brought a civil rights class action against Roadway Express, Inc. (Roadway), alleging that Roadway's employment policies discriminated against employees based on race. During the discovery process, the plaintiffs served Roadway with an interrogatory. Roadway answered and served the plaintiffs with an interrogatory. Thereafter, the trial process was stalled by the plaintiffs' uncooperative behavior. Plaintiffs failed to (1) produce answers to the interrogatory, (2) appear at a motion hearing for an order compelling answers to the interrogatory, (3) meet a court ordered deadline for answering the interrogatories, (4) appear at a deposition, and (5) file court ordered briefs. Roadway then moved to dismiss the suit under Federal Rule of Civil Procedure 37 which allows courts to dismiss cases and impose sanctions and costs upon parties that, in bad faith, fail to cooperate in the discovery process.

The District Court dismissed the suit and ordered the plaintiffs to pay Roadway $17,000 for costs and attorney's fees. The District Court found justification for its ruling in the confluence of several statutes, including civil rights statutes that allow the prevailing party to recover attorney's fees as "part of the costs" of litigation and 28 U.S.C. § 1927, that permits a court to tax the excess "costs" of a proceeding against a lawyer "who so multiplies the proceedings . . . as to increase costs unreasonably and vexatiously . . . ." Read together, the District Court concluded, the statutes authorize the assessment of costs and attorney's fees against the respondents. The respondents appealed.

The Appellate Court rejected the District Court's conclusion that civil rights statutes could be read into § 1927 and concluded that § 1927 only deals with attorney conduct and attorney liability for costs. The Court held that the plaintiffs to the original suit would not be held liable for attorney's fees, vacated the District Court's order and remanded for recalculation of costs. Roadway appealed. The Supreme Court granted certiorari on the question of taxing attorney's fees to a party that has engaged in attorney misconduct, resulting in a frivolous suit.

MR. JUSTICE POWELL delivered the opinion of the Court.

This case presents the question whether federal courts have statutory or inherent power to tax attorney's fees directly against counsel who have abused the processes of the courts.

Two specific provisions have been said to be controlling in this case: 28 U.S.C. § 1927, and Federal Rule of Civil Procedure 37... Due to sloth, inattention, or desire to seize tactical advantage, lawyers have long indulged in dilatory practices. Cf. C. Dickens, *Bleak House* 2-5 (1948). A number of factors legitimately may lengthen a lawsuit, and the parties themselves may cause some of the delays. Nevertheless, many actions are extended unnecessarily by lawyers who exploit or abuse judicial procedures, especially the liberal rules for pretrial discovery. The glacial pace of much litigation breeds frustration with the federal courts and, ultimately, disrespect for the law.

Section 1927 provides that lawyers who multiply court proceedings vexatiously may be assessed the excess "costs" they create. The provision, however, does not define the critical word. Only if "costs" includes attorney's fees can § 1927 support the sanction in this case... Congress returned to the problems of the federal courts in 1853... The 1853 Act specified the costs recoverable in federal litigation and also allowed the award of excess "costs" against counsel who vexatiously multiply litigation. The most reasonable construction is that the Act itself defined those costs that may be recovered from counsel. Congress, of course, may amend those provisions that derive from the 1853 Act. In the absence of express modification of those provisions by Congress, however, we should not look beyond the Act for the definition of costs under § 1927. Congress in 1853 prescribed taxable costs for the same reasons it authorized the assessment of costs against dilatory attorneys: "[T]o prevent abuses arising from ingenious constructions . . . to discourage unnecessary prolixity, old useless forms, and the multiplication of proceedings, and the prosecutions of several suits which might better be joined in one."

> **"THE GLACIAL PACE** of much litigation breeds frustration with the federal courts and, ultimately, disrespect for the law.

Federal Rule of Civil Procedure 37(b) authorizes sanctions for failure to comply with discovery orders. The District Court may bar the disobedient party from introducing certain evidence, or it may direct that certain facts shall be "taken to be established for the purposes of the action. . . ." The Rule also permits the trial court to strike claims from the pleadings, and even to "dismiss the action ... or render a judgment by default against the disobedient party." ... Both parties and counsel may be held personally liable for expenses, "including attorney's fees," caused by the failure to comply with discovery orders. Rule 37 sanctions must be applied diligently both "to penalize those whose conduct may be deemed to warrant such a sanction, [and] to deter those who might be tempted to such conduct in the absence of such a deterrent."...

The respondents in this case never have complied with the District Court's order that they answer Roadway's interrogatories. That failure was the immediate ground for dismissing the case, and it also exposed respondents and their clients to liability under Rule 37(b) for the resulting costs and attorney's fees. Indeed, Roadway's motion for dismissal sought recovery of those expenses under Rule 37. On the remand of this action, the District Court will have the authority to act upon that request.

IN NARROWLY DEFINED circumstances federal courts have inherent power to assess attorney's fees against parties who have acted in bad faith, resulting in a frivolous suit. The general rule is that a litigant cannot recover his counsel fees, but that rule does not apply when the opposing party has acted in bad faith, including bad faith in the conduct of the litigation. In view of a court's power over members of its bar, if it may tax counsel fees against a party who has litigated in bad faith, it certainly may assess those expenses against counsel who willfully abuse judicial processes.

Assessing costs against the party frivolously filing the case or obstructing the hearing of the case is but one option. In the following case, the court throws out the case itself.

Link v. Wabash R. Co.

U.S. Supreme Court, 1962 370 U.S. 626

The action, growing out of a collision between petitioner's automobile and one of respondent's trains, was commenced on August 24, 1954. Some six years later, and more than three years after petitioner had finally prevailed on respondent's motion for judgment on the pleadings (during which time two fixed trial dates had been postponed), the District Court, on September 29, 1960, duly notified counsel for each side of the scheduling of a pretrial conference to be held at the courthouse in Hammond, Indiana, on October 12, 1960, at 1 p.m. During the preceding morning, October 11, petitioner's counsel telephoned respondent's lawyer from Indianapolis, stating that 'he was doing some work on some papers,' that he expected to be at the pretrial conference, but that he might not attend the taking of a deposition of the plaintiff scheduled for the same day. At about 10:45 on the morning of October 12 petitioner's counsel telephoned the Hammond courthouse from Indianapolis (about 160 miles away), and after asking for the judge, who then was on the bench, requested the judge's secretary to convey to him this message: 'that he (counsel) was busy preparing papers to file with the (Indiana) Supreme Court,' that 'he couldn't be here by 1:00 o'clock, but he would be here either Thursday afternoon (October 13) or any time Friday (October 14) if it (the pretrial conference) could be reset.'

When petitioner's counsel did not appear at the pretrial conference the District Court, after reviewing the history of the case and finding that counsel had failed 'to indicate... a reasonable reason' for his nonappearance, dismissed the action 'for failure of the plaintiff's counsel to appear at the pretrial, for failure to prosecute this action.' The court, acting two hours after the appointed hour for the conference, stated that the dismissal was in the 'exercise (of) its inherent power.' The Court of Appeals affirmed by a divided vote. The Supreme Court granted certiorari.

MR. JUSTICE HARLAN delivered the opinion of the Court.

The authority of a federal trial court to dismiss a plaintiff's action with prejudice because of his failure to prosecute cannot seriously be doubted. The power to invoke this sanction is necessary in order to prevent undue delays in the disposition of pending cases and to avoid congestion in the calendars of the District Courts. The power is of ancient origin, having its roots in judgments of nonsuit and *non prosequitur* entered at common law, e.g., 3 Blackstone, *Commentaries* (1768), 295-296, and dismissals for want of prosecution of bills in equity, e.g., id., at 451. It has been expressly recognized in Federal Rule of Civil Procedure 41(b), which provides, in pertinent part:

> **Involuntary Dismissal: Effect Thereof.** For failure of the plaintiff to prosecute or to comply with these rules or any order of court, a defendant may move for dismissal of an action or of any claim against him. * * * Unless the court in its order for dismissal otherwise specifies, a dismissal under this subdivision and any dismissal not provided for in this rule, other than a dismissal for lack of jurisdiction or for improper venue, operates as an adjudication upon the merits.'

Petitioner contends that the language of this Rule, by negative implication, prohibits involuntary dismissals for failure of the plaintiff to prosecute except upon motion by the defendant. In the present case there was no such motion.

We do not read Rule 41(b) as implying any such restriction. Neither the permissive language of the Rule-which merely authorizes a motion by the defendant-nor its policy requires us to conclude that it was the purpose of the Rule to abrogate the power of courts, acting on their own initiative, to clear their calendars of cases that have remained dormant because of the inaction or dilatoriness of the parties seeking relief.

Nor does the absence of notice as to the possibility of dismissal or the failure to hold an adversary hearing necessarily render such a dismissal void. It is true, of course, that 'the fundamental requirement of due process is an opportunity to be heard upon such notice and proceedings as are adequate to safeguard the right for which the constitutional protection is invoked.' But this does not mean that every order entered without notice and a preliminary adversary hearing offends due process.

On this record we are unable to say that the District Court's dismissal of this action for failure to prosecute, as evidenced only partly by the failure of petitioner's counsel to appear at a duly scheduled pretrial conference, amounted to an abuse of discretion. It was certainly within the bounds of permissible discretion for the court to conclude that the telephone excuse offered by petitioner's counsel was inadequate to explain his failure to attend. And it could reasonably be inferred from his absence, as well as from the drawn-out history of the litigation, that petitioner had been deliberately proceeding in dilatory fashion.

There is certainly no merit to the contention that dismissal of petitioner's claim because of his counsel's unexcused conduct imposes an unjust penalty on the client. Petitioner voluntarily chose this attorney as his representative in the action, and he cannot now avoid the consequences of the acts or omissions of this freely selected agent. Any other notion would be wholly inconsistent with our system of representative litigation, in which each party is deemed bound by the acts of his lawyer-agent and is considered to have 'notice of all facts, notice of which can be charged upon the attorney.'

———————————

Though Justice Harlan referred to the problem of frivolous cases as needing to avoid "congestion in the calendars," that congestion is not simply one of time management and delay. As Justice Powell indicated in the *Roadway Express* case, such delay would cause disrespect for the law and the legal system itself.

Assuming that the plaintiff has not filed a frivolous case, there are four key elements of a negligence case:

DUTY: Did the defendant have a duty to conform his conduct to a specific standard of care?	**BREACH:** Did the defendant's conduct fall below the applicable standard of care?
CAUSATION: Did the defendant's failure to meet the applicable standard of care cause the plaintiff's harm, either directly or proximately?	**DAMAGE:** Did the plaintiff suffer harm that can be compensated monetarily?

Using the *Roadway* case, we can apply these key elements as follows:

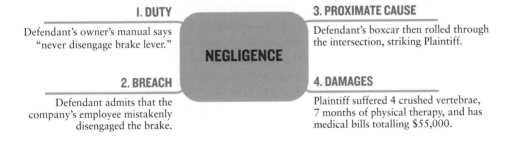

1. DUTY
Defendant's owner's manual says "never disengage brake lever."

2. BREACH
Defendant admits that the company's employee mistakenly disengaged the brake.

NEGLIGENCE

3. PROXIMATE CAUSE
Defendant's boxcar then rolled through the intersection, striking Plaintiff.

4. DAMAGES
Plaintiff suffered 4 crushed vertebrae, 7 months of physical therapy, and has medical bills totalling $55,000.

Source: http://www.mindmeister.com/95034339/negligence

I. Duty

For a judge to hold that the plaintiff is entitled to damages for a negligence case, the defendant must have breached a duty. How do you know if you have a duty or not? How do you know if you have breached a duty? Three sources of duty exist. One sets out clear definitions of duty, though the downside is that you actually have to read the law in order to know it. It exists in statutes, ordinances, and other legislation. A second exists in common law precedents that help one identify the duty. Here too, unless one has read legal cases, one may not know that one has a duty. A third set is more based on common sense, though some people may argue just how common and just how sensible some of the duties may be.

In common law, the duties of landowners differ depending on whether the plaintiff is a licensee, an invitee, or a trespasser. A landowner owes a licensee—a social guest who enters the premises with permission—the duty to warn of discovered hidden dangers (not overt and not natural conditions). To an invitee, a person who is on the premises by invitation (public area or business), a landowner owes the duty to warn of dangers and to take reasonable measures to make the premises safe. Generally, there are no duties owed to trespassers, with the exception of attractive nuisances and anticipated or discovered trespassers. In those special circumstances, there is only a duty to exercise reasonable care for artificial conditions likely to cause death or serious bodily injury.

> A LANDOWNER owes a licensee—a social guest who enters the premises with permission—the duty to warn of discovered hidden dangers (not overt and not natural conditions). To an invitee, a person who is on the premises by invitation (public area or business), a landowner owes the duty to warn of dangers and to take reasonable measures to make the premises safe.

Tort law is specific to each state and changes over time. In *Heins v. Webster County*, for instance, the Supreme Court of Nebraska wrestled with state court precedents that mandated different duties to those coming to visit a hospital. If one was visiting socially, one set of laws applied that provided minimal duties from the hospital to the visitor. If one was visiting as a volunteer—for instance, who might play Santa Claus at a holiday event—another, stricter set of duties applied. The court discusses the different duties owed and comes to the decision to get rid of the distinctions between duties owed to invitees and those owed to licensees with a more general balancing test, thus illustrating that even in 1996, tort law doctrine continues to evolve.

Imposing duties on landowners for people using the property, whether licensee or invitee, is one thing. It does seem to be common sense to impose duties to keep such visitors reasonably safe. But cases have not stopped at the issue of guests. In some cases, courts have found that the duty owed by businesses includes the duty to take reasonable protective measures against foreseeable criminal acts of third parties.

Claxton v. Atlantic Richfield Co.

Court of Appeals, Second District,
2003 108 Cal.App.4th 327

A gas station customer who was subjected to a racially motivated assault on the gas station premises brought an action against the owners and operators of the station, alleging that defendants failed to take reasonable steps to secure their premises against foreseeable criminal acts of third parties. The trial court granted defendants' nonsuit motion on the ground that the prior incidents on the premises, which were not racially motivated, were insufficiently similar to the attack on plaintiff to give rise to a duty to prevent the type of attack that occurred.

Under the circumstances, the appropriate test in determining foreseeability was prior similar incidents, not prior identical incidents. The station's manager had earlier been robbed at knifepoint by the same party who attacked plaintiff, and this had been reported both to defendant oil company and to the manager's supervisor. Additionally, there had been other robberies and assaults, an altercation between gangs of different races, and numerous crimes in the adjacent park. These incidents amounted to substantial evidence of a reasonably foreseeable risk of violent criminal assaults at the station.

The determination of duty in a given situation "involves the balancing of a number of considerations; the major ones are the foreseeability of harm to the plaintiff, the degree of certainty that the plaintiff suffered injury, the closeness of the connection between the defendant's conduct and the injury suffered, the moral blame attached to the defendant's conduct, the policy of preventing future harm, the extent of the burden to the defendant and consequences to the community of imposing a duty to exercise care with resulting liability for breach, and the availability, cost, and prevalence of insurance for the risk involved."

With respect to the question of the scope of a landowner's duty to provide protection from foreseeable third party crime, "the scope of the duty is determined in part by balancing the foreseeability of the harm against the burden of the duty to be imposed." [I]n cases where the burden of preventing future harm is great, a high degree of foreseeability may be required. On the other hand, in cases where there are strong policy reasons for preventing the harm, or the harm can be prevented by simple means, a lesser degree of foreseeability may be required... [D]uty in such circumstances is determined by a balancing of 'foreseeability' of the criminal acts against the 'burdensomeness, vagueness, and efficacy' of the proposed security measures."

A high degree of foreseeability is required in order to find that the scope of a landowner's duty of care includes the hiring of security guards, and the requisite degree of foreseeability rarely, if ever, can be proven in the absence of prior similar incidents of violent crime on the landowner's premises. The trial court's ruling that in the absence of any previous racially-motivated robberies or assaults, there were no prior similar incidents is without legal support. As set forth in *Ann M. and*

Sharon P., the test is prior "similar" incidents, not prior *identical* incidents. Therefore, it is immaterial whether any prior robberies or assaults at the station were motivated by racial animus, or were merely garden-variety antisocial behavior. Claxton presented substantial evidence of prior robberies and assaults, as well as other indications of a reasonably foreseeable risk of violent criminal assaults at the station. Therefore, the nonsuit motion should have been summarily denied.

The Court of Appeal reversed, holding that the trial court erred in granting nonsuit for defendants.

-----

a. Statutory Duty The duties that are most straightforward are those where a legislature, city council, county board, or some other body with law-making powers has enacted a law that specifies what a person's duty is. For example, in the United States, all 50 states have enacted laws of the road that specify that we drive on the right side of a divided highway. This duty goes as far back as 1792, when Pennsylvania passed the first law requiring all traffic to keep right. Since then, each state has passed a similar law. If you drive on the left side of a divided highway, except of course to pass a car in a permitted passing zone, you are driving the car negligently. This is also sometimes known as negligence *per se*. In *Jones v. Inmont Corporation*, the Federal District for the Southern District of Ohio held that an agent of the company was dumping waste in an open pit or ditch in Kentucky that had no license to receive such waste.

How would we know that the company violated a duty? In this case, because of several statutes such as the Comprehensive Environmental Response Compensation and Liability Act of 1980, 42 U.S.C. § 9601 (CERCLA) and the Resource Conservation and Recovery Act of 1976, 42 U.S.C. § 6901 (RCRA). The court, therefore, did not have to look at common law precedent or custom to determine duty; the legislature preemptive prescribed it.

Legislators actively enact provisions such as these on a regular basis. Such laws apply to, for instance, product liability laws, joint and several liability, respondeat superior laws, strict liability for ultra-hazardous activities, landlord-tenant laws, the Consumer Protection Act, Fair Labor Standards Act, Title VII of the Civil Rights Act, the Equal Pay Act, Comprehensive Environmental Response, Clean Up and Liability Act, Occupational Safety and Health Act, Family and Medical Leave Act, Employee Retirement Income Security Act, Immigration and Nationality Act, Contract Work Hours and Safety Standards Act, and Migrant and Seasonal Worker Protection Act. These are simply a few examples; the list could be extended much further. For someone going into business, it would make very good sense to ask an attorney or to research the specific area to make sure one knows what legislation already pertains to the business.

b. Duty via Precedent As we have already seen, once a court has determined a case, there is precedent that other courts turn to in order to resolve their own cases, either by holding that the case is similar to the earlier precedent or can be somehow distinguished. One of the more famous cases—also a products liability case—is when an elderly woman spilled hot coffee on her lap after paying for it at a drive-through McDonalds' window.[1] The damages were later reduced, but the principle of the case provides precedent for the duty sellers of hot coffee have so that it protects, "the reasonably foreseeable plaintiff."

Indeed, once one is outside of the statutory-duty kinds of cases, the test for whether a person (including a company) has a duty is whether the defendant acted in a way to protect the reasonably foreseeable plaintiff. All of us have duties, whether we know about them or acknowledge them. We are to act in a way that does not endanger other people. Moreover, the definition of a person's duty also depends on the kind of person the (potential) defendant may be.

For example, suppose you are a blind person who, in order to navigate the street, uses a walking stick. When walking down the street, your walking stick accidently strikes another person on the ankle. It is not likely that this will constitute a breach of duty. You are acting as a prudent person with the disability of being blind. At least as described—a blind person walking down the street at a reasonable pace and using a walking stick as one would typically do as a blind person—you have not breached any kind of duty.

However, what if you are instead swinging the walking stick above your head like a cowboy would twirl a lasso and, in doing so, hit the same person on the street in the head? Could that person have just cause to sue you? The answer is yes, because now you are not acting as a reasonably prudent blind person who is conducting themselves in a way to protect a reasonably foreseeable plaintiff. Thus, what constitutes duty can vary.

i. Duty Dependent Upon Age

There are some differentiations of duties based on age. A five year old must behave as a reasonably prudent five year old. Such beings, of course, may not exist. The more interesting cases are those where the person is closer to being an adult. A fifteen year old must behave as a reasonably prudent fifteen year old and if she doesn't, then the fifteen year old, and perhaps her parents, may have to pay damages.

---

1   *Liebeck vs. McDonalds Restaurants, P.T.S., Inc.* District Court of New Mexico, 1994 CV-93- 02419.

The following case sets out the duties (or lack thereof) of young children:

Howland v. Sears, Roebuck & Co.

United States Court of Appeals, Sixth Circuit, 1971 438 F.2d 725

A mother took her two sons, Timothy (eight years old) and Thomas (nine years old) to a local Sears, Roebuck and Company retail store. Thomas was looking at bicycles when he noticed a shelf across from the bicycle rack that stored small arms ammunition.

Thomas testified that he noticed an open drawer in the base table and he took out a box of bullets which had written upon it '.22 long, keep out of reach of children.' Thomas put the box of bullets in his pocket. He testified he did not attempt to pay for the box of bullets he had taken from the store and did not tell his mother that he had taken the bullets. However, he did show the bullets to Timothy.

When the boys were at home, they began playing with the bullets and at one point put the bullets on concrete and started hitting the bullets with hammers. Mr. Howland testified that he had told both Thomas and Timothy not to play with bullets because they were dangerous. Timothy testified his father had told him on an occasion previous to the day in question that he could be blinded playing with bullets. Mr. Howland was unaware his children were playing with bullets and did not specifically warn them on the evening of the injury. At about 6:00, Thomas and Timothy went outside to play and Timothy immediately began exploding bullets. The second bullet which Timothy exploded sent a piece of metal into his left eye. He was rushed to a hospital. But after initial surgery, it was determined necessary to remove his left eye. Timothy's left eye was replaced with a permanent artificial eye.

The family sued Sears, Roebuck & Co. for negligence in leaving the ammunition drawer open so that his minor brother could remove ammunition and Timothy, a minor, could subsequently explode a bullet and blind himself. At trial, the District Court gave standard charges as to the issues of Burden of Proof, Negligence and Ordinary Care, Proximate Cause, Contributory Negligence and Assumption of the Risk. On Contributory Negligence, the District Court did not permit Timothy a rebuttable presumption that he was incapable of committing negligence or contributory negligence because he was between the ages of 7 and 14. A jury verdict rendered judgment for Sears, Roebuck & Co. and Timothy appealed.

On appeal, the primary question is whether the District Court properly charged the jury on the jury questions of negligence, contributory negligence, assumption of the risk and proximate cause. On the issue of contributory negligence... Federal jurisdiction is premised on diversity of the parties. Hence the issue of Appellant's contributory negligence is controlled by Ohio law. As a general rule, the defense of contributory negligence of the complaining party may be raised even when the complaining party is a minor. This is so because, except where a child is incapable of understanding and appreciating the perils threatening him, a minor is required to exercise ordinary care for his own safety and protection. In that minors, however, have less capacity for self care and judgment than an adult, children are generally accorded a special status in applying the rules of contributory negligence.

The State of Ohio has had great difficulty in fashioning a judicial standard to make the delicate judgment of when a minor has the capacity for self care in the conduct of his activities. At very early ages, of course, this determination is not difficult. Just as a child of very tender years may not be held criminally responsible at the common law... he also does not have the capacity to form sufficiently intelligent judgments from his observations so that one may equitably hold him responsible for the protection of his own safekeeping. In *Holbrock v. Hamilton* Distributing, Inc. the Supreme Court of Ohio held 'as a matter of law that a child under seven years of age is incapable of contributory negligence, (and that) the submission of that issue to the jury constituted error.' In creating a conclusive presumption of 'general incapacity * * * (where a child is) under seven years of age,' the Ohio Supreme Court provided in their own words, 'a clear and simple rule which we believe will reach just and accurate results while also achieving a desirable judicial economy.'

In the instant case we are concerned with the capacity and judgment of a child who was two weeks less than nine years old, but who had repeated a year of school...

In *Lake Erie & W. Railroad Co. v. Mackey*, (a case which involved the alleged negligence and contributory negligence of a nine year old child) the rule... was modified for infants between seven and fourteen years of age. The *Mackey* court... held that a child is presumed to possess only such discretion as is common to children, and is, therefore, held only to the exercise of such care as is reasonably expected from children of his own age and capacity. But the *Mackey* court observed that by analogy to the principles of capacity in criminal law, there is a rebuttable legal presumption that a child of nine years of age is incapable of being contributorily negligent. This presumption may be rebutted by a factual showing that the child is of sufficient maturity and capacity to avoid danger and make intelligent judgments with regard to the particular activities in which he had engaged.

We determine it is Ohio law that minors are generally chargeable with the capacity for committing contributory negligence, except where they are under seven years of age. And further we determine that where a minor is between seven and fourteen years of age a rebuttable presumption arises that the minor involved is 'incapable' of forming the necessary judgments for self care. The charge by the District Court to the jury did not give the Appellant the benefit of the rebuttable presumption that a child of his age and maturity was entitled to under the law of the State of Ohio. We find such error prejudicial. The judgment of the District Court is reversed and the cause is remanded for a new trial.

ACCORDING TO STATE LAWS, the ages at which minors are exempt from arguments of negligence or contributory negligence will differ. If a child is exempt from the defenses of negligence or contributory negligence, he cannot be found at fault for his injury, despite his behavior leading up to the injury. This protection afforded to minors leaves open the possibility that businesses such as Sears, Roebuck & Co. could be found wholly responsible for a child's injury. As a general rule, however, the responsible child standard seen in *Howland v. Sears, Roebuck & Co.* is not applied when a child is engaged in adult activity. Here is a case where the court held a minor to an adult standard of care.

Robinson v. Lindsay

Supreme Court of Washington, 1979 92 Wash.2d 410

Kelly Robinson, the plaintiff, lost full use of a thumb in a snowmobile accident when she was 11 years of age. The defendant, Billy Anderson, 13 years of age at the time of the accident, was the driver of the snowmobile. After a jury verdict in favor of Anderson, the trial court ordered a new trial. The defendant appealed.

The single issue on appeal is whether a minor operating a snowmobile is to be held to an adult standard of care. The trial court failed to instruct the jury as to that standard and ordered a new trial because it believed the jury should have been so instructed. We agree and affirm the order granting a new trial.

The trial court instructed the jury to use the following standard of care of negligence in reaching its decision:

> In considering the claimed negligence of a child, you are instructed that it is the duty of a child to exercise the same care that a reasonably careful child of the same age, intelligence, maturity, training and experience would exercise under the same or similar circumstances.

Respondent properly excepted to the giving of this instruction and to the court's failure to give an adult standard of care.

Traditionally, a flexible standard of care has been used to determine if children's actions were negligent. Under some circumstances, however, courts have developed a rationale for applying an adult standard. In the courts' search for a uniform standard of behavior to use in determining whether or not a person's conduct has fallen below minimal acceptable standards, the law has developed a fictitious person, the "reasonable man of ordinary prudence."

In the past we have always compared a child's conduct to that expected of a reasonably careful child of the same age, intelligence, maturity, training and experience. This case is the first to consider the question of a child's liability for injuries sustained as a result of his or her operation of a motorized vehicle or participation in an inherently dangerous activity.

Such a rule protects the need of children to be children but at the same time discourages immature individuals from engaging in inherently dangerous activities. Children will still be free to enjoy traditional childhood activities without being held to an adult standard of care. Although accidents sometimes occur as the result of such activities, they are not activities generally considered capable of resulting in "grave danger to others and to the minor himself if the care used in the course of the activity drops below that care which the reasonable and prudent adult would use . . ."

Other courts adopting the adult standard of care for children engaged in adult activities have emphasized the hazards to the public if the rule is otherwise. The operation of a snowmobile likewise requires adult care and competence. Currently 2.2 million snowmobiles are in operation in the United States. Studies show that collisions and other snowmobile accidents claim hundreds of casualties each year and that the incidence of accidents is particularly high among inexperienced operators.

At the time of the accident, the 13-year-old petitioner had operated snowmobiles for about 2 years. When the injury occurred, petitioner was operating a 30-horse-power snowmobile at speeds of 10-20 miles per hour. The record indicates that the machine itself was capable of 65 miles per hour. Because petitioner was operating a powerful motorized vehicle, he should be held to the standard of care and conduct expected of an adult.

The order granting a new trial is affirmed.

---

ii. Duty Dependent Upon Nature of Disability

As indicated earlier, people are held to a standard of reasonableness. The same standards of reasonableness apply to people with disabilities. Ordinary care is such that an ordinarily prudent person with a like infirmity would have exercised the same precautions under similar circumstances. For example, a blind person must behave as a reasonably prudent blind person. The same test holds true for other kinds of disability as well.

Roberts v. Ring

Supreme Court of Minnesota, 1919 142 Minn. 151

Defendant, seventy-seven years old with defective sight and hearing, was driving an automobile on a city street. He drove over a seven year old boy. The street was crowded and the boy ran from behind another conveyance. Defendant was driving four or five miles an hour. He testified that he saw the boy at a distance of four or five feet from the car. On other occasions he is alleged to have said he did not see the boy at all. His automobile passed clear over the boy. The evidence raised an issue of fact as to his negligence. The court charged the jury that in determining the contributory negligence of the boy they should take his age into account and that in determining the negligence of defendant they might take into account his age and infirmities. The jury found for the defendant and the plaintiff appealed. Defendant contended that the charge was without error and further contends that as a matter of law, defendant was without negligence and that the boy was negligent.

In instructing the jury as to contributory negligence of the boy the court said:

> 'A person may not go blindly across the street, especially where there is no street crossing. He must use the care which an ordinarily prudent person uses under those circumstances.'

Plaintiff promptly at the conclusion of the charge excepted to this language and asked the court to charge:

> 'That the care required of the boy is only such as is usually exercised by children of his age and mental capacity under similar circumstances.'

This the court declined to do. The charge of the court did not give the jury the proper standard of care to be applied to this boy of seven. It is true that in another part of the charge the court stated to the jury that in determining whether the boy was negligent they should take his age into account. If it can be said that this particular statement cured the general erroneous one then we encounter another difficulty as follows: As to the negligence of defendant the court charged:

> 'In determining whether the defendant was guilty of negligence you may take into consideration * * * the age of the defendant * * * and whether or not the defendant had any physical infirmities.'

> "WHEN ONE, by his acts or omissions causes injury to others, his negligence is to be judged by the standard of care usually exercised by the ordinarily prudent normal man."

If it can be said that the instruction that the age of the boy should be taken into consideration in determining his negligence can be considered as an instruction that his age could be considered in extenuation of his conduct, then the same must be said of the similar instruction that they should consider the age and infirmities of the man in determining the question of his negligence. We think the charge would be so understood by a jury. As above indicated, defendant's infirmities did not tend to relieve him from the charge of negligence. On the contrary they weighed against him. Such infirmities, to the extent that they were proper to be considered at all, presented only a reason why defendant should refrain from operating an automobile on a crowded street where care was required to avoid injuring other travelers. When one, by his acts or omissions causes injury to others, his negligence is to be judged by the standard of care usually exercised by the ordinarily prudent normal man.

iii. Common Carriers

Commercial aviation as well as trains, buses, and other forms of transportation open to the general public carry very high duties of care. Common carriers are responsible for even the slightest negligence and are required to do all that human care, vigilance, and foresight could reasonably do under all circumstances. Furthermore, common carriers may even be held liable for intentional infliction of emotional distress if an insult causes a patron to suffer mental distress. The traditional requirements for the insult to be extreme or outrageous and for the distress to be extreme are not applied.

Andrews v. United Airlines, Inc.

United States Court of Appeals, Ninth Circuit, 1994 24 F.3d 39

During the mad scramble that usually follows hard upon an airplane's arrival at the gate, a briefcase fell from an overhead compartment and seriously injured plaintiff Billie Jean Andrews. No one knows who opened the compartment or what caused the briefcase to fall, and Andrews doesn't claim that airline personnel were involved in stowing the object or opening the bin. Her claim, rather, is that the injury was foreseeable and the airline didn't prevent it. The district court dismissed the suit on summary judgment, and we review *de novo*. This is a diversity action brought in California, whose tort law applies.

> **"WHILE THE SKIES are friendly enough, the ground can be a mighty dangerous place when heavy objects tumble from overhead compartments."**

We are called upon to determine whether United Airlines took adequate measures to deal with that elementary notion of physics—what goes up, must come down. For, while the skies are friendly enough, the ground can be a mighty dangerous place when heavy objects tumble from overhead compartments. The parties agree that United Airlines is a common carrier and as such "owe[s] both a duty of utmost care and the vigilance of a very cautious person towards [its] passengers." Though United is "responsible for any, even the slightest, negligence and [is] required to do all that human care, vigilance, and foresight reasonably can do under all the circumstances," "[T]he degree of care and diligence which [it] must exercise is only such as can reasonably be exercised consistent with the character and mode of conveyance adopted and the practical operation of [its] business...."

To show that United did not satisfy its duty of care toward its passengers, Ms. Andrews presented the testimony of two witnesses. The first was Janice Northcott, United's Manager of Inflight Safety, who disclosed that in 1987 the airline had received 135 reports of items falling from overhead bins. As a result of these incidents, Ms. Northcott testified, United decided to add a warning to its arrival announcements, to wit, that items stored overhead might have shifted during flight and passengers should use caution in opening the bins. This announcement later became the industry standard.

Ms. Andrews's second witness was safety and human factors expert Dr. David Thompson, who testified that United's announcement was ineffective because passengers opening overhead bins couldn't see objects poised to fall until the bins were opened, by which time it was too late. Dr. Thompson also testified that United could have taken additional steps to prevent the hazard, such as retrofitting its overhead bins with baggage nets, as some airlines had already done, or by requiring passengers to store only lightweight items overhead.

United argues that Andrews presented too little proof to satisfy her burden under One hundred thirty-five reported incidents, United points out, are trivial when spread over the millions of passengers travelling on its 175,000 flights every year. Even that number overstates the problem, according to United, because it includes events where passengers merely observed items falling from overhead bins but no one was struck or injured. Indeed, United sees the low incidence of injuries as incontrovertible proof that the safety measures suggested by plaintiff's expert would not merit the additional cost and inconvenience to airline passengers.

It is a close question, but we conclude that plaintiff has made a sufficient case to overcome summary judgment. United is hard-pressed to dispute that its passengers are subject to a hazard from objects falling out of overhead bins, considering the warning its flight crews give hundreds of times each day. The case then turns on whether the hazard is serious enough to warrant more than a warning. Given the heightened duty of a common carrier, even a small risk of serious injury to passengers may form the basis of liability if that risk could be eliminated "consistent with the character and mode of [airline travel] and the practical operation of [that] business...." United has demonstrated neither that retrofitting overhead bins with netting (or other means) would be prohibitively expensive, nor that such steps would grossly interfere with the convenience of its passengers. Thus, a jury could find United has failed to do "all that human care, vigilance, and foresight reasonably can do under all the circumstances." Reversed and remanded.

Because of the heightened duty of a common carrier, even a small risk of injury to passengers may form the basis of liability. However, the courts will also consider the costs and convenience of preventing the injury.

----

iv. Superior Skills

Doctors, lawyers, accountants, and other professionals can be sued under a negligence theory for malpractice. Specialists can be found guilty of malpractice if they have not exercised the degree of care and skill that an average person in their profession would have used. In exercising this heightened degree of care and skill, specialists have an additional duty of disclosure and can be sued for not disclosing material risks before acting. However, the duty to disclose is not too strict, as there is no duty to ensure that their clients or patients have full comprehension of the disclosure.

The majority rule concerning the duty of specialists is that the specialist is required to use the degree of care and skill which the average specialist in his field would use. While the rule used to be that courts would look to the standard set in the local community of specialists, courts have since abandoned that view. One exception to the locality argument is considered when it comes to equipment and resources.

Anytime one faces a medical procedure, there is risk. A patient must determine whether it is worth facing those risks and to make that decision, depends on disclosures provided by the doctor or hospital. Duties come with such disclosure and the following case examines some of the issues pertaining to them.

Canterbury v. Spence

United States Court of Appeals, District of Columbia Circuit, 1972 464 F.2d 772

At the time of the events which gave rise to this litigation, appellant was nineteen years of age, a clerk-typist employed by the Federal Bureau of Investigation. In December, 1958, he began to experience severe pain between his shoulder blades. He consulted two general practitioners, but the medications they prescribed failed to eliminate the pain. Thereafter, appellant secured an appointment with Dr. Spence, who is a neurosurgeon. Dr. Spence examined appellant in his office at some length but found nothing amiss. On Dr. Spence's advice appellant was x-rayed, but the films did not identify any abnormality. Dr. Spence then recommended that appellant undergo a myelogram—a procedure in which dye is injected into the spinal column and traced to find evidence of disease or other disorder-at the Washington Hospital Center.

Appellant explained to Dr. Spence that his mother was a widow of slender financial means living in Cyclone, West Virginia, and that she could be reached through a neighbor's telephone. Appellant called his mother the day after the myelogram was performed and, failing to contact her, left Dr. Spence's telephone number with the neighbor. When Mrs. Canterbury returned the call, Dr. Spence told her that the surgery was occasioned by a suspected ruptured disc. Mrs. Canterbury then asked if the recommended operation was serious and Dr. Spence replied "not anymore than any other operation." He added that he knew Mrs. Canterbury was not well off and that her presence in Washington would not be necessary. The testimony is contradictory as to whether during the course of the conversation Mrs. Canterbury expressed her consent to the operation. Appellant himself apparently did not converse again with Dr. Spence prior to the operation.

Dr. Spence performed the laminectomy on February 11 at the Washington Hospital Center. Mrs. Canterbury traveled to Washington, arriving on that date but after the operation was over, and signed a consent form at the hospital. Neither the appellant or his mother were told of the one percent possibility of paralysis resulting from laminectomy.

A day after the operation he fell from his hospital bed after having been left without assistance while voiding. A few hours after the fall, the lower half of his body was paralyzed, and he had to be operated on again. Despite extensive medical care, he has never been what he was before. The patient brought action against the surgeon and the hospital. At the end of the patient's case in chief, the United States District Court for the District of Columbia directed verdicts for the surgeon and hospital, and the patient appealed.

> **"THUS THE TEST for determining whether a particular peril must be divulged is its materiality to the patient's decision: all risks potentially affecting the decision must be unmasked."**

The Court of Appeals held that evidence presented a jury issue as to sufficiency of the surgeon's disclosure, i.e., whether a one percent possibility of paralysis resulting from laminectomy was peril of sufficient magnitude to bring a disclosure duty into play; evidence also presented an issue as to whether the operation was negligently performed. The Court also held that evidence including evidence that the patient progressed after the operation until he fell while unattended but, a few hours thereafter, his condition had deteriorated and testimony that there were complaints of paralysis and respiratory difficulty and medical testimony that paralysis can be brought on by trauma or shock presented an issue whether there was dereliction of the hospital's duty to exercise reasonable care for the safety and well-being of the patient, and an issue of causality.

Once the circumstances give rise to a duty on the physician's part to inform his patient, the next inquiry is the scope of the disclosure the physician is legally obliged to make. The courts have frequently confronted this problem but no uniform standard defining the adequacy of the divulgence emerges from the decisions. Some have said "full" disclosure, a norm we are unwilling to adopt literally. It seems obviously prohibitive and unrealistic to expect physicians to discuss with their patients every risk of proposed treatment-no matter how small or remote-and generally unnecessary from the patient's viewpoint as well. Indeed, the cases speaking in terms of "full" disclosure appear to envision something less than total disclosure, leaving unanswered the question of just how much.

In our view, the patient's right of self-decision shapes the boundaries of the duty to reveal. That right can be effectively exercised only if the patient possesses enough information to enable an intelligent choice. The scope of the physician's communications to the patient, then, must be measured by the patient's need, and that need is the information material to the decision. Thus the test for determining whether a particular peril must be divulged is its materiality to the patient's decision: all risks potentially affecting the decision must be unmasked. And to safeguard the patient's interest in achieving his own determination on treatment, the law must itself set the standard for adequate disclosure.

Of necessity, the content of the disclosure rests in the first instance with the physician. Ordinarily it is only he who is in position to identify particular dangers; always he must make a judgment, in terms of materiality, as to whether and to what extent revelation to the patient is called for. He cannot know with complete exactitude what the patient would consider important to his decision, but on the basis of his medical training and experience he can sense how the average, reasonable patient expectably would react. Indeed, with knowledge of, or ability to learn, his patient's background and current condition, he is in a position superior to that of most others-attorneys, for example-who are called upon to make judgments on pain of liability in damages for unreasonable miscalculation....

The scope of the standard is not subjective as to either the physician or the patient; it remains objective with due regard for the patient's informational needs and with suitable leeway for the physician's situation. In broad outline, we agree that "[a] risk is thus material when a reasonable person, in what the physician knows or should know to be the patient's position, would be likely to attach significance to the risk or cluster of risks in deciding whether or not to forego the proposed therapy."

---

v. Other Examples of Duty: "Common Sense" Duties, Reasonability, and "Taking the Plaintiff As You Find Him"

The above examples do not exhaust the possible definitions of duty. Remember, the idea of negligence law is for an individual to act as a reasonably prudent person who will protect against a reasonably foreseeable plaintiff. This test can be applied to new kinds of negligence cases quite easily. Thus, even if a person memorized all the statutes pertaining to negligence and read all the court cases on negligence, one would not have exhausted the possible range of negligence cases.

The linchpin of these cases is the "reasonability" standard. How does a "reasonable" person act? What constitutes a "reasonably foreseeable plaintiff?" The reasonability test is meant to be objective. Subjectively speaking, we can all think of something another person did that made us angry. We may even think that they should be sued for it. But the test of reasonableness is meant for us to take a step back and look at the action a bit more objectively. That is what courts will do. Some may object that reasonability is simply the subjective view of a given judge. There is some truth to this, since two judges may see something differently, but bear in mind that a trial judge is not the final word on the determination of a case for several reasons.

The linchpin of these cases is the "reasonability" standard. How does a "reasonable" person act? What constitutes a "reasonably foreseeable plaintiff?" The reasonability test is meant to be objective.

One reason is that there are two sides to a case and so a judge, regardless of what she first might think about a case, will end up having to hear from both sides and that tends to make judgments less subjective. Second, if there is a statute or precedent, then the judge, whatever he personally thinks, still has to follow the law and precedent or to find a way to argue that previous law is not controlling. Third, regardless of what a trial judge (or jury) holds, the case can be appealed. Thus, while some decisions may seem absurd to an outsider, there are several checks within the system to assure that an objective standard, flexible as it is, does still apply.

A further complication is the adage of "taking the plaintiff as you find him." The defendant may not know the vulnerabilities of the plaintiff in advance but be held liable for them. A further elucidation of this point will be made in the section on causation, below, and the issues that arise with an "eggshell plaintiff."

2. Breach of Duty

Once one has determined the existence of a duty relevant to the situation, the next step of breach of duty is very straightforward: did they adhere to the duty? If the alleged defendant adhered to the duty, then there is no case. The plaintiff would need to find some other theory to hold the defendant liable.

3. Causation

There are two types of causation in a tort case: actual and proximate. While lawyers and law students love to analyze the difference between the two, the cause that really matters is proximate cause. The difference between the two mainly goes to providing an analytical category for those things that lead up to an injury while keeping them separate from the particular aspect that did cause the plaintiff's injury. Whatever is the proximate cause will also be an actual cause, but there are some actual causes that are not proximate causes.

For example, suppose you are standing on an urban street corner and a bus comes thundering by and, edging toward the curb to make a scheduled stop, rolls over your foot which is on the sidewalk. The proximate cause—the thing that caused your smashed foot—is the bus driver's negligent driving of the bus. But there are many actual causes. "But for" (a way lawyers sometimes characterize the actual cause test) the fact that you were on the corner at that moment rather than five minutes earlier (because the line at Starbucks was longer than you expected), you would not have been hurt. So does that mean that you can sue Starbucks or the people lined up in front of you for having caused your injury? Of course not, but they are in the chain of events that led up to the injury.

Here are two cases that set out the differences between actual and proximate cause.

Stubbs v. City of Rochester

Court of Appeals of New York, 1919 226 N.Y. 516

During the year 1910 and for many years prior thereto the defendant under legislative authority was engaged in the business of selling water to its inhabitants. A duty was imposed on the commissioner of public works to provide an abundant supply of wholesome water for public and private use, to devise plans and sources of water supply, to plan and supervise the distribution of water through the city and to protect it against contamination. The city has two systems of water supply. One for potable water brought by it from Hemlock Lake some distance south of the city to reservoirs near the city and thence distributed by gravity to consumers. That system is known as the Hemlock system.

The plaintiff, a resident of the city of Rochester and a machinist, was employed by a firm whose place of business was at the corner of Allen and Platt streets, about one block from the Brown street bridge. The factory was supplied with Hemlock lake water for drinking purposes. Plaintiff drank the water from time to time, using his individual drinking glass. He was taken ill September 6, 1910, with typhoid fever and was sick in bed for six weeks and unable to work for some twelve weeks. Asserting that his illness was caused by reason of drinking contaminated water supplied by the city, the plaintiff sought to recover damages by reason thereof. This case is on appeal from a judgment entered September 13, 1916, upon an order of the Appellate Division of the Supreme Court in the fourth judicial department, overruling plaintiffs' exceptions, ordered to be heard in the first instance by the Appellate Division, denying a motion for a new trial and directing judgment in favor of defendant upon the nonsuit granted at the Trial Term.

The evidence disclosed upon the trial clearly established that the water furnished by the defendant for potable purposes in the locality of the Brown street bridge was contaminated. The important question in this case is—did the plaintiff produce evidence from which inference might reasonably be drawn that the cause of his illness was due to the use of contaminated water furnished by defendant. Counsel for respondent argues that even assuming that the city may be held liable to plaintiff for damages caused by its negligence in furnishing contaminated water for drinking purposes, (a) that the evidence adduced by plaintiff fails to disclose that he contracted typhoid fever by drinking contaminated water; (b) that it was incumbent upon the plaintiff to establish that his illness was not due to any other cause to which typhoid fever may be attributed for which defendant is not liable. The evidence does disclose several causes of typhoid fever which is a germ disease, the germ being known as the typhoid bacillus, which causes may be classified as follows:

■ HEMLOCK LAKE, ROCHESTER, NY

First. Drinking of polluted water. *Second*. Raw fruits and vegetables in certain named localities where human excrement is used to fertilize the soil are sometimes sources of typhoid infection. *Third*. The consumption of shell fish, though not a frequent cause. *Fourth*. The consumption of infected milk and vegetables. *Fifth*. The house fly in certain localities. *Sixth*. Personal contact with an infected person by one who has a predilection for typhoid infection and is not objectively sick with the disease. *Seventh*. Ice if affected with typhoid bacilli. *Eighth*. Fruits, vegetables, etc., washed in infected water. *Ninth*. The medical authorities recognize that there are still other causes and means unknown. This fact was developed on cross-examination of physicians called by plaintiff.

Counsel for respondent asserts that there was a failure of proof on the part of plaintiff in that he did not establish that he contracted disease by drinking contaminated water and in support of his argument cites a rule of law, that when there are several possible causes of injury for one or more of which a defendant is not responsible, plaintiff cannot recover without proving that the injury was sustained wholly or in part by a cause for which defendant was responsible. He submits that it was essential for plaintiff to eliminate all other of seven causes from which the disease might have been contracted. If the argument should prevail and the rule of law stated is not subject to any limitation the present case illustrates the impossibility of a recovery in any case based upon like facts.

The plaintiff was employed in the immediate locality where the water was contaminated. He drank the water daily. The consumption of contaminated water is a very frequent cause of typhoid fever. In the locality there were a large number of cases of typhoid fever and near to sixty individuals who drank the water and had suffered from typhoid fever in that neighborhood appeared as witnesses on behalf of plaintiff. The plaintiff gave evidence of his habits, his home surroundings and his method of living, and the medical testimony indicated that his illness was caused by drinking contaminated water. Without reiteration of the facts disclosed on the trial I do not believe that the case on the part of plaintiff was so lacking in proof as matter of law that his complaint should be dismissed. On the contrary the most favorable inferences deducible from the plaintiff were such as would justify a submission of the facts to a jury as to the reasonable inferences to be drawn therefrom, and a verdict rendered thereon for either party would rest not in conjecture but upon reasonable possibilities.

The judgment should be reversed and a new trial granted, costs to abide the event.

———————————

IN A CLAIM OF ACTUAL CAUSE, a plaintiff must show that the defendant's negligence actually caused the injury. However, the possibility that there may be other causes for the injury does not compel the plaintiff to prove that none of the other possible factors was actually the cause. The plaintiff only has to prove that under a reasonable inference, the defendant's negligence caused the injury. In some cases, it is only necessary to prove that the defendant's negligence increased the chances of injury.

Benn v. Thomas

Supreme Court of Iowa, 1994 512 N.W.2d 537

On February 15, 1989, on an icy road in Missouri, a semi-tractor and trailer rear-ended a van in which Loras J. Benn was a passenger. In the accident, Loras suffered a bruised chest and a fractured ankle. Six days later he died of a heart attack.

Subsequently, Carol A. Benn, as executor of Loras's estate, filed suit against defendants Leland R. Thomas, the driver of the semi-tractor, K-G Ltd., the owner of the semi-tractor and trailer, and Heartland Express, the permanent lessee of the semi-tractor and trailer. The plaintiff estate sought damages for Loras's injuries and death. At trial, the estate's medical expert, Dr. James E. Davia, testified that Loras had a history of coronary disease and insulin-dependent diabetes. Loras had a heart attack in 1985 and was at risk of having another. Dr. Davia testified that he viewed "the accident that [Loras] was in and the attendant problems that it cause[d] in the body as the straw that broke the camel's back" and the cause of Loras's death. Other medical evidence indicated the accident did not cause his death. Based on Dr. Davis's testimony, the estate requested an instruction to the jury based on the "e The district court denied this request. The jury returned a verdict for the estate in the amount of $17,000 for Loras's injuries but nothing for his death. In the special verdict, the jury determined the defendant's negligence in connection with the accident did not proximately cause Loras's death.

The main question here is whether the trial court erred in refusing to instruct the jury on the "eggshell plaintiff" rule in view of the fact that plaintiff's decedent, who had a history of coronary disease, died of a heart attack six days after suffering a bruised chest and fractured ankle in a motor vehicle accident caused by defendant's negligence. The court of appeals concluded that the trial court's refusal constituted reversible error. We agree with the court of appeals and reverse the judgment of the trial court and remand for a new trial.

The estate claims that the court erred in failing to include, in addition to its proximate cause instruction to the jury, a requested instruction on the eggshell plaintiff rule. Such an instruction would advise the jury that it could find that the accident aggravated Loras's heart condition and caused his fatal heart attack.

A tortfeasor whose act, superimposed upon a prior latent condition, results in an injury may be liable in damages for the full disability. This rule deems the injury, and not the dormant condition, the proximate cause of the plaintiff's harm. *Id*. This precept is often referred to as the "eggshell plaintiff" rule, which has its roots in cases such as where the court observed:

■ EGGSHELL SKULL (OR THIN SKULL) DOCTRINE STATES THAT IF A PERSON HAD A SKULL AS FRAGILE AS AN EGG SHELL, AND A DEFENDANT'S ACTIONS CAUSED A SKULL FRACTURE, THE DEFENDANT WOULD STILL BE HELD LIABLE FOR ALL THE DAMAGES, EVEN IF THERE WAS NO INTENT TO CAUSE SEVERE INJURY.

> If a man is negligently run over or otherwise negligently injured in his body, it is no answer to the sufferer's claim for damages that he would have suffered less injury, or no injury at all, if he had not had an unusually thin skull or an unusually weak heart.

The proximate cause instruction in this case provided:

> The conduct of a party is a proximate cause of damage when it is a substantial factor in producing damage and when the damage would not have happened except for the conduct.

"Substantial" means the party's conduct has such an effect in producing damage as to lead a reasonable person to regard it as a cause... The eggshell plaintiff rule rejects the limit of foreseeability that courts ordinarily require in the determination of proximate cause. Once the plaintiff establishes that the defendant caused some injury to the plaintiff, the rule imposes liability for the full extent of those injuries, not merely those that were foreseeable to the defendant. Defendant nevertheless maintains that an eggshell plaintiff instruction would draw undue emphasis and attention to Loras's prior infirm condition. We have, however, explicitly approved such an instruction in two prior cases.

Moreover, the other jurisdictions that have addressed the issue have concluded that a court's refusal to instruct on the eggshell plaintiff rule constitutes a failure to convey the applicable law. To deprive the plaintiff estate of the requested instruction under this record would fail to convey to the jury a central principle of tort liability.

The record in this case warranted an instruction on the eggshell plaintiff rule. We therefore affirm the decision of the court of appeals. We reverse the judgment of the district court and remand the cause to the district court for a new trial consistent with this opinion.

THE EGGSHELL THIN SKULL DOCTRINE leads Courts to "take their plaintiffs as they find them." If the plaintiff suffers a foreseeable injury (given his existing condition) resulting from the defendant's conduct, the defendant's actions are the proximate cause. Once proximate cause is shown, the defendant may be liable to the full extent of the injury.

4. Damages

While negligence (and other tort) cases can cause controversy, especially among businesspeople, damages, we might say, are the "proximate cause" of the anger. When a person goes to court, she has to ask the judge or jury to do something. Occasionally, all a plaintiff wants is a public determination of poor behavior on the part of the defendant. Some people actually only want an apology. But the vast majority of people initiate tort suits to ask for monetary damages and, in a tort case, that is what a court can order. There are two categories of damages: compensatory and punitive.

a. Compensatory Compensatory damages attempt to make an injured plaintiff whole, or put another way, to make up for what the plaintiff lost as a result of being hurt. Examples would include lost wages or income from having to take time off work because of the injury. Expenses for medical care would be another example. This is worth thinking about. When a person signs up for health insurance coverage, they "subrogate" their rights to the insurance company for recovering health care costs in case of an injury. Thus, even if you have no interest in suing someone who injured you because your expenses were covered by insurance, your health insurance company would be able to do so in order to get the money it paid for your medical care back from the defendant. The following case illustrates subrogation rights.

*Allstate Insurance Co. v. Mazzola

United States Court of Appeals, Ninth Circuit, 1999 175 F.3d 255

The automobile insurer, as subrogee of insured, sued the driver and owner of an automobile involved in an accident, to recover first-party medical benefits paid for insured's injuries. The United States District Court for the Southern District of New York granted summary judgment for defendants based on release they obtained from insured. Insurer appealed.

The Court of Appeals held that the insurer could maintain equitable subrogation claim. "Subrogation is the right one party has against a third party following payment, in whole or in part, of a legal obligation that ought to have been met by the third party." The doctrine of equitable subrogation allows insurers to "stand in the shoes" of their insured to seek indemnification by pursuing any claims that the insured may have had against third parties legally responsible for the loss. In short, one party known as the subrogee is substituted for and succeeds to the rights of another party, known as the subrogor. The doctrine of subrogation, which is based upon principles of equity has a dual objective as stated by New York courts:

> The doctrine of EQUITABLE SUBROGATION allows insurers to "stand in the shoes" of their insured to seek indemnification.

> It seeks, first, to prevent the insured from recovering twice for one harm, as it might if it could recover from both the insurer and from a third person who caused the harm, and second, to require the party who has caused the damage to reimburse the insurer for the payment the insurer has made.

The first issue concerns whether Allstate's inability to recover under New York Insurance Law §§ 5104(b) and 5105(a)3 bars a remedy under the doctrine of equitable subrogation as applied by New York courts. Allstate does not quarrel with the district court's ruling in so far as it held that the company may not recover no-fault medical benefits paid on behalf of Kevin Hall from the defendants under these statutes.[2] (In addition, the plaintiff acknowledges that sections 5104(b) and 5105(a) provide the exclusive remedy for insurers seeking to bring an action to recoup "first party benefits" or the first $50,000 of no-fault benefits paid to their insured. However, Allstate contends that sections 5104(b) and 5105(a) do not bar an equitable subrogation claim to recover the remaining amount of $83,637.22 in excess of the nonrecoverable $50,000. We agree.

As a creature of equity, the right of subrogation does not arise from, nor is it dependent upon, statute or the terms of a contract of insurance." One court stated this axiom in the following manner:

> "If the insured were permitted to keep the payment from [the insurer] under his additional endorsement and recover from [the tortfeasor] for extended economic loss, he would sustain a double recovery. Such result is clearly not contemplated under the no-fault statutory scheme. Subrogation is the principle which exists to prevent double recovery by the insured and to force the wrongdoer to bear the ultimate costs. The purpose of the statutory scheme is to make whole an injured party, not to provide him with a windfall. *** As a corollary, the doctrine of equitable subrogation must be liberally applied for the protection of insurers, its intended beneficiaries.
>
> *Source:(http://bjs.gov/content/pub/pdf/pdasc05.pdf*

ANOTHER KIND OF COMPENSATORY DAMAGES, standing in between medical damages and the following category of pain and suffering, is a price placed on loss of a physical capability. If a person has been in an accident that left them paralyzed, the courts, after hearing evidence, will place a price on the loss of the ability to walk or the loss of a limb. In a wrongful death case, Courts have placed a value on "loss of consortium" which means the loss of having sex with one's spouse.

---

2   The district court concluded that Allstate could not recover pursuant to section 5104(b) because the statute provides relief only in actions brought against a "noncovered person." Since Mazzola was insured by Royal at a level above that required by New York law, he constituted a covered person, rather than a non-covered person as required by section 5104(b). The district court also found that the requirements of section 5105(a) were not satisfied because the vehicles involved in the accident each weighed less than six thousand five hundred pounds unloaded and were not used principally for the transportation of persons or property for hire.

Seffert v. Los Angeles Transit Lines

Supreme Court of California, 1961 56 Cal. 2d

Defendants appeal from a judgment for plaintiff for $187,903.75 entered on a jury verdict. Their motion for a new trial for errors of law and excessiveness of damages was denied.

At the trial plaintiff contended that she was properly entering defendants' bus when the doors closed suddenly catching her right hand and left foot. The bus started, dragged her some distance, and then threw her to the pavement. Defendants contended that the injury resulted from plaintiff's own negligence, that she was late for work and either ran into the side of the bus after the doors had closed or ran after the bus and attempted to enter after the doors had nearly closed.

The evidence supports plaintiff's version of the facts. Several eyewitnesses testified that plaintiff started to board the bus while it was standing with the doors wide open. Defendants do not challenge the sufficiency of the evidence. They do contend, however, that prejudicial errors were committed during the trial and that the verdict is excessive. ***

The evidence most favorable to the plaintiff shows that prior to the accident plaintiff was in good health, and had suffered no prior serious injuries. She was single, and had been self-supporting for 20 of her 42 years. The accident happened on October 11, 1957. The trial took place in July and August of 1959.

As already pointed out, the injury occurred when plaintiff was caught in the doors of defendants' bus when it started up before she had gained full entry. As a result she was dragged for some distance. The record is uncontradicted that her injuries were serious, painful, disabling and permanent.

Since the accident, and because of it, plaintiff has undergone nine operations and has spent eight months in various hospitals and rehabilitation centers. These operations involved painful skin grafting and other painful procedures. Although plaintiff has gone back to work, she testified that she has difficulty standing, walking or even sitting, and must lie down frequently; that the leg is still very painful; that she can, even on her best days, walk not over three blocks and that very slowly; that her back hurts from walking; that she is tired and weak; that her sleep is disturbed; that she has frequent spasms in which the leg shakes uncontrollably; that she feels depressed and unhappy, and suffers humiliation and embarrassment.

Plaintiff claims that there is evidence that her total pecuniary loss, past and future, amounts to $53,903.75. This was the figure used by plaintiff's counsel in his argument to the jury, in which he also claimed $134,000 for pain and suffering, past and future. Since the verdict was exactly the total of these two estimates, it is reasonable to assume that the jury accepted the amount proposed by counsel for each item.

The summary of plaintiff as to pecuniary loss, past and future, is as follows:

PAST MEDICAL EXPENSES:

Doctor and Hospital Bills	$10,330.50
Drugs and other medical expenses stipulated to in the amount of	2,273.25
	5,500.00
	$18,103.75

FUTURE MEDICAL EXPENSES:

$2,000 per year for next 10 years	20,000.00
$200 per year for the 24 years thereafter	4,800.00
Drugs for 34 years	1,000.00
	25,800.00
	43,903.75
Possible future loss of earnings	10,000.00
Total Pecuniary Loss	**$53,903.75**

There is substantial evidence to support these estimates. The amounts for past doctor and hospital bills, for the cost of drugs, and for a past loss of earnings, were either stipulated to, evidence was offered on, or is a simple matter of calculation. These items totaled $18,103.75. While the amount of $25,800 estimated as the cost of future medical expense, for loss of future earnings and for the future cost of drugs, may seem high, there was substantial evidence that future medical expense is certain to be high. There is also substantial evidence that plaintiff's future earning capacity may be substantially impaired by reason of the injury. The amounts estimated for those various items are not out of line, and find support in the evidence.

This leaves the amount of $134,000 presumably allowed for the nonpecuniary items of damage, including pain and suffering, past and future. It is this allowance that defendants seriously attack as being excessive as a matter of law.

While the appellate court should consider the amounts awarded in prior cases for similar injuries, obviously, each case must be decided on its own facts and circumstances. Such examination demonstrates that such awards vary greatly. Injuries are seldom identical and the amount of pain and suffering involved in similar physical injuries varies widely. These factors must be considered. (*Leming v. Oilfields Trucking Co., supra,* 44 Cal.2d 343, 356; *Crane v. Smith,* 23 Cal.2d 288, 302 [144 P.2d 356].) Basically, the question that should be decided by the appellate courts is whether or not the verdict is so out of line with reason that it shocks the conscience and necessarily implies that the verdict must have been the result of passion and prejudice.

In the instant case, the nonpecuniary items of damage include allowances for pain and suffering, past and future, humiliation as a result of being disfigured and being permanently crippled, and constant anxiety and fear that the leg will have to be amputated. While the amount of the award is high, and may be more than we would have awarded were we the trier of the facts, considering the nature of the injury, the great pain and suffering, past and future, and the other items of damage, we cannot say, as a matter of law, that it is so high that it shocks the conscience and gives rise to the presumption that it was the result of passion or prejudice on the part of the jurors.

WITH PAIN AND SUFFERING, the courts try to determine a price on how much a plaintiff is hurting. The court would likely hear evidence of how much pain and suffering the plaintiff is in with the plaintiff's lawyer then asking the jury: "wouldn't it be worth $5 an hour not to be in this kind of pain? Or $10 an hour?" The lawyer might try to read body language and jurors' minds to see how much further to push the question. But if the lawyer thinks that $10 has stuck, approvingly, in the jurors' mind, then one can do the math from there: that means $240 a day or $87,600 a year. Say the person has a remaining life expectancy of 50 years, and you have a pain and suffering amount of $4,380,000. That would have to be discounted back to the net present value of the total in order to make a current damage award, but one can see how breaking pain and suffering into small, discrete amounts that seem very reasonable to a juror's mind can add up into large damage awards for pain and suffering. Courts will also consider damages for loss of enjoyment of life as part of pain and suffering.

b. Punitive In some cases, a plaintiff may not only get compensatory damages, but punitive damages as well. Punitive damages, as the name suggests, are meant not to compensate a victim-plaintiff but instead to punish the "tortfeasor" (defendant). These damages are also known as exemplary damages because they are meant to make an example of the defendant who has engaged in problematic behavior. The idea is to make the punishment for the wrongdoing so significant that the defendant will have the incentive to change his behavior or production process or whatever was the proximate cause that triggered the injury.

In *Taylor v. Superior Court*, the Court held an alcoholic, who was aware of the seriousness of his problem and the danger driving while intoxicated posted, was forced to pay punitive damages even though the theory against the defendant was based in negligence rather than intentional torts. In this and in many other instances, courts have found various ways to impose punitive damages on defendants.

B. TWO LATIN WRINKLES

I. Res Ispa Loquitor

Res ipsa loquitor is a term applied to negligence cases where it is very difficult for the plaintiff to determine how and what exactly caused the injury. It means "the thing speaks for itself." *Res ipsa loquitor* is not a separate theory of liability; instead it is simply a shifting of the normal burden of proof from the plaintiff (who normally has to prove the case with a preponderance of the evidence) to the defendant to prove that they were not negligent.

Res Ispa Loquitor:
"The thing speaks for itself"

Respondeat Superior:
"Let the master answer."

For example, think of days gone by when a person is walking by another's barn and a bale of hay comes flying out of the barn, landing on the person's head. Bales of hay do not typically come flying out of barns and hitting bystanders without some degree of negligence (unless the bystander happens to be climbing into a horse's or cow's eating area). But how is that bystander able to prove the negligence? These were the kinds of cases where *res ipsa loquitor* began to be used because the thing—bales of haying flying out of farms and hitting people—speaks for itself. In such situations, the burden of proof of establishing the duty and the breach of duty shifts from the plaintiff to the defendant.

The tests for applying res ipsa loquitor are:

1. Does the action typically happen only with a party's negligence;

2. Was the item causing the damage solely within the defendant's control with the damages occurred; and

3. Was the plaintiff innocent of any contributing negligence.

Today, *res ipsa* cases primarily apply to products liability cases, and more will be covered at that point of the text. For now, it is well to situate it within its origins in negligence.

2. Respondeat Superior

Sometimes, a third party is liable for the negligent actions of another person. This happens when one person (an agent) is working for another person (a principal), especially when that agent is a regular employee of the principal/employer. If the agent injures someone while on the job, working for the employer, then the employer as well as the employee could be held liable for damages caused by the employee's negligence. The subsequent chapter on agency law will cover this issue in more detail.

C. DEFENSES

Historically, contributory negligence significantly limited the likelihood that a plaintiff would recover damages from the defendant. Contributory negligence held that any negligence of the plaintiff would bar recovery, no matter how negligent the defendant's conduct was. For example, suppose the plaintiff and the defendant were driving their respective cars on a two-lane highway. The speed limit stands at 55 miles per hour. The plaintiff is travelling at 57 MPH and the defendant, driving drunk, is travelling 110. The defendant drifts over the center lane and hits the plaintiff's car, which is still squarely in its own lane. Fault here seems straightforward, but because the plaintiff is driving above the speed limit, he is negligent too. At least in theory, this could historically be used to bar recovery.

Courts modified the harshness of this approach with theories such as "last clear chance." This theory asks, even if the plaintiff was negligent, did the defendant have the last chance to avoid the injury (for instance, by not drifting over the center line)? Courts may also look to see if a defendant has voluntarily assumed the risk. Both of these mitigating theories, especially assumption of risk, still can be utilized in a case, but the modern rule tends to look at comparative rather than contributory negligence.

> "...THE PLAINTIFF driving 57 miles per hour might be two percent negligent for driving over the speed limit, but the defendant driving 110 miles per hour, while drunk and drifting over the center line would likely be 98 percent negligent."

With comparative negligence, the Court looks to see how much each party is negligent. In the above scenario, the plaintiff driving 57 miles per hour might be two percent negligent for driving over the speed limit, but the defendant driving 110 miles per hour, while drunk and drifting over the center line would likely be 98 per cent negligent (or more). With a 98-2 negligence factor, the plaintiff's recover would be reduced by his 2 percent of negligence. The comparative negligence rule thus simplifies analysis of fault and recovery.

Assumption of risk remains an important defense. If a fan goes to a major league baseball game and sits in the lower seats down the third base/left field line, gets hit by a line drive, and then sues the baseball team for negligence, the baseball team has a strong case to argue that the fan assumed the risk of being hit at a game, especially given the choice of seats that might be available. If a fan wanted to have more protection, she could sit behind home plate (where in all major league stadiums, there is netting to prevent being hit by a foul ball) or in more remote seats less likely to have a blistering line drive hit toward them. Of course, the hard issues come when one tries to determine whether a fan fully knew of the risk she was incurring.

II. Strict Liability

A. HISTORICAL ANTECEDENTS

Strict liability is sometimes also referred to as absolute duty. This concept behind it is simple: some activities are so dangerous that the person who introduces them to the public is absolutely liable in case something goes wrong. One cannot be careful. One cannot exercise such prudence so as to avoid a charge of negligence. Simply by introducing the activity or product, the opportunity for reasonable care has been lost. One is strictly liable for anything that goes wrong.

■ UNDER STRICT LIABILITY THE IDEA IS THAT THERE IS NO WAY TO INTRODUCE A MOUNTAIN LION INTO A COMMUNITY SAFELY.

For example, suppose a person kept a mountain lion cub as a pet. When the owner first got the cub, the neighborhood was a small, sparsely populated neighborhood. But with population growth, that neighborhood became well within a heavily congested urban area. The lion grew and although it was de-fanged and de-clawed, it was still a 350 pound animal. One day, the lion got out and jumped on an elderly neighbor. De-fanged or not, it still bruised the neighbor.

If negligence was the only theory of liability, then the owner might claim that he had been reasonably prudent in keeping the lion in an enclosure and de-fanging and de-clawing him. It doesn't matter with strict liability. Under strict liability the idea is that there is no way to introduce a mountain lion into a community safely.

The following case illustrates this historical example.

Collins v. Otto

Supreme Court of Colorado, 1962 369 P.2d 564

The plaintiff was a four year old child who alleged defendants owned and wrongfully harbored a coyote, a wild animal of vicious propensities. On May 22, 1960, the child was attacked and bitten by the coyote and seriously injured. The Ottos admitted ownership of the animal for a period of about two years. They had fitted it with a collar and kept it on a chain about 15 ft. long. At the time of the attack on plaintiff, the coyote had recently been delivered of a litter and some of her puppies were still with her. Mr. Otto admitted that he gave one of the puppies to David to pet in the presence of the coyote.

Although the Ottos denied that they knew the coyote was vicious, they both testified that it was their custom not to let children approach it to pet it unless in their presence. Mrs. Otto testified that all of the neighborhood children had been warned not to go close to the coyote unless she or her husband were present. Mrs. Otto further testified that she worried about it and kept a very strong chain on the animal, and she did not tell the children that the coyote might hurt them but just warned the children to stay away unless she or her husband were present.

That the coyote attacked the boy is not disputed. An eye witness testified as to the viciousness of the attack, and the medical testimony established that lacerations of the forehead, eyelid, face, ears, and back of head were the result of the bites of the coyote. The injuries were quite extensive, leaving scars requiring at least two operations by a plastic surgeon.

The Ottos defended on the theory of the contributory negligence of this four year old child and on the basis that they had no prior knowledge of the viciousness of the animal.

The law is virtually universal that one who harbors a wild animal, which by its very nature is vicious and unpredictable, does so at his peril, and liability for injuries inflicted by such animal is absolute. ***

As a universal rule of torts, those who harbor wild animals, which by their nature are vicious and unpredictable, are strictly liable for the any injuries caused by those animals. While other tort liability requires previous knowledge, it is not a defense to claim that one had no knowledge of the vicious nature of a wild animal. However, the strict liability rule for owning wild animals is not absolute. In cases where the injured party assumed a "primary assumption of risk," the owners may not be strictly liable.

———————————

IN THE FOLLOWING CASE, a specialist hired to clean a shark tank lost on a claim of strict liability when he was bitten by one of the defendant's sharks.

Rosenbloom v. Hanour Corp.

Court of Appeals, Fourth District, 1998 66 Cal.App.4th 1477

The trial court entered summary judgment in favor of defendant, a club that kept a shark in an aquarium, in a personal injury action brought by an individual who was bitten while attempting to remove the shark from the tank. Plaintiff was an employee of the company that built and maintained the aquarium, and the trial court found that the doctrine of assumption of the risk barred the action.

The Court of Appeal affirmed. It held that defendant was not liable as a matter of law. Strict liability is generally imposed upon one who keeps a naturally dangerous animal such as a shark, but liability is not absolute. The owner of a naturally dangerous animal may be excused from the usual duty of care in cases involving the doctrine of primary assumption of risk, where by virtue of the nature of the activity

"**THE OWNER** of a naturally dangerous animal may be excused from the usual duty of care in cases involving the doctrine of primary assumption of risk."

and the parties' relationship to the activity, the defendant owes no legal duty to protect the plaintiff from the particular risk of harm that caused the injury. The doctrine operates as a complete bar to recovery. In this case, the defendant recognized the expertise necessary for the dangerous task of handling a shark and accordingly hired a known expert in the field to do the work. Shark bites were the company's occupational hazard, and no duty was owed to protect the shark handler from the very danger that he or she was employed to confront.

———

STRICT LIABILITY TOOK A STEP into the business world when commerce introduced new ways of doing business that were determined to be ultra-hazardous. Two examples of this were dynamite blasting (for instance, to clear areas for new roads) or crop-dusting for farmland. The courts determined that these were such dangerous activities that strict liability was the appropriate standard to be applied. In a case involving an accident that occurred during the transportation of toxic chemicals, *Indiana Harbor Belt Railroad Co. v. American Cyanamid Co.*, 916 f.2d 1174 (7th Cir. 1990), Judge Posner laid out six factors that should be considered in determining whether an activity is ultra-hazardous:

Factors in Ultra-Hazardous Activities	
1. How great the risk of harm was.	4. Whether the activity is commonly engaged in.
2. The seriousness of the harm that could result.	5. Whether the activity is appropriate for the location.
3. Whether the risk could be prevented with the exercise of due care.	6. Whether the social value of the activity outweighs the risks.

B. CONTEMPORARY EXAMPLES

I. "One Free Bite"

If the owner of a mountain lion is strictly liable for any damages caused by the lion, what about the owner of a domesticated animal? The answer is, as is usually the case in law, that it depends. It depends on the history of the animal and also on the breed of the animal. A dog owner will be aware that a Pit Bull has a greater dangerous propensity, on the whole, than a Basset Hound. For the most part, a commonly domesticated dog or cat will not be considered to be unreasonably dangerous. As a result, the liability theory that attaches to domesticated animals is one of negligence rather than strict liability.

That changes, however, if an owner becomes aware of the dangerous propensity of the pet. Whimsically put, your dog gets one free bite. After that—once you are aware of the pet's dangerous propensity—strict liability applies.

Rules are also a bit different with respect to animals that trespass. The courts hold that owners of animals that trespass are strictly liable for the damages inflicted by the trespass. Furthermore, depending on state law, owners may be held strictly liable for damages incurred on public property. The following case sketches these issues.

> Whimsically put, your dog gets one free bite. After that—once you are aware of the pet's dangerous propensity—strict liability applies.

Vanderwater v. Hatch

United States Court of Appeals, Tenth Circuit, 1987 835 F.2d 239

Plaintiff, Dee Dee Vanderwater, brought this diversity action seeking damages for injuries she suffered in a collision between a motorcycle on which she was a passenger and a yearling cow owned by defendant, Roger Hatch. The collision occurred at approximately 10:00 p.m. on a stretch of rural highway in northern Utah, adjacent to a fenced pasture owned by Hatch in which he was then keeping approximately twenty-five yearling cattle. Beginning one-half to three-fourths of a mile west of the accident scene, the highway crosses a five-mile stretch of open range in which cattle are permitted to wander without restriction. *See* Utah Code Ann. § 41-6-38. Hatch kept about 120 cows on this open range, where there were also 400 to 500 cows belonging to other area ranchers. Hatch testified that most of his range cattle were cows with calves, but that he also kept a few yearlings on open range. Two witnesses travelling the opposite direction from plaintiff reported passing through a group of dark-colored cattle on the road seconds before the collision. One, Arthur DeSorcy, remembered seeing five or six cattle standing in the road. The other witness, Rennie DeSorcy, remembered seeing "ten to as many as 15" cattle, which he described as "half way between a calf and an adult cow as far as the size of them." II R. 124-25. The yearling cow involved in the accident was killed; there was no clear testimony concerning where the other cattle went or were taken following the accident.

Plaintiff argues that Utah Code Ann. § 41-6-38 violates the Equal Protection Clause of the Fourteenth Amendment to the United States Constitution because it imposes a greater burden of proof on her than Utah Code Ann. § 4-25-8 imposes on other plaintiffs similarly situated. Section 4-25-8 generally imposes strict liability on the owner of any livestock "that trespasses upon the premises of another person ... to the owner or occupant of such premises for any damage inflicted by the trespass." *Id.; see Nelson v. Tanner*, 113 Utah 293, 194 P.2d 468, 470 (1948) (interpreting former code section). Vanderwater construes such damage to include personal injuries. *See Restatement (Second) of Torts* § 504(2) (1977) (possessor of trespassing livestock is strictly liable for harm "to the land or to its possessor or a member of his household"). We conclude that plaintiff's equal protection challenge is without merit. Because the statutes in issue do not employ suspect classifications or implicate fundamental rights, they "must be upheld against equal protection attack [if] the legislative means are rationally related to a legitimate governmental purpose. Moreover, such legislation carries with it a presumption of rationality that can only be overcome by a clear showing of arbitrariness and irrationality." *Hodel v. Indiana*, 452 U.S. 314, 331-32 (1981). We cannot find it irrational for the Utah legislature to treat persons injured on public highways differently from those injured on their own lands. The legislature reasonably could have concluded that people's interest in the crops, fences, and even personal security on their own land is both greater and different in kind than travelers' interest in safety on the highway. We need not agree with the different burden of proof imposed by the statute in order to uphold its constitutionality; nor need we inquire further into the actual, subjective motivation of the Utah legislature. *See United States Railroad Retirement Board v. Fritz*, 449 U.S. 166, 179, 101 S.Ct. 453, 461 66 L.Ed.2d 368 (1980). The interests involved are sufficiently dissimilar to reasonably warrant the different degrees of protection provided by §§ 4-25-8 and 41-6-38.

----

2. Abnormally Dangerous Activities

Unless you take your dog to the office, have an office at home, or are in the pet business, pets may not be a major concern in the workplace. The theories of liability established with wild, domesticated and dangerous animals, however, apply to commercial issues. The application of these strict liability theories commercially tend to apply to products liability cases, where the absolute standard applies. More about this application will be reviewed in the chapter on product liability.

C. DEFENSES

When applied to product liability cases, there are some defenses a defendant can raise. It is, however, very difficult for the defendant to raise effective defenses in a strict liability case because the nature of the liability is that the defendant has introduced something to society that is unreasonably dangerous and, thus, is liable for any damages that result from that animal, practice, or thing.

III. Intentional Torts

NEGLIGENCE AND STRICT LIABILITY proceed on the basis that the tortfeasor—the person causing the injury—did not mean to injure the plaintiff, but either because the defendant was not careful (did not act as a reasonably prudent person) or because she introduced an unreasonably danger into society, they are held liable. Intentional torts are much more straightforward and can also trigger criminal charges.

With intentional torts, the defendant "meant" or intended to do a prohibited act. The duty and its breach are not analytically quite the same as they are in a negligence case. Causation and damages are the same, with punitive damages more likely in an intentional tort case.

In an intentional tort case, the first step is to define whether there is a prohibited act (analogous to the duty step in a negligence case) and then whether the defendant performed the prohibited act. Here are some examples of prohibited acts.

> With intentional torts, the defendant "meant" or intended to do a prohibited act.

- Unauthorized touching
- Reasonable apprehension that a battery is about to occur
- Interfering with another person's property
- Making false statements that damage another person in their work

- Harassing or otherwise verbally abusing another person
- Battery
- Assault
- Trespass
- Defamation
- Intentional infliction of emotional harm

Wishnatsky v. Huey

Court of Appeals of North Dakota, 1998 584 N.W.2d 859

On January 10, 1996, Huey, an assistant attorney general, was engaged in a conversation with attorney Peter B. Crary in Crary's office. Without knocking or announcing his entry, Wishnatsky, who performs paralegal work for Crary, attempted to enter the office. Huey pushed the door closed, thereby pushing Wishnatsky back into the hall. Wishnatsky reentered the office and Huey left.

Wishnatsky brought an action against Huey, seeking damages for battery. Huey moved for summary judgment of dismissal. The trial court granted Huey's motion and a judgment of dismissal was entered. Wishnatsky moved to alter the judgment. The trial court denied Wishnatsky's motion.

Wishnatsky appealed, contending the evidence he submitted in response to Huey's motion for summary judgment satisfies the elements of a battery claim and the trial court erred in granting Huey's motion. Wishnatsky also contends Huey is not entitled to prosecutorial or statutory immunity.

"In its original conception [battery] meant the infliction of physical injury." VIII Sir William Holdsworth, *A History of English Law* 422 (2d Impression 1973). By the Eighteenth Century, the requirement of an actual physical injury had been eliminated:

> At Nisi Prius, upon evidence in trespass for assault and battery, Holt, C.J. declared, 1. That the least touching of another in anger is a battery. 2. If two or more meet in a narrow passage, and without any violence or design of harm, the one touches the other gently, it is no battery. 3. If any of them use violence against the other, to force his way in a rude inordinate manner, it is a battery; or any struggle about the passage, to that degree as may do hurt, is a battery. ***

We certainly agree with the Supreme Court's determination that when Wishnatsky attempted to enter the room in which Huey was conversing with Crary, "Huey apparently reacted in a rude and abrupt manner in attempting to exclude Wishnatsky from that conversation." As a matter of law, however, Huey's "rude and abrupt" conduct did not rise to the level of battery.

To find battery, the plaintiff must prove that the act (1) was intentional, (2) caused contact with the plaintiff and (3) was harmful or offensive. Showing harm requires physical impairment, pain or illness. For an act to be offensive, the act would have to offend a reasonable sense of personal dignity.

A. ASSAULT

Acts intending to cause a harmful or offensive contact with the person or a third person, or an imminent apprehension of such a contact, and the other is thereby put in such imminent apprehension.

Spider-Man Arrested for Battery

www.loweringthebar.net/2010/05/spiderman-arrested-for-battery.html

MANY HAVE RIGHTLY PRAISED Spider-Man for foiling that comic-book-store robbery in Australia last week (with the aid of a few super-friends), but some still question whether his brand of vigilante justice is always a good thing.

The robbery story reminded me of one from last November, when Spider-Man was arrested in Los Angeles after allegedly hitting a man on Hollywood Boulevard. On that occasion, the masked crimefighter attempted to blend into the crowd after the assault. That's not as far-fetched as it sounds, given that Hollywood Boulevard is probably one of the few places in the world where somebody could blend in while wearing a Spider-Man outfit.

More specifically, police did not have trouble finding Spider-Man, but they did have trouble finding the right Spider-Man—when they arrived, they found at least four Spider-Men lurking among the crowd of costumed characters that works the boulevard hoping for tips from tourists. The second one they unmasked was the suspect.

> "A few years ago, the police had a 'super-hero' summit to try to reduce tensions."

Police said that the victim decided not to press charges, but Spider-Man was booked anyway because it turned out there were existing warrants out for his arrest. Bail for Spider-Man was set at $5,500.

According to the report, the crowd of celebrity/character impersonators normally gets along reasonably well, but tempers have flared from time to time. "A few years ago," the report said, "the police had a 'super-hero' summit to try to reduce tensions."

Picard v. Barry Pontiac-Buick, Inc.

Supreme Court of Rhode Island, 1995 654 A.2d 690

The plaintiff, Victorie A. Picard, brought her mother's car to Barry Pontiac-Buick, Inc. (Barry Pontiac), where the car had been purchased, to have the light repaired. The car failed an annual inspection because, according to a Barry Pontiac representative, the brakes needed to be replaced. The plaintiff brought the car to Kent's Alignment Service (Kent's Alignment), where the car passed inspection. The plaintiff then contacted a local television news "troubleshooter" reporter, presumably to report her experience at the two inspection sites.

The plaintiff returned to Barry Pontiac for a reinspection, bringing a camera with her. The plaintiff began to take a picture of the defendant while he was inspecting the breaks. After the camera snapped, the events that gave rise to this case occurred.

The plaintiff testified that defendant "lunged" at her and "grabbed [her] around around [sic] the shoulders," although plaintiff did not experience any pain. The plaintiff then testified on cross-examination that after defendant grabbed her by both her shoulders, she and defendant "spun around wrestling." According to plaintiff, defendant released her after someone said, "let her go." The plaintiff then left the garage with her goddaughter. The plaintiff brought action against the automobile mechanic for assault and battery. The Superior Court, Newport County, entered judgment for plaintiff, and the defendant appealed.

The Supreme Court held that: (1) customer established reasonable apprehension of injury necessary for prima facie case of assault; (2) mechanic's contact with customer's camera was sufficient to constitute battery.

Assault and battery are separate acts, usually arising from the same transaction, each having independent significance. "An assault is a physical act of a threatening nature or an offer of corporal injury which puts an individual in reasonable fear of imminent bodily harm." It is a plaintiff's apprehension of injury which renders a defendant's act compensable.

> "[t]he damages recoverable for [assault] are those for the plaintiff's mental disturbance, including fright, humiliation and the like, as well as any physical illness which may result from them"). This apprehension must be the type of fear normally aroused in the mind of a reasonable person.

The plaintiff testified that she was frightened by defendant's actions. A review of the attendant circumstances attests that such a reaction was reasonable. The defendant admitted approaching plaintiff, and the photograph taken that day clearly showed defendant pointing his finger at plaintiff as defendant approached her. Because plaintiff's apprehension of imminent bodily harm was reasonable at that point, plaintiff has established a prima facie case of assault.

B. TRESPASS

A defendant may be found guilty of trespass to land if they intentionally enter or remain (if entry was legal) or places an object (or refuses to remove an object on the plaintiff's land without permission.

Martin v. Reynolds Metals Co.

Supreme Court of Oregon, 1959 342 P.2d 790

The plaintiffs allege that during the period from August 22, 1951 to January 1, 1956 the defendant, in the operation of its aluminum reduction plant near Troutdale, Oregon caused certain fluoride compounds in the form of gases and particulates to become airborne and settle upon the plaintiffs' land rendering it unfit for raising livestock during that period. Plaintiffs allege that their cattle were poisoned by ingesting the fluorides which contaminate the forage and water on their land. They sought damages in the amount of $450,000 for the loss of use of their land for grazing purposes and for the deterioration of the land through the growth of brush, trees and weeds resulting from the lack of use of the premises for grazing purposes. The plaintiffs also sought punitive damages in the amount of $30,000.

The plaintiffs and the defendant each moved for a directed verdict, whereupon the trial court found that the plaintiffs had suffered damage in the amount of $71,500 in the loss of use of their land and $20,000 for the deterioration of their land and entered judgment accordingly. The trial court rejected the plaintiffs' claim for punitive damages.

In the course of the pleadings the defendant raised the issue as to whether the complaint alleged a cause of action in trespass. The defendant contended that at most a cause of action in nuisance was stated.

We must determine... whether all or only a part of this damage may be shown; all, if the invasion constitutes a trespass, a part only (i. e., the damage which resulted within the two-year period of the statute of limitations) if the invasion was a nuisance and not a trespass.

The gist of the defendant's argument is as follows: a trespass arises only when there has been a 'breaking and entering upon real property,' constituting a direct, as distinguished from a consequential, invasion of the possessor's interest in land; and the settling upon the land of fluoride compounds consisting of gases, fumes and particulates is not sufficient to satisfy these requirements.

Before appraising the argument we shall first describe more particularly the physical and chemical nature of the substance which was deposited upon plaintiffs' land. In reducing alumina (the oxide of aluminum) to aluminum the alumina is subjected to an electrolytic process which causes the emanation of fluoridic compounds consisting principally of hydrogen fluoride, calcium fluoride, iron fluoride and silicon tetrafluoride. The individual particulates which form these chemical compounds are not visible to the naked eye. A part of them were captured by a fume collection system which was installed in November, 1950; the remainder became airborne and a part of the uncaptured particles eventually were deposited upon plaintiffs' land.

Trespass and private nuisance are separate fields of tort liability relating to actionable interference with the possession of land. They may be distinguished by comparing the interest invaded; an actionable invasion of a possessor's interest in the exclusive possession of land is a trespass; an actionable invasion of a possessor's interest in the use and enjoyment of his land is a nuisance. 4 Restatement, Torts 224, Intro. Note Chapter 40.

However, there are cases which have held that the defendant's interference with plaintiff's possession resulting from the settling upon his land of effluents emanating from defendant's operations is exclusively nontrespassory... Although in such cases the separate particles which collectively cause the invasion are minute, the deposit of each of the particles constitutes a physical intrusion and, but for the size of the particle, would clearly give rise to an action of trespass. The defendant asks us to take account of the difference in size of the physical agency through which the intrusion occurs and relegate entirely to the field of nuisance law certain invasions which do not meet the dimensional test, whatever that is. In pressing this argument upon us the defendant must admit that there are cases which have held that a trespass results from the movement or deposit of rather small objects over or upon the surface of the possessor's land.

The view recognizing a trespassory invasion where there is no 'thing' which can be seen with the naked eye undoubtedly runs counter to the definition of trespass expressed in some quarters. 1 Restatement, Torts § 158, Comment h (1934); Prosser, Torts § 13 (2d Ed.1955). It is quite possible that in an earlier day when science had not yet peered into the molecular and atomic world of small particles, the courts could not fit an invasion through unseen physical instrumentalities into the requirement that a trespass can result only from a *direct* invasion. But in this atomic age even the uneducated know the great and awful force contained in the atom and what it can do to a man's property if it is released. In fact, the now famous equation $E=mc^2$ has taught us that mass and energy are equivalents and that our concept of 'things' must be reframed. If these observations on science in relation to the law of trespass should appear theoretical and unreal in the abstract, they become very practical and real to the possessor of land when the unseen force cracks the foundation of his house. The force is just as real if it is chemical in nature and must be awakened by the intervention of another agency before it does harm.

If, then, we must look to the character of the instrumentality which is used in making an intrusion upon another's land we prefer to emphasize the object's energy or force rather than its size. Viewed in this way we may define trespass as any intrusion which invades the possessor's protected interest in exclusive possession, whether that intrusion is by visible or invisible pieces of matter or by energy which can be measured only by the mathematical language of the physicist.

We are of the opinion, therefore, that the intrusion of the fluoride particulates in the present case constituted a trespass.

C. DEFAMATION

The law defines defamation as a published communication that tends to harm the reputation of another as to lower him in the estimation of the community or to deter third persons from associating or dealing with him. The standards for defamation differ for certain groups. For example, there is a general rule that you cannot defame the deceased. Public officials and celebrities have a very high standard to meet in order to prove defamation: they must show that there was actual knowledge of falsehood or a reckless disregard for falsehood. Lastly, large groups generally cannot be defamed, while it is possible for small groups to be defamed. Here are some examples to demonstrate how the rules of defamation differ.

Milkovich v. Lorain Journal Co.

Supreme Court of the United States, 1990 497 U.S 1

Respondent J. Theodore Diadiun authored an article in an Ohio newspaper implying that petitioner Michael Milkovich, a local high school wrestling coach, lied under oath in a judicial proceeding about an incident involving petitioner and his team which occurred at a wrestling match. Petitioner sued Diadiun and the newspaper for libel, and the Ohio Court of Appeals affirmed a lower court entry of summary judgment against petitioner. This judgment was based in part on the grounds that the article constituted an "opinion" protected from the reach of state defamation law by the First Amendment to the United States Constitution. The case was appealed to the Supreme Court.

Chief Justice Rehnquist, held that: (1) separate constitutional privilege for "opinion" was not required in addition to established safeguards regarding defamation to ensure freedom of expression guaranteed by First Amendment, and (2) reasonable fact finder could conclude that statements in reporter's column implied assertion that high school coach perjured himself in judicial proceeding, and implication that coach committed perjury was sufficiently factual to be susceptible of being proved true or false and might permit defamation recovery.

Defamation law developed not only as a means of allowing an individual to vindicate his good name, but also for the purpose of obtaining redress for harm caused by such statements. As the common law developed in this country, apart from the issue of damages, one usually needed only allege an unprivileged publication of false and defamatory matter to state a cause of action for defamation. The common law generally did not place any additional restrictions on the type of statement that could be actionable. Indeed, defamatory communications were deemed actionable regardless of whether they were deemed to be statements of fact or opinion. See, *e.g.,* Restatement of Torts, *supra,* §§ 565-567. As noted in the 1977 Restatement (Second) of Torts § 566, Comment a:

> "Under the law of defamation, an expression of opinion could be defamatory if the expression was sufficiently derogatory of another as to cause harm to his reputation, so as to lower him in the estimation of the community or to deter third persons from associating or dealing with him.... The expression of opinion was also actionable in a suit for defamation, despite the normal requirement that the communication be false as well as defamatory.... This position was maintained even though the truth or falsity of an opinion-as distinguished from a statement of fact- is not a matter that can be objectively determined and truth is a complete defense to a suit for defamation."

However, due to concerns that unduly burdensome defamation laws could stifle valuable public debate, the privilege of "fair comment" was incorporated into the common law as an affirmative defense to an action for defamation. "The principle of 'fair comment' afford[ed] legal immunity for the honest expression of opinion on matters of legitimate public interest when based upon a true or privileged statement of fact." 1 F. Harper & F. James, *Law of Torts* § 5.28, p. 456 (1956) (*footnote omitted*). As this statement implies, comment was generally privileged when it concerned a matter of public concern, was based upon true or privileged facts, represented the actual opinion of the speaker, and was not made solely for the purpose of causing harm. See Restatement of Torts, *supra,* § 606. "According to the majority rule, the privilege of fair comment applied only to an expression of opinion and not to a false statement of fact, whether it was expressly stated or implied from an expression of opinion." Restatement (Second) of Torts, *supra,* § 566, Comment *a*. Thus under the common law, the privilege of "fair comment" was the device employed to strike the appropriate balance between the need for vigorous public discourse and the need to redress injury to citizens wrought by invidious or irresponsible speech.

"COMMENT WAS GENERALLY privileged when it concerned a matter of public concern, was based upon true or privileged facts, represented the actual opinion of the speaker, and was not made solely for the purpose of causing harm."

...The next step in this constitutional evolution was the Court's consideration of a private individual's defamation actions involving statements of public concern. Although the issue was initially in doubt, see *Rosenbloom v.Metromedia, Inc.,* 403 U.S. 29, 91 S.Ct. 1811, 29 L.Ed.2d 296 (1971), the Court ultimately concluded that the

New York Times malice standard was inappropriate for a private person attempting to prove he was defamed on matters of public interest. *Gertz v. Robert Welch, Inc., supra.* As we explained:

> "Public officials and public figures usually enjoy significantly greater access to the channels of effective communication and hence have a more realistic opportunity to counteract false statements than private individuals normally enjoy. . . . . ."[More important,] public officials and public figures have voluntarily exposed themselves to increased risk of injury from defamatory falsehood concerning them. No such assumption is justified with respect to a private individual." *Id.* 418 U.S., at 344-345, 94 S.Ct., at 3009...

Next, the *Bresler-Letter Carriers-Falwell* line of cases provides protection for statements that cannot "reasonably [be] interpreted as stating actual facts" about an individual. *Falwell*, 485 U.S., at 50, 108 S.Ct., at 879. This provides assurance that public debate will not suffer for lack of "imaginative expression" or the "rhetorical hyperbole" which has traditionally added much to the discourse of our Nation. See *id.*, at 53-55, 108 S.Ct., at 880-882.

We are not persuaded that, in addition to these protections, an additional separate constitutional privilege for "opinion" is required to ensure the freedom of expression guaranteed by the First Amendment. The dispositive question in the present case then becomes whether a reasonable factfinder could conclude that the statements in the Diadiun column imply an assertion that petitioner Milkovich perjured himself in a judicial proceeding. We think this question must be answered in the affirmative. As the Ohio Supreme Court itself observed: "[T]he clear impact in some nine sentences and a caption is that [Milkovich] 'lied at the hearing after ... having given his solemn oath to tell the truth.' " *Scott*, 25 Ohio St.3d, at 251, 496 N.E.2d, at 707. This is not the sort of loose, figurative, or hyperbolic language which would negate the impression that the writer was seriously maintaining that petitioner committed the crime of perjury. Nor does the general tenor of the article negate this impression.

D. INTENTIONAL INFLICTION OF EMOTIONAL DISTRESS (IIED)

IIED occurs when one intentionally or recklessly causes severe emotional damage to another through extreme and outrageous conduct. The standards for IIED are extremely difficult to meet and must be outrageous and extreme in order to qualify as an IIED.

ARTICLE: IIED

Man Claims Emotional Distress Due to Bird Insults
www.loweringthebar.net; January 16, 2011

THE AFP REPORTS that a Taiwanese man has sued his neighbors claiming that they trained their mynah bird to swear at him and that the bird's relentless taunting caused him serious emotional distress.

Few details were available, but it appeared that Wang Han-chin had previously complained to police that his neighbors were too loud, and he alleged that in revenge they had trained their bird to call him a "clueless big-mouthed idiot" when he left for work in the morning. Wang claimed that the bird's insults caused him serious distress, and had affected his concentration at work to the point that he had somehow burned himself. Prosecutors apparently declined to charge the neighbors with anything "due to insufficient evidence linking the bird to his injuries," and that seems to have led to a civil lawsuit.

In a similar case in 2006, which also shows that my database of "similar cases" is getting pretty comprehensive, a 78-year-old Pennsylvania woman charged one of her neighbors with repeatedly meowing at her in retaliation for complaining to police about their cat's infiltration of her flower garden. Alexandra Carasia also claimed the conduct had caused her emotional harm, and even used the word "torture" to describe her experience, completing the final degradation of that word from something that once meant "heinous war crime" into a term that can also encompass repeated meowing.

That case was also similar in that the charges were quickly dismissed.

As with all torts (including products liability, which is a combination of torts and contracts), there may be multiple charges for a particular incident. For example, suppose two drivers got into a road rage altercation, which resulted in one of them crashing his car into the other's. Then the two drivers got out, exchanged words and started to fight. There could be trespass, battery, assault, and perhaps even emotional harm charges from this one incident. Running a car into someone else intentionally is not only an intentional tort; it is also negligent operation of an automobile. In an actual lawsuit, the injured party (and that could be both parties in the scenario above), would sue the other side on alleged multiple theories or reasons why the other party should be held liable. Thus, one does not have to choose theories; one can take a shotgun approach. In the following chapter on products liability, we will also see another use of the shotgun approach in suing as many different people as possible.

E. DEFENSES

Defenses to intentional torts typically revolve around some notion of consent or self-defense. If the plaintiff consented to the intentional tort, either expressly or through her actions, then the defendant may raise that consent as a defense to a suit by the plaintiff against the defendant. To take an obvious example, if the plaintiff and defendant engage in a sport with physical contact involved—football, boxing, wrestling, etc.—then one of them cannot claim that the other committed a battery. It is part of the sport to touch the other party. Indeed, in such cases, one could further ask whether a batter struck by a pitch is at all in issue since it requires an unauthorized touching. In a football game, touching would be in a sense, authorized. One could imagine a possibility in which prior to a karate match, one of the soon-to-be participants hit the other. That could be a battery even though, a few minutes later, it might be consented to within the context of the actual match. Thus, the timing of the consent becomes important.

To stay with the battery example, the more serious cases concern issues of sexual assault. What may begin as a consensual act could turn into a non-consensual one; at the point it becomes non-consensual the act could then become a battery.

Self-defense constitutes another defense. A person has a right to defend themselves against another's attack. One's right to self-defense consists of using the amount of force necessary to repel the attack, thus significantly limiting a right to increase the amount of force. For example, if someone were to attack you with their fists, that is not likely to justify you pulling out a shotgun and shooting them. You could use your own fists and, if the other person was bigger or a more skilled fighter, you might be able to add a baseball bat to fend off the attack. But the more one adds weapons with fatal potential, the more risk one undertakes of losing the justification of self-defense.

The same rules apply to a third party who is under attack. As long as that person has a right to his own self-defense, an intervening third party can use the same reasonable measure on behalf of that person to repel the attack.

It is worth noting, in these rules, that the use of a watchdog or a spring-loaded gun bring significant risk to the person under attack. This becomes an even bigger issue in terms of defending one's property. The law nearly always sides with protection of the person or the protection of property, and so the range of defense one uses to protect property is much narrower.

NOTES AND COMMENTS

I. TORT LAW ALWAYS RAISES QUESTIONS ABOUT RESPONSIBILITY. Going back to the opening of this chapter, why does a landowner have any liability for a group of drunken students crossing his land? What about their responsibility? Often a property owner or a business does have a capability to prevent harm from happening. Whether that is considered fair by all parties or not, it is the way the law works in the United States and so businesses must manage their affairs with the specter of liability in mind.

In this chapter, the plight of the "eggshell plaintiff" was noted. A person committing a tort does not need to desire for his actions—say an unauthorized touching (a batter) as gentle as touching a shoulder—to cause tremendous damage to a victim. But if the victim is fragile, the tortfeasor does "take the plaintiff as he finds him." Is this a reasonable state of affairs? Is there a better rule of law to handle such cases? If so, what would it look like?

2. SHOULD A PERSON be able to use deadly force to protect property? What would be the pros and cons of that proposition?

PRODUCTS LIABILITY

PRODUCTS LIABILITY is a relatively modern invention. Legal commentator David

Brody has contrasted the historic adage, *caveat emptor* (buyer beware), with one

more aligned with a commercial age governed in part by products liability laws:

caveat venditor (seller beware). While historically, the buyer was to be aware, today
the seller needs to be. To be sure, products caused harms in the past, but the explosion of products liability cases arose from the Industrial Revolution and the
resulting increase in the variety and number of products, often from
mass production, that were sold to the public. Whether cars.
augurs, toasters, or hair driers, products sometimes don't
work the way they are supposed to. Sometimes, their
malfunctions cause injuries to others and lawsuits
get filed to obtain damages for those injuries. What
kinds of cases are these? Through the ingenuity
of litigating attorneys and the flexibility of the
common law court system, cases draw from
both torts and contracts theories of liability.

I. General Concepts and Classifications of Products Liability

PERHAPS THE KEY STEP in unleashing these kinds of cases was through the minimization of the obstacle called privity of contract. That legal rule allowed an injured plaintiff to sue a seller who had sold a defective product to him through tort or contract, but not other suppliers and manufacturers who had supplied component parts of manufactured items that the seller relied on to place the product into the market. Prior to the Industrial Revolution and the mass production of products, privity of contract made sense because transactions were far more one-to-one exchanges. Sellers

were much more likely to also be the manufacturer. But the complexity of contemporary manufacturing turns sellers into mere retailers who take a product made by someone else and then sell it to the customer. While the retailer is the seller, it is the parties making the product who construct it in ways that could be defective.

Cases chipped away at the privity doctrine, culminating in the 1916 landmark case, *MacPherson v. Buick Motor Co.* (217 N.Y. 382). In that case, one of the wheels of the vehicle was made of defective wood and while Mr. MacPhearson was operating the vehicle, one of the spokes crumbled, resulting in an accident. The famous judge, Benjamin Cardozo, writing before he became a Justice of the U.S. Supreme Court, wrote:

> If the nature of a thing is such that it is reasonably certain to place life and limb in peril when negligently made, it is then a thing of danger. Its nature gives warning of the consequences to be expected. If to the element of danger there is added knowledge that the thing will be used by persons other than the purchaser and used with now tests, then, irrespective of contra, the manufacturer of this thing of danger is under a duty to make it carefully. MacPherson, 217 N.Y. 382, 389 (1916)

Indeed, one thing to keep in mind is that there may be four or five theories of liability, drawing from both torts and contracts, that a plaintiff may use in a lawsuit. The plaintiff does not have to pick just one theory; he can use a shotgun approach and allege multiple reasons for liability.

Similarly, because manufacturing often entails a variety of companies from suppliers to designers to component manufacturers to final manufacturers to retailers, there could be multiple potential defendants in the chain of production and sale. One often sues them all, so in case one can get out of liability, several remain who could still be successfully sued.

It is even possible that if one does not know who caused an injury, one can sue them anyway. For instance, if a person takes a drug and dies or is harmed by the drug, it may be medically ascertained that a certain combination of chemicals caused the harm, but it may not be possible to prove which company produced the specific product that the consumer/plaintiff ingested. In such cases, a concept called "enterprise liability theory" could be used to sue all the manufacturers of the competing products, with damage awards divided according the market share in the geographical area at the time the product was used.

For these reasons, as well as due to fear that both punitive and compensatory damages might be awarded after a long, expensive trial, potential defendants are often motivated to settle cases. In some ways, this further incents lawsuits, because then an individual with a marginal case may sue simply in hopes of getting a significant settlement without having to go through the process of a trial.

Two other concepts also make products liability controversial generally and unpopular with businesspeople. One of those concerns the economics of lawsuits. Most product liability (and tort) litigation is driven with very little or no cost, except for the time invested, to the plaintiff. Lawyers accept these kinds of cases on a "contingent fee" arrangement. These call for the plaintiff/victim to forward no money to the lawyer, nor to pay the lawyer anything unless the lawyer obtains a settlement or trial verdict from the defendant. Lawyers may have a base contingent fee of 33.3% if they settle the case prior to trial. The fee may increase depending on whether the case goes to trial or to appeal, or it may be higher simply because of the complexity of the case. It is common for the contingent fee to go up to 40-45% for complex cases, such as products liability cases. To determine the enforceability of contingency fees set by lawyers, the American Bar Association set out its Model Rules of Professional Conduct, which exempt contingent fees for domestic dispute cases whose outcome is dependent upon securing a divorce, alimony, or support settlement and for criminal defense cases. Furthermore, applicable contingent fees must be considered reasonable. In *Venegas v. Mitchell*, a U.S. Supreme Court case decided in 1990, an attorney representing the plaintiff in a civil rights case sued his client for recovery of contingent fees.[1] In civil rights cases, the losing party is statutorily obligated to pay for the other side's attorney's costs and in this case, the court-calculated attorneys' costs amounted to $75,000. In the suit, the attorney claimed his client owed him an additional amount due to the agreed upon 40% contingent fee. The Supreme Court held that a statutory award of attorney's fees did not release a client from paying his attorney an additional contingent fee and that the 40% fee was reasonable. The attorney was eventually rewarded $406,000.

Another of these concerns relates to the size of compensatory damage awards. Indeed, there has been ongoing political debate for a number of years now calling for caps on damage awards, some of which have been adopted. In 2005, President George W. Bush proposed a nationwide cap of $250,000 on damage awards for medical malpractice suits. Since then, over half of the states have passed legislation

---

1   *Venegas v. Mitchell*, 495 U.S. 82 (1990).

limiting damages for malpractice suits. The caps range from $250,000 to $650,000. Some states have also passed legislation limiting compensatory damages for products liability cases. In Michigan, for example, the compensatory damages for products liability cases cannot exceed $500,000. In other states, such as California, proposed legislation to cap compensatory damages has been struck down.

Figure 2. Tort costs relative to GDP
(in billions)

Year	U.S. tort costs	U.S. GDP	Tort costs as % of GDP
1950	$ 1.8	$ 294	0.62%
1960	5.4	526	1.03
1970	13.9	1,038	1.34
1980	42.7	2,788	1.53
1990	130.2	5,801	2.24
2000	179.1	9,952	1.80
2003	245.7	11,142	2.21
2004	260.3	11,853	2.20
2005	261.4	12,623	2.07
2006	246.9	13,377	1.85
2007	252.0	14,029	1.80
2008	254.9	14,292	1.78
2009	251.8	13,939	1.81
2010	264.6	14,527	1.82

*Throughout this report, unadjusted, or nominal, GDP is used.
Most news releases on GDP rely on inflation-adjusted, or real, GDP.

As we saw in the chapter on torts, compensation for pain and suffering can add up to large damage awards. In North Carolina, the Kanahwa County jury awarded $11.5 million in compensatory damages to a family for the death of their mother, who was found severely dehydrated as the result of the negligence of a nursing home.

The even bigger issue, though, is punitive damages. The case of an elderly woman (initially successfully) suing McDonalds for over $1 million because coffee burned her legs after she placed the cup there after going through the fast food restaurant's drive-through has become popular culture folklore. The fact that damages were later reduced has been buried in the news and urban legend. Instead, what remains "known" is the (not necessarily misleading) perception that companies can be hit with huge punitive damage awards that appear to be far beyond the gravity of the injury in question.

"A FINE LIMITED to compensatory damages could well be swallowed as a cost of doing business by a huge multinational company. But the punitive damage weapon creates a different risk calculation. Punitive damages can change the ways companies manufacture and sell products."

Why would this be? If you remember the philosophy underlying punitive damages, it is that there needs to be a punishment significant enough so that the tortfeasor/defendant will wake up and change its ways. A fine limited to compensatory damages could well be swallowed as a cost of doing business by a huge multinational company. But the punitive damage weapon creates a different risk calculation. Punitive damages can change the ways companies manufacture and sell products. Thus, from a public policy standpoint, one rationale for punitive damages is that it provides incentives for the manufacture and sale of safer products.

Also part of the debate over the product liability system is the question of who should receive punitive damages. In most states, the current structure of the damage award system calls for the plaintiff to receive damage awards. With the exception of controversy over the amount of pain and suffering awards, this principle tends to be accepted by all parties to the debate. Once the party has been compensated for damages suffered, however, the debate kicks in as to whether the victim should also receive punitive damages. After all, punitive damages do not compensate the victim; punitive damages are awarded to punish the defendant for egregious conduct and to make an example of the defendant so others do not behave the same way in the future. Thus, why would the victim receive punitive damages? Why wouldn't the punitive portion of the damages go elsewhere?

And this is where the debate really becomes contentious and unsettled. According to the laws of some states, the state itself is entitled to a certain percentage of the punitive damages awarded. Such states include Colorado, Florida, Alaska, Oregon, Indiana, New York, Utah, Iowa, Georgia and Missouri. (http://www.atra. org/issues/punitive-damages-reform). The percentages range from 20% to 100%. The state of Illinois has taken another approach by giving the court discretion to allocate punitive awards to either the prevailing party, the plaintiff's attorney, or the state. The development of these laws is based upon the idea that punitive damages reflect an interest of the state to deter future misconduct rather than an interest in compensating the victim—that's what compensatory damages are for. Plaintiff attorneys, a strong lobbying force whose fees are contingent on the overall size of the awards, contend that they need incentives for plaintiffs to be willing to move forward on cases. The other side, comprised of business lobbyists and defense attorneys, raise constitutional issues. They claim that punitive damages are often so large and arbitrary that they violate the Due Process clause of the Fourteenth Amendment. They also argue that the current system amounts to a lottery and that the punitive damages component adds a significant cost of doing business to the companies, which in turn will either reduce shareholder profit or raise consumer prices as their costs are passed along into the marketplace. If, they argue, products need to be made safer, that should be done through the regulatory process rather than through the less predictable current system.

Having said all this, there have been laws passed in over half the states that do limit punitive damages. Some states tie compensatory damages together with punitive damages so that punitive damages cannot exceed a certain ratio to the compensatory element. For example, in Wisconsin, punitive damages cannot exceed twice the amount of compensatory damages or $200,000.00, whichever is greater. In New Jersey, punitive damages are capped at five times the compensatory damages or $350,000, whichever is greater. Another strategy is to have separate trials on damages so that the sympathies engendered by the determination of liability do not spill over into the computations of punitive damage awards. On a federal level, some defense attorneys employ Federal Rule of Civil Procedure 42(b) to bifurcate punitive damages issues, while some states have made this option available through state law. For example, in Texas, a defendant may move to have punitive damages determined in a separate trial from compensatory damages. However, in the interest of judicial efficiency, the court retains the discretion to determine whether a bifurcated trial is warranted. In Missouri, on the other hand, the right to a bifurcated trial concerning punitive damages is guaranteed by state law if requested by one of the parties. Other ways to limit punitive damages have included mandating a higher burden of proof from the plaintiff in justifying the amount of the punitive damage award. For example, in Ohio, a claim for punitive damages in a products liability case requires an elevated standard of "clear and convincing evidence" which is not required by common law.

As you can see, products liability raises many questions that are debated in public policy circles today. It is also worth recognizing that while each of the above argu-

ments are made today in public policy debates and reflected in the variety of state law concerning damage awards, they are also frequently presented in ethical terms. The arguments center around personal responsibility issues. What responsibilities do plaintiffs have for their own safety? A classic example comes from the manufacture and sale of ladders. Because plaintiffs frequently misuse ladders by standing too far up on the top of a ladder or reaching beyond where one can safely reach, ladder manufacturers attempt to make the product safer by placing warning labels on the product. If one purchases a ladder at a hardware store, you will see multiple warning labels exactly because companies fear being sued by a careless plaintiff.

While courts do allow for the consideration of many kinds of lawsuits, there are times when the personal responsibility of the victim is so obvious that courts will throw out the case. The following example demonstrates this point.

Wyda v. Makita Elec. Works, Ltd.

New York Supreme Court, Appellate Division, 1996
232 A.D.2d 407

A worker who was injured while using a saw brought action to recover for personal injuries based on negligence and strict products liability against the saw manufacturer. It is undisputed that when the accident occurred the plaintiff's employer, the third-party defendant, had wedged the saw's moveable blade guard open by placing a piece of wood between the guard and the body of the saw, removing the safety feature on the saw blade. The safety feature was designed to be a permanent fixture on the saw and was not designed to be removed. The Supreme Court, Westchester County, denied manufacturer's motion for summary judgment. Manufacturer appealed.

The Supreme Court, Appellate Division, held that removal of safety feature on saw blade by the worker's employer was substantial material alteration to saw, such that the worker could not maintain action against manufacturer. A manufacturer may not be cast in damages, either on a strict products liability or negligence cause of action, where, after the product leaves the possession and control of the manufacturer, there is a subsequent modification which "substantially alters the product and is the proximate cause of the plaintiff's injuries" Material alterations at the hand of a third party which work a substantial change in the condition in which the product was sold "by destroying the functional utility of a key safety feature, however foreseeable that modification may have been, are not within the ambit of a manufacturer's responsibility."

ANOTHER DIMENSION of personal responsibility goes to the issue of filing frivolous lawsuits, as we saw in the chapter on torts. Legislatures and courts have acted on this by creating penalties for plaintiffs who have no legitimate case, but who file suit either to harass another party or in hopes of getting an easy settlement.

In addition to themes centering on the personal responsibility of plaintiffs, there are also ethical arguments directed toward their attorneys, the so-called "ambulance chasers." Do plaintiffs want to sue, or is it their lawyers who convince them to sue? It is probably a bit of both, but there is little doubt that there is a sizeable group of attorneys whose career is based on this kind of litigation. Without nefarious motives, lawyers educate their clients on their legal options, and the lawsuits described in this chapter are, indeed, legal options. Thus, the ethical issue can be joined according to how different parties "see" what happens between lawyer and client: unethical manipulation or client education.

The responsibility of manufacturers is also, clearly, very much in play. The claim of all product liability cases is that the company not only caused damages, but did something wrong. They were negligent. They are strictly liability because they introduced something unreasonably dangerous into society. They breached a contractual promise. Thus there is always a dimension of wrongdoing being alleged and, if that is true, then logically, the wrongdoer should have liability.

Without exhausting the possible ethical issues, a final one for this discussion is one based on utilitarianism. What legal system of product liability creates the greatest good for the greatest number? All sides to this debate argue that their approach meets this standard.

II. Contractual Theories of Product Liability

IN TORT LAW, there often is no preexisting relationship between the plaintiff and the defendant. The plaintiff drives a car and is hit by the car driven by the defendant. The defendant's dog bites the plaintiff. A trespassing child drowns while swimming in the pool of someone in the child's subdivision who has never met the child's family. In all these cases, there was no contract between the parties. But in products liability cases, there is. The nature of that contractual relationship is important because, as noted in the beginning of this chapter, liability is clearer if there is "privity of contract." That is, the two parties directly contracting with each other—a retailer and consumer—generate clearer liability than the parties who made the product the retailer sold. But even in such cases, courts may find enough contractual relationship between the parties so that warranty theories could create liability. While there are four kinds of warranties used in product liability cases, this is particularly important.

In proving that a warranty theory applies, the plaintiff needs to prove that a warranty existed; show that the warranty was breached; demonstrate that the breach was the proximate cause of the plaintiff's injury; and prove that notice of the breach was given to the seller. In some cases, the seller/manufacturer must also give notice of a breach of the warranty to buyer(s), as in the case of a product recall or another announcement or warning of a potential product defect.

A. EXPRESS WARRANTY

Express warranties result when there is a statement or portrayal of a particular capability of the product. It could be in the form of an affirmation of a fact or promise or a description of the goods: "This drilling rig will pump up to one million barrels of oil a day," or "this copying machine will make thirty copies a minute." With statements like these, a warranty attaches pursuant to the Uniform Commercial Code, Section 2-313, which more specifically states:

(1) Express warranties by the seller are created as follows:

> (a) Any affirmation of fact or promise made by the seller to the buyer which relates to the goods and becomes part of the basis of the bargain

creates an express warranty that the goods shall conform to the affirmation or promise.

(b) Any description of the goods which is made part of the basis of the bargain creates an express warranty that the goods shall conform to the description.

(c) Any sample or model which is made part of the basis of the bargain creates an express warranty that the whole of the goods shall conform to the sample or model.

(2) It is not necessary to the creation of an express warranty that the seller use formal words such as "warrant" or "guarantee" or that he have a specific intention to make a warranty, but an affirmation merely of the value of the goods or a statement purporting to be merely the seller's opinion or commendation of the goods does not create a warranty.

A WARRANTY NEEDS TO BE A BASIS OF THE BARGAIN BETWEEN THE BUYER AND THE SELLER.

As the UCC provision indicates, the expression need not be in words. It can be in other forms, such as a portrayal or by providing a sample. The warranty needs to be a basis of the bargain between the buyer and the seller. The following case demonstrates the application of this kind of express warranty.

Bayliner Marine Corp. v. Crow

Supreme Court of Virginia, 1999
509 S.E.2d 499

In the summer of 1989, John R. Crow was invited by John Atherton, then a sales representative for Tidewater Yacht Agency, Inc. (Tidewater), to ride on a new model sport fishing boat known as a 3486 Trophy Convertible, manufactured by Bayliner Marine Corporation (Bayliner). During an excursion lasting about 20 minutes, Crow piloted the boat for a short period of time but was not able to determine its speed because there was no equipment on board for such testing.

When Crow asked Atherton about the maximum speed of the boat, Atherton explained that he had no personal experience with the boat or information from other customers concerning the boat's performance. Therefore, Atherton consulted two documents described as "prop matrixes," which were included by Bayliner in its dealer's manual. Atherton gave Crow copies of the "prop matrixes," which listed the boat models offered by Bayliner and stated the recommended propeller sizes, gear ratios, and engine sizes for each model. The "prop matrixes" also listed the maximum speed for each model. The 3486 Trophy Convertible was listed as having a maximum speed of 30 miles per hour when equipped with a size "20x20" or "2019" propeller. The boat Crow purchased did not have either size propeller but, instead, had a size "20x17" propeller.

At the bottom of one of the "prop matrixes" was the following disclaimer: "This data is intended for comparative purposes only, and is available without reference to weather conditions or other variables. All testing was done at or near sea level, with full fuel and water tanks, and approximately 600 lb. passenger and gear weight." Atherton also showed Crow a Bayliner brochure describing the 1989 boat models, including the 3486 Trophy Convertible. The brochure included a picture of that model fully rigged for offshore fishing, accompanied by the statement that this model "delivers the kind of performance you need to get to the prime offshore fishing grounds." In August 1989, Crow entered into a written contract for the purchase of the 3486 Trophy Convertible in which he had ridden. The purchase price was $120,000, exclusive of taxes. Crow did not test drive the boat after the additional equipment was installed or at any other time prior to taking delivery.

When Crow took delivery of the boat in September 1989, he piloted it onto the Elizabeth River. He noticed that the boat's speed measuring equipment, which was installed in accordance with the contract terms, indicated that the boat's maximum speed was 13 miles per hour. Crow immediately returned to Tidewater and reported the problem.

During the next 12 to 14 months, while Crow retained ownership and possession of the boat, Tidewater made numerous repairs and adjustments to the boat in an attempt to increase its speed capability. Despite these efforts, the boat consistently achieved a maximum speed of only 17 miles per hour... In July 1990, a representative from Bayliner wrote Crow a letter stating that the performance representations made at the time of purchase were incorrect, and that 23 to 25 miles per hour was the maximum speed the boat could achieve.

In 1992, Crow filed a motion for judgment against Tidewater, Bayliner, and Brunswick Corporation, the manufacturer of the boat's diesel engines. Crow alleged, among other things, that Bayliner breached express warranties, and implied warranties of merchantability and fitness for a particular purpose.

At a bench trial in 1994, Crow, Atherton, and Gordon W. Shelton, III, Tidewater's owner, testified that speed is a critical quality in boats used for offshore sport fishing in the Tidewater area of Virginia because of the distance between the coast and the offshore fishing grounds. According to these witnesses, a typical offshore fishing site in that area is 90 miles from the coast. Therefore, the speed at which the boat can travel to and from fishing sites has a major impact on the amount of time left in a day for fishing. Crow testified that because of the boat's slow speed, he could not use the boat for offshore fishing, that he had no other use for it, and that he would not have purchased the boat if he had known that its maximum speed was 23 to 25 miles per hour.

The trial court entered judgment in favor of Crow against Bayliner on the counts of breach of express warranty and breach of implied warranties of merchantability and fitness for a particular purpose. The court awarded Crow damages of $135,000, plus prejudgment interest from June 1993. The court explained that the $135,000 award represented the purchase price of the boat, and about $15,000 in "damages" for a portion of the expenses Crow claimed in storing, maintaining, insuring, and financing the boat.

On appeal, we review the evidence in the light most favorable to Crow, the prevailing party at trial. We will uphold the trial court's judgment unless it is plainly wrong or without evidence to support it.

Crow argues that the "prop matrixes" he received created an express warranty by Bayliner that the boat he purchased was capable of a maximum speed of 30 miles per hour. We disagree.

Code§ 8.2-313 provides, in relevant part: Express warranties by the seller are created as follows:

> (a) Any affirmation of fact or promise made by the seller to the buyer which relates to the goods and becomes part of the basis of the bargain creates an express warranty that the goods shall conform to the affirmation or promise.

> (b) Any description of the goods which is made a part of the basis of the bargain creates an express warranty that the goods shall conform to the description.

The issue whether a particular affirmation of fact made by the seller constitutes an express warranty is generally a question of fact. In *Daughtrey*, we examined whether a jeweler's statement on an appraisal form constituted an express warranty. We held that the jeweler's description of the particular diamonds being purchased as "v.v.s. quality" constituted an express warranty that the diamonds were, in fact, of that grade.

Unlike the representation in *Daughtrey*, however, the statements in the "prop matrixes" provided by Bayliner did not relate to the particular boat purchased by Crow, or to one having substantially similar characteristics. By their plain terms, the figures stated in the "prop matrixes" referred to a boat with different sized propellers that carried equipment weighing substantially less than the equipment on Crow's boat. Therefore, we conclude that the statements contained in the "prop matrixes" did not constitute an express warranty by Bayliner about the performance capabilities of the particular boat purchased by Crow. Crow also contends that Bayliner made an express warranty regarding the boat's maximum speed in the statement in Bayliner's sales brochure that this model boat "delivers the kind of performance you need to get to the prime offshore fishing grounds." While the general rule is that a description of the goods that forms a basis of the bargain constitutes an express warranty, Code§ 8.2-313(2) directs that "a statement purporting to be merely the seller's opinion or commendation of the goods does not create a warranty."

The statement made by Bayliner in its sales brochure is merely a commendation of the boat's performance and does not describe a specific characteristic or feature of the boat. The statement simply expressed the manufacturer's opinion concerning the quality of the boat's performance and did not create an express warranty that the boat was capable of attaining a speed of 30 miles per hour. Therefore, we conclude that the evidence does not support the trial court's finding that Bayliner breached an express warranty made to Crow...

... For these reasons, we will reverse the trial court's judgment and enter final judgment in favor of Bayliner.

WITH EXPRESS WARRANTIES, it is virtually impossible to disclaim them. After all, the idea of an express warranty is that the seller is trying to convince a buyer to purchase the product on the basis of the expression of the product's capability. One cannot promise the product to do something and then disclaim any responsibility if it doesn't deliver on what was promised.

From a business standpoint, express warranties can be a point of tension between the marketing department and the General Counsel's Office. Marketers have a strong interest in advertising the product as attractively as possible, whereas the legal office is interested in limiting potential risk.

Express warranties are different from what is known as "puffing." If a company says its product is the greatest thing in the world, the statement does not amount to an express warranty. Such a statement is merely "puffing." Or sometimes, an advertisement may suggest that if a customer uses its product, amazing and wonderful things would happen. Particularly in the 1980s and 1990s, there were beer advertisements that showed someone—always a male—drinking a can of Coors beer and suddenly, something called the Coors Bikini Team (very attractive women attired only in bikinis) appeared. Does this become an express warranty? Are there grounds for a lawsuit if a beer drinker opens a can of Coors and, disappointingly for the drinker, the Bikini Team does not materialize while he guzzles a Coors on his living room sofa? Obviously not; this advertisement is mere puffing.

The following case provides a more serious discussion of the parameters of express warranties.

Royal Indemnity Co. v. Tyco Fire Products, LP

Supreme Court of Virginia, 2011
704 S.E.2d 91

This case arose out of a fire that started on the exterior balcony of an apartment building on February 8, 2003. Two exterior sidewall sprinkler heads installed on two separate balconies where the fire originated failed to activate, which allowed the fire to spread to other parts of the building and adjoining buildings causing substantial damage.

Royal Indemnity Company and American Empire Surplus Lines Insurance Company (together, Royal) filed an amended motion for judgment in the amount of $10,317,083.78 against Tyco Fire Products (Tyco) and SimplexGrinnell, LP (Simplex) alleging that the sprinkler heads, which were manufactured by Tyco and installed by Simplex prior to June 1997, failed to properly activate causing substantial damage to the apartment complex. Royal asserted various negligence-based causes of action against both Tyco and Simplex, including negligent design and manufacture of the sprinkler heads, and post-sale duty to warn. Royal also asserted warranty claims against both defendants, claiming that the defendants breached an alleged warranty of future performance.

In its complaint, Royal alleged that the sprinkler heads failed to operate properly. Specifically, Royal asserted that "[s]cientific inspection of the pressure tested sprinkler heads ... determined that corrosion existed at the interface between the brass plug and O-ring assembly and inlet which ... prevented the inlet plugs from disengaging and operating as intended upon the breaking of the frangible bulbs."

Tyco and Simplex filed pleas in bar asserting that the negligence-based causes of action were barred by the statute of repose, Code§ 8.01–250. After an *ore tenus* hearing and receipt of stipulated evidence, the circuit court granted the defendants' pleas in bar ruling that the sprinkler heads were ordinary building materials under the statute of repose.

The defendants also filed pleas in bar arguing that Royal's warranty claims were barred by the statute of limitations. After a hearing, the circuit court sustained the pleas in bar ruling the warranty claims were barred by the applicable statutes of limitations. We awarded Royal this appeal.

In this product liability case, we address issues concerning the statute of repose and breach of warranty. We conclude that exterior sidewall sprinkler heads are "equipment" under Code § 8.01–250 and reverse the judgment of the circuit court that the sprinkler heads are ordinary building materials. We also hold that a manufacturer's description of how a sprinkler head functions does not constitute an express warranty of future performance...

Regarding Tyco's plea in bar, the circuit court ruled that the breach of warranty claims concerning the sprinkler heads were barred by the four-year statute of limitations per Code§ 8.2–725, which applies to contracts for the sale of goods.

In making this ruling, the circuit court rejected Royal's contention that the "technical data sheet," which is the accompanying literature to the sprinkler heads, contained an express warranty of future performance. Royal argues that the circuit court erred in ruling that the "technical data sheet" did not contain an express warranty of future performance. We disagree with Royal.

Code§ 8.2–725(1) provides that a breach of a contract for sale must be commenced within four years after the cause of action accrues. A cause of action for breach of a contract for the sale of goods accrues when the breach occurs. Code§ 8.2–725(2). In a contract for the sale of goods, the breach of warranty occurs when tender of delivery is made, except that where a warranty explicitly extends to future performance of the goods and discovery of the breach must await the time of such performance the cause of action accrues when the breach is or should have been discovered.

It is undisputed that Royal's breach of warranty claim was filed more than four years after delivery of the sprinkler heads. Thus, the issue is whether there was an express warranty of future performance. Code§ 8.2–313, titled "Express warranties by affirmation, promise, description, sample [,]" provides:

> (1) Express warranties by the seller are created as follows:
>
>> (a) Any affirmation of fact or promise made by the seller to the buyer which relates to the goods and becomes part of the basis of the bargain creates an express warranty that the goods shall conform to the affirmation or promise.
>>
>> (b) Any description of the goods which is made part of the basis of the bargain creates an express warranty that the goods shall conform to the description.
>>
>> (c) Any sample or model which is made part of the basis of the bargain creates an express warranty that the whole of the goods shall conform to the sample or model.
>
> (2) It is not necessary to the creation of an express warranty that the seller use formal words such as "warrant" or "guarantee" or that he have a specific intention to make a warranty, but an affirmation merely of the value of the goods or a statement purporting to be merely the seller's opinion or commendation of the goods does not create a warranty.

The "technical data sheet" contains a description of how the sprinkler heads work. The description, which Royal asserts is a warranty of future performance, states:

> When the F960/Q–46 is in service, water is prevented from entering the assembly by the Plug and O–Ring Seal in the Inlet of the Sprinkler. Upon exposure to a temperature sufficient to operate the Bulb, the Bulb shatters and the Bulb Seat is released. The compressed Spring is then able to expand and push the Water Tube as well as the Guide Tube outward. This action

simultaneously pulls outward on the Yoke, withdrawing the Plug and O–
Ring Seal from the Inlet and initiating water flow.

There is no evidence in the record showing that this language became "part of
the basis of the bargain" such that it may be an express warranty of future performance. Indeed, the language amounts
to nothing more than a simple description of how the sprinkler heads operate. Nowhere in the description of how the
sprinkler heads work does Tyco promise that the sprinkler
heads will operate correctly for a particular period of time.
Manufacturers of products often provide such information,
especially when the products are mechanical devices. To hold
that such language amounts to an express warranty of future
performance would result in Tyco insuring its sprinkler heads
indefinitely. It would be an absurd result to conclude that a
description given by a manufacturer as to how a device operates amounts to an express warranty of future performance
for an unlimited duration.

> **"IT WOULD BE an absurd result to conclude that a description given by a manufacturer as to how a device operates amounts to an express warranty of future performance for an unlimited duration."**

Additionally, the "technical data sheet" explicitly provided a one-year warranty
that the sprinkler head shall be "free from defects in material and workmanship."
The warranty language is under the heading "WARRANTY" in the "technical data
sheet." If Tyco wished to provide any further warranty, surely it would have put
additional language under this section. Considering the explicit one-year warranty
contained in the "technical data sheet," the product description cannot be said
to constitute an express warranty of future performance for an indefinite period
of time. For these reasons, we hold that the circuit court did not err in sustaining
Tyco's plea in bar.

Regarding the circuit court's ruling on Simplex' plea in bar, Royal argues that
the court erred by dismissing the "warranty cause of action on the grounds that the
statements concerning [the sprinkler heads'] future performance under the Virginia
Uniform Commercial Code did not constitute a warranty of future performance."
We cannot address this assignment of error because Royal alleges that the circuit
court erred in making a ruling that it did not make. The circuit court did not
sustain Simplex' plea in bar on the ground that there was no warranty of future
performance. In fact, the circuit court ruled that the Uniform Commercial Code
did not apply to Royal's warranty claim against Simplex because the underlying
contract, which was "for the 'design and installation of a fire protection system,' "
was not a contract " predominately [for] the sale of goods." Accordingly, we cannot
address Royal's argument that the circuit court erred in sustaining Simplex' plea
in bar. Rule 5:25.

In the appeal against Tyco, for the reasons stated, we will reverse in part, affirm
in part, and remand this case to the circuit court. On remand, the circuit court shall
address Royal's negligence-based causes of action against Tyco.

In the appeal against Simplex, for the reasons stated, we will affirm the judgment of the circuit court.

WHEN THERE IS EVIDENCE of two express warranties that cannot be read as consistent with each other, courts will apply evidence of exact language and the parties' intent over general descriptive language. Because there was explicit language describing the warranty of the product, the court did not read into the general description of how the product works to mean an additional express warranty.

B. IMPLIED WARRANTY OF MERCHANTABILITY

Perhaps the most commonly used warranty theory is the Implied Warranty of Merchantability. The following language from the Uniform Commercial Code sets out the provisions in Section 2-314:

(1) Unless excluded or modified (Section 2-316), a warranty that the goods shall be merchantable is implied in a contract for their sale if the seller is a merchant with respect to goods of that kind. Under this section the serving for value of food or drink to be consumed either on the premises or elsewhere is a sale.

(2) Goods to be merchantable must be at least such as

      (a) pass without objection in the trade under the contract description; and

      (b) in the case of fungible goods, are of fair average quality within the description; and

      (c) are fit for the ordinary purposes for which such goods are used; and

      (d) run, within the variations permitted by the agreement, of even kind, quality and quantity within each unit and among all units involved; and

      (e) are adequately contained, packaged, and labeled as the agreement may require; and

      (f) conform to the promises or affirmations of fact made on the container or label if any.

(3) Unless excluded or modified (Section 2-316) other implied warranties may arise from course of dealing or usage of trade.

The idea behind this warranty is that new products are supposed to work for their normal, ordinary purposes. If one buys a dishwasher, it is supposed to wash dishes. If one buys a coffee pot, it is supposed to brew coffee. There is an automatic, implied warranty without any particular expression of capability.

Frantz v. Cantrell

Court of Appeals of Indiana, 1999
711 N.E.2d 856

In the summer of 1994, Cantrell entered into a contractual arrangement with Frantz, whereby Frantz agreed to install a new shingled roof on Cantrell's residence. At that time, Cantrell's only specification was that the shingles be of a good quality asphalt, as opposed to fiberglass shingles. The representative of Frantz obliged by selecting a particular brand of three-tabbed asphalt shingles which the lumber company routinely dealt with and which carried a twenty-year warranty from the manufacturer. The agreed upon price for the shingles and the installation of the new roof was $1,985.15.

Frantz completed the roof later that summer. Cantrell was initially satisfied with the work and with the shingles which had no apparent defects and paid Frantz for the work. However, in the winter months following the installation, Cantrell noticed that some of the shingles were curling up at the edges and that the tabs of many of the shingles had failed to seal down properly. This caused Cantrell concern not only for the integrity of the roof, but its appearance as well.

Cantrell notified Frantz of the problem and a representative of Frantz came to Cantrell's home to inspect the shingles. Upon examining the roof, the representative noted that while the workmanship was competent, there was a problem with the shingles which he had never encountered before. The representative indicated he would contact the manufacturer of the shingles in an effort to determine an appropriate course of action.

In the months following Cantrell's initial inquiries, Frantz mailed a document to Cantrell which detailed a phenomenon known as "cold curl," a peculiarity to the type of asphalt shingles which had been used on Cantrell's roof. The document advised that this occurrence should correct itself when the roof warms up either by sunlight or an increase in the ambient temperature, but did not address the failure of a number of the shingles' tabs to seal down.

In light of this information, Cantrell waited until the summer of 1995 to see if the warmer weather would in fact remedy the problem. However, when the cold curl and defective sealing did not rectify itself with the increase in temperature, Cantrell again contacted Frantz in an attempt to resolve these issues. When that attempt failed, Cantrell filed his Complaint For Damages against Frantz, claiming breach of implied warranty for the sale of the defective shingles. Following a bench trial, the court entered its order of judgment against Frantz in the amount of $3,904.97, the cost of repair or replacement less the value and use of the installed roof. Frantz appealed.

Frantz contends that absent evidence of a special relationship between Frantz and the manufacturer of the shingles, there can be no basis for a breach of implied warranty suit against Frantz. We cannot agree.

Under the Uniform Commercial Code as enacted in Indiana, IC 26-1-1-101 to -10-104, there are two implied warranties, that of merchantability and that of fitness for a particular purpose. Because the implied warranty of merchantability is the only type implicated under the facts in the present case, we limit our review to that warranty only.

Unless excluded or modified, a warranty that goods shall be merchantable is implied in *all* sales contracts if the seller is a merchant with respect to goods of that kind. IC 26-1-2-314(1). The warranty of merchantability arises out of the relationship between the buyer and the seller who is a merchant. *Richards*, 384 N.E.2d at 1091.

> "UNLESS EXCLUDED or modified, a warranty that goods shall be merchantable is implied in *all* sales contracts if the seller is a merchant with respect to goods of that kind."

An implied warranty of merchantability is imposed by operation of law for the protection of the buyer and must be liberally construed in favor of the buyer. To exclude this warranty, one must exercise special care. There is no requirement that any specific relationship between the seller and the manufacturer exist for the warranty to be implied.

Frantz next argues that it is not a "merchant" within the meaning of IC 26-1-2-314. A seller who makes casual or occasional sales of goods of a particular kind is not a merchant in those goods. Because a person making an isolated sale of goods is not a "merchant" within the scope of the Indiana UCC provision, no warranty of merchantability applies.

IC 26-1-2-104(1) defines "merchant" as "a person who deals in goods of the kind or otherwise by his occupation holds himself out as having knowledge or skill peculiar to the practices or goods involved in the transaction...." Applying this definition here, we note that the Frantz family has been affiliated with the lumber company since 1910, and during those eighty-nine years it has sold more than just lumber. Indeed, its business accounting statements bear the phrase "ALL KINDS OF BUILDING MATERIAL" directly beneath the company logo. By Cantrell's own testimony, Frantz was the only establishment he approached to install the new roof on his house, because he had heard of the company's local reputation to do good construction and roofing work. Cantrell also testified that upon specifying he wanted asphalt shingles for his new roof, the representative from Frantz promptly advised that the lumber company did deal with an asphalt shingle which carried a twenty-year warranty. Moreover, the Record as a whole demonstrates Frantz to be extremely knowledgeable about the construction and installation of new roofs, and in turn, the shingles which are used during the course of such work, and supports the trial court's finding that Frantz was a merchant.

Frantz next invokes IC 26-1-2-316(3)(c) for the argument that it is excused from liability under the implied warranty of merchantability because of certain usages of trade prevalent in the roofing business. This statute provides in pertinent part that an implied warranty may be excluded or modified by usage of trade. A usage of trade is "any practice or method of dealing having such regularity of observance in a place, vocation or trade as to justify an expectation that it will be observed with respect to the transaction in question." In support of its position, Frantz notes that Cantrell's own expert witness testified that a roofer traditionally does not provide any warranties as to the shingles themselves, and as such, argues that the implied warranty of merchantability is inapplicable in the instant case.

In *Martin Rispens & Son v. Hall Farms, Inc.*, our supreme court held that in order for the exception to be applicable, the usage of trade must be used in the vocation or trade in which *both* the contracting parties are engaged or be one of which *both* parties are or should be aware. Here, the parties in the present case are not in the same trade and there is no evidence that Cantrell was or should have been aware of the asserted usage of trade.

Because we find that the trial court did not err in its determination that an implied warranty of merchantability arose out of Frantz's sale of the asphalt shingles to Cantrell, the question becomes whether the evidence is sufficient to support the trial court's finding of a breach of that warranty. "Any action based on breach of warranty requires evidence showing not only the existence of the warranty but that the warranty was broken and that the breach of warranty was the proximate cause of the loss sustained." Frantz contends that the Record in this case does not contain any evidence to sustain a judgment against it for breach of implied warranty of merchantability. Again, we cannot agree...

Here, the court determined that "[t]he shingles were defective in that they would not seal properly causing curling of the edges. This curling of the edges resulted in a very unsightly roof with a great potential for failure at an early age." In opposition to the court's findings, Frantz contends that the sole purpose of shingles is to roof a house thereby securing the structure from the elements, and that because none of the shingles ever blew off or the roof had never leaked, there was no breach.

In *Travel Craft*, our supreme court stated that a good may be defective as the result of some sort of imperfection or dereliction. The trial court's finding that the shingles in this case were defective is more than adequately supported by the evidence of their imperfections, namely, the curling and failure to seal. Shingles which fail to seal and which curl in an unsightly manner even in warm weather cannot be said to "conform to ordinary standards and ... be of the same average grade, quality, and value as similar goods sold under similar circumstances. In addition, a roof which is not flat and smooth and whose shingles curl up at the edges and fail to seal cannot be said to "pass without objection in the trade," IC 26-1-2-314(2)(a), even if it does shield the structure from the elements. As such, the trial court's determination that Frantz breached the implied warranty of merchantability in its sale of shingles to Cantrell is supported by the Record and was not clearly erroneous.

...As such, the court's judgment against Frantz for its breach of implied warranty of merchantability in the amount of $3,904.97 was reasonable and comports with UCC guidelines. The evidence in the Record is more than sufficient to support such an award and the trial court's determination was not clearly erroneous.

We affirm.

Crowe v. CarMax Auto Superstores, Inc.

Court of Appeals of Georgia, 2005
612 S.E.2d 90

Tina and Thad Crowe appeal from the trial court's order granting summary judgment to defendant CarMax Auto Superstores, Inc....The Crowes purchased a 1999 Dodge Durango automobile from CarMax on October 5, 2002. They received a 30-day/1,000 mile express warranty from CarMax, and they purchased an 18-month/18,000 mile "Mechanical Repair Agreement" (MRA). The obligor on this extended warranty was Consumer Program Administrators, Inc., not CarMax. Over the course of the next year, the Crowes brought the vehicle to CarMax and other repair facilities numerous times for a variety of repairs. All repairs made within the original and extended warranty periods were made without cost to the Crowes, except for deductibles, although those were sometimes waived. Nevertheless, the Crowes contend they lost confidence in the vehicle, and on May 30, 2003, the Crowes filed a complaint against CarMax, asserting claims for breach of implied and express warranties under the Magnuson-Moss Warranty Act and Georgia law. The trial court granted summary judgment to CarMax on both the express and implied warranty claims, and the Crowes do not challenge that ruling insofar as it pertains to their express warranty claims. However, the Crowes challenge the grant of summary judgment on their implied warranty claim, contending that they have established a viable claim under the Magnuson-Moss Warranty Act.

The Magnuson-Moss Warranty Act allows "a consumer who is damaged by the failure of a supplier, warrantor, or service contractor to comply with any obligation under ... (an) implied warranty ... (to) bring suit for damages and other legal and equitable relief." The Act defines "implied warranty" as "an implied warranty arising under State law ... in connection with the sale by a supplier of a consumer product." [To recover, therefore, [the Crowes] must show that [CarMax] breached the implied warranty of merchantability arising under Georgia law.

Under OCGA§ 11-2-314(1), "a warranty that the goods shall be merchantable is implied in a contract for their sale if the seller is a merchant with respect to goods of that kind." "This warranty protects consumers from defects or conditions existing at the time of sale." In *Jones v. Marcus*, this court held that "it is obvious that the alleged defect or condition must have existed at the time of the sale." This is logical, because it is clear that "the implied warranties warrant against defects or conditions existing at the time of sale, but [they] do not provide a warranty of continuing serviceability." It follows that proof that the vehicle was defective *when it was sold* is an essential element of the Crowes' claim for breach of the implied warranty of merchantability.

The Crowes contend the trial court erred by finding that they did not meet their burden of showing that a jury question exists concerning whether the vehicle was defective at the time of sale. We find no error. Although the vehicle was first returned to CarMax just five days after it was sold, the record shows that those repairs were primarily to remedy cosmetic defects that CarMax agreed to fix at the time of sale. The Crowes returned the car again on October 22, after what they contend was 11 days of actual use. The problems noted on that visit were that the vehicle was consuming massive amounts of oil, that the instrument panel lights were flickering, and that the four-wheel-drive illumination light was not working. Tina Crowe testified that the problems were fixed on that visit.

The vehicle was returned to CarMax on November 13, 2002, because the check engine light was on. The repair ticket indicated that "false codes" were detected and removed. However, the problem with the check engine light reappeared in January 2003, and the vehicle was returned to CarMax. At this time a broken ground wire was found, and Tina Crowe testified the problem was fixed to her satisfaction, as was a problem with the rear windshield wiper, which was remedied by replacing the wiper motor.

On the January visit, it was also noted that the vehicle was jerking and the engine was revving up to 6,000 rpm when driving. Tina Crowe testified that the problem with the engine revving persisted for several months and that she returned the car for repairs several times before the control module was replaced and the problem fixed in April 2003. The record shows that during this same period the engine was running rough, but that problem was attributed to carbon build-up in the cylinders and was also remedied. Tina Crowe testified she did not take the vehicle back to CarMax after the MRA expired, but instead took it to another facility for repair when it began stalling out in June 2003. At that time a fuel system tune-up was performed. A low out speed sensor was replaced in August, and a ball bearing was replaced on the front of the car in October 2003. At that time the Crowes had owned the vehicle a little over a year, and the odometer reading was at 65,621 miles, indicating the car had been driven over 25,000 miles during that time. Tina Crowe testified that at the time of her deposition in December 2003 there were no current problems with the car.

Based on this evidence, the trial court found that the Crowes failed to establish that the vehicle was defective when sold. We agree that this evidence does not present a jury question on this essential element of their claim. Although the vehicle was repaired on numerous occasions over the course of the first year of ownership, as the trial court noted, for the most part these repairs were for different items or concerns on each occasion, and the problems were all remedied at the time the car was first brought in or on a subsequent visit. And although the Crowes argue strenuously that at least some evidence of a defect at the time of sale is shown by the fact that

THE MAGNUSON-MOSS WARRANTY ACT ALLOWS A CONSUMER WHO IS DAMAGED BY THE FAILURE OF A SUPPLIER, WARRANTOR, OR SERVICE CONTRACTOR TO BRING SUIT FOR DAMAGES AND EQUITABLE RELIEF.

the car had to be returned for repairs after it was driven for just 11 days, the record shows that the primary complaint at that time was that the vehicle was consuming massive amounts of oil and that problem was remedied on that repair visit and did not recur. Moreover, although the vehicle had only been owned for a short period, it had already been driven in excess of 1,100 miles. The recurring problem with the engine revving was not detected until about three months later, and at that time the car had been driven almost 5,000 more miles. Although it took several attempts, that problem was also fixed. We note also that by the time the bearings had to be replaced in October 2003, the car had been driven over 25,000 miles since it was purchased about 13 months previously. Moreover, at the time of Tina Crowe's deposition in December 2003, there were no current problems with the car. Under these facts, we agree that no defect has been shown to exist at the time of purchase, and to find otherwise would require the jury to rely on speculation or conjecture, improper bases for imposing liability. The trial court did not err in granting summary judgment on the implied warranty claim.

Judgment affirmed.

A KEY QUESTION that arises with implied warranties of merchantability is whether the seller can disclaim the warranty that goes with the product. With used products, this can be done with a conspicuous statement of disclaimer in the contract. The following case products an example of the effectiveness of this kind of situation.

Bevard v. Ajax Mfg. Co.

United States District Court, Eastern District of Michigan, 1979
473 F.Supp. 35

This case involves a Motion for Summary Judgment made by one of multiple Defendants, Aluminum Forge Division of Altamil Corporation (hereinafter Altamil). Altamil purchased a press from Defendant, Ajax Manufacturing Company, in or around 1966, and it was used by them for approximately five years. Through a used equipment dealer, Altamil sold this press in 1971 to Plaintiff's employer, Webb Forging Company. While in the employment of Webb, and while working on the press in question, Plaintiff sustained the injury which is the subject of this lawsuit.

Under Michigan law, there are three potential theories of recovery if someone sustains personal injury by means of defective product: Uniform Commercial Code warranty remedies, common-law warranty remedies and negligence. Implied warranty of merchantability applied only as to merchants, and one-time seller who was not engaged in business of selling goods in question, or holding himself out as person who deals in such goods, was not "merchant" for purposes of implied warranty of merchantability. An occasional, one time seller, such as the Defendant, who is not engaged in the business of selling the goods in question, or holding himself out as a person who deals in such goods, is not a "merchant."

In addition, it seems clear... that the Complaint could fairly be interpreted to allege breach of the Code's implied warranty of fitness for a particular purpose under U.C.C. § 2-315. Although one need not be a "merchant" to extend this warranty to the buyer, it can be expressly disclaimed. As Defendant indicated, words such as "as is" or "with all faults" are adequate disclaimer of all implied warranties. However, this disclaimer must be in writing and conspicuous, a fact left out of the Movant's brief. Movant's discussion and affidavits regarding the "as is" nature of the agreement are, therefore, irrelevant as to disclaimer under the Code.

Nevertheless, the evidence of the "as is" nature of the transaction is useful for other purposes. The following quote from R. Anderson's work on the U.C.C. is helpful:

> With respect to a warranty of fitness for a particular purpose, there is no requirement that the seller be a merchant. As a practical matter, however, the seller will ordinarily be a merchant for the reason that the implied warranty of fitness for a particular purpose does not arise unless the buyer relies on the seller's skill and judgment and that when the facts are such as support the conclusion that the seller possesses "skill and judgment" it is more than likely that the seller will come within the description of "merchant."

1 R. Anderson, Uniform Commercial Code § 2-315: 15 (1970).

Anderson suggests that, in most instances, the seller will be a merchant because the warranty requires reliance on the seller's skill and judgment. He then proceeds to hypothesize the existence of a fact-pattern where the warranty applies to a non-merchant. The reliance by the buyer upon the skill and judgment of the seller is wholly lacking in our case. In fact, there was never any allegation or claim of skill or judgment on Altamil's part the " as is" nature of the transaction conclusively establishes that. In addition, the "as is" nature of the transaction, albeit oral and inadequate for disclaimer purposes, negates the existence of any reliance by the buyer. Also, the Complaint makes no allegation of reliance...

Defendant Altamil's Motion for Summary Judgment is granted in part and denied in part.

———————————

IT IS MUCH HARDER to disclaim an implied warranty for a new product, but the procedures to do so are the same as for a used product. In order to effectively disclaim the implied warranty of merchantability from a new product, the seller must mention the word "merchantability" in the disclaimer in a conspicuous way. The test for whether a seller effectively does this is based on whether a reasonable person who is buying the product, and thus to whom the seller is directing the disclaimer, should have noticed it. This would require that the disclaimer be in capital letters that are as large or larger than the text surrounding the disclaimer and/or appears in a font color and size intended to catch the buyer's attention. Placing the words "AS IS" in the same, stand-out font size or color is important too. These requirements suggest that disclaiming an implied warranty of merchantability is no easy task, and the following case shows just how difficult it can be.

Woodruff v. Clark County Farm Bureau Co-op. Ass'n

Court of Appeals of Indiana, Second District, 1972
286 N.E.2d 188

From 1945 until 1960 Woodruff was engaged in the business of raising broiler chickens near Remington, Indiana. In 1960 he phased out his broiler business and began raising chickens for the production of eggs... In July of 1964, Ken Bowlin (Bowlin), a Farm Bureau representative, discovered that Woodruff intended to replace his flock of chickens. Farm Bureau did not have any chickens in Woodruff's area, but Bowlin contacted Woodruff in an attempt to persuade him to try Farm Bureau chickens.

As a consequence of this initial conversation, Woodruff met with Searcy and other Farm Bureau representatives at Indianapolis and travelled to the Clark County Farm Bureau to observe its flock of chickens. While at the Clark County Farm, Woodruff observed that the chickens were out of feed and that they were 'congested'... After viewing these conditions Woodruff testified that he was assured by Farm Bureau that he would get only the good chickens and that 'they would do a good job in my chicken-house.'

Woodruff further noted that he did not raise any questions at the Clark County farm regarding vaccination or mortality rates because he had confidence in Farm Bureau and that it was customary for chicken farmers to vaccinate against coccidiosis at an early stage. He presumed that 'they had been in it for a long time and they certainly had brains enough to know what to do, and it was not for me to ask about it.'

Following the examination of the Clark County chickens, Woodruff and the Farm Bureau representatives travelled to Jackson County, where they viewed another flock of chickens. Woodruff again observed that the chicken feeders were empty, the chickens were badly stunted and their feathers were ruffled. While he generally condemned the Jackson County operation, the response to his comments at Jackson

County was much the same as at the Clark County farm—that he would get only the good chickens, 'that the chickens would be culled' and he 'would get only good birds.'

After observing the Jackson County birds, Woodruff and the Farm Bureau representatives drove back to Indianapolis. At some time during the return trip to Indianapolis, Farm Bureau and Woodruff entered into an oral agreement whereby Woodruff agreed to purchase chickens from Farm Bureau for $1.55 per chicken.

On July 23, 1964 the chickens were delivered to Woodruff with Mr. Wayne Isaacs, of the Farm Bureau, present. Woodruff himself culled approximately 1,400 chickens out of the total delivered... Woodruff did understand that he could return any of them that appeared to be unacceptable. At the time of delivery Woodruff was advised that the chickens would develop in the proper manner i.e. that they would 'bloom out or straighten up and fly right.'

As the chickens progressed in age many of them were dying, so in the early part of August 1964, Woodruff contacted Bowlin concerning the mortality rate. At Bowlin's insistence, Woodruff called the Indianapolis Farm Bureau office and requested that someone examine the chickens. Subsequently, Searcy and two other Farm Bureau representatives visited Woodruff and concluded that the chickens were in no great danger. Nevertheless, the high mortality rate continued, so Woodruff again contacted Farm Bureau representatives, who returned a second time to examine the chickens. At the second meeting, Woodruff was asked if he was using anything in his feed for coccidiosis. Woodruff replied:

'I've got nothing in my feed for coccidiosis; when chickens get this age you are not supposed to have anything in your feed for coccidiosis. Any normal chicken from any reputable company will have their immunity by the time they are twenty weeks old.'

The Farm Bureau representatives then departed without giving Woodruff any indication as to the condition of the birds.

Woodruff began feeding the birds a special feed, but the mortality rate continued at the same pace. The condition did not improve and eventually Woodruff's poultry business was destroyed. Woodruff testified that he lost approximately $45,000.00 of gross income because the chickens never exceeded sixty percent of production capabilities. Woodruff also testified that ultimately approximately 2500 chickens died and probably 1600 more were condemned because of their condition.

In August 1966, Woodruff filed a Complaint against Farm Bureau for damages for breach of warranty, misrepresentation and fraud.

In the sale of the chickens by Farm Bureau to Woodruff, implied warranties of merchantability and fitness for a particular purpose arose as a matter of law. In 1963 Indiana adopted the Uniform Commercial Code (UCC) as part of its statutory law on commercial transactions.

Where the seller at the time of contracting has reason to know any particular purpose for which the goods are required and that the buyer is relying on the seller's skill or judgment to select or furnish suitable goods, there is unless excluded or modified under the next section an implied warranty that the goods shall be fit for such purpose.

The facts before us indicate no dispute that Farm Bureau is a merchant with respect to the chickens it sold Woodruff—it is in the business of selling chickens, among other things, for the purpose for which Woodruff purchased them. Consequently, an implied warranty of merchantability did arise by operation of law from the sole fact that Farm Bureau was a regular merchant with respect to the sale of chickens. Moreover, Farm Bureau knew the particular purpose for which Woodruff intended to use these chickens, i.e., production of eggs. This knowledge is indicated by the fact that Farm Bureau initially contacted Woodruff hoping to persuade him to purchase Farm Bureau chickens for the production of eggs.

While Woodruff had raised broiler chickens for some fifteen years he was relatively new to the egg production business. His deposition indicates that he had confidence in the people he was dealing with and that he relied on their skill and judgment to select and furnish suitable chickens for the production of eggs. Thus, a material issue of fact existed as to whether the implied warranties of merchantability and fitness for a particular purpose were violated. Unless otherwise excluded or modified, they remained in full force at the time of the sale and delivery of the chickens by Farm Bureau to Woodruff. The effect of the disclaimers then becomes paramount.

It is our opinion that the disclaiming language in the Receipts is insufficient as a matter of law to negate the implied warranties of merchantability and fitness for a particular purpose.

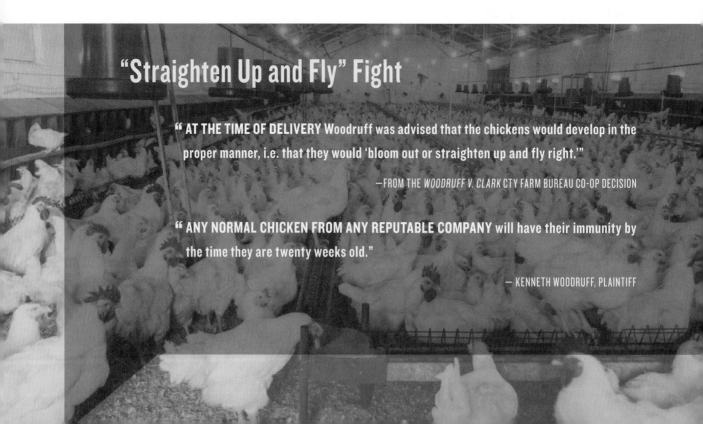

"Straighten Up and Fly" Fight

" **AT THE TIME OF DELIVERY** Woodruff was advised that the chickens would develop in the proper manner, i.e. that they would 'bloom out or straighten up and fly right.'"

—FROM THE *WOODRUFF V. CLARK* CTY FARM BUREAU CO-OP DECISION

" **ANY NORMAL CHICKEN FROM ANY REPUTABLE COMPANY** will have their immunity by the time they are twenty weeks old."

— KENNETH WOODRUFF, PLAINTIFF

Ind.Ann.Stat. § 19-2-316 (Burns 1964), IC 1971, 26-1-2-316 provides for the exclusion or modification of express and implied warranties:

> Exclusion or modification of warranties: (1) Words or conduct relevant to the creation of an express warranty and words or conduct tending to negate or limit warranty shall be construed wherever reasonable as consistent with each other; but subject to the provisions of this Article on parol or extrinsic evidence negation or limitation is inoperative to the extent that such construction is unreasonable. (2) Subject to subsection (3), to exclude or modify the implied warranty of merchantability or any part of it the language must mention merchantability and in case of a writing must be conspicuous, and to exclude or modify any implied warranty of fitness the exclusion must be by a writing and conspicuous. Language to exclude all implied warranties of fitness is sufficient if it states, for example, that 'There are no warranties which extend beyond the description on the face hereof.' (3) Notwithstanding subsection (2)

> (a) unless the circumstances indicate otherwise, all implied warranties are excluded by expressions like 'as is', 'with all faults' or other language which in common understanding calls the buyer's attention to the exclusion of warranties and makes plain that there is no implied warranty; and (b) when the buyer before entering into the contract has examined the goods or the sample or model as fully as he desired or has refused to examine the goods there is no implied warranty with regard to defects which an examination ought in the circumstances to have revealed to him; and (c) an implied warranty can also be excluded or modified by course of dealing or course of performance or usage of trade.

Disclaimers of implied warranties… are not favored and are strictly construed against the sellers for reasons of public policy. In order to exclude or modify an implied warranty of merchantability under § 19-2-316(2), (herein referred to as Number 2), the disclaimer 'must mention merchantability' and the written exclusionary language 'must be conspicuous.' The disclaiming language in the Receipts omits any such reference, and further none of the language of the disclaimer is in any way made 'conspicuous.'

By the unmistakable language of Number 2, neither of the implied warranties of merchantability and fitness are excluded or negated by the attempted disclaimer. The exclusionary language must be written and it must be conspicuous. 'Conspicuous,' as used within the meaning of § 19-2-316, supra, is defined in Ind.Ann.Stat. § 19-1-201(10) (Burns 1964), IC 1971, 26-1-1-201(10) thusly:

> "Conspicuous:' A term or clause is conspicuous when it is so written that a reasonable person against whom it is to operate ought to have noticed it. A printed heading in capitals (as: Non-negotiable Bill of Lading) is

conspicuous. Language in the body of a form is 'conspicuous' if it is in larger or other contrasting type or color. But in a telegram any stated term is 'conspicuous.' Whether a term or clause is 'conspicuous' or not is for decision by the court.'

Number 3 provides that if expressions like 'as is' are used in the exclusionary language any implied warranties are negated. It also provides other conditions which must exist in order to negate implied warranties, none of which are applicable here because of the conclusion we reach requiring exclusionary language to be conspicuous. The exclusionary language of the Receipts does contain a clause that pullets accepted by a purchaser 'shall be deemed to be accepted in an 'as is' condition.' While this disclaiming language is set out in quotation marks, it is hardly conspicuous.

The problem is to determine whether the conspicuous requirement of Number 2 is carried over to and becomes a part of Number 3 so that implied warranties are not negated unless expressions like 'as is' are conspicuous. The close interrelation of these two sections is manifested by their like intent to call the buyer's attention to the exclusion of implied warranties and it would do violence to their stated purpose to do otherwise than imply that excluding expressions like 'as is' must be conspicuous. This interpretation harmonizes with the basic purpose of the UCC which is designed to protect purchasers from surprise.

Bringing the buyer's attention to exclusion of implied warranties is frequently emphasized by the cases in interpreting the UCC... Since the exclusionary language contained in the 'Delivery Receipts' in the case before us was not drawn to the attention of Woodruff at the time of delivery, and since there was nothing contained within the body of the purported disclaimers drawing Woodruff's attention to the exclusionary language or making that language conspicuous in and of itself, these 'Delivery Receipts' were insufficient as a matter of law to negate any implied warranties.

Disclaimers of implied warranties are not favored and are strictly construed against the sellers for reasons of public policy.

C. IMPLIED WARRANTY FOR PARTICULAR PURPOSE

An Implied Warranty for a Particular Purpose, UCC Section 2-315, has elements of both express warranty and implied warranty of merchantability. In an actual case, it would not be at all surprising that a plaintiff suing primarily on the basis of an implied warranty for a particular purpose would not also include the previously two mentioned theories. With an implied warranty for a particular purpose, the seller knows of the particular need or purpose of the buyer and designs a product that will satisfy that need. Indeed, the tests for this kind of warranty are that:

1. The seller has reason to know of the particular purpose
    of the buyer; and

2. The seller also knows that the buyer is relying on the seller's
    skill and judgment.

Implied with the contract will be a warranty that with that amount of cus-
tomization, the product will actually do what the buyer asked for. Further, if a
product is being designed for the particular purpose of the buyer, it would be very
likely that the seller states that the product will satisfy the buyer's needs, thus
making it an express warranty. Following is the relevant except from the Uniform
Commercial Code:

> Where the seller at the time of contracting has reason to know any partic-
> ular purpose for which the goods are required and that the buyer is relying
> on the seller's skill or judgment to select or furnish suitable goods, there is
> unless excluded or modified under the next section an implied warranty
> that the goods shall be fit for such purpose. (UCC§ 2-315)

Matter of Clements and Van Wagnen Const. Co.

United States Bankruptcy Court, Eastern District of Michigan, 1982
23 B.R. 617

Plaintiff filed its complaint on June 11, 1981, praying for damages resulting from
defective cement supplied by defendant. Defendant filed this motion for summary
judgment on March 24, 1982. Pursuant to a contract between the parties defendant
delivered cement to plaintiff to be used in the construction of sidewalks on a project
being carried out by plaintiff. According to the express terms of the contract it was
specified that the cement delivered to plaintiff was to have an air-void content between three and six percent of the concrete volume. The parties agree that the air-void
content of the cement delivered pursuant to their contract was 4.2% of the concrete
volume. 4.2% air-void content is within the specification set forth in the contract.
Despite the contractually proper air-void content, the sidewalks constructed with
defendant's cement became cracked. Plaintiff has presented no evidence, nor alleged,
that the air-void specifications set forth in the contract were those of the defendant.

The existence of an implied warranty of fitness for a particular purpose is contingent on two general facts. First, the seller must be aware at the time of contracting
of a particular purpose for which the buyer intends to use the goods. Second, the
buyer must rely on the seller's skill or judgment to select or furnish goods suitable
for that particular purpose.

No warranty of fitness for a particular purpose can be implied unless the buyer is relying on the seller's skill and judgment to select or manufacture suitable goods for a particular purpose for which the seller knows the goods are required.

In the case of *Price Brothers Co. v. Philadelphia Gear Co.* the court had occasion to rule on the very issue before this court today. Price Brothers submitted a purchase order to Philadelphia Gear specifying certain performance characteristics of the components ordered, apparently arrived at with Philadelphia Gear's assistance. The components were produced in conformance with the specifications of the buyer set forth in its purchase order. Price Brothers later experienced difficulties with a machine built with components produced by seller, attributing the problems to an alleged failure of the Philadelphia Gear components to perform as warranted.

The 6th Circuit reversed the trial court on the following basis: The trial court's conclusion that Philadelphia Gear breached an implied warranty of fitness for a particular purpose must be reversed because of the degree of specificity of Price Brothers' purchase order and Price Brothers' own undisputed high degree of knowledge regarding the mechanical requirements of its own pipe wrapping machine make any finding that Price Brothers relied on Philadelphia Gear's selection clearly erroneous.

In the present case Price Brothers ordered components from Philadelphia Gear by use of a purchase order specifying performance criteria. It is of no avail to Price Brothers that Philadelphia Gear may have assisted Price Brothers in arriving at these specifications. The fact that the specifications were jointly arrived at by Price Brothers engineers and Philadelphia Gear representatives only emphasizes the fact that Price Brothers exercised its own judgment in selecting the components ordered and did not rely on Philadelphia Gear to supply components.

It is the view of this court that the specification of air-void parameters by plaintiff in this matter is sufficient, standing alone, to warrant summary judgment on the issue of an implied warranty of fitness in favor of the defendant. Plaintiff has made no showing, nor advanced any facts which would indicate a positive reliance on defendant's expertise on the part of plaintiff. Indeed, plaintiff is a construction contractor, not without some expertise in such matters.

The overriding fact, however, is that in spite of any expertise defendant had, plaintiff simply did not rely on that expertise. The fact that defendant was in the business of producing concrete, and knew of the particular manner in which its concrete was to be employed, does not give rise to a finding of reliance. The specification of allowable air-void percentages in the contract indicates a lack of reliance on the part of the plaintiff.

There is, as a matter of law, no implied warranty of fitness for a particular purpose when goods are manufactured in accordance with specifications provided by the buyer. Where no evidence has been advanced by plaintiff that the specifications of air-void content were those of the defendant, no question of fact exists as to reliance.

It is therefore ordered that summary judgment is granted in favor of the movant-defendant, and plaintiff's cause of action based upon breach of an implied warranty of fitness for a particular purpose is hereby dismissed.

D. WARRANTY OF TITLE

The three warranties discussed above comprise the vast majorities of product liability usages. But a fourth can play a role on occasion. This is the warranty of title.
With this warranty, the seller is guaranteeing that she has good and rightful title
(or ownership) of a product and the product is not subject to some kind of security
agreement (such as being collateral for a loan). Here is an example of a case where a
buyer alleges that the seller breached an implied warranty of title.

Lawson v. Turner

District Court of Appeals of Florida, First District, 1981
404 So.2d 424

In 1973, Cox purchased a 1970 GMC dump truck from a Mr. Tyson. Turner was
guarantor on Cox's note at the bank for the purchase price. Turner, in fact, handled
most of the negotiations of the purchase for Cox. Cox drove the truck for several
months but was unable to earn enough money driving the truck to pay the note at
the bank. Cox returned the truck to Turner's place of business and explained the
situation to Willis, his stepfather, and Turner.

Willis then took over the truck and began driving it, hoping to earn enough money to pay the note. After several months Willis decided to sell the truck to Lawson for
$7,500.00. In September 1973, Lawson, Willis, and Turner met at the bank to take
care of the paper work for the transfer of the truck to Lawson. Lawson paid Willis
for the equity in the truck and assumed payments. Turner remained guarantor on the
bank note for Lawson also. Title to the truck was not transferred at that time, but
Turner told Lawson that as soon as the title arrived from Tyson, he would guarantee
delivery of it to Lawson.

Subsequently, the truck was discovered to be stolen and Lawson surrendered it to its rightful owner. Lawson brought suit for damages. At trial, the parties stipulated: (1) the truck was stolen; (2) none of the parties knew the truck was stolen; (3) Cox was a seller of the truck; and (4) the truck was surrendered to its rightful owner when it was discovered to be stolen. At trial, Willis also testified he was seller of the truck. Turner denied being a seller, arguing he was merely the guarantor of the bank note for Cox and Lawson. Lawson brought suit against Turner, Cox, and Willis seeking damages for breach of implied warranty of title resulting from his purchase of a used dump truck which was subsequently discovered to be a stolen vehicle. Lawson appeals the trial court's denial of his motion for a directed verdict.

Section 672.312, Florida Statutes (1973) states: (1) Subject to subsection (2) there is in a contract for sale a warranty by the seller that: (a) The title conveyed shall be good, and its transfer rightful; and (b) The goods shall be delivered free from any security interest or other lien or encumbrance of which the buyer at the time of contracting has no knowledge. (2) A warranty under subsection (1) will be excluded or modified only by specific language or by circumstances which give the buyer reason to know that the person selling does not claim title in himself or that he is purporting to sell only such right or title as he or a third person may have.

Accordingly, under the statute there was an implied warranty of title by the sellers of the truck to Lawson. In the absence of a specific exclusion, a third party defendant who sold a semi-trailer to the defendant and the defendant who sold it to the plaintiff both impliedly warranted good title. Although a defendant had no knowledge that an automobile which he purchased from a third party and ultimately sold to the plaintiff was stolen, he was nevertheless liable to the plaintiff for breach of the warranty of title. The damages for breach of the implied warranty of title are set forth in Section 672.714(2) and (3), Florida Statutes (1973). Therefore, in the absence of an exclusion of the implied warranty, the sellers are liable to Lawson for breach of the implied warranty of title.

In order to exclude the implied warranty of title, the seller must do so in very precise and unambiguous language. In *Sunseri v. RKO-Stanley Warner Theaters, Inc.*, the following language in a bill of sale for recreational equipment was held insufficiently specific to exclude the implied warranty of title:

It is expressly understood and agreed that seller shall in nowise be deemed or held to be obligated, liable, or accountable upon or under guaranties (sic.) or warranties, in any manner or form including, but not limited to, the implied warranties of title, merchantability, ...

> The evidence in the case below in no way approached the attempted disclaimer in Sunseri. The only language which could be construed as an attempted disclaimer is Turner's statement to Lawson that he did not have the title, but he would guarantee Lawson would get it as soon as he received it from Tyson. We hold, therefore, as a matter of law, this language is insufficient to exclude the implied warranty of title in the transaction below.

The evidence adduced at trial was insufficient to prove that Turner was a seller of the truck, but based upon the parties' stipulations and Willis' admissions, we find that Cox and Willis were sellers. They, therefore, breached the implied warranty of title when they sold the stolen truck to Lawson. The trial judge should have granted Lawson's motion for directed verdict as to Cox and Willis.

Accordingly, the judgment is affirmed as to Turner and is reversed as to Cox and Willis. This cause is remanded with instructions that the trial court enter a directed verdict in favor of Lawson against Cox and Willis.

III. Tort Theories of Product Liability

A. NEGLIGENCE

The most basic of tort liability theories, nearly every products liability case will contain a charge of negligence. If the defendant was more careful, the injury would not have occurred. But that simple rendition of negligence underplays the scope of negligence theories available in a products liability case. One might be negligent in terms of product design, in the selection of component parts, in the manufacturing process, in the quality review process, or in many other facets. At any step of the manufacture and sale of the product, there could be a negligence issue and so in a given products liability case, one may have a half dozen or more negligence charges.

In just about every one of these negligence charges, the plaintiff will also seek to utilize res ipsa loquitor so that the plaintiff does not have to prove negligence, but instead, that the defendant will have to prove that it was not negligent. The reason courts believe this makes sense is that, pursuant to the tests for res ipsa loquitor, each step (of design, selection of component parts, manufacturing, quality review, etc.) is in the control of the defendant with no input from the plaintiff, and it would be very difficult for the plaintiff to obtain the records from the defendant necessary to establish negligence.

Thus, a products liability case will trigger significant costs for the defendant even if the defendant ends up prevailing on the case itself. And so, there is incentive for a company to settle the case rather than proving that they were not negligent in each of these steps. Further, because court cases are generally of public record, companies may not want a great deal of inside information to be made available. Unless a trade secret is involved that would allow for consideration of evidence only among the litigants and decision makers of the case, anyone—including competitors or other parties interested in finding grounds to file suit—could obtain this company information.

The following cases demonstrate the operation of negligence in product liability suits.

MacPherson v. Buick Motor Co.

New York Court of Appeals, 1916
217 N.Y. 382

The defendant is a manufacturer of automobiles. It sold an automobile to a retail dealer. The retail dealer resold to the plaintiff. While the plaintiff was in the car, it suddenly collapsed. He was thrown out and injured. One of the wheels was made of defective wood, and its spokes crumbled into fragments. The wheel was not made by the defendant; it was bought from another manufacturer. There is evidence, however, that its defects could have been discovered by reasonable inspection, and that inspection was omitted. There is no claim that the defendant knew of the defect and willfully concealed it. The charge is one, not of fraud, but of negligence.

The question to be determined is whether the defendant owed a duty of care and vigilance to any one but the immediate purchaser. The foundations of this branch of the law, at least in this state, were laid in *Thomas v. Winchester* (6 N. Y. 397). A poison was falsely labeled. The sale was made to a druggist, who in turn sold to a customer. The customer recovered damages from the seller who affixed the label. 'The defendant's negligence,' it was said, 'put human life in imminent danger.' A poison falsely labeled is likely to injure any one who gets it. Because the danger is to be foreseen, there is a duty to avoid the injury. Cases were cited by way of illustration in which manufacturers were not subject to any duty irrespective of contract. The distinction was said to be that their conduct, though negligent, was not likely to result in injury to any one except the purchaser. We are not required to say whether the chance of injury was always as remote as the distinction assumes. Some of the illustrations might be rejected to-day. The *principle* of the distinction is for present purposes the important thing.

Thomas v. Winchester became quickly a landmark of the law.... There has never in this state been doubt or disavowal of the principle itself. The chief cases are well known, yet to recall some of them will be helpful. *Loop v. Litchfield* (42 N. Y. 351) is the earliest. It was the case of a defect in a small balance wheel used on a circular saw. The manufacturer pointed out the defect to the buyer, who wished a cheap article and was ready to assume the risk. The risk can hardly have been an imminent one, for the wheel lasted five years before it broke. In the meanwhile the buyer had made a lease of the machinery. It was held that the manufacturer was not answerable to the lessee. *Loop v. Litchfield* was followed in *Losee v. Clute*, the case of the explosion of a steam boiler. That decision has been criticized... but it must be confined to its special facts. It was put upon the ground that the risk of injury was too remote. The buyer in that case had not only accepted the boiler, but had tested it. The manufacturer knew that his own test was not the final one. The finality of the test has a bearing on the measure of diligence owing to persons other than the purchaser...

These early cases suggest a narrow construction of the rule. Later cases, however, evince a more liberal spirit. First in importance is *Devlin v. Smith*. The defendant, a contractor, built a scaffold for a painter. The painter's servants were injured. The contractor was held liable. He knew that the scaffold, if improperly constructed, was a most dangerous trap. He knew that it was to be used by the workmen. He was building it for that very purpose. Building it for their use, he owed them a duty, irrespective of his contract with their master, to build it with care.

From *Devlin v. Smith* we pass over intermediate cases and turn to the latest case in this court in which *Thomas v. Winchester* was followed. That case is *Statler v. Ray Mfg. Co.* The defendant manufactured a large coffee urn. It was installed in a restaurant. When heated, the urn exploded and injured the plaintiff. We held that the manufacturer was liable. We said that the urn 'was of such a character inherently that, when applied to the purposes for which it was designed, it was liable to become a source of great danger to many people if not carefully and properly constructed.' It may be that *Devlin v. Smith and Statler v. Ray Mfg. Co.* have extended the rule of *Thomas v. Winchester.* If so, this court is committed to the extension. The defendant argues that things imminently dangerous to life are poisons, explosives, deadly weapons—things whose normal function it is to injure or destroy. But whatever the rule in *Thomas v. Winchester* may once have been, it has no longer that restricted meaning. A scaffold (*Devlin v. Smith, supra*) is not inherently a destructive instrument. It becomes destructive only if imperfectly constructed. A large coffee urn (*Statler v. Ray Mfg. Co., supra*) may have within itself, if negligently made, the potency of danger, yet no one thinks of it as an implement whose normal function is destruction. What is true of the coffee urn is equally true of bottles of aerated water...

The rule has received a like extension in our courts of intermediate appeal. In *Burke v. Ireland* it was applied to a builder who constructed a defective building; in *Kahner v. Otis Elevator Co.* to the manufacturer of an elevator; in *Davies v. Pelham Hod Elevating Co.* to a contractor who furnished a defective rope with knowledge of the purpose for which the rope was to be used. We are not required at this time either to approve or to disapprove the application of the rule that was made in these cases. It is enough that they help to characterize the trend of judicial thought.

We hold, then, that the principle of *Thomas v. Winchester* is not limited to poisons, explosives, and things of like nature, to things which in their normal operation are implements of destruction. If the nature of a thing is such that it is reasonably certain to place life and limb in peril when negligently made, it is then a thing of danger. Its nature gives warning of the consequences to be expected. If to the element of danger there is added knowledge that the thing will be used by persons other than the purchaser, and used without new tests, then, irrespective of contract, the manufacturer of this thing of danger is under a duty to make it carefully. That is as far as we are required to go for the decision of this case. There must be knowledge of a danger, not merely possible, but probable. It is *possible* to use almost anything in a way that will make it dangerous if defective. That is not enough to charge the manufacturer with a duty independent of his contract.

Whether a given thing is dangerous may be sometimes a question for the court and sometimes a question for the jury.

There must also be knowledge that in the usual course of events the danger will be shared by others than the buyer. Such knowledge may often be inferred from the nature of the transaction. But it is possible that even knowledge of the danger and of the use will not always be enough. The proximity or remoteness of the relation is a factor to be considered. We are dealing now with the liability of the manufacturer of the finished product, who puts it on the market to be used without inspection by his customers. If he is negligent, where danger is to be foreseen, a liability will follow. We are not required at this time to say that it is legitimate to go back of the manufacturer of the finished product and hold the manufacturers of the component parts. To make their negligence a cause of imminent danger, an independent cause must often intervene; the manufacturer of the finished product must also fail in *his* duty of inspection. It may be that in those circumstances the negligence of the earlier members of the series is too remote to constitute, as to the ultimate user, an actionable wrong. We leave that question open. We shall have to deal with it when it arises. The difficulty which it suggests is not present in this case. There is here no break in the chain of cause and effect. In such circumstances, the presence of a known danger, attendant upon a known use, makes vigilance a duty. We have put aside the notion that the duty to safeguard life and limb, when the consequences of negligence may be foreseen, grows out of contract and nothing else. We have put the source of the obligation where it ought to be. We have put its source in the law.

> "BEYOND ALL QUESTION, the nature of an automobile gives warning of probable danger if its construction is defective. This automobile was designed to go fifty miles an hour. Unless its wheels were sound and strong, injury was almost certain."

From this survey of the decisions, there thus emerges a definition of the duty of a manufacturer which enables us to measure this defendant's liability. Beyond all question, the nature of an automobile gives warning of probable danger if its construction is defective. This automobile was designed to go fifty miles an hour. Unless its wheels were sound and strong, injury was almost certain. It was as much a thing of danger as a defective engine for a railroad. The defendant knew the danger. It knew also that the car would be used by persons other than the buyer. This was apparent from its size; there were seats for three persons. It was apparent also from the fact that the buyer was a dealer in cars, who bought to resell. The maker of this car supplied it for the use of purchasers from the dealer just as plainly as the contractor in *Devlin v. Smith* supplied the scaffold for use by the servants of the owner. The dealer was indeed the one person of whom it might be said with some approach to certainty that by him the car would not be used. Yet the defendant would have us say that he was the one person whom it was under a legal duty to protect. The law does not lead us to so inconsequent a conclusion. Precedents drawn from the days of travel by stage coach do not fit the conditions of travel to-day. The principle that the danger must be imminent does not change, but the things subject to the principle do change. They are whatever the needs of life in a developing civilization require them to be.

We think the defendant was not absolved from a duty of inspection because it bought the wheels from a reputable manufacturer. It was not merely a dealer in automobiles. It was a manufacturer of automobiles. It was responsible for the finished product. It was not at liberty to put the finished product on the market without subjecting the component parts to ordinary and simple tests. Under the charge of the trial judge nothing more was required of it. The obligation to inspect must vary with the nature of the thing to be inspected. The more probable the danger, the greater the need of caution… Both by its relation to the work and by the nature of its business, it is charged with a stricter duty.

The judgment should be affirmed with costs.

IF THE NATURE of a finished product placed on the market by a manufacturer to be used without inspection by his customers is such that it is reasonably certain to place life and limb in peril if the product is negligently made, it is then a thing of danger. Its nature gives warning of the consequences to be expected. If, to the element of danger, there is added knowledge that the thing will be used by persons other than the purchaser, and used without new tests, then, irrespective of contract, the manufacturer of this thing of danger is under a duty to make it carefully. This principle is not limited to poisons, explosives and things of like nature, which in their normal operation are implements of destruction.

The following case provides an example of *res ipsa loquitur* being applied.

Escola v. Coca Cola Bottling Co. of Fresno

California Supreme Court, 1944
24 Cal. 2d 453

Plaintiff, a waitress in a restaurant, was injured when a bottle of Coca Cola broke in her hand. She alleged that defendant company, which had bottled and delivered the alleged defective bottle to her employer, was negligent in selling "bottles containing said beverage which on account of excessive pressure of gas or by reason of some defect in the bottle was dangerous … and likely to explode." This appeal is from a judgment upon a jury verdict in favor of plaintiff.

Defendant's driver delivered several cases of Coca Cola to the restaurant, placing them on the floor, one on top of the other, under and behind the counter, where they remained at least thirty-six hours. Immediately before the accident, plaintiff picked up the top case and set it upon a near-by ice cream cabinet in front of and about three feet from the refrigerator. She then proceeded to take the bottles from the case with her right hand, one at a time, and put them into the refrigerator. Plaintiff testified that after she had placed three bottles in the refrigerator and had moved the fourth bottle about eighteen inches from the case "it exploded in my hand." The bottle broke into two jagged pieces and inflicted a deep five-inch cut, severing blood vessels, nerves and muscles of the thumb and palm of the hand...

One of defendant's drivers, called as a witness by plaintiff, testified that he had seen other bottles of Coca Cola in the past explode and had found broken bottles in the warehouse when he took the cases out, but that he did not know what made them blow up. Plaintiff then rested her case, having announced to the court that being unable to show any specific acts of negligence she relied completely on the doctrine of *res ipsa loquitur*. Defendant contends that the doctrine of *res ipsa loquitur* does not apply in this case, and that the evidence is insufficient to support the judgment.

> "RES IPSA LOQUITUR does not apply unless (1) defendant had exclusive control of the thing causing the injury and (2) the accident is of such a nature that it ordinarily would not occur in the absence of negligence by the defendant."

Res ipsa loquitur does not apply unless (1) defendant had exclusive control of the thing causing the injury and (2) the accident is of such a nature that it ordinarily would not occur in the absence of negligence by the defendant.

Many authorities state that the happening of the accident does not speak for itself where it took place some time after defendant had relinquished control of the instrumentality causing the injury. Under the more logical view, however, the doctrine may be applied upon the theory that defendant had control at the time of the alleged negligent act, although not at the time of the accident, *provided* plaintiff first proves that the condition of the instrumentality had not been changed after it left the defendant's possession.

As said in *Dunn v. Hoffman Beverage Co.*, "defendant is not charged with the duty of showing affirmatively that something happened to the bottle after it left its control or management; ... to get to the jury the plaintiff must show that there was due care during that period." Plaintiff must also prove that she handled the bottle carefully. The reason for this prerequisite is set forth in *Prosser on Torts*, where the author states: "Allied to the condition of exclusive control in the defendant is that of absence of any action on the part of the plaintiff contributing to the accident. Its purpose, of course, is to eliminate the possibility that it was the plaintiff who was responsible. If the boiler of a locomotive explodes while the plaintiff engineer is operating it, the inference of his own negligence is at least as great as that of the defendant, and *res ipsa loquitur* will not apply until he has accounted for his own conduct."

It is not necessary, of course, that plaintiff eliminate every remote possibility of injury to the bottle after defendant lost control, and the requirement is satisfied if there is evidence permitting a reasonable inference that it was not accessible to extraneous harmful forces and that it was carefully handled by plaintiff or any third person who may have moved or touched it. If such evidence is presented, the question becomes one for the trier of fact and, accordingly, the issue should be submitted to the jury under proper instructions.

In the present case no instructions were requested or given on this phase of the case, although general instructions upon *res ipsa loquitur* were given. Defendant, however, has made no claim of error with reference thereto on this appeal. Upon an examination of the record, the evidence appears sufficient to support a reasonable inference that the bottle here involved was not damaged by any extraneous force after delivery to the restaurant by defendant. It follows, therefore, that the bottle was in some manner defective at the time defendant relinquished control, because sound and properly prepared bottles of carbonated liquids do not ordinarily explode when carefully handled.

The next question, then, is whether plaintiff may rely upon the doctrine of *res ipsa loquitur* to supply an inference that defendant's negligence was responsible for the defective condition of the bottle at the time it was delivered to the restaurant. Under the general rules pertaining to the doctrine, as set forth above, it must appear that bottles of carbonated liquid are not ordinarily defective without negligence by the bottling company. In *1 Shearman and Redfield on Negligence*, it is stated that: "The doctrine ... requires evidence which shows at least the probability that a particular accident could not have occurred without legal wrong by the defendant."

An explosion such as took place here might have been caused by an excessive internal pressure in a sound bottle, by a defect in the glass of a bottle containing a safe pressure, or by a combination of these two possible causes. The question is whether under the evidence there was a probability that defendant was negligent in any of these respects. If so, the doctrine of *res ipsa loquitur* applies.

The bottle was admittedly charged with gas under pressure, and the charging of the bottle was within the exclusive control of defendant. As it is a matter of common knowledge that an overcharge would not ordinarily result without negligence, it follows under the doctrine of *res ipsa loquitur* that if the bottle was in fact excessively charged an inference of defendant's negligence would arise. If the explosion resulted from a defective bottle containing a safe pressure, the defendant would be liable if it negligently failed to discover such flaw. If the defect were visible, an inference of negligence would arise from the failure of defendant to discover it. Where defects are discoverable, it may be assumed that they will not ordinarily escape detection if a reasonable inspection is made, and if such a defect is overlooked an inference arises that a proper inspection was not made. A difficult problem is presented where the defect is unknown and consequently might have been one not discoverable by a reasonable, practicable inspection. In the Honea case we refused to take judicial notice of the technical practices and information available to the bottling industry for finding defects which cannot be seen. In the present case, however, we are supplied with evidence of the standard methods used for testing bottles.

A chemical engineer for the Owens-Illinois Glass Company and its Pacific Coast subsidiary, maker of Coca Cola bottles, explained how glass is manufactured and the methods used in testing and inspecting bottles. He testified that his company is the largest manufacturer of glass containers in the United States, and that it uses the standard methods for testing bottles recommended by the glass containers association. A pressure test is made by taking a sample from each mold every three hours-approximately one out of every 600 bottles-and subjecting the sample to an internal pressure of 450 pounds per square inch, which is sustained for one minute. (The normal pressure in Coca Cola bottles is less than 50 pounds per square inch.) The sample bottles are also subjected to the standard thermal shock test. The witness stated that these tests are "pretty near" infallible.

It thus appears that there is available to the industry a commonly-used method of testing bottles for defects not apparent to the eye, which is almost infallible. Since Coca Cola bottles are subjected to these tests by the manufacturer, it is not likely that they contain defects when delivered to the bottler which are not discoverable by visual inspection. Both new and used bottles are filled and distributed by defendant. The used bottles are not again subjected to the tests referred to above, and it may be inferred that defects not discoverable by visual inspection do not develop in bottles after they are manufactured. Obviously, if such defects do occur in used bottles there is a duty upon the bottler to make appropriate tests before they are refilled, and if such tests are not commercially practicable the bottles should not be re-used. This would seem to be particularly true where a charged liquid is placed in the bottle. It follows that a defect which would make the bottle unsound could be discovered by reasonable and practicable tests.

Although it is not clear in this case whether the explosion was caused by an excessive charge or a defect in the glass, there is a sufficient showing that neither cause would ordinarily have been present if due care had been used. Further, defendant had exclusive control over both the charging and inspection of the bottles. Accordingly, all the requirements necessary to entitle plaintiff to rely on the doctrine of *res ipsa loquitur* to supply an inference of negligence are present.

It is true that defendant presented evidence tending to show that it exercised considerable precaution by carefully regulating and checking the pressure in the bottles and by making visual inspections for defects in the glass at several stages during the bottling process. It is well settled, however, that when a defendant produces evidence to rebut the inference of negligence which arises upon application of the doctrine of *res ipsa loquitur*, it is ordinarily a question of fact for the jury to determine whether the inference has been dispelled.

The judgment is affirmed.

THE DOCTRINE OF *RES IPSA LOQUITUR* may be applied on the theory that defendant had control of the instrumentality causing the injury at the time of the alleged negligent act, although not at the time of the accident, provided plaintiff first proves that the condition of the instrumentality had not been changed after it left defendant's possession. The doctrine of *res ipsa loquitur* does not apply unless defendant had exclusive control of the thing causing the injury and the accident is of such a nature that it ordinarily would not occur in the absence of negligence by defendant.

B. STRICT LIABILITY

Strict liability is awkwardly named for a product liability case because in some respects, courts view some manufacturing issues as satisfying the strict liability requirement that the company is introducing an unreasonably dangerous—or ultra-hazardous—product into the market. If this is true, then following the logic of strict liability, any damages caused by the product would make the company liable. The following case demonstrates the application of this aspect of strict (product) liability.

Brewer v. Oriard Powder Co.

Supreme Court of Washington, 1965
401 P.2d 844

This is an action to recover damages for personal injuries suffered by plaintiffs while employed by Murphy Brothers, who had contracted for construction work on a United States missile site. The injuries, which were very serious, were caused by a premature explosion of dynamite which had been issued to them by their employer to be used in blasting holes for the construction. The plaintiffs' employer had purchased the dynamite from Oriard Powder Company. The dynamite had been manufactured by Atlas Chemical Industries. The dynamite and essential detonating components were sold and delivered by Atlas to Oriard and, in turn, to Murphy Brothers in the original containers.

The plaintiffs alleged that Atlas had manufactured and sold dangerous, unfit and defective dynamite explosives, primers, blasting caps, related components and accessories which were unfit and dangerous for normal use. They further alleged that Atlas had failed to adequately test or inspect these explosives prior to sale and had knowledge that they were defective and dangerous. The plaintiffs' complaint stated that Oriard was engaged in the sale of these unfit, defective and dangerous products and that it 'had notice of circumstances of the dangers relating to said products and their use by the public and was negligent in failing to test and experiment with said explosives before its products were sold to the public.'

Their third cause of action was that the defendants breached their express and implied warranties of fitness in the manufacture, distribution and sale of the products involved. In a fourth cause of action, the plaintiffs alleged that defendants are absolutely liable to plaintiffs for the injuries and damages sustained. The defendants' answers to this complaint contain general denials and allegations of contributory negligence and assumption of risk. The defendant Oriard asks in the event the plaintiffs recover judgment against Oriard that it, in turn, be awarded judgment against Atlas.

The trial court declined to grant Oriard's motion for summary judgment but dismissed plaintiffs' complaint with prejudice and awarded judgment in favor of the defendants at the conclusion of the opening statement of counsel for the plaintiffs. This is an appeal from the judgment of dismissal.

The question to be resolved by us in this case is: Is the theory of breach of implied warranty of fitness applicable under the facts and circumstances of this case?

The right of an injured person to recover from a manufacturer or retailer for breach of implied warranty in the absence of privity of contract presents what might well be described as the Sargasso Sea of the law. It is filled with entangling theories, rules and doctrines from which courts throughout the United States and England have been attempting to extricate themselves for decades… There is a certain and steady trend in the direction of fixing greater responsibility in manufacturers and sellers.

This court was in the vanguard of the movement to solve these vexing problems when we decided the case of *Mazetti v. Armour & Co.* In that case, it was held that a manufacturer may be liable for damages, irrespective of privity of contract, in the manufacture and sale of food products. The Mazetti case extended that liability to a restaurateur who had purchased from a retail grocer contaminated and impure canned meat manufactured by the defendant. This court discussed the various theories upon which other courts had reached similar conclusions and stated as a basis of the decision: 'Our holding is that, in the absence of an express warranty of quality, a manufacturer of food products under modern conditions impliedly warrants his goods when dispensed in original packages, and that such warranty is available to all who may be damaged by reason of their use in the legitimate channels of trade.' It has been well established by this court that privity of contract is not required in order that there be an implied warranty of fitness where the article involved is food, clothing, drugs, or cosmetics. The reason for these exceptions would appear to be that these items are manufactured and sold with knowledge that they will come into direct contact with the human body either externally or internally.

We held in *LaHue v. Coca Cola Bottling, Inc.*, that, in an action by a remote vendee against the manufacturer of bottled beverages, privity of contract was not an essential element and this was an exception to the general rule of nonliability. Although that suit was based upon the theory of breach of implied warranty, the court pointed out that the liability rests more upon a theory of violation of duty to members of the general public to protect them from injuries due to the wrongful manufacture or distribution of food products or beverages.

In *Esborg v. Bailey Drug Co., supra*, we extended the doctrine of implied warranty without privity of contract to a cosmetic intended for application to the hair, scalp or skin. In the carefully considered opinion in *Freeman v. Navarre*, this court recognized the changes which have appeared in the law relative to the privity rule.

We stated: 'The exception to the privity of contract doctrine has been extended in our state to so-called inherently dangerous instrumentalities.'

This court emphasized the continuing trend away from the privity rule in warranty cases... 'The seller's warranty is a curious hybrid of tort and contract. It has not lost its original tort character. Of course, if breach of actual representations can be proved and there is privity of parties, the action may be in contract; but primarily, a manufacturer's liability for having furnished an inherently dangerous product to the public sounds in tort. That the action is a product of the common-law decisions has been recognized in a variety of situations.

The *Greenman* case, cited in Dipangrazio, undoubtedly goes beyond anything necessary for disposition of the case now before the court, since it is based upon strict liability without negligence or privity... It seems that a searching judicial review of the privity rule is in order, but that such is not necessary for the disposition of the appeal in the case at bar. If impure food, flammable clothing, and toxic cosmetics are so inherently dangerous to the consumer or ultimate user that we waive the requisite of privity of contract, the exception certainly must be extended to dynamite or explosives. The manufacturer knows that dynamite and its components and accessories will finally be touched, handled and used by employees of the retail purchaser and, being aware of this, must be held to impliedly warrant the fitness of his product. Few commodities are more dangerous than dynamite and it can be far more lethal than canned food, housedresses, toothpaste, or lipstick.

Consequently, we now hold that a manufacturer of dynamite is liable to the ultimate user for breach of implied warranty of fitness without regard to privity of contract. The appellants alleged in their complaint that Oriard had notice of the circumstances of the dangers relating to these explosives and their use by the public and was negligent in failing to test them before they were sold. The appellants further mentioned in their opening statement that they had never been warned of the possibility of premature explosion. Under these circumstances, we do not feel that Oriard is entitled to dismissal of the complaint against it and award of summary judgment at this time.

The judgment of the trial court dismissing appellants' claim with prejudice is reversed and the cause remanded for trial.

> "IF IMPURE FOOD, flammable clothing, and toxic cosmetics are so inherently dangerous to the consumer or ultimate user that we waive the requisite of privity of contract, the exception certainly must be extended to dynamite or explosives."

LIKE NEGLIGENCE, strict liability can apply to a number of different parts of the manufacturing process. For example, a manufacturer can be found subject to strict liability for defects present in the actual manufacturing process, or for defects in the design of the product. A defect in the manufacturing process is proven by showing that the product did not meet the manufacturer's own specifications. A design is considered defective if it makes the product unreasonably dangerous—the argument is that there was a reasonable, alternative design that would have made the product safer. The courts consider different factors on a case-by-case basis to determine what is "reasonable" or "unreasonable." The following case demonstrates how the courts apply strict liability to manufacturing defects and design defects.

Transue v. Aesthetech Corp.

United States Court of Appeals, Ninth Circuit, 2003
341 F.3d 911

In 1985, Transue received silicone-gel filled breast implants manufactured by Medical Engineering Corporation, Inc., a wholly-owned subsidiary of Bristol-Myers Squibb Company (collectively, "BMS"). The implantation was performed by Dr. Hobart J. White of Tacoma, Washington. Transue alleges that the implants ruptured inside of her body, causing tissue death, scarring, pain, and permanent silicone contamination of her body. BMS claims that a 1993 mammogram, a 1994 ultrasound, the opinion of the only plastic surgeon who testified at trial, Dr. Stevens, and a 1995 xerogram all indicate that the implants did not rupture while inside Transue's body. In 1995, Transue underwent explant surgery to remove the implants and replaced them with saline implants, which she currently uses. Transue alleges that her injuries are permanent and that she will have to undergo periodic implant and explant surgery for her lifetime.

■ SILICONE
BREAST IMPLANTS.

Image: Thinkstock

On October 18, 1994, Transue filed suit against BMS in state court in Seattle, Washington, seeking damages caused by the allegedly defective breast implant devices. BMS filed a Motion for Summary Judgment or in the Alternative for Summary Adjudication. The district court granted BMS summary judgment as to all of Transue's claims except her claims under the Washington Product Liability Act ("WPLA"). The district court also disallowed Transue's claim for punitive damages.

Transue's remaining claims, after summary judgment, arise under the WPLA, which consolidated the previously used common law theories of product liability. Specifically, the surviving claims were the standard product liability claims, alleging manufacturing defects, design defects, and a failure to adequately warn, as well as a claim alleging that BMS breached express and implied warranties. In the Joint Pretrial Order, BMS responded to Transue's claims by denying that its products were defective in design, manufacture, or warning, and denying that it breached any warranty or made any misrepresentation regarding the implants. Further, BMS asserted the learned intermediary doctrine as an affirmative defense, and also asserted the defense that Transue assumed the risk of the injuries she alleges and/or that others contributed to causing her injuries, and therefore, that the fault should be distributed proportionally.

After a ten-day jury trial, the jury returned a verdict for the defendants on all of Transue's claims. Instructed on negligence, and not strict liability, the jury found that (1) BMS manufactured Transue's breast implants; (2) BMS did not fail to use ordinary care in designing the implants; (3) BMS did not fail to use ordinary care in manufacturing the implants; and (4) BMS did not fail to use ordinary care in issuing warnings or instructions. Transue filed a notice of appeal.

Transue contends that the district court committed reversible error by failing to issue strict liability jury instructions, and instead issuing negligence jury instructions with regard to the manufacturing and design defect claims. BMS contends that Comment *K* to the Restatement (Second) of Torts,§ 402A governs manufacturing and design defect claims in this case, and exempts from strict liability medical devices, such as breast implants, that are available only through a prescribing physician. Transue argues that BMS "lead[s] the trial court into error by arguing that Comment K completely eviscerates strict liability in any medical device case, which it does not." Transue essentially argues that Comment *K* does not apply to breast implant devices, and, even if it does, it does not provide blanket immunity from strict liability, but only exempts design defect claims. Transue states that the district court "did not give Plaintiff a chance to prove her manufacturing defect claim under the correct law," which is strict liability, and that the negligence instruction misdirected the jury.

Given the conclusion that Comment *K* mandates different jury instructions with respect to design and manufacturing defect claims, the discussion below evaluates Comment *K* in the context of different product liability theories.

A. *Under Washington law, Comment K affords a blanket exemption from strict liability for design defects in medical devices or products.*

Despite Transue's argument to the contrary, "[t]here is no debate" that Washington courts have expressly adopted the Comment *K* exception to strict liability in the case of unavoidably unsafe products. Moreover, as discussed below, the Washington Supreme Court has indicated that Comment *K* provides an exemption for medical products generally.

The Washington Supreme Court treated the issue in three cases leading up to its recent opinion in *Ruiz-Guzman*. First, in *Terhune v. A.H. Robins Co.*, the court found that the Dalkon Shield implanted contraceptive device qualified for Comment *K* exemption because of its availability only through a physician. Second, in *Rogers v. Miles Laboratories, Inc.*, the court held that blood and blood products qualify for Comment *K* exemption. Third, a plurality of the court in *Young v. Key Pharmaceuticals, Inc.*, held that "a separate determination of whether a product is unavoidably unsafe need not be made on a case-by-case basis if that product is a prescription drug." Finally, in its recent opinion in *Ruiz-Guzman*, the court held that "[b]y its own terms, Comment *K* is especially applicable to medical products. The exceptions for medical products recognize the unique protection provided to the consumers of such products by the prescribing physician (and/ or pharmacist) intermediary." The court held that a "product-by-product" determination is to be made with regard to whether pesticides are governed by Comment *K*, "as opposed to a *blanket exemption* like that for medical products." While this statement in *Ruiz-Guzman* appears to be dicta, the Washington Supreme Court expressed its belief that all medical products receive blanket Comment *K* exemption.

It appears that the issue of whether a breast implant, specifically, is a "medical device or product" that is unavoidably unsafe and therefore receives Comment *K* exemption has not been directly addressed by Washington courts. However, breast implants fall within the rationale of *Ruiz-Guzman* for providing Comment *K* immunity for medical devices and products. This rationale emphasizes the presence of physicians as intermediaries between manufacturers and consumers, and recognizes that "[a] physician possesses the medical training to assess adverse health effects of a medical product and to tailor that assessment to a particular patient."

The California appellate courts have addressed the issue more directly and concluded that breast implants, along with other implanted medical products or devices, are within the ambit of Comment *K*.

B. *Comment K does not permit a negligence instruction with respect to a manufacturing defect claim.*

Despite the conclusion above that Comment K applies to breast implants, Comment *K* should not be construed to provide protection for manufacturing defect claims based on unavoidably unsafe products. For the purposes of manufacturing defects, the relevant portion of Comment *K* states: "Such a product, *properly prepared*, and accompanied by proper directions and warning, is not defective, nor is it unreasonably dangerous.... The seller of such products, again with the qualification that they are *properly prepared* and marketed, and proper warning is given, where the situation calls for it, is not to be held to strict liability...."

At trial, Transue argued that the proper standard for a manufacturing defect, even under Comment *K*, is strict liability. The district court, however, read the word "properly," italicized above, to indicate that a negligence standard is appropriate... Indeed, a number of authorities from other jurisdictions persuasively indicate that such a jump is not warranted and that, in fact, Comment *K* is not intended to apply a negligence standard to manufacturing defect claims in the context of unavoidably unsafe products. As the Idaho Supreme Court wrote:

> By its terms, Comment K excepts unavoidably unsafe products from strict liability only where the plaintiff alleges a design defect, and not where the

plaintiff alleges a manufacturing flaw or an inadequate warning. Comment K intends to shield from strict liability products which cannot be designed more safely; however, if such products are mismanufactured or unaccompanied by adequate warnings, then the seller may be liable even if the plaintiff cannot establish the seller's negligence. Courts and commentators universally agree to this limitation on Comment K's grant of immunity from strict liability.

The point was reiterated recently by a California court in the context of a breast implant case. The *Artiglio* court explained *Brown* as holding that:

> Liability for defective design [of prescription drugs] could not be premised on strict liability, but would require proof of negligence. Strict liability would continue applicable for manufacturing defects; and liability for failure to warn of known or reasonably knowable risks in the use of the product remains viable "under general principles of negligence."

This understanding of Comment *K* is further supported by commentary in the Restatement (Third) of Torts: Product Liability, discussing a section analogous to§ 402A of the Restatement (Second) of Torts. "Limitations on the liability for prescription drug and medical-device designs do not support treating drug and medical-device manufacturers differently from commercial sellers of other products with respect to manufacturing defects. Courts have traditionally subjected manufacturers of prescription products to liability for harm caused by manufacturing defects." Rest. (3d) Torts: Prod. Liab.§ 6 (1998) Comment C.

Therefore, the district court erred in denying Transue's request that a strict liability jury instruction be given with respect to her claim alleging a manufacturing defect.

BMS argues that, even if Washington law recognizes strict liability for manufacturing defects where Comment *K* applies, the plaintiff did not present sufficient evidence to entitle her to a manufacturing defect instruction. The district court issued jury instructions covering Transue's manufacturing defect claim. While the district court noted that BMS was challenging the appellant's contention that a manufacturing defect existed and the appellant's theory of causation, there was no indication by the district court that there was insufficient evidence to support a jury instruction on the alleged manufacturing defect... Instead, the district court indicated that the manufacturing defect instruction was simply to employ the same standard as the design defect instruction. The district court gave these manufacturing defect instructions: Jury Instruction No. 11: "Plaintiff claims that defendants were negligent ... by failing to use ordinary care in the manufacturing of plaintiff's implants...."; Jury Instruction No. 14: "With regard to plaintiff's claim that the manufacturer was negligent in designing and/or manufacturing her breast implants, the plaintiff has the burden of proving each of the following propositions...." Because circumstantial evidence may be a sufficient basis for instructing a jury, we are satisfied that BMS has failed to demonstrate that the error relating to the manufacturing defect instruction was more probably than not harmless.

Based on the erroneous jury instructions given by the district court, the case is reversed and remanded.

Unavoidably unsafe products, as in Comment K, are excepted from strict liability only where the plaintiff alleges a design defect, and not where the plaintiff alleges a manufacturing flaw or an inadequate warning.

As seen in the case above, Section 402A of the Restatement (Second) of Torts, Comment K, provides a blanket exception for unavoidably unsafe products in strict liability product defect claims. Comment K states:

> There are some products which, in the present state of human knowledge, are quite incapable of being made safe for their intended and ordinary use. These are especially common in the field of drugs. An outstanding example is the vaccine for the Pasteur treatment of rabies, which not uncommonly leads to very serious and damaging consequences when it is injected. Since the disease itself invariably leads to a dreadful death, both the marketing and the use of the vaccine are fully justified, notwithstanding the unavoidable high degree of risk which they involve. Such a product, properly prepared, and accompanied by proper directions and warning, is not defective, nor is it unreasonably dangerous. The same is true of many other drugs, vaccines, and the like, many of which for this very reason cannot legally be sold except to physicians, or under the prescription of a physician. It is also true in particular of many new or experimental drugs as to which, because of lack of time and opportunity for sufficient medical experience, there can be no assurance of safety, or perhaps even of purity of ingredients, but such experience as there is justifies the marketing and use of the drug notwithstanding a medically recognizable risk. The seller of such products, again with the qualification that they are properly prepared and marketed, and proper warning is given, where the situation calls for it, is not to be held to strict liability for unfortunate consequences attending their use, merely because he has undertaken to supply the public with an apparently useful and desirable product, attended with a known but apparently reasonable risk.

The conventional application of strict liability tends to differ from what we see in products liability cases because in products liability cases, the courts allow some negligence-like testing of manufacturing processes to determine liability. For example, remember from the chapter on torts, if one keeps a pet mountain lion, one is liable for the damages caused by the mountain lion no matter how "careful" or "prudent" the lion owner has been. A lion is simply too dangerous. There is no testing as to whether one has exercised proper prudence.

Yet, in products liability cases, courts do allow companies to demonstrate that the costs associated by making a product safer would be so expensive so as to make the product unable to compete in the market. Thus, there are balancing tests within the strict liability framework that do look much like a negligence case. The following case demonstrates these kinds of balancing tests in a strict products liability case.

Barker v. Lull Engineering Co.

Supreme Court of California, 1978
573 P.2d 443

In August 1970, plaintiff Ray Barker was injured at a construction site at the University of California at Santa Cruz while operating a high-lift loader manufactured by defendant Lull Engineering Co. and leased to plaintiff's employer by defendant George M. Philpott Co., Inc. Claiming that his injuries were proximately caused, *inter alia*, by the alleged defective design of the loader, Barker instituted the present tort action seeking to recover damages for his injuries. The jury returned a verdict in favor of defendants, and plaintiff appeals from the judgment entered upon that verdict, contending primarily that... the trial court erred in instructing the jury "that strict liability for a defect in design of a product is based on a finding that the product was unreasonably dangerous for its intended use . . . ."

As numerous recent judicial decisions and academic commentaries have recognized, the formulation of a satisfactory definition of "design defect" has proven a formidable task; trial judges have repeatedly confronted difficulties in attempting to devise accurate and helpful instructions in design defect cases. Aware of these problems, we have undertaken a review of the past California decisions which have grappled with the design defect issue, and have measured their conclusions against the fundamental policies which underlie the entire strict product liability doctrine.

As we explain in more detail below, we have concluded from this review that a product is defective in design either (1) if the product has failed to perform as safely as an ordinary consumer would expect when used in an intended or reasonably foreseeable manner, or (2) if, in light of the relevant factors discussed below, the benefits of the challenged design do not outweigh the risk of danger inherent in such design. In addition, we explain how the burden of proof with respect to the latter "risk-benefit" standard should be allocated.

This dual standard for design defect assures an injured plaintiff protection from products that either fall below ordinary consumer expectations as to safety, or that,

> **"THE FORMULATION of a satisfactory definition of 'design defect' has proven a formidable task; trial judges have repeatedly confronted difficulties in attempting to devise accurate and helpful instructions in design defect cases."**

on balance, are not as safely designed as they should be. At the same time, the standard permits a manufacturer who has marketed a product which satisfies ordinary consumer expectations to demonstrate the relative complexity of design decisions and the trade-offs that are frequently required in the adoption of alternative designs. Finally, this test reflects our continued adherence to the principle that, in a product liability action, the trier of fact must focus on the product, not on the manufacturer's conduct, and that the plaintiff need not prove that the manufacturer acted unreasonably or negligently in order to prevail in such an action.

Plaintiff's principal expert witness initially testified that by reason of its relatively narrow base the loader was unstable and had a tendency to roll over when lifting loads to considerable heights... Evidence at trial revealed that cranes and some high lift loader models are either regularly equipped with outriggers or offer outriggers as optional equipment. Plaintiff's expert testified that the availability of outriggers would probably have averted the present accident. The expert additionally testified that the loader was defective in that it was not equipped with a roll bar or seat belts. He stated that such safety devices were essential to protect the operator in the event that the machine rolled over. Plaintiff theorized that the lack of such safety equipment was a proximate cause of his injuries because in the absence of such devices he had no reasonable choice but to leap from the loader as it began to tip. If a seat belt and roll bar had been provided, plaintiff argued, he could have remained in the loader and would not have been struck by the falling lumber. Finally, plaintiff's experts testified that the absence of a "park" position on the loader's transmission, that could have been utilized to avoid the possibility of the loader's movement during a lift, constituted a further defect in design which may have caused the accident.

Defendants explain that in a manufacturing defect case, a jury may find a product defective because it deviates from the manufacturer's intended result, but may still decline to impose liability under the Restatement test on the ground that such defect did not render the product unreasonably dangerous. In a design defect case, by contrast, defendants assert that a defect is defined by reference to the "unreasonably dangerous" standard... In essence, defendants argue that under the instruction which the trial court gave in the instant case, plaintiff was not required to prove both that the loader was defective and that such defect made the loader unreasonably dangerous, but only that the loader was defectively designed by virtue of its unreasonable dangerousness.

First, our cases establish that a product may be found defective in design if the plaintiff demonstrates that the product failed to perform as safely as an ordinary consumer would expect when used in an intended or reasonably foreseeable manner. When a product fails to satisfy such ordinary consumer expectations as to safety in its intended or reasonably foreseeable operation, a manufacturer is strictly liable for resulting injuries...

The expectations of the ordinary consumer cannot be viewed as the exclusive yardstick for evaluating design defectiveness because "(i)n many situations . . . the consumer would not know what to expect, because he would have no idea how safe the product could be made." Numerous California decisions have implicitly recognized this fact and have made clear, through varying linguistic formulations, that a product may be found defective in design, even if it satisfies ordinary consumer expectations, if through hindsight the jury determines that the product's design embodies "excessive preventable danger," or, in other words, if the jury finds that the risk of danger inherent in the challenged design outweighs the benefits of such design.

A review of past cases indicates that in evaluating the adequacy of a product's design pursuant to this latter standard, a jury may consider, among other relevant factors, the gravity of the danger posed by the challenged design, the likelihood that such danger would occur, the mechanical feasibility of a safer alternative design, the financial cost of an improved design, and the adverse consequences to the product and to the consumer that would result from an alternative design.

If a jury in determining liability for a defect in design is instructed only that it should decide whether or not there is "a defective design," it may reach to the extreme conclusion that the plaintiff, having suffered injury, should without further showing, recover; on the other hand, it may go to the opposite extreme and conclude that because the product matches the intended design the plaintiff, under no conceivable circumstance, could recover. The submitted definition eschews both extremes and attempts a balanced approach.

We hold that a trial judge may properly instruct the jury that a product is defective in design (1) if the plaintiff demonstrates that the product failed to perform as safely as an ordinary consumer would expect when used in an intended or reasonably foreseeable manner, or (2) if the plaintiff proves that the product's design proximately caused his injury and the defendant fails to prove, in light of the relevant factors discussed above, that on balance the benefits of the challenged design outweigh the risk of danger inherent in such design.

Because the jury may have interpreted the erroneous instruction given in the instant case as requiring plaintiff to prove that the high-lift loader was ultrahazardous or more dangerous than the average consumer contemplated, and because the instruction additionally misinformed the jury that the defectiveness of the product must be evaluated in light of the product's "intended use" rather than its "reasonably foreseeable use," we cannot find that the error was harmless on the facts of this case.

The judgment in favor of defendants is reversed.

TO DETERMINE IF A PRODUCT is "unreasonably dangerous" for purposes of a strict liability claim, fact finders should consider a number of factors, including whether the product's design represents a fair balance between the cost of designing a safer product, the risk of injury, and whether the product satisfies consumer expectations.

IV. Special Issues of Damages

AS INDICATED AT THE BEGINNING of this chapter, damages can be large in product liability cases. Some part of this is, as previously indicated with punitive damages, the theory that the damage award needs to be high enough to get the attention of a large, wealthy company. If the award is small, it will be ignored, the argument goes, and simply be viewed as a cost of doing business. No changes will be made. The idea of punitive damages is that it is an opportunity to make products safer. Thus, there is a built-in logic to any kind of punitive damage award, at least against a large company. However, as seen in the case below, the Supreme Court has attempted to mitigate the trend towards grossly excessive punitive damages that it considers unconstitutional.

BMW of North America, Inc. v. Gore

Supreme Court of the United States, 1996
517 U.S. 559

After Dr. Gore purchased a new BMW automobile from an authorized Alabama dealer, he discovered that the car had been repainted. He brought this suit for compensatory and punitive damages against petitioner, the American distributor of BMW's, alleging, *inter alia*, that the failure to disclose the repainting constituted fraud under Alabama law. At trial, BMW acknowledged that it followed a nationwide policy of not advising its dealers, and hence their customers, of pre-delivery damage to new cars when the cost of repair did not exceed 3 percent of the car's suggested retail price. Gore's vehicle fell into that category. The jury returned a verdict finding BMW liable for compensatory damages of $4,000, and assessing $4 million in punitive damages.

The Due Process Clause of the Fourteenth Amendment prohibits a State from imposing a "grossly excessive" punishment on a tortfeasor. The wrongdoing involved in this case was the decision by a national distributor of automobiles not to advise its dealers, and hence their customers, of pre-delivery damage to new cars when the cost of repair amounted to less than 3 percent of the car's suggested retail price. The question presented is whether a $2 million punitive damages award to the purchaser of one of these cars exceeds the constitutional limit.

Punitive damages may properly be imposed to further a State's legitimate interests in punishing unlawful conduct and deterring its repetition. In our federal system, States necessarily have considerable flexibility in determining the level of punitive damages that they will allow in different classes of cases and in any particular case. Most States that authorize exemplary damages afford the jury similar latitude, requiring only that the damages awarded be reasonably necessary to vindicate the State's legitimate interests in punishment and deterrence. Only when an award can fairly be categorized as "grossly excessive" in relation to these interests does it enter the zone of arbitrariness that violates the Due Process Clause of the Fourteenth

Amendment. For that reason, the federal excessiveness inquiry appropriately begins with an identification of the state interests that a punitive award is designed to serve. We therefore focus our attention first on the scope of Alabama's legitimate interests in punishing BMW and deterring it from future misconduct.

No one doubts that a State may protect its citizens by prohibiting deceptive trade practices and by requiring automobile distributors to disclose presale repairs that affect the value of a new car. But the States need not, and in fact do not, provide such protection in a uniform manner. Some States rely on the judicial process to formulate and enforce an appropriate disclosure requirement by applying principles of contract and tort law. Other States have enacted various forms of legislation that define the disclosure obligations of automobile manufacturers, distributors, and dealers. The result is a patchwork of rules representing the diverse policy judgments of lawmakers in 50 States.

We may assume, *arguendo,* that it would be wise for every State to adopt Dr. Gore's preferred rule, requiring full disclosure of every presale repair to a car, no matter how trivial and regardless of its actual impact on the value of the car. But while we do not doubt that Congress has ample authority to enact such a policy for the entire Nation, it is clear that no single State could do so, or even impose its own policy choice on neighboring States. Similarly, one State's power to impose burdens on the interstate market for automobiles is not only subordinate to the federal power over interstate commerce... We think it follows from these principles of state sovereignty and comity that a State may not impose economic sanctions on violators of its laws with the intent of changing the tortfeasors' lawful conduct in other States. Before this Court Dr. Gore argued that the large punitive damages award was necessary to induce BMW to change the nationwide policy that it adopted in 1983. But by attempting to alter BMW's nationwide policy, Alabama would be infringing on the policy choices of other States. To avoid such encroachment, the economic penalties that a State such as Alabama inflicts on those who transgress its laws, whether the penalties take the form of legislatively authorized fines or judicially imposed punitive damages, must be supported by the State's interest in protecting its own consumers and its own economy. Alabama may insist that BMW adhere to a particular disclosure policy in that State. Alabama does not have the power, however, to punish BMW for conduct that was lawful where it occurred and that had no impact on Alabama or its residents. Nor may Alabama impose sanctions on BMW in order to deter conduct that is lawful in other jurisdictions.

In this case, we accept the Alabama Supreme Court's interpretation of the jury verdict as reflecting a computation of the amount of punitive damages "based in large part on conduct that happened in other jurisdictions." As the Alabama Supreme Court noted, neither the jury nor the trial court was presented with evidence that any of BMW's out-of-state conduct was unlawful. "The only testimony touching the issue showed that approximately 60% of the vehicles that were refinished were sold in states where failure to disclose the repair was not an unfair trade practice." The Alabama Supreme Court therefore properly eschewed reliance on BMW's out-of-state conduct and based its remitted award solely on conduct that occurred within

Alabama. The award must be analyzed in the light of the same conduct, with consideration given only to the interests of Alabama consumers, rather than those of the entire Nation. When the scope of the interest in punishment and deterrence that an Alabama court may appropriately consider is properly limited, it is apparent—for reasons that we shall now address—that this award is grossly excessive.

Elementary notions of fairness enshrined in our constitutional jurisprudence dictate that a person receive fair notice not only of the conduct that will subject him to punishment, but also of the severity of the penalty that a State may impose. Three guideposts, each of which indicates that BMW did not receive adequate notice of the magnitude of the sanction that Alabama might impose for adhering to the nondisclosure policy adopted in 1983, lead us to the conclusion that the $2 million award against BMW is grossly excessive: the degree of reprehensibility of the nondisclosure; the disparity between the harm or potential harm suffered by Dr. Gore and his punitive damages award; and the difference between this remedy and the civil penalties authorized or imposed in comparable cases.

The sanction imposed in this case cannot be justified on the ground that it was necessary to deter future misconduct without considering whether less drastic remedies could be expected to achieve that goal. The fact that a multimillion dollar penalty prompted a change in policy sheds no light on the question whether a lesser deterrent would have adequately protected the interests of Alabama consumers. The fact that BMW is a large corporation rather than an impecunious individual does not diminish its entitlement to fair notice of the demands that the several States impose on the conduct of its business. Indeed, its status as an active participant in the national economy implicates the federal interest in preventing individual States from imposing undue burdens on interstate commerce. While each State has ample power to protect its own consumers, none may use the punitive damages deterrent as a means of imposing its regulatory policies on the entire Nation.

The judgment is reversed, and the case is remanded for further proceedings not inconsistent with this opinion.

A SECOND REASON FOR LARGE DAMAGE AWARDS is attributable to the ways trials proceed. There is an old trial law adage called "waving the bloody foot." This means that the more a plaintiff has been injured, the more the lawyer wants that injured plaintiff in plain view, even right in front of a jury. By "waving the bloody foot," the plaintiff's lawyer will generate sympathy for the client. Jury members will then, the tactic assumes, be more sympathetic to the injured plaintiff and be more prone to making an award. That is particularly true if the contrast with the plaintiff is a wealthy, anonymous corporation that has deep pockets and probably a lot of insurance as well. While some of these attributes are, in theory, inadmissible as evidence, lawyers find ways of making this contrast clear in the courtroom and, thus, compensatory damages may tend to be higher as well.

The following case demonstrates the high cost that can come with compensatory damage awards.

Harley-Davidson Motor Co., Inc. v. Wisniewski

Court of Special Appeals of Maryland, 1981
437 A.2d 700

Michael S. Wisniewski, plaintiff below and appellee herein, purchased a new Harley-Davidson motorcycle from Garrett's Harley-Davidson in April of 1978. On September 16, 1978, appellee was riding his motorcycle at approximately 25 m.p.h. on an "S" shaped curve along Key Highway in South Baltimore when the throttle slipped off the handlebar. He lost control of the bike, crossed into the lanes of on-coming traffic and collided with a car traveling in the opposite lane at approximately the same speed.

The throttle control mechanism of the motorcycle was the type which operates the throttle by rotating the right handgrip on the handlebar. The alleged defect in this case was stated as an improper assembly of the throttle control clamp causing a clamp screw to suddenly fracture. This, it is contended, permitted the throttle control mechanism to come off the handlebar while the appellee was operating his motorcycle.

Appellee's principal injuries consisted of leg fractures of the right tibia and left femur. He required hospitalization for slightly less than two months and his total expenses for medical care and hospitalization were $14,786.20. In addition, he lost $11,152 in income. Repairs to his motorcycle cost $2,964.09. The stipulated total of medical bills, lost income and property damage was $28,902.29.

The Superior Court granted seller partial summary judgment as to punitive damages, but denied manufacturer's motions for summary judgment on punitive damages, and, after trial, entered judgment on jury verdict awarding rider $544,604 for compensatory damages and $1,900,000 punitive damages against manufacturer. After judgment was entered in favor of seller against manufacturer for indemnity for full amount of seller's liability to rider, both seller and manufacturer appealed.

Harley-Davidson raises the following two issues to be determined by this Court:

> I. Whether the trial court erred in denying appellant's motion for a directed verdict on the issue of punitive damages?

> II. Whether the trial court should have granted a new trial on the issue of compensatory damages because of the claimed prejudice by the allegedly erroneous submission of the punitive damage issue to the jury?

In our consideration of the issues raised by the appellants in this case, we note initially that appellants do not challenge the jury's specific finding of negligence on the part of the appellants. The question then remains whether there was sufficient evidence to require the trial judge to submit to the jury the question of the assessment of punitive damages against the appellant. Maryland has adhered to the principle that a manufacturer is required to compensate a consumer for all injuries proximately caused by products either defectively designed or manufactured.

We have carefully considered the voluminous record extract filed in this case and we find no evidence that Harley-Davidson was aware of the cross-threaded throttle clamps. Nor does the evidence reveal the existence of a design defect which would inherently present the probability of recurrence of the danger to the consumer. There was more than sufficient evidence to establish negligence on the part of Harley-Davidson. It was obvious from the testimony that the appellant had used less than an ideal assembly process which involved the complete tightening of each of the throttle screws separately, rather than alternating each to the desired level of torque. There was, however, no evidence to establish the manufacturer's substantial knowledge of the existence of the danger to the plaintiff.

> **"IN ORDER to find "recklessness" in such circumstances there must be a readily perceptible danger and a conscious choice by the manufacturer to market the product despite the risk."**

In order to find "recklessness" in such circumstances there must be a readily perceptible danger and a conscious choice by the manufacturer to market the product despite the risk. We find nothing in the record to substantiate knowledge of the existence of the danger by the manufacturer or gross indifference to its existence. Under all the circumstances, we conclude that the trial court erred when it denied Harley-Davidson's motions for directed verdict on the issue of punitive damages.

Appellant finally urges that it is entitled to a new trial on the issue of compensatory damages because it was substantially prejudiced by the trial court's erroneous submission of the punitive damage issue to the jury. It points out that Maryland has never had occasion to evaluate the prejudicial impact on compensatory damages of an erroneous denial of a motion for directed verdict on a claim for punitive damages. This Court, however, has held that evidence of a defendant's wealth is probative and admissible only where a *prima facie* case for punitive damages has been established. Appellant suggests that the evidence of wealth of the defendant and the impassioned plea by plaintiff's counsel for punishment of Harley-Davidson created an obvious potential for prejudice and resulted in an improper verdict for compensatory damages. It suggests the only cure for this prejudicial potential is, in effect, the adoption of a per se rule that where such error occurs, a new trial as to compensatory damages must be allowed. We do not agree that such a rigid rule is mandated. We prefer to examine the evidence, on a case-by-case basis, and to determine whether a new trial on the issue of compensatory damages is required where a case has been erroneously submitted to the jury on the issue of punitive damages.

Our examination of the evidence in this case convinces us that there is no proof that the verdict for compensatory damages in this case was based on prejudice or bias. The appellee, a comparatively young man, sustained serious injuries to both legs which resulted in the permanent shortening of one of his limbs. The plaintiff, without objection, submitted to the jury a per diem calculation of what plaintiff considered an appropriate award for pain and suffering of $465,702. The plaintiff requested $615,000 as compensatory damages. The trial judge specifically instructed the jury not to consider the defendant's financial circumstances in reaching its decision of an appropriate award for compensatory damages. The only response of Harley-Davidson to plaintiff's request for assessment of compensatory damages was an assertion that the jury did not necessarily have to accept the figures of the plaintiff but could put in their own, and a disclosure to the jury that the plaintiff's top pretrial demand was for the sum of $250,000. In the light of all these circumstances we do not find that the jury's award of compensatory damages in the amount of $544,604 was influenced by a desire to punish the appellant, particularly since the jury returned a verdict against the defendant in the amount of $1,900,000 as punitive damages.

Judgment for punitive damages vacated, judgment for compensatory damages affirmed.

V. Defenses

THERE ARE FEW MORE POTENT DISCUSSIONS in the law pertaining to ethical issues today than the question of whether the plaintiffs bringing suit should have a greater sense of personal responsibility. After all, shouldn't plaintiffs realize some of the dangers they are getting themselves into? Another approach is to note that life is not lived without risk, so why place manufacturers into a position of insuring against times when things go awry?

Courts do take these kinds of arguments into account when they consider possible defenses to a case. That is, there are reasons why we should not hold a manufacturer/seller liable for the damages their product caused. Courts are more willing to cut off liability if the plaintiff is a commercial interest, such as another business. It is harder, though certainly not impossible, to find defenses for defendants when the victim is a consumer or bystander.

A. CONTRACT THEORIES

As has already been indicated, product liability suits became possible largely because of the undermining of the legal theory of privity of contract. That continues to be the case with respect to the ordinary consumer of the product or a bystander. It does remain an issue with commercial plaintiffs. Courts continue to eliminate privity concerns vertically. This means that when considering the chain of manufacturers, it makes no difference to the injured party as to who among them is liable.

While privity is not much help these days, defendants can obtain some protection by putting time limits for the warranty—whether implied or express—that run with the product. It is one thing to say that a new dishwasher won't wash dishes. It is hard to justify a seller disclaiming a warranty such as this. But it is not unreasonable for a seller to say that the warranty on the dishwasher ends in three years, or five years, or whatever the time may be. After the expiration of that time, then it is possible that a dishwasher might not wash dishes well. Thus, limitations of warranty based on time may protect the seller and manufacturer. Furthermore, as seen in the case below, there may also be a statute of limitations for claims of breach of warranty.

Trans-Spec Truck Service, Inc. v. Caterpillar Inc.

United States Court of Appeals, First Circuit, 2008
524 F.3d 315

In March 1999, Trans-Spec and Sterling Truck Corporation prepared a "specification proposal" for twenty-two heavy-duty, custom-built trucks that Trans-Spec intended to purchase from Sterling for use in Trans-Spec's oil delivery and dump trailer operations. The proposal called for installation of Caterpillar's C-12 model engines in each of the trucks. Trans-Spec allegedly decided upon Caterpillar engines after extensive conversations with Caterpillar's employees and agents regarding engine specifications and performance, the terms of the warranty, and which engine manufacturer would "stand behind their warranty the best." After finalizing the agreement, Caterpillar shipped completely assembled engines to Sterling for installation in the trucks. In December 1999 and January 2000, Trans-Spec took delivery of the trucks and put them into service.

By late 2001, serious problems had begun to develop with the flywheel housing on the Caterpillar engines in several of Trans-Spec's trucks. The housings loosened and cracked, leading to disruptions in the use of the trucks and time-consuming repair efforts. Caterpillar reimbursed Trans-Spec for the cost of the repairs to the first six trucks that experienced these flywheel housing failures in 2001 and 2002. When a seventh truck became inoperable, Caterpillar refused to pay for additional repairs. Since that time, Trans-Spec avers that an average of six, and as many as ten, of the twenty-two trucks have been inoperable at any given time due to engine-related issues.

Trans-Spec claims that the flywheel housing failures were caused by a major design defect in the C-12 engine, and that Caterpillar knew or should have known of this defect. Trans-Spec contends that the housing failures fell under the Caterpillar warranty and that Caterpillar should have rectified the problems. Trans-Spec also avers that, at meetings in June and August 2004, Caterpillar acknowledged responsibility for the flywheel housing failures and promised to "make [Trans-Spec] whole." In August 2004, apparently unpersuaded by this promise, Trans-Spec filed this suit against Caterpillar.

Trans-Spec's initial complaint alleged breach of warranty (Count I) and violations of Massachusetts General Laws chapter 93A (Count II). Its second amended complaint added a negligence claim (Count III) as well. Caterpillar moved to dismiss the second amended complaint on the grounds that Counts I and II were time-barred and that Count III was barred by the economic loss doctrine.

We begin with the district court's determination that Counts I and II of Trans-Spec's complaint are time-barred. We review the grant of a motion to dismiss de novo, accepting as true the factual allegations of the complaint and drawing all reasonable inferences in favor of the plaintiff.

The Uniform Commercial Code ("U.C.C."), as adopted in Massachusetts, provides that an action for breach of warranty must be commenced within four years of the date when the cause of action accrues. The code section then specifies when the cause of action accrues:

A breach of warranty occurs when tender of delivery is made, except that where a warranty explicitly extends to future performance of the goods and discovery of the breach must await the time of such performance the cause of action accrues when the breach is or should have been discovered.

Thus, the default rule in§ 2-725(2) is that the cause of action for breach of warranty is time-barred if brought more than four years after tender of delivery. However, if the warranty explicitly extends to future performance, "the four-year clock begins to tick when the breach is discovered or should have been discovered, or when the explicit time period expires, whichever occurs first."

Trans-Spec's complaint stated that Trans-Spec accepted delivery of the trucks containing Caterpillar's allegedly defective flywheel housing in December 1999 and January 2000. Trans-Spec filed suit for breach of warranty in August 2004. Thus, on its face, Trans-Spec's complaint is not timely unless the warranty on which its claims are based is one that "explicitly extend[s] to future performance of the goods" and the circumstances are such that the "'discovery of the breach must await'" the time of the promised future performance.

The Supreme Judicial Court of Massachusetts has not discussed the proper application of the future performance requirement in § 2-725(2) of the U.C.C. Thus we must make "an informed prophecy of what the court would do in the same situation." In making such a prophecy, we look to analogous cases decided by other courts in the forum state, persuasive reasoning in cases from other states, and learned treatises. To determine whether a warranty is one of future performance, we must look to the language of the warranty itself to determine whether it *explicitly* guarantees the future performance of the goods.

The only warranty language properly before us in considering Caterpillar's motion to dismiss is contained in the "On-Highway Vehicle Engine Extended Service Coverage" ("ESC") document, which was appended to Trans-Spec's complaint. The ESC states: "This service contract ... provides full components and labor coverage for covered components failures due to defects in Caterpillar materials or workmanship under normal use." The ESC guarantees that "Caterpillar will pay 100% of the components and labor charges for covered failures, with no deductible charges" for failures occurring within the first 60 months or 500,000 miles. It specifies Caterpillar's responsibility to "restore the engine to its operating condition prior to failure by repairing/replacing only the defective components and consequential damaged components necessary to remove/repair/install the defective components."

The ESC thus never guaranteed that Caterpillar's engines would not fail; it merely warranted that Caterpillar would pay to repair them if they did fail. As such, the warranty provided in the ESC is not a warranty that explicitly extends to the future performance of the goods, and the later accrual date specified in§ 2-725(2) does not apply. Thus, Trans-Spec's claims are time-barred by the four-year statute of limitations that began to run on the date of delivery of the trucks... If Trans-Spec finds itself without an adequate remedy here, it is because, as we describe above, Trans-Spec did not assert its contract remedies in a timely fashion.

So too could a situation that arises if the buyer inspects the product prior to actually purchasing it. If this has happened, then an implied warranty of merchantability could be more successfully disclaimed unless, of course, the defect was latent and the buyer unable to ascertain whether or not there were any product defects.

Seattle Flight Service, Inc. v. City of Auburn

Court of Appeals of Washington, 1979
604 P.2d 975

Seattle Flight Service, Inc., which owns and operates aircraft based at the Auburn airport, regularly purchased aircraft fuel from the City, the operator of the only fuel service at the airport. When it was learned that the fuel was contaminated, Seattle Flight Service cleaned the fuel systems of its aircraft at considerable expense. The City appeals from a judgment awarding Seattle Flight Service the cost it incurred in cleaning out the fuel systems.

In order for Seattle Flight Service to prevail in its action for breach of the warranty of merchantability, it was required to prove: (1) that a merchant sold goods, (2) which were not "merchantable" at the time of sale, and (3) injury and damages to the plaintiff or his property (4) caused proximately and in fact by the defective nature of the goods, and (5) notice to seller of injury. Whether a particular defect is patent or latent relates to the affirmative defense of whether the warranty was excluded pursuant to RCW 62A.2-316(3)(b), which provides:

> When the buyer before entering into the contract has examined the goods
> or the sample or model as fully as he desired or has refused to examine

the goods there is no implied warranty with regard to defects which an examination ought in the circumstances to have revealed to him; . . .

Because the City had the affirmative burden of proving that the warranty was excluded, the absence of findings is tantamount to a finding against the City.

The City further contends that the trial court erred in refusing to enter proposed findings that (1) Seattle Flight Service inspected the aircraft fuel prior to each aircraft's flight; (2) Seattle Flight Service was informed of the fuel contamination by the City; (3) despite its knowledge of the fuel contamination, Seattle Flight Service continued to purchase the contaminated fuel for its aircraft; and (4) Seattle Flight Service was a professional buyer of aircraft fuel. We find no merit to this contention. The refusal of the trial court to enter the proposed findings is tantamount to a determination that the City did not sustain its burden of proving the affirmative defenses.

Further, the proposed findings are not determinative of the issue of whether the warranty of merchantability was excluded. Under RCW 62A.2-316(3)(b), the implied warranty of merchantability is excluded if the buyer inspects the goods prior to sale and discovers a defect or fails to discover a defect that is reasonably apparent, or refuses to examine the goods after a demand by the seller and an inspection would have revealed a defect. Any inspection must be made prior to the sale.

There is no evidence that Seattle Flight Service inspected the fuel prior to each sale or that the City required an inspection prior to each sale. Although Seattle Flight Service conducted a preflight inspection and learned that the fuel may have contained some contaminants, there was evidence that it did not know the type, level or degree of contamination. Under these circumstances, the trial court could reasonably reject the City's affirmative defense that the warranty of merchantability was excluded or the transaction was "as is."

B. TORT THEORIES

Historically, one defense a defendant had was contributory negligence. This was a harsh defense. As we saw in the chapter on torts, if the plaintiff was in any way negligent, that negligence eliminated defendant liability. This is an idea that runs contrary to the entire theory of products liability and, indeed, is one that no longer can be used successfully. A less draconian version of the idea is called comparative negligence, which is still very much in use. Under this defense, courts compare how negligent each party is, and then reduces the award received by the plaintiff to reflect his percentage of fault. So, if the judge or jury determined a plaintiff was 25% negligent and the award was for $10,000,000, then the amount actually going to the plaintiff would be $7,500,000 rather than $10,000,000. The $2,500,000 difference is accounted for by the plaintiff's negligence.

In the following case, the court found that though there was a design defect, the total award to the plaintiff should be reduced because the plaintiff was comparatively negligent.

General Motors Corporation v. Sanchez

Supreme Court of Texas, 1999
997 S.W.2d 584

Lee Sanchez, Jr. left his home to feed a pen of heifers in March 1993. The ranch foreman found his lifeless body the next morning and immediately called Sanchez's father. Apparently, Sanchez's 1990 Chevy pickup had rolled backward with the driver's side door open pinning Sanchez to the open corral gate in the angle between the open door and the cab of the truck. Sanchez suffered a broken right arm and damaged right knee where the gate crushed him against the door pillar, the vertical metal column to which the door is hinged. He bled to death from a deep laceration in his right upper arm.

The Sanchez family, his estate, and his wife sued General Motors Corporation and the dealership that sold the pickup for negligence, products liability, and gross negligence based on a defect in the truck's transmission and transmission-control linkage. The plaintiffs presented circumstantial evidence to support the following theory of how the accident happened. Sanchez drove his truck into the corral and stopped to close the gate. He mis-shifted into what he thought was Park, but what was actually an intermediate, "perched" position between Park and Reverse where the transmission was in "hydraulic neutral." Expert witnesses explained that hydraulic neutral exists at the intermediate positions between the denominated gears, Park, Reverse, Neutral, Drive, and Low, where no gear is actually engaged. Under this scenario, as Sanchez walked toward the gate, the gear shift slipped from the perched position of hydraulic neutral into Reverse and the truck started to roll backwards. It caught Sanchez at or near the gate and slammed him up against it, trapping his right arm and knee. He was pinned between the gate and the door pillar by the pressure the truck exerted while idling in Reverse. Struggling to free himself, Sanchez severed an artery in his right arm and bled to death after 45 to 75 minutes.

In the trial court, G.M. offered alternative theories explaining the cause of the accident, all of which directed blame at Sanchez. It suggested that Sanchez left his truck in Reverse either accidentally or in a conscious attempt to prevent cattle from escaping the corral. Alternatively, G.M. suggested that Sanchez simply left the truck in Neutral and it rolled down the five degree slope toward the gate. Finally, G.M. argued that even if the accident was caused by a mis-shift as alleged by the plaintiffs, the mis-shift was a result of operator error, and not a defect in design.

The jury rejected G.M.'s theories and found that G.M. was negligent, the transmission was defectively designed, and G.M.'s warning was so inadequate as to constitute a marketing defect. The jury also found that Sanchez was fifty percent responsible for the accident, but the trial court disregarded this finding. The trial court rendered judgment for actual and punitive damages of $8.5 million for the plaintiffs. A panel of the court of appeals affirmed the trial court's judgment with one justice dissenting.

G.M. argues that there is no evidence to support liability for negligence or strict liability. Alternatively, G.M. challenges the trial court's refusal to apply the comparative responsibility statute. The plaintiffs respond that evidence supports both the negligence and strict liability findings, and that Sanchez's negligence was nothing more than a failure to discover or guard against a product defect. Thus, they contend, comparative responsibility does not apply here as a defense to strict liability.

Here, G.M. does not dispute that Sanchez's fatal injury was caused when he mis-shifted the truck's transmission into hydraulic neutral, which then migrated into Reverse. The parties agree that all transmissions made today can mis-shift, that no design eliminates the possibility of a mis-shift, and that a mis-shifted car is dangerous. As G.M. puts it, a "[m]is-shift is just physics." G.M. contends that it has no liability, even if its product is defective, because the plaintiffs failed to present evidence of a safer alternative design.

> "A PLAINTIFF must prove that there is a safer alternative design in order to recover under a design defect theory."

We consider first the evidence of strict liability. We will sustain G.M.'s no evidence point only if there is no more than a scintilla of evidence to prove the existence of a product defect.

A design defect renders a product unreasonably dangerous as designed, taking into consideration the utility of the product and the risk involved in its use. A plaintiff must prove that there is a safer alternative design in order to recover under a design defect theory. An alternative design must substantially reduce the risk of injury and be both economically and technologically feasible. We first examine the evidence concerning the operation of the transmission in Sanchez's truck and then determine whether the plaintiffs have proven a safer alternative design.

Most of the plaintiff's design evidence came in through the testimony of the plaintiffs' expert, Simon Tamny, who testified about the operation of the 700R4 transmission in Sanchez's truck. He opined that the G.M. transmission and transmission-control linkage presented a particular risk. All transmissions have an intermediate position between Reverse and Park. It is impossible, under federal standardization guidelines, to design a gear shift without an intermediate position between Reverse and Park. However, Tamny testified that G.M.'s transmission has the added danger that internal forces tend to move the gear selector toward Reverse rather than Park when the driver inadvertently leaves the lever in this intermediate position. Tamny explained how G.M. could alter the design to make the operation of the 700R4 safer.

Tamny admitted that his design change would not totally eliminate the possibility of leaving the gearshift in the intermediate position of hydraulic neutral. However, according to Tamny, his design change would totally eliminate the possibility of slipping into Reverse from hydraulic neutral. Tamny described his design change as a "99% solution" to the mis-shift problem. While his design change would not eliminate the risk that the car might roll in hydraulic neutral, it would eliminate the most dangerous risk of migration to Reverse and powered movement without a driver.

G.M. does not challenge that Tamny's design was technically and economically feasible. Instead, G.M. argues that, as a matter of law, Tamny's design is inadequate to prove a substantial reduction in the risk of injury because: (1) the design was not proved safer by testing; (2) the design was not published and therefore not subjected to peer review; and (3) G.M.'s statistical evidence proved that other manufacturers, whose designs incorporated some of Tamny's suggestions, had the same accident rate as G.M. These arguments however, go to the reliability and therefore the admissibility of expert evidence rather than the legal sufficiency of the evidence of a product defect.

However, the plaintiffs did not have to build and test an automobile transmission to prove a safer alternative design. A design need only prove "capable of being developed." The *Restatement (Third) of Torts: Products Liability* takes the position that "qualified expert testimony on the issue suffices, even though the expert has produced no prototype, if it reasonably supports the conclusion that a reasonable alternative design could have been practically adopted at the time of sale." Furthermore, assuming we could consider evidence contrary to the verdict, no manufacturer has incorporated Tammy's design into an existing transmission. For that reason alone, G.M.'s statistical evidence comparing the safety of different existing designs could not conclusively establish the safety of Tamny's design.

The evidence supporting Tamny's conclusion that his design is safer raises a fact question that the jury resolved in favor of the plaintiffs. We conclude that the plaintiffs have presented more than a scintilla of evidence that Tamny's alternative design substantially reduced the risk of injury.

Having determined that the plaintiffs met their burden of proving some evidence of design defect, we need not consider G.M.'s challenge to the findings of a marketing defect or negligence. We next consider whether to give effect to the jury's comparative responsibility findings.

The jury found that Sanchez was fifty percent responsible for his accident. in negligence or strict liability. However, the plaintiffs argue that Sanchez's actions amounted to no more than a failure to discover or guard against a product defect and, because of our decision in *Keen v. Ashot Ashkelon, Ltd.*,28 such negligence does not constitute a defense to strict liability... Implicit in this Court's holding in *Keen* was that a consumer has no duty to discover or guard against a product defect. We believe that a duty to discover defects, and to take precautions in constant anticipation that a product might have a defect, would defeat the purposes of strict liability. Thus, we hold that a consumer has no duty to discover or guard against a product defect, but a consumer's conduct other than the mere failure to discover or guard against a product defect is subject to comparative responsibility. Public policy favors reasonable conduct by consumers regardless of whether a product is defective. A consumer is not relieved of the responsibility to act reasonably nor may a consumer fail to take reasonable precautions regardless of a known or unknown product defect... we next determine whether the decedent's conduct in this case was merely the failure to discover or guard against a product defect or some other negligence unrelated to a product defect.

The truck's owner's manual describes safety measures designed to ensure that the truck would not move when parked: (1) set the parking brake; (2) place the truck completely in Park; (3) turn off the engine; (4) remove the key from the ignition; and (5) check that Park is fully engaged by pulling down on the gear shift. Sanchez's father testified that his son probably read the entire owner's manual. The plaintiff's own experts agreed at trial that Sanchez failed to perform any of the safety measures described in the owner's manual and that performing any one of them would have prevented the accident. This evidence is sufficient to support the jury's negligence finding.

Regardless of any danger of a mis-shift, a driver has a duty to take reasonable precautions to secure his vehicle before getting out of it. The danger that it could roll, or move if the engine is running, exists independently of the possibility of a mis-shift. For instance, the driver could inadvertently leave a vehicle in gear or a mechanical problem unrelated to a product defect could prevent Park from fully engaging. A moving vehicle without a driver is a hazard to public safety. The state licenses drivers who have demonstrated the minimum knowledge and skill necessary to safely operate a motor vehicle. Many, perhaps most, consumer products may be operated without a license, including lawn and garden equipment, household appliances, and powered hand tools. It follows then that, because of this licensing requirement, as well as other special duties imposed on drivers, more is expected of an operator of a motor vehicle than of users of most other consumer products. Thus, although we do not expect the average driver to have the engineering background to discover defects in their car's transmission, we do expect the reasonably prudent driver to take safety precautions to prevent a runaway car. Sanchez had a responsibility to operate his truck in a safe manner. The fact that the precautions demanded of a driver generally would have prevented this accident does not make Sanchez's negligence a mere failure to discover or guard against a mis-shift. We hold as a matter of law that such conduct must be scrutinized under the duty to use ordinary care or other applicable duty. We conclude that there was legally sufficient evidence to support the jury's verdict that Sanchez breached the duty to use ordinary care and was fifty percent responsible for the accident.

In conclusion, we hold that (1) there is some evidence of a product defect; (2) comparative responsibility applies because there was evidence of negligence beyond the mere failure to discover or guard against a product defect; and (3) there is no evidence supporting the gross negligence finding. Accordingly, we reverse the court of appeals judgment and render judgment that the plaintiffs recover their actual damages reduced by the jury's finding of fifty percent comparative responsibility.

ANOTHER TORT DEFENSE is assumption of risk. Here the notion is that if the plaintiff discovers a defect and then continues to use the product, then she has assumed a risk that the defect may cause harm. The test for assumption of risk is whether the plaintiff actually knew and understood the risk or danger from a product defect, yet continued to use it; the plaintiff voluntarily encountered the risk while realizing the danger, and the plaintiff's decision to encounter the risk was unreasonable.

Johnson v. Clark Equipment Co.

Supreme Court of Oregon, 1976
547 P.2d 132

Plaintiff was employed as a forklift operator at the Warrenton Lumber Company in Warrenton. His job entailed moving bundles of lumber about the Warrenton plant. Because of his various responsibilities, the job was a rather hectic one. The accident occurred on June 24, 1971, shortly after plaintiff's shift began and while he was engaged in feeding the random planer. Plaintiff was in a hurry and was carrying two banded bundles of 2 4's which were to be placed on the chains leading into the planer. Before the bundles could be placed on the chains, it was necessary to cut the metal bands around them. Normally, these bands were cut either by the forklift driver himself or by another Warrenton employee. On the day of the accident, plaintiff had no one to help him by cutting the bands. Although he normally dismounted his machine and moved to the front to cut the bands on this occasion plaintiff remained in the cab of the forklift and reached through the uprights with the cutters. While he was cutting the bands, his body came in contact with the ascent/descent lever controlling the movement of the forks. The forklift carriage descended and severed his arms just below the elbows.

In his complaint, plaintiff alleged faulty design and manufacture of the forklift. He charged that the forklift was defective and unreasonably dangerous in that (a) the uprights and cross members were positioned in a manner which allowed them to sever plaintiff's arms; (b) no guard or screen was placed between the cab and the uprights; (c) the ascent/descent lever was located so as to permit the operator's body to unintentionally come in contact with it; (d) the lever was not designed to remain in a neutral position until manually released; and (e) no adequate signs were included to warn the operator of the dangers posed by the machine.

As a preliminary matter, we note defendants' contention that any error committed in the instructions given concerning the concept of strict liability and the defense of assumption of risk was harmless because defendants' motions for a directed verdict and for an involuntary nonsuit should have been granted... We believe that there was a jury question as to the existence of the alleged defects and as to whether such defects rendered the forklift dangerously defective.

The concept of assumption of risk in a products liability case differs somewhat from the traditional tort doctrine of assumption of risk. Accordingly, in *Findlay v. Copeland Lumber Co.*, we adopted the definition of assumption of risk for products liability cases which is contained in Comment N to § 402A of the Restatement of Torts 2d (1965). In contrast to the more traditional defense which includes only two elements—subjective knowledge and voluntary encounter—Comment N sets forth three elements which must be shown before the plaintiff can be barred from recovery. The defendant must show, first, that the plaintiff Himself actually knew and appreciated the particular risk or danger created by the defect; second, that plaintiff voluntarily encountered the risk while realizing the danger; and, third, that plaintiff's decision to voluntarily encounter the known risk was unreasonable. If the trier of fact finds that any one of these elements did not exist in a particular case, the defense cannot be sustained.

In this case, although the trial court properly began by distinguishing assumption of risk from contributory negligence, the court's definition of assumption of risk was not complete. There was no discussion of the element of unreasonableness as it relates to plaintiff's decision to encounter the risk. Although the court did not least mention the other two elements, proof of all three elements is essential to the assumption of the risk defense outlined in Comment N, and adopted by this court in *Findlay v. Copeland Lumber*, supra.

The reasonableness of any decision to encounter a known danger must depend upon the circumstances surrounding that decision as well as on the relative probability and gravity of the risk incurred. Whenever the jury attempts to ascertain whether a plaintiff's decision to encounter a known risk was reasonable, it will be necessary for them to consider the conditions which motivated the decision, the pressures which were operating on the plaintiff, and the amount of time which he had to make the decision.

"We feel that working conditions and related circumstances are a particularly relevant consideration in an inquiry into the reasonableness of a decision to encounter a job-related danger. Such factors often will have a strong influence on that decision, and, in some cases, they may represent the most important motivational factors."

Image: thinkstock.com

It should be emphasized that this element of unreasonableness pertains only to the nature of plaintiff's decision to encounter the known danger. We are not concerned with the apparent reasonableness or unreasonableness of the physical conduct through which plaintiff encountered the danger, but rather the reasonableness of his decision to do so. This distinction, while seemingly theoretical, is significant. The actions through which one encounters a known danger may appear unreasonable—such as reaching through the uprights of a forklift—and yet the decision to so act still could be found to be reasonable when the circumstances surrounding the incident are considered.

We feel that working conditions and related circumstances are a particularly relevant consideration in an inquiry into the reasonableness of a decision to encounter a job-related danger. Such factors often will have a strong influence on that decision, and, in some cases, they may represent the most important motivational factors. For example, a worker might fear that a slowdown in his individual production would slow down the entire production team and thereby draw the attention of his boss. If he has a history of such slow-downs, or of causing excessive spoilage or ruining machine parts, he may have good cause to fear dismissal. The job market could be tight, and he may have little hope of being able to find a new job. Moreover, the situation may demand an immediate, hurried decision. It is certainly possible that, under such circumstances, a reasonable jury could find that his decision to encounter a known risk was not unreasonable.

Hindsight is always better than foresight, and the reasonableness of a decision to encounter a risk should be determined as of the time that decision is made. In this case there was considerable testimony about the hectic nature of the forklift driver's job from both the plaintiff himself and from a former driver who had been doing the same work plaintiff was doing at the time of the injury, and who had asked for another position when he found that he was no longer able to keep up that job's demands. Plaintiff indicated that if his forklift had been able to keep up with the heavy loads and the fast pace which he was required to maintain, he would not have been in a rush, time would not have been so important, and he would have been able to get off the machine to cut the wire bands. Plaintiff testified that all he was thinking of at the time of the accident was '(t)he time that I had to do the job in, and the job I was doing.' He also stated that if he had had time to think about it he would not have reached through the uprights. Significantly, the defendants' brief concedes that plaintiff encountered the risk only because of his working conditions, and at trial defendants even argued that such factors were the sole cause of plaintiff's injury.

Therefore, even if the jury disbelieved plaintiff's testimony and concluded that he knew and appreciated the danger that the carriage might somehow start to descend while his arms were through the uprights, and, further, that his actions in reaching through the uprights were voluntary, there would still remain an issue for the jury's consideration—whether, under the evidence in this case, his decision to do so was unreasonable. The issue is not whether it might have been more reasonable to have selected another method of cutting the bands around the lumber but rather, whether it was unreasonable, under all the circumstances, for plaintiff to have selected the method he did. Thus, considering all these circumstances, we find that the requested instruction should have been given.

Reversed and remanded for a new trial.

——————————————

ANOTHER DEFENSE that may be used is one of product misuse. Here is where the plaintiff used the product in a way unintended by the seller and in a way that the seller could not have reasonably anticipated, but where the plaintiff did not directly appreciate the risk itself (which would be more akin to assumption of risk). Related to this is the defense of alteration of a product, where the plaintiff was injured due to a subsequent alteration to a product that was otherwise without defect.

Jones v. Ryobi, Ltd.

Court of Appeals for the Eighth Circuit, 1994
37 F.3d 423

Jennifer Jones was employed at Business Cards Tomorrow (BCT) as the operator of a small printing press known as an offset duplicator. Jones seriously injured her left hand when she caught it in the moving parts of the press. The press involved in Jones's injury operates by passing blank paper through several moving parts, imprinting an image on the paper, and dispensing the printed paper through upper and lower "eject wheels." To avoid streaking the freshly printed image, on each job the operator must adjust the eject wheels to ensure the wheels do not touch the freshly printed area. The press was manufactured and sold to BCT equipped with both a plastic guard that prevented the operator from reaching into the moving parts to adjust the eject wheels, and an electric interlock switch that automatically shut off the press if the guard was opened. Sometime after the press was manufactured and delivered to BCT, the guard was removed and the interlock switch was disabled to allow the press to run without the guard. Because this modification increased production by saving the few seconds required to stop and to restart the press when the operator adjusted the eject wheels, the modification was a common practice in the printing industry.

Jones learned to operate the press by watching other BCT employees. Jones testified she knew the guard was missing and knew it was dangerous to have her hands near the unguarded moving parts, but her supervisor pressured her to save time by adjusting the eject wheels while the press was running. Jones feared she would be fired if she took the time to stop the press. While Jones was adjusting the eject wheels on the running press, a noise startled her. Jones jumped and her left hand was caught in the press's moving parts and crushed.

In granting the manufacturer's and the distributor's motions for judgment as a matter of law (JAML), the district court relied on the open and obvious nature of the asserted danger. *See* Restatement (Second) of Torts§ 402A cmt. i (1965) (consumer expectation test). The district court did not reach the manufacturer's and the distributor's other grounds for JAML. We review the district court's grant of JAML de novo; thus, we may affirm on another ground.

To recover on a theory of strict liability for defective design under Missouri law, Jones must prove she was injured as a direct result of a defect that existed when the press was sold. *Jasinski v. Ford Motor Co.*, Jones had the burden to show the press had not been modified to create a defect that could have proximately caused her injury. *Id.* Jones failed to meet this burden because her evidence showed the press had been substantially modified by removing the safety guard and disabling the interlock switch, and showed the modification caused her injury. When a third party's modification makes a safe product unsafe, the seller is relieved of liability even if the modification is foreseeable. Jones did not show who modified the press, but her evidence clearly showed that a third party, not the manufacturer or the distributor, was responsible for the modification. Although the manufacturer provided tools for general maintenance of the press that could also be used to remove the guard, we do not believe this made the manufacturer responsible for the guard's removal. Jones produced no evidence that any representative of the manufacturer or the distributor removed the guard or instructed BCT to remove the guard from the press involved in Jones's injury. Indeed, the distributor's service representative testified he told BCT's owner several times the guard should be replaced, but BCT's owner shrugged off the suggestion. Because BCT knew the guard was missing and the interlock switch was disabled, but did not follow the distributor's advice to repair the disabled safety features, the distributor's service work on the press did not extend the distributor's liability to defects that were not present when the press was sold. Because Jones's evidence showed a third party's modification, not a defect existing when the press was sold, was the sole cause of her injury, her strict product liability claim for defective design fails as a matter of law.

The district court thus properly granted the manufacturer's and the distributor's JAML motions.

Accordingly, we affirm.

BECAUSE THE EMPLOYER KNEW there was an alteration and disabled safety features, but did not follow the distributor's advice to repair these alterations, the alteration of the press did not extend the distributor's liability for defective design to defects that were not present when the press was sold.

Finally, as with limitations on warranties on the basis of time, so too legislatures will enact statutes of repose that provide a time frame within which one must bring a suit for a defective product.

NOTES AND COMMENTS

1. ONE THING TO KEEP IN MIND about product liability is that, perhaps more so than many other branches of the law, it is continuing to rapidly develop before our eyes today. Some reform efforts now seek to make tests of times when products vary from design defects be more akin to strict liability standards, even if the manufacturer used all possible care. [see Restatement of Torts 3] At the same time, reformers have proposed that design defects themselves be treated more on a negligence standard. Other proposals pertain to issues of warnings and how they increase or decrease the safety of products.

2. THE ATTEMPT TO REIGN IN DAMAGE AWARDS, especially punitive damage awards, remains a hotly contested issue, and there is little reason to believe that it will suddenly be resolved. What do you think the proper mix of punitive and compensatory damage should be? Should there be limits on the amount of punitive damages? On the amount of pain and suffering? What kind of rules would you propose? Do you think damages should all go to the injured party or should some be paid to a public fund?

3. DO YOU BELIEVE that tort judgments reflect societal values as to how to assign fault and responsibility? Do you think such judgments assess such fault fairly?

CORPORATE CRIMINAL ISSUES

IN THE WAKE OF the turn-of-the-century corporate scandals, many called for increased emphasis on ethics instruction in business schools. University of Texas law professor Robert Prentice, however, wrote a *New York Times* op-ed in which he argued that ethics wasn't really the problem. The problem was the outright flouting of the law. It is a good point. Many corporate ethics issues are legal issues. Moreover, what is called "ethics" in the press, government, and business are often laws concerning things like conflicts of interest. The law is not the only thing one has to concern oneself with in making ethical judgments, but law and ethics do interact in significant ways.

This chapter focuses on certain legal provisions that create unique criminal or civil liabilities. These provisions also provide a basis for a significant amount of corporate attention to ethics issues today. For example, prior to 1991, few companies had corporate mission statements, educational programs, ombudspersons, and other forms of ethical guidance mechanisms. Since that year's amendments to the Federal Sentencing Guidelines, however, nearly every company has these things and because the 2004 amendments to these same Guidelines call for corporations to attend to building "organizational cultures" that attend to "ethics" as well as law, this procedural, criminal, and regulatory mechanism has made it necessary for companies to adopt ethics and compliance programs. The lack of such a program has even been held to be grounds for a shareholders' derivative lawsuit. Thus, law and ethics can blend in many ways, and that is particularly true as pertains to criminal business issues. This chapter does not pretend to be a comprehensive treatment of ethics, but it will identify some important connections.

I. General Notions of Corporate Liability

CRIMINAL PROSECUTIONS are brought by some government entity against a person (a natural person or an artificial one, such as a corporation) for violating a law enacted to protect the public. In a tort case, the "prosecutor" is an individual plaintiff who seeks monetary damages or other forms of equitable relief, such as an injunction in nuisance cases, for injuries caused by the defendant. In a criminal case, the prosecutor really is one: an Attorney General, a States' Attorney, a District Attorney, etc. Because the prosecutor acts on behalf of the state, it is the state and the system of justice that is in a sense the plaintiff and victim in a criminal case. It is possible that a criminal defendant will also be subject to suit by the by victim through a related civil suit. One famous example of this is the O.J. Simpson civil and criminal trial, where he was acquitted for criminal charges but still found liable for civil damages. In this chapter, I will focus on criminal law, though occasionally I will reference tort law.

Tort vs. Criminal Law

	TORT LAW	**CRIMINAL LAW**
DEFINITION	Civil law deals with the disputes between individuals, organizations, or between the two, in which compensation is awarded to the victim.	Criminal law is the body of law that deals with crime and the legal punishment of criminal offenses.
BURDEN OF PROOF	"Preponderance of evidence" The burden of proof falls on the plaintiff.	"Beyond a reasonable doubt": Burden of proof is always on the state/government.
EXAMPLES	Landlord/tenant disputes, divorce proceedings, child custody proceedings, property disputes, personal injury, etc.	Theft, assault, robbery, trafficking in controlled substances, murder, etc.
TYPE OF PUNISHMENT	Civil litigation usually involves some type of compensation for injuries or damages as well as disposition of property and other disputes.	A guilty defendant is punished by incarceration and/or fines, or in exceptional cases, the death penalty. Crimes are divided into two broad classes: Felonies and Misdemeanors.
CASE FILED BY	Private party	Government

A. BASIC COMPONENTS

A subjective intent standard requires the alleged criminal to either know what she is doing or be reckless in her actions. If the intent is purposeful (willful), knowing or reckless, then a higher level of punishment is warranted because what the defendant is doing is no accident. Someone trying to blackmail (or extort) another person doesn't do so accidentally; the perpetrator purposefully devises a scheme to try to extort money from another person. Embezzlement is another example of a purposeful crime because it would be nearly impossible to achieve without the actual purpose to embezzle.

An objective intent standard applies when the subjective intent of the defendant cannot be known, or at least not proven, yet the actions of the defendant indicate a disregard for others. This is a negligence standard and would apply to issues such as careless or drunken driving. Sometimes negligence may err into gross negligence and even recklessness. The defendant may not have set out to drive carelessly, but objectively speaking, he can be determined to have driven negligently by expressing a lack of regard for others through his choices. If so, he still may be guilty of a crime, though it may result in a lesser offense and involve a more lenient punishment because of the lack of provable, subjective intent.

ARTICLE: PURPOSEFUL CRIME

Embezzlement versus Larceny: Ice Cream Truck?

http://www.forensicaccountingservices.com/2012/05/embezzlement-versus-larceny-ice-cream-truck/

LARCENY IS A LEGAL TERM for theft or stealing, the taking of another's property for personal gain with no intent to return the property (permanently deprive rightful owner of their property).

- **Embezzlement** is a form of larceny, with some unique characteristics. Embezzlement involves an individual using (and exploiting) a position of trust and opportunity, committing theft acts over time, with or without intention of returning what was stolen, and the activity is concealed (covered up) so as to avoid detection, allowing the suspect to continue perpetrating future theft acts.

- **Stealing the end of day deposit** rather than taking it to the bank to be deposited into an organization's bank account would be larceny.

- **Stealing (skimming)** $100 from each day's deposit, and altering the bank deposit slip to reflect the reduced amount to be deposited, would be along the lines of an embezzlement.

In a recent article, it appeared the driver of an ice cream truck stole the truck's contents. One event, discovered all at once, and not well concealed. Larceny, not embezzlement.

Had the driver skimmed cash or ice cream from the truck and deposits, and concealed the short (theft) by altering his records, that would have been an embezzlement.

Then, there are some crimes that require no intent at all; these cases are known as strict liability crimes since merely committing the *actus reus* with no intent results in a violation. In these cases, the defendant may not have intended any criminal violation at all, but still ended up violating a statute. One example of strict liability that arises with relative frequency is in the context of statutory rape crimes because the crime does not require that the defendant have any knowledge of the victim's age. Age restrictions on pornography and child pornography crimes are also strict liability. Each state has laws against pornography and the Supreme Court has given great deference to how local communities set their own standards for what constitutes pornography. Yet, the Internet crosses state lines by its very nature. So, what happens when someone under the age of eighteen accesses pornography?

The following case illustrates that issue and the issue of criminal violations with no intent. It deals with a unique kind of business—pornography—which often raises new legal and ethical issues as new technologies become available for its distribution. In the following case, what may be most interesting is the Court's determination of "community" and how new technology can create unforeseen liability because of the community one unexpectedly finds oneself in.

U.S. v. Thomas

EDMUNDS, District Judge.

* * *

I.

Robert Thomas and his wife Carleen Thomas began operating the Amateur Action Computer Bulletin Board System ("AABBS") from their home in Milpitas, California in February 1991. The AABBS was a computer bulletin board system that operated by using telephones, modems, and personal computers. Its features included e-mail, chat lines, public messages, and files that members could access, transfer, and download to their own computers and printers.

Information loaded onto the bulletin board was first converted into binary code, i.e., 0's and 1's, through the use of a scanning device. After purchasing sexually-explicit magazines from public adult book stores in California, Defendant Robert Thomas used an electronic device called a scanner to convert pictures from the magazines into computer files called Graphic Interchange Format files or "GIF" files. The AABBS contained approximately 14,000 GIF files. Mr. Thomas also purchased, sold, and delivered sexually-explicit videotapes to AABBS members. Customers ordered the tapes by sending Robert Thomas an e-mail message, and Thomas typically delivered them by use of the United Parcel Service ("U.P.S.").

Persons calling the AABBS without a password could view the introductory screens of the system which contained brief, sexually-explicit descriptions of the GIF files and adult videotapes that were offered for sale. Access to the GIF files, however, was limited to members who were given a password after they paid a membership fee and submitted a signed application form that Defendant Robert Thomas reviewed. The application form requested the applicant's age, address, and telephone number and required a signature.

Members accessed the GIF files by using a telephone, modem and personal computer. A modem located in the Defendants' home answered the calls. After they established membership by typing in a password, members could then select, retrieve, and instantly transport GIF files to their own computer. A caller could then view the GIF file on his computer screen and print the image out using his printer. The GIF files contained the AABBS name and access telephone number; many also had "Distribute Freely" printed on the image itself.

In July 1993, a United States Postal Inspector, Agent David Dirmeyer ("Dirmeyer"), received a complaint regarding the AABBS from an individual who resided in the Western District of Tennessee. Dirmeyer dialed the AABBS' telephone number. As a non-member, he viewed a screen that read "Welcome to AABBS, the Nastiest Place On Earth," and was able to select various "menus" and read graphic descriptions of the GIF files and videotapes that were offered for sale.

Subsequently, Dirmeyer used an assumed name and sent in $55 along with an executed application form to the AABBS. Defendant Robert Thomas called Dirmeyer at his undercover telephone number in Memphis, Tennessee, acknowledged receipt of his application, and authorized him to log-on with his personal password. Thereafter, Dirmeyer dialed the AABBS's telephone number, logged-on and, using his computer/modem in Memphis, downloaded the GIF files listed in counts 2–7 of the Defendants' indictments. These GIF files depicted images of bestiality, oral sex, incest, sado-masochistic abuse, and sex scenes involving urination. Dirmeyer also ordered six sexually-explicit videotapes from the AABBS and received them via U.P.S. at a Memphis, Tennessee address. Dirmeyer also had several e-mail and chat-mode conversations with Defendant Robert Thomas.

On January 10, 1994, a search warrant was issued by a U.S. Magistrate Judge for the Northern District of California. The AABBS' location was subsequently searched, and the Defendants' computer system was seized.

On January 25, 1994, a federal grand jury for the Western District of Tennessee returned a twelve-count indictment charging Defendants Robert and Carleen Thomas with the following criminal violations: one count under 18 U.S.C. § 371 for conspiracy to violate federal obscenity laws—18 U.S.C. §§ 1462, 1465, six counts under 18 U.S.C. § 1465 for knowingly using and causing to be used a facility and means of interstate commerce—a combined computer/telephone system—for the purpose of transporting obscene, computer-generated materials (the GIF files) in interstate commerce, three counts under 18 U.S.C. § 1462 for shipping obscene videotapes via U.P.S., one count of causing the transportation of materials depicting minors engaged in sexually explicit conduct in violation of 18 U.S.C. § 2252(a)(1) as to Mr. Thomas only, and one count of forfeiture under 18 U.S.C. § 1467.

...

B.

Defendants ... challenge venue in the Western District of Tennessee for counts 2–7 of their indictments. They argue that even if venue was proper under count 1 (conspiracy) and counts 8–10 (videotapes sent via U.P.S.), counts 2–7 (GIF files) should have been severed and transferred to California because Defendants did not cause the GIF files to be transmitted to the Western District of Tennessee. Rather, Defendants assert, it was Dirmeyer, a government agent, who, without their knowledge, accessed and downloaded the GIF files and caused them to enter Tennessee. We disagree. To establish a Section 1465 violation, the Government must prove that a defendant knowingly used a facility or means of interstate commerce for the purpose of distributing obscene materials. Contrary to Defendants' position, Section 1465 does not require the Government to prove that Defendants had specific knowledge of the destination of each transmittal at the time it occurred.

> "Venue lies in any district in which the offense was committed," and the Government is required to establish venue by a preponderance of the evidence. This court examines the propriety of venue by taking "'into account a number of factors—the site of the defendant's acts, the elements and nature of the crime, the locus of the effect of the criminal conduct, and the suitability of each district for accurate fact finding ...'"

Section 1465 is an obscenity statute, and federal obscenity laws, by virtue of their inherent nexus to interstate and foreign commerce, generally involve acts in more than one jurisdiction or state. Furthermore, it is well-established that "there is no constitutional impediment to the government's power to prosecute pornography dealers in any district into which the material is sent."

...

2. The Community Standards to be Applied When Determining Whether the GIF Files Are Obscene

In *Miller v. California*, 413 U.S. 15 (1973), the Supreme Court set out a three-prong test for obscenity. It inquired whether (1) "'the average person applying contemporary community standards' would find that the work, taken as a whole appeals to the prurient interest;"(2) it "depicts or describes, in a patently offensive way, sexual conduct specifically defined by applicable state law;"and (3) "the work, taken as a whole, lacks serious literary, artistic, political, or scientific value."

Under the first prong of the *Miller* obscenity test, the jury is to apply "contemporary community standards." Defendants acknowledge the general principle that, in cases involving interstate transportation of obscene material, juries are properly instructed to apply the community standards of the geographic area where the materials are sent. Nonetheless, Defendants assert that this principle does not apply here for the same reasons they claim venue was improper. As demonstrated above, this argument cannot withstand scrutiny. The computer-generated images described in counts 2–7 were electronically transferred from Defendants' home in California to the Western District of Tennessee. Accordingly, the community standards of that judicial district were properly applied in this case.

Issues regarding which community's standards are to be applied are tied to those involving venue. It is well-established that:

> [v]enue for federal obscenity prosecutions lies "in any district from, through, or into which" the allegedly obscene material moves, according to 18 U.S.C. § 3237. This may result in prosecutions of persons in a community to which they have sent materials which is obscene under that community's standards though the community from which it is sent would tolerate the same material.

Prosecutions may be brought either in the district of dispatch or the district of receipt, and obscenity is determined by the standards of the community where the trial takes place. Moreover, the federal courts have consistently recognized that it is not unconstitutional to subject interstate distributors of obscenity to varying community standards.

3. The Implications of Computer Technology on the Definition of "Community"

Defendants and *Amicus Curiae* appearing on their behalf argue that the computer technology used here requires a new definition of community, i.e., one that is based on the broad-ranging connections among people in cyberspace rather than the geographic locale of the federal judicial district of the criminal trial. Without a more flexible definition, they argue, there will be an impermissible chill on protected speech because BBS operators cannot select who gets the materials they make available on their bulletin boards. Therefore, they contend, BBS operators like Defendants will be forced to censor their materials so as not to run afoul of the standards of the community with the most restrictive standards.

Defendants' First Amendment issue, however, is not implicated by the facts of this case. This is not a situation where the bulletin board operator had no knowledge or control over the jurisdictions where materials were distributed for downloading or printing. Access to the Defendants' AABBS was limited. Membership was necessary and applications were submitted and screened before passwords were issued and materials were distributed. Thus, Defendants had in place methods to limit user access in jurisdictions where the risk of a finding of obscenity was greater than that in California. They knew they had a member in Memphis; the member's address and local phone number were provided on his application form. If Defendants did not wish to subject themselves to liability in jurisdictions with less tolerant standards for determining obscenity, they could have refused to give passwords to members in those districts, thus precluding the risk of liability.

This result is supported by the Supreme Court's decision in *Sable Communications of Cal., Inc. v. F.C.C.* where the Court rejected Sable's argument that it should not be compelled to tailor its dial-a-porn messages to the standards of the least tolerant community. The Court recognized that distributors of allegedly obscene materials may be subjected to the standards of the varying communities where they transmit their materials, citing *Hamling,* and further noted that Sable was "free to tailor its messages, on a selective basis, if it so chooses, to the communities it chooses to serve." The Court also found no constitutional impediment to forcing Sable to incur some costs in developing and implementing a method for screening a customer's location and "providing messages compatible with community standards."

Thus, under the facts of this case, there is no need for this court to adopt a new definition of "community" for use in obscenity prosecutions involving electronic bulletin boards. This court's decision is guided by one of the cardinal rules governing the federal courts, i.e., never reach constitutional questions not squarely presented by the facts of a case.

...

III.

For the foregoing reasons, this court *AFFIRMS* Robert and Carleen Thomas' convictions and sentences.

THE *THOMAS* CASE tends to surprise readers in at least two ways. One way is with respect to free speech. Aren't individuals allowed to have whatever materials they wish in their own homes? In an omitted section of the above opinion, the Court indeed affirmed that the Thomases could do so. However, once it is being distributed, they are liable for laws that exist where it is, in fact, being distributed. That means that California businesspeople have to concern themselves about the laws of Tennessee, or Turkey for that matter. Modern communications does change things and creates blowback based on local community norms.

Do you think that the *Thomas* case was decided correctly? What implications does this have in terms of other businesses and the consequences of local laws and other norms on doing business?

The tug of war between home community and where business is done can play out in the opposite direction. Sometimes, a country passes a law that requires "its" companies (a phrase itself pregnant with ambiguity) to follow certain laws no matter where they go. The U.S. Foreign Corrupt Practices Act provides an example of this.

II. Legislative & Regulatory Prohibitions

A. FOREIGN CORRUPT PRACTICES.

One of the most controversial laws applicable to international business is the Foreign Corrupt Practices Act ("FCPA"). Passed into law in 1977, after the discovery that hundreds of U.S. companies were paying bribes, the FCPA makes it illegal for any U.S. company to offer to pay—or indeed to pay—a bribe to a foreign official in order to obtain or retain business. It also prohibits making a payment to a foreign political party or to a candidate for political office. The law also applies to foreign corporations that have securities listed on a U.S. securities exchange. The following case provides an example of the enforcement of the FCPA.

U.S. v. Kozeny

638 F.Supp.2d 348 (S.D.N.Y. 2009):

SHIRA A. SCHEINDLIN, District Judge.

I. INTRODUCTION

Defendant Frederic Bourke moves pursuant to Federal Rule of Criminal Procedure 29 for an entry of a judgment of acquittal. For the reasons that follow, his motion is denied.

II. BACKGROUND

The Government's allegations in this case are complex, and it is unnecessary to recite them here. The relevant facts are as follows: SOCAR is the state-owned oil company of the Republic of Azerbaijan ("Azerbaijan"). In the mid-1990s, Azerbaijan began a program of privatization. The program gave the President of Azerbaijan, Heydar Aliyev, discretionary authority as to whether and when to privatize SOCAR. Bourke and others allegedly conspired to violate the FCPA by agreeing to make payments to Azeri officials to encourage the privatization of SOCAR and to permit them to participate in that privatization.

* * *

IV. DISCUSSION

A. Count Two-Money Laundering Conspiracy

Bourke argues that the Government has presented no evidence (1) "showing that [he] entered into any agreement with the specific intent of transporting money overseas for the purpose of promoting a violation of the FCPA;" and (2) "demonstrating that the scope of any such conspiracy extended into the statute of limitations period." I will address each of these arguments in turn.

1. Lack of Intent

Bourke contends that the Government has failed to prove that Bourke's intent in agreeing to transfer money overseas was to violate the FCPA rather than to purchase vouchers and options, which he notes is lawful.

As an initial matter, there is no dispute that Bourke invested in Oily Rock in March and July 1998. In order to sustain the money laundering conspiracy charge against Bourke, the Government must present evidence that Bourke had the "knowledge or awareness of the illegal nature of the charged activity and [that he intended] to advance the illegal objective." After a review of the evidence admitted at trial, I conclude that a reasonable jury could draw the inference that Bourke agreed with others that the intended use of his investment would be, in part, for the purpose of bribing Azeri officials.

Hans Bodmer, attorney to co-defendant Viktor Kozeny during the period of the privatization scheme, testified that he had a conversation with Bourke in early February 1998 regarding the bribery of Azeri officials. Bodmer testified that during one trip to Azerbaijan, Bourke asked him, "what is the arrangement, what are the Azeri interests." After obtaining Kozeny's approval to speak to Bourke about the specifics of the "arrangement," Bodmer then met with Bourke the following day. He testified that he then told Bourke that two-thirds of the vouchers had been issued to the Azeri officials under credit facility agreements at no risk to them. He also identified the Azeri officials who received these vouchers as Barat Nuriyev and his family and Nadir Nasibov and his family. It would certainly be reasonable for the jury to conclude that Bourke was aware of the bribery arrangements as early as February 1998.

In addition to Hans Bodmer, the Government also called Thomas Farrell, one of Kozeny's employees, as a witness. Farrell testified that some time after Bourke had invested in Oily Rock, Bourke requested that Farrell leave his office with him so that they might have a conversation. During that conversation, Bourke asked about the status of the privatization venture and whether President Aliyev or Barat Nuriyev had given any indications to Farrell about possible approval. Farrell testified that at one point in the conversation, Bourke had asked: "Has Viktor given them enough money?"

Farrell testified that Bourke raised the subject with him a second time during a trip to celebrate the opening of the Minaret offices in Baku, Azerbaijan in April 1998. Farrell testified that Bourke asked him about privatization and whether Farrell had heard anything from the officials in charge, such as Nuriyev. After Farrell gave Bourke a short status report, Bourke asked: "Well are—is Viktor giving enough to them?"

The testimony of Bodmer and Farrell, when considered in the light most favorable to the Government, is sufficient to prove beyond a reasonable doubt that Bourke agreed and intended that his investment not only be used for the purpose of purchasing vouchers and options, but also to ensure that the privatization of SOCAR occurred, by bribing the officials involved in the decision-making process. At oral argument, Bourke argued that proof that he knew that the investment money was being used partly to bribe officials is not enough; intent is required to sustain a conviction for conspiracy. However, even if *Bodmer's testimony shows only knowledge* of the bribery arrangements, a reasonable jury could infer from *Farrell's testimony* of Bourke's statements that Bourke *intended* that part of his July 1998 investment money be used to bribe officials.

* * *

B. Count One-Conspiracy to Violate the FCPA and Travel Act

Bourke next argues that he should be acquitted of Count One because "[n]o rational juror could find beyond a reasonable doubt that the post-July 22, 1998 payments (and other alleged overt acts) furthered the FCPA conspiracy, as opposed to the options fraud conspiracy." Bourke argues that by July 1998, the privatization venture was a "pipe dream," but that the options fraud conspiracy continued at "full speed." Bourke further notes that it would be "nothing but 'speculation and conjecture' to conclude that any such payments furthered the FCPA conspiracy-and that cannot be the basis for finding guilt beyond a reasonable doubt."

However, there is ample evidence to suggest that the purpose of many of the payments was to obtain assistance from the Azeri officials in the privatization venture. Farrell testified that bribes had been paid to the officials for the purpose of "help[ing] us purchase and obtain vouchers and options to [use in the] privatization auction." There is also testimony connecting specific bribes to the privatization venture. For instance, Farrell testified that at the meeting in which Kozeny agreed to give the officials a two-thirds share of the vouchers, he had also agreed to pay an "entry fee" of eight to twelve million dollars to President Aliyev in order to participate in the privatization of SOCAR, which was subsequently transferred in cash and by wire. A reasonable jury could properly conclude that any bribes made after July 22, 1998 were also made for the purpose of encouraging privatization rather than facilitating Kozeny's options fraud scheme.

Bourke's argument is also unpersuasive for another reason. As noted, there is sufficient evidence from which a reasonable jury could infer that Bourke knew of payments being made to Azeri officials by February 1998 and that he intended for similar payments to be made as of April 1998. In addition, there is evidence that he was involved in referring Nuriyev to a doctor in the United States and obtaining a visa for him to travel to the United States in August 1998. But there is also evidence that Bourke had no knowledge of the options fraud scheme until later-sometime around October 1998. It would therefore be plausible for a jury to infer that the purpose of the bribes—including some that were made after July 22, 1998—was to encourage the privatization of SOCAR, in which Bourke participated, rather than to facilitate the options fraud scheme, of which Bourke had no knowledge. Because this inference is supported by the evidence, it would not be the result of "speculation or conjecture." Bourke's motion with respect to Count One must therefore also be denied.

C. Count Three-False Statements Charge

* * *

Bourke's argument that he had not made a false statement because he "expressly stated his belief that Kozeny was 'paying off Azeri officials' (including Nuriyev) as part of the options fraud scheme" is of no moment. As noted, a reasonable jury could find, based on the evidence offered at trial, that Bourke had no knowledge of the options fraud scheme until approximately October 1998. Therefore, Bourke's statement that Kozeny was bribing officials in furtherance of Kozeny's options fraud scheme would not explain Bourke's denial of knowledge of the bribery that had already occurred by April 1998. Bourke's motion with respect to Count Three is denied.

BRIBERY IS NOT LIKELY TO OCCUR by one person handing over a suitcase full of money to a foreign governmental official over lunch. Instead, it is more likely to occur by an agreement to hire a "local consultant to advise on local business matters." That advice is to convey money and questions of what the bribe-maker intended become important. If it can be shown that the bribe-maker should reasonably know that money or other valuable resources will be conveyed to a governmental official in a way that is tantamount to paying a bribe, then it will be treated as such.

The FCPA does allow for what are known as "grease payments." These are payments made to a foreign official to expedite the performance of duties the person is already bound to perform. But the exact nature of what constitutes a grease payment that would fall outside of the scope of the FCPA seems to be in flux itself as the following case demonstrates.

U.S. v. Kay

359 F.3d 738 (5th Cir. 2004)

WIENER, Circuit Judge:

PROCEEDINGS

American Rice, Inc. ("ARI") is a Houston-based company that exports rice to foreign countries, including Haiti. Rice Corporation of Haiti ("RCH"), a wholly owned subsidiary of ARI, was incorporated in Haiti to represent ARI's interests and deal with third parties there. As an aspect of Haiti's standard importation procedure, its customs officials assess duties based on the quantity and value of rice imported into the country. Haiti also requires businesses that deliver rice there to remit an advance deposit against Haitian sales taxes, based on the value of that rice, for which deposit a credit is eventually allowed on Haitian sales tax returns when filed.

In 2001, a grand jury charged Kay with violating the FCPA and subsequently returned the indictment, which charges both Kay and Murphy with 12 counts of FCPA violations.

* * *

Although it recites in great detail the discrete facts that the government intends to prove to satisfy each other element of an FCPA violation, the indictment recites no particularized facts that, if proved, would satisfy the "assist" aspect of the business nexus element of the statute, i.e., the nexus between the illicit tax savings produced by the bribery and the assistance such savings provided or were intended to provide in *obtaining or retaining business* for ARI and RCH. Neither does the indictment contain any factual allegations whatsoever to identify just *what* business in Haiti (presumably some rice-related commercial activity) the illicit customs and tax savings assisted (or were intended to assist) in obtaining or retaining, or just *how* these savings were supposed to assist in such efforts. In other words, the indictment recites no facts that could demonstrate an actual or intended cause-and-effect nexus between reduced taxes and obtaining identified business or retaining identified business opportunities.

* * *

II. ANALYSIS

A. *Standard of Review*

We review *de novo* questions of statutory interpretation, as well as "whether an indictment sufficiently alleges the elements of an offense."

* * *

Because an offense under the FCPA requires that the alleged bribery be committed for the purpose of inducing foreign officials to commit unlawful acts, the results of which will assist in obtaining or retaining business in their country, the questions before us in this appeal are (1) whether bribes to obtain illegal but favorable tax and customs treatment can ever come within the scope of the statute, and (2) if so, whether, in combination, there are minimally sufficient facts alleged in the indictment to inform the defendants regarding the nexus between, on the one hand, Haitian taxes avoided through bribery, and, on the other hand, assistance in getting or keeping some business or business opportunity in Haiti.

B. *Words of the FCPA*

* * *

The FCPA prohibits payments to foreign officials for purposes of:

> (i) influencing any act or decision of such foreign official in his official capacity, (ii) inducing such foreign official to do or omit to do any act in violation of the lawful duty of such official, or (iii) securing any improper

advantage ... in order to assist [the company making the payment] in obtaining or retaining business for or with, or directing business to, any person.

* * *

C. *FCPA Legislative History*

As the statutory language itself is amenable to more than one reasonable interpretation, it is ambiguous as a matter of law. We turn therefore to legislative history in our effort to ascertain Congress's true intentions.

1. *1977 Legislative History*

Congress enacted the FCPA in 1977, in response to recently discovered but widespread bribery of foreign officials by United States business interests. Congress resolved to interdict such bribery, not just because it is morally and economically suspect, but also because it was causing foreign policy problems for the United States. In particular, these concerns arose from revelations that United States defense contractors and oil companies had made large payments to high government officials in Japan, the Netherlands, and Italy. Congress also discovered that more than 400 corporations had made questionable or illegal payments in excess of $300 million to foreign officials for a wide range of favorable actions on behalf of the companies.

In deciding to criminalize this type of commercial bribery, the House and Senate each proposed similarly far-reaching, but non-identical, legislation. In its bill, the House intended "broadly [to] prohibit transactions that are *corruptly* intended to induce the recipient to use his or her influence to affect *any* act or decision of a foreign official...." Thus, the House bill contained no limiting "business nexus" element. Reflecting a somewhat narrower purpose, the Senate expressed its desire to ban payments made for the purpose of inducing foreign officials to act "so as to direct business to any person, maintain an established business opportunity with any person, divert any business opportunity from any person or influence the enactment or promulgation of legislation or regulations of that government or instrumentality."

At conference, compromise language "clarified the scope of the prohibition by requiring that the purpose of the payment must be to influence any act or decision of a foreign official ... so as to assist an issuer in obtaining, retaining or directing business to any person." In the end, then, Congress adopted the Senate's proposal to prohibit only those payments designed to induce a foreign official to act in a way that is intended to facilitate ("assist") in obtaining or retaining of business.

Congress expressly emphasized that it did not intend to prohibit "so-called grease or facilitating payments," such as "payments for expediting shipments through customs or placing a transatlantic telephone call, securing required permits, or obtaining adequate police protection, transactions which may involve even the proper performance of duties." Instead of making an express textual exception for these types of non-covered payments, the respective committees of the two chambers sought to distinguish permissible grease payments from prohibited bribery by only prohibiting payments that induce an official to act "corruptly," i.e., actions requiring him "to misuse his official position" and his discretionary authority, not those "essentially ministerial" actions that "merely move a particular matter toward an eventual act or decision or which do not involve any discretionary action."

In short, Congress sought to prohibit the type of bribery that (1) prompts officials to misuse their discretionary authority and (2) disrupts market efficiency and United States foreign relations, at the same time recognizing that smaller payments intended to expedite ministerial actions should remain outside of the scope of the statute. The Conference Report explanation, on which the district court relied to find a narrow statutory scope, truly offers little insight into the FCPA's precise scope, however; it merely parrots the statutory language itself by stating that the purpose of a payment must be to induce official action "so as to assist an issuer in obtaining, retaining or directing business to any person."

* * *

In short, the 1977 legislative history, particularly the Senate's proposal and the SEC Report on which it relied, convinces us that Congress meant to prohibit a range of payments wider than only those that directly influence the acquisition or retention of government contracts or similar commercial or industrial arrangements. On the other end of the spectrum, this history also demonstrates that Congress explicitly excluded facilitating payments (the grease exception). In thus limiting the exceptions to the type of bribery covered by the FCPA to this narrow category, Congress's intention to cast an otherwise wide net over foreign bribery suggests that Congress intended for the FCPA to prohibit all other illicit payments that are intended to influence non-trivial official foreign action in an effort to aid in obtaining or retaining business for some person. The congressional target was bribery paid to engender assistance in improving the business opportunities of the payor or his beneficiary, irrespective of whether that assistance be direct or indirect, and irrespective of whether it be related to administering the law, awarding, extending, or renewing a contract, or executing or preserving an agreement. In light of our reading of the 1977 legislative history, the subsequent 1988 and 1998 legislative history is only important to our analysis to the extent it confirms or conflicts with our initial conclusions about the scope of the statute.

2. 1988 Legislative History

After the FCPA's enactment, United States business entities and executives experienced difficulty in discerning a clear line between prohibited bribes and permissible facilitating payments. As a result, Congress amended the FCPA in 1988, expressly to clarify its original intent in enacting the statute. Both houses insisted that their proposed amendments only clarified ambiguities "without changing the basic intent or effectiveness of the law."

In this effort to crystallize the scope of the FCPA's prohibitions on bribery, Congress chose to identify carefully two types of payments that are not proscribed by the statute. It expressly excepted payments made to procure "routine governmental action" (again, the grease exception), and it incorporated an affirmative defense for payments that are legal in the country in which they are offered or that constitute bona fide expenditures directly relating to promotion of products or services, or to the execution or performance of a contract with a foreign government or agency.

We agree with the position of the government that these 1988 amendments illustrate an intention by Congress to identify very limited exceptions to the kinds of bribes to which the FCPA does not apply. A brief review of the types of routine governmental actions enumerated by Congress shows how limited Congress wanted to make the grease exceptions. Routine governmental action, for instance, includes "obtaining permits, licenses, or other official documents to qualify a person to do business in a foreign country," and "scheduling inspections associated with contract performance or inspections related to transit of goods across country." Therefore, routine governmental action does not include the issuance of *every* official document or *every* inspection, but only (1) documentation that qualifies a party to do business and (2) scheduling an inspection—very narrow categories of largely non-discretionary, ministerial activities performed by mid—or low-level foreign functionaries. In contrast, the FCPA uses broad, general language in prohibiting payments to procure assistance for the payor in obtaining or retaining business, instead of employing similarly detailed language, such as applying the statute only to payments that attempt to secure or renew particular government contracts. Indeed, Congress had the opportunity to adopt narrower language in 1977 from the SEC Report, but chose not to do so.

* * *

3. 1998 Legislative History

In 1998, Congress made its most recent adjustments to the FCPA when the Senate ratified and Congress implemented the Organization of Economic Cooperation and Development's Convention on Combating Bribery of Foreign Public Officials in International Business Transactions (the "Convention"). Article 1.1 of the Convention prohibits payments to a foreign public official to induce him to "act or refrain from acting in relation to the performance of official duties, in order to obtain or retain business *or other improper advantage* in the conduct of international business." When Congress amended the language of the FCPA, however, rather than inserting "any improper advantage" immediately following "obtaining or retaining business" within the business nexus requirement (as does the Convention), it chose to add the "improper advantage" provision to the original list of abuses of discretion in consideration for bribes that the statute proscribes. Thus, as amended, the statute now prohibits payments to foreign officials not just to buy any act or decision, and not just to induce the doing or omitting of an official function "to assist ... in obtaining or retaining business for or with, or directing business to, any person," but also the making of a payment to such a foreign official to secure an "improper advantage" that will assist in obtaining or retaining business.

The district court concluded, and defendants argue on appeal, that merely by adding the "improper advantage" language to the two existing kinds of prohibited acts acquired in consideration for bribes paid, Congress "again declined to amend the 'obtain or retain' business language in the FCPA." In contrast, the government responds that Congress's choice to place the Convention language elsewhere merely shows that Congress already intended for the business nexus requirement to apply broadly, and thus declined to be redundant.

The Convention's broad prohibition of bribery of foreign officials likely includes the types of payments that comprise defendants' alleged conduct. The commentaries to the Convention explain that "'[o]ther improper advantage' refers to something to which the company concerned was not clearly entitled, for example, an operating permit for a factory which fails to meet the statutory requirements." Unlawfully reducing the taxes and customs duties at issue here to a level substantially below that which ARI was legally obligated to pay surely constitutes "something [ARI] was not clearly entitled to," and was thus potentially an "improper advantage" under the Convention.

As we have demonstrated, the 1977 and 1988 legislative history already make clear that the business nexus requirement is not to be interpreted unduly narrowly. We therefore agree with the government that there really was no need for Congress to add "or other improper advantage" to the requirement. In fact, such an amendment might have inadvertently swept grease payments into the statutory ambit—or at least created new confusion as to whether these types of payments were prohibited—even though this category of payments was excluded by Congress in 1977 and remained excluded in 1988; and even though Congress showed no intention of adding this category when adopting its 1998 amendments. That the Convention, which the Senate ratified without reservation and Congress implemented, would also appear to prohibit the types of payments at issue in this case only bolsters our conclusion that the kind of conduct allegedly engaged in by defendants can be violative of the statute.

4. Summary

Given the foregoing analysis of the statute's legislative history, we cannot hold as a matter of law that Congress meant to limit the FCPA's applicability to cover only bribes that lead directly to the award or renewal of contracts. Instead, we hold that Congress intended for the FCPA to apply broadly to payments intended to assist the payor, either directly or indirectly, in obtaining or retaining business for some person, and that bribes paid to foreign tax officials to secure illegally reduced customs and tax liability constitute a type of payment that can fall within this broad coverage. In 1977, Congress was motivated to prohibit rampant foreign bribery by domestic business entities, but nevertheless understood the pragmatic need to exclude innocuous grease payments from the scope of its proposals. The FCPA's legislative history instructs that Congress was concerned about both the kind of bribery that leads to discrete contractual arrangements and the kind that more generally helps a domestic payor obtain or retain business for some person in a foreign country; and that Congress was aware that this type includes illicit payments made to officials to obtain favorable but unlawful tax treatment.

Furthermore, by narrowly defining exceptions and affirmative defenses against a backdrop of broad applicability, Congress reaffirmed its intention for the statute to apply to payments that even indirectly assist in obtaining business or maintaining existing business operations in a foreign country. Finally, Congress's intention to implement the Convention, a treaty that indisputably prohibits any bribes that give an advantage to which a business entity is not fully entitled, further supports our determination of the extent of the FCPA's scope.

Thus, in diametric opposition to the district court, we conclude that bribes paid to foreign officials in consideration for unlawful evasion of customs duties and sales taxes *could* fall within the purview of the FCPA's proscription. We hasten to add, however, that this conduct does not automatically constitute a violation of the FCPA: It still must be shown that the bribery was intended to produce an effect—here, through tax savings—that would "assist in obtaining or retaining business."

* * *

THE FCPA HAS BEEN CRITICIZED by many businesses as creating a competitive disadvantage for American companies vis-à-vis foreign competitors who are legally able to pay bribes to secure business. On the other hand, some businesses claim that FCPA actually works to their benefit by removing ongoing demands for money from foreign governments. By removing bribes from the negotiating table, companies can more squarely focus on issues of price and quality. What do you think about the efficacy and fairness of the FCPA? Given the narrowing of "grease payments" in the above case, how far would you go in proposing to "assist" government officials in making decisions affecting your business? Do you think that the U.S. forcing companies to abide by FCPA imperialistically forces business to change according to an "American Way" of doing business? Or, what would you make of Wharton Law Professor Phil Nichols' research that shows that every government in the world outlaws corruption and every major religion condemns it as to whether FCPA only does what legal and moral consensus already demands?

B. OTHER EXAMPLES OF WHITE COLLAR CRIME

There are numerous examples of "white collar" crimes. The following is an illustrative, but certainly not exhaustive list:

- **Bank Fraud:** Engaging in an activity with the purpose of defrauding a bank.

- **Computer Fraud:** Hacking into databases holding information such as credit card numbers, social security numbers, or proprietary company information.

- **Credit Card Fraud:** Unauthorized use of a credit card, usually via theft.

- **Environmental Fraud:** Overbilling government contracts by claiming to do environmental work.

- **Health Care/Medicaid/Insurance Fraud:** Overbilling for health care treatment in excess of the treatments provided.

- **Insider Trading:** Use of securities information inaccessible to the public (inside information, advance notice of an announcement that will affect stock price) to inform trading decisions.

- **Money Laundering:** Hiding illegal commercial activities by making them appear to be part of a legitimate business enterprise.

- **Ponzi Scheme:** An investment scheme where the originator encourages investment with the promise of very high rates of return. The originator does not invest the money, but uses newly invested money to pay the large returns to the earlier investors. Eventually, the scheme falls apart when an insufficient number of new investors can be recruited to continue to pay the large returns.

CREDIT CARD THEFT COSTS BANKS $11 BILLION PER YEAR, AND CUSTOMERS LOSE ABOUT $4.8 BILLION.
Source: forbes.com

- **Pyramid Scheme:** Similar to a Ponzi scheme except while Ponzi schemes are associated with investments, pyramid schemes generally are associated with businesses such as franchise arrangements.

C. RICO

Sometimes these white collar crimes can be compiled and prosecuted together, at least in the United States, under the Racketeer Influenced and Corrupt Organizations Act ("RICO"). RICO was designed as a tool to fight organized crime. Enacted in 1970, RICO imposes stiff civil and criminal penalties for an organization found guilty under it.

The Ten Nastiest Ponzi Schemes Ever

by Drea Knufken, for businesspundit.com

PONZIFICATING—perpetuating a fraud by paying off early investors with new investors' money—is a concept as old as the hills. Honoring everyone involved in the act would be like writing a history of cheating itself. So we narrowed the Ponzi criminals down to the more recent, more nasty ilk, including Bernard Madoff himself:

10. The Fraudulent Feminist

In 1880, Boston Ponzian **SARAH HOWE** promised women 8% interest on a "Ladies Deposit." She said it was only for women, selling an implicit assumption of safety. She took the money and ran.

NASTINESS FACTOR: BAD. Way to break the sisterhood of trust, Sarah.

9. The Haiti Haters

Ponzi schemes popped up all over **HAITI** in the early 2000s. These schemes sold themselves as government-backed "cooperatives." They ran mainstream-sounding ads, some of which featured Haitian pop stars. As a result, people felt safe investing more than $240 million–60% of Haitian GDP in 2001–into the schemes, which ended up being a massive swindle.

NASTINESS FACTOR: BAD. Haiti is already one of the poorest countries in the world. People there eat mud cakes when times get bad. Cheating them out of their meager savings is sick; alas, it also appears to be systemic.

8. The Scientologist Snake

Earthlink co-founder and Scientology minister **REED SLATKIN** posed as a brilliant investment advisor for A-list Hollywood residents and corporate bosses. Working out of his garage, Slatkin cheated the rich and famous out of roughly $593 million, creating fake statements referring back to fake brokerage firms to prove his mettle. He fed the Church of Scientology with millions of his winnings. In 2000, the SEC caught wind that Slatkin wasn't licensed, and busted the scheme.

NASTINESS FACTOR: MILD. Cheating the rich and famous usually results in fewer bankruptcies than, say, chiseling seniors out of their retirement funds.

7. The Lottery Uprising

When **ALBANIA** was moving out from behind the Iron Curtain in the mid-1990s, a powerful government and environment of questionable ethics resulted in a financial system dominated by pyramid schemes. The government endorsed various Ponzis, which robbed the majority of the population and netted more than $1 billion in losses. Albanians rioted and overthrew the government.

NASTINESS FACTOR: DEPLORABLE. Don't government officials realize that endorsing Ponzi schemes might get them overthrown?

6. The Costa Rica Crooks

Three Costa Rican brothers, ENRIQUE, OSVALDO AND **FREDDY VILLALOBOS**, defrauded clients–mostly American and Canadian retirees—out of $400 million in a 20-odd-year unregulated loan scheme that started in the late 1980s. They promised interest rates of 3% per month on a minimum investment of $10,000. Villalobos moved money through shell companies before paying investors. Its staying power had to do with the fact that margins were low, the brothers were disciplined, and the outfit just barely skirted past laws.

NASTINESS FACTOR: MILD. The size of the operation gives it a place on this list, but the brothers also had real assets to back them up. It's Ponzi Lite, but that doesn't ease the burden on people who lost everything.

5. The Biblical Bilker

In fraud-rich Florida, the Greater Ministries International church used Bible-speak to cheat its flock out of $500 million. Starting in the early 1990s, the church, led by gun-toting minister **GERALD PAYNE**, offered worshippers investments in gold coins. Payne then created an investment plan that would "double the 'blessings' that people invested" by funneling money towards the church's fake precious metals investments. According to the Anti-Defamation League, Payne said that God had modernized the multiplication of the loaves and fishes and asked him to share the secret. $500 million later, the Feds caught Payne, but most investors never got their money back.

NASTINESS FACTOR: DISGUSTING. Anyone who uses holy speak to bilk people out of their retirement savings is disgusting, plain and simple.

4. The Boy Band Bandit

Beginning in the late 1980s, **LOU PEARLMAN**, Art Garfunkel's cousin and former manager of 'N Sync and the Backstreet Boys, offered attractive returns through his FDIC-insured Trans Continental Savings Program. The scheme was neither a savings and loan nor FDIC-approved, but that didn't stop Pearlman from bilking investors out of nearly $500 million, with which he planned on funding three MTV shows and an entertainment complex.

NASTINESS FACTOR: DEPLORABLE. Pearlman was already a multimillionaire. The fact that he became a compulsive criminal after that means he should sit in a cell for a very long time.

3. The Retiree Plunderer

Mexican resort owner **MICHAEL EUGENE KELLY** schemed retirees and senior citizens out of $428 million. He offered them timeshare investments in Cancun hotels that he called "Universal Leases." The timeshares came with rental agreements promising investors a nice fixed rate of return. Most of his victims used their retirement savings, thinking they would get solid, low-risk returns. The SEC says that "more than $136 million of the funds invested (came) from IRA accounts."

Kelly, meanwhile, bought himself a private jet, racetrack, and four yachts.

NASTINESS FACTOR: DISGUSTING. Defrauding senior citizens out of their retirement savings is just about as low as you can go.

2. Madman Madoff

BERNARD MADOFF's scam is still unfolding. The facts as we know them now are that Madoff spent decades building the biggest Ponzi scheme in history, bilking nonprofits, famous people, funds, banks, and countless others out of $50 billion.

NASTINESS FACTOR: DEPLORABLE. The man single-handedly destroyed charities, life savings, and other organizations yet to be named. The amount of money involved earns him a spot just below Charles Ponzi himself.

1. The Namesake

The King of Get Rich Quick, **CHARLES PONZI** (pictured above) became a millionaire in six months by promising investors 50% return in 45 days on international postal coupon investments. He earned $15 million, which in 1920s terms was serious money. After Ponzi was caught, investors only received $5 million back.

NASTINESS FACTOR: MYTHICAL. This ancestor of fraudulent men passed his name on to the many schemes that would follow his own. His legacy, and his scheme, are forever memorialized, earning them a unique Nastiness Factor label.

There are nine categories of state crimes and more than criminal offenses under RICO. Consistent with the aim of fighting organized crime, these offenses include drug dealing, extortion, bribery, mail fraud, kidnapping, murder, and arson. If within a ten year window, an organization has violated two of these criminal statutes (known as "predicate acts") then RICO can be triggered and criminal penalties of up to $25,000 and prison terms of up to twenty years per violation can be applied. Though designed for organized crime, regular businesses sometimes fall into committing two predicate acts, and so RICO has been applied to them as well.

D. ALIEN TORT STATUTE

Enacted in the 1700s, the Alien Tort Statute ("ATS") has become a major concern for multinational corporations. The ATS has been used by human rights groups to require corporations doing business overseas to adhere to certain U.S. and/or international laws. Companies respond that they have an obligation—a humbly respectful one, painted in the best light—of obeying local laws and customs. Those using the ATS claim that companies use this as an excuse to violate basic human rights standards. The ATS has been used in litigation against Chevron, for instance, for abuses in complicity with the local government of Myanmar; Exxon too, has faced similar litigation, as have companies working in Iraq.

Internet companies such as Yahoo and Google faced challenge from human rights groups for giving personal information of users to the government of China, which did not like postings that included words like democracy.

III. Reflexive Use of Criminal Law

IN 1984, Congress passed the Federal Sentencing Guidelines. These guidelines provide instructions to federal judges as to the severity of sentences that should be handed down to those convicted of a federal crime. If you listen to CNN when a famous or notorious criminal is sentenced, you will likely hear a commentator saying that the expected sentence in such a case would be such and such. His or her prediction is most likely coming from the Federal Sentencing Guidelines. They are the topic of the next section.

A. LEGAL INCENTIVES FOR ORGANIZATIONAL CULTURE & ETHICS

Intuitively, one thinks of criminal law in terms of the government prosecuting wrongdoers. But increasingly, both Congress and the courts have sought to find ways to achieve governmental purposes without creating more cases to be heard in court. They have created incentives for corporations to be actively involved in the administration of public policy, including criminal issues. As one commentator said of the

Federal Sentencing Guidelines, the law amounts to the deputization of corporations.[1] The Federal Sentencing Guidelines ("Guidelines") are not the only reflexive law to do this, but they are among the most important and are illustrative.

The Sentencing Commission, established by Congress, established the Guidelines. It is important to note that these Guidelines are exactly that: guidelines. Judges need not follow them with every "I dotted" and "T crossed." The same is true for corporations with respect to the organizational aspect—the deputization part—of the Guidelines.

In 1991, Congress amended the Guidelines to create provisions applicable to organizations. These provisions extend to a wide variety of organizations, including non-profit as well as for-profit corporations. They provide incentives for a corporation to set up compliance programs that make it less likely for employees in the organization to violate the law. These include a statement of the standards and mission of the corporations, which typically results in a Mission Statement or a Code of Conduct. A high-level official in the organization is to oversee the program. There should be a forum—such as a hotline or an ombudsperson—where employees can safely report a violation without fear of reprisal. Corporations are benefitted by self-reporting violations rather than waiting for a violation to be discovered. There should be training programs so that employees understand the specifics of the laws applicable to them and the methods for compliance.

These steps comprise a compliance program. The incentives for a corporation to set these up are the major monetary issues involved. If a company violates a criminal law, a judge can see the relevant base fine that applies to it based on the severity of the offense, as demonstrated in the following chart (U.S. Sentencing Guidelines Manual § 8C2.4(d)):

Offense Level	Amount	Offense Level	Amount
6 or less	$5,000	7	$7,500
8	$10,000	9	$15,000
10	$20,000	11	$30,000
12	$40,000	13	$60,000
14	$85,000	15	$125,000
16	$175,000	17	$250,000
18	$350,000	19	$500,000
20	$650,000	21	$910,000
22	$1,200,000	23	$1,600,000

---

1 *See*, David Hess et al., *The 2004 Amendments to the Federal Sentencing Guidelines and Their implicit Call for a Symbiotic Integration of Business Ethics*, 11.4 Fordham J. Corp. & Fin. L. 725, 726 (2006).

Offense Level	Amount	Offense Level	Amount
24	$2,100,000	25	$2,800,000
26	$3,700,000	27	$4,800,000
28	$6,300,000	29	$8,100,000
30	$10,500,000	31	$13,500,000
32	$17,500,000	33	$22,000,000
34	$28,500,000	35	$36,000,000
36	$45,500,000	37	$57,500,000
38 or more	$72,500,000.		

The amount of the fine will decrease if the judge sees that the corporation has made a good faith effort to implement the compliance program pursuant to the Guidelines. On the other hand, a fine could increase if there is no program or if there is no evidence that there has been a good faith effort to comply with the Guidelines. The Guidelines actually use a series of criteria to determine a culpability score, which is then added to the number of violations to determine the fine. (The actual language is set out in the Appendix)

These differences in monetary punishment can become significant and so, while not formally mandated as a law to follow, every major company has implemented a corporate compliance system. Indeed, in the *Caremark* case, 698 A.2d 959 (Del. Ch. 1996), the court held that it was a breach of fiduciary duty to shareholders to not have a compliance program in place. Under examination by the court as to whether the directors met their duties to monitor employee actions and comply with their fiduciary duties as well as the Sentencing Guidelines, the Directors came out rather well. But the important aspect of the case was not that the Directors breached their duty, but instead, that failure to institute a compliance program in accord with the Federal Sentencing Guidelines could be held to be a breach of their fiduciary obligations. That legal point provides a precedent for future shareholders to hold directors liable to the corporation itself. In *Caremark*, the Court said

"Modernly this question has been given special importance by an increasing tendency, especially under federal law, to employ the criminal law to assure corporate compliance with external legal requirements, including environmental, financial, employee and product safety as well as assorted other health and safety regulations. In 1991, pursuant to the Sentencing Reform Act of 1984, the United States Sentencing Commission adopted Organizational Sentencing Guidelines which impact importantly on the prospective effect these criminal sanctions might have on business corporations. The Guidelines set forth a uniform sentencing structure for organizations to be sentenced for violation of federal criminal statutes and provide for penalties that equal or often massively exceed those previously imposed on corporations. The Guidelines offer powerful incentives for corporations today to have in place compliance programs to detect violations of law, promptly to report violations to appropriate public officials when discovered, and to take prompt, voluntary remedial efforts. * * *

[A] corporate board has no responsibility to assure that appropriate information and reporting systems are established by management-would not, in any event, be accepted by the Delaware Supreme Court in 1996, in my opinion. In stating the basis for this view, I start with the recognition that in recent years the Delaware Supreme Court has made it clear-especially in its jurisprudence concerning takeovers, from *Smith v. Van Gorkom* through *Paramount Communications v. QVC*, the seriousness with which the corporation law views the role of the corporate board. Secondly, I note the elementary fact that relevant and timely *information* is an essential predicate for satisfaction of the board's supervisory and monitoring role under Section 141 of the Delaware General Corporation Law. Thirdly, I note the potential impact of the federal organizational sentencing guidelines on any business organization. Any rational person attempting in good faith to meet an organizational governance responsibility would be bound to take into account this development and the enhanced penalties and the opportunities for reduced sanctions that it offers.

* * *

[I]t is important that the board exercise a good faith judgment that the corporation's information and reporting system is in concept and design adequate to assure the board that appropriate information will come to its attention in a timely manner as a matter of ordinary operations, so that it may satisfy its responsibility.

> Thus, I am of the view that a director's obligation includes a duty to attempt in good faith to assure that a corporate information and reporting system, which the board concludes is adequate, exists, and that failure to do so under some circumstances may, in theory at least, render a director liable for losses caused by non-compliance with applicable legal standards. * * * * "

Through a reflexive legal measure, governments can provide incentives so significant for corporations to follow that management really has little choice but to implement them. Empirical studies have also now been undertaken to determine what makes for effective compliance programs. In a series of articles written by Linda Trevino, Gary Weaver and Phillip Cochran, the authors identify two key factors as crucial to an effect compliance program.[2]

The first concerned whether a common set of standards was applied throughout the organization. If employees perceived that there were a set of standards for

---

2   See, Cochran et al., *Corporate Ethics Programs As Control Systems* 42.1 Academy of Management J. 41 (Feb. 1999); Cochran et al., *Integrated and Decoupled Corporate Social Performance* 42.5 Academy of Management J 539 (Oct. 1999); Cochran et al., *Corporate Ethics Practices in the Mid-1990's: An Empirical Study of the Fortune 1000* 18.3 J. Business Ethics 283 (Feb. 1999).

high-ranking officials in the organization and another set of standards for the rank-and-file, the compliance program was not as effective. This led to a second, related, finding that procedural justice issues were the most important factors in creating an effective compliance program. That is, whatever the particulars of a company's program, its effectiveness mainly depending on whether the standards were enforced.

Effective compliance, then, is not simply the drafting of rules and having employees sign a statement that they have received and read the applicable rules, though that may be a step in the compliance process. Effective compliance has been empirically shown to be dependent on other factors as well. Complicating things further were a set of amendments to the Guidelines in 2004 that mandated that these programs should create "organizational cultures" leading to "ethics" as well as legal compliance. With these, the ante was further upped for companies to go beyond legal minimums and to consider how to create ethical corporate cultures in order to meet the applicable legal requirement of creating effective compliance programs.

> If employees perceived that there were a set of standards for high-ranking officials in the organization and another set of standards for the rank-and-file, the compliance program was not as effective.

Before discussing what ethical corporate culture may mean, it is worth noting that the Guidelines are not an aberration. A similar, reflexive model was implemented with respect to sexual harassment cases in a 1998 U.S. Supreme Court case, *Burlington Industries v. Ellerth*, 524 U.S. 742 (1998). That case clarified a point, previously mentioned in this chapter, that employers could be vicariously liable for the actions of their employees. In a sexual harassment case, that means that a company could be liable for the sexually harassing actions of one of its employees. While the case confirmed that rule, it also provided a way for employers to reduce the likelihood of having such cases go through the long, expensive court process. That alternative was to provide a compliance program directed toward sexual harassment issues that included training programs, as well as a forum for resolving the cases.

In short, these reflexive methods of having corporations improve their culture in order to head off legal and ethical indiscretions create significant pressures on corporations to address issues of culture and ethics as well as compliance. That then requires a consideration of the relationship between ethics, law, and business.

IV. Ethics, the Law, and Corporations

ON THE ONE HAND, the idea of businesses having ethical obligations is very old. Legal historian Reuven Avi-Yonah has shown that social obligations of business, grounded in the law, date back to Roman antiquity.[3] In early American legal history, one could

---

3   See, Reuven S. Avi-Yonah, *The Cyclical Transformations of the Corporate Form* (2005).

only obtain a corporate charter if a legislature determined that the corporate purpose served some kind of public good. In smaller towns and urban neighborhoods around the country, the currency of a businessperson very much depended on the extent to which that person was a leading citizen in the community.

For a variety of reasons, the connection between ethical, social engagement of businesses and their profit-making function became perceived to be more tenuous. Part of that reason may have been because the rise of large corporations made it difficult for any one person in the organization, except perhaps the CEO, to see her own obligations extended beyond her job performance. One of the prominent philosophers of the twentieth century, Alasdair MacIntyre, has decried "managerialism" that does not ask ultimate questions of whether a business action is bad or good, but simply whether one has completed one's job description.[4]

Liquid markets also play a role because today, a stockholder who has a computer can change positions in the market a dozen or more times a day. Many academic studies—and meta-studies of those studies—conclude that there is a slight correlation between good ethics/social performance and good business/financial performance.[5] But those studies look at long-term business performance. In the long term, concepts such as reputation, goodwill, and social capital have genuine economic value. In the short term, it is much harder to calculate the value of goodwill when determining the company's quarterly forecast on which basis shareholders will make decisions to buy and sell, as well as to retain or fire a CEO.

A third factor has been the rise, both in law and in business, of an economics movement, primarily drawing on the Chicago School of Economics, that sidelines notions of corporate responsibility. As Milton Friedman argued, a CEO who spends corporate assets on philanthropic purposes commits theft: stealing shareholder money. Unless that philanthropy leads to a measureable economic benefit (which Friedman acknowledges could happen) then executives should maximize profit and let the shareholders choose what to do with their own money. Similar economic models, especially within finance, have developed precise statistics models that measure mechanisms that enhance profitability while leaving hard-to-measure issues of ethics and social goods out of the equation.

These factors triggered a reaction. Depending on where one begins the history, that reaction could be located in a famous debate between Adolf Berle and E.M. Dodd in the *Harvard Law Review* where they debated whether corporate leaders should manage for the benefit of the shareholders or for the benefit of the general public.[6] In the 1960s, one began to see studies by academics of what businesspeople

---

4   *See*, Alasdair MacIntyre *After Virtue* 75 (2007).

5   *See*, Joshua D. Margolis, Hillary Anger Elfenbein, and James P. Walsh, *Do Well by Doing Good? Don't Count on It* 86.1 *Harvard Business Review* 19 (Jan. 2008).

6   A.A. Berle, *Corporate Powers as Powers in Trust* 44 Harv. L. Rev 1049 (1931); E. Merrick Dodd, *For Whom are Corporate Managers Trustees* 45 Harv. L. Rev. 1145 (1932).

say about ethics.[7] In the 1970s, in the aftermath of political scandals such as Watergate and then with corporate scandals like the bribery scandals of Lockheed (see William Hartung, *Prophets of War: Lockheed Martin and the Making of the Military-Industrial Complex* 115 (2011)), public and institutional pressure built on business schools to address ethical issues.

In the 1980s, that gave rise to the major effort of philosophers entering into business schools who took classic philosophical frameworks and applied them to business. This included scholars such as Ed Freeman, who brought to life the idea of Stakeholder Theory, a play on the more traditional focus on Shareholders. Following principles of the German philosopher, Immanuel Kant, Freeman argued that all people should be treated as ends, not as means to an end (a corollary of Kant's Categorical Imperative), and so, businesses should not look at employees as "labor inputs," but as flesh-and-blood beings with dignity to be treated as an end. The same logic applied to anyone else who was affected by a corporate action (Freeman's definition of a stakeholder). Kant was also followed by those who advocated for a human rights standard within business. Some such philosophers have already been mentioned in this book, such as Patricia Werhane. Thomas Donaldson invoked the work of social contractarian John Rawls and argued for a meta-bargain between businesses and society with businesses owing obligations to society in exchange for its existence. Donaldson later partnered with Thomas Dunfee to expand that social contract to consider not only philosophical social contracts, but practical, political, and legal social contracts that already exist around the world. Robert Solomon and Edwin Hartman drew on Aristotle to argue for a virtue-based philosophy of business ethics and a community-based one, respectively. William Frederick drew upon naturalist notions and applied them to business to create a more pragmatic version of business ethics; drawing on different sources, Richard DeGeorge similarly articulated a pragmatic model.

Though these rich formulations were being developed, notions of ethics and social responsibility were fairly marginalized in business schools until the mid-to-late 1990s. At that point, more scandals erupted, especially just after the turn of the century with Enron, Worldcom, and others. This placed more pressure on business schools. Their accrediting body, the AACSB, responded with a requirement that all business schools have some method of teaching ethics. Perhaps more influentially, cell phones and the Internet appeared. When those technological tools became available, it became quickly apparent that a corporate indiscretion could be captured on a hand-held cell phone and placed for worldwide view on the Internet within a matter of seconds.

Suddenly corporations realized that actions matter, just as they might for a business in a small town or in an urban neighborhood. Corporations began to create public relations departments that focused on issues of corporate responsibility.

7　*See*, Raymond Baumhart *Ethics is Business* (1968).

Perhaps as or more importantly, business school students drove the faculty and deans to address the issue of ethics, corporate social responsibility, and environmental responsibility. Thus, by 2005 or so, business schools had been pushed by students and businesses to address corporate responsibility issues by technology, scandals, and accrediting bodies. One more thing added to this mix, the previously mentioned Federal Sentencing Guidelines. By 2005, studies were showing that paper programs and legal-only based compliance programs were ineffective. Amendments to the Guidelines were, in light of the scandals of Enron and others, requiring that attention be given to "organizational culture" and "ethics."

With this history in mind, one has an answer to the question of why a company would bother to undertake an ethics initiative or social responsibility project. One reason is economic. No less an authority than former Federal Reserve Chairman Alan Greenspan testified before Congress that in today's economy, the only thing a business may bring to the market is its reputation; if that reputation is damaged, so is the company.[8] Protection of reputation has become a vital issue of today's modern businesses whether in the form of a public relationship campaign, partnering with an NGO to address social ills, or hiring employees or consultants to "scrub" damaging statements about the company placed on the Internet.

IN TODAY'S ECONOMY, the only thing a business may bring to the market is its reputation; if that reputation is damaged, so is the company.

The economic calculus is not merely that of damage control. It also brings with it opportunity. Some firms seek to differentiate themselves in the market by appealing to a segment that values identifiable corporate reputation. Ben and Jerry's ice cream was the forerunner of this, but today that niche—and it can be a big niche—is filled with companies such as Whole Foods, Timberland, and Starbucks. Without canonizing these companies, other companies have had more mixed results in achieving this niche, but their effort in trying to do so is indicative of the value reputation has in today's market. Thus, one sees extractives such as Chevron, Shell, and even Exxon touting their corporate social responsibility programs, even though each has been the target of major, public demonization in the not-so-recent past. Diamond companies, such as Tiffany's and DeBeers, embraced a certification program (the Kimberly Protocol) that attempted to assure a customer that diamonds were not mined with the assistance of child soldiers. Wal-Mart gets hammered in the press for its labor practices one day and then is touted for its environmental programs the next. Johnson & Johnson was one of the great champions of ethical conduct in the 1980s, but its reputation suffered under continuous recalls and lawsuits so much that its shareholders filed a derivative lawsuit demanding that the board of directors bring the company back to its moral roots. In short, companies today see an opportunity to maintain or gain market share by being a company that seeks to do good while also doing well.

---

8   Alan Greenspan, *The Assault on Integrity*, 2.8 *The Objectivist Newsletter* 31(1963).

These considerations spill over into two other reasons for why a company might take ethics and social responsibility seriously. Legal reasons also are important. Companies get sued for breaches of conduct. To get out ahead of potential litigation, one might adopt an ethically driven policy. Studies also show that sexually harassing workplaces, for instance, tend to be less productive. After all, the harasser isn't working; he is harassing. And targets of the harassment aren't working either; they are trying to get away from the harasser. Neither lends itself to economic productivity.[9]

That leads to the a third reason for why one might bother: identity reasons. Continuing with the sexual harassment example, most companies would prefer not to be known as the sexual harassment company. It also leads to some of the earlier examples of wanting to be known as a clean diamond company or a shoe company that gives its employees forty hours a year off from work to do volunteer work in the community (as Timberland does). In an Internet age where reputation is important, so is identity. Indeed, companies recruit on the basis of their identity and so if a company does not consistently manage with that identity in mind, it can have an impact on the morale of the employees recruited to work in "that kind" of company.

A final reason to bother with ethical issues is simply a moral one. At the end of the day, human beings, even at work, have moral sentiments. They have a hardwired desire to want to help those in need and they take pride, even joy, in treating others well. At times, organizational incentives do not reward such actions; they may even punish such considerations. But there is an aspect of human nature that wants to be proud of the ethical content of the work one does.

---

9   *See,* Roy Whitehead, Jr. and Walter Block, *Sexual Harassment in the Workplace: A Property Rights Perspective* 4 J. L. & Fam. Stud. 229, 243 (2002).

NOTES AND COMMENTS

I. WITH CASES SUCH AS *THOMAS* and regulations such as the Federal Sentencing Guidelines, one sees criminal enactments that draw upon ethical standards in order to determine whether an individual is in compliance with the law. With *Thomas,* the Court appealed to the relevant community standards on obscenity; with the FSG, courts look at "organizational culture" leading to "ethics and compliance." If you are a businessperson, how do you determine the ethical standards that help you comply with the law? What sources might you look to? Do you think it is fair to bring in ethical standards that are not define *per se* by a legal authority that could have legal implications?

2. ONE OF THE ARGUMENTS for applying criminal sanctions for business misconduct is to get the attention of corporations with fines and bad publicity. Another reason is to make more accountable those that might hide under the guise of bureaucracy where it seems no one is truly accountable. Do either of these arguments persuade you? Is increasing criminalization of business misconduct a good idea or a bad idea?

3. TAKE A LOOK in a newspaper or magazine over the past year (or do an Internet search over that time frame) and see what kinds of criminal charges were brought by prosecutors against businesses. Do you see any trends or areas that seem to cause more problems than others?

Part 3

Agency, Partnerships & Limited Liability Entities

Moses Takes His Leave of Jethro, by Jan Victors, c. 1635

(An early and notable instance of a principal delegating a task to an agent.)

12

THE LAW
OF AGENCY

AGENCY, AS A PART OF BUSINESS LAW, is that body of law that determines when one person ("the principal") is legally responsible for the acts of another (the "agent"). The law of agency also determines the duty which the agent owes to the principal.

Without the law of Agency complex business organizations would be impossible, and we may regard it as a fundamental building block of business law, just as are the doctrines of property, torts, and contracts, which we have previously explored. For our purposes, then, there are two main questions to explore: (1) when is the agency relationship created, and (2) what duties does the agent owe the principal?

I. When Is the Agency Relationship Created?

ACCORDING TO § 1.01 OF THE RESTATEMENT OF AGENCY (3RD) "Agency is the fiduciary relationship that arises when one person (a 'principal') manifests assent to another person (an 'agent') that the agent shall act on the principal's behalf and subject to the principal's control, and the agent manifests assent or otherwise consents so to act." We will soon explore what is meant by "fiduciary relationship," but let's first explore how the law determines whether the manifestation of assent to create the agency relationship is found. The principal will be liable to third parties for the acts of an agent, so long as the agent is acting within the scope of the authority the principal has granted the agent. This question, whether the principal gives the agent the proper "authority" to act on the principal's behalf, is not quite as straightforward as we might think. Consider the following intriguing agency case.

Croisant v. Watrud

Supreme Court of Oregon.
248 Ore. 234, 432 P.2d 799 (1967).

* * *

[O'CONNELL, Justice, for the court]

This is a [lawsuit] brought against [some] partners in a firm of certified public accountants and the [estate] of a deceased partner, LaVern Watrud. Plaintiff appeals from a decree in favor of defendants. * * * The defendants engaged in the accounting practice with their principal office in Klamath Falls and their branch office in Medford. Watrud was in charge of the Medford office. Plaintiff was the owner of a sawmill, timberlands, and other property over which she exercised general control, delegating the details of management of the business to others.

In 1955 plaintiff employed the defendant partnership to advise her on tax matters and to prepare income tax returns for her business enterprises. All of these services were performed by Watrud * * *. In 1956 plaintiff sold her sawmill. Thereafter her business activities consisted almost entirely of making collections under the contract for the sale of the mill, collections on the sale of timber, collections of rents, and various disbursements from the moneys so collected.

In 1957 plaintiff moved to California. She made arrangements with Watrud to make the collections referred to above, to make certain disbursements, to keep her financial books and records, and to prepare her financial statements and tax returns. The moneys collected by Watrud were deposited in the account of the Lloyd Timber Company (plaintiff's business name in Oregon) in a Grants Pass bank.

In 1957 plaintiff learned that her husband, Glenn Lloyd, had induced Watrud to make unauthorized payments out of the Lloyd Timber Company account to him. Plaintiff instructed Watrud not to make any further payments to her husband, but Watrud violated her instructions. Plaintiff was informed of these subsequent misappropriations by Watrud on behalf of Glenn Lloyd in 1958. She also learned that her husband was unfaithful to her. Plaintiff again excused Watrud's breach of trust and her husband's infidelity. After their reconciliation, plaintiff and her husband took a trip to Europe. When they returned, plaintiff discovered that her husband had forged checks on her California bank account and had also forged her signature upon a $75,000 note and negotiated it. Plaintiff also became aware of the fact that Watrud had continued to pay money to Glenn Lloyd out of plaintiff's Oregon account. In addition, she learned that Watrud, without authorization, had drawn a check payable to himself. When Watrud was confronted with this evidence he finally acknowledged his abuse of his trust. Soon thereafter Watrud died from gunshot wounds while hunting.

Plaintiff then filed this suit . . . against [Watrud's] surviving partners [of the firm of accountants].

* * *

It is undisputed that plaintiff's initial business arrangements for tax advice and the preparation of tax returns were with the partnership and not simply with Watrud individually. After the partnership was employed, Watrud individually performed all of the services sought by plaintiff. As time went on plaintiff called upon Watrud to perform additional services in connection with her business including the collection and disbursements of funds. The initial question is whether these subsequent services performed by Watrud are to be regarded as having been performed as a part of the partnership business or under a separate arrangement calling only for the services of Watrud personally.

The record suggests that plaintiff, Watrud, and defendants considered all of Watrud's services to the plaintiff as services performed by a member of a partnership on behalf of that firm. The partnership received a check each month for all of Watrud's services including the services involved in handling plaintiff's business affairs. Had the parties viewed the services in making collections and disbursements for plaintiff as independent activities separate compensation would have been in order. Although the partnership's Medford office was geographically separated from the Klamath Falls office, both operations constituted one autonomous business enterprise and consequently defendants cannot insulate themselves from liability on the ground that the Medford office was a separate business operation. Defendants are liable, therefore, if Watrud can be regarded as the agent of the partnership in performing the fund-handling services for plaintiff.

It is clear that Watrud had no express authority from defendants to perform these services. And there was no evidence from which an authority implied in fact could be derived. If it were common knowledge that accountants frequently act as trustees in the collection and disbursement of funds, we would be in a position to take judicial notice of the common practice and thus find an implied authority or an apparent authority. But we have no basis for saying that accountants commonly or frequently perform fund-handling services. Thus we conclude that liability cannot be rested upon a manifestation by defendants that they assented to be bound for such services. However, an agent can impose liability upon his principal even where there is no actual or apparent authority or estoppel. An agent may have an "inherent agency power" to bind his principal. Such power is defined in *Restatement (Second), Agency § 8A* as "the power of an agent which is derived not from authority, apparent authority or estoppel, but solely from the agency relation and exists for the protection of persons harmed by or dealing with a servant or other agent." When an agent has acted improperly in entering into a contract the inherent agency power "is based neither upon the consent of the principal nor upon his manifestations."

* * * The scope of the principal's liability under an inherent agency power is stated in Section 161 [of the *Restatement (Second), Agency]:*"A general agent for a disclosed or partially disclosed principal subjects his principal to liability for acts done on his account which usually accompany or are incidental to transactions which the agent is authorized to conduct if, although they are forbidden by the principal, the other party reasonably believes that the agent is authorized to do them and has no notice that he is not so authorized." *Restatement (Second), Agency § 161*, p. 378 (1958).

It will be noted that Section 161 states that the principal is liable only for his agent's acts "which *usually accompany* or are *incidental* to transactions which the agent is authorized to conduct * * *." (Emphasis added.) As we have previously observed, we have neither evidence nor judicial knowledge of the practice of accountancy from which to decide whether the collection and disbursement of accounts is commonly undertaken by accountants. We cannot say, therefore, that the fund-handling services performed by Watrud in this case were the type which "usually accompany" the transactions which accountants ordinarily conduct viewed from the standpoint of those engaged in accountancy. Upon similar reasoning we are unable to say that the services here were "incidental" to the transactions Watrud was authorized to conduct. But this does not conclude the matter. Assuming that accountants do not regard the collection and disbursement of funds as a part of the services usually offered by members of their profession, what significance should this have if, in the particular circumstances, a person dealing with a member of an accounting partnership reasonably believes that accountants perform the kind of service which he seeks to have performed? If the phrase "acts * * * which usually accompany * * * transactions which the agent is authorized to conduct" is to be tested solely from the viewpoint of accountants in describing the kind of services they usually perform then, of course, *Section 161 of the Restatement (Second) of Agency* would not be applicable even though a client of an accounting firm mistakenly but reasonably believed that the services he requested were not alien to the work of accountants. The basis for the principal's liability under these circumstances is best explained by the comments appended to Section 8A and related sections of the Restatement; whether the theory is categorized as one of apparent authority (treating the circumstances as a manifestation of authority by principal), or as arising out of an inherent agency power is immaterial. The rationale begins with the idea that:

"The principles of agency have made it possible for persons to utilize the services of others in accomplishing far more than could be done by their unaided efforts. * * * [The] primary function in modern life is to make possible the commercial enterprises which could not exist otherwise. * * * Partnerships and corporations, through which most of the work of the world is done today, depend for their existence upon agency principles. The rules designed to promote the interests of these enterprises are necessarily accompanied by rules to police them.

It is inevitable that in doing their work, either through negligence or excess of zeal, agents will harm third persons or will deal with them in unauthorized ways. It would be unfair for an enterprise to have the benefit of the work of its agents without making it responsible to some extent for their excesses and failures to act carefully. The answer of the common law has been the creation of special agency powers or, to phrase it otherwise, the imposition of liability upon the principal because of unauthorized or negligent acts of his servants and other agents. * * * " *Restatement (Second) Agency, § 8A*, comment *a* (1958).

The basis for principal's liability under this section is further explained in the comment as follows: "* * * His liability exists solely because of his relation to the agent. It is based primarily upon the theory that, if one appoints an agent to conduct a series of transactions over a period of time, it is fair that he should bear losses which are incurred when such an agent, although without authority to do so, does something which is usually done in connection with the transactions he is employed to conduct. Such agents can properly be regarded as part of the principal's organization in much the same way as a servant is normally part of the master's business enterprise. In fact most general agents are also servants, such as managers and other persons continuously employed and subject to physical supervision by the employer. The basis of the extended liability stated in this Section is comparable to the liability of a master for the torts of his servant. * * * In the case of the master,

it is thought fair that one who benefits from the enterprise and has a right to control the physical activities of those who make the enterprise profitable, should pay for the physical harm resulting from the errors and derelictions of the servants while doing the kind of thing which makes the enterprise successful.

The rules imposing liability upon the principal for some of the contracts and conveyances of a general agent, whether or not a servant, which he is neither authorized nor apparently authorized to make, are based upon a similar public policy. Commercial convenience requires that the principal should not escape liability where there have been deviations from the usually granted authority by persons who are such essential parts of his business enterprise. In the long run it is of advantage to business, and hence to employers as a class, that third persons should not be required to scrutinize too carefully the mandates of permanent or semi-permanent agents who do no more than what is usually done by agents in similar positions." *Restatement (Second), Agency § 161* at p. 379–380.

If a third person reasonably believes that the services he has requested of a member of an accounting partnership is undertaken as a part of the partnership business, the partnership should be bound for a breach of trust incident to that employment even though those engaged in the practice of accountancy would regard as unusual the performance of such service by an accounting firm. The reasonableness of a third person's belief in assuming that a partner is acting within the scope of the partnership should not be tested by the profession's own description of the function of its members. Those who seek accounting services may not understand the refinements made by accountants in defining the services they offer to the public. Whether a third person's belief is reasonable in assuming that the service he seeks is within the domain of the profession is a question which must be answered upon the basis of the facts in the particular case.

We are of the opinion that the facts in the present case are sufficient to establish a reasonable belief on the part of plaintiff that Watrud had undertaken all of the work assigned to him by plaintiff as a continuation of the original employment of the partnership firm. The initial work for which defendants were engaged was the preparation of income tax returns. Thereafter plaintiff sought Watrud's advice on tax matters and continued to have him prepare income tax returns for her business ventures. Watrud did not do the actual bookkeeping for plaintiff's business activities when the partnership was first employed, but eventually he prepared and kept in his own custody the financial books and records of plaintiff's enterprises. This service was assumed by Watrud when plaintiff decided to move to California permanently. When plaintiff left Grants Pass she also arranged with Watrud to have him receive all the income from her Oregon and California properties and to make disbursements from the money so collected. Before she employed him to handle her funds she asked him if he was bonded and he assured her that he was. We think it is important to note that the increased responsibilities directed to Watrud coincided with plaintiff's departure for California.

Thereafter, Watrud was the only person who drew checks on the account set up pursuant to the arrangement with plaintiff, although the bank signature card included the names of plaintiff and others. Watrud handled a very substantial amount of plaintiff's money during the course of his employment, drawing as many as 1500 checks per year. The bank statements and cancelled checks were sent directly to Watrud; he collected her business mail at her post office box in Grants Pass and in other respects acted in her behalf after her departure for California. As we have already mentioned, the partnership received compensation for these services at the rate of $800 per month. As plaintiff testified, nothing was ever said or done by Watrud which might have indicated to her that he was acting on his account as distinguished from acting for the partnership. It was reasonable for plaintiff to assume that the added assignment of collecting and disbursing funds delegated to Watrud was an integral part of the function of one employed to keep the accounts reflecting the income and disbursement of those funds. This assumption, we think, is even more likely in circumstances such as we have here where there is trust and confidence reposed in the person employed. * * * This is not a case in which a person deals with an ordinary commercial partnership. Accountants stand in a fiduciary relation to their clients and out of that relationship there is generated a trust and confidence which invites the client to rely upon the advice and guidance of the one she employs. * * * The fiduciary character of the relationship in these circumstances is clearly explained in *Cafritz v. Corporation Audit Co., 60 F. Supp. 627* (D.C. Dist., 1945). In that case the defendant, an accounting firm, was employed by the plaintiff to maintain and audit the records of his enterprises. The defendant was authorized to perform a variety of services for plaintiff including the preparation of checks for plaintiff's signature and the deposit of checks to the plaintiff's account. * * * Defendant's general manager misappropriated some of the checks deposited with defendant and the plaintiff brought suit for an accounting. In holding the defendant liable for the defalcation the court emphasized the fiduciary relation which arose between the plaintiff and the defendant accounting firm. The court said: "It is well established that when the defendant is an accounting party, and stands as one occupying a fiduciary relation toward the plaintiff, because of money or property entrusted to him, the burden is upon him to show that he has performed his trust and the manner of its performance. He owes this duty because of the confidential relation he bears to his principal, and because he is presumed to know how he has performed his duty. * * * The burden of proof is on the accountant after he has admitted the relation and the receipt of a certain sum, to prove that he had disposed properly of the amount for which he is accountable, and to show what that amount is." * * *

In the present case defendants owed a similar duty for the defalcation of Watrud.

* * *

NOTES AND QUESTIONS

1. THIS CASE SERVES many purposes for us, but the primary one is to introduce you to the doctrines of agency, and, indeed, those of partnership. To begin with the basics, as indicated earlier, an *agent* is someone who acts on behalf of and subject to the control of another, known as the *principal*. While acting on behalf of a principal, an agent possesses a *fiduciary duty* to the principal, which means that he or she must place the principal's financial interests above the agent's own. As this case makes clear, enunciating another basic principle of agency, the principal is bound by the acts of the agent, that is the principal is liable to third parties as a result of obligations created by the agent's interaction with the third party, if the agent was acting according to the directions of the principal, within the scope of his employment, or, as the law puts it, if the agent acted pursuant to sufficient *authority* given by the principal.

As you will have discerned from the case, there are several different kinds of authority the principal can grant the agent. These include, among others, *actual* authority, *apparent* authority, agency by *estoppel*, and, finally, the elusive kind of authority discussed in the *Croisant* case, "inherent" authority.

Can you understand from the case when a court ought to find such authority present? A principal is also liable for the acts of his or her agent even if no authority was present when the acts purportedly binding the principal were done, if the principal later *ratifies* the acts of the agent, that is, agrees to accept liability for them.

As agency law is an important body of doctrines for both partnerships and corporations, it is worth going into a bit more detail about the agent's authority. As you may have discerned from the case, in a partnership, absent a contrary agreement, all of the partners are regarded as agents of the partnership. This is why the other partners of the accounting partnership in the case were held liable for the results of Watrud's conduct. In a corporation or other forms of business organizations, various persons (officers, directors, employees) may, if given the proper authority, act as agents for those business organizations. It is important, then, to understand the various types of authority a principal can grant to an agent. Consider the following types of authority and the situations in which they apply. Do these rules make sense to you?

. . . .

2. ACTUAL AUTHORITY: An agent exercises *actual authority* if the agent reasonably believes from the principal's conduct or words that the principal has authorized him to act. Even when the principal's subjective intention may have been otherwise, if an agent reasonably understands that the principal intended to confer authority, then the agent has actual authority and the principal will be liable for the acts of the agent. Actual authority can be either *express,* when a principal specifies exactly what the agent is to do or not do, or *implied*, when a principal specifies what an agent is to do, but the power to choose the method or other acts incidental to the specified act can be reasonably inferred by the agent. A common type of implied actual authority is *incidental authority* in which the agent is authorized to do acts reasonably or usually necessary to accomplish the principal's desired objectives. Note that the determination of whether an agent has actual authority is done with reference to what the *agent* reasonably believed, and does not turn on what the third party knew regarding the agent's authority. Unless otherwise specified, actual authority terminates when either the agent or the principal provides notice to the other of his wish to terminate their relationship.

> ■ *Example:* P leaves a note on the desk of a stockbroker, A, saying, "I authorize you to purchase 100 shares of Intel for me today." When A acts on P's behalf in accordance with the note, A has *actual* authority to serve as a stockbroker for P, *express* authority to purchase the shares, perhaps *implied* authority to wait until the price drops in the afternoon before buying, and *incidental* authority to pay the transactional fees for purchasing the shares. Would A have been acting within a grant of authority from P if he sold the shares mid-day and repurchased them when the price dropped again? What if A used the profits from that transaction to purchase additional shares of Intel?

3. APPARENT AUTHORITY: An agent acts with *apparent authority* if the principal's manifestations led the involved third party reasonably to conclude that the principal had authorized the agent to act in a specified manner. Here it is not the understanding of the agent that is at issue, but the understanding of the *third party*. Nevertheless, you can probably understand why apparent authority often coincides with actual authority. Note that apparent authority can be present even if a principal does not intend to authorize the agent to act, in a manner similar to how actual authority can be found. Frequently an officer's position within a corporation provides apparent authority, if a third party reasonably believes the agent's authority to be consistent with his position. This is called *authority by position*.

> ■ *Example:* A is the President and Chairman of the Board, the Chief Executive Officer (CEO) of XYZ, Inc. In his position, A is the agent of corporation. T, a third party who signs a contract with A, could reasonably believe from the corporation's Board of Directors (which body selects the officers) appointing of A to a high position within the corporation that the Board had implicitly or expressly authorized A to sign contracts on behalf of XYZ, especially if that is the usual practice for executives in his position. In this situation, A would have apparent authority to sign a contract with T, and XYZ, Inc. would be liable for A's actions, even if no one else involved in the corporation had wished for A to sign a contract with T.

4. AGENCY BY ESTOPPEL: A would-be principal can be *estopped* [a technical term of art, which means "prevented by the law," in order to promote justice] from denying an agency relationship and become liable to a third party if the third party relied to his detriment on his belief in an agent's authority. The third party's belief must have been caused either by intentional or careless behavior of the would-be principal, or a failure of the principal to take reasonable steps to notify the third party of the error of such belief.

(Restatement (3rd) of Agency § 2.05). Although agency by estoppel usually involves false representations by an actor purporting to be an agent, a would-be principal will still be found liable because it was his acts or his failure reasonably to act to deny authority which enabled the purported agent to misrepresent his or her authority to third parties. Agency by estoppel, like apparent authority, rests on the *third party's* understanding. Unlike apparent authority, in order to be invoked, agency by estoppel requires detrimental reliance on the part of the third party.

■ *Example:* T enters a store called "P's Stereos" and is approached by A, wearing a "P's Stereos" shirt and otherwise acting like a salesman. Although T doesn't know it, A had found the shirt and a P's Stereos receipt book on the sidewalk, where P had negligently left them the day before. A induces T to purchase a stereo, and, in exchange for cash, gives T an official-looking receipt and explains that the stereo will be delivered later in the day. T never receives his stereo, nor does P ever receive the cash from the transaction. A is neither an agent nor employee of P, and does not have actual or apparent authority to sell from P's inventory. Even so, P may be liable for T's detrimental reliance through the creation of agency by estoppel because P's carelessness with identifying materials and lack of surveillance over the store's sales force facilitated T's reasonable belief that A was authorized as an agent of P.

5. AUTHORITY BY RATIFICATION: An agent who acts on behalf of a principal, but without actual or apparent authority, can still bind the principal to third parties if the principal, who later acquires knowledge of the material facts regarding the agent's dealings with the third party, either objectively manifests his consent to being liable for the agent's conduct, or behaves in such a way that consent can be inferred. The legal consequence of the principal's *ratification* is that the agency relationship is treated as if the agent possessed *actual authority* at the time of the relevant acts.

6. INHERENT AUTHORITY: According to Restatement (Second) of Agency and, as you saw in *Croisant v. Watrud*, even when an agent acts without actual authority or apparent authority, a principal can still be liable through the application of the doctrine of inherent authority. Somewhat similar to apparent authority, inherent authority turns on the beliefs of the particular involved third party. The difference between apparent and inherent authority has not always been easy for courts or commentators to discern. Inherent authority exists when a particular third party has an actual and reasonable belief that the agent possesses authority to act in a specified manner on behalf of the principal, even if that third party's belief is not based on particular manifestations by the principal (as is true for apparent authority). Inherent authority arises solely from the agency relationship itself, and, as the Croisant court indicates, is based on the theory that if a principal appoints an agent to conduct a series of transactions, it is only fair that the principal should bear losses that are incurred when the agent, although not authorized to do so, does something that is closely connected with the transactions he is employed to conduct. As in Croisant, a principal is liable for his agent's actions that "usually accompany or are incidental to transactions which the agent is authorized to conduct," even if no authority is given or implied. Because inherent agency imposes liability on a principal in an indefinite variety of circumstances, potentially beyond those when actual or apparent authority are present, the existence of the doctrine purportedly encourages principals to exercise more caution in selecting agents, thereby minimizing their potential liability and perhaps avoiding harm to third persons.

....

7. DON'T WORRY if you're having trouble figuring out exactly what inherent authority is and how it differs from apparent authority. *Inherent authority* has recently been eliminated in drafts of the Restatement (Third) of Agency. The drafters of this Third Restatement (as the law develops, the Restatements have gone through subsequent drafts) removed the distinction between inherent authority and apparent authority by expanding the definition of the principal's manifestations to include situations without verbal communications by the principal, such as appointments of agents to certain positions. The confusion between apparent and inherent authority explains the suggestion in *Croisant* that "whether the theory is characterized as one of apparent authority . . . or as arising out of an inherent agency power is immaterial." In the reporter's notes for the Third Restatement, the authors argue that as the Restatements are designed to simplify the law and create a more unified, concise statement of the law of the states, elimination of inherent agency is needed.

In an important law review article, one critic of the Third Restatement's elimination of inherent authority argues that apparent authority ought to be conceptualized as only a small subset of inherent authority, and thus it should not be expanded to replace inherent authority. This critic explains the distinction between the two kinds of authority by suggesting that inherent authority requires only that the third party's belief be actual and reasonable, whereas apparent authority requires that the third party's belief be actual, reasonable, and based on the principal's manifestations. Inherent authority thus becomes the most useful in cases, such as *Croisant*, where the third party's beliefs are reasonable but cannot be traced to manifestations by the principal. Because of this narrow but useful difference between inherent authority and actual authority, it is suggested that elimination of inherent authority breaks with precedent cases like *Croisant* and constitutes an inappropriate substantive change of the law.[1] Remember that Restatements are not supposed to change the law, just to reflect it. Having read a case in which apparent authority and inherent authority both

_____

1   Matthew P. Ward, *Note: A Restatement or a Redefinition: Elimination of Inherent Agency in the Tentative Draft of the Restatement (Third) of Agency,* 59 Wash & Lee L. Rev. 1585, 1626 2002).

play a large role, do you agree with the new Restatement's elimination of inherent authority? Do you think this change potentially makes the law clearer or does the new Restatement increase confusion?

8. WHY ALL THIS FUSS about different kinds of authority in the first place? Does having multiple types of authority benefit business? Does it further fairness? Do you think it adds certainty and predictability to the law? Is there an economic benefit to allowing agents to act on behalf of principals, and bind the principals (whether individuals, partnerships (as in *Croisant*), or corporations) without requiring more formal, explicit grants of authority? What would happen if courts required a showing of express actual authority before they would allow a principal to be bound by an agent's acts?

9. WHAT DIFFERENCE DOES IT MAKE, if any, that the purported principal in Croisant is a *partnership*? What can you infer about the nature of partnerships from the case? See if your inferences are borne out by the consideration of partnership law which follows this chapter on Agency.

II. What Are the Fiduciary Duties of the Agent?

SURELY ONE OF THE MOST REMARKABLE THINGS about the law of agency is the manner in which the law attempts to ensure that the agent (for whose actions the principal is liable) serves the interests of the principal. This is accomplished by the enforcement of the agent's fiduciary duty to the principal. The extent to which this will be done is illustrated by the following case. Does it seem to you that the law of agency goes too far, not far enough, or just the right distance?

Tarnowski v. Resop

Supreme Court of Minnesota, 236 Minn. 33, 51 N.W.2d 801 (1952).

* * *

[KNUTSON, J.]

Plaintiff * * * engaged defendant as his agent to investigate and negotiate for the purchase of a route of coin-operated music machines. On June 2, 1947, relying upon the advice of defendant * * * plaintiff purchased such a business from Phillip Loechler and Lyle Mayer of Rochester, Minnesota, who will be referred to hereinafter as the sellers. The business was located at La Crosse, Wisconsin, and throughout the surrounding territory. Plaintiff alleges that defendant represented to him that he had made a thorough investigation of the route; that it had 75 locations in operation; that one or more machines were at each location; that the equipment at each location was not more than six months old; and that the gross income from all locations amounted to more than $3,000 per month. As a matter of fact, defendant had made only a superficial investigation and had investigated only five of the locations. Other than that, he had adopted false representations of the sellers as to the other locations and had passed them on to plaintiff as his own. Plaintiff was to pay $30,620 for the business. He paid $11,000 down. About six weeks after the purchase, plaintiff discovered that the representations made to him by defendant were false, in that there were not more than 47 locations; that at some of the locations there were no machines and at others there were machines more than six months old, some of them being seven years old; and that the gross income was far less than $3,000 per month. Upon discovering the falsity of defendant's representations and those of the sellers, plaintiff rescinded the sale. He offered to return what he had received, and he demanded the return of his money. The sellers refused to comply, and he brought suit against them in the district court of Olmsted county. The action was tried, resulting in a verdict of $10,000 for plaintiff. Thereafter, the sellers paid plaintiff $9,500, after which the action was dismissed with prejudice pursuant to a stipulation of the parties.

In this action, brought in Hennepin county, plaintiff alleges that defendant, while acting as agent for him, collected a secret commission from the sellers for consummating the sale, which plaintiff seeks to recover under his first cause of action. In his second cause of action, he seeks to recover damages [besides the side-payment to the agent, incidental to the case.] The case was tried to a jury, and plaintiff recovered a verdict of $5,200. This appeal is from the judgment entered pursuant thereto.

Defendant contends that after recovery of a verdict by plaintiff in his action for rescission against the sellers he cannot maintain this action against defendant. Principally, defendant argues that recovery in the action against the sellers is a bar to this action * * *.

1. With respect to plaintiff 's first cause of action, the principle that all profits made by an agent in the course of an agency belong to the principal, whether they are the

fruits of performance or the violation of an agent's duty, is firmly established and universally recognized. * * * It matters not that the principal has suffered no damage or even that the transaction has been profitable to him. * * *

The rule and the basis therefor are well stated in *Lum v. McEwen, 56 Minn. 278, 282, 57 N.W. 662*, where, speaking through Mr. Justice Mitchell, we said: "Actual injury is not the principle the law proceeds on, in holding such transactions void. Fidelity in the agent is what is aimed at, and, as a means of securing it, the law will not permit him to place himself in a position in which he may be tempted by his own private interests to disregard those of his principal. * * * It is not material that no actual injury to the company [principal] resulted, or that the policy recommended may have been for its best interest. Courts will not inquire into these matters. It is enough to know that the agent in fact placed himself in such relations that he might be tempted by his own interests to disregard those of his principal. "The transaction was nothing more or less than the acceptance by the agent of a bribe to perform his duties in the manner desired by the person who gave the bribe. Such a contract is void.

> **"FIDELITY IN** the agent is what is aimed at, and, as a means of securing it, the law will not permit him to place himself in a position in which he may be tempted by his own private interests to disregard those of his principal.

"This doctrine rests on such plain principles of law, as well as common business honesty, that the citation of authorities is unnecessary." The right to recover profits made by the agent in the course of the agency is not affected by the fact that the principal, upon discovering a fraud, has rescinded the contract and recovered that with which he parted. Restatement, Agency, § 407(2). *Comment e on Subsection* (2) reads:

"If an agent has violated a duty of loyalty to the principal so that the principal is entitled to profits which the agent has thereby made, the fact that the principal has brought an action against a third person and has been made whole by such action does not prevent the principal from recovering from the agent the profits which the agent has made. Thus, if the other contracting party has given a bribe to the agent to make a contract with him on behalf of the principal, the principal can rescind the transaction, recovering from the other party anything received by him, or he can maintain an action for damages against him; in either event the principal may recover from the agent the amount of the bribe."

It follows that, insofar as the secret commission of $2,000 received by the agent is concerned, plaintiff had an absolute right thereto, irrespective of any recovery resulting from the action against the sellers for rescission.

2. Plaintiff's second cause of action is brought to recover damages for (1) losses suffered in the operation of the business prior to rescission; (2) loss of time devoted to operation; (3) expenses in connection with rescission of the sale and investigation therewith; (4) nontaxable expenses in connection with the prosecution of the suit against the sellers; and (5) attorneys' fees in connection with the suit.

* * * Our inquiry is limited to a consideration of the question whether a principal may recover [from] an agent who has breached his trust the items of damage mentioned after a successful prosecution of an action for rescission against the third parties with whom the agent dealt for his principal.

The general rule is stated in Restatement, Agency, § 407(1), as follows:

> "If an agent has received a benefit as a result of violating his duty of loyalty, the principal is entitled to recover from him what he has so received, its value, or its proceeds, and also the amount of damage thereby caused, except that if the violation consists of the wrongful disposal of the principal's property, the principal cannot recover its value and also what the agent received in exchange therefor."

> In *Comment a on Subsection* (1) we find the following:

> " * * * In either event, whether or not the principal elects to get back the thing improperly dealt with or to recover from the agent its value or the amount of benefit which the agent has improperly received, he is, in addition, entitled to be indemnified by the agent for any loss which has been caused to his interests by the improper transaction. Thus, if the purchasing agent for a restaurant purchases with

> the principal's money defective food, receiving a bonus therefor, and the use of the food in the restaurant damages the business, the principal can recover from the agent the amount of money improperly expended by him, the bonus which the agent received, and the amount which will compensate for the injury to the business."

The general rule with respect to damages for a tortious act is that— "The wrong-doer is answerable for all the injurious consequences of his tortious act which, according to the usual course of events and general experience, were likely to ensue and which, therefore, when the act was committed, he may reasonably be supposed to have foreseen and anticipated." 1 Sutherland, Damages (4 ed.) § 45 * * *.

The general rule is given in Restatement, Torts, § 910, as follows: "A person injured by the tort of another is entitled to recover damages from him for all harm, past, present and prospective, legally caused by the tort." *Bergquist v. Kreidler, 158 Minn. 127, 196 N.W. 964,* involved an action to recover attorneys' fees expended by plaintiffs in an action seeking to enforce and protect their right to the possession of real estate. Defendant, acting as the owner's agent, had falsely represented to plaintiffs that they could have possession on August 1, 1920. It developed after plaintiffs had purchased the premises that a tenant had a lease running to August 1, 1922, on a rental much lower than the actual value of the premises. Defendant (the agent) conceded that plaintiffs were entitled to recover the loss in rent, but contended that attorneys' fees and disbursements expended by plaintiffs in testing the validity of the tenant's lease were not recoverable. In affirming plaintiffs' right to recover we said *(158 Minn. 132, 196 N.W. 966):* " * * * the litigation in which plaintiffs became involved was the direct, legitimate and a to-be-expected result of appellant's misrepresentation. The loss sustained by plaintiffs in conducting that litigation 'is plainly traceable' to appellant's wrong and he should make compensation accordingly."

So far as the right to recover attorneys' fees is concerned, the same may be said in this case. Plaintiff sought to return what had been received and demanded a return of his down payment. The sellers refused. He thereupon sued to accomplish this purpose, as he had a right to do, and was successful. His attorneys' fees and expenses of suit were directly traceable to the harm caused by defendant's wrongful act. As such, they are recoverable. * * * The same is true of the other elements of damage involved. See, generally, 15 Am. Jur., Damages, § 138.

3. Defendant contends that plaintiff had an election of remedies and, having elected to proceed against the sellers to recover what he had paid, is now barred from proceeding against defendant. It is true that upon discovery of the fraud plaintiff had an election of remedies against the sellers. It is not true, however, that, having elected to sue for recovery of that with which he had parted, he is barred from proceeding against his agent to recover damages for [the agent's] tortious conduct. While some of the allegations in plaintiff's complaint against the sellers are similar to or identical with those in his complaint in this case, insofar as the fraud is concerned, the right of recovery here against the agent goes much further than the action against the sellers. Many of the elements of damage against the agent are not available to plaintiff against the sellers. For instance, he has no right to recover attorneys' fees and expenses of the litigation against the sellers. He has that right against the agent. * * *

Losses directly flowing from the agent's tortious conduct are not recoverable against the sellers in an action for rescission, but they may be recovered against the agent, whose breach of faith has caused such losses.

4. Nor is the settlement and dismissal of the action against the sellers a bar to an action against the agent, for the same reasons as stated above. The sellers and agent are not joint tortfeasors in the sense that their wrongful conduct necessarily grows out of the same wrong. Their individual torts may have been based on the same fraud, but their liabilities to plaintiff do not have the same limitations. In simple terms, the causes of action are not the same. * * *

NOTES AND QUESTIONS

I. SO FAR YOU HAVE LEARNED that agents are authorized to conduct business for a principal and can enter into contracts which bind the principal, if they act with sufficient authority. The *Tarnowski* case is your introduction to an equally important aspect of agency law, the *fiduciary responsibility* of the agent to the principal. As indicated, the essence of this fiduciary responsibility is that the agent is required to put the principal's interests ahead of his own. Why should this be so? Because many business entities, particularly corporations, can only act through agents (can you understand why this is the case?) regulating their behavior is tremendously important. Can you understand why the fiduciary principle is necessary given the enormous discretion that agents may have not only to make binding contracts for their principals, but also to negotiate and execute them?

2. GIVEN HUMAN NATURE, one will want to look out for one's own interests ahead of those of others. Agency law must come to grips with the fact that the inevitable agency relationship will require some mechanisms so that the principal can minimize the temptation of the agent to betray the principal's interests in favor of the agent's own. There is a vast economic literature on this problem, but for our purposes it is enough to note that without legal restraints on the agent, and even with them, principals will often expend "monitoring costs" to ensure that their agents act according to the principal's wishes. The principal might also require that the agent enter into some kind of security arrangement so that funds are forfeited if the agent acts in a manner contrary to the principal's interest. The costs of such an arrangement are known as "bonding costs." Finally, as we have seen in *Tarnowski*, if the agent does fail to perform according to the wishes and interests of the principal, the principal may face some loss, either of lost opportunity, or of money expended for inferior goods. This is generally referred to as "residual loss."

The economic literature explains that "agency costs" the costs to all concerned of employing agents to carry out transactions, is the sum of the monitoring expenses expended by the principal, the bonding expenditures of the agent, and the residual loss faced by the principal. Can you understand how imposing a fiduciary duty on the agent serves to reduce "agency costs?"

3. IN *TARNOWSKI* the agent, Resop, took a bribe and bound his principal in a business deal that featured fraud on the part of the sellers (the third parties) and also on the part of the agent. The principal, Tarnowski, sued the sellers, and essentially recovered his losses from the fraudulent transaction, and then Tarnowski proceeded to bring a second lawsuit against his disloyal agent. Because he had previously been made virtually whole as a result of the favorable settlement of the lawsuit against the sellers, it might be said that Tarnowski was no longer financially harmed by his agent's taking of a bribe, yet the court rules that he is still entitled to that bribe, or "side payment" made by the sellers to the agent. Why? The court writes in its decision, "all profits made by an agent in the course of an agency belong to the principal, whether they are the fruits of performance or the violation of an agent's duty." The court continues "it matters not that the principal has suffered no damage or even that the transaction has been profitable to him." How can this be? Is it wise policy? If side-payments from third parties to agents can be recovered by principals will this result in principals taking less care to hire trustworthy agents?

....

4. AS YOU MAY KNOW, Courts rarely and reluctantly award attorney's fees, particularly in private disputes, unless such remedy is set forth in a statute. In this case, the court awarded attorneys fees expended by Tarnowski. In the logic of the court, "the attorneys' fees and expenses of suit were directly traceable to the harm caused by defendant's wrongful act." Does this decision seem fair to you, given the usual reluctance to award attorney's fees?

Note that the court reaches this decision after consulting authorities regarding the law of torts. Is this a torts case or a contracts case? Should it make a difference? For further thoughts on the fiduciary duty as it applies to agents in a variety of contexts, *see* Victor Brudney, *Contract and Fiduciary Duty in Corporate Law*, 38 B.C.L. Rev. 595 (1997), and, for an analysis of the problem of agency from a literary perspective, *see* Allen D. Boyer, *Agents, Lovers, and Institutions: John Le Carre as Legal Critic*, 65 Notre Dame L. Rev. 78 (1989).

THE LAW
OF PARTNERSHIP

THE PARTNERSHIP MAY BE the most ancient form of business organization. It is generally defined simply as "an association of two or more persons jointly engaged in a business for profit." The partnership was, formerly, one of the most

common forms used for business (along with the corporation), but it is now rapidly being replaced by newer forms such as the Limited Liability Company (LLC), or the Limited Liability Partnership (LLP). We can best appreciate these newer forms by spending some time studying the older or "classic" partnership form. Bear in mind, as you begin this study, why it is that the partnership form is now being eclipsed. Would you have wanted to be a partner? Why or why not?

I. When Is There a Partnership?

Martin v. Peyton

Court of Appeals of New York.
246 N.Y. 213, 158 N.E. 77 (1927).

[ANDREWS, J.]

* * * Partnership results from contract, express or implied. If denied it may be proved by the production of some written instrument; by testimony as to some conversation; by circumstantial evidence. If nothing else appears the receipt by the defendant of a share of the profits of the business is enough. * * *

Assuming some written contract between the parties the question may arise whether it creates a partnership. If it be complete; if it expresses in good faith the full understanding and obligation of the parties, then it is for the court to say whether a partnership exists. It may, however, be a mere sham intended to hide the real relationship. Then other results follow. In passing upon it effect is to be given to each provision. Mere words will not blind us to realities. Statements that no partnership is intended are not conclusive. If as a whole a contract contemplates an association of two or more persons to carry on as co-owners a business for profit a partnership there is. * * * On the other hand, if it be less than this no partnership exists. Passing on the contract as a whole, an arrangement for sharing profits is to be considered. It is to be given its due weight. But it is to be weighed in connection with all the rest. It is not decisive. It may be merely the method adopted to pay a debt or wages, as interest on a loan or for other reasons.
       * * *

In the case before us the claim that the defendants became partners in the firm of Knauth, Nachod & Kuhne, doing business as bankers and brokers, depends upon the interpretation of certain instruments. * * * "The plaintiff's position is not," we are told, "that the agreements of June 4, 1921, were a false expression or incomplete expression of the intention of the parties. We say that they express defendants' intention and that that intention was to create a relationship which as a matter of law constitutes a partnership." Nor may the claim of the plaintiff be rested on any question of estoppel. "The plaintiff's claim," he stipulates, "is a claim of actual partnership, not of partnership by estoppel * * *."

Remitted then, as we are, to the documents themselves, we refer to circumstances surrounding their execution only so far as is necessary to make them intelligible. And we are to remember that although the intention of the parties to avoid liability as partners is clear, although in language precise and definite they deny any design to then join the firm of K. N. & K.; although they say their interests in profits should be construed merely as a measure of compensation for loans, not an interest in profits as such; although they provide that they shall not be liable for any losses or treated as partners, the question still remains whether in fact they agree to so associate themselves with the firm as to "carry on as co-owners a business for profit."

In the spring of 1921 the firm of K. N. & K. found itself in financial difficulties. John R. Hall was one of the partners. He was a friend of Mr. Peyton. From him he obtained the loan of almost $500,000 of Liberty bonds, which K. N. & K. might use as collateral to secure bank advances. This, however, was not sufficient. The firm and its members had engaged in unwise speculations, and it was deeply involved. Mr. Hall was also intimately acquainted with George W. Perkins, Jr., and with Edward W. Freeman. He also knew Mrs. Peyton and Mrs. Perkins and Mrs. Freeman. All were anxious to help him. He, therefore, representing K. N. & K., entered into negotiations with them. While they were pending a proposition was made that Mr. Peyton, Mr. Perkins and Mr. Freeman or some of them should become partners. It met a decided refusal. Finally an agreement was reached. It is expressed in three documents, executed on the same day, all a part of the one transaction. * * * We shall refer to them as "the agreement," "the indenture" and "the option."

We have no doubt as to their general purpose. The respondents were to loan K. N. & K. $2,500,000 worth of liquid securities, which were to be returned to them on or before April 15, 1923. The firm might hypothecate them to secure loans totalling $2,000,000, using the proceeds as its business necessities required. To insure respondents against loss K. N. & K. were to turn over to them a large number of their own securities which may have been valuable, but which were of so speculative a nature that they could not be used as collateral for bank loans. In compensation for the loan the respondents were to receive 40 per cent of the profits of the firm until the return was made, not exceeding, however, $500,000 and not less than $100,000. Merely because the transaction involved the transfer of securities and not of cash does not prevent its being a loan * * *. The respondents also were given an option to join the firm if they or any of them expressed a desire to do so before June 4, 1923.

Many other detailed agreements are contained in the papers. Are they such as may be properly inserted to protect the lenders? Or do they go further? Whatever their purpose, did they in truth associate the respondents with the firm so that they and it together thereafter carried on as co-owners a business for profit? * * *

As representing the lenders, Mr. Peyton and Mr. Freeman are called "trustees." The loaned securities when used as collateral are not to be mingled with other securities of K. N. & K., and the trustees at all times are to be kept informed of all transactions affecting them. To them shall be paid all dividends and income accruing therefrom. They may also substitute for any of the securities loaned securities of equal value. With their consent the firm may sell any of its securities held by the respondents, the proceeds to go, however, to the trustees. In other similar ways the trustees may deal with these same securities, but the securities loaned shall always be sufficient in value to permit of their hypothecation for $2,000,000. If they rise in price the excess may be withdrawn by the defendants. If they fall they shall make good the deficiency.

So far there is no hint that the transaction is not a loan of securities with a provision for compensation. Later a somewhat closer connection with the firm appears. Until the securities are returned the directing management of the firm is to be in the hands of John R. Hall, and his life is to be insured for $1,000,000, and the policies are to be assigned as further collateral security to the trustees. These requirements are not unnatural. Hall was the one known and trusted by the defendants. Their acquaintance with the other members of the firm was of the slightest. These others had brought an old and established business to the verge of bankruptcy. As the respondents knew, they also had engaged in unsafe speculation. The respondents were about to loan $2,500,000 of good securities. As collateral they were to receive others of problematical value. What they required seems but ordinary caution. Nor does it imply an association in the business.

The trustees are to be kept advised as to the conduct of the business and consulted as to important matters. They may inspect the firm books and are entitled to any information they think important. Finally they may veto any business they think highly speculative or injurious. Again

we hold this but a proper precaution to safeguard the loan. The trustees may not initiate any transaction as a partner may do. They may not bind the firm by any action of their own. Under the circumstances the safety of the loan depended upon the business success of K. N. & K. This success was likely to be compromised by the inclination of its members to engage in speculation. * * * The trustees, therefore, might prohibit it, and that their prohibition might be effective, information was to be furnished them. Not dissimilar agreements have been held proper to guard the interests of the lender.

As further security each member of K. N. & K. is to assign to the trustees their interest in the firm. No loan by the firm to any member is permitted and the amount each may draw is fixed. No other distribution of profits is to be made. So that realized profits may be calculated the existing capital is stated to be $700,000, and profits are to be realized as promptly as good business practice will permit. In case the trustees think this is not done, the question is left to them and to Mr. Hall, and if they differ then to an arbitrator. There is no obligation that the firm shall continue the business. It may dissolve at any time. Again we conclude there is nothing here not properly adapted to secure the interest of the respondents as lenders. If their compensation is dependent on a percentage of the profits still provision must be made to define what these profits shall be.

The "indenture" is substantially a mortgage of the collateral delivered by K. N. & K. to the trustees to secure the performance of the "agreement." It certainly does not strengthen the claim that the respondents were partners.

Finally we have the "option." It permits the respondents or any of them or their assignees or nominees to enter the firm at a later date if they desire to do so by buying 50 per cent or less of the interests therein of all or any of the members at a stated price. Or a corporation may, if the respondents and the members agree, be formed in place of the firm. Meanwhile, apparently with the design of protecting the firm business against improper or ill-judged action which might render the option valueless, each member of the firm is to place his resignation in the hands of Mr. Hall. If at any time he and the trustees agree that such resignation should be accepted, that member shall then retire, receiving the value of his interest calculated as of the date of such retirement.

This last provision is somewhat unusual, yet it is not enough in itself to show that on June 4, 1921, a present partnership was created nor taking these various papers as a whole do we reach such a result. It is quite true that even if one or two or three like provisions contained in such a

contract do not require this conclusion, yet it is also true that when taken together a point may come where stipulations immaterial separately cover so wide a field that we should hold a partnership exists. As in other branches of the law a question of degree is often the determining factor. Here that point has not been reached. * * *

NOTES AND QUESTIONS

I. AS INDICATED EARLIER, the partnership is one of the oldest and simplest ways for multiple parties to organize a business. The law of partnerships was originally part of the common law, but these business forms are now more commonly regulated by the Uniform Partnership Act (UPA), a statute drafted in 1914, and since passed in many jurisdictions. The UPA was itself substantially revised in 1994, and is now denominated as the Revised Uniform Partnership Act (RUPA). The UPA and the RUPA provide the basic definitions and governing rules for partnerships, but for our purposes the UPA, and the RUPA can be understood as simply restating the basic principles of the common law of partnership. Note, in particular, as indicated in the opening paragraphs of *Martin v. Peyton*, that partnership is primarily regarded as a creature of contract. Because partners are personally jointly and severally liable for the debts of the partnership, it is important that all parties understand what they are doing, and understand the consequences of creating a partnership. Still, as ought to be the clear implication from *Martin v. Peyton*, just as agency (another creature of contract) can be determined to be present even if it was not the intention of the parties involved, a partnership will exist whenever a court determines that it has before it "An association of two or more persons to carry on, as co-owners, a business for profit." UPA Sec. 6(1). This will be true whatever may have been the expressed intention of the putative partners. When do you suppose a court will determine that a partnership exists (and impose liability on partners to third persons) in spite of clear expressions to the contrary by those associated in the business?

2. IN *MARTIN*, THE DISTINCTION between creditor and partner is of crucial importance. The bargain between Hall and his friends is an elaborate one, featuring three different documents, the "agreement," the "indenture," and the "option." Do you understand the purposes of each of them? If you had to come up with a single purpose or set of purposes of the three, what would it be? Do these six friends of Mr. Hall strike you as having more control over the workings of the K,N, & K firm than your average creditor? Do you agree with Judge Andrews's opinion that the six friends were only creditors and not partners?

In a recent excellent treatment of *Martin v. Peyton*, longtime UCLA Law Professor William Klein, a distinguished practitioner of law and economics analysis, argues that when one examines "each of the deal points—most notably, modified profit share (40 Percent of profit, with a minimum of $100,000 and a maximum of $500,000) and control (designation of the managing partner (Hall), veto, and resignations)–with an effort to determine whether each element pointed more to partnership or to debt" then the case "could have gone either way." William A. Klein, "The Story of *Martin v. Peyton*: Rich Investors, Risky Investment, and the Line Between Lenders and Undisclosed Partners," in J. Mark Ramseyer, Ed., *Corporate Law Stories* 77, 91 (2009). Which way do you think the case should have gone, and why? Is the outcome of the case explainable in part because of the extraordinary social prominence of the Hall, Peyton, Perkins, and Freeman families? Which result in the case, imposing partnership liability on those families, or treating them as creditors, is most consonant with economic efficiency? Which with fairness? On these points generally, consult Klein, *supra*.

3. WHY DO YOU SUPPOSE we impose unlimited personal liability on partners? Why not on creditors? Based on what you know of the law of agency, for example, is it likely that there is a real possibility of harm to innocent third parties? Consider the situation where A and B agree to go into business together. A, who is very wealthy, provides all the capital, while B provides industry know-how and contacts, but has no personal net worth to speak of. A and B agree to share the profits of their business equally (which, by the way, is the default rule for partnerships). If C, a third party, is injured by a product produced by the partnership of A and B, C could go after the assets of both partners. If, however, A, having read *Martin v. Peyton*, had set up the business agreement to look as though he loaned the money to B, C is left with only the assets of the business and the meager personal assets of B to compensate him for any injury. You can see that those who can afford to hire attorneys to draft sophisticated agreements such as those in *Martin v. Peyton* may be able to exercise a great deal of control over the business while still facing no personal financial risks other than losing their initial investment. Does this seem fair to you?

4. THE "CLASSIC" FORM OF partnership, where all the partners are liable for all the debts of the partnership, and where all the partners have a fiduciary duty to each other, is known as a "general" partnership. Other forms of "partnership" have arisen to combat the perceived shortcomings and potential liability issues in general partnerships. One alternative form, of fairly ancient vintage, is a limited partnership, in which one or more general partners are active in managing the business and are personally liable for the partnership's debts and obligations. The limited partner or partners have limited liability, that is, under normal circumstances their liability is limited to their investment in the firm, and, in turn, the limited partners have no right to control the day-to-day operations of the partnership, and usually cannot act as agents of the partnership. Most states also offer *limited liability partnerships* (LLP's) which are like general partnerships, in terms of giving each partner an equal right to participate in management, but which give limited liability protection to all partners. Generally speaking, there are filing and other requirements (such as the provision of indemnification to at least some extent for third parties who deal with these entities) for limited partnerships or LLP's. LLP's are popular with law and accounting firms, but not widely used in commercial business. The newest and most generally successful business form to emerge is the *limited liability company* (LLC) which, in the space of a very few years, became accepted in virtually all the states. We will have more to say about LLC's soon, but for now we need only remark that an LLC provides limited liability for all participants, whether or not they are active in the management of the business. Given the availability of Limited Partnerships, LLP's, and LLC's, why would any firm now choose the partnership form? Why do many businesses now choose to avoid that venerable form? Do the following cases provide any clues?

II. What Is The Nature Of Partnership Governance?

National Biscuit Co., Inc. v. Stroud

Supreme Court of North Carolina.
249 N.C. 467, 106 S.E.2d 692 (1959)

[PARKER, J.]

C. N. Stroud and Earl Freeman entered into a general partnership to sell groceries under the firm name of Stroud's Food Center. There is nothing in the agreed statement of facts to indicate or suggest that Freeman's power and authority as a general partner were in any way restricted or limited by the articles of partnership in respect to the ordinary and legitimate business of the partnership. Certainly, the purchase and sale of bread were ordinary and legitimate business of Stroud's Food Center during its continuance as a going concern.

Several months prior to February 1956 Stroud advised plaintiff that he personally would not be responsible for any additional bread sold by plaintiff to Stroud's Food Center. After such notice to plaintiff, it from 6 February 1956 to 25 February 1956, at the request of Freeman, sold and delivered bread in the amount of $171.04 to Stroud's Food Center.

In *Johnson v. Bernheim*, 76 N.C. 139, this Court said: "A and B are general partners to do some given business; the partnership is, by operation of law, a power to each to bind the partnership in any manner legitimate to the business. If one partner go to a third person to buy an article on time for the partnership, the other partner cannot prevent it by writing to the third person not to sell to him on time; or, if one party attempt to buy for cash, the other has no right to require that it shall be on time. And what is true in regard to buying is true in regard to selling. What either partner does with a third person is binding on the partnership. It is otherwise where the partnership is not general, but is upon special terms, as that purchases and sales must be with and for cash. There the power to each is special, in regard to all dealings with third persons at least who have notice of the terms." * * *

The General Assembly of North Carolina in 1941 enacted a Uniform Partnership Act, which became effective 15 March 1941. G.S. Ch. 59, Partnership, Art. 2. G.S. 59–39 is entitled PARTNER AGENT OF PARTNERSHIP AS TO PARTNERSHIP BUSINESS, and subsection (1) reads: "Every partner is an agent of the partnership for the purpose of its business, and the act of every partner, including the execution in the partnership name of any instrument, for apparently carrying on in the usual way the business of the partnership of which he is a member binds the partnership, unless the partner so acting has in fact no authority to act for the partnership in the particular matter, and the person with whom he is dealing has knowledge of the fact that he has no such authority." *G.S. 59–39(4)* states: "No act of a partner in con-travention of a restriction on authority shall bind the partnership to persons having knowledge of the restriction." *G.S. 59–45* provides that "all partners are jointly and severally liable for the acts and obligations of the partnership." *G.S. 59–48* is captioned RULES DETERMINING RIGHTS AND DUTIES OF PARTNERS. Subsection (e) thereof reads: "All partners have equal rights in the management and conduct of the partnership business." Subsection (h) thereof is as follows:

> "Any difference arising as to ordinary matters connected with the partnership business may be decided by a majority of the partners; but no act in contravention of any agreement between the partners may be done rightfully without the consent of all the partners."

Freeman as a general partner with Stroud, with no restrictions on his authority to act within the scope of the partnership business so far as the agreed statement of facts shows, had under the Uniform Partnership Act "equal rights in the manage-ment and conduct of the partnership business." Under *G.S. 59–48(h)* Stroud, his co-partner, could not restrict the power and authority of Freeman to buy bread for the partnership as a going concern, for such a purchase was an "ordinary matter connected with the partnership business," for the purpose of its business and within its scope, because in the very nature of things Stroud was not, and could not be, a majority of the partners. Therefore, Freeman's purchases of bread from plaintiff for Stroud's Food Center as a going concern bound the partnership and his co-partner Stroud. * * *

In *Crane on Partnership*, 2nd Ed., p. 277, it is said: "In cases of an even division of the partners as to whether or not an act within the scope of the business should be done, of which disagreement a third person has knowledge, it seems that logically no restriction can be placed upon the power to act. The partnership being a going concern, activities within the scope of the business should not be limited, save by the expressed will of the majority deciding a disputed question; half of the members are not a majority." *Sladen v. Lance, 151 N.C. 492, 66 S.E. 449*, is distinguishable. That was a case where the terms of the partnership imposed special restrictions on the power of the partner who made the contract.

At the close of business on 25 February 1956 Stroud and Freeman by agreement dissolved the partnership. By their dissolution agreement all of the partnership as-sets, including cash on hand, bank deposits and all accounts receivable, with a few exceptions, were assigned to Stroud, who bound himself by such written dissolution agreement to liquidate the firm's assets and discharge its liabilities. It would seem a fair inference from the agreed statement of facts that the partnership got the benefit of the bread sold and delivered by plaintiff to Stroud's Food Center, at Freeman's request, from 6 February 1956 to 25 February 1956. *See Guano Co. v. Ball, 201 N.C. 534, 160 S.E. 769*. But whether it did or not, Freeman's acts, as stated above, bound the partnership and Stroud.

* * *

NOTES AND QUESTIONS

I. AS YOU HAVE PROBABLY BEEN able to discern by now, generally, absent an agreement to the contrary, every partner has an equal share in the operation of the partnership, including decision making power, profit sharing and liability for the partnership's debts. Should partners wish to create a different set-up, including unequal divisions of authority, profits and liability, or even requirements for super-majorities, they must specify any variations in a *partnership agreement* when forming their original partnership, or unanimously modify the agreement at a later date. Contracts explicitly detailing the management of the partnership will then govern future disputes. Can you think of situations in which adjusting partners' liability and power is beneficial to the partnership? What about situations in which requiring unanimity of partners is more desirable than requiring a simple majority of partners?

2. THE RULE APPLIED IN *National Biscuit Company, Inc. v. Stroud* is that although neither partner in two-person partnership constitutes a majority, absent a previous agreement to the contrary, "no restriction can be placed on the power" of one partner to act. Does this make sense to you? Who is protected by such a rule? The result in National Biscuit Company would not occur in some jurisdictions, at least with regard to matters of hiring employees. In another leading case, *Summers v. Dooley*, 94 *Id*.ho 87, 481 P.2d 318 (1971), the Supreme Court of *Id*.ho held that where there are only two partners, and one objects to the hiring of an employee, since the will of the majority ought to govern, and one party does not constitute a majority when partners are equally divided, the party who forbids a change must have his way. Would you have applied this rule under the facts of *National Biscuit Company*? There is a hint, at the end of *National Biscuit*, that a relevant question might be if one partner acted contrary to the wishes of the other, and still the partnership benefited, the dissenting partner might not be able to escape liability for the action taken. Is this the kind of an argument you have seen before? Does it make sense?

3. ONE OF THE WORST DILEMMAS of partnership law is what to do when the partners are divided, especially where there are only two partners. You will have noticed that the partnership in question in *National Biscuit Company, Inc. v. Stroud* ended in dissolution. Generally speaking, and absent contrary agreement, any partner may dissolve the partnership at will, and the assets of the partnership are then divided, usually with one partner buying out the other. Is this any way to run a business?

Another feature of the common law of partnership (and also the default position of the UPA) is that absent contrary agreement, the profits of the partnership are divided equally among the members, and, as you have already understood, each partner is jointly and severally liable for the debts of the partnership. Do you understand why it is one of the oldest old saws of business that partnership is the "worst ship?"

Why did the form persist for so long? One reason is the tax treatment of partnerships, where income and losses are annually allocated directly to the partners, thus avoiding the so-called "double-taxation" of the corporate form, where, for most corporations, revenues are first taxed to the corporation, and then, when profits are distributed as dividends to the shareholders, these dividends are taxed as ordinary income to the individual shareholders receiving the dividends. Are there, or were there once, other reasons for favoring the partnership form, or for embracing the message being partners suggests? Consider the implications of the next case, not, strictly speaking, a partnership case, but one that is frequently cited in the partnership context. It is a bit longer than many of the cases we consider, but you should be aware that it is one of the most famous decisions in all of the law of business organizations. Why do you suppose it has garnered such fame?

III. The Fiduciary Duty Of Partners (And "Coadventurers")

YOU ARE ABOUT TO READ ONE OF the most famous cases in all of business law. It is a bit longer than most of the cases in this book, because we wanted you to get the full flavor of both the majority and the dissenting opinions. Why do you suppose the case became so important, and do you agree with the majority opinion or the dissent?

Meinhard v. Salmon

Court of Appeals of New York.
249 N.Y. 458, 164 N.E. 545, 62 A.L.R. 1 (1928)

[Cardozo, Ch. J.]

On April 10, 1902, Louisa M. Gerry leased to the defendant Walter J. Salmon the premises known as the Hotel Bristol at the northwest corner of Forty-second street and Fifth avenue in the city of New York. The lease was for a term of twenty years, commencing May 1, 1902, and ending April 30, 1922. The lessee undertook to change the hotel building for use as shops and offices at a cost of $200,000. * * *

Salmon, while in course of treaty with the lessor as to the execution of the lease, was in course of treaty with Meinhard, the plaintiff, for the necessary funds. The result was a joint venture with terms embodied in a writing. Meinhard was to pay to Salmon half of the moneys requisite to reconstruct, alter, manage and operate the property. Salmon was to pay to Meinhard 40 per cent of the net profits for the first five years of the lease and 50 per cent for the years thereafter. If there were losses, each party was to bear them equally. Salmon, however, was to have sole power to "manage, lease, underlet and operate" the building. * * *

The two were coadventurers, subject to fiduciary duties akin to those of partners * * *. As to this we are all agreed. The heavier weight of duty rested, however, upon Salmon. He was a coadventurer with Meinhard, but he was manager as well. During the early years of the enterprise, the building, reconstructed, was operated at a loss. If the relation had then ended, Meinhard as well as Salmon would have carried a heavy burden. Later the profits became large with the result that for each of the investors there came a rich return. For each, the venture had its phases of fair weather and of foul. The two were in it jointly, for better or for worse.

When the lease was near its end, Elbridge T. Gerry had become the owner * * *. He owned much other property in the neighborhood, one lot adjoining the Bristol Building on Fifth avenue and four lots on Fortysecond street. He had a plan to lease the entire tract for a long term to some one who would destroy the buildings then existing, and put up another in their place. In the latter part of 1921, he submitted such a project to several capitalists and dealers. He was unable to carry it through with any of them. Then, in January, 1922, with less than four months of the lease to run, he approached the defendant Salmon. The result was a new lease to the Midpoint Realty Company, which is owned and controlled by Salmon, a lease covering the whole tract, and involving a huge outlay. The term is to be twenty years, but successive covenants for renewal will extend it to a maximum of eighty years at the will of either party. The existing buildings may remain unchanged for seven years. They are then to be torn down, and a new building to cost $3,000,000 is to be placed upon the site. The rental, which under the Bristol lease was only $55,000, is to be from $350,000 to $475,000 for the properties so combined.

Salmon personally guaranteed the performance by the lessee of the covenants of the new lease until such time as the new building had been completed and fully paid for. The lease between Gerry and the Midpoint Realty Company was signed and delivered on January 25, 1922. Salmon had not told Meinhard anything about it. * * * The first that he knew of it was in February when the lease was an accomplished fact. He then made demand on the defendants that the lease be held in trust as an asset of the venture, making offer upon the trial to share the personal obligations incidental to the guaranty. The demand was followed by refusal, and later by this suit. A referee gave judgment for the plaintiff, limiting the plaintiff's interest in the lease, however, to 25 percent. The limitation was on the theory that the plaintiff's equity was to be restricted to one-half of so much of the value of the lease as was contributed or represented by the occupation of the Bristol site. Upon cross-appeals to the Appellate Division, the judgment was modified so as to enlarge the equitable interest to one-half of the whole lease. With this enlargement of plaintiff's interest, there went, of course, a corresponding enlargement of his attendant obligations. The case is now here on an appeal by the defendants.

Joint adventurers, like copartners, owe to one another, while the enterprise continues, the duty of the finest loyalty. Many forms of conduct permissible in a workaday world for those acting at arm's length, are forbidden to those bound by fiduciary ties. A trustee is held to something stricter than the morals of the market place. Not honesty alone, but the punctilio of an honor the most sensitive, is then the standard of behavior. As to this there has developed a tradition that is unbending and inveterate. Uncompromising rigidity has been the attitude of courts of equity when petitioned to undermine the rule of undivided loyalty by the "disintegrating erosion" of particular exceptions * * *. Only thus has the level of conduct for fiduciaries been kept at a level higher than that trodden by the crowd. It will not consciously be lowered by any judgment of this court.

The owner * * *, Mr. Gerry, had vainly striven to find a tenant who would favor his ambitious scheme of demolition and construction. Baffled in the search, he turned to the defendant Salmon in possession of the Bristol, the keystone of the project. He figured to himself beyond a doubt that the man in possession would prove a likely customer. To the eye of an observer, Salmon held the lease as owner in his own right, for himself and no one else. In fact he held it as a fiduciary, for himself and another, sharers in a common venture. If this fact had been proclaimed, if the lease by its terms had run in favor of a partnership, Mr. Gerry, we may fairly assume, would have laid before the partners, and not merely before one of them, his plan of reconstruction. The pre-emptive privilege, or, better, the pre-emptive opportunity, that was thus an incident of the enterprise, Salmon appropriated to himself in secrecy and silence. He might have warned Meinhard that the plan had been submitted, and that either would be free to compete for the award. If he had done this, we do not need to say whether he would have been under a duty, if successful in the competition, to hold the lease so acquired for the benefit of a venture then about to end, and thus prolong by indirection its responsibilities and duties. The trouble about his conduct is that he excluded his coadventurer from any chance to compete, from any chance to enjoy the opportunity for benefit that had come to him alone by virtue of his agency. This chance, if nothing more, he was under a duty to concede. The price of its denial is an extension of the trust at the option and for the benefit of the one whom he excluded.

No answer is it to say that the chance would have been of little value even if seasonably offered. Such a calculus of probabilities is beyond the science of the chancery. Salmon, the real estate operator, might have been preferred to Meinhard, the woolen merchant. On the other hand, Meinhard might have offered better terms, or reinforced his offer by alliance with the wealth of others. Perhaps he might even have persuaded the lessor to renew the Bristol lease alone, postponing for a time, in return for higher rentals, the improvement of adjoining lots. We know that even under the lease as made the time for the enlargement of the building was delayed for seven years. All these opportunities were cut away from him through another's intervention. He knew that Salmon was the manager. As the time drew near for the expiration of the lease, he would naturally assume from silence, if from nothing else, that the lessor was willing to extend it for a term of years, or at least to let it stand as a lease from year to year. Not impossibly the lessor would have done so, whatever his protestations of unwillingness, if Salmon had not given assent to a project more attractive. At all events, notice of termination, even if not necessary, might seem, not unreasonably, to be something to be looked for, if the business was over and another tenant was to enter. In the absence of such notice, the matter of an extension was one that would naturally be attended to by the manager of the enterprise and not neglected altogether. At least, there was nothing in the situation to give warning to any one that while the lease was still in being, there had come to the manager an offer of extension which he had locked within his breast to be utilized by himself alone. The very fact that Salmon was in control with exclusive powers of direction charged him the more obviously with the duty of disclosure, since only through disclosure could opportunity be equalized. If he might cut off renewal by a purchase for his own benefit when four months were to pass before the lease would have an end, he might do so with equal right while there remained as many years * * *. He might steal a march on his comrade under cover of the darkness, and then hold the captured ground. Loyalty and comradeship are not so easily abjured.

Little profit will come from a dissection of the precedents. None precisely similar is cited in the briefs of counsel. What is similar in many, or so it seems to us, is the animating principle. Authority is, of course, abundant that one partner may not appropriate to his own use a renewal of a lease, though its term is to begin at the expiration of the partnership (*Mitchell v. Reed, 61 N. Y. 123; 84 N. Y. 556*). The lease at hand with its many changes is not strictly a renewal. Even so, the standard of loyalty for those in trust relations is without the fixed divisions of a graduated scale. There is indeed a dictum in one of our decisions that a partner, though he may not renew a lease, may purchase [the property itself] if he acts openly and fairly (*Anderson v. Lemon, 8 N. Y. 236 * * *). It is a dictum, and no more, for on the ground that he had acted slyly he was charged as a trustee. The holding is thus in favor of the conclusion that a purchase as well as a lease will succumb to the infection of secrecy and silence. Against the dictum in that case, moreover, may be set the opinion of Dwight, C., in *Mitchell v. Read*, where there is a dictum to the contrary *(61 N. Y. at p. 143)*. To say that a partner is free without restriction to buy * * * the [leased] property where the business is conducted is to say in effect that he may strip the good will of its chief element of value, since good will is largely dependent upon continuity of possession * * * Equity refuses to confine within the bounds of classified transactions its precept of a loyalty that is undivided and unselfish. Certain at least it is that a "man obtaining his *locus standi* [literally "place of standing"], and his opportunity for making such arrangements, by the position he occupies as a partner, is bound by his obligation to his co-partners in such dealings not to separate his interest from theirs, but, if he acquires any benefit, to communicate it to them." * * *

We have no thought to hold that Salmon was guilty of a conscious purpose to defraud. Very likely he assumed in all good faith that with the approaching end of the venture he might ignore his coadventurer and take the extension for himself. He had given to the enterprise time and labor as well as money. He had made it a success. Meinhard, who had given money, but neither time nor labor, had already been richly paid. There might seem to be something grasping in his insistence upon more. Such recriminations are not unusual when coadventurers fall out. They are not without their force if conduct is to be judged by the common standards of competitors. That is not to say that they have pertinency here. Salmon had put himself in a position in which thought of self was to be renounced, however hard the abnegation. He was much more than a coadventurer. He was a managing coadventurer * * * For him and for those like him, the rule of undivided loyalty is relentless and supreme * * *. A different question would be here if there were lacking any nexus of relation between the business conducted by the manager and the opportunity brought to him as an incident of management.* * * For this problem, as for most, there are distinctions of degree. If Salmon had received from Gerry a proposition to lease a building at a location far removed, he might have held for himself the privilege thus acquired, or so we shall assume. Here the subject-matter of the new lease was an extension and enlargement of the subject-matter of the old one. A managing coadventurer appropriating the benefit of such a lease without warning to his partner might fairly expect to be reproached with conduct that was underhand, or lacking, to say the least, in reasonable candor, if the partner were to surprise him in the act of signing the new instrument. Conduct subject to that reproach does not receive from equity a healing benediction.

A question remains as to the form and extent of the equitable interest to be allotted to the plaintiff. The trust as declared has been held to attach to the lease which was in the name of the defendant corporation. We think it ought to attach at the option of the defendant Salmon to the shares of stock which were owned by him or were under his control. The difference may be important if the lessee shall wish to execute an assignment of the lease, as it ought to be free to do with the consent of the lessor. On the other hand, an equal division of the shares might lead to other hardships. It might take away from Salmon the power of control and management which under the plan of the joint venture he was to have from first to last. The number of shares to be allotted to the plaintiff should, therefore, be reduced to such an extent as may be necessary to preserve to the defendant Salmon the expected measure of dominion. To that end an extra share should be added to his half.

Subject to this adjustment, we agree with the Appellate Division that the plaintiff's equitable interest is to be measured by the value of half of the entire lease, and not merely by half of some undivided part. A single building covers the whole area. Physical division is impracticable along the lines of the Bristol site, the keystone of the whole. Division of interests and burdens is equally impracticable. Salmon, as tenant under the new lease, or as guarantor of the performance of the tenant's obligations, might well protest if Meinhard, claiming an equitable interest, had offered to assume a liability not equal to Salmon's, but only half as great. He might justly insist that the lease must be accepted by his coadventurer in such form as it had been given, and not constructively divided into imaginary fragments. What must be yielded to the one may be demanded by the other. The lease as it has been executed is single and entire. If confusion has resulted from the union of adjoining parcels, the trustee who consented to the union must bear the inconvenience * * *.

* * *

ANDREWS, J. (dissenting). * * *

* * * Fair dealing and a scrupulous regard for honesty is required. But nothing more. It may be stated generally that a partner may not for his own benefit secretly take a renewal of a firm lease to himself. * * * Yet under very exceptional circumstances this may not be wholly true. * * *

Where the trustee, or the partner or the tenant in common, takes no new lease but buys the [property] in good faith a somewhat different question arises. Here is no direct appropriation of the expectancy of renewal. Here is no offshoot of the original lease. We so held in *Anderson v. Lemon (8 N.Y. 236)* * * * The issue then is whether actual fraud, dishonesty, unfairness is present in the transaction. If so, the purchaser may well be held as a trustee. * * *

With this view of the law I am of the opinion that the issue here is simple. Was the transaction in view of all the circumstances surrounding it unfair and inequitable? I reach this conclusion for two reasons. There was no general partnership, merely a joint venture for a limited object, to end at a fixed time. The new lease, covering additional property, containing many new and unusual terms and conditions, with a possible duration of eighty years, was more nearly the purchase of the[property] than the ordinary [lease] renewal with which the authorities are concerned.

The findings of the referee are to the effect that before 1902, Mrs. Louisa M. Gerry was the owner of a plot on the corner of Fifth avenue and Forty-second street, New York, containing 9,312 square feet. On it had been built the old Bristol Hotel.

Walter J. Salmon was in the real estate business, renting, managing and operating buildings. On April 10th of that year Mrs. Gerry leased the property to him for a term extending from May 1, 1902, to April 30, 1922. The property was to be used for offices and business, and the design was that the lessee should so remodel the hotel at his own expense as to fit it for such purposes, all alterations and additions, however, at once to become the property of the lessor. The lease might not be assigned without written consent.

Morton H. Meinhard was a woolen merchant. At some period during the negotiations between Mr. Salmon and Mrs. Gerry, so far as the findings show without the latter's knowledge, he became interested in the transaction. Before the lease was executed he advanced $5,000 toward the cost of the proposed alterations. Finally, on May 19th he and Salmon entered into a written agreement. "During the period of twenty years from the 1st day of May, 1902," the parties agree to share equally in the expense needed "to reconstruct, alter, manage and operate the Bristol Hotel property;" and in all payments required by the lease, and in all losses incurred "during the full term of the lease, i.e., from the first day of May, 1902, to the 1st day of May, 1922." During the same term net profits are to be divided. Mr. Salmon has sole power to "manage, lease, underlet and operate" the premises. If he dies, Mr. Meinhard shall be consulted before any disposition is made of the lease, and if Mr. Salmon's representatives decide to dispose of it, and the decision is theirs, Mr. Meinhard is to be given the first chance to take the unexpired term upon the same conditions they could obtain from others.

The referee [the person employed to determine the facts of the case and render an initial judgment] finds that this arrangement did not create a partnership between Mr. Salmon and Mr. Meinhard. In this he is clearly right. He is equally right in holding that while no general partnership existed the two men had entered into a joint adventure and that while the legal title to the lease was in Mr. Salmon, Mr. Meinhard had some sort of an equitable interest therein. Mr. Salmon was to manage the property for their joint benefit. He was bound to use good faith. He could not willfully destroy the lease, the object of the adventure, to the detriment of Mr. Meinhard.

Mr. Salmon went into possession and control of the property. The alterations were made. At first came losses. Then large profits which were duly distributed. At all times Mr. Salmon has acted as manager.

Some time before 1922 Mr. Elbridge T. Gerry became the owner of the reversion. He was already the owner of an adjoining lot on Fifth avenue and of four lots adjoining on Forty-second street, in all 11,587 square feet, covered by five separate buildings. Obviously all this property together was more valuable than the sum of the value of the separate parcels. Some plan to develop the property as a whole seems to have occurred to Mr. Gerry. He arranged that all leases on his five lots should expire on the same day as the Bristol Hotel lease. Then in 1921 he negotiated with various persons and corporations seeking to obtain a desirable tenant who would put up a building to cover the entire tract, for this was the policy he had adopted. These negotiations lasted for some months. They failed. About January 1, 1922, Mr. Gerry's agent approached Mr. Salmon and began to negotiate with him for the lease of the entire tract. Upon this he insisted as he did upon the erection of a new and expensive building covering the whole. He would not consent to the renewal of the Bristol lease on any terms. This effort resulted in a lease to the Midpoint Realty Company, a corporation entirely owned and controlled by Mr. Salmon. For our purposes the paper may be treated as if the agreement was made with Mr. Salmon himself.

In many respects, besides the increase in the land demised, the new lease differs from the old. Instead of an annual rent of $55,000 it is now from $350,000 to $475,000. Instead of a fixed term of twenty years it may now be, at the lessee's option, eighty. Instead of alterations in an existing structure costing about $200,000 a new building is contemplated costing $3,000,000. Of this sum $1,500,000 is to be advanced by the lessor to the lessee, "but not to its successors or assigns," and is to be repaid in installments. Again no assignment or sale of the lease may be made without the consent of the lessor.

This lease is valuable. In making it Mr. Gerry acted in good faith without any collusion with Mr. Salmon and with no purpose to deprive Mr. Meinhard of any equities he might have. But as to the negotiations leading to it or as to the execution of the lease itself Mr. Meinhard knew nothing. Mr. Salmon acted for himself to acquire the lease for his own benefit.

Under these circumstances the referee has found and the Appellate Division agrees with him, that Mr. Meinhard is entitled to an interest in the second lease, he having promptly elected to assume his share of the liabilities imposed thereby. This conclusion is based upon the proposition that under the original contract between the two men "the enterprise was a joint venture, the relation between the parties was fiduciary and governed by principles applicable to partnerships," therefore, as the new lease is a graft upon the old, Mr. Salmon might not acquire its benefits for himself alone.

Were this a general partnership between Mr. Salmon and Mr. Meinhard I should have little doubt as to the correctness of this result assuming the new lease to be an offshoot of the old. * * *

We have here a different situation governed by less drastic principles. I assume that where parties engage in a joint enterprise each owes to the other the duty of the utmost good faith in all that relates to their common venture. Within its scope they stand in a fiduciary relationship. I assume *prima facie* that even as between joint adventurers one may not secretly obtain a renewal of the lease of property actually used in the joint adventure where the possibility of renewal is expressly or impliedly involved in the enterprise. I assume also that Mr. Meinhard had an equitable interest in the Bristol Hotel lease. Further, that an expectancy of renewal inhered in that lease. Two questions then arise. Under his contract did he share in that expectancy? And if so, did that expectancy mature into a graft of the original lease? To both questions my answer is "no."

The one complaint made is that Mr. Salmon obtained the new lease without informing Mr. Meinhard of his intention. Nothing else. There is no claim of actual fraud. No claim of misrepresentation to any one. Here was no movable property to be acquired by a new tenant at a sacrifice to its owners. No good will, largely dependent on location, built up by the joint efforts of two men. Here was a refusal of the landlord to renew the Bristol lease on any terms; a proposal made by him, not sought by Mr. Salmon, and a choice by him and by the original lessor of the person with whom they wished to deal shown by the covenants against assignment or underletting, and by their ignorance of the arrangement with Mr. Meinhard.

What then was the scope of the adventure into which the two men entered? It is to be remembered that before their contract was signed Mr. Salmon had obtained the lease of the Bristol property. Very likely the matter had been earlier discussed between them. The $5,000 advance by Mr. Meinhard indicates that fact. But it has been held that the written contract defines their rights and duties.

Having the lease Mr. Salmon assigns no interest in it to Mr. Meinhard. He is to manage the property. It is for him to decide what alterations shall be made and to fix the rents. But for twenty years from May 1, 1902, Salmon is to make all advances from his own funds and Meinhard is to pay him personally on demand one-half of all expenses incurred and all losses sustained "during the full term of said lease," and during the same period Salmon is to pay him a part of the net profits. There was no joint capital provided.

It seems to me that the venture so inaugurated had in view a limited object and was to end at a limited time. There was no intent to expand it into a far greater undertaking lasting for many years. The design was to exploit a particular lease. Doubtless in it Mr. Meinhard had an equitable interest, but in it alone. This interest terminated when the joint adventure terminated. There was no intent that for the benefit of both any advantage should be taken of the chance of renewal—that the adventure should be continued beyond that date. Mr. Salmon has done all he promised to do in return for Mr. Meinhard's undertaking when he distributed profits up to May 1, 1922. Suppose this lease, non-assignable without the consent of the lessor, had contained a renewal option. Could Mr. Meinhard have exercised it? Could he have insisted that Mr. Salmon do so? Had Mr. Salmon done so could he insist that the agreement to share losses still existed or could Mr. Meinhard have claimed that the joint adventure was still to continue for twenty or eighty years? I do not think so. The adventure by its express terms ended on May 1, 1922. The contract by its language and by its whole import excluded the idea that the tenant's expectancy was to subsist for the benefit of the plaintiff. On that date whatever there was left of value in the lease reverted to Mr. Salmon, as it would had the lease been for thirty years instead of twenty. Any equity which Mr. Meinhard possessed was in the particular lease itself, not in any possibility of renewal. There was nothing unfair in Mr. Salmon's conduct.

I might go further were it necessary. Under the circumstances here presented had the lease run to both the parties I doubt whether the taking by one of a renewal without the knowledge of the other would cause interference by a court of equity. An illustration may clarify my thought. A and B enter into a joint venture to resurface a highway between Albany and Schenectady. They rent a parcel of land for the storage of materials. A, unknown to B, agrees with the lessor to rent that parcel and one adjoining it after the venture is finished, for an iron foundry. Is the act unfair? Would any general statements, scattered here and there through opinions dealing with other circumstance, be thought applicable? In other words, the mere fact that the joint venturers rent property together does not call for the strict rule that applies to general partners. Many things may excuse what is there forbidden. Nor here does any possibility of renewal exist as part of the venture. The nature of the undertaking excludes such an idea.

So far I have treated the new lease as if it were a renewal of the old. As already indicated, I do not take that view. Such a renewal could not be obtained. Any expectancy that it might be had vanished. What Mr. Salmon obtained was not a graft springing from the Bristol lease, but something distinct and different—as distinct as if for a building across Fifth avenue. I think also that in the absence of some fraudulent or unfair act the secret purchase of the reversion even by one partner is rightful. Substantially this is such a purchase. Because of the mere label of a transaction we do not place it on one side of the line or the other. Here is involved the possession of a large and most valuable unit of property for eighty years, the destruction of all existing structures and the erection of a new and expensive building covering the whole. No fraud, no deceit, no calculated secrecy is found. Simply that the arrangement was made without the knowledge of Mr. Meinhard. I think this not enough. * * *

NOTES AND QUESTIONS

1. THIS IS A CASE THAT TURNS on its facts, but it has also come to be renowned as the leading case on fiduciary responsibility, widely applicable to the duty not only of joint adventurers and partners, but also to corporate officers and directors. Do you understand what is meant by "fiduciary" responsibility, as Cardozo outlines it? It is also a case involving "equity," which for our purposes we can define as the power of the court to remake the legal relationship between parties when one of them has engaged in conduct which is found to be unfair or unethical. A court exercising equitable powers, for example, can set aside a contract for fraud. Generally speaking, as law students know, remedies in equity are exceptional, and may only be granted where legal remedies (e.g. monetary remedies for breach of contract) are inadequate. Do you understand why an equitable remedy might be appropriate in *Meinhard v. Salmon*?

2. THE PRINCIPAL TECHNICAL LEGAL issue in *Meinhard v. Salmon*, or at least the one that seems to divide the majority from the dissenters, is the legal effect of the distinction between a joint venture and a partnership. A joint venture can involve individuals, as in *Meinhard v. Salmon*, or it can involve giant corporations. This joint venture case is of interest to us not only to read two opinions from two of the greatest New York common law judges (Cardozo and Andrews), but also to understand the precise nature of the fiduciary duty of partners, since, as both Cardozo and Andrews make clear, while the joint venture is ongoing, and with regard to the specific task of the joint venture, the parties owe each other the same fiduciary duty as that owed by partners to each other. Judge Andrews's opinion is particularly good at laying out the differences between joint ventures and partnerships. Why does he dissent from Cardozo's opinion, which opinion, by the way, is the one that has gained lasting fame? Is this fame deserved? Who got it right, Cardozo or Andrews?

3. ROBERT B. THOMPSON, A LAW professor at Vanderbilt, and one of the country's leading experts on fiduciary duties, has formulated an intriguing hypothetical in connection with *Meinhard v. Salmon*. Suppose, he suggests, that Salmon, before making his agreement with Gerry, had said to Meinhard, "I know we haven't talked in a long time, but I wanted you to know that Mr. Gerry is looking to develop a large new building on the Bristol property plus some additional land he owns at 5th Avenue and 42nd and I am talking to him about a[n] eighty-year lease for the construction of a new skyscraper. You are welcome to pursue the opportunity on your own, but as for us, I have done the lion's share of the work for twenty years and I am not interested in entering into a similar relationship going forward. I am tired of carrying you."

If Salmon had said that to Meinhard, would Cardozo have decided the case differently? Would you? See generally, for this hypothetical and an informative study of the background of the case, Robert B. Thompson, "The Story of *Meinhard v. Salmon*: Fiduciary Duty's Punctilio," in J. Mark Ramseyer, Ed., Corporate Law Stories 105, 126–127 (2009).

---

4. WHAT HAPPENED IN *MEINHARD v. SALMON* can perhaps be a bit better appreciated if one knows a bit more about Judge Benjamin Cardozo. Apart from being widely regarded as one of the greatest legal minds in American history both from his distinguished service on the Court of Appeals of New York (that state's highest court) and later on the US Supreme Court, Cardozo is considered one of our greatest legal writers. Several of Cardozo's decisions are a staple part of the law school canon, and are regularly included in casebooks. Because of his stature in the pantheon of American jurisprudence, Cardozo's life has long been a subject of scholarly interest. Harvard Law Professor Andrew L. Kaufman, a Cardozo clerk, and the author of the leading Cardozo biography, Cardozo (1998), examines Cardozo's early life, in particular Cardozo's relationship with his father, Albert.

Albert Cardozo was a New York state judge with strong ties to the notoriously corrupt Democratic political organization, Tammany Hall. Albert conducted his court in a highly unorthodox manner, including occasionally meeting with only one side's counsel before issuing a decision. He eventually found himself facing proceedings to remove him from the bench, involving five charges, among them one for refusing to block an order which denied alimony to the wife of a New York State Senator, Thomas C. Fields. *Id.*, at 17. Albert Cardozo eventually resigned from the bench rather than enduring the proceedings for removal before the state senate. Professor Kaufman examines how Cardozo's father's misconduct led Benjamin Cardozo to pursue a career in the law. Kaufman reports that according to E.R.A. Seligman, a Columbia University professor and close family friend, Cardozo "felt that he had to clear up the disgrace to his family name and could do this only as a lawyer." Similarly, according to Judge Abram Elkus, a friend and brief colleague on the Court of Appeals, "Cardozo once mentioned to him a desire to 'work away' his father's disgrace." *Id.*, at 40. Given Judge Cardozo's family background, does it make sense that his decision in *Meinhard* places such a heavy weight on the "punctilio of honor most sensitive"?

5. PROFESSOR KAUFMAN ALSO POINTS out that critics have often disagreed as to the level of candor in Judge Cardozo's decisions. While some critics praise Cardozo for his honesty and seemingly morally driven decisions, others have called him a master of deception. Kaufman writes "Cardozo was fundamentally honest in his opinions. He said what he meant, and he meant what he said." *Id.*, at 445. Kaufman goes on to write "sometimes. . . he left out some facts that now seem important to a full understanding of the problem, especially from the perspective of the losing party. This situation did not happen often, and I see no evidence that Cardozo was being manipulative. Either his literary bent may have led him astray, or he may simply have made a mistake in assuming that he had stated everything he needed for the reader to understand the case." Ibid. Reading *Meinhard*, did you find Cardozo's opinion completely candid with the facts, especially compared to the account given by Judge Andrews? Do you agree with Kaufman, that Cardozo was essentially honest, although his literary style sometimes got the better of him?

6. PROFESSOR KAUFMAN AND MANY other legal scholars generally praise what we might describe as the delightfully florid prose of Judge Cardozo, but one other prominent liberal legal theorist, United States Court of Appeals Judge Jerome Frank, published an anonymous scathing critique of Cardozo's decisions shortly after Cardozo died. Beginning with a biographical interpretation and relying on psychoanalysis, Frank writes of a Cardozo "[d]eeply hurt, in his youth" who "retreat[ed] from 20th Century living" and "re-entered it disguised as an 18th Century scholar and gentleman." Frank goes on to describe Cardozo's writing as having "an alien grace." Anon Y. Mous [Jerome Frank]. "The Speech of Judges: A Dissenting Opinion." 29 Va. L. Rev. 625, 630 (1942–1943). Said Frank, Cardozo's writing style is "an unmitigated nuisance to the lawyer who must, in a work-a-day world, make use of his judicial opinions. They sometimes obscure where there is need for clarity." *Id.* at 637–638. Frank indicates that he prefers the writing style of Justices Black, Douglas, and Jackson, because "[t]hey write much as they talk, as their fellow Americans talk." *Id.*, at 639. Given all this fuss about Cardozo's style, what importance do you give to the manner in which a judge explains the reasoning behind a decision? Is it more important to be clear and concise? Do judges have to persuade as well as explain, and is style important for that purpose? Judge Frank was a notoriously scrappy individual. Is he barking up the wrong tree here?

7. SITUATED SOMEWHERE BETWEEN THE many members in the legal academy of the Cardozo fan club and more dyspeptic scholars like Jerome Frank is Judge Richard Posner, formerly chief judge of the United States Court of Appeals for the Seventh Circuit, and formerly a law professor at the University of Chicago. Posner, the most famous practitioner of the law and economics school, now a leading legal pragmatist, wrote in his book Cardozo: *A Study in Reputation* (1990), that Cardozo's decision in *Meinhard* is "the most famous of Cardozo's moralistic opinions." *Id.,* at 104. Referring to the punctilio passage, Posner writes "it is possible to object that these are just words, and florid ones at that. But they are memorable words, and they set a tone. They make the difference between an arm's length relationship and a fiduciary relationship vivid, unforgettable." *Id.,* at 105. Posner continues, "a more informative description of the concept would be that, while normally a party to a contract is entitled, with certain exceptions, to take advantage of the other party's ignorance, a fiduciary is not; he must treat the other party's interests as if they were his own. But this is awfully dry." Ibid. Posner argues that there is a "halo effect" surrounding Cardozo's opinion, and concludes that it is "the power of the vivid statement" that lifts Cardozo's opinions "out of the swarm of humdrum, often numbing, judicial opinions, rivets attention, crystallizes relevant concerns and considerations, [and] provokes thoughts." *Id.,* at 136. For Posner, the success of Judge Cardozo's opinions comes as much from his rhetoric as it does from his logic. Does all this scholarly attention to the rhetorical skills, and psychological underpinnings of Cardozo's decision make sense to you? After reading about Cardozo, do you have more or less faith in the wisdom of *Meinhard v. Salmon*?

8. THERE WAS A TIME WHEN whole courses in agency and whole courses in partnership were required parts of the law school curriculum, but for a short course in business law, where our concentration is on the form of the business entity that will most probably concern most of you, the corporation, we can limit our consideration of agency and partnership to the fundamental principles of authority, equality, and fiduciary duty that the cases you have so far studied have explored. Before going on to study corporations, and to contrast them with other legal entities, however, we should pause to recognize an increasingly popular hybrid form, the limited liability company, or LLC.

THE LIMITED LIABILITY COMPANY

I. The Nature Of LLCs

Elf Atochem North America, Inc. v. Jaffari and Mallek, LLC.

Supreme Court of Delaware

727 A.2d 286 (1999).

VEASEY, Chief Justice:

This is a case of first impression before this Court involving the Delaware Limited Liability Company Act (the "Act"). The limited liability company ("LLC") is a relatively new entity that has emerged in recent years as an attractive vehicle to facilitate business relationships and transactions. The wording and architecture of the Act is somewhat complicated, but it is designed to achieve what is seemingly a simple concept-to permit persons or entities ("members") to join together in an environment of private ordering to form and operate the enterprise under an LLC agreement with tax benefits akin to a partnership and limited liability akin to the corporate form.

  This is a purported derivative suit brought on behalf of a Delaware LLC calling into question whether: (1) the LLC, which did not itself execute the LLC agreement in this case ("the Agreement") defining its governance and operation, is nevertheless bound by the Agreement; and (2) contractual provisions directing that all disputes be resolved exclusively by arbitration or court proceedings in California are valid under the Act. * * *

We hold that: (1) the Agreement is binding on the LLC as well as the members; and (2) since the Act does not prohibit the members of an LLC from vesting exclusive subject matter jurisdiction in arbitration proceedings (or court enforcement of arbitration) in California to resolve disputes, the contractual forum selection provisions must govern.

* * *

FACTS

Plaintiff below-appellant Elf Atochem North America, Inc., a Pennsylvania Corporation ("Elf"), manufactures and distributes solvent-based maskants to the aerospace and aviation industries throughout the world. Defendant below-appellee Cyrus A. Jaffari is the president of Malek, Inc., a California Corporation. Jaffari had developed an innovative, environmentally-friendly alternative to the solvent-based maskants that presently dominate the market.

For decades, the aerospace and aviation industries have used solvent-based maskants in the chemical milling process. [Manufactures of airplanes and missiles use maskants in the process of chemical milling in order to reduce the weight of their products. Chemical milling is a process where a caustic substance is placed on metal parts in order to dissolve the metal with which it comes into contact. Maskants are used to protect those areas of metal intended to be preserved.] Recently, however, the Environmental Protection Agency ("EPA") classified solvent-based maskants as hazardous chemicals and air contaminants. To avoid conflict with EPA regulations, Elf considered developing or distributing a maskant less harmful to the environment.

In the mid-nineties, Elf approached Jaffari and proposed investing in his product and assisting in its marketing. Jaffari found the proposal attractive since his company, Malek, Inc., possessed limited resources and little international sales expertise. Elf and Jaffari agreed to undertake a joint venture that was to be carried out using a limited liability company as the vehicle.

On October 29, 1996, Malek, Inc. caused to be filed a Certificate of Formation with the Delaware Secretary of State, thus forming Malek LLC, a Delaware limited liability company under the Act. The certificate of formation is a relatively brief and formal document that is the first statutory step in creating the LLC as a separate legal entity.[1] The certificate does not contain a comprehensive agreement among the parties, and the statute contemplates that the certificate of formation is to be complemented by the terms of the Agreement.

Next, Elf, Jaffari and Malek, Inc. entered into a series of agreements providing for the governance and operation of the joint venture. Of particular importance to this litigation, Elf, Malek, Inc., and Jaffari entered into the Agreement,

---

1 *See 6 Del.C.* § 18-201.

a comprehensive and integrated document[2] of 38 single-spaced pages setting forth detailed provisions for the governance of Malek LLC, which is not itself a signatory to the Agreement. Elf and Malek LLC entered into an Exclusive Distributorship Agreement in which Elf would be the exclusive, worldwide distributor for Malek LLC. The Agreement provides that Jaffari will be the manager of Malek LLC. Jaffari and Malek LLC entered into an employment agreement providing for Jaffari's employment as chief executive officer of Malek LLC.

* * * Under the Agreement, Elf contributed $1 million in exchange for a 30 percent interest in Malek LLC. Malek, Inc. contributed its rights to the water-based maskant in exchange for a 70 percent interest in Malek LLC.

The Agreement contains an arbitration clause covering all disputes. The clause, Section 13.8, provides that "any controversy or dispute arising out of this Agreement, the interpretation of any of the provisions hereof, or the action or inaction of any Member or Manager hereunder shall be submitted to arbitration in San Francisco, California...." Section 13.8 further provides: "No action ... based upon any claim arising out of or related to this Agreement shall be instituted in any court by any Member except (a) an action to compel arbitration ... or (b) an action to enforce an award obtained in an arbitration proceeding...." The Agreement also contains a forum selection clause, Section 13.7, providing that all members consent to: "exclusive jurisdiction of the state and federal courts sitting in California in any action on a claim arising out of, under or in connection with this Agreement or the transactions contemplated by this Agreement, provided such claim is not required to be arbitrated pursuant to Section 13.8"; and personal jurisdiction in California. * * *

ELF'S SUIT IN THE COURT OF CHANCERY

On April 27, 1998, Elf sued Jaffari and Malek LLC, individually and derivatively on behalf of Malek LLC, in the Delaware Court of Chancery * * *. Among other claims, Elf alleged that Jaffari breached his fiduciary duty to Malek LLC, pushed Malek LLC to the brink of insolvency by withdrawing funds for personal use, interfered with business opportunities, failed to make disclosures to Elf, and threatened to make poor quality maskant and to violate environmental regulations. Elf also alleged breach of contract, tortious interference with prospective business relations, and (solely as to Jaffari) fraud.

The Court of Chancery granted defendants' motion to dismiss * * *. The court held that Elf's claims arose under the Agreement, or the transactions contemplated by the agreement, and were directly related to Jaffari's actions as manager of Malek LLC. Therefore, the court found that the Agreement governed the question of jurisdiction and that only a court of law or arbitrator in California is empowered to decide these claims. Elf now appeals * * *.

---

2 *See* the definition section of the statute, 6 *Del.C.* § 18-101(7), defining the term "limited liability company agreement" as "any agreement ... of the ... members as to the affairs of a limited liability company and the conduct of its business," and setting forth a nonexclusive list of what it may provide.

CONTENTIONS OF THE PARTIES

Elf claims that the Court of Chancery erred in holding that the arbitration and forum selection clauses in the Agreement governed, and thus deprived that court of jurisdiction to adjudicate all of Elf's claims, including its derivative claims made on behalf of Malek LLC. Elf contends that, since Malek LLC is not a party to the Agreement, it is not bound by the forum selection provisions. Elf also argues that the court erred in failing to classify its claim as derivative on behalf of Malek LLC against Jaffari as manager. Therefore, Elf claims that the Court of Chancery should have adjudicated the dispute. Finally, Elf argues that the dispute resolution clauses of the Agreement are invalid under Section 109(d) of the Act, which, it alleges, prohibits the parties from vesting exclusive jurisdiction in a forum outside of Delaware.[3]

Defendants claim that Elf contracted with Malek, Inc. and Jaffari that all disputes that arise out of, under, or in connection with the Agreement must be resolved exclusively in California by arbitration or court proceedings. Defendants allege that the characterization of Elf's claim as direct or derivative is irrelevant, as the Agreement provides that the members would not institute "any" action at law or equity except one to compel arbitration, and that any such action must be brought in California. Defendants also argue that, in reality, Elf's claims are direct, not derivative, claims against its fellow LLC members, Malek, Inc. and Jaffari.

With regard to the validity of Section 13.7, defendants argue that Section 18-109(d) of the Act is a permissive statute and does not prohibit the parties from vesting exclusive jurisdiction outside of Delaware. Thus, defendants assert that the Court of Chancery correctly held that the dispute resolution provisions of the Agreement are valid and apply to bar Elf from seeking relief in Delaware.

GENERAL SUMMARY OF BACKGROUND OF THE ACT

The phenomenon of business arrangements using "alternative entities" has been developing rapidly over the past several years. Long gone are the days when business planners were confined to corporate or partnership structures.

Limited partnerships date back to the 19th Century. They became an important and popular vehicle with the adoption of the Uniform Limited Partnership Act in 1916. Sixty years later, in 1976, the National Conference of Commissioners on Uniform State Laws approved and recommended to the states a Revised Uniform Limited Partnership Act ("RULPA"), many provisions of which were modeled after the innovative 1973 Delaware Limited Partnership (LP) Act. Difficulties with the workability of the 1976 RULPA prompted the Commissioners to amend RULPA in 1985.

To date, 48 states and the District of Columbia have adopted the RULPA in either its 1976 or 1985 form. Delaware adopted the RULPA with innovations designed to

---

3   *See* 6 *Del.C.* § 18-109(d), which provides:

In a written limited liability company agreement or other writing, a manager or member *may* consent to be subject to the nonexclusive jurisdiction of the courts of, or arbitration in, a specified jurisdiction, or the exclusive jurisdiction of the courts of the State of Delaware, or the exclusivity of arbitration in a specified jurisdiction or the State of Delaware....(Emphasis Added.)

improve upon the Commissioners' product. Since 1983, the General Assembly has amended the LP Act eleven times, with a view to continuing Delaware's status as an innovative leader in the field of limited partnerships.

The Delaware [LLC] Act was adopted in October 1992. The Act is codified in Chapter 18 of Title 6 of the Delaware Code. To date, the Act has been amended six times with a view to modernization. The LLC is an attractive form of business entity because it combines corporate-type limited liability with partnership-type flexibility and tax advantages. The Act can be characterized as a "flexible statute" because it generally permits members to engage in private ordering with substantial freedom of contract to govern their relationship, provided they do not contravene any mandatory provisions of the Act. Indeed, the LLC has been characterized as the "best of both worlds."

The Delaware Act has been modeled on the popular Delaware LP Act. In fact, its architecture and much of its wording is almost identical to that of the Delaware LP Act. Under the Act, a member of an LLC is treated much like a limited partner under the LP Act. The policy of freedom of contract underlies both the Act and the LP Act.

* * *

POLICY OF THE DELAWARE ACT

The basic approach of the Delaware Act is to provide members with broad discretion in drafting the Agreement and to furnish default provisions when the members' agreement is silent. The Act is replete with fundamental provisions made subject to modification in the Agreement (*e.g.* "unless otherwise *provided* in a limited liability company agreement....").[4]

* * *

FREEDOM OF CONTRACT

Section 18-1101(b) of the Act, like the essentially identical Section 17-1101(c) of the LP Act, provides that "[i]t is the policy of [the Act] to give the maximum effect to the principle of freedom of contract and to the enforceability of limited liability company agreements." Accordingly, the following observation relating to limited partnerships applies as well to limited liability companies:

The Act's basic approach is to permit partners to have the broadest possible discretion in drafting their partnership agreements and to furnish answers only in situations where the partners have not expressly made provisions in their partnership agreement. Truly, the partnership agreement is the cornerstone of a Delaware limited

---

4   *See, e.g.,* 6 *Del.C.* §§ 18-107, 18-204(b), 18-209(b), 18-301(d), 18-302(d),18-304(a) & (b), 18-402, 18-403, 18-404(d), 18-502(a) & (b), 18-503, 18-504,18-605, 18-606, 18-702(a), (b) & (d), 18-704(b), 18-801(a)(4) & (b), 18-803(a), and 18-804(a)(2) & (3). For example, members are free to contract among themselves concerning management of the LLC, including who is to manage the LLC, the establishment of classes of members, voting, procedures for holding meetings of members, or considering matters without a meeting. * * *

partnership, and effectively constitutes the entire agreement among the partners with respect to the admission of partners to, and the creation, operation and termination of, the limited partnership. Once partners exercise their contractual freedom in their partnership agreement, the partners have a great deal of certainty that their partnership agreement will be enforced in accordance with its terms.

In general, the commentators observe that only where the agreement is inconsistent with mandatory statutory provisions will the members' agreement be invalidated. Such statutory provisions are likely to be those intended to protect third parties, not necessarily the contracting members. As a framework for decision, we apply that principle to the issues before us, without expressing any views more broadly.

* * *

Malek LLC's Failure to Sign the Agreement Does Not Affect the Members' Agreement Governing Dispute Resolution

Elf argues that because Malek LLC, on whose behalf Elf allegedly brings these claims, is not a party to the Agreement, the derivative claims it brought on behalf of Malek LLC are not governed by the arbitration and forum selection clauses of the Agreement.

Elf argues that Malek LLC came into existence on October 29, 1996, when the parties filed its Certificate of Formation with the Delaware Secretary of State. The parties did not sign the Agreement until November 4, 1996. Elf contends that Malek LLC existed as an LLC as of October 29, 1996, but never agreed to the Agreement because it did not sign it. Because Malek LLC never expressly assented to the arbitration and forum selection clauses within the Agreement, Elf argues it can sue derivatively on behalf of Malek LLC pursuant to 6 *Del.C.* § 18-1001.[5]

We are not persuaded by this argument. Section 18-101(7) defines the limited liability company agreement as "any agreement, written or oral, *of the member or members* as to the affairs of a limited liability company and the conduct of its business."[6] Here, Malek, Inc. and Elf, the members of Malek LLC, executed the Agreement to carry out the affairs and business of Malek LLC and to provide for arbitration and forum selection.

Notwithstanding Malek LLC's failure to sign the Agreement, Elf's claims are subject to the arbitration and forum selection clauses of the Agreement. The Act is a statute designed to permit members maximum flexibility in entering into an

---

5   6 *Del.C.* § 18-1001 provides: "Right to bring action. A member may ... bring an action in the Court of Chancery in the right of a limited liability company to recover a judgment in its favor if managers or members with authority to do so have refused to bring the action or if an effort to cause those managers or members to bring the action is not likely to succeed."

6   6 *Del.C.* § 18-101(7) (emphasis added).

agreement to govern their relationship.[7] It is the members who are the real parties in interest. The LLC is simply their joint business vehicle. * * *

Classification by Elf of its Claims as Derivative is Irrelevant

Elf argues that the Court of Chancery erred in failing to classify its claims against Malek LLC as derivative. Elf contends that, had the court properly characterized its claims as derivative instead of direct, the arbitration and forum selection clauses would not have applied to bar adjudication in Delaware.

In the corporate context, "the derivative form of action permits an individual shareholder to bring 'suit to enforce a corporate cause of action against officers, directors and third parties.' " The derivative suit is a corporate concept grafted onto the limited liability company form. The Act expressly allows for a derivative suit, providing that "a member ... may bring an action in the Court of Chancery in the right of a limited liability company to recover a judgment in its favor if managers or members with authority to do so have refused to bring the action or if an effort to cause those managers or members to bring the action is not likely to succeed."[8] Notwithstanding the Agreement to the contrary, Elf argues that Section 18-1001 permits the assertion of derivative claims of Malek LLC against Malek LLC's manager, Jaffari.

Although Elf correctly points out that Delaware law allows for derivative suits against management of an LLC, Elf contracted away its right to bring such an action in Delaware and agreed instead to dispute resolution in California. That is, Section 13.8 of the Agreement specifically provides that the parties (*i.e.*, Elf) agree to institute "[n]o action at law or in equity based upon *any* claim arising out of or related to this Agreement" except an action to compel arbitration or to enforce an arbitration award. Furthermore, under Section 13.7 of the Agreement, each member (*i.e.*, Elf) "consent[ed] to the exclusive jurisdiction of the state and federal courts sitting in California in *any* action on a claim arising out of, under or in connection with this Agreement or the transactions contemplated by this Agreement."

Sections 13.7 and 13.8 of the Agreement do not distinguish between direct and derivative claims. They simply state that the members may not initiate any claims outside of California. Elf initiated this action in the Court of Chancery in contravention of its own contractual agreement. ***

This prohibition is so broad that it is dispositive of Elf's claims (counts IV, V and VI of the amended complaint) that purport to be under the Distributorship Agreement that has no choice of forum provision. Notwithstanding the fact that the Distributorship Agreement is a separate document, in reality these counts are all

---

7   *See* 6 *Del.C.* § 18-1101(b); Lubaroff & Altman, *supra* note 14, at § 20.4.

8   6 *Del.C.* § 18-1001.

subsumed under the rubric of the Agreement's forum selection clause for any claim "arising out of" and those that are "in connection with" the Agreement or transactions "contemplated by" or "related to" that Agreement under Sections 13.7 and 13.8. * * *

* * *

The Argument that Chancery Has "Special" Jurisdiction for Derivative Claims Must Fail

Elf claims that 6 *Del.C.* §§ 18-110(a), 18-111 and 18-1001 vest the Court of Chancery with subject matter jurisdiction over this dispute. According to Elf, the Act grants the Court of Chancery subject matter jurisdiction over its claims for breach of fiduciary duty and removal of Jaffari, even though the parties contracted to arbitrate all such claims in California. In effect, Elf argues that the Act affords the Court of Chancery "special" jurisdiction to adjudicate its claims, notwithstanding a clear contractual agreement to the contrary.

Again, we are not persuaded by Elf's argument. Elf is correct that 6 *Del.C.* §§ 18-110(a) and 18-111 vest jurisdiction with the Court of Chancery in actions involving removal of managers and interpreting, applying or enforcing LLC agreements respectively. As noted above, Section 18-1001 provides that a party may bring derivative actions in the Court of Chancery. Such a grant of jurisdiction may have been constitutionally necessary if the claims do not fall within the traditional equity jurisdiction. Nevertheless, for the purpose of designating a more convenient forum, we find no reason why the members cannot alter the default jurisdictional provisions of the statute and contract away their right to file suit in Delaware.

* * *

Our conclusion is bolstered by the fact that Delaware recognizes a strong public policy in favor of arbitration. Normally, doubts on the issue of whether a particular issue is arbitrable will be resolved in favor of arbitration. In the case at bar, we do not believe there is any doubt of the parties' intention to agree to arbitrate *all* disputed matters in California. If we were to hold otherwise, arbitration clauses in existing LLC agreements could be rendered meaningless. By resorting to the alleged "special" jurisdiction of the Court of Chancery, future plaintiffs could avoid their own arbitration agreements simply by couching their claims as derivative. Such a result could adversely affect many arbitration agreements already in existence in Delaware.

VALIDITY OF SECTION 13.7 OF THE AGREEMENT UNDER 6 DEL.C. § 18-109(D)

Elf argues that Section 13.7 of the Agreement, which provides that each member of Malek LLC "consents to the exclusive jurisdiction of the state and federal courts sitting in California in any action on a claim arising out of, under or in connection with this Agreement or the transactions contemplated by this Agreement ..." is invalid under Delaware law. Elf argues that Section 13.7 is invalid because it violates 6 *Del.C.* § 18-109(d).

Subsection 18-109(d) is part of Section 18-109 relating to "Service of process on managers and liquidating trustee." It provides:

In a written limited liability company agreement or other writing, a manager or member *may* consent to be subject to the nonexclusive jurisdiction of the courts of, or arbitration in, a specified jurisdiction, or the exclusive jurisdiction of the courts of the State of Delaware, or the exclusivity of arbitration in a specified jurisdiction or the State of Delaware....

Section 18-109(d) does not expressly state that the parties are prohibited from agreeing to the *exclusive* subject matter jurisdiction of the courts or arbitration for a of a foreign jurisdiction. Thus, Elf contends that Section 18-109(d) prohibits vesting exclusive jurisdiction in a court outside of Delaware, which the parties have done in Section 13.7.

We decline to adopt such a strict reading of the statute. * * * Section 109(d) * * * is permissive in that it provides that the parties "may" agree to the non-exclusive jurisdiction of the courts of a foreign jurisdiction or to submit to the exclusive jurisdiction of Delaware. In general, the legislature's use of "may" connotes the voluntary, not mandatory or exclusive, set of options.[9] The permissive nature of Section 18-109(d) complements the overall policy of the Act to give maximum effect to the parties' freedom of contract. Although Section 18-109(d) fails to mention that the parties may agree to the *exclusive* jurisdiction of a foreign jurisdiction, the Act clearly does not state that the parties must agree to either one of the delineated options for subject matter jurisdiction. Had the General Assembly intended to prohibit the parties from vesting exclusive jurisdiction in arbitration or court proceedings in another state, it could have proscribed such an option. * * *

CONCLUSION

We affirm the judgment of the Court of Chancery dismissing Elf Atochem's amended complaint for lack of subject matter jurisdiction.

---

9 *See Delaware Citizens for Clean Air v. Water and Air Resources Comm'n*, Del.Super., 303 A.2d 666, 667, *aff'd*, Del.Supr., 310 A.2d 128 (1973) ("While the words 'shall' and 'may' do not always by themselves determine the mandatory or permissive character of a statute, it is generally presumed that the word 'shall' indicates a mandatory requirement.")

NOTES AND QUESTIONS

I. THIS IS A COMPLEX CASE, involving as it does obscure questions about subject matter jurisdiction, arbitration, derivative lawsuits, and the nature of the Limited Liability Company (LLC). You are not expected, on first reading, to be able to grasp all of these subtleties, but the case serves as an interesting introduction to the LLC and its nature, as well as an example of the careful approach of the Delaware Supreme Court, which you will be encountering in many of the cases that follow.

2. AS THE COURT MENTIONS, this case is one of first impression regarding the Delaware Limited Liability Company Act. Note the court's sensitivity to the notion that LLC's are supposed to encompass "the best of both worlds," referring to LLC's purported combination of the advantages of both the partnership and the corporate forms. As the court notes, if LLC's are to achieve this, it is paramount that "maximum effect [is given] to the principle of freedom of contract and to the enforceability of limited liability company agreements." Is the court's reading of the statute and its action of forgoing jurisdiction in order to give full effect to the agreement of the parties in keeping with this principle? Would you have read the statute differently? For the argument that this case ought to have been decided differently, see Leigh A. Bacon, *"Freedom of" or "Freedom from"? The Enforceability of Contracts and the Integrity of the LLC*, 50 Duke L.J. 1087 (2001).

3. YOU WILL HAVE NOTICED THAT in bolstering its reading of the statute, the Court relies in part on the oft repeated provision "unless otherwise provided in the LLC agreement." The court uses this to stress the pervasiveness of the contractual freedom principle woven into the statute. Even so, in *R&R Capital, LLC v. Buck & Doe Run Valley farms, LLC*, CA # 3803-CC (Del. Ch. Aug. 19, 2008), the Chancery Court held as a matter of first impression that LLC members can contractually waive their statutory right to seek judicial dissolution of a Delaware LLC, notwithstanding the absence of the provision "unless otherwise provided in the LLC agreement" from the relevant part of the statute. Given the case you just read, does this strike you as an odd development of the law?

4. THE NEAR-BOUNDLESS CONTRACTUAL freedom afforded LLC's in light of *Elf Atochem* resulted in a good deal of uncertainty. Indeed, some even speculated that the reason the Delaware Supreme Court ruled as it did was to avoid deciding the tricky question of what fiduciary duties are owed by parties to an LLC. For an overview of that uncertainty, and a summary of the opposing camps at the time, see J. William Callison, *Blind Men and Elephants: Fiduciary Duties Under the Revised Uniform Partnership Act, Uniform Limited Liability Company Act, and Beyond*, 1 J. Small & Emerging Bus. L. 109, 111 (1997). For a more updated state of the law, see Sandra K. Miller, *What Fiduciary Duties Should Apply to the LLC Manager After More Than A Decade of Experimentation?*, 32 J. Corp. L. 565, 569 (2007).

5. FOR FURTHER READING ON the nature of LLCs and their rise to stardom, see generally Larry E. Ribstein, *The Uncorporation and Corporate Indeterminacy*, 2009 U. Ill. L. Rev. 131, 157 (2009)

II. Fiduciary Duties In LLCs

AN OVERVIEW

Fiduciary law serves to induce investment through assurances that investor assets will be protected. This is primarily achieved through the imposition of duties of loyalty, care, and good faith.

Corporations enjoy the most-developed fiduciary law, and constitute a natural jumping-off point for other entity law. Nowhere is the risk to investors from misconduct by officers more obvious than in corporations, and so the justification for imposing fiduciary duties in the corporate context is also obvious. The investors (shareholders) have little to no bargaining power, and are entirely at the mercy of corporate officers and directors when it comes to the security and maximization of their investments. Directors and officers, in turn, may have little incentive to maximize shareholder wealth in the absence of clear impositions of duty. As a result, "corporations need fiduciary duties, despite their indeterminacy, to address the misalignment of manager's incentives with those of their owners."[10]

In partnerships the justification for imposing fiduciary duties is somewhat less obvious; after all, the partners are personally liable for the partnership's debts, and this ought to be a good enough incentive to properly manage the partnership. Despite this, there is a sense in which partners are at each other's mercy, because of their ability to delegate authority.[11] Hence, fiduciary duties are imposed upon partners in order to ensure that delegation is responsibly executed.

Nowhere has fiduciary law caused more grief than in the LLC context. As one author observes, "while a cloud of confusion has always hovered over the application of fiduciary duties, in no context do they cause more head-scratching than LLCs."[12] Indeed, it is not difficult to understand the confusion when one reflects on the fact that part of the justification for affording wide latitude and freedom of contract principles to LLC's is that unlike in corporations and partnerships, parties to LLC's are assumed to be sophisticated businesspersons with near-equal bargaining positions. With this in mind, and assuming one believes the justifications offered in favor of fiduciary laws, one might expect to find that such laws are absent in the LLC context (unless, of course, the parties contract for such responsibilities). Nonetheless, the law seems to have developed in an odd direction, as explained in the following article:

---

10   Larry E. Ribstein, *The Uncorporation and Corporate Indeterminacy*, 2009 U. Ill. L. Rev. 131, 142-43 (2009).

11   See Larry E. Ribstein, *Are Partners Fiduciaries?*, 2005 U. Ill. L. Rev. 209, 240 (2005).

12   Larry E. Ribstein, *Are Partners Fiduciaries?*, 2005 U. Ill. L. Rev. 209 at 211-212 (2005).

Judicial Scrutiny of Fiduciary Duties in Delaware Limited Partnerships and Limited Liability Companies

32 Del. J. Corp. L. I (2007)

MYRON T. STEELE[13]

I. Introduction

* * * Much has been written recently about statutory and judicial approaches to fiduciary duties in unincorporated business organizations. This article cannot begin to cover all of the statutory nuances and differing judicial approaches that have resulted. The article, therefore, is necessarily limited to analyzing the State of Delaware'sspecific statutory provisions for limited partnerships and limited liability companies and examining its unique judicial culture. * * * I suggest that although current judicial analysis seems to imply that fiduciary duties engrained in the corporate law readily transfer to limited partnerships and limited liability companies as efficiently and effectively as they do to corporate governance issues, that conclusion is flawed.

* * *

II. Some Necessary Predicates for a Frame of Reference

Certain fundamental assumptions compel comment * * *. First, this discussion concerns the rational and efficient mechanism for resolving tensions in the governance framework of limited partnerships and limited liability companies. It is widely recognized that fiduciary duty principles currently operate within statutory parameters generally thought to be "enabling," and thus are flexible in a way that enhances wealth building. Second, there are at least two agreed-upon, well-defined fiduciary duties and an arguable, if incompletely defined, third. The first two are, of course, loyalty and care; the third is the highly enigmatic "good faith."

Third, limited partnerships and limited liability companies, like corporations, are creatures of statute, and do not exist at common law. The policy direction from the legislature-for the purpose of this article, the Delaware General Assembly-carries the day over even the most clearly defined doctrinal common law principles. Interestingly, no relevant Delaware statute names, numbers, or defines any fiduciary duty or refers to the famous "triad."

* * *

Instruments creating limited partnerships and limited liability companies can easily be structured to carve out safe harbors for self-dealing by managers where the parties, fully informed about the scope of those safe harbors, agree in writing.

---

13   Chief Justice, Delaware Supreme Court. B.A., J.D., University of Virginia, LL.M. Thesis, University of Virginia School of Law, spring 2005. The views and opinions expressed herein are solely those of the author and not of the Delaware Supreme Court or its other members. * * *

Barring any evidence to the contrary, courts should restrain themselves from reaching any conclusions other than those that the parties, who are perceived to have understood the terms of the written agreement and bargained for and negotiated the relationship created by the contract in exchange for consideration. Courts should assume, absent clear and convincing evidence to the contrary, that implicit in that process were considerations of fee arrangements and investment entry costs.

It is important to note that this article is limited to an examination of Delaware law, and that Delaware has not codified the model standards of conduct of directors or officers. Over forty states have adopted statutory standards, however. Delaware does, however, have an extensive body of common law addressing fiduciary duties imposed on managers, i.e., directors and officers, in the corporate structure. In the words of a prolific and thoughtful Delaware vice chancellor, this may be because:

> the continued importance of the common law of corporations is not the result of happenstance, but reflects a policy choice made by the Delaware General Assembly. That choice deliberately deploys Delaware's judiciary to guarantee the integrity of our corporate law through the articulation of common law principles of equitable behavior for corporate fiduciaries.[14]

Delaware's primary court for applying these principles is its court of equity—the Delaware Court of Chancery. That court reviews the exercise of the vast array of powers the Delaware General Corporation Law grants directors and officers. Equity provides the tools for ensuring that corporate directors do not abuse their statutory authority to act outside of the best interest of the corporation that they serve. Otherwise lawful actions may be "tainted" by a fiduciary breach, justifying a court-imposed equitable remedy. In essence, under Delaware's scheme, the fact that managers may lawfully take action does not mean the action is equitable, as it may not comport with the actors' fundamental fiduciary duties.

III. Fiduciary Obligations in Corporate, Limited Partnership, and Limited Liability Company Internal Governance

Although the above-described scheme operates reasonably effectively and efficiently in resolving daily tensions in corporate governance, it is reasonable to ask: should it be the model for resolving governance issues in limited partnerships and limited liability companies as representative unincorporated business entities created by statute and unrecognized at common law?

Traditionally, courts and draftsmen have reasoned from fiduciary relationships recognized in one context to impose fiduciary duties in what they believe to be analogous contexts. * * *

---

14   Leo E. Strine, If Corporate Action Is Lawful, Presumably There Are Circumstances in Which It's Equitable to Take That Action: The Important Corollary to the Rule of Schnell v. Chris-Craft 4 (Regents Lecture, UCLA School of Law, Mar. 31, 2005) * * *.

* * *

For purposes of this article, it must be accepted that fiduciary duties will be developed in each new business context by drawing analogies from duties recognized in already existing contexts. The alternative is to develop fiduciary duties in these new statutory entities as an entirely new body of law, recognizing all business fiduciaries as a single group with a distinct body of principles and rules. The latter is an unlikely and unwise course for Delaware, given its rich common law of corporations readily adaptable, when appropriate, to limited partnerships and limited liability companies. But given their rapid growth and continued variety, there is also a danger in continuing to analogize principles of fiduciary duty as used in the corporate governance context to the internal governance of limited partnerships and limited liability companies. * * *

IV. The Left Hand May Not Know
What the Right Hand Is Doing: Fiduciary Defaults

When deciding to draw analogies from corporation law, Delaware courts need to be mindful of the distinction between status relationships and contractual relationships. At present, it can be argued that the Delaware Supreme Court focuses on status relationships, while the Delaware Court of Chancery, and perhaps the General Assembly, focus on contractual relationships.

This premise is best illustrated by contrasting the Delaware Supreme Court's view that the common law fiduciary duties of loyalty and good faith cannot be eliminated by the agreement of the parties, with the view of the court of chancery that, given an expressed waiver in the agreement establishing the limited partnership or limited liability company, they can. The court of chancery and the supreme court, however, do appear to agree on at least one proposition: default rules for judicial intervention apply where the parties to the agreement have not set out, in writing, their own preferred rules.[15]

Absent evidence to the contrary, it must be assumed that passive investors who authorize, in the unincorporated business entities' enabling documents, the elimination or restriction of one or more fiduciary duties are fully informed of the risks and benefits. Because the passive investor is ordinarily in no position to supervise the fiduciary, it must be assumed that the passive investor has bargained for a power-sharing relationship that serves his or her best interests. It must further be assumed that the

---

15   In at least one opinion, the court of chancery has been bold enough to state that when the terms of the agreement are inconsistent with traditional common law fiduciary duties, the inconsistency alone establishes the parties' intent to restrict, eliminate, or at least modify the default to the common law fiduciary duties. See, e.g., *R.S.M. Inc. v. Alliance Capital Mgmt. Holdings* L.P., 790 A.2d 478, 497-98 (Del. Ch. 2001). Another decision implies that to supplant the default provisions of law, the agreement must expressly state the parties' intent, i.e., no elimination by implication. *Miller v. Am. Real Estate Partners, L.P.,* No. 16,788, 2001 Del. Ch. LEXIS 116, at *29 (Del. Ch. Sept. 6, 2001).

passive investor knows that once the limited partnership or limited liability company becomes active, again absent court intervention, there is little the passive investor can do to determine the ongoing risk of abuse of authorized power or the potential loss the passive investor might suffer. One would assume the contract negotiations, or a review of the documents generated before the LLP or LLC agreement has been signed, would enable a reviewing court to conclude who the contracting partners agreed would bear the costs of monitoring the fiduciary's compliance with whatever duties or risks the documents impose.

A. The Statutory Framework

* * *

In August 2004, the General Assembly amended the Delaware Revised Uniform Limited Partnership Act to express its intent to establish legislative policy in derogation of the common law's fiduciary duty principles and to give maximum effect to the principle of freedom of contract.[16] A partner who acts in "good faith" reliance on the provisions of the agreement escapes liability at law or in equity. Whatever duties or liabilities that would potentially flow from a breach of those duties "may be expanded or restricted or eliminated by provision in the partnership agreement; provided that the partnership agreement may not eliminate the implied contractual covenant of good faith and fair dealing."[17]

The August 2004 amendment to section 17-1101(d) is arguably the General Assembly's response to the Delaware Supreme Court's restrictive interpretation of the earlier version of that statute. In *Gotham Partners, L.P. v. Hallwood Realty Partners, L.P.,*[18] the Delaware Supreme Court held that, while a limited partnership agreement could provide for contractually created fiduciary duties substantially mirroring corporate common law fiduciary duties, a limited partnership agreement could not "eliminate" the fiduciary duties or liabilities of a general partner. Before the August 2004 amendment specifically authorized the "elimination" of a partner's duties, the court of chancery had interpreted the earlier language of section 17-1101—"the partner's. . . duties may be expanded or restricted"[19]—to include the ability to eliminate one or more of the traditional fiduciary duties analogized from the corporate law.[20]

Apparently concerned by the court of chancery's overreliance on the policy to "give maximum effect to the principle of freedom of contract" announced clearly in the statute, the supreme court pointedly criticized the court of chancery for its expansive interpretation of the statute. Both courts no doubt believed that they were giving

---

16   Del. Code Ann. tit. 6, § 17-1101(b)-(d) (2005) (as amended by 74 Del. Laws, c. 265).

17   Id. § 17-1101(d).

18   817 A.2d 160 (Del. 2002)

19   Del. Code Ann. tit. 6, § 17-1101(d) (2005).

20   Gotham Partners, L.P. v. Hallwood Realty Partners, L.P., 795 A.2d 1, 31 (Del. Ch. 2001).

effect to the General Assembly's intent, though in so doing they reached different results. The court of chancery found the term "restrict[ion]" of the application of corporate law fiduciary principles to be consistent with eliminating one or more of those duties when such an intent appeared in the limited partnership agreement. The supreme court rejected that broad construction.

It is fair to say that the Delaware Supreme Court, following our earlier reference to the "triad" of fiduciary duties at common law, failed to recognize a clear legislative intent to enable parties to negotiate contractual relationships based upon free exchange of consideration for a set of rights and risks unfettered by common law fiduciary duty principles. The supreme court apparently found it difficult to abandon the view that judicial oversight of disputes within the governance structure of limited liability unincorporated entities must invariably be from the perspective of a set of freestanding non-waivable equitable principles, drawn from the common law of corporate governance.

B. Precursors to Legislative Action

* * *

Commentators knowledgeable about Delaware law were...already of the view, even before the August 2004 amendment, that a reviewing court should first look to the agreement of the parties. They suggested that courts should employ analogies drawn from the vast body of fiduciary duty common law only when necessary to address the scope of a party's duties and liabilities for its breach of those duties.

Thus, in determining the scope of the fiduciary duties owed by a general partner of a limited partnership, a partnership agreement must be consulted since any definition of fiduciary duty whether or not arrived at by analogy to corporate law may have been modified in the partnership agreement. * * *

The Delaware Supreme Court's singular focus on status relationships, treating the parties to all limited partnership or limited liability company agreements as having a dependency relationship (e.g., a trustee to beneficiary or agent to principal), rather than a contractual relationship, appears to have drawn Gotham's rationale. One must conclude that the Delaware Supreme Court's analysis resulted in the General Assembly's August 2004 amendment which reaffirmed the policy that parties may contract away common law fiduciary duties with contractual language that addresses expansion, restriction, or elimination of a partner's duties-"(including fiduciary duties)." The General Assembly clearly established, in response to Gotham, that contractual relationships and not status relationships control the duties and liabilities of parties to a contractual entity agreement.

V. Reacting to the Delaware Revised Uniform
Limited Partnership Act's August 2004 Amendment

If the import of the language of the August 2004 amendment, by its reference to "restricted or eliminated by provisions in the partnership agreement," was not clear enough, the quintessential contract reference, "provided that the partnership agreement may not eliminate the implied contractual covenant of good faith and fair dealing," should make the legislature'sintent abundantly clear. This language, carefully borrowed from contract law, as distinguished from corporate law, to set the parameters of action deemed to be in "good faith," must be read as an affirmation that the three-legged stool-the "triad" or "troika" of corporate fiduciary duty-is not the lens through which the action of parties to a limited partnership or limited liability company agreement will be viewed.

For example, if a limited partnership agreement provides expressly and unequivocally that all three fiduciary duty principles found in the common law of corporations are to be eliminated, then a partner's act in furtherance of his duties as a manager would be scrutinized first to determine whether the agreement authorized or empowered the partner to so act, and second, whether the action did or did not breach the implied contractual covenant of good faith and fair dealing. * * *

The August 2004 amendment leaves little, if any, room for argument over whether the contract relationship has triumphed over the status relationship in Delaware limited partnership and limited liability company internal governance scrutiny. What the amendment potentially does is takes away from the courts a well-developed framework of doctrine from the corporate law arena and requires the courts to delve into an area of ex post scrutiny where Delaware has little developed law. Few Delaware cases address the concept of the implied contractual covenant of good faith and fair dealing outside of the subject matter of employment contracts.

What, then, would be the approach taken by Delaware courts when confronting the issue of a limited partnership agreement, created after August 2004, that (1) purports to eliminate the application of all common law fiduciary duties to a party in a limited partnership or a limited liability company; (2) purports to restrict or eliminate one or modify another of those duties; or (3) is silent about the application of common law fiduciary duties to the acts of a party?

* * *

A. The Inferential Impact of the Cases

First, to date there are no Delaware cases addressing the contractual relationship or status relationship of a general partner, member, or manager where the agreement purported expressly to eliminate all fiduciary duties of the party occupying fiduciary status-the acting managing partner, member, or manager. Nevertheless, it is helpful to predict how a Delaware court might react to a claim that a general partner, member, or manager has violated the statutorily mandated implied contractual covenant of good faith and fair dealing, and what liability scheme might be imposed for harm caused by any act or omission that constitutes a bad faith violation of the implied contractual covenant of good faith and fair dealing. In anticipating the (admittedly hypothetical) court's approach, one must examine Delaware case law that addresses the implied contractual covenant of good faith and fair dealing.

Second, one must further contrast the concept of good faith as derived from a contractual relationship as opposed to the status relationship viewed through the prism of the fiduciary duty of "good faith." * * *

As we examine the covenant of good faith in the context of the contractual relationship between partners and limited partners and manager and members, three factors should be considered. First, there is no current Delaware case law addressing the implied contractual covenant of good faith and fair dealing in this context. Second, the case law that does address the covenant of good faith and fair dealing does so in employment, commercial, and insurance contract scenarios, not in the context of allocating power or liability within a governance structure of a business entity. And third, the lure of the case law from the corporate governance context may tend to cause the courts to misfocus, particularly in a vacuum, especially where the conduct of the defendant may appear so inequitable that the court will look to the fiduciary relationship between the parties and not their contractual arrangement. Delaware courts repeatedly claim to expand the application of the implied covenant cautiously, but seem much less reluctant to identify and then apply "unremitting" and "inviolable" fiduciary duties when the results of an otherwise lawful act by a fiduciary appears inequitable.[21]

B. The Implied Contractual Covenant of Good Faith and Fair Dealing: Background in Delaware Jurisprudence

Although bad faith is invariably described in the case law and secondary literature as the absence of good faith, the covenant itself is a freestanding regulator of conduct. The Delaware Supreme Court has recognized, reluctantly, "the occasional necessity" of implying contract terms to ensure that the parties' "reasonable expectations" are honored. This quasi reformation remedy, however, "should be [a] rare and fact-intensive" exercise, governed solely by "issues of compelling fairness." Only when it is clear from the writing that the contracting parties "would have agreed to proscribe the act later complained of . . . had they thought to negotiate with respect to that matter" may a party invoke the covenant's protections.[22]

---

21   See, e.g., *Omnicare, Inc. v. NCS Healthcare, Inc.*, 818 A.2d 914, 938 (Del. 2003) ("The fiduciary duties of a director are unremitting and must be effectively discharged in the specific context of the actions that are required with regard to the corporation or its stockholders as circumstances change.") (emphasis added); *McMullin v. Beran*, 765 A.2d 910, 920 (Del. 2000) ("[A]lthough the [defendant] Board could not effectively seek an alternative to the proposed Lyondell sale by auction or agreement, and had no fiduciary responsibility to engage in either futile exercise, its ultimate statutory duties under [the DGCL] and attendant fiduciary obligations remained inviolable.") (emphasis added).

22   *Katz v. Oak Indus., Inc.*, 508 A.2d 873, 880 (Del. Ch. 1986).

Stated in general terms, the covenant requires "a party in a contractual relationship to refrain from arbitrary or unreasonable conduct which has the effect of preventing the other party to the contract from receiving the fruits" of the bargain. Thus, parties are liable when their conduct frustrates the "overarching purpose" of the contract "by taking advantage of their position to control" implementation of the agreement's terms. Traditional contract principles still control, however, as parties may bargain away covenant protections. Furthermore, only parties to the contract can breach the covenant.

* * *

C. How Do the Cases Express a Policy Bias?

The Delaware Supreme Court's holding in Gotham illustrates, quite effectively, the lure of analogizing to the corporate law (i.e., the status relationship analysis) as opposed to employing a contractual relationship analysis that supports a freedom of contract policy and redress for overstepping the bounds of lawful activity only where a partner or manager has breached an implied contractual covenant of good faith and fair dealing.

I submit this reluctance to recognize a clearly articulated legislative policy stems from two sources: (1) the relative certainty of, and long experience with, the application of fiduciary duty concepts in the common law of corporate governance in many different contexts; and, (2) the desire to proceed cautiously in expanding the application of an implied contractual covenant of good faith and fair dealing in any context outside employment.

* * *

[In Gotham,] on a motion for summary judgment, the court of chancery dismissed the traditional breach-of-fiduciary-duty claims on the basis that the partnership agreement supplemented traditional fiduciary duties and provided for contractual fiduciary duties by which the conduct of the defendants, including the general partner, would be measured. In doing so, the vice chancellor recognized that he should analyze the claims based on the contractual relationship between the parties, not their status relationship.* * *

At the time of the court's summary judgment opinion, the Limited Partnership Act provided that its policy was to "give maximum effect to the principle of freedom of contract," and that the partner's duties "may be expanded or restricted by provisions in a partnership agreement." The vice chancellor interpreted those provisions together and concluded the power to restrict fiduciary duties, interpreted broadly consistent with freedom of contract, would include the ability to eliminate one or more of the "triad" of traditional common law fiduciary duties. Although the precise word "eliminate" did not appear in the statute at the time of his opinion, the vice chancellor'sdictum seems entirely consistent with both the policy of the statute and a contractual relationship analysis.

On appeal, while apparently understanding that the vice chancellor'slanguage constituted dictum, the Delaware Supreme Court nonetheless took pains to emphasize that the vice chancellor'sstatements "create[d] a separate problem."[23] The court stated:

> [I]n the interest of avoiding the perpetuation of a questionable statutory interpretation that could be relied upon adversely by courts, commentators[,] and practitioners in the future, we are constrained to draw attention to the statutory language and the underlying general principle in our jurisprudence that scrupulous adherence to fiduciary duties is normally expected.

What could the supreme court have meant, other than to express its intent to continue to draw on common law corporate principles of fiduciary duty to address governance issues, even where it had to be clear that such an approach was at odds with statutory policy favoring freedom of contract and freedom from the constriction of the common law?

The court avoided the statutory language that recognized the right of the contracting partner to abrogate the common law by contract and "restrict" fiduciary duties not welcome by the parties to the agreement. One could argue that the supreme court merely interpreted the word restrict narrowly, properly noting that to "restrict" did not mean to "eliminate" fiduciary duties completely. To accept this view, however, one must over-look the clearly announced legislative intent that the statute be construed broadly, and to abrogate the common law, and that freedom of contract would guide its purpose. The supreme court'srestrictive interpretation, at least in hindsight, neither advanced the policy of the statute nor recognized the status relationship of the parties in the trust, agency, and corporate governance arenas rather than explicit contractual language, dictated the imposition of traditional fiduciary duties.* * *

Even more interestingly, at least to this author, is that the Delaware Supreme Court in Gotham held that the partnership agreement "supplanted fiduciary duty and became the sole source of protection for the public unitholders of the Partnership," just as the vice chancellor had ruled.[24] Nevertheless, expressing its continued reluctance to depart from corporate governance fiduciary duty law, the court imposed a fairness-standard overlay "akin to the common law one applicable to self-dealing transactions by fiduciaries." The court reached that result despite the clear language of then section 17-1101: "The rule that statutes in derogation of the common law are to be strictly construed shall have no application to this chapter."

Gotham thus teaches that first, Delaware courts remain reluctant to leave the secure ground of fiduciary duty common law so well fleshed out in corporate

---

23 *Gotham Partners, L.P. v. Hallwood Realty Partners*, L.P., 817 A.2d 160, 167 (Del. 2002).

24 See id. at 171 (quoting *Gotham Partners, L.P. v. Hallwood Realty Partners, L.P.*, 795 A.2d 1, 24 (Del. Ch. 2001).

governance decisions even in the face of a statute instructing them to do so. Second, Gotham teaches that even when the courts hold that common law duties are "supplanted" by the language of a valid partnership agreement as authorized by statute, absent a clearly articulated standard, the courts will default to the tried (and occasionally, true) method of judicial scrutiny utilized in equity as if the parties were in a status, rather than a contractual, relationship.

Gotham teaches that the General Assembly remains poised to correct the courts when they get it wrong. The August 2004 amendment makes it clear that "practitioners," if not "commentators" and "courts," knew what the General Assembly originally intended even though the supreme court in Gotham suggested that court of chancery opinions to that point in time might mislead them.

* * *

NOTES AND QUESTIONS

I. IN *ELF ATOCHEM*, we saw a Delaware Supreme Court that clearly recognized the nature of LLCs as creatures of contract, the core of which is supposed to be freedom and flexibility. Yet, as Chief Justice Steele correctly highlights, in *Gotham Partners*, the same Court seemed to take a step back from the *Elf Atochem* reasoning. Though the part of the opinion chastising the Chancery Court for its "questionable statutory interpretation" was merely dicta, the court took pains to highlight its position that in general, common law fiduciary principles normally apply. Why do you suppose that is? Chief Justice Steele seems to suggest that the reason the court did so was to express its intention to draw on settled principles even where doing so would fly in the face of statutory authority. Do you find this convincing? A more likely explanation might be that the Court was trying to mend a split between the lower courts. More specifically, given what you have read in the preceding article, what would a Delaware court do in a case where an LLC agreement made no mention of fiduciary duties? Do they apply by default, or are they only applicable when parties make them so through agreement? According to Chief Justice Steele, the "amendment leaves little, if any, room for argument over whether the contract relationship has triumphed over the status relationship in Delaware limited partnership and limited liability company internal governance scrutiny." Chief Justice Steele seems to think that common law fiduciary principles have no place in the LLC context; rather, he advocates that the general assembly, in carefully choosing contractual language in the 2004 amendment, intended that courts use the implied covenant of good faith and fair dealing to police these bargains. However, both contract theory and the Delaware LLC act itself teach that the implied covenant cannot be eliminated from any agreement. Since the implied covenant cannot be eliminated, the general assembly must have intended that some minimal protection be left in place in every LLC agreement. Most troubling, by Justice Steele's own admission, it is uncetain what this implied covenant might look like in the LLC context. At the same time, the Chief Justice notes that it would be unwise for Delaware courts to create new law when they have such a well-developed common law to rely on.

Another puzzle is, if the general assembly did intend for courts to use the implied covenant of good faith and fair dealing to police LLC agreements, and the covenant cannot be eliminated, then was the general assembly being self-contradictory in stating that fiduciary duties can be eliminated?

2. THE CHIEF JUSTICE is impressed by the General Assembly's quick amendment to correct the Supreme Court in *Gotham*. What, then, should we make of the fact that the General Assembly has not reacted to the "overlay" of common law equitable principles? Does that imply that the General Assembly approves of the direction the courts are taking?

3. THE ARTICLE DRAWS attention to the fact that "one must ... contrast the concept of good faith as derived from a contractual relationship as opposed to the status relationship viewed through the prism of the fiduciary duty of 'good faith,' " indicating also that "perhaps only in Delaware would one have to undertake such an inquiry." For a stimulating exploration of this predicament of the possible conflict between status and contract, see generally David Rosenberg, *Making Sense of Good Faith in Delaware Corporate Fiduciary Law: A Contractarian Approach*, 29 Del. J. Corp. L. 491 (2004). Do you have a sense of the difference after reading the article? Do you understand why it is important for courts to separate the two concepts?

Part of the worry here is that the implied covenant might be used as a back door through which contractually eliminated fiduciary duty of good faith might be revived. The argument would be that even though the duty of good faith was eliminated contractually, that duty cannot be eliminated pursuant to prohibition on eliminating the implied covenant. Responding to this danger, courts have very narrowly interpreted the implied covenant.[25] Perhaps the most enlightening articulation of the difference

---

25   To compare the courts' strategy with an alternative one holding that there should exist some core duties that are unwaivable, see Sandra K. Miller, *What Fiduciary Duties Should Apply to the LLC Manager after More than a Decade of Experimentation?*, 32 J. CORP. L. 565. For more on fiduciary duties, see generally Larry E. Ribstein, *Fiduciary Duty Contracts in Unincorporated Firms*, 54 Wash. & Lee L. Rev. 537, 583 (1997).

has been recently articulated by the Delaware Supreme Court, in *Gerber v. Enter. Products Holdings*, LLC, 67 A.3d 400, 418-19 (Del. 2013):

> The implied covenant seeks to enforce the parties' contractual bargain by implying only those terms that the parties would have agreed to during their original negotiations if they had thought to address them. Under Delaware law, a court confronting an implied covenant claim asks whether it is clear from what was expressly agreed upon that the parties who negotiated the express terms of the contract would have agreed to proscribe the act later complained of as a breach of the implied covenant of good faith—had they thought to negotiate with respect to that matter. While this test requires resort to a counterfactual world—what if—it is nevertheless appropriately restrictive and commonsensical.

> The temporal focus is critical. Under a fiduciary duty or tort analysis, a court examines the parties as situated at the time of the wrong. The court determines whether the defendant owed the plaintiff a duty, considers the defendant's obligations (if any) in light of that duty, and then evaluates whether the duty was breached. Temporally, each inquiry turns on the parties' relationship as it existed at the time of the wrong. The nature of the parties' relationship may turn on historical events, and past dealings necessarily will inform the court's analysis, but liability depends on the parties' relationship when the alleged breach occurred, not on the relationship as it existed in the past.

> An implied covenant claim, by contrast, looks to the past. It is not a free-floating duty unattached to the underlying legal documents. It does not ask what duty the law should impose on the parties given their relationship at the time of the wrong, but rather what the parties would have agreed to themselves had they considered the issue in their original bargaining positions at the time of contracting. "Fair dealing" * * * is * * * a commitment to deal "fairly" in the sense of consistently with the terms of the parties' agreement and its purpose. Likewise "good faith" does not envision loyalty to the contractual counterparty, but rather faithfulness to the scope, purpose, and terms of the parties' contract. Both necessarily turn on the contract itself and what the parties would have agreed upon had the issue arisen when they were bargaining originally.

The retrospective focus applies equally to a party's discretionary rights. The implied covenant requires that a party refrain from arbitrary or unreasonable conduct which has the effect of preventing the other party to the contract from receiving the fruits of its bargain. When exercising a discretionary right, a party to the contract must exercise its discretion reasonably. The contract may identify factors that the decision-maker can consider, and it may provide a contractual standard for evaluating the decision. Express contractual provisions always supersede the implied covenant, but even the most carefully drafted agreement will harbor residual nooks and crannies for the implied covenant to fill. In those situations, what is "arbitrary" or "unreasonable"—or conversely "reasonable"—depends on the parties' original contractual expectations, not a "free-floating" duty applied at the time of the wrong.

Given this articulation, now adopted as law, does it seem likely that Chief Justice Steele's article has had the desired impact? In any event, does it seem wise to integrate contract theory with concerns of corporate governance? Part of the lesson here is that the law tends to specialize as it develops. Thus, common law fiduciary duty principles evolve with an eye to encouraging investment—or "enabling," as the Chief Justice puts it—while contract theory must remain sufficiently broad to govern all manner of contract disputes, not just those arising out of LLC agreements. As such, one might be leery of taking a contractual principle such as the implied covenant, whose breadth is literally as varied as contracts themselves, and trying to infuse it with considerations for specific relationships.

4. THE ARTICLE RELIES heavily on the idea that statutory authority has proclaimed its preference for contractual resolution of disputes over common law principles, in part because the general assembly authorized the elimination of fiduciary duties, but prohibits parties from eliminating the implied covenant. Do you find this convincing? What about the words of the "prolific and thoughtful vice chancellor," who argues that "the continued importance of the common law of corporations ... reflects a policy choice made by the Delaware General Assembly. That choice deliberately deploys Delaware's judiciary to guarantee the integrity of our corporate law through the articulation of common law principles of equitable behavior for corporate fiduciaries"?

The case that follows tries to reconcile the competing policies of contract and the common law. Does it succeed, in your opinion?

Auriga Capital Corp., v. Gatz Properties, LLC

40 A.3d 839 (2012) (aff'd, 59 A.3d 1206 (2013))
Court of Chancery of Delaware.

OPINION

STRINE, Chancellor.

I. INTRODUCTION

The manager of an LLC and his family ["Gatz"] acquired majority voting control over * * * the LLC's equity during the course of its operations and thereby held a veto over any strategic option. The LLC was an unusual one that held a long-term lease on a valuable property owned by the manager and his family. The leasehold allowed the LLC to operate a golf course on the property.

The LLC intended to act as a passive operator by subleasing the golf course for operation by a large golf management corporation. A lucrative sublease to that effect was entered in 1998. The golf management corporation, however, was purchased early in the term of the sublease by owners that sought to consolidate its operations. Rather than invest in the leased property and put its full effort into making the course a success, the management corporation took short cuts, let maintenance slip, and evidenced a disinterest in the property. By as early as 2004, it was clear to the manager that the golf management corporation would not renew its lease.

This did not make the manager upset. The LLC and its investors had invested heavily in the property, building on it a first-rate Robert Trent Jones, Jr.—designed golf course and a clubhouse. If the manager and his family could get rid of the investors in the LLC, they would have an improved property, which they had reason to believe could be more valuable as a residential community. Knowing that the golf management corporation would likely not renew its sublease, the manager failed to take any steps at all to find a new strategic option for the LLC that would protect the LLC's investors. Thus, the manager did not search for a replacement management corporation, explore whether the LLC itself could manage the golf course profitably, or undertake to search for a buyer for the LLC. Indeed, when a credible buyer for the LLC came forward on its own and expressed a serious interest, the manager failed to provide that buyer with the due diligence that a motivated seller would typically provide to a possible buyer. Even worse, the manager did all it could to discourage a good bid, frustrating and misleading the interested buyer.

The manager then sought to exploit the opportunity provided by the buyer's emergence to make low-ball bids to the other investors in the LLC on the basis of materially misleading information. Among other failures, the manager made an offer at $5.6 million for the LLC without telling the investors that the buyer had expressed a willingness to discuss a price north of $6 million. The minority investors refused the manager's offer. When the minority investors asked the manager to go back and negotiate a higher price with the potential buyer, the manager refused.

This refusal reflected the reality that the manager and his family were never willing to sell the LLC. Nor did they desire to find a strategic option for the LLC that would allow it to operate profitably for the benefit of the minority investors. The manager and his family wanted to be rid of the minority investors, whom they had come to regard as troublesome bothers.

Using the coming expiration of the golf management corporation's sublease as leverage, the manager eventually conducted a sham auction to sell the LLC. The auction had all the look and feel of a distress sale * * *. Ridiculous postage stamp-sized ads were published and unsolicited junk mail was sent out. Absent was any serious marketing to a targeted group of golf course operators by a responsible, mature, respected broker on the basis of solid due diligence materials. * * * Worst of all, interested buyers could take no comfort in the fact that the manager—who controlled the majority of the voting power of the LLC—was committed to selling the LLC to the highest bidder, as the bidding materials made clear that the manager was also planning to bid and at the same time reserved the right to cancel the auction for any reason.

When the results of this incompetent marketing process were known and the auctioneer knew that no one other than the manager was going to bid, the auctioneer told the manager that fact. The manager then won with a bid of $50,000 in excess of the LLC's debt, on which the manager was already a guarantor. Only $22,777 of the bid went to the minority investors. For his services in running this ineffective process, the auctioneer received a fee of $80,000, which was greater than the cash component of the winning bid. * * *

A group of minority investors have sued for damages, arguing the manager breached his contractual and fiduciary duties through this course of conduct. The manager, after originally disclaiming that he owed a fiduciary duty of loyalty to the minority, now rests his defense on two primary grounds. The first is that the manager and his family were able to veto any option for the LLC as their right as members. As a result, they could properly use a chokehold over the LLC to pursue their own interests and the minority would have to live with the consequences of their freedom of action. The second defense is that by the time of the auction, the LLC was valueless.

In this post-trial decision, I find for the plaintiffs. For reasons discussed in the opinion, I explain that the LLC agreement here does not displace the traditional duties of loyalty and care that are owed by managers of Delaware LLCs to their investors in the absence of a contractual provision waiving or modifying those duties. The Delaware Limited Liability Company Act (the "LLC Act") explicitly applies equity as a default[26] and our Supreme Court, and this court, have consistently held that default fiduciary duties apply to those managers of alternative entities who would qualify as fiduciaries under traditional equitable principles, including managers of LLCs. Here, the LLC agreement makes clear that the manager could only enter into

---

26   6 *Del. C.* § 18–1104: In any case not provided for in this chapter, the rules of law and equity, including the rules of law and equity relating to fiduciary duties and the law merchant, shall govern.

a self-dealing transaction, such as its purchase of the LLC, if it proves that the terms were fair. In other words, the LLC agreement essentially incorporates a core element of the traditional fiduciary duty of loyalty. Not only that, the LLC agreement's exculpatory provision makes clear that the manager is not exculpated for bad faith action, willful misconduct, or even grossly negligent action, *i.e.*, a breach of the duty of care.

The manager's course of conduct here breaches both his contractual and fiduciary duties. Using his control over the LLC, the manager took steps to deliver the LLC to himself and his family on unfair terms. When the LLC had a good cushion of cash from the remaining years of the lease, it was in a good position to take the time needed to responsibly identify another strategic option to generate value for the LLC and all of its investors. Although the economy was weakening, the golf course was well-designed and located in a community that is a good one for the profitable operation of a golf course. With a minimally competent and loyal fiduciary at the helm, the LLC could have charted a course that would have delivered real value to its investors. * * *

The manager himself is the one who has created evidentiary doubt about the LLC's value by failing to pursue any strategic option for the LLC in a timely fashion because he wished to squeeze out the minority investors. The manager's defense that his voting power gave him a license to exploit the minority fundamentally misunderstands Delaware law. The manager was free not to vote his membership interest for a sale. But he was not free to create a situation of distress by failing to cause the LLC to explore its market alternatives and then to buy the LLC for a nominal price. The purpose of the duty of loyalty is in large measure to prevent the exploitation by a fiduciary of his self-interest to the disadvantage of the minority. The fair price requirement of that duty, which is incorporated in the LLC agreement here, makes sure that if the conflicted fiduciary engages in self-dealing, he pays a price that is as much as an arms-length purchaser would pay.

The manager is in no position to take refuge in uncertainties he himself created by his own breaches of duty. * * * Because the manager has made this litigation far more cumbersome and inefficient than it should have been by advancing certain frivolous arguments, I award the plaintiffs one-half of their reasonable attorneys' fees and costs. This award is justified * * * and also ensures that the disloyal manager is not rewarded for making it unduly expensive for the minority investors to pursue their legitimate claims to redress his serious infidelity. I do not award full-fee shifting because I have not adopted all of the plaintiffs' arguments and because the manager's litigation conduct, while sanctionably disappointing, was not so egregious as to justify that result.

* * *

IV. ANALYSIS

A. What Duties Did Gatz Owe To The [minority] Members Of [the LLC]?

At points in this litigation, Gatz has argued that his actions were not subject to any fiduciary duty analysis because the LLC Agreement * * * displaced any role for the use of equitable principles in constraining the LLC's Manager. As I next explain, that is not true.

The Delaware LLC Act starts with the explicit premise that "equity" governs any case not explicitly covered by the Act.[27] But the Act lets contracting parties modify or even eliminate any equitable fiduciary duties, a more expansive constriction than is allowed in the case of corporations.[28] For that reason, in the LLC context, it is typically the case that the evaluation of fiduciary duty claims cannot occur without a close examination of the LLC agreement itself, which often tailors the traditional fiduciary duties to address the specific relationship of the contracting parties.

* * *

1. Default Fiduciary Duties Do Exist In The LLC Context

The Delaware LLC Act does not plainly state that the traditional fiduciary duties of loyalty and care apply by default as to managers or members of a limited liability company. In that respect, of course, the LLC Act is not different than the DGCL ["Delaware General Corporations Law"], which does not do that either. In fact, the absence of explicitness in the DGCL inspired the case of *Schnell v. Chris–Craft*.[29] Arguing that the then newly-revised DGCL was a domain unto itself, and that compliance with its terms was sufficient to discharge any obligation owed by the directors to the stockholders, the defendant corporation in that case won on that theory at the Court of Chancery level.[30] But our Supreme Court reversed and made emphatic that the new DGCL was to be read in concert with equitable fiduciary duties just as had always been the case, stating famously that "inequitable action does not become legally permissible simply because it is legally possible."[31]

The LLC Act is more explicit than the DGCL in making the equitable overlay mandatory. Specifically, § 18–1104 of the LLC Act provides that "[i]n any case not provided for in this chapter, *the rules of law and equity ... shall govern.*"[32] In this way, the LLC Act provides for a construct similar to that which is used in the corporate context. But unlike in the corporate context, the rules of equity apply in the LLC context *by statutory mandate*, creating an even stronger justification for application of fiduciary duties grounded in equity to managers of LLCs to

---

27   See *Id.*

28   *Compare 6 Del. C.* § 18–1101(c), *with 8 Del. C.* § 102(b)(7).

29   *Schnell v. Chris–Craft Indus., Inc.*, 285 A.2d 437 (Del.1971).

30   *Schnell v. Chris–Craft Indus., Inc.*, 285 A.2d 430, 437 (Del.Ch.1971).

31   *Schnell*, 285 A.2d at 439 (Del.1971).

32   *6 Del. C.* § 18–1104 (emphasis added).

the extent that such duties have not been altered or eliminated under the relevant LLC agreement.

It seems obvious that, under traditional principles of equity, a manager of an LLC would qualify as a fiduciary of that LLC and its members. Under Delaware law, "[a] fiduciary relationship is a situation where one person reposes special trust in and reliance on the judgment of another or where a special duty exists on the part of one person to protect the interests of another." Corporate directors, general partners and trustees are analogous examples of those who Delaware law has determined owe a "special duty."[33] Equity distinguishes fiduciary relationships from straightforward commercial arrangements where there is no expectation that one party will act in the interests of the other.

The manager of an LLC—which is in plain words a limited liability "company" having many of the features of a corporation—easily fits the definition of a fiduciary. The manager of an LLC has more than an arms-length, contractual relationship with the members of the LLC. Rather, the manager is vested with discretionary power to manage the business of the LLC.[34]

Thus, because the LLC Act provides for principles of equity to apply, because LLC managers are clearly fiduciaries, and because fiduciaries owe the fiduciary duties of loyalty and care, the LLC Act starts with the default that managers of LLCs owe enforceable fiduciary duties.

This reading of the LLC Act is confirmed by the Act's own history. Before 2004, § 18–1101(c) of the LLC Act provided that fiduciary duties, to the extent they existed, could only be "expanded or restricted" by the LLC agreement.[35] Following our Supreme Court's holding in *Gotham Partners*,[36] which questioned whether default fiduciary duties could be fully eliminated in the limited partnership context when faced with similar statutory language and also affirmed our law's commitment to protecting investors who have not explicitly agreed to waive their fiduciaries' duties and therefore expect their fiduciaries to act in accordance with their interests, the General Assembly amended not only the Delaware Revised Limited Uniform Partnership Act ("DRULPA"), but also the LLC Act to permit the "eliminat[ion]" of default fiduciary duties in an LLC agreement.[37] At the same time, the General Assembly added a provision to the LLC Act (the current § 18–1101(e)) that permits

---

33   *See Metro Ambulance*, 1995 WL 409015, at *3; *McMahon v. New Castle Assocs.*, 532 A.2d 601, 604–05 (Del.Ch.1987).

34   See 6 *Del. C.* § 18–402. In this regard, managers of an LLC bear resemblance to directors of a corporation, who are charged with managing "the business and affairs" of the corporation. 8 *Del. C.* § 141(a).

35   6 *Del. C.* § 18–1101(c) (2003).

36   *Gotham Partners, L.P. v. Hallwood Realty Partners, L.P.*, 817 A.2d 160 (Del.2002).

37   74 Del. Laws ch. 275, § 13 (2004).

full contractual exculpation for breaches of fiduciary and contractual duties, except for the implied contractual covenant of good faith and fair dealing.[38]

If the equity backdrop I just discussed did not apply to LLCs, then the 2004 "Elimination Amendment" would have been logically done differently. Why is this so? Because the Amendment would have instead said something like: "The managers, members, and other persons of the LLC shall owe no duties of any kind to the LLC and its members except as set forth in this statute and the LLC agreement." Instead, the Amendment only made clear that an LLC agreement could, if the parties so chose, "eliminat[e]" default duties altogether, thus according full weight to the statutory policy in favor of giving "maximum effect to the principle of freedom of contract and to the enforceability of [LLC] agreements."[39] The General Assembly left in place the explicit equitable default in § 18–1104 of the Act. Moreover, why would the General Assembly amend the LLC Act to provide for the elimination of (and the exculpation for) "something" if there were no "something" to eliminate (or exculpate) in the first place? The fact that the legislature enacted these liability-limiting measures against the backdrop of case law holding that default fiduciary duties did apply in the LLC context, and seemed to have accepted the central thrust of those decisions to be correct, provides further weight to the position that default fiduciary duties do apply in the LLC context to the extent they are not contractually altered.

* * *

There are two issues that would arise if the equitable background explicitly contained in the statute were to be judicially excised now. The first is that those who crafted LLC agreements in reliance on equitable defaults that supply a predictable structure for assessing whether a business fiduciary has met his obligations to the entity and its investors will have their expectations disrupted. The equitable context in which the contract's specific terms were to be read will be eradicated, rendering the resulting terms shapeless and more uncertain. The fact that the implied covenant of good faith and fair dealing would remain extant would do little to cure this loss.

The common law fiduciary duties that were developed to address those who manage business entities were, as the implied covenant, an equitable gap-filler. If, rather than well thought out fiduciary duty principles, the implied covenant is to be used as the sole default principle of equity, then the risk is that the certainty of contract law itself will be undermined. The implied covenant has rightly been narrowly interpreted by our Supreme Court to apply only "when the express terms of the contract indicate that the parties would have agreed to the obligation had they negotiated the issue." The implied covenant is to be used "cautious[ly]" and does not apply to situations that could be anticipated, which is a real problem in the business context, because fiduciary duty review typically addresses actions that are

---

38   *Id.* § 14; *see also id.* at ch. 265, § 16 (amending DRULPA in same way).

39   6 *Del. C.* § 18–1101(b).

anticipated and permissible under the express terms of the contract, but where there is a potential for managerial abuse. For these reasons, the implied covenant is not a tool that is designed to provide a framework to govern the discretionary actions of business managers acting under a broad enabling framework like a barebones LLC agreement. In fact, if the implied covenant were used in that manner, the room for subjective judicial oversight could be expanded in an inefficient way. The default principles that apply in the fiduciary duty context of business entities are carefully tailored to avoid judicial second-guessing. A generalized "fairness" inquiry under the guise of an "implied covenant" review is an invitation to, at best, reinvent what already exists in another less candid guise, or worse, to inject unpredictability into both entity and contract law, by untethering judicial review from the well-understood frameworks that traditionally apply in those domains.

The second problem is a related one, which is that a judicial eradication of the explicit equity overlay in the LLC Act could tend to erode our state's credibility with investors in Delaware entities. To have told the investing public that the law of equity would apply if the LLC statute did not speak to the question at issue, and to have managers of LLCs easily qualify as fiduciaries under traditional and settled principles of equity law in Delaware, and then to say that LLC agreements could "expan[d] or restric[t] or eliminat [e]" these fiduciary duties, would lead any reasonable investor to conclude the following: the managers of the Delaware LLC in which I am investing owe me the fiduciary duties of loyalty and care except to the extent the agreement "expand [s]," "restrict[s]," or "eliminate[s]" these duties. That expectation has been reinforced by our Supreme Court in decisions like *William Penn Partnership v. Saliba*, where it stated that "[t]he parties here agree that managers of a Delaware [LLC] owe traditional fiduciary duties of loyalty and care to the members of the LLC, unless the parties expressly modify or eliminate those duties in an operating agreement;"[40] in a consistent line of decisions by this court affirming similar principles; in the reasoning of *Gotham Partners* in the analogous limited partnership context; and culminating with legislative reinforcement in the 2004 Elimination Amendment inspired by *Gotham Partners* that allowed LLC agreements to eliminate fiduciary duties altogether. Reasonable investors in Delaware LLCs would, one senses, understand even more clearly after the Elimination Amendment that they were protected by fiduciary duty review unless the LLC agreement provided to the contrary, because they would of course think that there would have been no need for our General Assembly to pass a statute authorizing the elimination of something that did not exist at all.

Reasonable minds can debate whether it would be wise for the General Assembly to create a business entity in which the managers owe the investors no duties at all except as set forth in the statute and the governing agreement. Perhaps it would

---

40   *William Penn P'ship v. Saliba*, 13 A.3d 749, 756 (Del.2011) (citing *Bay Ctr. Apartments Owner, LLC v. Emery Bay PKI, LLC*, 2009 WL 1124451, at *8 (Del.Ch. Apr. 20, 2009)).

be, perhaps it would not. That is a policy judgment for the General Assembly. What seems certain is that the General Assembly, and the organs of the Bar who propose alteration of the statutes to them, know how to draft a clear statute to that effect and have yet to do so. * * *

With that statement of the law in mind, let us turn to the relevant terms of Peconic Bay'sLLC Agreement.

2. The Relevant Provisions Of The LLC Agreement

I note at the outset that the Peconic Bay LLC Agreement contains no general provision stating that the only duties owed by the manager to the LLC and its investors are set forth in the Agreement itself. Thus, before taking into account the existence of an exculpatory provision, the LLC Agreement does not displace the traditional fiduciary duties of loyalty and care owed to the Company and its members by Gatz Properties and by Gatz, in his capacity as the manager of Gatz Properties. And although LLC agreements may displace fiduciary duties altogether or tailor their application, by substituting a different form of review, here § 15 of the LLC Agreement contains a clause reaffirming that a form akin to entire fairness review [a judicial standard which requires "arms-length" bargaining] will apply to "Agreements with Affiliates," a group which includes Gatz Properties, that are not approved by a majority of the unaffiliated members' vote. In relevant part, § 15 provides:

> 15. *Neither the Manager nor any other Member shall be entitled to cause the Company to enter ... into any additional agreements with affiliates on terms and conditions which are less favorable to the Company than the terms and conditions of similar agreements which could be entered into with arms-length third parties, without the consent of a majority of the non-affiliated Members * * *.*[41]

This court has interpreted similar contractual language supplying an "arm's length terms and conditions" standard for reviewing self-dealing transactions, and has read it as imposing the equivalent of the substantive aspect of entire fairness review, commonly referred to as the "fair price" prong.[42] This interpretation is confirmed by the defendants' own understanding of § 15 as requiring that Gatz pay a "fair price" to the Minority Members if Gatz were to acquire Peconic Bay, as reflected by a letter sent from Gatz'scounsel to the Minority Members.

Importantly, however, entire fairness review'sprocedural inquiry into "fair dealing" does not completely fall away, because the extent to which the process leading

---

41 JX–2 § 15 (emphasis added).

42 *See Gotham Partners, L.P. v. Hallwood Realty Partners, L.P.*, 795 A.2d 1, 27 (Del.Ch.2001), *aff'd in relevant part,*817 A.2d 160 (Del.2002); *Flight Options Int'l, Inc. v. Flight Options*, LLC, 2005 WL 2335353, at *7–8 (Del.Ch. Sept. 20, 2005).

to the self-dealing either replicated or deviated from the behavior one would expect in an arms-length deal bears importantly on the price determination. Where a self-dealing transaction does not result from real bargaining, where there has been no real market test, and where the self-interested party's own conduct may have compromised the value of the asset in question or the information available to assess that value, these factors bear directly on whether the interested party can show that it paid a fair price. Thus, as written, § 15 permits Affiliate Agreements without the approval of the majority of the Minority Members, subject to a proviso that places the burden on the Manager (here, Gatz) to show that the price term of the Affiliate Agreement was the equivalent of one in an agreement negotiated at arms-length. But, "[i]mplicit in this proviso is the requirement that the [defendants] *undertake some effort* to determine the price at which a transaction with [Gatz] could be effected through a deal with a third party." In other words, in order to take cover under the contractual safe harbor of § 15, Gatz bears the burden to show that he paid a fair price to acquire Peconic Bay, a conclusion that must be supported by a showing that he performed, in good faith, a responsible examination of what a third-party buyer would pay for the Company. * * * Gatz has failed to meet the terms of this proviso.

Because the terms of § 15 only apply to Affiliate Agreements, and because these terms address the duty owed by Gatz to the Minority Members as to Affiliate Agreements, they distill the traditional fiduciary duties as to the portion of the Minority Members' claims that relates to the fairness of the Auction and Merger into a burden to prove the substantive fairness of the economic outcome. * * *

The LLC Agreement does, however, contain an exculpatory provision, which is functionally akin to an exculpatory charter provision authorized by 8 *Del. C.* § 102(b)(7). In relevant part, § 16, governing "Exculpation and Indemnification," reads as follows:

> 16. *No Covered Person* [defined to include "the Members, Manager and the officers, equity holders, partners and employees of each of the foregoing"] *shall be liable to the Company, [or] any other Covered Person* or any other person or entity who has an interest in the Company *for any loss, damage or claim incurred by reason of any act or omission performed or omitted by such Covered Person in good faith* in connection with the formation of the Company or *on behalf of the Company and in a manner reasonably believed to be within the scope of the authority conferred on such Covered Person by this Agreement, except that a Covered Person shall be liable for any such loss, damage or claim incurred by reason of such Covered Person's gross negligence, willful misconduct or willful misrepresentation.*

Thus, by the terms of § 16, Gatz may escape monetary liability for a breach of his default fiduciary duties if he can prove that his fiduciary breach was not: (1) in bad faith, or the result of (2) gross negligence, (3) willful misconduct or (4) willful misrepresentation. Also, in order to fall within the terms of § 16, a Covered Person must first be acting "on behalf of the company" and "in a manner reasonably believed to be within the scope of authority conferred on [him] by [the LLC Agreement]." Thus, § 16 only insulates a Covered Person from liability for authorized actions; that is, actions taken in accordance with the other stand-alone provisions of the LLC Agreement. So, to the extent that the Auction and the follow-on Merger were effected in violation of the arms-length mandate set forth in § 15 (which, as I shall find, they were), such a breach would not be exculpated by § 16. Moreover, even if I were to find that § 16 operated to limit Gatz's liability for actions taken in contravention of the terms of § 15, I find that his actions related to and in consummation of the Auction and follow-on Merger were taken in bad faith such that he would not be entitled to exculpation anyway.

* * *

I now analyze the Minority Members' claim that Gatz breached his fiduciary and contractual duties as the Manager of Peconic Bay. Specifically, I conclude that Gatz breached his fiduciary duties of loyalty and care, and the fair price requirement of § 15. He has not proven that these breaches are exculpated, and * * * he acted in bad faith and with gross negligence. I detail the reasons for those conclusions now.

B. Did Gatz Breach His Contractual and Fiduciary Duties to the Minority Members?

The record convinces me that Gatz pursued a bad faith course of conduct to enrich himself and his family without any regard for the interests of Peconic Bay or its Minority Members. His breaches may be summarized as follows: (1) failing to take any steps for five years to address in good faith the expected loss of American Golf as an operator; (2) turning away a responsible bidder which could have paid a price beneficial to the LLC and its investors in that capacity; (3) using the leverage obtained by his own loyalty breaches to play "hardball" with the Minority Members by making unfair offers on the basis of misleading disclosures; and (4) buying the LLC at an auction conducted on terms that were well-designed to deter any third-party buyer, and to deliver the LLC to Gatz at a distress sale price.

* * *

VI. Conclusion

For all these reasons, I find for the Minority Members and will enter a final judgment for them. * * *

NOTES AND QUESTIONS

I. THIS CASE INCLUDES conceptual, historical, analogical and prudential arguments for the conclusion that default fiduciary duties do apply to LLCs. You have now been exposed to arguments on both sides of the debate regarding fiduciary duties in LLCs. Both purport to arrive at their conclusions based on the 2004 amendment, practical considerations, as well as the nature of the relationship between parties to LLCs. Which do you find more convincing, Chief Justice Steele's contractual approach, or Vice Chancellor Strine's equitable approach?

This case focuses on the default rules that govern when LLC Member Agreements are silent. Yet, as you no doubt have gathered, what fiduciary duties apply to each case is a function of the LLC agreement itself. In this case, for example, even though the vice chancellor found that equity is the default where LLC agreements are silent, he still embarked on a contractual analysis prior to deciding that fiduciary duties were not eliminated by the agreement, and consequently applying principles of equity. This approach seems very consistent with what the Chief Justice identified as the correct approach for LLCs and LLPs. With that in mind, do you think the Chief Justice would be happy with the result of this case? In any case, part of the takeaway here is that when it comes to LLC fiduciary law, one must embark on a case-by-case analysis. A result of that approach that is perhaps unfortunate is that one must take special care when relying on case law. This because, it is rare that any two relevant agreements will be identical, and to any extent that they are not judges have ample room to navigate precedent as they see fit. With that in mind, do you think investors prefer the equitable overlay?

....

2. WHAT DOES THE VICE chancellor mean in quoting the supreme court's language that "inequitable action does not become permissible simply because it is legally possible"? That phrase is the supreme court's response to a defendant-corporation's management's argument that it abided by all laws and by-laws in advancing the date of the annual shareholder meeting. Because the annual meeting was the designated time for challenging the reelection of incumbent management, and because the court perceived the advancement as an attempt by management to procure an unfair advantage over potential challengers by giving them less time to prepare, the supreme court struck down the action, even though it was technically "legal." What do you think of the supreme court's action in that case? Why do you think the vice chancellor invoked it here?

....

3. YOU HAVE UNDOUBTEDLY noticed the discussion surrounding the "entire fairness standard," both in the article, and in the case you just read. In general, Delaware courts apply three different standards of review to breach of fiduciary duty claims in the corporate context. "Entire fairness" is the most stringent level of review, and applies when a majority of the officers approving a transaction are interested, or where a majority stockholder stands on both sides of the transaction. Directors are "interested" if they "appear on both sides of a transaction [or] expect to derive any personal financial benefit from it in the sense of self-dealing as opposed to a benefit which devolves upon the corporation or all stockholders generally." Given this definition of entire fairness, do you think the vice chancellor was warranted in applying it to the case, or do you think, along with the Chief Justice, that parties to LLCs factor these considerations in when drafting the agreement, and so the consideration reflects the costs of dropping these protections?

4. ONE THING YOU MIGHT find surprising is that the ruling of this case was affirmed by Justice Steele's supreme court. Perhaps less remarkable is the fact that in the supreme court's *per curiam* opinion, vice chancellor Strine was criticized for venturing beyond what the supreme court thought necessary to decide the case, and proclaiming that default fiduciary duties apply to LLCs:

> Where, as here, the dispute over whether fiduciary standards apply could be decided solely by reference to the LLC Agreement, it was improvident and unnecessary for the trial court to reach out and decide, *sua sponte*, the default fiduciary duty issue as a matter of statutory construction. The trial court did so despite expressly acknowledging that the existence of fiduciary duties under the LLC Agreement was "no longer contested by the parties." For the reasons next discussed, that court's statutory pronouncements must be regarded as dictum without any precedential value ... The court's excursus on this issue strayed beyond the proper purview and function of a judicial opinion. "Delaware law requires that a justiciable controversy exist before a court can adjudicate properly a dispute brought before it." We remind Delaware judges that the obligation to write judicial opinions on the issues presented is not a license to use those opinions as a platform from which to propagate their individual world views on issues not presented. A judge's duty is to resolve the issues that the parties present in a clear and concise manner. To the extent Delaware judges wish to stray beyond those issues and, without making any definitive pronouncements, ruminate on what the proper direction of Delaware law should be, there are appropriate platforms, such as law review articles, the classroom, continuing legal education presentations, and keynote speeches.

Gatz Properties, LLC v. Auriga Capital Corp., 59 A.3d 1206, 1218 (Del. 2012) (internal citations omitted).

III. LLC Veil Piercing

Soroof Trading Development Co., Ltd. v. GE Fuel Cell Systems, LLC

United States District Court, S.D. New York.

842 F.Supp.2d 502

LAURA TAYLOR SWAIN, District Judge.

Plaintiff Soroof Trading Development Company Ltd. ("Plaintiff" or "Soroof") brings this action against GE Fuel Cell Systems, LLC ("GEFCS"), GE Microgen, Inc., and Plug Power, Inc. (collectively, "Defendants"), for breach of contract, misrepresentation, conversion, constructive trust, unjust enrichment and an accounting under New York state law. The claims arise from disputes regarding a contract that the parties entered into in 2000, under which Soroof was to have exclusive distribution rights in Saudi Arabia for a fuel cell product (the "Contract"). Soroof commenced this action, seeking an estimated three million dollars in compensatory damages, after GEFCS failed to produce the fuel cells. * * *

Defendants have moved for judgment on the pleadings * * *. The parties have cross-moved for summary judgment, and Soroof has moved for sanctions. * * * For the reasons that follow, Defendants' motion for judgment on the pleadings will be granted and Plaintiff will be permitted to replead its claims for breach of contract and misrepresentation. Plaintiff's motion for sanctions and Defendants' application for attorneys' fees and costs will both be denied. Plaintiff's motion for partial summary judgment will be granted as to the request to pierce the veil of GEFCS and denied in all other respects. Defendants' summary judgment motion for dismissal of all claims will be granted with respect to GEFCS and denied with respect to GE Microgen and Plug Power.

BACKGROUND

For the purposes of evaluating Defendants' motion for judgment on the pleadings, all of the non-conclusory factual allegations of Plaintiff's Complaint are assumed to be true. Soroof is a company organized under the laws of the Kingdom of Saudi Arabia. Defendant GEFCS was a limited liability company made up of two members: GE Microgen and Plug Power. GEFCS was dissolved in 2006. On June 6, 2000, Soroof and GEFCS entered into a contract whereby Soroof was to distribute in Saudi Arabia GEFCS–produced Proton Exchange Membrane Fuel Cells, which were to meet specific contractual standards. Under the terms of the Contract, Soroof was required to pay GEFCS an up-front "non-refundable distributor fee" of one million U.S. dollars. Soroof was also required to use its "best efforts to sell, advertise and promote" the fuel cells in Saudi Arabia and to purchase a minimum number of fuel cells from GEFCS each year, including 100 units in the first year that commercial units became available,

300 units the second year and 500 units the third year. GEFCS was not, however, obligated to fulfill every Soroof order. Rather, the Contract obligated GEFCS to "use reasonable efforts to supply" the fuel cells to Soroof and to satisfy any "firm purchase orders" that were "accepted by GEFCS." GEFCS was also obligated to "share promptly [with Soroof] relevant information, including but not limited to product performance, failure and liability issues." The Contract specified further that GEFCS was not liable for any "incidental ... or consequential damages" that Soroof incurred, even in the event of tortious conduct or breach of contract and, also, that "[t]he total liability for GEFCS ... whether in contract, warranty, indemnity, tort (including negligence), strict liability, or otherwise, arising out of or related to this Agreement ... shall not exceed the amount that has been paid to GEFCS by [Soroof] under this Agreement." In the Contract, both parties represented that they had the "full authority and capacity to enter into and perform [their] obligations" under the Contract.

The Contract includes a merger clause, providing that the written document "contains the entire and only agreement between [Soroof] and GEFCS.... Any representations or terms and conditions relating to transactions within the scope of this Agreement which are not incorporated or referenced herein shall not be binding upon either Party." On December 31, 2005, the Contract expired on its own terms.

During discussions prior to the execution of the Contract, GEFCS officials told Soroof that they "stood ready to deliver the Product to Soroof within six months." However, no such delivery timetable was included in the Contract. In November of 2000, GEFCS informed Soroof that the fuel cells did not yet meet quality standards and thus were not ready for distribution. Over the remaining years of the Contract, GEFCS continued to tell Soroof that the product was not yet ready but would nevertheless be forthcoming. As a result, Soroof did not place any firm orders for the duration of the Contract, but maintained offices and employees and engaged in third-party negotiations in preparation for eventually distributing the fuel cells, spending an estimated two million U.S. dollars on these preparations. In 2005, GEFCS informed Soroof that it was unable to make fuel cells meeting the Contract's specifications and, in 2006, GE Microgen and Plug Power dissolved GEFCS.

On July 1, 2008, Soroof initiated arbitration proceedings against GEFCS, alleging that GEFCS had breached the Contract and misrepresented its ability to bring the fuel cells to market. Soroof moved to compel GE Microgen and Plug Power to join the arbitration. GEFCS moved to dismiss Soroof's claims, arguing that suit could not be brought against a dissolved LLC or its former member companies, that the terms of the Contract barred Soroof from recovering the consequential damages and one million dollar non-refundable payment, that GEFCS never breached the terms of the Contract and that the claims were, in any event, barred by New York's six-year statute of limitations. On November 9, 2009, the American Arbitration Association Panel (the "Arbitration Panel") denied GEFCS's motion, stating: "Respondent's motion to dismiss the claims in this arbitration is denied without prejudice to the filing of a motion for summary disposition at the close of discovery on the issues raised in the motion to dismiss and the merits of the arbitration claims."

Shortly thereafter, Soroof, GE Microgen and Plug Power entered into a Venue Agreement, discontinuing the arbitration and agreeing to litigate the controversy in this Court. * * *

DISCUSSION

* * *

Plaintiff's Motion for Partial Summary Judgment Nullifying GEFCS's Certificate of Cancellation and Defendants' Motion for Summary Judgment Dismissing Claims Against GEFCS

A limited liability company cannot be sued under Delaware law once the company's certificate of cancellation has been filed unless the plaintiff successfully seeks to have the company's certificate of cancellation nullified on the ground that the company was not "wound up" in compliance with Delaware law. * * * Plaintiff moves for partial summary judgment nullifying GEFCS's certificate of cancellation, asserting that GEFCS was wound up in contravention of Delaware law when GEFCS failed to make provision sufficient to provide compensation to Soroof for claims likely to arise at the time of dissolution. Defendants cross-move for summary judgment dismissing all claims against GEFCS, asserting that GEFCS had no obligation to make provision for Plaintiff's claims because GEFCS had no available assets at the time of dissolution. The applicable section of the Delaware LLC Act provides that:

> If there are sufficient assets, such claims and obligations [against an LLC] shall be paid in full and any such provision for payment made shall be made in full. If there are insufficient assets, such claims and obligations shall be paid or provided for according to their priority and, among claims of equal priority, ratably *to the extent of assets available therefor* (emphasis added).

LLC Act § 18–804(b). It is undisputed that GEFCS had no assets available to pay potential claims at the time of dissolution. * * * Because an LLC is obligated to make provision for claims only "to the extent of assets available therefor," GEFCS was not wound up in contravention of Delaware law when, lacking any real assets, it did not make adequate provision for Soroof's claims. Therefore, Plaintiff's motion for partial summary judgment nullifying GEFCS's certificate of cancellation will be denied, and Defendants' motion for summary judgment dismissing all claims against GEFCS will be granted.

* * *

PLAINTIFF'S MOTION TO PIERCE THE VEIL OF GEFCS

Plaintiff moves for partial summary judgment to pierce the veil of GEFCS, thereby enabling Plaintiff to pursue its claims against GE Microgen and Plug Power. Defendants argue in their cross-motion that Plaintiff has not proffered facts adequate to pierce the veil of GEFCS and that, therefore, all claims should be dismissed as against GE Microgen and Plug Power. "Delaware law permits a court to pierce the corporate veil where there is fraud or where [the corporation] is in fact a mere instrumentality or alter ego of its owner." *NetJets Aviation, Inc. v. LHC Commc'ns LLC*, 537 F.3d 168, 177 (2d Cir.2008) (citations and internal quotation marks omitted). "To prevail under the alter-ego theory of piercing the veil, a plaintiff need not prove that there was actual fraud but must show a mingling of the operations of the entity and its owner plus an overall element of injustice or unfairness." *Id.* (citation and internal quotation marks omitted). The factors that a court must consider when evaluating an alter-ego argument for veil piercing include:

> whether the corporation was adequately capitalized for the corporate undertaking; whether the corporation was solvent; whether dividends were paid, corporate records kept, officers and directors functioned properly, and other corporate formalities were observed; whether the dominant shareholder siphoned corporate funds; and whether, in general, the corporation simply functioned as a facade for the dominant shareholder.

Id. at 176–77. "These principles are generally applicable as well where one of the entities in question is an LLC rather than a corporation," except that "somewhat less emphasis is placed on whether the LLC observed internal formalities because fewer such formalities are legally required." *Id.* at 178. Overall, "no single factor can justify a decision to disregard the corporate entity, but ... some combination of them is required, and ... an overall element of injustice or unfairness must always be present, as well." *Id.* at 177.

Plaintiff has proffered evidence that GEFCS had no cash assets at the time of dissolution; that GEFCS had no employees and that the individuals working at GE-FCS were actually employees of Plug Power, Microgen or GE; and that GEFCS did not lease its office space but, instead, GE Microgen leased the office space from Plug Power. The office space did not have a plaque or other sign indicating the presence of GEFCS; instead, the space "was identified as GE Microgen." Plaintiff's uncontroverted proffers demonstrate an extensive "mingling of the operations" of GEFCS and its owners, such that GEFCS was a mere instrumentality or alter ego of GE Microgen and Plug Power, as well as an overall element of unfairness to Soroof. Defendants' proffers have not created a genuine issue of material fact such that a rational jury could find that piercing GEFCS's corporate veil is not warranted.

Plaintiff's motion for partial summary judgment piercing the veil of GEFCS will be granted so that Soroof may proceed with its claims against GE Microgen and Plug Power. Defendants' motion for summary judgment dismissing all claims against GE Microgen and Plug Power will be denied.

* * *

In Re BH S & B Holdings LLC[43]

United States Bankruptcy Court, S.D. New York.
420 B.R. 112, 52 Bankr.Ct.Dec. 125 (2009)

MARTIN GLENN, Bankruptcy Judge.

Pending before the Court are all of the defendants' motions to dismiss this adversary proceeding brought by the Official Committee of Unsecured Creditors (the "Committee"). Repeat corporate bankruptcies, sometimes by the same debtor and sometimes by a successor entity, particularly under current economic conditions, are, unfortunately, not uncommon. This case stands out, however, by the rapidity with which the debtors here, successors through a chapter 11, section 363 purchase in July 2008 of the Steve & Barry's women's clothing business for $163 million, subject to various adjustments, descended into their own chapter 11 cases in November 2008. The debtors' filing here was followed immediately by a court-approved going-out-of-business sale and the shuttering of 153 stores that the debtors' business plan had hoped to maintain, with the resulting loss of many jobs. The debtors are hopelessly insolvent. * * *

As explained below, Steve & Barry's assets were acquired from the Stone Barn LLC Chapter 11 estate by a group of private equity investors, and a firm specializing in the liquidation of retail stores, as well as by several owners of the Stone Barn LLC debtors. Initially capitalized by $225 million, including a $125 million first lien loan provided by Abelco Finance LLC ("Abelco"), an affiliate of Cerberus, a $75 million loan provided by a subordinated second lien facility from Defendant BH S & B Finco, LLC ("Finco"), and $25 million in equity from defendant BHY S & B Holdco LLC ("Holdco"). In three months of operation, in August, September and October, 2008, the acquired business rapidly burned through its available capital and the new owners declined to invest additional funds. This bankruptcy case followed.

The Committee commenced this adversary proceeding against the entities and individuals that were involved in the purchase and short-lived operations of the debtors, seeking to recover money for the estate, based on claims of piercing the corporate veil, breach of fiduciary duty and equitable subordination or recharacterization. The defendants have all moved to dismiss the Complaint. One thing that stands out here is the absence of any allegation that, during the debtors' short-lived and rapid path to bankruptcy, any of the defendants did anything to recover the money they invested or loaned to the debtors. In other words, the defendants too lost a lot of money as this venture failed.

For the reasons explained below, with the exception of the equitable subordination claim against defendant Finco, the Court concludes that the Complaint must be

---

43   Aff'd., In re BH S & B Holdings LLC, 807 F. Supp. 2d 199 (S.D.N.Y. 2011).

dismissed with prejudice. With respect to the equitable subordination claim against Finco, the Complaint is dismissed with leave to amend within 30 days of entry of this Opinion and Order.

BACKGROUND

The facts below are taken from the Complaint and the original, first, Second and Third Amended and Restated LLC Agreements of BH S & B Holdings, LLC ("Holdings"), and the Amended and Restated LLC Agreement of Holdings's indirect parent, BH S & B Holdco LLC ("Holdco") (collectively, the "LLC Agreements").

A. The First Bankruptcy and Sale of Steve & Barry's

This case arises out of the Bankruptcy Code § 363 sale of the bankrupt Steve & Barry's line of clothing stores and the subsequent bankruptcy filing by the purchaser, Holdings, and its operating subsidiaries (together with Holdings, the "Debtors"). * * * Steve & Barry's sold licensed university apparel and lifestyle brands, private label casual clothing and accessories for men, women and children, and exclusive celebrity branded lines of apparel and accessories. At the time it filed for bankruptcy on July 9, 2008, Steve & Barry's, through its parent corporation, S & B Industries, Inc., operated 276 stores. Steve & Barry's filed for bankruptcy due to a liquidity crisis caused by a host of reasons, including: delayed store openings, delayed receipts of tenant allowances, and reduced borrowing capacity arising from inventory appraisal reductions, all exacerbated by the instability in the credit markets.

On August 21, 2008, Holdings purchased a majority of the assets and liabilities of S & B Industries, Inc. in a § 363 sale in the Steve & Barry's bankruptcy proceeding. The purchase price for the acquisition was $163 million, subject to various adjustments. The Bankruptcy Court for the Southern District of New York approved the sale in an order on August 22, 2008.

* * *

DISCUSSION

* * *

B. Choice of Law

Since Holdings, Holdco and most of the other corporate entities here are based in Delaware, Delaware law applies to the veil-piercing and fiduciary-breach claims. * * * The parties also agreed in their briefs that Delaware law controlled. The Court will therefore apply Delaware law to the veil piercing and breach of fiduciary duty claims. * * *

C. Piercing the Corporate Veil

1. Standard

In general, the corporate form is sacrosanct and courts will not disturb it to hold shareholders of a corporation, or members of an LLC, liable. "There is, of course, no doubt that upon a proper showing corporate entities as between parent and subsidiary may be disregarded and the ultimate party in interest, the parent, be regarded in law and fact as the sole party in a particular transaction." *Pauley Petroleum Inc. v. Continental Oil Co.*, 239 A.2d 629, 633 (Del.1968). "Persuading a Delaware court to disregard the corporate entity is a difficult task." *LaSalle Nat'l Bank v. Perelman,* 82 F.Supp.2d 279, 295 (D.Del.2000) (citing *Harco Nat'l Ins. Co. v. Green Farms, Inc.,* 1989 WL 110537, at *9–10 (Del.Ch. Sept.19, 1989)). Piercing the corporate veil "may be done only in the interest of justice, when such matters as fraud, contravention of law or contract, public wrong, or where equitable consideration among members of the corporation require it...." *Pauley Petroleum,* 239 A.2d at 633.

Under Delaware law, to pierce the corporate veil and establish alter-ego liability, a plaintiff must show (1) that the parent and subsidiary "operated as a single economic entity," and (2) that an "overall element of injustice or unfairness is present." * * *

With respect to the first factor, determining whether the parent and subsidiary acted as a single economic entity, courts look to numerous factors, identified by the Third Circuit in *United States v. Pisani,* 646 F.2d 83, 88 (3d Cir.1981):(1) undercapitalization, (2) failure to observe corporate formalities, (3) nonpayment of dividends, (4) insolvency of the debtor corporation at the time, (5) siphoning off of the corporation'sfunds by the dominant parent, (6) absence of corporate records, and (7) the fact that the corporation is merely a façade for the operations of the dominant parent. * * * Examples of "corporate formalities" include "whether dividends were paid, corporate records kept, [and] officers and directors functioned properly." * * * "While no single factor justifies a decision to disregard the corporate entity, some combination of the above is required, and an overall element of injustice or unfairness must always be present, as well." * * * The Committee alleges that factors (1), (2) and (7) support piercing the corporate veil here.

With respect to the second factor required to pierce the corporate veil—a showing of unfairness or injustice—while a showing of fraud is not necessary, "the requisite injustice or unfairness ... is also not simple in nature but rather something that is similar in nature to fraud or a sham." * * * The "fraud or similar injustice ... must, in particular, 'be found in the defendants' use of the corporate form.' " * * * In other words, "the underlying cause of action, at least by itself, does not supply the necessary fraud or injustice. To hold otherwise would render the fraud or injustice element meaningless, and would sanction bootstrapping." * * * "A court shall only pierce the corporate veil in order to prevent fraud, illegality, or injustice, or the adverse effects thereof." * * *

Furthermore, at the motion to dismiss stage, it is insufficient to make conclusory "[a]llegations of mere domination or control by one entity over another.... Rather, the extent of the domination and control must preclude the controlled entity from having legal or independent significance of its own. There must be an abuse of the corporate form to effect a fraud or an injustice—some sort of elaborate shell game." * * *

* * *

3. Application of the Standard to the Committee's Complaint

The Committee argues that the following allegations in the Complaint support a finding that Bay Harbour and York, through Holdco, totally dominated Holdings and treated Holdings as a mere instrumentality: (a) Holdings was inadequately capitalized; (b) corporate formalities were not observed in that Holdings had no management or board of directors; and (c) Holdings functioned as a façade for Bay Harbour and York. Evaluating each of these allegations separately shows that they are insufficient to pierce the corporate veil.

a. Inadequate Capitalization

The Committee argues that Holdings was inadequately capitalized from its inception, since Holdings's business plan required the purchase of $100 million of merchandise, but Holdings only had $40 million in unencumbered cash on-hand. The Committee argues that this supports an inference that Holdings was established for a sham purpose and its corporate veil should be pierced.

As an initial matter, undercapitalization is rarely sufficient to pierce the corporate veil, because otherwise "the veil of every insolvent subsidiary or failed start-up corporation could be pierced." * * * The inquiry "is most relevant for the inference it provides into whether the corporation was established to defraud its creditors or other improper purpose such as avoiding the risks known to be attendant to a type of business." * * * When determining whether a subsidiary was adequately capitalized, courts focus on the initial capitalization: "whether a corporate entity was or was not set up for financial failure." *George Hyman Constr. Co. v. Gateman*, 16 F.Supp.2d 129, 152–53 (D.Mass.1998).

The Committee concedes in the Complaint that Holdings was established for a legitimate business purpose. [Holdings was established "for the purpose of entering into the APA, liquidating a portion of Steve and Barry'sretail stores, and continuing to operate the remaining stores and related business as a going concern".] Therefore, the defendants argue, even if the allegations regarding undercapitalization were true, it could not support the inference that Holdings was formed for an illegitimate business purpose, because such an inference would be contradicted by the Complaint itself. Further, the defendants argue that the allegations in the Complaint could not support a finding of undercapitalization in any event, because Holdings was initially capitalized with $225 million, with $55 million cash on-hand to operate its business ($40 million for inventory, plus a $15 million cash-cushion).

The Committee responds by arguing that the undercapitalization test focuses on unencumbered assets, not just cash available on hand. * * * The Committee argues that because the Abelco Loan, which represented $125 million of the $225 million initial capitalization, was subject to reductions based on inventory levels, there was no adequate capitalization for running the business beyond a couple of months. The defendants respond by arguing that with $55 million in cash on hand, Holdings had enough cash to purchase inventory.

The Court need not reach the question whether Holdings was adequately capitalized, because it finds that the allegations in the Complaint do not support a finding that Holdings was established as a sham entity. As noted above, the Complaint concedes that Holdings was initially a legitimate business. Therefore, even if it were true that Holdings was inadequately capitalized at the time, it could not support the inference that Holdings served an illegitimate purpose. In addition, the undercapitalization would be insufficient to pierce the corporate veil for the same reason articulated by Judge Gropper in [a prior decision]: it is a rare instance that the veil should be pierced because of undercapitalization, because otherwise every insolvent subsidiary would have its veil pierced. * * * Here, even if the allegations were true, the circumstances would not be unusual enough to support veil-piercing. Holdings had cash on hand, and, by the Complaint's own admission, sufficient funds to operate for at least a few months. Without any more unusual facts or circumstances, the facts as alleged, even if true, would not support disregarding the corporate form. * * *

b. Failure to Observe Corporate Formalities

The Committee alleges that Holdings failed to observe certain corporate formalities, further supporting piercing the corporate veil, including that Holdings had no Board meetings. Though the Committee failed to mention it, Holdings had a single Manager at all times—Bay Harbour, Holdco and then Intermediate Holdco; however, the Holdings LLC Agreements, which, as noted *supra*, the Court is considering for purposes of the motions to dismiss, make this clear. Furthermore, though the Committee failed to point it out, the Holdings LLC Agreements provide that each respective Manager had "all of the powers and authority of a managing member under the [Delaware Limited Liability Company] Act, including, without limitation all necessary authority to conduct the business of the [c]ompany, to open bank or brokerage accounts, to place orders for the purchase or sale of securities, to exercise all rights with respect thereto and to enter into and execute and deliver agreements and other instruments on behalf of the [c]ompany."

The Committee, did, however, allege that Holdings had no CEO until a few weeks before the bankruptcy filing; its CFO was a consulting firm reporting directly to the Bay Harbour and York members of Holdco's Board; all major (and many minor) strategic and financial decisions were made by Bay Harbour and York directly; and Holdings's management was generally kept in the dark. As a result of these allegations, and the fact that there were no Board meetings, the Committee argues that Holdings's corporate independence was illusory and was interposed to protect Bay Harbour and York from the consequences of their own actions.

While Bay Harbour and York put a lot of stock in the fact that Holdings was an LLC, and so corporate formalities need not be observed, "emerging caselaw illustrates that situations that result in a piercing of the limited liability veil are similar to those that warrant piercing the corporate veil." *NetJets Aviation, Inc. v. LHC Commc'ns, LLC,* 537 F.3d 168, 176 (2d Cir.2008). Indeed, as one treatise put it: "Every state that has enacted LLC piercing legislation has chosen to follow corporate law standards and not develop a separate LLC standard." *Id.* (citing J. Leet, J. Clarke, P. Nollkamper & P. Whynott, *The Limited Liability Company* § 11:130 at 11–9 (rev. ed.2007)). Nevertheless, in the LLC context, "somewhat less emphasis is placed on whether the LLC observed internal formalities because fewer such formalities are legally required." *Id.* at 178. Indeed, the Delaware Limited Liability Company Act (DLLCA) requires little more than that an LLC execute a proper certificate of formation, maintain a registered office in Delaware, have a registered agent for service of process in Delaware, and maintain certain records for membership and tax purposes. DEL.CODE ANN. tit. 6, § 18–101 *et seq.* (2009). Furthermore, whereas the Delaware General Corporations Law requires a corporation to be managed by a Board of Directors, unless the certificate of incorporation otherwise provides, the director of a corporation must be a "natural person." 8 Del.Code Ann. § 141 * * *. However, the DLLCA permits non-natural persons (including another limited liability company or a corporation) to serve as Managers of an LLC. See 6 Del.Code Ann. tit. 6 §§ 18–101; 18–401.

It is well-established that wholly-owned subsidiaries may share officers, directors and employees with their parent, without requiring the court to infer that the subsidiary is a mere instrumentality for the parent and without requiring the court to conclude that those officers and directors were not functioning properly. * * * As the Supreme Court recognized, "it is entirely appropriate for directors of a parent corporation to serve as directors of its subsidiary, and that fact alone may not serve to expose the parent corporation to liability for its subsidiary's acts." *United States v. Bestfoods*, 524 U.S. 51, 69, 118 S.Ct. 1876, 141 L.Ed.2d 43 (1998) * * *.

That Holdings'sparents retained decision-making authority is also insufficient to pierce the corporate veil. "Since courts generally presume that the directors are wearing their 'subsidiary hats' and not their 'parent hats' when acting for the subsidiary ... it cannot be enough to establish liability here that dual officers and directors made policy decisions and supervised activities at the facility." *Id.* at 69–70, 118 S.Ct. 1876 * * *. Courts refuse to pierce the veil just because parent corporations retain decision-making authority over subsidiaries. * * *

At the same time, in *Valley Finance, Inc. v. United States* * * * the corporation was solely owned by a single individual, who made all major corporate decisions, there was doubt as to whether a Board of Directors existed for part of the corporation's existence, the Board "played no meaningful role," directors met infrequently and approved corporate decisions and policies without discussion or question, but the individual owner also used corporate funds and staff for his own private purposes, the court permitted veil-piercing. *Valley Finance, Inc. v. United States*, 629 F.2d 162, 172 (D.C.Cir.1980). * * *

Here, Holdings is an LLC, not a closely held corporation. Furthermore, even though at all relevant times the only Manager of Holdings was the direct parent, Intermediate Holdco, or the indirect parent, Holdco, and thus, there was no board of managers, at least one court has determined that the lack of officers and directors in a subsidiary LLC is not a "persuasive veil-piercing factor." *Capricorn Investors*

III, L.P. v. Coolbrands Intern., Inc., 2009 WL 2208339 at *5 (N.Y.Sup.2009) (applying New York law). In *Capricorn Investors, III, L.P.,* the court determined that "Plaintiff's assertion that [the LLCs] have no officers or directors, and did not hold board or executive committee meetings are not persuasive veil piercing factors for an LLC, where plaintiff does not argue that management was required to be centralized in a board." Id. While presumably it was impossible for the sole managing member of Holdings (Holdco or Intermediate Holdco) to make decisions wearing anything other than their "parent hats," because of their own duties to their members * * *, the DLLCA permits "Members" to be other LLCs or corporations, impliedly permitting those LLCs or corporations to serve in an entity capacity in which they continue to owe fiduciary duties to their own Members.

Other allegations made by the Committee do not support an inference that Holdings did not observe corporate formalities. None of the allegations suggest impropriety or abuse of the corporate form. The failure to hold board meetings does not support piercing, because under the DLLCA, Holdings did not have to hold board meetings or observe other formalities. Indeed, it is not at all odd that a board meeting was not held in Holdings's brief life between the August 2008 acquisition and the November 2008 bankruptcy.

The remaining allegations with respect to the officers of Holdings—that Holdings lacked a CEO until a few weeks before the bankruptcy filing, that CFO functions were outsourced to a company that reported directly to Bay Harbour, and that management was generally kept in the dark—are either (1) not required under the DLLCA, and so are insufficient to support a finding of total domination and control sufficient to pierce the corporate veil, or (2) too conclusory to survive a motion to dismiss. * * *

c. Whether Holdings Was a Façade for Its Parents and Equity and Fairness Require Piercing the Corporate Veil

Finally, the Committee alleges generally that Holdings was but a mere façade for Bay Harbour and York to achieve a quick profit while protecting themselves from a downturn by secretly planning to liquidate as quickly as possible should things go wrong. The Committee appears to make this allegation to comply with both factors required to pierce the veil—that there was a "single economic entity," and an "overall element of fraud or injustice."

Under Delaware law, the corporate veil will be pierced only if the defendants used the corporate structure itself to further the fraud or injustice; the "underlying cause of action, at least by itself, does not supply [it]." * * * In other words, "the plaintiff must plead facts showing that the corporation is a sham and exists for no other purpose than as a vehicle for fraud." * * * "The extent of the domination and control must preclude the controlled entity from having legal or independent significance of its own. There must be an abuse of the corporate form to effect a fraud or an injustice—some sort of elaborate shell game. To survive a motion to dismiss, a plaintiff must allege facts that the controlling owners operated the company as an 'incorporated pocketbook' and used the corporate form to shield themselves from liability." * * *

The Committee's allegations here are virtually identical to the allegations that numerous courts have found insufficient and dismissed. For example, in [one case], the plaintiffs relied on the following factors to argue that the corporate subsidiary was a sham and that its corporate veil should be pierced: (1) the subsidiary was undercapitalized and insolvent since its inception; (2) there was significant overlap in management between the parent and the subsidiary; (3) directors of the parent had ownership interests in the subsidiary; (4) the subsidiary never had a sustainable financial business, and was reliant on the parent for financing; (5) the parent provided managerial services and its officers directed the day-to-day operations of the subsidiary, exercising "de facto" or "effective control" over the affairs of the subsidiary and its directors; and (6) the subsidiary served as a tool to further the interests of the defendants. [In deciding that case,] Judge Gropper noted: "[A]bsent an allegation of direct injury to the corporation, or a diversion of goods or services from the company, it cannot be presumed that the alleged wrongful concealment of [the subsidiary's] insolvency harmed or injured [the subsidiary]." * * *

Judge Gropper pointed out that there was no "de facto control" of the subsidiary by the parents to pierce the veil because "at least several directors for [the subsidiary] were not directors of either [parent]." * * * In [another case,] the Delaware Chancery Court determined that a majority shareholder did not exercise de facto control over the board of directors of a corporation in such a manner as to "frustrate or foil" the corporation's efforts to raise needed financing or capital, in order to protect its position as controlling shareholder. * * * The court noted that board members were, among other things, a former officer of the majority shareholder and its designee, had a "consulting agreement" with the majority shareholder by which the compensation was not significant and generous, participated in lobbying efforts with respect to a proposal of the majority shareholder and scheduled meetings at the majority shareholder's offices. * * * Also, in *Aronson v. Lewis*, the Court found that a 47% stockholder did not exercise control over the board with respect to the plaintiff's claim of demand futility in the context of a derivative action where plaintiff alleged the stockholder "personally selected" each director, and the board approved an agreement which the plaintiff alleged constituted a breach of fiduciary duty. *Aronson*, 473 A.2d at 815 (internal citation omitted). The court determined "a plaintiff charging domination and control of one or more directors must allege particularized facts manifesting a direction of corporate conduct in such a way as to comport with the wishes or interests of the corporation (or persons) doing the controlling." * * * Here, [it does not] matter whether Holdco or Intermediate Holdco, through their boards, were exercising de facto control of the subsidiary; the DLLCA did not require the Holdings to have a board of managers made of independent natural persons; it permitted Holdings's parents, Holdco and then Intermediate Holdco, to be the sole Manager.

Similarly, in *Trevino*, conclusory allegations that (1) a subsidiary was not wholly independent of its parent, (2) that it was under the utter and complete domination and control of its parent, and (3) that it was formed for the purpose of facilitating the parents' business and limiting their liability were found insufficient to survive a motion to dismiss, because they did not show how the defendants abused or caused in an injustice with the use of the corporate form. *Trevino*, 583 F.Supp.2d at 529–31. Finally, in *Ticketplanet.com*, the chapter 7 trustee alleged that (1) there was significant overlap in the directors of the parents and debtor and other subsidiaries; (2) the parent'sprincipal had an ownership interest in all of the entities; (3) the parent'sprincipals were affiliated with an intermediate company, and became involved in the debtor'soperations; and (4) the parent'sprincipals, through an intermediary, dominated and controlled the debtor for their own personal gain and used the debtor and another subsidiary as an incorporated pocketbook. *Ticketplanet.com*, 313 B.R. at 71. Judge Gropper dismissed the complaint because the allegations did not demonstrate that "there was an overall element of injustice or unfairness present that arose from abuse of the corporate form. An overlap in ownership, officers and directors and responsibilities is not uncommon or impermissible." *Id.*

These cases all show that allegations such as the Committee's here are insufficient to survive a motion to dismiss, because even if true they would not rise to the level of injustice or fraud that would justify disregarding the corporate form. Here, the Committee merely alleges "deception of creditors concerning the Debtor's plans and prospects for operating as a going concern." In addition, the Complaint's allegations—specifically, that Holdings was formed for a legitimate business purpose and that it had $55 million in cash-on-hand to fund operations—undermine any veil-piercing claim the Committee could come up with. Therefore, the veil-piercing claim is dismissed with prejudice.

*   *   *

NOTES AND QUESTIONS

I. YOU HAVE NOW READ two cases regarding LLC veil piercing, with opposite outcomes. Despite that, both cases purport to apply Delaware law to the issue of whether the LLC veil ought to be pierced, and both cases were decided by non-Delaware courts; one was a decision from the Southern District of New York, and the other was affirmed on appeal by that same district. LLC veil piercing is a very closely monitored issue, by practitioners and academics alike. Part of the difficulty enveloping this issue is—as has been the case with other aspects of LLCs—whether the law of corporations applies to LLCs by analogy. Some states' LLC statutes explicitly provide that the veils of LLCs may be pierced in appropriate circumstances, but Delaware is not among them. Hence, much of the debate used to center on whether veil piercing even had a place in Delaware LLC law. More recently, however, courts have found that veil piercing does apply to LLCs in appropriate circumstances. Of course, the debate then shifted focus to what these enigmatic "appropriate circumstances" might be. By this point, you have been extensively exposed to the careful approach of Delaware courts—they seem especially mindful of the central importance their decisions have in relation to Delaware's position as the central source of much of American corporate law. Given your experience, which case would you guess is more true to Delaware law? The length of the analysis ought to give you a hint in answering this question, as "persuading a Delaware court to disregard the corporate entity is a difficult task." In fact, *Soroof*, the first case you read, marks the first time that a Delaware LLC veil has been pierced by a court purporting to apply Delaware law. Did it seem to you like the plaintiffs in that case faced "a difficult task"? Do you find the court's analysis in that case satisfactory? *Soroof* has sent shockwaves throughout the legal community, with several commentators claiming that no Delaware court would have pierced the veil under the fact presented in that case. Given the much more careful and thorough approach of the *BH S & B* court, you ought to be able to discern why.

For one, as the *BH S & B* court noted, "at the motion to dismiss stage...the extent of the domination and control must preclude the controlled entity from having legal or independent significance of its own. There must be an abuse of the corporate form to effect a fraud or an injustice—some sort of elaborate shell game." Are you convinced that GEFCS had no independent significance? Note that even if the sole purpose behind GEFCS was to limit liability, that alone is not sufficient to sustain a veil-peircing claim, as the *BH S & B* court takes pains to highlight. What about the fact that "in the LLC context, 'somewhat less emphasis is placed on whether the LLC observed internal formalities because fewer such formalities are legally required'...It is well-established that wholly-owned subsidiaries may share officers, directors and employees with their parent, without requiring the court to infer that the subsidiary is a mere instrumentality for the parent"? The *Soroof* court focused on the fact that GEFCS employees were actually employees of the parents; that GEFCS did not lease its office space but, instead, GE Microgen leased the office space, which did not have a plaque or other sign indicating the presence of GEFCS. Do you find these facts significant?

. . . .

2. WHY, THEN, did the Soroof court pierce the veil? You only read parts of the case; in those parts you didn't read, the plaintiff made several claims; among them, count one, a breach of contract claim, on the grounds that GEFCS did not deliver any fuel cells. Count two was a misrepresentation claim, on the grounds that GEFCS did not communicate to Soroof that they were unable to provide the fuel cells, even though they allegedly knew they could not deliver the fuel cells as early as four years prior to letting the plaintiff know. These first two claims were dismissed because they were insufficiently pled, but the court dismissed those without prejudice, so that the plaintiff could replead. Given that, and given that GEFCS had since been cancelled, it is likely the court saw that without piercing the veil, the plaintiffs would not be able to recover on the two counts even if successful. So it may be that the court was merely facilitating what it believed to be potentially meritorious claims in the future. If this is the case, was the *Soroof* court wise in deciding the way it did? Before you answer, it is worth noting that veil piercing "is not a separate and independent cause of action, but rather is merely a procedure to enforce an underlying judgment." Thus, without an underlying liability, there is no basis for piercing the veil of limited liability. Was there an underlying judgment in Soroof, or merely the potential for one? Could the court have been worried that potentially meritorious claims might have been defeated on account of GEFCS having been dissolved?

3. AMONG THE DANGERS of wanton veil-piercing you read in *BH S & B*, was that "the underlying cause of action, at least by itself, does not supply the necessary fraud or injustice. To hold otherwise would render the fraud or injustice element meaningless, and would sanction bootstrapping." Do you understand what this means? As you have gathered, veil piercing is supposed to be an exceptional remedy. As such, courts are reluctant to make it readily available, and that is effectuated by adding elements that must be satisfied. The fraud element, were it allowed to be satisfied by garden-variety fraud, would essentially make veil piercing available anytime fraud is claimed successfully. In demanding that the fraud stem from the misuse of the corporate form itself, courts are signaling that limited liability will be honored unless it is abused, and in no other circumstance. The *Soroof* court found, in rather conclusory a fashion, "an overall element of unfairness to Soroof." Does this strike you as the requisite unfairness sufficient to pierce a veil? What exactly was the unfairness to Soroof? That they drafted a bad contract, perhaps?

4. COMPLICATING THIS PIERCING issue further is a new form, dubbed the "series LLCs." As is usually the case, Delaware spearheaded this innovation in 1996.[44] You have noticed that courts are responsive to the reality that part of what makes LLCs appealing is their convenience—this is why courts relax the corporate formalities factor, for example. In the same vein, the Delaware legislature provided a mechanism to make LLCs even easier to manage and maintain. Under an addition to the

---

44   Carol R. Goforth, The Series LLC, and A Series of Difficult Questions, 60 Ark. L. Rev. 385, 387 (2007).

Delaware Limited Liability Company Act, LLCs observing certain requirements can set up a series under a single LLC, where each member of the series can have independent ownership, management, and control and own distinct assets, to which limited liability attaches. By way of example, instead of having to set up ten different LLCs to keep liability compartmentalized, an owner can opt to set up a single LLC with 10 series subsumed under it. The motivation seems to be to further simplify LLC filing and keep costs associated with it at a minimum. A drawback is that this theoretical separation of liability amongst the series is so far untested. We don't yet know how veil-piercing attempts in series LLC's will be treated by the courts. Presumably, all members within a series will have a near-identical factor analysis as far as veil piercing is concerned. This is because it seems safe to assume that a common owner will treat all members of the series very similarly. But then, if a successful veil piercing claim is made against one member of the series, it is possible that one has made a successful argument to pierce all the veils in the series. For more on series LLCs and different states' approach to them, see Carol R. Goforth, The Series LLC, and A Series of Difficult Questions, 60 Ark. L. Rev. 385, 387 (2007).

- -

5. THE *SOROOF* COURT also cited undercapitalization as one of the grounds for piercing GEFCS veil. Yet, "undercapitalization is rarely sufficient to pierce the corporate veil, because otherwise 'the veil of every insolvent subsidiary or failed start-up corporation could be pierced.' " If limited liability is intended to protect a company when it becomes insolvent, then why is it that undercapitalization is a factor when considering a veil piercing claim? Is this consistent? Is it wise?

IV. Why Corporations?

IF THERE IS A SINGLE OVERARCHING TAKEAWAY from this chapter, it is that LLCs are the rising stars of the business associations' world. In fact, the numbers suggest that in Delaware, over three new LLCs are formed for every one new corporation.[45] LLCs essentially permit the parties involved to do whatever they deem best suits their needs. In terms of attractiveness, their adaptability is rivaled perhaps only by their tax benefits. Of course, their success is perhaps not correctly attributed entirely to the flexibility of LLCs, but also to the erosion of the benefits of rival entities. At any rate, one thing you might naturally wonder, is why corporations at all?

As a threshold matter, consider that that drafting specialized LLC member agreements entails considerable expense, and spending money to create something that already exists in standard form does not seem always to make sense. In addition to the added costs of drafting among multiple parties, there are other considerations we have seen, such as the fact that the LLC Agreement defines the scope and existence of fiduciary duties. Of course, this also means that only parties to the agreement can be found to have breached such duties, unlike in corporations. Moreover, as suggested in this chapter, LLC law is largely unsettled on fairly central matters.

It is widely thought that another drawback of LLCs is that only Corporations have the ability to go public. This is not true, strictly speaking. LLCs can be publicly traded.[46] However, this is rare, and seemingly for good reasons. For one, corporations offer a far more established and well understood legal platform. Second, a startup company seeking to have an IPO will find that venture capitalists will rarely invest in anything that is not a Delaware corporation. A further discouragement is the limitations on transferability in LLCs, that do not generally occur in corporations.[47] Further, corporations offer perpetual existence, while some LLC statutes provide for mandatory liquidation provisions at a set date.

Trying to delve deeper into this question, one author—a titan in alternative entity law—suggested political reasons for the enduring prevalence of corporations. He wrote:

> The main problem with trying to get corporate features without incorporating is not that firms have been expressly prohibited from doing so, but the risk that courts may not enforce novel contracts without statutory

---

[45]   Rodney D. Chrisman, Llcs Are the New King of the Hill: An Empirical Study of the Number of New Llcs, Corporations, and Lps Formed in the United States Between 2004-2007 and How Llcs Were Taxed for Tax Years 2002-2006, 15 Fordham J. Corp. & Fin. L. 459, 460 (2010)

[46]   See, e.g., In re Atlas Energy Res., LLC, CIV.A. 4589-VCN, 2010 WL 4273122 (Del. Ch. Oct. 28, 2010).

[47]   See Larry E. Ribstein, Why Corporations?, 1 Berkeley Bus. L.J. 183, 188-89 (2004)

authorization. Courts and legislators historically have been hostile to non-corporate limited liability. * * * Thus, although limited liability is now widely available ... the historical constraints on the spread of limited liability may help explain why non-corporate limited liability forms have not been developed or widely used for publicly held firms. Parties who attempt to create new forms of limited liability risk judicial non-enforcement of the liability shield.

Even if a state recognizes a novel form of limited liability, another state might not enforce the shield. Although the internal affairs rule enforcing formation-state law generally applies to established business associations, in other contexts interstate enforcement would be subject to the general rules on contractual choice of law. Applying those rules, a court might not enforce contractual choice of a state limited liability rule, particularly if no party resides in the forum state and limited liability in novel contexts is considered contrary to local public policy.

* * *The move to publicly held [non-corporate forms also] presents a kind of chicken-egg problem. Like starting a new telephone network or computer operating system, the new system may not take hold until the network is established, which cannot happen until the system is accepted.

There may be other reasons for continued dominance of the corporate form that relate neither to its efficiency nor to politics. For example, the switch into [forms other than the corporation] depends both on suitable ... forms being developed and firms getting adequate legal advice about the availability of these alternatives. Lawyers may have reputational incentives to participate in making "wholesale" changes. However, in order to make these changes on the retail level of individual clients, lawyers have to be willing to learn about the new forms and advise on their use. They may be concerned that their investments in the new learning will not pay off in higher fees or that the increased risk of malpractice in giving such advice exceeds any additional fees.

Larry E. Ribstein, *Why Corporations?*, 1 Berkeley Bus. L.J. 183, 226-231 (2004).

Part 4

Corporations

The Iron Rolling Mill (Modern Cyclopes), by Adolph Friedrich Erdmann von Menzel (c. 1872–1875)

15

BASICS OF THE CORPORATION

I. Choice of Entity

ALTHOUGH MOST OF OUR TIME IN THIS CHAPTER will be spent studying aspects of the corporation, it is still important to understand the basics of the other business associations, how they differ from corporations, and why a business might choose one form over another. Although each state has authorized different forms of business associations, the same types of organizations exist throughout the nation, and the laws governing them are similar. Three basic business forms were widely used in Britain and pre-Revolutionary America—the general partnership, the limited partnership, and the corporation.[1] The other business forms available to modern enterprises include a variety of hybrid forms in which some benefits of partnerships are combined with some characteristics of corporations. The following is an outline of the currently most-popular business organizations.

> **THREE BASIC BUSINESS FORMS** were widely used in Britain and pre-Revolutionary America—the general partnership, the limited partnership, and the corporation.

---

1   Robert W. Hamilton, *Entity Proliferation*, 37 Suffolk U. L. Rev. 859, 862 (2004).

A. SOLE PROPRIETORSHIP

A *sole proprietorship*, the simplest business organization to start and maintain, is an unincorporated business owned by one individual. There is no separate existence of the business apart from the owner, so all liabilities of the proprietorship are personal liabilities, and all income or expenses of the business must be included on the owner's personal tax return.

Advantages of the sole proprietorship include ease of creation and termination—states do not require any organizational documents to be filed—and operational flexibility, as the business is operated entirely at the discretion of the owner, without required formalities such as shareholder meetings. The principal disadvantage is the unlimited liability that results because there is no separate existence of the business apart from the owner.[2]

B. GENERAL PARTNERSHIP

A *general partnership*, which is the type of partnership you have studied, for example, in the *Croisant and National Biscuit Company* cases, is the simplest business organization for two or more people jointly carrying on a trade or business. General partnerships can be formed by nothing more than a verbal agreement among the partners that each party will contribute and expects to share in the profits and losses of the business. Frequently, however, written agreements and contracts will be drafted by lawyers to ensure that the organization is precisely as the partners want it. Until very recently, in most jurisdictions, a partnership was not actually a legally separate entity, so the partnership could not hold property, sue or be sued, and (as is still true) was not taxed as a separate entity.

Advantages of general partnerships include the ease of formation and, as indicated earlier, avoidance of the "double tax" corporations and their shareholders must pay. This feature is sometimes referred to as "flow-through" taxation. Income and expenses of the partnership are taxed only once, on individual partners' personal tax returns. The disadvantages of partnerships include joint and several liability on the part of individual partners for the entirety of the partnership's obligations and the fact that each partner is potentially an agent of the partnership able to bind all the others. In addition, ownership of a partnership is generally not transferable and partnerships are not perpetual, dissolving when one partner dies or withdraws from the business.[3]

C. LIMITED PARTNERSHIP

While the general partnership emerged from the common law, the *limited partnership* is a creature of statute. Still, a limited partnership is in many respects similar to a general partnership, the primary difference being that a limited partnership involves

---

2   Small Business Opportunity Clinic, Northwestern University School of Law. "Comparison of Business Entities Overview," (privately distributed paper prepared by David Gaffin, used by permission of the author).

3   Id.

limited liability for one or more of the partners. A limited partnership must have at least one *general partner*, which general partner will be personally liable for the limited partnership's debts and obligations and will actively manage the business. This general partner can be an individual or a corporation. The other partners, called, not surprisingly, *limited partners*, are not liable for partnership obligations, do not control the day-to-day operations of the partnership, and are not authorized to act as agents of the limited partnership. When limited partners withdraw or transfer their interest in the business, the limited partnership does not dissolve.

As in general partnerships, the partner's share of the income and expenses of the limited partnership are reported on each partner's personal tax returns. Another advantage of limited partnerships is that the law of limited partnerships is well established and well settled, unlike that of other more recently-developed business associations. The law governing limited partnerships is more complex than that of general partnerships, however, and several state and federal requirements must be fulfilled to set up this type of partnership. Another disadvantage of limited partnership is the fragility of a limited partner's liability shield. In the past, a limited partner could be personally liable for the partnership's debts if he participated in the control and management of the business. This "control rule" was eliminated in the Uniform Limited Partnership Act of 2001, which made it easier for a limited partner to participate in business as a limited partner, and allowed for a limited partner to become a general partner with the implied consent of the other partners, instead of requiring written consent.[4]

D. LIMITED LIABILITY PARTNERSHIP (LLP)

A *limited liability partnership* is organized as a general partnership but allows for all partners to avoid personal liability for firm obligations, whether or not they are active in the management of the business. This is a relatively new business form, authorized first in Texas in the late 1980s, and now adopted in virtually all states.[5] LLPs are popular business organizations for law and accounting firms, but not widely used in commercial businesses. LLPs are essentially hybrids of the general partnership and corporate forms, including the tax and control advantages of a partnership and the limited liability advantage of a corporation. One disadvantage of the LLP is that, as in a partnership, ownership is not transferable. Another disadvantage of the LLP form is increased formalities—LLPs must register with the permitting state, and many states require that a minimum amount of liability insurance be carried by the firm or that the firm segregate client funds from its own.

---

4   Carter G. Bishop, *The New Limited Partner Liability Shield: Has the Vanquished Control Rule Unwittingly Resurrected Lingering Limited Partner Estoppel Liability as well as Full General Partner Liability?*, 37 Suffolk U. L. Rev. 667, 668 (2004).

5   Hamilton, 37 Suffolk U. L. Rev. at 863.

E. LIMITED LIABILITY LIMITED PARTNERSHIP (LLLP)

A *limited liability limited partnership* is permitted by statute in something less than half of the states. This business organization applies the limited liability partnership concept of limited personal liability to the limited partnership concept of general and limited partners. In an LLLP, there is still a distinction between general and limited partners' roles in the organization, as in a limited partnership, but all general partners have the protection of an LLP—no personal liability. Because the name serves as a beacon to third parties that they may not rely upon the credit and personal liability of any partner in the firm, this organization theoretically eliminates liability through estoppel against partners, as may have been a problem in limited partnerships.[6] As with all other partnerships, the business is not a separate legal entity, and individual partners must report their share of the firm's expenses and income on their personal tax returns.

F. CORPORATION

The most significant features of a *corporation* include (1) limited liability for share-holders, (2) free transferability of ownership interest, (3) perpetual existence, (4) separation of ownership and management ("centralized control"), and (5) legal status of the corporation as a separate entity ("artificial personality"). As a legally separate entity, a corporation can sue and be sued, can own property, and can generally exercise rights as a person would, including enjoying the benefits of some Constitutional protections. A corporation must generally pay income taxes as a separate entity, and shareholders must pay taxes on the dividends or distributions they receive from their corporations (this is the so-called "double taxation" applicable to corporations and their shareholders).

Corporations were originally permitted only if the King granted a charter, and after American independence the state legislatures took the place of the King in making the decision whether corporations would be permitted to exist. During the course of the Nineteenth century, instead of requiring a separate legislative act, incorporation became routinely available if certain state requirements were met and certain information was filed with a state official, usually the Secretary of State. Each of the fifty states has its own separate corporations though there are increasing similarities. Generally speaking, corporations are statutorily required to have a three-tiered structure, including shareholders, directors and officers.

Shareholders are the owners of the corporation, but they have limited managerial control. Their primary power is to elect and remove directors, although they must also vote on major decisions of the corporation, such as the amendment of the corporate charter, mergers or sale of substantially all of the assets of the corporation.

Directors have general management power, and depending on the size of the corporation, the directors either monitor the management or act as managers themselves.

---

6   Bishop, supra, 37 Suffolk U. L. Rev. at 716.

Large corporations often have professional managers to conduct the day-to-day business operations, and the Board of Directors, who are legally required to meet at least once a year, are responsible for voting on major decisions, and for conducting votes by shareholders when those are required. Directors may be paid for their services, or may be compensated by stock or stock options in the corporation. Directors, like partners, are fiduciaries, who must place the interests of the corporation above their own. Directors are agents of the *corporation*, not of its shareholders. More, as has been held in some cases, they are bound to exercise their independent judgment and cannot simply take orders from shareholders.

Officers of the corporation are selected and terminated by the board of directors. Typical officers might include a Chairman of the Board, a President, a Secretary, a Treasurer, a Comptroller, and assorted Vice Presidents. Generally officers and their responsibilities are not spelled out in statutes, but will vary with the individual corporate charter or bylaws The precise nature of the officers' duties and powers will thus vary across corporations, but an officer's position may carry with it certain generally understood powers, giving rise to apparent or inherent authority. For example, Presidents can usually enter into contracts on behalf of the corporation, treasurers and comptrollers have broad power to monitor the financial activity of the corporation, and secretaries will have custody over the shareholder lists and the books and records of the corporation. In theory, at least, the officers carry out the directors' decisions, rather than setting policy for the corporation.

There are two main types of corporations we will be considering. One is the "publicly-held" corporation, so-called because share ownership is widely dispersed among members of the public. A second is the "closely-held" or "close" corporation, the most notable feature of which is that ownership is in a smaller number of shareholders. In close corporations, the divisions between shareholders, directors, and officers may not be as distinct as in larger, publicly traded, publicly held corporations, and some states, most notably Delaware, permit close corporations entirely to dispense with the three-tiered structure of publicly-held corporations, and have shareholders manage the corporation as if they were partners. When they choose to do so, they assume a fiduciary liability akin to that of partners. In all the states, close corporations generally are operated more informally, although they must still meet some formal statutory requirements. Other significant characteristics of close corporations are that they are often family-run businesses, there is generally not a significant public market for their shares, and the transferability of those shares is often limited by shareholders' agreements. A third type of corporation, the charitable corporation, is not, strictly speaking, a business organization, and is beyond the scope of this book.

Corporations are similarly divided into two types under the United States Internal Revenue Code, called subchapter "S" and subchapter "C" corporations.

In Subchapter "S" corporations (sometimes called "S-corps") the shareholders are treated like partners for tax purposes, and profits or losses of the S-corp are taxed directly to shareholders. Small corporations may elect subchapter S status only if they meet certain requirements: the corporation must have no more than 75 shareholders, only one class of stock is permitted, all shareholders must be US residents, and all shareholders must be individuals and not other corporate entities. The number of shareholders allowed in an S corporation changed from 35 to 75 in 1996.[7] The basic advantage of S corporation election is to avoid double taxation. An S corporation is generally exempt from federal income tax, so shareholders include on their personal tax returns their share of the corporation's income, deductions and losses.

A "C corporation," on the other hand, is any corporation which does not meet the criteria for S corporation election or has not chosen to become an S corporation. A C corporation can have an unlimited number of shareholders, non-US resident shareholders, and can be owned by S or C corporations or any other business form. A C corporation, is, of course, subject to "double" taxation.

It is likely that the primary advantage of the corporate form is shareholder limited liability. A corporation is also the entity through which shares can most easily be marketed to the public (except for close corporations), which market availability is often essential for raising large amounts of capital. Other advantages of the corporate form include free transferability of interest, and potentially perpetual existence. This is to be contrasted with the partnership form, where ownership interests cannot change hands without the agreement of all the partners, and where the business ends if any partner wishes to end it.[8]

The process of incorporation is also more formalized, regulated and expensive than the process required of partnerships or sole practitioners, where normally nothing must be filed with the state. All states require a filing procedure for corporations, require a filing fee that may amount to several hundred dollars or more, and often require regular reports as well as the filing of corporate tax returns. An important feature of corporate law is that the internal affairs of the corporation (the relationship among officers, directors, and shareholders) will be governed by the state of incorporation, and one can choose to incorporate in any state, even if corporate headquarters will be in another state, and business will be conducted in still other states. Some states require that any corporations operating in their jurisdiction must make certain filings or pay certain fees, but all states recognize that when they deal with corporations it is the law of the state of incorporation that governs internal matters, the so-called "internal affairs" doctrine.

A closely held corporation will generally choose to incorporate in the state in which it expects to do business. As a corporation must pay taxes on both its income and a franchise tax to the state for the privilege of conducting business in the state, limiting the number of states in which a small corporation must pay taxes is seen as an advantage. For larger, publicly held corporations, on the other hand, state taxes

---

7   26 USCS § 1361 (2004).

8   Comparison of Business Entities Overview, Small Business Opportunity Clinic, Northwestern University School of Law.

and filings are frequently inconsequential compared to overall revenues. Considerations for choosing where to incorporate publicly-held companies often include how state laws affect business organization or shareholder voting. States generally wish to encourage incorporation, because of the revenue from filing fees, and some states have crafted their corporate law governing internal affairs to encourage such incorporation. As we will see, of all the states, Delaware has been so successful in crafting its corporate law, that most large publicly-held United States corporations now choose to incorporate in Delaware.

After choosing a state of incorporation, a corporation must file a "certificate of incorporation," "articles of incorporation" or a "charter" with the state (the three terms refer to the same document), which charter contains provisions meeting statutory requirements. The certificate of incorporation designates the classes of stock and the number of shares that the corporation is authorized to issue, as well as other important corporate specifications, including such matters as the number of Board Members, the kinds of officers, the corporation's purpose, and the location of its headquarters. The "bylaws" of the corporation, which specify the manner in which the corporation will conduct its ongoing operations, including such matters as how vacancies in the board are to be filled, how many members of the board constitute a quorum, which officers can perform which functions, etc., must generally also be filed with the state of incorporation.

G. LIMITED LIABILITY COMPANY (LLC)

A *limited liability company*, as we have seen in the preceding case, is a relatively new business form, developed since the late 1970s, which provides the limited liability and tax benefits of an S corporation, commonly called "partnership-tax status," without the restrictions placed on S corporation ownership.[9] Like a corporation and unlike a partnership, an LLC is treated as a legally separate entity, distinct from its members. As such, the LLC members are shielded from personal liability for the business's obligations, whether or not they are active in management. Another benefit of an LLC is the breadth of flexibility in management—it can be managed as if it were a sole proprietorship, partnership or corporation. The manner in which the LLC will be managed will be set out in a "Members Agreement" which might be regarded as analogous to the Corporate Charter, or the Partnership Agreement. Members can also transfer their interest in an LLC without causing dissolution, an advantage over partnerships and LLPs.

LLCs are becoming the most popular form for new small businesses; over 697,000 were formed in 2002, as compared to 63,000 partnerships.[10] LLCs are primarily replacing general and limited partnerships, although they provide a good

---

9   Hamilton, supra, 37 Suffolk U. L. Rev. at 863

10   2002 Report of International Association of Commercial Administrators (IACA), *www.iaca.org*, as cited by Daniel S. Kleinberger, *A User's Guide to the New Uniform Limited Partnership Act*, 37 Suffolk U. L. Rev. 583, 588 n31–32. (Fall, 2004).

alternative to closely-held corporations as well. The law governing LLCs is not yet well established, and can vary greatly between states. In Florida and Texas, for example, LLCs are taxed as corporations for purposes of the state corporate franchise tax, eliminating some incentive for forming this type of organization in those states. In Illinois and some other states LLCs are more expensive to form than corporations due to higher initial filing fees and annual report filing fees.[11] We will occasionally refer to the LLC in what follows, but, again, our primary interest is in the corporation. While LLC case law is still in its infancy, it does appear that for many matters, most prominently shareholder liability for entity debts when shareholders abuse their power to the detriment of third parties ("piercing the corporate veil"), the law of LLC's tracks that of corporations.

II. A Short History of the Corporation

AS WE WILL SOON SEE, there is now and has been for some time considerable debate about the social responsibility of American corporations. At one time it might have been said that there was a burden of proof that incorporators had to meet before the monarch, or the legislature, as a matter of discretion, would confer what was then regarded as the *privilege* of incorporation. That privilege was only to be granted if incorporation served the public good, and that notion is not completely absent from the law even today. Still, it is more common to view incorporation as a ministerial act, one to which any incorporators meeting simple and formal registration requirements can claim a right. The view of incorporation as a privilege granted to serve the public interest, however, was central to corporate existence through many centuries, and a full understanding of the law of corporations and the policies it seeks to implement is impossible without some consideration of this history.

The corporate form dates back to the early Roman Empire, but its use for private commercial enterprise is considerably more recent. Blackstone attributed the idea for the corporate form to Numa Pompilius, a Roman who helped the warring factions of Sabines and Romans incorporate as separate municipal entities, believing that if the groups could govern and view themselves as independent, it would reduce bloodshed.[12]

The life of the corporation as a creature of English law began in England during the twelfth and thirteenth centuries, as towns sought independence from feudal and ecclesiastical control and were incorporated as self-governing municipalities. During the same era, general merchant or crafts guilds were the most important form of

---

11   Small Business Opportunity Clinic, Northwestern University School of Law. "Comparison of Business Entities Overview," supra note 2.

12   Douglas Arner, *Article in Tribute: Development of the American Law of Corporations to 1832*, 55 SMU L. Rev. 23, 25 (2002).

commercial organization, and in exchange for substantial fees to the crown, enjoyed a monopoly of their trade within a city's walls.[13] These merchant guilds were perhaps more like trade unions than modern corporations, as they were principally concerned with supervising apprenticeships, determining who ought to be admitted to the trade, and taking other steps to protect guild members' interests and their exclusive right to carry on trade. In the manner in which they functioned, however, the guilds can properly be viewed as prototypical corporate forms. The Guilds were governed by a council, similar to the modern corporate board of directors, and as early as 1437, the guilds had to be registered with and approved by the town where they were established.[14] Beginning in the fifteenth century, the crafts guild and the municipal borough were viewed as distinct in function, with the municipal corporation acting as a governing body while the crafts guild served as an economic tool only for its members, although the corporate forms of the two types of entities were identical and both ensured survival of the institutions themselves, even though the governing persons and the individual members would eventually pass on. Both types of corporations could include either natural members or "bodies incorporate and political," indicating that corporations could be part of other corporations.[15]

Nineteenth century American legal scholars Joseph K. Angell and Samuel Ames and English economist Adam Smith divided early economic corporations into two classes: regulated companies and joint stock companies.[16] Regulated companies were state-chartered monopolies authorized to pursue interests beneficial to the state and were dependent on the state for their continued power and success. The most successful of the regulated companies was the Staple of London, founded in 1248 to control wool exports and granted power in 1357 to collect taxes on wool exports in return for helping finance Edward III's French wars.[17] Joint stock companies, which emerged during the sixteenth and seventeenth centuries, more closely resemble the modern business corporation, as they involved owners who left the management of the business entirely to a body of directors.[18] Joint stock companies did not invent the selling of shares on the open market—an idea that dates back to at least the thirteenth century when shares in mines and ships were commonly sold—but they did substantially advance the technique of selling shares as a means of raising large amounts of corporate capital.[19]

---

13   John Micklethwait & Adrian Wooldridge, *The Company: A Short History of a Revolutionary Idea* 23 (Weidenfeld and Nicolson 2003).

14   Arner, *supra* n. 12 at 26

15   *Id.* at 29–30, citing Coke 5. Co. Rep. 23, 29b (1526–1616).

16   *Id.* at 26 and 38.

17   Mickelthwait and Wooldridge, *supra* n. 13 at 24.

18   Arner, *supra* n. 12 at 26, citing Joseph K. Angell and Samuel Ames, *Treatise on the Law of Private Corporations Aggregate* 32 (reprint N.Y. Arno Press 1972) (1832).

19   Mickelthwait and Wooldridge, *supra* n. 13 at 26.

Shareholders in joint stock companies also enjoyed some limited liability, enhanced by the fact that the company itself usually held substantial assets in land, and exposure to tort liability during this period was rare. Generally, shareholders would agree to be responsible for the contribution of a certain amount of total capital, even though they would customarily not pay the entire amount as an initial investment. The result was that even though the shareholder could be liable for more than his initial investment, his liability was capped at that agreed-upon amount.[20] Joint stock companies appear to have gradually developed due to the activities of wealthy merchants, property owners, and successful tradesmen who combined their resources to undertake ventures beyond their individual means or tolerance for risk, and utilizing the now available corporate form in a manner very different from that of the early incorporated towns and guilds. This development reflects the general expansion of markets and private capital investment, which became as important to commerce as the specialized skills of merchant craftsmen had been earlier.[21]

In the first two decades of the seventeenth century, forty joint stock "colonizing" companies were granted charters and trading monopolies in exchange for the crown's rights to the land discovered or settled by the corporations. The trade monopolies granted to these corporations encouraged shareholders to invest in these high risk ventures, even though their liability was not fully limited.[22] In addition, the shares held in these corporations were not fully protected as an individual property right, since the monarch retained the prerogative to refuse to renew or to withdraw the corporate charter. Nevertheless, interests in those corporations were widely traded on a stock exchange, much in the manner they are now.[23] As with earlier regulated corporations, the division between those that ought to be regarded as purely private and those that might be classified as "public" was often difficult to determine—directors of the British East India Company, for example, a concern that made many of its individual investors wealthy men, reported that "the Company traded more for the benefit of the nation [England] than for itself."[24]

The English "Bubble Act" of 1720 marks a definitive point in the history of modern business corporations. When the South Sea Company took over the British national debt in an attempt to retire it by selling shares on the open market to individuals, other corporations fought to participate in this emerging public debt market.

---

20   Arner, *supra* n. 12 at 39.

21   *Id.* at 27.

22   Janet McLean, *The Transnational Corporation in History: Lessons for Today?*, 79 Ind. L.J. 363, 365–66 (2004).

23   *Id.* at 370 n.43

24   *Id.* at 369 n, 33, citing K.N Chaudhuri, *The Trading World of Asia and the English East India Company, 1660–1760* 121 (1978).

The South Sea Company lobbied for the Bubble Act to be passed, in an attempt to restrict competing enterprises. The act, among other things, made it clearly illegal for any joint stock company to operate without a charter from parliament or the king.[25] As formalized charters were relatively difficult to obtain for most businesses, the act essentially cut off the growth of the private corporation in England until the nineteenth century, leaving contract-formed partnerships to emerge as the preferred vehicle of business in England.[26] The Bubble Act was extended to the colonies in 1741 and, along with the general political unrest that characterized the colonies in the eighteenth century, slowed the development of the corporation there. To circumvent the Bubble Act, many colonial businesses were formed according to private articles of agreement, and although legally partnerships, these businesses were able to approximate the joint stock form.[27]

After the American Revolution, it was commonly understood that the power to grant corporate charters, which in England had eventually come to be shared by the king and parliament, was possessed in America solely by the state legislatures.[28] Colonial legislatures had made frequent use of the corporate form to organize religious congregations and units of local government, and general incorporation statutes for creating these organizations were passed in many states shortly after the Revolution.[29] Forming a private business corporation, however, required more formalities. State legislatures had to pass a special act of incorporation for each new entity, which was required first to demonstrate that its operation would confer a public benefit. A charter might then be granted, which gave legal standing to the corporation and might also confer special franchise rights such as monopolies. As a result, the majority of early American corporations might be characterized as close to "public utilities," and included banks, insurance companies, universities, and companies engaged in constructing turnpikes, bridges and canals.[30] These early American corporations were usually limited to 5 to 30-year terms, with perpetual duration of corporations remaining rare until after the Civil War.[31]

---

25   Mickelthwait and Wooldridge, *supra* n. 13 at 40–41.

26   Arner, *supra* n. 12 at 33–34.

27   *Id.* at 43, citing Shaw Livermore, Unlimited Liability in Early American Corporations, 43 J. of Pol. Econ. 674, 674 n.2 (1935).

28   E. Dodd, *American Business Corporations Until 1860* 196 (1954).

29   Ronald E. Seavoy, *The Origins of the American Business Corporation, 1784–1855: Broadening the Concept of Public Service During Industrialization* 4–5 (1982).

30   James Willard Hurst, *The Legitimacy of the Business Corporation in the Law of the United States 1780–1970* 18 (U. Press of Va. 1970).

31   Lawrence Friedman, *A History of American Law* 188–192 (2d ed. 1985).

In the nineteenth century, four important developments in American business and politics combined to produce changes that led to the form of business corporation we have today, which entity does, perhaps, represent American law's greatest contribution to world commerce.

The first important event was a clarification of the Constitutional status of the American corporation, through one of the most important decisions ever rendered by the United States Supreme Court. In *Dartmouth College v. Woodward*, 17 U.S. (4 Wheat.) 518, 4 L.Ed. 629 (1819), the Court held that the charter of Dartmouth College (organized as a corporation) was a contract conferring private rights on the incorporators and their successors. The charter, then, was understood to be the valuable private property of the corporation, rather than property held in trust for the state, as had previously been the more commonly accepted view. Prior to *Dartmouth College*, it was understood that the granting of a corporate charter by a state legislature was no different from any other legislative act, and that as was true for any other law, the grant of a charter might be amended or repealed if the operation of the corporation was deemed by the legislature no longer to be in the public interest.[32] Because the corporate charter was held to be a contract in *Dartmouth College*, this brought into play Article I, Section 10, clause 1 of the United States Constitution, which provides in pertinent part that "No State [legislature] shall . . . pass any . . . Law impairing the Obligation of Contracts." This meant, then, that no state legislature could alter any corporate charter unless it had reserved the right to do so in the original grant. Writing for the Court in *Dartmouth College*, Chief Justice John Marshall observed that private colleges were essential in America, and that no one would ever found or invest in a college or other corporation while "believing that it is immediately to be deemed a public institution, whose funds are to be governed and applied, not by the will of the donor, but by the will of the legislature."[33] Justice Story, in his concurrence in the case, suggested that private colleges were like privately-funded banks, and that while both performed functions that were beneficial to the public, neither should be regarded as "public corporations," but rather as private entities, the private property of which required insulation from legislative interference. As Story put it, "the mere act of incorporation will not change the charity from a private to a public one."[34]

The second important development was the rise of the railroads, the first national-scale businesses. Administering these enterprises required the creation of a complex hierarchy of managers who, although they did not own the businesses with which they were involved, came to stake their professional careers on enabling enterprise to grow and prosper. This separation of management and ownership also further accelerated the development of large-scale public markets for the sale of shares,

---

32   See, for the leading case expressing this view, *Currie's Administrators v. The Mutual Assurance Society*, 14 Va. 315 (1809).

33   17 U.S. (4 Wheat.) at 647.

34   *Id.* at 671.

since it was now possible for investors passively to reap the rewards of investment in corporations without participating in management. By 1898, railroads accounted for over 60% of the publicly-issued stock in the US.[35]

The third development was the formation of large-scale manufacturing, mining and other industrial concerns which created a rapid increase in the number of charters granted to businesses that did not directly perform a public benefit. As requests for such charters became more frequent and were granted, the understanding that corporate charters were a privilege granted only to those who served the public began to erode. As corporations became more common and legislators became more familiar with the corporation as an instrument of private business, political, legal and structural changes followed. In what, as you will see, has been characterized as a "race to the bottom" that began in the 1820s and purportedly continues today, states began to loosen their regulation of corporations and to make it easier to incorporate. This occurred not only because the economic operations of corporations might be beneficial to the state of incorporation, but also because incorporators began to understand that they had some choice in determining in which state they might incorporate, and states found that incorporation and franchise fees could be an important source of state income.[36]

These changes led to the passage of general incorporation laws that removed the requirement of the legislature's individual approval for each entity and, eventually, evolved into a system that made incorporation an option for almost any enterprise. The standard general incorporation acts of the 1880s made corporate status available through simple administrative procedures, but required very strict compliance with limits on capitalization, corporate organization and share structure.[37] By the1930s, a more liberalized type of general incorporation had been put in place throughout the country, providing a standard corporate structure but allowing variations as the drafters of individual corporate bylaws desired.[38] Throughout the twentieth century, general incorporation statutes came to grant expansive power for incorporators to vary, through contracts, charter or bylaws, the terms that the law might otherwise impose for corporate organization and governance.[39]

Finally, in what may have been the most important of these developments, limited shareholder liability became commonplace during the nineteenth century. Some firms chartered in the eighteenth and early nineteenth centuries were granted a form of limited liability, perhaps in exchange for the firms' building of public improvements

---

35 Mickelthwait and Wooldridge, *supra* n. 13 at 66.

36 Hurst, *supra* n. 30 at 18.

37 *Id.* at 69.

38 *Id.* at 70.

39 *Id.* at 120.

without the expenditure of public funds.[40] Although limited liability was thus not unknown in the eighteenth century, there is at least one instance of a corporate charter's dictating that shareholders had *unlimited* liability for the enterprise's debts.[41] Unlimited liability became even more common in the first part of the nineteenth century, as a legislative policy of protecting corporate creditors took hold in many American jurisdictions.[42] This policy was based, at least in part, on the belief that corporations could more easily amass the necessary capital from creditors' loans if creditors knew that there was recourse against the individuals involved. Making capital more easily available from creditors, so the argument ran, would itself benefit fledgling entrepreneurs, and this would ultimately benefit the public. By 1840, however, perhaps as private equity investment became a preferred means of raising capital, many states' legislators amended their corporate laws to provide for limited shareholder liability. This legislative change was supported not only by the economic argument that lowering liability would lead to additional investment in the state's businesses, but also by the notion that by removing the threat of unlimited liability, shareholders of modest means would be able to invest in corporations, thus democratizing corporate ownership.[43]

The notion of limited liability is not without controversy today.[44] Critics claim that limited liability encourages corporations to make risky and dangerous investments; because their potential losses are limited to the amount of their investments, owners have the incentive to skimp on precautions and prudent safeguards while over-investing in hazardous industries. Thus society, rather than the offending corporation, pays the cost for massive torts whose damages exceed corporate equity. Proponents of unlimited liability believe that corporations would become more responsible without the shield of limited liability. As you might imagine, criticisms of this view abound. Perhaps the most obvious objection is that a regime of unlimited liability would have a severe chilling effect on investment in equity, making it extremely difficult for companies to raise money. Secondly, critics charge that unlimited liability would make securities markets illiquid: it would be many times more difficult to sell a security when a buyer knows she would be personally liable for the torts of a corporation over which she may exert minimal influence. Recently, there have been some calls to institute unlimited corporate liability in certain cases, often concerning environmental damage. However, large-scale changes to the doctrine of corporate limited liability are unlikely to come to pass in the foreseeable future. There is one

---

40   Seavoy, *supra* n. 29 at 257–58.

41   Dodd, *supra* n. 28 at 227.

42   *E.g.*, Handlin and Handlin, *Origins of the American Business Corporation*, 5 J. Econ. Hist. 1, 10 (1945).

43   Seavoy, *supra* n. 29 at 115.

44   For a modern criticism of limited liability for corporate shareholders (including a proposed model for unlimited liability), see Henry Hansmann & Reinier Kraakman, "Toward Unlimited Shareholder Liability for Corporate Torts," 100 Yale L.J. 1879 (1991).

long-standing exception to the doctrine of corporate limited liability, known as "piercing the corporate veil," which you will read about in Chapter 16.

One of most recent and most important developments in the operations of private corporations, one that has led to an explosion of corporate development in the twentieth and on into the twenty-first century, is the increasing prevalence of subsidiary and affiliated corporations. These are corporations owned by each other, or sister corporations for whom ownership is identical, often in another corporation. Giant global business entities, many incorporated in the state of Delaware, now function all over the world through separately-incorporated subsidiaries and affiliates. As we will see in Chapter Four, it is now universally accepted that absent an abuse of the corporate form, a corporate shareholder has the same limited liability for the debts of its subsidiaries and affiliates as does an individual investing in a corporation. The rise of operation through subsidiaries and affiliates appears to have come about in tandem with the wide dispersal of passive shareholder investors, and the rise of professional managers. The number of individuals owning shares in corporations rose from two million in 1920 to over ten million in 1930. Current estimates suggest that approximately sixty percent of American households can be regarded as investors in corporations, and, during the 2004 Presidential election, some commentators suggested that "investor interests" were important in the reelection of the Republican candidate, George W. Bush.

In the 1960s, diversified conglomerate corporate entities emerged and grew to be a powerful economic force by taking over divisions of other corporations, either through friendly negotiated buyouts or hostile "takeovers." By 1973, fifteen of the top 200 American manufacturing corporations were conglomerates, but by then this particular wave of mergers and acquisitions was ending, as the conglomerates failed to deliver expected returns and the stock value of these huge businesses declined.[45]

Even so, the urge to merge grew again as financing became more generally available in the 1980s. Large corporations grew even larger and more diverse through the "merger boom" of the 1980s, but all was not well.[46] From 1970 to 1990, the rate at which large American companies left the Fortune 500 increased four times, and many large conglomerates found it more profitable to slim down and focus on core businesses.[47] The business of many American corporations also changed radically toward the turn of the Century. By 1999, the most valuable American export was probably intellectual capital, as old-style manufacturing gave way to the "information age" and the "service economy" and new groups of entrepreneurs found success in small, flexible upstart corporations.[48]

---

45   *Id*. at 120.

46   *Id*. at 138.

47   *Id*. at 125.

48   *Id*. at 139.

By the end of the twentieth century, there seemed to be a discernable trend for state and national governments to set the corporation free by deregulating markets, simplifying general incorporation procedures, and loosening trade barriers. At the same time, however, and somewhat paradoxically, the state legislatures and Congress increasingly regulated the ongoing operations of corporations through laws governing accounting procedures, the health and safety of workers, the environment, affirmative action, and the protection of employee, consumer and even investor rights.[49] Although general incorporation statutes had been simplified and streamlined such that the act of incorporation seemed little more than a formality, modern corporations still needed some form of government authorization to exist, and the corporate laws and other regulatory measures of particular states continued to have great influence on where businesses chose to incorporate. In 1999, most of the largest American companies were incorporated in Delaware, a state whose laws favored the discretion of managers and majority shareholders over the purported corporate governance rights of minority shareholders.

We will explore several of the implications of this brief history of corporations, but this whistle-stop tour should give you enough information to reach some preliminary conclusions. Are you comfortable with the ubiquity of the corporation (and other similar business vehicles such as the limited liability company (LLC))? Is the history of the development of the corporation, and the emergence of the modern American business corporation (the model for the rest of the world) an unqualifiedly noble human achievement? How should the corporation be regulated in the public interest? Consider the implications of *Ford v. Dodge* and *Smith v. Barlow*, which follow.

III. The Purpose of the Corporation

Dodge v. Ford Motor Co.

Supreme Court of Michigan.
204 Mich. 459, 170 N.W. 668, 3 A.L.R. 413 (1919).

OSTRANDER, J.

* * * [T]he case for plaintiffs must rest upon the claim, and the proof in support of it, that the proposed expansion of the business of the corporation, involving the further use of profits as capital, ought to be enjoined because inimical to the best interests of the company and its shareholders, and upon the further claim that in any event the withholding of the special dividend asked for by plaintiffs is arbitrary action of the directors requiring judicial interference.

---

49   *Id.* at 146.

The rule which will govern courts in deciding these questions is not in dispute. It is, of course, differently phrased by judges and by authors, and, as the phrasing in a particular instance may seem to lean for or against the exercise of the right of judicial interference with the actions of corporate directors, the context, or the facts before the court, must be considered. This court, in *Hunter v. Roberts, Throp & Co., 83 Mich. 63, 71*, recognized the rule in the following language:

> "It is a well-recognized principle of law that the directors of a corporation, and they alone, have the power to declare a dividend of the earnings of the corporation, and to determine its amount. * * * Courts of equity will not interfere in the management of the directors unless it is clearly made to appear that they are guilty of fraud or misappropriation of the corporate funds, or refuse to declare a dividend when the corporation has a surplus of net profits which it can, without detriment to its business, divide among its stockholders, and when a refusal to do so would amount to such an abuse of discretion as would constitute a fraud or breach of that good faith which they are bound to exercise towards the stockholders."

In 2 *Cook on Corporations* (7th Ed.), § 545, it is expressed as follows:

> "The board of directors declare the dividends, and it is for the directors, and not the stockholders, to determine whether or not a dividend shall be declared.

> "When, therefore, the directors have exercised this discretion and refused to declare a dividend, there will be no interference by the courts with their decision, unless they are guilty of a willful abuse of their discretionary powers, or of bad faith or of a neglect of duty. It requires a very strong case to induce a court of equity to order the directors to declare a dividend, inasmuch as equity has no jurisdiction, unless fraud or a breach of trust is involved. There have been many attempts to sustain such a suit, yet, although the courts do not disclaim jurisdiction, they have quite uniformly refused to interfere. The discretion of the directors will not be interfered with by the courts, unless there has been bad faith, willful neglect, or abuse of discretion.

> "Accordingly, the directors may, in the fair exercise of their discretion, invest profits to extend and develop the business, and a reasonable use of the profits to provide additional facilities for the business cannot be objected to or enjoined by the stockholders."

In 1 *Morawetz on Corporations* (2d Ed.), § 447, it is stated:

> "Profits earned by a corporation may be divided among its shareholders; but it is not a violation of the charter if they are allowed to accumulate

and remain invested in the company's business. The managing agents of a corporation are impliedly invested with a discretionary power with regard to the time and manner of distributing its profits. They may apply profits in payment of floating or funded debts, or in development of the company's business; and so long as they do not abuse their discretionary powers, or violate the company's charter, the courts cannot interfere.

"But it is clear that the agents of a corporation, and even the majority, cannot arbitrarily withhold profits earned by the company, or apply them to any use which is not authorized by the company's charter. The nominal capital of a company does not necessarily limit the scope of its operations; a corporation may borrow money for the purpose of enlarging its business, and in many instances it may use profits for the same purpose. But the amount of the capital contributed by the shareholders is an important element in determining the limit beyond which the company's business cannot be extended by the investment of profits. If a corporation is formed with a capital of $100,000 in order to carry on a certain business, no one would hesitate to say that it would be a departure from the intention of the founders to withhold profits, in order to develop the company's business, until the sum of $500,000 had been amassed, unless the company was formed mainly for the purpose of accumulating the profits from year to year. The question in each case depends upon the use to which the capital is put, and the meaning of the company's charter. If a majority of the shareholders or the directors of a corporation wrongfully refuse to declare a dividend and distribute profits earned by the company, any shareholder feeling aggrieved may obtain relief in a court of equity.

"It may often be reasonable to withhold part of the earnings of a corporation in order to increase its surplus fund, when it would not be reasonable to withhold all the earnings for that purpose. The shareholders forming an ordinary business corporation expect to obtain the profits of their investment in the form of regular dividends. To withhold the entire profits merely to enlarge the capacity of the company's business would defeat their just expectations. After the business of a corporation has been brought to a prosperous condition, and necessary provision has been made for future prosperity, a reasonable share of the profits should be applied in the payment of regular dividends, though a part may be reserved to increase the surplus and enlarge the business itself."

One other statement may be given from *Park v. Grant Locomotive Works, 40 N.J. Eq. 114 (3 Atl. 162, 45 N.J. Eq. 244, 19 Atl. 621):*

"In cases where the power of the directors of a corporation is without limitation, and free from restraint, they are at liberty to exercise a very liberal discretion as to what disposition shall be made of the gains of the business of the corporation. Their power over them is absolute as long as they act in the exercise of their honest judgment. They may reserve of them whatever their judgment approves as necessary or judicious for repairs or improvements, and to meet contingencies, both present and prospective. And their determination in respect of these matters, if made in good faith and for honest ends, though the result may show that it was injudicious, is final, and not subject to judicial revision."

It is not necessary to multiply statements of the rule.

* * *

When plaintiffs made their complaint and demand for further dividends the Ford Motor Company had concluded its most prosperous year of business. The demand for its cars at the price of the preceding year continued. It could make and could market in the year beginning August 1, 1916, more than 500,000 cars. Sales of parts and repairs would necessarily increase. The cost of materials was likely to advance, and perhaps the price of labor, but it reasonably might have expected a profit for the year of upwards of $60,000,000. It had assets of more than $132,000,000, a surplus of almost $112,000,000, and its cash on hand and municipal bonds were nearly $54,000,000. Its total liabilities, including capital stock, was a little over $20,000,000. It had declared no special dividend during the business year except the October, 1915, dividend. It had been the practice, under similar circumstances, to declare larger dividends. Considering only these facts, a refusal to declare and pay further dividends appears to be not an exercise of discretion on the part of the directors, but an arbitrary refusal to do what the circumstances required to be done. These facts and others call upon the directors to justify their action, or failure or refusal to act. In justification, the defendants have offered testimony tending to prove, and which does prove, the following facts. It had been the policy of the corporation for a considerable time to annually reduce the selling price of cars, while keeping up, or improving, their quality. As early as in June, 1915, a general plan for the expansion of the productive capacity of the concern by a practical duplication of its plant had been talked over by the executive officers and directors and agreed upon, not all of the details having been settled and no formal action of directors having been taken. The erection of a smelter was considered, and engineering and other data in connection therewith secured. In consequence, it was determined not to reduce the selling price of cars for the year beginning August 1, 1915, but to maintain the price and to accumulate a large surplus to pay for the proposed expansion of plant and equipment, and perhaps to build a plant for smelting ore. It is hoped, by Mr. Ford, that eventually 1,000,000 cars will be annually produced. The contemplated changes will permit the increased output.

The plan, as affecting the profits of the business for the year beginning August 1, 1916, and thereafter, calls for a reduction in the selling price of the cars. It is true that this price might be at any time increased, but the plan called for the reduction in price of $80 a car. The capacity of the plant, without the additions thereto voted to be made (without a part of them at least), would produce more than 600,000 cars annually. This number, and more, could have been sold for $440 instead of $360, a difference in the return for capital, labor and materials employed of at least $48,000,000. In short, the plan does not call for and is not intended to produce immediately a more profitable business but a less profitable one; not only less profitable than formerly but less profitable than it is admitted it might be made. The apparent immediate effect will be to diminish the value of shares and the returns to shareholders.

It is the contention of plaintiffs that the apparent effect of the plan is intended to be the continued and continuing effect of it and that it is deliberately proposed, not of record and not by official corporate declaration, but nevertheless proposed, to continue the corporation henceforth as a semi-eleemosynary institution and not as a business institution. In support of this contention they point to the attitude and to the expressions of Mr. Henry Ford.

Mr. Henry Ford is the dominant force in the business of the Ford Motor Company. No plan of operations could be adopted unless he consented, and no board of directors can be elected whom he does not favor. One of the directors of the company has no stock. One share was assigned to him to qualify him for the position, but it is not claimed that he owns it. A business, one of the largest in the world, and one of the most profitable, has been built up. It employs many men, at good pay.

> "My ambition," said Mr. Ford, "is to employ still more men, to spread the benefits of this industrial system to the greatest possible number, to help them build up their lives and their homes. To do this we are putting the greatest share of our profits back in the business."

> "With regard to dividends, the company paid sixty per cent. on its capitalization of two million dollars, or $1,200,000, leaving $58,000,000 to reinvest for the growth of the company. This is Mr. Ford's policy at present, and it is understood that the other stockholders cheerfully accede to this plan."

He had made up his mind in the summer of 1916 that no dividends other than the regular dividends should be paid, "for the present."

> "Q. For how long? Had you fixed in your mind any time in the future, when you were going to pay—

> "A. No.

"*Q*. That was indefinite in the future?

"*A*. That was indefinite, yes, sir."

The record, and especially the testimony of Mr. Ford, convinces that he has to some extent the attitude towards shareholders of one who has dispensed and distributed to them large gains and that they should be content to take what he chooses to give. His testimony creates the impression, also, that he thinks the Ford Motor Company has made too much money, has had too large profits, and that although large profits might be still earned, a sharing of them with the public, by reducing the price of the output of the company, ought to be undertaken. We have no doubt that certain sentiments, philanthropic and altruistic, creditable to Mr. Ford, had large influence in determining the policy to be pursued by the Ford Motor Company—the policy which has been herein referred to.

It is said by his counsel that—

> "Although a manufacturing corporation cannot engage in humanitarian works as its principal business, the fact that it is organized for profit does not prevent the existence of implied powers to carry on with humanitarian motives such charitable works as are incidental to the main business of the corporation."

And again:

> "As the expenditures complained of are being made in an expansion of the business which the company is organized to carry on, and for purposes within the powers of the corporation as hereinbefore shown, the question is as to whether such expenditures are rendered illegal because influenced to some extent by humanitarian motives and purposes on the part of the members of the board of directors."

[The decision in this case, as in other similar cases, must] turn finally upon * * * whether it appears that the directors were not acting for the best interests of the corporation. We do not draw in question, nor do counsel for the plaintiffs do so, the validity of the general propositions stated by counsel nor the soundness of the opinions delivered in the cases cited [by them, which uphold expenditures of some corporate funds for charitable purposes which benefit employees]. The case presented here is not like any of them. The difference between an incidental humanitarian expenditure of corporate funds for the benefit of the employees, like the building of a hospital for their use and the employment of agencies for the betterment of their condition, and a general purpose and plan to benefit mankind at the expense of others, is obvious. There should be no confusion (of which there is evidence) of the duties which Mr. Ford conceives that he and the stockholders owe to the general public and the duties which in law he and his codirectors owe to protesting, minority stockholders. A business corporation is organized and carried on primarily for the profit of the stockholders. The powers of the directors are to be employed for that end. The discretion of directors is to be exercised in the choice of means to attain that end and does not extend to a change in the end itself, to the reduction of profits or to the nondistribution of profits among stockholders in order to devote them to other purposes.

There is committed to the discretion of directors, a discretion to be exercised in good faith, the infinite details of business, including the wages which shall be paid to employees, the number of hours they shall work, the conditions under which labor shall be carried on, and the prices for which products shall be offered to the public. It is said by appellants that the motives of the board members are not material and will not be inquired into by the court so long as their acts are within their lawful powers. As we have pointed out, and the proposition does not require argument to sustain it, it is not within the lawful powers of a board of directors to shape and conduct the affairs of a corporation for the merely incidental benefit of shareholders and for the primary purpose of benefiting others, and no one will contend that if the avowed purpose of the defendant directors was to sacrifice the interests of shareholders it would not be the duty of the courts to interfere.

We are not, however, persuaded that we should interfere with the proposed expansion of the business of the Ford Motor Company. In view of the fact that the selling price of products may be increased at any time, the ultimate results of the larger business cannot be certainly estimated. The judges are not business experts. It is recognized that plans must often be made for a long future, for expected competition, for a continuing as well as an immediately profitable venture. The experience of the Ford Motor Company is evidence of capable management of its affairs. It may be noticed, incidentally, that it took from the public the money required for the execution of its plan and that the very considerable salaries paid to Mr. Ford and to certain executive officers and employees were not diminished. We are not satisfied that the alleged motives of the directors, in so far as they are reflected in the conduct of the business, menace the interests of shareholders. It is enough to say, perhaps, that the court of equity is at all times open to complaining shareholders having a just grievance.

Assuming the general plan and policy of expansion and the details of it to have been sufficiently, formally, approved at the October and November, 1917, meetings of directors, and assuming further that the plan and policy and the details agreed upon were for the best ultimate interest of the company and therefore of its shareholders, what does it amount to in justification of a refusal to declare and pay a special dividend, or dividends? The Ford Motor Company was able to estimate with nicety its income and profit. It could sell more cars than it could make. Having ascertained what it would cost to produce a car and to sell it, the profit upon each car depended upon the selling price. That being fixed, the yearly income and profit was determinable, and, within slight variations, was certain.

There was appropriated-voted-for the smelter $11,325,000. As to the remainder voted there is no available way for determining how much had been paid before the action of directors was taken and how much was paid thereafter, but assuming that the plans required an expenditure sooner or later of $9,895,000 for duplication of the plant, and for land and other expenditures $3,000,000, the total is $24,220,000. The company was continuing business, at a profit—a cash business. If the total cost of proposed expenditures had been immediately withdrawn in cash from the cash surplus (money and bonds) on hand August 1, 1916, there would have remained nearly $30,000,000.

Defendants say, and it is true, that a considerable cash balance must be at all times carried by such a concern. But, as has been stated, there was a large daily, weekly, monthly, receipt of cash. The output was practically continuous and was continuously, and within a few days, turned into cash. Moreover, the contemplated expenditures were not to be immediately made. The large sum appropriated for the smelter plant was payable over a considerable period of time. So that, without going further, it would appear that, accepting and approving the plan of the directors, it was their duty to distribute on or near the first of August, 1916, a very large sum of money to stockholders.

In reaching this conclusion, we do not ignore, but recognize, the validity of the proposition that plaintiffs have from the beginning profited by, if they have not lately, officially, participated in, the general policy of expansion pursued by this corporation. We do not lose sight of the fact that it had been, upon an occasion, agreeable to the plaintiffs to increase the capital stock to $100,000,000 by a stock dividend of $98,000,000. These things go only to answer other contentions now made by plaintiffs and do not and cannot operate to estop them to demand proper dividends upon the stock they own. It is obvious that an annual dividend of sixty per cent. upon $2,000,000, or $1,200,000, is the equivalent of a very small dividend upon $100,000,000, or more.

The decree of the court below fixing and determining the specific amount to be distributed to stockholders is affirmed. * * * Plaintiffs will recover interest at five per cent. per annum upon their proportional share of said dividend from the date of the decree of the lower court. * * *

NOTES AND QUESTIONS

I. *DODGE* v. *FORD MOTOR CORP.* is presented as a means of studying why we allow corporations, and what their purpose ought to be. What is the view of the court, and what was the view of Mr. Henry Ford on this question? Which do you find most congenial? By the way, are the Court's assumptions about what shareholders are looking for consistent with how you understand the expectations of shareholders today? Consider the facts of the case. *Ford v. Dodge* centers on the fiduciary duties of corporate managers and whether such duties allow for the consideration of the interests of non-shareholders, such as workers or consumers. By 1919, when the case arose, Henry Ford had become the Bill Gates of his era; he was a phenomenally-successful businessman, and as the Court observes, he had increased the wealth of his investors, including the plaintiffs in this case, the Dodge brothers (is that name familiar to you?), many times over. What do you understand to be the nature of the debate between Ford and the Dodge brothers? The dispute is over how the profits of the company should be distributed. Ford wants to reinvest in the company, lower the production price of his cars, and ultimately pass the savings on to the buyers of Fords. The Dodge brothers believe the amount of money Ford is reinvesting is excessive and that the money should be distributed to the investors in the form of a special dividend. To whom do you think Ford owes the greater duty, the consumers whose expenditures have allowed him to build his fortune, and increase the wealth of the corporation, or the investors who have originally financed his enterprise? The court rules in favor of the Dodge brothers, holding that Ford should distribute the earnings in the form of a special dividend. One reason is that "[t]he purpose of any [corporate] organization under the law is earnings." Should corporations be guided by anything other than making profits for their investors? If so, what outside concerns should be considered? Is the Court's view of the limited purposes of corporations persuasive?

2. WE WILL RETURN TO this particular theme later in the course, but consider, for a moment, how the court views its role in intervening in a dispute between corporate directors and their President on the one hand, and shareholders on the other. Note that the court begins by indicating the rule of the common law that it is inappropriate to interfere with directors' discretion to declare a dividend "unless they are guilty of a willful abuse of their discretionary powers, or of bad faith or of a neglect of duty." Furthermore there must be "a very strong case to induce a court of equity to order the directors to declare a dividend." In your view, was *Dodge v. Ford* such a case? If the same factual situation arose today, would it be appropriate for a court to intervene? Are there any other remedies for shareholders in such a situation of refusal to pay dividends besides a lawsuit to compel their payment? To determine whether this situation merits intervention, the court looks to the profit history of the company. Ford had been making large profits and was in the habit of declaring large dividends. Furthermore, Ford's business plan which would ultimately reduce production costs had the immediate effect of "diminish[ing] the value of shares and the returns to shareholders." Is it fair to help non-shareholders at the expense of corporate investors? If you are an investor, do you want Ford as a CEO? If you are a CEO, should you consider non-shareholder interests at all?

3. THE COURT ULTIMATELY views the testimony of Henry Ford as evincing "the attitude towards shareholders of one who has dispensed and distributed to them large gains and that they should be content to take what he chooses to give." Should a corporate officer or director have this attitude? Do you agree that Ford's desire to reduce the cost of cars to consumers, presumably enabling more people to purchase the company's product, is the arbitrary action of a wealthy tycoon who feels insufficient concern for his investors? Could it be dangerous for a corporate director to distribute profits as he or she sees fit? On the other hand, the Dodge brothers have been given large returns on their initial investment. If the corporate directors and shareholders have already made large amounts of money, do they have less of a claim on future profits? Should the amount of money already distributed affect a corporation's duties to non-shareholders?

4. IN HIS TESTIMONY, Ford says his ambition "is to employ still more men, to spread the benefits of this industrial system to the greatest possible number, to help them build up their lives and their homes." In 1918, Ford's workers were paid $6 for an eight hour day, which at the time was quite a substantial wage, one almost unheard of for laborers. Ford also allowed his employees to enter into an innovative profit-sharing program. Is there an extra-legal obligation among managers to enable more people than shareholders to reap the benefits of the industrial system? Even if there is not an implicit obligation, should the courts allow or encourage this type of benefit sharing? Did the court's decision help or harm capitalism?

5. THE COURT'S DECISION does not prevent corporations from undertaking philanthropic endeavors. However, as we will see in the next case, such philanthropic undertakings must be connected to the interests of the corporation. In *Dodge v. Ford*, the court holds "[t]he difference between an incidental humanitarian expenditure of corporate funds for the benefit of the employees, like the building of a hospital for their use and the employment of agencies for the betterment of their condition, and a general purpose and plan to benefit mankind at the expense of others, is obvious." Does it make sense that a corporation can use some of its profits to help its workers, but not reduce its profits to benefit non-shareholders in general? How closely related does the use of corporate funds need to be to the interests of the corporation?

....

6. THE COURT IS ULTIMATELY persuaded that it should interfere in the management of Ford's corporate assets. The judges recognize the capability of Ford Motor Company to manage its own affairs, yet still feel compelled to second-guess the board's decision on dividend policy. Although the court's members are "not business experts" they cite the fact that "the very considerable salaries paid to Mr. Ford and to certain executive officers and employees were not diminished" as evidence of wrongdoing to support their intervention. Is it generally appropriate for judges, based on their assessment of what is good for the business or the business community, to overrule the business decision of a board selected by shareholders? Should judges substitute their knowledge for the knowledge of business experts? Given that Mr. Ford's own earnings were not reduced, do you agree that this is a case where judicial intervention was warranted?

....

7. PROFESSOR STEPHEN M. BAINBRIDGE writes in the *Northwestern Law Review* that "*Dodge's* theory of shareholder wealth maximization has widely been accepted by the courts." Professor Bainbridge continues "shareholder wealth maximization is not only the law, but also is a basic feature of corporate ideology."[50] Is this an ideology to which you subscribe? Is there an alternative? Given that such a high percentage of Americans have portions of their earnings, or retirement or pension funds invested in the stock market, either directly through their purchase of stocks or mutual funds, or indirectly through the purchase of insurance underwritten by entities invested in the market, or through their participation as students attending endowed universities, is the *Dodge* theory of shareholder primacy with regards to the distribution of corporate assets the fairest method to the largest group of people? To what extent should corporate officers and directors be able to act on the basis of the interests of other constituencies or stakeholders such as creditors, employees, workers, consumers

---

50 Stephen M. Bainbridge, *Director Primacy: The Means and Ends of Corporate Governance*, 97 NW. U.L. Rev. 547, 575–576 (2003).

or the community generally? As the economy is increasingly global, do American corporations owe any obligations to their overseas workers? Do corporations have a duty to be ambassadors for capitalism? Should American corporations be more considerate of how Americans will be perceived in the era of a war on terrorism? Remember these issues as you read through the next case.

8. **IN A VERY PROVOCATIVE** piece, law Professor Lynn A. Stout, Professor Bainbridge's colleague at UCLA, has argued that it is a mistake to continue to teach *Dodge v. Ford Motor Co.*, because, she asserts, it is now no longer true (if it ever was) that the legally-sanctioned purpose of corporations is to make money for shareholders. Lynn A. Stout, "Why We Should Stop Teaching *Dodge v. Ford*," Chapter 1 of Jonathan R. Macey, ed., *The Iconic Cases in Corporate Law* 1 (2008). Is this correct? Bear this question in mind as you continue to work your way through this course. If making money for shareholders is not the *raison d'etre* of corporations, what is? For further background on *Dodge v. Ford Motor Co.*, including biographical information on Henry Ford and the Dodge brothers, and for the suggestion that what happened in that case foreshadowed current battles for corporate control and shareholder influence on corporate boards, see M. Todd Henderson, "The Story of Dodge v. Ford Motor Company: Everything Old is New Again," in J. Mark Ramseyer, Ed., *Corporate Law Stories* 37 (2009). Professor Henderson argues, among other things, that the case would be decided differently today, and that, in particular, a court would be more likely to defer to Ford's decision to reinvest, to pay his workers more, and to sell more cars, instead of using revenues to pay dividends. Do you agree?

9. **WHEN IS IT APPROPRIATE** for a corporation to issue dividends? Corporate dividends and distributions are matters that we will not explore in any detail in this course, leaving these and other such issues for you to explore, should you choose to do so, on your own, or in a future course in corporate finance. Even so, a few brief sentences on the topic may help put *Dodge v. Ford* in further perspective.

The decision about whether or not to issue dividends, or to use corporate funds for other corporate purposes, for example to expand the productive capacity of the corporation, as you may have been able to discern from *Dodge v. Ford*, is normally a matter of the "business judgment" of directors, and, absent obvious conflicts of interest, as seems to have been found in that case, the courts will leave the matter to the decision of the directors. Still, there are some legal limits that state legislatures have placed on the situations in which dividends may be declared. These statutes are currently in a state of flux, but all share a common perspective that dividends should not be permitted where they would unduly endanger the continuing operations of the corporation.

Thus, in many states, dividends may not be declared unless the corporation's Balance Sheet (the accountants' report on the financial health of the corporation) reveals that the corporation's capital accounts (which reflect initial investment in the corporation) are undiminished, and that there is a capital surplus (a condition where accrued earnings result in an amount over and above the amount initially invested). When studying capital accounts, you may encounter the notion of a stock's "par value." While once meant to reflect some initial value of the stock, par value is an increasingly irrelevant idea, and many stocks have a par value of one cent or none at all. It remains worthy of notice, however, as the cumulative sum of a stock's par value can limit the amount of legally payable dividends (as in Delaware).

Because the Balance Sheet is based on initial valuations of assets, and because some assets (for example accounts receivable), may not be reliable indicators of positive value, the "Balance Sheet" test for declaration of dividends has been replaced in some states by newer means of evaluating the financial health of the corporation. These include, for example, evaluations based on the corporation's cash flow, requirements that corporate assets be valued at their present worth, and that this value be higher (sometimes by a specified ratio) than the liabilities of the corporation after any proposed dividends are paid, or simply that dividends may not be paid if the corporation will be rendered incapable of meeting its expected debts as they mature.

For further reading on the law and economics of dividend payments see, e.g., Stephen M. Bainbridge, *Corporation Law and Economics* 768–796 (2002), William A. Klein, and John C. Coffee, Jr., *Business Organization and Finance: Legal and Economic Principles* 218–220 (8th ed. 2002), Jeffrey J. Haas, *Corporate Finance in a Nutshell*, 331–358 (2004). These three paperback volumes contain a wealth of information relevant to all economic issues we will consider, and are worthy additions to the library of any student seriously interested in economic analysis of the law of business organizations.

A.P. Smith Manufacturing Co. v. Barlow

Supreme Court of New Jersey.
13 N.J. 145, 98 A.2d 581 (1953).

[JACOBS, J.] The Chancery Division

* * * determined that a donation by the plaintiff The A.P. Smith Manufacturing Company to Princeton University was *intra vires* ["within the powers of the corporation"]. Because of the public importance of the issues presented, the appeal duly taken to the Appellate Division has been certified directly to this court * * *.

The company was incorporated in 1896 and is engaged in the manufacture and sale of valves, fire hydrants and special equipment, mainly for water and gas industries. Its plant is located in East Orange and Bloomfield and it has approximately 300 employees. Over the years the company has contributed regularly to the local community chest and on occasions to Upsala College in East Orange and Newark University, now part of Rutgers, the State University. On July 24, 1951 the board of directors adopted a resolution which set forth that it was in the corporation's best interests to join with others in the 1951 Annual Giving to Princeton University, and appropriated the sum of $1,500 to be transferred by the corporation's treasurer to the university as a contribution towards its maintenance. * * *

Mr. Hubert F. O'Brien, the president of the company, testified that he considered the contribution to be a sound investment, that the public expects corporations to aid philanthropic and benevolent institutions, that they obtain good will in the community by so doing, and that their charitable donations create favorable environment for their business operations. In addition, he expressed the thought that in contributing to liberal arts institutions, corporations were furthering their self-interest in assuring the free flow of properly trained personnel for administrative and other corporate employment. Mr. Frank W. Abrams, chairman of the board of the Standard Oil Company of New Jersey, testified that corporations are expected to acknowledge their public responsibilities in support of the essential elements of our free enterprise system. He indicated that it was not "good business" to disappoint "this reasonable and justified public expectation," nor was it good business for corporations "to take substantial benefits from their membership in the economic community while avoiding the normally accepted obligations of citizenship in the social community." Mr. Irving S. Olds, former chairman of the board of the United States Steel Corporation, pointed out that corporations have a self-interest in the maintenance of liberal education as the bulwark of good government. He stated that "Capitalism and free enterprise owe their survival in no small degree to the existence of our private, independent universities" and that if American business does not aid in their maintenance it is not "properly protecting the long-range interest of its stockholders, its employees and its customers." Similarly, Dr. Harold W. Dodds, President of Princeton University, suggested that if private institutions of higher learning were replaced by governmental institutions our society would be vastly different and private enterprise in other fields would fade out rather promptly. Further on he stated that "democratic society will not long endure if it does not nourish within itself strong centers of non-governmental fountains of knowledge, opinions of all sorts not governmentally or politically originated. If the time comes when all these centers are absorbed into government, then freedom as we know it, I submit, is at an end."

The objecting stockholders have not disputed any of the foregoing testimony nor the showing of great need by Princeton and other private institutions of higher learning and the important public service being rendered by them for democratic government and industry alike. Similarly, they have acknowledged that for over two decades there has been state legislation on our books which expresses a strong public policy in favor of corporate contributions such as that being questioned by them. Nevertheless, they have taken the position that (1) the plaintiff's certificate of incorporation does not expressly authorize the contribution and under common-law principles the company does not possess any implied or incidental power to make it, and (2) the New Jersey statutes which expressly authorize the contribution may not constitutionally be applied to the plaintiff, a corporation created long before their enactment. * * *

In his discussion of the early history of business corporations Professor Williston refers to a 1702 publication where the author stated flatly that "The general intent and end of all civil incorporations is for better government." And he points out that the early corporate charters, particularly their recitals, furnish additional support for the notion that the corporate object was the public one of managing and ordering the trade as well as the private one of profit for the members. See 3 *Select Essays on Anglo-American Legal History* 201 (1909); 1 *Fletcher, Corporations* (rev. ed. 1931), 6. See also *Currie's Administrators v. The Mutual Assurance Society, 4 Hen. & M. 315, 347 (Va. Sup. Ct. App. 1809)*, where Judge Roane referred to the English corporate charters and expressed the view that acts of incorporation ought never to be passed "but in consideration of services to be rendered to the public." However, with later economic and social developments and the free availability of the corporate device for all trades, the end of private profit became generally accepted as the controlling one in all businesses other than those classed broadly as public utilities. *Cf. Dodd, For Whom Are Corporate Managers Trustees?, 45 Harv. L. Rev. 1145, 1148 (1932)*. As a concomitant the common-law rule developed that those who managed the corporation could not disburse any corporate funds for philanthropic or other worthy public cause unless the expenditure would benefit the corporation. *Hutton v. West Cork Railway Company, 23 Ch. D. 654 (1883); Dodge v. Ford Motor Co., 204 Mich. 459, 170 N.W. 668, 3 A.L.R. 413 (Sup. Ct. 1919). Ballantine, Corporations* (rev. ed. 1946), 228; 6A *Fletcher, supra*, 667. During the 19th Century when corporations were relatively few and small and did not dominate the country's wealth, the common-law rule did not significantly interfere with the public interest. But the 20th Century has presented a different climate. *Berle and Means, The Modern Corporation and Private Property* (1948). Control of economic wealth has passed largely from individual entrepreneurs to dominating corporations, and calls upon the corporations for reasonable philanthropic donations have come to be made with increased public support. In many instances such contributions have been sustained by the courts within the common-law doctrine upon liberal findings that the donations tended reasonably to promote the corporate objectives. * * *

Thus, in the leading case of *Evans v. Brunner, Mond & Company, Ltd. [1921] 1 Ch. 359,* the court held that it was within the incidental power of a chemical company to grant $100,000 to universities or other scientific institutions selected by the directors "for the furtherance of scientific education and research." The testimony indicated that the company desired to encourage and assist men who would devote their time and abilities to scientific study and research generally, a class of men for whom the company was constantly on the lookout. This benefit was not considered by the court to be so remote as to bring it outside the common-law rule. Similarly, in *Armstrong Cork Co. v. H.A. Meldrum Co., 285 F. 58 (D.C.W.D.N.Y. 1922),* the court sustained contributions made by the corporation to the University of Buffalo and Canisius College. In the course of its opinion the court quoted the familiar comment from *Steinway v. Steinway & Sons, 17 Misc. 43, 40 N.Y.S. 718 (Sup. Ct. 1896),* to the effect that as industrial conditions change business methods must change with them and acts become permissible which theretofore were considered beyond the corporate powers; and on the issue as to whether the corporation had received any corporate benefit it said:

"It was also considered, in making the subscriptions or donations, that the company would receive advertisement of substantial value, including the good will of many influential citizens and of its patrons, who were interested in the success of the development of these branches of education, and, on the other hand, suffer a loss of prestige if the contributions were not made, in view of the fact that business competitors had donated and shown a commendable public spirit in that relation. In the circumstances the rule of law that may fairly be applied is that the action of the officers of the company was not *ultra vires* ["outside the powers of the corporation"], but was in fact within their corporate powers, since it tended to promote the welfare of the business in which the corporation was engaged."

In *American Rolling Mill Co. v. Commissioner of Internal Revenue, 41 F. 2d 314 (C.C.A. 6 1930),* the corporation had joined with other local industries in the creation of a civic improvement fund to be distributed amongst community enterprises including the Boy Scouts and Girl Scouts, the Y.M.C.A., the Hospital, etc. The court readily sustained the contribution as an ordinary and necessary expense of the business within the Revenue Act. And in *Greene County Nat. Farm Loan Ass'n v. Federal Land Bank of Louisville, 57 F. Supp. 783, 789 (D.C.W.D. Ky. 1944),* affirmed *152 F. 2d 215 (6th Cir. 1945),* cert. denied *328 U.S. 834, 66 S. Ct. 978, 90 L. Ed. 1610 (1946),* the court in dealing with a comparable problem said:

"But it is equally well established that corporations are permitted to make substantial contributions which have the outward form of gifts where the activity being promoted by the so-called gift tends reasonably to promote the goodwill of the business of the contributing corporation. Courts recognize in such cases that although there is no dollar and cent supporting consideration, yet there is often substantial indirect benefit accruing to the corporation which supports such action. So-called contributions by corporations to churches, schools, hospitals, and civic improvement funds, and the establishment of bonus and pension plans with the payment of large sums flowing therefrom have been upheld many times as reasonable business expenditures rather than being classified as charitable gifts. * * *"

The foregoing authorities illustrate how courts, while adhering to the terms of the common-law rule, have applied it very broadly to enable worthy corporate donations with indirect benefits to the corporations. In *State ex rel. Sorensen v. Chicago B. & Q.R. Co., 112 Neb. 248, 199 N.W. 534, 537 (1924)*, the Supreme Court of Nebraska, through Justice Letton, went even further and without referring to any limitation based on economic benefits to the corporation said that it saw "no reason why if a railroad company desires to foster, encourage and contribute to a charitable enterprise, or to one designed for the public weal and welfare, it may not do so" * * *. Similarly, the court in *Carey v. Corporation Commission of Oklahoma, 168 Okla. 487, 33 P. 2d 788, 794 (Sup. Ct. 1934)*, while holding that a public service company was not entitled to an increase in its rates because of its reasonable charitable donations, broadly recognized that corporations, like individuals, have power to make them. * * * In the course of his opinion for the court in the *Carey* case Justice Bayless said:

> "Next is the question of dues, donations, and philanthropies of the Company. It is a matter for the discretion of corporate management in making donations and paying dues. In that respect a corporation does not occupy a status far different from an individual. An individual determines the propriety of joining organizations, and contributing to their support by paying dues, and all contribution to public charities, etc., according to his means. He does not make such contributions above his means with the hope that his employer will increase his compensation accordingly. A corporation likewise should not do so. Its ultimate purpose, from its own standpoint, is to earn and pay dividends. If, as a matter of judgment, it desires to take part of its earnings, just as would an individual, and contribute them to a worthy public cause, it may do so; but we do not feel that it should be allowed to increase its earnings to take care thereof."

Over 20 years ago Professor Dodd, *supra, 45 Harv. L. Rev., at 1159, 1160*, cited the views of Justice Letton in *State ex rel. Sorensen v. Chicago B. & Q.R. Co., supra*, with seeming approval and suggested the doctrine that corporations may properly support charities which are important to the welfare of the communities where they do business as soundly representative of the public attitude and actual corporate practice. Developments since he wrote leave no doubts on this score.

When the wealth of the nation was primarily in the hands of individuals they discharged their responsibilities as citizens by donating freely for charitable purposes. With the transfer of most of the wealth to corporate hands and the imposition of heavy burdens of individual taxation, they have been unable to keep pace with increased philanthropic needs. They have therefore, with justification, turned to corporations to assume the modern obligations of good citizenship in the same manner as humans do. Congress and state legislatures have enacted laws which encourage corporate contributions, and much has recently been written to indicate the crying need and adequate legal basis therefor. * * * In actual practice corporate giving has correspondingly increased. Thus, it is estimated that annual corporate contributions throughout the nation aggregate over 300 million dollars with over 60 million dollars thereof going to universities and other educational institutions. Similarly, it is estimated that local community chests receive well over 40% of their contributions from corporations; these contributions and those made by corporations to the American Red Cross, to Boy Scouts and Girl Scouts, to 4–H Clubs and similar organizations have almost invariably been unquestioned.

During the first world war corporations loaned their personnel and contributed substantial corporate funds in order to insure survival; during the depression of the '30s they made contributions to alleviate the desperate hardships of the millions of unemployed; and during the second world war they again contributed to insure survival. They now recognize that we are faced with other, though nonetheless vicious, threats from abroad which must be withstood without impairing the vigor of our democratic institutions at home and that otherwise victory will be pyrrhic indeed. More and more they have come to recognize that their salvation rests upon sound economic and social environment which in turn rests in no insignificant part upon free and vigorous non-governmental institutions of learning. It seems to us that just as the conditions prevailing when corporations were originally created required that they serve public as well as private interests, modern conditions require that corporations acknowledge and discharge social as well as private responsibilities as members of the communities within which they operate. Within this broad concept there is no difficulty in sustaining, as incidental to their proper objects and in aid of the public welfare, the power of corporations to contribute corporate funds within reasonable limits in support of academic institutions. But even if we confine ourselves to the terms of the common-law rule in its application to current conditions, such expenditures may likewise readily be justified as being for the benefit of the corporation; indeed, if need be the matter may be viewed strictly in terms of actual survival of the corporation in a free enterprise system. The genius of our common law has been its capacity for growth and its adaptability to the needs of the times. Generally courts have accomplished the desired result indirectly through the molding of old forms. Occasionally they have done it directly through frank rejection of the old and recognition of the new. But whichever path the common law has taken it has not been found wanting as the proper tool for the advancement of the general good. Cf. Holmes, *The Common Law*, 1, 5 (1951); Cardozo, *Paradoxes of Legal Science, Hall, Selected Writings*, 253 (1947).

In 1930 a statute was enacted in our State which expressly provided that any corporation could cooperate with other corporations and natural persons in the creation and maintenance of community funds and charitable, philanthropic or benevolent instrumentalities conducive to public welfare, and could for such purposes expend such corporate sums as the directors "deem expedient and as in their judgment will contribute to the protection of the corporate interests." *L. 1930, c. 105; L. 1931, c. 290; R.S. 14:3–13.* * * * Under the terms of the statute donations in excess of 1% of the capital stock required 10 days' notice to stockholders and approval at a stockholders' meeting if written objections were made by the holders of more than 25% of the stock; in 1949 the statute was amended to increase the limitation to 1% of capital and surplus. * * * In 1950 a more comprehensive statute was enacted. *L. 1950, c. 220; N.J.S.A. 14:3–13.1 et seq.* In this enactment the Legislature declared that it shall be the public policy of our State and in furtherance of the public interest and welfare that encouragement be given to the creation and maintenance of institutions engaged in community fund, hospital, charitable, philanthropic, educational, scientific or benevolent activities or patriotic or civic activities conducive to the betterment of social and economic conditions; and it expressly empowered corporations acting singly or with others to contribute reasonable sums to such institutions, provided, however, that the contribution shall not be permissible if the donee institution owns more than 10% of the voting stock of the donor and provided, further, that the contribution shall not exceed 1% of capital and surplus unless the excess is authorized by the stockholders at a regular or special meeting. To insure that the grant of express power in the 1950 statute would not displace preexisting power at common law or otherwise, the Legislature provided that the "act shall not be construed as directly or indirectly minimizing or interpreting the rights and powers of corporations, as heretofore existing, with reference to appropriations, expenditures or contributions of the nature above specified." N.J.S.A. 14:3–13.3. It may be noted that statutes relating to charitable contributions by corporations have now been passed in 29 states. * * *

The appellants contend that the foregoing New Jersey statutes may not be applied to corporations created before their passage. Fifty years before the incorporation of The A.P. Smith Manufacturing Company our Legislature provided that every corporate charter thereafter granted "shall be subject to alteration, suspension and repeal, in the discretion of the legislature." L. 1846, p. 16; R.S. 14:2–9. A similar reserved power was placed into our State Constitution in 1875 (*Art. IV, Sec. VII, par.* 11), and is found in our present Constitution. *Art.* IV, *Sec.* VII, *par.* 9. In the early case of *Zabriskie v. Hackensack and New York Railroad Company, 18 N.J. Eq. 178 (Ch. 1867),* the court was called upon to determine whether a railroad could extend its line, above objection by a stockholder, under a legislative enactment passed under the reserve power after the incorporation of the railroad. Notwithstanding the breadth of the statutory language and persuasive authority elsewhere * * *, it was held that the proposed extension of the company's line constituted a vital change of its corporate object which could not be accomplished without unanimous consent. See *Lattin, A Primer on Fundamental Corporate Changes, 1 West. Res. L. Rev. 3, 7 (1949).* The court announced the now familiar New Jersey doctrine that although the reserved power permits alterations in the public interest of the contract between the state and the corporation, it has no effect on the contractual rights between the corporation and its stockholders and between stockholders * * *. Unfortunately, the court did not consider whether it was not contrary to the public interest to permit the single minority stockholder before it to restrain the railroad's normal corporate growth and development as authorized by the Legislature and approved, reasonably and in good faith, by the corporation's managing directors and majority stockholders. Although the later cases in New Jersey have not disavowed the doctrine of the *Zabriskie* case, it is noteworthy that they have repeatedly recognized that where justified by the advancement of the public interest the reserved power may be invoked to sustain later charter alterations even though they affect contractual rights between the corporation and its stockholders and between stockholders * * *. See *Berger v. United States Steel Corporation, 63 N.J. Eq. 809, 824 (E. & A. 1902); Murray v. Beattie Manufacturing Co., 79 N.J. Eq. 604, 609 (E. & A. 1912); Grausman v. Porto Rican–American Tobacco Co., 95 N.J. Eq. 155 (Ch. 1923)* * * * *Bingham v. Savings Investment & Trust Co., 101 N.J. Eq. 413, 415 (Ch. 1927),* affirmed *102 N.J. Eq. 302 (E. & A. 1928); In re Collins–Doan Co., 3 N.J. 382, 391 (1949). Cf. State v. Miller, 30 N.J.L. 368, 373 (Sup. Ct. 1863),* affirmed *31 N.J.L. 521 (E. & A. 1864); Montclair v. New York & Greenwood Lake Railway Co., 45 N.J. Eq 436, 444 (Ch. 1889),* * * * *Moore v. Conover, 123 N.J. Eq. 61, 74 (Ch. 1937).*

Thus, in the *Berger* case the Court of Errors and Appeals sustained the applicability under the reserved power of provisions relating to corporate borrowing and the purchase of corporate stock, and in considering the doctrine of the *Zabriskie* case noted that the rights of the stockholders * * * may not be impaired "except in so far as impairment may result from an alteration required by the public interest." And later in its opinion the court, referring to the provision in the Corporation Act of 1896 that the act and all amendments shall be a part of the charter of every corporation formed theretofore or thereafter, said: "It is difficult to perceive how any substantial force can be accorded to it, unless some amendment may be made which may affect the rights of stockholders *inter sese* ['among themselves'] to some extent." In the *Murray* case the court sustained a statute substituting a discretionary power to pay dividends for a pre-existing duty; in the course of his opinion Justice Swayze indicated that even apart from stockholders' consent the statutory alteration could be sustained since it was "a matter of state concern that a corporation should be permitted to accumulate a sufficient fund to secure its credit and make permanent its successful operation." And in the *Bingham* case the court sustained a bank merger under the authority of legislation enacted after the incorporation of the bank, with Vice-Chancellor Backes pointing out that the office of the reserve power in our organic and statutory law "is to safeguard the public interests in corporate grants."

This court had recent occasion to deal with the problem in *In re Collins-Doan Co., supra.* There it appeared that the board of directors was hopelessly deadlocked and application was duly made under *L. 1938, c. 303 (N.J.S.A. 14:13–15)* by the plaintiffs, representing half the directors and stockholders, for dissolution of the corporation. The defendants representing the other half resisted the application, contending that since the corporation was formed in 1916 it could not be dissolved except with the consent of two-thirds of the stockholders. This court, while recognizing that the later enactment did affect the rights between the corporation and its stockholders and between the stockholders *inter se* ["among themselves"], nevertheless held that it was applicable to the pre-existing corporation as a proper exercise of the reserved power. In the course of his opinion for the court Justice Heher pointed out that "the contractual rights of the stockholders *inter se* are not proof against 'alteration required by the public interest.' " It may be noted that the later enactment not only affected the relations between the corporation and stockholders and the stockholders *inter se*, but also enabled complete termination of the original corporate objectives; yet this court found little difficulty in subordinating these considerations to the paramount public interest in avoiding the indefinite continuance of a corporation which could not function with propriety because of the "stalemate in corporate management." * * * The legislative function recognized here may be considered somewhat akin to that under the police power generally where private interests frequently are called upon to give way to the paramount public interest. See * * * *Lakewood Express Service, Inc. v. Board of Public Utility Commissioners, 1 N.J. 45, 50 (1948)*, where Justice Oliphant, in discussing the police power, said:

> "This power extends to all great public needs and the constitutional interdictions as to due process and the protection of property rights does not prevent a state from exercising such powers as are vested in it for the promotion of the common weal or are necessary for the general good of the public even though property or contract rights are affected. * * * "

State legislation adopted in the public interest and applied to pre-existing corporations under the reserved power has repeatedly been sustained by the United States Supreme Court above the contention that it impairs the rights of stockholders and violates constitutional guarantees under the Federal Constitution. Thus, in *Looker v. Maynard, 179 U.S. 46, 21 S. Ct. 21, 45 L. Ed. 79 (1900)*, the court sustained the application to pre-existing corporations of later legislation designed to secure minority representation on boards of directors by permitting cumulative voting by stockholders; in *Polk v. Mutual Reserve Fund Life Association of New York, 207 U.S. 310, 28 S. Ct. 65, 52 L. Ed. 222 (1907)*, the court sustained state legislation which permitted reorganizations of existing corporations involving changes in their corporate purposes * * * and in *Sutton v. New Jersey, 244 U.S. 258, 37 S. Ct. 508, 61 L. Ed. 1117 (1917)*, a New Jersey statute which required pre-existing street railway corporations to carry police officers without charge was upheld as a proper exercise of the reserve power. * * *

It seems clear to us that the public policy supporting the statutory enactments under consideration is far greater and the alteration of pre-existing rights of stockholders much lesser than in the cited cases sustaining various exercises of the reserve power. In encouraging and expressly authorizing reasonable charitable contributions by corporations, our State has not only joined with other states in advancing the national interest but has also specially furthered the interests of its own people who must bear the burdens of taxation resulting from increased state and federal aid upon default in voluntary giving. It is significant that in its enactments the State had not in anywise sought to impose any compulsory obligations or alter the corporate objectives. And since in our view the corporate power to make reasonable charitable contributions exists under modern conditions, even apart from express statutory provision, its enactments simply constitute helpful and confirmatory declarations of such power, accompanied by limiting safeguards.

In the light of all of the foregoing we have no hesitancy in sustaining the validity of the donation by the plaintiff. There is no suggestion that it was made indiscriminately or to a pet charity of the corporate directors in furtherance of personal rather than corporate ends. On the contrary, it was made to a preeminent institution of higher learning, was modest in amount and well within the limitations imposed by the statutory enactments, and was voluntarily made in the reasonable belief that it would aid the public welfare and advance the interests of the plaintiff as a private corporation and as part of the community in which it operates. We find that it was a lawful exercise of the corporation's implied and incidental powers under common-law principles and that it came within the express authority of the pertinent state legislation. As has been indicated, there is now widespread belief throughout the nation that free and vigorous non-governmental institutions of learning are vital to our democracy and the system of free enterprise and that withdrawal of corporate authority to make such contributions within reasonable limits would seriously threaten their continuance. Corporations have come to recognize this and with their enlightenment have sought in varying measures, as has the plaintiff by its contribution, to insure and strengthen the society which gives them existence and the means of aiding themselves and their fellow citizens. Clearly then, the appellants, as individual stockholders whose private interests rest entirely upon the well-being of the plaintiff corporation, ought not be permitted to close their eyes to present-day realities and thwart the long-visioned corporate action in recognizing and voluntarily discharging its high obligations as a constituent of our modern social structure.

* * *

NOTES AND QUESTIONS

I. AT ISSUE IN *SMITH v. BARLOW* is a $1500 donation to Princeton University that plaintiffs argue the corporate charter does not grant the directors the power to authorize. The defendant corporation argues that such philanthropic donations obtain good-will from the community, create a "favorable environment for their business," and further the corporation's "self-interest in assuring the free flow of properly trained personnel for . . . corporate employment." To resolve the dispute the court looks to the common law rule that corporations cannot "disburse any corporate funds for philanthropic or other worthy public cause[s] unless the expenditure would benefit the corporation." The court holds that a contribution to Princeton does benefit the corporation. Do you agree? Where would you draw the line? If a contribution to a university benefits the corporation, what kind of contributions would not? Even if you think the judges applied the rule correctly, does it make sense that corporations can only act in their own self-interest?

2. TO SUPPORT THE CLAIM that corporations should be allowed to make public donations, the defendants offer testimony from various industry leaders such as the chairmen of Standard Oil and U.S. Steel. The President of Princeton University goes so far as to suggest that "democratic society will not long endure" if corporations cannot make charitable contributions. Is this correct? The court observes that "we are faced with other . . . threats from abroad which must be withstood without impairing the vigor of our democratic institutions at home." The court continues, indicating that corporate "survival rests upon [a] sound economic and social environment which in turn rests in no insignificant part upon free and vigorous non-governmental institutions of learning." What threats do you suppose the court had in mind? Do they continue? Have other "threats" taken their place? Is protecting a $1500 donation to Princeton really saving the democratic cause? On the other hand, after the collapse of the Berlin Wall and the demise of Soviet-style communism, do you think decisions like *Barlow* did in fact help promote and protect capitalism?

3. WHAT DO YOU MAKE of the Court's analysis and exposition of the manner of operation of the common law? You will have noted that the Court, citing, *inter alia*, Holmes and Cardozo, suggests that it is part of the task of the common law judge to mold the common law to fit the needs of the times. Is this what judges are supposed to do? From an historical perspective, the Supreme Court of New Jersey seems to have decided the case correctly. They accurately note that the common-law rule has been applied "very broadly to enable worthy corporate donations with indirect benefits to the corporations." The court observes that early 19th century corporations would most likely not have been allowed to make such a contribution to Princeton, but the court suggests that changes in wealth patterns should alter the common-law rule. The court points out that "[c]ontrol of economic wealth has passed largely from individual entrepreneurs to dominating corporations, and calls upon the corporation for reasonable philanthropic donations have come to be made with increased public support." Because wealth was no longer held by a limited number of individuals who, under the old rule, could distribute their income to any source they desired, but instead by a limited number of corporations who cannot donate under the old rule, the court believed that the rule had already been relaxed according to widespread public interest and desire. The court is correct in its analysis of wealth distribution. Still, if some of the profits of a corporation that might have been used for charitable contributions are distributed to its shareholders, as dividends, is it clear that they would only use those funds for personal purposes, or might the individuals donate to the charities of their choice, possibly not including Princeton? If there really are social problems that require public donations to private institutions to ameliorate, would shareholders not also be sensitive to these needs and wish to contribute as individuals? If the court holds true to the principle of shareholder primacy, does that really spell doom for charities and public institutions, or would it enable a more democratic selection of charitable donations, in which individuals may select which charities and causes they wish to support? Is the *Smith v. Barlow* case undemocratic?

....

4. AS WE SAW IN *Ford v. Dodge*, the issue of the social responsibilities and duties of corporations is a complicated one. Debates over to whom corporations owe obligations have no doubt existed since the first corporation, but one important debate in American legal circles, alluded to by the court in *Smith v. Barlow*, took place in the pages of the *Harvard Law Review* between A.A. Berle and E. Merrick Dodd in 1932.

Writing in 2002, Professor C.A. Harwell Wells[51] argued that all subsequent debates over corporate responsibility "shar[e] conceptual foundations" with the debate between Berle and Dodd.[52] Professor Wells indicates that like the controversy

---

51   C.A. Harwell Wells, "The Cycles of Corporate Social Responsibility: An Historical Retrospective for the Twenty-first century," 51 Kan L.Rev. 77 (2002).

52   Id., at 79.

between Berle and Dodd, all subsequent controversies share four characteristic premises. The first is that corporate "social responsibility is about big business" and that legal scholars writing about corporate responsibility always "really mean the responsibility of giant corporations." The second premise is that the goal is "to reform corporate power, not eliminate it," and because of this goal, no "proponents of corporate social responsibility were genuinely radical." Third, the general form of the debate, regardless of the period when it took place, always remains "duty to owners alone versus duties to many constituencies." The final premise, according to Wells, is that "each decade supplies its own reason why corporations should assume greater responsibility," which Wells calls "an unchanging solution to an ever-new problem."[53]

The publication of E. Merrick Dodd's "For Whom Are Corporate Managers Trustees?"[54] helped to begin the still-ongoing modern debate regarding corporate social responsibility. Dodd saw the 1920s, before the crash of 1929, as "a moment in time when corporations had finally begun to take responsibility for their employees and communities."[55] Both Dodd and his principal adversary, A.A. Berle, were responding to the fact, noted earlier, that by the first third of the twentieth century, at least with regard to large publicly-held corporations, there had come to be an increasing separation between ownership and management, as corporations were controlled by their officers and directors, and shareholders had become, essentially, passive investors.

A.A. Berle saw this separation as something that should be reflected by changes in the law, that the law had formerly given too much deference to corporate owners, and that since they were now removed from control, managers should be regulated, to make them act more like responsible owners, and, in particular, to get them to assume responsibility not just to line the pockets of their passive shareholders, but also to assume some of the social burdens of the time.[56] Dodd, while sympathizing somewhat with Berle's desire for social responsibility, saw Berle's solution—increased regulation—as too radical.

Dodd argued that appropriate rules were already in place, and that added regulation would probably halt or, at best, slow economic progress. Dodd wanted managers, instead of being subject to regulation, to have the flexibility to respond to the times as they saw fit. He wrote "many conservatives . . . believe that capitalism is worth

---

53   Id., at 80–81.

54   E. Merrick Dodd, Jr., *For Whom Are Corporate Managers Trustees?*, 45 Harv. L. Rev. 1145 (1932).

55   Wells, supra note 50, at 92.

56   This argument was most fully elaborated in A.A. Berle and Gardner Means, *The Corporation and Private Property* (1932), a modern classic.

saving but that it can not permanently survive under modern conditions unless it treats the economic security of the worker as one of its obligations and is intelligently directed so as to attain that object."[57] Dodd argued, however, that regulations passed in the interests of employees and consumers "may increasingly limit the methods which managers of incorporated business enterprises may employ in seeking profits for their stockholders without in any way affecting the proposition that the sole function of such managers is to work for the best interests of the stockholders."

Dodd saw business as "a profession of public service, not primarily because the law had made it such but because a public opinion shared by business men themselves had brought about a professional attitude."[58] Dodd believed that if corporate managers were to be left to their own devices, they would come up with solutions to problems more efficiently than if government regulations mandated charitable contributions or safe workplaces—that public outcry would direct the actions of those at the top of corporations more efficiently than federal regulation. Dodd wrote "power over the lives of others tends to create on the part of those most worthy to exercise it a sense of responsibility."[59] Do you agree? Are those in charge often those most "worthy"?

A.A. Berle was much less sanguine. As did many American academics, he believed that the Great Depression and the stock market crash came about because of widespread misconduct. He saw the 1920s as a time rife with corporate wrongdoing and stock market fraud. Writing in response to Dodd, Berle suggested that leaving management unfettered by outside regulation "might be unsafe" and was "an invitation not to law or orderly government, but to a process of economic civil war."[60] Berle believed that corporate management had accomplished a "seizure of power without recognition of responsibility-ambition without courage."[61] According to Professor Wells, Berle's "problem with Dodd's proposal was not that it replaced shareholder primacy with broader responsibilities, but that it replaced shareholder primacy with nothing at all."[62] Does *Smith v. Barlow* follow the principle of "shareholder primacy," or does it replace it with something else?

---

57   Dodd, *For Whom Are Corporate Managers Trustees?*, 45 Harv. L. Rev 1145.

58   Dodd, supra note 56, at 1154.

59   Id., at 1157.

60   A.A. Berle, Jr., *For Whom Corporate Managers Are Trustees: A Note*, 45 Harv. L. Rev. 1365, 1369 (1932).

61   Ibid.

62   Wells, supra, note 50, at 95.

6. PROFESSOR CYNTHIA A. WILLIAMS nicely suggests that what Dodd and Berle were arguing about was "the extent to which the corporation should be thought of primarily as an economic entity, versus the extent to which it should be thought of primarily as a social entity."[63] Professor Williams argues that globalization "undermines sovereigns' power to regulate corporate activity . . . companies can, and do, move their productive processes to different countries or 'outsource' to independent producers in other countries to take advantage of competitive opportunities."[64] Williams wonders whether the principle of shareholder primacy with its attendant lack of regulation in the interest of non-shareholder constituencies is appropriate for our age of globalization. She suggests that we should require greater "transparency" in the international activities of our corporations, primarily through mandating increased disclosure of corporate activities. One could, of course, go further, and suggests that American courts, realizing the problem of there being no appropriate international body to regulate corporations, should, once they shake off the purportedly archaic notions of shareholder primacy, offer themselves as a forum to aid non-shareholder plaintiffs from all over the world in getting corporations to operate in their interests. Would this sort of a change in the common law be appropriate? Would the judges in *Smith v. Barlow* have approved? Is the notion of "shareholder primacy" archaic, or is there still much to be said for it? And what of Delaware, the state that has done more than any other to facilitate the operation of and the investment in the management-run modern American corporation?

---

63 Cynthia A. Williams "Symposium: Corporations Theory and Corporate Governance Law: Corporate Social Responsibility in an Era of Economic Globalization." 35 U.C. Davis L. Rev. 705. 707 (2002).

64 Id. at 726.

IV. A Note on Delaware Incorporation

Over 50% of all publicly-traded American corporations and 58% of Fortune 500 corporations are incorporated in Delaware. According to the state's webpage, "[b]usinesses choose Delaware because we provide a complete package of incorporation services including modern and flexible corporate laws, our highly-respected Court of Chancery, a business-friendly State Government, and the customer service oriented Staff of the Delaware Division of Corporations."

At first blush, it seems surprising that a tiny state on the Eastern Seaboard should be the nominal home to so many great American corporations. How did this come about? As already indicated, towards the end of the 19th century, many states began to relax their general incorporation laws in an attempt to attract more corporations and acquire more revenue from franchise taxes and fees associated with incorporation. Initially, it was Delaware's neighbor, New Jersey, which won this battle. In 1896, New Jersey enacted the most liberal general incorporation law in the nation. Soon, however, Woodrow Wilson, then governor of New Jersey, spearheaded an effort to change the policies of the state, and New Jersey passed the "Seven Sisters Act" in 1913, effectively outlawing trusts (a device by which a very small number of persons could control a large number of corporations) and holding companies (corporations that owned other corporations). Soon after, Delaware, which still permitted such devices, found itself the nation's leading haven for incorporation.

After the stock market crash of 1929, and the passage of significant federal legislation to regulate the issuance and trading in the stock of corporations, the wave of incorporations in Delaware subsided somewhat, and after the close of World War II, many states revised their laws to compete more effectively with Delaware. In 1967 the Delaware Bar Association, with the aid of many leading corporate law experts, substantially revised Delaware's General Corporation Law in order once again to make the state the most attractive for incorporation. One of the most important changes to come out of that revision is a speedy amendment process for the Delaware Corporations statutes, which "allows the Delaware General Assembly to keep ahead of legal developments, fix ambiguities in the law, and correct problems noted by judicial decisions."

Delaware's Corporate legislation, and the process whereby the state seeks to be the premier site for incorporation, are not without their critics. Over the years, many scholars, politicians and even some judges have blasted Delaware and other states that have purportedly loosened restrictions on corporations. One of the most famous such critiques came from Supreme Court Associate Justice LOUIS BRANDEIS writing in dissent in *Louis K. Liggett Co. v. Lee*. Said the great Justice and former prototype of the public interest lawyer,

> "[t]he removal by the leading industrial states of the limitations upon the size and powers of business corporations appears to have been due, not to their conviction that maintenance of the restrictions was undesirable

in itself, but to the conviction that it was futile to insist upon them; because local restriction would be circumvented by foreign incorporation. Indeed, local restriction seemed worse than futile. Lesser states, eager for the revenue derived from the traffic in charters, had removed safeguards from their own incorporation laws. Companies were early formed to provide charters for corporations in states where the cost was lowest and the laws least restrictive. The states joined in advertising their wares. *The race was one not of diligence but of laxity.* Incorporation under such laws was possible; and the great industrial States yielded in order not to lose wholly the prospect of the revenue and the control incident to domestic incorporation." [Emphasis supplied][65]

BRANDEIS thus regarded Delaware's attempts to liberalize corporate law as a cynical ploy by the state to raise and protect revenue associated with incorporation. Was Brandeis correct, or are there more benign explanations for Delaware's success as a haven for incorporation?

In a manner similar to the assertions of BRANDEIS, after the 1967 revisions of Delaware's Corporations Law, in a seminal piece for the Yale Law Journal,[66] Professor William L. Cary stated that "Delaware is both the sponsor and the victim of a system contributing to the deterioration of corporation standards." Professor Cary argued that the competition among the states to attract incorporation was "a race to the bottom," in which the states tried to outdo each other in creating the most lenient business laws, to attract incorporations in order to raise funds through fees, while failing to protect shareholders, workers and consumers.

Professor Cary did not level all of his fire on Delaware for the race to the bottom phenomenon, noting that "other states would have joined in to attract the lucrative business of incorporating." Still, Cary challenged Delaware's claim to be acting in the best interests of its corporations, as he observed that at the time his article was published, Delaware derived approximately a quarter of its state revenue from incorporations and franchise taxes. In Delaware, Cary stated, "both the courts and the legislature may be said to lack the neutrality and detachment 'to hold the balance nice, clear, and true' required in passing upon the complaints of shareholders." Cary thought that Delaware's corporate law unduly favored management and thus posed a danger to shareholders. He thought it wrong that one tiny state should possess such power to "set social policy in the corporate field." His solution was to advocate federal chartering of corporations, with more stringent regulatory standards.

Consider Professor Cary's thesis. Do you think that because Delaware raises large amounts of revenue through incorporations that the state has lost its impartiality, and cannot be trusted to come up with a system that is fair to shareholders, managers, and the rest of the corporate constituencies or stakeholders? Do you think

---

65   *Louis K. Liggett Co. v. Lee*, 288 U.S. 517, 557–560, 53 S.Ct. 481, 77 L.Ed. 929 (1933).

66   William L. Cary, Federalism and Corporate Law: Reflections upon Delaware, 83 Yale L.J. 663 (1974).

if Delaware's laws were dangerous to shareholders that shareholders would invest in Delaware corporations, instead of corporations incorporated in states with laws that may be more favorable? Professor Cary argues that management decisions "should be disclosed and monitored by outside groups" to protect investors. Cary favors a federally supervised plan requiring frequent shareholder approval of corporate transactions, the abolition of nonvoting shares and federal fiduciary standards. Do you agree with Professor Cary as to the extent of the threat states like Delaware pose to shareholders' rights? Do you think that increased federal regulation would better protect shareholders' rights? As we will soon see, ever since Cary's piece there has been substantial federal intervention further to regulate corporations, on the theory that state law does not adequately protect shareholders. The solution endorsed by many critics of the current system of corporate management continues to be to give shareholders more explicitly-protected rights and more opportunities for corporate control. Do you think investors desire this level of involvement or do more investors prefer a passive role in the management of corporate affairs? Would changes such as those Cary advocates (changes, by the way, that seem to be the thrust of modern federal legislation) solve the problem that Berle perceived because of the separation of corporate ownership from management?

Professor Cary's "race to the bottom" thesis was attacked by equally passionate defenders of Delaware. They argued that Delaware and other states were engaged not in a "race to the bottom," but rather in a "race to the top" to find the optimal form of corporate regulation. According to this view Delaware's success in attracting incorporators is the result of Delaware's success in crafting legislation which permitted more profitable corporate operation, thus benefiting shareholders, who otherwise would not stand for incorporation or reincorporation (moving one's state of incorporation) in Delaware. The fact that the traffic in reincorporation seemed to run virtually only one way (into Delaware) is often cited as evidence of Delaware's positive achievement, as is the fact that the stock market prices shares higher once corporations reincorporate in Delaware. Nevertheless, although no general federal incorporation statute, along the lines advocated by Cary was ever passed, his "race to the bottom thesis" still survives, especially in some parts of the legal academy. Professor John C. Coffee, Jr. wrote in a response to critics of Cary that Cary's article, among other effects, "embarrassed and infuriated the Delaware bench and bar, may have been responsible for a surprising string of pro-shareholder decisions in Delaware over the next decade, provoked the then adolescent 'law and economics' movement to argue that the race was to the top, not the bottom, and motivated Ralph Nader and similar corporate reformers to join Cary in recommending federal chartering of corporations."[67]

---

67 John C. Coffee, Jr., Commentary on William L. Cary, Federalism and Corporate Law: Reflections Upon Delaware, 83 YALE L.J. 663 (1974), 100 Yale L.J. 1449 (1991) (Part of commentary on the most-cited law review articles from the Yale Law Journal. Cary's article was number fourteen).

Catherine Holst has pointed out that "the American debate over the 'race to the bottom' thesis assumes as a starting point that regulatory competition has beneficial effects."[68] Holst believes that federal minimum standards could be designed to place limits on the extent to which states could favor management over shareholders. Holst concludes that while Professor Cary's article has advanced the debate over the nature of competition for corporate charters, "his conclusions are arguably not self-evident and indeed, his call for federal regulatory intervention has gone unheeded in the U.S." See if you agree with Ms. Holst after considering the federal law to which will soon turn.

It may still be true, however, that state law is still the primary regulator of corporations. Why do you suppose, then, that Cary's call for federal regulation has been unsuccessful? Who gets it right, Cary or his critics? Cary singled out several purportedly pernicious provisions of the Delaware Corporate law, some of which we will return to later, but which might be quickly summarized.

(1) Cary observed that it was easier to accomplish organic change (mergers, sale of substantially all of the assets, amending of the corporate charter, etc.) in Delaware than in any other state, since all that was required was a vote of the majority of the board followed by a vote of the majority of the shareholders. Other states often required super-majority votes to accomplish such matters. (2) Cary suggested that it was easier to declare dividends in Delaware than in any other state, and (3) Cary observed that Delaware did not require cumulative voting for shareholders (which procedure made it easier for shareholder minorities to be represented on the Board), that (4) Delaware did not require that all members of the Board be subject to election each year, that (5) Delaware did not require pre-emptive rights (allowing shareholders the first option of purchasing an aliquot share of new issues of corporate stock), and that (6) Delaware went further than any other state in allowing corporations to hold officers and directors harmless for action taken in good faith, but which later proved deleterious to the corporation. Looking at all of this, in a famous metaphor, Cary stated that Delaware "waters down the rights of shareholders to a thin gruel." Do you agree?

One way of trying to understand whether Delaware law is good or bad for shareholders is to try to discern how Delaware law orders the relationship among shareholders, directors, and officers. A fine vehicle for seeking to achieve this understanding is the great case of *Campbell v. Loews*, which follows. Would you say that the opinion of Judge SEITZ in that case seeks admirably to protect shareholders or not?

---

68   Catherine Holst, *European Company Law after Centros: Is the EU on the Road to Delaware?*, 8 Colum. J. Eur. L. 323 (2002).

V. The Players in the Corporation: Shareholders, Directors, and Officers

RECALL THE THREE CATEGORIES of participants in the ownership and management of a corporation: stockholders, officers, and directors. Stockholders are the owners of the corporation, and vote on major corporate actions and to fill the board of directors. Officers are high-ranking employees of the corporation who direct its day-to-day business activity. Finally, directors have control of the business and determine its strategy. While directors are under no obligation to follow the wishes of stockholders, they can be voted out of office, and always owe fiduciary duties to the stockholders. The following classic case examines a fight for the control of a great American film company.

Campbell v. Loew's Inc.

Court of Chancery of Delaware, New Castle County.
36 Del.Ch. 563, 134 A.2d 852 (1957).

SEITZ, CHANCELLOR:

* * *

* * * Two factions have been fighting for control of Loew's. One faction is headed by Joseph Tomlinson (hereafter "Tomlinson faction") while the other is headed by the President of Loew's, Joseph Vogel (hereafter "Vogel faction"). At the annual meeting of stockholders last February a compromise was reached by which each nominated six directors and they in turn nominated a thirteenth or neutral director. * * * Passing by much of the controversy, we come to the July 17–18 period of this year when two of the six Vogel directors and the thirteenth or neutral director resigned. A quorum is seven.

On the 19th of July the Tomlinson faction asked that a directors' meeting be called for July 30 to consider, *inter alia*, the problem of filling director vacancies. On the eve of this meeting one of the Tomlinson directors resigned. This left five Tomlinson directors and four Vogel directors in office. Only the five Tomlinson directors attended the July 30 meeting. They purported to fill two of the director vacancies and to take other action. This Court has now ruled that for want of a quorum the two directors were not validly elected and the subsequent action taken at that meeting was invalid. * * *

On July 29, the day before the noticed directors' meeting, Vogel, as president, sent out a notice calling a stockholders' meeting for September 12 for the following purposes:

1. to fill director vacancies.

2. to amend the by-laws to increase the number of the board from 13 to 19; to increase the quorum from 7 to 10 and to elect six additional directors.

3. to remove Stanley Meyer and Joseph Tomlinson as directors and to fill such vacancies.

Still later, another notice for a September 12 stockholders' meeting as well as a proxy statement went out over the signature of Joseph R. Vogel, as president. It was accompanied by a letter from Mr. Vogel dated August 9, 1957, soliciting stockholder support for the matters noticed in the call of the meeting, and particularly seeking to fill the vacancies and newly created directorships with "his" nominees. Promptly thereafter, plaintiff began this action. An order was entered requiring that the stockholders' meeting be adjourned until October 15, to give the Court more time to decide the serious and novel issues raised. * * *

          *   *   *

Plaintiff contends that the president had no authority in fact to call a special meeting of stockholders to act upon policy matters which have not been defined by the board of directors. Defendant says that the by-laws specifically authorize the action taken.

It is helpful to have in mind the pertinent by-law provisions:

Section 7 of *Article* I provides:

"Special meetings of the stockholders for any purpose or purposes, other than those regulated by statute, may be called by the President * * * "

Section 2 of *Article* IV reads:

"The President * * * shall have power to call special meetings of the stockholders * * * for any purpose or purposes * * * "

It is true that *Section* 8(11) of *Article* II [of the bylaws] also provides that the board of directors may call a special meeting of stockholders for any purpose. But, in view of the explicit language of the by-laws above quoted, can this Court say that the president was without authority to call this meeting for the purposes stated? I think not. I agree that the purposes for which the president called the meeting were not in furtherance of the routine business of the corporation. Nevertheless, I think the stockholders, by permitting the quoted by-laws to stand, have given the president the power to state these broad purposes in his call. Moreover, it may be noted that at least one other by-law (*Article* V, § 2) makes certain action of the president subject to board approval. The absence of such language in connection with the call [of a shareholders' meeting] provision, while not conclusive, is some evidence that it was intended that the call provision should not be so circumscribed.

The plaintiff argues that if this by-law purports to give the president the power to call special stockholders' meetings for the purposes here stated, then it is contrary to *8 Del.C. § 141(a)*, which provides:

> "The business of every corporation organized under the provisions of this chapter shall be managed by a board of directors, except as hereinafter or in its certificate of incorporation otherwise provided."

I do not believe the call of a stockholders' meeting for the purposes mentioned is action of the character which would impinge upon the power given the directors by the statute. I say this because I believe a by-law giving the president the power to submit matters for stockholder action presumably only embraces matters which are appropriate for stockholder action. * * *

Plaintiff's next argument is that the president has no authority, without board approval, to propose an amendment of the by-laws to enlarge the board of directors. Admittedly this would be a most radical change in this corporate management. Indeed, it may well involve the determination of control. However, as I have already indicated, I believe the wording of the by-laws authorizes such action.

Plaintiff next argues that the president had no power to call a stockholders' meeting to fill vacancies on the board. As I understand plaintiff's argument it is that the existence of *Article* V, § 2 of the by-laws, which provides that the stockholders or the remaining directors may fill vacancies, by implication, precludes the president from calling a stockholders' meeting for that purpose, that provision being intended for stockholder use only at the initiative of the stockholders. First of all, the by-laws permit the president to call a meeting for any purpose. This is broad and all-embracing language and I think it must include the power to call a meeting to fill vacancies. * * *

Plaintiff points to the "extraordinary state of affairs" which the recognition of such power in the president would create. Obviously it gives the president power which may place him in conflict with the members of the board. But such consequences inhere in a situation where those adopting the by-laws grant such broad and concurrent power to the board and to the president. * * *

     * * *

I therefore conclude that the president had the power to call the meeting for the purposes noticed. * * *

Plaintiff next argues that the stockholders have no power between annual meetings to elect directors to fill newly created directorships.

Plaintiff argues in effect that since the Loew's by-laws provide that the stockholders may fill "vacancies", and since our Courts have construed "vacancy" not to embrace "newly created directorships" * * * the attempted call by the president for the purpose of filling newly created directorships was invalid.

Conceding that "vacancy" as used in the by-laws does not embrace "newly created directorships", that does not resolve this problem. I say this because in *Moon v. Moon Motor Car Co., 17 Del. Ch. 176, 151 A. 298*, it was held that the stockholders had the inherent right between annual meetings to fill newly created directorships. * * * There is no basis to distinguish the *Moon* case unless it be because the statute has since been amended to provide that not only vacancies but newly created directorships "may be filled by a majority of the directors then in office * * * unless it is otherwise provided in the certificate of incorporation or the by-laws * * * ". *8 Del.C.* § 223. Obviously, the amendment to include new directors is not worded so as to make the statute exclusive. It does not prevent the stockholders from filling the new directorships.

* * *

Plaintiff next argues that the shareholders of a Delaware corporation have no power to remove directors from office even for cause and thus the call for that purpose is invalid. * * *

While there are some cases suggesting the contrary, I believe that the stockholders have the power to remove a director for cause. * * * This power must be implied when we consider that otherwise a director who is guilty of the worst sort of violation of his duty could nevertheless remain on the board. It is hardly to be believed that a director who is disclosing the corporation's trade secrets to a competitor would be immune from removal by the stockholders. Other examples, such as embezzlement of corporate funds, etc., come readily to mind.

But plaintiff correctly states that there is no provision in our statutory law providing for the removal of directors by stockholder action. In contrast he calls attention to § 142 of 8 *Del.C.*, dealing with officers, which specifically refers to the possibility of a vacancy in an office by removal. He also notes that the Loew's by-laws provide for the removal of officers and employees but not directors. From these facts he argues that it was intended that directors not be removed even for cause. I believe the statute and by-law are of course some evidence to support plaintiff's contention. But when we seek to exclude the existence of a power by implication, I think it is pertinent to consider whether the absence of the power can be said to subject the corporation to the possibility of real damage. * * * Considering the damage a director might be able to inflict upon his corporation, I believe the doubt must be resolved by construing the statutes and by-laws as leaving untouched the question of director removal for cause. This being so, the Court is free to conclude on reason that the stockholders have such inherent power.

* * *

Plaintiff next argues that the removal of Tomlinson and Meyer as directors would violate the right of minority shareholders to representation on the board and would be contrary to the policy of the Delaware law regarding cumulative voting. Plaintiff contends that where there is cumulative voting, as provided by the Loew's certificate, a director cannot be removed by the stockholders even for cause.

It is true that the Chancellor noted in [an earlier case] that the provision for cumulative voting in the Delaware law was one reason why directors should not be considered to have the power to remove a fellow director even for cause. And it is certainly evident that if not carefully supervised the existence of a power in the stockholders to remove a director even for cause could be abused and used to defeat cumulative voting. * * *

Does this mean that there can be no removal of a director by the stockholders for cause in any case where cumulative voting exists? The conflicting considerations involved make the answer to this question far from easy. Some states have passed statutes dealing with this problem but Delaware has not. The possibility of stockholder removal action designed to circumvent the effect of cumulative voting is evident. This is particularly true where the removal vote is, as here, by mere majority vote. On the other hand, if we assume a case where a director's presence or action is clearly damaging the corporation and its stockholders in a substantial way, it is difficult to see why that director should be free to continue such damage merely because he was elected under a cumulative voting provision.

On balance, I conclude that the stockholders have the power to remove a director for cause even where there is a provision for cumulative voting. I think adequate protection is afforded not only by the legal safeguards announced in this opinion but by the existence of a remedy to test the validity of any such action, if taken.

* * *

I turn next to plaintiff's charges relating to procedural defects and to irregularities in proxy solicitation by the Vogel group.

Plaintiff's first point is that the stockholders can vote to remove a director for cause only after such director has been given adequate notice of charges of grave impropriety and afforded an opportunity to be heard.

Defendant raises a preliminary point that plaintiff, being only a stockholder, has no standing to make the contention that the foregoing requirements have not been met. * * * [O]n reason, there would seem no basis for telling a stockholder, particularly where cumulative voting is involved, that he has no right to challenge the legal propriety of action proposed to be taken to remove a member of the board of directors. After all, the board is managing the corporation for all the stockholders and while a director may have sufficient standing to attack the action himself, I cannot believe that a stockholder is lacking a sufficient interest to warrant legal recognition.

I am inclined to agree that if the proceedings preliminary to submitting the matter of removal for cause to the stockholders appear to be legal and if the charges are legally sufficient on their face, the Court should ordinarily not intervene. The sufficiency of the evidence would be a matter for evaluation in later proceedings. But where the procedure adopted to remove a director for cause is invalid on its face, a stockholder can attack such matters before the meeting. This conclusion is dictated both by the desirability of avoiding unnecessary and expensive action and by the importance of settling internal disputes, where reasonably possible, at the earliest moment. * * * Otherwise a director could be removed and his successor could be appointed and participate in important board action before the illegality of the removal was judicially established. This seems undesirable where the illegality is clear on the face of the proceedings.

* * *

Turning now to plaintiff's contentions, it is certainly true that when the share-holders attempt to remove a director for cause, " * * * there must be the service of specific charges, adequate notice and full opportunity of meeting the accusation * * * ". * * * While it involved an invalid attempt by directors to remove a fellow director for cause, nevertheless, this same general standard was recognized in *Bruch v. National Guarantee Credit Corp. [13 Del. Ch. 180, 116 A. 738].* The Chancellor said that the power of removal could not "be exercised in an arbitrary manner. The accused director would be entitled to be heard in his own defense".

Plaintiff asserts that no specific charges have been served upon the two directors sought to be ousted; that the notice of the special meeting fails to contain a specific statement of the charges; that the proxy statement which accompanied the notice also failed to notify the stockholders of the specific charges; and that it does not inform the stockholders that the accused must be afforded an opportunity to meet the accusations before a vote is taken.

Matters for stockholder consideration need not be conducted with the same formality as judicial proceedings. The proxy statement specifically recites that the two directors are sought to be removed for the reasons stated in the president's ac-companying letter. Both directors involved received copies of the letter. Under the circumstances I think it must be said that the two directors involved were served with notice of the charges against them. It is true, as plaintiff says, that the notice and the proxy statement failed to contain a specific statement of charges. But as indicated, I believe the accompanying letter was sufficient compliance with the notice requirement.

* * *

I next consider plaintiff's contention that the charges against the two directors do not constitute "cause" as a matter of law. It would take too much space to narrate in detail the contents of the president's letter. I must therefore give my summary of its charges. First of all, it charges that the two directors (Tomlinson and Meyer) failed to cooperate with Vogel in his announced program for rebuild-ing the company; that their purpose has been to put themselves in control; that they made baseless accusations against him and other management personnel and attempted to divert him from his normal duties as president by bombarding him with correspondence containing unfounded charges and other similar acts; that they moved into the company's building, accompanied by lawyers and accoun-tants, and immediately proceeded upon a planned scheme of harassment. They called for many records, some going back twenty years, and were rude to the personnel. Tomlinson sent daily letters to the directors making serious charges directly and by means of innuendos and misinterpretations.

Are the foregoing charges, if proved, legally sufficient to justify the ouster of the two directors by the stockholders? I am satisfied that a charge that the directors desired to take over control of the corporation is not a reason for their ouster. Standing alone, it is a perfectly legitimate objective which is a part of the very fabric of corporate existence. Nor is a charge of lack of cooperation a legally sufficient basis for removal for cause.

The next charge is that these directors, in effect, engaged in a calculated plan of harassment to the detriment of the corporation. Certainly a director may examine books, ask questions, etc., in the discharge of his duty, but a point can be reached when his actions exceed the call of duty and become deliberately obstructive. In such a situation, if his actions constitute a real burden on the corporation then the stockholders are entitled to relief. The charges in this area made by the Vogel letter are legally sufficient to justify the stockholders in voting to remove such directors. * * *

I therefore conclude that the charge of "a planned scheme of harassment" as detailed in the letter constitutes a justifiable legal basis for removing a director.

I next consider whether the directors sought to be removed have been given a reasonable opportunity to be heard by the stockholders on the charges made.

The corporate defendant freely admits that it has flatly refused to give the five Tomlinson directors or the plaintiff a stockholders' list. Any doubt about the matter was removed by the statement of defendant's counsel in open court at the argument that no such list would be supplied. The Vogel faction has physical control of the corporate offices and facilities. By this action the corporation through the Vogel group has deliberately refused to afford the directors in question an adequate opportunity to be heard by the stockholders on the charges made. This is contrary to the legal requirements which must be met before a director can be removed for cause.

At the oral argument the defendant's attorney offered to mail any material which might be presented by the Tomlinson faction. This falls far short of meeting the requirements of the law when directors are sought to be ousted for cause. Nor does the granting of the statutory right to inspect and copy some 26,000 names fulfill the requirement that a director sought to be removed for cause must be afforded an opportunity to present his case to the stockholders before they vote.

When Vogel as president caused the notice of meeting to be sent, he accompanied it with a letter requesting proxies granting authority to vote for the removal of the two named directors. It is true that the proxy form also provided a space for the stockholder to vote against such removal. However, only the Vogel accusations accompanied the request for a proxy. Thus, while the stockholder could vote for or against removal, he would be voting with only one view-point presented. This violates every sense of equity and fair play in a removal for cause situation.

While the directors involved or some other group could mail a letter to the stockholders and ask for a proxy which would revoke the earlier proxy, this procedure does not comport with the legal requirement that the directors in question must be afforded an opportunity to be heard before the shareholders vote. This is not an ordinary proxy contest case and a much more stringent standard must be invoked, at least at the initial stage, where it is sought to remove a director for cause. This is so for several reasons. Under our statute the directors manage the corporation and each has a somewhat independent status during his term of office. This right could be greatly impaired if substantial safeguards were not afforded a director whose removal for cause is sought. The possibility of abuse is evident. Also, as the Chancellor pointed * * * the power of removal can be a threat to cumulative voting rights. This is particularly true where, as here, the removal is by mere majority vote.

* * *[T]o the extent the matter is to be voted upon by the use of proxies, such proxies may be solicited only after the accused directors are afforded an opportunity to present their case to the stockholders. This means, in my opinion, that an opportunity must be provided such directors to present their defense to the stockholders by a statement which must accompany or precede the initial solicitation of proxies seeking authority to vote for the removal of such director for cause. If not provided then such proxies may not be voted for removal. And the corporation has a duty to see that this opportunity is given the directors at its expense. Admittedly, no such opportunity was given the two directors involved. Indeed, the corporation admittedly refused to supply them with a stockholders' list.

To require anything less than the foregoing is to deprive the stockholders of the opportunity to consider the case made by both sides before voting and would make a mockery of the requirement that a director sought to be removed for cause is entitled to an opportunity to be heard before the stockholders vote. * * *

I therefore conclude that the procedural sequence here adopted for soliciting proxies seeking authority to vote on the removal of the two directors is contrary to law. The result is that the proxy solicited by the Vogel group, which is based upon unilateral presentation of the facts by those in control of the corporate facilities, must be declared invalid insofar as they purport to give authority to vote for the removal of the directors for cause.

A preliminary injunction will issue restraining the corporation from recognizing or counting any proxies held by the Vogel group and others insofar as such proxies purport to grant authority to vote for the removal of Tomlinson and Meyer as directors of the corporation.

* * *

Plaintiff seeks a preliminary injunction restraining the defendant from using the corporate funds, employees and facilities for the solicitation of proxies for the Vogel group and from voting proxies so solicited. Plaintiff bases this request upon the contention that Vogel and his group, by calling the meeting and by using corporate funds and facilities, are usurping the authority of the board of directors. Plaintiff says that the president in effect is using his corporate authority and the corporate resources to deny the will of the board of directors and to maintain himself in office.

This brings the Court to an analysis of this most unusual aspect of this most unusual case. The by-laws provide for thirteen directors. Seven is a quorum. Due to four resignations there are now nine directors in office. Five of the nine are of the Tomlinson faction while the remaining four are of the Vogel faction. Since the

Vogel faction will not attend directors' meetings, or at least will not attend directors meetings at which matters may possibly be considered which they do not desire to have considered, it follows that the Tomlinson faction is unable to muster a quorum of the board and thus is unable to take action on behalf of the board. * * * In this setting, where a special stockholders' meeting for the election of directors is pending, it becomes necessary to determine the status of each faction in order to resolve the issues posed. And it must be kept in mind that this election can determine which faction will control the corporation.

We start with the basic proposition that the board of directors acting as a board must be recognized as the only group authorized to speak for "management" in the sense that under the statute they are responsible for the management of the corporation. *8 Del.C. § 141(a).* In substance that was the holding of the Court in *Empire Southern Gas Co. v. Gray, 29 Del. Ch. 95, 46 A.2d 741.* However, we are not here confronted with the situation in the *Gray* case because Loew's board as such cannot act for want of a quorum. Thus, there is no board policy as such with respect to the matters noticed for stockholder consideration. I am nevertheless persuaded that at least where a quorum of directors is in office the majority thereof are not "outsiders" merely because they cannot procure the attendance of a quorum at a meeting. By this I mean that they are not like the customary opposition which is seeking to take control of corporate management. To hold otherwise would be to set a most undesirable legal precedent in connection with the allocation of corporate powers.

Since the Vogel group, being in physical possession of the records and facilities of the corporation, treated the request of the directors for a stockholders' list as though it were to be judged by standards applicable to a mere stockholder's request, I think they violated the duty owed such directors as directors. I need not decide how far the rights of such directors go but I am satisfied that they are not less than the rights of the four "in" directors insofar as the right to have a stockholders' list is concerned. The fact that Vogel, as president, had the power to call a stockholders' meeting to elect directors, and is, so to speak, in physical control of the corporation, cannot obscure the fact that the possible proxy fight is between two sets of directors. Vogel, as president, has no legal standing to make "his" faction the exclusive voice of Loew's in the forthcoming election.

On balance, I believe the conclusion on this point should not result in the absolute nullification of all proxies submitted by the Vogel group. However, I believe it does require that their use be made subject to terms. I say this because they should not be permitted to benefit merely because they have physical control of the corporate facilities when they represent less than a majority of the directors in office.

I conclude that the Vogel group should be enjoined from voting any proxies unless and until the Tomlinson board members are given a reasonable period to solicit proxies after a stockholders' list is made available to them without expense by the corporation.

* * *

I next consider how these two groups should be classified for purposes of determining the rights of the Vogel group in connection with the use of corporate money and facilities for proxy solicitation at a stockholders' meeting duly called by the president. Basically, the stockholders are being asked whether they approve of a record made by one group and perhaps opposed by another. While the Tomlinson faction has five of the nine directors, it would be most misleading to have them represent to the stockholders that they are "management" in the sense that they have been responsible for the corporate policy and administration up to this stage. Resignations of directors have created the unusual situation now presented.

Viewing the situation in the light of what has just been said, it is apparent that the Vogel group is entitled to solicit proxies, not as representing a majority of the board, but as representing those who have been and are now responsible for corporate policy and administration. Whereas, the Tomlinson group, while not management in the sense that it is able on its own to take effective director action, is representative of the majority of the incumbent directors and is entitled to so represent to the stockholders if it decides to solicit proxies.

Since the stockholders will, in the event of a proxy fight, be asked to determine which group should run the corporation in the future, the Vogel faction, because it symbolizes existing policy, has sufficient status to justify the reasonable use of corporate funds to present its position to the stockholders. I am not called upon to decide whether the Tomlinson board members would also be entitled to have the corporation pay its reasonable charges for proxy solicitation.

* * *

I next consider whether the Vogel faction is entitled to use corporate facilities and employees in connection with its solicitation. Because such action would carry the intra-corporate strife even deeper within the corporation and because there is no practical way, if there is a proxy contest, to assure equal treatment for both factions in this area when only one is in physical control of such facilities and personnel, I conclude that the defendant should be preliminarily enjoined from using corporate facilities and personnel in soliciting proxies. I emphasize that this conclusion is based upon the corporate status of the two factions herein involved.

Plaintiff next claims that the Vogel group should be enjoined from voting any proxies obtained as a result of the material sent out by Vogel. He argues that Vogel's letter to the stockholders, the proxy statement and the form of proxy deceived and misled the stockholders into believing that the matters noticed for consideration by the stockholders were proposed by the company or its management, whereas the Vogel group is not authorized to speak as "management".

* * *

I turn now to the various factors which, according to plaintiff, show that the Vogel faction represented, contrary to fact, that it was soliciting proxies as management.

1. The letter of Mr. Vogel to the shareholders is reproduced on the letterhead of Loew's, Incorporated and comes from the "Office of the President".

I have already pointed out that this is not the case of a working majority of the board versus the president. Indeed, in this case Vogel's administration as president symbolizes one choice in the policy dispute. This dispute is evident from a reading of the material in its entirety. I therefore conclude that by sending the letter on Loew's stationery from the office of the president, Vogel, was not misleading the stockholders.

2. The notice of the special meeting is reproduced on the letterhead of Loew's, Incorporated, signed, by order of the president, by Irving H. Greenfield, Secretary.

The fact is that there was no misrepresentation when the notice of the special meeting was reproduced on Loew's letterhead and signed by the order of the president. I say this because the president was authorized as president to call such a meeting.

3. I assume that plaintiff had now abandoned this point which deals with the power to close the transfer books.

4. The proxy statement recites that "it is considered to be in the best interest of Loew's and the stockholders to remove * * * [Mr. Meyer and Mr. Thomlinson] as a director".

This is nothing more than a statement of belief of Vogel and his group. I cannot see how it is misleading.

5. The proxy material states that Loew's will bear all costs in connection with the solicitation of proxies; that Loew's will reimburse the brokerage houses for expenses incident to the solicitation of proxies; that Loew's has entered into contracts with certain firms to solicit proxies and has agreed to pay them a fee for their services, and that the costs to be paid by Loew's for proxy solicitation will be approximately $100,000.

Plaintiff is here saying in effect that Vogel's group was representing to the stockholders that the corporation would pay for the expenses of proxy solicitation for the Vogel group and thus leading the reader to believe that it was a management solicitation. First of all, such was the intention of the Vogel group and thus it did not constitute a misrepresentation as to their intention. But, in any event, I have now held that reasonable expenses of such solicitation are properly chargeable to the corporation and so no factual misrepresentation was involved. In any event, since the Vogel group was synonymous with management in the policy sense, I cannot see how a stockholder would be misled.

6. The proxy material states that the officers and employees of Loew's will solicit and request the return of proxies.

This is not a misrepresentation in the sense that it was contrary to the intention of the Vogel group. The Court has now determined that the officers and employees in such capacity, cannot solicit proxies. This does not mean that the representation is so material that it can be said to influence stockholders to the extent that the proxies should be voided.

7. The proxy statement is signed by Joseph R. Vogel, as president.

There is no merit to this contention. Vogel as president was certainly authorized to sign the statement in view of the fact that he had the authority to call the meeting.

8. The business reply envelope included with the proxy has on it that postage will be paid by the secretary of Loew's Inc., and is addressed to him in his official capacity. The permit on the envelope is Loew's permit.

The foregoing facts are true but I do not believe that they are so misleading as to void the proxies. After all, the Vogel group is soliciting proxies on the basis of its record in administering the corporation.

Plaintiff contends that in any event the cumulative effect of the various statements mentioned is to lead the ordinary reader to believe that the solicitation is by management.

Plaintiff recognizes that the proxy statement and the form of proxy both recite that "this proxy is solicited by the President and George L. Killion [of the Vogel group] who are members of the executive committee of Loew's, Inc., and in view of the circumstances, not by the management". However, he argues that the import of this statement is lost in the overall impact of the material. Since the meeting was validly called by the president, there was nothing misleading in the creation of the impression that the meeting and material were initiated by the company. I think the whole impact of the proxy material conveyed to the average reader the impression that there is a bitter fight between the president and his faction and another faction on the board.

While I have no doubt that it would have been better for the material to have contained a more explicit factual narrative of the status of the board personnel at the time of the proxy solicitation, I cannot believe that the overall result is so misleading as to justify this Court in concluding that the proxies may not be used for any purpose. * * * This is particularly so in view of the statement made that it was not solicited by management. Indeed, I think the statement * * * may have been somewhat misleading in the sense that it may have suggested to the reader that the Vogel group was not responsible for the corporate policy up to that date. To this extent, it was more prejudicial to the Vogel group than the Tomlinson group, if a stockholder desired to vote for "management" in the policy sense.

* * *

Plaintiff next seeks a mandatory injunction to compel the individual defendants (four Vogel directors) to attend directors' meetings. He argues that Vogel and his associates acted unlawfully in attempting to cause the absence of a quorum at meetings of the board of directors for the purpose of preventing the board from exercising its powers.

While a concerted plan to abstain from attending directors' meetings may be improper under some circumstances, I cannot find that the fact that the so-called Vogel directors did not attend directors' meetings called to take action which would give an opposing faction an absolute majority of the board—solely because of director resignations—is such a breach of their fiduciary duty that they should be judicially compelled to attend board meetings. This is particularly so where stockholder action is in the offing to fill the board.

*   *   *

NOTES AND QUESTIONS

1. *CAMPBELL* v. *LOEW'S* WAS part of the fall-out of a titanic struggle for control of Loews, Inc. the owner of MGM, the once-peerless great American movie studio. In particular, it involved an attempt by the recently-resigned movie mogul, Louis B. Mayer, to take back the company he had originally built. The story, worthy itself of a Hollywood epic picture, is wonderfully (if not particularly objectively) told in the autobiography of Louis B. Nizer, *My Life in Court* 427–524 (1961). Nizer was the lawyer hired by Joseph Vogel, Loew's President, and his book does a splendid job of illuminating the legal issues and explaining how a brilliant corporate counsel can also work as a corporate strategist. Our use of the case is a bit more prosaic, however, and our principal concerns are with the respective roles of shareholders, directors, and officers, and, in particular, how they share and exercise power in the corporation. We are also concerned with the role of formalities and bylaws in the operation of the corporation.

2. ON THE POINT OF THE corporate bylaws, consider an earlier stage in the litigation, *Tomlinson v. Loew's* Inc., 134 A.2d 518 (Del.Ch.1957). As the court in *Campbell v. Loew's* notes, there was a struggle among Board factions, which emerged after the creation of a thirteen-member Board of Directors, six of whom were chosen by the "Tomlinson faction," six of whom were chosen by the "Vogel faction," and one of whom was a "neutral," acceptable to both sides. Following ceaseless bickering

between the factions over the competence of Vogel as President, and whether he ought to be replaced, two of the Vogel-friendly directors, and the neutral director, Reid, resigned. Shortly thereafter one of the Tomlinson-friendly directors also resigned. This left four vacancies on the Board of Directors. The Vogel faction (then at 4 directors) wanted to call a special shareholders' meeting to fill the vacancies, but the Tomlinson faction (then at 5 directors), since it held a one-vote majority, wanted to fill the vacancies by a vote of the remaining Board members, not the shareholders. Accordingly it scheduled a Board meeting to fill the vacancies. As you might be able to infer from your reading of the case, the Vogel faction decided not to attend that Board meeting, which meant that the Tomlinson faction was deprived of a quorum, which the bylaws provided was to be 7 directors. Nevertheless the 5 Tomlinson directors met, and, taking advantage of a Delaware statute, 8 Del. C. § 223, which stated in pertinent part that "Unless otherwise provided in the certificate of incorporation or bylaws, when 1 or more directors shall resign from the board, effective at a future date, a majority of the directors then in office. . . . shall have power to fill such vacancy or vacancies . . . " they filled two of the vacancies, giving themselves a quorum to act on other matters. The Vogel faction challenged this action.

The question for the Delaware court to decide then became whether Loew's bylaws "otherwise provided" that what the Tomlinson faction had done was impermissible. In the relevant portions of the bylaws, one stated that "seven (7) of the directors shall constitute a quorum for the transaction of business, and the act of a majority of directors present at a meeting in the presence of a quorum, shall constitute the act of the Board of Directors . . . " while another enumerated "some 14 specified powers granted 'the directors' and number (14) grants power to the directors 'to fill vacancies in the Board of Directors.' " (Quoting from the court's opinion in *Tomlinson v. Loews*, 134 A.2d, at 522). Would that mean that only a quorum of the Board of Directors could fill vacancies? There was one more bylaw dealing with the problem. That bylaw provided, in pertinent part, that "A vacancy in the Board of Directors may be filled by the stockholders or by the directors in office (although less than a quorum)." Should the presence of that bylaw mean that what the Tomlinson faction did (filling the vacancies through a vote of only the five of them) was permissible? The Delaware Chancellor concluded that this last bylaw referred to was not applicable (do you understand why?) and he nullified the election of the two new directors, leaving the matter for Loew's shareholders to decide. Who can do a better job filling vacancies on the Board, the shareholders or the remaining directors? Was it legitimate for the 4 directors from the Vogel faction to refuse to attend Board meetings? One of the reasons the Vogel faction wanted to deprive the Tomlinson faction of a quorum was to prevent it from firing Vogel. The Board has the power to hire and fire officers, and what the Vogel faction did deprived the Board of this power, and every other power of the Board. Was this appropriate? What does Chancellor Seitz say on this issue? Do you agree?

3. WITH THIS BACKGROUND, let's further consider the actual issues raised in the *Campbell v. Loew's* case. We should note, at the outset, the key statutory provision Delaware § 141, which provides that "The business of every corporation organized under the provisions of this chapter shall be managed by a board of directors, except as hereinafter or in its certificate of incorporation otherwise provided." How, exactly, should Directors charged with the management of the corporation carry out their task? Tomlinson, one of the directors, as you may have discerned, believed that it was his job to ferret out information as to how the corporation was being run, and, in his efforts to gather data (which he hoped would demonstrate the incompetence of Vogel and that he ought to be replaced by Mayer) he brought the operations of the corporation to a virtual standstill. Was this an abuse of his powers as director? Chancellor Seitz suggested that there is nothing wrong with a Director seeking to take over control, or being unwilling to cooperate with other directors on the Board. Do you agree? What should be the role of corporate officers, as distinguished from those of Directors? Is it wise for corporate officers to be members of the Board of Directors? This last is a sorely-contended modern point of dispute among corporate scholars, by the way.

....

4. NOTE THAT CONSIDERING the possibility of abuses by directors such as those suggested in the last question, Chancellor Seitz decides, without benefit of relevant statute, that "the Court is free to conclude on reason that the stockholders have . . . [an] inherent power" to remove directors for cause. What does he mean by "on reason?" Do you agree with his conclusion?

....

5. WE HAVE EARLIER ALLUDED to the fact that Delaware law does not require cumulative voting, and that some critics of Delaware's corporate law believe that this provides insufficient protection to shareholders. Delaware law does permit a corporation to institute cumulative voting if it so desires, however, and Loew's, Inc., at the time of this case, did provide for cumulative voting in its Articles of Incorporation. Note that this presents a difficulty for Chancellor Seitz, because he sees some inconsistency between the provision of cumulative voting and permitting shareholders, by majority vote, to remove a director elected through cumulative voting. Do you understand why this is a problem? Cumulative voting is not a particularly easy procedure to grasp, but, for our purposes, it can be considered to be a form of proportional representation, more easily permitting minorities among the shareholders to be represented on the Board. Without wishing to get too bogged down in numbers (law students, unlike management students, tend to be frightened by matters of calculation), where there is no cumulative voting (the default position in Delaware), sometimes referred to as a "straight voting" regime, each share of stock may cast one vote for each open position on the Board of Directors. So that if one owns 100 shares, for example, and there are nine open slots on the Board, one may cast 100 votes for one's favored candidate for each of the nine slots. A little reflection should allow even law students to understand how in a "straight voting" regime, if one owns a majority of the shares, one can dictate the entire composition of the Board of Directors.

Where there is cumulative voting, however, a shareholder with 100 shares is not restricted to casting only 100 votes for each Board vacancy, but can multiply his or her number of shares by seats up for election on the Board of Directors, and "cumulate" or aggregate votes for any one or more seats on the Board. So that, if there are nine seats on the board up for election, our holder of 100 shares will have 900 votes to cast in any manner he or she sees fit. 900 may be cast for one seat on the board, 450 may be cast for each of two seats, 300 may be cast for each of three seats, or 100 may be cast for each of nine seats, and so on. While this point is a little tougher to grasp, you may be able to understand how this allows a shareholder with less than a majority of shares to obtain representation on the Board. If your brain has not yet seized up, you may realize that there are mathematical formulae that will yield how many shares must be owned in order to fill any particular number of seats on the Board.

One formula for determining the minimum number of shares needed to elect a particular number of directors, where X is the minimum number of shares needed, S is the total number of shares that will be voted at a shareholders' meeting, N is the number of directors one desires to elect, and D is the total number of directors to be elected is:

$$X = (S \times N)/(D + 1) + 1$$

So that, for example, if there are 900 total shares that will be voted, one desires to elect only 1 director, and there are 9 directors up for election, the number of shares that one will need is $(900 \times 1)/(9 + 1) + 1$ or $900/10 + 1$ or 91 shares. Can you understand Seitz's concern better? Do you favor cumulative voting or not? After the controversy that resulted in *Campbell v. Loew's*, Loew's shareholders voted to amend Loew's charter to eliminate cumulative voting. Can you understand why? If this is a subject you'd like to pursue further see Randall S. Thomas & Catherine T. Dixon's *Aranow & Einhorn, Proxy Contests for Corporate Control* 10.04[B] (3d ed. 1998), quoted from and discussed in Melvin Aron Eisenberg, *Corporations and Other Business Organizations* 159–162 (8th concise ed. 2000).

6. THERE ARE SEVERAL OTHER interesting procedural and substantive issues raised in *Campbell v. Loew's*. The first is a problem lawyers call "standing," the legal requirement that someone attempting to bring a lawsuit have a sufficient interest in the outcome of the case for the court to be certain that it will have all the facts brought before it, and that it will be dealing with a real legal problem. Here the "standing" question was whether a shareholder has standing to bring a lawsuit complaining about procedural irregularities in an attempt to remove a director for cause, specifically that the director had not received adequate notice of charges and an adequate opportunity to be heard in his defense. This would seem, at first blush anyway, to be a cause of action that belongs to the Director, not the shareholder. Why does Chancellor Seitz rule that the shareholder-plaintiff has standing? What exactly is the nature of the relationship between Directors and Shareholders? Are Directors the agents of shareholders? It is clear that Directors have a fiduciary responsibility to the shareholders, or at least to the corporation, but it does appear that the weight of authority on this issue, as indicated earlier, is that the Directors are agents of the corporation and not exactly agents of the shareholders. In a leading case on the subject the New York Court of Appeals stated that the directors "hold such office charged with the duty to act for the corporation according to their best judgment, and in so doing they cannot be controlled [by the shareholders] in the reasonable exercise and performance of such duty. . . . The relation of the directors to the stockholders is essentially that of trustee and *cestui que trust* ['the beneficiary for whom the trustee acts'] . . . The corporation is the owner of the property, but the directors in the performance of their duty possess it, and act in every way as if they owned it." People ex rel. *Manice v. Powell*, 201 N.Y. 194, 200–01, 94 N.E. 634, 637 (1911). Would you want to be a corporate director?

. . . .

7. MUCH OF *CAMPBELL v. LOEW'S* is concerned with the proxy vote. We will explore this in a bit more detail later, when we consider the federal regulation of proxy voting, but for now we can observe that large publicly-held corporations, that is those whose shares are dispersed among hundreds, thousands, or even millions of stockholders, can only have their shareholders vote by deputizing corporate officials to vote for them. Conducting such voting, or asking for the votes of shareholders, is called *soliciting proxies*, and at issue in *Campbell v. Loew's* is whether proxies to remove Tomlinson as a director were properly solicited. What does the Court decide on this issue? Note that the court observes that there is a difference between corporate proceedings and judicial proceedings, but precisely how much of a difference is there? In any event, you will have observed that Chancellor Seitz does say that whatever the difference, there is still a need to make sure that proxy battles are conducted pursuant to notions of equity and fair play. Did the Vogel faction so conduct itself? You will have noticed that Seitz states that the Vogel faction refused to supply a shareholder list to the Tomlinson faction, that it initially refused to mail out a statement from Tomlinson, and that the Vogel faction sought to use corporate funds and corporate personnel to wage a proxy battle against the Tomlinson faction. Was this appropriate?

You will have observed that, in the end, Seitz did rule that it was appropriate for the Vogel faction to make use of the corporation's funds. Was this decision correct? Is it appropriate for a corporate officer to use the funds of the corporation to solicit proxies to remove one of the directors when that director is seeking to fire that officer? The issue wasn't before Judge Seitz, but should the Tomlinson faction have been permitted to use the corporation's funds to solicit proxies against the removal of Tomlinson as director? Officers are hired and fired by the Board. Does that mean that officers owe a fiduciary duty to the Board or to the corporation? If the duty is to the corporation, is such a duty different from a duty owed to the shareholders? If you were a shareholder of Loew's, would you have been happy with the decision in this case? It appears to be a strong rule of Delaware law that a Board which seeks to prevent a shareholder vote bears a heavy burden of demonstrating a compelling justification for such action, and that it is rare that the Delaware courts will sustain such Board action. While the Board (with the aid of the officers it appoints) is supposed to manage the corporation, the Board may not deliberately frustrate the exercise of the shareholders' right ultimately to control. Was the Vogel faction or the Tomlinson faction seeking to do that? For important Delaware cases addressing this frustration of shareholder control issue, *see Schnell v. Chris–Craft Industries, Inc.*, 285 A.2d 437 (Del. 1971), *Blasius Industries, Inc. v. Atlas Corp.*, 564 A.2d 651 (Del. Ch. 1988), and *Stroud v. Grace*, 606 A.2d 75 (Del. 1992).

We have now learned a little bit about the interaction among officers, directors, and shareholders, and we have sought to begin to understand who is recognized as ultimately in control of the corporation. We next turn to some instances of the manner that such control can be abused, and the consequences to the abuser.

PIERCING THE CORPORATE VEIL

NO ISSUE of state corporate law is more frequently litigated than that of imposing liability for the debts of a corporation on its shareholders, or, as it is also known "piercing the corporate veil." You have already been introduced to this issue in the context of LLC's. In this chapter we will go somewhat more deeply into the elements required in order to pierce the corporate veil, and the resumptions that govern the approach taken by both state and federal courts. It is generally understood by both state and federal courts that there is a presumption that shareholders or parent corporations enjoy "limited liability" for their corporations' debts, and beyond their initial investment in those corporations they should not be called upon for further financial exposure, but this presumption of limited liability can be overcome, if a court finds that there has been an "abuse" of the corporate form sufficient to rebut the general rule. Just what the nature of that "abuse" is, or indeed, what sort of showing of "abuse" will be required is elusive, and the reading in this chapter is designed to suggest the contours of this fundamentally difficult area. Generalizations are quite risky here, but we will briefly take a look at two key jurisdictions, New York, which will serve as our paradigmatic state approach to piercing the corporate veil, and federal jurisprudence (in the form of the leading Supreme Court decision), which will suggest the possibilities that the aims of the state and federal government may lead to different approaches to this problematic area of corporate law.

I. State Law

THE FIRST OF THE CASES WE WILL consider in this chapter is by that most famous and controversial judge, Benjamin Cardozo, whom you have already encountered. In your opinion, does he illuminate or obfuscate the law?

Minnie B. Berkey v. Third Avenue Railway Company

Court of Appeals of New York.
244 N.Y. 84, 155 N.E. 58, 50 A.L.R. 599 (1926).

[Opinion by CARDOZO, J.]

The plaintiff boarded a street car at Fort Lee Ferry and One Hundred and Twenty-fifth street on October 4, 1916, in order to go east on One Hundred and Twenty-fifth street to Broadway, and thence south on Broadway to Columbia University at One Hundred and Seventeenth street. She was hurt in getting out of the car through the negligence of the motorman in charge of it. The franchise to operate a street railroad along the route traveled by the plaintiff belongs to the Forty-second Street, Manhattanville and Saint Nicholas Avenue Railway Company (described for convenience as the Forty-second Street Company) and no one else. Substantially all the stock of that company is owned by the Third Avenue Railway Company, the defendant, which has its own franchise along other streets and avenues. Stock ownership alone would be insufficient to charge the dominant company with liability for the torts of the subsidiary * * *. The theory of the action is that under the screen of this subsidiary and others, the defendant does in truth operate for itself the entire system of connected roads, and is thus liable for the torts of the consolidated enterprise * * *.

We are unable to satisfy ourselves that such dominion was exerted. The Forty-second Street Company deposits in its own bank account the fares collected on its route. It pays out of that account and no other the wages of the motormen and conductors engaged in the operation of its cars. It was not organized by the defendant as a decoy or a blind. It was not organized, so far as the record shows, by the defendant at all. There is no evidence that at the time of its formation the defendant had any interest in it as shareholder or otherwise. Its franchise goes back to the year 1884, and through all the intervening years it has preserved its corporate organization with property adequate to the maintenance of life. Its balance sheet for the year ending July, 1917, shows assets of $12,456,847.86. The values there stated are much in excess of the debts and liabilities, including in the reckoning of liabilities the outstanding capital stock. In no possible view * * * are they unsubstantial or nominal. True the subsidiary lost money that year, but so also did its parent. The fact remains that it was functioning as a corporation continuously and actively. It was so functioning at the trial in 1924. There is no evidence or suggestion that it has ceased to function since.

The question is whether other circumstances yet to be noted neutralize these indicia of separate life and operation. The defendant, as we have seen, was the owner in 1916 of substantially all the stock of the subsidiary corporation. Its president in reporting to the stockholders the financial situation at the end of the fiscal year informed them that to make the picture accurate, the statement must exhibit the consolidated income, and this was obviously true. Other ties must be shown in addition to the one resulting from ownership of shares. The members of the two boards of directors were nearly, though not quite the same. Each road had the same executive officers, i.e., the same president, treasurer, general manager, paymaster and counsel. The parent has made loans to the subsidiary from time to time, sometimes for construction, sometimes for operating expenses. * * * The parent is also the holder of the second mortgage bonds, $1,487,000, the first mortgage bonds, however ($1,200,000), being issued to the public. The operating loans are temporary advances for electric power, for materials or supplies and for the salaries of executive officers. As a matter of convenience these are made in the first instance out of the treasury of the parent company. They are then charged to the account of the subsidiary, and repaid generally the following month, and not later than the following year. Repayment is inconsistent with an understanding that the parent in making the advances was operating on its own account the cars of a connecting line. The charges are more than book entries, mere devices of an accountant. Drafts are drawn upon the subsidiary and paid with its own money. * * * We are not to confuse the salaries of the executive officers with the wages of motormen and conductors. The latter, as already pointed out, were paid in the first instance as well as ultimately by the subsidiary itself. So were many other expenses for maintenance and repair. So were the many judgments for personal injuries recovered in the past.

* * * The defendant was the dominant stockholder, not only in this subsidiary, but also in many others. The routes when connected cover an area from the lower part of Manhattan at the south to Yonkers and other points in Westchester at the north. All the cars, wherever used, are marked "Third Avenue System." On the other hand, the transfer slips bear the name in each instance of the company that issues them. The cars, when new ones become necessary, are bought by the defendant, and then leased to the subsidiaries, including, of course, the Forty-second Street Company, for a daily rental which is paid. The cars leased to one road do not continue along the routes [of] others. The motormen and conductors do not travel beyond their respective lines. With the approval of the Public Service Commission, transfer slips are issued between one route and another, but transfers could have been required by the Commission if not voluntarily allowed * * *.

Upon these facts we are to say whether the parent corporation, the owner of a franchise to operate a street railroad on Third avenue and the Bowery and a few connected streets, has in truth operated another railroad on Broadway and Forty-second street, and this in violation of the statutes of the State. The plaintiff 's theory of the action requires us to assume the existence of a contract between the defendant on the one side and the Forty-second Street Company on the other. The several circumstances relied upon—community of interest and in a sense community of management—are important only in so far as they are evidence from which the existence of a contract may fairly be inferred. The contract in the plaintiff 's view was one between the two corporations by which the defendant was to use and operate the other's franchise as its own. If such a contract was made, it was not only ultra vires, but illegal, because prohibited by statute. By Public Service Commissions Law (§ 54), "no franchise nor any right to or under any franchise, to own or operate a railroad or street railroad shall be assigned, transferred or leased, nor shall any contract or agreement with reference to or affecting any such franchise or right be valid or of any force or effect whatsoever, unless the assignment, transfer, lease, contract or agreement shall have been approved by the proper commission." By section 56 any violation of the provisions of the statute exposes the offending corporation to continuing fines of large amounts, and its officers and agents to prosecution and punishment as guilty of a misdemeanor. If a written contract had been made for the operation by the defendant of the subsidiary's line no one would doubt that such contract would fall within the condemnation of section 54 of the act. The contract is not the less illegal because made by word of mouth.

We cannot bring ourselves to believe that an agreement, criminal in conception and effect, may be inferred from conduct or circumstances so indefinite and equivocal. Community of interest there must obviously be between a subsidiary corporation and a parent corporation, the owner of its stock. This community of interest would prompt the parent, not unnaturally, to make advances for operating expenses to the subsidiary when convenience would be thus promoted. The advances so made have for the most part been repaid, and in so far as they remain unpaid have been carried as a debt. During all this time the cars have been manned by the subsidiary's servants, who are paid for their work out of the subsidiary's fares. We do not stop to inquire whether the inference of unified operation would be legitimate in a case where a contract for such an extension of the area of activity would be permitted by the law. We feel assured that no such inference is to be drawn from acts so uncertain in their suggestions where the inference is also one of the commission of a crime.

The law prohibits a contract for operation by the parent of a franchise other than its own without the consent of the appropriate commission. It does not prohibit stock ownership, or at least did not, so far as the record shows, when the defendant bought the shares. We are now asked to draw from conduct appropriate to the ownership of stock, and fairly explicable thereby, the inference of a contract prohibited by law. We do not obviate the difficulty when we say that the stockholders by acquiescence have ratified any departure from the restrictions of the charter. They could do this so as to wipe out the transgression of their officers if the act constituting the transgression were ultra vires only. They could not do so where the act was one prohibited by law * * *. The statute is aimed at more than the protection of the stockholders. It protects the creditors also, and beyond the creditors the public. Creditors are to be guarded against an increase of liabilities and an impairment of assets by an extension of corporate activities not approved by the Public Service Commission, the representative of the State. The public is to be guarded against like consequences, for the public which rides upon the cars has an interest, not to be ignored, in cheap, continuous and efficient operation. These benefits cannot be enjoyed if a road has been plunged into insolvency by improvident extensions. "The business of a railroad [i.e., a street railroad] is to run its own lines. The law does not permit it at its pleasure to run the lines of others" (*Doran v. N. Y. City Int. Ry. Co.*, 239 N. Y. 448).

We do not mean that a corporation which has sent its cars with its own men over the route of another corporation may take advantage of the fact that its conduct in so doing is illegal to escape liability for the misconduct of its servant * * *. There is no room for varying constructions when operation results from acts so direct and unequivocal. A defendant in such circumstances is liable for the tort, however illegitimate the business, just as much as it would be if its board of directors were to order a motorman to run a traveler down. We do mean, however, that an intention to operate a route in violation of a penal statute is not to be inferred from acts which reasonably interpreted are as compatible with innocence as with guilt * * *. Such, it seems to us, whether viewed distributively or together, are the acts relied on here to establish an agreement between two corporations that the business of one shall be the business of the other. Many arrangements for economy of expense and for convenience of administration may be made between carriers without subjecting them to liability as partners or as coadventurers "either inter sese or as to third persons" (*Ins. Co. v. Railroad Co.*, 104 U.S. 146, 158). For like reasons such arrangements may be made without establishing a relation of principal and agent. Where the coadventure or the agency, if created, carries consequences along with it that are offensive to public policy, the law will not readily imply the relation it condemns. The basis for the implication must be either intention or estoppel. We perceive no evidence sufficient to support a finding of estoppel. Intention is presumed, unless the inference of innocence is belied with reasonable certainty, to be conformable to law.

* * *

* * * [I]n *Davis v. Alexander* [269 U.S. 114] the case was submitted to the jury upon the theory that the proceeds of operation over the two routes were commingled in a single fund. Not only that, but engines and cars were used indiscriminately, and so also were the crews. The jury were told that all these facts must be found to coexist before the wrong of the subsidiary could be charged against the parent. The Supreme Court in its opinion does not catalogue the circumstances supporting the inference of unity of control. The opinion is confined to the statement that "the shippers introduced substantial evidence in support of their allegations." The facts are disclosed when we examine the record on appeal. So in *Wichita Falls Ry. Co. v. Puckett* [53 Okla. 463] the same employees worked on the entire route, and a common treasury received the proceeds of the system. Between such cases and the one before us there

exists a distinction plain upon the surface. * * * Liability of the parent has never been adjudged when the subsidiary has maintained so consistently and in so many ways as here the separate organization that is the mark of a separate existence, and when the implication of a contract for unity of operation would be the implication of a contract for the commission of a crime.

The whole problem of the relation between parent and subsidiary corporations is one that is still enveloped in the mists of metaphor. Metaphors in law are to be narrowly watched, for starting as devices to liberate thought, they end often by enslaving it. We say at times that the corporate entity will be ignored when the parent corporation operates a business through a subsidiary which is characterized as an "alias" or a "dummy." All this is well enough if the picturesqueness of the epithets does not lead us to forget that the essential term to be defined is the act of operation. Dominion may be so complete, interference so obtrusive, that by the general rules of agency the parent will be a principal and the subsidiary an agent. Where control is less than this, we are remitted to the tests of honesty and justice (Ballantine, Parent & Subsidiary Corporations, 14 Calif. Law Review, 12, 18, 19, 20). The logical consistency of a juridical conception will indeed be sacrificed at times when the sacrifice is essential to the end that some accepted public policy may be defended or upheld. This is so, for illustration, though agency in any proper sense is lacking, where the attempted separation between parent and subsidiary will work a fraud upon the law (Chicago, etc., *Ry. Co. v. Minn. Civic Assn.*, 247 U.S. 490; *United States v. Reading Company*, 253 U.S. 26, 61, 63). At such times unity is ascribed to parts which, at least for many purposes, retain an independent life, for the reason that only thus can we overcome a perversion of the privilege to do business in a corporate form. We find in the case at hand neither agency on the one hand, nor on the other abuse to be corrected by the implication of a merger. On the contrary, merger might beget more abuses than it stifled. Statutes carefully framed for the protection, not merely of creditors, but of all who travel upon railroads, forbid the confusion of liabilities by extending operation over one route to operation on another. In such circumstances, we thwart the public policy of the State instead of defending or upholding it, when we ignore the separation between subsidiary and parent, and treat the two as one.

* * *

CRANE, J. (dissenting). The United States Supreme Court in *Davis v. Alexander (269 U.S. 114)* said: "Where one railroad company actually controls another and operates both as a single system, the dominant company will be liable for injuries due to the negligence of the subsidiary company." This court decided in *Stone v. Cleveland, C., C. & St. L. Ry. Co. (202 N.Y. 352)* "that the ownership of a majority of the stock of a corporation, while it gives a certain control of the corporation, does not give that control of corporate transactions which makes the holder of the stock responsible for the latter."

These two decisions are not inconsistent. Each depends upon the particular facts and the nature and extent of the control by the dominant company of the subsidiary.

It is largely a question of degree. This was recognized in the opinion in the *Stone* case when referring to the Federal authorities. We there said (p. 361) that the facts in those cases were stronger for the plaintiff than in the *Stone* action.

* * *

The plaintiff was injured on the evening of October 4, 1916, by stepping into an unlighted excavation in the street, while alighting from a car at the corner of Broadway and One Hundred and Seventeenth street. The proof of negligence for this appeal is unquestioned and need not be further mentioned, so that we may turn our attention at once to the corporation responsible.

The Forty-second Street Railway Company is a street railroad corporation having a franchise to operate passenger cars through Broadway at the point in question. Its authorized capital stock is $2,500,000, of which $2,494,900 is outstanding, and of this the Third Avenue Railway Company owns $2,471,300. The Third Avenue Railway Company is also a duly authorized and chartered railroad, operating surface lines in the city of New York connecting with and transferring to the cars running on the Forty-second Street line. Its system, which includes the Third Avenue and Amsterdam line, the One Hundred and Twenty-fifth Street Crosstown line, Broadway-Kingsbridge line as well as the branches of the Forty-second Street Railway, was termed and called "The Third Avenue Railway System." The car from which the plaintiff fell had on it the words, "Third Avenue Railway System."

The report of the president to the stockholders for the year ending June 30, 1917, stated: "The Third Avenue Railway System is composed of the Third Avenue Railway Company and the following subsidiary companies."

The Forty-second Street Railway Company was one of these named subsidiary companies.

"The Third Avenue Railway Company," says the report, "controls all the above companies through ownership of stock and to arrive at the result of the operations it is necessary to consolidate the income accounts and the balance sheets of all the corporations and eliminate the inter-company transactions so that all duplications may be avoided. This explanation is made in order that there may be no misunderstanding in considering the statements appearing in this report."

The outstanding second mortgage bonds, amounting to $1,487,000, were entirely owned by the Third Avenue Railway Company. This second mortgage was past due. $6,415,152.98 was due for construction. It was represented by a note of the Forty-second Street Railway Company given years ago to the Third Avenue Railway Company. It is a demand note.

The officers for both companies were the same. Edward A. Maher, Jr., was the assistant manager of the Third Avenue Railway Company and of the Forty-second Street Railway Company. His father, Edward A. Maher, was the general manager of both. Each railway company had the same president, treasurer, secretary and the same board of directors with some slight variation. "They were practically all the same directors." The following question was asked of Edward A. Maher, Jr.:

> "Q. Take the Third Avenue Railroad Company and the Forty-second Street
> and Manhattanville Railroad Company, were they identical?
>
> A. They were."

The general auditor, Walter Farrington, was asked:

> "Q. I notice on page 6 of this report this statement: The Employees As-
> sociation—the statement is as follows: 'The Association on June 30th,
> 1917, had a membership of 3,412, and had to its credit on that date New
> York City bonds valued at $79,833.30, and cash on deposit amounting
> to $13,285.51, the total of $93,116.81.' These employees were employees
> of the entire system?
>
> A. Yes.
>
> "Q. The next item to which I would call your attention is on page 6: 'It is
> most gratifying to contrast the attitude of some of the employees of the
> company with the strikes, was the response of the men to the company's
> invitation to subscribe to the Liberty Loan of 1917 within two weeks of
> the announcement of the company's partial payment plan of 3,265 sub-
> scriptions which have been received from 73%, and investment of bonds
> to the value of $200,000.' That refers to the employees of the subsidiary
> companies as well as of the others; as well as of the Third Avenue?
>
> A. May I see what you are reading from?
>
> "Q. Yes. 'Subscription to Liberty Loan Bonds.'
>
> A. It does.
>
> "Q. They are all treated as employees of the Third Avenue, with reference
> to that loan?
>
> A. Employees of all the companies."

The company referred to, of which these men were the employees, was the Third
Avenue Railway Company. In its report the company did not discriminate.

Again, the Third Avenue Railway Company had a printing plant, referred to as
follows:

> "Q. I find on page 9 of this report this expression: 'The economical ef-
> fect to the operation of its own printing plant has continued during the
> past year. All of the company's printing has been done in its own plant.'
> That refers to the printing plant which was used for printing matter of

not only the Third Avenue Railway Company, but of the subsidiary Companies?

A. It does, yes."

As to pensions for employees, the report of the president said: "Under this plan, any employees who have reached the age of seventy years after at least twenty years service with the company, or who have reached the age of sixty-five and have been incapacitated are eligible for pensions," etc. That the company referred to was the Third Avenue Railway Company appears from this testimony:

"Q. You had a system of pensions for the employees, didn't you?

A. Yes.

"Q. That was entirely under the control of the Third Avenue Railway Company, wasn't it?

A. Yes.

"Q. Which handled that entirely; is that right?

A. Yes."

The executive officers, above referred to, were paid by the checks of the Third Avenue Railway Company; the general manager of the entire system had charge of the superintendents of operation, who in turn had control of the conductors and motormen, all of whom reported to a central school for instruction; repairs and construction were operated from a single department; the cars of both the Third Avenue Railway Company and the Forty-second Street Railway Company were marked "Third Avenue Railway System;" the Third Avenue Railway Company contracted and paid for the electricity to be used in the system; there was one common purchasing agent, and it is conceded that the Third Avenue Railway Company in the first instance paid the bills for all general and miscellaneous expenses, including salaries of claim agents and expenses for services and for material purchased. The Third Avenue Company owned all the cars which were operated over the lines of the system. One paymaster for the entire system, with assistants, paid the motormen and conductors of the Forty-second Street Railway Company with cash obtained at the bank by checks drawn by Mr. Sage, who was the treasurer of the Third Avenue Railway Company and the Forty-second Street Railway Company. The testimony of this point is as follows:

"Q. How many paymasters were there for the whole system?

A. I think there was one so-called paymaster, possibly two assistants.

"Q. And they were employees of the Third Avenue Railway Company?

A. They were paid out of the Third Avenue Railway Company's general fund.

"Q. Was there any such department in the Forty-second Street and Manhattan Railway Company pay department?

A. No. * * * They were employees just as much of the 42nd Street company as they were of the Third Avenue. * * *

"Q. Who pays that paymaster and his subordinates?

A. The paymaster was paid out of the Third Avenue Company's fund."

The legal department for the adjustment and settlement of claims and the claims themselves were paid by the Third Avenue Railway Company. So, too, the accounting department was for the entire system paid by the Third Avenue Railway Company. Walter Farrington, the general auditor, testified as to the advertising:

"Q. Do you know where the money for that advertising came from, from the various advertisements?

A. Yes.

"Q. Who was it paid to?

A. It was paid to the Third Avenue Railway."

Ely M. T. Ryder, engineer of the Forty-second Street Railway Company, swore that the annual report of that company states that the road was held in joint title by the Third Avenue Railway Company and the Forty-second Street Railway Company.

"Q. What does that mean, joint title?

A. That is the title to the ownership of the road, which has nothing to do with maintenance.

"Q. Then the ownership of the road is jointly in the two companies; is that right?

A. It is so stated.

"Q. Will you go a little further and read the next section, 'Operated jointly with,' and say whether the same statement is not made there?

A. It states, 'Operated jointly with.'

"Q. That means the joint operation of the two, does it not?

A. Yes.

"Q. Do you still adhere to your former statement that it was operated alone by the Forty-second Street and Manhattanville Railway Company?

A. I did not say that it was operated alone, but it was maintained by the Forty-second Street.

"Q. You admit that it is jointly owned, jointly operated, but that you say that it is jointly—it is maintained solely by the one road?

A. Correct."

These being the facts regarding the maintenance and operation of the Third Avenue Railway System, what is our conclusion? Is it that the Forty-second Street Railway Company maintained a separate and distinct existence as a corporation operating its railroad as a corporate entity under the guidance and control of its own officers and board of directors? Such to my mind would be an absurd conclusion, especially in the face of the declarations of the Third Avenue Railway Company through its officers. They certainly know the facts, and it is the facts, and the facts alone which the law seizes upon to form and to justify its conclusion. These facts are that the Third Avenue Railway Company owned and controlled the Forty-second Street Railway. It dominated its entire existence. It not only owned the majority of the stock; it owned nearly all of its bonded and floating indebtedness. It officered it with its own officers; it executed the work and the service by its own executives; it paid the employees, including motormen and conductors, by and through its own paymaster; it bought and paid for all materials, supplies and operating facilities. Every activity as an operating railroad was dominated, controlled and executed by the Third Avenue Railway Company, its officers and employees. Ryder, the engineer, had it right when he said that both railroads jointly owned and operated this branch of the system.

These are the facts which cannot be changed by mere bookkeeping entries. It is true that the Forty-second Street Railway Company made out separate reports required by law; that it existed as a corporation; that it owned the street franchise; that upon the books of the Third Avenue Company charges were made for the various services and expenses to the Forty-second Street Railway Company as though it were in reality an independent, vital organism. But all these things cannot hide the reality or cover up the fact that the Third Avenue Railway Company in operation, in control, in dominance, in execution and in the furnishing of service to the city of New York was the Forty-second Street Railway Company.

No facts could exist which would justify the application of the statement in the *Davis Case (supra)*, if these facts did not. "Where one railroad company actually controls another and operates both as a single system, the dominant company will be liable for injuries due to the negligence of the subsidiary company." Such was the rule with which I commenced this opinion, as laid down in *Davis v. Alexander* by the United States Supreme Court, and such is the law which must be applied to the Third Avenue Railway Company in this case. Its activities fit it exactly. * * * A quotation may not be inapt at this point.

> "Much emphasis is laid upon statements made in various decisions of this court that ownership, alone, of capital stock in one corporation by another, does not create an identity of corporate interest between the two companies, or render the stockholding company the owner of the property of the other, or create the relation of principal and agent or representative between the two. * * *

>> "While the statements of the law thus relied upon are satisfactory in the connection in which they were used, they have been plainly and repeatedly held not applicable where stock ownership has been resorted to, not for the purpose of participating in the affairs of a corporation in the normal and usual manner, but for the purpose, as in this case, of controlling a subsidiary company so that it may be used as a mere agency or instrumentality of the owning company or companies." [*Chicago, M. & S. P. R. Co. v. Minneapolis Civic & Commerce Ass'n*, 247 U.S. 490, 500–501 (1918)].

* * *

Walkovszky v. Carlton

Court of Appeals of New York.
18 N.Y.2d 414, 223 N.E.2d 6, 276 N.Y.S.2d 585 (1966).

* * *

[FULD, J.]

This case involves what appears to be a rather common practice in the taxicab industry of vesting the ownership of a taxi fleet in many corporations, each owning only one or two cabs.

The complaint alleges that the plaintiff was severely injured four years ago in New York City when he was run down by a taxicab owned by the defendant Seon Cab Corporation and negligently operated at the time by the defendant Marchese. The individual defendant, Carlton, is claimed to be a stockholder of 10 corporations, including Seon, each of which has but two cabs registered in its name, and it is implied that only the minimum automobile liability insurance required by law (in the amount of $10,000) is carried on any one cab. Although seemingly independent of one another, these corporations are alleged to be "operated * * * as a single entity, unit and enterprise" with regard to financing, supplies, repairs, employees and garaging, and all are named as defendants. * * * The plaintiff asserts that he is also entitled to hold their stockholders personally liable for the damages sought because the multiple corporate structure constitutes an unlawful attempt "to defraud members of the general public" who might be injured by the cabs.

* * *

The law permits the incorporation of a business for the very purpose of enabling its proprietors to escape personal liability (see, e.g., *Bartle v. Home Owners Coop., 309 N. Y. 103, 106)* but, manifestly, the privilege is not without its limits. Broadly speaking, the courts will disregard the corporate form, or, to use accepted terminology, "pierce the corporate veil", whenever necessary "to prevent fraud or to achieve equity". *(International Aircraft Trading Co. v. Manufacturers Trust Co., 297 N. Y. 285, 292.)* In determining whether liability should be extended to reach assets beyond those belonging to the corporation, we are guided, as Judge Cardozo noted, by "general rules of agency". *(Berkey v. Third Ave. Ry. Co., 244 N. Y. 84, 95.)* In other words, whenever anyone uses control of the corporation to further his own rather than the corporation's business, he will be liable for the corporation's acts "upon the principle of *respondeat superior* applicable even where the agent is a natural person". *(Rapid Tr. Subway Constr. Co. v. City of New York, 259 N. Y. 472, 488.)* Such liability, moreover, extends not only to the corporation's commercial dealings * * * but to its negligent acts as well. * * *

In the *Mangan* case ([*Mangan v. Terminal Transp. System*], *247 App. Div. 853,* mot. for lv. to app. den. *272 N. Y. 676)*, the plaintiff was injured as a result of the negligent operation of a cab owned and operated by one of four corporations affiliated with the defendant Terminal. Although the defendant was not a stockholder of any of the operating companies, both the defendant and the operating companies were owned, for the most part, by the same parties. The defendant's name (Terminal) was conspicuously displayed on the sides of all of the taxis used in the enterprise and, in point of fact, the defendant actually serviced, inspected, repaired and dispatched them. These facts were deemed to provide sufficient cause for piercing the corporate veil of the operating company—the nominal owner of the cab which injured the plaintiff—and holding the defendant liable.

The operating companies were simply instrumentalities for carrying on the business of the defendant without imposing upon it financial and other liabilities incident to the actual ownership and operation of the cabs. * * *

In the case before us, the plaintiff has explicitly alleged that none of the corporations "had a separate existence of their own" and, as indicated above, all are named as defendants. However, it is one thing to assert that a corporation is a fragment of a larger corporate combine which actually conducts the business. (See Berle, The Theory of Enterprise Entity, *47 Col. L. Rev. 343, 348–350.*) It is quite another to claim that the corporation is a "dummy" for its individual stockholders who are in reality carrying on the business in their personal capacities for purely personal rather than corporate ends. * * * Either circumstance would justify treating the corporation as an agent and piercing the corporate veil to reach the principal but a different result would follow in each case. In the first, only a larger *corporate* entity would be held financially responsible * * * while, in the other, the stockholder would be personally liable. * * * Either the stockholder is conducting the business in his individual capacity or he is not. If he is, he will be liable; if he is not, then, it does not matter—insofar as his personal liability is concerned—that the enterprise is actually being carried on by a larger "enterprise entity". * * *

* * *

The individual defendant is charged with having "organized, managed, dominated and controlled" a fragmented corporate entity but there are no allegations that he was conducting business in his individual capacity. Had the taxicab fleet been owned by a single corporation, it would be readily apparent that the plaintiff would face formidable barriers in attempting to establish personal liability on the part of the corporation's stockholders. The fact that the fleet ownership has been deliberately split up among many corporations does not ease the plaintiff's burden in that respect. The corporate form may not be disregarded merely because the assets of the corporation, together with the mandatory insurance coverage of the vehicle which struck the plaintiff, are insufficient to assure him the recovery sought. If Carlton were to be held individually liable on those facts alone, the decision would apply equally to the thousands of cabs which are owned by their individual drivers who conduct their businesses through corporations organized pursuant to * * * the Business Corporation Law and carry the minimum insurance required by subdivision 1 (par. [a]) of *section 370* of the Vehicle and Traffic Law. These taxi owner-operators are entitled to form such corporations * * * and we agree with the court at Special Term that, if the insurance coverage required by statute "is inadequate for the protection of the public, the remedy lies not with the courts but with the Legislature." It may very well be sound policy to require that certain corporations must take out liability insurance which will afford adequate compensation to their potential tort victims.

However, the responsibility for imposing conditions on the privilege of incorporation has been committed by the Constitution to the Legislature (N. Y. Const., art. X, § 1) and it may not be fairly implied, from any statute, that the Legislature intended, without the slightest discussion or debate, to require of taxi corporations that they carry automobile liability insurance over and above that mandated by the Vehicle and Traffic Law.

> This is not to say that it is impossible for the plaintiff to state a valid cause of action against the defendant Carlton. However, the simple fact is that the plaintiff has just not done so here. While the complaint alleges that the separate corporations were undercapitalized and that their assets have been intermingled, it is barren of any "sufficiently [particularized] statements" * * * that the defendant Carlton and his associates are actually doing business in their individual capacities, shuttling their personal funds in and out of the corporations "without regard to formality and to suit their immediate convenience." (*Weisser v. Mursam Shoe Corp., 127 F. 2d 344, 345, supra.*) Such a "perversion of the privilege to do business in a corporate form" (*Berkey v. Third Ave. Ry. Co., 244 N. Y. 84, 95, supra*) would justify imposing personal liability on the individual stockholders. * * * Nothing of the sort has in fact been charged, and it cannot reasonably or logically be inferred from the happenstance that the business of Seon Cab Corporation may actually be carried on by a larger corporate entity composed of many corporations which, under general principles of agency, would be liable to each other's creditors in contract and in tort. * * *

In point of fact, the principle relied upon in the complaint to sustain the imposition of personal liability is not agency but fraud. Such a cause of action cannot withstand analysis. If it is not fraudulent for the owner-operator of a single cab corporation to take out only the minimum required liability insurance, the enterprise does not become either illicit or fraudulent merely because it consists of many such corporations. The plaintiff's injuries are the same regardless of whether the cab which strikes him is owned by a single corporation or part of a fleet with ownership fragmented among many corporations. Whatever rights he may be able to assert against parties other than the registered owner of the vehicle come into being not because he has been defrauded but because, under the principle of *respondeat superior*, he is entitled to hold the whole enterprise responsible for the acts of its agents.

> In sum, then, the complaint falls short of adequately stating a cause of action against the defendant Carlton in his individual capacity. * * *

* * *

KEATING, J. (dissenting). The defendant Carlton, the shareholder here sought to be held for the negligence of the driver of a taxicab, was a principal shareholder and organizer of the defendant corporation which owned the taxicab. The corporation was one of 10 organized by the defendant, each containing two cabs and each cab having the "minimum liability" insurance coverage mandated by *section 370* of the Vehicle and Traffic Law. The sole assets of these operating corporations are the vehicles themselves and they are apparently subject to mortgages. [It appears that the [taxicab] medallions, which are of considerable value, are judgment proof. (Administrative Code of City of New York, § 436–2.0.)]

From their inception these corporations were intentionally undercapitalized for the purpose of avoiding responsibility for acts which were bound to arise as a result of the operation of a large taxi fleet having cars out on the street 24 hours a day and engaged in public transportation. And during the course of the corporations' existence all income was continually drained out of the corporations for the same purpose.

The issue presented by this action is whether the policy of this State, which affords those desiring to engage in a business enterprise the privilege of limited liability through the use of the corporate device, is so strong that it will permit that privilege to continue no matter how much it is abused, no matter how irresponsibly the corporation is operated, no matter what the cost to the public. I do not believe that it is.

Under the circumstances of this case the shareholders should all be held individually liable to this plaintiff for the injuries he suffered. * * *

> "If a corporation is organized and carries on business without substantial capital in such a way that the corporation is likely to have no sufficient assets available to meet its debts, it is inequitable that shareholders should set up such a flimsy organization to escape personal liability. The attempt to do corporate business without providing any sufficient basis of financial responsibility to creditors is an abuse of the separate entity and will be ineffectual to exempt the shareholders from corporate debts. It is coming to be recognized as the policy of law that shareholders should in good faith put at the risk of the business unincumbered capital reasonably adequate for its prospective liabilities. If capital is illusory or trifling compared with the business to be done and the risks of loss, this is a ground for denying the separate entity privilege." (Ballantine, Corporations [rev. ed., 1946], § 129, pp. 302–303.)

In *Minton v. Cavaney (56 Cal. 2d 576)* the Supreme Court of California had occasion to discuss this problem in a negligence case. The corporation of which the defendant was an organizer, director and officer operated a public swimming pool. One afternoon the plaintiffs' daughter drowned in the pool as a result of the alleged negligence of the corporation.

Justice ROGER TRAYNOR, speaking for the court, outlined the applicable law in this area. "The figurative terminology 'alter ego' and 'disregard of the corporate entity' ", he wrote, "is generally used to refer to the various situations that are an abuse of the corporate privilege * * * The equitable owners of a corporation, for example, are personally liable when they treat the assets of the corporation as their own and add or withdraw capital from the corporation at will * * *; when they hold themselves out as being personally liable for the debts of the corporation * * *; *or when they provide inadequate capitalization and actively participate in the conduct of corporate affairs*". *(56 Cal. 2d, p. 579;* italics supplied.)

Examining the facts of the case in light of the legal principles just enumerated, he found that "[it was] undisputed that there was no attempt to provide adequate capitalization. [The corporation] never had any substantial assets. It leased the pool that it operated, and the lease was forfeited for failure to pay the rent. Its capital was 'trifling compared with the business to be done and the risks of loss' ". *(56 Cal. 2d, p. 580.)*

It seems obvious that one of "the risks of loss" referred to was the possibility of drownings due to the negligence of the corporation. And the defendant's failure to provide such assets or any fund for recovery resulted in his being held personally liable.

In *Anderson v. Abbott (321 U.S. 349)* the defendant shareholders had organized a holding company and transferred to that company shares which they held in various national banks in return for shares in the holding company. The holding company did not have sufficient assets to meet the double liability requirements of the governing Federal statutes which provided that the owners of shares in national banks were personally liable for corporate obligations "to the extent of the amount of their stock therein, at the par value thereof, in addition to the amount invested in such shares" (U. S. Code, tit. 12, former § 63).

The court had found that these transfers were made in good faith, that other defendant shareholders who had purchased shares in the holding company had done so in good faith and that the organization of such a holding company was entirely legal. Despite this finding, the Supreme Court, speaking through Mr. Justice Douglas, pierced the corporate veil of the holding company and held all the shareholders, even those who had no part in the organization of the corporation, individually responsible for the corporate obligations as mandated by the statute.

"Limited liability", he wrote, "is the rule, not the exception; and on that assumption large undertakings are rested, vast enterprises are launched, and huge sums of capital attracted. But there are occasions when the limited liability sought to be obtained through the corporation will be qualified or denied. Mr. Justice Cardozo stated that a surrender of that principle of limited liability would be made 'when the sacrifice is essential to the end that some accepted public policy may be defended or upheld.' * * * The cases of fraud make up part of that exception * * * But they do not exhaust it. *An obvious inadequacy of capital, measured by the nature and magnitude of the corporate undertaking, has frequently been an important factor in cases denying stockholders their defense of limited liability * * * That rule has* *been invoked even in absence of a legislative policy which undercapitalization would defeat. * * * It has often been held that the interposition of a corporation will not be allowed to defeat a legislative policy, whether that was the aim or only the result of the arrangement * * * 'the courts will not permit themselves to be blinded or deceived by mere forms of law' but will deal 'with the substance of the transaction involved as if the corporate agency did not exist and as the justice of the case may require.' "* (*321 U.S., pp. 362–363; emphasis added.*)

The policy of this State has always been to provide and facilitate recovery for those injured through the negligence of others. The automobile, by its very nature, is capable of causing severe and costly injuries when not operated in a proper manner. The great increase in the number of automobile accidents combined with the frequent financial irresponsibility of the individual driving the car led to the adoption of *section 388* of the Vehicle and Traffic Law which had the effect of imposing upon the owner of the vehicle the responsibility for its negligent operation. It is upon this very statute that the cause of action against both the corporation and the individual defendant is predicated.

In addition the Legislature, still concerned with the financial irresponsibility of those who owned and operated motor vehicles, enacted a statute requiring minimum liability coverage for all owners of automobiles. The important public policy represented by both these statutes is outlined in *section 310* of the Vehicle and Traffic Law. That section provides that: "The legislature is concerned over the rising toll of motor vehicle accidents and the suffering and loss thereby inflicted. The legislature determines that it is a matter of grave concern that motorists shall be financially able to respond in damages for their negligent acts, so that innocent victims of motor vehicle accidents may be recompensed for the injury and financial loss inflicted upon them."

The defendant Carlton claims that, because the minimum amount of insurance required by the statute was obtained, the corporate veil cannot and should not be pierced despite the fact that the assets of the corporation which owned the cab were "trifling compared with the business to be done and the risks of loss" which were certain to be encountered. I do not agree.

The Legislature in requiring minimum liability insurance of $10,000, no doubt, intended to provide at least some small fund for recovery against those individuals and corporations who just did not have and were not able to raise or accumulate assets sufficient to satisfy the claims of those who were injured as a result of their negligence. It certainly could not have intended to shield those individuals who organized corporations, with the specific intent of avoiding responsibility to the public, where the operation of the corporate enterprise yielded profits sufficient to purchase additional insurance. Moreover, it is reasonable to assume that the Legislature believed that those individuals and corporations having substantial assets would take out insurance far in excess of the minimum in order to protect those assets from depletion. Given the costs of hospital care and treatment and the nature of injuries sustained in auto collisions, it would be unreasonable to assume that the Legislature believed that the minimum provided in the statute would in and of itself be sufficient to recompense "innocent victims of motor vehicle accidents * * * for the injury and financial loss inflicted upon them".

The defendant, however, argues that the failure of the Legislature to increase the minimum insurance requirements indicates legislative acquiescence in this scheme to avoid liability and responsibility to the public. In the absence of a clear legislative statement, approval of a scheme having such serious consequences is not to be so lightly inferred.

The defendant contends that the court will be encroaching upon the legislative domain by ignoring the corporate veil and holding the individual shareholder. This argument was answered by Mr. Justice Douglas in *Anderson v. Abbot (supra, pp. 366–367)* where he wrote that: "In the field in which we are presently concerned, judicial power hardly oversteps the bounds when it refuses to lend its aid to a promotional project which would circumvent or undermine a legislative policy. To deny it that function would be to make it impotent in situations where historically it has made some of its most notable contributions. If the judicial power is helpless to protect a legislative program from schemes for easy avoidance, then indeed it has become a handy implement of high finance. *Judicial interference to cripple or defeat a legislative policy is one thing; judicial interference with the plans of those whose corporate or other devices would circumvent that policy is quite another.* Once the purpose or effect of the scheme is clear, once the legislative policy is plain, we would indeed forsake a great tradition to say we were helpless to fashion the instruments for appropriate relief." (Emphasis added.)

The defendant contends that a decision holding him personally liable would discourage people from engaging in corporate enterprise.

What I would merely hold is that a participating shareholder of a corporation vested with a public interest, organized with capital insufficient to meet liabilities which are certain to arise in the ordinary course of the corporation's business, may be held personally responsible for such liabilities. Where corporate income is not sufficient to cover the cost of insurance premiums above the statutory minimum or where initially adequate finances dwindle under the pressure of competition, bad times or extraordinary and unexpected liability, obviously the shareholder will not be held liable. * * *

The only types of corporate enterprises that will be discouraged as a result of a decision allowing the individual shareholder to be sued will be those such as the one in question, designed solely to abuse the corporate privilege at the expense of the public interest.

* * *

NOTES AND QUESTIONS

I. IT IS NOW ACCEPTED AS ONE of the first principles of American law that those who own shares in corporations, whether such shareholders are individuals or are themselves corporations, normally are not liable for the debts of their corporations.[1] As you noted in the *Bartle* case above, it is further accepted as perfectly legal to incorporate for the express purpose of limiting the liability of the corporation's owners.

Indeed, there has been an almost romantic aspect about American law when some scholars have considered the doctrine of shareholder limited liability. This view is rarely expressed today, but when one consults an early twentieth century treatise on the corporate entity one can find it said that "This attribute of limited liability is regarded by most persons as the greatest advantage of incorporation. Indeed many immigrants doubtless possess full knowledge of this fact before coming within hailing distance of the Statute of Liberty."[2] As indicated earlier, in the early part of the twentieth century the then President of Columbia University declared that:

> [T]he limited liability corporation is the greatest single discovery of modern times [and that] even steam and electricity are far less important than the limited liability corporation, and they would be reduced to comparative impotence without it. . . . It substitutes co-operation on a large scale for individual, cut-throat, parochial competition. It makes possible huge economy in production and in trading . . . it means the only possible engine for carrying on international trade on a scale commensurate with modern needs and opportunities.[3]

---

1   For the evolution of the acceptance of this "first principle," see, e.g., Dodd, "The Evolution of Limited Liability in American Industry: Massachusetts," 61 Harv. L. Rev. 1351 (1948).

For some typical examples of statutory treatment see Delaware General Corporate Law Section 102(b)(6), which provides that the certificate of incorporation may contain "A provision imposing personal liability for the debts of the corporation on its stockholders or members to a specified extent and upon specified conditions; *otherwise, the stockholders or members of a corporation shall not be personally liable for the payment of the corporation's debts except as they may be liable by reason of their own conduct or acts.*" (emphasis supplied), or the Revised Model Business Corporation Act, § 6.22(b), which states that "Unless otherwise provided in the articles of incorporation *a shareholder of a corporation is not personally liable for the acts or debts of the corporation except that he may become personally liable by reason of his own acts or conduct.*" (Emphasis supplied).

2   M. Wormser, Disregard of the Corporate Fiction and Allied Corporation Problems 14 (New York: Baker, Voorhis and Co. 1927). See also Barber, "Piercing the Corporate Veil," 17 Willamette L. Rev. 371–372 (1981): "This incentive to business investment has been called the most important legal development of the nineteenth century."

3   Quoted by M. Wormser, D*isregard of the Corporate Fiction and Allied Corporation Problems 2–3* (New York: Baker, Voorhis and Co. 1927). To strikingly similar effect see the comments from the Economist of 18 December 1926 quoted by Halpern, Trebilcock & Turnbull, "An Economic Analysis of Limited Liability in Corporation Law," 30 U. of Toronto L.J. 117, 118 (1980): "The economic historian of the future may assign to the nameless inventor of the principle of limited liability, as applied to trading corporations, a place of honor with Watt and Stephenson, and other pioneers of the Industrial Revolution."

Would you agree with these sentiments? Do these four New York cases lead you to believe that limited shareholder liability is a good idea? Why or why not?

. . . .

2. YOU SHOULD UNDERSTAND, though, that even in jurisdictions where this "first principle" of shareholder limited liability exists, there are exceptions to the rule of no liability of shareholders for corporate debts. For example, it is commonly true that shareholders will be liable to the corporation or to its creditors if they fail to pay the full consideration for their shares.[4] Some states impose liability on shareholders of small corporations for certain debts to corporate employees.[5] There is also criminal or civil liability for shareholders or officers who commit crimes or torts on behalf of their corporations, where they personally possess the requisite intent to cause harm.

We are now concerned with still another exception to the rule absolving shareholders from liability for the debts of their corporations. This exception, known as the "piercing the veil" doctrine, has long been a rule, equitable in nature, applied by American and foreign courts to fasten liability on shareholders of corporations of varying size and character for corporate debts of all kinds.

. . . .

3. THE "VEIL" OF THE "CORPORATE FICTION," or the "artificial personality" of the corporation, is "pierced," and the individual or corporate shareholder exposed to personal or corporate liability, as the case may be, when a court determines that the debt in question *is not really a debt of the corporation*, but ought, in fairness, *to be viewed as a debt of the individual or corporate shareholder or shareholders*. While it can probably be stated that what is involved in veil-piercing is a paradigm case of a judgment call on the part of judge or jury,[6] the articulation of the doctrine is usually in terms that suggest that more than mere equitable discretion is involved.

The most commonly quoted general rule is probably that stated by Judge SANBORN in *United States v. Milwaukee Refrigerator Transit Co.*:

> [A] corporation will be looked upon as a legal entity as a general rule, and until sufficient reason to the contrary appears; but, when the notion of legal entity is used to defeat public convenience, justify wrong, protect fraud, or defend crime, the law will regard the corporation as an association of persons.

---

4   See, e.g., Delaware General Corporation Law § 162, Revised Model Business Corporation Act § 6.22(a).

5   At least as of 1987 this was the situation in New York and Wisconsin. See P. Blumberg, The Law of Corporate Groups: Tort, Contract, and Other Common Law Problems in the Substantive Law of Parent and Subsidiary Corporations 50 (1987).

6   *United States v. Milwaukee Refrigerator Transit Co.*, 142 F. 247, 255 (C.C.E.D. Wis. 1905).

Applying this general rule, do you believe it was appropriate to pierce the corporate veil in any of the four cases you have just read? Note that there is a majority and dissenting opinion in the first three of these cases, which should give you some sense of the difficulty of the area. Who gets it right in each of those cases, the majority or the dissent?

....

4. UNTIL ABOUT THE LAST TWO decades of the twentieth century there was relatively little theoretical or scholarly work done on the issue of "piercing the veil," considering that any brief perusal of the state or federal reporters is likely to show as many corporation law cases on piercing the veil as those devoted to any other issue, and occasionally more than the other various issues combined. The explanation for the reluctance of scholars to tackle the issue is probably to be found in the doctrine's frustrating fluidity, of which you have already had a glimpse. As the general language of Judge Sanborn suggests, there has been a real reluctance on the part of courts clearly to define piercing the veil standards.

Scholars who have examined the piercing the veil doctrine have seemed almost in despair, remarking that the rationales for piercing the veil are "vague and illusory," and that the jurisprudence of veil-piercing is a "legal quagmire."[7] As it was stated in a relatively recent attempt to impose order on the field, the law of piercing the veil "like lightning . . . is rare, severe, and unprincipled. There is a consensus that the whole area of limited liability, and conversely of piercing the corporate veil, is among the most confusing in corporate law."[8] One leading scholar of corporations, taking all of this into consideration has simply thrown up his hands and declared that we should do away with the piercing the veil doctrine altogether, at least in the case of individual shareholder liability for corporate debts.[9]

Veil-piercing is a doctrine that often incorporates and bears a strong resemblance to fraud, and thus it is not too difficult to understand why courts have been reluctant, just as they have been in fraud cases, to enunciate hard and fast rules, lest the ingenuity of man (or woman) find a way to pervert the spirit while sticking to the letter of the law.[10] Piercing the veil has thus remained one of the great tightly-held possessions

---

7   Ballantine on "Parent and Subsidiary Corporations," 14 Cal. L. Rev., at 15 (1925). Ballantine on Private Corporations, p. 34, quoted in Frederick J. Powell, Parent and Subsidiary Corporations: Liability of a Parent Corporation for the Obligations of Its Subsidiary (Chicago, Callaghan and Co. 1931), at iv.

8   Easterbrook & Fischel, "Limited Liability and the Corporation," 52 U. Chi. L. Rev. 89 (1985). Easterbrook and Fischel's arguments have been reprinted in their book, The Economic Structure of Corporate Law 40–62 (1991).

9   Stephen M. Bainbridge, "Abolishing Veil Piercing," 26 Journal of Corporation Law 479 (2001).

10   Cf. Krendl & Krendl, "Piercing the Corporate Veil: Focusing the Inquiry," 55 Denver L. J. 1, 22 (1978) ("In this equitable area [of piercing the corporate veil] involving as wide a variety of situations as foolishness or deviousness can contrive, there appears to be no single determinative factor."), and Thompson, "Piercing the

of what one of the first commentators called "Our lady of the common law."[11] It is a doctrine applied by courts in an extremely discretionary manner, in accordance with the individual consciences of judges. In an age dominated by statutes, piercing the veil remains a vital and robust common-law doctrine. Do you see evidence of this vitality or robustness in these four cases?

....

5. THESE TWO CASES, *Berkey* and *Walkovsky* are two of the most important cases decided by the highest New York Court, the Court of Appeals (New York's "Supreme Court," somewhat paradoxically, unlike the situation in many states, is an intermediate appellate court. Go figure.). New York, as the commercial capital of the country, has had more than its share of veil-piercing cases, and it could probably be characterized as the leading jurisdiction for veil-piercing law. Would you characterize New York as a jurisdiction in which it is difficult or easy to pierce the corporate veil? Note that the majority opinion in *Berkey* is by Judge CARDOZO, whom you encountered earlier in *Meinhard v. Solomon*. Does this seem like the work of the same judge? Why or why not? Note CARDOZO's caution that when we are thinking about whether it is proper to pierce the corporate veil of a subsidiary corporation to reach a parent we should be careful lest our way be obscured by the "mists of metaphor." What do you suppose that means?

Note that Cardozo is reluctant to apply agency doctrine to find the controlling parent liable for the acts of the subsidiary. Is this reluctance justified? Why doesn't the dissent go along? *Berkey* is a case involving an attempt to pierce the corporate veil of a subsidiary to reach a parent corporation, while *Walkovsky* is an attempt to fasten liability on an individual shareholder. Should there be a difference in the manner of treatment between corporations and individuals when veil-piercing is at issue? Generally speaking the law says "no." Do you agree?

Corporate Veil: An Empirical Study," 76 Cornell L. Rev. 1043 (1991) ("As with insider trading and much of the law of directors' fiduciary duties, additional specification may not be possible without inviting greater abuse, as investors and their lawyers plan transactions to avoid specific terms of the law." (footnotes omitted)).

11   M. Wormser, *Disregard of the Corporate Fiction and Allied Corporation Problems* (New York: Baker, Voorhis and Co. 1927). For an examination of that common-law ethos, as practiced by some leading common lawyers, see R. Cosgrove, *Our Lady The Common Law: An Anglo–American Legal Community, 1870–1930* (1987).

6. *BERKEY* AND *WALKOVSKY* ARE cases in which plaintiffs seek to recover for torts committed by the agents of defendant corporations, and to impute these torts to the shareholders through the principle of *respondeat superior* (literally "let the master answer," a broad principle in the law of torts which provides that the employer is liable for the acts of employees under his or her direction, or, if you like, that the principal is responsible for the torts committed by his or her agent). Plenty of other cases involve plaintiffs suing in breach of contract. Which plaintiffs should be entitled to easier piercing of the veil—voluntary creditors who agree to enter into agreement with corporations, or involuntary creditors injured by the acts of agents of corporations? Most courts suggest that it should be easier for tort creditors to recover. Do you understand why? It is not clear, however, that as far as actual cases are concerned, it is easier to pierce for tort creditors than it is for contract creditors. The leading empirical study reached a contrary conclusion, but this may be because the vast majority of cases settle before they can be tried.[12]

While there was relatively little scholarly interest in the piercing issue until recently, it is now a red-hot topic in the law reviews. The thrust of such scholarship seems to be the suggestion that we should eliminate the protection of limited liability for parent corporations in the case of torts committed by their subsidiaries. Would you agree? Henry Hansmann and Reinier Kraakman fired the opening shot in the academic war over limited liability in their article *Toward Unlimited Shareholder Liability for Corporate Torts*, 100 Yale L.J. 1879 (1991). Professor Kraakman's casebook with William T. Allen, Allen & Kraakman, *Commentaries and Cases of the Law of Business Organization* 169 (2003), identifies the following articles as providing "subsequent and related contributions to the debate": Janet Alexander, *Unlimited Shareholder Liability Through a Procedural Lens*, 106 Harv. L. Rev. 387 (1992); Peter Z. Grossman, *The Market for Shares of Companies with Unlimited Liability*, 24 J. Leg. Stud. 63 (1995); Joseph Grundfest, *The Limited Future of Unlimited Liability* 102 Yale L. Rev. 387 (1992); Hansmann & Kraakman, *A Procedural Focus on Unlimited Liability*, 106 Harv. L. Rev. 446 (1992); Hansmann & Kraakman, *Do the Capital Markets Compel Limited Liability? A Response to Professor Grundfest*, 102 Yale L. Rev. 427 (1992); David Leebron, *Limited Liability, Tort Victims, and Creditors*, 91 Colum. L. Rev. 1565 (1991); Jonathan R. Macey & Geoffrey P. Miller, *Double Liability of Bank Shareholders: History and Implications*, 27 Wake Forest L.Rev. 31 (1992); *Note, In Defense of Limited Liability: A Reply to Hansmann & Kraakman*, 1 Geo. Mason U.L.Rev. 59 (1994); and Stephen B. Presser, *Thwarting the Killing of the Corporation: Limited Liability, Democracy and Economics*, 87

---

12   For that empirical study see Robert Thompson, "Piercing the Corporate Veil: An Empirical Study," 76 Cornell L. Rev. 1036 (1991). See also, for further data, Robert Thompson, The Limits of Liability in the New Limited Liability Entities, 32 Wake Forest L. Rev. 1–29 (1997), where Professor Thompson reports that with regard to individual shareholders piercing the corporate veil has never occurred in a corporation with more than nine shareholders and usually occurs as to shareholders who are also managers of the entity. Would you have expected this?

Nw. U. L. Rev. 148 (1992). *See also* Stephen M. Bainbridge, *Abolishing Veil Piercing*, 26 Iowa J. Corp. L. 479 (2001); Richard A. Booth, *Limited Liability and the Efficient Allocation of Resources*, 89 Nw. U. L. Rev. 140 (1994); Rebecca J. Huss, *Revamping Veil-Piercing for all Limited Liability Entities: Forcing the Common Law Doctrine into the Statutory Age*, 70 U. Cinn. L. Rev. 95 (2001); Lynn M. LoPucki, *The Death of Liability*, 106 Yale L.J. 1 (1996); Nina A. Mendelson, *A Control-Based Approach to Shareholder Liability for Corporate Torts*, 102 Colum. L. Rev. 1203 (2002); and Robert B. Thompson, *Unpacking Limited Liability: Direct and Vicarious Liability of Corporate Participants for Torts of the Enterprise*, 47 Vand. L. Rev. 1 (1994).

Is limited liability for torts likely to be abolished, as many of these scholars suggest? Consider the opinion of the United States Supreme Court, which follows.

II. Federal Law

United States v. Bestfoods et al.

Supreme Court of the United States.
524 U.S. 51, 118 S.Ct. 1876, 141 L.Ed.2d 43 (1998).

JUSTICE SOUTER delivered the opinion of [a unanimous] Court.

The United States brought this action for the costs of cleaning up industrial waste generated by a chemical plant. The issue before us, under the Comprehensive Environmental Response, Compensation, and Liability Act of 1980 (CERCLA), 94 Stat. 2767, as amended, *42 U.S.C. § 9601 et seq.*, is whether a parent corporation that actively participated in, and exercised control over, the operations of a subsidiary may, without more, be held liable as an operator of a polluting facility owned or operated by the subsidiary. We answer no, unless the corporate veil may be pierced. But a corporate parent that actively participated in, and exercised control over, the operations of the facility itself may be held directly liable in its own right as an operator of the facility.

I

In 1980, CERCLA was enacted in response to the serious environmental and health risks posed by industrial pollution. * * * "As its name implies, CERCLA is a comprehensive statute that grants the President broad power to command government agencies and private parties to clean up hazardous waste sites." * * * If it satisfies certain statutory conditions, the United States may, for instance, use the "Hazardous Substance Superfund" to finance cleanup efforts, see *42 U.S.C. § § 9601(11), 9604; 26 U.S.C. § 9507,* which it may then replenish by suits brought under § 107 of the Act against, among others, "any person who at the time of disposal of any hazardous substance owned or operated any facility." *42 U.S.C. § 9607*(a)(2). So, those actually "responsible for any damage, environmental harm, or injury from chemical poisons [may be tagged with] the cost of their actions," S. Rep. No. 96–848, p. 13 (1980). * * * The term "person" is defined in CERCLA to include corporations and other business organizations, see *42 U.S.C. § 9601*(21), and the term "facility" enjoys a broad and detailed definition as well, see § 9601(9).[13] The phrase "owner or operator" is defined only by tautology, however, as "any person owning or operating" a facility, § 9601(20) (A)(ii), and it is this bit of circularity that prompts our review. Cf. *Exxon Corp. v. Hunt, supra, at 363* (CERCLA, "unfortunately, is not a model of legislative draftsmanship").

II

In 1957, Ott Chemical Co. (Ott I) began manufacturing chemicals at a plant near Muskegon, Michigan, and its intentional and unintentional dumping of hazardous substances significantly polluted the soil and ground water at the site. In 1965, respondent CPC International Inc. [CPC has recently changed its name to Bestfoods. Consistently with the briefs and the opinions below, we use the name CPC herein.] incorporated a wholly owned subsidiary to buy Ott I's assets in exchange for CPC stock. The new company, also dubbed Ott Chemical Co. (Ott II), continued chemical manufacturing at the site, and continued to pollute its surroundings. CPC kept the managers of Ott I, including its founder, president, and principal shareholder, Arnold Ott, on board as officers of Ott II. Arnold Ott and several other Ott II officers and directors were also given positions at CPC, and they performed duties for both corporations.

In 1972, CPC sold Ott II to Story Chemical Company, which operated the Muskegon plant until its bankruptcy in 1977. Shortly thereafter, when respondent Michigan Department of Natural Resources (MDNR) * * * examined the site for environmental damage, it found the land littered with thousands of leaking and even exploding drums of waste, and the soil and water saturated with noxious chemicals. MDNR sought a buyer for the property who would be willing to contribute toward its cleanup, and after extensive negotiations, respondent Aerojet-General Corp. arranged for transfer of the site from the Story bankruptcy trustee in 1977. Aerojet created a wholly owned California subsidiary, Cordova Chemical Company (Cordova/California), to purchase the property,

---

13   "The term 'facility' means (A) any building, structure, installation, equipment, pipe or pipeline (including any pipe into a sewer or publicly owned treatment works), well, pit, pond, lagoon, impoundment, ditch, landfill, storage container, motor vehicle, rolling stock, or aircraft, or (B) any site or area where a hazardous substance has been deposited, stored, disposed of, or placed, or otherwise come to be located; but does not include any consumer product in consumer use or any vessel."

and Cordova/California in turn created a wholly owned Michigan subsidiary, Cordova Chemical Company of Michigan (Cordova/Michigan), which manufactured chemicals at the site until 1986. * * *

By 1981, the federal Environmental Protection Agency had undertaken to see the site cleaned up, and its long-term remedial plan called for expenditures well into the tens of millions of dollars. To recover some of that money, the United States filed this action * * * in 1989, naming five defendants as responsible parties: CPC, Aerojet, Cordova/California, Cordova/Michigan, and Arnold Ott.[14] (By that time, Ott I and Ott II were defunct.) After the parties (and MDNR) had launched a flurry of contribution claims, counterclaims, and cross-claims, the District Court consolidated the cases for trial * * * [and] in 1991, the District Court held a 15-day bench trial [a trial conducted without a jury] on the issue of liability. * * * [T]he trial focused on the issues of whether CPC and Aerojet, as the parent corporations of Ott II and the Cordova companies, had "owned or operated" the facility within the meaning of § 107(a)(2).

The District Court said that operator liability may attach to a parent corporation both directly, when the parent itself operates the facility, and indirectly, when the corporate veil can be pierced under state law. See *CPC Int'l, Inc. v. Aerojet–General Corp., 777 F. Supp. 549, 572 (W.D. Mich. 1991).* The court explained that, while CERCLA imposes direct liability in situations in which the corporate veil cannot be pierced under traditional concepts of corporate law, "the statute and its legislative history do not suggest that CERCLA rejects entirely the crucial limits to liability that are inherent to corporate law." *Id., at 573.* As the District Court put it,

> "a parent corporation is directly liable under section 107(a)(2) as an operator only when it has exerted power or influence over its subsidiary by actively participating in and exercising control over the subsidiary's business during a period of disposal of hazardous waste. A parent's actual participation in and control over a subsidiary's functions and decision-making creates 'operator' liability under CERCLA; a parent's mere oversight of a subsidiary's business in a manner appropriate and consistent with the investment relationship between a parent and its wholly owned subsidiary does not." *Ibid.*

Applying that test to the facts of this case, the District Court held both CPC and Aerojet liable under § 107(a)(2) as operators. As to CPC, the court found it particularly telling that CPC selected Ott II's board of directors and populated its executive ranks with CPC officials, and that a CPC official, G.R.D. Williams, played a significant role in shaping Ott II's environmental compliance policy.

After a divided panel of the Court of Appeals for the Sixth Circuit reversed in part, *United States v. Cordova/Michigan, 59 F.3d 584,* that court granted rehearing en banc and vacated the panel decision, *67 F.3d 586 (1995).* This time, 7 judges to

---

14   Arnold Ott settled out of court with the Government on the eve of trial.

6, the court again reversed the District Court in *part.* 113 F.3d 572 (1997). The majority remarked on the possibility that a parent company might be held directly liable as an operator of a facility owned by its subsidiary: "At least conceivably, a parent might independently operate the facility in the stead of its subsidiary; or, as a sort of joint venturer, actually operate the facility alongside its subsidiary." *Id.,* at 579. But the court refused to go any further and rejected the District Court's analysis with the explanation:

> "Where a parent corporation is sought to be held liable as an operator *
> * * based upon the extent of its control of its subsidiary which owns the
> facility, the parent will be liable only when the requirements necessary
> to pierce the corporate veil [under state law] are met. In other words, . .
> . whether the parent will be liable as an operator depends upon whether
> the degree to which it controls its subsidiary and the extent and manner
> of its involvement with the facility, amount to the abuse of the corporate
> form that will warrant piercing the corporate veil and disregarding the
> separate corporate entities of the parent and subsidiary." *Id., at 580.*

Applying Michigan veil-piercing law, the Court of Appeals decided that neither CPC nor Aerojet * * * was liable for controlling the actions of its subsidiaries, since the parent and subsidiary corporations maintained separate personalities and the parents did not utilize the subsidiary corporate form to perpetrate fraud or subvert justice.

We granted certiorari * * * to resolve a conflict among the Circuits over the extent to which parent corporations may be held liable under CERCLA for operating facilities ostensibly under the control of their subsidiaries. * * *

III

It is a general principle of corporate law deeply "ingrained in our economic and legal systems" that a parent corporation (so-called because of control through ownership of another corporation's stock) is not liable for the acts of its subsidiaries. Douglas & Shanks, Insulation from Liability Through Subsidiary Corporations, *39 Yale L. J. 193 (1929)* (hereinafter Douglas); * * * cf. *Anderson v. Abbott, 321 U.S. 349, 362, 88 L. Ed. 793, 64 S. Ct. 531 (1944)* ("Limited liability is the rule, not the exception"); *Burnet v. Clark, 287 U.S. 410, 415, 77 L. Ed. 397, 53 S. Ct. 207 (1932)* ("A corporation and its stockholders are generally to be treated as separate entities"). Thus it is hornbook law that "the exercise of the 'control' which stock ownership gives to the stockholders . . . will not create liability beyond the assets of the subsidiary. That 'control' includes the election of directors, the making of by-laws . . . and the doing of all other acts incident to the legal status of stockholders. Nor will a duplication of some or all of the directors or executive officers be fatal." Douglas 196 (footnotes omitted). Although this respect for corporate distinctions when the subsidiary is a polluter has been severely criticized in the literature, see, *e.g., Note, Liability of Parent Corporations for Hazardous Waste Cleanup and Damages, 99 Harv. L. Rev. 986 (1986),* nothing in CERCLA purports to reject this bedrock principle, and against this venerable common-law backdrop, the congressional silence is audible. Cf. *Edmonds v. Compagnie Generale Transatlantique, 443 U.S. 256, 266–267, 61 L. Ed. 2d 521, 99 S. Ct. 2753 (1979)* ("silence is most eloquent, for such reticence while contemplating an important and controversial change in existing law is unlikely"). The Government has indeed made no claim that a corporate parent is liable as an owner or an operator under § 107 simply because its subsidiary is subject to liability for owning or operating a polluting facility.

But there is an equally fundamental principle of corporate law, applicable to the parent-subsidiary relationship as well as generally, that the corporate veil may be pierced and the shareholder held liable for the corporation's conduct when, *inter alia*, the corporate form would otherwise be misused to accomplish certain wrongful purposes, most notably fraud, on the shareholder's behalf. See, *e.g., Anderson v. Abbott, supra, at 362* ("there are occasions when the limited liability sought to be obtained through the corporation will be qualified or denied"); *Chicago, M. & St. P. R. Co. v. Minneapolis Civic and Commerce Assn., 247 U.S. 490, 501, 62 L. Ed. 1229, 38 S. Ct. 553 (1918)* (principles of corporate separateness "have been plainly and repeatedly held not applicable where stock ownership has been resorted to, not for the purpose of participating in the affairs of a corporation in the normal and usual manner, but for the purpose . . . of controlling a subsidiary company so that it may be used as a mere agency or instrumentality of the owning company") * * *. Nothing in CERCLA purports to rewrite this well-settled rule, either. CERCLA is thus like many another congressional enactment in giving no indication "that the entire corpus of state corporation law is to be replaced simply because a plaintiff's cause of action is based upon a federal statute," *Burks v. Lasker, 441 U.S. 471, 478, 60 L. Ed. 2d 404, 99 S. Ct. 1831 (1979)*, and the failure of the statute to speak to a matter as fundamental as the liability implications of corporate ownership demands application of the rule that "in order to abrogate a common-law principle, the statute must speak directly to the question addressed by the common law," *United States v. Texas, 507 U.S. 529, 534, 123 L. Ed. 2d 245, 113 S. Ct. 1631 (1993)* (internal quotation marks omitted). The Court of Appeals was accordingly correct in holding that when (but only when) the corporate veil may be pierced,[15] may a parent corporation be charged with derivative CERCLA liability for its subsidiary's actions. * * *

---

15   There is significant disagreement among courts and commentators over whether, in enforcing CERCLA's indirect liability, courts should borrow state law, or instead apply a federal common law of veil piercing. Compare, *e.g.,* * * * *Lansford–Coaldale Joint Water Auth. v. Tonolli Corp., 4 F.3d at 1225* ("given the federal interest in uniformity in the application of CERCLA, it is federal common law, and not state law, which governs when corporate veil-piercing is justified under CERCLA") * * * with, e.g., Dennis, Liability of Officers, Directors and Stockholders under CERCLA: The Case for Adopting State Law, *36 Vill. L. Rev. 1367 (1991)* (arguing that state law should apply). Cf. *In re Acushnet River & New Bedford Harbor Proceedings, 675 F. Supp. 22, 33 (Mass. 1987)* (noting that, since "federal common law draws upon state law for guidance, . . . the choice between state and federal [veil-piercing law] may in many cases present questions of academic interest, but little practical significance"). But cf. Note, Piercing the Corporate Law Veil: The Alter Ego Doctrine Under Federal Common Law, *95 Harv. L. Rev. 853 (1982)* (arguing that federal common law need not mirror state law, because "federal common law should look to federal statutory policy rather than to state corporate law when deciding whether to pierce the corporate veil"). Since none of the parties challenges the Sixth Circuit's holding that CPC and Aerojet incurred no derivative liability, the question is not presented in this case, and we do not address it further.

IV

A

If the act rested liability entirely on ownership of a polluting facility, this opinion might end here; but CERCLA liability may turn on operation as well as ownership, and nothing in the statute's terms bars a parent corporation from direct liability for its own actions in operating a facility owned by its subsidiary. As Justice (then-Professor) Douglas noted almost 70 years ago, derivative liability cases are to be distinguished from those in which "the alleged wrong can seemingly be traced to the parent through the conduit of its own personnel and management" and "the parent is directly a participant in the wrong complained of." Douglas 207, 208. * * * In such instances, the parent is directly liable for its own actions. See H. Henn & J. Alexander, Laws of Corporations 347 (3d ed. 1983) (hereinafter Henn & Alexander) ("Apart from corporation law principles, a shareholder, whether a natural person or a corporation, may be liable on the ground that such shareholder's activity resulted in the liability"). The fact that a corporate subsidiary happens to own a polluting facility operated by its parent does nothing, then, to displace the rule that the parent "corporation is [itself] responsible for the wrongs committed by its agents in the course of its business," *Mine Workers v. Coronado Coal Co., 259 U.S. 344, 395, 66 L. Ed. 975, 42 S. Ct. 570 (1922)*, and whereas the rules of veil-piercing limit derivative liability for the actions of another corporation, CERCLA's "operator" provision is concerned primarily with direct liability for one's own actions. * * *

Under the plain language of the statute, any person who operates a polluting facility is directly liable for the costs of cleaning up the pollution. See *42 U.S.C. § 9607*(a)(2). This is so regardless of whether that person is the facility's owner, the owner's parent corporation or business partner, or even a saboteur who sneaks into the facility at night to discharge its poisons out of malice. If any such act of operating a corporate subsidiary's facility is done on behalf of a parent corporation, the existence of the parent-subsidiary relationship under state corporate law is simply irrelevant to the issue of direct liability. See *Riverside Market Dev. Corp. v. International Bldg. Prods., Inc., 931 F.2d 327, 330* (CA5) ("CERCLA prevents individuals from hiding behind the corporate shield when, as 'operators,' they themselves actually participate in the wrongful conduct prohibited by the Act") * * * *United States v. Kayser-Roth Corp., 910 F.2d 24, 26 (CA1 1990)* ("a person who is an operator of a facility is not protected from liability by the legal structure of ownership").[16]

---

16   See Oswald, Bifurcation of the Owner and Operator Analysis under CERCLA, *72 Wash. U. L. Q. 223, 257 (1994)* ("There are . . . instances . . . in which the parent has not sufficiently overstepped the bounds of corporate separateness to warrant piercing, yet is involved enough in the facility's activities that it should be held liable as an operator. Imagine, for example, a parent who strictly observed corporate formalities, avoided intertwining officers and directors, and adequately capitalized its subsidiary, yet provided active, daily supervision and control over hazardous waste disposal activities of the subsidiary. Such a parent should not escape liability just because its activities do not justify a piercing of the subsidiary's veil").

This much is easy to say; the difficulty comes in defining actions sufficient to constitute direct parental "operation." Here of course we may again rue the uselessness of CERCLA's definition of a facility's "operator" as "any person . . . operating" the facility, *42 U.S.C. § 9601(20)(A)(ii)*, which leaves us to do the best we can to give the term its "ordinary or natural meaning." * * * In a mechanical sense, to "operate" ordinarily means "to control the functioning of; run: *operate a sewing machine*." American Heritage Dictionary 1268 (3d ed. 1992); see also Webster's New International Dictionary 1707 (2d ed. 1958) ("to work; as, to *operate* a machine"). And in the organizational sense more obviously intended by CERCLA, the word ordinarily means "to conduct the affairs of; manage: *operate a business*." American Heritage Dictionary, *supra,* at 1268; see also Webster's New International Dictionary, *supra,* at 1707 ("to manage"). So, under CERCLA, an operator is simply someone who directs the workings of, manages, or conducts the affairs of a facility. To sharpen the definition for purposes of CERCLA's concern with environmental contamination, an operator must manage, direct, or conduct operations specifically related to pollution, that is, operations having to do with the leakage or disposal of hazardous waste, or decisions about compliance with environmental regulations.

B

With this understanding, we are satisfied that the Court of Appeals correctly rejected the District Court's analysis of direct liability. But we also think that the appeals court erred in limiting direct liability under the statute to a parent's sole or joint venture operation, so as to eliminate any possible finding that CPC is liable as an operator on the facts of this case.

1

By emphasizing that "CPC is directly liable under section 107(a)(2) as an operator because CPC actively participated in and exerted significant control over Ott II's business and decision-making," *777 F. Supp. at 574*, the District Court applied the "actual control" test of whether the parent "actually operated the business of its subsidiary," *id., at 573*, as several Circuits have employed it * * *.

The well-taken objection to the actual control test, however, is its fusion of direct and indirect liability; the test is administered by asking a question about the relationship between the two corporations (an issue going to indirect liability) instead of a question about the parent's interaction with the subsidiary's facility (the source of any direct liability). If, however, direct liability for the parent's operation of the *facility* is to be kept distinct from derivative liability for the *subsidiary's own operation*, the focus of the enquiry must necessarily be different under the two tests. [emphasis supplied.] "The question is not whether the parent operates the subsidiary, but rather whether it operates the facility, and that operation is evidenced by participation in the activities of the facility, not the subsidiary. Control of the subsidiary, if extensive enough, gives rise to indirect liability under piercing doctrine, not direct liability under the statutory language." *Oswald* 269 * * *. The District Court was therefore mistaken to rest its analysis on CPC's relationship with Ott II, premising liability on little more than "CPC's 100-percent ownership of Ott II" and "CPC's active participation in, and at times majority control over, Ott II's board of directors." *777 F. Supp. at 575.* The analysis should instead have rested on the relationship between CPC and the Muskegon facility itself.

In addition to (and perhaps as a reflection of) the erroneous focus on the relationship between CPC and Ott II, even those findings of the District Court that might be taken to speak to the extent of CPC's activity at the facility itself are flawed, for the District Court wrongly assumed that the actions of the joint officers and directors are necessarily attributable to CPC. The District Court emphasized the facts that CPC placed its own high-level officials on Ott II's board of directors and in key management positions at Ott II, and that those individuals made major policy decisions and conducted day-to-day operations at the facility: "Although Ott II corporate officers set the day-to-day operating policies for the company without any need to obtain formal approval from CPC, CPC actively participated in this decision-making because high-ranking CPC officers served in Ott II management positions." *Id., at 559; see also id., at 575* (relying on "CPC's involvement in major decision-making and day-to-day operations through CPC officials who served within Ott II management, including the positions of president and chief executive officer," and on "the conduct of CPC officials with respect to Ott II affairs, particularly Arnold Ott"); *id., at 558* ("CPC actively participated in, and at times controlled, the policy-making decisions of its subsidiary thorough its representation on the Ott II board of directors"); *id., at 559* ("CPC also actively participated in and exercised control over day-to-day decision-making at Ott II through representation in the highest levels of the subsidiary's management").

In imposing direct liability on these grounds, the District Court failed to recognize that "it is entirely appropriate for directors of a parent corporation to serve as directors of its subsidiary, and that fact alone may not serve to expose the parent corporation to liability for its subsidiary's acts." *American Protein Corp. v. AB Volvo, 844 F.2d 56, 57 (CA2)* * * see also *Kingston Dry Dock Co. v. Lake Champlain Transp. Co., 31 F.2d 265, 267 (CA2 1929)* (L. Hand, J.) ("Control through the ownership of shares does not fuse the corporations, even when the directors are common to each"); Henn & Alexander 355 (noting that it is "normal" for a parent and subsidiary to "have identical directors and officers").

This recognition that the corporate personalities remain distinct has its corollary in the "well established principle [of corporate law] that directors and officers holding positions with a parent and its subsidiary can and do 'change hats' to represent the two corporations separately, despite their common ownership." *Lusk v. Foxmeyer Health Corp., 129 F.3d 773, 779 (CA5 1997)* * * * Since courts generally presume "that the directors are wearing their 'subsidiary hats' and not their 'parent hats' when acting for the subsidiary," P. Blumberg, Law of Corporate Groups: Procedural Problems in the Law of Parent and Subsidiary Corporations § 1.02.1, at 12 (1983) * * * it cannot be enough to establish liability here that dual officers and directors made policy decisions and supervised activities at the facility. The Government would have to show that, despite the general presumption to the contrary, the officers and directors were acting in their capacities as CPC officers and directors, and not as Ott II officers and directors, when they committed those acts.[17] The District Court made no such enquiry here, however, disregarding entirely this time-honored common law rule.

In sum, the District Court's focus on the relationship between parent and subsidiary (rather than parent and facility), combined with its automatic attribution of the actions of dual officers and directors to the corporate parent, erroneously, even if unintentionally, treated CERCLA as though it displaced or fundamentally altered common law standards of limited liability. Indeed, if the evidence of common corporate personnel acting at management and directorial levels were enough to support a finding of a parent corporation's direct operator liability under CERCLA, then the possibility of resort to veil piercing to establish indirect, derivative liability for the subsidiary's violations would be academic. There would in essence be a relaxed, CERCLA-specific rule of derivative liability that would banish traditional standards and expectations from the law of CERCLA liability. But, as we have said, such a rule does not arise from congressional silence, and CERCLA's silence is dispositive.

We accordingly agree with the Court of Appeals that a participation-and-control test looking to the parent's supervision over the subsidiary, especially one that assumes that dual officers always act on behalf of the parent, cannot be used to identify operation of a facility resulting in direct parental liability. Nonetheless, a return to the ordinary meaning of the word "operate" in the organizational sense will indicate why we think that the Sixth Circuit stopped short when it confined its examples of direct parental operation to exclusive or joint ventures, and declined to find at least the possibility of direct operation by CPC in this case.

In our enquiry into the meaning Congress presumably had in mind when it used the verb "to operate," we recognized that the statute obviously meant something more than mere mechanical activation of pumps and valves, and must be read to contemplate "operation" as including the exercise of direction over the facility's activities. * * * The Court of Appeals recognized this by indicating that a parent can be held directly liable when the parent operates the facility in the stead of its subsidiary or alongside the subsidiary in some sort of a joint venture. * * * We anticipated a further possibility above, however, when we observed that a dual officer or director might depart so far from the norms of parental influence exercised through dual officeholding as to serve the parent, even when ostensibly acting on behalf of the subsidiary in operating the facility. *See* n. [18], *supra.* Yet another possibility, suggested by the

---

17   We do not attempt to recite the ways in which the Government could show that dual officers or directors were in fact acting on behalf of the parent. Here, it is prudent to say only that the presumption that an act is taken on behalf of the corporation for whom the officer claims to act is strongest when the act is perfectly consistent with the norms of corporate behavior, but wanes as the distance from those accepted norms approaches the point of action by a dual officer plainly contrary to the interests of the subsidiary yet nonetheless advantageous to the parent.

facts of this case, is that an agent of the parent with no hat to wear but the parent's hat might manage or direct activities at the facility.

Identifying such an occurrence calls for line drawing yet again, since the acts of direct operation that give rise to parental liability must necessarily be distinguished from the interference that stems from the normal relationship between parent and subsidiary. Again norms of corporate behavior (undisturbed by any CERCLA provision) are crucial reference points. Just as we may look to such norms in identifying the limits of the presumption that a dual officeholder acts in his ostensible capacity, so here we may refer to them in distinguishing a parental officer's oversight of a subsidiary from such an officer's control over the operation of the subsidiary's facility. "Activities that involve the facility but which are consistent with the parent's investor status, such as monitoring of the subsidiary's performance, supervision of the subsidiary's finance and capital budget decisions, and articulation of general policies and procedures, should not give rise to direct liability." *Oswald* 282. The critical question is whether, in degree and detail, actions directed to the facility by an agent of the parent alone are eccentric under accepted norms of parental oversight of a subsidiary's facility.

There is, in fact, some evidence that CPC engaged in just this type and degree of activity at the Muskegon plant. The District Court's opinion speaks of an agent of CPC alone who played a conspicuous part in dealing with the toxic risks emanating from the operation of the plant. G.R.D. Williams worked only for CPC; he was not an employee, officer, or director of Ott II, see Tr. of Oral Arg. 7, and thus, his actions were of necessity taken only on behalf of CPC. The District Court found that "CPC became directly involved in environmental and regulatory matters through the work of . . . Williams, CPC's governmental and environmental affairs director. Williams . . . became heavily involved in environmental issues at Ott II." *777 F. Supp. at 561* He "actively participated in and exerted control over a variety of Ott II environmental matters," *ibid.*, and he "issued directives regarding Ott II's responses to regulatory inquiries," *id., at 575.*

> We think that these findings are enough to raise an issue of CPC's operation of the facility through Williams's actions, though we would draw no ultimate conclusion from these findings at this point. Not only would we be deciding in the first instance an issue on which the trial and appellate courts did not focus, but the very fact that the District Court did not see the case as we do suggests that there may be still more to be known about Williams's activities. Indeed, even as the factual findings stand, the trial court offered little in the way of concrete detail for its conclusions about Williams's role in Ott II's environmental affairs, and the parties vigorously dispute the extent of Williams's involvement. Prudence thus counsels us to remand, on the theory of direct operation set out here, for reevaluation of Williams's role, and of the role of any other CPC agent who might be said to have had a part in operating the Muskegon facility. * * *

* * *

NOTES AND QUESTIONS

1. *U.S. v. BESTFOODS* **OFFERS** an opportunity to consider whether the rules for piercing the corporate veil should be different for federal law and state law. Should they? Note that the position of the United States Supreme court, clearly articulated in the *Bestfoods* case, is that if Congress wants to remove the traditional corporate law protection for limited liability it needs to do so in clear unequivocal language, and that courts should not otherwise place federal goals ahead of the traditional limited liability for shareholders. Do you agree with this perspective? Should there be different treatment accorded in the case of individual or corporate shareholders?

2. **MOST OF THE CASES THAT** we have considered have been those involving corporate shareholders, that is, the case of parent and subsidiary corporations. Probably there has been more scholarly writing on this topic than that of the topic of piercing the corporate veil to reach individual shareholders, and it remains true, as Professor Thompson noted in his earlier-cited empirical study, that there does not seem to be a single example of individual shareholders being held liable in a veil-piercing action concerning a large publicly-held corporation. This is not the case, however, with shareholders in small, closely-held corporations, such as those involved in the *Walkovszky v. Carlton* case, *supra*. Another excellent example of a court specifying what is required before a corporate veil can be pierced to reach an individual shareholder is *Sea–Land Services, Inc. v. Pepper Source*, 993 F.2d 1309 (7th Cir. 1993), where the federal court, applying Illinois law, observed that it was appropriate to fasten liability on an individual shareholder where he treated as "playthings" corporations he controlled, including manipulating and diverting funds among them so that debtor entities were left with insufficient funds to pay their creditors, and where he used corporate funds to pay his personal expenses rendering corporations in question unable to pay their monetary obligations to vendors, creditors, and federal and state tax authorities.

3. **AS YOU HAVE ALREADY SEEN**, there are a variety of formulations of the test for piercing the corporate veil, although all seem to involve, as the *Bestfoods* Court indicates, an "abuse" of the corporate form in order to favor the controlling shareholder at the expense of creditors or the government. Put slightly differently:

> Although some courts do not require actual fraud, the language they use
> suggests that something close to common-law fraud is required. See, e.g.,

Hystro Prods. v. MPN Corp., 18 F.3d 1384, 1390 (7th Cir. 1994) (noting that the [element in addition to showing control, the] "promote injustice" test requires something less than an affirmative showing of fraud, but it requires something more than the mere prospect of an unsatisfied judgment); *Sea–Land Servs., Inc. v. Pepper Source*, 941 F.2d 519, 523 (7th Cir. 1991) ("Some element of unfairness, something akin to fraud or deception or the existence of a compelling public interest must be present in order to disregard the corporate fiction." (internal quotation marks omitted)); *Associated Vendors, Inc. v. Oakland Meat Co.*, 26 Cal.Rptr. 806, 813 (Ct. App. 1963) ("While the doctrine does not depend on the presence of actual fraud, it is designed to prevent what would be fraud or injustice if accomplished. Accordingly, bad faith in one form or another is an underlying consideration and will be found . . . in those cases wherein the trial court was justified in disregarding the corporate entity.").

Timothy P. Glynn, Beyond "Unlimiting" *Shareholder Liability: Vicarious Tort Liability for Corporate Officers*, 57 Vand. L. Rev. 329, n.84 (2004).

Just what such an "abuse" is, or what constitutes such "bad faith" is a bit elusive. Faced with the problem, some courts have sought to provide extensive laundry lists of what may constitute abuse, with a notable one appearing in *Associated Vendors, Inc. v. Oakland Meat Co.*, 26 Cal.Rptr. at 814–815 (Ct. App. 1963):

> [1]   Commingling of funds and other assets, [2] failure to segregate funds of the separate entities, and [3]the unauthorized diversion of corporate funds or assets to other than corporate uses * * * [4] the treatment by an individual of the assets of the corporation as his own * * *; [5] the failure to obtain authority to issue stock or to subscribe to or issue the same * * *; [6] the holding out by an individual that he is personally liable for the debts of the corporation * * *; [7] the failure to maintain minutes or adequate corporate records, and [8] the confusion of the records of the separate entities * * *; [9] the identical equitable ownership in the two entities; [10] the identification of the equitable owners thereof with the domination and control of the two entities; [11] identification of the directors and officers of the two entities in the responsible supervision and management; [12] sole ownership of all of the stock in a corporation by one individual or the members of a family * * *; [13] the use of the same office or business location; [14] the employment of the same employees and/or attorney * * *; [15] the failure to adequately capitalize a corporation; [16] the total absence of corporate assets and undercapitalization [17] the use of a corporation as a mere shell, instrumentality or conduit

for a single venture or the business of an individual or another corporation * * *; [18] the concealment and misrepresentation of the identity of the responsible ownership, management and financial interest, or [19] concealment of personal business activities * * *; [20] the disregard of legal formalities and [21] the failure to maintain arm's length relationships among related entities * * *; [22] the use of the corporate entity to procure labor, services or merchandise for another person or entity * * *; [23] the diversion of assets from a corporation by or to a stockholder or other person or entity, to the detriment of creditors, or [24] the manipulation of assets and liabilities between entities so as to concentrate the assets in one and the liabilities in another * * * [25] the contracting with another with intent to avoid performance by use of a corporate entity as a shield against personal liability, or [26] the use of a corporation as a subterfuge of illegal transactions * * *; and [27] the formation and use of a corporation to transfer to it the existing liability of another person or entity * * *. A perusal of these cases [for which citations were omitted here] reveals that in all instances several of the factors mentioned were present. It is particularly significant that while it was held, in each instance, that the trial court was warranted in disregarding the corporate entity, the factors considered by it were not deemed to be conclusive upon the trier of fact but were found to be supported by substantial evidence.

How many of these *Associated Vendors, Inc.* factors strike you as serious instances of "abuse" of the corporate form, and how many do not? Which ones have you already encountered, and how seriously have they been treated? By now you will understand that the question of whether or not to pierce the corporate veil in any given situation is heavily dependent on the facts, on the discretion of the individual judge, or on the sympathies of particular juries (there is not even universal agreement over whether the question of piercing the corporate veil ought to be one for the judge or for the jury). Do you understand why some commentators would like to do away with the doctrine altogether and others regard "piercing the corporate veil," as "unprincipled" or capricious as lightning?

- -

4. AS YOU HAVE LEARNED, the various veil-piercing tests are designed to ensure that shareholders do not shift corporate resources to themselves in a manner that unfairly cheats creditors, although the motive for incorporation of limiting shareholder liability is always and everywhere recognized as legitimate. Limiting liability, in other words, is perfectly appropriate, but manipulating corporations to avoid liability is something else again. Similar doctrines in corporate law seek to achieve the same effect of fastening liability on those who manipulate corporations for their own advantage, including for example, *fraudulent conveyance*, where assets of an insolvent corporation are wrongly transferred to shareholders or others, see generally Robert C. Clark, The Duties of the Corporate Debtor to Its Creditors, 90 Harv. L. Rev. 505 (1977), or *equitable subordination*, where corporate debts to shareholders of insolvent corporations are to be paid only out of assets remaining after non-affiliated creditors are paid. See, e.g., *Taylor v. Standard Gas & Electric Co.*, 306 U.S. 307, 59 S.Ct. 543, 83 L.Ed. 669 (1939).

. . . .

5. WE HAVE CONCENTRATED, in our review of piercing the corporate veil, in this chapter, on the corporation. As you discovered, generally speaking, the same sort of analysis applies in the case of the limited liability company (LLC), when creditors seek to impose liability for LLC debts on individual members of the LLC, although, generally speaking, LLC's are not expected to adhere to the same degree of formalities as are corporations so that a lack of corporate formalities may not be as much of a risk factor for veil-piercing in the case of an LLC as it is in a corporation. *See, e.g.,* David L. Cohen, *Theories of the Corporation and the Limited Liability Company: How Should Courts and Legislatures Articulate Rules for Piercing the Veil, Fiduciary Responsibility and Securities Regulation for the Limited Liability Company?,* 51 Okla. L. Rev. 427, 429 (1998), Eric Fox, *Piercing the Veil of Limited Liability Companies,* 62 Geo. Wash. L. Rev. 1143 (1994), and Emily A. Lackey, COMMENT: *Piercing the Veil of Limited Liability in the Non-Corporate Setting,* 55 Ark. L. Rev. 553 (2002).

. . . .

6. IN THIS CHAPTER WE HAVE been concerned with the problem of shareholders abusing the corporation to the detriment of third parties, including contract, tort, and governmental creditors. We return in the next chapter to our principal issue, regulating the conduct of those controlling the corporation to protect the owners of the corporation.

CHAPTER

17

STATE LAW ON FIDUCIARY DUTY OF DIRECTORS & OFFICERS

I. Nonfeasance

Francis v. United Jersey Bank

Supreme Court of New Jersey.
87 N.J. 15, 432 A.2d 814 (1981).

[POLLOCK, J.]

The primary issue on this appeal is whether a corporate director is personally liable in negligence for the failure to prevent the misappropriation of trust funds by other directors who were also officers and shareholders of the corporation.

Plaintiffs are trustees in bankruptcy of Pritchard & Baird Intermediaries Corp. (Pritchard & Baird), a reinsurance broker * * *. At the time of her death, Mrs. Pritchard was a director and the largest single shareholder of Pritchard & Baird. * * *

This litigation focuses on payments made by Pritchard & Baird to Charles Pritchard, Jr. and William Pritchard, who were sons of Mr. and Mrs. Charles Pritchard, Sr., as well as officers, directors and shareholders of the corporation. * * *

* * *

* * * [T]he initial question is whether Mrs. Pritchard was negligent in not noticing and trying to prevent the misappropriation of funds * * *. A further question is whether her negligence was the proximate cause of the plaintiffs' losses. * * *

* * * Reinsurance involves a contract under which one insurer agrees to indemnify another for loss sustained under the latter's policy of insurance. Insurance companies * * * seek at times to minimize their exposure by sharing risks with other insurance companies. * * * The selling insurance company is known as a ceding company. The entity that assumes the obligation is designated as the reinsurer.

The reinsurance broker arranges the contract between the ceding company and the reinsurer. * * * The broker negotiates the sale of portions of the risk to the reinsurers. In most instances, the ceding company and the reinsurer do not communicate with each other, but rely upon the reinsurance broker. The ceding company pays premiums due a reinsurer to the broker, who deducts his commission and transmits the balance to the appropriate reinsurer. When a loss occurs, a reinsurer pays money due a ceding company to the broker, who then transmits it to the ceding company.

The reinsurance business was described by an expert at trial as having "a magic aura around it of dignity and quality and integrity." * * * Though separate bank accounts are not maintained for each [reinsurance contract] the industry practice is to segregate the insurance funds from the broker's general accounts. * * *

* * * [This reinsurance brokerage,] Pritchard & Baird Intermediaries Corp. (Pritchard & Baird) * * * operated as a close family corporation with Mr. and Mrs. Pritchard and their two sons [Charles, Jr. and William] as the only directors. After the death of Charles, Sr. in 1973, only the remaining three directors continued to operate as the board. Lillian Pritchard inherited 72 of her husband's 120 shares in Pritchard & Baird, thereby becoming the largest shareholder in the corporation with 48% of the stock.

The corporate minute books reflect only perfunctory activities by the directors * * * . None of the minutes for any of the meetings contain a discussion of the loans to Charles, Jr. and William or of the financial condition of the corporation. Moreover, upon instructions of Charles, Jr. that financial statements were not to be circulated to anyone else, the company's statements for the fiscal years beginning February 1, 1970, were delivered only to him.

Charles Pritchard, Sr. was the chief executive and controlled the business [from 1964 to 1966]. Beginning in 1966, he gradually relinquished control over the operations of the corporation. In 1968, Charles, Jr. became president and William became executive vice president. Charles, Sr. apparently became ill in 1971 and during the last year and a half of his life was not involved in the affairs of the business. He continued, however, to serve as a director until his death on December 10, 1973. * * * Charles, Jr. dominated the management of the corporation and the board from 1968 until the bankruptcy in 1975.

Contrary to the industry custom of segregating funds, Pritchard & Baird commingled the funds of reinsurers and ceding companies with its own funds. All monies

* * * were deposited in a single account. Charles, Sr. began the practice of withdrawing funds from the commingled account in transactions identified on the corporate books as "loans." As long as Charles, Sr. controlled the corporation, the "loans" correlated with corporate profits and were repaid at the end of each year. Starting in 1970, however, Charles, Jr. and William begin to siphon ever-increasing sums from the corporation under the guise of loans. As of January 31, 1970, the "loans" to Charles, Jr. were $230,932 and to William were $207,329. At least by January 31, 1973, the annual increase in the loans exceeded annual corporate revenues. By October 1975, the year of bankruptcy, the "shareholders' loans" had metastasized to a total of $12,333,514.47.

The trial court rejected the characterization of the payments as "loans." * * * No corporate resolution authorized the "loans," and no note or other instrument evidenced the debt. Charles, Jr. and William paid no interest on the amounts received. The "loans" were not repaid or reduced * * * rather, they increased annually.

The designation of "shareholders' loans" on the balance sheet was an entry to account for the distribution of the premium and loss money to Charles, Sr., Charles, Jr. and William. As the trial court found, the entry was part of a "woefully inadequate and highly dangerous bookkeeping system." * * * .

The "loans" to Charles, Jr. and William far exceeded their salaries and financial resources. If the payments to Charles, Jr. and William had been treated as dividends or compensation, then the balance sheets would have shown an excess of liabilities over assets. If the "loans" had been eliminated, the balance sheets would have depicted a corporation not only with a working capital deficit, but also with assets having a fair market value less than its liabilities. The balance sheets for 1970–1975, however, showed an excess of assets over liabilities. This result was achieved by designating the misappropriated funds as "shareholders' loans" and listing them as assets offsetting the deficits. * * * [T]he "loans" represented a massive misappropriation of money belonging to the clients of the corporation.

* * *

[The] financial statements showed working capital deficits increasing annually in tandem with the amounts that Charles, Jr. and William withdrew as "shareholders' loans." In the last complete year of business (January 31, 1974, to January 31, 1975), "shareholders' loans" and the correlative working capital deficit increased by approximately $3,200,000.

The funding of the "loans" left the corporation with insufficient money to operate. Pritchard & Baird could defer payment on accounts payable because its clients allowed a grace period, generally 30 to 90 days, before the payment was due. During this period, Pritchard & Baird used the funds entrusted to it as a "float" to pay current accounts payable. By recourse to the funds of its clients, Pritchard & Baird not only paid its trade debts, but also funded the payments to Charles, Jr. and William. Thus, Pritchard & Baird was able to meet its obligations as they came due only through the use of clients' funds.

* * *   This led ultimately to the filing in December, 1975, of an involuntary petition in bankruptcy and the appointments of the plaintiffs as trustees in bankruptcy of Pritchard & Baird.

Mrs. Pritchard was not active in the business of Pritchard & Baird and knew virtually nothing of its corporate affairs. She briefly visited the corporate offices in Morristown on only one occasion, and she never read or obtained the annual financial statements. She was unfamiliar with the rudiments of reinsurance and made no effort to assure that the policies and practices of the corporation, particularly pertaining to the withdrawal of funds, complied with industry custom or relevant law. Although her husband had warned her that Charles, Jr. would "take the shirt off my back," Mrs. Pritchard did not pay any attention to her duties as a director or to the affairs of the corporation. * * *

After her husband died in December 1973, Mrs. Pritchard became incapacitated and was bedridden for a six-month period. She became listless at this time and started to drink rather heavily. Her physical condition deteriorated, and in 1978 she died. The trial court rejected testimony seeking to exonerate her because she "was old, was grief-stricken at the loss of her husband, sometimes consumed too much alcohol and was psychologically overborne by her sons." * * * That court found that she was competent to act and that the reason Mrs. Pritchard never knew what her sons "were doing was because she never made the slightest effort to discharge any of her responsibilities as a director of Pritchard & Baird." * * *

* * *

III

Individual liability of a corporate director for acts of the corporation is a prickly problem. Generally directors are accorded broad immunity and are not insurers of corporate activities. The problem is particularly nettlesome when a third party asserts that a director, because of nonfeasance, is liable for losses caused by acts of insiders, who in this case were officers, directors and shareholders. Determination of the liability of Mrs. Pritchard requires findings that she had a duty to the clients of Pritchard & Baird, that she breached that duty and that her breach was a proximate cause of their losses.

The New Jersey Business Corporation Act, * * * section, N.J.S.A. 14A:6–14, concerning a director's general obligation * * * makes it incumbent upon directors to discharge their duties in good faith and with that degree of diligence, care and skill which ordinarily prudent men would exercise under similar circumstances in like positions. * * *

* * *

A leading New Jersey opinion is *Campbell v. Watson*, 62 N.J.Eq. 396 (Ch.1901), which, like many early decisions on director liability, involved directors of a bank that had become insolvent. A receiver of the bank charged the directors with negligence that allegedly led to insolvency. In the opinion, Vice Chancellor Pitney explained that bank depositors have a right to rely upon the character of the directors and officers [and upon the representation] that they will perform their sworn duty to manage the affairs of the bank according to law and devote to its affairs the same diligent attention which ordinary, prudent, diligent men pay to their own affairs; and . . . such diligence and attention as experience has shown it is proper and necessary that bank directors should give to that business in order to reasonably protect the bank and its creditors against loss. [*Id.* at 406]

* * * New York courts, like those of New Jersey [have] espoused the principle that directors owed that degree of care that a businessman of ordinary prudence would exercise in the management of his own affairs. * * * In addition to requiring that directors act honestly and in good faith, the New York courts recognized that the nature and extent of reasonable care depended upon the type of corporation, its size and financial resources. Thus, a bank director was held to stricter accountability than the director of an ordinary business. * * *

* * *

As a general rule, a director should acquire at least a rudimentary understanding of the business of the corporation. Accordingly, a director should become familiar with the fundamentals of the business in which the corporation is engaged. * * * Because directors are bound to exercise ordinary care, they cannot set up as a defense lack of the knowledge needed to exercise the requisite degree of care. If one "feels that he has not had sufficient business experience to qualify him to perform the duties of a director, he should either acquire the knowledge by inquiry, or refuse to act." * * *

Directors are under a continuing obligation to keep informed about the activities of the corporation. Otherwise, they may not be able to participate in the overall management of corporate affairs. * * * Directors may not shut their eyes to corporate misconduct and then claim that because they did not see the misconduct, they did not have a duty to look. * * *

Directorial management does not require a detailed inspection of day-to-day activities, but rather a general monitoring of corporate affairs and policies. * * * Accordingly, a director is well advised to attend board meetings regularly. * * * Regular attendance does not mean that directors must attend every meeting, but that directors should attend meetings as a matter of practice. A director of a publicly held corporation might be expected to attend regular monthly meetings, but a director of a small, family corporation might be asked to attend only an annual meeting. * * *

While directors are not required to audit corporate books, they should maintain familiarity with the financial status of the corporation by a regular review of financial statements. * * * In some circumstances, directors may be charged with assuring that bookkeeping methods conform to industry custom and usage. * * * The extent of review, as well as the nature and frequency of financial statements, depends not only on the customs of the industry, but also on the nature of the corporation and the business in which it is engaged. Financial statements of some small corporations may be prepared internally and only on an annual basis; in a large publicly held corporation, the statements may be produced monthly or at some other regular interval. Adequate financial review normally would be more informal in a private corporation than in a publicly held corporation.

Of some relevance in this case is the circumstance that the financial records disclose the "shareholders' loans". Generally directors are immune from liability if, in good faith, they rely upon the opinion of counsel for the corporation or upon written reports setting forth financial data concerning the corporation and prepared by an independent public accountant or certified public accountant or firm of such accountants or upon financial statements, books of account or reports of the corporation represented to them to be correct by the president, the officer of the corporation having charge of its books of account, or the person presiding at a meeting of the board. * * *

The review of financial statements, however, may give rise to a duty to inquire further into matters revealed by those statements. * * * Upon discovery of an illegal course of action, a director has a duty to object and, if the corporation does not correct the conduct, to resign. * * *

In certain circumstances, the fulfillment of the duty of a director may call for more than mere objection and resignation. Sometimes a director may be required to seek the advice of counsel. * * * The duty to seek the assistance of counsel can extend to areas other than the interpretation of corporation instruments. Modern corporate practice recognizes that on occasion a director should seek outside advice. A director may require legal advice concerning the propriety of his or her own conduct, the conduct of other officers and directors or the conduct of the corporation. * * * Sometimes the duty of a director may require more than consulting with outside counsel. A director may have a duty to take reasonable means to prevent illegal conduct by co-directors; in an appropriate case, this may include threat of suit. * * * .

A director is not an ornament, but an essential component of corporate governance. Consequently, a director cannot protect himself behind a paper shield bearing the motto, "dummy director." * * * The New Jersey Business Corporation Act, in imposing a standard of ordinary care on all directors, confirms that dummy, figurehead and accommodation directors are anachronisms with no place in New Jersey law. * * * See [also] *Kavanaugh v. Gould*, 223 N.Y. at 111–117, 119 N.E. at 240–241 (the fact that bank director never attended board meetings or acquainted himself with bank's business or methods held to be no defense, as a matter of law, to responsibility for speculative loans made by the president and acquiesced in by other directors). * * *

* * *

* * * In general, the relationship of a corporate director to the corporation and its stockholders is that of a fiduciary. * * * Shareholders have a right to expect that directors will exercise reasonable supervision and control over the policies and practices of a corporation. The institutional integrity of a corporation depends upon the proper discharge by directors of those duties.

While directors may owe a fiduciary duty to creditors also, that obligation generally has not been recognized in the absence of insolvency. * * * With certain corporations, however, directors are deemed to owe a duty to creditors and other third parties even when the corporation is solvent. Although depositors of a bank are considered in some respects to be creditors, courts have recognized that directors may owe them a fiduciary duty. * * * Directors of nonbanking corporations may owe a similar duty when the corporation holds funds of others in trust. * * *

* * *

Courts in other states have imposed liability on directors of non-banking corporations for the conversion of trust funds, even though those directors did not participate in or know of the conversion. *Preston-Thomas Constr. Inc. v. Central Leasing Corp.*, 518 P.2d 1125 (Okl.Ct.App.1973) (director liable for conversion of funds entrusted to corporation for acquisition of stock in another corporation); *Vujacich v. Southern Commercial Co.*, 21 Cal.App. 439, 132 P. 80 (Dist.Ct.App.1913) (director of wholesale grocery business personally liable for conversion by corporation of worker's funds deposited for safekeeping). The distinguishing circumstances in regard to banks and other corporations holding trust funds is that the depositor or beneficiary can reasonably expect the director to act with ordinary prudence concerning the funds held in a fiduciary capacity. Thus, recognition of a duty of a director to those for whom a corporation holds funds in trust may be viewed as another application of the general rule that a director's duty is that of an ordinary prudent person under the circumstances.

The most striking circumstances affecting Mrs. Pritchard's duty as a director are the character of the reinsurance industry, the nature of the misappropriated funds and the financial condition of Pritchard & Baird. The hallmark of the reinsurance industry has been the unqualified trust and confidence reposed by ceding companies and reinsurers in reinsurance brokers. Those companies entrust money to reinsurance intermediaries with the justifiable expectation that the funds will be transmitted to the appropriate parties. Consequently, the companies could have assumed rightfully that Mrs. Pritchard, as a director of a reinsurance brokerage corporation, would not sanction the commingling and the conversion of loss and premium funds for the personal use of the principals of Pritchard & Baird.

As a reinsurance broker, Pritchard & Baird received annually as a fiduciary millions of dollars of clients' money which it was under a duty to segregate. * * * To this extent, it resembled a bank rather than a small family business. Accordingly, Mrs. Pritchard's relationship to the clientele of Pritchard & Baird was akin to that of a director of a bank to its depositors. * * * That trust relationship gave rise to a fiduciary duty to guard the funds with fidelity and good faith. * * *

As a director of a substantial reinsurance brokerage corporation, she should have known that it received annually millions of dollars of loss and premium funds which it held in trust for ceding and reinsurance companies. Mrs. Pritchard should have obtained and read the annual statements of financial condition of Pritchard & Baird. * * * [T]hose statements disclosed on their face the misappropriation of trust funds.

From those statements, she should have realized that, as of January 31, 1970, her sons were withdrawing substantial trust funds under the guise of "Shareholders' Loans." * * * Detecting a misappropriation of funds would not have required special expertise or extraordinary diligence; a cursory reading of the financial statements would have revealed the pillage. * * * When financial statements demonstrate that insiders are bleeding a corporation to death, a director should notice and try to stanch the flow of blood.

* * *

IV

Nonetheless, the negligence of Mrs. Pritchard does not result in liability unless it is a proximate cause of the loss. * * * Analysis of proximate cause requires an initial determination of cause-in-fact. Causation-in-fact calls for a finding that the defendant's act or omission was a necessary antecedent of the loss, i.e., that if the defendant had observed his or her duty of care, the loss would not have occurred. * * *

Cases involving nonfeasance present a much more difficult causation question than those in which the director has committed an affirmative act of negligence leading to the loss. Analysis in cases of negligent omissions calls for determination of the reasonable steps a director should have taken and whether that course of action would have averted the loss.

Usually a director can absolve himself from liability by informing the other directors of the impropriety and voting for a proper course of action. * * * Conversely, a director who votes for or concurs in certain actions may be "liable to the corporation for the benefit of its creditors or shareholders, to the extent of any injuries suffered by such persons, respectively, as a result of any such action." N.J.S.A. 14A:6–12 (Supp.1981–1982). * * *

Even accepting the hypothesis that Mrs. Pritchard might not be liable if she had objected and resigned, there are two significant reasons for holding her liable. First, she did not resign until just before the bankruptcy. Consequently, there is no factual basis for the speculation that the losses would have occurred even if she had objected and resigned. Indeed, the trial court reached the opposite conclusion: "The actions of the sons were so blatantly wrongful that it is hard to see how they could have resisted any moderately firm objection to what they were doing." * * * Second, the nature of the reinsurance business distinguishes it from most other commercial activities in that reinsurance brokers are encumbered by fiduciary duties owed to third parties. In other corporations, a director's duty normally does not extend beyond the shareholders to third parties.

In this case, the scope of Mrs. Pritchard's duties was determined by the precarious financial condition of Pritchard & Baird, its fiduciary relationship to its clients and the implied trust in which it held their funds. Thus viewed, the scope of her duties encompassed all reasonable action to stop the continuing conversion. Her duties extended beyond mere objection and resignation to reasonable attempts to prevent the misappropriation of the trust funds. * * *

A leading case discussing causation where the director's liability is predicated upon a negligent failure to act is *Barnes v. Andrews*, 298 F. 614 (S.D.N.Y.1924). In that case the court exonerated a figurehead director who served for eight months on a board that held one meeting after his election, a meeting he was forced to miss because of the death of his mother. Writing for the court, Judge Learned Hand distinguished a director who fails to prevent general mismanagement from one such as Mrs. Pritchard who failed to stop an illegal "loan":

> When the corporate funds have been illegally lent, it is a fair inference that a protest would have stopped the loan, and that the director's neglect caused the loss. But when a business fails from general mismanagement, business incapacity, or bad judgment, how is it possible to say that a single director could have made the company successful, or how much in dollars he could have saved? [*Id.* at 616–617]

* * *

Other courts have refused to impose personal liability on negligent directors when the plaintiffs have been unable to prove that diligent execution of the directors' duties would have precluded the losses. * * *

Other courts have held directors liable for losses actively perpetrated by others because the negligent omissions of the directors were considered a necessary antecedent to the defalcations. [See, e.g.] *Ringeon v. Albinson*, 35 F.2d 753 (D.Minn.1929) (negligent director not excused from liability for losses that could have been prevented by supervision and prompt action); *Heit v. Bixby*, 276 F.Supp. 217, 231 (E.D. Mo.1967) (directors liable for 40% commissions taken by co-directors because directors' "lackadaisical attitude" proximately caused the loss); *Ford v. Taylor*, 176 Ark. 843, 4 S.W.2d 938 (1928) (bank directors liable for losses due to misappropriations of cashier who "felt free to pursue [misconduct] without fear of detection by the directors through their failure to discharge the functions of their office"). * * *

In assessing whether Mrs. Pritchard's conduct was a legal or proximate cause of the conversion, * * *judicial determination involves not only considerations of causation-in-fact and matters of policy, but also common sense and logic. * * *

Within Pritchard & Baird, several factors contributed to the loss of the funds: commingling of corporate and client monies, conversion of funds by Charles, Jr. and William and dereliction of her duties by Mrs. Pritchard. The wrongdoing of her sons, although the immediate cause of the loss, should not excuse Mrs. Pritchard from her negligence which also was a substantial factor contributing to the loss. * * * Her sons knew that she, the only other director, was not reviewing their conduct; they spawned their fraud in the backwater of her neglect. Her * * * failure to act contributed to the continuation of that corruption. Consequently, her conduct was a substantial factor contributing to the loss.

* * * We conclude that even if Mrs. Pritchard's mere objection had not stopped the depredations of her sons, her consultation with an attorney and the threat of suit would have deterred them. That conclusion flows as a matter of common sense and logic from the record. Whether in other situations a director has a duty to do more than protest and resign is best left to case-by-case determinations. In this case, we are satisfied that there was a duty to do more than object and resign. Consequently, we find that Mrs. Pritchard's negligence was a proximate cause of the misappropriations.

* * *

II. The Business Judgment Rule

Nursing Home Building Corporation v. DeHart

Court of Appeals of Washington, Division One.
13 Wn. App. 489, 535 P.2d 137 (1975).

[SWANSON, J.]

Nursing Home Building Corporation, doing business as Arden Nursing Home (hereinafter referred to as "the corporation"), appeals from a judgment which awarded it only $9,914.85 of its $121,865 claim based upon alleged fraudulent misappropriation of corporate funds by Richard L. and Phoebe DeHart, the former sole shareholders of the corporation. * * *

The factual context in which this appeal arose is as follows: Two Seattle doctors, Dr. H. P. Clausing and Dr. G. E. Deer, were the sole owners of the corporation which in turn owned and operated the Arden Nursing Home located on Aurora Avenue in the city of Seattle. On January 20, 1970, the two doctors sold all of the outstanding stock (3,000 shares) of the corporation to the DeHarts on an installment contract for $700,000. The DeHarts made an initial down payment of $80,000 from their own resources and made subsequent payments on the stock purchase contract by checks totaling $34,089.64 drawn on the corporation checking account. In addition, as required by the terms of the stock purchase agreement, they transferred to Clausing and Deer a $29,099 account receivable asset of the corporation known as the "Southside Receivable." The payments from the corporate bank account and the transfer of the account receivable to Clausing and Deer were reflected in a loan account known as "Owner's Receivable." This account had a $45,563.45 loan balance due the corporation when the DeHarts were dispossessed of the nursing home in May 1971.

During the 15–month period of the DeHarts' management of the corporation, it had serious cash flow problems so that by March 1971, the corporation was unable to pay its creditors and keep current the payments on the building mortgage due the Bank of California as required by the sales contract. The DeHarts' breach of the mortgage obligation resulted in an action by Clausing and Deer to forfeit [that is, nullify] the stock purchase contract. * * *

On August 6, 1971, Robert Thompson, who was named receiver [by the court] to manage the nursing home and to maintain the forfeiture action, sued the DeHarts to recover $121,865 in corporate funds he alleged were "fraudulently misappropriated" and diverted to the DeHarts' personal use and benefit. At the outset of this litigation, the receiver obtained a writ of attachment* * * to secure his claimed creditor's lien the DeHarts' real estate. * * * The receiver Thompson was discharged prior to the trial of this action but the corporation, which was once again owned by the original owners Clausing and Deer, remained as a party plaintiff. After a trial to the court in which the DeHarts conceded an obligation to reimburse the corporation for $9,914.85 of corporate funds used for personal purposes unrelated to any corporate benefit, judgment was entered in that amount, but the court denied the corporation's claim for additional funds allegedly "fraudulently misappropriated" as is reflected in the following conclusions of law:

> The business expenses, salary, fringe benefits and reimbursed expenses were reasonable and proper exercises of business judgment by the DeHarts except as set forth in Finding of Fact VII. [Finding of Fact No. 7 contains the $9,914.85 item upon which judgment was rendered.]

Conclusion of Law No. 2.

> The payments to Drs. Clausing and Deer were authorized by all shareholders and, in addition, Drs. Clausing, Deer and the corporation ratified and accepted the payments. The corporation is not entitled to recover these payments from the DeHarts.

Conclusion of Law No. 3.

> The transfer of the Southside Receivable was pursuant to a contract which the corporation approved when Drs. Clausing and Deer controlled the corporation. In addition, the transfer was approved by the sole shareholders of the corporation at the time the transfer took place and was ratified and accepted by the present shareholders, Drs. Clausing and Deer. The corporation is not entitled to recover the value of the [Southside Receivable] from the DeHarts.

Conclusion of Law No. 4.

On appeal, the corporation contends the trial court erred in failing to enter judgment for $92,996.61 in additional funds which it contends were misappropriated by the DeHarts. The corporation assigns error to the quoted conclusions of law and to these findings of fact:

All other disbursements presented to the Court were proper business expenses.

Finding of Fact No. 12.

> The funds which would have been used for taxes were applied to other business expenses, such as staff salaries and trade accounts necessary to keep the nursing home open and provide patient care.

Finding of Fact No. 14, in part. The corporation's assignments of error focus primarily upon three categories of alleged misappropriation of funds: (1) Loans by the corporation to the DeHarts as reflected by the $45,563.45 balance shown in the Owner's Receivable; (2) corporate funds totaling $21,000 used in the management of the corporation; and (3) corporate funds totaling $26,433.16 which the corporation claims should have been used by the DeHarts to pay federal taxes.

In considering the first category, we note that the $45,563.45 loan balance item primarily consists of two items, (1) the corporate funds used to make the installment payments to Clausing and Deer on the stock purchase contract, and (2) the transfer to Clausing and Deer pursuant to the stock purchase contract of the Southside Receivable. The corporation asserts that such payments from corporate funds or by transfer of corporate assets amounts to money borrowed from the corporation for a personal obligation which must be repaid. As to the first item, the court found in an unchallenged finding that the obligation to make the installment payments was the personal obligation of the DeHarts but also found that

> [i]t was understood by all parties at the time the contract was signed that payments would probably come from the earnings of the business distributed to DeHarts if possible.

Finding of Fact No. 9, in part. In addition, the court entered the following significant findings to which no error is assigned:

> Payments were made to Drs. Clausing and Deer by checks dated April 16, 1970, of $5,000.00 each, drawn on the account of Arden Nursing Home at The Bank of California; and checks dated January 20, 1971, of $7,500.00 each, February 8, 1971, of $2,272.41 each, and March 3, 1971, of $4,544.82 total, all drawn on the account of Nursing Home Building Corporation, d/b/a Arden Nursing Home at Pacific National Bank, Everett Banking Center. Drs. Clausing and Deer received and cashed all such checks. On March 30, 1971, Dr. Clausing wrote [the] DeHarts formally demanding that all future payments be paid by [the] DeHarts from their personal funds.

Finding of Fact No. 10.

> All existing shareholders of the corporation, being the DeHarts, approved and ratified the payment of the above amounts to Drs. Clausing and Deer from corporate funds.

Finding of Fact No. 11. The trial court concluded that because all shareholders of the corporation approved the payments and Clausing and Deer ratified and accepted them, there can be no recovery by the corporation. We agree.

The corporation argues that the receipt by Clausing and Deer of these payments could not operate as an estoppelagainst it because they had no control over it but were merely creditors of the DeHarts with a pledgee's interest in the corporate stock.

* * * Thus, it is the corporation's theory of recovery that despite the facts that the DeHarts were the sole owners of the corporation when the payments were made and that Clausing and Deer, the recipients of the funds, had regained sole ownership of the corporation at the time of trial, the corporation's identity remained separate and apart from that of the individual stockholders and therefore it could recover the payments from the DeHarts through its right to an accounting and repayment of loans. In support of this argument, the corporation cites the following rule governing the conduct of corporate officers:

> As a general rule, the corporate officers or agents have no right or authority to use, divert, or appropriate corporate funds or property for their own individual interests or purposes, and they are responsible for the wrongful use or diversion of the corporate property and are accountable for any profits made thereby. Thus, it is generally held that a corporate officer has no authority to use corporate funds for payment of his own debts. . . .

(*Footnotes omitted.*) *19 Am. Jur. 2d Corporations § 1235 (1965).*

Further, the corporation contends that ownership by a borrower of all the shares of stock in a corporation does not prevent the corporation from recovering the balance due on a loan to the corporation. * * *

> Although it cannot be doubted that a corporation's separate legal identity is not lost merely because all of its stock is held by the members of a single family or by one person and thus the fact of sole ownership does not of itself immunize a sole shareholder from liability to the corporation, it is just as firmly established that the corporate entity will be disregarded when justice so requires. * * *

Here, as previously noted, the trial court found that all parties understood at the time the contract for the purchase of stock was signed that the payments probably would come from the earnings of the business distributed to the DeHarts. * * * Moreover, it is undisputed that at the time the contract was executed Clausing and Deer were the sole owners of the corporate stock. It is also unchallenged that after execution of the contract the payments from corporate funds were approved and ratified by all of the shareholders of the corporation, namely, the DeHarts. We are of the opinion that to permit the corporation to recover the amount of such payments from the DeHarts on the theory of misappropriation of corporate funds would be to require us to close our eyes to the realities of the situation. An award in favor of the corporation in the amount of the corporate funds previously paid to Clausing and Deer, who are now the present owners of the corporation, would amount to a double recovery. A corporation's separate identity cannot be preserved at the expense of fostering an obvious injustice; however, in this case, it is not necessary to disregard the corporate entity in order to uphold the trial court because the record reveals that the trial court's findings are supported by substantial evidence.

The court below properly found that the disbursements of corporate assets to Clausing and Deer were ratified by all of the shareholders and therefore the challenged transactions are governed by the general rule that limitations on corporate action can be waived by informed and unanimous consent by corporate shareholders. * * * As is stated in W. Fletcher [*Private Corporations*] § 1104 at page 725 [(perm. ed. 1974) (hereinafter cited as "W. Fletcher")]:

> If all the stockholders of a corporation consent, and it is not detrimental to creditors, officers may appropriate corporate assets. It follows that if there are no stockholders except the directors and officers, the latter may, of course, by unanimous consent, give away corporate property, where the rights of creditors are not impaired.

(Footnotes omitted.) * * * In the case at bar, there is no showing or claim that the rights of any creditors of the corporation were impaired. * * * Clausing and Deer, who make no argument that the corporation's identity ought to be disregarded were only creditors of the DeHarts individually and not of the corporation. The rule governing the management of solely-owned corporations which we apply here is stated as follows in W. Fletcher at page 724:

> If an officer is the owner of all the stock of a corporation, it seems that he may use the corporate assets as he sees fit, and there can be no misappropriation of corporate assets by him; but if there is even one share of stock outstanding he cannot use the corporate assets to pay his individual debts without the consent of the holder of such one share of stock.

(Footnotes omitted.) * * *

We conclude that the trial court did not err in declining to hold the DeHarts liable to the corporation for installment payments made with corporate assets to Clausing and Deer. Similarly, as to the claim that the DeHarts are liable for the transfer of the Southside Receivable, the trial court's unchallenged finding of fact No. 8 states:

> The contract for the sale of stock was executed by all parties to this action, including Nursing Home Building Corporation. It provided that an asset of the corporation, known as the Southside Receivable and worth approximately $29,099.00 would be assigned to Drs. Clausing and Deer and not later than January 1971, and earlier if the corporation was dissolved. The corporation approved this contract at a time when Drs. Clausing and Deer were the sole shareholders and were a majority of the Board of Directors. The contract was assigned in April 1970. All parties consented to and ratified that assignment by their execution of the contract and by their subsequent acts in assigning or accepting assignment of the receivable.

The trial court properly concluded that the ratification of this transaction by all parties in accordance with the stock purchase contract is binding on the corporation.

Directing our attention to the second category of alleged "fraudulent misappro-priation," the corporation asserts that such expenditures as management fees to the DeHarts, leased automobiles, and miscellaneous fringe benefits amounted to a waste of corporate assets and that the DeHarts failed to sustain the burden of proving that the expenditures were made in good faith. We disagree. Courts are reluctant to inter-fere with the internal management of corporations and generally refuse to substitute their judgment for that of the directors. See *Sanders v. E–Z Park, Inc.*, 57 Wn.2d 474, 358 P.2d 138 (1960). The "business judgment rule" immunizes management from liability in a corporate transaction undertaken within both the power of the corporation and the authority of management where there is a reasonable basis to indicate that the transaction was made in good faith. An excellent statement of the "business judgment rule" is found in W. Fletcher § 1039 at pages 621–25:

> It is too well settled to admit of controversy that ordinarily neither the directors nor the other officers of a corporation are liable for mere mistake or errors of judgment, either of law or fact. In other words, directors of a commercial corporation may take chances, the same kind of chances that a man would take in his own business. Because they are given this wide latitude, the law will not hold directors liable for honest errors, for mistakes of judgment, when they act without corrupt motive and in good faith, that is, for mistakes which may properly be classified under the head of honest mistakes. And that is true even though the errors may be so gross that they may demonstrate the unfitness of the directors to manage the corporate affairs. This rule is commonly referred to as the "business judgment rule."

(Footnotes omitted.) * * *

In this connection, the trial court entered detailed findings of fact which are not disputed and state as follows:

> Mr. and Mrs. DeHart were experienced in the operation of businesses of various types, including nursing home. Both were involved in the day-to-day management of Arden Nursing Home on a full-time or greater than full-time basis; most of the time they were in possession of Arden Nursing Home. Each was licensed by the State of Washington as nursing home administrators. Each performed a variety of duties and responsibilities in addition to the day-to-day management.

Finding of Fact No. 5.

> Mr. and Mrs. DeHart each received a management fee of $1,000.00 a month, plus certain fringe benefits such as a leased car, car operation expenses and key man life insurance. The cars were used predominantly for corporate purposes. The DeHarts used credit cards for such items as lunch conferences with staff, for entertainment of doctors and nurses who

might refer patients to Arden. While some of these expenses may not have been necessary or wise in retrospect, all of these expenses were reasonable expenditures for proper business purposes.

Finding of Fact No. 6. As we have noted previously, finding of fact No. 12 states:

> All other disbursements presented to the Court were proper business expenses.

This finding, though disputed, is properly supported by substantial evidence and must be upheld. The quoted findings support the trial court's conclusion of law that the challenged expenditures were made by the DeHarts within the scope of the proper exercise of their business judgment. This is especially so in view of the unchallenged finding of fact No. 16 which states:

> There is no evidence of any fraud or conspiracy to remove corporate assets wrongfully.

The corporation's third major argument centers upon the DeHarts' failure to pay federal withholding taxes and social security contributions which had accumulated to a sum in excess of $20,000 by the time the DeHarts' ownership of the corporation was forfeited. Again, the "business judgment rule" is controlling. Phoebe DeHart explained why the taxes were not paid in her testimony at trial, stating in part:

> We did not have the funds to pay them. We were using the money for food and heat and light, for patient care.

The trial court specifically found:

> The funds which would have been used for taxes were applied to other business expenses, such as staff salaries and trade accounts necessary to keep the nursing home open and provide patient care.

Finding of Fact No. 14, in part. This finding of fact, though challenged, is supported by substantial evidence and therefore must be sustained. Thus, the trial court was entitled to conclude that the use of corporate funds for the payment of expenses other than taxes constituted a valid exercise of business judgment with which the courts will not interfere in the absence of bad faith or fraud. There was no error.

* * *

Judgment affirmed.

NOTES AND QUESTIONS

I. **YOU HAVE JUST READ** two cases which involve "shareholder loans." Why do they result in liability for a defendant in one case, and not in the other? Consider *Francis v. United Jersey Bank*. This case has recently been called "[t]he paradigm case of director liability for breach of the fiduciary duty of care in the oversight context." Andrew D. Shaffer, *The Fiduciary Relationship Your Corporate Law Professor (Should Have) Warned You About*, 8 Am. Bankr. Inst. L. Rev. 479, 501 (2000). Until relatively recently, however, it was almost unheard of for a director to be held liable for losses to a corporation or to its shareholders—much less to its creditors— for director misconduct that did not involve bad faith. Why, precisely, is Lillian Pritchard found to have breached her duty as a director, and why did that breach of duty result in liability? Are you convinced that, even if Mrs. Prichard failed in her duty as a director she should have been found liable to her corporation's creditors?

If the standard of due care for a director is that of a reasonably-prudent similarly-situated person, is it reasonable to expect that, as the court suggests, she should have engaged in conduct up to and over the point of litigating with her own children? Is it significant that Mrs. Pritchard is no longer with us, and that only her estate would be liable? A typical comment in praise of this decision was that of the trial court judge whose opinion in the case was affirmed in the decision you read. That judge declared that "I wish I had had the wit, the time, and the skill to write the thorough, sophisticated, yet simple lesson on the responsibility of corporate directors contained in Justice Pollock's opinion." Reginald Stanton, Stewart G. Pollock— *As Seen from the Perspective of a Lawyer and Trial Judge*, 74 N.Y.U.L. Rev. 1215, 1216 (1999). Do you share Judge Stanton's views? For a powerful argument that Judge Pollock got it quite wrong in Francis, with information on the unsuccessful criminal trial against Charles, Jr. and William, on the social background of the Pritchards, and on the currently evolving liability of directors for failure to monitor, see Reinier Kraakman & Jay Kesten, "The Story of Francis v. United Jersey Bank: When A Good Story Makes Bad Law," Chapter 6 in J. Mark Ramseyer, ed. *Corporate Law Stories* 163 (2009).

....

2. ***NURSING HOME BUILDING CORPORATION v. DEHART*** is notable primarily because of the manner it which it lucidly sets forth what has come to be called the "business judgment rule." Note that the case also has something to say to us about the distinctions to be made between the owners of the corporation and the corporation itself. Is the court correct that since the "shareholder loans" in question were made with the knowledge of the once and future owners of the corporation there should be no liability to pay back the loans? Is this something like a "piercing the corporate veil"

case? Do you understand why the result would have been different if there were other creditors who might suffer?

What do you understand the "business judgment rule" to be? It has been suggested from time to time that the "business judgment rule" is really not a rule of law at all, but rather ought to be viewed as "a rebuttable evidentiary presumption that business decisions are made by disinterested and independent directors * * * on an informed basis and with a good faith belief that the decision is in the best interest of the corporation and its shareholders." Shaffer, supra, 8 Am. Bankr. Inst. L. Rev., at 498. If a plaintiff can successfully demonstrate that the directors were not disinterested or independent, that they were uninformed, or that they acted in bad faith, liability may still attach to the directors if it turns out that their actions were harmful to the corporation. What is necessary to rebut the presumption?

....

3. CONSIDER ANOTHER FAMOUS "business judgment case," *Kamin v. American Express,* 86 Misc.2d 809, 383 N.Y.S.2d 807 (Sup. Ct. 1976), aff'd, 54 A.D.2d 654, 387 N.Y.S. 2d 993 (App. Div. 1976), as described in a recent law review article:

> In 1972, American Express bought almost two million shares of Donaldson, Lufkin & Jenrette, Inc. ("DLJ") common stock for about $30 million. In 1975, when the value of that stock had declined to about $4 million, American Express announced that it would distribute the stock to its shareholders as a dividend.
>
> Two American Express shareholders urged the company to sell the DLJ stock, rather than distribute it as a dividend. They pointed out that if American Express sold the DLJ stock, it could reduce otherwise taxable capital gains by an amount equal to the roughly $26 million loss it would incur on the sale of its DLJ stock and thus save approximately $8 million in federal income taxes. On the other hand, by distributing the DLJ stock as a dividend, American Express would lose this potential tax saving and would provide no significant tax benefits to its shareholders. Put differently, if the board wanted to pay a dividend to shareholders, by selling the DLJ stock it would be able to distribute $12 million (the sale price plus the tax savings) in cash, which shareholders surely would prefer to receiving DLJ stock worth $4 million.
>
> The American Express board of directors considered the shareholders' argument and then rejected it. The board had previously been advised by American Express's CPAs that if American Express distributed the DLJ stock as a dividend, instead of selling it, American Express could

account for the transaction by reducing its retained earnings by the $30 million it had paid for the DLJ stock—the value at which American Express continued to carry that stock on its books. The advantage of this treatment, from the board's point of view, was that it allowed American Express to avoid reporting a loss of $26 million on its investment in DLJ and reducing its reported earnings by a like amount. The board was concerned that reporting such a loss, and a resulting reduction in American Express's income, would have a serious negative effect on the market value of American Express stock.

Elliott J. Weiss, *Accounting and Taxation: Teaching Accounting and Valuation in the Basic Corporation Law Course*, 19 Cardozo L. Rev. 679, 689–690 (1997).[1] The two shareholders later brought suit against the directors arguing that they had breached their fiduciary duty to the corporation. The court upheld the directors' decision as a proper exercise of "business judgment," and *Kamin v. American Express* is now a leading "business judgment" precedent. Was it correctly decided?

....

4. HOW, PRECISELY, are we to determine when we are confronted with a situation where the "business judgment" rule governs, and when we are in an area where directors are liable for their misconduct, even when they are acting in good faith? Consider the next famous (or, if you like, notorious) case, *Smith v. Van Gorkom.*

---

1   Reprinted with the kind permission of Mr. Weiss.

III. Nonfeasance or the Business Judgment Rule?

Smith v. Van Gorkom

Supreme Court of Delaware.
488 A.2d 858 (1985).

[HORSEY, J.]

This appeal from the Court of Chancery involves a class action brought by shareholders of the defendant Trans Union Corporation ("Trans Union" or "the Company"), * * * against the defendant members of the Board of Directors of Trans Union * * *.

Following trial, the former Chancellor granted judgment for the defendant directors * * * based on two findings: (1) that the Board of Directors had acted in an informed manner so as to be entitled to protection of the business judgment rule in approving the cash-out merger; and (2) that the shareholder vote approving the merger should not be set aside because the stockholders had been "fairly informed" by the Board of Directors before voting thereon. The plaintiffs appeal. * * *

Speaking for the [three-person] majority of the Court, we conclude that both rulings of the Court of Chancery are clearly erroneous. * * *

I.

* * *

A

Trans Union was a publicly-traded, diversified holding company, the principal earnings of which were generated by its railcar leasing business. During the period here involved, the Company had a cash flow of hundreds of millions of dollars annually. However, the Company had difficulty in generating sufficient taxable income to offset increasingly large investment tax credits (ITCs). Accelerated depreciation deductions had decreased available taxable income against which to offset accumulating ITCs. * * *

* * *.

B

On August 27, 1980, [Jerome W. Van Gorkom, Trans Union's Chairman and Chief Executive Officer] met with Senior Management of Trans Union. Van Gorkom reported * * * his desire to find a solution to the tax credit problem* * *. Various alternatives were suggested and discussed preliminarily, including the sale of Trans Union to a company with a large amount of taxable income.

> Donald Romans, Chief Financial Officer of Trans Union, stated that his department had done a "very brief bit of work on the possibility of a leveraged buy-out." * * * The work consisted of a "preliminary study" of the cash which could be generated by the Company if it participated in a leveraged buy-out. * * *

On September 5, at another Senior Management meeting which Van Gorkom attended, Romans again brought up the idea of a leveraged buy-out as a "possible strategic alternative" to the Company's acquisition program. Romans and Bruce S. Chelberg, President and Chief Operating Officer of Trans Union * * * "ran the numbers" at $50 a share and at $60 a share with the "rough form" of their cash figures at the time. Their "figures indicated that $50 would be very easy to do but $60 would be very difficult to do under those figures." * * *

At this meeting, Van Gorkom stated that he would be willing to take $55 per share for his own 75,000 shares. He vetoed the suggestion of a leveraged buy-out by Management, however, as involving a potential conflict of interest for Management. Van Gorkom, a certified public accountant and lawyer, had been an officer of Trans Union for 24 years, its Chief Executive Officer for more than 17 years, and Chairman of its Board for 2 years. It is noteworthy in this connection that he was then approaching 65 years of age and mandatory retirement.

* * *

Van Gorkom decided to meet with Jay A. Pritzker, a well-known corporate takeover specialist and a social acquaintance. * * *Van Gorkom assembled a proposed per share price for sale of the Company and a financing structure by which to accomplish the sale. Van Gorkom did so without consulting either his Board or any members of Senior Management except * * * Carl Peterson, Trans Union's Controller. Telling Peterson that he wanted no other person on his staff to know what he was doing, but without telling him why, Van Gorkom directed Peterson to calculate the feasibility of a leveraged buy-out at an assumed price per share of $55. Apart from the Company's historic stock market price,[2] and Van Gorkom's long association with Trans Union, the record is devoid of any competent evidence that $55 represented the per share intrinsic value of the Company.

* * *

Van Gorkom arranged a meeting with Pritzker at the latter's home on Saturday, September 13, 1980. Van Gorkom prefaced his presentation by stating to Pritzker: "Now as far as you are concerned, I can, I think, show how you can pay a substantial premium over the present stock price and pay off most of the loan in the first five years. * * * If you could pay $55 for this Company, here is a way in which I think it can be financed."

* * * Although Pritzker mentioned $50 as a more attractive figure, no other price was mentioned. However, Van Gorkom stated that to be sure that $55 was the best price obtainable, Trans Union should be free to accept any better offer. Pritzker

---

2   * * * Over the five year period from 1975 through 1979, Trans Union's stock had traded within a range of a high of $39 1/2 and a low of $24 1/4. Its high and low range for 1980 through September 19 (the last trading day before announcement of the merger) was $38 1/4–$29 1/2.

demurred, stating that his organization would serve as a "stalking horse" for an "auction contest" only if Trans Union would permit Pritzker to buy 1,750,000 shares of Trans Union stock at market price which Pritzker could then sell to any higher bidder. After further discussion on this point, Pritzker told Van Gorkom that he would give him a more definite reaction soon.

On Monday, September 15, Pritzker advised Van Gorkom that he was interested in the $55 cash-out merger proposal and requested more information on Trans Union. Van Gorkom agreed to meet privately with Pritzker, accompanied by Peterson, Chelberg, and Michael Carpenter, Trans Union's consultant from the Boston Consulting Group. The meetings took place on September 16 and 17. Van Gorkom was "astounded that events were moving with such amazing rapidity."

On Thursday, September 18, Van Gorkom met again with Pritzker. * * * Pritzker instructed his attorney, a merger and acquisition specialist, to begin drafting merger documents. There was no further discussion of the $55 price. However, the number of shares of Trans Union's treasury stock to be offered to Pritzker was negotiated down to one million shares; the price was set at $38–75 cents above the per share price at the close of the market on September 19. At this point, Pritzker insisted that the Trans Union Board act on his merger proposal within the next three days, stating to Van Gorkom: "We have to have a decision by no later than Sunday [evening, September 21] before the opening of the English stock exchange on Monday morning." * * *

On Friday, September 19, Van Gorkom, Chelberg, and Pritzker consulted with Trans Union's lead bank regarding the financing of Pritzker's purchase of Trans Union. The bank indicated that it could form a syndicate of banks that would finance the transaction. On the same day, Van Gorkom retained James Brennan, Esquire, to advise Trans Union on the legal aspects of the merger. Van Gorkom did not consult with * * * Trans Union's [in-house] legal staff.

On Friday, September 19, Van Gorkom called a special meeting of the Trans Union Board for noon the following day. He also called a meeting of the Company's Senior Management to convene at 11:00 a.m.* * * . No one, except Chelberg and Peterson, was told the purpose of the meetings. Van Gorkom did not invite Trans Union's investment banker, Salomon Brothers or its Chicago-based partner, to attend.

* * * Van Gorkom disclosed the offer and described its terms, but he furnished no copies of the proposed Merger Agreement. Romans announced that his department had done a second study which showed that, for a leveraged buy-out, the price range for Trans Union stock was between $55 and $65 per share. * * *

Senior Management's reaction to the Pritzker proposal was completely negative. No member of Management, except Chelberg and Peterson, supported the proposal. Romans objected to the price as being too low;[3] he was critical of the

---

3   Van Gorkom asked Romans to express his opinion as to the $55 price. Romans stated that he "thought the price was too low in relation to what he could derive for the company in a cash sale, particularly one which enabled us to realize the values of certain subsidiaries and independent entities."

timing and suggested that consideration should be given to the adverse tax consequences of an all-cash deal for low-basis shareholders; and he took the position that the agreement to sell Pritzker one million newly-issued shares at market price would inhibit other offers, as would the prohibitions against soliciting bids and furnishing inside information to other bidders. Romans argued that the Pritzker proposal was a "lock up" and amounted to "an agreed merger as opposed to an offer." Nevertheless, Van Gorkom proceeded to the Board meeting as scheduled without further delay.

Ten directors served on the Trans Union Board, five inside * * * and five outside * * * . All directors were present at the meeting, except [one] who was ill. Of the outside directors, four were corporate chief executive officers and one was the former Dean of the University of Chicago Business School. None was an investment banker or trained financial analyst. All members of the Board were well informed about the Company and its operations as a going concern. * * *

Van Gorkom began the Special Meeting of the Board with a twenty-minute oral presentation. Copies of the proposed Merger Agreement were delivered too late for study before or during the meeting. * * * He reviewed the Company's ITC and depreciation problems and the efforts theretofore made to solve them. He discussed his initial meeting with Pritzker * * *. Van Gorkom did not disclose to the Board, however, the methodology by which he alone had arrived at the $55 figure, or the fact that he first proposed the $55 price in his negotiations with Pritzker.

Van Gorkom outlined the terms of the Pritzker offer as follows: Pritzker would pay $55 in cash for all outstanding shares of Trans Union stock * * * for a period of 90 days, Trans Union could receive, but could not actively solicit, competing offers; the offer had to be acted on by the next evening, Sunday, September 21; Trans Union could only furnish to competing bidders published information, and not proprietary information; the offer was subject to Pritzker obtaining the necessary financing by October 10, 1980; if the financing contingency were met or waived by Pritzker, Trans Union was required to sell to Pritzker one million newly-issued shares of Trans Union at $38 per share.

Van Gorkom took the position that putting Trans Union "up for auction" through a 90–day market test would validate a decision by the Board that $55 was a fair price. He told the Board that the "free market will have an opportunity to judge whether $55 is a fair price." Van Gorkom framed the decision before the Board not as whether $55 per share was the highest price that could be obtained, but as whether the $55 price was a fair price that the stockholders should be given the opportunity to accept or reject. * * *

Attorney Brennan advised the members of the Board that they might be sued if they failed to accept the offer and that a fairness opinion was not required as a matter of law.

Romans * * * told the Board that he had not been involved in the negotiations with Pritzker and knew nothing about the merger proposal until the morning of the meeting; that his studies did not indicate either a fair price for the stock or a valuation of the Company; that he did not see his role as directly addressing the fairness issue; and that he and his people "were trying to search for ways to justify a price in connection with such a [leveraged buy-out] transaction, rather than to say what the shares are worth." * * *

Romans told the Board that, in his opinion, $55 was "in the range of a fair price," but "at the beginning of the range."

Chelberg, Trans Union's President, supported Van Gorkom's presentation and representations. * * *

* * * Based solely upon Van Gorkom's oral presentation, Chelberg's supporting representations, Romans' oral statement, Brennan's legal advice, and their knowledge of the market history of the Company's stock, * * * the directors approved the proposed Merger Agreement. However, the Board later claimed to have attached two conditions to its acceptance: (1) that Trans Union reserved the right to accept any better offer that was made during the market test period; and (2) that Trans Union could share its proprietary information with any other potential bidders. * * * [T]he Board did not reserve the right to actively solicit alternate offers.

The Merger Agreement was executed by Van Gorkom during the evening of September 20 at a formal social event that he hosted for the opening of the Chicago Lyric Opera. Neither he nor any other director read the agreement prior to its signing and delivery to Pritzker.

* * *

On Monday, September 22, the Company issued a press release announcing that Trans Union had entered into a "definitive" Merger Agreement with an affiliate of the Marmon Group, Inc., a Pritzker holding company. Within 10 days of the public announcement, dissent among Senior Management over the merger had become widespread. Faced with threatened resignations of key officers, Van Gorkom met with Pritzker who agreed to several modifications of the Agreement. Pritzker was willing to do so provided that Van Gorkom could persuade the dissidents to remain on the Company payroll for at least six months after consummation of the merger.

Van Gorkom reconvened the Board on October 8 and secured the directors' approval of the proposed amendments—sight unseen. The Board also authorized the employment of Salomon Brothers, its investment banker, to solicit other offers for Trans Union during the proposed "market test" period.

The next day, October 9, Trans Union issued a press release announcing: (1) that Pritzker had obtained "the financing commitments necessary to consummate" the merger with Trans Union; (2) that Pritzker had acquired one million shares of Trans Union common stock at $38 per share; (3) that Trans Union was now permitted to actively seek other offers and had retained Salomon Brothers for that purpose; and (4) that if a more favorable offer were not received before

February 1, 1981, Trans Union's shareholders would thereafter meet to vote on the Pritzker proposal.

It was not until the following day, October 10, that the actual amendments to the Merger Agreement were prepared by Pritzker and delivered to Van Gorkom for execution. [T]he amendments were considerably at variance with Van Gorkom's representations of the amendments to the Board on October 8; and the amendments placed serious constraints on Trans Union's ability to negotiate a better deal and withdraw from the Pritzker agreement. Nevertheless, Van Gorkom proceeded to execute what became the October 10 amendments to the Merger Agreement without conferring further with the Board members and apparently without comprehending the actual implications of the amendments.

* * *

Salomon Brothers' efforts over a three-month period from October 21 to January 21 produced only one serious suitor for Trans Union-General Electric Credit Corporation ("GE Credit") * * * However, GE Credit was unwilling to make an offer for Trans Union unless Trans Union first rescinded its Merger Agreement with Pritzker. When Pritzker refused, GE Credit terminated further discussions with Trans Union in early January.

In the meantime, in early December, the investment firm of Kohlberg, Kravis, Roberts & Co. ("KKR"), the only other concern to make a firm offer for Trans Union, withdrew its offer * * * .

On December 19, this litigation was commenced * * * . On January 21, Management's Proxy Statement for the February 10 shareholder meeting was mailed to Trans Union's stockholders. On January 26, Trans Union's Board met and, after a lengthy meeting, voted to proceed with the Pritzker merger. The Board also approved for mailing, "on or about January 27," a Supplement to its Proxy Statement. The Supplement purportedly set forth all information relevant to the Pritzker Merger Agreement, which had not been divulged in the first Proxy Statement.

* * *

On February 10, the stockholders of Trans Union approved the Pritzker merger proposal. Of the outstanding shares, 69.9% were voted in favor of the merger; 7.25% were voted against the merger; and 22.85% were not voted.

II.

We turn to the issue of the application of the business judgment rule to the September 20 meeting of the Board. * * *

The Court of Chancery [found] that the Board's conduct over the entire period from September 20 through January 26, 1981 was not reckless or improvident, but informed. * * * The Court's explicit finding was that Trans Union's Board was "free to turn down the Pritzker proposal" not only on September 20 but also on October 8, 1980 and on January 26, 1981. The Court's implied, subordinate findings were: (1) that no legally binding agreement was reached by the parties until January 26;

and (2) that if a higher offer were to be forthcoming, the market test would have produced it, * * * and Trans Union would have been contractually free to accept such higher offer. However, the Court offered no factual basis or legal support for any of these findings; and the record compels contrary conclusions.

* * *

The plaintiffs contend that the Court of Chancery erred as a matter of law by exonerating the defendant directors under the business judgment rule without first determining whether the rule's threshold condition of "due care and prudence" was satisfied. * * *

* * * Under Delaware law, the business judgment rule is the offspring of the fundamental principle, * * * that the business and affairs of a Delaware corporation are managed by or under its board of directors. * * * In carrying out their managerial roles, directors are charged with an unyielding fiduciary duty to the corporation and its shareholders. * * * The business judgment rule exists to protect and promote the full and free exercise of the managerial power granted to Delaware directors. * * * The rule itself "is a presumption that in making a business decision, the directors of a corporation acted on an informed basis, in good faith and in the honest belief that the action taken was in the best interests of the company." * * * Thus, the party attacking a board decision as uninformed must rebut the presumption that its business judgment was an informed one.

* * *

Under the business judgment rule there is no protection for directors who have made "an unintelligent or unadvised judgment." * * * A director's duty to inform himself [of all material information reasonably available] in preparation for a decision derives from the fiduciary capacity in which he serves the corporation and its stockholders. * * * Such obligation does not tolerate faithlessness or self-dealing. But fulfillment of the fiduciary function requires more than the mere absence of bad faith or fraud. Representation of the financial interests of others imposes on a director an affirmative duty to protect those interests and to proceed with a critical eye in assessing information of the type and under the circumstances present here. * * *

* * *

* * * We think the concept of gross negligence is * * * the proper standard for determining whether a business judgment reached by a board of directors was an informed one. * * *

In the specific context of a proposed merger of domestic corporations, a director has a duty * * * along with his fellow directors, to act in an informed and deliberate manner in determining whether to approve an agreement of merger before submitting the proposal to the stockholders. Certainly in the merger context, a director may not abdicate that duty by leaving to the shareholders alone the decision to approve or disapprove the agreement. * * *

III.

* * *

A

On the record before us, we must conclude that the Board of Directors did not reach an informed business judgment on September 20, 1980 in voting to "sell" the Company for $55 per share pursuant to the Pritzker cash-out merger proposal. Our reasons, in summary, are as follows:

The directors (1) did not adequately inform themselves as to Van Gorkom's role in forcing the "sale" of the Company and in establishing the per share purchase price; (2) were uninformed as to the intrinsic value of the Company; and (3) given these circumstances, at a minimum, were grossly negligent in approving the "sale" of the Company upon two hours' consideration, without prior notice, and without the exigency of a crisis or emergency.

* * *

Without any documents before them concerning the proposed transaction, the members of the Board were required to rely entirely upon Van Gorkom's 20-minute oral presentation of the proposal. No written summary of the terms of the merger was presented; the directors were given no documentation to support the adequacy of $55 price per share for sale of the Company; and the Board had before it nothing more than Van Gorkom's statement of his understanding of the substance of an agreement which he admittedly had never read, nor which any member of the Board had ever seen.

[Pursuant to the Corporations statutes in Delaware] "directors are fully protected in relying in good faith on reports made by officers." * * *   * * * However, there is no evidence that any "report," * * * concerning the Pritzker proposal, was presented to the Board on September 20. Van Gorkom's oral presentation of his understanding of the terms of the proposed Merger Agreement, which he had not seen, and Romans' brief oral statement of his preliminary study regarding the feasibility of a leveraged buy-out of Trans Union do not qualify as * * * "reports" for these reasons: The former lacked substance because Van Gorkom was basically uninformed as to the essential provisions of the very document about which he was talking. Romans' statement was irrelevant to the issues before the Board since it did not purport to be a valuation study. * * * Considering all of the surrounding circumstances—hastily calling the meeting without prior notice of its subject matter, the proposed sale of the Company without any prior consideration of the issue or necessity therefor, the urgent time constraints imposed by Pritzker, and the total absence of any documentation whatsoever—the directors were duty bound to make reasonable inquiry of Van Gorkom and Romans, and if they had done so, the inadequacy of that upon which they now claim to have relied would have been apparent.

The defendants rely on the following factors to sustain the Trial Court's finding that the Board's decision was an informed one: (1) the magnitude of the premium or spread between the $55 Pritzker offering price and Trans Union's current market price of $38 per share; (2) the amendment of the Agreement as submitted on September 20 to permit the Board to accept any better offer during the "market test" period; (3) the collective experience and expertise of the Board's "inside" and "outside" directors; and (4) their reliance on Brennan's legal advice that the directors might be sued if they rejected the Pritzker proposal. * * *

(1)

A substantial premium may provide one reason to recommend a merger, but in the absence of other sound valuation information, the fact of a premium alone does not provide an adequate basis upon which to assess the fairness of an offering price. * * *

The record is clear that before September 20, Van Gorkom and other members of Trans Union's Board knew that the market had consistently undervalued the worth of Trans Union's stock, despite steady increases in the Company's operating income in the seven years preceding the merger. The Board related this occurrence in large part to Trans Union's inability to use its ITCs as previously noted. Van Gorkom testified that he did not believe the market price accurately reflected Trans Union's true worth; and several of the directors testified that, as a general rule, most chief executives think that the market undervalues their companies' stock. Yet, on September 20, Trans Union's Board apparently believed that the market stock price accurately reflected the value of the Company for the purpose of determining the adequacy of the premium for its sale.

* * *

The parties do not dispute that a publicly-traded stock price is solely a measure of the value of a minority position and, thus, market price represents only the value of a single share. * * *

* * * As of September 20, the Board had made no evaluation of the Company designed to value the entire enterprise * * * .

* * *

We do not imply that an outside valuation study is essential to support an informed business judgment; nor do we state that fairness opinions by independent investment bankers are required as a matter of law. Often insiders familiar with the business of a going concern are in a better position than are outsiders to gather relevant information; and under appropriate circumstances, such directors may be fully protected in relying in good faith upon the valuation reports of their management. * * *

Here, the record establishes that the Board did not request its Chief Financial Officer, Romans, to make any valuation study or review of the proposal to determine the adequacy of $55 per share for sale of the Company.   * * *

* * *

The record also establishes that the Board accepted without scrutiny Van Gorkom's representation as to the fairness of the $55 price per share for sale of the

Company * * * The Board thereby failed to discover that Van Gorkom had suggested the $55 price to Pritzker and, most crucially, that Van Gorkom had arrived at the $55 figure based on calculations designed solely to determine the feasibility of a leveraged buy-out. * * *

* * *

None of the directors, Management or outside, were investment bankers or financial analysts. Yet the Board did not consider recessing the meeting until a later hour that day (or requesting an extension of Pritzker's Sunday evening deadline) to give it time to elicit more information as to the sufficiency of the offer, either from inside Management (in particular Romans) or from Trans Union's own investment banker, Salomon Brothers * * * .

* * *

(2)

This brings us to the post-September 20 "market test" * * * . In this connection, the directors present a two-part argument: (a) that by making a "market test" of Pritzker's $55 per share offer a condition of their September 20 decision to accept his offer, they cannot be found to have acted impulsively or in an uninformed manner on September 20; and (b) that the adequacy of the $17 premium for sale of the Company was conclusively established over the following 90 to 120 days by the most reliable evidence available—the marketplace. * * * .

Again, the facts of record do not support the defendants' argument. There is no evidence: (a) that the Merger Agreement was effectively amended to give the Board freedom to put Trans Union up for auction sale to the highest bidder; or (b) that a public auction was in fact permitted to occur. * * *

The Merger Agreement, specifically identified as that originally presented to the Board on September 20, has never been produced by the defendants, notwithstanding the plaintiffs' several demands for production before as well as during trial. No acceptable explanation of this failure to produce documents has been given to either the Trial Court or this Court. * * *

Van Gorkom states that the Agreement as submitted incorporated the ingredients for a market test by authorizing Trans Union to receive competing offers over the next 90–day period. However, he concedes that the Agreement barred Trans Union from actively soliciting such offers and from furnishing to interested parties any information about the Company other than that already in the public domain. * * * Van Gorkom, conceding that he never read the Agreement, stated that he was relying upon his understanding that, under corporate law, directors always have an inherent right, as well as a fiduciary duty, to accept a better offer notwithstanding an existing contractual commitment by the Board. * * *

Several of Trans Union's outside directors resolutely maintained that the Agreement as submitted was approved on the understanding that, "if we got a better deal, we had a right to take it." * * * The only clause in the Agreement as finally executed to which the defendants can point as "keeping the door open" is the following [italicized] statement found in subparagraph (a) of section 2.03 of the Merger Agreement as executed:

The Board of Directors shall recommend to the stockholders of Trans Union that they approve and adopt the Merger Agreement ('the stockholders' approval') and to use its best efforts to obtain the requisite votes therefor. GL acknowledges that Trans Union directors may have a competing fiduciary obligation to the shareholders under certain circumstances.

Clearly, this language on its face cannot be construed as incorporating either of the two "conditions" described above * * *.

The defendants attempt to downplay the significance of the prohibition against Trans Union's actively soliciting competing offers by arguing that the directors "understood that the entire financial community would know that Trans Union was for sale upon the announcement of the Pritzker offer, and anyone desiring to make a better offer was free to do so." Yet, the press release issued on September 22, with the authorization of the Board, stated that Trans Union had entered into "definitive agreements" with the Pritzkers; and the press release did not even disclose Trans Union's limited right to receive and accept higher offers. * * *

* * *

(3)

The directors' unfounded reliance on both the premium and the market test as the basis for accepting the Pritzker proposal undermines the defendants' remaining contention that the Board's collective experience and sophistication was a sufficient basis for finding that it reached its September 20 decision with informed, reasonable deliberation. * * *

[The court observes in a footnote that] Trans Union's five "inside" directors had backgrounds in law and accounting, 116 years of collective employment by the Company and 68 years of combined experience on its Board. Trans Union's five "outside" directors included four chief executives of major corporations and an economist who was a former dean of a major school of business and chancellor of a university. The "outside" directors had 78 years of combined experience as chief executive officers of major corporations and 50 years of cumulative experience as directors of Trans Union. Thus, defendants argue that the Board was eminently qualified to reach an informed judgment on the proposed "sale" of Trans Union notwithstanding their lack of any advance notice of the proposal, the shortness of their deliberation, and their determination not to consult with their investment banker or to obtain a fairness opinion. [But the court rejects this experience as a significant factor because of its belief that there wasn't enough information on which to base a decision.]

(4)

Part of the defense is based on a claim that the directors relied on legal advice rendered at the September 20 meeting by James Brennan, Esquire, who was present at Van Gorkom's request. Unfortunately, Brennan did not appear and testify at trial even though his firm participated in the defense of this action. There is no contemporaneous evidence of the advice given by Brennan on September 20, only the later deposition and trial testimony of certain directors as to their recollections or understanding of what was said at the meeting. Since counsel did not testify, and the advice attributed to Brennan is hearsay received by the Trial Court over the plaintiffs' objections, we consider it only in the context of the directors' present claims. In fairness to counsel, we make no findings that the advice attributed to him was in fact given. We focus solely on the efficacy of the defendants' claims, made months and years later, in an effort to extricate themselves from liability.

Several defendants testified that Brennan advised them that Delaware law did not require a fairness opinion or an outside valuation of the Company before the Board could act on the Pritzker proposal. If given, the advice was correct. However, that did not end the matter. Unless the directors had before them adequate information regarding the intrinsic value of the Company, upon which a proper exercise of business judgment could be made, mere advice of this type is meaningless; and, given this record of the defendants' failures, it constitutes no defense here. * * *

* * *

A second claim is that counsel advised the Board it would be subject to lawsuits if it rejected the $55 per share offer. It is, of course, a fact of corporate life that today when faced with difficult or sensitive issues, directors often are subject to suit, irrespective of the decisions they make. However, counsel's mere acknowledgement of this circumstance cannot be rationally translated into a justification for a board permitting itself to be stampeded into a patently unadvised act. * * *

* * *

B

We now examine the Board's post-September 20 conduct for the purpose of determining first, whether it was informed and not grossly negligent; and second, if informed, whether it was sufficient to legally rectify and cure the Board's derelictions of September 20.

(1)

First, as to the Board meeting of October 8: Its purpose arose in the aftermath of the September 20 meeting: (1) the September 22 press release announcing that Trans Union "had entered into definitive agreements to merge with an affiliate of Marmon Group, Inc.;" and (2) Senior Management's ensuing revolt.

Trans Union's press release stated:

FOR IMMEDIATE RELEASE:

CHICAGO, IL—Trans Union Corporation announced today that it had entered into definitive agreements to merge with an affiliate of The Marmon Group, Inc. * * *

The merger is subject to approval by the stockholders of Trans Union at a special meeting expected to be held sometime during December or early January.

Until October 10, 1980, the purchaser has the right to terminate the merger if financing that is satisfactory to the purchaser has not been obtained* * *.

In a related transaction, Trans Union has agreed to sell to a designee of the purchaser one million newly-issued shares of Trans Union common stock at a cash price of $38 per share. * * *

Completing of the transaction is also subject to the preparation of a definitive proxy statement and making various filings and obtaining the approvals or consents of government agencies.

The press release made no reference to provisions allegedly reserving to the Board the rights to perform a "market test" and to withdraw from the Pritzker Agreement if Trans Union received a better offer before the shareholder meeting. * * *

The public announcement of the Pritzker merger resulted in an "en masse" revolt of Trans Union's Senior Management. The head of Trans Union's tank car operations (its most profitable division) informed Van Gorkom that unless the merger were called off, fifteen key personnel would resign.

Instead of reconvening the Board, Van Gorkom again privately met with Pritzker, informed him of the developments, and sought his advice. Pritzker then made the following suggestions for overcoming Management's dissatisfaction: (1) that the Agreement be amended to permit Trans Union to solicit, as well as receive, higher offers; and (2) that the shareholder meeting be postponed from early January to February 10, 1981. In return, Pritzker asked Van Gorkom to obtain a commitment from Senior Management to remain at Trans Union for at least six months after the merger was consummated.

Van Gorkom then advised Senior Management that the Agreement would be amended to give Trans Union the right to solicit competing offers through January, 1981, if they would agree to remain with Trans Union. Senior Management was temporarily mollified; and Van Gorkom then called a special meeting of Trans Union's Board for October 8.

Thus, the primary purpose of the October 8 Board meeting was to amend the Merger Agreement, in a manner agreeable to Pritzker, to permit Trans Union to conduct a "market test." * * * Van Gorkom understood that the proposed amendments were intended to give the Company an unfettered "right to openly solicit offers down through January 31." * * * In a brief session, the directors approved Van Gorkom's oral presentation of the substance of the proposed amendments, the terms of which were not reduced to writing until October 10. * * *[T]he Board again approved them sight unseen and adjourned, giving Van Gorkom authority to execute the papers when he received them. * * *.

The next day, October 9, and before the Agreement was amended, Pritzker moved swiftly to off-set the proposed market test amendment. First, Pritzker informed Trans Union that he had completed arrangements for financing its acquisition and that the parties were thereby mutually bound to a firm purchase and sale arrangement. Second, Pritzker announced the exercise of his option to purchase one million shares of Trans Union's treasury stock at $38 per share * * * .

The next day, October 10, Pritzker delivered to Trans Union the proposed amendments to the September 20 Merger Agreement. Van Gorkom promptly proceeded to countersign all the instruments on behalf of Trans Union without reviewing the instruments to determine if they were consistent with the authority previously granted him by the Board. * * *

The October 10 amendments to the Merger Agreement did authorize Trans Union to solicit competing offers, but the amendments had more far-reaching effects. The most significant change was in the definition of the third-party "offer" available to Trans Union as a possible basis for withdrawal from its Merger Agreement with Pritzker. Under the October 10 amendments, a better offer was no longer sufficient to permit Trans Union's withdrawal. Trans Union was now permitted to terminate the Pritzker Agreement and abandon the merger only if, prior to February 10, 1981, Trans Union had either consummated a merger (or sale of assets) with a third party or had entered into a "definitive" merger agreement more favorable than Pritzker's and for a greater consideration—subject only to stockholder approval.   * * *

In our view, the record compels the conclusion that the directors' conduct on October 8 exhibited the same deficiencies as did their conduct on September 20 * * * .

We conclude that the Board acted in a grossly negligent manner on October 8. * * *

The October 9 press release, coupled with the October 10 amendments, had the clear effect of locking Trans Union's Board into the Pritzker Agreement. Pritzker had thereby foreclosed Trans Union's Board from negotiating any better "definitive" agreement * * * .

(2)

Next, as to the "curative" effects of the Board's post-September 20 conduct, we review in more detail the reaction of Van Gorkom to the KKR proposal and the results of the Board-sponsored "market test."

The KKR proposal was the first and only offer received subsequent to the Pritzker Merger Agreement. The offer resulted primarily from the efforts of Romans and other senior officers to propose an alternative to Pritzker's acquisition of Trans Union. In late September, Romans' group contacted KKR about the possibility of a leveraged buy-out by all members of Management, except Van Gorkom. By early October, Henry R. Kravis of KKR gave Romans written notice of KKR's "interest in making an offer to purchase 100% of Trans Union's common stock."

Thereafter, and until early December, Romans' group worked with KKR to develop a proposal. It did so with Van Gorkom's knowledge and apparently grudging consent. On December 2, Kravis and Romans hand-delivered to Van Gorkom a formal letter-offer to purchase all of Trans Union's assets and to assume all of its liabilities for an aggregate cash consideration equivalent to $60 per share. The offer was contingent upon completing equity and bank financing of $650 million, which Kravis represented as 80% complete. The KKR letter made reference to discussions with major banks regarding the loan portion of the buy-out cost and stated that KKR was "confident that commitments for the bank financing * * * can be obtained within two or three weeks." The purchasing group was to include certain named key members of Trans Union's Senior Management * * * and a major Canadian company. Kravis stated that they were willing to enter into a "definitive agreement" under terms and conditions "substantially the same" as those contained in Trans Union's agreement with Pritzker. * * *

Van Gorkom's reaction to the KKR proposal was completely negative; he did not view the offer as being firm because of its financing condition. It was pointed out, to no avail, that Pritzker's offer had not only been similarly conditioned, but accepted on an expedited basis. Van Gorkom refused Kravis' request that Trans Union issue a press release announcing KKR's offer, on the ground that it might "chill" any other offer. * * * Romans and Kravis left with the understanding that their proposal would be presented to Trans Union's Board that afternoon.

Within a matter of hours and shortly before the scheduled Board meeting, Kravis withdrew his letter-offer. He gave as his reason a sudden decision by the Chief Officer of Trans Union's rail car leasing operation to withdraw from the KKR purchasing group. Van Gorkom had spoken to that officer about his participation in the KKR proposal immediately after his meeting with Romans and Kravis. However, Van Gorkom denied any responsibility for the officer's change of mind.

At the Board meeting later that afternoon, Van Gorkom did not inform the directors of the KKR proposal because he considered it "dead." * * *

GE Credit Corporation's interest in Trans Union did not develop until November; and it made no written proposal until mid-January. Even then, its proposal was not in the form of an offer. Had there been time to do so, GE Credit was prepared to offer between $2 and $5 per share above the $55 per share price which Pritzker offered. But GE Credit needed an additional 60 to 90 days; and it was unwilling to make a formal offer without a concession from Pritzker extending the February 10 "deadline" for Trans Union's stockholder meeting. * * *

* * *

* * * Our review of the record compels a finding that confirmation of the appropriateness of the Pritzker offer by an unfettered or free market test was virtually meaningless in the face of the terms and time limitations of Trans Union's Merger Agreement with Pritzker as amended October 10, 1980.

(3)

Finally, we turn to the Board's meeting of January 26, 1981. The defendant directors rely upon the action there taken to refute the contention that they did not reach an informed business judgment in approving the Pritzker merger. * * *

The Board's January 26 meeting was the first meeting following the filing of the plaintiffs' suit in mid-December and the last meeting before the previously-noticed shareholder meeting of February 10. * * * At that meeting the following facts, among other aspects of the Merger Agreement, were discussed:

(a) The fact that prior to September 20, 1980, no Board member or member of Senior Management, except Chelberg and Peterson, knew that Van Gorkom had discussed a possible merger with Pritzker;

(b) The fact that the price of $55 per share had been suggested initially to Pritzker by Van Gorkom;

(c) The fact that the Board had not sought an independent fairness opinion;

(d) The fact that, at the September 20 Senior Management meeting, Romans and several members of Senior Management indicated both concern that the $55 per share price was inadequate and a belief that a higher price should and could be obtained;

(e) The fact that Romans had advised the Board at its meeting on September 20, that he and his department had prepared a study which indicated that the Company had a value in the range of $55 to $65 per share, and that he could not advise the Board that the $55 per share offer made by Pritzker was unfair.

* * * On the basis of this evidence, the defendants argue that whatever information the Board lacked to make a deliberate and informed judgment on September 20, or on October 8, was fully divulged to the entire Board on January 26. Hence, the argument goes, the Board's vote on January 26 to again "approve" the Pritzker merger must be found to have been an informed and deliberate judgment.

* * * Following this review and discussion, [three attorneys who were present] advised the Directors that in light of their discussions, they could (a) continue to recommend to the stockholders that the latter vote in favor of the proposed merger, (b) recommend that the stockholders vote against the merger, or (c) take no position with respect to recommending the proposed merger and simply leave the decision to stockholders. After further discussion, it was moved, seconded, and unanimously voted that the Board of Directors continue to recommend that the stockholders vote in favor of the proposed merger * * * .

On the basis of this evidence, the defendants assert: (1) that the Trial Court was legally correct in widening the time frame for determining whether the defendants' approval of the Pritzker merger represented an informed business judgment to include the entire four-month period during which the Board considered the matter from September 20 through January 26; and (2) that, given this extensive evidence of the Board's further review and deliberations on January 26, this Court must affirm the Trial Court's conclusion that the Board's action was not reckless or improvident.

We cannot agree. * * *

[The evidence indicates] recognition that the question of the alternative courses of action, available to the Board on January 26 with respect to the Pritzker merger, was a legal question, presenting to the Board (*after* its review of the full record developed through pre-trial discovery) *three* options: (1) to "continue to recommend" the Pritzker merger; (2) to "recommend that the stockholders vote against" the Pritzker merger; or (3) to take a noncommittal position on the merger and "simply leave the decision to [the] shareholders."

We must conclude from the foregoing that the Board was mistaken as a matter of law regarding its available courses of action on January 26, 1981. Options (2) and (3) were not viable or legally available to the Board * * * . The Board could not remain committed to the Pritzker merger and yet recommend that its stockholders vote it down; nor could it take a neutral position and delegate to the stockholders the unadvised decision as to whether to accept or reject the merger. Under § 251 (b) [of the Delaware Corporations Code], the Board had but two options: (1) to proceed with the merger and the stockholder meeting, with the Board's recommendation of approval; or (2) to rescind its agreement with Pritzker, withdraw its approval of the merger, and notify its stockholders that the proposed shareholder meeting was cancelled. There is no evidence that the Board gave any consideration to these * * * .

But the second course of action would have clearly involved a substantial risk— that the Board would be faced with suit by Pritzker for breach of contract based on its September 20 agreement as amended October 10. As previously noted, under the terms of the October 10 amendment, the Board's only ground for release from its agreement with Pritzker was its entry into a more favorable definitive agreement to sell the Company to a third party. Thus, in reality, the Board was not "free to turn down the Pritzker proposal" as the Trial Court found. * * *

Therefore, the Trial Court's conclusion that the Board reached an informed business judgment on January 26 in determining whether to turn down the Pritzker "proposal" on that day cannot be sustained. * * *

* * *

[SECTION IV IS OMITTED]

V.

The defendants ultimately rely on the stockholder vote of February 10 for exoneration. The defendants contend that the stockholders' "overwhelming" vote approving the Pritzker Merger Agreement had the legal effect of curing any failure of the Board to reach an informed business judgment in its approval of the merger.

* * *

On this issue the Trial Court summarily concluded "that the stockholders of Trans Union were fairly informed as to the pending merger. . . . " The Court provided no supportive reasoning nor did the Court make any reference to the evidence of record.

* * *

The settled rule in Delaware is that "where a majority of fully informed stockholders ratify action of even interested directors, an attack on the ratified transaction normally must fail." * * * The question of whether shareholders have been fully informed such that their vote can be said to ratify director action, "turns on the fairness and completeness of the proxy materials submitted by the management to the . . . shareholders."

[C]orporate directors owe to their stockholders a fiduciary duty to disclose all facts germane to the transaction at issue in an atmosphere of complete candor. We defined "germane" in the tender offer context as all "information such as a reasonable stockholder would consider important in deciding whether to sell or retain stock." * * * In reality, "germane" means material facts.

Applying this standard to the record before us, we find that Trans Union's stockholders were not fully informed of all facts material to their vote on the Pritzker Merger and that the Trial Court's ruling to the contrary is clearly erroneous. We list the material deficiencies in the proxy materials:

(1) The fact that the Board had no reasonably adequate information indicative of the intrinsic value of the Company, other than a concededly depressed market price, was without question material to the shareholders voting on the merger. * * *

Accordingly, the Board's lack of valuation information should have been disclosed. * * *

(2) We find false and misleading the Board's characterization of the Romans report in the Supplemental Proxy Statement. The Supplemental Proxy stated:

> At the September 20, 1980 meeting of the Board of Directors of Trans Union, Mr. Romans indicated that while he could not say that $55.00 per share was an unfair price, he had prepared a preliminary report which reflected that the value of the Company was in the range of $55.00 to $65.00 per share.

Nowhere does the Board disclose that Romans stated to the Board that his calculations were made in a "search for ways to justify a price in connection with" a leveraged buy-out transaction, "rather than to say what the shares are worth," and that he stated to the Board that his conclusion thus arrived at "was not the same thing as saying that I have a valuation of the Company at X dollars." * * *

(3) We find misleading the Board's references to the "substantial" premium offered. The Board gave as their primary reason in support of the merger the "substantial premium" shareholders would receive. But the Board did not disclose its failure to assess the premium offered in terms of other relevant valuation techniques, thereby rendering questionable its determination as to the substantiality of the premium over an admittedly depressed stock market price.

(4) We find the Board's recital in the Supplemental Proxy of certain events preceding the September 20 meeting to be incomplete and misleading. It is beyond dispute that a reasonable stockholder would have considered material the fact that Van Gorkom not only suggested the $55 price to Pritzker, but also that he chose the figure because it made feasible a leveraged buy-out. * * *

* * *

The burden must fall on defendants who claim ratification based on shareholder vote to establish that the shareholder approval resulted from a fully informed electorate. On the record before us, it is clear that the Board failed to meet that burden. * * *.

* * *

VI.

* * *

We hold, therefore, that the Trial Court committed reversible error in applying the business judgment rule in favor of the director defendants in this case.

On remand, the Court of Chancery shall conduct an evidentiary hearing to determine the fair value of the shares represented by the plaintiffs' class, based on the intrinsic value of Trans Union on September 20, 1980. * * * Thereafter, an award of damages may be entered to the extent that the fair value of Trans Union exceeds $55 per share. * * *

DISSENT:

MCNEILLY, Justice, dissenting:

The majority opinion reads like an advocate's closing address to a hostile jury. * * * Throughout the opinion great emphasis is directed only to the negative, with nothing more than lip service granted the positive aspects of this case. In my opinion Chancellor Marvel (retired) should have been affirmed. The Chancellor's opinion was the product of well reasoned conclusions, based upon a sound deductive process, clearly supported by the evidence and entitled to deference in this appeal. Because of my diametrical opposition to all evidentiary conclusions of the majority, I respectfully dissent.

* * *

* * * At the time the merger was proposed the inside five directors had collectively been employed by the Company for 116 years and had 68 years of combined experience as directors. * * * With the exception of [outside director, Dr.] Wallis, these were all chief executive officers of Chicago based corporations that were at least as large as Trans Union. The five "outside" directors had 78 years of combined experience as chief executive officers, and 53 years cumulative service as Trans Union directors.

* * *

Directors of this caliber are not ordinarily taken in by a "fast shuffle". I submit they were not taken into this multi-million dollar corporate transaction without being fully informed and aware of the state of the art as it pertained to the entire corporate panorama of Trans Union. * * * These men knew Trans Union like the back of their hands and were more than well qualified to make on the spot informed business judgments concerning the affairs of Trans Union including a 100% sale of the corporation. Lest we forget, the corporate world of then and now operates on what is so aptly referred to as "the fast track". These men were at the time an integral part of that world, all professional business men, not intellectual figureheads.

* * *

At the time of the September 20, 1980 meeting the Board was acutely aware of Trans Union and its prospects. The problems created by accumulated investment tax credits and accelerated depreciation were discussed repeatedly at Board meetings, and all of the directors understood the problem thoroughly. * * *

At the September 20 meeting Van Gorkom reviewed all aspects of the proposed transaction and repeated the explanation of the Pritzker offer he had earlier given to senior management. Having heard Van Gorkom's explanation of the Pritzker's offer, and Brennan's explanation of the merger documents the directors discussed the matter. Out of this discussion arose an insistence on the part of the directors that two modifications to the offer be made. First, they required that any potential competing bidder be given access to the same information concerning Trans Union that had been provided to the Pritzkers. Second, the merger documents were to be modified to reflect the fact that the directors could accept a better offer and would not be required to recommend the Pritzker offer if a better offer was made. * * *

At a subsequent meeting on October 8, 1981 the directors, with the consent of the Pritzkers, amended the Merger Agreement so as to establish the right of Trans Union to solicit as well as to receive higher bids * * *.

Following the October 8 board meeting of Trans Union, the investment banking firm of Salomon Brothers was retained by the corporation to search for better offers than that of the Pritzkers, Salomon Brothers being charged with the responsibility of doing "whatever possible to see if there is a superior bid in the marketplace over a bid that is on the table for Trans Union". In undertaking such project, it was agreed that Salomon Brothers would be paid the amount of $500,000 to cover its expenses as well as a fee equal to 3/8ths of 1% of the aggregate fair market value of the consideration to be received by the company in the case of a merger or the like, which meant that in the event Salomon Brothers should find a buyer willing to pay a price of $56.00 a share instead of $55.00, such firm would receive a fee of roughly $2,650,000 plus disbursements.

* * * As matters transpired, no firm offer which bettered the Pritzker offer of $55 per share was ever made.

On January 21, 1981 a proxy statement was sent to the shareholders of Trans Union advising them of a February 10, 1981 meeting in which the merger would be voted. On January 26, 1981 the directors held their regular meeting. At this meeting the Board discussed the instant merger as well as all events, including this litigation, surrounding it. At the conclusion of the meeting the Board unanimously voted to recommend to the stockholders that they approve the merger. Additionally, the directors reviewed and approved a Supplemental Proxy Statement which, among other things, advised the stockholders of what had occurred at the instant meeting and of the fact that General Electric had decided not to make an offer. On February 10, 1981 the stockholders of Trans Union met pursuant to notice and voted overwhelmingly in favor of the Pritzker merger, 89% of the votes cast being in favor of it.

I have no quarrel with the majority's analysis of the business judgment rule. It is the application of that rule to these facts which is wrong. An overview of the entire record, rather than the limited view of bits and pieces which the majority has exploded like popcorn, convinces me that the directors made an informed business judgment which was buttressed by their test of the market.

* * * At the September 20 meeting Van Gorkom presented the Pritzker offer, and the board then heard from James Brennan, the company's counsel in this matter, who discussed the legal documents. Following this, the Board directed that certain changes be made in the merger documents. These changes made it clear that the Board was free to accept a better offer than Pritzker's if one was made. The above facts reveal that the Board did not act in a grossly negligent manner in informing themselves of the relevant and available facts before passing on the merger. To the contrary, this record reveals that the directors acted with the utmost care in informing themselves of the relevant and available facts before passing on the merger.

* * *

Overall, my review of the record leads me to conclude that the proxy materials adequately complied with Delaware law in informing the shareholders about the proposed transaction and the events surrounding it.

* * *

CHRISTIE, Justice, dissenting:

I respectfully dissent.

* * * I believe that the record taken as a whole supports a conclusion that the actions of the defendants are protected by the business judgment rule. * * * I also am satisfied that the record supports a conclusion that the defendants acted with * * * complete candor * * * . * * *

NOTES AND QUESTIONS

1. WHO GOT IT RIGHT, the majority or the dissent in *Smith v. Van Gorkom*? The consensus among corporations scholars is probably that one of their number got it right when he called this case, "one of the worst decisions in the history of corporate law." Daniel R. Fischel, *The Business Judgment Rule and the Trans Union Case*, 40 Bus. Law. 1437, 1455 (1985). Still, even the dissenters seem to indicate that the majority got the law right, but their application of the law to the facts seems to be the difficulty. Why, precisely, does the majority feel that the Board failed in their duty, and, why, precisely, doesn't the business judgment rule cover? In other words, is this really the same case as *Francis v. United Jersey Bank*, as the majority seems to think, or is it a case more like *Kamin v. American Express*, discussed in the last set of notes and questions? For something of a dissent to Professor Fischel's view of *Smith v. Van Gorkom*, and a fascinating study of the background and the personalities of the case, see Stephen M. Bainbridge, "The Story of Smith v. Van Gorkom," in J. Mark Ramseyer, ed., Corporate Law Stories 198 (2009). Professor Bainbridge observes that the Delaware Supreme Court's decision in *Smith v. Van Gorkom* "encourages inquiry, deliberation, care, and process. The decision strongly encourages boards to seek outside counsel and financial advice, which is consistent with evidence that groupthink can be prevented by outside expert advice and evaluations. [footnote omitted]" *Id.*, at 221. The implication is that the decision was a wise one. Do you agree?

2. IT IS CERTAINLY OF INTEREST that shortly after the Delaware Court's decision in *Smith v. Van Gorkom* the Delaware legislature amended its corporate law to provide that the charter of a corporation in Delaware may contain

> A provision eliminating or limiting the personal liability of a director to the corporation or its stockholders for monetary damages for breach of fiduciary duty as a director, provided that such provision shall not eliminate or limit the liability of a director: (i) For any breach of the director's duty of loyalty to the corporation or its stockholders; (ii) for acts or omissions not in good faith or which involve intentional misconduct or a knowing violation of law; (iii) under § 174 of this title; or (iv) for any transaction from which the director derived an improper personal benefit. * * *

Del. Corp. Code 102(b)(7). What would have been the effect on the Directors in *Smith v. Van Gorkom* if Trans Union's charter contained such a provision? Would you have voted for the adoption of 102(b)(7)? Can you understand how it can be said that, in effect, 102(b)(7) overrules *Smith v. Van Gorkom*? Note, however, that *Smith v. Van Gorkom* is still, technically speaking, good law, and that if a Delaware corporation fails to take advantage of 102(b)(7), liability of a kind that was imposed in Smith is still a possibility. You will not be surprised to learn that since the passage of 102(b)(7) the great majority of Delaware corporations have amended their charters accordingly if they were in existence before 102(b)(7)'s passage, and those formed subsequently have routinely incorporated provisions authorized by 102(b)(7). Is it becoming clearer to you why Delaware is such an attractive state for incorporation?

3. WHAT DO YOU MAKE OF THE FACTS (and the law) of *Smith v. Van Gorkom*? It is a lengthy case, and, believe it or not, the version presented here has been severely edited. We have exceeded our usual page limits for cases because this very famous case (even in light of Section 102(b)(7)), offers a splendid opportunity to distinguish between acts of nonfeasance and what we might label acts of misfeasance, the one giving rise to liability if there is director negligence or director gross negligence, and the other generally creating no liability if the directors act consistently with the provisions of the business judgment rule. Again, the majority of three justices in Smith believes it is confronted with a situation involving director gross negligence, and the dissenters believe they are examining a classic business judgment rule situation. Does the analysis in the case help you sort out which is which? Chancellor Allen, perhaps the pre-eminent Delaware Chancellor of our era, remarked in his opinion in the case of *In re RJR Nabisco, Inc. Shareholders Litigation*, 1989 WL 7036 (Del.Ch. 1989), "that the amount of information that it is prudent to have before a decision is made is itself a business judgment of the very type that courts are institutionally poorly equipped to make." *Id.*, at *19, quoted in Bainbridge, supra at 217–218, n. 121. How does that suggest *Smith v. Van Gorkom* should have been decided?

Have we made an error in forcing you to read this lengthy case? Virtually every corporations casebook compiled since 1985 includes *Smith v. Van Gorkom*, but in an intriguing recent essay, Lawrence A. Hamermesh, Fiduciary Duty, Limited Liability and the Law of Delaware: Why I do not teach *Smith v. Van Gorkom*, 34 Ga. L. Rev. 477 (2000), a law professor at Widener University in Delaware, argues that it is a mistake to teach the case to law students. Professor Hamermesh states that "The case is simply too involved factually, too dependent upon knowledge of complex factual and legal matters concerning mergers and acquisitions and valuation, and too light on good legal reasoning to justify an extended effort by students, especially when most students have no intention of representing business clients at all, let alone engaging in a mergers and acquisitions practice." *Id.*, at 479. How would you respond to each of Hamermesh's points? Most important, says Hamermesh, "*Van Gorkom*'s greatest vice is that it conveys the inaccurate impression that claims for money damages against corporate managers for failure of attention constitute a common and viable form of litigation. Nothing could be further from the truth. Exculpatory charter provisions adopted pursuant to statutes, almost universally enacted since *Van Gorkom*, have rendered the damages claim for breach of the duty of care essentially non-existent." *Ibid.* Do you suppose he is correct about that? Does *Francis v. United Jersey Bank* suggest otherwise? It is intriguing to observe that from 1985 to 1994, Professor Hamermesh was a partner in the leading Wilmington, Delaware law firm of Morris, Nichols, Arsht & Tunnell, which represented the corporate defendants in *Smith v. Van Gorkom*, though he had no personal role in the litigation.

....

4. IN ANOTHER LINE OF CASES the Delaware courts have also indicated that the Directors' obligations include a "duty to monitor." In key language from the most important of this line of cases, *In re Caremark International Inc. Derivative Litigation* 698 A.2d 959 (Del.Ch. 1996), the then Chancellor Allen, stated that "A director's obligation includes a duty to attempt in good faith to assure that a corporate information and reporting system, which the board concludes is adequate, exists, and that failure to do so under some circumstances may, in theory at least, render a director liable for losses." The duty to monitor, a duty enacted into federal law in the Sarbanes–Oxley Act of 2002, which we will encounter later, is particularly important in regulated industries, such as banks, utility companies, or, as in Caremark itself, the provision of health-care services.

Precisely how the duty to monitor is carried out seems to be a subject of some controversy. For example, it is a nice question whether the inside directors can be trusted effectively to monitor the conduct of the officers of the corporation. To meet this problem, in the Caremark case, as part of the settlement, Caremark agreed to form a "Compliance and Ethics Committee," made up of four directors, two of whom were to be outside directors. The Compliance and Ethics Committee was to "report to the Caremark board on monitoring and compliance systems." On the Caremark settlement, see generally Hillary A. Sale, "Good Faith's Procedure and Substance: In re Caremark International Inc., Derivative Litigation," Chapter 14 in Jonathan R. Macey, Ed., *The Iconic Cases in Corporate Law* 278, 282 (2008).

As Ms. Sale notes, quoting from Chancellor Allen's opinion, when a court is reviewing whether the board did an adequate job performing its duty to monitor, the standard to be used is the business judgment rule, and the question to be asked is whether the board undertook a good faith effort "to be informed to exercise appropriate judgment." *Id.*, at 283, quoting 698 A.2d, at 968. (Is this standard of "good faith" consistent with the Court's holding in *Smith v. Van Gorkom*?) An earlier case on the duty to monitor had held that "absent cause for suspicion there is no duty upon the directors to install and operate a corporate system of espionage to ferret out wrongdoing which they have no reason to suspect exists." *Graham v. Allis-Chalmers Manufacturing Co.*, 188 A.2d 125, 130 (Del. 1963), but Ms. Sale quite correctly observes that Chancellor Allen found this exculpatory language too broad, and that, given the requirements of the times, it was better to mandate that "directors needed to establish information and reporting systems to satisfy their good-faith obligations to be reasonably informed." Sale, supra, at 285.

For further guidance on the requirements of good faith in fulfilling directors' oversight and monitoring roles see *Stone v. Ritter*, 911 A.2d 362 (Del. 2006), discussed in Sale, supra at 289–292. Ms. Sale concludes that Stone "clarifies that a board that fails to either implement the appropriate [monitoring] system or fails to respond to red flags, is not a good-faith or loyal monitor." *Id.*, at 293 (emphasis in original). Such "red flags" might include "problematic practices revealed in audit reports," "newspaper of other media reports of specific company problems" or "pending governmental investigations," or "general media stories of significant industry or broad-based governance or accounting issues." *Id.*, at 293–294. Similar "red flags" might be raised by "negative government inspections of companies in a regulated industry," or "resignations of fellow directors." *Id.*, at 293.

For another penetrating study of the duty to monitor cases, and another appreciation of the manner in which Chancellor Allen sought to balance the requirements for the Delaware courts to monitor director conduct with the need to allow business persons the freedom to manage their firms in a manner to serve the interests of shareholders, see Jennifer Arlen, "The Story of Allis-Chalmers, Caremark, and Stone: Directors' Evolving Duty to Monitor," Chapter 11 in J. Mark Ramseyer, ed., *Corporate Law Stories* 323 (2009).

IV. Duty of Loyalty

Holden v. Construction Machinery Co.

Supreme Court of Iowa.
202 N.W.2d 348 (1972).

[RAWLINGS, J.]

* * *

[Construction Machinery Co. ("CMC")] is a Waterloo-based corporation engaged primarily in the manufacture of tools and equipment for concrete and construction industries. About 1936, L.S. Holden became the sole owner of CMC. He and his first wife, now Mrs. Leona Hansen, had three children, Herle, Warren and a younger daughter, Mrs. Melva Davey. * * * Except for the last few months of his life L.S. Holden ran the business, but gradually accorded Warren more authority in the management area.

During his lifetime L.S. Holden made substantial gifts of CMC stock to his three children. The father also engineered a series of transactions by which Herle and Warren acquired additional stock from other family shareholders. [At the] time of the father's death July 3, 1955, he possessed 544 shares, Herle and Warren each then owning 2028 shares.

[The father's will] bequeathed 25 percent of his stock in CMC to Herle, 75 percent to Warren.

Herle * * * was extremely disappointed upon learning his father's will gave majority control of CMC to Warren. There followed several months of frequent discussions between the brothers during which Herle vainly explored possible courses which would make him an equal stockholder with Warren. The latter remained firm in his resolution not to relinquish control. The problem was compounded by the fact that [their mother,] Carmen elected to take her statutory dower interest in the estate instead of the share provided under terms of the will. This meant, among other things, if her dower interest was to be monetarily satisfied some method must be employed which would make cash available to the estate for that purpose.

[An accord was reached whereby] Melva received $42,510, Warren $26,924.73, and Carmen $56,060.66. Furthermore, 540 shares of CMC stock were passed by the estate to Carmen, which she then transferred to CMC in consideration of its agreement to pay her a total of $93,484.80 in five equal payments. The $26,924.73 check to Warren was apparently an adjustment for the fact that since the will left him with 272 shares more than Herle, an agreement had been reached which retired 540 shares. Consequently, Warren held 2031 shares, Herle 2029 shares.

Herle testified all of this was resolved between himself and Warren during a discussion early in 1956. That under this agreement (1) Herle consented to the arrangement giving Warren "control" of CMC (2) Herle promised to keep all of his

CMC stock, fulfill his contractual commitments to Carmen and Melva, and remain in CMC's employ; (3) Warren agreed in return that both of them would have employment with CMC of equal duration, and their compensation, salaries and bonuses, would always be the same. Warren denies any discussion regarding duration of employment or equal recompense.

After the father's death Warren became president of CMC and continued as general manager. Herle remained vice-president in charge of manufacturing. From 1955 through 1963 they received equal remuneration. There appears, however, to have been a noticeable deterioration in their relationship during that period of time.

In December 1960, the board of directors had been expanded to include five key employees, along with Warren and Herle. Active monthly meetings followed for a period of time. This regularity was discontinued by Warren not long after the board out-voted him regarding expansion of research and development facilities. Abandonment of the regular board meeting program served to deprive Herle of an appropriate forum in which he could, and often did, take issue with Warren.

In early 1964, CMC engaged Batten and Associates (Batten), a management consultant organization, to effect a survey of CMC's operations. Joe McBride was then working for Batten. The first report of that study (Batten I) was submitted April 22, 1964. Based upon problems there disclosed a second study was suggested and undertaken in mid-1964 primarily to (1) evaluate management personnel by tests and interviews, and (2) propose a plan of organization. Batten II was made available August 27, 1964. One of the major recommendations there advanced was that manufacturing be placed directly under Warren rather than Herle as in the past. It also suggested Herle retain responsibility only in the areas of purchasing and design engineering. In any event, the organizational formula proposed in Batten II was never followed. Warren shortly announced a plan putting Herle in charge of engineering only, with production, purchasing, industrial engineering, research and development being under Warren's control. The result was a further deterioration of the brothers' relationship.

Near the end of 1964, Warren paid himself a supplemental bonus of $1500 which Herle did not receive. When salaries were fixed for 1965, Warren got a $50 per month increase but Herle's pay remained at the 1964 level.

[Herle] became aware of the bonus and salary differential sometime after the first of the year 1965, and in March or April contacted Mr. Beecher, a Waterloo attorney, seeking advice concerning violation of his claimed equal compensation agreement * * * and other related problems. Beecher realized Herle's very substantial estate was "locked" in the minority interest of a closely held family corporation. A series of meetings followed among Warren, Herle and their respective attorneys. Mr. Beecher asserted Herle's claimed violation of an equal compensation agreement. Counsels' efforts were directed, however, toward possible solution of the larger overall problems. The relationship between Warren and Herle had then seriously deteriorated and they were communicating almost entirely through their attorneys and by memos passed or placed on the other's desk.

In June 1965, Joe McBride was hired as vice-president of operations, a position comparable to that held by Herle prior to Batten II. Herle was replaced as head of engineering and given the title vice-president in charge of corporate development with no management authority. Being no longer involved in operations he was not participating in meetings and discussions relative to CMC's operations, but continued to report for work regularly and attended those board meetings irregularly held.

In the spring of 1966 Herle was relieved of all duties and advised [that] a Stock Purchase Agreement which existed between him and CMC was being cancelled, as were life insurance policies on Herle's life, owned by CMC. Although then also told his salary was being reduced, this did not actually occur until later. Upon advice of counsel Herle continued to report for work but had nothing to do.

At the annual stockholders' meeting in early 1968, Herle was reelected to the board of directors, but not made an officer. In April 1968, came a letter from Mr. Hoxie, corporation secretary, proposing Herle's early retirement. This was effectuated by board action in late May. Herle was thereby allowed retirement compensation equivalent to half the average of his highest five years pay within the last ten years. That has continued to date. After Herle's forced retirement he was required to vacate his office, and allowed only limited access to restricted corporate records. * * *

* * *

* * * First to be considered is defendants' proposition to the effect [that the] trial court erroneously found for Herle regarding the Chamberlain [a local corporation] stock transaction. More specifically they take issue with the finding that such stock was purchased by Warren in 1959 as an investment on behalf of CMC, being thereafter held by him in constructive trust for the corporation.

The record reveals, while Warren was president of the Waterloo Chamber of Commerce in 1954, a successful Chamberlain stock subscription campaign was undertaken. Warren actively participated in that program. His election as a Chamberlain director followed.

In 1959, 2000 shares of Chamberlain stock, restricted to board members, were issued in Warren's name, but paid for by a $10,000 check from CMC. This transaction was shown on CMC books as a purchase of "Stock in Other Corporations", and so remained until 1964. Warren claims, on April 6 of that year he gave CMC his personal no-interest-note for $10,000. In any event, a journal voucher dated April 30, 1964, was then entered debiting "Secured Loans to Officers" account; crediting "Stock in Other Corporations" account for $10,000, with an explanatory memo reciting "to show transfer of 2000 shares common stock of CC (Chamberlain) to W.A. Holden. Note for $10,000 given CMC by W.A. Holden secured by 6500 shares Chamberlain Stock".

[Herle] alleges the Chamberlain stock was at all times an asset of CMC and the transfer to Warren in 1964 was for less than its fair value, thus a fraud on CMC.

In an attempt to support their opposing position defendants, and more particularly Warren, attempted to show (a) the transaction was first mistakenly entered upon CMC books as "Stock in Other Corporations"; (b) the 1964 paper transaction was merely a correction of an original error; (c) Warren gave CMC his personal note for $10,000 when the stock was purchased in 1959, and then delivered to Mr. Ries, head of CMC accounting department, a memo directing the transaction be recorded to show the $10,000 payment as a loan to Warren, both instruments being since lost; (d) purchase of the Chamberlain stock was at all times his personal investment.

The testimony with regard thereto is so intermittently protracted and involved as to preclude any summarization. We can do no more than observe that defense counsel endeavored to explain Warren's testimonial statements as being, even to them, a belatedly revealed and self-initiated reconstruction of past events effort on Warren's part. It still remains, however, [that] Warren's testimony on the subject at hand, and that of his quasi-corroborative associate, Leonard Ries, is so replete with inconsistent, improbable and paralogistic statements as to be of no evidential weight or value. * * *

* * *

* * * [The] corporate records disclose, and Herle established by a preponderance of evidence, in support of the instantly considered derivative action, [that] Warren breached his fiduciary duties as a corporate director of CMC. On that matter several well established legal principles come into full play.

> "Where it appears a corporate director is dealing on behalf of the corporation with another corporation of which he is also a director he is required to make a full disclosure and obtain the consent of all concerned. When it appears he has not done so the burden is on him to establish the good faith, honesty and fairness of the transaction * * *.

> "This rule and burden should also apply in dealings between directors who are stockholders, especially in a relatively small corporation in which the stock is closely held.'

> "Such director is not liable merely for failure to make full disclosure and to obtain consent but because the transaction is not in good faith, honest and fair." * * *

[In] *Gord v. Iowana Farms Milk Co.*, 245 Iowa at 16–17, 60 N.W.2d at 829, this court said:

> "And bearing upon the fiduciary relation of corporate directors and officers, * * * 'It is the policy of the courts to put such fiduciaries beyond the reach of temptation and the enticement of illicit profit. These principles are founded on the soundest morality and have received the clearest recognition in all courts'.

> "A director is required to act in the utmost good faith and not for his own personal interest. * * *

"And in *Hoyt v. Hampe*, 206 Iowa 206, 220, 214 N.W. 718, 724, * * * this court stated:" * * * 'The policy of the law is to put fiduciaries beyond the reach of temptation, by making it unprofitable for them to yield to it. To that end an act by the fiduciary in which personal interest and duty conflict is voidable at the mere option of the beneficiary, regardless of good faith or results. The court will not inquire into its profitableness to the trustee or prejudice to the beneficiary * * *. "

* * *

From all this flows the conclusion * * * [that] Warren must be held strictly accountable to CMC for the Chamberlain stock or its fair market value, and for all increases, income, proceeds or dividends realized therefrom.

* * *

* * * On cross-appeal Herle contends [the] trial court erred in holding exemplary damages were not allowable against Warren by reason of (1) his intentional acts of fraud in connection with the Chamberlain stock transaction, (2) his malicious attempt to "freeze" Herle out of CMC.

* * *

Ordinarily, actual damage must be established as a condition precedent to an allowance of punitive damages. * * *

On the other hand, in a stockholder's derivative action an equity court may, in its discretion, award exemplary damages upon a showing that some legally protected right has been invaded, such as an intentional act of fraud or other wrongful conduct. * * *

Turning now to the matter of Warren's alleged fraudulent conduct, trial court was:

> " * * * not sufficiently satisfied that an intentionally fraudulent act was committed in transferring the asset in April, 1964, the finding heretofore made being only that the transfer constituted a 'legal fraud' upon CMC. The fact that Warren might well have felt that he was entitled to the advantage of the CC (Chamberlain) stock transaction because his position as a board member made its original acquisition possible adds further to the Court's conclusion that exemplary damages should not be awarded for that act."

We cannot agree.

An intentional act of fraud, as the term is here used, does not mean actionable fraud or deceit. * * *

On the contrary, an intentional act of fraud in a court of equity includes all acts, omissions and concealments which involve a breach of either legal or equitable duties, trust or confidence, justly reposed, which are injurious to another or by which an undue or unconscionable advantage is taken. * * *

For reasons heretofore disclosed, we find Warren's acts and conduct embracing the entire Chamberlain transaction were dedicated to his own personal gain or advantage, to the detriment of CMC. In this regard the record reveals he, as managing president of the corporation, (1) personally engineered every phase of the Chamberlain deal, (2) appropriated to his own use all dividends issued upon the Chamberlain stock, (3) directed a falsification of corporate records and other documents when exposed by Herle's instant action, (4) aggravated the aforesaid deception by attempted use of a "reconstruction" stratagem which included the giving of his no-interest-note to CMC, absent board authorization, and (5) subsequently endeavored to impress upon the whole transaction a coloration of honesty by liquidating the no-interest-note prior to commencement of the trial of this case.

Also, as previously determined, Warren unquestionably did all in his power to isolate Herle from any rights or privileges pertaining to CMC management, even to the point of removing him from any corporate office, save as a director. This was patently a wrongful if not malicious "freeze-out".

In sum total the foregoing constituted conduct which * * * compels an assessment of exemplary damages.

We therefore reverse on this issue and direct that on remand trial court shall enter a $10,000 judgment against defendant, Warren A. Holden, in favor of defendant corporation, Construction Machinery Company.

* * *

* * * Defendants, more particularly Warren, have borrowed from CMC without board authorization, and squeezed Herle out of any effective corporate management activities. It may therefore be reasonably assumed, practices of like nature would be continued in the future if not enjoined. There is nothing in the record which can be said to indicate otherwise.

In any event, Herle established a sound premise upon which trial court acted within the ambit of its discretion in [granting an injunction ordering Warren not to engage in such conduct the future.] * * *

* * * By his petition Herle individually alleges:

> "In 1955, defendant Warren A. Holden, acting on behalf of defendant corporation and as controlling stockholder, made an oral agreement with plaintiff which by its terms, gave to plaintiff lifetime employment with defendant corporation. Said oral agreement further provided that the salary, bonuses and other compensation paid to plaintiff would always be equal to that paid to defendant Warren A. Holden."

Defendants, in resisting, first contend the asserted employment agreement was lacking in consideration and not sufficiently specific to permit a measure of damages, therefore invalid, unenforceable and terminable at the will of either party.

* * * [We have previously held that] extrinsic evidence may be admitted for the

limited purpose of interpreting any language or terms of a contract, and promise for promise creates a mutually legal duty, the breach thereof by one giving rise to a cause of action by the other.

[A case relevant on this point] is *LaFontaine v. Developers and Builders, Inc.*, 261 Iowa 1177, 156 N.W.2d 651 (1968). There the parties entered into a written installment agreement for the sale and purchase of corporate stock. Plaintiff-purchaser claimed he and defendant-seller simultaneously entered into an oral agreement by which the former was to be employed by the latter for the equivalent of 25 years. As in the instant case, the oral agreement was effected on behalf of defendant corporation by its managing president. Upholding plaintiff-employee's action for breach of contract we said, *261 Iowa at 1182–1183, 156 N.W.2d at 655*:

> "The parties are entitled to the benefit of that interpretation of their evidence, and of all reasonable inferences most favorable to their case, in an effort to prove the real intent of the parties to an agreement, and if reasonable minds may differ as to the conclusions to be drawn from that evidence, a question of fact exists. 'The existence of a contract, 'meeting of the minds', intention to assume an obligation, the understanding, is to be determined not alone from words used, but in the situation, acts, and conduct of the parties, and from their situation and the attending circumstances, and by the inferences which mankind would ordinarily and reasonably draw therefrom.' (Authorities cited)."

This court also aptly stated in LaFontaine, *261 Iowa at 1185–1186, 156 N.W.2d at 657*:

> "Equity courts will not hesitate to indulge in inferences which will avoid unfair or inequitable results. On this matter we have stated, ' * * * that an agreement will not be construed so as to give one party an unfair, oppressive or inequitable advantage over the other, that unless the terms of the contract clearly require it, an interpretation will not be given which places one party at the mercy of the other, that courts will endeavor to give the contract that interpretation most equitable to the parties, * * * .' * * *

* * *

As previously disclosed, L.S. Holden's will served to give Warren 75 percent and Herle 25 percent of all CMC stock held by the father at time of his death. Repeated discussions followed between Herle and Warren. The former was bent upon an equalization of stock holdings, the latter being resolutely determined to retain majority control. In other words corporate control was at stake. After several stormy months had passed an agreement was formulated by which Warren was permitted to have two more shares of stock than Herle. At the same time Herle was promised employment with CMC of the same duration and with compensation equal to that enjoyed by Warren. * * *

Surely defendants cannot successfully contend the agreement between Warren and Herle, sole CMC stockholders, was not made and entered into on behalf of the corporation. Unquestionably, the rising tension between Warren and Herle posed a threat to efficient corporate operations, if not to its very existence. Thus the employment agreement was ultimately, albeit arduously, reached with the common thought that such was beneficial to CMC, a closely held corporation. * * *

The record also discloses that from 1956, date of the subject agreement, through 1963, the brothers did receive equal compensation. Under these circumstances it appears all parties here concerned accorded full recognition to the agreement until it was breached in 1964. * * *

* * *

Trial court found Herle entitled to affirmative relief and judgment should be entered in his favor against CMC for the amount of variance in compensation received by Herle and Warren from 1964 to date of the decree, with interest. * * *

* * * June 24, 1970, the [trial] court * * * ordered that the first of each year, commencing January 1971, and continuing for the life of the employment period, plaintiff be required to file a verified statement of earnings for personal services, including those received from CMC, and that the corporation likewise file verified statements regarding all compensation paid to Warren. If either party disputed the verified statements, request for hearing could be made. Also, in such event, if CMC contended Herle had not exercised reasonable diligence in finding other employment of the same general character it should thereupon file an appropriate pleading, the burden of proof being then on CMC to prove its contention by a preponderance of the evidence. Judgment is to be entered accordingly.

In resisting this decree defendants assert there is no precedent for same. We find that argument nonpersuasive.

"Wherever a situation exists which is contrary to the principles of equity and which can be redressed within the scope of judicial action, a court of equity will devise a remedy to meet the situation, though no similar relief has been given before." McClintock on Equity, § 29 at 76 (2d ed. 1948). * * *

Furthermore, mere difficulty in ascertaining and measuring damages does not alone constitute a cause for denial of recovery. * * *

We are satisfied trial court equitably tailored the relief accorded to the exigent circumstances peculiar to this case. * * *

* * * Countering, defendants take the position all compensatory relief is precluded because Herle's conduct was hostile to CMC's interests and was a breach of the employment agreement, all of which constituted a good cause for his discharge.

Unquestionably a corporate officer, employee or agent is required to obey all reasonable rules, orders and instructions issued by the employer and to at all times act in the best interests of the corporation. * * *

The record here discloses:

(1) In 1964 Warren breached the employment agreement;

(2) at all times prior to January 1, 1965, Herle efficiently performed all work assigned him at CMC in such manner as to give no cause for his discharge;

(3) to the extent Herle may have precipitated any disagreements or contributed to disunity between himself and Warren prior to January 1, 1965, he was acting reasonably as an officer, director and holder of a 49.98 percent interest in the corporation;

(4) Warren's violation of the equal compensation agreement in 1964 and 1965 invited and provoked any absence of work efficiency by Herle;

(5) regardless of Warren's violation of the employment agreement, Herle continued to report for work and performed acceptably until placed on early retirement and directed to vacate his office in 1968; and

(6) Warren was at all times the dominant personality, his actions were adverse to Herle's and CMC's best interests as is well demonstrated by the "freeze-out" tactics employed by Warren and his co-defendants.

The burden was on defendants to prove the alleged justification for Herle's discharge and removal from any corporate position. * * * They failed to meet or carry that burden.

Moreover, there was no such conduct on Herle's part which justified his arbitrary removal as a CMC officer or employee.

We hereby affirm (1) trial court's judgment in favor of Herle against CMC in the sum of $86,742.38 as the amount owing for compensation due him from 1964 to April 3, 1970; (2) trial court's in futuro judgment with jurisdiction retained to annually determine and adjudicate the compensation owing to Herle by CMC in accord with the employment agreement and applicable standards. * * *

* * *

Total Of All Reasonable Attorneys' Fees And Expenses Incurred By Said Defendants In Connection With The Trial Of This Case And Appeal Here Taken.

We affirm trial court in holding the individual defendants are entitled to indemnification from CMC for reasonable attorneys' fees and expenses incurred in defense of Herle's nonderivative action, but modify as to the basis upon which computation was effected, and remand for further proceedings.

* * *

NOTES AND QUESTIONS

I. THIS CASE IS PRIMARILY offered at this point in the text for what it teaches us about what is usually referred to as the "duty of loyalty," but it raises two other issues, one of which, the nature of closely held corporations, that we will treat in a subsequent chapter, and another, the nature of derivative lawsuits, which is often a subject in corporations casebooks, and which we encountered in the *Elf Atochem* case, in Chapter Two.

Do you understand what a "derivative lawsuit" is? Generally speaking, it is one brought in the name of the corporation, by a shareholder, in order to recover for damages done to the corporation. Whether to allow such a lawsuit is discretionary with the court, in the exercise of its equitable powers. Usually, if there is any recovery in a derivative lawsuit it goes to the corporation, although the court has the discretion to allow attorney's fees to the plaintiff-shareholder who brings the lawsuit, and the court may, in some limited circumstances, allow "pro-rata recovery" to go directly to the plaintiff shareholder/s where there is a likelihood that if there is full recovery by the corporation wrongdoers controlling the corporation will misappropriate the funds or be wrongly rewarded for their misconduct. See, e.g., Richard A. Booth, "Derivative Suits and Pro Rata Recovery," 61 Geo. Wash. L. Rev. 1274 (1993), and Note, Individual Pro Rata Recovery in Stockholders' Derivative Suits, 69 Harv. L. Rev. 1314 (1956).

There is a disagreement among lawyers, courts, and commentators about whether the derivative lawsuit really is a useful tool to police officer, director, or majority shareholder misconduct, or whether it actually does more harm than good because it encourages "strike suits," litigation brought for the purpose of compelling a settlement favorable to plaintiff or plaintiff's lawyers, settlements that, because of indemnity provisions, may end up being paid out of the corporate treasury. There is also controversy about (1) whether shareholders should be required to make a demand on the directors or other shareholders to deal with the problem before actually bringing a derivative lawsuit (particularly in closely held corporations), (2) which shareholders can bring such suits, (3) whether incumbent managers or board members should be able to decide to intervene to seek dismissal of derivative lawsuits on the grounds that they are not brought in the best interest of the corporation, and (4) precisely what procedures ought to be followed in seeking such a dismissal. For further reading on the debate over derivative lawsuits, see, e.g., *Ross v. Bernhard*, 396 U.S. 531, 90 S.Ct. 733, 24 L.Ed.2d 729 (1970).

There is no doubt that the topic of shareholder derivative lawsuits is one of the most complex in corporate law, but those subtle complexities need not concern us here, other than to try and understand why the court in *Holden v. Construction Machinery Co.*, indicates that some of the plaintiff's claims are derivative in nature and some are "individual" in nature. A shareholder's claim that he or she suffers a particular injury apart from an injury done to the corporation as an entity is an "individual" claim, and, of course, requires no exercise of court discretion or demand on the directors before it may be heard. To avoid the procedural hurdles of a derivative suit, plaintiffs often try to get their claims characterized as "individual" or "direct" (which means the same thing) rather than "derivative." In 12B W. Fletcher, *Cyclopedia of the Law of Private Corporations* section 5911 (rev. perm. ed. 1984), a leading authority, the author indicates that a given action is a derivative one, one enforcing a corporate right, "if the gravamen of the complaint is injury to the corporation, or to the whole body of its stock or property without any severance or distribution among individual holders." "A direct action," on the other hand, "can be brought either when there is a special duty, such as a contractual duty, between the wrongdoer and the shareholder, or when the shareholder suffers injury separate and distinct from that suffered by other shareholders." *Sax v. World Wide Press, Inc.*, 809 F.2d 610, 614 (9th Cir. 1987), citing Fletcher, supra. Do you understand which aspects of the lawsuit brought by Herle Holden are characterized as "direct" or "individual" claims, and which are characterized as "derivative?" Do you understand how Herle's lawsuit spotlights potential problems in the small, closely held corporation?

. . . .

2. HERLE SUGGESTED THAT Warren breached the fiduciary duty of loyalty that Warren owed to the corporation. How exactly did Warren do so? What is the standard for evaluating a claim that a director or officer has breached his duty of loyalty because of self-dealing? The case you have just read is a common-law case, but this is a matter dealt with in many jurisdictions by statute, although the statutes tend not really to depart from the common law rules. An excellent such case of purported director/officer self-dealing is *Cookies Food Products v. Lakes Warehouse*, 430 N.W.2d 447 (Iowa 1988). That was a derivative action brought against a majority shareholder of Cookies Food Products, Duane "Speed" Herrig, and two of his family owned corporations, Lakes Warehouse Distributing, Inc. and Speed's Automotive Co., Inc. Herrig had used his control of the board of directors of Cookies to engage in contracts with his family-owned corporations in order to store and market Cookies' principal products, barbecue and taco sauce. Herrig had turned Cookies Food Products from a failing business into an enormously profitable enterprise, although the deals with his family-owned corporations were also quite profitable to Herrig. Worse, in spite of the profits that inured to Cookies, no money had been paid out in dividends to other shareholders because of restrictions in the financing agreement Cookies had with the Small Business Administration. The minority shareholder plaintiffs sought to argue in their derivative suit that Herrig's large personal profits were "unfair," that they breached his fiduciary duty to the corporation, and that the difference between the fair market value of his and his family corporations' services and what the Cookies Food Products Corporation actually paid to Herrig and his corporations ought to be recovered by the Corporation, presumably for eventual distribution to all the shareholders. The relevant rule was that specified by the Iowa Corporate Code Section 496A.34, quoted by the Court in pertinent part:

> No contract or other transaction between a corporation and one or more of its directors or any other corporation, firm, association or entity in which one or more of its directors are directors or officers or are financially interested, shall be either void or voidable because of such relationship or interest . . . if any of the following occur:
>
> 1. The fact of such relationship or interest is disclosed or known to the board of directors or committee which authorizes, approves, or ratifies the contract or transaction . . . without counting the votes . . . of such interested director.
>
> 2. The fact of such relationship or interest is disclosed or known to the shareholders entitled to vote [on the transaction] and they authorize . . . such contract or transaction by vote or written consent.
>
> 3. The contract or transaction is fair and reasonable to the corporation.

Applying this statute, the court in Cookies Food Products decided that there had been full disclosure as required by paragraph (1) of 496A.34 (even though the precise amount of the profits to Herrig were not revealed), but that since Herrig controlled the Board and was the majority shareholder, though he might avoid the statutory possibility of having the transaction made voidable, he still had the burden of proving the transaction fair to the corporation. As the court put it, indicating that the statute was not intended to change the common law fiduciary duty of directors, "We * * * require directors who engage in self-dealing to establish the additional element that they have acted in good faith, honesty and fairness." *Id.*, at 452–453. The majority of the court affirmed the trial court's determination that because of Herrig's nearly superhuman efforts to render the corporation profitable he had demonstrated that his self-dealing was fair to the corporation. The dissent, evaluating the same evidence, thought that the trial court had improperly discounted testimony which suggested that Herrig and his corporations had charged more than was fair. There seemed also to be an implication in the dissenting opinion that Herrig had failed to meet his burden of proof by demonstrating that any profits he had received were not unreasonable. Is *Cookies Food Products* an easier or harder case than *Holden v. Construction Machinery Co.?*

3. YOU MAY HAVE DISCERNED, by now, that there are essentially four aspects, requirements, or tests to be employed in the determination of whether the duty of loyalty has been violated, and a transaction should therefore be set aside or damages should be collected. They are:

(1) The duty fully to disclose the fact of a conflict of interest, as well as the material facts regarding the transaction that may be known to the person with the conflict of interest, but may not be known to the corporation.

(2) The requirement that the transaction be approved by a disinterested corporate decision-maker, such as a disinterested majority of the board, or a disinterested majority of the shareholders, or perhaps a corporate official or outside advisors specifically designated for the purpose.

(3) The requirement that the transaction be fair to the corporation.

(4) That if the requirements of (1) and (2) are met, the burden of proving that the transaction does not meet the requirement of (3) is on any party challenging the transaction, while if the requirement of (2) is not met, the burden is on the party with the conflict of interest to prove the transaction fair. It is fairly common for courts reviewing transactions involving a conflict of interest to find that if the requirements of (1) are not met, this means that the transaction should be deemed not to meet the requirements of (3). In other words, it is inherently unfair if there is a failure to disclose.

If you were drafting a statute to cover matters of director or officer conflict of interest, what additional requirements would you impose, or what additional determinations would you suggest?

No doubt you have also realized that the interested director or officer transaction (the problem in Cookies Food Products, and to some extent, at least, the problem in *Holden v. Construction Machinery Co.*) is not the only factual situation that may give rise to conflict of interest problems. The most notable other such situations are the taking of a "corporate opportunity" by an officer or director (see, e.g., *Klinicki v. Lundren*, 298 Or. 662, 695 P.2d 906 (Or. 1985)), the setting of executive compensation (see, e.g., *Lewis v. Vogelstein*, 699 A.2d 327 (Del. Ch. 1997)), and the sale of a controlling interest in the corporation (see, e.g., *Perlman v. Feldmann*, 219 F.2d 173 (2nd Cir. 1955), cert. den. 349 U.S. 952, 75 S.Ct. 880, 99 L.Ed. 1277 (1955)). Perhaps because of the difficulty of proving a violation of the duty of loyalty pursuant to state corporate law, there has been a felt need to supplement the state law rules of self-dealing with federal ones, to which we will soon turn.

V. Note on "The Duty to Act in Good Faith": The *Disney* Case

The nature and scope of the fiduciary duties of directors and officers of Delaware corporations was somewhat amplified and clarified by the Delaware Supreme Court's important opinion, *In re The Walt Disney Company Derivative Litigation*, 906 A.2d 27 (2006). The case arose out of the hiring and relatively rapid firing of Disney President Michael Ovitz. Ovitz, one of the top talent agents in Hollywood, was brought in by Disney Chairman Michael Eisner, a friend of Ovitz. Ovitz had been earning around $20 million per year in his position at the agency he headed before assuming the Disney job. When Ovitz was hired, the stock of Disney, which had formerly been passing through a troubled period, shot up approximately $1 billion in value.

Ovitz's employment agreement with Disney stipulated that if he were fired by Disney without cause he was entitled to a substantial severance payment. Unfortunately, Ovitz seems to have had some difficulty adapting to the "Disney Culture," and he eventually fell out with his former friend Eisner, and Eisner eventually terminated Ovitz's employment fourteen months after he had been hired. Disney's lawyers could find no legal cause to support this termination, which triggered the severance pay provisions of Ovitz's employment agreement, resulting in an eventual payout to him of more than $130 million. This was, at the time, the highest such payment ever recorded in the corporate world, and a number of Disney's stockholders sued the directors and officers, alleging that they had breached their fiduciary duties both in acquiescing in such a lucrative severance arrangement for Ovitz, and in failing to determine a "cause" to fire Ovitz and avoid this payment. The Supreme Court of Delaware, affirming an earlier decision by the Delaware Chancellor, rejected the stockholders' argument and held that there was no breach of fiduciary duty.

The Court began by noting the "presumptions that cloak director action" under the business judgment rule. Said the Court, "Our law presumes that 'in making a business decision the directors of a corporation acted on an informed basis, in good faith, and in the honest belief that the action taken was in the best interests of the company.' " 906 A.2d, at 52. The Court went on to observe that "Those presumptions can be rebutted if the plaintiff shows that the directors breached their fiduciary duty of care or of loyalty or acted in bad faith. If that is shown, the burden then shifts to the director defendants to demonstrate that the challenged act or transaction was entirely fair to the corporation and its shareholders." *Ibid*. Quoting from its earlier decision in *Brehm v. Eisner*, 746 A.2d 244, 264, n. 66 (Del. 2000) the Court remarked in a footnote that "Thus, directors' decisions will be respected by courts unless the directors are interested or lack independence relative to the decision, do not act in good faith, act in a manner that cannot be attributed to a rational business purpose or reach their decision by a grossly negligent process that includes the failure to consider all material facts reasonably available." *Ibid*. Note 62.

The Court took special note of the provisions of Section 102 (b) (7) of the Delaware Corporate Code, which, as indicated earlier, was passed in the wake of the *Smith v. Van Gorkom* decision. To reiterate, that Section provides, in pertinent part, that Delaware corporations may place in their charter "A provision eliminating or limiting the personal liability of a director to the corporation or its stockholders for monetary damages for breach of fiduciary duty as a director, provided that such provision shall not eliminate or limit the liability of a director: (i) For any breach of the director's duty of loyalty to the corporation or its stockholders; (ii) for acts or omissions not in good faith or which involve intentional misconduct or a knowing violation of law . . . or (iv) for any transaction from which the director derived an improper personal benefit. . . . " (emphasis supplied).

Disney had placed a provision of the type authorized by 102(b)(7) in its charter, and the real question in the case was whether the directors or officers had forfeited the liability shield of 102(b)(7) because they had failed to act with "good faith," in their transactions with Eisner. Ovitz's compensation arrangement had been approved by a committee of the Board, to which the other members of the Board deferred. This was fine, said the Delaware Supreme court, as the committee or at least some of its members spent a significant amount of time discussing the question of appropriate compensation and even retained an expert to help in that determination. Furthermore, the Compensation Committee was well aware that Ovitz had left "a very lucrative and secure position" at his talent agency, where he had been a controlling partner, "to join a publicly held corporation to which Ovitz was a stranger, and that had a very different culture and an environment which prevented him from completely controlling his destiny." *Id.*, at 57–58. The Court further observed that "The committee members knew that by leaving [his talent agency] and coming to Disney, Ovitz would be sacrificing 'booked' [agency] commissions of $150 to $200 million—an amount that Ovitz demanded as protection against the risk that his employment relationship with Disney might not work out." *Id.*, at 58. This suggested that the financial arrangement the Board had approved for Ovitz was reasonable under the circumstances, and this appeared to be, to the Delaware Supreme Court, evidence of the "good faith" of the Board.

The Supreme Court, for the first time in Delaware Jurisprudence, appeared to make clear that the duty to act in "good faith" of the Officers and Board could be viewed as a third obligation in addition to the two other fiduciary duties of Care and Loyalty. The Court proceeded to define "good faith," quoting a definition previously offered by the Chancellor for the absence of good faith. This was "the concept of intentional dereliction of duty, a conscious disregard for one's responsibilities. . . . Deliberate indifference and inaction in the face of a duty to act is, in my mind, conduct that is clearly disloyal to the corporation. It is the epitome of faithless conduct." *Id.*, at 62. (Is there a clear difference between the duty of good faith and the duty of loyalty?). The Court indicated that there was a wealth of scholarship recently published on the purported duty of "good faith," citing, in its footnote 99, *Id.*, at 64, "See, e.g., Hillary A. Sale, *Delaware's Good Faith*, 89 Cornell L. Rev. 456 (2004); Matthew R. Berry, *Does Delaware's Section 102(b)(7) Protect Reckless Directors From Personal Liability? Only if Delaware Courts Act in Good Faith*, 79 Wash. L. Rev. 1125 (2004); John L. Reed and Matt Neiderman, *Good Faith and the Ability of Directors to Assert § 102(b)(7) of the Delaware Corporation Law as a Defense to Claims Alleging Abdication, Lack of Oversight, and Similar Breaches of Fiduciary Duty,* 29 DEL. J. CORP. L. 111 (2004); David Rosenberg, *Making Sense of Good Faith in Delaware Corporate Fiduciary Law: A Contractarian Approach,* 29 DEL. J. CORP. L. 491 (2004); Sean J. Griffith, *Good Faith Business Judgment: A Theory of Rhetoric in Corporate Law Jurisprudence,* 55 Duke L. J. 1 (2005) . . . Melvin A. Eisenberg, *The Duty of Good Faith in Corporate Law,* 31 DEL. J. CORP. L. 1 (2005); Filippo Rossi, *Making Sense of the Delaware Supreme Court's Triad of Fiduciary Duties* (June 22, 2005), available at http://ssrn.com/abstract=755784; Christopher M. Bruner, *"Good Faith," State of Mind, and the Outer Boundaries of Director Liability in Corporate Law* (Boston Univ. Sch. of Law Working Paper No. 05–19), available at http://ssrn.com/abstract=832944; Sean J. Griffith & Myron T. Steele, *On Corporate Law Federalism Threatening the Thaumatrope,* 61 Bus. LAW. 1 (2005)," all of which might be consulted by anyone wishing further to research the topic.

Still, the Court recognized that "to date" the duty of good faith "is not a well-developed area of our corporate fiduciary law," and "the duty to act in good faith is, up to this point relatively uncharted." *Id.,* at 64. Indeed, the Court stated that the Chancellor, in the opinion below, "observed, after surveying the sparse case law on the subject, that both the meaning and the contours of the duty to act in good faith were 'shrouded in the fog of . . . hazy jurisprudence." *Id.,* at 64, note 98. Trying to remove the fog, the Delaware Supreme Court declared that there were actually three different categories that had been discerned in Delaware jurisprudence on the duty of good faith.

"The first category," said the Court, "involves so-called 'subjective bad faith,' that is, fiduciary conduct motivated by an actual intent to do harm. That such conduct constitutes classic, quintessential bad faith is a proposition so well accepted in the liturgy of fiduciary law that it borders on axiomatic." *Id.,* at 64. (But does this actually sound more like the Duty of Loyalty, rather than the Duty to Act in Good Faith?) Continuing, the Court stated that "The second category of conduct, which is at the opposite end of the spectrum, involves lack of due care—that is, fiduciary action taken solely by reason of gross negligence and without any malevolent intent." *Ibid.* (But is this, then, strictly speaking, a matter of "good faith," or really a question of whether the requisite Duty of Care has been met?). In any event, the Delaware Supreme Court seemed to reject this purported Second category as actually relevant to the inquiry into good faith. Commenting on what the Chancellor below had found, the Court stated: "Although the Chancellor found, and we agree, that the appellants failed to establish gross negligence, to afford guidance we address the issue of whether gross negligence (including a failure to inform one's self of available material facts), without more, can also constitute bad faith. The answer is clearly no." *Id.,* at 64–65.

Having then rejected the second category, the Court observed that "That leaves the third category of fiduciary conduct, which falls in between the first two categories of (1) conduct motivated by subjective bad intent and (2) conduct resulting from gross negligence. This third category is what the Chancellor's definition of bad faith—

intentional dereliction of duty, a conscious disregard for one's responsibilities—is intended to capture." *Id.*, at 66. (Is it now clear to you what is required by the Duty to Act in Good Faith?) Surely this is something less than a model of clarity, and perhaps that explains why the Supreme Court went on once again to quote the Chancellor below, "The good faith required of a corporate fiduciary includes not simply the duties of care and loyalty . . . but all actions required by a true faithfulness and devotion to the interests of the corporation and its shareholders." *Id.*, at 67. (Do you recall anything written by Benjamin Cardozo on fiduciary duty that sounds similar?) Further quoting from the Chancellor, the Delaware Supreme Court observed that "A failure to act in good faith may be shown, for instance, [1] where the fiduciary intentionally acts with a purpose other than that of advancing the best interests of the corporation, [2] where the fiduciary acts with the intent to violate applicable positive law, or [3] where the fiduciary intentionally fails to act in the face of a known duty to act, demonstrating a conscious disregard for his duties. There may be other examples of bad faith yet to be proven or alleged, but these three are the most salient." *Ibid.* (Now can you distinguish the Duty to Act in Good Faith from the Duty of Loyalty and the Duty of Care?).

The plaintiffs in the Disney case had also argued that the Directors and Officers who approved the generous severance package for Mr. Ovitz had engaged in "waste" of corporate assets. The Delaware Supreme Court rather summarily rejected that claim. Said the Court, "To recover on a claim of corporate waste, the plaintiffs must shoulder the burden of proving that the exchange was 'so one sided that no business person of ordinary, sound judgment could conclude that the corporation has received adequate consideration.' " *Id.*, at 74. The Court continued by stating that "A claim of waste will arise only in the rare, 'unconscionable case where directors irrationally squander or give away corporate assets.' " *Ibid.* (You have seen unconscionability before, in a contracts context. Is this like that?) The Court concluded by stating that "This onerous standard for waste is a corollary of the proposition that where business judgment presumptions are applicable, the board's decision will be upheld unless it cannot be 'attributed to any rational business purpose.' " *Ibid.* Since it was rational to believe that Ovitz could not have been persuaded to leave his talent agency without a substantial severance package, the Court decided, there was no "waste" and the plaintiffs were entitled to no relief.

Smith v. Van Gorkom was clearly a case where the Supreme Court of Delaware imposed a rigid requirement that the Board be fully informed before it acted, and many believed that the Court had substituted its business judgment for that of the Board. What do you suppose the Court was doing in Disney?

FEDERAL LAW REGARDING DUTIES TO SHAREHOLDERS

I. Introduction To Federal Securities Regulation[1]

SPECULATION IN SECURITIES has existed for centuries. The history of eighteenth-century England, for example, is filled with economic booms and busts linked directly to securities trading. Thus for centuries have governments attempted to regulate the trading of these investment products; such efforts became even more important as the corporation became the dominant force in economic life around the turn of the twentieth century. In the United States, securities regulation was originally a matter of state law. These state provisions, known as "blue sky laws,"[2] were concerned with stopping fraud in securities sales. While these laws still exist, most attention is now paid to the dominant arena of securities regulation, that of federal law and the U.S. Securities and Exchange Commission (SEC).

Questions about the efficacy of these state laws abounded, and calls for federal intervention in the securities market grew in volume. Even so, no permanent federal

---

1 Information in this section was drawn from numerous sources. *See* GARY M. BROWN, SECURITIES LAW AND PRACTICE DESKBOOK (Practising Law Institute, 2013); THOMAS LEE HAZEN, SECURITIES REGULATION 1–22 (2011).

2 Various explanations for this colloquial term exist: some claim it refers to unscrupulous securities vendors selling "everything but the blue sky."

legislation was passed in the wake of several stock market crashes throughout the late nineteenth and early twentieth centuries. The great crash of 1929 provided the incentive for significant federal action, although it had to wait for Franklin D. Roosevelt's election and inauguration (in 1932 and 1933, respectively). Almost immediately after his inauguration, Roosevelt began pressing for significant securities legislation. After some initial drafting, Roosevelt appointed his friend and future Supreme Court justice Felix Frankfurter to lead a team in completing the legislation which would become the Securities Act of 1933.

The Securities Act of 1933 and the Securities Exchange Act of 1934 are creatures of the New Deal, reflecting a shift away from *laissez faire* attitudes towards a growing acceptance of government regulation of the markets. Roosevelt's express goal in passing the legislation was spurring the economy via increased investor confidence in the securities of the companies they were purchasing. Put simply, the 1933 Act regulates primary markets, concerned with the initial offering of securities to the public, while the 1934 Act regulates secondary markets, the trading in securities that occur after an initial offering. Both statutes are still in force today, with some amendments, and are explored in the following article.

ARTICLE: THE SECURITIES ACT

A Historical Introduction to the Securities Act of 1933 and the Securities Exchange Act of 1934

Elizabeth Keller and Gregory A. Gehlmann, 49 Оню Sт. L.J. 329 (1988).

* * *

THE GENERAL PURPOSE of the Securities Act is to regulate the initial distribution of securities by issuers to public investors. The Act compels the filing of a registration statement for securities sold through the instrumentalities of interstate commerce or the mails. The goal of registration is the full disclosure of truthful information regarding the character of the securities offered to the public. The Exchange Act provides for the regulation of the securities exchange markets and the operations of the corporations listed on the various national securities exchanges (such as the New York and American stock exchanges). The Exchange Act also created the federal agency in charge of securities regulation, the Securities and Exchange Commission.

* * *

While promises of 'getting rich quick' were made to investors, the typical offering circular prior to 1933 contained little of the information needed to estimate the worth of a security. A circular usually included 'very little information as to the use of the proceeds, a rather brief description of the securities themselves, and very few if any material facts relating to the business of the issuer.' The public, however, was caught up in a current of optimistic speculation. * * * Accounts of the swindles and fraudulent practices perpetrated on the public, including bankers and other businessmen, were numerous. For example, George Graham Rice defrauded investors of over $200,000,000 through the sale of securities for bogus corporations. Rice 'touted the stock of Idaho Copper, a corporation which he formed. He had its stock listed on the Boston Curb. Its property consisted of a water-filled, abandoned mine, the entrance to which was so overgrown that the federal investigators had difficulty locating it.' He later wrote a book entitled *My Adventures with Your*

Money, dedicated 'to the American Damphool Speculator, surnamed the American Sucker, otherwise described herein as The Thinker, Who Thinks He knows But He Doesn't—Greetings!'

* * *

The opening gun in the campaign to enact securities regulation was sounded by President Roosevelt in his message to Congress in March 1933. He recommended 'legislation for Federal supervision of traffic in investment securities in interstate commerce.' This legislation was not to be construed as a guarantee 'that newly issued securities are sound in the sense that their value will be maintained or that the properties which they represent will earn profit.' The major safeguard was to be full disclosure of information to the potential buyer. The aim was to be 'full publicity and information, and that no essentially important element attending the issue shall be concealed from the buying public.' Roosevelt asserted that his proposal adds to the ancient rule of caveat emptor, the further doctrine 'let the seller beware."

The principle underlying Roosevelt's regulatory philosophy had been expressed earlier by Brandeis in his book, Other People's Money. He wrote, 'publicity is justly commended as a remedy for social and industrial diseases. Sunlight is said to be the best of disinfectants; electric light the most efficient policeman . . . The potent force of publicity must . . . be utilized in many ways as a continuous remedial measure.'

* * *

III. Key Provisions Of The Securities Act of 1933 and the Securities Exchange Act of 1934 as Originally Enacted

A. The Securities Act of 1933

Despite various conflicting viewpoints, the drafters produced a bill with an underlying policy of disclosure through registration of securities unless the securities

or the transaction are exempt. * * * The drafters of the Act were concerned primarily with providing adequate information to potential purchasers and holding those filing the registration statement liable for any misstatements or omissions.

The Securities Act is designed to regulate the new issuing of securities by any issuer. A corporation cannot use the mails or instruments of interstate and foreign commerce to sell or offer to sell a security before it files with the Commission the appropriate registration statement, and includes the prospectus relating to the security to which a registration statement applies, unless it complies with the requirements of the Act.

* * *

A part of the registration statement is the prospectus. Section 10 of the Securities Act prescribes what shall be included in every prospectus used in the sale of securities over which the Commission has jurisdiction. Again, the purpose of this section is to give potential buyers an effective means to understand the intricacies of the transaction in which they are asked to invest.

* * *

The informational requirements of the registration statement are set forth in section 7 of the Securities Act. Over thirty-two items concerning the corporation and its finances are required to be included in the statement. The registration statement provides information to the prospective buyer and supplies a foundation for civil liability for false or misleading information.

* * *

The registration statement does not become effective until the twentieth day after it is filed, and any amendment to the statement will trigger another twenty day period. The twenty day waiting period was not merely an administrative provision; the drafters were concerned with high pressure sales techniques inducing stock purchases before the purchaser could adequately review the securities' merit. In addition to giving the Commission time to review the registration statement, the waiting period serves as a 'cooling-off' period, allowing investors time to examine the statements and make informed decisions. The Commission, although not making a merit review, can refuse to allow the statement to become effective until the proper amendments to cure any inaccuracies are completed. Additionally, the Commission, at any time after filing, can suspend a registration statement if the statement contains 'any untrue statement of a material fact required to be stated therein or necessary to make the statement therein not misleading.'

Although full and fair disclosure has been the cornerstone of the Securities Act, the drafters realized they needed additional weapons to ensure successful regulation. The Act imposes criminal liability on anyone who: (1) attempts to sell a security prior to filing a registration statement; (2) transmits a prospectus related to a security that does not comply with the Act; or (3) makes any misrepresentation to a prospective purchaser contrary to the provisions of the Act. These criminal penalties are only partially effective because injured investors are not compensated and prosecution is difficult.

Civil sanctions included in both the Acts effectively complete federal regulation, enabling injured investors to recover lost funds. In adopting the federal securities laws, Congress recognized that private actions for damages could play an important role in assuring compliance. Although there was some opposition to the civil liability sections, the atmosphere in 1933 was not conducive to restraint.

* * *

Liability arising out of the filing of a registration statement is predicated on an untrue statement of a material fact or on an omission of a material fact that was necessary in order to make other statements not misleading. Various individuals, including every person who signs the registration statement, every director, every expert preparing the registration statement, and every underwriter, are jointly and severally liable. Section 11 acts as an '*in terrorem*' remedy to deter violations by encouraging careful preparations.

* * *

To recover, the purchaser need only establish that the assertion or assertions in the registration statement omitted material information required to be included. At common law there is no duty to disclose all information in an arm's length relationship; however, 'a duty to speak may arise from partial disclosure, so that the speaker, although not under a duty to speak, has a duty to tell the whole truth if he does speak.'

The liability of the issuer for violations of section 11 of the Securities Act is almost absolute. The issuer's only two defenses available are that the purchaser knew the statement was not true at the time of the sale or that the statute of limitations has run. Individual defendants are treated differently. In addition to the defenses available to the issuer, individual defendants are not liable if they can prove one or all of the following: (1) reliance on experts as to that section of the statement; (2) reasonable investigation and reasonable grounds for belief, and belief that the registration statement was true, complete, and not misleading; or (3) that the part of the registration statement sued on was allegedly made by an official person or is extracted from an official document and the defendant had reason to believe it was not misleading and fairly represented the statement made by the official.

* * *

Section 12 imposes liability on any person who sells a security in violation of section 5 or sells a security by means of 'a prospectus or oral communication, which includes an untrue statement of material fact or omits to state a material fact necessary in order to make the statements, in light of the circumstances under which they were made, not misleading . . ."

* * *

When a prospectus or registration statement is in violation of the Securities Act, anyone who purchases a security can rescind the transaction or sue to recover damages if the purchaser has sold the security. The purchaser must bring an action within one year of discovery of the untrue statement or within one year of when the untrue statement should reasonably have been discovered. In any event no suit may be brought under sections 11 or 12(2) of the Securities Act three years after the security was offered to the public.

B. The Securities Exchange Act of 1934

The many complexities and inadequacies of the Securities Act and the need for an independent administrative body to enforce the federal securities laws, regulate stock market practices, and curb the evils in the stock exchanges themselves led Congress to enact the Securities Exchange Act of 1934. * * *

The Exchange Act intended to reach various exchange abuses: notably speculation and market manipulation. The most common forms of speculation are short selling and margin trading. A short sale 'is made when a trader sells on the market shares of stock he does not . . . own, but . . . expects to acquire later when the market price shall reach a lower level.' In order to meet the delivery requirements, the seller 'borrows through his broker the requisite number of shares from another broker.' The seller then 'covers' by purchasing the shares in the market, hopefully at a lower price. Margin trading 'involves the process by which a portion of the capital required by a customer in buying or in selling short any given number of shares of stock is supplied by loans made to him by the broker.' Although speculation in certain circumstances is acceptable, the deliberate efforts of a dishonest trader to artificially raise or lower the price of a particular security to make profits at the expense of the investing public is not allowed.

Section 10(a) of the Exchange Act addresses short sales, prohibiting such sales except those in accordance with such rules and regulations as the Commission may deem 'necessary or appropriate in the public interest or for the protection of investors.' Similarly, margin trading is effectively regulated by section 7(a), preventing 'excessive use of credit in purchasing or carrying securities.' Speculation is further limited as capital requirements prevent brokers from extending 'excessive

amounts of credit for the purpose of speculation.' Those opposing margin and capital requirements had argued that any requirement was too inflexible, but again the proponents of strict regulation carried the day.

Congress was quite concerned about market manipulation. Various sections of the Exchange Act prohibit manipulative devices, prohibit manipulative pricing, and regulate broker and dealer activities.

* * *

In addition to Commission regulation, the Exchange Act provides individual purchasers the right to sue those who willfully violate its manipulative prohibitions. Those who willfully violate any provision of the Exchange Act or any rule or regulation thereunder, or are responsible for making a statement false or misleading are subject to criminal liability.

* * *

Section 18(a) of the Exchange Act provides purchasers an express private right of action if they have been injured due to reliance on documents required to be filed under the Exchange Act. Although section 18(a) of the Exchange Act parallels section 11 of the Securities Act, it is less effective because, unlike sections 11 and 12, section 18(a) requires the buyer to prove that she read the statement, and actually relied on the material misrepresentation.

The Exchange Act reached securities listed on the exchange by prohibiting trading unless registered pursuant to the Act. Rather than specific regulations, the Commission was directed to make a study and report to Congress concerning unlisted securities traded on the exchange, and over-the-counter securities were to be regulated by rules and regulations promulgated by the Commission. In effect, section 12 of the Exchange Act requires securities listed on the national securities exchanges to be registered and to contain information similar to the information requirements of new issues under the Act.

The Exchange Act also requires periodic reports necessary to keep reasonably current the information on material filed pursuant to section 12. * * * Proxies are similarly regulated, as they are prohibited unless they comply with the regulations of the Commission.

From the outset, Congress was concerned with insider trading. * * *

The drafters supplied section 16 of the Exchange Act with a three-fold attack on the problem. First, the Exchange Act requires reporting by certain insiders of their stock holdings and transactions in the company's securities. Second, it makes it unlawful for the same insiders to engage in short sales of their company's equity securities. Third, it permits the corporation or security holder bringing an action on behalf of the corporation to disgorge and recover for the benefit of the corporation any short-swing profits arising from the purchase and sale or sale and purchase by insiders within any six month period. This section allows disgorgement within the six month period regardless of fault. The *in terrorem* approach is used because it is difficult for the corporation or shareholder to prove actual intent of the insider. Beneficial owners of more than ten percent of a corporation's shares are similarly regulated.

This chapter will go on to explore a number of Exchange Act Rules, including some of those discussed above. It should be noted that many rules are now promulgated directly by the SEC, as opposed to being passed in Congress. The 1934 Act controversially provided broad rule-making powers to the new Commission, allowing them to make not only procedural rules but also to fill in the meanings of some statutory terms. Furthermore, the SEC has informal rulemaking authority in the form of its "Releases," documents explaining the SEC's views on particular matters. While these and other advisory opinions lack the force of law, securities lawyers are well advised to take them seriously. Finally, in some areas the common law of judicial decisions has "filled out" the meanings of statutory promulgations.

Perhaps the most prominent area of securities regulation (at least in popular culture) is that combating insider trading.

II. Insider Trading

TO WHAT DOES THE TERM "insider trading" actually refer? In its original meaning, insider trading was the sale or purchase of securities by a corporate insider based on the knowledge of material nonpublic information. For instance, a director of Acme Corporation, knowing that Acme was about to be acquired by XYZ Conglomerate, purchases shares of Acme in the expectation that its price will rise upon public announcement of the merger. "Material" matters are those that a reasonable shareholder would deem significant in considering a purchase or sale of a security, while an "insider" was a director, senior officer, or large shareholder. These insiders, when trading on such information, were considered to be violating their fiduciary duties to the company. This is the definition of the "classical theory" of insider trading. Today, however, the definition of insider has been expanded to "temporary insiders" such as lawyers, consultants, accountants, or other professionals who, in their work for a client, are privy to material nonpublic information. Furthermore, the theory of insider trading has been, in places, expanded to include "outsiders": individuals with no relationship to the company whose securities are in question. This is called the "misappropriation theory" of insider trading and will be explored in detail below.

Insider trading was not always illegal, and until the New Deal no federal statute forbade it. The basis for this liability is most often found in Rule 10b-5 of the 1934 Exchange Act. 10b-5 was not in the original Act, but was added by the SEC when, in 1942, it discovered that the president of a publicly-traded company was lying about the company's earnings while purchasing its stock. Rule 10b of the Act gave the SEC the authority to create rules related to "deceptive practices . . . in connection with the purchase or sale of any security." 10b-5 (the fifth rule promulgated under 10b) states:

It shall be unlawful for any person, directly or indirectly, by the use of any means or instrumentality of interstate commerce, or of the mails or of any facility of any national securities exchange,

> (a) To employ any device, scheme, or artifice to defraud,

> (b) To make any untrue statement of a material fact or to omit to state a material fact necessary in order to make the statements made, in the light of the circumstances under which they were made, not misleading, or

> (c) To engage in any act, practice, or course of business which operates or would operate as a fraud or deceit upon any person, in connection with the purchase or sale of any security.

17 C.F.R. § 240.10b–5. You may not be surprised to learn that the relatively vague language of this statute has required a long line of judicially-created case law to flesh out its meaning and sources of liability.

This line can arguably be traced to the 1961 SEC administrative opinion of In re Cady, Roberts & Co. Here, the SEC announced its interpretation of Rule 10b-5 to be that an insider must "disclose or abstain" from trading when knowing material nonpublic information about the company. The first great court case addressing this rule was *SEC v. Texas Gulf Sulphur Co.*, 401 F.2d 833 (2d Cir. 1968).

Securities and Exchange Commission v. Texas Gulf Sulphur Co.

United States Court of Appeals Second Circuit
401 F.2d 833 (1968)

[The Texas Gulf Sulphur Company was taking ore samples from land in Canada when it obtained a very promising extraction, evidence of a massive and valuable mineral deposit. Examination of the drill core confirmed that the land was likely rich with minerals. While the company downplayed any knowledge of such a discovery in public statements, various insiders purchased stock and options, and tipped outsiders who subsequently made purchases as well. When the company finally announced the discovery, its stock price nearly tripled.]

* * *

The core of Rule 10b-5 is the implementation of the Congressional purpose that all investors should have equal access to the rewards of participation in securities transactions. It was the intent of Congress that all members of the investing public should be subject to identical market risks,— which market risks include, of course the risk that one's evaluative capacity or one's capital available to put at risk may exceed another's capacity or capital. The insiders here were not trading on an equal footing with the outside investors. They alone were in a position to evaluate the probability and magnitude of what seemed from the outset to be a major ore strike; they alone could invest safely, secure in the expectation that the price of TGS stock would rise substantially in the event such a major strike should materialize, but would decline little, if at all, in the event of failure, for the public, ignorant at the outset of the favorable probabilities would likewise be unaware of the unproductive exploration, and the additional exploration costs would not significantly affect TGS market prices. Such inequities based upon unequal access to knowledge should not be shrugged off as inevitable in our way of life, or, in view of the congressional concern in the area, remain uncorrected.

We hold, therefore, that all transactions in TGS stock or calls by individuals apprised of the drilling results of K-55-1 [the mineral extraction] were made in violation of Rule 10b-5. Inasmuch as the visual evaluation of that drill core (a generally reliable estimate though less accurate than a chemical assay) constituted material information, those advised of the results of the visual evaluation as well as those informed of the chemical assay traded in violation of law. * * *

[Important] is the realization which we must again underscore at the risk of repetition, that the investing public is hurt by exposure to false or deceptive statements irrespective of the purpose underlying their issuance. It does not appear to be unfair to impose upon corporate management a duty to ascertain the truth of any statements the corporation releases to its shareholders or to the investing public at large. Accordingly, we hold that Rule 10b-5 is violated whenever assertions are made, as here, in a manner reasonably calculated to influence the investing public." * * *

WHILE THE SEC PREVAILED, and had a federal appellate court endorse its doctrine of "disclose or abstain," the federal courts did not always agree with the SEC's interpretation of 10b-5. The following case serves as an example of the Supreme Court rejecting the SEC's broad interpretation of the rule, refusing to hold an *outsider* liable for trading on material nonpublic information.

Chiarella v. United States

Supreme Court of the United States.

45 U.S. 222, 100 S. Ct. 1108 (1980).

MR. JUSTICE **POWELL** delivered the opinion of the Court.

The question in this case is whether a person who learns from the confidential documents of one corporation that it is planning an attempt to secure control of a second corporation violates § 10(b) of the Securities Exchange Act of 1934 if he fails to disclose the impending takeover before trading in the target company's securities.

I

Petitioner is a printer by trade. In 1975 and 1976, he worked as a "markup man" in the New York composing room of Pandick Press, a financial printer. Among documents that petitioner handled were five announcements of corporate takeover bids. When these documents were delivered to the printer, the identities of the acquiring and target corporations were concealed by blank spaces or false names. The true names were sent to the printer on the night of the final printing.

The petitioner, however, was able to deduce the names of the target companies before the final printing from other information contained in the documents. Without disclosing his knowledge, petitioner purchased stock in the target companies and sold the shares immediately after the takeover attempts were made public. By this method, petitioner realized a gain of slightly more than $30,000 in the course of 14 months. Subsequently, the Securities and Exchange Commission (Commission or SEC) began an investigation of his trading activities. In May 1977, petitioner entered into a consent decree with the Commission in which he agreed to return his profits to the sellers of the shares. On the same day, he was discharged by Pandick Press.

In January 1978, petitioner was indicted on 17 counts of violating § 10(b) of the Securities Exchange Act of 1934 (1934 Act) and SEC Rule 10b–5. After petitioner unsuccessfully moved to dismiss the indictment, he was brought to trial and convicted on all counts.

The Court of Appeals for the Second Circuit affirmed petitioner's conviction. 588 F.2d 1358 (1978). We granted certiorari, 441 U.S. 942, 99 S.Ct. 2158, 60 L.Ed.2d 1043 (1979), and we now reverse.

II

* * *

The SEC took an important step in the development of § 10(b) when it held that a broker-dealer and his firm violated that section by selling securities on the basis of undisclosed information obtained from a director of the issuer corporation who was also a registered representative of the brokerage firm. In *Cady, Roberts & Co.,* 40 S.E.C. 907 (1961), the Commission decided that a corporate insider must abstain from trading in the shares of his corporation unless he has first disclosed all material inside information known to him. The obligation to disclose or abstain derives from

"[a]n affirmative duty to disclose material information[, which] has been traditionally imposed on corporate 'insiders,' particular officers, directors, or controlling stockholders. We, and the courts have consistently held that insiders must disclose material facts which are known to them by virtue of their position but which are not known to persons with whom they deal and which, if known, would affect their investment judgment." *Id.,* at 911.

The Commission emphasized that the duty arose from (i) the existence of a relationship affording access to inside information intended to be available only for a corporate purpose, and (ii) the unfairness of allowing a corporate insider to take advantage of that information by trading without disclosure. *Id.,* at 912, and n. 15.

* * *

[A]dministrative and judicial interpretations have established that silence in connection with the purchase or sale of securities may operate as a fraud actionable under § 10(b) despite the absence of statutory language or legislative history specifically addressing the legality of nondisclosure. But such liability is premised upon a duty to disclose arising from a relationship of trust and confidence between parties to a transaction. Application of a duty to disclose prior to trading guarantees that corporate insiders, who have an obligation to place the shareholder's welfare before their own, will not benefit personally through fraudulent use of material, nonpublic information.

III

In this case, the petitioner was convicted of violating § 10(b) although he was not a corporate insider and he received no confidential information from the target company. Moreover, the "market information" upon which he relied did not concern the earning power or operations of the target company, but only the plans of the acquiring company. Petitioner's use of that information was not a fraud under § 10(b) unless he was subject to an affirmative duty to disclose it before trading. In this case, the jury instructions failed to specify any such duty. * * *

The Court of Appeals, like the trial court, failed to identify a relationship between petitioner and the sellers that could give rise to a duty. Its decision thus rested solely upon its belief that the federal securities laws have "created a system providing equal access to information necessary for reasoned and intelligent investment decisions." *Id.,* at 1362. The use by anyone of material information not generally available is fraudulent, this theory suggests, because such information gives certain buyers or sellers an unfair advantage over less informed buyers and sellers.

This reasoning suffers from two defects. First not every instance of financial unfairness constitutes fraudulent activity under § 10(b). See *Santa Fe Industries, Inc. v. Green*, 430 U.S. 462 * * * (1977). Second, the element required to make silence fraudulent—a duty to disclose—is absent in this case. No duty could arise from petitioner's relationship with the sellers of the target company's securities, for petitioner had no prior dealings with them. He was not their agent, he was not a fiduciary, he was not a person in whom the sellers had placed their trust and confidence. He was, in fact, a complete stranger who dealt with the sellers only through impersonal market transactions.

We cannot affirm petitioner's conviction without recognizing a general duty between all participants in market transactions to forgo actions based on material, nonpublic information. Formulation of such a broad duty, which departs radically from the established doctrine that duty arises from a specific relationship between two parties, see n. 9, *supra*, should not be undertaken absent some explicit evidence of congressional intent.

As we have seen, no such evidence emerges from the language or legislative history of § 10(b). * * *

We see no basis for applying such a new and different theory of liability in this case. As we have emphasized before, the 1934 Act cannot be read " 'more broadly than its language and the statutory scheme reasonably permit.' " *Touche Ross & Co. v. Redington*, 442 U.S. 560 (1979), quoting *SEC v. Sloan*, 436 U.S. 103, 116 (1978). Section 10(b) is aptly described as a catchall provision, but what it catches must be fraud. When an allegation of fraud is based upon nondisclosure, there can be no fraud absent a duty to speak. We hold that a duty to disclose under § 10(b) does not arise from the mere possession of nonpublic market information. The contrary result is without support in the legislative history of § 10(b) and would be inconsistent with the careful plan that Congress has enacted for regulation of the securities markets. Cf. *Santa Fe Industries, Inc. v. Green*, 430 U.S., at 479.

NOTES AND COMMENTS

I. WHY IS INSIDER TRADING ILLEGAL? The Second Circuit in *Texas Gulf Sulphur* seemed to think that it has something to do with investors having fair access to all relevant information. But the Supreme Court in *Chiarella* emphasized that insider trading was illegal due to a breach of the insider's fiduciary duty owed to her company. As we shall see, some commentators reject the notion of insider trading laws entirely. Do you think they should be enforced? If so, on what grounds? And how strictly?

2. THE SEC PRESENTED an alternative theory of liability in this case, that of misappropriation. The majority contended that due to issues with the jury instructions at the trial court, it would not consider the misappropriation theory's merits. Chief Justice Burger filed a dissent, stating that he would have found against the defendant on grounds of misappropriation. "I would read § 10(b) and Rule 10b-5 to encompass and build on this principle: to mean that a person who has misappropriated nonpublic information has an absolute duty to disclose that information of refrain from trading." Do you agree with this extension of liability? The Supreme Court returned to the question of misappropriation theory in *U.S. v. O'Hagan*, which you will read shortly.

3. AFTER THE *CHIARELLA* DECISION, the SEC promulgated Rule 14e-3 in order to further regulate tender offers. Under 14e-3, it is illegal for *anyone* to trade securities based on material nonpublic information regarding expected tender offers. This liability-expanding rule is considered in *O'Hagan*, infra. As you will see, its adoption was not uncontroversial.

4. IN *CHIARELLA*, the outsider defendant learned of the material information on his own; but what about outsiders who are tipped directly by an insider? Today, liability for insider trading extends to outsiders who were tipped off by insiders in most circumstances. The question of who is liable in such a case is fraught with problems (consider when a tippee tips a third party, and she tips another, etc.) and, again, varying theories and justifications for the answers abound. The following case explores tipper/tippee liability in depth.

Dirks v. Security and Exchange Commission

Supreme Court of the United States.
463 U.S. 646, 103 S. Ct. 3255 (1983).

Justice **POWELL** delivered the opinion of the Court.

Petitioner Raymond Dirks received material nonpublic information from "insiders" of a corporation with which he had no connection. He disclosed this information to investors who relied on it in trading in the shares of the corporation. The question is whether Dirks violated the antifraud provisions of the federal securities laws by this disclosure.

I

In 1973, Dirks was an officer of a New York broker-dealer firm who specialized in providing investment analysis of insurance company securities to institutional investors. On March 6, Dirks received information from Ronald Secrist, a former officer of Equity Funding of America. Secrist alleged that the assets of Equity Funding, a diversified corporation primarily engaged in selling life insurance and mutual funds, were vastly overstated as the result of fraudulent corporate practices. Secrist also stated that various regulatory agencies had failed to act on similar charges made by Equity Funding employees. He urged Dirks to verify the fraud and disclose it publicly.

Dirks decided to investigate the allegations. He visited Equity Funding's headquarters in Los Angeles and interviewed several officers and employees of the corporation. The senior management denied any wrongdoing, but certain corporation employees corroborated the charges of fraud. Neither Dirks nor his firm owned or traded any Equity Funding stock, but throughout his investigation he openly discussed the information he had obtained with a number of clients and investors. Some of these persons sold their holdings of Equity Funding securities, including five investment advisers who liquidated holdings of more than $16 million.

* * *

During the two-week period in which Dirks pursued his investigation and spread word of Secrist's charges, the price of Equity Funding stock fell from $26 per share to less than $15 per share. This led the New York Stock Exchange to halt trading on March 27. Shortly thereafter California insurance authorities impounded Equity Funding's records and uncovered evidence of the fraud. Only then did the Securities and Exchange Commission (SEC) file a complaint against Equity Funding and only then, on April 2, did the *Wall Street Journal* publish a front-page story based largely on information assembled by Dirks. Equity Funding immediately went into receivership.

* * *

[Dirks was charged with and convicted of several securities violations, including Rule 10b-5.] The SEC concluded: "Where 'tippees'—regardless of their motivation or occupation—come into possession of material 'information that they know is confidential and know or should know came from a corporate insider,' they must either publicly disclose that information or refrain from trading." * * *

II

* * * [The Chiarella] requirement of a specific relationship between the shareholders and the individual trading on inside information has created analytical difficulties for the SEC and courts in policing tippees who trade on inside information. Unlike insiders who have independent fiduciary duties to both the corporation and its shareholders, the typical tippee has no such relationships. In view of this absence, it has been unclear how a tippee acquires the Cady, Roberts duty to refrain from trading on inside information.

A

The SEC's position, as stated in its opinion in this case, is that a tippee "inherits" the Cady, Roberts obligation to shareholders whenever he receives inside information from an insider * * *

> **"DETERMINING WHETHER** an insider personally benefits from a particular disclosure, a question of fact, will not always be easy for courts."

In effect, the SEC's theory of tippee liability in both cases appears rooted in the idea that the antifraud provisions require equal information among all traders. This conflicts with the principle set forth in Chiarella that only some persons, under some circumstances, will be barred from trading while in possession of material nonpublic information. Judge Wright correctly read our opinion in Chiarella as repudiating any notion that all traders must enjoy equal information before trading: "[T]he 'information' theory is rejected. Because the disclose-or-refrain duty is extraordinary, it attaches only when a party has legal obligations other than a mere duty to comply with the general antifraud proscriptions in the federal securities laws." * * * We reaffirm today that "[a] duty [to disclose] arises from the relationship between parties ... and not merely from one's ability to acquire information because of his position in the market. * * *

Imposing a duty to disclose or abstain solely because a person knowingly receives material nonpublic information from an insider and trades on it could have an inhibiting influence on the role of market analysts, which the SEC itself recognizes is necessary to the preservation of a healthy market. It is commonplace for analysts to "ferret out and analyze information," 21 S.E.C., at 1406, and this often is done by meeting with and questioning corporate officers and others who are insiders. And information that the analysts obtain normally may be the basis for judgments as to the market worth of a corporation's securities. The analyst's judgment in this respect is made available in market letters or otherwise to clients of the firm. It is the nature of this type of information, and indeed of the markets themselves, that such information cannot be made simultaneously available to all of the corporation's stockholders or the public generally.

B

The conclusion that recipients of inside information do not invariably acquire a duty to disclose or abstain does not mean that such tippees always are free to trade on the information. The need for a ban on some tippee trading is clear. Not only are insiders forbidden by their fiduciary relationship from personally using undisclosed corporate information to their advantage, but they may not give such information to an outsider for the same improper purpose of exploiting the information for their personal gain. * * *

Thus, some tippees must assume an insider's duty to the shareholders not because they receive inside information, but rather because it has been made available to them *improperly*. And for Rule 10b–5 purposes, the insider's disclosure is improper only where it would violate his *Cady, Roberts* duty. Thus, a tippee assumes a fiduciary duty to the shareholders of a corporation not to trade on material nonpublic information only when the insider has breached his fiduciary duty to the shareholders by disclosing the information to the tippee and the tippee knows or should know that there has been a breach. * * *

C

In determining whether a tippee is under an obligation to disclose or abstain, it thus is necessary to determine whether the insider's "tip" constituted a breach of the insider's fiduciary duty. All disclosures of confidential corporate information are not inconsistent with the duty insiders owe to shareholders. * * * Whether disclosure is a breach of duty therefore depends in large part on the purpose of the disclosure. This standard was identified by the SEC itself in *Cady, Roberts*: a purpose of the securities laws was to eliminate "use of inside information for personal advantage." 40 S.E.C., at 912, n. 15. * * * Thus, the test is whether the insider personally will benefit, directly or indirectly, from his disclosure. Absent some personal gain, there has been no breach of duty to stockholders. And absent a breach by the insider, there is no derivative breach. * * *

Determining whether an insider personally benefits from a particular disclosure, a question of fact, will not always be easy for courts. But it is essential, we think, to have a guiding principle for those whose daily activities must be limited and instructed by the SEC's inside-trading rules, and we believe that there must be a breach of the insider's fiduciary duty before the tippee inherits the duty to disclose or abstain. In contrast, the rule adopted by the SEC in this case would have no limiting principle.

IV

Under the insider-trading and tipping rules set forth above, we find that there was no actionable violation by Dirks. It is undisputed that Dirks himself was a stranger to Equity Funding, with no pre-existing fiduciary duty to its shareholders. He took no action, directly or indirectly, that induced the shareholders or officers of Equity Funding to repose trust or confidence in him. There was no expectation by Dirk's sources that he would keep their information in confidence. Nor did Dirks misappropriate or illegally obtain the information about Equity Funding. Unless the insiders breached their *Cady, Roberts* duty to shareholders in disclosing the nonpublic information to Dirks, he breached no duty when he passed it on to investors as well as to the *Wall Street Journal*.

It is clear that neither Secrist nor the other Equity Funding employees violated their *Cady, Roberts* duty to the corporation's shareholders by providing information to Dirks. The tippers received no monetary or personal benefit for revealing Equity Funding's secrets, nor was their purpose to make a gift of valuable information to Dirks. As the facts of this case clearly indicate, the tippers were motivated by a desire to expose the fraud. * * * In the absence of a breach of duty to shareholders by the insiders, there was no derivative breach by Dirks. * * * Dirks therefore could not have been "a participant after the fact in [an] insider's breach of a fiduciary duty." *Chiarella*, 445 U.S., at 230, n. 12.

V

We conclude that Dirks, in the circumstances of this case, had no duty to abstain from use of the inside information that he obtained. The judgment of the Court of Appeals therefore is reversed.

ALTHOUGH *CHIARELLA* AND *DIRKS* were defeats for the SEC, the Commission gained a significant victory in 1997 with the decision in *United States v. O'Hagan*. The majority of the Supreme Court accepted the misappropriation theory of insider trading, and thus liability was widely extended beyond the traditional duty-based understanding. The case also considers the SEC's rule-making authority in reference to Rule 14e-3.

United States v. O'Hagan

Supreme Court of the United States.
521 U.S. 642, 117 S.Ct. 2199, 138 L.Ed.2d 724 (1997).

Opinion By: GINSBURG

* * *

I

Respondent James Herman O'Hagan was a partner in the law firm of Dorsey & Whitney in Minneapolis, Minnesota. In July 1988, Grand Metropolitan PLC (Grand Met), a company based in London, England, retained Dorsey & Whitney as local counsel to represent Grand Met regarding a potential tender offer for the common stock of the Pillsbury Company, headquartered in Minneapolis. Both Grand Met and Dorsey & Whitney took precautions to protect the confidentiality of Grand Met's tender offer plans. O'Hagan did no work on the Grand Met representation. Dorsey & Whitney withdrew from representing Grand Met on September 9, 1988. Less than a month later, on October 4, 1988, Grand Met publicly announced its tender offer for Pillsbury stock.

On August 18, 1988, while Dorsey & Whitney was still representing Grand Met, O'Hagan began purchasing call options for Pillsbury stock. * * * Later in August and in September, O'Hagan made additional purchases of Pillsbury call options. By the end of September, he owned 2,500 unexpired Pillsbury options, apparently more than any other individual investor. . . . O'Hagan also purchased, in September 1988, some 5,000 shares of Pillsbury common stock, at a price just under $39 per share. When Grand Met announced its tender offer in October, the price of Pillsbury stock rose to nearly $60 per share. O'Hagan then sold his Pillsbury call options and common stock making a profit of more than $4.3 million.

The Securities and Exchange Commission (SEC or Commission) initiated an investigation into O'Hagan's transactions, culminating in a 57-count indictment The indictment alleged that O'Hagan defrauded his law firm and its client, Grand Met, by using for his own trading purposes material, nonpublic information regarding Grand Met's planned tender offer * * *. O'Hagan was charged with * * * 17 counts of securities fraud, in violation of § 10(b) of the Securities Exchange Act of 1934 (Exchange Act) * * * and SEC Rule 10b–5, [and] 17 counts of fraudulent trading in connection with a tender offer, in violation of § 14(e) of the Exchange Act, * * * and SEC Rule 14e–3(a) * * * A jury convicted O'Hagan on all * * * counts, and he was sentenced to a 41–month term of imprisonment.

* * *A divided panel of the Court of Appeals for the Eighth Circuit reversed all of O'Hagan's convictions. . . . Liability under § 10(b) and Rule 10b–5, the Eighth Circuit held, may not be grounded on the "misappropriation theory" of securities fraud on which the prosecution relied.* * * The Court of Appeals also held that Rule

14e–3(a)—which prohibits trading while in possession of material, nonpublic information relating to a tender offer—exceeds the SEC's § 14(e) rulemaking authority because the rule contains no breach of fiduciary duty requirement.

＊ ＊ ＊

II

We address first the Court of Appeals' reversal of O'Hagan's convictions under § 10(b) and Rule 10b–5. Following the Fourth Circuit's lead, see *United States v. Bryan, 58 F.3d 933, 943–959 (1995),* the Eighth Circuit rejected the misappropriation theory as a basis for § 10(b) liability. We hold, in accord with several other Courts of Appeals, that criminal liability under § 10(b) may be predicated on the misappropriation theory.

A

In pertinent part, § 10(b) of the Exchange Act provides:

"It shall be unlawful for any person, directly or indirectly, by the use of any means or instrumentality of interstate commerce or of the mails, or of any facility of any national securities exchange—

. . . . .

"(b) To use or employ, in connection with the purchase or sale of any security registered on a national securities exchange or any security not so registered, any manipulative or deceptive device or contrivance in contravention of such rules and regulations as the [Securities and Exchange] Commission may prescribe as necessary or appropriate in the public interest or for the protection of investors."

The statute thus proscribes (1) using any deceptive device (2) in connection with the purchase or sale of securities, in contravention of rules prescribed by the Commission. The provision, as written, does not confine its coverage to deception of a purchaser or seller of securities ＊ ＊ ＊ rather, the statute reaches any deceptive device used "in connection with the purchase or sale of any security."

Pursuant to its § 10(b) rulemaking authority, the Commission has adopted Rule 10b–5, which, as relevant here, provides:

> "It shall be unlawful for any person, directly or indirectly, by the use of any means or instrumentality of interstate commerce, or of the mails or of any facility of any national securities exchange,
>
> "(a) To employ any device, scheme, or artifice to defraud, [or]
>
> ＊ ＊ ＊
>
> "(c) To engage in any act, practice, or course of business which operates or would operate as a fraud or deceit upon any person, in connection with the purchase or sale of any security."

* * *Under the "traditional" or "classical theory" of insider trading liability, § 10(b) and Rule 10b–5 are violated when a corporate insider trades in the securities of his corporation on the basis of material, nonpublic information. Trading on such information qualifies as a "deceptive device" under § 10(b), we have affirmed, because "a relationship of trust and confidence [exists] between the shareholders of a corporation and those insiders who have obtained confidential information by reason of their position with that corporation." * * * That relationship, we recognized, "gives rise to a duty to disclose [or to abstain from trading] because of the 'necessity of preventing a corporate insider from . . . taking unfair advantage of * * * uninformed . . . stockholders.' " * * * The classical theory applies not only to officers, directors, and other permanent insiders of a corporation, but also to attorneys, accountants, consultants, and others who temporarily become fiduciaries of a corporation. * * *

The "misappropriation theory" holds that a person commits fraud "in connection with" a securities transaction, and thereby violates § 10(b) and Rule 10b–5, when he misappropriates confidential information for securities trading purposes, in breach of a duty owed to the source of the information. * * * Under this theory, a fiduciary's undisclosed, self-serving use of a principal's information to purchase or sell securities, in breach of a duty of loyalty and confidentiality, defrauds the principal of the exclusive use of that information. In lieu of premising liability on a fiduciary relationship between company insider and purchaser or seller of the company's stock, the misappropriation theory premises liability on a fiduciary-turned-trader's deception of those who entrusted him with access to confidential information.

* * *In this case, the indictment alleged that O'Hagan, in breach of a duty of trust and confidence he owed to his law firm, Dorsey & Whitney, and to its client, Grand Met, traded on the basis of nonpublic information regarding Grand Met's planned tender offer for Pillsbury common stock. * * * This conduct, the Government charged, constituted a fraudulent device in connection with the purchase and sale of securities. * * *

B

We agree with the Government that misappropriation, as just defined, satisfies § 10(b)'s requirement that chargeable conduct involve a "deceptive device or contrivance" used "in connection with" the purchase or sale of securities. We observe, first, that misappropriators, as the Government describes them, deal in deception. * * * A fiduciary who "[pretends] loyalty to the principal while secretly converting the principal's information for personal gain," * * * "dupes" or defrauds the principal * * *

Deception through nondisclosure is central to the theory of liability for which the Government seeks recognition. As counsel for the Government stated in explanation of the theory at oral argument: "To satisfy the common law rule that a trustee may not use the property that [has] been entrusted [to] him, there would have to be consent. To satisfy the requirement of the Securities Act that there be no deception, there would only have to be disclosure." * * *

We turn next to the § 10(b) requirement that the misappropriator's deceptive use of information be "in connection with the purchase or sale of [a] security." This element is satisfied because the fiduciary's fraud is consummated, not when the fiduciary gains the confidential information, but when, without disclosure to his principal, he uses the information to purchase or sell securities. The securities transaction and the breach of duty thus coincide. This is so even though the person or entity defrauded is not the other party to the trade, but is, instead, the source of the nonpublic information. * * * A misappropriator who trades on the basis of material, nonpublic information, in short, gains his advantageous market position through deception; he deceives the source of the information and simultaneously harms members of the investing public. * * *

The misappropriation theory targets information of a sort that misappropriators ordinarily capitalize upon to gain no-risk profits through the purchase or sale of securities. Should a misappropriator put such information to other use, the statute's prohibition would not be implicated. The theory does not catch all conceivable forms of fraud involving confidential information; rather, it catches fraudulent means of capitalizing on such information through securities transactions.

* * *The misappropriation theory comports with § 10(b)'s language, which requires deception "in connection with the purchase or sale of any security," not deception of an identifiable purchaser or seller. The theory is also well-tuned to an animating purpose of the Exchange Act: to insure honest securities markets and thereby promote investor confidence. * * * Although informational disparity is inevitable in the securities markets, investors likely would hesitate to venture their capital in a market where trading based on misappropriated nonpublic information is unchecked by law. * * *

* * *

III

We consider next the ground on which the Court of Appeals reversed O'Hagan's convictions for fraudulent trading in connection with a tender offer, in violation of § 14(e) of the Exchange Act and SEC Rule 14e–3(a). A sole question is before us as to these convictions: Did the Commission, as the Court of Appeals held, exceed its rulemaking authority under § 14(e) when it adopted Rule 14e–3(a) without requiring a showing that the trading at issue entailed a breach of fiduciary duty? We hold that the Commission, in this regard and to the extent relevant to this case, did not exceed its authority.

The governing statutory provision, § 14(e) of the Exchange Act, reads in relevant part:

> "It shall be unlawful for any person . . . to engage in any fraudulent, deceptive, or manipulative acts or practices, in connection with any tender offer * * *. The [SEC] shall, for the purposes of this subsection, by rules and regulations define, and prescribe means reasonably

designed to prevent, such acts and practices as are fraudulent, deceptive, or manipulative." * * *

Section 14(e)'s first sentence prohibits fraudulent acts in connection with a tender offer. * * * The section's second sentence delegates definitional and prophylactic rulemaking authority to the Commission. * * *

Relying on § 14(e)'s rulemaking authorization, the Commission, in 1980, promulgated Rule 14e–3(a). That measure provides:

> "(a) If any person has taken a substantial step or steps to commence, or has commenced, a tender offer (the 'offering person'), it shall constitute a fraudulent, deceptive or manipulative act or practice within the meaning of section 14(e) of the [Exchange] Act for any other person who is in possession of material information relating to such tender offer which information he knows or has reason to know is nonpublic and which he knows or has reason to know has been acquired directly or indirectly from:

> "(1) The offering person,

> "(2) The issuer of the securities sought or to be sought by such tender offer, or

> "(3) Any officer, director, partner or employee or any other person acting on behalf of the offering person or such issuer, to purchase or sell or cause to be purchased or sold any of such securities or any securities convertible into or exchangeable for any such securities or any option or right to obtain or to dispose of any of the foregoing securities, unless within a reasonable time prior to any purchase or sale such information and its source are publicly disclosed by press release or otherwise." . . .

As characterized by the Commission, Rule 14e–3(a) is a "disclose or abstain from trading" requirement. . . . The Second Circuit concisely described the rule's thrust:

> "* * * It creates a duty in those traders who fall within its ambit to abstain or disclose, without regard to whether the trader owes a pre-existing fiduciary duty to respect the confidentiality of the information." *United States v. Chestman*, 947 F.2d 551, 557 (1991) * * * (emphasis added) * * *.

* * *In the Eighth Circuit's view, because Rule 14e–3(a) applies whether or not the trading in question breaches a fiduciary duty, the regulation exceeds the SEC's § 14(e) rulemaking authority * * *

We need not resolve in this case whether the Commission's authority under § 14(e) to "define . . . such acts and practices as are fraudulent" is broader than the Commission's fraud-defining authority under § 10(b), for we agree with the United States that Rule 14e–3(a), as applied to cases of this genre, qualifies under § 14(e) as a "means reasonably designed to prevent" fraudulent trading on material, nonpublic information in the tender offer context. A prophylactic measure, because its mission is to prevent, typically encompasses more than the core activity prohibited. * * *

The United States emphasizes that Rule 14e–3(a) reaches trading in which "a breach of duty is likely but difficult to prove." * * * "Particularly in the context of a tender offer," as the Tenth Circuit recognized, "there is a fairly wide circle of people with confidential information," * * *, notably, the attorneys, investment bankers, and accountants involved in structuring the transaction. The availability of that information may lead to abuse, for "even a hint of an upcoming tender offer may send the price of the target company's stock soaring." * * * Individuals entrusted with nonpublic information, particularly if they have no long-term loyalty to the issuer, may find the temptation to trade on that information hard to resist in view of "the very large short-term profits potentially available [to them]." * * *

In sum, it is a fair assumption that trading on the basis of material, nonpublic information will often involve a breach of a duty of confidentiality to the bidder or target company or their representatives. The SEC, cognizant of the proof problem that could enable sophisticated traders to escape responsibility, placed in Rule 14e–3(a) a "disclose or abstain from trading" command that does not require specific proof of a breach of fiduciary duty. That prescription, we are satisfied, applied to this case, is a "means reasonably designed to prevent" fraudulent trading on material, nonpublic information in the tender offer context.* * * Therefore, insofar as it serves to prevent the type of misappropriation charged against O'Hagan, Rule 14e–3(a) is a proper exercise of the Commission's prophylactic power under § 14(e).

* * *The judgment of the Court of Appeals for the Eighth Circuit is reversed, and the case is remanded for further proceedings consistent with this opinion.

It is so ordered.

* * *

JUSTICE THOMAS, with whom THE CHIEF JUSTICE joins, concurring in the judgment in part and dissenting in part.

* * * Central to the majority's holding is the need to interpret § 10(b)'s requirement that a deceptive device be "used or employed, in connection with the purchase or sale of any security." * * * Because the Commission's misappropriation theory fails to provide a coherent and consistent interpretation of this essential requirement for liability under § 10(b), I dissent.

The majority also sustains respondent's convictions under § 14(e) of the Securities Exchange Act, and Rule 14e–3(a) promulgated thereunder, regardless of whether respondent violated a fiduciary duty to anybody. I dissent too from that holding because, while § 14(e) does allow regulations prohibiting nonfraudulent acts as a prophylactic against certain fraudulent acts, neither the majority nor the Commission identifies any relevant underlying fraud against which Rule 14e–3(a) reasonably provides prophylaxis . . .

* * *

II

* * *

As the majority acknowledges, Rule 14e–3(a) prohibits a broad range of behavior regardless of whether such behavior is fraudulent under our precedents. * * *

The Commission offers two grounds in defense of Rule 14e–3(a). First, it argues that § 14(e) delegates to the Commission the authority to "define" fraud differently than that concept has been defined by this Court, and that Rule 14e–3(a) is a valid exercise of that "defining" power. Second, it argues that § 14(e) authorizes the Commission to "prescribe means reasonably designed to prevent" fraudulent acts, and that Rule 14e–3(a) is a prophylactic rule that may prohibit nonfraudulent acts as a means of preventing fraudulent acts that are difficult to detect or prove.

The majority declines to reach the Commission's first justification, instead sustaining Rule 14e–3(a) on the ground that

> "under § 14(e), the Commission may prohibit acts, not themselves fraudulent under the common law or § 10(b), if the prohibition is 'reasonably designed to prevent . . . acts and practices [that] are fraudulent.' " * * *

According to the majority, prohibiting trading on nonpublic information is necessary to prevent such supposedly hard-to-prove fraudulent acts and practices as trading on information obtained from the buyer in breach of a fiduciary duty.* * *

* * * With regard to the Commission's claim of authority to redefine the concept of fraud, I agree with the Eighth Circuit that the Commission misreads the relevant provision of § 14(e).

> "Simply put, the enabling provision of § 14(e) permits the SEC to identify and regulate those 'acts and practices' which fall within the § 14(e) legal definition of 'fraudulent,' but it does not grant the SEC a license to redefine the term." * * *

This conclusion follows easily from our similar statement in *Schreiber v. Burlington Northern, Inc., 472 U.S. 1, 11, n.11 (1985),* that § 14(e) gives the "Commission latitude to regulate nondeceptive activities as a 'reasonably designed' means of preventing manipulative acts, without suggesting any change in the meaning of the term 'manipulative' itself."

Insofar as the Rule 14e–3(a) purports to "define" acts and practices that "are fraudulent," it must be measured against our precedents interpreting the scope of fraud. The majority concedes, however, that Rule 14e–3(a) does not prohibit merely trading in connection with fraudulent nondisclosure, but rather it prohibits trading in connection with *any* nondisclosure, regardless of the presence of a pre-existing duty to disclose. * * * The Rule thus exceeds the scope of the Commission's authority to define such acts and practices as "are fraudulent." * * *

Turning to the Commission's second justification for Rule 14e–3(a), although I can agree with the majority that § 14(e) authorizes the Commission to prohibit non-fraudulent acts as a means reasonably designed to prevent fraudulent ones, I cannot agree that Rule 14e–3(a) satisfies this standard. As an initial matter, the Rule, on its face, does not purport to be an exercise of the Commission's prophylactic power, but rather a redefinition of what "constitutes a fraudulent, deceptive, or manipulative act or practice within the meaning of § 14(e)." That Rule 14e–3(a) could have been "conceived and defended, alternatively, as definitional or preventive," * * * misses the point. We evaluate regulations not based on the myriad of explanations that could have been given by the relevant agency, but on those explanations and justifications that were, in fact, given. * * * Rule 14e–3(a) may not be "sensibly read" as an exercise of "preventive" authority * * * it can only be differently so read, contrary to its own terms. * * *

Finally, even further assuming that the Commission's misappropriation theory is a valid basis for direct liability, I fail to see how Rule 14e–3(a)'s elimination of the requirement of a breach of fiduciary duty is "reasonably designed" to prevent the underlying "fraudulent" acts. The majority's primary argument on this score is that in many cases " 'a breach of duty is likely but difficult to prove.' " * * * Although the majority's hypothetical difficulties involved in a tipper-tippee situation might have some merit in the context of "classical" insider trading, there is no reason to suspect similar difficulties in "misappropriation" cases. In such cases, Rule 14e–3(a) requires the Commission to prove that the defendant "knows or has reason to know" that the nonpublic information upon which trading occurred came from the bidder or an agent of the bidder. Once the source of the information has been identified, it should be a simple task to obtain proof of any breach of duty. After all, it is the bidder itself that was defrauded in misappropriation cases, and there is no reason to suspect that the victim of the fraud would be reluctant to provide evidence against the perpetrator of the fraud. * * * There being no particular difficulties in proving a breach of duty in such circumstances, a rule removing the requirement of such a breach cannot be said to be "reasonably designed" to prevent underlying violations of the misappropriation theory. * * *

* * *

NOTES AND QUESTIONS

I. **THERE IS ALWAYS PRESSURE** on the federal government to act when state law seems inadequately to be performing its regulatory function, particularly when that regulatory function is perceived as the protection of investors. There are at least five main areas in which the federal government has acted to protect investors in publicly traded corporations 1) insider trading, 2) proxy voting, 3) new issues, 4) tender offers and takeovers, and 5) executive misconduct. We will treat proxy voting in the following case, *J.I. Case v. Borak*, and you have already caught a glimpse of the problems in that area through your study of *Campbell v. Loew's* in Chapter Three. We will treat federal regulation of tender offers and takeovers in Chapter Twenty. Federal regulation of executive misconduct will be examined in a note on the Sarbanes/Oxley and Dodd-Frank Acts, the controversial federal statutes which deal with such matters, which concludes this Chapter.

2. *UNITED STATES v. O'HAGAN*, which you have just read, was the culmination of a long line of securities fraud cases, and it clearly established the viability of three different theories of liability under the 1934 Securities Exchange Act, and, in particular, Sections 10(b) and 14(e) of that act, as amended, and two important regulations thereunder, Rule 10b–5 and Rule 14e–3. Were you able to glean an understanding of the misconduct against which they were targeted? Would you be surprised to learn that of all the areas of federal law this one is probably the one that encourages the most litigation? Much of it has been in the form of civil actions brought by individuals who claim to have been damaged by corporate insiders or corporate management acting in violation of Section 10(b) and Rule 10b–5. Section 10(b) does not expressly permit private persons to bring actions based on violations of the section, but that has been the practice since at least the 1940's, and Congress has made clear that such actions will be permitted to continue, although it has sought, in such measures as the Private Securities Litigation Reform Acts of 1995 and 1997 to diminish somewhat the overabundance of such lawsuits by eliminating so-called "professional plaintiffs" and by specifying stricter pleading standards. It is perhaps significant that the 1995 Act is the only measure ever successfully passed by the requisite two-thirds majority of both houses of Congress over the veto of President Clinton. Can you understand why President Clinton might choose to veto such a measure, and why Congress might pass it over his veto? Are you comfortable with providing a private remedy through litigation for those injured by violations of the securities law? Consider the explanation provided for the practice in *J.I. Case v. Borak*, which appears in the next section.

3. THE PRIVATE SECURITIES Litigation Reform Act of 1995 (PSLRA) was passed one year after an important Supreme Court decision, *Central Bank of Denver, N. A. v. First Interstate Bank Of Denver, N. A.*, 511 U.S. 164 114 S.Ct. 1439, 128 L.Ed.2d 119 (1994), in which the Court ruled that private actions could not be brought under 10(b) and 10b–5 against persons who "<fill>aided and abetted" securities fraud, but only against those who directly engaged in such fraudulent conduct. In Section 104 of the PSLRA, however, the SEC, was directed to prosecute persons guilty of such secondary liability. In 2008, in *Stoneridge Investment Partners v. Scientific–Atlanta, Inc.*, 552 U.S. 148 128 S.Ct. 761, 169 L.Ed.2d 627 (2008) the Court reaffirmed its holding in *Central Bank of Denver*, and made clear that it would not permit "scheme liability," whereby a plaintiff seeks to impose liability on parties doing business with parties guilty of securities fraud. "Scheme liability" would have created a bonanza for trial lawyers bringing securities-fraud class actions, particularly since the pressure to settle such cases and avoid expensive discovery and other proceedings would have been difficult to resist even for innocent parties who were contractually involved with violators of Rule 10b–5. Writing for the Court, in a 5 to 3 decision (Justice Breyer had recused himself because he had investments in the parent corporation of one of the parties to the case), Justices Stevens, Ginsberg, and Souter dissenting, Justice Kennedy observed in *Stoneridge* that to have ruled for the plaintiffs would have been to authorize "a private cause of action against the entire marketplace in which the issuing company [that allegedly making a false or misleading statement] operates," 552 U.S., at 162, and, further, that if Congress had wanted to open the floodgates to such private actions, it could have done so instead of just directing the SEC to bring actions against "aiders and abetters" in the PSLRA. The trial lawyers and their friends in Congress, in November 2009, however, had drafted legislation as part of a broader effort to impose greater financial regulation on the market, expressly to permit private actions against those who "aided and abetted" securities law violators, thus reversing *Central Bank of Denver*. It is possible that by the time you read this, it will have been enacted into law. See generally "Dodd's Lawsuit Makeover," The *Wall Street Journal*, Friday, November 13, at A22 (Editorial opposing the return of private actions for "aiding and abetting" securities fraud).

....

4. WHAT THEN, were the three theories of liability examined (or at least mentioned) in *O'Hagan*? The first is the "classical" theory of liability under Section 10(b). This applies only to corporate fiduciaries, such as officers or directors, and suggests, simply, that such officials may not trade in their corporation's securities without disclosing any material facts that a shareholder with whom they might deal would want to know. It is the most basic form of the "disclose or abstain from trading" rule.

The second is the "misappropriation" theory, which applies to persons who are entrusted with information to be used for a particular purpose and then misuse that information in order to take advantage by trading in the market with shareholders who are unaware of the information. In *O'Hagen* the information was the fact that a tender offer for Pillsbury stock was forthcoming. A "misappropriator" has a fiduciary duty to his or her employer not to misuse the information, although the duty does not actually run to the stockholder with whom the misappropriator trades. Do you understand why the dissenters in *O'Hagan* had trouble with finding liability under the misappropriation theory when no duties ran to shareholders? Nevertheless, *O'Hagan* makes clear that the misappropriation theory is now a permissible basis for finding a violation of the securities laws has taken place.

The third theory is occasionally referred to as the "equal playing field" theory. Its notion is that *any* person who trades in the securities market should not be able to take advantage of inside information whether or not that person has a fiduciary duty or whether or not that person has a duty not to misappropriate information. If you consult the language of Section 10(b) and Rule 10b–5 which refer to "any person" using any "manipulative device or contrivance," you will be tempted to believe that the "equal playing field" theory has a firm statutory basis, and this was the position both the Justice Department and the SEC had argued for. At least one Supreme Court Justice, Harry Blackmun, was sympathetic to the theory, but, as you know, a majority of the Supreme Court rejected it in the *Chiarella* case, holding that 10(b) and Rule 10b–5 were limited to cases in which persons were under a duty to shareholders to disclose or abstain from trading, as was true, for example in the case of corporate fiduciaries. Foiled in their use of the "equal playing field" theory under Section 10(b) and Rule 10b–5, the SEC tried again by promulgating Rule 14e–3, pursuant to the authority granted it by Section 14(e) of the Securities Exchange Act. This time, in *O'Hagan*, the "equal playing field" theory was accepted, but limited only to the problem of inside information regarding tender offers.

. . . .

5. ANOTHER FORM OF LIABILITY for insider trading does not involve any of these subtle distinctions, and simply imposes a penalty of possible disgorgement of profits on any officer, director, or 10% beneficial shareholder who buys and sells his or her corporation's stock within a six month (called a "short swing") period. This is pursuant to Section 16(b) of the Securities Exchange Act of 1934, which you first read about in the law review excerpt which began the chapter. 16(b) provides that:

> For the purpose of preventing the unfair use of information which may have been obtained by such beneficial owner, director, or officer by reason of his relationship to the issuer, any profit realized by him from any purchase

and sale, or any sale and purchase, of any equity security of such issuer
* * * within any period of less than six months * * * shall inure to and be
recoverable by the issuer, irrespective of any intention on the part of such
beneficial owner, director, or officer in entering into such transaction of
holding the security * * * for a period exceeding six months. Suit to recover
such profit may be instituted at law or in equity in any court of competent
jurisdiction by the issuer, or by the owner of any security of the issuer in
the name and in behalf of the issuer if the issuer shall fail or refuse to bring
such suit within sixty days after request or shall fail diligently to prosecute the same thereafter; but no such suit shall be brought more than two
years after the date such profit was realized. This subsection shall not be
construed to cover any transaction where such beneficial owner was not
such both at the time of the purchase and sale, or the sale and purchase,
of the security * * *.

Would you have voted for Section 16(b) if you were a member of Congress?
Does it represent a different sort of theory of legislation than does Section 10(b)?

....

6. IN 2000, the SEC promulgated Regulation FD (for Fair Disclosure). Previously,
companies could meet their disclosure requirements by announcing material information to a group of invited parties, including other financial organizations, some
investors, and journalists. Smaller investors complained about this treatment, as it
allowed certain favored parties to gain a temporary trading advantage based on the
information. Regulation FD instituted strict new rules about disclosure: material
information must be disclosed to *all* investors simultaneously. Regulation FD does
not create a fraud cause of action, and private parties cannot sue under it, but it does
allow the SEC to penalize and enjoin violating companies.

....

7. TWO OTHER STATUTES concerning remedies for insider trading are worth considering: the Insider Trading Sanctions Act of 1984 (ITSA) and the Insider Trading and
Securities Fraud Enforcement Act of 1988 (ITSFEA). ITSA allows the SEC to levy
sanctions against anyone convicted of violating the Exchange Act or its associated
rules, as well as non-trading tippers. These sanctions can be up to three times the
amount of ill-gotten gains, which are also required to be disgorged. ITSFEA requires
businesses (such as broker-dealers) to maintain a "Chinese Wall" between sections of
its business in order to prevent the misappropriation of inside information. ITSFEA
also increases the criminal sanctions for securities acts violations from five years

imprisonment and fines of $100,000 to ten years and $1,000,000. Finally, it creates an explicit private right-of-action for contemporaneous traders against the insider.

---

8. CONSIDER THE FOLLOWING HYPOTHETICAL. Domestic Diva has a thriving business which provides household management and decorating tips to American women. Ms. Diva has made millions and has invested much of her cash in other corporations. One of these is a drug company, which has an application before the FDA seeking approval for a cancer drug. Ms. Diva is also a personal friend of the CEO of the drug company, and the CEO and Diva share a Broker at Merrill Lynch. The CEO receives advance word that in two days the FDA is going formally to deny the application to approve the cancer drug. The CEO knows that when this information becomes public the drug company's stock will plummet in price. CEO proceeds to alert his family members to sell their holdings in the drug company, and seeks to sell some of his own shares, but Broker advises him that to do so would violate the federal securities laws. The family members, through Broker, sell their drug company shares. One day before the public FDA announcement of disapproval of the cancer drug Broker calls up Diva and tells her that CEO's family has been selling their shares in the drug company. Diva tells Broker to sell her shares in the drug company. Has anyone violated Section 10(b) and Rule 10b–5? On what theories?

---

9. NOT ALL LEGAL THEORISTS believe that insider trading should be illegal. A number of scholars have sustained a lively academic debate on the subject for decades; proponents of the permissive view include Judge Frank Easterbrook of the Seventh Circuit, economist Milton Friedman, and academics such as Henry Manne and Daniel Fischel.[3] These writers propose various justifications for accepting the practice of insider trading, including the difficulty of consistent enforcement and its potential use as a compensation device. Perhaps the leading defense is that in an efficient market securities will already reflect the reality of insider knowledge; that is, buyers of securities will pay less for them than they would were information perfectly and widely shared. Insider trading regulations are thus superfluous, as the market already is acting upon the assumption of insider knowledge and use of material nonpublic information. Do you find this argument compelling?

---

3   For detailed defenses of this view, see HENRY MANNE, INSIDER TRADING AND THE STOCK MARKET (1966); Frank Easterbrook, *Insider Trading, Secret Agents, Evidentiary Privileges, and the Production of Information,* 1981 SUP. CT. L. REV. 309 (1981); and Dennis Carlton & Daniel Fischel, *The Regulation of Insider Trading,* 35 STAN. L. REV. 857 (1983).

10. THE SEC HAS STEPPED UP its enforcement of insider trading laws following the financial crisis of 2007–08, with a number of high-profile indictments and convictions. Perhaps the most prominent has been the 2012 conviction of Rajat Gupta for insider trading. Gupta was, at one point, the chief executive of the McKinsey & Co. consulting firm and served on the board of Goldman Sachs. At the time of publication, he was serving a two-year prison sentence and had been ordered to pay a $5 million fine. His co-conspirators, including hedge-fund founder Raj Rajaratnam, were also sentenced to prison in what has been described by Bloomberg News as "the most extensive insider-trading case in U.S. history."

III. The Federal Proxy Rules

AS INDICATED EARLIER, the aims of federal regulation of securities transactions are the promotion of disclosure and the prevention of fraud. To that end, the SEC is authorized to require that certain information be provided shareholders when they are asked to authorize that their votes be cast by "proxy." Because in large publicly-held corporations there may be millions of shareholders it is impossible that they all cast their votes at shareholder meetings in person, and so whenever shareholder meetings are necessary (as they are, for example, to elect directors or remove directors for cause—or for other major changes in the corporation, such as Amendments of the Charter, mergers, dissolution, or sale of substantially all of the assets) the method that has evolved is for shareholders to grant a "proxy" allowing someone else, usually a member of corporate management, to cast their votes at the shareholder meeting for them. Management or others may solicit proxies from shareholders, but the SEC requires that such solicitations not be misleading, and that shareholders are supplied with information at the time proxies are solicited, or on an ongoing basis by the corporation (in Annual Reports, quarterly reports and supplemental reports when major economic changes occur to the corporation) so that they can authorize proxies in an informed manner. When management solicits proxies it will usually recommend a course of action for the shareholder, indicating that management recommends that the proxies be cast to authorize a vote in the manner approved by management, but shareholders are free to vote against management proposals when they cast proxy votes, and this is always clearly indicated in the proxy solicitations. These days one can cast proxies (that is, authorize the manner in which one's shares are to be voted at shareholder meetings) by mail, by phone, or even over the internet. You may not be surprised to learn that the vast majority of proxy votes cast favor management, but it is not uncommon for large institutional shareholders to contest recommendations of management, and occasionally management proposals are defeated.

There are four general themes in U.S. proxy regulation. They encompass (1) requirements of detailed disclosure to shareholders regarding the corporation and proposed actions, (2) requiring non-fraudulent or misleading proxy materials, (3) providing opportunities for shareholders to submit their own proposals, and (4) regulation of takeover attempts via proxy contest. Because the potential for proxy fraud implicates shareholder suffrage, proxies are closely regulated by the SEC. The following are two cases concerning § 14 of the Exchange Act, which governs proxies.

J.I. Case Co. et al. v. Borak

Supreme Court of the United States.
377 U.S. 426, 84 S.Ct. 1555, 12 L.Ed.2d 423 (1964).

MR. JUSTICE CLARK delivered the opinion of the Court.

This is a civil action brought by respondent, a stockholder of petitioner J. I. Case Company, charging deprivation of the pre-emptive rights of respondent and other shareholders by reason of a merger between Case and the American Tractor Corporation. It is alleged that the merger was effected through the circulation of a false and misleading proxy statement by those proposing the merger. The complaint was in two counts, the first based on diversity and claiming a breach of the directors' fiduciary duty to the stockholders. The second count alleged a violation of § 14 (a)[4] of the Securities Exchange Act of 1934 with reference to the proxy solicitation material. The trial court held that as to this count it had no power to redress the alleged violations of the Act but was limited solely to the granting of declaratory relief thereon under § 27 of the Act.[5] The court held Wis. Stat., 1961, § 180.405 (4), which requires

---

4   Section 14 (a) of the Securities Exchange Act of 1934, 48 Stat. 895, 15 U. S. C. § 78n (a), provides: "It shall be unlawful for any person, by the use of the mails or by any means or instrumentality of interstate commerce or of any facility of any national securities exchange or otherwise to solicit or to permit the use of his name to solicit any proxy or consent or authorization in respect of any security (other than an exempted security) registered on any national securities exchange in contravention of such rules and regulations as the [Securities and Exchange] Commission may prescribe as necessary or appropriate in the public interest or for the protection of investors."

5   Section 27 of the Act, 48 Stat. 902–903, 15 U. S. C. § 78aa, provides in part: "The district courts of the United States, the Supreme Court of the District of Columbia, and the United States courts of any Territory or other place subject to the jurisdiction of the United States shall have exclusive jurisdiction of violations of this title or the rules and regulations thereunder, and of all suits in equity and actions at law brought to enforce any liability or duty created by this title or the rules and regulations thereunder. Any criminal proceeding may be brought in the district wherein any act or transaction constituting the violation occurred. Any suit or action to enforce any liability or duty created by this title or rules and regulations thereunder, or to enjoin any violation of such title or rules and regulations, may be brought in any such district or in the district wherein the defendant is found or

posting security for expenses in derivative actions, applicable to both counts, except that portion of Count 2 requesting declaratory relief. It ordered the respondent to furnish a bond in the amount of $75,000 thereunder and, upon his failure to do so, dismissed the complaint, save that part of Count 2 seeking a declaratory judgment. On interlocutory appeal the Court of Appeals reversed on both counts, holding that the District Court had the power to grant remedial relief and that the Wisconsin statute was not applicable. * * * We consider only the question of whether § 27 of the Act authorizes a federal cause of action for rescission or damages to a corporate stockholder with respect to a consummated merger which was authorized pursuant to the use of a proxy statement alleged to contain false and misleading statements violative of § 14(a) of the Act. * * *

I.

Respondent, the owner of 2,000 shares of common stock of Case acquired prior to the merger, brought this suit based on diversity jurisdiction seeking to enjoin a proposed merger between Case and the American Tractor Corporation (ATC) on various grounds, including breach of the fiduciary duties of the Case directors, self-dealing among the management of Case and ATC and misrepresentations contained in the material circulated to obtain proxies. The injunction was denied and the merger was thereafter consummated. Subsequently successive amended complaints were filed and the case was heard on the aforesaid two-count complaint. The claims pertinent to the asserted violation of the Securities Exchange Act were predicated on diversity jurisdiction as well as on § 27 of the Act. They alleged: that petitioners, or their predecessors, solicited or permitted their names to be used in the solicitation of proxies of Case stockholders for use at a special stockholders' meeting at which the proposed merger with ATC was to be voted upon; that the proxy solicitation material so circulated was false and misleading in violation of § 14(a) of the Act and Rule 14a–9[6] which the Commission had promulgated thereunder; that the merger was approved at the meeting by a small margin of votes and was thereafter consummated; that the merger would not have been approved but for the false and misleading statements in the proxy solicitation material; and that Case stockholders were damaged thereby. The respondent sought judgment holding the merger void and damages for himself and all other stockholders similarly situated, as well as such further relief "as equity shall require." The District Court ruled that the Wisconsin security for expenses statute did not apply to Count 2 since it arose under federal law. However, the court

---

is an inhabitant or transacts business, and process in such cases may be served in any other district of which the defendant is an inhabitant or wherever the defendant may be found."

6   17 CFR § 240.14a–9 provides: "False or misleading statements. No solicitation subject to § § 240.14a–1 to 240.14a–10 shall be made by means of any proxy statement, form of proxy, notice of meeting, or other communication written or oral containing any statement which at the time and in the light of the circumstances under which it is made, is false or misleading with respect to any material fact, or which omits to state any material fact necessary in order to make the statements therein not false or misleading or necessary to correct any statement in any earlier communication with respect to the solicitation of a proxy for the same meeting or subject matter which has become false or misleading."

found that its jurisdiction was limited to declaratory relief in a private, as opposed to a government, suit alleging violation of § 14(a) of the Act. Since the additional equitable relief and damages prayed for by the respondent would, therefore, be available only under state law, it ruled those claims subject to the security for expenses statute. After setting the amount of security at $75,000 and upon the representation of counsel that the security would not be posted, the court dismissed the complaint, save that portion of Count 2 seeking a declaration that the proxy solicitation material was false and misleading and that the proxies and, hence, the merger were void.

II.

It appears clear that private parties have a right under § 27 to bring suit for violation of § 14(a) of the Act. Indeed, this section specifically grants the appropriate District Courts jurisdiction over "all suits in equity and actions at law brought to enforce any liability or duty created" under the Act. The petitioners make no concessions, however, emphasizing that Congress made no specific reference to a private right of action in § 14(a) * * *.

III.

The purpose of § 14 (a) is to prevent management or others from obtaining authorization for corporate action by means of deceptive or inadequate disclosure in proxy solicitation. The section stemmed from the congressional belief that "fair corporate suffrage is an important right that should attach to every equity security bought on a public exchange." H. R. Rep. No. 1383, 73d Cong., 2d Sess., 13. It was intended to "control the conditions under which proxies may be solicited with a view to preventing the recurrence of abuses which . . . [had] frustrated the free exercise of the voting rights of stockholders." Id., at 14. "Too often proxies are solicited without explanation to the stockholder of the real nature of the questions for which authority to cast his vote is sought." S. Rep. No. 792, 73d Cong., 2d Sess., 12. These broad remedial purposes are evidenced in the language of the section which makes it "unlawful for any person . . . to solicit or to permit the use of his name to solicit any proxy or consent or authorization in respect of any security . . . registered on any national securities exchange in contravention of such rules and regulations as the Commission may prescribe as necessary or appropriate in the public interest *or for the protection of investors.*" (Italics supplied.) While this language makes no specific reference to a private right of action, among its chief purposes is "the protection of investors," which certainly implies the availability of judicial relief where necessary to achieve that result.

The injury which a stockholder suffers from corporate action pursuant to a deceptive proxy solicitation ordinarily flows from the damage done the corporation, rather than from the damage inflicted directly upon the stockholder. The damage suffered results not from the deceit practiced on him alone but rather from the deceit practiced on the stockholders as a group. To hold that derivative actions are not within the sweep of the section would therefore be tantamount to a denial of private relief. Private enforcement of the proxy rules provides a necessary supplement to Commission action. As in antitrust treble damage litigation the possibility of civil damages or injunctive relief serves as a most effective weapon in the enforcement of the proxy requirements. The Commission advises that it examines over 2,000 proxy statements annually and each of them must necessarily be expedited. Time does not permit an independent examination of the facts set out in the proxy material and this results in the Commission's acceptance of the representations contained therein at their face value, unless contrary to other material on file with it. Indeed, on the allegations of respondent's complaint, the proxy material failed to disclose alleged unlawful market manipulation of the stock of ATC, and this unlawful manipulation would not have been apparent to the Commission until after the merger.

We, therefore, believe that under the circumstances here it is the duty of the courts to be alert to provide such remedies as are necessary to make effective the congressional purpose. As was said in *Sola Electric Co. v. Jefferson Electric Co., 317 U.S. 173, 176 (1942):*

> "When a federal statute condemns an act as unlawful, the extent and nature of the legal consequences of the condemnation, though left by the statute to judicial determination, are nevertheless federal questions, the answers to which are to be derived from the statute and the federal policy which it has adopted."

* * * It is for the federal courts "to adjust their remedies so as to grant the necessary relief" where federally secured rights are invaded. "And it is also well settled that where legal rights have been invaded, and a federal statute provides for a general right to sue for such invasion, federal courts may use any available remedy to make good the wrong done." *Bell v. Hood, 327 U.S. 678, 684 (1946).* Section 27 grants the District Courts jurisdiction "of all suits in equity and actions at law brought to enforce any liability or duty created by this title. . . . " In passing on almost identical language found in the Securities Act of 1933, the Court found the words entirely sufficient to fashion a remedy to rescind a fraudulent sale, secure restitution and even to enforce the right to restitution against a third party holding assets of the vendor. *Deckert v. Independence Shares Corp., 311 U.S. 282 (1940).* This significant language was used:

> "The power *to enforce* implies the power to make effective the right of recovery afforded by the Act. And the power to make the right of recovery effective implies the power to utilize any of the procedures or actions normally available to the litigant according to the exigencies of the particular case." At 288. * * *

Nor do we find merit in the contention that such remedies are limited to prospective relief. This was the position taken in *Dann v. Studebaker-Packard Corp., 288 F.2d 201,* where it was held that the "preponderance of questions of state law which would have to be interpreted and applied in order to grant the relief sought . . . is so great that the federal question involved . . . is really negligible in comparison." At 214. But we believe that the overriding federal law applicable here would, where the facts required, control the appropriateness of redress despite the provisions of state corporation law, for it "is not uncommon for federal courts to fashion federal law where federal rights are concerned." *Textile Workers v. Lincoln Mills, 353 U.S. 448, 457 (1957)*. In addition, the fact that questions of state law must be decided does not change the character of the right; it remains federal. As Chief Justice Marshall said in *Osborn v. Bank of the United States, 9 Wheat. 738 (1824)*:

> "If this were sufficient to withdraw a case from the jurisdiction of the federal Courts, almost every case, although involving the construction of a law, would be withdrawn. . . . " At 819–820.

Moreover, if federal jurisdiction were limited to the granting of declaratory relief, victims of deceptive proxy statements would be obliged to go into state courts for remedial relief. And if the law of the State happened to attach no responsibility to the use of misleading proxy statements, the whole purpose of the section might be frustrated. Furthermore, the hurdles that the victim might face (such as separate suits, as contemplated by *Dann v. Studebaker–Packard Corp., supra*, security for expenses statutes, bringing in all parties necessary for complete relief, etc.) might well prove insuperable to effective relief.

IV.

Our finding that federal courts have the power to grant all necessary remedial relief is not to be construed as any indication of what we believe to be the necessary and appropriate relief in this case. We are concerned here only with a determination that federal jurisdiction for this purpose does exist. Whatever remedy is necessary must await the trial on the merits.

* * *

Virginia Bankshares, Inc. v. Sandberg

Supreme Court of the United States.
501 U.S. 1083, 111 S. Ct. 2749, (1964).

Justice SOUTER delivered the opinion of the Court.

Section 14(a) of the Securities Exchange Act of 1934, 48 Stat. 895, 15 U.S.C. § 78n(a), authorizes the Securities and Exchange Commission (SEC) to adopt rules for the solicitation of proxies, and prohibits their violation. In *J.I. Case Co. v. Borak*, 377 U.S. 426, 84 S.Ct. 1555, 12 L.Ed.2d 423 (1964), we first recognized an implied private right of action for the breach of § 14(a) as implemented by SEC Rule 14a-9, which prohibits the solicitation of proxies by means of materially false or misleading statements.

The questions before us are whether a statement couched in conclusory or qualitative terms purporting to explain directors' reasons for recommending certain corporate action can be materially misleading within the meaning of Rule 14a-9, and whether causation of damages compensable under § 14(a) can be shown by a member of a class of minority shareholders whose votes are not required by law or corporate bylaw to authorize the corporate action subject to the proxy solicitation. We hold that knowingly false statements of reasons may be actionable even though conclusory in form, but that respondents have failed to demonstrate the equitable basis required to extend the § 14(a) private action to such shareholders when any indication of congressional intent to do so is lacking.

I

In December 1986, First American Bankshares, Inc. (FABI), a bank holding company, began a "freeze-out" merger, in which the First American Bank of Virginia (Bank) eventually merged into Virginia Bankshares, Inc. (VBI), a wholly owned subsidiary of FABI. VBI owned 85% of the Bank's shares, the remaining 15% being in the hands of some 2,000 minority shareholders. FABI hired the investment banking firm of Keefe, Bruyette & Woods (KBW) to give an opinion on the appropriate price for shares of the minority holders, who would lose their interests in the Bank as a result of the merger. Based on market quotations and unverified information from FABI, KBW gave the Bank's executive committee an opinion that $42 a share would be a fair price for the minority stock. The executive committee approved the merger proposal at that price, and the full board followed suit.

Although Virginia law required only that such a merger proposal be submitted to a vote at a shareholders' meeting, and that the meeting be preceded by circulation of a statement of information to the shareholders, the directors nevertheless solicited proxies for voting on the proposal at the annual meeting set for April 21, 1987. In their solicitation, the directors urged the proposal's adoption and stated they had approved the plan because of its opportunity for the minority shareholders to achieve a "high" value, which they elsewhere described as a "fair" price, for their stock.

Although most minority shareholders gave the proxies requested, respondent Sandberg did not, and after approval of the merger she sought damages in the United States District Court for the Eastern District of Virginia from VBI, FABI, and the directors of the Bank. She pleaded two counts, one for soliciting proxies in violation of § 14(a) and Rule 14a-9, and the other for breaching fiduciary duties owed to the minority shareholders under state law. Under the first count, Sandberg alleged, among other things, that the directors had not believed that the price offered was high or that the terms of the merger were fair, but had recommended the merger only because they believed they had no alternative if they wished to remain on the board. At trial, Sandberg invoked language from this Court's opinion in *Mills v. Electric Auto-Lite*

Co., 396 U.S. 375, 385, 90 S.Ct. 616, 622, 24 L.Ed.2d 593 (1970), to obtain an instruction that the jury could find for her without a showing of her own reliance on the alleged misstatements, so long as they were material and the proxy solicitation was an "essential link" in the merger process.

The jury's verdicts were for Sandberg on both counts, after finding violations of Rule 14a-9 by all defendants and a breach of fiduciary duties by the Bank's directors. The jury awarded Sandberg $18 a share, having found that she would have received $60 if her stock had been valued adequately. * * *

On appeal, the United States Court of Appeals for the Fourth Circuit affirmed the judgments, holding that certain statements in the proxy solicitation were materially misleading for purposes of the Rule, and that respondents could maintain their action even though their votes had not been needed to effectuate the merger. 891 F.2d 1112 (1989). We granted certiorari because of the importance of the issues presented. * * *

II

The Court of Appeals affirmed petitioners' liability for two statements found to have been materially misleading in violation of § 14(a) of the Act, one of which was that "The Plan of Merger has been approved by the Board of Directors because it provides an opportunity for the Bank's public shareholders to achieve a high value for their shares." App. to Pet. for Cert. 53a. Petitioners argue that statements of opinion or belief incorporating indefinite and unverifiable expressions cannot be actionable as misstatements of material fact within the meaning of Rule 14a-9, and that such a declaration of opinion or belief should never be actionable when placed in a proxy solicitation incorporating statements of fact sufficient to enable readers to draw their own, independent conclusions.

A

We consider first the actionability per se of statements of reasons, opinion, or belief. Because such a statement by definition purports to express what is consciously on the speaker's mind, we interpret the jury verdict as finding that the directors' statements of belief and opinion were made with knowledge that the directors did not hold the beliefs or opinions expressed, and we confine our discussion to statements so made. That such statements may be materially significant raises no serious question. * * * We think there is no room to deny that a statement of belief by corporate directors about a recommended course of action, or an explanation of their reasons for recommending it, can take on just that importance. Shareholders know that directors usually have knowledge and expertness far exceeding the normal investor's resources, and the directors' perceived superiority is magnified even further by the common knowledge that state law customarily obliges them to exercise their judgment in the shareholders' interest. Cf. *Day v. Avery*, 179 U.S.App.D.C. 63, 71, 548 F.2d 1018, 1026 (1976) (action for misrepresentation). Naturally, then, the shareowner faced with a proxy request will think it important to know the directors' beliefs about the course they recommend and their specific reasons for urging the stockholders to embrace it.

B

1

But, assuming materiality, the question remains whether statements of reasons, opinions, or beliefs are statements "with respect to ... material fact [s]" so as to fall within the strictures of the Rule. Petitioners argue that we would invite wasteful litigation of amorphous issues outside the readily provable realm of fact if we were to recognize liability here on proof that the directors did not recommend the merger for the stated reason * * *

It is no answer to argue, as petitioners do, that the quoted statement on which liability was predicated did not express a reason in dollars and cents, but focused instead on the "indefinite and unverifiable" term, "high" value, much like the similar claim that the merger's terms were "fair" to shareholders. The objection ignores the fact that such conclusory terms in a commercial context are reasonably understood to rest on a factual basis that justifies them as accurate, the absence of which renders them misleading. * * * In this case, whether $42 was "high," and the proposal "fair" to the minority shareholders, depended on whether provable facts about the Bank's assets, and about actual and potential levels of operation, substantiated a value that was above, below, or more or less at the $42 figure, when assessed in accordance with recognized methods of valuation.

Respondents adduced evidence for just such facts in proving that the statement was misleading about its subject matter and a false expression of the directors' reasons. Whereas the proxy statement described the $42 price as offering a premium above both book value and market price, the evidence indicated that a calculation of the book figure based on the appreciated value of the Bank's real estate holdings eliminated any such premium. The evidence on the significance of market price showed that KBW had conceded that the market was closed, thin, and dominated by FABI, facts omitted from the statement. There was, indeed, evidence of a "going concern" value for the Bank in excess of $60 per share of common stock, another fact never disclosed. However conclusory the directors' statement may have been, then, it was open to attack by garden-variety evidence, subject neither to a plaintiff's control nor ready manufacture, and there was no undue risk of open-ended liability or uncontrollable litigation in allowing respondents the opportunity for recovery on the allegation that it was misleading to call $42 "high." * * *

2

* * * The question arises, then, whether disbelief, or undisclosed belief or motivation, standing alone, should be a sufficient basis to sustain an action under § 14(a), absent proof by the sort of objective evidence described above that the statement also expressly or impliedly asserted something false or misleading about its subject matter. We think that proof of mere disbelief or belief undisclosed should not suffice

for liability under § 14(a), and if nothing more had been required or proven in this case, we would reverse for that reason.

On the one hand, it would be rare to find a case with evidence solely of disbelief or undisclosed motivation without further proof that the statement was defective as to its subject matter. While we certainly would not hold a director's naked admission of disbelief incompetent evidence of a proxy statement's false or misleading character, such an unusual admission will not very often stand alone, and we do not substantially narrow the cause of action by requiring a plaintiff to demonstrate something false or misleading in what the statement expressly or impliedly declared about its subject.

On the other hand, to recognize liability on mere disbelief or undisclosed motive without any demonstration that the proxy statement was false or misleading about its subject would authorize § 14(a) litigation confined solely to what one skeptical court spoke of as the "impurities" of a director's "unclean heart." * * * We therefore hold disbelief or undisclosed motivation, standing alone, insufficient to satisfy the element of fact that must be established under § 14(a).

C

* * * [P]etitioners argue that even if conclusory statements of reason or belief can be actionable under § 14(a), we should confine liability to instances where the proxy material fails to disclose the offending statement's factual basis. There would be no justification for holding the shareholders entitled to judicial relief, that is, when they were given evidence that a stated reason for a proxy recommendation was misleading and an opportunity to draw that conclusion themselves.

The answer to this argument rests on the difference between a merely misleading statement and one that is materially so. While a misleading statement will not always lose its deceptive edge simply by joinder with others that are true, the true statements may discredit the other one so obviously that the risk of real deception drops to nil. Since liability under § 14(a) must rest not only on deceptiveness but materiality as well (*i.e.*, it has to be significant enough to be important to a reasonable investor deciding how to vote, see *TSC Industries,* 426 U.S., at 449, 96 S.Ct., at 2132), petitioners are on perfectly firm ground insofar as they argue that publishing accurate facts in a proxy statement can render a misleading proposition too unimportant to ground liability.

But not every mixture with the true will neutralize the deceptive. If it would take a financial analyst to spot the tension between the one and the other, whatever is misleading will remain materially so, and liability should follow. * * *

Suffice it to say that the evidence invoked by petitioners in the instant case fell short of compelling the jury to find the facial materiality of the misleading statement neutralized. The directors claim, for example, to have made an explanatory disclosure of further reasons for their recommendation when they said they would keep their seats following the merger, but they failed to mention what at least one of them admitted in testimony, that they would have had no expectation of doing so without supporting the proposal, App. 281-282. And although the proxy statement did speak factually about the merger price in describing it as higher than share prices in recent sales, it failed even to mention the closed market dominated by FABI. None of these disclosures that the directors point to was, then, anything more than a half-truth, and the record shows that another fact statement they invoke was arguably even worse. The claim that the merger price exceeded book value was controverted, as we have seen already, by evidence of a higher book value than the directors conceded, reflecting appreciation in the Bank's real estate portfolio. Finally, the solicitation omitted any mention of the Bank's value as a going concern at more than $60 a share, as against the merger price of $42. There was, in sum, no more of a compelling case for the statement's immateriality than for its accuracy. [The second argument, concerning the causation issue, is omitted].

Justice SCALIA, concurring in part and concurring in the judgment.

I

As I understand the Court's opinion, the statement "In the opinion of the Directors, this is a high value for the shares" would produce liability if in fact it was not a high value and the directors knew that. It would not produce liability if in fact it was not a high value but the directors honestly believed otherwise. The statement "The Directors voted to accept the proposal *because* they believe it offers a high value" would not produce liability if in fact the directors' genuine motive was quite different-except that it would produce liability if the proposal in fact did not offer a high value and the Directors knew that.

I agree with all of this. However, not every sentence that has the word "opinion" in it, or that refers to motivation for directors' actions, leads us into this psychic thicket. Sometimes such a sentence actually represents facts as facts rather than opinions-and in that event no more need be done than apply the normal rules for § 14(a) liability. I think that is the situation here. In my view, the statement at issue in this case is most fairly read as affirming *separately* both the fact of the Directors' opinion *and* the accuracy of the facts upon which the opinion was assertedly based. It reads as follows:

> "The Plan of Merger has been approved by the Board of Directors because it provides an opportunity for the Bank's public shareholders to achieve a high value for their shares." App. to Pet. for Cert. 53a.

Had it read "because *in their estimation* it provides an opportunity, etc.", it would have set forth nothing but an opinion. As written, however, it asserts both that the board of directors acted for a particular reason *and* that that reason is correct. This interpretation is made clear by what immediately follows: "The price to be paid is about 30% higher than the [last traded price immediately before announcement of the proposal].... [T]he $42 per share that will be paid to public holders of the common stock represents a premium of approximately 26% over the book value.... [T]he bank earned $24,767,000 in the year ended December 31, 1986...." *Id.*, at 53a-54a.

These are all facts that support and that are obviously introduced for the *purpose* of supporting-the factual truth of the "because" clause, *i.e.,* that the proposal gives shareholders a "high value."

If the present case were to proceed, therefore, I think the normal § 14(a) principles governing misrepresentation of fact would apply. * * *

NOTES AND QUESTIONS

I. **WHAT SORT OF** information must be supplied when proxies are solicited, what is involved in the solicitation of proxies, and when is a statement by management or others to be construed as a solicitation? Some of the answers to these questions are suggested by *J.I. Case v. Borak*. It observes that Section 14(a) of the Securities Exchange Act of 1934 authorizes the SEC to promulgate rules regarding proxy solicitation "for the protection of investors," and that solicitation of proxies in violation of those rules is "unlawful," and, because unlawful conduct under the securities act can virtually always be the subject of criminal prosecution by the Justice Department or a civil proceeding brought by the SEC, the consequences of non-compliance with the proxy rules can be severe. You will have noticed that *J.I. Case v. Borak* holds that violations of the proxy rules can also lead to civil actions being brought by individuals who allege injury as a result of such non-compliance. Do you agree with the court's reasoning on this point? Is the reasoning weakened by the suggestion, made by the defendant in the case, and often repeated since then, that other sections of the Securities Laws expressly permit private actions, and if none is expressly permitted in Section 14(a) then the courts should not grant such permission? You will remember that similar issues were raised by the courts' permitting private actions grounded on violations of Section 10(b), though such actions are now expressly acknowledged as valid by Congressional statute.

A brief review of some of the provisions of the proxy rules may help clarify the issues in this area. These are collected in the SEC's Regulation 14A, and can be found on the web, at http://www.sec.gov/divisions/corpfin/forms/14a.htm. We ought to begin with the definition of a proxy "solicitation," from Regulation 14a–1(l):

(l) Solicitation.

(1) The terms "solicit" and "solicitation" include:

(i) Any request for a proxy whether or not accompanied by or included in a form of proxy;

(ii) Any request to execute or not to execute, or to revoke, a proxy; or

(iii) The furnishing of a form of proxy or other communication to security holders under circumstances reasonably calculated to result
in the procurement, withholding or revocation of a proxy.

Does this definition strike you as too broad? Would it conflict, for example, with
the First Amendment? Would a corporation's press release, extolling the performance
of the company, or of particular director who might be standing for reelection come
within the definition? Consider what is required if a given communication is deemed
to be a "solicitation." This is covered by Rule 14a–3, which provides, in pertinent part:

(a) No solicitation subject to this regulation shall be made unless each
person solicited is concurrently furnished or has previously been furnished
with a publicly-filed preliminary or definitive written proxy statement
containing the information specified in Schedule 14A * * * or with a publicly-filed preliminary or definitive written proxy statement included in a
registration statement filed under the Securities Act of 1933 * * *

(b) If the solicitation is made on behalf of the registrant other than an
investment company registered under the Investment Company Act of
1940, and relates to an annual (or special meeting in lieu of the annual)
meeting of security holders, or written consent in lieu of such meeting, at
which directors are to be elected, each proxy statement furnished pursuant
to paragraph (a) of this section shall be accompanied or preceded by an
annual report to security holders as follows:

* * *(1) The report shall include, for the registrant and its subsidiaries
consolidated, audited balance sheets as of the end of each of the two most
recent fiscal years and audited statements of income and cash flows for
each of the three most recent fiscal years * * *

(2) (i) Financial statements and notes thereto shall be presented in roman
type at least as large and as legible as 10–point modern type. If
necessary for convenient presentation, the financial statements may
be in roman type as large and as legible as 8-point modern type. All
type shall be leaded at least 2 points.

(ii) Where the annual report to security holders is delivered through
an electronic medium, issuers may satisfy legibility requirements
applicable to printed documents, such as type size and font, by presenting all required information in a format readily communicated
to investors.

(3) The report shall contain the supplementary financial information required by Item 302 of Regulation S–K (§ 229.302 of this chapter).

(4) The report shall contain information concerning changes in and disagreements with accountants on accounting and financial disclosure required by Item 304 of Regulation S–K (§ 229.304 of this chapter).

(5) (i) The report shall contain the selected financial data required by Item 301 of Regulation S–K (§ 229.301 of this chapter).

(ii) The report shall contain management's discussion and analysis of financial condition and results of operations required by Item 303 of Regulation S–K (§ 229.303 of this chapter) or, if applicable, a plan of operation required by Item 303(a) of Regulation S–B (§ 228.303(a) of this chapter).

(iii) The report shall contain the quantitative and qualitative disclosures about market risk required by Item 305 of Regulation S–K (§ 229.305 of this chapter).

(6) The report shall contain a brief description of the business done by the registrant and its subsidiaries during the most recent fiscal year which will, in the opinion of management, indicate the general nature and scope of the business of the registrant and its subsidiaries.

(7) The report shall contain information relating to the registrant's industry segments, classes of similar products or services, foreign and domestic operations and exports sales required by paragraphs (b), (c)(1)(i) and (d) of Item 101 of Regulation S–K (§ 229.101 of this chapter).

(8) The report shall identify each of the registrant's directors and executive officers, and shall indicate the principal occupation or employment of each such person and the name and principal business of any organization by which such person is employed.

(9) The report shall contain the market price of and dividends on the registrant's common equity and related security holder matters required by Item 201(a), (b) and (c) of Regulation S–K (§ 229.201 of this chapter).

(10) The registrant's proxy statement, or the report, shall contain an undertaking in bold face or otherwise reasonably prominent type to provide without charge to each person solicited upon the written request of any such person, a copy of the registrant's annual report on Form 10–K and Form 10–KSB, including the financial statements and the financial statement schedules, required to be filed with the Commission pursuant to Rule 13a–1 under the Act for the registrant's most recent fiscal year, and shall indicate the name and address (including title or department) of the person to whom such a written request is to be directed. * * *

You will not, of course, be aware of the precise requirements of disclosure here required without consulting the other SEC forms or federal law referenced, but have you seen enough to determine the quality and quantity of information likely to be supplied in a proxy statement?

You can get some sense of the information required, by considering what must be in a Schedule 14A, which must be supplied for proxies not solicited at the time of the annual meeting (when an annual report must accompany proxies). Among the directions for filling out Schedule 14A are:

(1) Describe briefly any substantial interest, direct or indirect, by security holdings or otherwise, of each participant as defined in paragraphs (a)(ii), (iii), (iv), (v) and (vi) of Instruction 3 to Item 4 of this Schedule 14A, in any matter to be acted upon at the meeting, and include with respect to each participant the following information, or a fair and adequate summary thereof:

(i) Name and business address of the participant.

(ii) The participant's present principal occupation or employment and the name, principal business and address of any corporation or other organization in which such employment is carried on.

(iii) State whether or not, during the past ten years, the participant has been convicted in a criminal proceeding (excluding traffic violations or similar misdemeanors) and, if so, give dates, nature of conviction, name and location of court, and penalty imposed or other disposition of the case. A negative answer need not be included in the proxy statement or other soliciting material.

(iv) State the amount of each class of securities of the registrant which the participant owns beneficially, directly or indirectly.

(v) State the amount of each class of securities of the registrant which the participant owns of record but not beneficially.

(vi) State with respect to all securities of the registrant purchased or sold within the past two years, the dates on which they were purchased or sold and the amount purchased or sold on each such date.

(vii) If any part of the purchase price or market value of any of the shares specified in paragraph (b)(1)(vi) of this Item is represented by funds borrowed or otherwise obtained for the purpose of acquiring or holding such securities, so state and indicate the amount of the indebtedness as of the latest practicable date. If such funds were borrowed or obtained otherwise than pursuant to a margin account or bank loan in the regular course of business of a bank, broker or dealer, briefly describe the transaction, and state the names of the parties.

(viii) State whether or not the participant is, or was within the past year, a party to any contract, arrangements or understandings with any person with respect to any securities of the registrant, including, but not limited to, joint ventures, loan or option arrangements, puts or calls, guarantees against loss or guarantees of profit, division of losses or profits, or the giving or withholding of proxies. If so, name the parties to such contracts, arrangements or understandings and give the details thereof.

(ix) State the amount of securities of the registrant owned beneficially, directly or indirectly, by each of the participant's associates and the name and address of each such associate.

(x) State the amount of each class of securities of any parent or subsidiary of the registrant which the participant owns beneficially, directly or indirectly.

(xi) Furnish for the participant and associates of the participant the information required by Item 404(a) of Regulation S–K (§ 229.404(a) of this chapter).

(xii) State whether or not the participant or any associates of the participant have any arrangement or understanding with any person—

(A) with respect to any future employment by the registrant or its affiliates; or

(B) with respect to any future transactions to which the registrant or any of its affiliates will or may be a party. If so, describe such arrangement or understanding and state the names of the parties thereto.

Would this information help you in deciding whether or not to grant a proxy? Compliance with the proxy rules is required of corporations which are publicly traded and registered pursuant to the 1933 Securities Act, and not those close corporations which are privately held. Still, many publicly-held businesses are relatively small businesses. Can you understand how the costs of compliance might be substantial, and also how compliance is unlikely to be accomplished without the aid of professionals, at least lawyers and accountants? In general, forms for solicitation of proxies and proxy statements must be filed with the SEC before they are distributed to shareholders, and the SEC will review these documents, not necessarily for the truth contained therein, but the SEC may ask for explanations of particular statements, may suggest revisions, and may indicate where materials do not comply with SEC requirements. You may have inferred that proxy solicitors are well-advised to revise in line with SEC staff suggestions, or to decline to send out materials which the SEC has indicated are problematic. The SEC reviews many thousands of such documents, and whether or not the SEC comments on the materials the person or firm soliciting proxies remains responsible for their accuracy. As you have seen, Rule 14a–9 creates liability for false or misleading statements, and, as you have seen from *J.I. Case v. Borak*, violations of 14a–9 can lead to private actions by those purportedly injured by such false or misleading statements. One solicits proxies, then, at one's peril.

2. THIS FACT BECOMES especially clear in *Virginia Bankshares*. Those favoring the merger held 85% of the shares and could not have been defeated in a vote. Why do you think the directors solicited proxies when it was unnecessary to do so? How do you feel about the liability to which they were exposed? Note that because the minority shareholders could not have prevailed in a vote their claims were dismissed for lack of causation.

....

3. IN COURTS OF EQUITY there exists the long-standing doctrine of "clean hands." This doctrine requires that a plaintiff in equity not be at fault himself; that is, a plaintiff cannot recover if he enters the court with "unclean hands." A similar doctrine is known as *in pari delicto*, which requires that a plaintiff not be equally or more at fault than the defendant. The famous case of *Gaudiosi v. Mellon* considered the clean hands doctrine in a proxy fraud context. 269 F.2d 873 (3d Cir. 1959). The plaintiff Phillips and some of his fellow shareholders sought relief in the federal trial court, acting as a court of equity, which they asked to issue an injunction to prevent the management nominees of the Pennsylvania Railroad from being seated as directors, alleging that the proxies which management obtained and voted for those seats were somehow obtained in a manner that violated the securities law. The district court found for the defendants, and the appellate court refused to consider the merits of the plaintiffs' case because of the securities violations of Phillips himself: he had sent threatening telegrams to Swiss banks, shareholders in the company with an upcoming vote, falsely warning of their fraud liability. This caused the banks to not vote most of their proxies. The court was unmoved by plaintiffs' appeals.

We do not need to dwell further on the District Court's findings of 'unclean hands' on Phillips' part except to say that his dire threats to the Swiss banks in his April 30th telegrams of possible anti-trust action, and his invocation of the spectres of 'fraud', 'violation of American equitable and common law principles applicable to banks', violation of 'the rules of the Securities and Exchange Commission and New York Stock Exchange as well as American banking practices applicable to all stock exchange brokers and banks in this country' amply supported the District Court's fact-finding of 'deliberate and malicious' wrongdoing with intent to 'intimidate' in violation of the Rules of the Securities and Exchange Commission in proxy contests.

Clearly Phillips' conduct constituted the 'unclean hands' which barred his prayers for equitable relief. * * *

These principles are well-settled:

- One who comes into equity must come with clean hands and keep those hands clean throughout the pendency of the litigation even to the time of ultimate disposition by an appellate court. * * *

- Courts are concerned primarily with their own integrity in the application of the clean hands maxim and even though not raised by the parties the court will of its own motion apply it. * * *

- The clean hands maxim gives wide sweep to the equity court's exercise of discretion 'in refusing to aid the unclean litigant.' * * *

- The equity court 'is not bound by formula or restrained by any limitation that tends to trammel the free and just exercise of discretion.' * * *

'The doctrine (of unclean hands) is confessedly derived from the unwillingness of a court, originally and still nominally one of conscience, to give its peculiar relief to a suitor who in the very controversy has so conducted himself as to shock the moral sensibilities of the judge. It has nothing to do with the rights or liabilities of the parties; indeed the defendant who invokes it need not be damaged, and the court may even raise it sua sponte [on its own]. * * *

There remains for disposition Phillips' contention that 'the maxim of 'unclean hands' does not dispose of the rights of others', and that 'neither plaintiffs Gaudiosi or Schwartz participated in these acts of Phillips, thus the defense is totally inapplicable to them, as well as to the 23,000, or less, stockholders upon whose behalf all three plaintiffs sued.' * * *

[T]o subscribe to this last contention would require us to ignore the fact that plaintiffs' two actions (apart from the derivative claim in Count IV) were specifically instituted to further Phillips' candidacy for director. The startling result would be to permit Phillips to eat his apple with 'unclean hands'. Justice may be blind but it isn't 'dumb'.

Do you approve of the "clean hands" doctrine?

....

4. SO FAR WE HAVE BEEN examining the Regulations which relate to the solicitation of proxies, but we should also note one other means of shareholder communication and control, also covered in Regulation 14A. This is the federally-provided-for right of shareholders to put items on the agenda for the annual shareholder meeting, to be voted on by their fellow shareholders. The SEC regards this as a very important matter, and note that the language of this Rule, which is provided below, is carefully drafted in a form that shareholders can purportedly understand. Why do you suppose that the SEC has not done this for all of its Regulations?

Shareholder Proposals

§ 240.14a–8.

This section addresses when a company must include a shareholder's proposal in its proxy statement and identify the proposal in its form of proxy when the company holds an annual or special meeting of shareholders. In summary, in order to have your shareholder proposal included on a company's proxy card, and included along with any supporting statement in its proxy statement, you must be eligible and follow certain procedures. Under a few specific circumstances, the company is permitted to exclude your proposal, but only after submitting its reasons to the Commission. We structured this section in a question-and-answer format so that it is easier to under-stand. The references to "you" are to a shareholder seeking to submit the proposal.

(a) **Question 1:** What is a proposal?

A shareholder proposal is your recommendation or requirement that the company and/or its board of directors take action, which you intend to present at a meeting of the company's shareholders. Your proposal should state as clearly as possible the course of action that you believe the company should follow. If your proposal is placed on the company's proxy card, the company must also provide in the form of proxy means for shareholders to specify by boxes a choice between approval or disapproval, or abstention. Unless otherwise indicated, the word "proposal" as used in this section refers both to your proposal, and to your corresponding statement in support of your proposal (if any).

(b) **Question 2:** Who is eligible to submit a proposal, and how do I demonstrate to the company that I am eligible?

(1) In order to be eligible to submit a proposal, you must have continuously held at least $2,000 in market value, or 1%, of the company's securities entitled to be voted on the proposal at the meeting for at least one year by the date you submit the proposal. You must continue to hold those securities through the date of the meeting.

   *   *   *

(c) **Question 3:** How many proposals may I submit?

Each shareholder may submit no more than one proposal to a company for a particular shareholders' meeting.

(d) **Question 4:** How long can my proposal be?

The proposal, including any accompanying supporting statement, may not exceed 500 words.

   *   *   *

(f) **Question 6:** What if I fail to follow one of the eligibility or procedural require-ments explained in answers to Questions 1 through 4 of this section?

(1) The company may exclude your proposal, but only after it has notified you of the problem, and you have failed adequately to correct it. * * *

(2) If you fail in your promise to hold the required number of securities through the date of the meeting of shareholders, then the company will be permitted to exclude all of your proposals from its proxy materials for any meeting held in the following two calendar years.

(g) Question 7: Who has the burden of persuading the Commission or its staff that my proposal can be excluded?

Except as otherwise noted, the burden is on the company to demonstrate that it is entitled to exclude a proposal.

(h) Question 8: Must I appear personally at the shareholders' meeting to present the proposal?

(1) Either you, or your representative who is qualified under state law to present the proposal on your behalf, must attend the meeting to present the proposal. * * *

* * *(3) If you or your qualified representative fail to appear and present the proposal, without good cause, the company will be permitted to exclude all of your proposals from its proxy materials for any meetings held in the following two calendar years.

(i) Question 9: If I have complied with the procedural requirements, on what other bases may a company rely to exclude my proposal?

(1) *Improper under state law:* If the proposal is not a proper subject for action by shareholders under the laws of the jurisdiction of the company's organization; * * *

(2) *Violation of law:* If the proposal would, if implemented, cause the company to violate any state, federal, or foreign law to which it is subject; * * *

(3) *Violation of proxy rules:* If the proposal or supporting statement is contrary to any of the Commission's proxy rules, including § 240.14a–9, which prohibits materially false or misleading statements in proxy soliciting materials;

(4) *Personal grievance; special interest:* If the proposal relates to the redress of a personal claim or grievance against the company or any other person, or if it is designed to result in a benefit to you, or to further a personal interest, which is not shared by the other shareholders at large;

(5) *Relevance:* If the proposal relates to operations which account for less than 5 percent of the company's total assets at the end of its most recent fiscal year, and for less than 5 percent of its net earnings and gross sales for its most recent fiscal year, and is not otherwise significantly related to the company's business;

(6) *Absence of power/authority:* If the company would lack the power or authority to implement the proposal;

(7) *Management functions:* If the proposal deals with a matter relating to the company's ordinary business operations;

(8) *Relates to election:* If the proposal relates to an election for membership on the company's board of directors or analogous governing body;

(9) *Conflicts with company's proposal:* If the proposal directly conflicts with one of the company's own proposals to be submitted to shareholders at the same meeting; * * *

(10) *Substantially implemented:* If the company has already substantially implemented the proposal;

(11) *Duplication:* If the proposal substantially duplicates another proposal previously submitted to the company by another proponent that will be included in the company's proxy materials for the same meeting;

(12) *Resubmissions:* If the proposal deals with substantially the same subject matter as another proposal or proposals that has or have been previously included in the company's proxy materials within the preceding 5 calendar years, a company may exclude it from its proxy materials for any meeting held within 3 calendar years of the last time it was included if the proposal received:

    (i) Less than 3% of the vote if proposed once within the preceding 5 calendar years;

    (ii) Less than 6% of the vote on its last submission to shareholders if proposed twice previously within the preceding 5 calendar years; or

    (iii) Less than 10% of the vote on its last submission to shareholders if proposed three times or more previously within the preceding 5 calendar years; and

(13) *Specific amount of dividends:* If the proposal relates to specific amounts of cash or stock dividends.

* * *

(l) Question 12: If the company includes my shareholder proposal in its proxy materials, what information about me must it include along with the proposal itself?

(1) The company's proxy statement must include your name and address, as well as the number of the company's voting securities that you hold. However, instead of providing that information, the company may instead include a statement that it will provide the information to shareholders promptly upon receiving an oral or written request. * * *

(m) Question 13: What can I do if the company includes in its proxy statement reasons why it believes shareholders should not vote in favor of my proposal, and I disagree with some of its statements?

(1) The company may elect to include in its proxy statement reasons why it believes shareholders should vote against your proposal. The company is allowed to make arguments reflecting its own point of view, just as you may express your own point of view in your proposal's supporting statement.

(2) However, if you believe that the company's opposition to your proposal contains materially false or misleading statements that may violate our anti-fraud rule, § 240.14a–9, you should promptly send to the Commission staff and the company a letter explaining the reasons for your view, along with a copy of the company's statements opposing your proposal. To the extent possible, your letter should include specific factual information demonstrating the inaccuracy of the company's claims. Time permitting, you may wish to try to work out your differences with the company by yourself before contacting the Commission staff.

(3) We require the company to send you a copy of its statements opposing your proposal before it mails its proxy materials, so that you may bring to our attention any materially false or misleading statements, under the following timeframes:

> (i) If our no-action response requires that you make revisions to your proposal or supporting statement as a condition to requiring the company to include it in its proxy materials, then the company must provide you with a copy of its opposition statements no later than 5 calendar days after the company receives a copy of your revised proposal; or

> (ii) In all other cases, the company must provide you with a copy of its opposition statements no later than 30 calendar days before it files definitive copies of its proxy statement and form of proxy under § 240.14a–6.

Are shareholder proposals a beneficial means of furthering corporate goals, or are they, more often than not, a frivolous exercise, and an opportunity for imposing costs of compliance on the corporation? Like many other points involving the proxy rules this one is subject to some debate, although as institutional investors are coming to play more and more of a role at making shareholder proposals pursuant to Rule 14a–8, the passage of such proposals does become somewhat more likely, particularly if they have to do with ensuring transparency about the conduct of the corporation. Consider a number of possible proposals pursuant to Rule 14a–8, and determine whether you think they are appropriate for inclusion on the annual meeting agenda or not:

(1) a proposal that the corporation cease manufacturing napalm

(2) a proposal that the corporation increase the number of outside directors

(3) a proposal that the corporation speed up its already-existing plans to cease manufacturing which produces chlorofluorocarbons

(4) a proposal that the corporation cease the manufacturing of *fois gras*

(5) a proposal that the directors take action against a CEO who has a practice of showing up at the office inebriated

(6) a proposal that the corporation cease trade with nations known to be harboring terrorists

(7) a proposal that the corporation condemn the practice of the United States making war on other countries without UN Security Council authorization.

....

5. THE PROXY RULES that we have been considering in this section, as we have seen, were conceived as a means of making it easier for shareholders to cast their votes in an informed manner, and, in the case of the rules regarding shareholder proposals we have just reviewed, of giving them an enhanced ability to communicate with their fellow shareholders. There is no doubt that the law still conceives of the shareholders as the owners of corporations, and that the basic understanding of corporate law is that corporations are to be run primarily if not exclusively for the benefit of their shareholders (so long as corporations comply with applicable laws and regulations). Still, to what extent ought efforts be undertaken to encourage and expand "shareholder democracy?" In a provocative and perceptive Op-ed in the *Wall Street Journal* on September 27, 2007 entitled "Corporations Shouldn't Be Democracies," UCLA Law Professor Lynn Stout argued against a change to the proxy rules, proposed by the SEC's Democratic Commissioners (there are five SEC Commissioners, who are appointed by the President to serve for staggered five-year terms, and no more than three Commissioners may belong to the same political party) which would have required publicly-traded corporations to "pay the expenses of dissident shareholders seeking to replace the company's board of directors," in particular by requiring corporations to place on the annual ballots shareholder nominees for directors.

Ms. Stout suggested that this proposed rule "is driven by the emotional claim, unsupported by evidence, that American corporations benefit from 'shareholder democracy.' " Ms. Stout argued that "Successful corporations are not, and never have been, democratic institutions. Since the public corporation first evolved over a century ago, U.S. law has discouraged shareholders from taking an active role in corporate governance, and this 'hands off' approach has proven a recipe for tremendous success." "Companies seem to succeed best when they are controlled by boards of directors, not by shareholders," Ms. Stout explained, because "board control is more informed and efficient decision making. An even more important factor," she continued, "is that board control 'locks in' and protects corporate assets and investment capital." Because of the huge amount of sunk costs required for the kind of complex software and electronics, new drugs and medical treatments, valuable trademarks and brand names in which today's corporations traffic, said Ms. Stout, Board control over these assets is necessary because it "protects those assets and gives them time to work, allowing shareholders collectively to recoup the value of their initial investment (and then some) over the long haul."

Such long term-investment would be impossible, Ms. Stout believes, "if shareholders have the power to drain cash out of the firm at any time—say, by threatening to remove directors who refuse to cut expenses or sell assets in order to pay shareholders a special dividend or fund a massive share repurchase program." And these are not idle worries, according to Ms. Stout because "Whether out of ignorance, greed, or short-sightedness, these are exactly the sorts of threats that today's activist shareholders, usually at hedge funds, typically make." "By giving activists even greater leverage over boards," Ms. Stout concluded, the SEC's Democratic commissioners' proposed proxy access rule would "undermine American corporations' ability to do exactly what investors, and the larger society, want them to do: pursue big, long-term, innovative business projects."

In early December, 2007, the SEC, by a three to one vote (the lone Democrat then on the SEC was the dissenter) rejected the so-called "shareholder access" proposal against which Ms. Stout had argued. On December 7, 2007, the *Wall Street Journal*, in an editorial that could fairly be described as exulting in the rejection, wrote that "In the case of proxy challenges, the main agitators are unions and their political allies who run public pension funds." "These groups," said the *Journal* "have their own political agendas that they want companies to pursue, and those agendas may or may not serve the larger interest of increasing shareholder value. In the worst case, such agitation could empower special-interests on boards that reduce a company's value." A recent study by University of Chicago researcher Ashwini Agrawal, the *Journal* reported, suggested that "the dominant concern of . . . pension fund holders is union representation, not overall corporate performance."

The December 7, 2007, *Wall Street Journal* Editorial concluded by observing that "under current law, nothing stops a company from adopting by-laws that would provide for easier proxy access by shareholders. If there were an advantage in doing so—if a company received a stock-price premium—more companies would do it because more investors would insist on it. That no such premium exists explains why investors at large aren't clamoring for this kind of proxy 'reform.' " Is this persuasive? For further argument along the lines suggested by Ms. Stout, see the seminal article by her UCLA colleague, Stephen Bainbridge, Director Primacy and Shareholder Disempowerment, 119 Harv.L.Rev. 1735 (2006), which maintains that other academics' proposals for increased shareholder participation in corporate governance are misguided given that the marketplace does not seem to favor them. Is this the right reference for corporate governance policy? Would Randolph Phillips have favored the proposal to require publicly-held corporations to list shareholder-nominated contestants for the Board of Directors?

....

6. WHAT IS THE STATE LAW regarding shareholder participation in corporate governance, and, in particular, what measures might states take to ensure that shareholders have the requisite information intelligently to participate—assuming, that is, that participation in corporate governance is something appropriate for shareholders (it might not be if most investors wish passively to invest and sell their shares instead of seeking to change the corporation if they are unsatisfied with its performance)? Consider the next case, dealing with Delaware's law regarding shareholder examination of books and records. After you read the case ask yourself if you believe federal action in this area, such as Rule 14a–8, the other proxy rules, or shareholder access for director elections is warranted.

IV. State Law Regarding Inspection
of Books and Records (Delaware)

WHILE THE REST OF THIS CHAPTER deals with federal law, we turn briefly to the state law of Delaware regarding shareholders' rights of inspecting corporate records. As you know, a majority of the United States' largest companies are chartered in Delaware, making its law in this area controlling for vast swaths of the nation's corporate landscape.

Seinfeld v. Verizon Communications, Inc.

Supreme Court of Delaware.

909 A.2d 117 (2006).

Before STEELE, *Chief Justice,* HOLLAND, BERGER, JACOBS *and* RIDGELY, *Justices, constituting the Court en Banc.*

OPINION

HOLLAND, Justice.

The plaintiff-appellant, Frank D. Seinfeld ("Seinfeld"), brought suit under section 220 of the Delaware General Corporation Law to compel the defendant-appellee, Verizon Communications, Inc. ("Verizon"), to produce, for his inspection, its books and records related to the compensation of Verizon's three highest corporate officers from 2000 to 2002. Seinfeld claimed that their executive compensation, individually and collectively, was excessive and wasteful. On cross-motions for summary judgment, the Court of Chancery applied well-established Delaware law and held that Seinfeld had not met his evidentiary burden to demonstrate a proper purpose to justify the inspection of Verizon's records.

The settled law of Delaware required Seinfeld to present some evidence that established a credible basis from which the Court of Chancery could infer there were legitimate issues of possible waste, mismanagement or wrongdoing that warranted further investigation. Seinfeld argues that burden of proof "erects an insurmountable barrier for the minority shareholder of a public company." We have concluded that Seinfeld's argument is without merit.

We reaffirm the well-established law of Delaware that stockholders seeking inspection under section 220 must present "some evidence" to suggest a "credible basis" from which a court can infer that mismanagement, waste or wrongdoing may have occurred. The "credible basis" standard achieves an appropriate balance between providing stockholders who can offer some evidence of possible wrongdoing with access to corporate records and safeguarding the right of the corporation to deny requests for inspections that are based only upon suspicion or curiosity. Accordingly, the judgment of the Court of Chancery must be affirmed.

FACTS

Seinfeld asserts that he is the beneficial owner of approximately 3,884 shares of Verizon, held in street name through a brokerage firm. His stated purpose for seeking Verizon's books and records was to investigate mismanagement and corporate waste regarding the executive compensations of Ivan G. Seidenberg, Lawrence T. Babbio, Jr. and Charles R. Lee. Seinfeld alleges that the three executives were all performing in the same job and were paid amounts, including stock options, above the compensation provided for in their employment contracts. Seinfeld's section 220 claim for inspection is further premised on various computations he performed which indicate that the three executives' compensation totaled $205 million over three years and was, therefore, excessive, given their responsibilities to the corporation.

During his deposition, Seinfeld acknowledged he had no factual support for his claim that mismanagement had taken place. He admitted that the three executives did not perform any duplicative work. Seinfeld conceded he had no factual basis to allege the executives "did not earn" the amounts paid to them under their respective employment agreements. Seinfeld also admitted "there is a possibility" that the $205 million executive compensation amount he calculated was wrong.

The issue before us is quite narrow: should a stockholder seeking inspection under section 220 be entitled to relief without being required to show some evidence to suggest a credible basis for wrongdoing? We conclude that the answer must be no.

Stockholder Inspection Rights

Delaware corporate law provides for a separation of legal control and ownership. The legal responsibility to manage the business of the corporation for the benefit of the stockholder owners is conferred on the board of directors by statute. The common law imposes fiduciary duties upon the directors of Delaware corporations to constrain their conduct when discharging that statutory responsibility.

Stockholders' rights to inspect the corporation's books and records were recognized at common law because "[a]s a matter of self-protection, the stockholder was entitled to know how his agents were conducting the affairs of the corporation of which he or she was a part owner." The qualified inspection rights that originated at common law are now codified in Title 8, section 220 of the Delaware Code, which provides, in part:

(b) Any stockholder, in person or by attorney or other agent, shall, upon written demand under oath stating the purpose thereof, have the right during the usual hours for business to inspect for any proper purpose.

Section 220 provides stockholders of Delaware corporations with a "powerful right." By properly asserting that right under section 220, stockholders are able to obtain information that can be used in a variety of contexts. Stockholders may use information about corporate mismanagement, waste or wrongdoing in several ways. For example, they may: institute derivative litigation; "seek an audience with the board [of directors] to discuss proposed reform or, failing in that, they may prepare a stockholder resolution for the next annual meeting, or mount a proxy fight to elect new directors."

* * *

Seinfeld Denied Inspection

The Court of Chancery determined that Seinfeld's deposition testimony established only that he was concerned about the large amount of compensation paid to the three executives. That court concluded that Seinfeld offered "no evidence from which [it] could evaluate whether there is a reasonable ground for suspicion that the executive's compensation rises to the level of waste." * * *

Evidentiary Barrier Allegation

In this appeal, Seinfeld asserts that the "Court of Chancery's ruling erects an insurmountable barrier for the minority shareholder of a public company." Seinfeld argues that:

This Court and the Court of Chancery have instructed shareholders to utilize § 220 as one of the tools at hand. Yet, the Court of Chancery at bar, in requiring *evidence* makes a § 220 application a mirage. If the shareholder had evidence, a derivative suit would be brought. Unless there is a whistle blower, or a video cassette, the public shareholder, having no access to corporate records, will only have suspicions.

Seinfeld submits that "by requiring evidence, the shareholder is prevented from using the tools at hand." Seinfeld's brief concludes with a request for this Court to reduce the burden of proof that stockholders must meet in a section 220 action:

Plaintiff submits that in a case involving public companies, minority shareholders who have access only to public documents and without a whistle blower or corporate documents should be permitted to have limited inspection based upon suspicions, reasonable beliefs, and logic arising from public disclosures.

After oral arguments, this Court asked the parties for supplemental briefs that would address the following questions:

A. Should a stockholder with a proper purpose be entitled to inspect carefully limited categories of corporate books and records, pursuant to Section 220, upon a showing that the stockholder has a rational basis for the stated purpose and no other purpose that would militate against inspection?

B. If the standard in question "A" would not be appropriate, is there *any* reduced burden of proof under Section 220 that would improve stockholders' ability to obtain the "tools" to pursue derivative claims without disrupting corporations' orderly conduct of business and without inappropriately interfering with corporate decision-making? If so, articulate the reduced burden of proof. If not, explain why not.

We asked these questions in order to review the current balance between the rights of stockholders and corporations that is established by *Thomas & Betts Corp. v. Leviton Mfg. Co.* and *Security First Corp. v. U.S. Die Casting & Dev. Co.* and their progeny.

Credible Basis From Some Evidence

In a section 220 action, a stockholder has the burden of proof to demonstrate a proper purpose by a preponderance of the evidence. It is well established that a stockholder's desire to investigate wrongdoing or mismanagement is a "proper purpose." Such investigations are proper, because where the allegations of mismanagement prove meritorious, investigation furthers the interest of all stockholders and should increase stockholder return.

The evolution of Delaware's jurisprudence in section 220 actions reflects judicial efforts to maintain a proper balance between the rights of shareholders to obtain information based upon credible allegations of corporation mismanagement and the rights of directors to manage the business of the corporation without undue interference from stockholders. In *Thomas & Betts*, this Court held that, to meet its "burden of proof, a stockholder must present some *credible basis* from which the court can infer that waste or mismanagement may have occurred." Six months later, in *Security First*, this Court held "[t]here must be *some evidence* of possible mismanagement as would warrant further investigation of the matter."

Our holdings in *Thomas & Betts* and *Security First* were contemporaneous with our decisions that initially encouraged stockholders to make greater use of section 220. In *Grimes v. Donald*, decided just months before *Thomas & Betts*, this Court reaffirmed the salutary use of section 220 as one of the "tools at hand" for stockholders to use to obtain information. When the plaintiff in *Thomas & Betts* suggested that the burden of demonstrating a proper purpose had been attenuated by our encouragement for stockholders to use section 220, we rejected that argument:

Contrary to plaintiff's assertion in the instant case, this Court in *Grimes* did not suggest that its reference to a Section 220 demand as one of the "tools at hand" was intended to eviscerate or modify the need for a stockholder to show a proper purpose under Section 220.

In *Security First* and *Thomas & Betts*, we adhered to the Court of Chancery's holding in *Helmsman Mgmt. Servs., Inc. v. A & S Consultants, Inc.* that:

A mere statement of a purpose to investigate possible general mismanagement, without more, will not entitle a shareholder to broad § 220 inspection relief. There must be *some evidence* of possible mismanagement as would warrant further investigation of the matter.

Standard Achieves Balance

Investigations of meritorious allegations of possible mismanagement, waste or wrongdoing, benefit the corporation, but investigations that are "indiscriminate fishing expeditions" do not. "At some point, the costs of generating more information fall short of the benefits of having more information. At that point, compelling production of information would be wealth-reducing, and so shareholders would not want it produced." Accordingly, this Court has held that an inspection to investigate possible wrongdoing where there is no "credible basis," is a license for "fishing expeditions" and thus adverse to the interests of the corporation:

Stockholders have a right to at least a limited inquiry into books and records when they have established some credible basis to believe that there has been wrongdoing.... Yet it would invite mischief to open corporate management to indiscriminate fishing expeditions.

A stockholder is "not required to prove by a preponderance of the evidence that waste and [mis]management are actually occurring." Stockholders need only show, by a preponderance of the evidence, a credible basis from which the Court of Chancery can infer there is possible mismanagement that would warrant further investigation-a showing that "may ultimately fall well short of demonstrating that anything wrong occurred." That "threshold may be satisfied by a credible showing, through documents, logic, testimony or otherwise, that there are legitimate issues of wrongdoing."

Although the threshold for a stockholder in a section 220 proceeding is not insubstantial, the "credible basis" standard sets the lowest possible burden of proof. The only way to reduce the burden of proof further would be to eliminate any requirement that a stockholder show some evidence of possible wrongdoing. That would be tantamount to permitting inspection based on the "mere suspicion" standard that Seinfeld advances in this appeal. However, such a standard has been repeatedly rejected as a basis to justify the enterprise cost of an inspection. * * *

Requiring stockholders to establish a "credible basis" for the Court of Chancery to infer possible wrongdoing by presenting "some evidence" has not impeded stockholder inspections. Although many section 220 proceedings have been filed since we decided *Security First* and *Thomas & Betts*, Verizon points out that Seinfeld's case is only the second proceeding in which a plaintiff's demand to investigate wrongdoing was found to be *entirely* without a "credible basis." In contrast, there are a myriad of cases where stockholders have successfully presented "some evidence" to establish a "credible basis" to infer possible mismanagement and thus received some narrowly tailored right of inspection.

We remain convinced that the rights of stockholders and the interests of the corporation in a section 220 proceeding are properly balanced by requiring a stockholder to show "some evidence of *possible* mismanagement as would warrant further investigation." The "credible basis" standard maximizes stockholder value by limiting the range of permitted stockholder inspections to those that might have merit. Accordingly, our holdings in *Security First* and *Thomas & Betts* are ratified and reaffirmed.

CONCLUSION

The judgment of the Court of Chancery is affirmed.

———————————

NOTES AND QUESTIONS

1. WHAT IS MEANT BY THE TERM "PROPER PURPOSE" in Delaware Section 220? Why did the court deny Seinfeld's request? Do you agree with the court's assertion that its current standard "achieves balance"?

....

2. NOTE THAT SECTION 220 provides for inspection of corporate books and records by directors. Would this have helped Tomlinson in *Campbell v. Loew's*?

....

3. WOULD CONTACTING OTHER SHAREHOLDERS in order to get further participation in a class action lawsuit against the corporation accusing management of misconduct be a proper purpose for seeking a shareholder list? It is quite clear that investigating possible management misconduct is a proper purpose for a shareholder to examine the books and records of the corporation, and that such examination of records might properly serve as the foundation for a derivative lawsuit. *Security First Corp. v. U.S. Die Casting and Development Co.*, 687 A.2d 563 (Del. 1997). Although the Delaware Court did make clear that a "proper purpose" could not be one inimical to the interests of the corporation, the court did hold in *Compaq Computer Corp. v. Horton*, 631 A.2d 1 (Del. 1993), that "a shareholder states a proper purpose for inspection under our statute in seeking to solicit the participation of other shareholders in legitimate non-derivative litigation against the defendant corporation." The Delaware court seems prepared to encourage shareholder litigation, both derivative and individual, in order to prevent mismanagement by corporate fiduciaries, but is this an effective remedy? Given the apparent explosion in corporate wrongdoing by purported corporate miscreants and their advisors such as those running Enron, WorldCom, and the accounting firm Arthur A. Anderson, the United States Congress apparently thought not, and passed legislation known as Sarbanes/Oxley, to which we now turn.

C. Sarbanes/Oxley

A Note on Sarbanes/Oxley[7]

In the wake of the early twenty-first century scandals involving WorldCom, Enron, and the Arthur Anderson firm which had served as accountants to both

---

7   A principal source for this Note is the "Executive Summary of the Sarbanes-Oxley Act of 2002 P.L. 107–204," prepared for the Conference of State Bank Supervisors, and available at http://www.csbs.org/government/legislative/misc/2002_sarbanes-oxley_summary.htm. Materials in quotes are taken from that Executive Summary unless otherwise indicated.

corporations, pressure built on Congress to come up with some federal legislation to prevent further such misadventures. Conventional wisdom had it that the accountants did not do an adequate job policing expenditures at these and other corporations, and that had stricter internal controls been in place, the possible looting of these corporations by senior management, and the questionable business practices in which they engaged, might not have occurred, and thus the bankruptcies that eventually resulted might have been avoided. Congress appears to have believed that state law—the primary regulator of conduct among shareholders, officers, and directors—was failing to put in place sufficient safeguards against accounting and officer/director misconduct, and thus, for the first time, Congress was emboldened to try to dictate in more detail than it ever had before (1) how accounting ought to be done, (2) how corporate oversight ought to be conducted, and (3) how relations between corporations and their officers ought to be adjusted. Reminiscent of the time more than a century earlier when Congress felt it ought to come up with some bill "to punish the trusts," and the result was the Sherman Antitrust Act (1890), the Sarbanes/Oxley Act of 2002, P.L. 107–204 (hereafter "the Act"), might be described as a broad brush attempt to protect against or punish corporate miscreants and rogue accountants. At this point there has been little litigation challenging the provisions or the Constitutionality of Sarbanes/Oxley, but there have already been small fortunes spent by corporations in complying with its provisions. Only time will tell whether this act, like so many other provisions of federal law regulating securities, may have to be changed in light of realities in the corporate world, especially if its costs exceed its benefits, but for now it is necessary to review its main provisions, since they will, for the foreseeable future, have considerable impact on publicly-traded corporations.

Creation of the Public Company Accounting Oversight Board. Title I of the act establishes a five-member "Public Company Accounting Oversight Board" ("the Board"), which is subject to general oversight by the SEC, and which is given the responsibility of establishing audit report standards and rules. The Board is authorized to inspect and oversee the auditing of publicly-traded companies, and is given the power to enforce compliance with its standards and rules by registered public accounting firms, which are all of those conducting audits of any publicly-traded company. As well as being tasked with the establishment of general auditing standards, including quality control and ethics standards, there are several substantive regulations mandated by the statute, including a seven-year retention period for audit work papers (reflecting the fact that Anderson was accused of shredding documents involved in its audit of Enron), a requirement that a second accounting-firm partner review and approve audits (to prevent accountants from becoming too chummy with the clients, as again was perceived as the situation between Anderson and Enron), and assorted provisions requiring the evaluation of internal control structures regarding receipts and expenditures (presumably to prevent the kind of lavish lifestyle

WorldCom enabled its top executive to enjoy). The activities of the Board are funded through fees to be collected from issuers (thus imposing an indirect cost on their shareholders—who are thus required to pay for what the federal government believes is their own protection). The Board is given the power to impose disciplinary or remedial sanctions upon accountants for intentional misconduct or for repeated instances of negligent conduct.

In 2006, the constitutionality of the Board was challenged by a group of plaintiffs who claimed its creation violated the Appointments Clause and that the Board's members (removable only for cause) were too insulated from Executive branch control. The case eventually found its way to the Supreme Court. Free *Enter. Fund v. Pub. Co. Accounting Oversight Bd.*, 130 S. Ct. 3138 (2010). There, the Court held that the Board could remain in existence, but that its members had to be removable at will by the Executive in order to be constitutional.

Title I of the Act contemplates the creation of a "principles-based accounting system" under the auspices of the SEC, and a report on such a system to the Congress which is to be used in the preparation of federally-mandated financial reports such as corporations' annual reports to shareholders. It might be said, in summary, that Title I federalizes accounting for publicly-traded corporations. Given the somewhat wonderful departures from generally accepted accounting principles in some parts of the federal government (for example Social Security) one might be forgiven for lifting an eyebrow at the notion that we ought to have that government regulate accounting.

Ensuring Auditor Independence. Whether or not it was accurate, there was a widespread perception that one reason that accounting firms auditing publicly-traded companies may have failed to be sufficiently objective or independent was that the firms also had vigorous and lucrative consulting practices, and that maintaining consulting contracts may have led them to fail vigorously to question corporations' accounting or other practices. Accordingly, Title II of the Act prohibits firms conducting audits from simultaneously performing some specified consulting services. Other services are permitted by the Act, if they are approved by the corporation's audit committee, a body which is given other particular tasks by the Act. These include, for example, the receiving of reports on the accounting policies and practices used in the accountants' audits, the consideration of alternative accounting treatments of various matters, and a review of written communications between the auditors and senior management of the issuer (again, to avoid overly friendly or compromising arrangements, as was thought to have occurred in Enron and WorldCom). Accounting firms are prohibited from rendering audit services if any of the corporation's senior executives had been employed by the accounting firm and had participated in an audit in the prior year. Auditor rotation, the requirement that a partner in the accounting firm may not be the lead or reviewing auditor for more than five consecutive years, is now mandated.

Mandating Corporate Compliance Structures. Never before has the federal government sought so extensively to dictate the internal organization of publicly-traded corporations, but Title III of the Act now dictates the composition of a mandatory audit committee, composed of outside members of the board of directors who are not permitted to have any other affiliation with or compensation from the corporation. The audit committee is charged with ensuring that the auditors do their job, and is given the responsibility for hiring, paying for, and conducting oversight of the audit. The Act gives the audit committee the express authority to hire independent counsel or other advisors, and requires the corporation to pay for those consultants to the audit committee. This could, of course, involve substantial expenditures by the Corporation, over which the corporation's Board of Directors as a whole will have no control. It is a nice question, then, whether or not this substantially modifies the omnipresent state corporate law provisions that the entire Board of Directors is charged with monitoring the affairs of the corporation. Some scholars have identified Sarbanes-Oxley as evidence of further federal influence in the traditional state area of corporate governance.[8] Title III also directs the SEC to promulgate new rules which will require the CEO and CFO personally to certify matters in periodic financial reports. These include certifying that the reports contain no untrue statements or material omissions, that the reports fairly present the financial conditions of corporations, and that the officers have supervised internal controls so that the officers receive material information regarding the corporation and its consolidated subsidiaries, that the officers have reviewed the internal controls within 90 days prior to the report in question, and that the officers have reported any significant changes to the internal controls. Once again there is federal mandating of particular executive tasks, in an unprecedented manner.

Other provisions of Title III (1) forbid corporate personnel from attempting improperly to influence an audit, (2) require that CEO's and CFO's must forfeit specified bonuses and compensation received if the corporation must make an accounting restatement due to prior material non-compliance with the federally-mandated standards, (3) authorize the prohibiting of those who violate particular SEC rules from continuing to serve as officers or directors, and (4) ban trading by directors and executives in a public company's stock during pension fund blackout periods (conduct that purportedly took place during some of the contemporary scandals). Finally, and most controversially for the legal profession, Section 307 of the Act requires lawyers appearing before the SEC to report violations of securities laws or other corporation or officer misconduct to the chief legal counsel or to the CEO of the corporation. Further regulations were proposed, specifying that if a lawyer's advice in this regard is not acted upon by the corporation, the lawyer must make a

---

8   See Stephen M. Bainbridge, *The Creeping Federalization of Corporate Law*, REGULATION, Spring 2003, at 26.

"noisy withdrawal" and give public notice that he or she will no longer represent the corporation. Because such regulations raise questions about compromising the traditional lawyer-client privilege formulating these regulations has not been easy. The nations' most prominent law firms and various securities organizations petitioned the SEC to reconsider and clarify the proposal. The SEC eventually proposed a rule in which a lawyer representing a client before the SEC "may" disclose such evidence of wrongdoing.

Further Financial Disclosures. Title IV of the Act includes new requirements for financial disclosures for listed corporations, including that an issuer must disclose "on a rapid and current basis" material shifts in the company's operations and finances. One facet of the Enron imbroglio was that many of the company's projects which turned out to be massive money-losers were conducted through partnerships that were not carried on Enron's balance sheets. Accordingly, this Title of the Act now requires disclosure of all off-balance sheet transactions and relationships that may have a material effect on the corporation's financial status. Attempting to correct an abuse at WorldCom and other corporations this title also prohibits most personal loans extended by the corporation to executives and directors. Another new provision requires that within 2 business days following the transaction, officers, directors, and 10% beneficial shareholders must report changes in their stock ownership. The former requirement had been that such reports need not be made until ten days after the close of the month in which such transactions occurred. In other provisions of this Title corporations are required to include an "internal control report" in their annual reports stating that corporate management is responsible for oversight procedures, and assessing the effectiveness of the internal controls for the previous fiscal year. This section, 404, appears to have spawned a variety of new software programs, and a plethora of new consulting opportunities, and will probably require many millions, if not billions of dollars for effective compliance. "According to a survey of 321 companies by Financial Executives International, companies with more than $5 billion in revenue expect to spend on average $4.7 million implementing Section 404 controls and about $1.5 million annually to maintain this level of compliance."[9] Put slightly differently, this means that roughly for every billion dollars in revenues, compliance costs generated by Sarbanes/Oxley will be more than a million dollars. Finally, Title IV requires each registered corporation to indicate whether it has adopted a code of ethics for its senior financial officers and to indicate whether its audit committee includes at least one member who is a financial expert. While neither of these appears actually to be required by the law, it is a safe bet that virtually all publicly-traded corporations will adopt such codes and place such a person on

---

9   Paul Volker [former Chairman of the Board of Governors of the Federal Reserve System], and Arthur Levitt, Jr. [former Chairman of the SEC] "In Defense of Sarbanes-Oxley," Wall Street Journal, June 14, 2004, page A16.

their audit committees. Indeed, both the NYSE and NASDAQ now require all listed companies to have a code of ethics.

Expanding the Budget of the SEC. Given its new supervisory responsibilities, which practically amount to the SEC becoming something of a super-Board of Directors for all corporations, it is not surprising that Title VI of the act mandates a 77.21% increase over the appropriations for FY 2002, including amounts for "pay parity, information and technology, security enhancements, and recovery and mitigation activities related to the September 11th terrorist attacks." There is a $98 million authorization for the hiring of no fewer than 200 additional "qualified professionals to provide improved oversight of auditors and audit services."

Ratcheting Up the Penalties for Corporate and Criminal Fraud. Title VIII of the act imposes new penalties "for knowingly destroying, altering, concealing, or falsifying records with intent to obstruct or influence either a Federal investigation or a matter in bankruptcy and for failure of an auditor to maintain for a five year period all audit or review work papers" of a corporate audit. These penalties include up to ten years in federal prison. Title VIII also extends the statute of limitation for a private right of action for securities fraud violations to "not later than two years [after the discovery of such fraud] or five years after the date of the violation," (prior limits were 1 year and 3 years respectively) thus enhancing the ability of "private attorneys general" to litigate in the manner permitted by *J.I. Case v. Borak.* Another provision of Title VIII prohibits retaliatory action against "whistleblower" employees of listed corporations in connection with the investigation of fraud or other misconduct by "Federal regulators, Congress or supervisors," or in connection with the bringing of proceedings (presumably civil or criminal litigation) "relating to fraud against shareholders." Title VIII also increases the penalties formerly prevailing for securities fraud, to up to 25 years imprisonment. Provisions of Title IX increase penalties for mail and wire fraud from five to twenty years in prison, increase penalties for violations of the federal pension law (ERISA) up to $500,000 and ten years imprisonment, and "[E]stablishes criminal liability for failure of corporate officers to certify financial reports," including maximum imprisonment of twenty years for "willfully certifying a statement knowing it does not comply" with the Act. Title XI establishes a maximum 20 year sentence for "tampering with a record or otherwise impeding an official proceeding, and also authorizes the SEC to prohibit a corporate official who violates Section 10(b) from serving as an officer or director of a publicly traded corporation if the person's conduct demonstrates unfitness to serve." Finally, not only does Title XI increase penalties for violations of the Securities Exchange Act of 1934 up to $25 million dollars, it also provides for imprisonment for up to twenty years for violations of that Act.

If possible fines and imprisonments are the test of government seriousness about corporate misconduct, the federal government is now very serious indeed. A former Chairman of the Federal Reserve and a former Chairman of the SEC have written that Sarbanes/Oxley is "the most far-reaching corporate reform legislation in 60 years," and have observed that it was passed "with the support of all but three members of Congress who voted." They conclude that $5 million down and $1.5 million a year is not too much to pay for a multibillion-dollar international company when compared to how much investors have lost—and stand to lose—if internal controls are not improved. Put it in the context of the tens of millions of dollars paid to investment bankers to advise on a deal, or on legal fees when things go wrong—or think of the $90 billion investors lost just on the collapse of Enron alone. By that calculus, Sarbanes-Oxley clearly meets the cost-benefit test, and is worth every penny.[10]

Are you pleased with what appears to be an increasing federalization of corporate law? What do you think about the evolution of federal regulation from a theory of disclosure to active direction of operations? Would you have voted for Sarbanes/Oxley if you were a member of Congress?

A Note on Dodd-Frank

The financial crisis of 2007–08 spurred calls for new regulation of the financial industry. The result was another piece of legislation hailed as the most comprehensive financial reform since the New Deal: the Dodd-Frank Wall Street Reform and Consumer Protection Act, P.L. 111–203 (Dodd-Frank). This massive bill introduced new regulation to numerous aspects of the financial industry and publicly-traded corporations, with the express intention of discouraging excessive growth and over-complexity in financial institutions. The Act is written in the spirit of Sarbanes-Oxley, continuing a shift from a disclosure-based regulation regime to one of active interference in a corporation's internal operations. Dodd-Frank provides for new oversight in the areas of consumer protection, insurance, credit rating agencies, corporate whistleblowing, and financial institutions, among others. This section is concerned with the elements of Dodd-Frank affecting corporate governance and government oversight of the financial industry: (1) the creation of the Financial Stability Oversight Council, (2) the proposed "Volcker Rule," (3) new regulation of trading in derivatives, (4) new regulation of asset-backed securities, and (5) new shareholder rights in regard to corporate governance and executive compensation.

Title I of the Dodd-Frank Act authorizes the creation of the Financial Stability Oversight Council (FSOC). The Department of the Treasury describes FSOC as having "collective accountability for identifying risks and responding to emerging threats to financial stability." This broad mandate allows FSOC to coordinate

---

10   Volker and Leavitt, supra.

information sharing among regulatory agencies, identify individual companies for special oversight, recommend stricter standards for large corporations' operations, and break up financial companies at risk of becoming "too big to fail." Titles II through V concern the liquidation of large financial organizations, eliminate the Office of Thrift Supervision and transfer its authority, and increase the regulation of hedge funds and insurance companies.

Title VI is most notable for its promulgation of the so-called "Volcker Rule," names after the former Federal Reserve Chairman who championed the policy. The Volcker Rule prohibits proprietary trading by banks, meaning that standard retail and commercial banking operations must be separate from investment banking. Banking firms will no longer be able to offer standard services such as deposits and lending while investing on their own behalf. As of publication, the controversial rule has yet to be implemented, although pressure is mounting for its enforcement by the end of 2014.

Title VII concerns new regulation of trading in derivatives, which some commentators blamed for contributing to the 2007–08 financial crisis. The term "derivatives" refers to a broad array of financial instruments which *derive* their worth from another asset or value, such as stocks, bonds, interest rates, or the sale price of commodities. Derivatives include options, futures, and swaps. Because derivatives are just contracts between parties in reference to another asset or value, truly exotic products can be assembled and sold by creative market participants. This flexibility, and the fact that many derivatives were traded "over the counter" between parties (not on a listed market), made derivatives a special target of criticism in the wake of the financial crisis. Congress' intent in drafting Title VII was increased "transparency and accountability" on the part of traders in derivatives. The SEC and the Commodity Futures Trading Commission (CFTC) are identified as the primary regulators of the swaps market. Title VII requires certain swaps to be traded and recorded on centralized exchanges, while traders of significant numbers of derivatives must register with a regulatory authority for further oversight. Many aspects of this derivatives legislation are left undefined, allowing the SEC and CFTC to fill in its meanings and rules at a later time.

Title IX of the Dodd-Frank Act institutes new regulation of the credit rating agencies and asset-backed securities. Asset-backed securities are financial instruments which bundle products such as loans, debt, or accounts receivable to be bought and sold on the market. These sale of these products, like derivatives, were criticized in the wake of the 2007–08 financial crisis as many suffered significant losses in value. Dodd-Frank requires the institutions selling asset-backed securities to retain an increased amount of risk in the product, thereby keeping "skin in the game." Furthermore, issuers of asset-backed securities must disclose detailed information about the loans which make up the security themselves.

Finally, Title IX also introduces broad (some might say intrusive) measures to reform corporate governance for the alleged protection of investors. Besides providing for further regulation of the national credit rating agencies, Title IX provides for new shareholder rights in regard to executive compensation and corporate operations. The Act requires the board of directors to institute a compensation committee, which must be entirely composed of outside directors with compensation restrictions in order to maintain independence. Publicly-traded corporations must now allow a non-binding shareholder vote approving the overall compensation of its executive officers, and are required to hold a separate non-binding vote to decide whether the compensation-approval vote shall take place every one, two, or three years. Title IX's other new regulations require the disclosure of performance-based compensation for officers and institutes new compensation clawback provisions triggered when corporate financials are restated. Finally, Title IX allows the SEC to rule that a corporation's proxy solicitation must list a directorship nominee chosen by opposition shareholders against management. The remaining Titles institute a Bureau of Consumer Financial Protection and other miscellaneous regulations.

Do you feel that Dodd-Frank's regulations are necessary or prudent? What do you suppose their overall effect on the financial market has been and will be? The average cost of a company's compliance with the Sarbanes-Oxley Act has been many times greater than the government's estimates. What do you expect the cost of complying with Dodd-Frank to be? Consider the entire federal regulatory regime as sketched in this chapter. Are there certain aspects you find more compelling or useful than others? In the next chapter, we will consider important aspects of the closely-held corporation.

THE CLOSE CORPORATION

I. Fiduciary Responsibility in the Closely-Held Corporation

Euphemia Donahue v. Rodd Electrotype Company of New England, Inc.

Supreme Judicial Court of Massachusetts.
367 Mass. 578, 328 N.E.2d 505 (1975).

[TAURO, C.J.]

The plaintiff, Euphemia Donahue, a minority stockholder in the Rodd Electrotype Company of New England, Inc. (Rodd Electrotype), a Massachusetts corporation, brings this suit against the directors of Rodd Electrotype, Charles H. Rodd, Frederick I. Rodd and Mr. Harold E. Magnuson, against Harry C. Rodd, a former director, officer, and controlling stockholder of Rodd Electrotype and against Rodd Electrotype (hereinafter called defendants). The plaintiff seeks to rescind Rodd Electrotype's purchase of Harry Rodd's shares in Rodd Electrotype * * * and to compel Harry Rodd "to repay to the corporation the purchase price of said shares, $36,000, together with interest from the date of purchase." * * * The plaintiff alleges that the defendants caused the corporation to purchase the shares in violation of their fiduciary duty to her, a minority stockholder of Rodd Electrotype. * * *

The trial judge, after hearing oral testimony [denied relief to the plaintiff]. He found that the purchase was without prejudice to the plaintiff and implicitly * * * found that the transaction had been carried out in good faith and with inherent fairness. The Appeals Court affirmed with costs. * * * The case is before us on the plaintiff's application for further appellate review.

* * *

* * * In 1935, the defendant, Harry C. Rodd, began his employment with Rodd Electrotype, then styled the Royal Electrotype Company of New England, Inc. (Royal of New England). * * * Mr. Rodd's advancement within the company was rapId. The following year he was elected a director, and, in 1946, he succeeded to the position of general manager and treasurer.

In 1936, the plaintiff's husband, Joseph Donahue (now deceased), was hired by Royal of New England as a "finisher" of electrotype plates. His duties were confined to operational matters within the plant. Although he ultimately achieved the positions of plant superintendent (1946) and corporate vice president (1955), Donahue never participated in the "management" aspect of the business.

In the years preceding 1955, the parent company, Royal Electrotype, made available to Harry Rodd and Joseph Donahue shares of the common stock in its subsidiary, Royal of New England. Harry Rodd took advantage of the opportunities offered to him and acquired 200 shares for $20 a share. Joseph Donahue, at the suggestion of Harry Rodd, who hoped to interest Donahue in the business, eventually obtained fifty shares * * *. The parent company at all times retained 725 of the 1,000 outstanding shares. * * *

In June of 1955, Royal of New England purchased all 725 of its shares owned by its parent company. The total price amounted to $135,000. Royal of New England remitted $75,000 of this total in cash and executed five promissory notes of $12,000 each, due in each of the succeeding five years. * * * A substantial portion of Royal of New England's cash expenditures was loaned to the company by Harry Rodd, who mortgaged his house to obtain some of the necessary funds.

The stock purchases left Harry Rodd in control of Royal of New England. Early in 1955, before the purchases, he had assumed the presidency of the company. His 200 shares gave him a dominant eighty per cent interest. Joseph Donahue, at this time, was the only minority stockholder.

Subsequent events reflected Harry Rodd's dominant influence. In June, 1960 * * * the company was renamed the Rodd Electrotype Company of New England, Inc. In 1962, Charles H. Rodd, Harry Rodd's son (a defendant here), who had long been a company employee working in the plant, became corporate vice president. In 1963, he joined his father on the board of directors. In 1964, another son, Frederick I. Rodd (also a defendant), replaced Joseph Donahue as plant superintendent. By 1965, Harry Rodd had evidently decided to reduce his participation in corporate management. That year, Charles Rodd succeeded him as president and general manager of Rodd Electrotype.

From 1959 to 1967, Harry Rodd pursued what may fairly be termed a gift program by which he distributed the majority of his shares equally among his two sons and his daughter, Phyllis E. Mason. Each child received thirty-nine shares. * * *

* * * In May of 1970, Harry Rodd was seventy-seven years old. The record indicates that for some time he had not enjoyed the best of health and that he had undergone a number of operations. His sons wished him to retire. Mr. Rodd was not averse to this suggestion. However, he insisted that some financial arrangements be made with respect to his remaining eighty-one shares of stock. A number of conferences ensued. Harry Rodd and Charles Rodd (representing the company) negotiated terms of purchase for forty-five shares which, Charles Rodd testified, would reflect the book value and liquidating value of the shares.

A special board meeting convened on July 13, 1970. As the first order of business, Harry Rodd resigned his directorship of Rodd Electrotype. The remaining incumbent directors, Charles Rodd and Mr. Harold E. Magnuson (clerk of the company and a defendant and defense attorney in the instant suit), elected Frederick Rodd to replace his father. The three directors then authorized Rodd Electrotype's president (Charles Rodd) to execute an agreement between Harry Rodd and the company in which the company would purchase forty-five shares for $800 a share ($36,000).

The stock purchase agreement was formalized between the parties on July 13, 1970. Two days later, a sale pursuant to the July 13 agreement was consummated. At approximately the same time, Harry Rodd resigned his last corporate office, that of treasurer.

Harry Rodd completed divestiture of his Rodd Electrotype stock in the following year. * * * [By] March, 1971, the shareholdings in Rodd Electrotype were apportioned as follows: Charles Rodd, Frederick Rodd and Phyllis Mason each held fifty-one shares; the Donahues[1] held fifty.

A special meeting of the stockholders of the company was held on March 30, 1971. At the meeting, Charles Rodd, company president and general manager, reported the tentative results of an audit conducted by the company auditors and reported generally on the company events of the year. For the first time, the Donahues learned that the corporation had purchased Harry Rodd's shares. According to the minutes of the meeting, following Charles Rodd's report, the Donahues raised questions about the purchase. They then voted against a resolution, ultimately adopted by the remaining stockholders, to approve Charles Rodd's report. * * * [T]he trial judge found * * * that the Donahues did not ratify the purchase of Harry Rodd's shares. * * *

A few weeks after the meeting, the Donahues, acting through their attorney, offered their shares to the corporation on the same terms given to Harry Rodd. Mr. Harold E. Magnuson replied by letter that the corporation would not purchase the shares and was not in a financial position to do so. * * * This suit followed.

In her argument before this court, the plaintiff has characterized the corporate purchase of Harry Rodd's shares as an unlawful distribution of corporate assets

---

1   Joseph Donahue gave his wife, the plaintiff, joint ownership of his fifty shares in 1962. In 1968, they transferred five shares to their son, Dr. Robert Donahue. On Joseph Donahue's death, the plaintiff became outright owner of the forty-five share block. * * *

to controlling stockholders. She urges that the distribution constitutes a breach of the fiduciary duty owed by the Rodds, as controlling stockholders, to her, a minority stockholder in the enterprise, because the Rodds failed to accord her an equal opportunity to sell her shares to the corporation. The defendants reply that the stock purchase was within the powers of the corporation and met the requirements of good faith and inherent fairness imposed on a fiduciary in his dealings with the corporation. They assert that there is no right to equal opportunity in corporate stock purchases for the corporate treasury. For the reasons hereinafter noted, we agree with the plaintiff and reverse the decree of the Superior Court. However, we limit the applicability of our holding to "close corporations," as hereinafter defined. * * *

A. Close Corporations.

In previous opinions, we have alluded to the distinctive nature of the close corporation * * * but have never defined precisely what is meant by a close corporation. There is no single, generally accepted definition. Some commentators emphasize an "integration of ownership and management" * * * in which the stockholders occupy most management positions. * * * Others focus on the number of stockholders and the nature of the market for the stock. In this view, close corporations have few stockholders; there is little market for corporate stock. * * * We accept aspects of both definitions. We deem a close corporation to be typified by: (1) a small number of stockholders; (2) no ready market for the corporate stock; and (3) substantial majority stockholder participation in the management, direction and operations of the corporation.

As thus defined, the close corporation bears striking resemblance to a partnership. Commentators and courts have noted that the close corporation is often little more than an "incorporated" or "chartered" partnership.[2] * * * The stockholders "clothe" their partnership "with the benefits peculiar to a corporation, limited liability, perpetuity and the like." * * * In essence, though, the enterprise remains one in which ownership is limited to the original parties or transferees of their stock to whom the other stockholders have agreed,[3] in which ownership and management are in the same hands, and in which the owners are quite dependent on one another for the

---

2   The United States Internal Revenue Code gives substantial recognition to the fact that close corporations are often merely incorporated partnerships. The so called Subchapter S, 26 U. S. C. §§ 1371–1379 (1970), enables "small business corporations," defined by the statute (26 U. S. C. § 1371 [a] [1970]), to make an election which generally exempts the corporation from taxation (26 U. S. C. § 1372 [b] [1] [1970]) and causes inclusion of the corporation's undistributed, as well as distributed, taxable income in the gross income of the stockholders for the year (26 U. S. C. § 1373 [a] [1970]). This is essentially the manner in which partnership earnings are taxed. See 26 U. S. C. § 701 (1970).

3   The original owners commonly impose restrictions on transfers of stock designed to prevent outsiders who are unacceptable to the other stockholders from acquiring an interest in the close corporation. These restrictions often take the form of agreements among the stockholders and the corporation or by-laws which give the corporation or the other stockholders a right of "first refusal" when any stockholder desires to sell his shares. * * * In a partnership, of course, a partner cannot transfer his interest in the partnership so as to give his assignee a right to participate in the management or business affairs of the continuing partnership without the agreement of the other partners. * * *

success of the enterprise. * * * Just as in a partnership, the relationship among the stockholders must be one of trust, confidence and absolute loyalty if the enterprise is to succeed. Close corporations with substantial assets and with more numerous stockholders are no different from smaller close corporations in this regard. All participants rely on the fidelity and abilities of those stockholders who hold office. Disloyalty and self-seeking conduct on the part of any stockholder will engender bickering, corporate stalemates, and, perhaps, efforts to achieve dissolution. * * *

In *Helms v. Duckworth*, 249 F. 2d 482 (D. C. Cir. 1957), the United States Court of Appeals for the District of Columbia Circuit had before it a stockholders' agreement providing for the purchase of the shares of a deceased stockholder by the surviving stockholder in a small "two-man" close corporation. The court held the surviving stockholder to a duty "to deal fairly, honestly, and openly with . . . [his] fellow stockholders." *Id.* at 487. Judge Burger, now Chief Justice Burger, writing for the court, emphasized the resemblance of the two-man close corporation to a partnership: "In an intimate business venture such as this, stockholders of a close corporation occupy a position similar to that of joint adventurers and partners. While courts have sometimes declared stockholders 'do not bear toward each other that same relation of trust and confidence which prevails in partnerships,' this view ignores the practical realities of the organization and functioning of a small 'two-man' corporation organized to carry on a small business enterprise in which the stockholders, directors, and managers are the same persons" (footnotes omitted). *Id.* at 486.

Although the corporate form provides the above-mentioned advantages for the stockholders (limited liability, perpetuity, and so forth), it also supplies an opportunity for the majority stockholders to oppress or disadvantage minority stockholders. The minority is vulnerable to a variety of oppressive devices, termed "freeze-outs," which the majority may employ. * * * An authoritative study of such "freeze-outs" enumerates some of the possibilities: "The squeezers [those who employ the freeze-out techniques] may refuse to declare dividends; they may drain off the corporation's earnings in the form of exorbitant salaries and bonuses to the majority shareholder-officers and perhaps to their relatives, or in the form of high rent by the corporation for property leased from majority shareholders . . . ; they may deprive minority shareholders of corporate offices and of employment by the company; they may cause the corporation to sell its assets at an inadequate price to the majority shareholders . . . ." F. H. O'Neal and J. Derwin, *Expulsion or Oppression of Business Associates*, 42 (1961). In particular, the power of the board of directors, controlled by the majority, to declare or withhold dividends and to deny the minority employment is easily converted to a device to disadvantage minority stockholders. * * *

The minority can, of course, initiate suit against the majority and their directors. Self-serving conduct by directors is proscribed by the director's fiduciary obligation to the corporation. * * * However, in practice, the plaintiff will find difficulty in challenging dividend or employment policies. * * * Such policies are considered to be within the judgment of the directors. This court has said: "The courts prefer not to interfere . . . with the sound financial management of the corporation by its directors, but declare as a general rule that the declaration of dividends rests within the sound discretion of the directors, refusing to interfere with their determination unless a plain abuse of discretion is made to appear." *Crocker v. Waltham Watch Co.* 315 Mass. 397, 402 (1944). * * * Judicial reluctance to interfere combines with the difficulty of proof when the standard is "plain abuse of discretion" or bad faith, * * * to limit the possibilities for relief. Although contractual provisions in an "agreement of association and articles of organization" (*Crocker v. Waltham Watch Co.*, supra, at 401) or in by-laws * * * have justified decrees in this jurisdiction ordering dividend declarations, generally, plaintiffs who seek judicial assistance against corporate dividend or employment policies[4] do not prevail. * * *

Thus, when these types of "freeze-outs" are attempted by the majority stockholders, the minority stockholders, cut off from all corporation-related revenues, must either suffer their losses or seek a buyer for their shares. Many minority stockholders will be unwilling or unable to wait for an alteration in majority policy. Typically, the minority stockholder in a close corporation has a substantial percentage of his personal assets invested in the corporation. * * * The stockholder may have anticipated that his salary from his position with the corporation would be his livelihood. Thus, he cannot afford to wait passively. He must liquidate his investment in the close corporation in order to reinvest the funds in income-producing enterprises.

At this point, the true plight of the minority stockholder in a close corporation becomes manifest. He cannot easily reclaim his capital. In a large public corporation, the oppressed or dissident minority stockholder could sell his stock in order to extricate some of his invested capital. By definition, this market is not available for shares in the close corporation. In a partnership, a partner who feels abused by his fellow partners may cause dissolution by his "express will . . . at any time" (G. L. c. 108A, § 31 [1] [b] and [2]) and recover his share of partnership assets and accumulated profits. * * * If dissolution results in a breach of the partnership articles, the culpable partner will be liable in damages. G. L. c. 108A, § 38 (2) (a) II. By contrast, the stockholder in the close corporation or "incorporated partnership" may achieve dissolution and recovery of his share of the enterprise assets only by compliance with the rigorous terms of the applicable chapter of the General Laws. * * * "The dissolution of a corporation which is a creature of the Legislature is primarily a legislative function, and the only authority courts have to deal with this subject is the power conferred upon them by the Legislature." * * * To secure dissolution of the ordinary close corporation subject to G. L. c. 156B, the stockholder, in the absence of corporate deadlock, must own at least fifty per cent of the shares (G. L. c. 156B, § 99 [a]) or have the advantage of a favorable provision in the articles of organization (G. L. c. 156B, § 100 [a] [2]). The minority stockholder, by definition lacking fifty per cent of the corporate shares, can never "authorize"

---

4   Attacks on allegedly excessive salaries voted for officers and directors fare better in the courts. *See Stratis v. Andreson*, 254 Mass. 536 (1926); *Sagalyn v. Meekins, Packard & Wheat, Inc.* 290 Mass. 434 (1935). What is "reasonable compensation" is a question of fact. *Black v. Parker Mfg. Co.* 329 Mass. 105, 116 (1952). The proof which establishes an excess over such "reasonable compensation" appears easier than the proof which would establish bad faith or plain abuse of discretion.

the corporation to file a petition for dissolution under G. L. c. 156B, § 99 (a), by his own vote. He will seldom have at his disposal the requisite favorable provision in the articles of organization.

Thus, in a close corporation, the minority stockholders may be trapped in a disadvantageous situation. No outsider would knowingly assume the position of the disadvantaged minority. The outsider would have the same difficulties. To cut losses, the minority stockholder may be compelled to deal with the majority. This is the capstone of the majority plan. Majority "freeze-out" schemes which withhold dividends are designed to compel the minority to relinquish stock at inadequate prices. * * * When the minority stockholder agrees to sell out at less than fair value, the majority has won.

Because of the fundamental resemblance of the close corporation to the partnership, the trust and confidence which are essential to this scale and manner of enterprise, and the inherent danger to minority interests in the close corporation, we hold that stockholders[5] in the close corporation owe one another substantially the same fiduciary duty in the operation of the enterprise that partners owe to one another. In our previous decisions, we have defined the standard of duty owed by partners to one another as the "utmost good faith and loyalty." *Cardullo v. Landau*, 329 Mass. 5, 8 (1952). *DeCotis v. D'Antona*, 350 Mass. 165, 168 (1966). Stockholders in close corporations must discharge their management and stockholder responsibilities in conformity with this strict good faith standard. They may not act out of avarice, expediency or self-interest in derogation of their duty of loyalty to the other stockholders and to the corporation.

We contrast * * * this strict good faith standard with the somewhat less stringent standard of fiduciary duty to which directors and stockholders[6] of all corporations must adhere in the discharge of their corporate responsibilities. Corporate directors are held to a good faith and inherent fairness standard of conduct * * * and are not "permitted to serve two masters whose interests are antagonistic." *Spiegel v. Beacon Participations, Inc.* 297 Mass. 398, 411 (1937). "Their paramount duty is to the corporation, and their personal pecuniary interests are subordinate to that duty." *Durfee v. Durfee & Canning*, Inc. 323 Mass. 187, 196 (1948).

The more rigorous duty of partners and participants in a joint adventure * * * here extended to stockholders in a close corporation, was described by then Chief Judge Cardozo of the New York Court of Appeals in *Meinhard v. Salmon*, 249 N. Y. 458 (1928): "Joint adventurers, like copartners, owe to one another, while the enterprise continues, the duty of the finest loyalty. Many forms of conduct permissible in a workaday world for those acting at arm's length, are forbidden to those bound by fiduciary duties. . . . Not honesty alone, but the punctilio of an honor the most sensitive, is then the standard of behavior." Id. at 463–464. * * *

---

5   We do not limit our holding to majority stockholders. In the close corporation, the minority may do equal damage through unscrupulous and improper "sharp dealings" with an unsuspecting majority. * * *

6   The rule set out in many jurisdictions is: "The majority has the right to control; but when it does so, it occupies a fiduciary relation toward the minority, as much so as the corporation itself or its officers and directors." * * *

Application of this strict standard of duty to stockholders in close corporations is a natural outgrowth of the prior case law. In a number of cases involving close corporations, we have held stockholders participating in management to a standard of fiduciary duty more exacting than the traditional good faith and inherent fairness standard because of the trust and confidence reposed in them by the other stockholders. In *Silversmith v. Sydeman*, 305 Mass. 65 (1940), the plaintiff brought suit for an accounting of the liquidation of a close corporation which he and the defendant had owned. In assessing their relative rights in the discount of a note, we had occasion to consider the defendant's fiduciary duty with respect to the financial affairs of the company. We implied that, in addition to the fiduciary duty owed by an officer to the corporation, a more rigorous standard of fiduciary duty applied to the defendant by virtue of the relationship between the stockholders: "... it could be found that the plaintiff and the defendant were acting as partners in the conduct of the company's business and in the liquidation of its property even though they had adopted a corporate form as the instrumentality by which they should associate in furtherance of their joint venture." *Id.* at 68.

In *Samia v. Central Oil Co. of Worcester*, 339 Mass. 101 (1959), sisters alleged that their brothers had systematically excluded them from management, income and partial ownership of a close corporation formed from a family partnership. In rejecting arguments that the plaintiffs' suit was barred by the statute of limitations or laches, we stressed the familial relationship among the parties, which should have given rise to a particularly scrupulous fidelity in serving the interests of all of the stockholders * * *.

* * * In the instant case, we extend this strict duty of loyalty to all stockholders in close corporations. The circumstances which justified findings of relationships of trust and confidence in these particular cases exist universally in modified form in all close corporations. * * *

B. *Equal Opportunity in a Close Corporation.* Under settled Massachusetts law, a domestic corporation, unless forbidden by statute, has the power to purchase its own shares. * * * An agreement to reacquire stock "is enforceable, subject, at least, to the limitations that the purchase must be made in good faith and without prejudice to creditors and stockholders." * * * When the corporation reacquiring its own stock is a close corporation, the purchase is subject to the additional requirement, in the light of our holding in this opinion, that the stockholders, who, as directors or controlling stockholders, caused the corporation to enter into the stock purchase agreement, must have acted with the utmost good faith and loyalty to the other stockholders.

To meet this test, if the stockholder whose shares were purchased was a member of the controlling group, the controlling stockholders must cause the corporation to offer each stockholder an equal opportunity to sell a ratable number of his shares to the corporation at an identical price.[7] Purchase by the corporation confers substantial

---

7   Of course, a close corporation may purchase shares from one stockholder without offering the others an equal opportunity if all other stockholders give advance consent to the stock purchase arrangements through acceptance of an appropriate provision in the articles of organization, the corporate by-laws * * * or a stockholder's agreement. Similarly, all other stockholders may ratify the purchase. * * *

benefits on the members of the controlling group whose shares were purchased. These benefits are not available to the minority stockholders if the corporation does not also offer them an opportunity to sell their shares. The controlling group may not, consistent with its strict duty to the minority, utilize its control of the corporation to obtain special advantages and disproportionate benefit from its share ownership. * * *

The benefits conferred by the purchase are twofold: (1) provision of a market for shares; (2) access to corporate assets for personal use. By definition, there is no ready market for shares of a close corporation. The purchase creates a market for shares which previously had been unmarketable. * * * If the close corporation purchases shares only from a member of the controlling group, the controlling stockholder can convert his shares into cash at a time when none of the other stockholders can. Consistent with its strict fiduciary duty, the controlling group may not utilize its control of the corporation to establish an exclusive market in previously unmarketable shares from which the minority stockholders are excluded. * * *

The purchase also distributes corporate assets to the stockholder whose shares were purchased. Unless an equal opportunity is given to all stockholders, the purchase of shares from a member of the controlling group operates as a preferential distribution of assets. * * * The other stockholders benefit from no such access to corporate property and cannot withdraw their shares of the corporate profits and capital in this manner unless the controlling group acquiesces. Although the purchase price for the controlling stockholder's shares may seem fair to the corporation and other stockholders under the tests established in the prior case law * * * the controlling stockholder whose stock has been purchased has still received a relative advantage over his fellow stockholders, inconsistent with his strict fiduciary duty—an opportunity to turn corporate funds to personal use.

The rule of equal opportunity in stock purchases by close corporations provides equal access to these benefits for all stockholders. We hold that, in any case in which the controlling stockholders have exercised their power over the corporation to deny the minority such equal opportunity, the minority shall be entitled to appropriate relief. * * *

C. APPLICATION OF THE LAW TO THIS CASE. * * *

* * *

Because of the foregoing, we hold that the plaintiff is entitled to relief. Two forms of suitable relief are set out hereinafter. The judge below is to enter an appropriate judgment. The judgment may require Harry Rodd to remit $36,000 with interest at the legal rate from July 15, 1970, to Rodd Electrotype in exchange for forty-five shares of Rodd Electrotype treasury stock. * * * In the alternative, the judgment may require Rodd Electrotype to purchase all of the plaintiff's shares for $36,000 * * *. In the circumstances of this case, we view this as the equal opportunity which the plaintiff should have received. * * *

* * *

WILKINS, J. (concurring).

* * * I do not join in any implication * * * that the rule concerning a close corporation's purchase of a controlling stockholder's shares applies to all operations of the corporation as they affect minority stockholders. That broader issue, which is apt to arise in connection with salaries and dividend policy, is not involved in this case. The analogy to partnerships may not be a complete one.

NOTES AND QUESTIONS

I. THIS CASE IS our introduction to the problems of the close corporation. It is concerned with the duty that those in control of a close corporation owe to the minority shareholders. What was the purported breach of fiduciary duty here? Given that the company would not be what it was but for Harry Rodd's efforts, did the court reach the appropriate conclusion in the case? For a different approach to the question of selective purchases by the corporation of some but not all of shareholders' stock, see, e.g., *Toner v. Baltimore Envelope Co.*, 304 Md. 256, 498 A.2d 642 (1985) and *Delahoussaye v. Newhard*, 785 S.W.2d 609 (Mo.App. 1990). Delaware appears to permit selective redemption of shares in an appropriate situation, such as resistance to a coercive tender-offer, see e.g., *Unocal Corp. v. Mesa Petroleum Co.*, 493 A.2d 946 (Del.Supr.1985). But see the so-called "all holders rule" of federal law, a regulation of the Securities and Exchange Commission, which requires that when a tender offer is made for shares in a publicly-held corporation all shareholders holding the same class of shares must be treated equally. SEC Rule13e–4(f)(8)(i). Still, should that rule broadly apply in the case of privately-held corporations?

....

2. *DONAHUE* PROVIDES a concise definition of a close corporation: "We deem a close corporation to be typified by: (1) a small number of stockholders; (2) no ready market for the corporate stock; and (3) substantial majority stockholder participation in the management, direction and operations of the corporation." Do you understand how these characteristics of the close corporation pose the risk of breaches of fiduciary duties? Does it make sense, as did the court, to conclude that "stockholders in the close corporation owe one another substantially the same fiduciary duty in the operation of the enterprise that partners owe to one another?" Why do you suppose Justice Wilkins expressed some reservations on this point? Can you understand how the fiduciary duty imposed in Donahue is different from that owed to the publicly-held corporation by directors and officers? Should there be a difference? Where they have the potential to obstruct the business of the close corporation, do minority shareholders owe others the same fiduciary duty a majority shareholder has to the minority in a close corporation? For an affirmative answer see, e.g., *Wilkes v. Springside Nursing Home, Inc.* 370 Mass. 842, 353 N.E.2d 657 (Mass. 1976). For a superb discussion of the Donahue case, including some treatment of *Wilkes v. Springside Nursing Home, see* Douglas K. Moll, "Protection of Minority Shareholders in Closely–Held Corporations: Donahue v. Rodd Electrotype Co.," Chapter 6 in Jonathan R. Macey, ed., *The Iconic Cases in Corporate Law* 98 (2008). In his analysis, Professor Moll, one of the country's leading experts in the law of the close corporation, praises the Donahue case in general, but does offer some critical comments on the decision. He indicates that "Although the validity of the equal opportunity rule and the usefulness of the partnership analogy can be questioned, the significance of the Donahue decision lies less in its detail and more in its overall push for enhanced minority shareholder rights." *Id.*, at 105. Do you agree?

....

3. IT IS PROBABLY DIFFICULT to overstate the importance (or the recent importance) of the closely-held corporation. As late as 1990 it could be said that "close corporations account for most of American business." Steven C. Bahls, Resolving Shareholder Dissension: Selection of the Appropriate Equitable Remedy, 15 J. Corp. L. 285, 287 (1990) (observing that "family-owned businesses alone represent 95% of all United States businesses")(cited in Douglas Moll, *Shareholder Oppression in Close Corporations: The Unanswered Question of Perspective*, 53 Vand. L. Rev. 749, 754 (2000)). Some of these businesses are shifting to the Limited Liability Company (LLC) form, but it is likely that the questions of fiduciary duty will be similarly analyzed whatever the small business vehicle chosen. Is it important to keep much of American business in the hands of small groups of entrepreneurs? Do you sympathize with the plight of the Donahues? Clearly the Rodds were getting some remuneration from their position as officials of the corporation, and, indeed, as you may have discerned from the *Holden v. Construction Company* case we considered in Chapter Five, shareholders in a close corporation often cannot count on dividends, and may only expect to receive remuneration from salaries they receive as officials of the corporation. As nicely put in a recent article on the close corporation:

A characteristic of close corporations that has been central to many oppression cases is that distribution of business income to the owners is
commonly in the form of salary and employment benefits rather than
dividends. Federal income tax advantages are one major reason. For "C
corporations" (all corporations except those that qualify for and elect pass-
through "S" status), salary payments are taxable income to the recipient.
These payments, however, are a business deduction to the corporation, so
are effectively taxed just once. Dividend payments, in sharp contrast, are
income to the recipient but not deductible by the corporation. Therefore,
the dividend payments are double taxed.

Experts describe salary and other employment benefits, which may be at
the high end of a reasonable range of compensation for services, as "de
facto dividends." Moreover, some characterize employment by closely held
corporations of their shareholders as an investment interest of the shareholders, not a separate relationship as in other situations. A shareholder of
a close corporation who is terminated from employment with the company
may lose not only the job but also all income and all return on investment.
Though the person may continue to own shares, they produce no income in
the absence of employment and are not salable at fair value. The minority's
investment is locked in, producing no return to the minority, and serving
only to promote the interests of the controlling shareholders.

Robert C. Art, *Shareholder Rights and Remedies in Close Corporations:
Oppression, Fiduciary Duties, and Reasonable Expectations*, 28 Iowa J. Corp. L.
371, 383–384 (2003) (footnotes omitted). Does this give you a better sense of the
plight faced by the Donahues? How might one seek to plan around this possible
problem of oppression of the minority by the majority in a close corporation (or in
an LLC)? Consider the next case.

II. Shareholder Agreements in the Close Corporation

Galler v. Galler

Supreme Court of Illinois.

32 Ill.2d 16, 203 N.E.2d 577 (1964).

[UNDERWOOD, J.]

Plaintiff, Emma Galler, sued in equity for an accounting and for specific performance of an agreement made in July, 1955, between plaintiff and her husband, of one part, and defendants, Isadore A. Galler and his wife, Rose, of the other. Defendants appealed from a decree of the superior court of Cook County granting the relief prayed. The First District Appellate Court reversed the decree and denied specific performance * * *. That decision is appealed here * * *.

* * * From 1919 to 1924, Benjamin and Isadore Galler, brothers, were equal partners in the Galler Drug Company, a wholesale drug concern. In 1924 the business was incorporated under the Illinois Business Corporation Act, each owning one half of the outstanding 220 shares of stock. * * * For approximately one year prior to the entry of the decree by the chancellor in July of 1962, there were no outstanding minority shareholder interests.

In March, 1954, Benjamin and Isadore, on the advice of their accountant, decided to enter into an agreement for the financial protection of their immediate families and to assure their families, after the death of either brother, equal control of the corporation. In June, 1954, while the agreement was in the process of preparation by an attorney-associate of the accountant, Benjamin suffered a heart attack. Although he resumed his business duties some months later, he was again stricken in February, 1955, and thereafter was unable to return to work. During his brother's illness, Isadore asked the accountant to have the shareholders' agreement put in final form in order to protect Benjamin's wife, and this was done by another attorney employed in the accountant's office. On a Saturday night in July, 1955, the accountant brought the agreement to Benjamin's home, and 6 copies of it were executed there by the two brothers and their wives. * * * Between the execution of the agreement in July, 1955, and Benjamin's death in December, 1957, the agreement was not modified. Benjamin suffered a stroke late in July, 1955, and on August 2, 1955, Isadore and the accountant and a notary public brought to Benjamin for signature two powers of attorney which were retained by the accountant after Benjamin executed them with Isadore as a witness. The plaintiff did not read the powers and she never had them. One of the powers authorized the transfer of Benjamin's bank account to Emma and the other power enabled Emma to vote Benjamin's 104 shares. Because of the state of Benjamin's health, nothing further was said to him by any of the parties concerning the agreement. It appears from the evidence that some months after the agreement was signed, the defendants Isadore and Rose Galler and their son, the defendant, Aaron Galler, sought to have the agreements destroyed. The evidence is undisputed that defendants had decided prior to Benjamin's death they would not honor the agreement, but never disclosed their intention to plaintiff or her husband.

On July 21, 1956, Benjamin executed an instrument creating a trust naming his wife as trustee. The trust covered, among other things, the 104 shares of Galler Drug Company stock and the stock certificates were endorsed by Benjamin and delivered to Emma. When Emma presented the certificates to defendants for transfer into her name as trustee, they sought to have Emma abandon the 1955 agreement or enter into some kind of a noninterference agreement as a price for the transfer of the shares. Finally, in September, 1956, after Emma had refused to abandon the shareholders' agreement, she did agree to permit defendant Aaron to become president for one year and agreed that she would not interfere with the business during that year. The stock was then reissued in her name as trustee. During the year 1957 while Benjamin was still alive, Emma tried many times to arrange a meeting with Isadore to discuss business matters but he refused to see her.

Shortly after Benjamin's death, Emma went to the office and demanded the terms of the 1955 agreement be carried out. Isadore told her that anything she had to say could be said to Aaron, who then told her that his father would not abide by the agreement. He offered a modification of the agreement by proposing the salary continuation payment but without her becoming a director. When Emma refused to modify the agreement and sought enforcement of its terms, defendants refused and this suit followed.

During the last few years of Benjamin's life both brothers drew an annual salary of $42,000. Aaron, whose salary was $15,000 as manager of the warehouse prior to September, 1956, has since the time that Emma agreed to his acting as president drawn an annual salary of $20,000. In 1957, 1958, and 1959 a $40,000 annual dividend was paId. Plaintiff has received her proportionate share of the dividend.

The July, 1955, agreement in question here, entered into between Benjamin, Emma, Isadore and Rose, recites that Benjamin and Isadore each own 47 1/2% of the issued and outstanding shares of the Galler Drug Company, an Illinois corporation, and that Benjamin and Isadore desired to provide income for the support and main-tenance of their immediate families. No reference is made to the shares [which were then owned by a minority shareholder, Rosenberg, which shares were later acquired by the Gallers.] The essential features of the contested portions of the agreement are substantially * * * [1] that the bylaws of the corporation will be amended to provide for a board of four directors; [2] that the necessary quorum shall be three directors; and that no directors' meeting shall be held without giving ten days notice to all directors. [3] The shareholders will cast their votes for the above named persons (Isadore, Rose, Benjamin and Emma) as directors at said special meeting and at any other meeting held for the purpose of electing directors. [4] In the event of the death of either brother his wife shall have the right to nominate a director in place of the decedent. [5] Certain annual dividends will be declared by the corporation. The dividend shall be $50,000 payable out of the accumulated earned surplus in excess of $500,000. If 50% of the annual net profits after taxes exceeds the minimum $50,000, then the directors shall have discretion to declare a dividend up to 50% of the annual net profits. If the net profits are less than $50,000, nevertheless the minimum $50,000 annual dividend shall be declared, providing the $500,000 surplus is maintained. * * * [6] The certificates evidencing the said shares of Benjamin Galler and Isadore Galler shall bear a legend that the shares are subject to the terms of this agreement. [7] A salary continuation agreement shall be entered into by the corporation which shall authorize the corporation upon the death of Benjamin Galler or Isadore Galler, or both, to pay a sum equal to twice the salary of such officer, payable monthly over a five-year period. Said sum shall be paid to the widow during her widowhood, but should be paid to such widow's children if the widow remarries within the five-year period. [8] The parties to this agreement further agree and hereby grant to the corporation the authority to purchase, in the event of the death of either Benjamin or Isadore, so much of the stock of Galler Drug Company held by the estate as is necessary to provide sufficient funds to pay the federal estate tax, the Illinois inheritance tax and other administrative expenses of the estate. If as a result of such purchase from the estate of the decendent the amount of dividends to be received by the heirs is reduced, the parties shall nevertheless vote for directors so as to give the estate and heirs the same representation as before (2 directors out of 4, even though they own less stock), and also that the corporation pay an additional benefit payment equal to the diminution of the dividends.[9] In the event either Benjamin or Isadore decides to sell his shares he is required to offer them first to the remaining shareholders and then to the corporation at book value, according each six months to accept the offer.

The Appellate Court found the 1955 agreement void because "the undue duration, stated purpose and substantial disregard of the provisions of the Corporation Act outweigh any considerations which might call for divisibility" and held that "the public policy of this state demands voiding this entire agreement".

While the conduct of defendants towards plaintiff was clearly inequitable, the basically controlling factor is the absence of an adverse effect upon a minority interest, together with the absence of public detriment. * * *

Faulds v. Yates, 57 Ill. 416, decided by this court in 1870, established the general rule that the owners of the majority of the stock of a corporation have the right to select the agents for the management of the corporation. This court observed (57 Ill. 416, 421): "It is strange that a man can not, for honest purposes, unite with others in the protection and security of his property and rights without liability to the charge of fraud and inequity".

In *Higgins v. Lansingh*, 154 Ill. 301, 357, this court again recognized the right of majority owners of stock to combine to secure the board of directors in the management of the corporation. There, the court went further and denied the corporation and some of its stockholders the right to question the validity of an issue of preferred stock not provided for in the corporate charter, where the stockholders authorized the issue, the corporation paid dividends on it and all treated it as valid for 22 years.

In *Kantzler v. Bensinger*, 214 Ill. 589, decided in 1905, the issue of statutory violation was raised, and this court again followed *Faulds v. Yates*, emphasizing and quoting the following (p. 598):

> "In *Faulds v. Yates*, 57 Ill. 416, it was objected that an agreement between certain persons owning a majority of the stock of a corporation that they would elect the directors and manage the business was against public policy. There were other stockholders, but they made no objection. The court upheld the agreement, and on page 420 said: 'There was no fraud in the agreement which has been so bitterly assailed in the argument. There was nothing unlawful in it. There was nothing which necessarily affected the rights and interests of the minority. Three persons owning a majority of the stock had the unquestioned right to combine, and thus secure the board of directors and the management of the property. Corporations are governed by the republican principle that the whole are bound by the acts of the majority, when the acts conform to the law of their creation. The co-operation, then, of these parties in the election of the officers of the company, and their agreement not to buy or sell stock except for their joint benefit, cannot properly be characterized as dishonest and violative of the rights of others and in contravention of public policy. * * * The agreement complained of was entered into by *Faulds* and his partners. The shareholders whom he is so solicitous to defend and protect have not complained. He cannot invoke their shield to fight imaginary wrongs. The transaction which he, through his counsel, denounces as fraudulent and nefarious was conceived and consummated by him as much as by his partners. Every motive which could influence a man for good should have prompted him to silence. If this combination was fraudulent and intended for bad purposes, the stockholders who are in a minority and who may have suffered have ample redress. We prefer to listen to them before any decision as to their wrongs.' * * *."

Again, in 1913, this court in *Venner v. Chicago City Railway Co.* 258 Ill. 523, 539, followed the *Faulds* case and said:

> "There is no statute of this State which prohibits a trust of the stock of a corporation for the purpose of controlling its management. There is no rule of public policy in this State which prohibits the combination of the owners of the majority of the stock of a corporation for the purpose of controlling the corporation. On the contrary, it has been expressly held that a contract by the owners of more than one-half of the shares of stock of a corporation to elect the directors of the corporation so as to secure the management of its property, to ballot among themselves for directors and officers if they could not agree, to cast their vote as a unit as the majority should decide so as to control the election, and not to buy or sell stock except for their joint benefit is not dishonest, violative of the rights of others or in contravention of public policy * * *."

In *Thompson v. Thompson Carnation Co.* 279 Ill. 54, 58, we again approved a contract by which the owners of a majority of stock agreed to vote for certain persons for directors so as to secure to themselves the control and management of the corporation and held such an agreement not to be illegal or void so long as no fraud is committed on the corporation or wrong done to the other stockholders. In this case, as in the others, this court found that no fraud was practiced or intended to be practiced by the contract in question, and insofar as its validity was assailed on those grounds it was sustained as a valid exercise of the right of contract.

In *Schumann–Heink v. Folsom*, 328 Ill. 321, 330, we said:

> "In considering whether any contract is against public policy it should be remembered that it is to the interests of the public that persons should not be unnecessarily restricted in their freedom to make their own contracts. Agreements are not held to be void, as being contrary to public policy, unless they be clearly contrary to what the constitution, the statutes or the decisions of the courts have declared to be the public policy or unless they be manifestly injurious to the public welfare. Courts must act with care in extending those rules which say that a given contract is void because against public policy, since if there be one thing more than any other which public policy requires, it is that men of full age and competent understanding shall have the utmost liberty of contract, and that their contracts, when entered into fairly and voluntarily, shall be held sacred and shall be enforced by the courts."

* * *

The power to invalidate the agreements on the grounds of public policy is so far reaching and so easily abused that it should be called into action to set aside or annul the solemn engagement of parties dealing on equal terms only in cases where the corrupt or dangerous tendency clearly and unequivocally appears upon the face of the agreement itself or is the necessary inference from the matters which are expressed, and the only apparent exception to this general rule is to be found in those cases where the agreement, though fair and unobjectionable on its face, is a part of a corrupt scheme and is made to disguise the real nature of the transaction. * * *

Defendants have referred us to cases in other jurisdictions and the Appellate Courts of this State, particularly *Odman v. Oleson*, 319 Mass. 24, 64 N.E.2d 439, and *Teich v. Kaufman*, 174 Ill. App. 306. Neither is persuasive, for Odman exemplifies the public policy of Massachusetts whose courts, while not holding agreements such as we have here invalid per se, have not relaxed their requirements of strict statutory compliance when dealing with close corporations, at least where all the stockholders have not signed the agreement in question. * * * In any event, decisions setting forth the public policies of other jurisdictions will not be followed if not harmonious with the judicially declared public policy of Illinois. * * * *Teich* held the majority agreement void as benefitting the individual interests of the major shareholders at corporate expense and to the detriment of the minority who had no knowledge of the agreement.

At this juncture it should be emphasized that we deal here with a so-called close corporation. Various attempts at definition of the close corporation have been made. * * * For our purposes, a close corporation is one in which the stock is held in a few hands, or in a few families, and wherein it is not at all, or only rarely, dealt in by buying or selling. * * * Moreover, it should be recognized that shareholder agreements similar to that in question here are often, as a practical consideration, quite necessary for the protection of those financially interested in the close corporation. While the shareholder of a public-issue corporation may readily sell his shares on the open market should management fail to use, in his opinion, sound business judgment, his counterpart of the close corporation often has a large total of his entire capital invested in the business and has no ready market for his shares should he desire to sell. He feels, understandably, that he is more than a mere investor and that his voice should be heard concerning all corporate activity. Without a shareholder agreement, specifically enforceable by the courts, insuring him a modicum of control, a large minority shareholder might find himself at the mercy of an oppressive or unknowledgeable majority. Moreover, as in the case at bar, the shareholders of a close corporation are often also the directors and officers thereof. With substantial shareholding interests abiding in each member of the board of directors, it is often quite impossible to secure, as in the large public-issue corporation, independent board judgment free from personal motivations concerning corporate policy. For these and other reasons too voluminous to enumerate here, often the only sound basis for protection is afforded by a lengthy, detailed shareholder agreement securing the rights and obligations of all concerned. * * *

* * * [T]here has been a definite * * * trend toward eventual judicial treatment of the close corporation as sui generis. Several shareholder-director agreements that have technically "violated" the letter of the Business Corporation Act have nevertheless been upheld in the light of the existing practical circumstances, i.e., no apparent public injury, no apparent injury to a minority interest, and no apparent prejudice to creditors. However, we have thus far not attempted to limit these decisions as applicable only to close corporations and have seemingly implied that general considerations regarding judicial supervision of all corporate behavior apply.

The practical result of this series of cases, while liberally giving legal efficacy to particular agreements in special circumstances notwithstanding literal "violations" of statutory corporate law, has been to inject much doubt and uncertainty into the thinking of the bench and corporate bar of Illinois concerning shareholder agreements. * * *

It is therefore necessary, we feel, to discuss the instant case with the problems peculiar to the close corporation particularly in mind.

It would admittedly facilitate judicial supervision of corporate behavior if a strict adherence to the provisions of the Business Corporation Act were required in all cases without regard to the practical exigencies peculiar to the close corporation.

* * * However, courts have long ago quite realistically, we feel, relaxed their attitudes concerning statutory compliance when dealing with close corporate behavior, permitting "slight deviations" from corporate "norms" in order to give legal efficacy to common business practice. See, e.g., *Clark v. Dodge*, 269 N.Y. 410, 199 N.E. 641; *Benintendi v. Kenton Hotel*, 294 N.Y. 112, 60 N.E.2d 829 (dissenting opinion subsequently legislatively approved.) This attitude is illustrated by the following language in *Clark v. Dodge*:

> "Public policy, the intention of the Legislature, detriment to the corporation, are phrases which in this connection [the court was discussing a shareholder-director agreement whereby the directors pledged themselves to vote for certain people as officers of the corporation] mean little. Possible harm to bona fide purchasers of stock or to creditors or to stockholding minorities have more substance; but such harms are absent in many instances. If the enforcement of a particular contract damages nobody—not even, in any perceptible degree, the public—one sees no reason for holding it illegal, even though it impinges slightly on the broad provisions of [the relevant statute providing that the business of a corporation shall be managed by its board of directors.]. Damage suffered or threatened is a logical and practical test, and has come to be the one generally adopted by the courts. * * * "

—*Clark v. Dodge*, 199 N.E. 641, 642.

Again,

> "As the parties to the action are the complete owners of the corporation, there is no reason why the exercise of the power and discretion of the directors cannot be controlled by valid agreement between themselves, provided that the interests of creditors are not affected."

— *Clark v. Dodge*, 119 N.E. 641, 643* * *.

* * *

This court has recognized * * * the significant conceptual differences between the close corporation and its public-issue counterpart in, among other cases, *Kantzler v. Benzinger*, 214 Ill. 589, where an agreement quite similar to the one under attack here was upheld. Where, as in Kantzler and here, no injury to a minority interest appears, no fraud or apparent injury to the public or creditors is present, and no clearly prohibitory statutory language is violated, we can see no valid reason for precluding the parties from reaching any arrangements concerning the management of the corporation which are agreeable to all.

Perhaps, as has been vociferously advanced, a separate comprehensive statutory scheme governing the close corporation would best serve here. * * * Some states have enacted legislation dealing specifically with the close corporation. * * *

At any rate, however, the courts can no longer fail to expressly distinguish between the close and public-issue corporation when confronted with problems relating to either. What we do here is to illuminate this problem—before the bench, corporate bar, and the legislature, in the context of a particular fact situation. To do less would be to shirk our responsibility, to do more would, perhaps be to invade the province of the legislative branch.

We now, in the light of the foregoing, turn to specific provisions of the 1955 agreement.

The Appellate Court correctly found many of the contractual provisions free from serious objection, and we need not prolong this opinion with a discussion of them here. That court did, however, find difficulties in the stated purpose of the agreement as it relates to its duration, the election of certain persons to specific offices for a number of years, the requirement for the mandatory declaration of stated dividends (which the Appellate Court held invalid), and the salary continuation agreement.

Since the question as to the duration of the agreement is a principal source of controversy, we shall consider it first. The parties provided no specific termination date, and while the agreement concludes with a paragraph that its terms "shall be binding upon and shall inure to the benefits of" the legal representatives, heirs and assigns of the parties, this clause is, we believe, intended to be operative only as long as one of the parties is living. It further provides that it shall be so construed as to carry out its purposes, and we believe these must be determined from a consideration of the agreement as a whole. Thus viewed, a fair construction is that its purposes were accomplished at the death of the survivor of the parties. While these life spans are not precisely ascertainable, and the Appellate Court noted Emma Galler's life expectancy at her husband's death was 26.9 years, we are aware of no statutory or public policy provision against stockholder's agreements which would invalidate this agreement on that ground. * * * While defendants argue that the public policy evinced by the legislative restrictions upon the duration of voting trust agreements (Ill. Rev. Stat. 1963, chap. 32, par. 157.30a) should be applied here, this agreement is not a voting trust, but as pointed out by the dissenting justice in the Appellate Court, is a straight contractual voting control agreement which does not divorce voting rights from stock ownership. That the policy against agreements in which stock ownership and voting rights are separated, indicated in *Luthy v. Ream*, 270 Ill. 170, is inapplicable to voting control agreements was emphasized in [a prior case] wherein a control agreement was upheld as not attempting to separate ownership and voting power. While limiting voting trusts in 1947 to a maximum duration of 10 years, the legislature has indicated no similar policy regarding straight voting agreements although these have been common since prior to 1870. In view of the history of decisions of this court generally upholding, in the absence of fraud or prejudice to minority interests or public policy, the right of stockholders to agree among themselves as to the manner in which their stock will be voted, we do not regard the period of time within which this agreement may remain effective as rendering the agreement unenforceable.

The clause that provides for the election of certain persons to specified offices for a period of years likewise does not require invalidation. In *Kantzler v. Benzinger*, 214 Ill. 589, this court upheld an agreement entered into by all the stockholders providing that certain parties would be elected to the offices of the corporation for a fixed period. In *Faulds v. Yates*, 57 Ill. 416, we upheld a similar agreement among the majority stockholders of a corporation, notwithstanding the existence of a minority which was not before the court complaining thereof. * * *

We turn next to a consideration of the effect of the stated purpose of the agreement upon its validity. The pertinent provision is: "The said Benjamin A. Galler and Isadore A. Galler desire to provide income for the support and maintenance of their immediate families." Obviously, there is no evil inherent in a contract entered into for the reason that the persons originating the terms desired to so arrange their property as to provide post-death support for those dependent upon them. Nor does the fact that the subject property is corporate stock alter the situation so long as there exists no detriment to minority stock interests, creditors or other public injury. It is, however, contended by defendants that the methods provided by the agreement for implementation of the stated purpose are, as a whole, violative of the Business Corporation Act (Ill. Rev. Stat. 1963, chap. 32, pars. 157.28, 157.30a, 157.33, 157.34, 157.41) to such an extent as to render it void in toto.

The terms of the dividend agreement require a minimum annual dividend of $50,000, but this duty is limited by the subsequent provision that it shall be operative only so long as an earned surplus of $500,000 is maintained. It may be noted that in 1958, the year prior to commencement of this litigation, the corporation's net earnings after taxes amounted to $202,759 while its earned surplus was $1,543,270, and this was increased in 1958 to $1,680,079 while earnings were $172,964. The minimum earned surplus requirement is designed for the protection of the corporation and its creditors, and we take no exception to the contractual dividend requirements as thus restricted. * * *

The salary continuation agreement is a common feature, in one form or another, of corporate executive employment. It requires that the widow should receive a total benefit, payable monthly over a five-year period, aggregating twice the amount paid her deceased husband in one year. This requirement was likewise limited for the protection of the corporation by being contingent upon the payments being income tax-deductible by the corporation. The charge made in those cases which have considered the validity of payments to the widow of an officer and shareholder in a corporation is that a gift of its property by a noncharitable corporation is in violation of the rights of its shareholders and *ultra vires*. Since there are no shareholders here other than the parties to the contract, this objection is not here applicable, and its effect, as limited, upon the corporation is not so prejudicial as to require its invalidation.

* * *

NOTES AND QUESTIONS

1. WHAT DO YOU MAKE of the "shareholder agreement" entered into by the Gallers? Note that the appellate court voided the agreement. Do you understand why it did so? Why did the Supreme Court disagree? Do you understand how the shareholder agreement is a device that can alleviate the potential problems of the close corporation? An analogue to the shareholder agreement is the "operating agreement" now often employed for LLC's. *See, e.g.*, Sandra K. Miller, "The Role of the Court in Balancing Contractual Freedom with the Need for Mandatory Constraints on Opportunistic and Abusive Conduct in the LLC," 152 U.Pa. L. Rev. 1609 (2004).

2. THE KEY PROVISION of the shareholder agreement in this case was probably the one that fixed the selection of the directors of the corporation. Why might this be against public policy? There is a line of close corporation cases in New York that suggests that the shareholders may not enter into an agreement that they will manage the corporation, or certain aspects of its operation, in a manner that "sterilizes" the board of directors, see, e.g. *McQuade v. Stoneham*, 263 N.Y. 323, 189 N.E. 234 (1934), *Clark v. Dodge*, 269 N.Y. 410, 199 N.E. 641 (1936). Why do you suppose that is? Compare § 350 and § 351 of the Delaware corporations code, infra, which permit shareholders of a close corporation to enter into agreements restricting the operation of the Board of Directors, or even to dispense with the Board altogether and manage the corporation themselves. Is this wise? Does Homer's story (told in Book XII of the Odyssey) of Odysseus and the Sirens help suggest the role directors might play even in a close corporation?

3. NOTE THAT the *Galler v. Galler* Court indicates that the agreement before it is not a "voting trust," and thus does not conflict with the Illinois statutory policy limiting voting trusts to ten years. What is a "voting trust," and why might one be concerned with voting trusts that are not limited in duration?

A voting trust generally is a voluntary arrangement in which several stockholders of a corporation pool their stock into a trust for a specified period of time in order to control a corporation. All of the stock in the trust is voted by a third party trustee. Sometimes, the voting instructions for the trustee are spelled out in the trust document; other times, the trustee is given discretion concerning how to vote. Additionally, the trust beneficiaries may give voting instructions to the trustee. The primary purpose of the trust is to promote continuity of ownership and corporate direction for a period of time.

Richard L. Epling, *Fun With Non-Voting Stock*, 10 Bank. Dev. J. 17, n.6 (1993). A "voting trust" can also be created by a sole shareholder either to satisfy creditors (who may take stock as collateral and wish to vote it the better to secure their debt) or "to vest control of his business in managers." Melvin Aron Eisenberg, *Corporations and Other Business Organizations: Cases and Materials* 265 (Concise 8th ed., 2000). Can you discern a difference in the *Galler* court's attitude toward voting trusts and shareholder agreements? Is there a difference in your attitude toward the two?

....

4. YOU WILL HAVE NOTICED that the court in *Galler* suggested it might be a good thing for the Illinois legislature to pass special provisions for dealing with the close corporation. "In 1977, Illinois adopted The Close Corporation Act [ILL. REV. STAT. ch. 32, PP1201–1216 (1983)] which authorizes shareholders' agreements for the conduct of the affairs of corporations qualifying as close corporations under that Act. That statutory provision is consistent with *Galler* in that the statutorily-authorized agreement must be between all shareholders of the close corporation and the statutory grant of validity applies only 'as between the parties' to the agreement, without purporting to deal with the question of validity when third-party rights are involved." James M. Van Vliet, Jr., *The New Illinois Business Corporation Act Needs More Work*, 61 Chi.-Kent. L. Rev. 1, 30 (1985). There seems to be a trend for state legislatures to treat the special problems of the close corporation by special statutory provisions. For an evaluation of these efforts, see, e.g. George J. Seidel, *Close Corporation Law: Michigan, Delaware, and the Model Act*, 11 Del. J. Corp. L. 383 (1987). For some criticism of the Illinois statutory approach, especially insofar as it permits dissolution of the close corporation to prevent minority shareholder oppression, see Timothy J. Storm, "Remedies for Oppression of Non-Controlling Shareholders in Illinois Closely-Held Corporations: An Idea Whose Time Has Gone," 33 Loy. U. Chi. L.J. 379 (2002). For a more favorable evaluation of Illinois Law regarding close corporations, see, e.g., William R. Quinlan & John F. Kennedy, *Family Business Legal & Financial Advisor Conference: The Rights and Remedies of Shareholders in Closely Held Corporations Under Illinois Law*, 29 Loy. U. Chi. L.J. 585 (1998).

It is to the problem of oppression in the close corporation context, and appropriate remedies, that we next turn.

III. Oppression in the Close Corporation

Baker v. Commercial Body Builders, Inc.

Supreme Court of Oregon.
264 Ore. 614, 507 P.2d 387 (1973).

[TONGUE, J.]

This is a suit under ORS 57.595 by the owners of 49% of the stock in a "close corporation" to compel a dissolution of the corporation for alleged "illegal, oppressive and fraudulent" conduct by defendants . . . as directors of the corporation and for "misapplication and waste" of its assets.[8]

Plaintiffs appeal from a decree dismissing their complaint * * *. We affirm.

* * *

1. SUMMARY OF EVIDENCE.

A. Organization of corporation. Subsequent purchase of stock by Baker. Original agreement between parties. Defendant Commercial Body Builders, Inc., ("Commercial") was originally organized in August 1966 by defendants Charles Siler and his wife as a family corporation. Its purpose was to engage in the construction of truck bodies, lift gates, and related truck equipment—a business with which Siler was thoroughly familiar and experienced.

About a year later, in 1967, at the suggestion of defendant Siler, plaintiff Baker invested $14,210 in the corporation. Baker was not familiar with the business, but was engaged in the insurance and real estate business. At that time an additional 100 shares of stock were issued and Baker and his wife became owners of 98 shares of the corporation's stock, while Siler and his wife retained ownership of 102 shares. * * * Baker also signed a promissory note for $5,000, payable to Siler, with no time specified for payment, but with payment to be made from the "proceeds" of future bonuses to be paid to employees, including Baker.[9]

---

8   ORS 57.595 provides, in part, as follows:

"(1) The circuit courts shall have full power to liquidate the assets and business of a corporation:

"(a) In an action by a shareholder when it is established:

" * * *

"(B) That the acts of the directors or those in control of the corporation are illegal, oppressive or fraudulent; or

" * * *

"(D) That the corporate assets are being misapplied or wasted."

ORS 57.600 provides, in part, as follows:

"(1) In proceedings to liquidate the assets and business of a corporation the court shall have power to issue injunctions, to appoint a receiver or receivers * * * with such powers and duties as the court, from time to time, may direct, and to take such other proceedings as may be requisite to preserve the corporate assets wherever situated, and carry on the business of the corporation until a full hearing can be had."

9   The reason for this note, according to Siler, was that because he and his wife had started the business he was not willing to let Baker come in on the basis under which he would "match dollar for dollar" what Siler and his wife had "put in."

At the same time, Siler was elected president and his wife treasurer of the corporation, while Baker was elected vice-president and his wife secretary. Monthly salaries were also established, including a salary of $800 to Siler, $200 to his wife, and $100 to Baker. Siler, however, spent full time in the business and his wife worked approximately six hours each business day as bookkeeper, while it was agreed that Baker would spend one day each week at the office. At that time, however, he apparently devoted at least part of that day to the transaction of his insurance and real estate business. As stated by Baker, there was no "formal understanding" what he was to do for Commercial, but the monthly salary of $100 was used by him to pay off the mortgage loan by which he raised the money to purchase the stock.

Shortly afterwards, a buy-sell" agreement was prepared by Baker's attorney and was signed by the parties. By its terms, if either party desired to sell his stock he was required to first offer it to the other party "at the same price as offered on the market or at the book value of said shares as computed by the accounting methods regularly recognized for the computation of book value of corporate stock, whichever is less."

B. *Two Profitable Years Of Operation. Increase In Salaries And Bonuses.* At the end of the following fiscal year on June 30, 1968, the corporation showed a profit of $9,743.90. At that time the following bonuses were paid: Siler, $1,750; Baker, $1,000, and Mrs. Siler, $500. As of the same date salaries were increased as follows: Siler to $1,000 per month, his wife to $350 per month, and Baker to $250 per month.

Similarly, at the end of the next fiscal year on June 30, 1969, the corporation showed a further profit of $19,712.16. According to Siler, however, as of that date Baker, although "doing a satisfactory job," was not making any contacts or sales. Nevertheless, the following additional bonuses were then paid: Siler, $2,625; Baker, $1,500, and Mrs. Siler, $750. On October 6, 1969, Siler's salary was also increased to $1,500, as of July 1, 1969, with no corresponding increase to Baker or to Mrs. Siler. To provide for future expansion, the corporation also loaned $1,370.58 each to Siler and to Baker to provide funds for use as a down payment for the purchase of adjacent property. That property was then apparently purchased by them as partners, under the name of Dorpat Investment Co., and was leased to the corporation.

C. *Termination Of Baker And Negotiations For Purchase Of His Stock.* During the fiscal year 1969–1970, according to Siler, business was "terrible" and although sales increased by $50,000, labor costs increased even more. During that same year, as a result of the organization of Dorpat and the leasing of larger quarters from it, payments for rent, insurance, taxes, "moving in" expenses, and other items were increased. The profit for the fiscal year ending June 30, 1970, dropped to $269.52.

Also, according to both Siler and Baker, the relationship between them deteriorated in early 1970. Siler testified that Baker made only one small sale while he was with the company and that he was not "getting out and calling on the trade" or spending as much time as he should for the company.[10] Baker testified, however, that

---

10   Siler also testified that he was upset at Baker because Baker twice purchased new sets of tires for the

Siler told him not to contact large companies, such as the telephone company, because any resulting orders would be too large for the small business to handle and that relations deteriorated because Siler wanted him to sell out and because Siler thought that a Mr. Ahern could do more for the business than Baker could.

In early May 1970, Mr. Ahern tried to talk to Baker about purchasing his stock, but Baker refused to talk to him about a price for the sale of his stock. According to Baker, he was then offered $20,000 for his stock by Siler, who "intimated" that if Baker didn't sell he would get no profits from the business.

Siler denied that statement and denied making an offer to Baker for his stock, but said that Ahern also wanted to buy Siler's stock and had offered to pay $45,000 for it * * * and that Siler told Baker that if he sold out the purchaser might operate the business in such a way that it would show no profits. Siler also testified that he told Baker, apparently on another occasion, that Ahern would pay Baker $22,500 for his stock; that he talked to Baker about that offer; that Baker said he didn't know what to do, and that he told Baker that if Baker didn't sell to Ahern, Siler was going to do so. In addition, Siler testified that he tried to get Baker to buy him out, but that Baker would not do so and would not tell Ahern whether or not he would sell out to him.

On June 25, 1970, after these negotiations failed, Baker was terminated as a salesman "because of unsatisfactory work performance." According to Siler, this was done because Baker had made no sales and because Siler decided that Baker "was not doing the company any good." On July 10, 1970, Baker and his wife were "voted out" as directors and officers. After that date no notices were sent to Baker of any further stockholders' meetings and he was not consulted by Siler thereafter about the business. Baker also testified that he was also not permitted to see the company books and that he had to get "legal redress" in order to do so. This was denied by Siler.

Also, at the meeting on July 10, 1970, Siler's salary was increased to $1,800 per month and his wife's salary was increased to $500. There were no subsequent salary increases and no bonuses were paid to Siler or to his wife, however, either at the end of the 1969–70 fiscal year or at any later date.[11]

During the period of the years from 1967 to 1970, prior to Baker's "termination," he was paid $7,975 in salary for his services for one day each week, plus $2,500 in bonuses, for a total of $10,475, not including the value of medical insurance and the use of a company car at a somewhat nominal rental. As previously stated, he was offered $22,500 for the stock, for which he had paid $14,210. As also previously

---

company car which he rented from the company, at a somewhat nominal rental, and that he paid more for the tires than Siler could get them for and charged them to the corporation, contrary to instructions that such purchases were to be "cleared" through Siler.

11   Payment of a salary to Siler of $1,800 per month had previously been recommended by the CPA engaged by the company at the time when Siler's salary was increased to $1,500. In addition, Siler justified these salary increases by the savings resulting from the elimination of Baker's salary and automobile expenses. Siler and his wife continued, as in the past, to use a company owned pickup truck and car. Baker also complained that Siler employed his own son. Siler, however, justified this by saying that he paid his son less than previously paid to the employee who was replaced by his son.

noted, Baker also had given Siler a $5,000 note payable from the "proceeds" of the corporation, on which he subsequently paid $1,000 to Siler.

D. *Funds and Services Provided By Corporation to Advance Hydro Wreckers, Mfg., Inc.* In late 1970, a new corporation was organized named Advance Hydro Wreckers, Mfg., Inc. ("Hydro"). Siler was its president and was issued 30% of its stock, in return for his "ability to set the operation in motion." The remaining stock was apparently issued to Ahern, who was "to furnish the money," and to a man named Mr. Nowell, who claimed to own patents for certain wrecker equipment.

According to Siler, this corporation was organized because Commercial could not otherwise build such equipment in view of these patents. Siler did not consult Baker about the Hydro venture.

Hydro leased a portion of Commercial's unused shop space and also used Commercial's office. Prior to December 1, 1970 (when Hydro apparently acquired its own crew), the Commercial crew did work for Hydro. Commercial also furnished bookkeeping services to Hydro. As of May 1971, Hydro owed $10,700 to Commercial. Nevertheless, the Commercial financial statements for the fiscal year ending June 30, 1971, as prepared by a CPA, show a net profit of $15,772.53 and a net worth in the sum of $74,498.11, after including that profit as "retained earnings."

Hydro apparently ceased active operations after a few months and Commercial advanced $2,510 to pay a debt owed by Hydro for the purchase of a wrecker chassis. Commercial also billed $6,700 to Hydro for labor made available by the Commercial crew to build the wrecker on that chassis, which Commercial then took over in payment for these advances and was holding for sale at the time of trial. Commercial also billed Hydro for $1,500 for bookkeeping and managerial services. Hydro was also delinquent in some rental payments and at the time of trial owed a balance of approximately $5,000 to Commercial.

Although the Commercial accounts receivable increased substantially after the advent of Hydro and apparently included substantial amounts owed by Hydro, at least at one time, and although, as a result, Commercial had to borrow $7,000, and was Hydro's largest creditor, there was no direct proof that, as a result, Commercial had suffered any actual loss as of the time of trial in January 1972. As of that date it appears that Hydro had ceased active operations and that Commercial had ceased making any further "advances" to it. It also appears that Hydro then still owned some completed "wreckers," which it had for sale. In addition, Siler was apparently negotiating with Nowell to take over the assets of Hydro, including the alleged patent rights, for enough money to pay the balance owed by Hydro to Commercial.

Neither was there evidence whether Commercial made a profit or suffered a loss during the period between the end of the fiscal year on June 30, 1971, and at the time of trial in January 1972. According to Siler, Hydro did not compete with Commercial and the Commercial crew worked for Hydro during "slack periods," so as to keep the crew busy, rather than lay off men and risk losing them. Also, Baker testified on trial that he presumed that the last financial statements, which were prepared by a CPA and showed a net worth of $74,498, were accurate and that the corporation was worth more at the time of trial than when he was "terminated" in June 1970.

Indeed, at the conclusion of the trial plaintiffs' attorney stated that his "calculation [based upon that same amount] is that at the present time the book value of 49% is worth $36,504.07" and that was the amount for which plaintiffs demanded judgment in the trial court as the "value of their stock," and as an alternative to a forced dissolution of the corporation.

2. PLAINTIFFS' CONTENTIONS—*Browning v. C & C Plywood Corp.*

Plaintiffs' primary contentions are: (1) that the trial court erred when it failed to find that the conduct of defendants Siler was "oppressive" within the meaning of ORS 57.595, as construed by this court in *Browning v. C & C Plywood Corp.*, 248 Or. 574, 434 P.2d 339 (1967), and (2) that the trial court should have used its equitable powers to provide a remedy even if it felt that those provided in ORS 57.595 and 57.600 were inappropriate.

Plaintiffs say that this court formerly subscribed to the "robber baron" theory of corporation law to the effect that the majority stockholders who control the operation of a corporation can do "anything," including a "squeeze out" of minority stockholders, so long as they break no specific laws and commit no actual fraud and that they owe no fiduciary duty to minority stockholders, citing *McMunn v. ML & H Lumber*, 247 Or. 319, 429 P.2d 798 (1967), and *Jackson v. Nicolai-Neppach Co.*, 219 Or. 560, 348 P.2d 9 (1959), as our most recent decisions "reiterating the old 'robber baron' theory."

* * *

* * * [W]e do not mean to approve what plaintiff refers to as the "robber baron" theory of corporate operation, much less to give approval to "squeeze out" or "freeze out" tactics in "close" corporations.

3. *What is "oppressive" conduct for the purposes of ORS 57.595.*

In considering the meaning and application of the term "oppressive" conduct it is first to be noted that by the very terms of ORS 57.595 conduct need not be fraudulent or illegal to be "oppressive" within the meaning of that statute. * * *

* * * [P]erhaps the most widely quoted definitions are that "oppressive conduct" for the purposes of such a statute is:

> " 'burdensome, harsh and wrongful conduct; a lack of probity and fair dealing in the affairs of a company to the prejudice of some of its members; or a visual departure from the standards of fair dealing, and a violation of fair play on which every shareholder who entrusts his money to a company is entitled to rely.' " * * *[12]

---

12 Comment, 1965 Duke LJ 128, 134 * * *.

We agree, however, that the question of what is "oppressive" conduct by those in control of a "close" corporation as its majority stockholders is closely related to what we agree to be the fiduciary duty of a good faith and fair dealing owed by them to its minority stockholders. * * *

Thus, an abuse of corporate position for private gain at the expense of the stockholders is "oppressive" conduct. * * * Or the plundering of a "close" corporation by the siphoning off of profits by excessive salaries or bonus payments and the operation of the business for the sole benefit of the majority of the stockholders, to the detriment of the minority stockholders, would constitute such "oppressive" conduct as to authorize a dissolution of the corporation under the terms of ORS 57.595. * * *

On the other hand, it has been said that a single act in breach of such a fiduciary duty may not constitute such "oppressive" conduct as to authorize the dissolution of a corporation unless extremely serious in nature * * * and that even a continuing course of "oppressive" conduct may not be sufficient for that purpose unless it appears that, as a result, there has been a disproportionate loss to the minority * * * or that those in control of the corporation are so incorrigible that they can no longer be trusted to manage it fairly in the interests of its stockholders. * * *

In other words, although a showing of "imminent disaster" is not required, liquidation is not available upon a showing of mere vague apprehensions of possible future mischief or injury or to extricate minority stockholders from an investment that turns out to be a bad bargain. * * * We also reject the concept that a "close corporation" is like a partnership to the extent that a minority stockholder should have the same right as a partner to demand a dissolution of the business upon substantially the same showing as may be sufficient for the dissolution of a partnership. * * * After all, the remedy of a forced dissolution of a corporation may equally be "oppressive" * * * to the majority stockholders.

It has also been said that the decision by a court whether or not to require dissolution of a corporation for "oppressive" conduct requires an "appraisal of the future" of the corporation and that if the future appears to hold "no hope" or if the majority is "incorrigible" dissolution may be an appropriate remedy. * * *

In any event * * * while a showing of "oppressive" conduct may be sufficient to confer jurisdiction upon the court under ORS 57.595, such a showing does not require the court to exercise the power conferred upon it by that statute to require either the dissolution of a corporation or any other alternative equitable remedy. * * * We thus come to the question of what, if any, other remedies may be appropriate in such a case as an alternative to the forced dissolution of a corporation.

4. Remedies available for "oppressive" conduct as an alternative to dissolution.

We have already held in Browning, supra (at p 582), that in a suit under ORS 57.595 for "oppressive" conduct consisting of a "squeeze out" or "freeze out" in a "close" corporation the courts are not limited to the remedy of dissolution, but may, as an alternative, consider other appropriate equitable relief. * * * [V]arious alternative remedies may be appropriate. Among those suggested are the following:

(a) The entry of an order requiring dissolution of the corporation at a specified future date, to become effective only in the event that the stockholders fail to resolve their differences prior to that date; * * *

(b) The appointment of a receiver, not for the purposes of dissolution, but to continue the operation of the corporation for the benefit of all of the stockholders, both majority and minority, until differences are resolved or "oppressive" conduct ceases; * * *

(c) The appointment of a "special fiscal agent" to report to the court relating to the continued operation of the corporation, as a protection to its minority stockholders, and the retention of jurisdiction of the case by the court for that purpose; * * *

(d) The retention of jurisdiction of the case by the court for the protection of the minority stockholders without appointment of a receiver or "special fiscal agent"; * * *

(e) The ordering of an accounting by the majority in control of the corporation for funds alleged to have been misappropriated; * * *

(f) The issuance of an injunction to prohibit continuing acts of "oppressive" conduct and which may include the reduction of salaries or bonus payments found to be unjustified or excessive; * * *

(g) The ordering of affirmative relief by the required declaration of a dividend or a reduction and distribution of capital; * * *

(h) The ordering of affirmative relief by the entry of an order requiring the corporation or a majority of its stockholders to purchase the stock of the minority stockholders at a price to be determined according to a specified formula or at a price determined by the court to be a fair and reasonable price; * * *

(i) The ordering of affirmative relief by the entry of an order permitting minority stockholders to purchase additional stock under conditions specified by the court; * * *

(j) An award of damages to minority stockholders as compensation for any injury suffered by them as the result of "oppressive" conduct by the majority in control of the corporation.* * *

5. Analysis of plaintiffs' charges of "specific acts of wrongdoing."

As "specific acts of wrongdoing" upon which plaintiffs rely in support of its contention that Silers' conduct amount to "oppressive" conduct, plaintiffs list the following:

> "Defendants continued to pay themselves ever increasing salaries and fringe benefits while excluding the Bakers from corporate participation. They have paid money to a debtor corporation in which they own a 1/3 interest during the time that corporation owes Defendant corporation money. They have permitted the other corporation, Advanced Hydro Wreckers, to compete with the Defendant corporation and to use the facilities of the defendant corporation without just compensation * * *. Although the business is still profitable, Defendants have siphoned all profits off into their own pockets and have excluded the Plaintiffs from any corporate benefits and have openly and flagrantly applied the 'squeeze out-freeze out'. Defendants have failed to notify the Plaintiffs of corporate meetings on occasion and have falsified the records concerning those meetings. They have at all times treated the corporation as if it were the Silers' private property with which they can do as they see fit, to the exclusion of the Bakers."

[Nevertheless] * * * reference should also be made to the following facts as they appear from the record in this case:

(a) It is true that Siler and his wife excluded Baker and his wife from "corporate participation." It must be remembered, however, that Siler had started the business before Baker came in; that Siler was probably the only one with the knowledge and experience required for the successful operation, and that his wife had also worked some six hours per day, five days a week, as bookkeeper for the business, whereas it appears that Baker only purported to spend one day per week with the business and apparently contributed little, if anything, to its successful operation other than his monetary investment. Accordingly, while he could not be properly excluded from "corporate participation" as a stockholder, it is an entirely different question whether it was "oppressive" to terminate his salary as an employee, together with his use of a company car and his medical insurance as an employee, despite the fact that Siler and his wife retained such benefits as full time employees of the corporation.

(b) While this would not justify the Silers in "siphoning all profits into their own pocket" by the payment of "ever increasing salaries and fringe benefits," to the detriment of plaintiffs, as stockholders, the evidence in this case does not support that charge. During the two-year period of Baker's active "participation," Siler's monthly salary had been increased from $800 to $1,500 and his wife's salary from $200 to $350. In addition, Siler was paid bonuses of $1,750 and $2,625 and his wife received $500 and $750 in bonuses. During the period after Baker's termination on May 31, 1970, and continuing to the date of trial in January 1972, no further bonuses were paid, although Siler's salary was increased from $1,500 to $1,800 and his wife's salary from $350 to $500 per month. There was no evidence, however, that such salaries were excessive * * *. * * * In addition, the financial statement for the year ending June 30, 1971, as prepared by a CPA and conceded by plaintiffs to be accurate, showed a profit of $15,772.53 during that period. Plaintiffs also concede that the net worth of the business at the time of trial was at least as much as on that date.

(c) It is also true that the Bakers, as stockholders, had a legitimate interest in the participation in profits earned by the corporation. Plaintiffs do not, however, request the court in this proceeding to require the declaration of a dividend so as to distribute profits improperly withheld by the corporation. The question whether profits must be distributed as dividends, rather than "plowed back" into a business, is by no means a simple problem. * * *

(d) It may have been improvident for Siler to advance corporate funds to Hydro, in which he owned an interest. However, there was no evidence that Hydro's production of "wreckers," for which it apparently held some patents, improperly "competed" with Commercial or that Hydro was not charged "just compensation" for using corporate "facilities." It appears, however, that defendants have provided plaintiffs with the accounting demanded by them and that there is no evidence that as a result of any such conduct the corporation suffered financial loss in any ascertainable amount. On the contrary, the corporation apparently made a substantial profit during that same year. Moreover, the Hydro venture is now being liquidated and there was no evidence to indicate that it may be revived in the future.

(e) It was highly improper for defendants to prevent plaintiffs from examining the corporate records, to fail to notify plaintiffs of certain corporate meetings and to "falsify" records of such meetings so as to indicate that plaintiffs had been notified or were present. It appears, however, that plaintiffs have since been permitted to examine the records and that the meetings in question occurred in 1969 and 1970. There was also no evidence that there is any reason to believe that proper notice will not be given to them of future meetings.

(f) In evaluating plaintiffs' further charge that defendants' conduct has not only been "inequitable," but "will result in a severe financial loss" to plaintiffs, it must also be remembered that plaintiffs were offered $22,500 for their stock and that they apparently were not interested in any sale of their stock at that time. It is true this was less than what plaintiffs considered to be its book value of $36,504.07, which they demanded on trial as an alternative to a forced corporate dissolution. On the other hand, it is common knowledge that, as a practical matter, the stock acquired by one who purchases a 49% interest in a "close" family corporation, as in this case, is worth considerably less than 49% of the book value of such stock. Furthermore, considering the expenses of a receiver, as well as other expenses incurred in dissolution proceedings, as well as the fact that on such a dissolution the value of the assets of the corporation as a going concern might be destroyed, the result of a forced dissolution, as originally demanded by plaintiffs, might well result in a return to the stockholders, including plaintiffs, of considerably less than the book value of their stock.

Upon considering plaintiffs' charges of "specific acts of wrongdoing," in the light of the foregoing additional facts, we conclude that although some of the conduct of defendants Siler in 1970 was "oppressive" conduct within the meaning of ORS 57.595, we cannot say that the trial judge, who heard the witnesses and observed their demeanor, was in error in finding, in effect, that such conduct was not so serious as to require the relief prayed for by plaintiffs in this case and after examination of the entire record we agree with his finding to that effect. For the same reasons, we also conclude that none of the alternative equitable remedies listed above would be appropriate in this case. In that connection, it should again be noted that most of the conduct complained of by plaintiffs occurred in 1970 and did not continue after that year.

Affirmed, without costs to either party.

NOTES AND QUESTIONS

1. DO YOU SUBSCRIBE TO THE "ROBBER BARON" theory of corporation law? In your opinion was Baker "oppressed" by the Silers? What does constitute "oppression" in a close corporation context? If you were an Oregon legislator, would you have voted for the passage of ORS 57.595? Is dissolution of the corporation an appropriate remedy for majority shareholder misconduct, in your view? When dissolution of the corporation takes place, its official existence comes to an end, and its assets are sold (usually at an auction) to the highest bidder. After the debts of the corporation are paid, the proceeds (if any) are distributed to the shareholders in proportion to their share ownership. Do you agree with the Court's assertion that "the remedy of a forced dissolution of a corporation may equally be 'oppressive' * * * to the majority stockholders." When would this be the case? Who is likely to be the buyer of the corporate assets? If you were advising the Bakers, would you have suggested they ask for different relief (for example, a declaration of dividends)? Note that the court does conclude that some conduct of Siler's was "highly improper." Where is the line to be drawn between conduct that is "highly improper" and that which is so "oppressive" that dissolution is called for? Does the attitude of this court seem similar to, or different from, the attitude of the Massachusetts Court in the Donahue case, *supra*?

2. **NOTE THAT, AS WE SAW EARLIER,** the failure to pay dividends in the close corporation context can be a tactic to squeeze or freeze out a minority shareholder. When is it appropriate for a court to intervene and declare the payment of dividends? This is something courts are reluctant to do, but for some suggestions on when it is appropriate, see, e.g., Douglas K. Moll, "Shareholder Oppression & Dividend Policy in the Close Corporation," 60 Wash & Lee L. Rev. 841 (2003). As indicated earlier, Professor Moll observes that those in control of a close corporation are in a position to pay themselves "de facto dividends" such as high salary payments or other arrangements that favor them at the expense of the minority shareholders. Moll concludes that:

> With respect to disputes involving de facto dividends, a minority shareholder's expectation of dividends should be considered reasonable, and thus enforceable [by the courts], whenever the majority shareholder receives a disproportionate amount of the company's profits. Regardless of whether such disputes arise from the fault of the majority, the fault of the minority, or from no fault at all, such a position mirrors the understandings that the shareholders themselves likely would have reached had they contemplated the possibility of an exclusion from de facto dividends.

Id., at 923. For further reading on the close corporation and the problem of oppression of minority shareholders see generally the leading treatises in the field, cited by the Baker court in an earlier edition, F. Hodge O'Neal & Robert B. Thompson, *O'Neal's Close Corporations* (3d ed. 2003) and F. Hodge O'Neal & Robert B. Thompson, *O'Neal's Oppression of Minority Shareholders* (2d ed. 1999) and for O'Neal's co-author's take on oppression, see Robert B. Thompson, The Shareholder's Cause of Action for Oppression, 48 Bus. Law. 699 (1993). See also Robert B. Thompson, *Corporate Dissolution and Shareholders' Reasonable Expectations*, 66 Wash. U. L.Q. 193 (1988).

3. SHOULD OFFICERS IN A CLOSE CORPORATION have the same business judgment rule protection that is available to managers in a publicly held corporation? Professor Moll, exploring this question in the article cited in the last note, observes that several distinguished commentators have argued that this should not be the case. Moll, *supra* at n.88, citing, *inter alia*, Frank H. Easterbrook & Daniel R. Fischel, *Close Corporations and Agency Costs*, 38 Stan. L. Rev. 271 (1986), F. Hodge O'Neal, *Close Corporations: Existing Legislation and Recommended Reform*, 33 Bus. Law. 873 (1978), and Henry G. Manne, *Our Two Corporation Systems: Law and Economics*, 53 Va. L. Rev. 259 (1967). Why not?

    4. The Baker Court gives a list of things that it might be appropriate for a court to do in remedying an oppressive situation. Can a statutory scheme alleviate the problem? Consider that of Delaware, which follows. Statutes are not exactly light reading, but see if, as you read through, you can discern responses to the particular needs of shareholders in close corporations.

IV. Special Statutory Treatment of the Close Corporation

TITLE 8 CORPORATIONS

Chapter I. [Delaware] General Corporation Law Subchapter XIV.

CLOSE CORPORATIONS; SPECIAL PROVISIONS

* * *

§ 342. Close corporation defined; contents of certificate of incorporation.
    (a) A close corporation is a corporation organized under this chapter whose certificate of incorporation contains the provisions required by § 102 of this title[13] and, in addition, provides that:
        (1) All of the corporation's issued stock of all classes, exclusive of treasury shares, shall be represented by certificates and shall be held of record by not more than a specified number of persons, not exceeding 30; and

---

13   Section 102 requires that the charter of each corporation set forth its name, include the word "corporation," "association," "ltd.," or something similar in its title, set forth the address, the nature of the business, the types of stock it may issue, and a variety of optional provisions.

  (2) All of the issued stock of all classes shall be subject to 1 or more of the restrictions on transfer permitted by § 202 of this title;[14] and

  (3) The corporation shall make no offering of any of its stock of any class which would constitute a "public offering" within the meaning of the United States Securities Act of 1933, 15 U.S.C. § 77a et seq. as it may be amended from time to time.

(b) The certificate of incorporation of a close corporation may set forth the qualifications of stockholders, either by specifying classes of persons who shall be entitled to be holders of record of stock of any class, or by specifying classes of persons who shall not be entitled to be holders of stock of any class or both.

* * *

---

14 § 202. Restrictions on transfer and ownership of securities.

 (a) A written restriction or restrictions on the transfer or registration of transfer of a security of a corporation, or on the amount of the corporation's securities that may be owned by any person or group of persons, if permitted by this section and noted conspicuously on the certificate or certificates representing the security or securities so restricted * * *may be enforced against the holder of the restricted security or securities or any successor or transferee of the holder * * *. Unless noted conspicuously on the certificate or certificates representing the security or securities so restricted * * * a restriction, even though permitted by this section, is ineffective except against a person with actual knowledge of the restriction.

 (b) A restriction on the transfer or registration of transfer of securities of a corporation, or on the amount of a corporation's securities that may be owned by any person or group of persons, may be imposed by the certificate of incorporation or by the bylaws or by an agreement among any number of security holders or among such holders and the corporation. * * *

 (c) A restriction on the transfer * * * of securities of a corporation or on the amount of such securities that may be owned by any person or group of persons is permitted by this section if it:

 (1) Obligates the holder of the restricted securities to offer to the corporation or to any other holders of securities of the corporation or to any other person or to any combination of the foregoing, a prior opportunity, to be exercised within a reasonable time, to acquire the restricted securities; or

 (2) Obligates the corporation or any holder of securities of the corporation or any other person or any combination of the foregoing, to purchase the securities which are the subject of an agreement respecting the purchase and sale of the restricted securities; or

 (3) Requires the corporation or the holders of any class or series of securities of the corporation to consent to any proposed transfer of the restricted securities or to approve the proposed transferee of the restricted securities, or to approve the amount of securities of the corporation that may be owned by any person or group of persons; or

 (4) Obligates the holder of the restricted securities to sell or transfer an amount of restricted securities to the corporation or to any other holders of securities of the corporation or to any other person or to any combination of the foregoing, or causes or results in the automatic sale or transfer of an amount of restricted securities to the corporation or to any other holders of securities of the corporation or to any other person or to any combination of the foregoing; or

 (5) Prohibits or restricts the transfer of the restricted securities to, or the ownership of restricted securities by, designated persons or classes of persons or groups of persons, and such designation is not manifestly unreasonable.

 (d) Any restriction on the transfer or the registration of transfer of the securities of a corporation, or on the amount of securities of a corporation that may be owned by a person or group of persons, for any of the following purposes shall be conclusively presumed to be for a reasonable purpose:

 (1) Maintaining any local, state, federal or foreign tax advantage to the corporation or its stockholders * * *.

 (2) Maintaining any statutory or regulatory advantage or complying with any statutory or regulatory requirements under applicable local, state, federal or foreign law.

 (e) Any other lawful restriction on transfer or registration of transfer of securities, or on the amount of securities that may be owned by any person or group of persons, is permitted by this section. * * *

§ 343. *Formation of a close corporation.*

A close corporation shall be formed in accordance with §§ 101,[15] 102[16] and 103[17] of this title, except that:

> (1) Its certificate of incorporation shall contain a heading stating the name of the corporation and that it is a close corporation; and

> (2) Its certificate of incorporation shall contain the provisions required by § 342 of this title. * * *

§ 344. *Election of existing corporation to become a close corporation.*

Any corporation organized under this chapter may become a close corporation under this subchapter by executing, acknowledging and filing, in accordance with § 103 of this title, a certificate of amendment of its certificate of incorporation which shall contain a statement that it elects to become a close corporation, the provisions required by § 342 of this title to appear in the certificate of incorporation of a close corporation, and a heading stating the name of the corporation and that it is a close corporation. Such amendment shall be adopted in accordance with the requirements of § 241[18] or 242[19] of this title, except that it must be approved by a vote of the holders of record of at least two thirds of the shares of each class of stock of the corporation which are outstanding. * * *

§ 345. *Limitations on continuation of close corporation status.*

A close corporation continues to be such and to be subject to this subchapter until:

> (1) It files with the Secretary of State a certificate of amendment deleting from its certificate of incorporation the provisions required or permitted by § 342 of this title to be stated in the certificate of incorporation to qualify it as a close corporation; or

---

15   § 101. Incorporators; how corporation formed; purposes.

(a) Any person, partnership, association or corporation, singly or jointly with others, and without regard to such person's or entity's residence, domicile or state of incorporation, may incorporate or organize a corporation under this chapter by filing with the Division of Corporations in the Department of State a certificate of incorporation which shall be executed, acknowledged and filed in accordance with § 103 of this title.

(b) A corporation may be incorporated or organized under this chapter to conduct or promote any lawful business or purposes, except as may otherwise be provided by the Constitution or other law of this State.

16   See note 13, supra.

17   Section 103 specifies directions for filing articles of incorporation with the Delaware Secretary of State.

18   Section 241 provides for amendment of the certificate before any stock is sold by a vote of a majority of the incorporators.

19   Section 242 provides procedures for amending the certificate after stock has been issued, principally by requiring an affirmative vote of a majority of the board of directors, followed by an affirmative vote of a majority of the shareholders.

(2) Any 1 of the provisions or conditions required or permitted by § 342 of this title to be stated in a certificate of incorporation to qualify a corporation as a close corporation has in fact been breached and neither the corporation nor any of its stockholders takes the steps required by § 348 of this title to prevent such loss of status or to remedy such breach. * * *

§ 346. *Voluntary termination of close corporation status by amendment of certificate of incorporation; vote required.*

(a) A corporation may voluntarily terminate its status as a close corporation and cease to be subject to this subchapter by amending its certificate of incorporation to delete therefrom the additional provisions required or permitted by § 342 of this title to be stated in the certificate of incorporation of a close corporation. Any such amendment shall be adopted and shall become effective in accordance with § 242 of this title, except that it must be approved by a vote of the holders of record of at least two-thirds of the shares of each class of stock of the corporation which are outstanding.

(b) The certificate of incorporation of a close corporation may provide that on any amendment to terminate its status as a close corporation, a vote greater than two-thirds or a vote of all shares of any class shall be required; and if the certificate of incorporation contains such a provision, that provision shall not be amended, repealed or modified by any vote less than that required to terminate the corporation's status as a close corporation. * * *

§ 347. *Issuance or transfer of stock of a close corporation in breach of qualifying conditions.*

(a) If stock of a close corporation is issued or transferred to any person who is not entitled under any provision of the certificate of incorporation permitted by subsection (b) of § 342 of this title to be a holder of record of stock of such corporation, and if the certificate for such stock conspicuously notes the qualifications of the persons entitled to be holders of record thereof, such person is conclusively presumed to have notice of the fact of such person's ineligibility to be a stockholder.

(b) If the certificate of incorporation of a close corporation states the number of persons, not in excess of 30, who are entitled to be holders of record of its stock, and if the certificate for such stock conspicuously states such number, and if the issuance or transfer of stock to any person would cause the stock to be held by more than such number of persons, the person to whom such stock is issued or transferred is conclusively presumed to have notice of this fact.

(c) If a stock certificate of any close corporation conspicuously notes the fact of a restriction on transfer of stock of the corporation, and the restriction is one which is permitted by § 202 of this title, the transferee of the stock is conclusively presumed to have notice of the fact that such person has acquired stock in violation of the restriction, if such acquisition violates the restriction.

(d) Whenever any person to whom stock of a close corporation has been issued or transferred has, or is conclusively presumed under this section to have, notice either (1) that such person is a person not eligible to be a holder of stock of the corporation, or (2) that transfer of stock to such person would cause the stock of the corporation to be held by more than the number of persons permitted by its certificate of incorporation to hold stock of the corporation, or (3) that the transfer of stock is in violation of a restriction on transfer of stock, the corporation may, at its option, refuse to register transfer of the stock into the name of the transferee.

(e) Subsection (d) of this section shall not be applicable if the transfer of stock, even though otherwise contrary to subsection (a), (b) or (c), of this section has been consented to by all the stockholders of the close corporation, or if the close corporation has amended its certificate of incorporation in accordance with § 346 of this title.

(f) The term "transfer," as used in this section, is not limited to a transfer for value.

(g) The provisions of this section do not in any way impair any rights of a transferee regarding any right to rescind the transaction or to recover under any applicable warranty express or implied. * * *

§ 348. Involuntary termination of close corporation status; proceeding to prevent loss of status.

(a) If any event occurs as a result of which 1 or more of the provisions or conditions included in a close corporation's certificate of incorporation pursuant to § 342 of this title to qualify it as a close corporation has been breached, the corporation's status as a close corporation under this subchapter shall terminate unless:

(1) Within 30 days after the occurrence of the event, or within 30 days after the event has been discovered, whichever is later, the corporation files with the Secretary of State a certificate, executed and acknowledged in accordance with § 103 of this title, stating that a specified provision or condition included in its certificate of incorporation pursuant to § 342 of this title to qualify it as a close corporation has ceased to be applicable, and furnishes a copy of such certificate to each stockholder; and

(2) The corporation concurrently with the filing of such certificate takes such steps as are necessary to correct the situation which threatens its status as a close corporation, including, without limitation, the refusal to register the transfer of stock which has been wrongfully transferred as provided by § 347 of this title, or a proceeding under subsection (b) of this section.

(b) The Court of Chancery, upon the suit of the corporation or any stockholder, shall have jurisdiction to issue all orders necessary to prevent the corporation from losing its status as a close corporation, or to restore its status as a close corporation by enjoining or setting aside any act or threatened act on the part of the corporation or a stockholder which would be inconsistent with any of the provisions or conditions required or permitted by § 342 of this title to be stated in the certificate of incorporation of a close corporation, unless it is an act approved in accordance with § 346 of this title. The Court of Chancery may enjoin or set aside any transfer or threatened transfer of stock of a close corporation which is contrary to the terms of its certificate of incorporation or of any transfer restriction permitted by § 202 of this title, and may enjoin any public offering, as defined in § 342 of this title, or threatened public offering of stock of the close corporation. * * *

§ 349. Corporate option where a restriction on transfer of a security is held invalid.

If a restriction on transfer of a security of a close corporation is held not to be authorized by § 202 of this title, the corporation shall nevertheless have an option, for a period of 30 days after the judgment setting aside the restriction becomes final, to acquire the restricted security at a price which is agreed upon by the parties, or if no agreement is reached as to price, then at the fair value as determined by the Court of Chancery. In order to determine fair value, the Court may appoint an appraiser to receive evidence and report to the Court such appraiser's findings and recommendation as to fair value. * * *

§ 350. Agreements restricting discretion of directors.

A written agreement among the stockholders of a close corporation holding a majority of the outstanding stock entitled to vote, whether solely among themselves or with a party not a stockholder, is not invalid, as between the parties to the agreement, on the ground that it so relates to the conduct of the business and affairs of the corporation as to restrict or interfere with the discretion or powers of the board of directors. The effect of any such agreement shall be to relieve the directors and impose upon the stockholders who are parties to the agreement the liability for managerial acts or omissions which is imposed on directors to the extent and so long as the discretion or powers of the board in its management of corporate affairs is controlled by such agreement. * * *

§ 351. Management by stockholders.

The certificate of incorporation of a close corporation may provide that the business of the corporation shall be managed by the stockholders of the corporation rather than by a board of directors. So long as this provision continues in effect:

(1) No meeting of stockholders need be called to elect directors;

(2) Unless the context clearly requires otherwise, the stockholders of the

corporation shall be deemed to be directors for purposes of applying provisions of this chapter; and

(3) The stockholders of the corporation shall be subject to all liabilities of directors.

Such a provision may be inserted in the certificate of incorporation by amendment if all incorporators and subscribers or all holders of record of all of the outstanding stock, whether or not having voting power, authorize such a provision. An amendment to the certificate of incorporation to delete such a provision shall be adopted by a vote of the holders of a majority of all outstanding stock of the corporation, whether or not otherwise entitled to vote. If the certificate of incorporation contains a provision authorized by this section, the existence of such provision shall be noted conspicuously on the face or back of every stock certificate issued by such corporation. * * *

§ 352. *Appointment of custodian for close corporation.*

(a) In addition to § 226[20] of this title respecting the appointment of a custodian for any corporation, the Court of Chancery, upon application of any stockholder, may appoint 1 or more persons to be custodians, and, if the corporation is insolvent, to be receivers, of any close corporation when:

(1) Pursuant to § 351 of this title the business and affairs of the corporation are managed by the stockholders and they are so divided that the business of the corporation is suffering or is threatened with irreparable injury and any remedy with respect to such deadlock provided in the certificate of incorporation or bylaws or in any written agreement of the stockholders has failed; or

(2) The petitioning stockholder has the right to the dissolution of the corporation

---

20   § 226. Appointment of custodian or receiver of corporation on deadlock or for other cause.

(a) The Court of Chancery, upon application of any stockholder, may appoint 1 or more persons to be custodians, and, if the corporation is insolvent, to be receivers, of and for any corporation when:

(1) At any meeting held for the election of directors the stockholders are so divided that they have failed to elect successors to directors whose terms have expired or would have expired upon qualification of their successors; or

(2) The business of the corporation is suffering or is threatened with irreparable injury because the directors are so divided respecting the management of the affairs of the corporation that the required vote for action by the board of directors cannot be obtained and the stockholders are unable to terminate this division; or

(3) The corporation has abandoned its business and has failed within a reasonable time to take steps to dissolve, liquidate or distribute its assets.

(b) A custodian appointed under this section shall have all the powers and title of a receiver appointed under § 291 of this title, but the authority of the custodian is to continue the business of the corporation and not to liquidate its affairs and distribute its assets, except when the Court shall otherwise order and except in cases arising under paragraph (3) of subsection (a) of this section or paragraph (2) of subsection (a) of § 352 of this title. * * *

§ 291. Receivers for insolvent corporations; appointment and powers.

Whenever a corporation shall be insolvent, the Court of Chancery, on the application of any creditor or stockholder thereof, may, at any time, appoint 1 or more persons to be receivers of and for the corporation, to take charge of its assets, estate, effects, business and affairs, and to collect the outstanding debts, claims, and property due and belonging to the corporation, with power to prosecute and defend, in the name of the corporation or otherwise, all claims or suits, to appoint an agent or agents under them, and to do all other acts which might be done by the corporation and which may be necessary or proper. The powers of the receivers shall be such and shall continue so long as the Court shall deem necessary. * * *

under a provision of the certificate of incorporation permitted by § 355 of this title.

(b) In lieu of appointing a custodian for a close corporation under this section or § 226 of this title the Court of Chancery may appoint a provisional director, whose powers and status shall be as provided in § 353 of this title if the Court determines that it would be in the best interest of the corporation. Such appointment shall not preclude any subsequent order of the Court appointing a custodian for such corporation. * * *

§ 353. *Appointment of a provisional director in certain cases.*

(a) Notwithstanding any contrary provision of the certificate of incorporation or the bylaws or agreement of the stockholders, the Court of Chancery may appoint a provisional director for a close corporation if the directors are so divided respecting the management of the corporation's business and affairs that the votes required for action by the board of directors cannot be obtained with the consequence that the business and affairs of the corporation can no longer be conducted to the advantage of the stockholders generally.

(b) An application for relief under this section must be filed

    (1) by at least one half of the number of directors then in office,

    (2) by the holders of at least one third of all stock then entitled to elect directors, or,

    (3) if there be more than 1 class of stock then entitled to elect 1 or more directors, by the holders of two thirds of the stock of any such class; but the certificate of incorporation of a close corporation may provide that a lesser proportion of the directors or of the stockholders or of a class of stockholders may apply for relief under this section.

(c) A provisional director shall be an impartial person who is neither a stockholder nor a creditor of the corporation or of any subsidiary or affiliate of the corporation, and whose further qualifications, if any, may be determined by the Court of Chancery. A provisional director is not a receiver of the corporation and does not have the title and powers of a custodian or receiver appointed under §§ 226 and 291[21] of this title. A provisional director shall have all the rights and powers of a duly elected director of the corporation, including the right to notice of and to vote at meetings of directors, until such time as such person shall be removed by order of the Court of Chancery or by the holders of a majority of all shares then entitled to vote to elect directors or by the holders of two thirds of the shares of that class of voting shares which filed the application for appointment of a provisional director. A provisional director's compensation shall be determined by agreement between such person and the

---

21   See note 20, supra.

corporation subject to approval of the Court of Chancery, which may fix such person's compensation in the absence of agreement or in the event of disagreement between the provisional director and the corporation.

(d) Even though the requirements of subsection (b) of this section relating to the number of directors or stockholders who may petition for appointment of a provisional director are not satisfied, the Court of Chancery may nevertheless appoint a provisional director if permitted by subsection (b) of § 352 of this title. * * *

§ 354. Operating corporation as partnership.

No written agreement among stockholders of a close corporation, nor any provision of the certificate of incorporation or of the bylaws of the corporation, which agreement or provision relates to any phase of the affairs of such corporation, including but not limited to the management of its business or declaration and payment of dividends or other division of profits or the election of directors or officers or the employment of stockholders by the corporation or the arbitration of disputes, shall be invalid on the ground that it is an attempt by the parties to the agreement or by the stockholders of the corporation to treat the corporation as if it were a partnership or to arrange relations among the stockholders or between the stockholders and the corporation in a manner that would be appropriate only among partners. * * *

§ 355. Stockholders' option to dissolve corporation.

(a) The certificate of incorporation of any close corporation may include a provision granting to any stockholder, or to the holders of any specified number or percentage of shares of any class of stock, an option to have the corporation dissolved at will or upon the occurrence of any specified event or contingency. Whenever any such option to dissolve is exercised, the stockholders exercising such option shall give written notice thereof to all other stockholders. After the expiration of 30 days following the sending of such notice, the dissolution of the corporation shall proceed as if the required number of stockholders having voting power had consented in writing to dissolution of the corporation as provided by § 228[22] of this title.

---

22   § 228. Consent of stockholders or members in lieu of meeting.

(a) Unless otherwise provided in the certificate of incorporation, any action required by this chapter to be taken at any annual or special meeting of stockholders of a corporation, or any action which may be taken at any annual or special meeting of such stockholders, may be taken without a meeting, without prior notice and without a vote, if a consent or consents in writing, setting forth the action so taken, shall be signed by the holders of outstanding stock having not less than the minimum number of votes that would be necessary to authorize or take such action at a meeting at which all shares entitled to vote thereon were present and voted and shall be delivered to the corporation by delivery to its registered office in this State, its principal place of business or an officer or agent of the corporation having custody of the book in which proceedings of meetings of stockholders are recorded. Delivery made to a corporation's registered office shall be by hand or by certified or registered mail, return receipt requested.

(b) If the certificate of incorporation as originally filed does not contain a provision authorized by subsection (a) of this section, the certificate may be amended to include such provision if adopted by the affirmative vote of the holders of all the outstanding stock, whether or not entitled to vote, unless the certificate of incorporation specifically authorizes such an amendment by a vote which shall be not less than two thirds of all the outstanding stock whether or not entitled to vote.

(c) Each stock certificate in any corporation whose certificate of incorporation authorizes dissolution as permitted by this section shall conspicuously note on the face thereof the existence of the provision. Unless noted conspicuously on the face of the stock certificate, the provision is ineffective. * * *

§ 356. Effect of this subchapter on other laws.

This subchapter shall not be deemed to repeal any statute or rule of law which is or would be applicable to any corporation which is organized under this chapter but is not a close corporation.* * *

NOTES AND QUESTIONS

1. READING STATUTES is not an easy undertaking, but these are some of the most important ever passed in Delaware. Can you understand why? If you were a Delaware legislator, would you have voted for this special subchapter of the Delaware Corporations law, which sets out special rules for the close corporation?

2. CAN YOU EXPLAIN any of these provisions with reference to the cases you have studied?

3. WHAT DO YOU MAKE, in particular, of the remedy of a "provisional director" provided for in Section 353? One recent commentator on the concept suggested that:

The appointment of a provisional director is not the answer for all forms of deadlock within corporations. However, it can be an important and effective first step in resolving certain impasses in corporate enterprises. Perhaps courts should be more willing to grant the provisional director remedy as a first line of attack in corporate deadlock cases, even in situations in which the differences seem irreconcilable upon first glance.

Susanna M. Kim, "The Provisional Director Remedy for Corporate Deadlock: A Proposed Model Statute," 60 Wash & Lee L. Rev. 111, 181 (2003). Would you agree with Professor Kim?

4. NOTE THE POSSIBILITY of allowing stockholders in a Delaware close corporation to decide to dissolve the corporation, provided by section 355. We've touched on this before, but do you believe that dissolution is a good remedy for deadlock or oppression in a close corporation? See generally Harvey Gelb, "Fiduciary Duties and Dissolution in the Closely Held Business," 3 Wyo. L. Rev. 547 (2003).

5. BY NOW IT SHOULD BE CLEAR that careful planning on the part of counsel can avoid at least some possible close corporation problems, and that, in particular, a shareholder agreement might be a useful tool in preventing shareholder oppression or deadlock. Note that the Delaware statute seems to encourage such agreements, even if they restrict the traditional role of directors. On the usefulness of such agreements see, e.g., Manuel A. Utset, "A Theory of Self-Control Problems and Incomplete Contracting: The Case of Shareholder Contracts," 2003 Utah L. Rev. 1329. There is much more that might be said about the close corporation, and even more about the emerging issues involving Limited Liability Companies (LLC's) which bid fair to replace the close corporation vehicle. In an introductory course of this nature, though, we can stop here (making just one more set of comments on LLC's) and return to the general problems of corporations, specifically organic change that ends one phase of corporate life, and perhaps begins another.

A Note on the LLC and the Close Corporation

THE LIMITED LIABILITY COMPANY (LLC) is a relatively new business model compared to the close corporation. According to numerous sources and statistics, there has been rapid and continuous growth in the number of LLCs formed since it was first introduced in 1977 in Wyoming, and especially since the Internal Revenue Service recognized its federal tax advantages in 1988. *See* Susan Pace Hamill, *The Limited Liability Company: A Catalyst Exposing The Corporate Integration Question*, 95 Mich. L. Rev. 393, 393 – 94 (1996); David L. Cohen, *Theories Of The Corporation And The Limited Liability Company: How Should Courts and Legislatures Articulate Rules for Piercing the Veil, Fiduciary Responsibility and Securities Regulation for the Limited Liability Company?*, 51 Okla. L. Rev. 427, 447 (1998). In terms of the future of the LLC, there is some belief that the LLC will replace the close corporation and become "the dominant form of business for nonpublicly traded entities." Hamill, supra, at 395. Apart from the obvious advantages of limited liability and taxing, are there any other attractions you can think of that make the LLC so popular? One author has suggested that an additional factor to the LLC's revolutionary growth is its ability to allow investors to decrease their fiduciary duties. *See* Mary Siegel, *Fiduciary Duty Myths In Close Corporate Law*, 29 Del. J. Corp. L. 377 (2004). Because the LLC is more "contract-oriented," the courts tend to enforce the principle of freedom of contract. *Id.* at 464. As such, investors can use contracts to reduce their fiduciary obligations. Siegel also contends that "there is a trend toward eliminating at-will dissolution rights in limited liability entities," thereby reinforcing their limited liability characteristic, lessening fiduciary duties, and affording minority owners in an LLC even less protection available. *Id.* at 467 – 68. Moreover, while the statutory close corporation provides grounds for involuntary dissolution, the LLC, which does not provide such grounds, may lock in its minority members more so than those of a statutory close corporation. *Id.* at 467. Thus, it has been suggested that "legislatures used the LLC statutes to express their displeasure with judicial meddling in the affairs of close corporations." *Id.* What do you think of this proposition? Do you agree with it?

What are some other problems and concerns that might arise from the contractarian nature of the LLC? In terms of the doctrines of piercing the corporate veil, how well would those apply to the LLC? David L. Cohen points out that, in addition to fiduciary duties, "traditional piercing doctrines are very hard to apply to LLCs." Cohen, supra, at 429. As such, "the 'waivability' of many corporate laws that impose high transaction costs is luring would be entrepreneurs to use the LLC form." *Id.* LLCs are easy to create and do not have many rules compared to the corporation. Its flexibility and its ability to avoid regulations that would normally apply to corporations, allow for lower transaction costs, thus making the LLC such an attractive business form. *Id.* at 453. In particular, most state statutes do not state whether corporate piercing doctrines apply to the LLC. *Id.* at 455. Yet, even if corporate piercing doctrines applied to the LLC, the results would be somewhat absurd. Given that the LLC is such a flexible and simple entity by nature, it would be difficult to use the piercing doctrines such as disregard of corporate formalities and shareholder dominance on the LLC. *Id.* at 457. Do you understand why? For more comments on the advantages and potential future of the LLC, *see* Howard M. Friedman, *The Silent LLC Revolution – The Social Cost of Academic Neglect*,

38 Creighton L. Rev. 35 (2004); Jerome Kurtz, *The Limited Liability Company and the Future of Business Taxation: A Comment on Professor Berger's Plan*, 47 Tax L. Rev. 815 (1992).

One factor that might hinder the LLC's growth depends on whether the courts will decide to step in and implement certain management duties like they did for close corporations. More recently in *Pointer v. Catellani*, the Massachusetts Supreme Judicial Court, citing Donahue and Wilkes, "held that the president of an LLC, who also owned a forty-three percent interest in the LLC, was wrongfully frozen-out when the other members removed him from his position." Mark J. Loewenstein, *Wilkes v. Springside Nursing Home, Inc.: A Historical Perspective,* 33 W. New Eng. L. Rev. 339, 365–66 (2011). The court in this case simply concluded that the LLC could be defined as a close corporation and therefore its stockholders owe fiduciary duties to one another. *Id.* Such decisions pose a risk for the popularity of the LLC because it would mean that lawyers would have to be more careful and draft around these decisions when creating LLC contracts. *Id.* at 367. As such, the transaction costs of the LLC would increase, and its attractiveness as a flexible, contractual entity would decrease. *Id.* Do you agree that LLCs should be treated like close corporations by the courts? What are the pros and cons of courts taking the direction that the Massachusetts Supreme Judicial Court took in Pointer? What about the role of LLC statutes? What can these statutes do to help protect minority investors in an LLC? For a comment on this issue and how LLC statutes may help reduce agency costs between majority owners and minority investors, *see* James W. Lovely, *Agency Costs, Liquidity, and the Limited Liability Company as an Alternative to the Close Corporation,* 21 Stetson L. Rev. 377 (1992).

ASPECTS OF THE ENDGAME

I. The Discretion of the Board in an Endgame Situation

Unocal Corp. v. Mesa Petroleum Co.

Supreme Court of Delaware
493 A.2d 946 (Del. 1985).

OPINION

MOORE, Justice.

We confront an issue of first impression in Delaware—the validity of a corporation's self-tender for its own shares which excludes from participation a stockholder making a hostile tender offer for the company's stock.

The Court of Chancery granted a preliminary injunction to the plaintiffs, Mesa Petroleum Co., Mesa Asset Co., Mesa Partners II, and Mesa Eastern, Inc. (collectively "Mesa"), enjoining an exchange offer of the defendant, Unocal Corporation (Unocal) for its own stock. The trial court concluded that a selective exchange offer, excluding Mesa, was legally impermissible. We cannot agree with such a blanket rule. The factual findings of the Vice Chancellor, fully supported by the record, establish that Unocal's board, consisting of a majority of independent directors, acted in good faith, and after reasonable investigation found that Mesa's tender offer was both inadequate and coercive. Under the circumstances the board had both the power and duty to oppose a bid it perceived to be harmful to the corporate enterprise. On this record we are satisfied that the device Unocal adopted is reasonable in relation to the threat posed, and that the board acted in the proper exercise of sound business judgment. We will not substitute our views for those of the board if the latter's decision can be "attributed to any rational business purpose." *Sinclair Oil Corp. v. Levien*, Del. Supr., 280 A.2d 717, 720 (1971). Accordingly, we reverse the decision of the Court of Chancery and order the preliminary injunction vacated.

I.

* * * On April 8, 1985, Mesa, the owner of approximately 13% of Unocal's stock, commenced a two-tier "front loaded" cash tender offer for 64 million shares, or approximately 37%, of Unocal's outstanding stock at a price of $54 per share. The "back-end" was designed to eliminate the remaining publicly held shares by an exchange of securities purportedly worth $54 per share. However, pursuant to an order entered by the United States District Court for the Central District of California on April 26, 1985, Mesa issued a supplemental proxy statement to Unocal's stockholders disclosing that the securities offered in the second-step merger would be highly subordinated, and that Unocal's capitalization would differ significantly from its present structure. Unocal has rather aptly termed such securities "junk bonds".

Unocal's board consists of eight independent outside directors and six insiders. It met on April 13, 1985, to consider the Mesa tender offer. Thirteen directors were present, and the meeting lasted nine and one-half hours. The directors were given no agenda or written materials prior to the session. However, detailed presentations were made by legal counsel regarding the board's obligations under both Delaware corporate law and the federal securities laws. The board then received a presentation from Peter Sachs on behalf of Goldman Sachs & Co. (Goldman Sachs) and Dillon, Read & Co. (Dillon Read) discussing the bases for their opinions that the Mesa proposal was wholly inadequate. Mr. Sachs opined that the minimum cash value that could be expected from a sale or orderly liquidation for 100% of Unocal's stock was in excess of $60 per share.

* * *

Mr. Sachs also presented various defensive strategies available to the board if it concluded that Mesa's two-step tender offer was inadequate and should be opposed. One of the devices outlined was a self-tender by Unocal for its own stock with a reasonable price range of $70 to $75 per share. The cost of such a proposal would cause the company to incur $6.1—6.5 billion of additional debt, and a presentation was made informing the board of Unocal's ability to handle it. The directors were told that the primary effect of this obligation would be to reduce exploratory drilling, but that the company would nonetheless remain a viable entity.

The eight outside directors, comprising a clear majority of the thirteen members present, then met separately with Unocal's financial advisors and attorneys.

Thereafter, they unanimously agreed to advise the board that it should reject Mesa's tender offer as inadequate, and that Unocal should pursue a self-tender to provide the stockholders with a fairly priced alternative to the Mesa proposal. The board then reconvened and unanimously adopted a resolution rejecting as grossly inadequate Mesa's tender offer. Despite the nine and one-half hour length of the meeting, no formal decision was made on the proposed defensive self-tender.

On April 15, the board met again * * * This session lasted two hours. Unocal's Vice President of Finance and its Assistant General Counsel made a detailed presentation of the proposed terms of the exchange offer. A price range between $70 and $80 per share was considered, and ultimately the directors agreed upon $72. The board was also advised about the debt securities that would be issued. * * * Based upon this advice, and the board's own deliberations, the directors unanimously approved the exchange offer. Their resolution provided that if Mesa acquired 64 million shares of Unocal stock through its own offer (the Mesa Purchase Condition), Unocal would buy the remaining 49% outstanding for an exchange of debt securities having an aggregate par value of $72 per share. The board resolution also stated that the offer would be subject to other conditions that had been described to the board at the meeting, or which were deemed necessary by Unocal's officers, including the exclusion of Mesa from the proposal (the Mesa exclusion). * * *

Legal counsel advised that under Delaware law Mesa could only be excluded for what the directors reasonably believed to be a valid corporate purpose. The directors' discussion centered on the objective of adequately compensating shareholders at the "back-end" of Mesa's proposal, which the latter would finance with "junk bonds". To include Mesa would defeat that goal, because under the proration aspect of the exchange offer (49%) every Mesa share accepted by Unocal would displace one held by another stockholder. Further, if Mesa were permitted to tender to Unocal, the latter would in effect be financing Mesa's own inadequate proposal. * * *

II.

The issues we address involve these fundamental questions: Did the Unocal board have the power and duty to oppose a takeover threat it reasonably perceived to be harmful to the corporate enterprise, and if so, is its action here entitled to the protection of the business judgment rule?

Mesa contends that the discriminatory exchange offer violates the fiduciary duties Unocal owes it. Mesa argues that because of the Mesa exclusion the business judgment rule is inapplicable, because the directors by tendering their own shares will derive a financial benefit that is not available to all Unocal stockholders. Thus, it is Mesa's ultimate contention that Unocal cannot establish that the exchange offer is fair to all shareholders, and argues that the Court of Chancery was correct in concluding that Unocal was unable to meet this burden.

Unocal answers that it does not owe a duty of "fairness" to Mesa, given the facts here. Specifically, Unocal contends that its board of directors reasonably and in good faith concluded that Mesa's $54 two-tier tender offer was coercive and inadequate, and that Mesa sought selective treatment for itself. Furthermore, Unocal argues that the board's approval of the exchange offer was made in good faith, on an informed basis, and in the exercise of due care. Under these circumstances, Unocal contends that its directors properly employed this device to protect the company and its stockholders from Mesa's harmful tactics.

III.

We begin with the basic issue of the power of a board of directors of a Delaware corporation to adopt a defensive measure of this type. Absent such authority, all other questions are moot. Neither issues of fairness nor business judgment are pertinent without the basic underpinning of a board's legal power to act.

The board has a large reservoir of authority upon which to draw * * * [I]t s now well established that in the acquisition of its shares a Delaware corporation may deal selectively with its stockholders, provided the directors have not acted out of a sole or primary purpose to entrench themselves in office. * * *

Finally, the board's power to act derives from its fundamental duty and obligation to protect the corporate enterprise, which includes stockholders, from harm reasonably perceived, irrespective of its source. * * * Thus, we are satisfied that in the broad context of corporate governance, including issues of fundamental corporate change, a board of directors is not a passive instrumentality.

Given the foregoing principles, we turn to the standards by which director action is to be measured. In *Pogostin v. Rice,* Del.Supr., 480 A.2d 619 (1984), we held that the business judgment rule, including the standards by which director conduct is judged, is applicable in the context of a takeover. *Id.* at 627. The business judgment rule is a "presumption that in making a business decision the directors of a corporation acted on an informed basis, in good faith and in the honest belief that the action taken was in the best interests of the company." *Aronson v. Lewis,* Del.Supr., 473 A.2d 805, 812 (1984) (citations omitted). A hallmark of the business judgment rule is that a court will not substitute its judgment for that of the board if the latter's decision can be "attributed to any rational business purpose." *Sinclair Oil Corp. v. Levien,* Del.Supr., 280 A.2d 717, 720 (1971).

When a board addresses a pending takeover bid it has an obligation to determine whether the offer is in the best interests of the corporation and its shareholders. In that respect a board's duty is no different from any other responsibility it shoulders, and its decisions should be no less entitled to the respect they otherwise would be accorded in the realm of business judgment. * * * There are, however, certain caveats to a proper exercise of this function. Because of the omnipresent specter that a board may be acting primarily in its own interests, rather than those of the corporation and its shareholders, there is an enhanced duty which calls for judicial examination at the threshold before the protections of the business judgment rule may be conferred.

This Court has long recognized that:

We must bear in mind the inherent danger in the purchase of shares with corporate funds to remove a threat to corporate policy when a threat to control is involved.

The directors are of necessity confronted with a conflict of interest, and an objective decision is difficult.

Bennett v. Propp, Del.Supr., 187 A.2d 405, 409 (1962). In the face of this inherent conflict directors must show that they had reasonable grounds for believing that a danger to corporate policy and effectiveness existed because of another person's stock ownership. *Cheff v. Mathes*, 199 A.2d at 554–55. However, they satisfy that burden "by showing good faith and reasonable investigation...." *Id.* at 555. Furthermore, such proof is materially enhanced, as here, by the approval of a board comprised of a majority of outside independent directors who have acted in accordance with the foregoing standards. * * *

IV.

A.

In the board's exercise of corporate power to forestall a takeover bid our analysis begins with the basic principle that corporate directors have a fiduciary duty to act in the best interests of the corporation's stockholders. * * * As we have noted, their duty of care extends to protecting the corporation and its owners from perceived harm whether a threat originates from third parties or other shareholders. But such powers are not absolute. A corporation does not have unbridled discretion to defeat any perceived threat by any Draconian means available.

The restriction placed upon a selective stock repurchase is that the directors may not have acted solely or primarily out of a desire to perpetuate themselves in office. * * * Of course, to this is added the further caveat that inequitable action may not be taken under the guise of law. * * * The standard of proof established in *Cheff v. Mathes* * * * is designed to ensure that a defensive measure to thwart or impede a takeover is indeed motivated by a good faith concern for the welfare of the corporation and its stockholders, which in all circumstances must be free of any fraud or other misconduct. * * * However, this does not end the inquiry.

B.

A further aspect is the element of balance. If a defensive measure is to come within the ambit of the business judgment rule, it must be reasonable in relation to the threat posed. This entails an analysis by the directors of the nature of the takeover bid and its effect on the corporate enterprise. Examples of such concerns may include: inadequacy of the price offered, nature and timing of the offer, questions of illegality, the impact on "constituencies" other than shareholders (i.e., creditors, customers, employees, and perhaps even the community generally), the risk of nonconsummation, and the quality of securities being offered in the exchange. * * * While not a controlling factor, it also seems to us that a board may reasonably consider the basic stockholder interests at stake, including those of short term speculators, whose actions may have fueled the coercive aspect of the offer at the expense of the long term investor. Here, the threat posed was viewed by the Unocal board as a grossly inadequate two-tier coercive tender offer coupled with the threat of greenmail.

Specifically, the Unocal directors had concluded that the value of Unocal was substantially above the $54 per share offered in cash at the front end. Furthermore, they determined that the subordinated securities to be exchanged in Mesa's announced squeeze out of the remaining shareholders in the "back-end" merger were "junk bonds" worth far less than $54. It is now well recognized that such offers are a classic coercive measure designed to stampede shareholders into tendering at the first tier, even if the price is inadequate, out of fear of what they will receive at the back end of the transaction. Wholly beyond the coercive aspect of an inadequate two-tier tender offer, the threat was posed by a corporate raider with a national reputation as a "greenmailer".

In adopting the selective exchange offer, the board stated that its objective was either to defeat the inadequate Mesa offer or, should the offer still succeed, provide the 49% of its stockholders, who would otherwise be forced to accept "junk bonds", with $72 worth of senior debt. We find that both purposes are valid.

However, such efforts would have been thwarted by Mesa's participation in the exchange offer. First, if Mesa could tender its shares, Unocal would effectively be subsidizing the former's continuing effort to buy Unocal stock at $54 per share. Second, Mesa could not, by definition, fit within the class of shareholders being protected from its own coercive and inadequate tender offer. * * *

Thus, the board's decision to offer what it determined to be the fair value of the corporation to the 49% of its shareholders, who would otherwise be forced to accept highly subordinated "junk bonds", is reasonable and consistent with the directors' duty to ensure that the minority stockholders receive equal value for their shares.

V.

Mesa contends that it is unlawful, and the trial court agreed, for a corporation to discriminate in this fashion against one shareholder. It argues correctly that no case has ever sanctioned a device that precludes a raider from sharing in a benefit available to all other stockholders. However, as we have noted earlier, the principle of selective stock repurchases by a Delaware corporation is neither unknown nor unauthorized. * * * The only difference is that heretofore the approved transaction was the payment of "greenmail" to a raider or dissident posing a threat to the corporate enterprise. All other stockholders were denied such favored treatment, and given Mesa's past history of greenmail, its claims here are rather ironic.

However, our corporate law is not static. It must grow and develop in response to, indeed in anticipation of, evolving concepts and needs. Merely because the General Corporation Law is silent as to a specific matter does not mean that it is prohibited. * * *

More recently, as the sophistication of both raiders and targets has developed, a host of other defensive measures to counter such ever mounting threats has evolved and received judicial sanction. These include defensive charter amendments and other devices bearing some rather exotic, but apt, names: Crown Jewel, White Knight, Pac Man, and Golden Parachute. Each has highly selective features, the object of which is to deter or defeat the raider.

Thus, while the exchange offer is a form of selective treatment, given the nature of the threat posed here the response is neither unlawful nor unreasonable. If the board of directors is disinterested, has acted in good faith and with due care, its decision in the absence of an abuse of discretion will be upheld as a proper exercise of business judgment. * * *

Mesa also argues that the exclusion permits the directors to abdicate the fiduciary duties they owe it. However, that is not so. The board continues to owe Mesa the duties of due care and loyalty. But in the face of the destructive threat Mesa's tender offer was perceived to pose, the board had a supervening duty to protect the corporate enterprise, which includes the other shareholders, from threatened harm. * * *

VI.

In conclusion, there was directorial power to oppose the Mesa tender offer, and to undertake a selective stock exchange made in good faith and upon a reasonable investigation pursuant to a clear duty to protect the corporate enterprise. Further, the selective stock repurchase plan chosen by Unocal is reasonable in relation to the threat that the board rationally and reasonably believed was posed by Mesa's inadequate and coercive two-tier tender offer. Under those circumstances the board's action is entitled to be measured by the standards of the business judgment rule. Thus, unless it is shown by a preponderance of the evidence that the directors' decisions were primarily based on perpetuating themselves in office, or some other breach of fiduciary duty such as fraud, overreaching, lack of good faith, or being uninformed, a Court will not substitute its judgment for that of the board. * * *

Revlon, Inc. v. MacAndrews & Forbes Holdings, Inc.

Supreme Court of Delaware
506 A.2d 173 (Del. 1986).

OPINION

MOORE, Justice:

In this battle for corporate control of Revlon, Inc. (Revlon), the Court of Chancery enjoined certain transactions designed to thwart the efforts of Pantry Pride, Inc. (Pantry Pride) to acquire Revlon. The defendants are Revlon, its board of directors, and Forstmann Little & Co. and the latter's affiliated limited partnership (collectively, Forstmann). The injunction barred consummation of an option granted Forstmann to purchase certain Revlon assets (the lock-up option), a promise by Revlon to deal exclusively with Forstmann in the face of a takeover (the no-shop provision), and the payment of a $25 million cancellation fee to Forstmann if the transaction was aborted. The Court of Chancery found that the Revlon directors had breached their duty of care by entering into the foregoing transactions and effectively ending an active auction for the company. The trial court ruled that such arrangements are not illegal *per se* under Delaware law, but that their use under the circumstances here was impermissible. We agree. *See MacAndrews & Forbes Holdings, Inc. v. Revlon, Inc.,* Del.Ch., 501 A.2d 1239 (1985). Thus, we granted this expedited interlocutory appeal to consider for the first time the validity of such defensive measures in the face of an active bidding contest for corporate control. Additionally, we address for the first time the extent to which a corporation may consider the impact of a takeover threat on constituencies other than shareholders. *See Unocal Corp. v. Mesa Petroleum Co.,* Del.Supr., 493 A.2d 946, 955 (1985).

In our view, lock-ups and related agreements are permitted under Delaware law where their adoption is untainted by director interest or other breaches of fiduciary duty. The actions taken by the Revlon directors, however, did not meet this standard. Moreover, while concern for various corporate constituencies is proper when addressing a takeover threat, that principle is limited by the requirement that there be some rationally related benefit accruing to the stockholders. We find no such benefit here.

Thus, under all the circumstances we must agree with the Court of Chancery that the enjoined Revlon defensive measures were inconsistent with the directors' duties to the stockholders. Accordingly, we affirm.

I.

[In June 1985, Ronald Perelman (the Chairman and CEO of Pantry Pride) expressed interest in acquiring Revlon. Revlon's chief, Michael Bergerac, rejected Perelman's offer in the range of $40-50 per share. That August, Pantry Pride's board authorized an acquisition attempt, either friendly (at $42-43) or hostile (at $45). Bergerac again rejected Perelman's offer, and the Revlon board met to discuss the threat of Pantry Pride's takeover. Revlon's investment bankers stated that $45 was far too low a price per share, and that Pantry Pride might see a value of $60-70 per share in a post-takeover asset sale.

Revlon adopted two anti-takeover tactics: a stock repurchase of up to 5 million outstanding shares (out of 30 million), and a Note Purchase Rights Plan. This would allow shareholders, upon a hostile acquisition of 20% of shares, to exchange each share for a $65 one-year note with 12% interest.

On August 23, Pantry Pride made its hostile tender offer: $47.50 per common share, subject to financing and the Note Purchase Rights being cancelled. The Revlon board recommended shareholders reject the offer, and further commenced its own offer for 10 million shares in exchange for further notes (with conditions) and convertible preferred stock.

Frustrated, Pantry Pride made several increasing offers. Meanwhile, the Revlon board had chosen Forstmann Little & Co. as a white knight. Forstmann offered a leveraged buyout paying $56 cash per share and granting the board "golden parachutes" in stock of the new company, in exchange for waiving the Rights and Notes conditions. Pantry Pride responded with a final offer of $56.25 per share on October 7. During further negotiations between Revlon and Forstmann (who had access to

Revlon financial data Perelman did not), Pantry Pride announced it would beat any Forstmann bid.

Forstmann made a final offer of $57.25 per share, but with a restrictive lockup option and other demands including immediate acceptance. The Revlon board accepted the offer and Pantry Pride filed suit.]

II.

C.

The second defensive measure adopted by Revlon to thwart a Pantry Pride takeover was the company's own exchange offer for 10 million of its shares. The directors' general broad powers to manage the business and affairs of the corporation are augmented by the specific authority conferred under 8 *Del.C.* § 160(a), permitting the company to deal in its own stock. *Unocal*, 493 A.2d at 953–54; *Cheff v. Mathes*, 41 Del.Supr. 494, 199 A.2d 548, 554 (1964); *Kors v. Carey*, 39 Del.Ch. 47, 158 A.2d 136, 140 (1960). However, when exercising that power in an effort to forestall a hostile takeover, the board's actions are strictly held to the fiduciary standards outlined in *Unocal*. These standards require the directors to determine the best interests of the corporation and its stockholders, and impose an enhanced duty to abjure any action that is motivated by considerations other than a good faith concern for such interests. *Unocal*, 493 A.2d at 954–55; *see Bennett v. Propp*, 41 Del.Supr. 14, 187 A.2d 405, 409 (1962).

The Revlon directors concluded that Pantry Pride's $47.50 offer was grossly inadequate. In that regard the board acted in good faith, and on an informed basis, with reasonable grounds to believe that there existed a harmful threat to the corporate enterprise. The adoption of a defensive measure, reasonable in relation to the threat posed, was proper and fully accorded with the powers, duties, and responsibilities conferred upon directors under our law. *Unocal*, 493 A.2d at 954; *Pogostin v. Rice*, 480 A.2d at 627.

D.

However, when Pantry Pride increased its offer to $50 per share, and then to $53, it became apparent to all that the break-up of the company was inevitable. The Revlon board's authorization permitting management to negotiate a merger or buyout with a third party was a recognition that the company was for sale. The duty of the board had thus changed from the preservation of Revlon as a corporate entity to the maximization of the company's value at a sale for the stockholders' benefit. This significantly altered the board's responsibilities under the *Unocal* standards. It no longer faced threats to corporate policy and effectiveness, or to the stockholders' interests, from a grossly inadequate bid. The whole question of defensive measures became moot. The directors' role changed from defenders of the corporate bastion to auctioneers charged with getting the best price for the stockholders at a sale of the company.

III.

This brings us to the lock-up with Forstmann and its emphasis on shoring up the sagging market value of the Notes in the face of threatened litigation by their holders. Such a focus was inconsistent with the changed concept of the directors' responsibilities at this stage of the developments. The impending waiver of the Notes covenants had caused the value of the Notes to fall, and the board was aware of the noteholders' ire as well as their subsequent threats of suit. The directors thus made support of the Notes an integral part of the company's dealings with Forstmann, even though their primary responsibility at this stage was to the equity owners.

The original threat posed by Pantry Pride—the break-up of the company—had become a reality which even the directors embraced. Selective dealing to fend off a hostile but determined bidder was no longer a proper objective. Instead, obtaining the highest price for the benefit of the stockholders should have been the central theme guiding director action. Thus, the Revlon board could not make the requisite showing of good faith by preferring the noteholders and ignoring its duty of loyalty to the shareholders. The rights of the former already were fixed by contract. *Wolfensohn v. Madison Fund, Inc.*, Del.Supr., 253 A.2d 72, 75 (1969); *Harff v. Kerkorian*, Del. Ch., 324 A.2d 215 (1974). The noteholders required no further protection, and when the Revlon board entered into an auction-ending lock-up agreement with Forstmann on the basis of impermissible considerations at the expense of the shareholders, the directors breached their primary duty of loyalty.

The Revlon board argued that it acted in good faith in protecting the noteholders because *Unocal* permits consideration of other corporate constituencies. Although such considerations may be permissible, there are fundamental limitations upon that prerogative. A board may have regard for various constituencies in discharging its responsibilities, provided there are rationally related benefits accruing to the stockholders. *Unocal*, 493 A.2d at 955. However, such concern for non-stockholder interests is inappropriate when an auction among active bidders is in progress, and the object no longer is to protect or maintain the corporate enterprise but to sell it to the highest bidder.

Revlon also contended that by *Gilbert v. El Paso Co.*, Del. Ch., 490 A.2d 1050, 1054–55 (1984), it had contractual and good faith obligations to consider the noteholders. However, any such duties are limited to the principle that one may not interfere with contractual relationships by improper actions. Here, the rights of the noteholders were fixed by agreement, and there is nothing of substance to suggest that any of those terms were violated. The Notes covenants specifically contemplated a waiver to permit sale of the company at a fair price. The Notes were accepted by the holders on that basis, including the risk of an adverse market effect stemming from a waiver. Thus, nothing remained for Revlon to legitimately protect, and no rationally related benefit thereby accrued to the stockholders. Under such circumstances we must conclude that the merger agreement with Forstmann was unreasonable in relation to the threat posed.

A lock-up is not *per se* illegal under Delaware law. Its use has been approved in an earlier case. *Thompson v. Enstar Corp.*,[509 A.2d 578 (Del. Ch. 1984)]. Such options can entice other bidders to enter a contest for control of the corporation, creating an auction for the company and maximizing shareholder profit. Current economic conditions in the takeover market are such that a "white knight" like Forstmann might only enter the bidding for the target company if it receives some form of compensation to cover the risks and costs involved. Note, *Corporations-Mergers—"Lock-up" Enjoined Under Section 14(e) of Securities Exchange Act—Mobil Corp. v. Marathon Oil Co., 669 F.2d 366 (6th Cir.1981),* 12 Seton Hall L.Rev. 881, 892 (1982). However, while those lock-ups which draw bidders into the battle benefit shareholders, similar measures which end an active auction and foreclose further bidding operate to the shareholders' detriment. Note, *Lock-up Options: Toward a State Law Standard,* 96 Harv. L. Rev. 1068, 1081 (1983). * * *

The Forstmann option had a * * * destructive effect on the auction process. Forstmann had already been drawn into the contest on a preferred basis, so the result of the lock-up was not to foster bidding, but to destroy it. The board's stated reasons for approving the transactions were: (1) better financing, (2) noteholder protection, and (3) higher price. As the Court of Chancery found, and we agree, any distinctions between the rival bidders' methods of financing the proposal were nominal at best, and such a consideration has little or no significance in a cash offer for any and all shares. The principal object, contrary to the board's duty of care, appears to have been protection of the noteholders over the shareholders' interests.

While Forstmann's $57.25 offer was objectively higher than Pantry Pride's $56.25 bid, the margin of superiority is less when the Forstmann price is adjusted for the time value of money. In reality, the Revlon board ended the auction in return for very little actual improvement in the final bid. The principal benefit went to the directors, who avoided personal liability to a class of creditors to whom the board owed no further duty under the circumstances. Thus, when a board ends an intense bidding contest on an insubstantial basis, and where a significant by-product of that action is to protect the directors against a perceived threat of personal liability for consequences stemming from the adoption of previous defensive measures, the action cannot withstand the enhanced scrutiny which *Unocal* requires of director conduct. *See Unocal,* 493 A.2d at 954–55.

In addition to the lock-up option, the Court of Chancery enjoined the no-shop provision as part of the attempt to foreclose further bidding by Pantry Pride. *MacAndrews & Forbes Holdings, Inc. v. Revlon, Inc.,* 501 A.2d at 1251. The no-shop provision, like the lock-up option, while not *per se* illegal, is impermissible under the *Unocal* standards when a board's primary duty becomes that of an auctioneer responsible for selling the company to the highest bidder. The agreement to negotiate only with Forstmann ended rather than intensified the board's involvement in the bidding contest.

It is ironic that the parties even considered a no-shop agreement when Revlon had dealt preferentially, and almost exclusively, with Forstmann throughout the contest. After the directors authorized management to negotiate with other parties, Forstmann was given every negotiating advantage that Pantry Pride had been denied: cooperation from management, access to financial data, and the exclusive opportunity to present merger proposals directly to the board of directors. Favoritism for a white knight to the total exclusion of a hostile bidder might be justifiable when the latter's offer adversely affects shareholder interests, but when bidders make relatively similar offers, or dissolution of the company becomes inevitable, the directors cannot fulfill their enhanced *Unocal* duties by playing favorites with the contending factions. Market forces must be allowed to operate freely to bring the target's shareholders the best price available for their equity. Thus, as the trial court ruled, the shareholders' interests necessitated that the board remain free to negotiate in the fulfillment of that duty.

The court below similarly enjoined the payment of the cancellation fee, pending a resolution of the merits, because the fee was part of the overall plan to thwart Pantry Pride's efforts. We find no abuse of discretion in that ruling. . . .

V.

In conclusion, the Revlon board was confronted with a situation not uncommon in the current wave of corporate takeovers. A hostile and determined bidder sought the company at a price the board was convinced was inadequate. The initial defensive tactics worked to the benefit of the shareholders, and thus the board was able to sustain its *Unocal* burdens in justifying those measures. However, in granting an asset option lock-up to Forstmann, we must conclude that under all the circumstances the directors allowed considerations other than the maximization of shareholder profit to affect their judgment, and followed a course that ended the auction for Revlon, absent court intervention, to the ultimate detriment of its shareholders. No such defensive measure can be sustained when it represents a breach of the directors' fundamental duty of care. *See Smith v. Van Gorkom*, Del.Supr., 488 A.2d 858, 874 (1985). In that context the board's action is not entitled to the deference accorded it by the business judgment rule. The measures were properly enjoined. The decision of the Court of Chancery, therefore, is AFFIRMED.

NOTES AND QUESTIONS

I. WHAT, EXACTLY, are the fiduciary duties of officers and directors when the corporate existence, in effect, comes to an end, or transforms into something else? We will not explore each of these areas, but similar problems present themselves when the corporation is dissolved, when there is sale of substantially all of the assets of the corporation, or when the corporation merges with another. There is a simple procedure that must be followed in such cases; first the Board of Directors must vote on the transaction, and, second, the transaction must be ratified by vote of the shareholders. Still, because of the potential conflict of interest posed by the fact that officers, directors, or majority shareholders may have interests adverse to those of other corporate stakeholders courts, and particularly the Delaware Supreme Court, have applied close scrutiny to sale of control situations, particularly in the takeover context.

....

2. WHAT SHOULD BE THE STANDARD of law to guide directors and officers faced with a hostile takeover bid? Such bids are often made because the target's share prices are depressed, and there is one school of academic thought which holds that share prices of such companies are depressed because incumbent management is doing a poor job. A bidder for such a company believes, so the argument goes, that it can do a better job managing the company and thus is in a position to increase value not only for itself, as a new majority owner, but also for the remaining shareholders. If one accepts this theory, then incumbent management should not be able to resist a tender offer, and such resistance, in fact, would probably be an act manifesting a conflict of interest between those of the incumbent managers (who want to hold on to their jobs) and shareholders (who would theoretically see their shares increase in value if a new management team were in place). Following this theory, in a brilliant article, Frank Easterbrook (now Chief Judge of the United States Court of Appeals for the Seventh Circuit, in Chicago) and Daniel Fischel (now a Professor at Northwestern University School of Law) argued that the only proper position of incumbent managers when faced with a hostile tender offer was supine. See generally Frank Easterbook and Daniel Fischel, The Proper Role of a Target's Management In Responding to a Tender Offer, 94 Harv. L. Rev. 1161 (1981). Do you agree?

....

3. THOUGH THE DELAWARE SUPREME COURT noted Fischel and Easterbook's argument in its *Unocal* it chose not to accept it. Basing its opinion in part on empirical data that since has been more-or-less discredited, the Court took the position that resisting a tender offer could increase shareholder value, and gave target management some discretion to combat such an offer. Realizing, however, that such a situation could present a conflict of interest for incumbent management, the Court said that it would subject the board's decision to resist to "enhanced scrutiny." This meant that the normal manner of applying the business judgment rule was not enough, and that, instead, the Court would require incumbent managers, if challenged, to demonstrate that they reasonably perceived a threat to the corporation or its constituencies (employees, creditors, consumers, even the community), and that the action they took to resist the takeover was reasonable in light of the threat posed. In the next major takeover case, *Moran v. Household Int'l, Inc.*, 500 A.2d 1346, 1356 (Del.1985), the Supreme Court indicated that incumbent managers could put defensive tactics, such as "poison pills" or "shareholder rights plans" (as they are also known) in place even if there is no immediate takeover threat to the corporation, so long as it was reasonable to perceive such a threat, and the response chosen was reasonable in light of the threat perceived.

Revlon spun Delaware anti-takeover law in a new direction, when it indicated that there were certain situations where incumbent managers would no longer be free to erect or employ defensive measures, and when, in fact, their role would shift from protecting the integrity of the corporation against hostile bids to simply making sure that the shareholders received the highest possible price for their shares. In *Revlon* the court indicated that two such situations were when a corporate "bust-up" was inevitable (in *Revlon* this was the case since it was clear that some divisions of the company were inevitably going to be sold), or when the corporation was on the auction block (that is, when there were multiple bidders, as there were for *Revlon*). The Court further made clear in *Revlon* that when a corporation was in "*Revlon mode*," as it came to be called, the Board could not take steps to protect other corporate constituencies, and could only look to the welfare of the shareholders, by securing the highest price for their shares. The *Revlon* court also made clear that its earlier comments in *Unocal* about permitting Boards to take defensive tactics to protect corporate constituencies other than the shareholders should be limited to situations in which the long-term shareholder wealth was enhanced by such actions.

· ·

4. IN 1995, the Delaware Supreme Court further refined the *Unocal* test in *Unitrin, Inc. v. American General Corp.*, 651 A.2d 1361 (Del. 1995). The case involved a hostile takeover attempt of one insurance company (Unitrin) by another (American General). Unitrin's board approved a poison pill defense and a repurchase program, under which Unitrin bought back 5 million of 51.8 million outstanding shares. This repurchase increased the directors' ownership interest from 23% to 28% of shares. The court noted, contra Chancery, that even if the Unitrin board controlled 28% of shares American General could still succeed in a takeover via proxy contest.

The *Unitrin* court considered both aspects of the *Unocal* test, reasonableness and proportionality, focusing on the latter. The court claimed that the line of cases applying *Unocal* had found defensive responses disproportionate when they were coercive or preclusive, and proportionate when not.

> In *Time,* for example, this Court concluded that the Time board's defensive response was reasonable and proportionate since it was not aimed at "cramming down" on its shareholders a management-sponsored alternative, *i.e.,* was not coercive, and because it did not preclude Paramount from making an offer for the combined Time–Warner company, *i.e.,* was not preclusive.

Unitrin at 1387. The court then held that coercive or preclusive actions would meet the common law definition of draconian. If, however, an action was deemed to be neither coercive nor preclusive, "the focus of enhanced judicial scrutiny [must] shift to the 'range of reasonableness.'" *Id.* at 1388. The range of reasonableness test is, of course, deferential to board discretion; the court reversed one order which had been in favor of American General and remanded the case back to Chancery.

· ·

5. BEFORE *UNITRIN*, the Delaware Supreme Court decided two important cases, both involving Paramount Communications, the large entertainment company. Both decisions demonstrate the complex requirements courts apply to board discretion in endgame scenarios.

Paramount Communications, Inc. v. Time, Inc.

Supreme Court of Delaware
571 A.2d 1140 (Del. 1990).

Judges: Horsey, Moore, and Holland, JJ.

OPINION BY: HORSEY

Paramount Communications, Inc. ("Paramount") and two other groups of plaintiffs ("Shareholder Plaintiffs"), shareholders of Time Incorporated ("Time"), a Delaware corporation, separately filed suits in the Delaware Court of Chancery seeking a preliminary injunction to halt Time's tender offer for 51% of Warner Communication,

Inc.'s ("Warner") outstanding shares at $70 cash per share. The court below * * * denied plaintiffs' motion. * * * On July 14, 1989, the Chancellor refused to enjoin Time's consummation of its tender offer, concluding that the plaintiffs were unlikely to prevail on the merits. * * *

The principal ground for reversal, asserted by all plaintiffs, is that Paramount's June 7, 1989 uninvited all-cash, all-shares, "fully negotiable" (though conditional) tender offer for Time triggered duties under *Unocal Corp. v. Mesa Petroleum Co.*, Del.Supr., 493 A.2d 946 (1985), and that Time's board of directors, in responding to Paramount's offer, breached those duties. * * *

Shareholder Plaintiffs also assert a claim based on *Revlon v. MacAndrews & Forbes Holdings, Inc.*, Del.Supr., 506 A.2d 173 (1986). They argue that the original Time–Warner merger agreement of March 4, 1989 resulted in a change of control which effectively put Time up for sale, thereby triggering *Revlon* duties. Those plaintiffs argue that Time's board breached its *Revlon* duties by failing, in the face of the change of control, to maximize shareholder value in the immediate term. * * *

[W]e affirm the Chancellor's ultimate finding and conclusion under *Unocal*. We find that Paramount's tender offer was reasonably perceived by Time's board to pose a threat to Time and that the Time board's "response" to that threat was, under the circumstances, reasonable and proportionate. Applying *Unocal*, we reject the argument that the only corporate threat posed by an all-shares, all-cash tender offer is the possibility of inadequate value.

We also find that Time's board did not by entering into its initial merger agreement with Warner come under a *Revlon* duty either to auction the company or to maximize short-term shareholder value, notwithstanding the unequal share exchange. Therefore, the Time board's original plan of merger with Warner was subject only to a business judgment rule analysis. * * *

I

[Time was a longstanding publisher of magazines and books, but also provided television entertainment through premium cable channels and cable franchises. Its board was made up of twelve outside and four inside directors. As early as 1983, Time's board was considering expanding its entertainment offerings. Despite concerns of a threat to the "editorial integrity and journalistic focus" of the company, the board felt that an expanded video enterprise would allow it to better compete globally.

In 1987, the CEOs of Time and Warner Brothers met to discuss a possible joint venture, although this plan was eventually abandoned. Through the rest of that year, and into 1988, Time's board held in-depth discussions on the viability of a consolidation with Warner and other entertainment companies. Certain directors were concerned that these actions might cause others to perceive Time as up for sale. The board eventually authorized continued discussions with Warner, though under the conditions that any resulting company would be controlled by Time. Warner was seen as the ideal candidate, as its existing offerings neatly complemented those of Time.

Although Time preferred an all-cash purchase of Warner, Warner insisted on a stock-for-stock transfer so as to preserve its own shareholders' interest in the resulting company. Time eventually relented, but insisted that it control the new board. Talks eventually foundered, as the CEO of Warner (Steve Ross) refused to limit his time as chief of the new corporation at the outset. Time then began informal discussions with other entertainment companies.

In January 1989, Steve Ross had dinner with a Time outside director, who was able to convince Ross to serve a term limited to five years as CEO of the resulting company. The companies restarted negotiations, and settled on a stock exchange ratio that would leave Warner shareholders with about 62% of the resulting company's common stock. Both boards approved the merger, in which Warner would merge with a Time subsidiary, and Time would change its name to Time Warner, Inc.

In a March meeting Time's board approved several defensive strategies. First, either Time or Warner could trigger an automatic share exchange. Time also pursued "confidence" letters from lenders in which the banks agreed not to finance third-party takeover attempts of Time. Finally, Time agreed to a no-shop clause, meaning that it could not invite any other proposal; Warner, now in play, did not want to be left for the taking should the deal fall through.

Shareholder approval seemed to be in hand when, on June 7, 1989, Paramount surprised all parties by announcing a cash offer for outstanding Time shares at $175 per share; Time's share price exploded from $126 to $170. The Time board firmly opposed Paramount's offer, finding the price inadequate and believing that merger with Warner was still the best option. The board was also concerned that shareholders would not appreciate the long-term value of merging with Warner nor the risks Paramount posed to Time.

After rejecting Paramount's offer, the Time board recast its merger with Warner as an acquisition, thus avoiding the necessity of a shareholder vote which might favor Paramount's offer. In order to buy Warner shares in cash, Time would have to incur 7–10 billion dollars of debt. Warner agreed to the deal, with further conditions extracted from Time. Paramount responded with a $200 per share offer on June 23, which the Time board rejected as still inadequate and threatening. Paramount filed suit.]

II

The Shareholder Plaintiffs first assert a *Revlon* claim. They contend that the March 4 Time–Warner agreement effectively put Time up for sale, triggering *Revlon* duties, requiring Time's board to enhance short-term shareholder value and to treat all other interested acquirors on an equal basis. The Shareholder Plaintiffs base this argument on two facts: (i) the ultimate Time–Warner exchange ratio of .465 favoring Warner, resulting in Warner shareholders' receipt of 62% of the combined company; and (ii) the subjective intent of Time's directors as evidenced in their statements that the market might perceive the Time–Warner merger as putting Time up "for sale" and their adoption of various defensive measures.

The Shareholder Plaintiffs further contend that Time's directors, in structuring the original merger transaction to be "takeover-proof," triggered *Revlon* duties by foreclosing their shareholders from any prospect of obtaining a control premium. In short, plaintiffs argue that Time's board's decision to merge with Warner imposed a fiduciary duty to maximize immediate share value and not erect unreasonable barriers to further bids. * * *

Paramount asserts only a *Unocal* claim in which the shareholder plaintiffs join. Paramount contends that the Chancellor, in applying the first part of the *Unocal* test, erred in finding that Time's board had reasonable grounds to believe that Paramount posed both a legally cognizable threat to Time shareholders and a danger to Time's corporate policy and effectiveness. Paramount also contests the court's finding that Time's board made a reasonable and objective investigation of Paramount's offer so as to be informed before rejecting it. Paramount further claims that the court erred in applying *Unocal* 's second part in finding Time's response to be "reasonable." Paramount points primarily to the preclusive effect of the revised agreement which denied Time shareholders the opportunity both to vote on the agreement and to respond to Paramount's tender offer. Paramount argues that the underlying motivation of Time's board in adopting these defensive measures was management's desire to perpetuate itself in office.

The Court of Chancery posed the pivotal question presented by this case to be: Under what circumstances must a board of directors abandon an in-place plan of corporate development in order to provide its shareholders with the option to elect and realize an immediate control premium? As applied to this case, the question becomes: Did Time's board, having developed a strategic plan of global expansion to be launched through a business combination with Warner, come under a fiduciary duty to jettison its plan and put the corporation's future in the hands of its shareholders?

While we affirm the result reached by the Chancellor, we think it unwise to place undue emphasis upon long-term versus short-term corporate strategy. Two key predicates underpin our analysis. First, Delaware law imposes on a board of directors the duty to manage the business and affairs of the corporation. 8 *Del.C.* § 141(a). This broad mandate includes a conferred authority to set a corporate course of action, including time frame, designed to enhance corporate profitability. Thus, the question of "long-term" versus "short-term" values is largely irrelevant because directors, generally, are obliged to chart a course for a corporation which is in its best interests without regard to a fixed investment horizon. Second, absent a limited set of circumstances as defined under *Revlon*, a board of directors, while always required to act in an informed manner, is not under any *per se* duty to maximize shareholder value in the short term, even in the context of a takeover.[1] In our view, the pivotal question presented by this case is: "Did Time, by entering into the proposed merger with Warner, put itself up for sale?" A resolution of that issue through application of *Revlon* has a significant bearing upon the resolution of the derivative *Unocal* issue.

---

1   Thus, we endorse the Chancellor's conclusion that it is not a breach of faith for directors to determine that the present stock market price of shares is not representative of true value or that there may indeed be several market values for any corporation's stock. [footnotes are from the original opinion, though some have been omitted, and the remaining footnotes have been renumbered here]

A.

We first take up plaintiffs' principal *Revlon* argument, summarized above. * * * [W]e premise our rejection of plaintiffs' *Revlon* claim on * * * the absence of any substantial evidence to conclude that Time's board, in negotiating with Warner, made the dissolution or break-up of the corporate entity inevitable, as was the case in *Revlon*.

Under Delaware law there are, generally speaking and without excluding other possibilities, two circumstances which may implicate *Revlon* duties. The first, and clearer one, is when a corporation initiates an active bidding process seeking to sell itself or to effect a business reorganization involving a clear break-up of the company. * * * However, *Revlon* duties may also be triggered where, in response to a bidder's offer, a target abandons its long-term strategy and seeks an alternative transaction involving the breakup of the company.[2] Thus, in *Revlon*, when the board responded to Pantry Pride's offer by contemplating a "bust-up" sale of assets in a leveraged acquisition, we imposed upon the board a duty to maximize immediate shareholder value and an obligation to auction the company fairly. If, however, the board's reaction to a hostile tender offer is found to constitute only a defensive response and not an abandonment of the corporation's continued existence, *Revlon* duties are not triggered, though *Unocal* duties attach. * * *

The plaintiffs insist that even though the original Time–Warner agreement may not have worked "an objective change of control," the transaction made a "sale" of Time inevitable. Plaintiffs rely on the subjective intent of Time's board of directors and principally upon certain board members' expressions of concern that the Warner transaction *might* be viewed as effectively putting Time up for sale. Plaintiffs argue that the use of a lock-up agreement, a no-shop clause, and so-called "dry-up" agreements prevented shareholders from obtaining a control premium in the immediate future and thus violated *Revlon*.

We agree with the Chancellor that such evidence is entirely insufficient to invoke *Revlon* duties; and we decline to extend *Revlon*'s application to corporate transactions simply because they might be construed as putting a corporation either "in play" or "up for sale." * * * The adoption of structural safety devices alone does not trigger *Revlon*. Rather, as the Chancellor stated, such devices are properly subject to a *Unocal* analysis.

Finally, we do not find in Time's recasting of its merger agreement with Warner from a share exchange to a share purchase a basis to conclude that Time had either abandoned its strategic plan or made a sale of Time inevitable. The Chancellor found that although the merged Time–Warner company would be large (with a value approaching approximately $30 billion), recent takeover cases have proven that acquisition of the combined company might nonetheless be possible. * * * The legal

---

2   As we stated in *Revlon*, in both such cases, "[t]he duty of the board [has] changed from the preservation of ... [the] corporate entity to the maximization of the company's value at a sale for the stockholder's benefit.... [The board] no longer face[s] threats to corporate policy and effectiveness, or to the stockholders' interests, from a grossly inadequate bid." *Revlon v. MacAndrews & Forbes Holdings, Inc.*, Del.Supr., 506 A.2d 173, 182 (1986).

consequence is that *Unocal* alone applies to determine whether the business judgment rule attaches to the revised agreement. * * *

B.

We turn now to plaintiffs' *Unocal* claim. * * * Our task is simply to review the record to determine whether there is sufficient evidence to support the Chancellor's conclusion that the initial Time–Warner agreement was the product of a proper exercise of business judgment. * * *

Time's decision in 1988 to combine with Warner was made only after what could be fairly characterized as an exhaustive appraisal of Time's future as a corporation. After concluding in 1983–84 that the corporation must expand to survive, and beyond journalism into entertainment, the board combed the field of available entertainment companies. By 1987 Time had focused upon Warner; by late July 1988 Time's board was convinced that Warner would provide the best "fit" for Time to achieve its strategic objectives. The record attests to the zealousness of Time's executives, fully supported by their directors, in seeing to the preservation of Time's "culture," i.e., its perceived editorial integrity in journalism. We find ample evidence in the record to support the Chancellor's conclusion that the Time board's decision to expand the business of the company through its March 3 merger with Warner was entitled to the protection of the business judgment rule. * * *

In *Unocal*, we held that before the business judgment rule is applied to a board's adoption of a defensive measure, the burden will lie with the board to prove (a) reasonable grounds for believing that a danger to corporate policy and effectiveness existed; and (b) that the defensive measure adopted was reasonable in relation to the threat posed. *Unocal*, 493 A.2d 946. Directors satisfy the first part of the *Unocal* test by demonstrating good faith and reasonable investigation. We have repeatedly stated that the refusal to entertain an offer may comport with a valid exercise of a board's business judgment. * * *

Unocal involved a two-tier, highly coercive [front-end loaded] tender offer.[3] In such a case, the threat is obvious: shareholders may be compelled to tender to avoid being treated adversely in the second stage of the transaction. * * * In subsequent cases, the Court of Chancery has suggested that an all-cash, all-shares offer, falling within a range of values that a shareholder might reasonably prefer, cannot constitute a legally recognized "threat" to shareholder interests sufficient to withstand a *Unocal* analysis. *AC Acquisitions Corp. v. Anderson, Clayton & Co.*, Del.Ch., 519 A.2d 103 (1986); *see Grand Metropolitan, PLC v. Pillsbury Co.*, Del.Ch., 558 A.2d 1049 (1988); *City Capital Associates v. Interco, Inc.*, Del.Ch., 551 A.2d 787 (1988). In those cases, the Court of Chancery determined that whatever threat existed related only to the shareholders and only to price and not to the corporation.

---

3   In a front-end loaded two-tiered tender offer, such as the one threatened in the Unocal case, a bidder acquires a majority of the shares for cash (in the first stage, or "front end" of the transaction) and then uses its majority control to freeze-out the remaining shareholders (those left at the "back end") usually giving them, instead of cash, high-risk debt instruments, or as they are also known, "junk bonds."—Ed.

From those decisions by our Court of Chancery, Paramount and the individual plaintiffs extrapolate a rule of law that an all-cash, all-shares offer with values reasonably in the range of acceptable price cannot pose any objective threat to a corporation or its shareholders. Thus, Paramount would have us hold that only if the value of Paramount's offer were determined to be clearly inferior to the value created by management's plan to merge with Warner could the offer be viewed—objectively—as a threat.

Implicit in the plaintiffs' argument is the view that a hostile tender offer can pose only two types of threats: the threat of coercion that results from a two-tier offer promising unequal treatment for nontendering shareholders; and the threat of inadequate value from an all-shares, all-cash offer at a price below what a target board in good faith deems to be the present value of its shares. * * * Since Paramount's offer was all-cash, the only conceivable "threat," plaintiffs argue, was inadequate value. We disapprove of such a narrow and rigid construction of *Unocal,* for the reasons which follow.

Plaintiffs' position represents a fundamental misconception of our standard of review under *Unocal* principally because it would involve the court in substituting its judgment as to what is a "better" deal for that of a corporation's board of directors. To the extent that the Court of Chancery has recently done so in certain of its opinions, we hereby reject such approach as not in keeping with a proper *Unocal* analysis. * * *

The usefulness of *Unocal* as an analytical tool is precisely its flexibility in the face of a variety of fact scenarios. *Unocal* is not intended as an abstract standard; neither is it a structured and mechanistic procedure of appraisal. Thus, we have said that directors may consider, when evaluating the threat posed by a takeover bid, the "inadequacy of the price offered, nature and timing of the offer, questions of illegality, the impact on 'constituencies' other than shareholders ... the risk of nonconsummation, and the quality of securities being offered in the exchange." 493 A.2d at 955. The open-ended analysis mandated by *Unocal* is not intended to lead to a simple mathematical exercise: that is, of comparing the discounted value of Time–Warner's expected trading price at some future date with Paramount's offer and determining which is the higher. Indeed, in our view, precepts underlying the business judgment rule militate against a court's engaging in the process of attempting to appraise and evaluate the relative merits of a long-term versus a short-term investment goal for shareholders. * * *

In this case, the Time board reasonably determined that inadequate value was not the only legally cognizable threat that Paramount's all-cash, all-shares offer could present. Time's board concluded that Paramount's eleventh hour offer posed other threats. One concern was that Time shareholders might elect to tender into Paramount's cash offer in ignorance or a mistaken belief of the strategic benefit which a business combination with Warner might produce. Moreover, Time viewed the conditions attached to Paramount's offer as introducing a degree of uncertainty that skewed a comparative analysis. Further, the timing of Paramount's offer to follow issuance of Time's proxy notice was viewed as arguably designed to upset, if not confuse, the Time stockholders' vote. Given this record evidence, we cannot conclude that the Time board's decision of June 6 that Paramount's offer posed a threat to corporate policy and effectiveness was lacking in good faith or dominated by motives of either entrenchment or self-interest.

Paramount also contends that the Time board had not duly investigated Paramount's offer. Therefore, Paramount argues, Time was unable to make an informed decision that the offer posed a threat to Time's corporate policy. Although the Chancellor did not address this issue directly, his findings of fact do detail Time's exploration of the available entertainment companies, including Paramount, before determining that Warner provided the best strategic "fit." In addition, the court found that Time's board rejected Paramount's offer because Paramount did not serve Time's objectives or meet Time's needs. Thus, the record does, in our judgment, demonstrate that Time's board was adequately informed of the potential benefits of a transaction with Paramount. * * * Time's failure to negotiate cannot be fairly found to have been uninformed. The evidence supporting this finding is materially enhanced by the fact that twelve of Time's sixteen board members were outside independent directors. * * *

We turn to the second part of the *Unocal* analysis. The obvious requisite to determining the reasonableness of a defensive action is a clear identification of the nature of the threat. As the Chancellor correctly noted, this "requires an evaluation of the importance of the corporate objective threatened; alternative methods of protecting that objective; impacts of the 'defensive' action, and other relevant factors." * * * It is not until both parts of the *Unocal* inquiry have been satisfied that the business judgment rule attaches to defensive actions of a board of directors. *Unocal*, 493 A.2d at 954. As applied to the facts of this case, the question is whether the record evidence supports the Court of Chancery's conclusion that the restructuring of the Time–Warner transaction, including the adoption of several preclusive defensive measures, was a *reasonable response* in relation to a perceived threat.

Paramount argues that, assuming its tender offer posed a threat, Time's response was unreasonable in precluding Time's shareholders from accepting the tender offer or receiving a control premium in the immediately foreseeable future. Once again, the contention stems, we believe, from a fundamental misunderstanding of where the power of corporate governance lies. Delaware law confers the management of the corporate enterprise to the stockholders' duly elected board representatives. 8 *Del.C.* § 141(a). The fiduciary duty to manage a corporate enterprise includes the selection of a time frame for achievement of corporate goals. That duty may not be delegated to the stockholders. * * * Directors are not obliged to abandon a deliberately conceived corporate plan for a short-term shareholder profit unless there is clearly no basis to sustain the corporate strategy. * * *

Here, on the record facts, the Chancellor found that Time's responsive action to Paramount's tender offer was not aimed at "cramming down" on its shareholders a management-sponsored alternative, but rather had as its goal the carrying forward of a pre-existing transaction in an altered form. Thus, the response was reasonably related to the threat. The Chancellor noted that the revised agreement and its accompanying safety devices did not preclude Paramount from making an offer for the combined Time–Warner company or from changing the conditions of its offer so as not to make the offer dependent upon the nullification of the Time–Warner agreement. Thus, the response was proportionate. We affirm the Chancellor's rulings as clearly supported by the record. Finally, we note that although Time was required, as a result of Paramount's hostile offer, to incur a heavy debt to finance its acquisition of Warner, that fact alone does not render the board's decision unreasonable so long as the directors could reasonably perceive the debt load not to be so injurious to the corporation as to jeopardize its well being.

C.

CONCLUSION

Applying the test for grant or denial of preliminary injunctive relief, we find plaintiffs failed to establish a reasonable likelihood of ultimate success on the merits. Therefore, we affirm.

Paramount Communications Inc. v. QVC Network, Inc.

Supreme Court of Delaware
637 A.2d 34 (Del. 1994).

Before VEASEY, C.J., MOORE and HOLLAND, JJ.

OPINION

VEASEY, Chief Justice.

In this appeal we review an order of the Court of Chancery dated November 24, 1993 (the "November 24 Order"), preliminarily enjoining certain defensive measures designed to facilitate a so-called strategic alliance between Viacom Inc. ("Viacom") and Paramount Communications Inc. ("Paramount") approved by the board of directors of Paramount (the "Paramount Board" or the "Paramount directors") and to thwart an unsolicited, more valuable, tender offer by QVC Network Inc. ("QVC"). In affirming, we hold that the sale of control in this case, which is at the heart of the proposed strategic alliance, implicates enhanced judicial scrutiny of the conduct of the Paramount Board under *Unocal Corp. v. Mesa Petroleum Co.*, Del.Supr., 493 A.2d 946 (1985), and *Revlon, Inc. v. MacAndrews & Forbes Holdings, Inc.*, Del.

Supr., 506 A.2d 173 (1986). We further hold that the conduct of the Paramount Board was not reasonable as to process or result. * * *

This action arises out of a proposed acquisition of Paramount by Viacom through a tender offer followed by a second-step merger (the "Paramount–Viacom transaction"), and a competing unsolicited tender offer by QVC. The Court of Chancery granted a preliminary injunction * * * (the "December 9 Order").

The Court of Chancery found that the Paramount directors violated their fiduciary duties by favoring the Paramount–Viacom transaction over the more valuable unsolicited offer of QVC. * * *

Under the circumstances of this case, the pending sale of control implicated in the Paramount–Viacom transaction required the Paramount Board to act on an informed basis to secure the best value reasonably available to the stockholders. Since we agree with the Court of Chancery that the Paramount directors violated their fiduciary duties, we have AFFIRMED the entry of the order of the Vice Chancellor granting the preliminary injunction and have REMANDED these proceedings to the Court of Chancery for proceedings consistent herewith.

I. FACTS

* * * The majority of Paramount's stock is publicly held by numerous unaffiliated investors. Paramount owns and operates a diverse group of entertainment businesses, including motion picture and television studios, book publishers, professional sports teams, and amusement parks. [Paramount's board consists of 11 outside and 4 inside directors, led by Martin Davis] * * *

Viacom is controlled by Sumner M. Redstone ("Redstone"), its Chairman and Chief Executive Officer * * * Viacom has a wide range of entertainment operations, including a number of well-known cable television channels such as MTV, Nickelodeon, Showtime, and The Movie Channel. * * *

Barry Diller ("Diller"), the Chairman and Chief Executive Officer of QVC, is also a substantial stockholder. QVC sells a variety of merchandise through a televised shopping channel. * * *

Beginning in the late 1980s, Paramount investigated the possibility of acquiring or merging with other companies in the entertainment, media, or communications industry. Paramount considered such transactions to be desirable, and perhaps necessary, in order to keep pace with competitors in the rapidly evolving field of entertainment and communications. Consistent with its goal of strategic expansion, Paramount made a tender offer for Time Inc. in 1989, but was ultimately unsuccessful.
* * *

[Redstone and Davis met on April 20, 1993, to discuss a possible merger between Paramount and Viacom. Negotiations eventually broke down, and Davis learned of (and spurned) Diller's interest in QVC acquiring Paramount. Discussions between Paramount and Viacom resumed in August, and the Paramount board eventually approved the Original Merger Agreement, under which Viacom would acquire Paramount. The agreement contained (among others) three controversial defensive measures: a no-shop provision, a termination fee, and a stock option agreement.

Under the no-shop provision, Paramount could only discuss a third-party transaction if it were necessary in order to comply with the board's fiduciary duties. Under the termination fee, Viacom would receive $100 million if Paramount chose another bid, Paramount's stockholders disapproved the merger, or the board recommended another bid. Finally, the stock option agreement allowed Viacom the option to purchase 19.9% of outstanding Paramount common stock under any of the terminating conditions. Furthermore, Viacom could purchase these shares with questionable notes and require Paramount to pay the difference between the purchase and market price of the stock (the "Put Feature").]

After the execution of the Original Merger Agreement and the Stock Option Agreement on September 12, 1993, Paramount and Viacom announced their proposed merger. * * * [QVC then began some negotiation with Paramount, but it moved slowly. Paramount and Viacom executives publicly confirmed the merger and hailed its inevitability.]

On October 21, 1993, QVC filed this action and publicly announced an $80 cash tender offer for 51 percent of Paramount's outstanding shares (the "QVC tender offer"). * * *

Confronted by QVC's hostile bid, which on its face offered over $10 per share more than the consideration provided by the Original Merger Agreement, Viacom realized that it would need to raise its bid in order to remain competitive. * * *

At a special meeting on October 24, 1993, the Paramount Board approved the Amended Merger Agreement [with Viacom] and an amendment to the Stock Option Agreement. The Amended Merger Agreement was, however, essentially the same as the Original Merger Agreement, except that it included a few new provisions. * * * The Amended Merger Agreement also added a provision giving Paramount the right not to amend its Rights Agreement to exempt Viacom if the Paramount Board determined that such an amendment would be inconsistent with its fiduciary duties because another offer constituted a "better alternative."[6] Finally, the Paramount Board was given the power to terminate the Amended Merger Agreement if it withdrew its recommendation of the Viacom transaction or recommended a competing transaction.

Although the Amended Merger Agreement offered more consideration to the Paramount stockholders and somewhat more flexibility to the Paramount Board than did the Original Merger Agreement, the defensive measures designed to make a competing bid more difficult were not removed or modified. In particular, there is no evidence in the record that Paramount sought to use its newly-acquired leverage to eliminate or modify the No–Shop Provision, the Termination Fee, or the Stock Option Agreement when the subject of amending the Original Merger Agreement was on the table.

Viacom's tender offer commenced on October 25, 1993, and QVC's tender offer was formally launched on October 27, 1993. [Each company was forced to raise its bid in response to the other, with Viacom's final bid at $85 per share and QVC's at $90.] * * *

At its meeting on November 15, 1993, the Paramount Board determined that the new QVC offer was not in the best interests of the stockholders. The purported basis for this conclusion was that QVC's bid was excessively conditional. The Paramount Board did not communicate with QVC regarding the status of the conditions because it believed that the No–Shop Provision prevented such communication in the absence of firm financing. Several Paramount directors also testified that they believed the Viacom transaction would be more advantageous to Paramount's future business prospects than a QVC transaction.[4] * * *

The preliminary injunction hearing in this case took place on November 16, 1993. On November 19, Diller wrote to the Paramount Board to inform it that QVC had obtained financing commitments for its tender offer and that there was no antitrust obstacle to the offer. On November 24, 1993, the Court of Chancery issued its decision granting a preliminary injunction in favor of QVC and the plaintiff stockholders. This appeal followed.

II. APPLICABLE PRINCIPLES OF ESTABLISHED DELAWARE LAW

* * * [T]here are rare situations which mandate that a court take a more direct and active role in overseeing the decisions made and actions taken by directors. In these situations, a court subjects the directors' conduct to enhanced scrutiny to ensure that it is reasonable.[5] The decisions of this Court have clearly established the circumstances where such enhanced scrutiny will be applied. * * * The case at bar implicates two such circumstances: (1) the approval of a transaction resulting in a sale of control, and (2) the adoption of defensive measures in response to a threat to corporate control.

A. *The Significance of a Sale or Change of Control*

When a majority of a corporation's voting shares are acquired by a single person or entity, or by a cohesive group acting together, there is a significant diminution in the voting power of those who thereby become minority stockholders. Under the statutory framework of the General Corporation Law, many of the most fundamental corporate changes can be implemented only if they are approved by a majority vote of the stockholders. * * * Because of the overriding importance of voting rights, this Court and the Court of Chancery have consistently acted to protect stockholders from unwarranted interference with such rights.

---

4   [Note- footnote numbering will need fixing]. [Most footnotes have been omitted. Those that remain have been renumbered] This belief may have been based on a report prepared by Booz–Allen and distributed to the Paramount Board at its October 24 meeting. The report, which relied on public information regarding QVC, concluded that the synergies of a Paramount–Viacom merger were significantly superior to those of a Paramount–QVC merger. QVC has labelled the Booz–Allen report as a "joke."

5   Where actual self-interest is present and affects a majority of the directors approving a transaction, a court will apply even more exacting scrutiny to determine whether the transaction is entirely fair to the stockholders. *E.g., Weinberger v. UOP, Inc.*, Del. Supr., 457 A.2d 701, 710–11 (1983) * * *.

In the absence of devices protecting the minority stockholders, stockholder votes are likely to become mere formalities where there is a majority stockholder. * * * Absent effective protective provisions, minority stockholders must rely for protection solely on the fiduciary duties owed to them by the directors and the majority stockholder, since the minority stockholders have lost the power to influence corporate direction through the ballot. * * *

In the case before us, the public stockholders (in the aggregate) currently own a majority of Paramount's voting stock. Control of the corporation is not vested in a single person, entity, or group, but vested in the fluid aggregation of unaffiliated stockholders. In the event the Paramount–Viacom transaction is consummated, the public stockholders will receive cash and a minority equity voting position in the surviving corporation. Following such consummation, there will be a controlling stockholder who will have the voting power to: (a) elect directors; (b) cause a breakup of the corporation; (c) merge it with another company; (d) cash-out the public stockholders; (e) amend the certificate of incorporation; (f) sell all or substantially all of the corporate assets; or (g) otherwise alter materially the nature of the corporation and the public stockholders' interests. Irrespective of the present Paramount Board's vision of a long-term strategic alliance with Viacom, the proposed sale of control would provide the new controlling stockholder with the power to alter that vision.

Because of the intended sale of control, the Paramount–Viacom transaction has economic consequences of considerable significance to the Paramount stockholders. Once control has shifted, the current Paramount stockholders will have no leverage in the future to demand another control premium. As a result, the Paramount stockholders are entitled to receive, and should receive, a control premium and/or protective devices of significant value. There being no such protective provisions in the Viacom–Paramount transaction, the Paramount directors had an obligation to take the maximum advantage of the current opportunity to realize for the stockholders the best value reasonably available.

B. The Obligations of Directors in a Sale or Change of Control Transaction

The consequences of a sale of control impose special obligations on the directors of a corporation. In particular, they have the obligation of acting reasonably to seek the transaction offering the best value reasonably available to the stockholders. * * * The directors' fiduciary duties in a sale of control context are those which generally attach. In short, "the directors must act in accordance with their fundamental duties of care and loyalty." *Barkan v. Amsted Indus., Inc.*, Del.Supr., 567 A.2d 1279, 1286 (1989). * * *

In the sale of control context, the directors must focus on one primary objective—to secure the transaction offering the best value reasonably available for the stockholders—and they must exercise their fiduciary duties to further that end. The decisions of this Court have consistently emphasized this goal. *Revlon*, 506 A.2d at 182 ("The duty of the board ... [is] the maximization of the company's value at a sale for the stockholders' benefit."); *Macmillan*, 559 A.2d at 1288 ("[I]n a sale of corporate control the responsibility of the directors is to get the highest value reasonably attainable for the shareholders."); *Barkan*, 567 A.2d at 1286 ("[T]he board must act in a neutral manner to encourage the highest possible price for shareholders."). * * *

In pursuing this objective, the directors must be especially diligent. * * * In particular, this Court has stressed the importance of the board being adequately informed in negotiating a sale of control: "The need for adequate information is central to the enlightened evaluation of a transaction that a board must make." *Barkan*, 567 A.2d at 1287. This requirement is consistent with the general principle that "directors have a duty to inform themselves, prior to making a business decision, of all material information reasonably available to them." *Aronson*, 473 A.2d at 812. *See also* * * * *Smith v. Van Gorkom*, Del.Supr., 488 A.2d 858, 872 (1985). Moreover, the role of outside, independent directors becomes particularly important because of the magnitude of a sale of control transaction and the possibility, in certain cases, that management may not necessarily be impartial. * * *

Barkan teaches some of the methods by which a board can fulfill its obligation to seek the best value reasonably available to the stockholders. 567 A.2d at 1286–87. These methods are designed to determine the existence and viability of possible alternatives. They include conducting an auction, canvassing the market, etc. Delaware law recognizes that there is "no single blueprint" that directors must follow. * * *

In determining which alternative provides the best value for the stockholders, a board of directors is not limited to considering only the amount of cash involved, and is not required to ignore totally its view of the future value of a strategic alliance. * * * Instead, the directors should analyze the entire situation and evaluate in a disciplined manner the consideration being offered. Where stock or other non-cash consideration is involved, the board should try to quantify its value, if feasible, to achieve an objective comparison of the alternatives. In addition, the board may assess a variety of practical considerations relating to each alternative, including:

> [an offer's] fairness and feasibility; the proposed or actual financing for the offer, and the consequences of that financing; questions of illegality; ... the risk of non-consum[m]ation; ... the bidder's identity, prior background and other business venture experiences; and the bidder's business plans for the corporation and their effects on stockholder interests.

—*Macmillan*, 559 A.2d at 1282 n. 29. * * *

C. Enhanced Judicial Scrutiny of a Sale or Change of Control Transaction

Board action in the circumstances presented here is subject to enhanced scrutiny. * * * In *Macmillan*, this Court held:

> When *Revlon* duties devolve upon directors, this Court will continue to exact an enhanced judicial scrutiny at the threshold, as in *Unocal*, before the normal presumptions of the business judgment rule will apply.

* * * The key features of an enhanced scrutiny test are: (a) a judicial determination regarding the adequacy of the decisionmaking process employed by the directors, including the information on which the directors based their decision; and (b) a judicial examination of the reasonableness of the directors' action in light of the circumstances then existing. The directors have the burden of proving that they were adequately informed and acted reasonably. * * *

[A] court applying enhanced judicial scrutiny should be deciding whether the directors made **a reasonable** decision, not **a perfect** decision. If a board selected one of several reasonable alternatives, a court should not second-guess that choice even though it might have decided otherwise or subsequent events may have cast doubt on the board's determination. * * *

D. *Revlon* and *Time–Warner* Distinguished

The Paramount defendants and Viacom assert that the fiduciary obligations and the enhanced judicial scrutiny discussed above are not implicated in this case in the absence of a "break-up" of the corporation, and that the order granting the preliminary injunction should be reversed. This argument is based on their erroneous interpretation of our decisions in *Revlon* and *Time–Warner*.

In *Revlon*, we reviewed the actions of the board of directors of Revlon, Inc. ("Revlon"), which had rebuffed the overtures of Pantry Pride, Inc. and had instead entered into an agreement with Forstmann Little & Co. ("Forstmann") providing for the acquisition of 100 percent of Revlon's outstanding stock by Forstmann and the subsequent break-up of Revlon. Based on the facts and circumstances present in *Revlon*, we held that "[t]he directors' role changed from defenders of the corporate bastion to auctioneers charged with getting the best price for the stockholders at a sale of the company." 506 A.2d at 182. We further held that "when a board ends an intense bidding contest on an insubstantial basis, ... [that] action cannot withstand the enhanced scrutiny which *Unocal* requires of director conduct." *Id.* at 184.

It is true that one of the circumstances bearing on these holdings was the fact that "the break-up of the company ... had become a reality which even the directors embraced." *Id.* at 182. It does not follow, however, that a "break-up" must be present and "inevitable" before directors are subject to enhanced judicial scrutiny and are required to pursue a transaction that is calculated to produce the best value reasonably available to the stockholders. In fact, we stated in *Revlon* that "when bidders make relatively similar offers, or dissolution of the company becomes inevitable, the directors cannot fulfill their enhanced *Unocal* duties by playing favorites with the contending factions." *Id.* at 184 (emphasis added). *Revlon* thus does not hold that an inevitable dissolution or "break-up" is necessary.

The decisions of this Court following *Revlon* reinforced the applicability of enhanced scrutiny and the directors' obligation to seek the best value reasonably available for the stockholders where there is a pending sale of control, regardless of whether or not there is to be a break-up of the corporation * * *

[T]he Paramount defendants have interpreted our decision in *Time–Warner* as requiring a corporate break-up in order for that obligation to apply. The facts in *Time–Warner,* however, were quite different from the facts of this case, and refute Paramount's position here. In *Time–Warner,* the Chancellor held that there was no change of control in the original stock-for-stock merger between Time and Warner because Time would be owned by a fluid aggregation of unaffiliated stockholders both before and after the merger * * * Moreover, the transaction actually consummated in *Time–Warner* was not a merger, as originally planned, but a sale of Warner's stock to Time. * * *

[T]he Paramount defendants here have argued that a break-up is a requirement and have focused on the following language in our *Time–Warner* decision:

> However, we premise our rejection of plaintiffs' *Revlon* claim on different grounds, namely, the absence of any substantial evidence to conclude that Time's board, in negotiating with Warner, made the dissolution or break-up of the corporate entity inevitable, as was the case in *Revlon.*
>
> Under Delaware law there are, generally speaking and **without excluding other possibilities,** two circumstances which may implicate *Revlon* duties. The first, and clearer one, is when a corporation **initiates an active bidding process seeking to sell itself** or to effect a business reorganization involving a clear break-up of the company. However, *Revlon* duties may also be triggered where, in response to a bidder's offer, a target abandons its long-term strategy and seeks an alternative transaction involving the breakup of the company.

Id. at 1150 (emphasis added) (citation and footnote omitted).

The Paramount defendants have misread the holding of *Time–Warner.* Contrary to their argument, our decision in *Time–Warner* expressly states that the two general scenarios discussed in the above-quoted paragraph are not the **only** instances where "*Revlon* duties" may be implicated. The Paramount defendants' argument totally ignores the phrase "without excluding other possibilities." Moreover, the instant case is clearly within the first general scenario set forth in *Time–Warner.* The Paramount Board, albeit unintentionally, had "initiate[d] an active bidding process seeking to sell itself" by agreeing to sell control of the corporation to Viacom in circumstances where another potential acquiror (QVC) was equally interested in being a bidder.

The Paramount defendants' position that **both** a change of control **and** a break-up are **required** must be rejected. Such a holding would unduly restrict the application of *Revlon,* is inconsistent with this Court's decisions in *Barkan* and *Macmillan,* and has no basis in policy. There are few events that have a more significant impact on the stockholders than a sale of control or a corporate break-up. * * *

Accordingly, when a corporation undertakes a transaction which will cause: (a) a change in corporate control; **or** (b) a break-up of the corporate entity, the directors' obligation is to seek the best value reasonably available to the stockholders. This obligation arises because the effect of the Viacom–Paramount transaction, if consummated, is to shift control of Paramount from the public stockholders to a controlling stockholder, Viacom. Neither *Time–Warner* nor any other decision of this Court holds that a "break-up" of the company is essential to give rise to this obligation where there is a sale of control.

III. BREACH OF FIDUCIARY DUTIES BY PARAMOUNT BOARD

* * *

A. *The Specific Obligations of the Paramount Board*

Under the facts of this case, the Paramount directors had the obligation: (a) to be diligent and vigilant in examining critically the Paramount–Viacom transaction and the QVC tender offers; (b) to act in good faith; (c) to obtain, and act with due care on, all material information reasonably available, including information necessary to compare the two offers to determine which of these transactions, or an alternative course of action, would provide the best value reasonably available to the stockholders; and (d) to negotiate actively and in good faith with both Viacom and QVC to that end.

Having decided to sell control of the corporation, the Paramount directors were required to evaluate critically whether or not all material aspects of the Paramount–Viacom transaction (separately and in the aggregate) were reasonable and in the best interests of the Paramount stockholders in light of current circumstances, including: the change of control premium, the Stock Option Agreement, the Termination Fee, the coercive nature of both the Viacom and QVC tender offers,[6] the No–Shop Provision, and the proposed disparate use of the Rights Agreement as to the Viacom and QVC tender offers, respectively.

These obligations necessarily implicated various issues, including the questions of whether or not [the defensive provisions] and other aspects of the Paramount–Viacom transaction (separately and in the aggregate): (a) adversely affected the value provided to the Paramount stockholders; (b) inhibited or encouraged alternative bids; (c) were enforceable contractual obligations in light of the directors' fiduciary duties; and (d) in the end would advance or retard the Paramount directors' obligation to secure for the Paramount stockholders the best value reasonably available under the circumstances.

The Paramount defendants contend that they were precluded by certain contractual provisions, including the No–Shop Provision, from negotiating with QVC

---

6   Both the Viacom and the QVC tender offers were for 51 percent cash and a "back-end" of various securities, the value of each of which depended on the fluctuating value of Viacom and QVC stock at any given time. Thus, both tender offers were two-tiered, front-end loaded, and coercive. Such coercive offers are inherently problematic and should be expected to receive particularly careful analysis by a target board. *See Unocal,* 493 A.2d at 956.

or seeking alternatives. Such provisions, whether or not they are presumptively valid in the abstract, may not validly define or limit the directors' fiduciary duties under Delaware law or prevent the Paramount directors from carrying out their fiduciary duties under Delaware law. To the extent such provisions are inconsistent with those duties, they are invalid and unenforceable. *See Revlon*, 506 A.2d at 184–85.

Since the Paramount directors had already decided to sell control, they had an obligation to continue their search for the best value reasonably available to the stockholders. This continuing obligation included the responsibility, at the October 24 board meeting and thereafter, to evaluate critically both the QVC tender offers and the Paramount–Viacom transaction * * *

B. The Breaches of Fiduciary Duty by the Paramount Board

The Paramount directors made the decision [that] a strategic merger with Viacom on the economic terms of the Original Merger Agreement was in the best interests of Paramount and its stockholders. Those terms provided a modest change of control premium to the stockholders. The directors also decided at that time that it was appropriate to agree to certain defensive measures (the Stock Option Agreement, the Termination Fee, and the No–Shop Provision) insisted upon by Viacom as part of that economic transaction. Those defensive measures, coupled with the sale of control and subsequent disparate treatment of competing bidders, implicated the judicial scrutiny of *Unocal, Revlon, Macmillan,* and their progeny. We conclude that the Paramount directors' process was not reasonable, and the result achieved for the stockholders was not reasonable under the circumstances.

* * * [T]he Paramount Board clearly gave insufficient attention to the potential consequences of the defensive measures demanded by Viacom. The Stock Option Agreement had a number of unusual and potentially "draconian" provisions, including the Note Feature and the Put Feature. Furthermore, the Termination Fee, whether or not unreasonable by itself, clearly made Paramount less attractive to other bidders, when coupled with the Stock Option Agreement. Finally, the No–Shop Provision inhibited the Paramount Board's ability to negotiate with other potential bidders, particularly QVC which had already expressed an interest in Paramount. * * *

The Paramount directors had the opportunity * * *, when the Original Merger Agreement was renegotiated, to take appropriate action to modify the improper defensive measures as well as to improve the economic terms of the Paramount–Viacom transaction. Under the circumstances existing at that time, it should have been clear to the Paramount Board that the Stock Option Agreement, coupled with the Termination Fee and the No–Shop Clause, were impeding the realization of the best value reasonably available to the Paramount stockholders. Nevertheless, the Paramount Board made no effort to eliminate or modify these counterproductive devices, and instead continued to cling to its vision of a strategic alliance with Viacom. Moreover, based on advice from the Paramount management, the Paramount directors considered the QVC offer to be "conditional" and asserted that they were precluded by the No–Shop Provision from seeking more information from, or negotiating with, QVC.

By November 12, 1993, the value of the revised QVC offer on its face exceeded that of the Viacom offer by over $1 billion at then current values. This significant disparity of value cannot be justified on the basis of the directors' vision of future strategy, primarily because the change of control would supplant the authority of the current Paramount Board to continue to hold and implement their strategic vision in any meaningful way. * * *

When the Paramount directors met on November 15 to consider QVC's increased tender offer, they remained prisoners of their own misconceptions and missed opportunities to eliminate the restrictions they had imposed on themselves. * * * [T]he Paramount directors remained paralyzed by their uninformed belief that the QVC offer was "illusory." This final opportunity to negotiate on the stockholders' behalf and to fulfill their obligation to seek the best value reasonably available was thereby squandered.

IV. VIACOM'S CLAIM OF VESTED CONTRACT RIGHTS

Viacom argues that it had certain "vested" contract rights with respect to the No–Shop Provision and the Stock Option Agreement. In effect, Viacom's argument is that the Paramount directors could enter into an agreement in violation of their fiduciary duties and then render Paramount, and ultimately its stockholders, liable for failing to carry out an agreement in violation of those duties. Viacom's protestations about vested rights are without merit. This Court has found that those defensive measures were improperly designed to deter potential bidders, and that such measures do not meet the reasonableness test to which they must be subjected. They are consequently invalid and unenforceable under the facts of this case. * * *

V. CONCLUSION

The realization of the best value reasonably available to the stockholders became the Paramount directors' primary obligation under these facts in light of the change of control. That obligation was not satisfied, and the Paramount Board's process was deficient. * * * QVC's unsolicited bid presented the opportunity for significantly greater value for the stockholders and enhanced negotiating leverage for the directors. Rather than seizing those opportunities, the Paramount directors chose to wall themselves off from material information which was reasonably available and to hide behind the defensive measures as a rationalization for refusing to negotiate with QVC or seeking other alternatives. Their view of the strategic alliance likewise became an empty rationalization as the opportunities for higher value for the stockholders continued to develop. * * *

NOTES AND QUESTIONS

I. HOW MUCH DISCRETION does a board of directors have to wrap up a deal for the sale of a corporation? To answer this question requires coming to grips with what the former Chief Justice of the Delaware Supreme Court, Justice Veasey, who wrote the opinion in *Paramount v. QVC*, has called the "defining tension" in corporate governance today. For Justice Veazey this is "the tension between deference to directors' decisions and the scope of judicial review." E. Norman Veasey, *The Defining Tension in Corporate Governance in America*, 52 Bus. Law. 393, 403 (1997). Do you agree or disagree with the Delaware Supreme Court's resolution of these issues in *Time v. Paramount* and *Paramount v. QVC*? Can you explain why the discretion of the board is affirmed in the first case and overruled in the second?

Both of these cases were controversial, although, among scholars, there has probably been greater approval of what the Delaware Supreme Court did in *Paramount v. QVC*. Can you understand why this might be true? For an entertaining review of *Paramount v. QVC*, with some pointed criticisms of *Time v. Paramount*, see Ehud Kamar, "The Story of Paramount Communications v. QVC Network: Everything is Personal," Chapter 10 of J. Mark Ramseyer, ed. *Corporate Law Stories* 293 (2009)

....

2. FOLLOWING *REVLON*, the crucial determination was whether the corporation which was the target of a hostile bid was in "*Unocal Mode*," in which situation the Board could decide that resistance was appropriate, or in "*Revlon Mode*," when it could not. You have just read the two important cases attempting to elucidate this point. In the first, Time shareholders challenged Time's decision to form an alliance with Warner Brothers, rather than to accept a tender offer from Paramount, since Paramount was offering a price for Time shares much higher than market, and the deal with Warner, as it worked out, simply involved a purchase of Warner, putting Time 10 billion dollars in debt. There was, as you saw, some question whether Time was in "*Unocal*" or "*Revlon*" mode. Time had been courting strategic partners for a possible merger, and some Time shareholders argued that Time was, in fact, putting itself up for sale, thus triggering *Revlon* duties to garner the best price for shareholders. Paramount argued that even if Time was simply in *Unocal Mode*, Paramount's all-cash all-shares offer could not be perceived as presenting a threat to the corporation, and Time should not be permitted to consummate its deal with Warner, which would have precluded Paramount's purchase of Time.

The Delaware Court rejected the contention that Time was in *Revlon Mode*, ostensibly because it had never actually put itself on the auction block and because not only was no breakup of Time inevitable, it actually was following a strategy which enhanced rather than diminished its ongoing business. Considering that Time was in *Unocal Mode*, then, the Court declared that resisting Paramount's bid, and deciding to acquire Warner was a valid defensive strategy, and deferred to the Time Board's decision that an alliance with Warner was in Time's long-term best interests, and thus in the long term best interests of the shareholders. The Time Board, said the Delaware Court, could reasonably decide that a combination with Warner would result in the long term prospects for shareholder value being greater than the price Paramount was offering now. Do you agree?

In *Paramount v. QVC*, as you remember, the Delaware Supreme Court distinguished the situation from *Time v. Paramount*. Following its unsuccessful courtship of Time, Paramount sought a "strategic alliance" with Viacom, a corporation whose cable interests and other pursuits, in the opinion of Paramount management, maximized Paramount's prospects. This was to be accomplished through a tender offer by Viacom for Paramount. QVC then made a competing tender offer for Paramount, which Paramount rebuffed, on the grounds that even though QVC was offering a nominally higher price, a long-term alliance with Viacom would result in the most value for shareholders. Paramount pointed to the *Time v. Paramount* case, where the court had enthusiastically endorsed Time's similar strategic plan. The Delaware Supreme Court held, however, that since a new entity was to gain majority control of Paramount, this meant that Paramount was in *Revlon Mode* and its duty was to get the highest price for shareholders. Paramount had argued that no bust-up was contemplated, and that it had not put Paramount up for sale, and that, in prior cases, these two things seemed to have been required before *Revlon Mode* could exist. The Court rejected this argument, and held that any time majority control changes it is a "*Revlon*" rather than a "*Unocal*" situation. Does that make sense?

......

3. THE DELAWARE SUPREME COURT returned to a consideration of *Revlon* in 2009 in *Lyondell Chem. Co. v. Ryan*, 970 A.2d 235 (Del. 2009). Lyondell, a large chemical company, agreed to an acquisition by Basell AF after several rounds of negotiations. The merger agreement contained Basell's final offer for $48 per share (up from an initial $40), a fiduciary out provision, and a $385 million termination fee should Lyondell choose another bid. A shareholder filed suit, contending that the negotiation process was flawed and that the deal protection apparatus was unreasonable. The *Lyondell* court described the claims as "two aspects of a single claim, under *Revlon* . . . that the directors failed to obtain the best available price in selling the company." *Id.* at 239.

The Chancery court had found good grounds to believe that the Lyondell board had breached its duties due to its "slothful indifference"; the board had "languidly awaited overtures" from other bidders after Basell had announced its interest in the company, having taken a wait-and-see approach. The Delaware Supreme Court reversed, finding that Basell's announcement, although it put Lyondell on notice that it was in play, did not trigger *Revlon* duties. Rather, *Revlon* duties were only triggered when the Lyondell directors actively began negotiating the company's sale to Basell.

The problem with the trial court's analysis is that *Revlon* duties do not arise simply because a company is "in play." The duty to seek the best available price applies only when a company embarks on a transaction-on its own initiative or in response to an unsolicited offer-that will result in a change of control.

Lyondell at 242. The board's subsequent negotiations, which were well-informed and raised the per share offer by 20%, were found to have met *Revlon* requirements. *Lyondell* reiterates that *Revlon* does not require a specific course of action (such as an auction) to be taken; just that the board choose a method which maximizes shareholder value.

. . . .

4. FOLLOWING THESE TWO CASES the Delaware Supreme Court was confronted with another interesting endgame situation in *Omnicare, Inc. v. NCS Healthcare, Inc.*, 818 A.2d 914 (Del. 2003). NCS Healthcare ("NCS") was an insolvent pharmacy services provider, which for many months had been seeking a merger partner to bail it out of its financial difficulties. NCS had retained two different investment banks as advisors in its search for a merger partner, and it considered about fifty different entities. At one point it sought to sell itself to Omnicare, another corporation in the same line of business, but Omnicare indicated that it was not interested in anything but a purchase of NCS's assets in a bankruptcy proceeding. This meant that while there might be some relief for NCS's creditors through a deal with Omnicare, NCS's shareholders would receive no consideration for their stock. Still another corporation in the same line of business, Genesis Health Ventures ("Genesis"), however, did offer a transaction which appeared more advantageous to NCS's board, because it indicated it was willing not only to enter into a deal which would have provided full relief to the debt holders, but also would have provided $1.00 per share to the common shareholders. By this time NCS's fortunes had improved somewhat, and Omnicare abruptly changed its views, and proposed to acquire NCS and pay a higher rate, $3.00, for the NCS shares. In the words of the Court, however, "Omnicare's proposal . . . was expressly conditioned on negotiating a merger agreement, obtaining certain third party consents, and [Omnicare's] completing its due diligence." NCS was wary of Omnicare, however, and while NCS was able to use Omnicare's new interest as leverage to get Genesis to offer a higher price than the $3.00 for the common shareholders, Genesis insisted that if it was going to go forward with any deal with NCS, NCS had to agree to submit the NCS merger deal to a vote by its shareholders even if there were a competing offer which was more attractive to the Board, and Genesis also managed to get the two majority shareholders in NCS contractually to agree to vote their shares in support of the deal with Genesis. Finally, Genesis insisted that the NCS Board not have a "fiduciary out" clause in the merger agreement with Genesis. (Such a clause would have permitted the NCS Board to back out of the merger agreement if it determined that its fiduciary obligations required such a move.) Omnicare then launched a tender offer for NCS shares at a price slightly higher than that Genesis was offering, and asked the Delaware courts to invalidate the NCS/Genesis deal and the majority shareholder agreements.

NCS argued that its decision to go with the Genesis deal was a proper exercise of the directors' business judgment, especially in light of the fact that Genesis, at the time negotiations first began with NCS, was the only firm that was offering relief to NCS's shareholders, and Genesis had insisted on "lock-up" arrangements because Genesis had had a prior unpleasant experience where Omnicare bested it in a struggle to acquire another entity by coming in at the last moment, and offering a higher price. The Delaware Supreme Court, in a rare 3–2 decision, ruled for Omnicare, and declared that NCS's attempt to "lock-up" the deal with Genesis impermissibly violated the NCS board's fiduciary duties to its shareholders, and was impermissibly "draconian" and "preclusive."

Two very powerful dissents were filed in the Omnicare case. One was by then Chief Justice Veasey, himself, who stated that:

> The process by which this merger agreement came about involved a joint decision by the controlling stockholders and the board of directors to secure what appeared to be the only value-enhancing transaction available for a company on the brink of bankruptcy. The Majority adopts a new rule of law that imposes a prohibition on the NCS board's ability to act in concert with controlling stockholders to lock up this merger. The Majority reaches this conclusion by analyzing the challenged deal protection measures as isolated board actions. The Majority concludes that the board owed a duty to the NCS minority stockholders to refrain from acceding to the Genesis demand for an irrevocable lock-up notwithstanding the compelling circumstances confronting the board and the board's disinterested, informed, good faith exercise of its business judgment. Because we believe this Court must respect the reasoned judgment of the board of directors and give effect to the wishes of the controlling stockholders, we respectfully disagree with the Majority's reasoning that results in a holding that the confluence of board and stockholder action constitutes a breach of fiduciary duty. The essential fact that must always be remembered is that this agreement and the voting commitments of [the two majority shareholders] concluded a lengthy search and intense negotiation process in the context of insolvency and creditor pressure where no other viable bid had emerged.

The other dissent was by Justice Steele (who, as this volume is written, is now the Chief Justice), who observed that

> Delaware corporate citizens now face the prospect that in *every* circumstance, boards must obtain the highest price, even if that requires breaching a contract entered into at a time when no one could have reasonably foreseen a truly "Superior Proposal." The majority's proscriptive rule limits the scope of a board's cost benefit analysis by taking the bargaining chip of foregoing a fiduciary out "off the table" in all circumstances. For that new principle to arise from the context of this case, when Omnicare, after striving to buy NCS on the cheap by buying off its creditors, slinked back into the fray, reversed its historic antagonistic strategy and offered a conditional "Superior Proposal" seems entirely counterintuitive.

Who gets it right, in light of *Time v. Paramount* and *Paramount v. QVC*—the majority in *Omnicare*, who held that the Board's duty was to get the highest price for the shareholders, or the dissent, who believed that the Board ought to have the discretion to favor a bird in hand over a bird in the bush?

....

5. OMNICARE CREATED QUITE A STIR:

> "When the Delaware Supreme Court issued its opinion in *Omnicare Inc. v. NCS Healthcare Inc.* * * * some observers called the decision the court's most important in a generation [because by] holding that a target company couldn't irrevocably lock up an agreement to sell itself, *Omnicare* turned its back on Delaware's strong preference for vesting boards of directors with broad discretionary powers."

David Marcus, *Disney's Dudley Do-Wrong, Daily Deal*, June 16, 2003, available at 2003 WL 4169554, quoted in Wayne O. Hanewicz, Director Primacy, Omnicare, and the Function of Corporate Law, 71 Tenn. L. Rev. 511, 512 n.6 (2004). Mr. Marcus concluded that "The ruling may have a very short shelf life." As this book went to press, however, in 2013, *Omnicare* was still good law. Intriguingly, *Omnicare* has its defenders. For subtle appreciation of the majority's opinion, see Hanewicz, *supra*. Given the majority's decision in *Omnicare*, do you suppose those in corporate boardrooms will be more comfortable? Is there any similarity between the 3 to 2 *Omnicare* ruling and the 3 to 2 decision in *Smith v. Van Gorkom*?

In an informative piece posted on the web in August of 2005, "*Omnicare v. NCS Healthcare*—More Bark than Bite?", three lawyers from Morrison and Foerster,

Michael G. O'Bryan, Lawrence T. Yanowitch, and Jacob D. Bernstein argue that *Omnicare* "has ended up having relatively little impact on the M & A landscape, in part because parties to M & A transactions have discovered ways to work within its constraints." See http://www.mofo.com/news/updates/files/update02057.html (accessed 12 November 2009). Thus, these authors point out, it is possible to avoid the difficulties of *Omnicare* if, for example, stockholder approval follows immediately following execution of the merger agreement, although they imply that it might still be a wise move to insert a "fiduciary out provision in the merger agreement. In fact, fiduciary outs have become ubiquitous in post-*Omnicare* mergers. "Since 2003, this judicially-mandated put has been universally present in all merger agreements." Brian J.M. Quinn, *Optionality in Merger Agreements*, 35 Del. J. Corp. L. 789, 799 (2010).

The Morrison and Foerster authors also note that the only post-*Omnicare* "deal protection" case from the Delaware court, *Orman v. Cullman*, 2004 Del. Ch. LEXIS 150, upheld a majority shareholder agreement similar to the one in the *Omnicare* case where the board was still free to consider other unsolicited acquisition proposals, where the board reserved the right to withdraw their recommendation of the acquisition proposal in question, and where approval was still needed from a majority of the minority public shareholders. Thus, as the dissenters in *Omnicare* suggested, *Omnicare* may be limited to its facts, a situation where it is "mathematically certain" that a transaction that is the subject of a "lock-up" will occur. Finally, as Messrs. O'Bryan, Yanowitch, and Bernstein observed in passing, "Justice Joseph Walsh, whose vote was one of three comprising the Omnicare majority, has since retired. The swing vote now rests in the hands of the recently sworn-in Justice and former Vice-Chancellor Jack Jacobs. Nobody knows whether Justice Jacobs would support the *Omnicare* majority decision, but clearly the *Omnicare* majority is not as secure today as it was before Justice Walsh retired." Note, then, how important the identity of the particular five members of the Delaware Supreme Court is, just as is true for the nine members of the United States Supreme Court. See also, for an argument that the impact of *Omnicare* may be limited, Daniel C. Davis, "Omnicare v. NCS Healthcare: A Critical Appraisal," 4 Berkeley Business Law Journal 177, 203 (2007) which asserts that "If *Omnicare* is applied broadly, it would be reasonable to expect some level of legislative intervention, much like the addition of Section 102(b)(7) to the DGCL following the *Van Gorkom* decision."

If you're having a little trouble grasping just when "Revlon Mode" or "Unocal Mode" occurs, you're not alone. When there is no certainty that there will be competing bidders, how does one measure value, and when should a court upset the calculation made by incumbent management? We next take a brief detour from analyzing proper procedures for officers and directors, and consider this matter of substance, the value of shares in a corporation. How should courts figure value? This becomes especially relevant when minority shareholders, who have lost influence in a merger or acquisition, assert their right to have their shares appraised.

You have probably also observed that a major issue in these takeover defensive cases, an issue that we've touched on in earlier chapters, is for whom the directors and officers should act as trustees, or, if you like, what should be the social responsibility of corporations. For further thoughts on these matters, and for further evaluation of how contemporary theories of corporate responsibilities can be integrated with governance implications, see Timothy L. Fort, *Ethics and Governance: Business as Mediating Institution* (Oxford University Press, 2001). For a provocative analysis of how consensus notions of ethical business behavior might contribute to general conditions of social harmony, see Timothy L. Fort & Cindy A. Schipani, *The Role of Business in Fostering Peaceful Societies* (Cambridge University Press, 2004).

II. Valuation

UNTIL THE 1983 DECISION of *Weinberger v. UOP, Inc.* (which you will read in the next section), the Delaware Supreme Court exclusively used the so-called "Delaware Block Method" in appraisal proceedings. Using this tool, a judge would determine the relative weights of three factors in valuing a corporation's shares: its asset, market, and earnings values. *See* In Re *Radiology Assocs., Inc. Litigation*, 611 A.2d 486, 496 (Del. Ch. 1991). *Weinberger* released the Delaware courts from the exclusive use of this method in favor of "any techniques or methods which are generally considered acceptable in the financial community and otherwise admissible in court," subject to statute. *Weinberger v. UOP, Inc.*, 457 A.2d 701, 713 (Del. 1983). While the Delaware Block Method remains a valid test, and a wide array of others are available to the courts, one method has risen to pre-eminence: the discounted cash flow (DCF) analysis. DCF uses three factors to value shares: (1) cash flow projections over a certain period (often five years), (2) a terminal value, and (3) a discount rate. These could be described, over-simply, as (1) revenue less expenses, (2) the expected cash flows after the projection period, and (3) the rate of the company's costs in obtaining capital.

In other words, DCF can be used to determine the *current* value of *future* cash flows. See Balotti and Finkelstein's Del. L. of Corp. and Bus. Org. § 9.45 (2013). Furthermore, it analyzes this value at the time of the merger, helpfully ignoring subsequent events and influences to the share price. The next case is from the Delaware Chancery, and illustrates how a court might apply DCF.

In re Radiology Assocs., Inc. Litigation

Court of Chancery of Delaware, New Castle County
611 A.2d 485, (Del. Ch. 1991).

OPINION: CHANDLER, V.C.

[The DCF appraisal rose from a suit for breach of contract and fiduciary duties brought by a minority shareholder (Dr. Kurtz) in a medical company following a questionable merger. This order concerns formulating damages and appraising the value of the plaintiff's shares.]

II. THE FAIR VALUE OF DR. KURTZ'S SHARES

Plaintiff, Dr. Kurtz, challenges the fairness of the merger price. Plaintiff contends that Radiology's fair value was $2300 per share on May 6, 1987, the merger date. Plaintiff's conclusion rests primarily on the testimony of his valuation expert, Anne Danyluk, who is manager of Valuation Services at Coopers & Lybrand's Philadelphia office. Defendants dispute this conclusion and contend that the fair value was $457 per share on the merger date. Defendants' conclusion rests primarily on the testimony of their valuation expert, Charles Stryker, who is a business valuator for the "Benchmark" subsidiary of KPMG Peat Marwick. * * *

A. Plaintiff's Valuation Methodology

Plaintiff's expert attempted to value Radiology by using two different methods: (1) a comparable company approach and (2) a discounted cash flow approach. Further, after determining the outcomes from the methods, plaintiff's expert argued that adjustments to the results were necessary in order to account for Radiology's S corporation status; in order to include Radiology's non-operating assets; and in order to alleviate the minority discount implicit in its valuation methods.

1. The Comparable Company Method

The comparable company approach attempts to value companies first by finding comparable publicly-traded companies. *See Harris v. Rapid–American Corp.*, Del. Ch., C.A. No. 6462, 1990 WL 146488, Chandler, V.C. (Oct. 2, 1990), slip op. at 19. After identifying a comparable company, this approach calculates the value of the company through the use of earnings and other multiples. *See id.* at 19–20. This Court has affirmed the general validity of this approach. *See id.* at 21.

"The first step in doing a comparable companies analysis is to compile a list of comparative companies." *Id.* at 19. In this case, Ms. Danyluk chose two companies with which she wished to compare Radiology: MEDIQ Incorporated ("MEDIQ") and MMI Medical ("MMI"). The companies chosen for comparison by plaintiff's expert differ significantly from Radiology. First, MMI derives its revenue from the operation of mobile radiological units, from the leasing of such units and from providing maintenance and repair services for radiological equipment. MEDIQ derives only 24% of its revenues from diagnostic imaging services, and MEDIQ provided these services through mobile units. On the other hand, Radiology derives its revenue solely from providing non-mobile radiological services. Further, defendants point out significant differences in revenues, size, profitability, and growth rates * * *

The utility of the comparable company approach depends on the similarity between the company the court is valuing and the companies used for comparison. At some point, the differences become so large that the use of the comparable company method becomes meaningless for valuation purposes. * * * In this case, the differences between Radiology and MMI and MEDIQ as to product mix, revenues, profit margins, revenue and earnings growth rates, assets and geographic markets combine to make any comparison with Radiology meaningless.

2. The Discounted Cash Flow Method

The second method Ms. Danyluk used in attempting to value Radiology was the discounted cash flow method.

> In theory, the value of an interest in a business depends on the future benefits discounted back to a present value at some appropriate discount (capitalization) rate. Thus, the theoretically correct approach is to project the future benefits (usually earnings, cash flow, or dividends) and discount the projected stream back to a present value.

S. Pratt, *Valuing a Business* 25 (2d ed. 1989). The Delaware courts have affirmed the validity of this method of valuation repeatedly. *See Neal, supra,* at 16; *Cede & Co. v. Technicolor,* Del.Ch., C.A. No. 7129, 1990 WL 161084, Allen, C. (Oct. 19, 1990), slip op. at 17.

> The DCF model entails three basic components: an estimation of net cash flows that the firm will generate and when, over some period; a terminal or residual value equal to the future value, as of the end of the projection period, of the firm's cash flows beyond the projection period; and finally a cost of capital with which to discount to a present value both the projected net cash flows and the estimated terminal or residual value.

Cede & Co., supra, at 17–18. The quality of the projection as to the future benefits over some period and the residual or terminal value is central to the reliability of the underlying methodology of the discount cash flow method. * * *

(a) Projected Revenues and Terminal Value

* * * In this case, Ms. Danyluk used projections prepared by the Delaware Trust Company for its internal purposes of assessing an application for a multi-million dollar loan for an ESOP. It is not as important that management itself did not create the projections as much as management had input with their creation. * * * Also, Delaware Trust's projections began from fact: they created the projections by making

adjustments to and applying a growth rate to *historical* earnings. For all of these reasons, I believe that the projections are reliable and should be used in applying the discounted cash flow approach.

Ms. Danyluk, however, did not use the exact projections of the Delaware Trust Company. She adjusted the five-year revenue projection of 5% growth annually to 7% annually. Ms. Danyluk did use the 5% growth figure used by the Delaware Trust Company in her terminal year calculation.

Ms. Danyluk justified a change in the five year revenue projection by relying on three factors: historical earnings, an analysis of the industry and an analysis of other projections. The parties argue over exactly what the historical earnings growth rate was. However, the Delaware Trust Company had the information both sides put forth to argue their respective positions available when they made their projections. Thus, Ms. Danyluk's reliance on this factor for adjusting the growth rate upward is without merit since the Delaware Trust Company undoubtedly considered historical earnings in projecting a future earnings growth rate. Similarly, Ms. Danyluk's second factor, an industry analysis, reflects information available to the Delaware Trust Company when they made their projections and information to which they undoubtedly referred in creating the earnings growth rate projections. Finally, Ms. Danyluk relied on the fact that other projections predicted higher growth rates. Ms. Danyluk did not explain who made these projections, how they were different, and why they were different. The concept of "other projections," in my opinion, is too amorphous and insufficient to warrant a deviation from the Delaware Trust Company's projections as to the growth rate.

Since I have adjusted the proper growth rate in the discounted cash flow analysis down to 5%, I also must adjust expenses projected on a percentage of net sales basis (*e.g.*, general administrative expenses and adjusted depreciation). * * *

Having made the adjustments to the projected growth rate, the expenses as a percentage of net sales and "salary" expenses, I am able to determine the projected net cash flows for years 1987 through 1991 and the terminal year. These projections of net cash flow are $744,000 for 1987; $1,218,000 for 1988; $1,301,000 for 1989; $1,388,000 for 1990; $1,480,000 for 1991; and $1,556,000 for the terminal year.

(b) *Discount Rate*

Having decided what are the proper projected revenues for 1987 through 1991 and for the terminal year, the third element that this Court must calculate in applying the discounted cash flow method is the proper discount rate. The discount rate attempts to reduce the projected future revenues to present value. *See Cede & Co., supra,* at 68.

Ms. Danyluk applied a 14% discount rate. On the other hand, defendants argue that 17% or 16.5% is the proper discount rate. Ms. Danyluk arrived at her discount rate by using the Capital Asset Pricing Model ("CAPM"). "That model estimates the cost of company debt (on an after tax basis for a company expected to be able to utilize the tax deductibility of interest payments) by estimating the expected future cost of borrowing; it estimates the future cost of equity through a multi-factor equation and then proportionately weighs and combines the cost of equity and cost of debt to determine a cost of capital." *Id.* at 68. This Court has affirmed the general validity of this approach for estimating the cost of capital component in the discounted cash flow model. *See id.* at 70.

The first step in applying the CAPM is to determine the expected future cost of equity. Ms. Danyluk determined the expected future cost of equity (re) by utilizing the CAPM equation of: re = rf + B (rm-rf). The letters rf symbolize a risk free rate of return. Ms. Danyluk used 8.82% which was the U.S. government long-term bonds average for the week ending May 6, 1987, as her rf. The market risk premium, rm-rf, is equal to the excess of the market rate of return, rm, over the risk free rate of return. Ms. Danyluk used a market premium of 13.5% that research conducted at the University of Chicago by Ibbotson Associates determined to be the mean for small (*i.e.,* less than $100 million) capitalization stock interests for the period 1926 through 1986. (Pl.Exh. 74 at 13). Finally, the B is the Beta factor which represents "the nondiversified risk associated with the economy as a whole as it affects this firm." *Cede, supra,* at 69. In this case, Ms. Danyluk used a Beta of .95. After plugging these numbers into the equation, Ms. Danyluk calculated the cost of equity to be 21.6%.

The second step in applying the CAPM is to determine the after tax expected future cost of borrowing. Ms. Danyluk determined the future cost of debt by taking the interest rate of A-rated industrial bonds for the week of May 6, 1987, according to Standard & Poors' bond guide (9.8%) and reducing it by a tax rate (34%) in order to take account of the tax deductibility of interest expenses. The outcome of this calculation was 6.47%.

As discussed later, Radiology was a nontaxable entity. Thus, Radiology does not deserve its cost of debt to be reduced by taxes since it paid no taxes. Therefore, I use 9.8% as Radiology's cost of debt. To the extent plaintiff argues that I must adjust the Beta factor and the cost of equity if I make no deduction for taxes in determining the cost of debt, his arguments are, at best, conclusory and afford no basis for these adjustments.

The final step in the CAPM is to determine the weighted average cost of capital (WACC). The WACC is the weighted average of the cost of debt and equity which represents the average cost of capital. In this case, Ms. Danyluk determined that the cost of debt should carry a 49% weight and that the cost of equity should carry a 51% weight. However, Ms. Danyluk did not use Radiology's debt to equity ratio, which was 21% to 79%, in calculating the WACC. Instead, she used a hypothetical debt to equity ratio of 49% to 51%. Ms. Danyluk's justification for the use of the hypothetical ratio was that the hypothetical ratio reflected the industry average capital structure, that Radiology's deviation from the industry average reflects a hidden value (*i.e.,* underleveraging) in the company, and that the company could and should maximize shareholder value by attaining the optimal capital structure (*i.e.,* the industry average debt to equity ratio). Thus, Ms. Danyluk argued that this

Court should employ the hypothetical rather than the actual debt to equity ratio in attempting to value the company. * * *

Even if Ms. Danyluk's hypothetical capital structure represents a debt to equity ratio that is closer to the industry average, defendants argue (and I agree) that the use of the industry average rather than Radiology's actual capital structure was improper. The entire focus of the discounted cash flow analysis is to determine the fair value of Radiology. I am not attempting to determine the potential maximum value of the company. Rather, I must value Radiology, not some theoretical company. Plaintiff has introduced no evidence (*e.g.*, Radiology's debt to equity ratio trends or goals) that implies that Radiology will mimic the industry's debt to equity ratio. Given the lack of evidence as to the applicability of the industry average to Radiology, I will use Radiology's own debt to equity ratio in determining its WACC. Thus, I use 18% ([29.63% x 9.80%] + [70.37%x 21.65%] = 18.14%) as the discount rate in applying the discounted cash flow method.

In applying the discount rate to the terminal year, Ms. Danyluk subtracted her terminal growth rate (5%) from her discount rate (14%). Ms. Danyluk then reduced the terminal value to present value using her discount rate of 14%. The financial community and this Court recognizes these valuation mechanics for the terminal year as acceptable. *See* R. Brealy and S. Myers, *Principles of Corporate Finance* 64 (2d ed. 1988). Given my prior findings as to the growth rate, the net income adjustments and the discount rate, I adjust the terminal value to equal $6,020,000.

[Vice Chancellor Chandler goes on to reject two adjustments to the model proposed by the plaintiff's expert before accepting a third. He then proceeds to reject the defendants' model, the Delaware Block Method. This is not because the method is invalid, but because the expert's creation of each prong of the test (asset, market, and earnings) was fatally flawed.]

C. *Summary*

I conclude that Mr. Stryker's valuation analysis as to asset value and market value deserve no weight. I give no weight to his earnings valuation principally because of the availability of reliable projections of Radiology's earnings, and secondarily because of my doubts as to the credibility of the information supplied to him.

As far as Ms. Danyluk's analysis, I conclude that her comparable company valuation deserves no weight because of the noncomparability of the companies chosen. Thus, I am left to use Ms. Danyluk's discounted cash flow valuation. However, as discussed earlier, I use only a 5% growth rate and do not use her implicit minority discount adjustment. Also, I do not use her S–Corp. adjustment directly. Therefore, I find the fair value of plaintiff's shares [to be $271,000.00].

NOTES AND QUESTIONS

1. AS YOU MAY HAVE ALREADY DISCERNED, lawyers and judges are leery of numbers. Valuation presents a particular problem for them. You have encountered the valuation problem before, in *Smith v. Van Gorkom*. There, you may remember, the Board members of Trans Union, most notably the CEO, Jerome Van Gorkom, believed that the only manner in which value could really be discerned was a "market test." In other words, there may really be no such thing as "intrinsic value," contrary to the belief of the three-person majority of the Delaware Supreme Court in its opinion in the *Smith* case. Is believing in "intrinsic value" like believing in Santa Claus or the Easter Bunny? Do you believe in "intrinsic value?" How might you discern it? As you have seen, the problem often comes up in the case of thinly-traded stock in closely-held corporations, especially in merger situations, when dissenters (those who don't want to remain after the merger) seek valuation of their stock and a buy-out of their shares.

2. YOU MIGHT WONDER how a judge determines which valuation model to use in a particular case. Care is taken to ensure that the model chosen is appropriate to the industry or company in question, with the belief it will more accurately determine the share value than others. The chosen model can be proposed by the plaintiff, defendant, or independently by the judge herself. Furthermore, both the plaintiff and defendant might propose the same analysis, such as DCF. In such a case, the particulars of the analysis, its inputs and exceptions, can be disputed by the parties. In any valuation proceeding, each party will pit a financial expert witness against the opposition to argue in favor of their chosen model or parameters. As you might imagine, the details can become mind-bogglingly complex. Furthermore, judges prefer to use models that management had created in the process of the merger, rather than those created by litigants for the lawsuit, in the belief that the models relied upon in the transaction will be more accurate than those tailored in adversarial proceedings.

3. ALTHOUGH THE DELAWARE BLOCK METHOD is not used as often as in the past, it formed an extremely important part of mergers and acquisitions law for many years in many states. As you know, the method relies on three inputs: asset, market, and earnings values. A judge might create a "block" which weighted market value at 10% of share price, earnings value at 40%, and net asset value at 50%. As long as these ranges were "reasonable" (they are reviewable by higher courts), a judge's discretion would stand. For a good example for a court applying the Delaware Block Method to an actual case, see *Piemonte v. New Boston Garden Corp.*, 387 N.E.2d 1145 (Mass.

1979). Can you see why companies might prefer the more complex DCF method? Can you see why lawyers might appreciate the Delaware Block Method's parameters? Consider this language from the Delaware Supreme Court in a Block Method case:

> [S]ince intrinsic or true value is to be ascertained, the problem will not be settled by the acceptance as the sole measure of only one element entering into value without considering other elements. For example, * * * market value may not be taken as the sole measure of the value of the stock. So, also, since value is to be fixed on a going-concern basis, the liquidating value of the stock may not be accepted as the sole measure.

> *Tri-Cont'l Corp. v. Battye*, 74 A.2d 71, 72 (Del. 1950).

4. A PARTICULARLY ACUTE NEED for valuation comes for those practicing mergers and acquisitions law, when they may need to defend a client's behavior in resisting a tender offer, or, perhaps, defend a client's bid for a target. In a splendidly sophisticated study of such valuation techniques Dean Samuel Thompson, of the University of Miami School of Law, reports that:

> There are many techniques for determining the value of the assets or shares of a target corporation. These include: (1) valuation based on comparable target corporations—similar to the traditional technique for valuing real estate; (2) valuation based on comparable transactions—looking to transactions that are similar to the one in which the stock or assets of the target are being acquired; (3) valuation based on the liquidation value of the assets of the target corporation; (4) valuation based on the replacement value of the target's assets; (5) valuation based on a leveraged buyout (LBO) analysis by a financial buyer; and (6) valuation based on the discounting to present value of the target's expected future cash flows through the use of the discounted cash flow (DCF) technique, with the discount rate determined by the use of (a) the capital asset pricing model (CAPM), (b) arbitrage pricing theory (APT), or (c) the weighted average cost of capital (WACC). * * *

Samuel C. Thompson, Jr., *A Lawyer's Guide to Modern Valuation Techniques in Mergers and Acquisitions*, 21 Iowa J. Corp. L. 457, 460–461 (1996). For more detailed explanations of CAPM, APT, or WACC, you'll need to consult a financial analyst or Thompson's article, but can you understand from the brief excerpt from Thompson's piece and *Radiology* why a court might cling to the Delaware Block Method? DCF may now be the preferred method for sophisticated financial analysts, but do you see merit in any of the other techniques Thompson lists? Considering the difficulty of figuring out substantive value, is it any surprise that lawyers are more comfortable evaluating procedure? Is it this preference that helps explain the outcome of the following case?

III. Freezeouts and the Entire Fairness Test

Weinberger v. UOP

Supreme Court of Delaware.
457 A.2d 701 (1983).

* * *

[MOORE, J.]

This post-trial appeal was reheard en banc from a decision of the Court of Chancery. It was brought by the class action plaintiff below, a former shareholder of UOP, Inc., who challenged the elimination of UOP's minority shareholders by a cash-out merger between UOP and its majority owner, The Signal Companies, Inc. The present Chancellor held that the terms of the merger were fair to the plaintiff and the other minority shareholders of UOP. * * *

In ruling for the defendants, the Chancellor re-stated his earlier conclusion that the plaintiff in a suit challenging a cash-out merger must allege specific acts of fraud, misrepresentation, or other items of misconduct to demonstrate the unfairness of the merger terms to the minority. We approve this rule and affirm it.

The Chancellor also held that even though the ultimate burden of proof is on the majority shareholder to show by a preponderance of the evidence that the transaction is fair, it is first the burden of the plaintiff attacking the merger to demonstrate some basis for invoking the fairness obligation. We agree with that principle. However, where corporate action has been approved by an informed vote of a majority of the minority shareholders, we conclude that the burden entirely shifts to the plaintiff to show that the transaction was unfair to the minority. * * * But in all this, the burden clearly remains on those relying on the vote to show that they completely disclosed all material facts relevant to the transaction.

Here, the record does not support a conclusion that the minority stockholder vote was an informed one. Material information, necessary to acquaint those shareholders with the bargaining positions of Signal and UOP, was withheld under circumstances amounting to a breach of fiduciary duty. We therefore conclude that this merger does not meet the test of fairness * * * and no burden thus shifted to the plaintiff by reason of the minority shareholder vote. * * *

I.

* * *

Signal is a diversified, technically based company operating through various subsidiaries. Its stock is publicly traded on the New York, Philadelphia and Pacific Stock Exchanges. UOP, formerly known as Universal Oil Products Company, was a diversified industrial company * * * Its stock was publicly held and listed on the New York Stock Exchange.

In 1974 Signal sold one of its wholly-owned subsidiaries for $420,000,000 in cash. * * * While looking to invest this cash surplus, Signal became interested in UOP as a possible acquisition. Friendly negotiations ensued, and Signal proposed to acquire a controlling interest in UOP at a price of $19 per share. UOP's representatives sought $25 per share. In the arm's length bargaining that followed, an understanding was reached whereby Signal agreed to purchase from UOP 1,500,000 shares of UOP's authorized but unissued stock at $21 per share.

This purchase was contingent upon Signal making a successful cash tender offer for 4,300,000 publicly held shares of UOP, also at a price of $21 per share. This combined method of acquisition permitted Signal to acquire 5,800,000 shares of stock, representing 50.5% of UOP's outstanding shares. The UOP board of directors advised the company's shareholders that it had no objection to Signal's tender offer at that price. Immediately before the announcement of the tender offer, UOP's common stock had been trading on the New York Stock Exchange at a fraction under $14 per share.

The negotiations between Signal and UOP occurred during April 1975, and the resulting tender offer was greatly oversubscribed. However, Signal limited its total purchase of the tendered shares so that, when coupled with the stock bought from UOP, it had achieved its goal of becoming a 50.5% shareholder of UOP.

Although UOP's board consisted of thirteen directors, Signal nominated and elected only six. Of these, five were either directors or employees of Signal. The sixth, a partner in the banking firm of Lazard Freres & Co., had been one of Signal's representatives in the negotiations and bargaining with UOP concerning the tender offer and purchase price of the UOP shares.

However, the president and chief executive officer of UOP retired during 1975, and Signal caused him to be replaced by James V. Crawford, a long-time employee and senior executive vice president of one of Signal's wholly-owned subsidiaries. Crawford succeeded his predecessor on UOP's board of directors and also was made a director of Signal.

By the end of 1977 Signal basically was unsuccessful in finding other suitable investment candidates for its excess cash, and by February 1978 considered that it had no other realistic acquisitions available to it on a friendly basis. Once again its attention turned to UOP.

The trial court found that at the instigation of certain Signal management personnel, including William W. Walkup, its board chairman, and Forrest N. Shumway, its president, a feasibility study was made concerning the possible acquisition of the balance of UOP's outstanding shares. This study was performed by two Signal officers, Charles S. Arledge, vice president (director of planning), and Andrew J. Chitiea, senior vice president (chief financial officer). Messrs. Walkup, Shumway, Arledge and Chitiea were all directors of UOP in addition to their membership on the Signal board.

Arledge and Chitiea concluded that it would be a good investment for Signal to acquire the remaining 49.5% of UOP shares at any price up to $24 each. Their report was discussed between Walkup and Shumway who, along with Arledge, Chitiea and Brewster L. Arms, internal counsel for Signal, constituted Signal's senior management. In particular, they talked about the proper price to be paid if the acquisition was pursued, purportedly keeping in mind that as UOP's majority shareholder, Signal owed a fiduciary responsibility to both its own stockholders as well as to UOP's minority. It was ultimately agreed that a meeting of Signal's Executive Committee would be called to propose that Signal acquire the remaining outstanding stock of UOP through a cash-out merger in the range of $20 to $21 per share.

The Executive Committee meeting was set for February 28, 1978. As a courtesy, UOP's president, Crawford, was invited to attend, although he was not a member of Signal's executive committee. On his arrival, and prior to the meeting, Crawford was asked to meet privately with Walkup and Shumway. He was then told of Signal's plan to acquire full ownership of UOP and was asked for his reaction to the proposed price range of $20 to $21 per share. Crawford said he thought such a price would be "generous", and that it was certainly one which should be submitted to UOP's minority shareholders for their ultimate consideration. He stated, however, that Signal's 100% ownership could cause internal problems at UOP. He believed that employees would have to be given some assurance of their future place in a fully-owned Signal subsidiary. Otherwise, he feared the departure of essential personnel. Also, many of UOP's key employees had stock option incentive programs which would be wiped out by a merger. Crawford therefore urged that some adjustment would have to be made, such as providing a comparable incentive in Signal's shares, if after the merger he was to maintain his quality of personnel and efficiency at UOP.

Thus, Crawford voiced no objection to the $20 to $21 price range, nor did he suggest that Signal should consider paying more than $21 per share for the minority interests. Later, at the Executive Committee meeting the same factors were discussed, with Crawford repeating the position he earlier took with Walkup and Shumway. Also considered was the 1975 tender offer and the fact that it had been greatly oversubscribed at $21 per share. For many reasons, Signal's management concluded that the acquisition of UOP's minority shares provided the solution to a number of its business problems.

Thus, it was the consensus that a price of $20 to $21 per share would be fair to both Signal and the minority shareholders of UOP. Signal's executive committee authorized its management "to negotiate" with UOP "for a cash acquisition of the minority ownership in UOP, Inc., with the intention of presenting a proposal to [Signal's] board of directors . . . on March 6, 1978". Immediately after this February 28, 1978 meeting, Signal issued a press release stating: "The Signal Companies, Inc.

and UOP, Inc. are conducting negotiations for the acquisition for cash by Signal of the 49.5 per cent of UOP which it does not presently own, announced Forrest N. Shumway, president and chief executive officer of Signal, and James V. Crawford, UOP president." * * *

The announcement also referred to the fact that the closing price of UOP's common stock on that day was $14.50 per share.

Two days later, on March 2, 1978, Signal issued a second press release stating that its management would recommend a price in the range of $20 to $21 per share for UOP's 49.5% minority interest. This announcement referred to Signal's earlier statement that "negotiations" were being conducted for the acquisition of the minority shares.

Between Tuesday, February 28, 1978 and Monday, March 6, 1978, a total of four business days, Crawford spoke by telephone with all of UOP's non-Signal, i.e., outside, directors. Also during that period, Crawford retained Lehman Brothers to render a fairness opinion as to the price offered the minority for its stock. He gave two reasons for this choice. First, the time schedule between the announcement and the board meetings was short (by then only three business days) and since Lehman Brothers had been acting as UOP's investment banker for many years, Crawford felt that it would be in the best position to respond on such brief notice. Second, James W. Glanville, a long-time director of UOP and a partner in Lehman Brothers, had acted as a financial advisor to UOP for many years. Crawford believed that Glanville's familiarity with UOP, as a member of its board, would also be of assistance in enabling Lehman Brothers to render a fairness opinion within the existing time constraints.

Crawford telephoned Glanville, who gave his assurance that Lehman Brothers had no conflicts that would prevent it from accepting the task. Glanville's immediate personal reaction was that a price of $20 to $21 would certainly be fair, since it represented almost a 50% premium over UOP's market price. Glanville sought a $250,000 fee for Lehman Brothers' services, but Crawford thought this too much. After further discussions Glanville finally agreed that Lehman Brothers would render its fairness opinion for $150,000.

During this period Crawford also had several telephone contacts with Signal officials. In only one of them, however, was the price of the shares discussed. In a conversation with Walkup, Crawford advised that as a result of his communications with UOP's non-Signal directors, it was his feeling that the price would have to be the top of the proposed range, or $21 per share, if the approval of UOP's outside directors was to be obtained. But again, he did not seek any price higher than $21.

Glanville assembled a three-man Lehman Brothers team to do the work on the fairness opinion. These persons examined relevant documents and information concerning UOP * * * In addition, on Friday, March 3, 1978, two members of the Lehman Brothers team flew to UOP's headquarters in Des Plaines, Illinois, to perform a "due diligence visit, during the course of which they interviewed Crawford as well as UOP's general counsel, its chief financial officer, and other key executives and personnel.

As a result, the Lehman Brothers team concluded that "the price of either $20 or $21 would be a fair price for the remaining shares of UOP". They telephoned this impression to Glanville, who was spending the weekend in Vermont.

On Monday morning, March 6, 1978, Glanville and the senior member of the Lehman Brothers team flew to Des Plaines to attend the scheduled UOP directors meeting. Glanville looked over the assembled information during the flight. The two had with them the draft of a "fairness opinion letter" in which the price had been left blank. Either during or immediately prior to the directors' meeting, the two-page "fairness opinion letter" was typed in final form and the price of $21 per share was inserted.

On March 6, 1978, both the Signal and UOP boards were convened to consider the proposed merger. Telephone communications were maintained between the two meetings. Walkup, Signal's board chairman, and also a UOP director, attended UOP's meeting with Crawford in order to present Signal's position and answer any questions that UOP's non-Signal directors might have. Arledge and Chitiea, along with Signal's other designees on UOP's board, participated by conference telephone. All of UOP's outside directors attended the meeting either in person or by conference telephone.

First, Signal's board unanimously adopted a resolution authorizing Signal to propose to UOP a cash merger of $21 per share as outlined in a certain merger agreement and other supporting documents. This proposal required that the merger be approved by a majority of UOP's outstanding minority shares voting at the stockholders meeting at which the merger would be considered, and that the minority shares voting in favor of the merger, when coupled with Signal's 50.5% interest would have to comprise at least two-thirds of all UOP shares. Otherwise the proposed merger would be deemed disapproved.

UOP's board then considered the proposal. Copies of the agreement were delivered to the directors in attendance, and other copies had been forwarded earlier to the directors participating by telephone. They also had before them UOP financial data for 1974–1977, UOP's most recent financial statements, market price information, and budget projections for 1978. In addition they had Lehman Brothers' hurriedly prepared fairness opinion letter finding the price of $21 to be fair. Glanville, the Lehman Brothers partner, and UOP director, commented on the information that had gone into preparation of the letter.

Signal also suggests that the Arledge–Chitiea feasibility study, indicating that a price of up to $24 per share would be a "good investment" for Signal, was discussed at the UOP directors' meeting. The Chancellor made no such finding, and our independent review of the record, detailed *infra*, satisfies us by a preponderance of the evidence that there was no discussion of this document at UOP's board meeting. Furthermore, it is clear beyond peradventure that nothing in that report was ever disclosed to UOP's minority shareholders prior to their approval of the merger.

After consideration of Signal's proposal, Walkup and Crawford left the meeting to permit a free and uninhibited exchange between UOP's non-Signal directors. Upon their return a resolution to accept Signal's offer was then proposed and adopted. * * *

Despite the swift board action of the two companies, the merger was not submitted to UOP's shareholders until their annual meeting on May 26, 1978. In the notice of that meeting and proxy statement sent to shareholders in May, UOP's management and board urged that the merger be approved. The proxy statement also advised:

The price was determined after *discussions* between James V. Crawford, a director of Signal and Chief Executive Officer of UOP, and officers of Signal which took place during meetings on February 28, 1978, and in the course of several subsequent telephone conversations. (Emphasis added.)

In the original draft of the proxy statement the word "negotiations" had been used rather than "discussions". However, when the Securities and Exchange Commission sought details of the "negotiations" as part of its review of these materials, the term was deleted and the word "discussions" was substituted. The proxy statement indicated that the vote of UOP's board in approving the merger had been unanimous. It also advised the shareholders that Lehman Brothers had given its opinion that the merger price of $21 per share was fair to UOP's minority. However, it did not disclose the hurried method by which this conclusion was reached.

As of the record date of UOP's annual meeting, there were 11,488,302 shares of UOP common stock outstanding, 5,688,302 of which were owned by the minority. At the meeting only 56%, or 3,208,652, of the minority shares were voted. Of these, 2,953,812, or 51.9% of the total minority, voted for the merger, and 254,840 voted against it. When Signal's stock was added to the minority shares voting in favor, a total of 76.2% of UOP's outstanding shares approved the merger while only 2.2% opposed it.

By its terms the merger became effective on May 26, 1978, and each share of UOP's stock held by the minority was automatically converted into a right to receive $21 cash.

II.

A.

A primary issue mandating reversal is the preparation by two UOP directors, Arledge and Chitiea, of their feasibility study for the exclusive use and benefit of Signal. This document was of obvious significance to both Signal and UOP. Using UOP data, it described the advantages to Signal of ousting the minority at a price range of $21–$24 per share. Mr. Arledge, one of the authors, outlined the benefits to Signal:

Purpose Of The Merger
1) Provides an outstanding investment opportunity for Signal—(Better than any recent acquisition we have seen.)
2) Increases Signal's earnings.
3) Facilitates the flow of resources between Signal and its subsidiaries—(Big factor—works both ways.)
4) Provides cost savings potential for Signal and UOP.
5) Improves the percentage of Signal's 'operating earnings' as opposed to 'holding company earnings'.

6) Simplifies the understanding of Signal.

7) Facilitates technological exchange among Signal's subsidiaries.

8) Eliminates potential conflicts of interest.

Having written those words, solely for the use of Signal, it is clear from the record that neither Arledge nor Chitiea shared this report with their fellow directors of UOP. We are satisfied that no one else did either. This conduct hardly meets the fiduciary standards applicable to such a transaction. While Mr. Walkup, Signal's chairman of the board and a UOP director, attended the March 6, 1978 UOP board meeting and testified at trial that he had discussed the Arledge–Chitiea report with the UOP directors at this meeting, the record does not support this assertion. * * *

Mr. Crawford, UOP's president, could not recall that any documents, other than a draft of the merger agreement, were sent to UOP's directors before the March 6, 1978 UOP meeting. Mr. Chitiea, an author of the report, testified that it was made available to Signal's directors, but to his knowledge it was not circulated to the outside directors of UOP. He specifically testified that he "didn't share" that information with the outside directors of UOP with whom he served.

None of UOP's outside directors who testified stated that they had seen this document* * *

Actually, it appears that a three-page summary of figures was given to all UOP directors. Its first page is identical to one page of the Arledge–Chitiea report, but this dealt with nothing more than a justification of the $21 price. * * *

The Arledge–Chitiea report speaks for itself in supporting the Chancellor's finding that a price of up to $24 was a "good investment" for Signal. It shows that a return on the investment at $21 would be 15.7% versus 15.5% at $24 per share. This was a difference of only two-tenths of one percent, while it meant over $17,000,000 to the minority. Under such circumstances, paying UOP's minority shareholders $24 would have had relatively little long-term effect on Signal, and the Chancellor's findings concerning the benefit to Signal, even at a price of $24, were obviously correct. * * *

Certainly, this was a matter of material significance to UOP and its shareholders. Since the study was prepared by two UOP directors, using UOP information for the exclusive benefit of Signal, and nothing whatever was done to disclose it to the outside UOP directors or the minority shareholders, a question of breach of fiduciary duty arises. This problem occurs because there were common Signal-UOP directors participating, at least to some extent, in the UOP board's decision-making processes without full disclosure of the conflicts they faced.[7]

---

7 Although perfection is not possible, or expected, the result here could have been entirely different if UOP had appointed an independent negotiating committee of its outside directors to deal with Signal at arm's length. * * * Since fairness in this context can be equated to conduct by a theoretical, wholly independent, board of directors acting upon the matter before them, it is unfortunate that this course apparently was neither considered nor pursued. * * * Particularly in a parent-subsidiary context, a showing that the action taken was as though each of the contending parties had in fact exerted its bargaining power against the other at arm's length is strong evidence that the transaction meets the test of fairness.* * *

B.

In assessing this situation, the Court of Chancery was required to:

> examine what information defendants had and to measure it against what
> they gave to the minority stockholders, in a context in which 'complete
> candor' is required. In other words, the limited function of the Court was
> to determine whether defendants had disclosed all information in their
> possession germane to the transaction in issue. And by 'germane' we mean,
> for present purposes, information such as a reasonable shareholder would
> consider important in deciding whether to sell or retain stock.

* * *

. . . Completeness, not adequacy, is both the norm and the mandate under present
circumstances.

* * * This is merely stating in another way the long-existing principle of Delaware
law that these Signal designated directors on UOP's board still owed UOP and its
shareholders an uncompromising duty of loyalty. The classic language of *Guth v. Loft,
Inc., Del. Supr., 23 Del. Ch. 255, 5 A.2d 503, 510 (1939),* requires no embellishment:

A public policy, existing through the years, and derived from a profound knowledge of human characteristics and motives, has established a rule that demands of a
corporate officer or director, peremptorily and inexorably, the most scrupulous observance of his duty, not only affirmatively to protect the interests of the corporation
committed to his charge, but also to refrain from doing anything that would work
injury to the corporation, or to deprive it of profit or advantage which his skill and
ability might properly bring to it, or to enable it to make in the reasonable and lawful
exercise of its powers. The rule that requires an undivided and unselfish loyalty to the
corporation demands that there shall be no conflict between duty and self-interest.

Given the absence of any attempt to structure this transaction on an arm's length
basis, Signal cannot escape the effects of the conflicts it faced, particularly when its
designees on UOP's board did not totally abstain from participation in the matter.
There is no "safe harbor" for such divided loyalties in Delaware. When directors
of a Delaware corporation are on both sides of a transaction, they are required to
demonstrate their utmost good faith and the most scrupulous inherent fairness of the
bargain. * * * The requirement of fairness is unflinching in its demand that where
one stands on both sides of a transaction, he has the burden of establishing its entire
fairness, sufficient to pass the test of careful scrutiny by the courts. * * *

There is no dilution of this obligation where one holds dual or multiple directorships, as in a parent-subsidiary context. * * * Thus, individuals who act in a
dual capacity as directors of two corporations, one of whom is parent and the other
subsidiary, owe the same duty of good management to both corporations, and in the
absence of an independent negotiating structure (see note [35] *supra*), or the directors'
total abstention from any participation in the matter, this duty is to be exercised in

light of what is best for both companies. * * * The record demonstrates that Signal has not met this obligation.

C.

The concept of fairness has two basic aspects: fair dealing and fair price. The former embraces questions of when the transaction was timed, how it was initiated, structured, negotiated, disclosed to the directors, and how the approvals of the directors and the stockholders were obtained. The latter aspect of fairness relates to the economic and financial considerations of the proposed merger, including all relevant factors: assets, market value, earnings, future prospects, and any other elements that affect the intrinsic or inherent value of a company's stock. * * * However, the test for fairness is not a bifurcated one as between fair dealing and price. All aspects of the issue must be examined as a whole since the question is one of entire fairness. However, in a non-fraudulent transaction we recognize that price may be the preponderant consideration outweighing other features of the merger. Here, we address the two basic aspects of fairness separately because we find reversible error as to both.

D.

Part of fair dealing is the obvious duty of candor * * * Moreover, one possessing superior knowledge may not mislead any stockholder by use of corporate information to which the latter is not privy * * * Delaware has long imposed this duty even upon persons who are not corporate officers or directors, but who nonetheless are privy to matters of interest or significance to their company. * * * With the well-established Delaware law on the subject, and the Court of Chancery's findings of fact here, it is inevitable that the obvious conflicts posed by Arledge and Chitiea's preparation of their "feasibility study", derived from UOP information, for the sole use and benefit of Signal, cannot pass muster.

The Arledge–Chitiea report is but one aspect of the element of fair dealing. How did this merger evolve? It is clear that it was entirely initiated by Signal. The serious time constraints under which the principals acted were all set by Signal. It had not found a suitable outlet for its excess cash and considered UOP a desirable investment, particularly since it was now in a position to acquire the whole company for itself. For whatever reasons, and they were only Signal's, the entire transaction was presented to and approved by UOP's board within four business days. * * *

* * * So far as negotiations were concerned, it is clear that they were modest at best. Crawford, Signal's man at UOP, never really talked price with Signal, except to accede to its management's statements on the subject, and to convey to Signal the UOP outside directors' view that as between the $20–$21 range under consideration, it would have to be $21. The latter is not a surprising outcome, but hardly arm's length negotiations. Only the protection of benefits for UOP's key employees and the issue of Lehman Brothers' fee approached any concept of bargaining.

As we have noted, the matter of disclosure to the UOP directors was wholly flawed by the conflicts of interest raised by the Arledge–Chitiea report. All of those conflicts were resolved by Signal in its own favor without divulging any aspect of them to UOP.

This cannot but undermine a conclusion that this merger meets any reasonable test of fairness. The outside UOP directors lacked one material piece of information generated by two of their colleagues, but shared only with Signal. True, the UOP board had the Lehman Brothers' fairness opinion, but that firm has been blamed by the plaintiff for the hurried task it performed, when more properly the responsibility for this lies with Signal. There was no disclosure of the circumstances surrounding the rather cursory preparation of the Lehman Brothers' fairness opinion. Instead, the impression was given UOP's minority that a careful study had been made, when in fact speed was the hallmark, and Mr. Glanville, Lehman's partner in charge of the matter, and also a UOP director, having spent the weekend in Vermont, brought a draft of the "fairness opinion letter" to the UOP directors' meeting on March 6, 1978 with the price left blank. We can only conclude from the record that the rush imposed on Lehman Brothers by Signal's timetable contributed to the difficulties under which this investment banking firm attempted to perform its responsibilities. Yet, none of this was disclosed to UOP's minority.

Finally, the minority stockholders were denied the critical information that Signal considered a price of $24 to be a good investment. Since this would have meant over $17,000,000 more to the minority, we cannot conclude that the shareholder vote was an informed one. Under the circumstances, an approval by a majority of the minority was meaningless. * * *

Given these particulars and the Delaware law on the subject, the record does not establish that this transaction satisfies any reasonable concept of fair dealing, and the Chancellor's findings in that regard must be reversed.

E.

Turning to the matter of price, plaintiff also challenges its fairness. His evidence was that on the date the merger was approved the stock was worth at least $26 per share. In support, he offered the testimony of a chartered investment analyst who used two basic approaches to valuation: a comparative analysis of the premium paid over market in ten other tender offer-merger combinations, and a discounted cash flow analysis.

In this breach of fiduciary duty case, the Chancellor perceived that the approach to valuation was the same as that in an appraisal proceeding. Consistent with precedent, he rejected plaintiff's method of proof and accepted defendants' evidence of value as being in accord with practice under prior case law. This means that the so-called "Delaware block" or weighted average method was employed wherein the elements of value, i.e., assets, market price, earnings, etc., were assigned a particular weight and the resulting amounts added to determine the value per share. This procedure has been in use for decades. * * * However, to the extent it excludes other generally accepted techniques used in the financial community and the courts, it is now clearly outmoded. It is time we recognize this in appraisal and other stock valuation proceedings and bring our law current on the subject.

While the Chancellor rejected plaintiff's discounted cash flow method of valuing UOP's stock, as not corresponding with "either logic or the existing law" * * * it is significant that this was essentially the focus, i.e., earnings potential of UOP, of Messrs. Arledge and Chitiea in their evaluation of the merger. Accordingly, the standard "Delaware block" or weighted average method of valuation, formerly employed in appraisal and other stock valuation cases, shall no longer exclusively control such proceedings. We believe that a more liberal approach must include proof of value by any techniques or methods which are generally considered acceptable in the financial community and otherwise admissible in court * * *. This will obviate the very structured and mechanistic procedure that has heretofore governed such matters. * * *

Fair price obviously requires consideration of all relevant factors involving the value of a company. This has long been the law of Delaware as stated in *Tri-Continental Corp. [v. Battye], 74 A.2d[71,] 72 [Del.1950]*:

> The basic concept of value under the appraisal statute is that the stockholder is entitled to be paid for that which has been taken from him, viz., his proportionate interest in a going concern. By value of the stockholder's proportionate interest in the corporate enterprise is meant the true or intrinsic value of his stock which has been taken by the merger. * * *

This is not only in accord with the realities of present day affairs, but it is thoroughly consonant with the purpose and intent of our statutory law. Under *8 Del. C. § 262(h)*, the Court of Chancery:

> shall appraise the shares, determining their fair value exclusive of any element of value arising from the accomplishment or expectation of the merger, together with a fair rate of interest, if any, to be paid upon the amount determined to be the fair value. In determining such fair value, the Court shall take into account all relevant factors . . . (Emphasis added)

* * *

It is significant that section 262 now mandates the determination of "fair" value based upon "all relevant factors". Only the speculative elements of value that may arise from the "accomplishment or expectation" of the merger are excluded. We take this to be a very narrow exception to the appraisal process, designed to eliminate use of pro form data and projections of a speculative variety relating to the completion of a merger. But elements of future value, including the nature of the enterprise, which are known or susceptible of proof as of the date of the merger and not the product of speculation, may be considered. When the trial court deems it appropriate, fair value also includes any damages, resulting from the taking, which the stockholders sustain as a class. If that was not the case, then the obligation to consider "all relevant factors" in the valuation process would be eroded. * * *

* * *

Although the Chancellor received the plaintiff's evidence, his opinion indicates that the use of it was precluded because of past Delaware practice. While we do not suggest a monetary result one way or the other, we do think the plaintiff's evidence should be part of the factual mix and weighed as such. Until the $21 price is measured on remand by the valuation standards mandated by Delaware law, there can be no finding at the present stage of these proceedings that the price is fair. Given the lack of any candid disclosure of the material facts surrounding establishment of the $21 price, the majority of the minority vote, approving the merger, is meaningless.

* * *

While a plaintiff's monetary remedy ordinarily should be confined to the more liberalized appraisal proceeding herein established, we do not intend any limitation on the historic powers of the Chancellor to grant such other relief as the facts of a particular case may dictate. The appraisal remedy we approve may not be adequate in certain cases, particularly where fraud, misrepresentation, self-dealing, deliberate waste of corporate assets, or gross and palpable overreaching are involved. * * * Under such circumstances, the Chancellor's powers are complete to fashion any form of equitable and monetary relief as may be appropriate, including rescissory damages. Since it is apparent that this long completed transaction is too involved to undo, and in view of the Chancellor's discretion, the award, if any, should be in the form of monetary damages based upon entire fairness standards, i.e., fair dealing and fair price.

* * *

III.

* * *

The requirement of a business purpose is new to our law of mergers and was a departure from prior case law. * * *

In view of the fairness test which has long been applicable to parent-subsidiary mergers, * * * the expanded appraisal remedy now available to shareholders, and the broad discretion of the Chancellor to fashion such relief as the facts of a given case may dictate, we do not believe that any additional meaningful protection is afforded minority shareholders by the business purpose requirement of the trilogy of *Singer, Tanzer,* * * * *Najjar,* * * * and their progeny. Accordingly, such requirement shall no longer be of any force or effect.

The judgment of the Court of Chancery, finding both the circumstances of the merger and the price paid the minority shareholders to be fair, is reversed. The matter is remanded for further proceedings consistent herewith. * * *

NOTES AND QUESTIONS

I. TAKING INTO CONSIDERATION the result in this case, and also the result in such cases as *Omnicare* and *Smith v. Van Gorkom*, can it really truthfully be said that the law of Delaware waters down the rights of shareholders to a "thin gruel?" Did the UOP shareholders really need protection in this case? Given the fact that the original tender offer made by Signal for its minority stake in UOP was significantly oversubscribed, and given the further fact that UOP had been trading at $14.50 per share before Signal's attempt to acquire the remaining shares at that same $21 price, is it as clear as the Delaware Supreme Court makes out that the conduct of Signal's officials was unfair to the UOP minority shareholders? Note that the court does suggest a means by which Signal might have been able to buy the remaining shares of UOP and avoid having the transaction attacked by disgruntled shareholders. What was that means, and are you satisfied that it would adequately protect the interests of UOP minority shareholders?

2. AS INDICATED EARLIER, this case moves on from the Delaware Block method to suggest that other means of valuation might appropriately be employed in Delaware courts. Note that Discounted Cash Flow (DCF) and Comparative Premium Studies seem implicitly to be approved. Do you have more confidence in those means than in the Delaware Block method? Why? Note further that the Delaware Supreme Court reiterates its belief, expressed in *Smith v. Van Gorkom*, that there is such a thing as "intrinsic" or "fair" value that can be demonstrated or at least suggested by appropriate financial analysis. Do you share the court's confidence on this point? What do you make of the Court's intriguing suggestion, implicitly criticizing the conduct of Signal, when it stated that:

> The Arledge–Chitiea report speaks for itself in supporting the Chancellor's finding that a price of up to $24 was a "good investment" for Signal. It shows that a return on the investment at $21 would be 15.7% versus 15.5% at $24 per share. This was a difference of only two-tenths of one percent, while it meant over $17,000,000 to the minority. Under such circumstances, paying UOP's minority shareholders $24 would have had relatively little long-term effect on Signal, and the Chancellor's findings concerning the benefit to Signal, even at a price of $24, were obviously correct.

Is there any kind of slip in the Court's reasoning on this point?

3. *WEINBERGER v. UOP*, insofar as it rejects the "business purpose" test for "freezeout" mergers, makes such transactions easier to accomplish. Other states have not rejected the "business purpose," test and do not permit such "freezeouts," whereby the minority interest is terminated, usually through purchase of the minority's shares by the majority, unless there is a purpose for the merger apart from the simple desire to appropriate the entire enterprise for the majority holder. Such a "business purpose" might include such matters as taking the corporation "private," so as to avoid particular regulatory consequences, including adverse tax treatment or compliance with disclosure requirements of the Securities Exchange Commission. Why abandon the "business purpose" requirement? Does the "entire fairness" test, as explained in *Weinberger*, do an adequate job of protecting shareholders potentially subject to a "freezeout?" As a policy matter, should reducing the number of owners, or eliminating minority ownership in large-scale businesses be something we should encourage or discourage? Given what you now know about Delaware law and tender offers, would you believe that there is a need for the federal government to step in to protect minority (or even majority) shareholders who might be faced with a tender offer, particularly one made by a bidder hostile to incumbent management? What do you make of the "Williams Act," considered next, in which the Congress did respond to what it believed to be inadequacies in state law?

Why do we continue to rely on a corporate structure that gives primacy to director/officer decision making? In the last chapter, there was an off-hand suggestion that the tale of Ulysses and the Sirens had something to teach us about close corporations. For the suggestion that this is true for the publicly-held corporation as well *see* Lynn A. Stout, *The Shareholder as Ulysses: Some Empirical Evidence on Why Investors in Public Corporations Tolerate Board Governance*, 152 U. Pa. L. Rev. 667, 689 (2003). For a panoramic view of developments at the Delaware Supreme Court and at the federal level see the recent after-dinner speech of the Chief Justice of the Delaware Supreme Court, E. Norman Veasey, *Views from the Bench: Musings on the Dynamics of Corporate Governance Issues, Director Liability Concerns, Corporate Control Transactions, Ethics and Federalism*, 152 U. Pa. L. Rev. 1007 (2003).

IV. A Note on the Williams Act and State Statutes

"IN RECENT YEARS WE HAVE seen proud old companies reduced to corporate shells after white-collar pirates have seized control with funds from sources which are unknown in many cases, then sold or traded away the best assets, later to split up most of the loot among themselves. . . . "[37] So said Senator Harrison Williams, when he introduced the federal legislation designed to regulate tender offers, soon to be called the "Williams Act."[38] You will note that Senator Williams does not appear to be a great friend to takeovers, and while some legislative history of the Williams Act says it was designed to be neutral, neither favoring or discouraging hostile bids for companies, it is very difficult to read it as anything but raising the costs of such bids. The act regulates "tender offers," the procedure whereby a bidder indicates that he is willing, if a specified number of shareholders "tender" their shares to the bidder at a specified price, to purchase those shares. The bidder is free to decline to purchase any of the shares if an insufficient number of them are tendered to meet the bidder's stated requirements. Do you understand why a tender offer is a much more effective takeover strategy than open-market purchases? Do you favor or oppose tender offers? There are many provisions of the Williams Act, and many regulations authorized by it, but for our purposes we need only highlight some of the major provisions.

Disclosure. For example, the Williams Act provides that when one either acquires 5% or more of a corporation listed on a national stock exchange (a "toehold interest") or makes a tender offer for 5% or more of such a company, one is required to file with the issuer and the SEC a statement indicating, among other things, one's identity, the source of one's funding, and one's future plans with regard to acquisition of additional interests in the target and whether a bust-up of the target is contemplated. See generally § 14(d)(1) of the Securities Exchange Act of 1934, as amended, 15 U.S.C. § 78n(d)(1) (1988), and the regulations thereunder. Would you be in favor of such a provision?

Duration. There was a time, in the early days of regulation of tender offers and takeovers, when one could make an offer that would be open for only eight days (the so-called "Saturday Night Special,") but under the Williams Act Rule 14e–1(a), 17 C.F.R. § 240.14e–1(a) (1990), and other federal legislation, such as the Hart-Scott-Rodino Antitrust Improvements Act, Pub. L. 94–435 (1976), a tender offer must remain open for at least 20, and sometimes as long as 50 days, while the FTC examines whether there are anti-competitive implications and thus whether or not it should permit a

---

37   Pub. L. No. 90–439, 82 Stat. 454 (1968) (codified as amended at 15 U.S.C. §§ 78m(d)–(e), 78n(d)–(f) (1988)). The Williams Act provisions became § 13(d)–(e) and § 14(d)–(f) of the Exchange Act, 15 U.S.C. §§ 78a–78ll (1988).

38   Pub. L. No. 90–439, 82 Stat. 454 (1968) (codified as amended at 15 U.S.C. §§ 78m(d)–(e), 78n(d)–(f) (1988)). The Williams Act provisions became § 13(d)–(e) and § 14(d)–(f) of the Exchange Act, 15 U.S.C. §§ 78a–78ll (1988).

tender offer and associated merger to be accomplished. Who benefits when a tender offer must be kept open for a substantial period of time? Who bears the cost?

Pro-Rating. In the early days of employment of tender offers, a bidder had the freedom to make such an offer for a specified percentage of the shares of a target corporation, and offer cash for those shares, and then freeze-out the remaining shareholders in a shares for debt swap. Such a transaction is known in the trade as a "Front-End-Loaded Two-Tiered Tender Offer," and it is a fearsome device, indeed. At the "back-end," the hapless minority shareholders often receive "junk-bonds" (non-investment grade securities, debt instruments that carry a high rate of interest, but that are often highly subordinated (their interest will not be paid until other creditors of the corporation are paid), and bear a high risk of declining in value). Fear of being at the back end of such a transaction often stampeded shareholders into accepting the tender offer, even if the price might not have been as high as such shareholders would have expected or desired. In order to alleviate the problem, under the current Williams Act regulations, a bidder is required, instead of being able to accept tendered shares on a first-come first-served basis, to purchase an aliquot portion of all shares tendered during the period the offer is required to remain open. Rule 14d–8, 17 C.F.R. § 240.14d–8 (1990). Do you understand why this, combined with the duration provisions mentioned above, reduces the threat of the Front-End-Loaded Two-Tiered Tender Offer? For a case involving a Front-End-Loaded Two-Tiered Tender Offer, explaining why it is a coercive device, and approving tactics to defeat it, see, e.g., *Unocal Corp. v. Mesa Petroleum Co.*, 493 A.2d 946 (Del. 1985).

Upping the Ante. There was a time when one could make a tender offer for a specified number of shares, say $50 for 51% of the shares, and if, for example, only 40% of the shares were tendered, the bidder was free to lock in those shares at $50, and then issue an additional tender offer for 11% of the shares, at a higher price, perhaps $55. This is no longer possible, as the Williams Act now provides that if the price of a tender offer is raised, all shares (even those previously tendered) must be purchased at the higher price. § 14(d)(7) of the Securities Exchange Act of 1937, as amended, 15 U.S.C. § 78n(d)(7) (1988). Can this be interpreted as anything but an attempt to discourage tender offers?

Withdrawal. At one time it was possible for the bidder to exert control over shares tendered for a set period of time before the bidder made the decision (as a bidder may do) to accept the tender of those shares and purchase them. The period in which the bidder could lock up such tendered shares was at first fourteen days, and then it was reduced to seven days. At the present time, however, Williams Act regulations provide that a shareholder who has tendered shares may withdraw them at any time before they have been accepted for purchase by the bidder. Rule 14d–7, 17 C.F.R. § 240.14d–7 (1990). Such a non-withdrawal provision gave the bidder the opportunity to keep shares off the market, and thus made it more difficult for competing tender offers. Do you favor the ending of this lock-up period?

All-Holders Rule. Before the passage of this recent revision of the Williams Act, it was possible for a tender offeror to make a selective bid targeted only at some share-holders, but not others. Such a bid might be made, for example, to shareholders at the back end of a Front-End-Loaded Two-Tiered Tender Offer by the target itself (a "self-tender") in order to raise the cost and thereby defeat that coercive tactic. Do you understand how this might work? *See, e.g., Unocal Corp. v. Mesa Petroleum Co.,* 493 A.2d 946 (Del. 1985), where the Delaware Supreme Court approved of such a selective tender, as a defensive strategy. Now the "all-holders rule" provides that a tender offer must be open to all holders of a given class of stock. Rule 14d–10, 17 C.F.R. § 240.14d–10 (1990). Was this federal non-discrimination rule wise?

Advice from the Target to its Shareholders. Whether or not academic theorists believe that the position of target management should be supine, a relatively new regulation under the Williams Act, Rule14e–2, 17 C.F.R. § 240.14e–2 (1990), provides that within ten business days of the commencement of a tender offer, a target must publish or send to its shareholders a statement indicating that it recommends acceptance or rejection of the tender offer, has chosen to remain neutral, or is unable to take a position on the tender offer. The statements of the corporation are subject to the general and broad anti-fraud provisions of the Williams Act, which provide penalties for untrue or misleading statements made in connection with a tender offer. For further application of the anti-fraud rules under the Williams Act, see, e.g., *United States v. O'Hagan, supra.*

As well as the Williams Act, there are now state statutory provisions which have the effect of delaying or making takeovers more difficult. There was some doubt about whether such statutes could be permitted, or whether the area (at least that of large publicly-held corporations) ought to be left for federal law. This was settled by the United States Supreme Court, allowing some regulatory freedom for the states in this area. See generally, *CTS Corp. v. Dynamics Corp. of America,* 481 U.S. 69, 107 S.Ct. 1637, 95 L.Ed.2d 67 (1987), which permitted states to make rules regarding "control share acquisitions." Subsequent state legislation which seeks to protect shareholders at the back end of a front-end-loaded two-tiered tender offer, state legislation which imposes a waiting period for the exercise of control by a bidder, and state legislation which gives discretion to board members to consider the effects of a takeover on corporate constituencies other than shareholders in deciding what action to take in response to a hostile offer appear to have met constitutional muster. For a useful brief note on this state legislation, see Melvin Eisenberg, *Corporations and Other Business Organizations: Cases and Materials* 874–877 (Concise 8th ed., 2000).

It is important to carefully study the statutes and case law concerning takeovers in a particular state. While the Delaware courts and the DGCL are prominent authorities in this area, many states reject heightened scrutiny standards like those in *Unocal* and *Revlon* or allow for more extreme defensive tactics, while others provide more stringent protection of shareholder rights. A lawyer or manager must study the relevant law for each jurisdiction. For an overview of such state regulations, see Michael Barzuza, *The State of State Antitakeover Law,* 95 Va. L. Rev. 1973 (2009).

Index